Problems in Economic and Social Archaeology

Problems in Economic and Social Archaeology

Edited by G. de G. Sieveking,
I.H. Longworth and K.E. Wilson

Duckworth

First published in 1976 by
Gerald Duckworth & Co. Ltd
The Old Piano Factory
43 Gloucester Crescent, London NW1

ISBN 0 7156 0942 4

Designed by Derek Doyle

Filmset by
Specialised Offset Services Ltd, Liverpool
and printed in Great Britain by
Unwin Brothers Ltd, Old Woking

This book has been written by his former
pupils in honour of Grahame Clark, one of the pioneers and an
outstanding exponent of economic and social archaeology

What after all *is* order, or something systematic? I suppose it is a pattern, and a pattern has no objective existence anyway. A pattern is a pattern because some*one* declares a concatenation of items to be meaningful or cohesive. The onus for detecting systems, and for deciding how to describe them, is very much on ourselves. I do not think we can adequately regard a system as a fact of nature, truths about which can be gradually revealed by patient analytical research. A viable system is something we detect and understand when it is mapped into our brains, and I suppose the inevitable result is that our brains themselves actually impose a structure on reality.

(S. Beer on systems, quoted by W.C. Clarke in *Place & People*, 1971)

Contents

PART IV THE BRITISH ISLES

PART V CONTINENTAL EUROPE

Contributors

Peter Addyman, Director, York Archaeological Trust.

Peter Bellwood, Lecturer, Department of Prehistory and Anthropology, School of General Studies, The Australian National University.

Martin Biddle, Director, Winchester Research Unit of the Winchester Excavation Committee.

John Blacking, Professor of Social Anthropology, Queen's University of Belfast.

Warwick Bray, Lecturer in Latin American Archaeology, University of London Institute of Archaeology.

Ralph Bulmer, Professor of Anthropology, University of Auckland.

Charles Burney, Senior Lecturer in Near Eastern Archaeology, Victoria University of Manchester.

David Clarke, formerly Lecturer, Department of Archaeology, University of Cambridge.

Barry Cunliffe, Professor of European Archaeology, University of Oxford.

Iain Davidson, Lecturer, Department of Prehistory and Archaeology, University of New England, New South Wales.

John Dixon, Lecturer, Department of Geology, University of Edinburgh.

John Evans, Director, University of London Institute of Archaeology.

Brian M. Fagan, Professor of Anthropology, University of California at Santa Barbara.

Andrew Fleming, Lecturer, Department of Ancient History, University of Sheffield.

Peter Gathercole, Curator, University of Museum of Archaeology and Ethnology, Cambridge.

Jack Golson, Professor of Prehistory, Research School of Pacific Studies, The Australian National University.

Norman Hammond, Senior Lecturer in Archaeology, University of Bradford.

Anthony Harding, Lecturer, Department of Archaeology, University of Durham.

Charles Higham, Professor of Anthropology, University of Otago.

Ray Inskeep, Assistant Curator, Pitt Rivers Museum, Oxford.

Glynn Isaac, Professor of Anthropology, University of California at Berkeley.

Michael Jarman, Assistant Director, British Academy Major Research Project: The Early History of Agriculture.

Rhys Jones, Research Fellow, Department of Prehistory, Research School of Pacific Studies, The Australian National University.

Charles McBurney, Reader in Prehistory, University of Cambridge.

Paul Mellars, Lecturer, Department of Ancient History, University of Sheffield.

John Nandris, Lecturer on Prehistoric Archaeology, University of London Institute of Archaeology.

David Oates, Professor of Western Asiatic Archaeology, University of London Institute of Archaeology.

Joan Oates, Tutor at Girton College, Cambridge.

Nicolas Peterson, Research Fellow, Department of Anthropology, Research School of Pacific Studies, The Australian National University.

Merrick Posnansky, Professor of Archaeology, University of Ghana.

Colin Renfrew, Professor of Archaeology, University of Southampton.

Derek Roe, Department of Prehistory, University of Oxford.

Wilfred Shawcross, Senior Lecturer, Department of Prehistory and Anthropology, School of General Studies, The Australian National University.

Andrew Sherratt, Assistant Keeper, Department of Antiquities, Ashmolean Museum, Oxford.

Ann Sieveking, Fellow of the Society of Antiquaries of London.

Gale Sieveking, Deputy Keeper, Department of Prehistoric and Romano-British Antiquities, British Museum.

Ian Stead, Assistant Keeper, Department of Prehistoric and Romano-British Antiquities, British Museum.

Michael Thompson, Inspector of Ancient Monuments for Wales, Department of the Environment.

David Trump, Tutor, Board of Extra-mural Studies, University of Cambridge.

David M. Wilson, Professor of Mediaeval Archaeology, University College, London.

A tribute to Grahame Clark

Dear Grahame,

This short foreword is written by one who regards himself as your oldest pupil, on behalf of a younger generation of post-war Cambridge prehistorians, including those who completed their studies while you held the Disney Chair of Archaeology from 1952 to 1974. The book is intended by its editors and contributors as a tribute to the many papers and books you published during that time and, above all, to the stimulus and direction you brought to the Cambridge school of prehistory during the twenty-two years of your tenure. In it I think you can perceive, as I certainly do, the impact both of ideas and methods you pioneered yourself and of other new ideas, to which you gave generous support, from those who have now to maintain the progress of the study as mature workers.

If the range of papers here offered is almost bewilderingly wide, you will, I think, be the last to complain of that. During the nearly forty years that I have studied and worked with you in the Department, I can think of few aspects indeed of the subject that you have not touched on at one time or another in your works of synthesis, and a vast variety to which you have contributed in depth. One of the first excavations of yours that I remember working on was that of a Roman canal-side station in the Fens. Within a year or two, searching my memory at random, there was your study of Henge Monuments and another on Beakers, to say nothing of your continuing work on the Mesolithic which did so much to stimulate and broaden my own interest in Early Hunters.

Of innumerable stimulating, and often animated, conversations that we have had over the years, two come to my mind as I write. In one we were having a conversation with a prehistorian interested mainly (and perhaps rather narrowly) in one of the terminal periods of prehistory. You were, if I remember rightly, referring (to his evident satisfaction) to the struggle to free East Anglian prehistory from the sterile 'flintology' of an earlier age; but at that point you suddenly changed course to remind him that the basic and most significant task of the subject was to further understanding of human development as a whole, for which the scrutiny of the earliest periods was of the essence. On another occasion, on the other hand, I can remember your urging me not to neglect the high peaks of human achievement, lest I become so absorbed in the formative stages as to forget where they had led.

I hope I have not misquoted you, but in any case let me hasten to add my conviction that it is the cumulative effect of years, rather than any particular items, which lead to the fruitful association of minds in a happy Faculty, as ours most certainly was. To my thinking, such a Faculty is not so much a chance association of students and teachers as a continuously self-renewing team, comprising every stage from the complete beginner to the most experienced, but all sharing a common interest in assimilating and enlarging knowledge in their chosen field; in a word, all engaged in learning, in the fullest sense of the term.

When I first joined the Department in 1935, you had newly begun to lecture. Our first introduction to the subject at that time was given by Miles Burkitt; it consisted mainly of the traditional outline presented with admirable clarity. From you, we began to hear at the same time of new and exciting developments quite outside the scope of the classic text-books of the day. Outstanding among these new topics were the growing fields of Post-Glacial and environmental studies based on the then new and rapidly growing techniques of pollen analysis, varve dating, Post-Glacial sea-level change and many others, not a few indeed exemplified as near at hand as Peacock's Farm and in the activities of the Fenland Research Committee.

The publication of The Mesolithic Settlement of Northern Europe *followed soon after, then* Archaeology and Society *and* Prehistoric England, *though* Star Carr *and* Prehistoric Europe: the Economic Basis *lay far in the future. Meanwhile the earlier works of Gordon Childe, Crawford and, from the recent past, Cyril Fox were all part of the academic fare of the day. The intellectual climate, as I recall it, was one of new ideas characterized everywhere by an atmosphere of excitement and optimism. Discussion and criticism indeed abounded, but were constantly vivified and rendered fruitful by important new discoveries and often spectacular developments in method and technique.*

Then came the war with its moratorium on field research, but it was perhaps not altogether the disaster it seemed at first sight for, as it drew to an end, we began to take stock of the status quo *and plan for a new era in the future. Moreover, it enabled many of us to travel and widen our horizons in a way that might not have occurred under more normal conditions. When I returned to Cambridge, it was some seven years since Dorothy Garrod had taken over the Chair from Ellis Minns. Many new ideas and trends were beginning to stir. Dorothy was able to impart something of these in her courses, over the relatively short period of her effective tenure, interrupted as it had been by the war.*

When, finally, you took over the Department in 1952 there were already initial signs of expansion, both in the scope of teaching and in numbers, although I suppose not one of us at that time would have predicted the total that we have now reached and seem likely to exceed in the future. When I first listened to your lectures in 1935, if I remember correctly, the total numbers reading archaeology and anthropology, all years and options included, together with the occasional research student, did not exceed about fifteen. In 1974 the number of archaeologists reading Part I was forty-six, and Part II forty-five, while there were forty research students, making up a total of 131, excluding the anthropologists, who have now left us.

But more important than sheer numbers has been the continuous broadening of the scope of the course. First there were the new regional courses such as Africa (where we have drawn on the resources of the corresponding department at Oxford) and the U.S.S.R. (which I personally have been concerned with), different areas of the Near and Far East and the New World, and even some coverage for the entirely new fields in Australia and Oceania (already reflected in some of the papers in the present volume). Then again there has been the great expansion of teaching on more theoretical and technical aspects, such as those connected with the British Academy Major Research Project, techniques of dating, presentation, and the philosophical and logical principles underlying the subject as a whole. Yet another trend during your tenure has been the steady growth in the importance of practical field and laboratory work as part of ongoing research and teaching. This last began under Dorothy Garrod but, under the impetus of your personal work and your interest and involvement in the work of others, it has expanded until I imagine it must form one of the most vivid recollections, for many of the writers of these papers, of their time as students.

Moreover many of the contributors, as you will see, have been quick to acknowledge these and other new departures that sprang directly from ground first broken by yourself. In my own recollection a series of early papers, considerably before the publication of Prehistoric Europe, *began to turn my own and other minds specifically towards economic aspects of prehistory. I remember particularly the paper on seal-hunting in 1946, another on the Scandinavian flint trade in 1948, and interesting critical comments in reviews on over-simplistic deductions concerning trade as inferred from archaeological evidence.*

But, no doubt, the landmark in the history of the Department with which many of the contributors to this book are most immediately concerned is the development of the British Academy Major Research Project on the Early History of Agriculture. If this owes much of its present form to the persuasive teaching of Eric Higgs and also, to some extent, to new trends in geography, it certainly owes its inception and not a little of its subsequent growth to yourself.

Since my own approach to economic prehistory has been mainly concerned with immediate and experimental issues rather than with the more distant speculative and philosophical horizons, I have perhaps viewed this venture from a different angle from some other workers. If I may offer a simile, I would say that no tree grows without shedding branches and changing shape as its life-cycle unfolds. It has been true of many new scientific ventures in the past that they have suffered more from over-enthusiastic adherents than from any spokesmen of an earlier line of thought. One can think of innumerable famous examples. It is often not until new concepts have been examined from many different angles that their validity, or otherwise, begins to emerge at all clearly.

In the meantime, however, any scrupulously collected data are, of course, bound to retain their value, irrespective of the synthesis in which they were originally presented. Of this at least we may be certain with regard to the topographical and biological data on the contexts of prehistoric sites being collected at the present time. But I also feel that we must be careful that any models that we may design to accommodate new data can also accommodate the old, and any further facts that may emerge in the future as well, and not just those that offer an attractive fit at first sight.

Several papers in this book are concerned, directly or indirectly, with problems of subsistence, since this is one of the unifying themes of the work. Yet I imagine that no one, except perhaps the extreme enthusiast, would wish to claim that these are the only problems worth solving, so it is perhaps interesting to consider where they fit into the picture as a whole. Recently, you yourself have given us an interesting lead-in to this very problem. In your reappraisal, not long ago, of Star Carr you drew a fascinating picture of the pattern of trans-humance to which it seems to relate. More recently still, you examined some of the more specifically sociological issues raised by the geographical distribution of various tool types of a similar age in Northern Europe. To me, at least, the point is well taken. If what we aim at in prehistory however imperfectly is, as I have said, nothing less than an integrated picture of human emergence, then we must couple our investigations in depth with syntheses. These must, ideally, be concerned with all *aspects of cultural growth – not just its material basis, aesthetic or religious or sociological expression or any other aspect taken in isolation. In the last resort, to borrow a favourite term of one of your pupils, it is the 'feedback' process in its entirety that we should have in mind, if we are to make the fullest use of the extraordinary revelations of the past that archaeology provides.*

You yourself have made contributions to this very process on many occasions and, moreover, as a self-confessed 'optimist' rather than a 'pessimist' in archaeology. I like to feel that I am another of these, and that through all the shades of opinion expressed in this book you will find yet other optimists, some even among those who like to protest that they are not.

If I had time and opportunity, I should like to ask all the writers here represented what was their strongest single impression of the Cambridge school of prehistory as they knew it. I do not know if I should get any consensus of opinion, but at least I know what my personal view would be. There was, throughout my period of association with the Department, a continuing enthusiasm to examine new ideas, whatever their source; but it was always coupled with a healthy critical sense which prevented them from too quickly fossilizing into 'isms'.

This, indeed, was an abiding characteristic of your own teaching as I remember it, and I hope and think that it will long continue to inspire your pupils in the many different parts of the world to which they have spread.

Last, but not least, we all look forward to many more papers by you to shake us out of any middle-aged complacency into which we may fall, and to spark off new and exciting lines of thought.

Greetings from us all at Cambridge
Charles McBurney

GALE SIEVEKING

Progress in economic and social archaeology

When Grahame Clark's first major studies in the field of economic prehistory were published between twenty and thirty years ago, many specialists were unable to visualize their application to other fields of archaeology. Even in prehistoric studies the value of such work was held to be limited by the lack of suitable evidence at supposedly *key* archaeological sites. It required a major reorientation of archaeological thought to consider actually *choosing* sites because they produced evidence of economy rather than the more recognizable varieties of pottery, tools, weapons and architecture. Such a change had to take place before economic studies in archaeology could be given sufficient priority over studies in the history of style – studies of the development of decorative patterns, or functional shapes – of the types that previously served so well as a guide to the age and to the presumed interests or activities of their makers. In the trackless wastes of prehistory, it thus required the development of accurate methods of absolute dating – the radiocarbon revolution – before economic prehistory could achieve a proper place. It is a measure of the distance between Roman or mediaeval history and the field archaeology of these later and more complex archaeological periods that here also time has been required to achieve the necessary reorientation.

Today economic and ecological studies make a major contribution to many different archaeological fields, and social archaeology, a study Grahame Clark has himself emphasized in recent years, is beginning to make real headway.

A number of important current social and economic themes are discussed in this book. Among others, they include the development of agriculture in the Americas and the Old World; settlement patterns and land use at different periods; functional archaeology; seasonality; human origins and hominid behaviour patterns; trade and its motivation; the use of geographical models; ethnoarchaeology and the interpretation of archaeological evidence. While prehistoric archaeology, Grahame Clark's own field of study, is well represented, other contributors discuss evidence from the ancient empires of the Near East and of Rome, the evolution of the British landscape in mediaeval times and the building of manor houses. Several papers discuss the archaeology of the last two hundred years especially as it affects Africa, Australia, New Zealand and the Far East.

In many cases these are contributions to a continuing discussion. The themes or problems have been raised in a number of previous papers and perhaps summarised in conferences with published reports. However, many of these previous discussions have been concerned mainly to enunciate the principles which should govern particular investigations, or to describe in outline projects that have not reached the stage of detailed publication. Contributors to this volume have therefore been asked and given space for substantial contributions to knowledge, rather than the illustrated bibliographies, convenient summaries of knowledge, and students' introductions to the subject which characterize some recent conference proceedings. Many of the contributions are of considerable length, some are more than controversial, others represent surveys of whole fields of knowledge or the results of many years' study. Shorter contributions are limited to a single line of research. Emphasis has also been laid on the publication of evidence in full, where this is available, on the grounds that an ounce of practice is worth a pound of theory, and in order that each research paper can stand on its own feet, rather than leading to the nearest source of reference. The result of this pragmatic approach is that *Problems in Economic and Social Archaeology*, besides being a contribution to knowledge, is also a guide to current practice in many different archaeological fields. The methods that have been most valuable in one field are often carried over to another but seldom receive quite the same emphasis.

The book's value as a guide to current methodology is increased by the nature of the contributors. As these are all pupils of Grahame Clark and of one school – the Cambridge school of prehistoric archaeology – their contribution might be thought to show some basic similarity. However, in approaching our different contributors we naturally tried to find old pupils from all periods of Grahame Clark's influence at Cambridge from the late 1940s right up to the present day. The list of contributors includes archaeologists at all stages of their professional career from professors and heads of departments (15) to those holding their first professional appointment or still completing their first research. The extended age range of the contributors leads to differences in assimilation of, or emphasis on, different techniques and practices in economic and social archaeology which have themselves been developed in the same period. This in itself provides a valuable diversity of approach.

As hinted in an earlier paragraph, we hold the view that renewed emphasis on economic studies in archaelogy preceded the development of what is here called social archaelogy, though the latter can claim a varied and attenuated ancestry from social history in later periods, or from the writings of Gordon Childe, themselves deriving almost without alteration from the social evolutionary theories of Lewis Morgan and Tyler in the nineteenth century. The point to emphasize is not the continuity of such scholarly preoccupations, but the effect of the great increases in archaeological efficiency which have taken place in the last twenty years. It must always have been apparent that archaeology had more to tell one about the economic or social life of human groups at any period up to the present day than it could reveal about the historical individual and the particular event recognizable in contemporary written records – about the inspiration of Michelangelo or the motivation of Napoleon or Stalin. But for a long period before 1940 most archaelogists had lost faith in both economic and social studies, as the nature of the evidence for society provided by field archaeology was unsatisfactory and in many cases elusive.

The pioneering of new methods, and new disciplines of excavation and recording which led to an increase in archaeological efficiency sufficient to transform the basic data, would seem to have been carried out in Europe between 1920 and 1940, by the leaders in the field of settlement archaeology such as Buttler, Van Giffen and Bersu, and in Britain by a small group of people including notably Sir Mortimer Wheeler, Stuart Piggott and Grahame Clark himself. These men and others were responsible for tightening up the efficiency of the archaeological machine; for introducing new standards rather than for applying them wholesale. The small field of archaeological endeavour that they represented was left only partly transformed in 1940, or for that matter in 1950, and the principal theoretician in the European field, Gordon Childe, was able to pursue an enormously useful and productive career without ever taking part in the movement.

Though vague reflections are to be seen in pre-war Britain and the United States, the major advances which were to lead to a revolution in field archaeology took place, as with atomic physics, in continental Europe, in Holland, Germany and Scandinavia. Settlement archaeology, the practice of uncovering houses and their surroundings completely, rather than defining their position and dimensions by narrow vertical trenches placed at suitable intervals, followed the development of such methods on a smaller scale in the excavation of earthen burial mounds or tumuli and the recognition, on these and similar sites, of perishable elements of architecture such as wooden walling, stakes and posts, from the discoloured filling of holes which had once supported their bases. The study of settlements in this way developed where it was easiest to put into effect, on the loess plains of Holland and Central Europe, where prehistoric settlements formerly of wood were available for study and where the effect of dark soil stains could be most readily appreciated against the background of yellow loess. Though the news of these discoveries travelled fast, they were difficult to acclimatize to different soils and to regions with building traditions based on stone even in prehistoric times. It was only in 1938, for example, that the first attempts at the application of these principles took place in Great Britain, when Bersu himself undertook excavations on behalf of the Prehistoric Society, at Little Woodbury on the chalk lands of the Salisbury Plain.

What had been achieved by 1940 was the publication of a series of examples of the newer archaeological report, each of which emphasized the barrenness of the surrounding territory, either by contrast, or because the perspicacity of the archaeologist underlined even more fully the small amount of real evidence there was for any social or economic theorizing. Perhaps the most valuable insights that were gained at this time were those obtained by calling in the resources of natural science, to assist in the study and the interpretation of archaeological evidence.

The major figures in the movement to call biological science to the aid of archaeology were, on the continent, Van Giffen and Rust and in Britain, Sir Cyril Fox and Grahame Clark. Van Giffen must be mentioned as the founder of the Biological-Archaeological Institute in Groningen and as being competent in both fields; Rust for the scientific examination of his magnificent discoveries at Meiendorf and Stellmoor, and Fox for the reconstructed landscapes of his *Archaeology of the Cambridge Region* (1923) and for the implications of his geographical study. *The Personality of Britain* (1932) which had its origins in a report to the first International Congress of Prehistoric and Protohistoric Sciences held in London in 1932. But it was Grahame Clark above all who realized the archaeological implications of the evidence of the biological sciences, and the value of relating mapped distributions of finds or settlements not only to a geological or a soil base map, as Fox and others had done, to reconstruct a timeless landscape, but also to a climatic sequence like that worked out for Scandinavia on the basis of varves and palynology, which could be used to reconstruct that landscape differently at different periods, firstly on the basis of changes of vegetation and secondly on the basis of man's interference with this vegetational succession, as documented in the palaeobotanical record. It was Clark also who, from the beginning, emphasized that this botanical and zoological evidence did not merely provide a painted back-cloth for the previous inhabitants of the landscape, but could also be used to reconstruct a true record of their available economic resources and, after the evidence from settlements and tools had been related to the natural record, also to show in what manner and to what extent these resources were exploited by different archaeological groups. This line of interpretation can be traced in Clark's work in association with Godwin in the Cambridgeshire fenland, then in his reconstruction of the early Scandinavian prehistoric succession in *The Mesolithic Settlement of Northern Europe* (1936), in popular accounts such as *Archaeology and Society* (first edition 1939), as well as in the synthesis *Prehistoric Europe: The Economic Basis* (1952), and in a dozen or so professional papers on different resources available to man in prehistoric Europe which preceded its publication.

If this point of view is today part of the generally accepted background of archaeological studies, it is as the result of the educational process carried out by a small number of European archaeologists including Clark and by natural scientists working with them among whom Godwin (Great Britain) and Iverson (Denmark) are pre-eminent. It was as a result of the transformation of the Prehistoric Society of East Anglia into the Prehistoric Society (Great Britain) in 1933-5, itself largely the work of C.W. Phillips and of Clark, that a platform was made available in Britain for the publication of such views. The *Proceedings of the Prehistoric Society*, edited by Clark between 1935 and 1970, was notable, particularly in the early years, for editorial notes describing new advances in archaeological interpretation based on the natural sciences, as well as for solicited articles from specialists in those fields.

If pre-war settlement archaeology opened up the possibility of more comprehensive investigation of the pits and post holes filled with discoloured soil, which were all that was preserved of wooden structures under normal conditions after only a few centuries in the ground, co-operation with the biological sciences led to the investigation of sites where conditions of survival were better, as could be seen from many accidental discoveries during pre-war excavations, and was demonstrated in the immediate post-war period by Grahame Clark in his excavation of Star Carr, carried out for this purpose. For more than a decade Clark had advocated in publications such as *Archaeology and Society* (1939), that archaeologists should concentrate on the excavation of settlements where many possible types of perishable raw materials were likely to be preserved. The Mesolithic settlement of Star Carr in Yorkshire (England) fulfilled these conditions. It was on the margin of a fossil lake and was buried beneath waterlogged peat. Poorly preserved wood and bone occurred in field exposures in the margin of the settlement – the bone was like 'old bedroom slippers' in the famous phrase attributed to John Moore, the field archaeologist responsible for the discovery. The position of the fossil lake margin at the appropriate period (demonstrated by palaeobotanical investigation) and the present-day level of the water table showed that water-logged conditions and therefore well preserved remains were likely to occur on at least a part of the settlement. In the event nearly the entire settlement was excellently preserved. It was almost completely excavated. The subsequent reports, with detailed publication of all the scientific as well as the archaeological evidence, demonstrated, as Clark had suggested it might, just how much more could be learned of the economic background to settlements of this or any age, where the natural remains are well preserved and carefully studied. Since Star Carr was the only known site in Great Britain of a comparatively little known period of prehistory, this was demonstrated with stunning effect. The wealth of material remains could be used to show the season of the year that Star Carr was occupied, the purpose of the settlement, and the relatively minor importance in the economy of the flint implements, which were commonly the only traces of human activity on other less well preserved sites of the Mesolithic. It is notable that this well studied site has been capable of yielding still further evidence, and after twenty-five years of subsequent research, Clark has published a major reinterpretation of the economy of the site, *Star Carr: A Case Study* (1972a), and also of comparable sites in his Oliver Davies lecture *The Archaeology of Stone Age Settlement* (1972b), based on ethnographic evidence not available in 1954.

If the period before 1940 saw the production of newly efficient means of archaeological excavation and recording, and most of the new ideas which were to transform the study of the economic and social aspects of archaeology into independent subjects, I have suggested that even in the immediate post-war years, after 1950, the application of such ideas and techniques had still hardly begun to make a mark on the quality of the data generally available.

Today the situation has altered in a number of respects, though the effects of change are still greater in some archaeological fields than in others, and the causes of change are sometimes hard to isolate. There is no doubt that in Europe and North America the acceleration of industrial activity after 1938 led to the destruction of large numbers of archaeological sites and hence to the provision of adequate governmental financial support for their investigation. In Eastern Europe and in the newly independent countries of Africa and Asia there were political reasons for such support, as there had been in Germany before 1938, but the East European contribution to change is small. Though the concept of total excavation of settlements was supported in prehistoric and mediaeval excavations such as Bylany (Soudsky 1966) or Novgorod (Thompson 1967), the lines of communication were poor. It was in Western Europe, Scandinavia (Bruce-Mitford 1975) and in North America that the effects of a change in scale of operations were first logically worked out.

Modern large-scale excavation had been initiated before the War, but its techniques were expensive and required both trained excavators and supervisors in considerable quantities. Excavation with trained students, which became the rule in post-war Europe and North America, is still unfortunately rare if not unknown in Eastern Europe and in other countries where labour is still cheap. This contrast in labour costs or in the availability of trained labour is reinforced by the change which took place in excavation technique. The substitution of horizontal excavation of whole areas for the grid of narrow vertical trenches of stratigraphical excavation was characteristic of post-war field techniques. The availability of earth-moving equipment such as bulldozers made it possible to remove disturbed top soil more cheaply, and cut labour and organisational costs. Nevertheless, the vastly increased size of later and economically more complex settlements demanded greatly increased resources, once the necessity for the employment of modern techniques was accepted.

It is of course precisely these increases of scale, taken together with the use of modern field techniques and the documentation of the biological and scientific evidence in settlement sites, which has led to the production of good statistical samples of data of all kinds which can be processed in a standardized manner. This in its turn has led to the use of such data for interpretative and synthetic purposes in ways which were not possible when only one or two sites had been treated in this manner. In many cases a feed-back relationship has developed between the increase in data and the subject under investigation. From having been a necessary evil, an increase in the quantity of data is now seen as a positive requirement, if certain hypotheses are to be adequately demonstrated. One thinks, for example, of the transformation of faunal reports from simple taxonomic lists of animal species, often founded on the recovery of single specimens, to their present purposes as descriptions of ancient animal *populations* skewed by their exploitation by *Homo sapiens*.

While the application of skills and concepts first developed in the field of prehistoric studies to more recent, more complex and better preserved settlements, and the consequent changes in scale, provided much of the impetus for new developments in economic and social archaeology, the institutional revolution that has taken place in the gathering of archaeological data has been accompanied by the application of new theoretical tools and interpretative models adapted from those in use in cognate fields. Fortunately, these archaeological improvements coincided with a renewed interest among anthropologists and other social scientists in the application of generalized models to explain the relation between different social communities, or between communities and their environment, and also in the use of evolutionary models of change in society, of the type originally put forward in anthropology by Lewis Morgan.

The application of such models to archaeological data has provided a welcome increase in perspective, similar to the effect of isotopic dating methods. Radiocarbon and potassium argon, in addition to making dating more accurate, have generally stretched out the existing chronologies, and provided more elbow room for social and economic developments. The new social and environmental models have provided enlarged frameworks for interpreting archaeological evidence, in place of the constricted field provided by *ad hoc* comparisons between archaeological remains and existing societies, and the drawbacks of an admittedly imperfect archaeological record. Admittedly, no one could know what song the sirens sang, but new problems could be selected and the archaeological data could be ordered to solve these problems by the use of new conceptual tools.

Among these tools the most conspicuous have been the many diagrammatic representations of the regularities in human behaviour generated by the construction of various models. In the field of social and economic archaeology it is the diagrams or rather the models generated by systems analysis and those of general systems theory which provide the most food for thought. Both of these techniques attempt to identify a pattern or group of variables as a coherent system of interdependent parts, whose behaviour cannot be predicted outside the context of the system, but requires an understanding of their place and function within the whole. In systems analysis (a branch of statistics based on operational research) attention is focussed on the flows or links between the parts, illustrated by a flow chart, which should function as a working model, with input into the system, and output from it moving during a period of time. In this form of analysis, all systems are regarded as either closed or open. Closed systems consist of a set of elements and links. Open systems have links between the elements and an environment outside the system.

A similar but distinct conceptualization is provided by general systems theory, a discipline developed by cyberneticians, largely as an aid to ecological and biological studies. Here the systems are more abstract in conception. The system itself may be taken for granted or left unknown (as with the so-called black box), and its character merely argued from input or output. It is in relation to general systems theory that the notions of feed-back and homeostasis or equilibrium have been developed. Systems of these types are not visualized as working models, but as descriptive ways of illustrating the possible analogies between machines and biological systems and economic or social systems.

The working models provided by systems analysis have perhaps been the most attractive, because they can be made to manipulate bodies of actual data under certain alternative assumptions, and can by this means be altered and improved. But there is no doubt that general systems models are intellectually most exciting, as can be seen with the present day world models of Meadows and Taylor, showing how Western civilization is consuming resources and carrying a catastrophist message.

The literature of such concepts, models, and systems and their archaeological applications is too large to be reviewed here. Mention can merely be made of some characteristic applications. Possibly the most sustained value has been obtained from models derived from the biological field, particularly from the study of ecology and animal population studies and latterly from ethology. In some cases the archaeological use of these models antedates the present discussion. The ecosystem concept, first put forward by the botanist A.G. Tansley in

1935, was introduced to archaeology by Grahame Clark in 1952, as the underpinning of his principal theoretical synthesis *Prehistoric Europe: The Economic Basis*. Animal population studies have been popular in archaeology since the publication by Birdsell of a series of papers between 1953 and 1968 and of a particularly significant study by Wynn-Edwards (1962).

Objections have been put forward to the central concept of the ecosystem, the notion of a self-correcting mechanism or homeostat, which keeps the system in balance. This is widely used in archaeological models showing the relationship of early societies to their environments, as well as in anthropological studies such as that of Rappaport (1967) showing how ritual functions to balance relations between a contemporary society and its neighbours. Archaeologists have been familiar with this view of society since it was introduced to them by the so-called functional anthropologists in the 1920s, and the equilibrium model of society 'in a stable self-regulating state of perpetual equipoise', as Lawrence Stone (1972) has noted, goes back to Rousseau or even to Aquinas. Stone finds it unconvincing as a sociological phenomenon: 'It looks to a society without change, with universal consensus on values, with complete social harmony, and isolated from external threats; no approximation to such a society has ever been seen' (1972:5). W.C. Clark (1971) has criticized the ecological model in similar terms: 'Too much emphasis (is put) on homeostasis as a static condition and too much trust in the unfailing operation of systems of negative feedback. No life system is stable in the sense that it is unchanging. Cultural behaviour may act to counterbalance environmental changes, but there is always a net change in the system. Certainly ecosystems as evolutionary entities are self-maintaining, but they are self-transforming, too. Rather than a homeostat, a gyroscope may be the suitable analogy for regulating mechanisms in ecosystems.'

Though the homeostasis concept is still in general use, a number of attempts have been made to accommodate the effects of change in ecological models, utilizing open systems, including the cascading systems advocated by Chorley and Kennedy (1971) and also Wood and Matsen's (1973) 'complex adaptive system' model. The best known archaeological applications are fairly unsophisticated. Using Birdsell's animal population studies referred to above, Binford (1968) produced a typology of 'population systems' to show how human populations grow, remain stable, or migrate into uninhabited territory, and a series of more sophisticated models has since been produced to take possible social and economic causes of population stability or growth into account. A distinctive ecological model was used by Flannery, in his study of the development of agriculture in the Oxaco valley. Flannery suggests that the areas which can support the greatest variety of agricultural techniques retain their innovative position, whereas areas of an environmental type that can only support the older agricultural techniques decline in importance. As has been pointed out by Bray (1973), Flannery's model derives from the genetic principle that a population where several adaptive genotypes are favoured is suited to a number of different ecological niches.

Many ecological models like Binford's and Flannery's assume that all changes in population must be adaptive. Objection has been taken to this feature on the grounds that it leads to an unnecessarily deterministic view of economic and social development. In current jargon it assumes that man in society must always pursue 'an optimiser rather than a satisficer strategy'. Such a criticism is simply a matter of scale. Seen over a period of time the total effect of change is adaptive, as Darwin demonstrated, and the prehistoric and historic time scale is often sufficiently long for such a model to be valid.

If the general models provided by ecology are found unsatisfactory in some respects, they still continue to be fruitful in archaeological applications, as do other simpler concepts based on biological and anthropological models such as *scheduling* and *seasonality*, when used to explain the manner in which environmental resources are utilized by early human societies at different seasons. The notion that there are annual territories larger than those within reach of a single settlement and that these can be exploited by moving, nomadic or pastoral communities exploiting different biological resources in season is now well established. Such communities are said to have *home bases*, sites with many different community functions, and also sites devoted to particular economic strategies, and temporary camp sites or stopping places of various kinds. Though the basic model is zoological, it is from ethnography that such terms as these and the American 'kill site' and the English 'butchering site' have entered archaeological literature. The accessible territory within reach of such sites has been variously termed the *home range* (Jewell 1966), the exploitation territory, or the site catchment area. Models based on these concepts have been successfully applied to mediaeval and recent archaeological fields as well as to remote prehistory (Ellison & Harris 1972).

Another anthropological concept that has proved of particular value is that of social reciprocity, the so called 'gift exchange' relationship, known among many contemporary ethnographical societies, which was used by Grahame Clark to explain prehistoric trading patterns, in his paper on traffic in stone axes in the New Guinea Highlands (1965) and has since been widely adopted (for instance, by Sherratt in 1972).

The second major class of models now popular with social and economic archaeologists are those provided by the central place theory and similar devices of locational analyses. These are fairly abstract models based on formal patterns made by conventionalized data on maps and were developed by the Cambridge geographers Haggatt and Chorley for the study of spatial power relationships among modern business communities – though they have obvious political connotations. But the use of such models is not confined in archaeology to the more complex economies and societies, and both central place and set theory have been of value in explaining the relationships of peasant and hunter-gatherer communities.

Similar spatial techniques are in use in geography and the other social sciences so it is not always easy to verify the usage of archaeological applications. A particularly interesting explanation for discontinuities in the distribution of hunter-gatherer stone tools is put forward by Yellen and Harpending (1972) using a network analysis model, closely related to geographical forms of analysis but deriving immediately from sociology. Yellen and Harpending make use of data provided by demographic studies of the !Kung Bushmen, which suggest that hunter-gatherer families, though gregarious, do not permanently form part of a larger community. As different local resources are exploited, families move out from community centres or take up residence with different communities. A network model showing the relations between different families has relatively few links between the same pairs of families. The social consequences of this behaviour pattern are suggested by measurements of in-breeding levels, dialect differentiation, and local differentiation of tool traditions. In terms of these parameters local differentiation is much lower than in more closely knit and endogamous societies. Though spatially segregated clusters of archaeological sites within a single small land area suggest the existence of discrete groups, made up of different sets of individuals, this is not so, for instance, among !Kung Bushmen. A relatively undifferentiated distribution of stone tools and other material traits can, therefore, be taken to suggest that the prehistoric hunter-gatherers belonged to anucleate exogamous groups like the Bushmen, with much family interchange between groups and a consequently high rate of information flow, leading to increased uniformity in tool traditions. Similar measures of social distance to those quoted by Yellen and Harpending were adapted by Rowlands (1973) to a study of Bronze Age 'trading' relationships and have since seen other archaeological applications.

One advantage of locational models of the geographical type is meant to be that they are based on probabilistic trends rather than general laws, so that quantified data can be used in problem solving, if they are available, as they can with mathematical techniques such as simulation or critical path analysis. When the new archaeological models and 'deductive hypotheses' were first proposed, it was suggested that they should be rigorously tested against independent sets of data and some working models of the systems analysis type are in the course of being set up. But the principle of testing has been more broadly stated and there is general agreement today that archaeological propositions can only be valid if capable of being tested, though some authors prefer to say that propositions of this kind can only be disproved. This standpoint is obviously valuable as an aid to clear thinking. It is presumably when another more sophisticated model is proposed, or one based on different propositions, that such rigorous testing takes place. Until that occasion it may hold the field untested. But the whole line of argument is slightly unreal. A model – in particular a systems model, with components, sub-systems and systems – is merely a pattern imposed on reality by the observer, it is neither right or wrong in itself. Like the simpler and less sophisticated analogies which the archaeologist finds in contemporary life these models are there to be used as interpretative devices, until they are discarded or outworn.

Before leaving our discussion of theoretical advances, attention should be drawn to the effects of very simple changes of interpretation, or changes of emphasis, when communicated to archaeology from another related field study. Our example is taken from the anthropological study of the smallest contemporay societies. The *Man the Hunter* symposium (1968) was devoted to the ecological and economic behaviour of present day hunting froups, such as the Bushmen of the Kalahari, but carried a strong message to the effect that such groups throughout the world, and in particular those under apparently difficult desertic conditions, did not live a hand to mouth existence, never knowing where their next meal was coming from, as previous reports and travellers' tales had suggested. On the contrary they nearly always had a varied and sufficient diet. Also this diet was often, except in the arctic, found to consist largely of vegetables; man the hunter might more properly be called man the gatherer. The realization that some prehistoric hunting groups may possibly have been better fed and more stable than the agricultural societies of a later period (Sahlins 1968; *cf.* Hole & Flannery 1963), and the utilization by early human societies of such natural resources as plant foods, are both beginning to be taken into account by archaeologists.

For present purposes we may divide archaeology into theory – the discussion of aims and concepts and their application to the data – and practice – the processing and publication of excavation results and the results of collection. Even where these include deductions that may have considerable theoretical implications, their application is as part of a field report or catalogue. Recent advances in the *practice* of economic and social archaeology have been mainly science-based, and are generally undertaken in the laboratory rather than the field. The laboratory study of biological remains such as animal bones or plant seeds discarded on settlement sites, and their interpretation in economic or ecological terms, has become a considerable industry carried on both by scientists and by specially trained archaeologists. The terms zooarchaeology, palaeoethnobotany and bioarchaeology have been coined to cover some of these developments. One British school in this field, developed by E.S. Higgs at Cambridge, and represented in this volume by contributions from Jarman and Davidson, has sought to produce an overall theory, which they have called palaeoeconomy, based on the study of these biological materials, as seen in relation to the total resources available in the immediate vicinity of the settlement where they were discarded and a *presumed* seasonal pattern of land use.

The physical sciences have also continued to provide mainly economic insights into archaeology. Petrological studies of stone axes and building materials have been supplemented by the newer methods or trace element analysis, based on spectroscopy of neutron activation, and applied to flint and metalwork, pottery, glass, obsidian, faience and amber, mainly to provide evidence of long-distance communications or trading relationships. Many of these studies were first applied in prehistoric studies but today they are common in all fields. Microscopic and photomicrographic studies of archaeological finds form another group of science-derived techniques which are much used in present-day archaelogy. In this field preliminary studies were published by the Russian archaeologist S.A. Semenov in his *Prehistoric Technology* (English edition 1964), a volume illustrating systematic patterns of microscopic scratches on ancient and modern tools of metal, stone and bone, interpreted as marks of wear or damage characteristic of particular uses such as cutting, or chopping down trees. A considerable school of European and North American archaeologists are now engaged in similar attempts to identify the function, or the degree of use of the commoner implements. Photomicrography has meanwhile been applied by Marshack and others to the study of palaeolithic bone engravings and sculpture, especially those pieces with non-figurative schematic decoration which Marshack interprets as calendars. The technique, in this case, depends on the recognition, in the enlarged view of such engravings, of marks left by different engraving tools and on being able to demonstrate by superposition that one set of engraved marks precedes another. Such pieces are termed 'time-structured'.

These archaeological techniques and applications of scientific practice are mentioned here because they seem to bear a direct economic and social message. The same cannot be said of such scientific applications as modern techniques of dating, or methods of identification of settlement sites such as magnetic and aerial surveying. It seems likely that phosphate surveying and other chemical or physical field survey methods could have some economic implications, if they were used to demonstrate a relationship for example between population size and area of disturbance or pollution of an ancient settlement site, but results in this field have so far been disappointing.

Geographical and palaeobotanical studies of the immediate vicinities of ancient settlements are more promising. Site catchment analysis, the term used by Jarman, Vita-Finzi & Higgs (1972) for a local survey of the available natural resources within striking distance of a camp (Leeds 1961, pls 1 and 2, and Clarke 1971, Fig 10, illustrate ethnographic surveys of this sort) should provide a most useful picture of the micro-environment of each human settlement, particularly if it could be given a time dimension by the addition of suitable biological information. Another promising development in this respect has been the palaeobotanical studies of lake margin and similar sites in the vicinity of human settlements (Smith 1970). Studies of the absolute concentration of pollen in the lake sediments can illustrate the *local* vegetation, and the direction from which the pollen has been derived. By this technique, for example, Waterbolk has shown the direction of fields used for certain crops by the inhabitants of one Swiss lake settlement. A more advanced model of the micro-environmental survey involving the use of three-dimensional pollen diagrams illustrates varying forms of exploitation of different parts of the site catchment area at different periods of settlement (Turner 1975). Latterly, further means for estimating the character and extent of site catchment areas have been provided by meteorological techniques for describing local micro-environments (Taylor 1975, also Andrieux 1969 and Legge 1972), and also by studies of the extent of home range measured against body weight among the higher mammals (Milton & May 1976).

The only more recent developments in archaeological field techniques which deserve to be mentioned here concern the collection of unbiassed archaeological samples and the selection of sites for excavation. Various wet sieving and flotation techniques are now being adopted for many types of archaeological excavation, both those where seeds and bones or teeth of voles and other small mammals are to be found, and also as a routine on sites with microlithic flint implements to ensure that the smaller tools are not under-represented. Wet sieving techniques have had considerable success on their first application to Magdalenian sites in France by Bordes and members of his team. The microlithic blade element at one site was increased from 4% to 74% of the industry. Large numbers of salmon bones were also found in a deposit not known to contain them. Wet sieving and flotation techniques have also completely altered the comparative representation of wheat and barley on some early farming settlements in the Near East (Payne 1972) and apparently demonstrated the use of cultivated grain in Mesolithic and even Palaeolithic settlements in Israel (Noy *et al.* 1973). Recent excavations by Kerney and Sieveking at an Ipswichian interglacial site at Northfleet in Kent (England) made use of a flotation 'seed machine' of the type designed by the British Academy Project for the History of Agriculture, and recovered polished bone points only a few centimetres long in an apparently homogenous fine grained clay deposit.

Recent prehistoric excavations have also demonstrated the importance of excavating short term settlement sites. This was already apparent from excavations such as Star Carr, where it was possible to isolate activity areas by patterns of debris characteristic of certain occupations, such as bead manufacture or flint knapping, and where the time control was sufficiently accurate to demonstrate that the site was only occupied for a short period, possibly two or three winters at the most. Leroi-Gourhan's and Brézillon's excavations at the Late Magdalenian hunters' camps at Pincevent in Northern France have been particularly impressive in this respect. At these sites the articulation of the living area can be demonstrated, that is to say the relationship between hearth or fireplace and shelter, between sleeping and working areas and the ways of communication between them, all outlined by the mapping of structures and debris on the largest possible scale. One can see, for example, that the fireplace is typically outside the tent structure at Pincevent, but near the doorway; that the flint knapping is carried out near the fire but only on one side of the fireplace and with the workman's back or side to the fireplace. It is also possible to distinguish fireplaces (either full or empty of ashes) from the heaps of ashes (*vidanges*) removed and parked at a convenient distance from the fire.

The Pincevent publications demonstrate that the best approach to the function of different structures or of different parts of a settlement, or even to population size studies, lies in the careful and minute investigation of settlements occupied for a short period of time, where the repeated activities of one individual in a few hours, or on a small number of separate occasions, as demonstrated by the relationship between debris and structure, are not masked by a uniform cover of discarded remains of the type common in sites occupied for a more prolonged period. Some archaeologists have put their faith in statistical studies of the spatial distribution of implements or debris to produce similar evidence, on sites occupied over a longer period or by a larger population. But activity patterns are likely to vary over time and from season to season, and there is very little evidence so far that nearest neighbour analysis or some similar mathematical technique can produce more than a generalized and unreal picture of activities under these conditions.

Examination of short period occupations is most valuable when settlements are untidy or insanitary and rubbish is left to lie where it fell. Where the beginnings of order and tidiness appear in the archaeological record there is always the chance as at Pompeii that the latest event at any rate will be clearly distinguishable.

It is of course in the interpretation of such short period occupation sites that the value of modern comparative evidence is greatest; the last decade has seen expansion of ethnoarchaeology (Peterson 1971), the study of modern primitive settlements just after they have been abandoned, and while informants are still available; and also experimental archaeology, the reproduction of the techniques of manufacture and ways of life of prehistoric groups. Many of these, like the reproduction of primitive farming methods at Butser, Hampshire (England) or at Lejre in Denmark, are long term experiments, at present inadequately documented. But they have already demonstrated their value for interpretation of existing but fragmentary archaeological evidence.

Economic archaeology is today too well established to require further comment, but in the case of social archaeology we are faced with the uneven application of a number of the newer interpretative models. It is not yet possible to state which of these will prove to be the most valuable and the rules that apply to the study of small isolated settlements of peasants or hunters may meet with indifferent success in an urban situation. Also the boundary between economic and sociological interpretation is one that can shift unexpectedly. In this respect attention should be drawn to the two contributions in this volume from full-time social anthropologists. Blacking provides a model of the evolution of early human or hominid communities derived from the tenets of social anthropology and very different from the severely economic view of the development of the same communities put forward by Isaac in this volume and also in earlier papers.

Bulmer describes a manner of accumulation of animal trophies in present-day New Guinea, which might provide food for thought for those engaged in the interpretation of the animal bone 'food-remains' on prehistoric settlement sites. One is reminded of Fleming's suggestion (1972) that such animals might have been kept as a form of wealth rather than food (*cf.* Paine 1971, Ingold 1974).

One archaeological field in which the fauna is no longer regarded as of economic importance is that of Palaeolithic cave art. Since the publication of Leroi-Gourhan's monumental survey *Préhistoric de l'art occidentale* (1965), the case for regarding the animals painted in the caves as spatially organized and related in some manner has to be accepted. The old idea that the animals were painted on the cave wall one by one on a number of separate occasions without regard for their company has to be abandoned. The suggestion that the purpose of such single representations was to obtain, by sympathetic magic, economic success in hunting similar animals on a number of separate occasions, was in any case unlikely, for the cave sanctuaries were seldom used and the main food animal of the Magdalenian artists, the reindeer, is seldom depicted. Also this model of behaviour would seem to depend on a picture of the ancient hunter's struggle for survival, which is less acceptable since the *Man the Hunter* symposium showed that this was uncharacteristic of any modern hunting economy, and has always been particularly inappropriate in relation to what is known of the stable and well-established economy of the Magdalenians. If we accept that the paintings of animals and other signs found in a cave, or part of a cave, must be related, then they are related structurally, rather than pictorially or visually. They are not meant as scenes. Leroi-Gourhan would regard their structural relationship as mythographic rather than as having a representational purpose, and, when pressed, he has said that Palaeolithic cave art is a symbolic mythogram of the universe. In the context of our discussion it is pleasant to think that the message of cave art is that man does not live by bread alone.

REFERENCES

Andrieux, C. (1969) *Contribution à l'étude du climat des cavités naturelles des massifs Karstiques.* Thèse de Université 1-2 Bordeaux, Parts 1-6 published in *Annales de spéléologie*, 25-7 (1970-2).

Bartholomew, G.A. and Birdsell, J.B. (1953) Ecology and the protohominids. *American Anthropologist*, 55 (2), 481-98.

Binford, L.R. (1968) Post-Pleistocene adaptations. In Binford, S.F. and Binford, L.R. (eds.), *New Perspectives in Archaeology*, 313-41. Chicago.

Birdsell, J.B. (1953) Some environmental and cultural factors influencing the structuring of Australian aboriginal populations. *American Naturalist*, 87 (834), 171-207.

Birdsell, J.B. (1957) Some population problems involving Pleistocene man. *Cold Spring Harbor Symposia in Quantitative Biology*, 22, 47-69.

Birdsell, J.B. (1968) Some predictions for the Pleistocene based upon equilibrium systems among recent hunters. In Lee, R.B. and DeVore, I. (eds.), *Man the Hunter*. Chicago.

Bordes, F. and Fitte, P. (1964) Microlithes du Magdalénien supérieur de la Gare de Couze. In Ripoll-Perelló, E. (ed.), *Miscelenea en Homanaje al abate Henri Breuil*, 1, 259-67.

Bray, W. (1973) The biological basis of culture. In Renfrew, C., (ed.), *The Explanation of Culture Change*, 73-92. London.

Bruce-Mitford, R.L.S. (ed.) (1975) *Recent Archaeological Excavations in Europe*. London.

Chorley, R.J. and Haggatt, P. (eds.) (1967) *Models in Geography*. London.

Chorley, R.J. and Kennedy, B.A. (1971) *Physical Geography: A Systems Approach*. London.

Clark, J.G.D. (1936) *The Mesolithic Settlement of Northern Europe*. Cambridge.

Clark, J.G.D. (1939) *Archaeology and Society*. London.

Clark, J.G.D. (1951) Folk culture and European prehistory. In Grimes, W.F. (ed.), *Aspects of Archaeology in Britain and Beyond*, 49-65. London.

Clark, J.G.D. (1952) *Prehistoric Europe: The Economic Basis*. London.

Clark, J.G.D. (1953) The economic approach to prehistory. *Proceedings of the British Academy*, 39, 215-38.

Clark, J.G.D. (1965) Traffic in stone axes and axe blades. *Economic History Review*, 18, 1-28.

Clark, J.G.D. (1972a) Starr Carr: a case study. *Addison-Wesley Modular Publications in Anthropology*, 10. Reading, Mass.

Clark, J.G.D. (1972b) The archaeology of stone age settlement. *Ulster Journal of Archaeology*, 35, 3-16.

Clark, J.G.D., Walker, D., Godwin, H., Frazer, F.C. and King, J.E. (1954) *Excavations at Star Carr*. Cambridge.

Clarke, D.L. (1972) (ed.), *Models in Archaeology*. London.

Clarke, W.C. (1971) *Place and People: An Ecology of a New Guinean Community*. Berkeley.

Coleman, J. (1964). *Introduction to Mathematical Sociology*. Glencoe, Ill.

Ellison, A. and Harris, J. (1972) Settlement and land use in the prehistory and early history of Southern England: a study based on locational models. In Clarke, D.L. (ed.), *Models in Archaeology*, 911-62. London.

Flannery, K.V., Kirby, A.T.V., Kirkby, M.J. and Williams, A.W. (1967) Farming systems and political growth in ancient Oxaco. *Science*, 158, 445-54.

Fleming, A.M. (1972) The genesis of pastoralism in European prehistory. *World Archaeology*, 4 (2), 179-91.

Fox, C. (1923) *The Archaeology of the Cambridge Region*. Cambridge.

Fox, C. (1932) *The Personality of Britain*. Cardiff.

Haggatt, P. (1965) *Locational Analysis in Human Geography*. London.

Harris, D.R. (1969) Agricultural systems, ecosystems and the origins of agriculture. In Ucko, P.J. and Dimbleby, G.W. (eds.), *The Domestication and Exploitation of Plants and Animals*, 3-15, London.

Harriss, J.C. (1971) Explanation in prehistory. *P.P.S.*, 37 (1), 38-55.

Higgs, E.S. (1972) (ed.) *Papers in Economic Prehistory*. Cambridge.

Higgs, E.S. (1975), (ed.) *Palaeoeconomy*. Cambridge.

Hole, F. (1973) Questions of theory in the explanation of culture change. In Renfrew, C. (ed.), *The Explanation of Culture Change*, 19-34. London.

Hole, F. and Flannery, K. (1963) The prehistory of South-Western Iran: a preliminary report. *P.P.S.*, 33, 201-78.

Hole, F., Flannery, K.V. and Neely, J.A. (1969) Prehistory and human ecology of the Deh Luran plain. *Memoirs Univ. of Michigan, Museum of Anthropology*.

Ingold, T. (1974) On reindeer and men. *Man*, n.s. 9, 523-38.

Jarman, M.R., Vita-Finzi, C. and Higgs, E.S. (1972) Site catchment analysis in archaeology. In Ucko, P.J., Tringham, R. and Dimbleby, G.W. (eds.), *Man, Settlement and Urbanism*, 61-7. London.

Jewell, P.A. (1966) The concept of home range in mammals. *Symposia of the Zoological Society of London*, 18, 85-109.

Lee, R.B. and DeVore, I. (eds.) (1968) *Man the Hunter*. Chicago.

Leeds, A. (1961) Yaruro incipient tropical forest horticulture. In Wilbert, J. (ed.), *The Evolution of Horticultural Systems in Native South America. Antropologia*, Supp. pub. 2, 13-46.

Legge, A.J. (1972) Cave climates. In Higgs, E.S. (ed.), *Papers in Economic Prehistory*, 97-103. Cambridge.

Leroi-Gourhan, A. (1965) *Préhistoire de l'art occidentale*. Paris.

Leroi-Gourhan, A. and Brézillon, M. (1966) L'habitation Magdalénienne No 1 de Pincevent, près Montereau. *Gallia Préhistoire*, 9 (2), 263-385.

Leroi-Gourhan, A. and Brézillon, M. (1972) *Fouilles de Pincevent: Essai d'analyse éthnographique d'un habitat*

Magdalénien (2 vols.), VII Supplement *Gallia Préhistoire*, CNRS, Paris.

Marshack, A. (1972) *The Roots of Civilization*, New York.

Milton, K. and May, M.L. (1976) Body weight, diet and home range area in primates. *Nature*, 259 (Feb. 12, 1976), 459-62.

Minton, R.J.C. (1973) Systems analysis: a comment. In Renfrew, C. (ed.), *The Explanation of Culture Change*, 685-90. London.

Mulvaney, D.J. and Golson, J. (1971) (eds.) *Aboriginal Man and Environment in Australia*. Canberra.

Noy, T., Legge, A.J. and Higgs, E.S. (1973) Recent excavations at Nahal Oren. *P.P.S.*, 39, 100-28.

Paine, R. (1971) Animals as capital: Comparisons among northern nomadic herders and hunters. *Anthropological Quarterly*, 157-72.

Payne, S. (1972) Partial recovery and sample bias: the results of some sieving experiments. In Higgs, E.S. (ed.), *Papers in Economic Prehistory*, 49-64. Cambridge.

Peterson, N. (1971) Open sites and the ethnographic approach to the archaeology of hunter gatherers. In Mulvaney, D.J. and Golson, J. (eds.), *Aboriginal Man and Environment in Australia*, 239-48. Canberra.

Rappaport, R. (1967) *Pigs for the Ancestors: Ritual in the Ecology of a New Guinea People*. New Haven.

Renfrew, J.M. (1973) *Palaeoethnobotany: The Prehistoric Food Plants of the Near East and Europe*. London.

Rowlands, M.J. (1973) Modes of exchange and incentives for trade, with reference to later European prehistory. In Renfrew, C. (ed.), *The Explanation of Culture Change*, 589-600. London.

Rust, A. (1937) *Das altsteinzeitliche rentierjagerlager Meiendorf*. Neumünster.

Rust, A. (1943) *Die alt und mittel steinzeitlichen Funde von Stellmoor*. Neumünster.

Sahlins, M.D. (1968) Notes on the original affluent society. In Lee, R.B. and DeVore, I. (eds.), *Man the Hunter*. Chicago.

Semenov, S.A. (1964) *Prehistoric Technology*, English edition ed. M.W. Thompson. London.

Sherratt, A.G. (1972) Socio-economic and demographic models for the Neolithic and Bronze Ages of Europe. In Clarke, D.L. (ed.), *Models in Archaeology*, 477-542. London.

Smith, A.G. (1970) The influence of mesolithic and neolithic man on British vegetation: a discussion. In Walker, D. and West, R.G. (eds.), *Studies in the Vegetational History of the British Isles*. Cambridge.

Soudsky, B. (1966) *Bylany*. Prague.

Stone, L. (1972) *The Causes of the English Revolution 1529-1642*, London.

Tansley, A.G. (1935) The use and abuse of vegetational concepts and terms. *Ecology*, 16, 284-307.

Taylor, J.A. (1975) The role of climatic factors in environmental and cultural changes in prehistoric times. In Evans, J.G., Limbry, S. and Cleere, H. (eds.), *The Effect of Man on the Landscape: The Highland Zone*, 6-19. London.

Thompson, M.W. (1967) *Novgorod the Great*. New York.

Turner, J. (1975) The evidence for land use by prehistoric farming communties: the use of three dimensional pollen diagrams. In Evans, J.G., Limbry, S. and Cleere, H. (eds.), *The Effect of Man on the Landscape: The Highland Zone*, 74-85. London.

Wood, J.M. and Matson, R.G. (1973) Two models of social cultural systems and their implications for the archaeological study of change. In Renfrew, C. (ed.), *The Explanation of Culture Change*, 672-83. London.

Wynn-Edwards, V.C. (1962) *Animal Dispersion in Relation to Social Behaviour*. Edinburgh.

Yellen, J. and Harpending, H. (1972) Hunter-gatherer populations and archaeological inference. *World Archaeology*, 4 (2), 244-53.

PART I

Africa

JOHN BLACKING

Dance, conceptual thought and production in the archaeological record

When I was a student attending Professor Clark's courses in prehistory and early civilizations, there was a joke that recurred whenever we speculated about the uses of artefacts or prepared for practical examinations. Someone would suggest that hand-axes were cult objects or advise his fellow candidates, 'If you don't know what it is, say it's a cult object'.

At that time, I was much attracted by Grahame Clark's evolutionary approach and his emphasis on the evidence of economic life, though puzzled by his criticisms of Gordon Childe, who seemed to me to take a similar view. I found the archaeological concept of a culture more precise and manageable than the anthropological, and on the basis of my experience with the Sakai in the forests of Malaysia and my possession of a stone axe from New Caledonia, I argued that hand-axes had been hafted for practical, economic purposes, that the round ends and not the points were more often used as working edges, and that wooden tools may have been more important in the economy of Palaeolithic hunter-gatherers than the stone artefacts that survive.

Now, twenty-one years later, as a result of anthropological field-work and some experience of the variety and complexity of non-material culture, I am more interested in the forms than in the possible functions of stone tools. We shall never know which were cult objects and which were tools, but in this paper I want to suggest that many early stone artefacts were the consequences of cults or, at least, of behaviour that we associate with cults; and that this kind of behaviour distinguishes man from other primates and has motivated human social and economic developments. I am concerned with a process that could have once generated, and may continue to generate, conceptual thought and the production of artefacts. There is some evidence for it in the archaeological record, but conclusive proof is unlikely to be found; and observations of its operation in contemporary societies are inevitably qualified both by the passing of time and of different species of *Homo* since the Lower Pleistocene, and by the distortions of a biosocial process that different cultures may make. Nevertheless, application of the theory might shed some new light on archaeological evidence, since it explains some aspects of motivation and technological change in terms of corporate experience and discovery rather than purposeful invention and the satisfaction of economic needs.

The problem posed by a new tool or technique or invention is essentially a problem of design: where to begin and where to end; how long, how wide, how short, and so on. It is a problem of capturing the force of an idea or discovery with form. The most striking feature of early stone artefacts is their form, rather than their function. More remarkable than the fact that a creature could use a tool to make a tool, is the evidence of systematic, repeated body movements in space and time and a continuity of style that implies a common culture. Whatever their social and economic functions may have been, their manufacture presupposes a sense of order that may be called artistic or aesthetic.

The earliest evidence of human cultures, and most of the archaeological record until the advanced Palaeolithic, is dominated by artefacts that appear to have been used for subsistence, and so it is not surprising that most writers see cultural evolution motivated by the desire to promote security, physical comfort and the chances of survival, by improving techniques of food-gathering and hunting. The satisfaction of economic needs is therefore said to have been the chief concern of the earliest men, and other, 'higher' considerations assumed importance in human life only after the emergence of *Homo sapiens* or even later.

Now, supposing that all the earliest stone

artefacts were made and used for subsistence, I can see no reason why men should have needed them, or perceived a need for them, unless they had already developed creative and social capacities that surpassed the basic requirements of ecological adaptation. The appearance of cultures of stone tools is the product of a process that must include a development of collective consciousness and of aesthetic awareness sufficient to generate sustained conceptual thought. It is surely consistent with the laws of evolution that pre-human creatures did not *need* tools, kinship, co-operation in production, or even language. They were presumably as well-equipped for survival as any other animal, and so utilitarian explanations of the evolution of peculiarly human practices fail to account for the factor of motivation. The problem begins to resolve if we consider these features of human life, not as necessities but first as luxuries that were generated by more essential conditions of human existence. Later, because of population growth and competition for scarce resources in certain parts of the world, the cultural luxuries of technology became primary necessities, and the biological necessities of artistic experience and generalized social interaction were classed as cultural luxuries. To paraphrase Emile Durkheim, societies that were, biologically, systems of active forces became nominal beings created by reason, and natural bonds, between men who communicated in face-to-face relationships, developed into cultural bonds, generated by developments in technology and increases in the division of labour.

Although all known systems of gift-exchange are cultural, and although the principle 'that it is more blessed to give than to receive' can be seen as a rational mechanism for buying future security or bidding for political power with an economic surplus, there is much evidence to support the basic argument of Malinowski's *Argonauts of the Western Pacific* (which Frazer applauded) that purely economic motivation does not adequately explain human economic behaviour. Without further discussion of Mauss's *The Gift* or Lévi-Strauss's arguments about the humanizing consequences of the exchange of women, we may accept the principle of reciprocity, of altruistic exchange, as a characteristic of the human species, a rudimentary form of communication. This may account for the social conditions necessary for the conceptual thought that generates technological invention, and it may explain why purely economic motivation is not necessary, but it does not account for the mental conditions that must certainly have preceded the manufacture of core tools and, probably, of earlier pebble tools.

Emile Durkheim argued that conceptual thought is derived from a process that may be called religious, and he believed that it was not necessary to place man's distinctive attributes beyond social experience: the concept of time, for example, arose from awareness of the intervals marked by communal festivals. In this he questioned Kant's statement that although there 'can be no doubt that all our knowledge begins with experience . . . it does not follow that it all arises out of experience'. He has been criticized for going 'too far, since the operations of the mind and the laws of logic are not determined by, or given in, experience, even in social experience' (Lukes 1973:447).

Lévi-Strauss (1969a:170) has refuted Durkheim's claims to derive categories and abstract ideas from the social order, on the grounds that the most elementary social life 'presupposes an intellectual activity in man of which the formal properties . . . cannot be a reflexion of the concrete organization of the society'. It is true that the very phrase 'communal festivals', as we are accustomed to think of it, presupposes some thinking and communication (probably in language) about social and religious organization. But can we not envisage 'communal festivals' as times of intense social interaction in which dancing and music, and perhaps other artistic activities such as body-painting, were the only forms of communication?

The performance of ritual by specific social groups presupposes the development of concepts and of groups in conscious association, as Lévi-Strauss rightly argues. But Durkheim's theory suggests that rituals, whose content and context are not consciously organized, may generate both categories of thought and conceptualized social groups; it allows for a distinction between a *generalized communion* and *particular communities* of beings. The operations of the mind and the laws of logic are not revealed until a special kind of social interaction transforms a generalized communion of men into a particular community of men. The formal properties of man's intellectual activity are brought out by *rhythms* of social interaction. In order to emphasize the non-intellectual basis of conceptual thought, I would prefer to call the first kind of association *generalized sensori-motor communion.* In another context, Lévi-Strauss (1969b:18) has said that music may hold the key to the progress of the Science of Man; I agree with his claim, though not for the reasons that he gives (Blacking 1974), and I hope to show why music (which begins with dancing) provides an explanatory model of the process of transformation from sensori-motor communion to conceptual thought, and also throws light on the origin of man.

Underlying my discussion is the assumption that human behaviour is an extension of capabilities that are already in the human body, and that the forms and content of these extensions are generated by interaction between bodies in the context of different environments. Since the interaction of human bodies provides the model for human behaviour, we must know what are the distinctive features of the human body and of relationships between man and fellow man. The behaviour that ethologists, primatologists, anthropologists and sociologists describe in their studies of living species must have a genetic base in the species whose bodies and social activities are known only from fragmentary evidence in the archaeological record. Inevitably, there is some discontinuity between interpretations of the skeletal evidence of the bodies and of the material evidence of their social interaction that is expressed in cultural traditions. Some of these gaps in the interpretation of the past can, I believe, be partly bridged if more attention is given to cultures as products of the interaction of bodies, and to the bodily movements in time and space that may have been required to produce the material evidence. Ethnomusicology is a branch of social anthropology whose chief area of study is the expressive, social movement of bodies in time and space. Its evidence of the forms and functions of music and dance in different cultures can throw considerable light on relationships between man's biological evolution and cultural development.

The conditions of musical development in contemporary *Homo sapiens sapiens* can provide little information about its role in biological evolution because the current supremacy of language as a form of communication and the unequal uses of music in different societies mask its universal qualities. However, I have suggested that the capabilities necessary for dancing and music are species-specific, and that their gradual emergence may be maturationally controlled, like the onset of speech (see Blacking 1971a; 1973). The varied ages at which musical ability may be manifested within a single society and in different societies, and the many cases of its apparent absence in individuals, do not necessarily contradict this argument: in some cultures, early musical expression may be 'suppressed' altogether, while in others it may emerge uniformly at an early age or sporadically at different ages, depending on the role of music in social life. Besides, as in the case of language, the comprehension of musical structures seems to precede the capacity to produce them. To what extent capabilities for music and dancing are separate and independent of other articulatory skills and motor processes, as the development of language seems to be, and whether or not 'important . . . milestones are reached in a fixed sequence and at a relatively constant chronological age' (Lenneberg 1967:127), remain open questions. Even if there is a maturational sequence of 'musical' capacities that can be related to the development of language or conceptual thought, it will neither confirm nor contradict any theory about the historical evolutionary order of emergence of music and language. The course of ontogenetic development in modern man is not necessarily a record of the species' evolution: for example, it is almost certain that prehistoric species of men who had no language were able to perform basic motor co-ordination patterns that today emerge in children long after many stages of language-acquisition have been passed.

Studies of patterns of co-operation, play and gestural communication in primates and the 'dances' and 'songs' of birds and other animals, suggest all kinds of antecedents for ritual in man. But man is unique in that he combines so many of these forms of behaviour that are found independently amongst different species, and organizes his social interaction into cycles of corporate and sporadic movement, music and non-music, greater or lesser social intensity, 'sacred' and 'profane', and so on. Other animals use, and even make, tools; but man's tools, at least from Acheulean times onwards, reflect concentration, a feeling for form and a systematic pattern of execution. The chimpanzees Washoe and Sarah have learnt to communicate with their human teachers, but their efforts are qualitatively far removed even from man's most rudimentary use of language (Ploog & Melnechuk 1971).

Since the size of human brains is not an accurate indication of performance, and the brains of Neanderthal and Cro-Magnon men seem to have been as large as those of modern men, we cannot argue that man's distinctive anatomical feature is the chief cause of his uniqueness, although it is largely responsible for the differences between his linguistic competence and that of chimpanzees. The development of the human brain can be seen as an anatomical product, through natural selection, of behavioural processes by which man gradually made himself different from his fellow primates. On the basis of the theory that the hand drives the brain, it has been argued that in human evolution the need to make better tools hastened the emergence of modern man. I propose that technological 'improvements' were motivated not by economic need so much as by man's pleasure in his own physical 'skills', an essentially sensuous aesthetic experience, and in his association with others. Moreover, the evolution of the hand *and* changes in the manufacture of tools are surely better understood as products of the evolution of the whole body, which I maintain is a consequence of the emergence of new kinds of physical relationships between bodies, similar to the ritual behaviour of animals.

Sooner or later, all discussions of the origin of man come up against the crucial issue of a qualitative difference between man and non-human primates. Whatever this difference is, it must exist in the body of man and it must have been present at the time when a distinctly human species began to evolve. This rules out tool-making, which is not a purely human activity and exists outside the body. Moreover, since the human course was already set before the appearance of *Homo sapiens sapiens* and the evolution of language, I suggest that neither the exercise of reason nor language are basic to man's humanity. I believe that the most quintessentially human characteristic of man's behaviour should be that in which he is both most like an animal and least like an animal. In other words, it is behaviour that allows him to be either closest to the animals as an organism reacting to the forces of nature, or furthest from the animals by the exercise of a will that can transcend nature. The organized movement of human bodies, a generalized kind of ritual behaviour, is the only human activity that can be said to extend from unconscious bodily resonance with the environment to a conscious rejection of the world of nature in the stillness of prayer or meditation, or simply non-movement.

The theory that I am advancing hinges on the hypothesis that there is a relationship between movement and thought, and in particular between communal movement and conceptual thought. We know that conceptual thought does not depend on language, and that man possesses many effective pre-linguistic modes of communication, ranging from visible body language to possibly telepathy. We know also that language is not learned in an arbitrary fashion by stimulus-response training, but that it is one of many capabilities present in every normal human body (Lenneberg 1967). Whether or not man's capacity to think evolved before language, it requires similar conditions of social interaction to emerge and develop. Conceptual thought and language are based on innate mechanisms for the discrimination of categories and for transformation, which are modified and extended through experience of different patterns of social interaction.

Man's thought is profoundly affected by his experience of other people. Thinking conceptually is not simply isolating and grouping together the common characteristics of a certain number of objects; it is relating the variable to the permanent, and seeing patterns in life that transcend individual sensations. If we can understand how private sensations are transformed into concepts, which by definition must be shared and sharable, we may know how evolutionary animal instincts are extended into the conscious human strategies that are the basis of cultural 'evolution'. Durkheim suggested that private sensations can be transformed into concepts, and a more permanent pattern in life can be perceived, when men contrast their experience of periods of intense and sporadic social interaction. I would suggest that periods of intense social interaction are most deeply experienced, and most likely to generate conceptual thought, when inner feelings are publicly shared through a counterpoint of body movement.

This hypothesis can be tested in contemporary societies. Firstly, the patterns of movement and sound that people share in dance and music are expressions of conceptual thought. But the processes of thinking and creating are not always consciously worked out: they may themselves be the unconscious reflections of expressive communal movement (see Blacking 1973: Ch. 3). Secondly, experiments in group movement and in the uses of dance and music in therapy or in education, may show how and when the relationship works: for instance, when the somatic state of *generalized sensori-motor communion* is achieved by a group of people, a pattern of movement may emerge, whose form should be affected by the differences in the numbers involved; if the corporate movement generates a single collective thought, we may have something like the situation that Durkheim envisaged. I am simply proposing the corollary of what many teachers of dance or gymnastics reiterate: if 'the movement is in your thinking', I suggest also that the thinking may come from the movement. And just as the ultimate aim of dancing is to be able to move *without* thinking, to *be* danced, so I suggest that the ultimate aim of thinking is to be moved to think, to *be* thought. It is sometimes called inspiration, insight, genius, creativity and so on. But essentially it is a form of unconscious cerebration that is most evident in artistic creation: it is a movement of the body; we are moved into thinking.

Besides developing co-operation, communal dancing may also encourage restraint and the ability to attend to a single task, which are unique capacities of man amongst primates. The very repetition of movements may improve the memory, provide a base for productive thinking, and promote learning in the organism by prolonging the inhibitory actions that block unnecessary pathways (Young 1971:621).

Communal dancing could be described as a form of play that is more positively adaptive than any observed amongst non-human primates: in addition to 'motivation for exploration' and a 'context for learning locomotor and manipulative skills' (Dolhinow & Bishop 1971:193), dancing requires a much higher degree of social interaction and inter-personal co-ordination than play, and therefore 'selects' for the maximum of co-operative behaviour. 'It is possible to imagine that those groups of early men in which individuals were united by common ceremonies, and enjoyed satisfying rhythmic experiences, whether of visual pattern or dance, would have been more coherent and successful than less "cultured" neighbours' (Young 1971:523).

Writing has been described as an extra-somatic information store that accelerated the rate of evolutionary change (Young 1971:516). Communal dancing or music could be described similarly as the earliest 'substitute for a function that was previously performed in the body . . . by the chromosomes of the germ cells'. Similarly, Malinowski pointed out that the poetry of Trobriand spells made them easier to remember as collections of technological instructions. Edward de Bono has argued that the 'special memory-surface' of the brain resides in a body which 'needs certain things for its survival. It is a matter of reactions to the environment and needs from the environment. The reactions, such as pain, are internal responses to an external event. The needs, such as hunger, are internal events that require an external response' (De Bono 1969:130). It is often necessary for survival that the memory-surface should react immediately to external information, but in terms of maximizing information it may be limiting. Creative thinking requires that the memory-surface should deal with information for its own sake, freed from the immediate requirements of the environment. A shared experience in dancing can produce the necessary detachment from external stimuli, as well as enhance the other essential factor in creative thinking, reciprocal social interaction (Wertheimer 1945).

The idea of dance as a uniquely human shared experience that adds a new dimension to social co-operation and generates new forms of energy was forced on me by experiences of dance and music in African societies, as well as by my own experiences as a music-maker; it was further reinforced by reports of musical experience in Sri Lanka, India, Bali and many other cultures, and by the testimonies of European composers and performers. Aspects of the theory have often been discussed both in Hindu cosmogony and mythology, in Greek philosophy, and in *The New Science* of Giambattista Vico, as well as in such modern classics as John Dewey's *Art as Experience*. Most recently, in a biology textbook, *An Introduction to the Study of Man* (1971:520-1), Professor J.Z. Young has written:

> The very slow changes in methods of flint chipping may have contained the first elements of creative art. To make something for future use already argues a capacity for abstraction from the present. To make it so that it is sharper or otherwise does its job better than before is creative even if not 'artistic'. To chip it in such a way that

it shows patterns of symmetry or rhythm may make it a pleasure to see, to hold, and to use, and the result may therefore be *more practical because it is more 'beautiful'*. (Italics in original)

. . . there may have been rhythmical dances before religion, and simple language before that, all of which left no enduring remains.

Because I accept Professor Young's suggestions about the priority of aesthetic experience and of generalized dance, I question his assumption that thought for the future and simple language were their precursors. I argue that the thought and the simple language arise from the making and the doing, that they are not so much purposeful, immediately utilitarian inventions as the evolutionary consequences of a gradual discovery of individuality in community (Blacking 1969b:3-5). Human reason and the development of conceptual thought are the consequences of discoveries in the fields of sensory awareness and social interaction that were made corporately, and these discoveries were achieved through the mediation of a special kind of *sensori-motor communion* amongst men which generated, and generates, new forms of communication by dividing space and time into contrasting sequences of social experience. It is this co-ordination between man and time in space that distinguishes music from non-music in many cultures. For instance, 'in the musical system of the Venda, it is rhythm that distinguishes song (*u imba*) from speech (*u amba*), so that patterns of words that are recited to a regular meter are called "songs" . . . Venda music is founded not on melody, but on a rhythmical stirring of the whole body of which singing is but one extension' (Blacking 1973:27). Furthermore, the ultimate aim of much music-making, apart from its immediate use to enhance some cultural institution, is to re-create in men the shared experience of *sensori-motor communion* on which specifically human achievements seem to depend (*ibid.*:51-2).

Once again, I find myself broadly in agreement with Professor Young:

There is no body of facts that yet enables us to understand the origins of aesthetic creation or religious beliefs and practices. Presumably both sorts of activity were somehow of assistance to Palaeolithic man in the business of getting a living. This does not mean that carving, or painting, or offering prayers for the dead were crudely of 'practical' value, for instance, by improving hunting technique. Yet there is a case for saying that creation of new aesthetic forms, including those of worship, has been the most fundamentally productive of all forms of human activity. Whoever creates new artistic conventions has found methods of interchange between people about matters that were incommunicable before. The capacity to do this has been the basis of the whole of human history. (Young 1971:519)

The absence of appropriate archaeological evidence before the Upper Pleistocene does not give us a date for the origins of aesthetic creation and religious beliefs and practices, just as the frequency or absence of musical instruments may bear no relation to the amount of music that is made in a society. Moreover, little or no material evidence of the complex musical and religious life of a society like, say, the Aranda would survive in deposits. The appearance of religion and art in the archaeological record surely represents the externalization of behaviour that had hitherto been shared between organisms with, perhaps, the addition of perishable skin or wooden objects and cosmetics (I am sure that red ochre was used to paint the living body long before it was used for the dead). I disagree with Professor Young's timing of events for the same reason as in the earlier quotation: if the capacity to create new aesthetic forms has been the basis of human history, why should it not also have been the basis of human prehistory? If the crucial developments that marked the origins of man were purely practical and concerned with the business of getting a living, why should the course of human history suddenly undergo a radical qualitative change? – unless, of course, it is claimed that *Homo sapiens* has only cultural, but not close genetic, links with *Australopithecus* and *Homo erectus*.

It is precisely because the creation of aesthetic forms has been such a productive human activity, and because this capability is so dramatically externalized with the appearance of *Homo sapiens*, that it could well be the kind of social behaviour that has enabled man to 'make himself' biologically into *Homo sapiens*, as well as to produce external manifestations in the forms of concepts, artefacts and language. Although Professor Young talks of aesthetic creation in terms of individuals ('Whoever creates new artistic conventions has found . . .'), I suggest that in man it is basically a form of *social* behaviour, an expression of *collective* consciousness that is radically different from the aesthetic appreciation and self-expressive artistic behaviour of apes and monkeys (see, for instance, Morris 1962). If some art in modern industrial societies seems to be primarily a matter of self-expression, this is probably an artificial consequence of the division of labour and the role of art in society, rather than a faithful representation of the artistic nature of the human species. Moreover, some of the earliest examples of man's cultural, and hence collective, conventions are also evidence of his aesthetic expression. If Oldowan choppers and Chellean hand-axes are not qualitatively different from the tools of non-human primates, there is little doubt that Acheulean hand-axes are aesthetic forms as well as practical tools, and that they presuppose regular, rhythmical movements of the body as well as manual dexterity. This point has been noted by Robert Ascher, who has suggested that if the earliest stone implements at Olduvai are tools, they are not as significantly human as those in Acheulean times. He suggests 'that there may be something in the organization of the brain or in the way the brain organizes the outside world that makes certain shapes and forms more pleasing than others' (DeVore 1965:115). Perhaps the symmetry and rhythm expressed in early stone implements is not merely an optional, 'artistic' extra: it could be the first evidence of the essential human dimension, which depended on new forms of bodily interaction.

One can speculate on the origins of such forms in grooming practices; in increased contact between mothers and children; in pair-bonding and protracted, face-to-face confrontations in sexual intercourse; or in play. I am concerned here only with the possible effects on the body, and particularly the brain, of a kind of behaviour that would have been easy to learn and pleasurable to the individuals concerned, and would have become a fundamental adaptive mechanism because of its benefits for social life (*cf.* Washburn 1968:22). Available skeletal evidence suggests that the Australopithecine gait was more a run than a walk, and that the hand and the foot became human before the brain. The regularity and rhythmic requirements of communal 'dancing' would have assisted changes in motor behaviour from sporadic, short runs to a steady, walking stride. It is even possible that the rings of stones at Bed I at Olduvai and some Acheulean sites could have been the remains of dancing grounds: in Africa, I have seen rings of stones both where an area has been cleared for dancing and where stones have been brought and left as a sign of the numbers of people attending a ritual.

Hitherto, I have referred loosely to the uniquely human factor as cult, sensori-motor communion, communal dancing, music or ritual behaviour. It will be necessary to clarify the concept and to provide terms that will not create undue confusion with existing concepts. As a form of animal behaviour, it may first be considered as ritual behaviour.

If the ritual behaviour of an animal species is adaptive, it should be adaptive for the whole species and therefore be practised at some time or another by every member. This does not mean that all members of a species who are gathered together must necessarily carry out the species' ritual behaviour at the same time. Amongst most non-human animals, ritual behaviour is not generally performed by all members present on a particular occasion, but those who abstain are not adversely affected. Now it seems that there is, and has been, much human ritual behaviour (of which warfare is a classic example) that is not performed by all members of the species and cannot be described as adaptive for the species as a whole. I suggest that a more inclusive kind of participation is required for any human ritual behaviour that is to be described as adaptive. Exclusive rituals may seem to confer survival benefits on certain groups, but in the long run they are as disadvantageous to the exclusive group as to those who were excluded.

The kind of ritual behaviour that I believe is peculiar to the human species is more than an extension of the work routines of insects, the formal interaction of non-human primates, the displays of birds, or the mating dances that bond some animal pairs. It is basically a form of communion whose adaptive function is to generate greater sensory awareness and social co-operation: the sharper experience of individual consciousness that is felt in the context of collective ritual reinforces the co-operative conditions required for the experience.

Because we do not know how animals feel, we cannot say whether the content of human experiences of ritual interaction is qualitatively greater than the experiences of other animals, except in so far as the complex human brain and encephalated nervous system are likely to be more receptive to environmental stimuli and so to create greater sensory tensions in the body. But we can say that there is an important difference in the forms of adaptive ritual behaviour in man and other animals. It seems that in animals adaptive ritual behaviour is specialized and maturational, whereas in man it is generalized and situational. That is, the species-specific, and hence adaptive, ritual behaviour of man, as distinct from the ritualistic behaviour of some men, must co-ordinate in time all men who happen to be within an immediately observable and/or ultimately conceivable space (thus including the physical absence of other known people, alive or dead). Experiences in time and space are therefore externalized in an *externally* given situation, so that theoretically any number of members of the human species can interact ritually at any time of life. For most animal rituals, the choice of time and place seems to depend on *internal* factors such as the stages of maturation of those involved.

There is, of course, much human ritual that, like animal ritual, is restricted to certain members of the species at certain times of life, and it may be adaptive in the context of different cultures. But, as Van Gennep (1960:65ff.) and others have observed, the time of performance of a ritual may transcend the time of the maturational event that it celebrates (see also Blacking 1969b: 4-5), and distinctions between rites that all members of the society undergo at some time or another and those that affect only some members, are generally functions of class divisions within the society. Even in societies where 'animal-like', maturational rituals are performed by all members, the most highly valued ritual of all is invariably a 'human-type', situational ritual, in which all available people participate together in time and space. As Radcliffe-Brown implied, in developing Durkheim's theory in *The Andaman Islanders* (1922) and subsequent papers on ritual, the maturational rituals presuppose a more general situational ritual. They are not so much rationalizations of innate maturational processes, as subdivisions of a conceptualization of general, situational ritual behaviour. But although they may be associated with biological events in the life-cycle of the organism, they are not necessarily biologically adaptive, because the culture within which they are conceptualized may not be adaptive. They are therefore only culturally adaptive within the limits of particular cultures. This is an aspect of Durkheim's theory that Radcliffe-Brown did not pursue: he gave the nominal solidarity of a particular culture the same value as the biological solidarity of which Durkheim wrote. I would argue that social solidarity that might seem adaptive in the context of a particular culture could be biologically non-adaptive, owing to 'faulty' rationalizations of biosocial forces, and that this conflict between real and rationalized solidarity would be a force for change. It is in order to distinguish between generalized biologically adaptive ritual behaviour and ritual behaviour in the context of particular cultures that I describe human ritual behaviour as 'situational' rather than cultural. This obviates Lévi-Strauss's complaint, namely that Durkheim's 'religious situation' presupposes existence of the very concepts that he claimed it generated.

I realize that the terms 'maturational' and 'situational' are not strictly accurate as distinctions between non-human and human ritual behaviour, especially in primates. There is, of course, a sense in which all ritual behaviour is situational. But I want to highlight my proposal that the basic biological form of human ritual behaviour is a special kind of communion between fellow men that may take place anywhere at any time of life, and that must incorporate all available organisms. There are many modern attempts to replicate this primordial human situation, but they are partially restricted by the specialized recruitment of participants. I refer to events such as a celebration of Mass, a symphony concert, a Pop festival, or a Quaker meeting. I have shared experiences in Africa that may be more truly adaptive than their European counterparts, such as a Venda *tshikona* (Blacking 1971b:65-71) or a meeting of the Nazarites on the Holy Mountain of Nhlangakazi (Sundkler 1961:110-11).

Having used the term 'ritual behaviour' in order to contrast certain behavioural traits in man and animals, I shall now propose new terms that avoid some of the cultural connotations associated with words such as 'cult', 'ritual' and 'play'. 'Dance' is a less functional term that I have already used to describe a uniquely human process, but distinctions must be drawn between: dance as we know it in contemporary societies; dance as it may have been in societies before the evolution of language, *Homo sapiens*, and perhaps even tool-making; and dance as a species-specific characteristic of man. The last type might be called biological dance or bio-dance, to emphasize that it is generated by innate mechanisms; but these terms would not distinguish it from individual expressions of feeling in man and animals. Because it is a special form of social co-operation generated by sensori-motor communion, I call it *biosocial dance*.

Because the patterns of movement of biosocial dance reflect the shared somatic states of bodies in communion at a particular point in time and space, it follows that no two biosocial dances can ever be exactly the same. However, as I have already argued, certain patterns of movement may have become 'fixed' in man's earliest biosocial dances and have been replicated on more than one occasion. When in human history patterns of movement were first shared on a number of occasions, there emerged what I call *proto-dance* and *proto-music*.

Obviously we can never know exactly what forms proto-dance and proto-music took, because they were created by species less evolved than *Homo sapiens sapiens*. But I would argue that many movements that are now accepted as characteristics of the species, such as walking, were originally proto-dance; that many of the 'pure' movements of proto-dance developed into 'applied' rituals or routines, such as the manufacture of Acheulean hand-axes; and that proto-dance and proto-music played a crucial role in refining man's bodily control and range of perceptual discrimination, and in extending his sensibility, gentleness and the quality of his social relationships.

Finally, as language evolved and *Homo sapiens sapiens* became established in the world, there emerged culturally defined areas of *dance* and *music*, which in many societies are inseparable, and whose main purpose is suggested to be the attainment of the somatic state of sensori-motor communion that generates biosocial dance.

If 'through the feedback relation between behaviour and biology the human gene pool is the result of the behaviour of times past' (Washburn 1968:25), and 'the large size of the brain of certain hominids was a relatively late development due to new selection pressures *after* bipedalism and consequent upon the use of tools' (Washburn & Howell 1960:49ff.), bio-social dance, proto-dance, and possibly proto-music, may have played a crucial role in the evolution of a larger human brain. If 'the uniqueness of modern man is .... the result of a technical-social life which tripled the size of the brain, reduced the face, and modified many other structures of the body' (*ibid.*), it may also be argued that the technical-social life was founded on refinements of sensori-motor capacities as much as on the development of a hunting way of life. The nature of hunting is such that it lacks a routine: the repetitive element in proto-dance could have promoted speculation and strategy in stalking. Efficient hunting presupposes the capacity to relate remembered events systematically.

If we regard conceptual thought and language, technological skill and human intelligence as not in themselves peculiarly human processes, but the products of more fundamental processes by which early hominids set themselves apart from other primates, I believe we have a better framework for understanding the discrepancy between the very slow rate of technological development and the comparatively rapid rate of biological evolution during the Lower Pleistocene. Assuming that the life of early hunter-gatherers was comparatively affluent (Lee & DeVore 1968:85-9, 311-13), their most peculiarly human concern would have been 'sensori-motor communion'. Through biosocial dance they could have developed a variety of proto-dance and proto-music systems that would have extended their powers of sensori-motor discrimination and the quality of their social relationships: systems such as dance, song (without words), tool-making, and gestural communication, as well as the crystallization of these systems in conceptual thought.

In discussing the gestural origin of language, Hewes (1973:11) has argued that 'the ability to acquire propositional language based on gesture is not only an older innate character of man, but one which is shared, in rudimentary form at least, with the Pongidae. Manual communication may thus come closer to representing the deep cognitive structure on which not only language but all of our intellectual and technological achievements rest'. I would add the rider that extensive manual communication probably developed from proto-dance and that gesture would have first acquired socially accepted meanings not as group signals, but as shared emotions. Lenneberg has pointed out that communication and the exchange of information are by-products of language, that language knowledge is the capacity to relate in specified ways (Ploog & Melnechuk 1971:635), and that the important quality is to be able to 'analyse novel utterances through the application of structural principles' (Lenneberg 1967:330). It is precisely these features of language that almost certainly would have been promoted by the experience of social relationships and structural regularities in the repeated movements of proto-dance.

Just as proto-dance probably played an important role in the development of the visual-gestural channels of communication, so proto-music may have affected the vocal-auditory channels. In contemporary *Homo sapiens sapiens*, songs without words may emerge as part of the movements of biosocial dance, and there is evidence that song is an extension of dance that enhances emotional expression. It may be said that such vocal activities are, like glossolalia, a consequence of the possession of language rather than a prelude to it, and that the performance of modern man cannot provide evidence of a process in his biological evolution. But Livingstone (1973:25) has recently drawn attention to the fact that 'singing is a simpler system than speech, with only pitch as a distinguishing feature', and has suggested 'that man could sing long before he could talk and that singing was in fact a prerequisite to speech and hence language'.

It is not yet known precisely what capabilities are required for competence in dance and music, whether or not they are centred in certain parts of the brain, and how they are related to other functions of the brain. Language disorders due to lesions in the frontal lobe in Broca's area do not necessarily prevent an aphasic from singing 'a melody correctly and even elegantly' (Geschwind 1970:941); and lesions that isolated the speech area of one patient did not prevent her from learning both the words and melodies of new songs (*ibid.*: 943).

An enormous amount of research remains to be done on the physiology of music and dance. It has probably been inhibited by the notion that music is a kind of game, with arbitrary rules, that is to be played by 'musical' people, rather than an area of human behaviour based on species-specific capabilities.

It is worth considering whether the theory can be of any use in interpreting archaeological evidence, especially if there is nothing to show for the practice of dancing and music. Whether or not its evolutionary aspect can be proved correct, there is little doubt about the close relationship between processes of body movement and thought and their material products. In other fields, skeuomorphs provide abundant evidence of the continuity of forms, and of their slow rate of adaptation to the full possibilities of the new medium. We need to give equal consideration to skeuomorphic *processes*. For example, archaeology provides evidence of the close relationship between basketry and early pottery, both in form and in function. But as movements of the body and of the mind, there is a great difference between making a basket and moulding a pot. (This may be reflected even in the sound of words that signify the processes, such as *-luka* (plait, make a basket) and *-vhumba* (mould, make a pot) in Venda, as well as in concepts associated with them: metaphors of creation and installation are derived from the pottery process, but not from basketry.) The feel of a polished stone axe in the hand, or the experience of modelling a figurine in clay, are closer to the experience of pot-making than any technique of basketry, and even the aesthetic function of a figurine may be tactile rather than visual: Eskimo sculptures are made to be felt as much as seen. Again the shapes of objects may reflect social processes and the movements and postures associated with them: changes in the style of school and university furniture during the past 100 years tell us much about the social structure and values of these institutions: and even though some actors may choose to loll and lounge on thrones or sedilia, there is a close relationship between erect bodily posture, patterns of authority, and the forms of the trappings of authority.

Thus, careful analyses of the body movements related to the manufacture or uses of an object may contribute to our understanding of the social and mental processes of different cultures. Even when only the artefacts are available and they may not have been retrieved from the places where they were made, it should be possible to derive from them some idea of the sequences of *total* body movement involved in their manufacture. It is not enough to consider how the hands and arms were moved when making stone implements, since they are only parts of the whole body, whose shape and sensori-motor apparatus are affected by relationships with other bodies and the space of the environment. Again, studies in kinesics, proxemics, personal space and 'interaction ritual' tend to concentrate on the face-to-face relationships of individuals, thus presupposing the evolution of individuality in community that is a distinctive characteristic of human societies. Such refinements of interpersonal emotional expression, however, presuppose the more generalized capability for sensori-motor communion and its realization and development in the shared experience of dance.

When dance is understood as a uniquely human form of social behaviour that extends from the proto-dance of the Lower Pleistocene to all contemporary forms of dancing, includes rituals and routines of body movement, and derives from the species-specific capability that I call biosocial dance, it is possible to regard developments in thought, technology and economic life as products of more fundamental forms of human co-operation, and to say that the basic incentive to co-operation in production is not a negative fear of extinction combined with a rational decision to solve a problem, but a positive desire to extend and express the body in time and space and to share the experience mutually and equitably with other beings. In other words, the need to be human is no less a force in human evolution than the avoidance of hunger and discomfort: it is the source of the human energy with which man has harnessed all other forms of energy; and the mechanism by which it may have been achieved, and must therefore be replenished, was a special kind of situational behaviour that made possible more intense, but at the same time more general, relationships between organisms. Since its most important characteristic is the creation of social energy and the means must be present in the body, it follows that the basic transformation process must be a fusion of bodies that transcends the sexual and can be extended to any number of human bodies at any time. I cannot think of any way in which this might have been achieved except through the evolution of some kind of ritual behaviour which, since it is a formal, communal movement of bodies, is best called dance.

REFERENCES

Blacking, J. (1969a) *Process and Product in Human Society*. Johannesburg.

Blacking, J. (1969b) Songs, dances, mimes and symbolism of Venda girls' initiation schools. *African Studies*, 28, 3-35.

Blacking, J. (1971a) Towards a Theory of Musical Competence. In de Jager, E.J. (ed.), *Man: Anthropological Essays presented to O.F. Raum*, 19-34. Cape Town.

Blacking, J. (1971b) The value of music in human experience. In Ringer, L. (ed.), *Yearbook of the International Folk Music Council 1969*, 33-71. Urbana, Ill.

Blacking, J. (1973) *How Musical is Man?* Seattle.

Blacking, J. (1975) The study of man as music-maker. *World Anthropology*, vol. on performing arts (forthcoming).

De Bono, E. (1969) *The Mechanism of Mind*. London.

De Vore, P. (ed.) (1965) *The Origin of Man*. New York.

Dolhinow, P.J. and Bishop, N. (1971) The development of motor skills and social relationships among primates through play. In Hill, J.P. (ed.), *Minnesota symposia on child psychology*, 4, 141-98. Minneapolis.

Gennep, A. van (1960) (trans. M.B. Vizedom and G.L. Caffee) *The Rites of Passage*. London.

Geschwind, N. (1970) The organization of language and the brain. *Science*, 170, 940-4.

Hewes, G.W. (1973) Primate communication and the gestural origin of language. *Current Anthropology*, 14, 5-24.

Lee, R.B. and DeVore, I. (eds.) (1968) *Man the Hunter*. Chicago.

Lenneberg, E. (1967) *Biological Foundations of Language*. New York.

Lévi-Strauss, C. (1969a) (trans. R. Needham) *Totemism*. London.

Lévi-Strauss, C. (1969b) (trans. J. and D. Weightman). *The Raw and the Cooked*. New York.

Livingstone, F.B. (1973) Did the Australopithecines sing? *Current Anthropology*, 14, 25-9.

Lukes, S. (1973) *Emile Durkheim: His Life and Work*. London.

Morris, D. (1962) *The Biology of Art: A study of the picture-making behaviour of the great apes and its relationship to human art*. London.

Ploog, D. and Melnechuk, T. (1971) *Are Apes Capable of Language?* Neurosciences Research Program Bulletin, Vol. 9, No. 5.

Sundkler, B.G.M. (1961) *Bantu Prophets in South Africa*. London.

Washburn, S.L. (1968) Behaviour and the origin of man. *Proc. Roy. Anthr. Inst.* for 1967, 21-7.

Washburn, S.L. and Howell, F.C. (1960) Human evolution and culture. In Tax, S. (ed.), *Evolution after Darwin*, 2, 33-56. Chicago.

Wertheimer, M. (1945) *Productive Thinking*. New York.

Young, J.Z. (1971) *An Introduction to the Study of Man*. Oxford.

BRIAN M. FAGAN

The hunters of Gwisho: a retrospect

Grahame Clark has long been an advocate of the ecological approach to prehistory and the influence of his teachings and writings has spread far wider than the narrow purview of European archaeology. Many of Clark's students have worked in sub-Saharan Africa, a region so far neglected by the Disney Professor in his extensive travels. But ecological archaeology has taken a strong hold in African prehistory in recent years, both in studies of early man and in research into the economic life of the Late Stone Age hunters in Southern Africa.

Many years ago, George Stow (1905) commented on the rich abundance of the game and vegetable resources available to Bushman hunters in Southern Africa: 'That these huntsmen, as long as the game was comparatively undisturbed, had an abundance of food is proved by the testimony of every observant traveller, some of whom have noticed that the very dogs among the Bushmen were invariably fat and in good condition.' Stow went on to trace a connexion between the stone tools made by nineteenth-century hunters and those found in the rock shelters and open sites on the veldt. He also described the beautiful rock paintings executed by Bushman artists and identified animal bones in the deposits of Stone Age occupation sites. The last hundred years has seen a flood of monographs, papers and popular books on the Late Stone Age hunters of Southern Africa. Much of this literature has been concerned with rock paintings and generalized descriptions of Bushman life, many of them of a romanticized nature, extolling the virtues of a happy and unsophisticated hunting life among the plentiful game herds of South Africa (for a bibliography see Holm 1966).

Fortunately, serious archaeological research has kept pace with the spate of semi-popular literature, but most attention has been focussed on the typology of stone tools, rock art and the definition of cultural-stratigraphic units. In contrast, surprisingly little attention has been paid to economic evidence from Late Stone Age settlements, despite abundant indications of many different specialized adaptations to the rich and diverse environment of Southern Africa.

Over a decade ago, Professor J. Desmond Clark (1959) wrote an elegant and closely-reasoned account of what he called 'daily life' in the Late Stone Age of Southern Africa. He based his study on a close examination of activities depicted in rock paintings, amplifying with archaeological evidence the generalized accounts of Bushman hunting and gathering methods compiled by Stow, Isaac Schapera (1930) and others. Desmond Clark's essay sparked off great interest in Late Stone Age archaeology, at a time when the subject of modern hunter-gatherers was attracting attention among anthropologists and those concerned with the economic and social life of early man. Richard Lee's research concerning the !Kung Bushmen of the Kalahari desert has also had a profound influence on Late Stone Age archaeology in Southern Africa (Lee 1965; Lee & DeVore 1968). The research of John Yellen (Yellen & Harpending 1972) has shown that the living Bushmen have lasting and close relationships in economic practices, settlement patterns and material culture with Late Stone Age hunters and gatherers. In archaeological terms, however, the evidence from most sites is highly fragmentary.

Archaeological evidence for subsistence activities from Late Stone Age sites is confined for the most part to fragmentary animal and fish bones, carbonized vegetal remains, shells and occasional finds of organic materials. One reason for an apparent lack of emphasis on economic data has been the generally poor preservation conditions on Late Stone Age sites. Most excavated settlements are either scatters of stone artefacts, shell-middens or the deposits in caves and rock shelters where acid soils and poor survival conditions have destroyed most of the plant remains and faunal materials. But there are

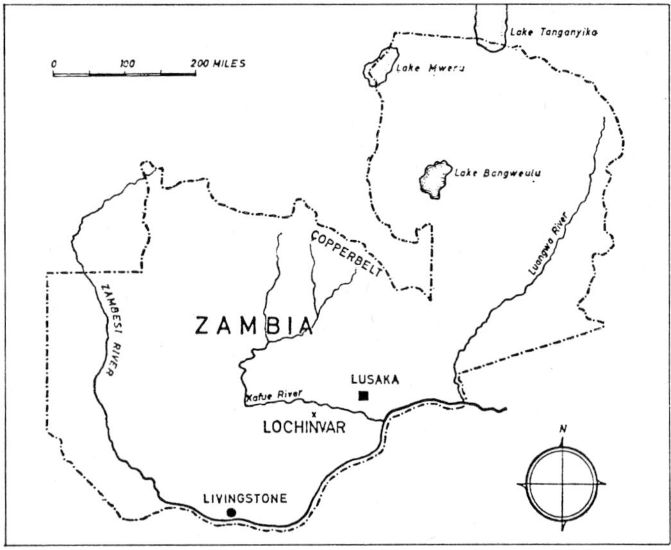

Figure 1a. Map of Zambia showing position of Lochinvar. After Fagan and Van Noten, 1971.

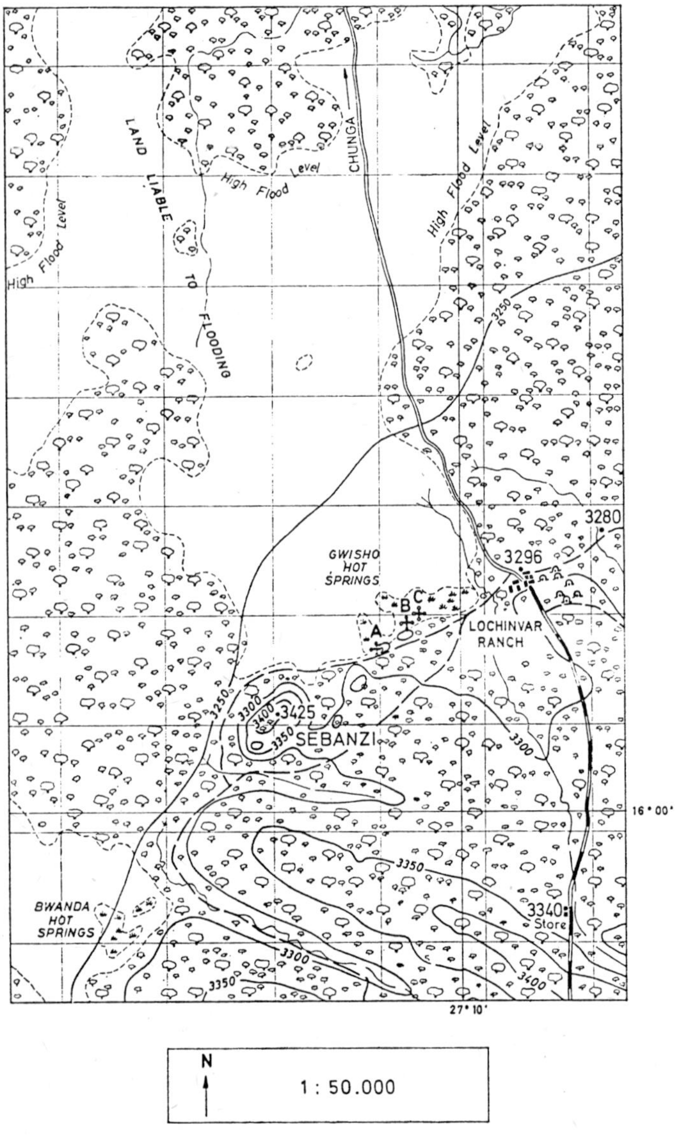

Figure 1b. The Lochinvar area with Gwisho hot-springs. The areas of land liable to flooding are indicated. After Fagan and Van Noten, 1971.

exceptions to the general pattern. The Gwisho hot-spring sites in Central Zambia have yielded spectacular organic materials and a wealth of economic data (Fagan & van Noten 1971). Coastal rock shelters in the Cape Province of South Africa contain comprehensive information on subsistence activities, including grasses, seeds, fish bones, shrubs, mammalian remains and occasional wooden artefacts (Deacon 1972; Klein 1974; Parkington 1972). But economic data from the majority of Late Stone Age sites is drawn from a handful of animal bones and a few seed fragments; hardly sufficient to give a clear picture of a sophisticated and highly effective series of hunting economies. In this paper, we consider some of the economic data from the Gwisho sites in the light of recent ecological research.

Gwisho

Recently, Francis van Noten and I (1971) published a basic description of two Late Stone Age hunting camps at Gwisho hot springs in Central Zambia (Figs. 1a, 1b). The monograph catalogued the various finds made at the settlements. We described the hunting and gathering economy at Gwisho, using a detailed study of the mammalian and fish bones as well as the vegetal remains from the settlement. In discussing the economic evidence, I wrote: 'The Gwisho hunters had a potentially very broad subsistence base, which they exploited on a very selective basis. The degree of sophistication in their subsistence strategy which they brought to bear on the food quest is difficult to determine from the archaeological evidence'. This statement, while bordering on the platitudinous, is one that can be qualified by examining in greater detail the economic evidence in the light of information about game movements and distributions, especially the important work of Sheppe & Osborne (1972) on the game populations of the Kafue Flats, kindly drawn to my attention by Professor Desmond Clark.

The Gwisho hot springs extend over a distance of 1.5 km. on the south edge of the Kafue Flats, 61 km. north-west of the town of Monze in the Southern Province of Zambia. Three Late Stone Age camps at the springs have been investigated: Gwisho A by Dr Creighton Gabel in 1960-61 (Gabel 1965), while Gwisho B and Gwisho C were excavated by Francis van Noten and myself in 1963-64 (Fagan & Van Noten 1971). Each consists of a low mound of earth and occupation debris surrounded by hot springs and dense stands of reeds. The springs are still active and have been so since prehistoric times, for clear traces of old spring eyes can be discerned in the deposits of the mounds. The water-table of the springs perennially floods the lowermost 2 m. of the sites. Organic remains abound in the lower levels of Gwisho A and B, while Gwisho C yielded a few wood fragments. The excavators at all three sites were richly rewarded. Enormous stone assemblages were associated with rich mammalian faunas, huge caches of vegetal remains, wooden artefacts, traces of brush structures and burials. As a result, we were able to build up a remarkably complete picture of the subsistence activities of the hunters.

Ecology

The Gwisho hot springs are situated in a large, shallow fault-determined valley, which is filled with extensive sand and recent alluvial deposits, the latter derived from the River Kafue. Hot and cold water springs are found in several parts of the fault valley. The Gwisho springs emanate from a breccia zone in the Karroo sands of the south side of the valley. They produce very hot water, undrinkable by modern standards, but probably used by the prehistoric inhabitants.

The dominant feature of this part of the Kafue valley is the vast river flood-plain, which extends from Iteshi Teshi in the north-west to the Kafue gorge in the east. The flood-plain is flat and topographically featureless except for the occasional shallow watercourse. For much of the year the waters of the Kafue inundate the flood-plain, providing a paradise of swamp and green grazing grass at the water's edge for the vast herds of game that teemed on the flood-plain in prehistoric times. Enormous herds of lechwe, zebra, buffalo and wildebeest flourished on the Kafue Flats until recently. They were joined at the water's edge by innumerable waterfowl feeding on catfish and other shallow-water species in the shallow pools and water-courses of the Flats.

Gwisho springs are some 22.5 km. south of the Kafue river itself and, except in years of exceptionally high flood waters, a considerable distance from the water's edge. About 11 km. north of the hot springs the ground rises slightly and the topography becomes less monotonous. The landscape is studded with ant-hills and a scatter of *Acacia* trees and bushes. Some denser woodland is found where soils are deeper and the drainage is of better quality. During the years of exceptional rainfall the game population of the Flats moves on to higher ground and congregates nearer the hot springs.

Older rocks emerge from the alluvial deposits of the flood-plain just to the south of the Gwisho hot springs, forming a higher plateau surface with some low hills. The hot springs lie on the boundary between the plain and the higher ground, at 977 m. above sea-level. The sporadic *Acacia* and high grasses of the alluvial plain give way to quite different savannah woodland vegetational patterns, including *Acacia, Combretum, Hyphaene* palm and many fruit-bearing trees. Edible fruit are also to be found in the trees surrounding the hot springs themselves. The savannah woodland fauna is rich and varied and includes such medium-sized antelope as the kudu and impala. Bushbuck, steenbuck and duiker are common. Many bushpig and warthog were to be found near Gwisho in prehistoric times, but warthog are now unknown in the reeds around the springs where they formerly abounded. Easily-snared birds such as the francolin and guinea-fowl still feed at the foot of the low hills behind the sites.

The inhabitants of Gwisho were able to draw on the resources of four major ecological zones (Sheppe & Osborne 1972):

(a) The *Brachystegia* woodland to the south of the hot springs, abundant in vegetable foods that came into season at intervals throughout most of the year and, importantly, during the late dry season. Water supplies are much less abundant in the dry season, except in the larger watercourses.

(b) The area of the hot springs themselves, where perennial water supplies form dense stands of reeds and allow some tree growth. Warthog made their burrows around the springs; game still drinks in the pools formed by the draining waters of the hot springs.

(c) The ant-hill studded 'termite zone', slightly higher ground immediately to the north of the hot springs, with its grass and *Acacia* cover. This merges into:

(d) The Kafue flood-plain itself with its abundant bird,. fish and game resources whose distribution varies with the flood-level.

The fluctuating water-level of the Kafue may have been of particular importance. Flood water is derived from three sources: rainfall, tributary streams and, most important of all, the Kafue river itself. The Kafue rises to a maximum height some time after the rains are over in March and spills over an enormous area of the flats, forming vast sheets of shallow water ponded on the impermeable soils of the flood-plain. From the point of view of game distribution and hunting strategies the horizontal distribution of water is critical. The extent of the flood varies greatly from year to year, the water falling much more slowly than it rises. Receding water-levels leave flooded depressions and small lagoons behind them that may persist long into the dry season. The amount of the termite zone covered by flood water varies from year to year, but in seasons of exceptionally high floods many acres of termite country, and even woodland, can be inundated. How close to Gwisho the flood waters have ever reached is a matter for conjecture. Certainly in high-flood years the game populations of the water's edge were much closer to the hunting camps than in drier years, at times conceivably within regular hunting distance of the home base.

The rising and falling flood waters leave distinct vegetational phenomena in their train. A variety of grasses cover the flood-plain, the most abundant being wild rice, *Oryza barthii*. *Sorghum verticilliflorum* occurs in dense stands, reaching a height of 2-4 m. Water-lilies (*Nymphaea*) are abundant in shallow water. As the flood recedes, it leaves behind it a dense growth of grasses which soon collapses into a blanket of dying vegetation. The game herds tend to follow the receding flood, feeding on the recently exposed vegetation. Throughout the year, the character of the vegetation in the Gwisho region is determined primarily by rain, floods, fire and grazing. Above all, the prolonged flooding of the Flats keeps them from being covered by woody vegetation and permits a dense primary growth of grasses and herbs. As a result, the game populations are larger than in the surrounding unflooded areas. Without question the height and extent of the flood waters of the Kafue profoundly affected the distribution of game resources available to the hunters of Gwisho in different years and from season to season. This statement is presumably true of Late Stone Age times as well, for there are no archaeological indications that climatic conditions in the Central

Kafue Basin have changed much over the past 5,000 years.

On superficial examination the environment of the Kafue valley seems to offer an over-abundance of economic resources for Stone Age hunters. Game on the hoof is always within easy reach. Birds could be snared with ease near the hunting camps. Fish abound in the shallow pools of the Kafue and its tributary streams. Vegetable foods are in season throughout much of the year. But to what extent was permanent settlement possible? Which of the four ecological zones available to the hunters of Gwisho did they exploit to the maximum extent? The second question is the one that provides the key to the answer to the first, and it lies in a comparison of the various economic finds at Gwisho relative to the probable hunting territory of the hot-spring settlements.

What range of ground did the hunters cover under normal circumstances, if they relied on Gwisho as their home base? The answer, to judge from Lee's work (1965), was about 8 km. distance from the camp, in other words the distance that a hunter could walk out and back from his home base in a day. Such a figure is in broad agreement with that proposed by Vita-Finzi & Higgs (1970) in a recent paper on site-catchment analysis. Such a theory ignores the occasional longer hunting or gathering expedition, where small groups of hunters might camp out while engaged in a specialized hunting or gathering activity, or small seasonal hunting camps, no trace of which has yet been located near Gwisho.

An 8 km. radius from Gwisho leaves the major centre of all economic activity within three ecological zones – the savannah woodland to the south of the hot springs, the vicinity of the springs themselves and the higher ground between Gwisho and the Kafue flood-plain. The flooded areas did not normally lie within the normal hunting range of the Gwisho people, except in years of higher flood levels. They may, however, have visited them on numerous occasions, perhaps visiting temporary camps near the water's edge.

The finds: mammals, fish, vegetable remains

Mammalian remains

The mammalian remains from Gwisho can be divided into a number of broad categories, both of size and of preferred ecological zones. We can summarize the data as in Table 1.

Table 1 Rough sub-division of observed Gwisho B fauna into users and non-users of the flood-plain

Flood-plain users	Users of flood-plain marginally (mainly in woods & termite zone)	Users of hot springs areas
Buffalo		Warthog
Zebra	frequently use other zones	
Lechwe*		
Wildebeest	frequently use other zones	
	Impala	
	Bushbuck	
	Bush-pig	Bush-pig
	Kudu	
Sometimes on Flats	Eland	
	Oribi	
	Roan	
	Hartebeest	
	Grysbok	
	Duiker	Hippopotamus (?)
Hippopotamus*	Rhinoceros	
Five	Eleven	Three

Data in part from Sheppe & Osborne (1972). The species range from amphibious mammals* (lechwe and hippopotamus), rarely observed away from the flood-plain, to terrestial animals (the remainder). All are listed in frequency of occurrence in the archaeological deposits (Fagan & Van Noten 1971). Game distributions are based on observations at Lochinvar, Zambia, and at other localities where this is possible.

Most species in Table 1 are either flood-plain users or prefer marginal or more wooded territory. Antelope, in the latter category, are present in considerable variety. We have listed the species in descending order of frequency in terms of number of specimens present. As Patricia Daly (1969) has shown, to estimate the number of individuals represented in any faunal collection is extremely difficult. Indeed, we were unable to devise an effective way of doing so. We suspect that large mammals such as the buffalo, for example, are almost certainly over-represented in the Gwisho collections, simply because their bones are more readily identified from small fragments. The conclusions that follow are based on specimen counts but should, with a large collection like that from Gwisho, at least allow us to make some broad generalizations.

Four of the five most common mammals at Gwisho B are listed by Sheppe & Osborne (1972) as flood-plain users. The lechwe is the only aquatic species among the five, and by far the most common large mammal in the Gwisho area today. Most lechwe rarely stray far from the water's edge on the Flats, except at high-flood time when they frequent the termite zone but never wooded territory. They stay within 1 km. from the water's edge. Lechwe are among the most amphibious of Zambian antelopes and were almost certainly hunted in their preferred grazing grounds close to the waters of the Kafue. Since the Kafue Flats lie well outside the normal range of a hunter based at Gwisho except at times of very high flood, we may reasonably assume that most of the lechwe in the collections were taken around April or May when the floods were at maximum extent, or during periods when the hunters were living away from the hot springs near the water's edge. The latter explanation requires that at least portions of carcases were carried back to the hot springs from the Flats, hardly a practical way of collecting meat when abundant game was at hand nearer home.

Zebra are said by Sheppe & Osborne (1972) to be next in what they call the 'water-table gradient'. They live on the flood-plain when it is dry but penetrate deeply into the termite and wooded zones at high flood. Seasonal movements of zebra herds vary from year to year, but some herds must have grazed within the normal hunting territory of the Gwisho people for most of the year. The same applies to the wildebeest, primarily a grassland species with a tolerance of woodland. Even today they can be sighted within easy hunting range of the Gwisho hot springs. Buffalo have a somewhat similar preference and live in the woodlands at high flood.

The total numbers of buffalo, wildebeest and zebra specimens recorded at Gwisho B are far higher than those for the aquatic lechwe, whose seasonal movements coincide so closely with the flood waters on the Flats. Except in years of unduly high floods, the grassland termite zone immediately to the north of the hot springs is not flooded, although it is said that flood waters have reached to within 3 km. of the sites (A. Fuller: personal communication). The Zambia Government Survey maps show land 'liable to flooding' within 6 km. of Gwisho, but gradients are so gradual that any precise estimates of flood-water distribution are bound to be inaccurate. With exceptionally high floods a comparative rarity, however, a predominance of grassland mammals over aquatic is entirely local. In all probability, most of the flood-plain users in Table 1, except for lechwe, were taken from the termite zone within the Gwisho territory, only a small proportion of the kill being carried to the hot springs from the water's edge. There is a danger that one can become preoccupied with the Kafue Flats as a factor in hunting economies. Buffalo, wildebeest and zebra all depend on readily available water supplies. Water was available all the year round at Gwisho itself. Indeed the hot springs may have generated their own concentration of game in prehistoric times. The presence of hippopotamus in the Gwisho B fauna suggests that there may have been large areas of water near the springs in which these animals flourished. No one would carry portions of hippopotamus carcase very far.

The importance of the springs themselves in the hunting quest is emphasized by the surprising quantities of warthogs found at Gwisho. Warthog is unknown in the region today, although formerly they were common at Gwisho itself and in the termite zone. The sample from Gwisho B is heavily weighted towards individuals of four years and older, which Graham Child (in Fagan & Van Noten 1971) feels is due to selective hunting rather than other factors such as drought. Warthog are good eating, and probably abounded in the immediate vicinity of the hot springs. Selective hunting strongly implies an abundance of warthog, with concentrations on larger individuals with a higher meat-yield from each kill. The absence of immature animals in the deposits may be explained by the fact that plains-mammals like the zebra and wildebeest calve on the Flats in the dry season. But immature bones preserve very badly and their absence at Gwisho B may equally well be explained by bad preservation or, as in the case of warthog, selective hunting of adult beasts.

With such sources of meat within easy reach, it is hardly surprising that the Gwisho people did not concentrate their main efforts on lechwe, whose main grazing grounds were at least 15 km. away for most of the year.

Species preferring the termite and woodland zones are found in smaller numbers, but a wide range of medium- and small-sized antelope is represented in the Gwisho collections. Bushbuck, kudu and eland still drink from the pools of the hot springs today. Duiker are still to be seen in thickets on Sebanzi Hill and elsewhere near the sites. The hartebeest, although difficult to distinguish osteologically from the wildebeest, flourishes in the *Brachystegia* woodland to the south of the hot springs. Today, the impala at Lochinvar live mostly in the open woodlands and go short distances into the termite zone.

The range of termite and woodland species is so wide that it seems to represent a random sampling of the game animals that commonly drank at the hot springs or ranged nearby. Most of the animals in this category were probably killed near the hot springs, and their meat combined in the diet with that obtained from lengthier forays into the termite zone. Undoubtedly most game could be obtained from an area within 8 km., or two hours' walk, from the site. Indeed, there can have been little incentive to move outside the immediate area of the settlements to obtain the meat that formed such a high proportion of the Gwisho diet.

Evidence for seasonal hunting is notoriously difficult to obtain from the bones of African *bovidae*, which lack the antlers used as seasonal indicators in other parts of the world. Our indications from animal bones can only be indirect. A substantial number of lechwe bones may mean that the hunters moved to the water's edge in search of lechwe in April or May; equally well, however, the lechwe may have been eaten when they could be killed at times of exceptionally high flood within easy walking distance of the hot springs. While some seasonal concentration on particular mammals is more than likely, we have an overwhelming impression of local exploitation of fauna with only occasional expeditions to the flood-plain.

Fishing

Elsewhere, we have described how fishing played a minor part in the Gwisho economy. This is, perhaps, rather surprising, with the abundant waters of the Kafue so relatively close to the hot springs (Fagan & Van Noten 1971). Nearly all the Gwisho fish bones are from *Clarias*, the barbel, a bottom species that flourishes in shallow water where the oxygen content is low, for it has an auxiliary breathing apparatus in the form of a bronchial organ. While barbel are abundant in the Kafue, the effort of carrying them, or drying the fish in the sun, seems quite out of proportion to the distance involved. Barbel do occur in shallow pools by the hot springs and could easily be dispatched with spears, or even trapped in rocky puddles. We can be virtually certain that the Gwisho fish came from the immediate vicinity of the hot springs, and not from the Kafue, purely because the effort involved in fishing the Kafue and its tributaries was of minimal value to the hunters of Gwisho.

Vegetal remains

The vegetal remains from Gwisho are unusually complete, because of the exceptional preservation conditions. Twelve species are represented in the Gwisho collections, 75% of which came from *Bauhinia* and *Hyphaene*, both plants with many economic uses. *Bauhinia* is today highly prized for its fruit and roots, which are in season between October and February. *Hyphaene* has little food value, except for the milk from the seed, but it is a constant source of matting, rope and thatch, all commodities conceivably used at Gwisho. Except for *Swartzia madagascariensis*, a source of arrow poison, and a few fragments of wild gourd, all the remaining vegetal materials are from edible species. The list includes the water-lily, *Nymphaea*, but not wild rice, so common at the edge of the flood waters. This species might, however, be detected in pollen samples, if ever palynological techniques could be applied to the Gwisho deposits. It is worth noting, however, that wild rice is rapidly trampled down by game and soon spoiled when the flood waters recede. With other vegetable foods close at hand, there may have been little incentive to collect wild rice.

The 10,000 Gwisho vegetal remains show major concentration on two species, the one an edible form, the other providing not only milk but fibres for many uses. Such specialized collection is a remarkable parallel to that practised by the !Kung Bushmen of the Kalahari desert (Lee 1965), who know of the existence of no less than 200 edible species, of which only nine are commonly eaten, including *Bauhinia*, although 74 are known to be used when the more commonly exploited plants are in short supply.

All the Gwisho plant species are to be found in comparative abundance in the vicinity of the hot springs today. Most of them occur in the *Brachystegia* woodlands, which extend southwards from the Gwisho hot springs. The fruiting seasons are comparatively long; the fruit are abundant; but only two were eaten regularly by the hunters of Gwisho.

The highly selective collection of vegetable foods might be explained by analogy with !Kung Bushman practice. Flesh is regarded by present-day Bushmen as the most desirable food. With an abundant meat diet, there is little incentive to broaden the subsistence base or the extent of the food quest, except under exceptional conditions. The archaeological remains represent, of course, only a small proportion of the vegetable resources available to, and used by, the Gwisho people. The food species at Gwisho are all well-known food sources. Their frequency at Gwisho presumably results from systematic and long-term exploitation of this small part of the wide spectrum of vegetable species available to the hunters.

The Gwisho economy

The hunters of Gwisho obtained almost all their food supplies from vegetable or animal resources within the immediate hunting territory around the hot springs. Vegetable foods came from the *Brachystegia* woodlands behind the sites and from trees growing at the springs themselves. Fish could be speared in tributary streams and in pools at Gwisho. Only in the case of the lechwe is there firm evidence for believing that the hunters moved far from their home base during the food quest. Even in this instance, the long occupation at Gwisho may mask many years of high flood when lechwe grazed closer to the sites than in normal years. To that extent we can state that lechwe were probably more intensively exploited in April and May of high-flood years, perhaps to the exclusion of other game.

Permanent water supplies and an abundant natural environment gave little incentive for regular seasonal mobility in the sense implied by Parkington (1972), nor does the 'flux' state defined by Turnbull (1968) pertain here. Parkington has made a brief summary of the characteristics of hunter-gatherer groups. We can expect such groups to have a detailed knowledge of the various game and vegetable foods available to them, which foods they will tend to maximize in season. Among hunter-gatherers, the rule seems to have been that women collect plant food and slow or immobile animal food, while men hunted more mobile animals with occasional assistance from women in mass hunts and other activities. Parkington argues that the bulk weight of consumed food supply was from plant sources, while animals may contribute most of the protein. The collecting of vegetable foods is in the hands of the women, an activity that tides the group over from day to day. Lee (1965) and others have repeatedly demonstrated that hunter-gatherers have so many viable alternative strategies in front of them that they rarely starve. In the case of the !Kung Bushmen, the women collect vegetable foods only two or three days a week. The !Kung do, however, like the Pygmies, live in a state of flux with constant movement of settlement sites on an annual 'beat' as different foods come into season. The social implications of this are flexible. Group size and composition is variable and changes constantly, helped by exogamous marriage ties and a flexible attitude towards the definitive territory upon which the hunters depend for their livelihood.

If Parkington's model is to apply to the hunters of Gwisho, we should look for evidence of ephemeral occupations of the hot-spring sites, a seasonal 'beat' of different settlements and an economic strategy in which plant foods play a major part. The archaeology of Gwisho provides no evidence of seasonal occupation beyond the possible instance of lechwe and some vegetable foods. Except for lechwe, all the game animals hunted by the inhabitants could be found within comfortable walking distance of the hot springs. The presence of vegetable foods that fruit during the dry season does not necessarily mean seasonal occupation, for other fruit are edible during the rains, even if they are absent from the archaeological record.

Without conclusive proof of seasonal occupation, one must ask whether hunters with perennial water supplies and abundant game and vegetable resources within their normal hunting territory had any incentive to move around at different seasons. Perhaps the archaeological evidence provides some indicators.

In the first place, the vegetal remains from Gwisho B prove that the hunters were concentrating on a limited range of vegetable foods. But, to judge from analogy with modern Bushmen, the Gwisho people were certainly aware of a huge range of vegetable foods that they could fall back on in times of stress or over-exploitation of standard forms. How important were vegetable foods? To what extent did their seasons determine the occupation of the hot springs? *Bauhinia* comes into fruit during the rains, *Hyphaene* in the dry season. The other vegetable foods found at Gwisho fruit at different times throughout the year. On the face of it, Gwisho was occupied all the year round. But it should be remembered that vegetable foods may have been of lesser importance than is sometimes assumed. Lee's often cited work on the !Kung Bushmen was carried out when the hunters were living under modern conditions. Over a century of rifle hunting had decimated their hunting territories, so they relied very heavily on vegetable foods although meat was prized above all foods. Even today, the game density on the Kafue Flats is amazing. The richness of the fauna even a hundred years ago must have far surpassed that of the 1970s, especially in the woodland and termite zones of the valley, which are more readily hunted out by riflemen than the swampy flats.

Meat was presumably a favourite food in Late Stone Age times as it is today. With much higher game densities, is it reasonable to assume that the Gwisho people relied heavily on vegetable foods when even scavenging from predator kills could provide some flesh without much effort? Questions such as this can be asked legitimately about many Late Stone Age settlements in Southern Africa where the natural environment is so rich that food supplies are almost embarrassingly abundant. In the case of Gwisho, I think that we can argue convincingly for an overwhelming importance of hunting in the diet, with meat supplies supplemented by vegetable foods in season and occasional fish protein. We can also assume a strong incentive towards more permanent settlement at Gwisho with seasonal movements confined to forays to the edge of the Flats in search of lechwe, especially in years of exceptionally high flood.

The Gwisho hot springs lie at the edge of two ecological zones, a classic example of a hunting camp sited on an ecotone, an area of contact between several ecosystems. With its abundant water supplies and readily available food resources from four ecological zones, Gwisho is a site which illustrates the viability of hunting and gathering as a highly effective human subsistence activity in Southern Africa, a way of life that continued into modern times. The archaeological finds of the hot springs provide, also, an instance of the importance of following lines of research opened up by Grahame Clark and other pioneers in ecological prehistory, to whom the writer, like many of his African colleagues, owes so much.

REFERENCES

Clark, J.D. (1959) *The Prehistory of Southern Africa.* Harmondsworth, Middlesex.

Daly, P. (1969) Approaches to faunal analysis in archaeology. *American Antiquity*, 34, 146-53.

Deacon, A.H. (1972) A review of the post-pleistocene in South Africa. *S.A. Arch. Bull.*, Goodwin series No. 1, 26-45.

Fagan, B.M. and van Noten, F. (1971) *The Hunter-Gatherers of Gwisho.* Tervuren.

Gabel, C. (1965) *Stone Age Hunters of the Kafue: the Gwisho A Site.* Boston.

Holm, S.E. (1966) *Bibliography of S.A. Pre- and Proto-historic Archaeology.* Pretoria.

Klein, R.G. (1974) Environment and subsistence of prehistoric man in the southern Cape Province, South Africa. *World Archaeology*, 5, 249-84.

Lee, R.B. (1965) *The Subsistence Ecology of !Kung Bushmen.* Ph.D. dissertation, University of California, Berkeley.

Lee, R.B. and DeVore, I. (eds.), 1968. *Man the Hunter.* Chicago.

Parkington, J.E. (1972) Seasonal mobility in the Late Stone Age. *African Studies*, 31, 223-44.

Schapera, I. (1930) *The Khoisan-Speaking Peoples of South Africa.* London.

Sheppe, W. and Osborne, T. (1972) Patterns of use of a flood plain by Zambian mammals. *Ecological Monographs*, 41, 179-205.

Stow, G.W. (1905) *The Native Races of South Africa.* London.

Turnbull, C.M. (1968) The importance of flux in two hunting societies. In Lee and DeVore (eds.), 1968, 132-7.

Vita-Finzi, C. and Higgs, E.S. (1970) Prehistoric economy in the Mount Carmel area of Palestine: site catchment analysis. *P.P.S.*, 36, 1-37.

Yellen, J. and Harpending, H. (1972) Hunter-gatherer populations and archaeological inference. *World Archaeology*, 4, 244-53.

RAY INSKEEP

The problem of 'Bantu origins'

It has repeatedly been stressed that the word *Bantu* is a linguistic term and, indeed, it was coined by W.H. Bleek, early in the second half of the last century, for those people speaking one or other of a number of more or less clearly defined, and apparently related, languages. By the end of the nineteenth century, however, the term was in general use for the black, or dark-skinned, peoples of southern Africa; and in the first publication on Mapungubwe (Fouché 1937) discussion ranged around the problem of the association of a non-negroid physical type with a typically 'Bantu *culture*'. It was very largely in an attempt to resolve this supposed enigma that a second series of excavations was carried out in the 1940s (Gardner 1963). It is probably true to say that, with one or two exceptions, there has remained ever since a tacit assumption that, in central and southern Africa, there is an overall equivalence between the terms 'Iron Age', 'Bantu' and 'negroid physical type'.

What seems to have impressed people, and demanded some explanation, was the contrast between the yellow-skinned hunter-gatherers (generally termed 'Bushmen') and the yellow-skinned herders (the 'Hottentots') in the south-west of the continent, on the one hand; and the darker-skinned mixed farmers, with their metal technology and ceramics, scattered over the rest of sub-Saharan Africa, on the other. It is in an attempt to explain this situation that, for a good many years, people have turned their minds to the problem of deciding *where* the Bantu-speakers came from, since it has always been tacitly assumed that they must be intrusive.

Sir Harry Johnston set the ball rolling sixty years ago (Johnston 1913) when he postulated hordes of Bantu invaders fanning out across Africa like so many hordes of nineteenth-century Zulus. He saw them sweeping into relatively thickly populated territory, and impressing 'with extraordinary rapidity and completeness their own type of language on the tribes they conquered'. Nearly fifty years later Wrigley (1960) saw them 'not as agriculturalists spreading out over a virtually empty land, but as a dominant minority, specialized to hunting with the spear, constantly attracting new adherents . . . by their fabulous prestige as suppliers of meat, constantly throwing off new bands of migratory adventurers until the whole southern sub-continent was iron-using and Bantu-speaking'.

In seeking an alternative to a Bantu 'conquest' theory, Roland Oliver (1966) has chosen the possibility of a population 'explosion', or rapid expansion. In doing so, he has suggested that the analogy of the European settlement of North America, or of Australia, might be more correct than that of the Teutonic invasions of Europe in the Dark Ages. Neither, however, is a very satisfactory analogy since, apart from extreme geographical and technological differences, European colonizations of the seventeenth and eighteenth centuries were intimately related to a vastly more complex economic structure and it is not at all easy to think of a documented analogy appropriate to the hypothesized Bantu expansion.

The first attempt to find an explanation other than pure speculation to account for the wide dispersion of Bantu-speakers, and one which has, to date, had the most profound effect on all subsequent work in this field comes, logically enough, from the study of African languages. By comparing the equivalents of about fifty common words in a large number of western-Sudanic and Bantu languages, Joseph Greenberg (1955) reached the conclusion that the Bantu languages were a part of the western-Sudanic language family, and that they did not form even a distinct sub-group within that family. He did, however, suggest that they formed a part of a sub-group that included most of the languages of the central Cameroons, and of east-central Nigeria. Greenberg was in no doubt as to the implications of this. He proposed that the speakers of the western-Sudanic language family had once lived further north, in the savannah belt, and for reasons and at a time, both unspecified, had moved southward to occupy the forest belt; those in the west halted when they reached the Atlantic Ocean, whereas those to the east carried on into the Congo basin, subsequently to fan out across the whole of what is now known as Bantu Africa.

On the basis of this hypothesis, one might suppose that the languages at the extremes of the area of dispersal would show the greatest differences from the parent stock, and that as one moved up the pathways of dispersion, back towards the parent area around Nigeria and the Cameroons, the evidence of common ancestry would become stronger. This, however, is not the conclusion reached by another African linguist who, at about the time that Greenberg was moving towards his conclusions on relationships between apparently different languages, began a most detailed comparative study of the languages commonly classed as Bantu.

Malcolm Guthrie's study (1970) involved collecting items into 'sets of cognates', each held together by completely regular rules of phonological correspondence, from some 350 of the 400 or more recorded Bantu languages. He derived some 2,400 sets of cognates from approximately 21,000 regular items, while for each set of cognates he postulated an ancestral 'root' from which each item in the set is ultimately derived. The words concerned are referred to as 'reflexes' of the postulated 'roots'. With some exceptions these sets of reflexes form three groups:

(1) having a distribution over the major part of the Bantu area, and referred to as 'general';
(2) sets with a predominantly western distribution; and
(3) sets with a predominantly eastern distribution.

The general sets are interpreted as deriving from roots present in the ancestor language. Those with a mainly western or eastern distribution are regarded as deriving from roots which themselves arose after the splitting of the hypothetical ancestor language into two dialects (east and west).

An examination of the occurrence of the 500 general sets of cognates in the languages concerned suggested to Guthrie that conclusions could be drawn as to the *location* and the *character* of the postulated ancestor language. Because the probability that a general root did belong to the ancestral language is, to some extent, proportionate to the part of the whole area that it covers, Guthrie allotted to each set of cognates a value which expressed the proportion of the whole field covered by each set. On the basis of these weighted figures, he proceeded to examine the distribution and content of the hypothesized ancestral language and its two dialects.

The procedure has resulted in the delineation of what has become known as the Bantu nuclear area (Fig. 1); a relatively small area, represented today by the territory of the Luba Lulua, the Luba Katanga, and the Bemba, in which the weighted count of general reflexes occurring in each language is more than 50% of the total for common Bantu. When the score is lowered to 45% the nuclear area becomes considerably extended, with Swahili forming a detached group on the east coast. As one moves away from the nuclear area, the percentage of common roots shared by the various languages decreases in all directions.

Thus, the picture of Bantu language origins emerging from Guthrie's work is substantially different from that of Greenberg's. But Guthrie seems also to have assumed that his Bantu-speakers had not always been there. Yet, for geographical reasons, he rejects the suggestion that they might have come through the forest from west Africa and, instead, proposes (not very enthusiastically) that there may have been a group of *pre*-Bantu-speakers somewhere near Lake Chad, some of whom migrated south along the eastern margin of the forest, to produce the proto-Bantu nuclear area, whilst a few spread west to provide the basis for the linguistic affinities noted by Greenberg. Roland Oliver's population explosion theory, to which we have already referred (see page 25), was really an attempt to wed the opposing linguistic observations by suggesting that 'a few dozens or hundreds' of pre-Bantu-speakers had migrated rapidly, using river craft, through the equatorial forest to produce a proto-Bantu nucleus (Oliver 1966:362).

Let us glance, for a moment, at one or two of Guthrie's observations on the content of his proto-Bantu language. The distribution of cog-

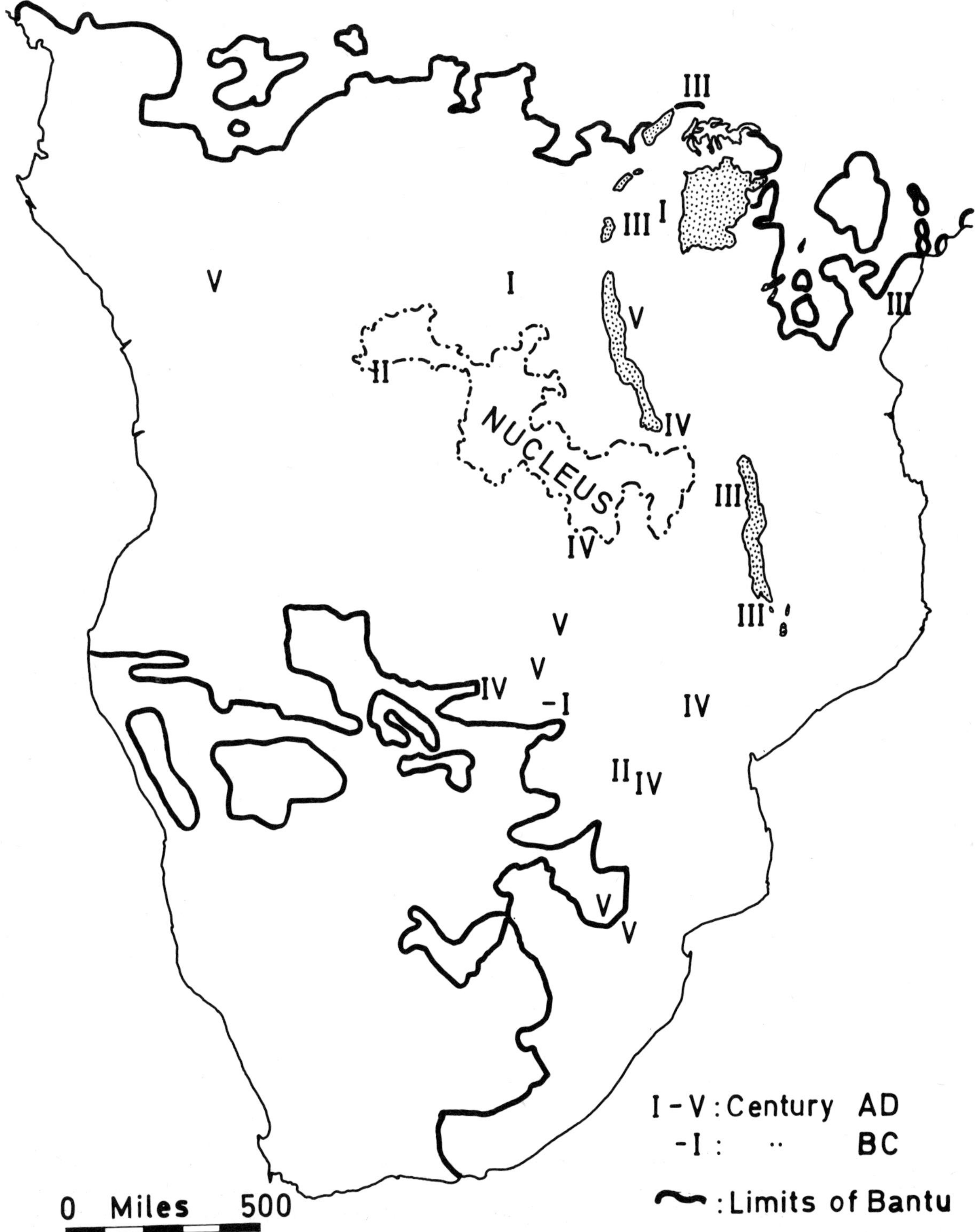

Figure 1. Part of Africa showing the limits of distribution of Bantu languages (after Guthrie), the hypothetical proto-Bantu nuclear area, and the earliest Iron Age dates within the area, expressed in centuries B.C. and A.D. to the fifth century A.D.

nates with the meaning 'to fish with a line' covers a major part of the Bantu field, with notable gaps in the east. Guthrie interprets this as implying that the meaning was present in the ancestral language, but was lost during the dispersal to the more arid regions in the east and south. The more broken distribution of the cognates for 'fish hook', on the other hand, suggests that proto-Bantu had no word for such objects and, presumably, did not use them. The root for canoe is extremely widely spread, and with no gaps, except for the eastern margin of the continent where a completely different root occurs, in five disparate regions, with the meaning 'dugout canoe with outriggers'.

The picture for 'metallic iron' seems curiously complex, and no less than three quite different roots are involved. It seems less easy to propose that any of these were necessarily present in the earliest ancestral language. That in the north-east of the area appears to represent the transfer of a meaning from a root implying 'something valuable', whilst the second most widely distributed root has the meaning 'iron stone', which might not necessarily imply an association with metallurgical process.

There is no set of cognates for the meaning 'to smelt', but there are three sets of cognates with the meaning 'to forge'. One of these is very wide-spread, and ought to imply its presence in the ancestral language, although the fact that one of the other sets of cognates is understood to derive from a root meaning 'to strike' does raise the question whether the very wide-spread set does not also represent a transfer of meaning of a similar kind. The third set of cognates very specifically implies an origin from a source other than proto-Bantu.

But the problem of Bantu origins involves more than language and culture; it involves physical anthropology, and less has been said on this subject. One major contribution comes from the pen of Professor Hiernaux (1968) who, using available data, has attempted to assess the degrees of similarity or difference that exist between each of the pairs of populations included in his study, which included both Bantu- and non-Bantu-speakers. One of the difficulties facing Hiernaux was the unevenness of the physical anthropological record, particularly for the southern Bantu-speakers. It is, of course, inherent in the whole problem of Bantu origins that a variety of complex subjects are involved, the intricacies of which no single scholar can hope to master and, in this case as in others, it is necessary to limit oneself to comments on some of the observations made and the conclusions drawn therefrom.

Hiernaux was concerned with examining and explaining what he called anthropo-biological distance. He stated three conditions as requisite for a low anthropo-biological distance, and these in themselves invite comment. The first condition is 'a relatively recent common origin', but we may well enquire whether, in a biological context, we have any yardstick for measuring the chronological distance of the 'relatively recent' past. The second requirement involves remaining in a not too different biotope. This seems a quite logical postulate, but once again one is inclined to ask just how different a biotope has to be, and how long does a population have to live in it before it experiences measurable genetic change? The third requirement is the absence of an important mixture with genetically large different populations. Since Hiernaux's conclusions favour the Greenberg/Oliver hypothesis of movement followed by expansion, we may well ask what happened to the gene pools of the Stone Age populations which, one must suppose, were replaced by the expanding Bantu population?

According to Hiernaux's anthropo-biological evidence, the twelve populations showing the least mean distances (i.e. biologically most similar to one another) include no less than three important language groups: Niger-Congo, Bantu (held by Greenberg to be a part of the former) and an eastern Sudanic language. The evidence is interpreted as indicating that the speakers of these several language groups are, in Hiernaux's words, 'relatively little modified descendants of an old African stock'. If this really is so, then we must allow sufficient time, and provide a mechanism, not only for the differentiation and spread of the Bantu languages over a vast area, but also for the differentiation of Greenberg's remaining Niger-Congo speakers *and* the eastern Sudanic language speakers who, linguistically speaking, are said to be much more distant from each other. One might expect that the time needed for these events would be considerably longer than the *c.* 2,000 years generally allotted to the 'Bantu Iron Age'.

It has been proposed that the process of

dispersion for the Bantu-speakers involved a movement from the Cross River area or, alternatively, the Ubangi-Shari watershed, along the rivers of the Congo/Zambesi basins. The rapid movement of iron-using farmers in such a way, over such great distances, through the equatorial forest, seems difficult to explain. Yet, if a much slower movement is postulated, chronological problems relating to iron-using arise. A rapid and purposeful movement of hunter-fisher-gatherers is equally difficult to sustain; but a gradual diffusion along waterways of groups exploiting fish resources seems a more acceptable proposition, and might permit of a much more ancient setting for Hiernaux's 'old African stock', and a correspondingly long period for dispersion. It may not be entirely without relevance that, among the general roots published by Guthrie with the widest distribution, we find the meanings *canoe, paddle* and *to fish with a line.*

Finally, it is noteworthy that anthropobiological similarity, as outlined by Hiernaux, groups together Bantu and non-Bantu speakers separated by as much as 3,500 miles, as well as Bantu and non-Bantu speaking hunter-gatherers such as the Mbuti pigmies, the Sandawe and the Hadza. On the face of it, this would not seem to provide particularly strong support for the general thesis that small groups of proto-Bantu speakers moved through the forest, from southern Nigeria or the Cameroons, to Guthrie's 'nuclear area' and expanded thence to the present area of Bantu distribution. If Hiernaux's work suggests the connexions indicated by him, it would seem more plausible to assign to them a more general degree of relationship and at a far deeper time level than *c.* 2,000 years.

So far we have remarked only on the contributions of linguistic and biological studies, and it is necessary to speak briefly of the evidence resulting from archaeological studies. The particular field of enquiry is generally referred to, archaeologically, as the 'Iron Age', and culturally it generally involves an association of ceramics and metallurgy (most commonly iron) with villages of more or less substantial houses. Not infrequently there is evidence of domestic livestock (sheep, goats or cattle) and agriculture is commonly assumed, although the evidence is almost invariably indirect. Recognition of occurrences lying at the early end of the time range, and of affinities between occurrences, is based almost entirely on the study of ceramic typology, aided intermittently by a little stratigraphy. Radiocarbon dating provides a valuable general indication of the chronological framework, but the margin of error, on a 95% probability at 1,500 to 2,000 years ago, is commonly in the order of 100 to 300 years. If we add to this the rather sparse number of occurrences of what the archaeologist might refer to as 'the earliest Iron Age' in any given region, we may see that our knowledge of events within the apparently crucial period between 1,500 and 2,500 years ago cannot be very refined. The importance of this state of affairs is that it makes it very difficult to say whether the various culture traits just mentioned appeared all together at the same time in an area, or whether they arrived at different times, in various combinations.

For east, central and southern Africa, a reasonably coherent picture is emerging, at least as far as pottery traditions are concerned. In the north, in the vicinity of Lake Victoria and the eastern Congo (Rwanda), the very striking and unmistakable Dimple-based (Urewe) pottery tradition is generally dated to the third and fourth centuries A.D. and it is worth noting that a date of A.D. 290 ± 125 (Sutton 1972:8) has been obtained for an occurrence of this pottery on the extreme northern edge of the area of Bantu language distribution. Two sites in fairly close proximity to each other in the interlacustrine area have yielded a number of dates, including three in the second half of the first millennium B.C. and two in the first century A.D.; however, the spread of dates from one of the sites is very wide, and they should be treated with some reserve.

East of this area, in central Tanzania and across towards the coast, is another ceramic tradition, named after the locality at Kwale which, although different, is none the less clearly related to the Dimple-based pottery tradition. The few dates available suggest a commencement in the second century. The early Iron Age occupation at Kalambo Falls (at the southern end of Lake Tanganyika), for all its distance from the main area of occurrence, may belong to the Kwale tradition, or it might represent a third member of a related triad. What is, perhaps, remarkable about Kalambo is that the pottery is said to display no apparent change throughout a 1200-year period spanning

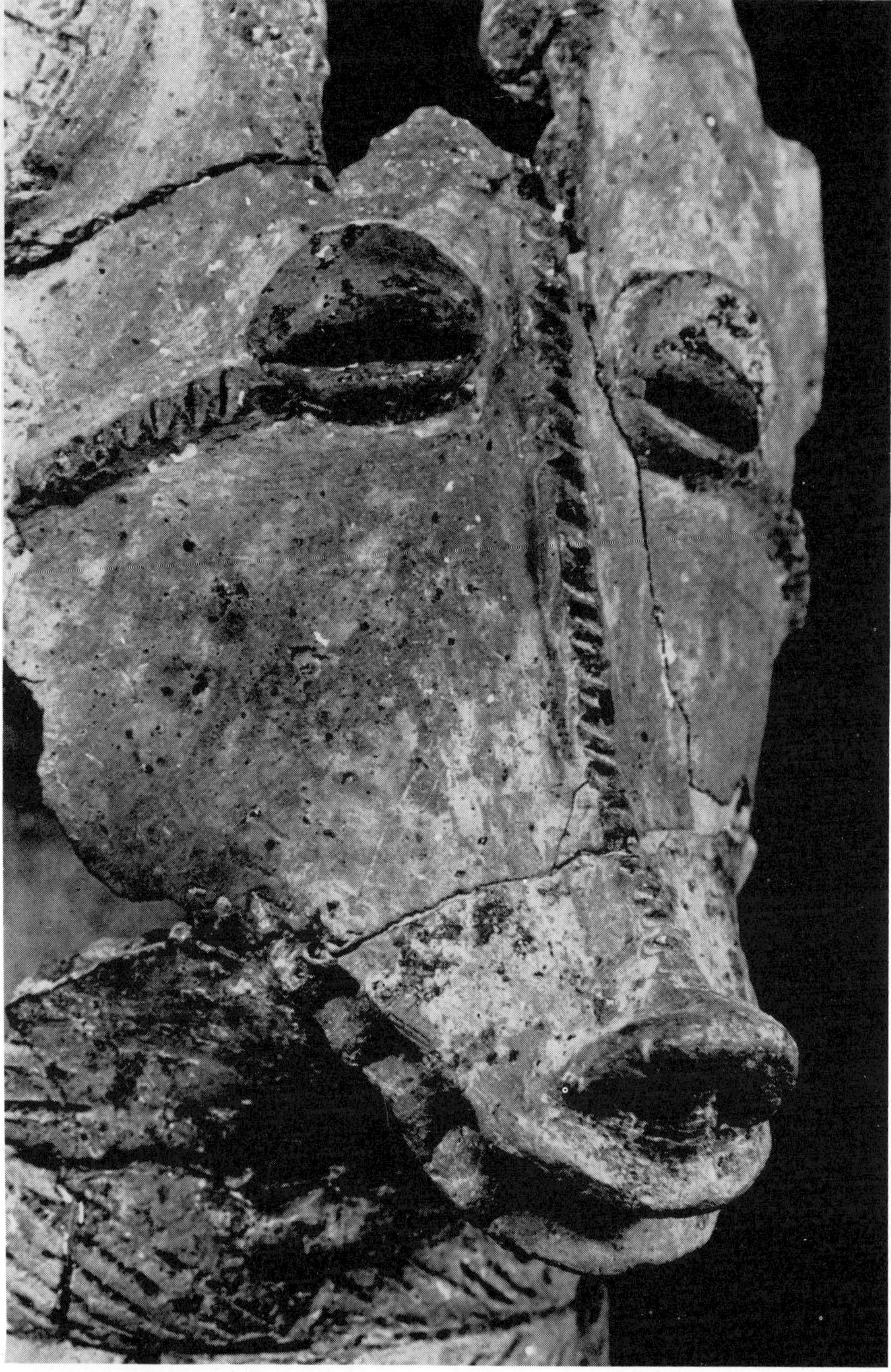

Figure 2. (above and right). Two of the pottery heads from Lydenburg, Transvaal.

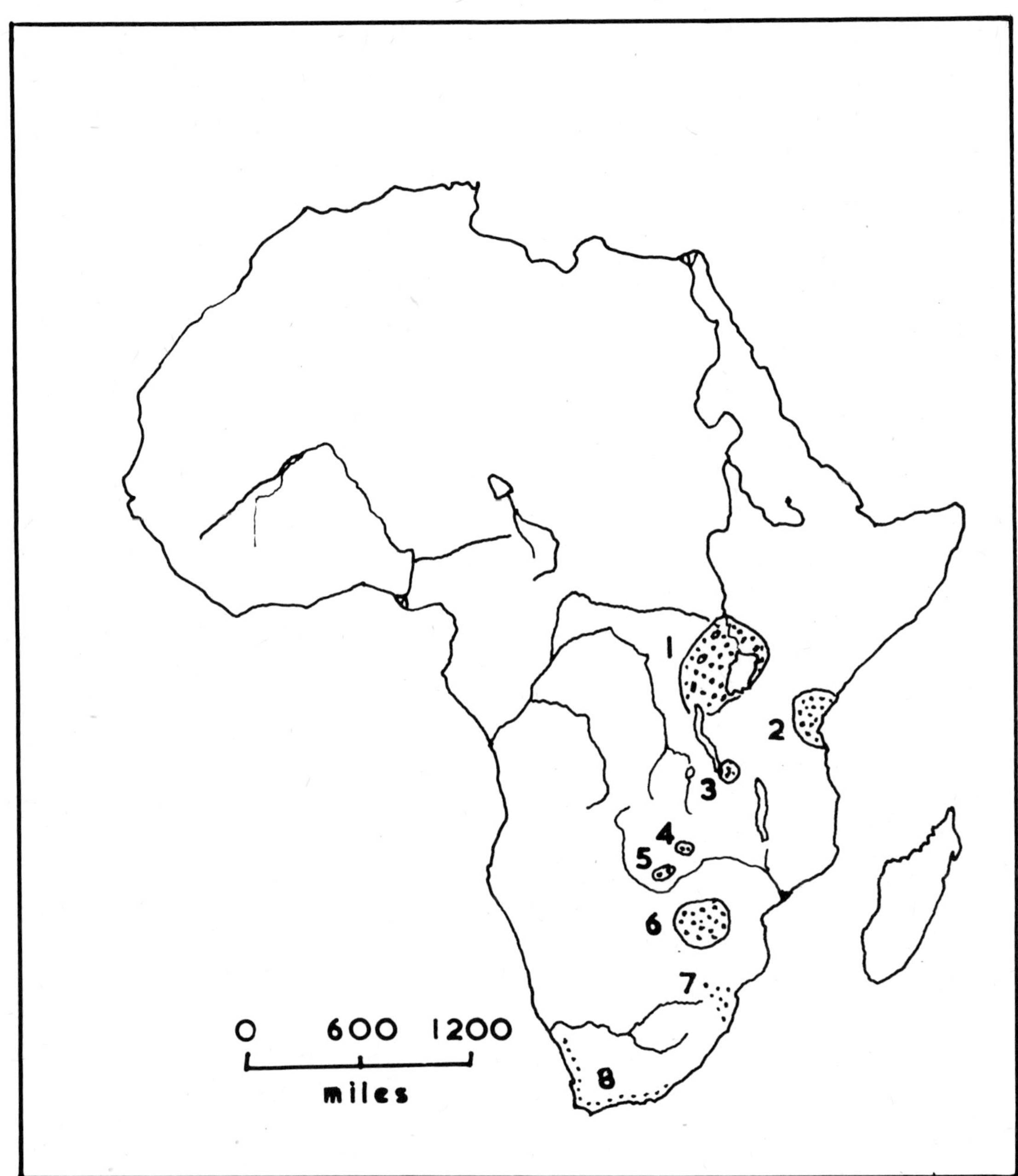

Figure 3. Distribution of main pottery traditions mentioned in the text. Based on Huffman, with additions. 1. Dimple base; 2. Kwale; 3. Kalambo; 4. Kapwirimbwe; 5. Kalundu; 6. Gokomere; 7. NC3 and related; 8. Coastal L.S.A.

the fourth to the sixteenth centuries. As one moves south through Zambia to the Lusaka region and Kalomo, two more ceramic traditions are encountered, Kapwirimbwe and Kalundu, which belong to the fifth/sixth and fourth/fifth centuries, respectively. In the region of the Victoria Falls, the earliest pottery, dated to the fifth to ninth centuries, seems to have affinities with Gokomere ware extending across Rhodesia almost to the Limpopo, with dates embracing the second to the eighth centuries. Eastwards, in Malawi, the earliest pottery in the north, related to Kwale and Kalambo Falls, has two dates in the third century A.D. and in the south, where the pottery shows closer affinities with Rhodesian Gokomere ware, dates span the third to the tenth centuries (Robinson 1973).

South of the Limpopo, most available data relate to later Iron Age events, with only a few discoveries relating to the early Iron Age. Mining and smelting of iron and copper were practised at Phalaborwa from at least the eighth century A.D. (van der Merwe & Scully 1971), and there is a third-century date from the northern Transvaal (Soutpansberg) and two fifth-century dates from close to Johannesburg.[1]

There is a fifth-century date from some remarkable pottery heads (Fig. 2) from Lydenburg, in the eastern Transvaal, and whilst the association of the date is not as sound as might be hoped for (Inskeep 1971:492), it finds some support in the fifth-century date from Castle Cavern in Swaziland (Sutton 1972:16), where the pottery is apparently somewhat similar (Maggs: *in lit.*).

With the possible exception of the Lydenburg and Swaziland pottery, the various ceramic traditions mentioned (Fig. 3), whilst displaying sufficient differences to justify separation from each other, have often been remarked to display a broad family resemblance; so much so that, although the traditions in the extreme north and south are very different, the intermediate occurrences provide a kind of bridge which, theoretically, could permit the construction of a typological series leading from one to the other. However, the radiocarbon datings do not support the suggestion of movement in either direction for, if the margins of error are noted, there is little justification for suggesting other than a broad contemporaneity throughout the entire area. This has led to the suggestion that somewhere there must be a co-tradition source area from which the traditions noted are all more or less contemporaneously derived (Huffman 1970). Regrettably, nothing has so far been found which, typologically or chronologically, could represent the hypothetical co-tradition source.

Now, since the followers of Greenberg have proposed that the proto-Bantu speakers, and by implication the bearers and initiators of early Iron Age culture, come from the Nigeria/Cameroons area, it is necessary to look briefly at that region and particularly at the Nok culture, Ife and Benin.

Very little material belonging to the Nok culture has come to light from archaeological contexts, but the yield includes domestic pottery, stone axes and adzes, possible stone hoes, grindstones, oil palm nuts, beads of tin and quartz and, above all, magnificent terracotta figures of human beings and other animals. The terracottas themselves have provided a wealth of data on dress, ornaments and hair styles, which in a remarkable number of instances find close parallels among the living peoples of Nigeria (Fagg 1962; Willett 1967). The site of Taruga has provided clear evidence of iron smelting in association with typical Nok material in the third to the fifth centuries B.C.

The tradition of modelling in clay is continued at Ife, in which place the heads assume a beautifully naturalistic form, and are later executed in brass, including pieces that are known to be associated with the ritual sacrifice of animals and human beings (Willett 1967). The tradition of brass-casting is continued at Benin.

The inhabitants of Ife preserve a tradition that the world originated at Ife when the children of the high god came down a chain from heaven, with a five-toed chicken and a bowl of sand, which the chicken scattered across the oceans to create the land. The senior descendant became the ruler (Oni) of Ife and, in due course, he sent out sixteen sons to found kingdoms of their own, including the kingdom of Benin.

The terracotta and brass heads of Ife and Benin are related to the practice of second burial of the ruler, and a beautiful example of this was seen recently in the form of an unused effigy in wood, found discarded in the courtyard of the royal palace at Ife. The effigy was like a life-sized wooden puppet, but the head was a naturalistic portrait of the dead queen, which would have been glimpsed briefly through heavy veils of beads below an ornate head-dress, whilst the body would have been completely obscured by robes.

In the town of Ife the archaeology is difficult because of extensive digging of clay pits for material to build or plaster walls and houses, but several dates in the tenth and eleventh centuries have been obtained. More importantly, Benin traces its present dynasty of rulers from Ife and, up to the fourteenth century when brass heads began to be made in Benin, it was the custom to send a token of a dead ruler for burial in Ife, in return for which Ife sent a modelled head for the second burial ceremony. A group of royal Bini burial pits has been found at Ife, yielding five dates ranging from A.D. 560 to A.D. 990, thus extending considerably the known chronology of Ife (Willett 1971). The chronological gap between Ife and Nok has been partly closed by the discovery of the site at Yelwa, some 300 miles north of Ife, from which terracottas reported to be in the style of Nok have been recovered, together with radiocarbon dates ranging from A.D. 100 to 700.

The importance of all this is that it creates a picture of a vigorous tradition of modelling and sculpture extending, in all probability, in unbroken succession from the fifth century B.C. to the present day in Nigeria, within the general region from which Greenberg would derive his pre- or proto-Bantu speakers. If we add to this the very clear evidence from anthropology and archaeology that the sculptures are an integral and vital part of deep-rooted religious and ritual beliefs and behaviour, we are left with what seems to be an important conclusion; since there is not the slightest trace of comparable ritual practices in the early Iron Age of east, central and southern Africa, it seems hard to derive our earliest Iron Age populations in these regions from an area in which such practices are so strong, and apparently have been so for two-and-a-half thousand years.

In a recent discussion of the problem of Bantu origins Clark (1970:214), apparently following Greenberg and Hiernaux, concludes that 'a large part of the ancestral Bantu stock comes from the savannah lands north of the rain forest'. 'From here', he continues, 'groups crossed the forest, rather than moving round its eastern borders, to a similar habitat in the southern Congo, from where there later began the wide-spread expansion into east and southern Africa.' Clark's following paragraph, however, leaves the reader with a feeling of uncertainty: 'The rapidity of the movement from this nuclear centre finds ample support in the archaeological evidence, though this is still very incomplete.' From this it appears that he has in mind the nuclear area defined by Guthrie on linguistic grounds; an area lying well south of the equatorial forest. The rapid movement into east and southern Africa attested by the archaeological evidence is presumably based on the apparently related early Iron Age pottery groups mentioned earlier. He goes on to say: 'It may not be too far from the truth to suggest . . . that the ancestors of the "proto-Bantu" speakers, who were primarily cultivators of root crops, sorghums and millets, made their way into the western and north-eastern parts of the Congo basin, perhaps in the second, but more likely in the first millennium B.C. when there is some evidence for forest clearance. . . . Then, around the beginning of the present era, the introduction of metallurgy and, in particular, an iron technology, triggered off rapid and wide-spread movements from the heartland south of the forests.'

The main difference, between this most recent statement of Clark's and those of Roland Oliver and earlier writers, is that whilst the latter envisage small groups of proto-Bantu speakers moving rapidly through the forest already equipped with an iron technology, Clark seems to favour an altogether slower movement, of what might legitimately be called a Neolithic culture, to the nuclear area, with subsequent acculturation in the form of iron working. What Clark does not discuss is how the knowledge of iron working may have reached the hypothetical nuclear area, nor does he point to any archaeological evidence for his Neolithic farmers south of the forest. Nothing has, as yet, been suggested as intervening between the Later Stone Age cultures and the fully fledged Iron Age cultures of the same regions. The one area in which a Neolithic may intervene, in east Africa, lies far from the apparent Bantu nuclear area.

A great, and apparently unnatural, grassland belt intervenes between the equatorial forest and the brachystegia woodland to the south of it (Gray 1962:184). Geographers maintain that this should be an area of mixed deciduous and evergreen forest, and that the grassland represents a secondary growth resulting from agriculture. They have suggested that it was chosen because the rain forest to the north presented too many difficulties for simple agriculturalists, whilst further south the rainfall is lower and there is a six-month dry season each year. It has also been noted that this grassland area coincides almost exactly with Guthrie's Bantu nuclear area. Unfortunately, we have no precise knowledge of how old the grassland area is, but it may not be entirely fortuitous that pollen analyses of cores from the bed of Lake Victoria show a sharp drop in forest pollens, with a corresponding increase in grasses, accompanied by an early-stage pioneer in the regeneration of abandoned gardens at about 3,000 years ago (Kendall & Livingstone 1972). Somewhat similar indications come from lake-bed borings in the central part of northern Zambia (Livingstone 1971) while in north-east Angola, Clark (1968) has noted marked erosion of sand from the valley slopes of streams, tentatively ascribed to the clearing of woodland for cultivation in the first millennium B.C.

How, then, may we sum up this evidence, so fleetingly reviewed? The palaeo-botanical and geological evidence, scant though it is, does suggest that there was some kind of agricultural activity south and east of the equatorial rain forest, during the first millennium B.C. Within the Bantu language area, with the exception of three isolated and suspect dates in the third to sixth centuries B.C. in the Lakes region (Sutton 1972:11) and another below Kilimanjaro (*ibid*:12), the quite large series of radiocarbon determinations points to the beginnings of iron technology in the area as commencing only after the turn of the Christian era. Only two or three dates lie in the first century A.D. and the bulk of Early Iron Age dates fall in the third to sixth centuries A.D.

If we insist on linking the Bantu 'nucleus' envisaged by Guthrie with the archaeologists' earliest Iron Age societies, regarding them as the introducers of ironworking into the area (*vide* Greenberg 1955; Oliver 1966), we meet with a number of problems. There is a possible gap of 500 to 1,000 years between the earliest inferred farming activities and the appearance of the proto-Bantu ironworkers. It also involves bringing an unknown number of proto-Bantu speakers from an unknown source to Guthrie's 'nuclear area' and expanding them from there, almost to the present limits of Bantu distribution, within a century or two. This would represent a very considerable achievement in even the most generous agricultural environment; in the territories concerned, cultivable land (in terms of traditional farming methods) may be as low as 5% over large areas, and for Zambia as a whole has been calculated to lie between 7.5% and 13.5% (Allan 1967).

Is there any alternative to this rather difficult hypothesis? It is not the aim of this essay to propose an alternative solution to a problem that will probably tax us for decades to come. It does, however, seem desirable to make an exploratory move away from an old hypothesis that has proved so unsatisfactory in so many ways, and to examine other possibilities.

Clark has come part-way to a new viewpoint by proposing that we may have to deal with *Neolithic* proto-Bantu speakers moving from north of the equatorial forest to the nuclear area and then, with the introduction of iron, undergoing a dramatic expansion. But we are still left with the problem of the absence of any convincing Neolithic 'culture' in the areas concerned, and with the improbably rapid expansion after the introduction of iron. Perhaps we should go one step further and suggest that the proto-Bantu speakers may represent a long-established Stone Age population basically, at least, hunter-gatherers, already dispersed over a considerable part of the Bantu language area several thousand years ago. They might, indeed, have practised intensive plant collection, or even incipient vegeculture, as Clark (1959:186; 1962:215, 227) has hinted, without leaving much evidence of the fact in the archaeological record.

Such a proposal would, at least, avoid the problems of deriving a proto-Bantu group from north of the forest, and its remarkably rapid growth and dispersion. It would also eliminate the difficulty of the absence of genetic disturbance, by the indigenous Stone Age populations, of the hypothetical Bantu groups suggested by Hiernaux, and would remove the problem of the gap in Clark's latest proposal. It would, however, require solutions to the problems of how such Bantu-speaking Later Stone Age populations might have received the various culture traits that make up the archaeological Iron Age.

Is there any positive justification for seeking such a radically different explanation? Not much; but at least there are a few scraps of evidence that encourage one to explore the possibility. Cultivated sorghums are an important food crop over much of Africa (held to be the home of all cultivated sorghums), and the wild forms from which the cultivated varieties are derived are wide-spread (Doggett 1965). In at least one area in the southern province of Zambia, the local Bantu population regularly harvests wild grass seeds (presumably a sorghum), which apparently form a staple part of the diet, being stored in granaries and used both for meal and for brewing.[2] The availability of such a staple might well make possible a relatively sedentary existence, conducive to the reception of crafts and behaviour patterns associated with Iron Age economy.

In the extreme south, in Later Stone Age contexts from the Atlantic coast to the Indian Ocean, pottery has long been recorded (Rudner 1968), but has only recently been dated. Although quite unlike any modern Bantu or Iron Age pottery in the central or southern regions of the continent, it has always been supposed to have been derived in some way or other from contact with Iron Age peoples to the north, or to be derived directly from somewhat similar forms in the Kenya highlands. The latter possibility was eliminated when the supposedly ancestral pottery was dated to the sixteenth century (Inskeep 1969:23-4), and it now seems that chronological considerations, as well as typology, eliminate the former. Pottery is firmly dated at about 2,000 years ago at Die Kelders, just east of Capetown (Sutton 1972:21) and slightly earlier on the Cape peninsula (Grindley *et al.* 1970). A less satisfactory date of the same order is recorded for a site 350 miles east of Capetown (Inskeep 1972:247). These dates appear to be too early to allow derivation from Iron Age ceramics to the north, and it looks as though we have to deal with a locally invented pottery tradition, unless the stimulus came independently of the African Iron Age, *via* some coastal trading contacts. If this is admitted for the ceramic tradition of the southern coastal regions, it must surely also be admitted as a *possibility* for other parts of Africa.

Finally, it may be necessary to take a fresh look at the evidence for the introduction of livestock to the southern part of the continent. Some circumstantial evidence suggests that sheep and cattle may have been introduced to South Africa at different times, and perhaps from different sources, with sheep appearing earlier than cattle (Inskeep 1969:29-31). The suggestion may find some support in the recent report of sheep remains on the south-west coast in the fourth or fifth century A.D. (Schweitzer & Scott 1973). As with the pottery, this date is early enough to raise the question whether the sheep represent a derivation from Iron Age sources to the north, or whether they might have been acquired independently by way of south-east-coast trading contacts.

The question of the date at which east-coast trading began is still an open one, and there is no reason why it should not antedate the *Periplus of the Erythraean Sea* by at least a century. Scholars seem agreed that the Indonesian colonization of Madagascar occurred before A.D. 400 and yet we do not know how much earlier it might have been (Gray 1962:182).

The question of Bantu origins may well prove to be a problem quite separate from that of Iron Age origins in central and southern Africa. It would be naive to suppose that solutions will come easily, and the present essay is not an attempt to provide answers; it is rather a plea to leave aside for a while an hypothesis that has proved rather unsatisfactory, and to consider the possibility of other, and perhaps more complex, explanations.

REFERENCES

Allan, W. (1967) *The African husbandman.* London.

Clark, J.D. (1959) *The Prehistory of Southern Africa.* Harmondsworth, Middlesex.

Clark, J.D. (1962) The spread of food-production in sub-Saharan Africa. *Jour. African Hist.*, 3, 211-28.

Clark, J.D. (1968) *Further Palaeo-Anthropological Studies in Northern Lunda* (Museu do Dundo, Publicações culturais, No. 78). Lisbon.

Clark, J.D. (1970) *The Prehistory of Africa.* London.

Doggett, H. (1965) The development of the cultivated sorghums. In Hutchinson, Sir J. (ed.), *Essays on Crop Plant Evolution*, 50-69. London.

Fagg, B.E.B. (1962) The Nok terracottas in west African art history. *Actes du IVe Congrès panafricain de préhistoire,* Sect. III, 445-50. Tervuren.

Fouché, L. (1937) *Mapungubwe.* Cambridge.

Gardner, G.A. (1963) *Mapungubwe*, Vol. 2. Pretoria.

Gray, R. (1962) Third conference on African history and archaeology: a report on the conference. *Jour. African Hist.*, 3, 175-91.

Greenberg, J.H. (1955) *Studies in African linguistic classification.* New Haven.

Grindley, J.R., Speed, E. and Maggs, T. (1970) The age of the Bonteberg shelter deposits, Cape Peninsula. *S. African Arch. Bull.*, 25, 24.

Guthrie, M. (1970) Contributions from comparative Bantu studies to the prehistory of Africa. In Dalby, D., *Language and History in Africa*, 20-49. London.

Hiernaux, J. (1968) Bantu expansion: the evidence from physical anthropology confronted with linguistic and archaeological evidence. *Jour. African Hist.*, 9, 505-15.

Huffman, T.N. (1970) The early iron age and the spread of the Bantu. *S. African Arch. Bull.*, 25, 3-21.

Inskeep, R.R. (1969) The archaeological background. In Wilson, M. and Thompson, L. (eds.), *The Oxford History of South Africa*, Vol. I, 1-39. Oxford.

Inskeep, R.R. (1971) Terracotta heads. *S. African Jour. Sci.*, 67, 492-3.

Inskeep, R.R. (1972) Nelson's Bay cave, Robberg Peninsula, Plettenberg Bay. In Bakker, E.M. van Z. (ed.), *Palaeoecology of Africa, the surrounding islands and Antarctica.* Cape Town.

Johnston, Sir H.H. (1913) A survey of the ethnography of Africa: and the former racial and tribal migrations in that continent. *Jour. R. Anthrop. Inst.*,43, 375-421.

Kendall, R.L. and Livingstone, D.A. (1972) Palaeo-ecological studies on the east African plateau. In Hugot, H.J. (ed.), *Congrès panafricain de préhistoire: Dakar 1967.* Chambéry.

Livingstone, D.A. (1971) A 22,000 year pollen record from the plateau of Zambia. *Limnology and Oceanography*, 16, 349-56.

Oliver, R. (1966) The problem of the Bantu expansion. *Jour. African Hist.*, 7, 361-76.

Robinson, K.R. (1973) The pottery sequence of Malawi briefly compared with that already established south of the Zambezi. *Arnoldia* (Rhodesia), 6, 1-12.

Rudner, J. (1968) Strandloper pottery from South and South West Africa. *Annals of the S. African Museum*, 49, (2).

Schweitzer, F.R. and Scott, K.J. (1973) Early occurrence of domestic sheep in sub-Saharan Africa. *Nature*, 241, 547.

Sutton, J.E.G. (1972) New radiocarbon dates for eastern and southern Africa. *Jour. African Hist.*, 13, 1-24.

Van der Merwe, N.J. and Scully, R.T.K. (1971) The Phalaborwa story. *World Arch.*, 3, 178-96.

Willett, F. (1967) *Ife in the History of West African Sculpture.* New York.

Willett, F. (1971) Nigeria. In Shinnie, P.L. (ed.), *The African Iron Age*, 1-35. Oxford.

Wrigley, C. (1960) Speculations on the economic history of Africa. *Jour. African Hist.*, 1, 189-203.

NOTES

1. These three dates were reported by Professor R.J. Mason at a meeting of the South African Association of Archaeologists in Johannesburg in September 1972, and communicated to me *in lit.* by T. Maggs, to whom I am most grateful.

2. I am indebted to Dr W. Bainbridge for this information, recorded during his service in the Provincial Forestry Department in Zambia.

GLYNN ISAAC

Early stone tools – an adaptive threshold?

Hominid evolution involved a series of transformations in behaviour which had the effect, not only of bringing mankind into existence, but also of creating an unconscious record of the process. The self-recording actions of hominids that make archaeology possible are as peculiar to man as language: transport of food to a central locale or 'camp' where refuse accumulates; consumption of food with a durable residue, as in meat with bone; manufacture of durable equipment and its by-products, the stone 'industries' of early man. It is salutary to reflect that the behaviour of our closest living relative, the chimpanzee, lacks these features and therefore, however interested one might be in the history of chimpanzee behaviour, there is no possibility of an archaeological study being made. Conversely, when archaeological traces are detectable one can be confident that they represent behaviour that was organized in a human pattern, at least to an incipient degree.

Among these several self-recording behaviour-types, the manufacture of artefacts has been the principal preoccupation of Palaeolithic archaeologists, but in recent years Mary Leakey and other workers have shown that even the very earliest assemblages need not be studied merely as sequences of technological fossils. If one seeks out localities where preservation is good, it is possible to study the proto-human activity of two or more million years ago with the same kind of holistic approach shown in Grahame Clark's classic research on the Mesolithic at Star Carr.

In this essay, I wish to offer a review of certain aspects of the latest evidence from East Africa concerning very early stone tools, seen from a behavioural and ecological point of view, rather than from the more familiar standpoint of morphology. I do so here in recognition of the fact that the example provided by Grahame Clark's work has been one of the crucial strands in the fabric of my own anthropological interests.

If we accept that mankind is derived by evolution from animals that had effectively zero material culture and much simpler patterns of socially-learned behaviour, then it follows that information on the ways in which our ancestral lineage became involved with 'equipment' is of considerable importance for evolutionary theory. We tend to assume that involvement must have proceeded in 'stages', marked initially by man's increasing intensity of dependence on tools and also by increasing degrees of technical and design complexity amongst the artefacts. Most of the information that we are ever likely to have on this subject will come from stone artefacts, and fortunately there are already sufficient samples of these from early Pleistocene time-ranges, for us at least to start formulating our questions more precisely. This paper is concerned with certain aspects of a pilot study of two Lower Pleistocene assemblages, carried out by the author.

In studies of early stone tools, we strive to obtain information on the following primary topics:

1. The specific recurrent craft-practices of the craftsman, as represented by each assemblage; this is described as 'technology';
2. The design-concepts or rules of these craftsmen, as indicated by recurrent artefact features (often miscalled 'typology');[1]
3. Patterns of use and function (as ascertained from morphology, damage, wear or context).

Various secondary inferences can also be made, based on data relating to the primary technical concepts:

1. Degrees of similarity in technique and design can be taken as indicative of culture-historic relationships;
2. Patterns of variation (or change) in technique and/or design may be treated as symptomatic of certain kinds of socio-cultural or economic arrangements;
3. Degrees of 'complexity' perceived in the

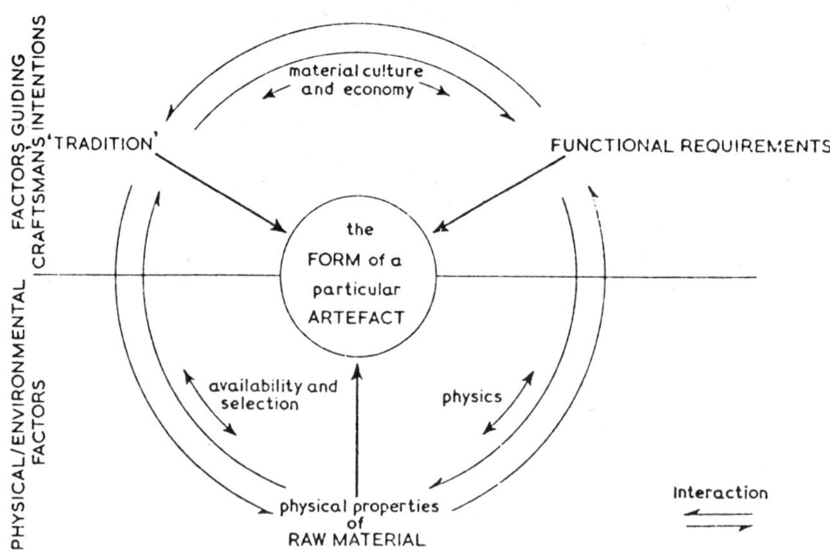

Figure 1. Diagrammatic representation of the interaction of factors that determine the form of a flaked stone artefact (from Isaac 1972b, in *Models in Archaeology*, edited by D.L. Clarke).

technique or design of artefacts may be regarded as indicative of the degrees of complexity in the material culture as a whole.

Nearly all Palaeolithic archaeology consists of comparative studies made for culture-historic purposes. However, when we come to deal with the early part of the Pleistocene, even if we accept these objectives, we run into difficulties with the normal assumptions of the culture taxonomic approach. Of particular interest are questions concerning 'levels of complexity' but with these, too, there are as yet unresolved methodological problems.

Fig. 1 illustrates schematically some of the factors that combine together to influence the final form of a stone tool. It can be seen that in trying to make inferences about the specific 'design norms', or 'traditions', manifest in a set of artefacts, it is necessary to resolve and subtract other factors, such as those that can be attributed to the physics of conchoidal fracture or to the primary form of the raw material. Now, for complex artefacts such as refined hand-axes or tanged points, each involving a great many technical acts (e.g. flake removals), the role of a specific tradition in determining form may be quite clear. However, the shorter the sequence of technical acts, the more decisive will be those aspects of form imposed by 'physics' and 'geology' rather than by design. Thus, there is a limited range of forms that can result from the simple sharpening of common, naturally occurring, stone fragments. This situation creates difficulties in the study of early tool-kits: it is hard to distinguish separate 'intentions' or 'traditions' from opportunism, and there is a continual danger of over-interpreting the material.

Models of the development of stone technology

Perhaps the majority of descriptions of very early stone tools, until recently, were based on a tacit assumption that the development of technological complexity and design-elaboration was initially a very prolonged and gradual process. It is possible to parody this view-point as follows:

> Stage I began when an early hominid genius knocked off one flake from a pebble and 'discovered' the small sharp edge thus produced.
>
> Several tens or hundreds of millennia later, stage II began when another accident occurred, leading to the removal of two flakes from the pebble, thus providing a unifacially worked chopper.
>
> Then, at intervals, it was found that three or four flakes could be removed until eventually, in stage III, it was discovered that flakes could

be knocked off in both directions, thereby producing bifacial choppers (chopping tools) – and so on.

This simplified developmental picture of early stone tool technology seems very improbable and, in fact, Mary Leakey's study of the artefacts from Bed I at Olduvai Gorge shows it to be misleading, since there are strong indications that the oldest assemblages known contain a far wider diversity of forms than would be predicted by our model (Leakey 1971).

One alternative to this 'gradual creep' theory of early technological development is what we may describe as the 'big bump' hypothesis: that is to say, the notion that there may have been 'thresholds' in man's involvement with stone tool manufacture and use. The possible threshold under discussion in this paper is that of the empirical discovery of conchoidal fracture of stone. It is conceivable that the knack of shaping stone by means of conchoidal fracture immediately gave rise to a fairly wide range of forms that were inherent in the combination of physics and stone-particle morphology. If there is any validity in this view, then such a range of forms must not be used to imply any specific tradition, nor need it necessarily imply any important duration of prior development. This alternative view-point is fairly widely held, though seldom explicitly stated. It is implicit, for example, in Grahame Clark's classification of industries into modes 1, 2, 3 etc. (Clark 1970).

On the basis of such threshold models, one might expect early phases in stone-craft to be of great duration and to involve subtle variation, without transcending the 'levels' or 'grades'. While it is beyond the scope of this paper, there are possibilities of extending the threshold concept to cope with various later transformations of stone industries (see Isaac 1972b).

Clearly, the notion of a threshold as a useful concept falls short of informing one as to what range of forms may be inherent consequences of such a discovery as that of conchoidal fracture. This range would have to be determined by experiment and by the analysis of the archaeological record. Moreover, gradual development and threshold models are not mutually exclusive: rather, they can best be seen as extremes in a continuum in which both gradual shift and rapid transformations were involved.

Tools and adaptation

In addition to questions regarding the processes of technological development, there is a whole series of other questions that relate to the role of early stone tools in the lives of the hominids. What were the functions of these objects? What part did they play in changing adaptations? We can, perhaps, best organize enquiry into these questions if we consider the part played by equipment in establishing contrasts between the behaviour of recent men and of non-human primates. Peoples such as the !Kung or the Australian aboriginals provide a suitable standard of reference for non-agricultural men, and the chimpanzee is probably the primate with behaviour patterns most relevant to the problem.

Chimpanzees are now known to engage in tool-use and even to carry out simple modifications of their equipment, but tools are not crucial to the basic subsistence pattern, that of individual feeding on fruits and to a lesser extent on leaf-shoots, insects, eggs and nestlings (Lawick-Goodall 1971). Chimpanzees do add a very small supplement to their diet by hunting but, as far as we know, their prey consists entirely of small animals that are caught by hand and then torn apart and chewed. Intra-specific aggression and defence against predators may involve branch-waving and throwing displays, but as far as is known, the fighting itself is done with hands and teeth.

By contrast, human groups are dependent on tools and equipment in carrying out their subsistence strategy. All non-agricultural groups consume more animal protein than do chimpanzees, and the acquisition of such protein ordinarily involves spears, clubs, missiles, nets or lines. Very often the quarry of human hunters are as large as, or larger than, the hunter, and such prey cannot readily be dismembered and consumed without the aid of cutting tools. Human societies have, as an integral part of their fabric, the sharing of foods between adults. Now, while meat can easily be carried without equipment and shared, this can only be done with most vegetable foods with the aid of bags, baskets or trays. Finally, amongst all human groups, both intra-specific aggression and defence against predators involve weapons and most men feel helpless if caught without them.

This contrast in degree of dependence on

artefacts surely arose in the course of evolution and the question can be formulated afresh: do the available samples of early Pleistocene equipment help us to understand the evolutionary origins of the present contrast between man and chimpanzee? Do we know anything about the relationships between the activities of Plio-Pleistocene hominids and the tools that have been recovered? These questions can best be answered after a summary of the character of the early assemblages.

Available samples of early stone tools

The best studied series of early Pleistocene stone artefacts is that recovered by Mary Leakey from Beds I and Lower II at Olduvai Gorge (Leakey 1971). The sample from below the Lemuta Member comprises about 6,000 artefacts derived from fifteen levels at five different sites. It was until recently supposed that the sample extended over a long span of time, but the latest palaeomagnetic data show clearly that all these occurrences belong within the Olduvai Normal Event (Gilsa event of some authors) of the Matuyama Reversed Epoch (Leakey 1971). The mean potassium-argon age for the whole implementiferous part of Bed I is 1.8 ± 0.13 million years (Curtis & Hay 1972), while the palaeomagnetic evidence makes the interval 1.8 – 1.65 the best estimate of age and duration. To this body of data we can now add the information from archaeological sites discovered in 1969 in the area east of Lake Rudolf (R.E. Leakey 1970; M.D. Leakey 1970). The artefact occurrences in question are stratified within the top part of the Lower Member of the Koobi Fora Formation, where they are associated with a volcanic tuff containing pumice cobbles with an age estimated as 2.6 ± 0.26 million years (Fitch & Miller 1970). Palaeomagnetic determinations lend support to this date (Brock & Isaac 1974), but further cross-checks are essential. Only a few sites have been found so far and, at all of these, the densities of artefacts were comparatively low, so that the technological and behavioural system represented is less well known than that of Olduvai (Isaac *et al.* 1971).

Other very early artefact assemblages have recently been recovered from Member F of the Shungara Formation in the lower Omo Valley (Coppens *et al.* 1973; Merrick *et al.* 1973). An age of about two million years was suggested for these assemblages and information has recently become available which suggests that both the East Rudolf and the Shungura samples may be of similar age. These samples span the time of the Pliocene-Pleistocene boundary according to many authorities (i.e. about two million years B.P.) and they can conveniently be referred to as 'Plio-Pleistocene' assemblages.

Assemblage composition (see Table 1)

At Koobi Fora and Olduvai, the artefact assemblages comprise two inherently distinct series, namely:

1. Comparatively chunky (i.e. thick relative to length and breadth) pieces of stone from which flakes have been removed;
2. Comparatively thin, sliver-like fragments of broken stone which are usually *flakes*, in the technical sense of that word, but which comprise also broken flakes and other shattered stone specimens.

The material so far reported from the Omo, on the other hand, involves only the second of these series. It appears that only very small quartz and other silicious pebbles were available at this site and that these were smashed to produce flakes and fragments, which are therefore difficult to compare with those of the other sites.

Series 1 artefacts are *cores*, in the sense of being the parent blocks from which flakes have been removed. However, if one judges that the flakes were knocked off primarily in order to shape the block for use as an implement, then the parent block must be classified as a *tool* and not as a *core*. In the Olduvai series Mary Leakey has shown strong reasons for regarding the majority of these 'flaked blocks' as choppers. There is a disproportion of raw material frequencies between the flakes and choppers and there are signs of damage on the relevant edges of the 'implements'. Equivalent evidence for the use of the chunky flaked objects has not so far been discovered at Koobi Fora. One can perhaps use an old-fashioned generic term, *core tools*, for the objects in this series.

Series 2 artefacts include flakes, flake-fragments and angular fragments of supposed artefactual origin. When present, 'light duty' tools such as scrapers, *becs* etc., are normally made

Table 1 Percentage composition of assemblages (to first decimal place)

	East Rudolf sites			*Olduvai I (selected sites)*			
	KBS excavation	*HAS excavation*	*KBS+HAS (total)*	*DKE*	*FLK Zinjanthropus*	*FLKN Levels 1-2*	*FLKN Level 3*
Total assemblage							
Tools	5.0	2.5		12.8	2.4	12.4	16.4
Utilized	2.1	0.8		15.6	5.4	17.7	28.6
Debitage	93.0	96.7		71.5	92.1	69.9	55.0
Numbers	*139*	*119*		*1198*	*2470*	*1205*	*171*
Tools							
Choppers			45.8	30.4	28.3	57.8	67.8
Broken/irregular choppers			16.9	–	–	3.3	3.6
Polyhedra			12.5	20.8	15.0	3.4	10.7
Discoids			8.3	17.5	5.0	5.4	7.1
Light duty scrapers			8.3	13.0	30.0	8.0	–
Sundry tools			8.3	5.2	–	2.0	–
Subspheroids & spheroids			–	4.5	–	8.0	7.1
Heavy duty scrapers			–	6.5	15.0	8.7	3.6
Burins			–	2.0	6.6	–	–
Protobifaces			–	–	–	3.4	–
Numbers	*7*	*3*	*24*	*154*	*60*	*149*	*28*
Debitage							
Whole flakes	32.0	29.5		28.2	11.3	21.1	29.8
Core resharpening flakes	2.0	0.9		1.8	–	0.3	–
Broken flakes	66.0	69.6		56.1	81.8	68.3	64.9
Core fragments	–	–		13.8	6.8	10.3	5.3
Numbers	*129*	*115*		*857*	*2275*	*842*	*94*
% of lava debitage	99.2	99.1		64.0	3.4	15.0	17.4

on pieces assignable to series 2. 'Heavy duty' scrapers etc. are, in some senses, intermediate between series 1 and series 2, but are comparatively rare. For present purposes, they are included with the chopper/cores.

Small scrapers are virtually absent from the early East Rudolf assemblages, being represented only by rare, poorly characterized and dubious examples. If this turns out to be a recurrent feature of the industry, then it will differ in this respect from almost all later stone industries, although almost half of the Olduvai Bed I assemblages also lack small tools. Fig. 2 shows the frequency distribution patterns for chopper/cores and 'small tools' in the Olduvai Bed I and Koobi Fora site samples. Fig. 3 shows the composition of the assemblages for these, not by category, but in relation to size, as expressed by the maximum dimension of each piece. It can be seen that the modal class of all the assemblages comprises comparatively small objects – namely pieces between 10 and 20 mm., except for DK which has a mode in the 20-30 mm. range. Of the four samples so far analysed in this way, DK and KBS show bi-modality with a diffuse minor second mode for larger pieces: 50-100 mm. This second mode reflects the presence of small, but significant, numbers of core-tools in these assemblages. Most of the core-tools can be categorized as choppers, discoids or polyhedra, and all of these categories are common to both the KBS sample and the Olduvai samples (Table 1). The characteristics and inter-relations of these form-categories have been well reported for the Olduvai sample (Leakey 1971). The flakes and flake-fragments at both Olduvai and East Rudolf show similar technical attributes and may fairly be regarded as the products of rather generalized opportunistic stone-knapping (Isaac, in preparation).

In summary, the available geophysically-dated samples of Plio-Pleistocene stone artefacts share

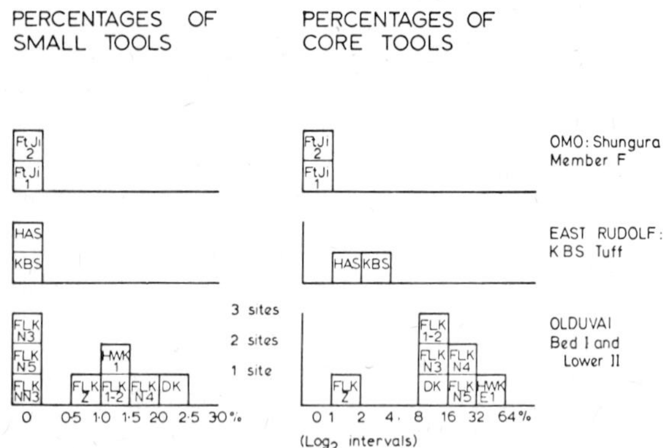

Figure 2. Histograms showing the frequency distribution of observations of the percentage frequency of each of the two major tool families: small tools (light-duty scrapers and burins); core tools (choppers, discoids, polyhedra, heavy-duty scrapers). All percentages are relative to the entire set of artefacts recovered. Olduvai Bed I and Lower II from M.D. Leakey (1971: 265). Omo from Merrick *et al.* 1973.

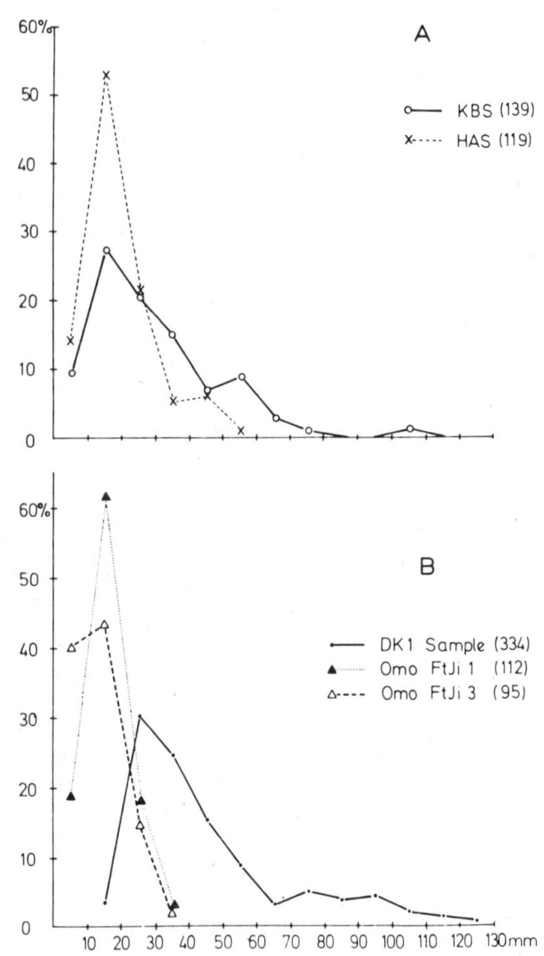

Figure 3. Frequency distributions for the size of all artefacts in early stone-tool assemblages. A. East Rudolf. B. Olduvai DK and the Omo. Data for the Omo from Merrick *et al.* 1973.

only one feature. Smallish flakes and flake-fragments predominate in all of them and this is, in fact, a generalized feature that they share with most other stone industries. As already shown, the Shungura samples differ markedly from the other two by the small modal size of the industry and the virtual absence of core-tools; but one suspects that both of these differences were determined, or at least very strongly influenced, by the restrictions of having only very small pebbles available. As long as we suspect that the differences were induced by the raw materials, we cannot make simple inferences about cultural or activity contrasts for this assemblage.

Preliminary comparisons between the lava artefacts of Koobi Fora and those of Olduvai Bed I suggest that the former fall entirely within the morphological range of the latter, and that the basic patterns of forms present are similar. Apparent differences include smaller modal size for the Koobi Fora samples and, perhaps, the absence of well-characterized small scrapers. The size-difference could well be a function of raw material availability, though it may not be due to this.

Function

We have, as yet, no direct evidence of the functions of early stone tools, but there is strong circumstantial evidence for associating them with some activities that would have been facilitated by their use. At both Olduvai and Koobi Fora, the early artefacts form scatters, coincident with patches of broken-up mammal bones, which would seem to constitute evidence for the division and consumption of a number of different animals, ranging in size from rodents to pachyderms. As discussed above, it is hard to conceive of a large carcase being dismembered by smallish primates without cutting tools, so that tools may fairly be regarded as an integral part of an adaptive complex that also involved hunting and food-sharing. In this connexion, it should be pointed out that there has been a growing awareness of the tendency for animal butchery to involve small, comparatively simple, tools (Clark & Haynes 1969). To be useful, a sharp or pointed piece need only be large enough to be held between index finger and thumb with the point or edge projecting. Sharp pieces from 10 to 15 mm. in diameter are

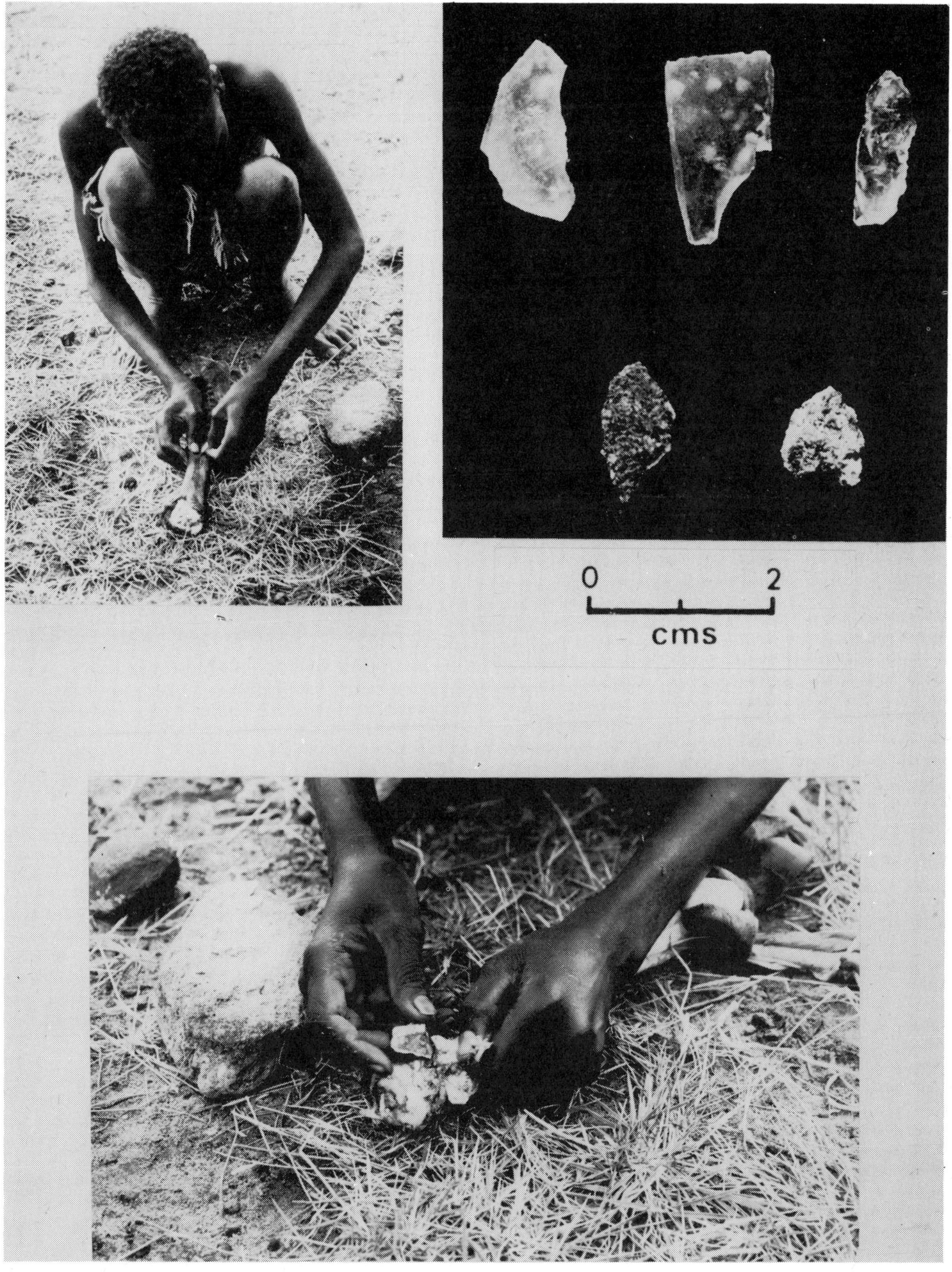

Figure 4. A Shangilla youth slits the skin of an antelope limb using only very small 'waste' flakes (c).

potentially most useful for this purpose. This realization received dramatic reinforcement during field-work at Lake Rudolf. In our presence, a young Shangilla pastoralist found himself without a metal knife while confronted by a fresh lion-killed antelope carcase. Spontaneously he tapped off a very small flake from a lava cobble and proceeded to slit the skin covering a cannon bone, which he then peeled and cracked open to obtain the marrow (see Fig. 4). Clearly, such minute flakes would have been equally effective for cutting articular sinews. From this and related observations (Gould 1967) it emerges that the small sharp flakes and flake-fragments, which by convention we label as 'waste' or 'debitage', may well have had crucial adaptive importance. Perhaps it is significant that this is, in fact, the preponderant class of material in all the early sites that we have discussed.

It seems unlikely that any of the early stone artefacts were actually fashioned as weapons. However, if improvements were made to the suitability of sticks and branches for use as spears or clubs, then presumably the sharp edges of the flakes would have served to notch and whittle, while the stouter jagged chopper-edges may have been effective for hacking. It is not inconceivable that the acquisition of bark trays, such as those found at Kalambo Falls (Clark 1962), would have been facilitated by the use of flakes and core tools.

In the regrettable absence of more direct evidence, these assemblages can also be looked at in another way. The known stone tool-kit of Plio-Pleistocene sites would be quite adequate to perform all of the essential tasks of tropical non-agricultural peoples: to butcher carcases, to make wooden weapons and to make containers. These are the integral parts of human adaptation.

Conclusion

Returning to the questions raised at the outset, one can ask: what does the available information contribute to our understanding of the processes whereby man's ancestors became involved in technology?

Firstly, if the current dating of the assemblages is sustained, then it appears that there was minimal change in the main features of the tool-kits between 2.6 and 1.6 million years. This may tentatively be seen as being more readily compatible with a 'threshold' model of development than with a 'gradualistic' one – though the proposition cannot be regarded as finally proven.

Secondly, it seems that we have positive evidence for the close involvement of the early stone tools in at least one economic arrangement that probably had crucial adaptive significance; namely, a hunting/food-sharing behavioural pattern. It seems likely that this complex within the hominids' behaviour pattern was novel in relation to that of their immediate ancestors and that it, in turn, induced formative selection pressures on social mechanisms such as emotional control, co-operation, reciprocal relations and communication.

If one follows the example of Grahame Clark by taking a holistic view of the meaning of even such scanty scraps as the earliest known artefacts, then one sees that these are indeed, in some sense, 'foundation stones' for the whole edifice of human organization.

REFERENCES

Brock, A. and Isaac, G. Ll. (1974) Palaeomagnetic stratigraphy and chronology of hominid-bearing sediments east of Lake Rudolf, Kenya. *Nature*, 247, 344-8.

Clark, J.D. (1962) The Kalambo Falls prehistoric site: an interim report. In Mortelmans, G. and Nenquin, J. (eds.), *Actes du IVe Congrès Pan-Africain de Préhistoire et de l'Étude du Quaternaire*, Vol. 2, 195-201. Tervuren.

Clark, J.D. and Haynes, C.V. (1969) An elephant butchery site at Mwanganda's Village, Karonga, Malawi, and its relevance for Palaeolithic archaeology. *World Arch.*, 1, 390-411.

Clark, J.G.D. (1970) *Aspects of Prehistory*. Berkeley.

Coppens, Y., Chavaillon, J. and Beden, M. (1973) Résultats de la nouvelle mission de l'Omo (campagne 1972). Découverte de restes d'Hominides et d'une industrie sur éclats. *C.R. Acad. Science, Paris*, Série D, 276, 161-4.

Curtis, G.H. and Hay, R.L. (1972) Further geological studies and potassium-argon dating at Olduvai Gorge and Ngorongoro Crater. In Bishop, W.W. and Miller, J.A. (eds.), *Calibration of Hominoid Evolution*, 289-301. Edinburgh.

Fitch, F.J. and Miller, J.A. (1970) Radioisotopic age determinations of Lake Rudolf artefact site. *Nature*, 226, 226-8.

Goodall, J. (1971) *In the Shadow of Man.* Glasgow.

Gould, R.A. (1967) *Notes on the hunting, butchering and sharing of game among the Ngatatjara and their neighbours in the West Australia Desert.* Kroeber Anthropological Papers No. 36, Berkeley.

Isaac. G.Ll. (1972a) Chronology and the tempo of cultural change during the Pleistocene. In Bishop, W.W. and Miller, J.A. (eds.), *Calibration of Hominoid Evolution,* 381-430. Edinburgh.

Isaac, G.Ll. (1972b) Early phases of human behaviour: models for Lower Palaeolithic archaeology. In Clarke, D.L. (ed.), *Models in Archaeology,* 167-99. London.

Isaac, G.Ll. (in preparation) Plio-Pleistocene artefact assemblages from East Rudolf, Kenya.

Isaac, G.Ll., Leakey, R.E.F. and Behrensmeyer, A.K. (1971) Archaeological traces of early hominid activities, east of Lake Rudolf, Kenya. *Science,* 173, 1129-34.

Lawick-Goodall, Baroness J. van (1971) *In the Shadow of Man.* Glasgow.

Leakey, M.D. (1970) Early artefacts from the Koobi Fora area. *Nature,* 226, 228-30.

Leakey, M.D. (1971) *Olduvai Gorge.* Vol. 3, *Excavations in Beds I and II.* London.

Leakey, R.E.F. (1970) New Hominid remains and early artefacts from Northern Kenya. *Nature,* 226, 223-4.

Merrick, H.V., Heinzelin, J. de, Haesaerts, P. and Howell, F.C. (1973) Archaeological occurrences of Early Pleistocene age from the Shungura formation, Lower Omo Valley, Ethiopia. *Nature,* 242, 572-5.

NOTES

1. Although these distinctions are useful, craft-practice in the sense of 'technology' and design-concepts in the sense of socially sanctioned 'mental templates' are inextricably interpenetrating concepts, since design involves choice of technique and techniques influence and limit the scope of design. Similarly, form and function are inter-related in an intricate fashion.

MERRICK POSNANSKY

Archaeology and the origins of the Akan society in Ghana

One of the central problems in the historiography of Ghana has been the origin of the Akan peoples. The Akan, distinguished on the basis of linguistic and cultural criteria, are the dominant ethnic group in Ghana and, at the present day, comprise more than forty per cent of the population. It was amongst the Akan groups that kingship developed with elaborate court rituals: their states became well known to the earliest European visitors to the West African coast, whose accounts, from the last quarter of the fifteenth century A.D., provide the earliest literary sources for Ghanaian history. The last major Akan state to arise, that of Asante which established a hegemony from 1701, both in the forest and to the north of it, is one of the most widely known of the so-called West African 'Forest states'. It is characterized by its panoply of gold-plated regalia, ceremonial umbrellas, finely woven *kente* cloth, intricate and aesthetically attractive brass weights for weighing gold, carved wooden stools and its famous golden stool that was the embodiment of the state itself. Linguistically, the Akan belong to the Niger-Khordofanian language-family of J.H. Greenberg (1953); sociologically, they are distinguished by their complex system of exogamous matrilineal and patrilineal clans that cut across tribal and political boundaries and have been described in detail by the social anthropologists. Basically, there are two schools of thought on Akan origins. The older school, with its roots in nineteenth-century scholarship, is diffusionist in opinion and claims that the Akan came from outside Ghana, either from the ancient kingdom of Ghana, whose capitals probably lay in southern Mauretania, or from the Nile Valley, north Africa, the Sahara (Meyerowitz 1960) or even as far afield as Mesopotamia (Danquah 1957). The more modern viewpoint, cogently summarized by Boahen (1966), locates the immediate focus of development of Akan society in the forest belt of Ghana itself and their ultimate origins in the Sudanic belt to the north-east. This paper is intended to indicate the archaeological contribution to this unresolved controversy. The writer is fully aware that many of the conclusions drawn are speculative due to the small amount of archaeological data available at present. These speculative ideas are here put forward in the belief that research approaches can be adequately planned only by critically examining hypotheses about problems in social and economic archaeology.

Archaeology in Ghana, as in most of tropical Africa, is in its infancy. The first Department of Archaeology dates from 1951 and the National Museum and Monuments Board from 1957. It is only in the last dozen years that a continuing programme of archaeological field investigation has proved feasible. Large areas are relatively unexplored and interpretative syntheses are difficult. The present state of knowledge is summarized in Calvocoressi and York (1971) and Posnansky (1970). Basically, the picture that is emerging is of a relatively late and sparse Stone Age settlement that, on present evidence, does not begin much before the end of the mid-Pleistocene. The earliest probable agricultural societies, characterized by the curious, oval-sectioned, round-ended pieces of soft stone or terracotta up to 30 cm. long and 5 cm. wide, termed 'cigars' by Davies (1961) and 'rasps' by Flight (1967), date from the second millennium B.C. Grouped together as the Kintampo 'Neolithic' tradition, they include within their material culture artefacts such as stone bracelets, harpoons and hollow-based arrow-points (at Ntereso), and impressed decorated pottery reminiscent of Saharan Neolithic traditions. Suggestions have been made by Davies (1963:383-5) of an independent development of vegeculture based on yams in the West African forest, dating to perhaps as early as the fifth millennium B.C. (Birmingham 1966:1), but there is neither direct nor circumstantial evidence in support of this

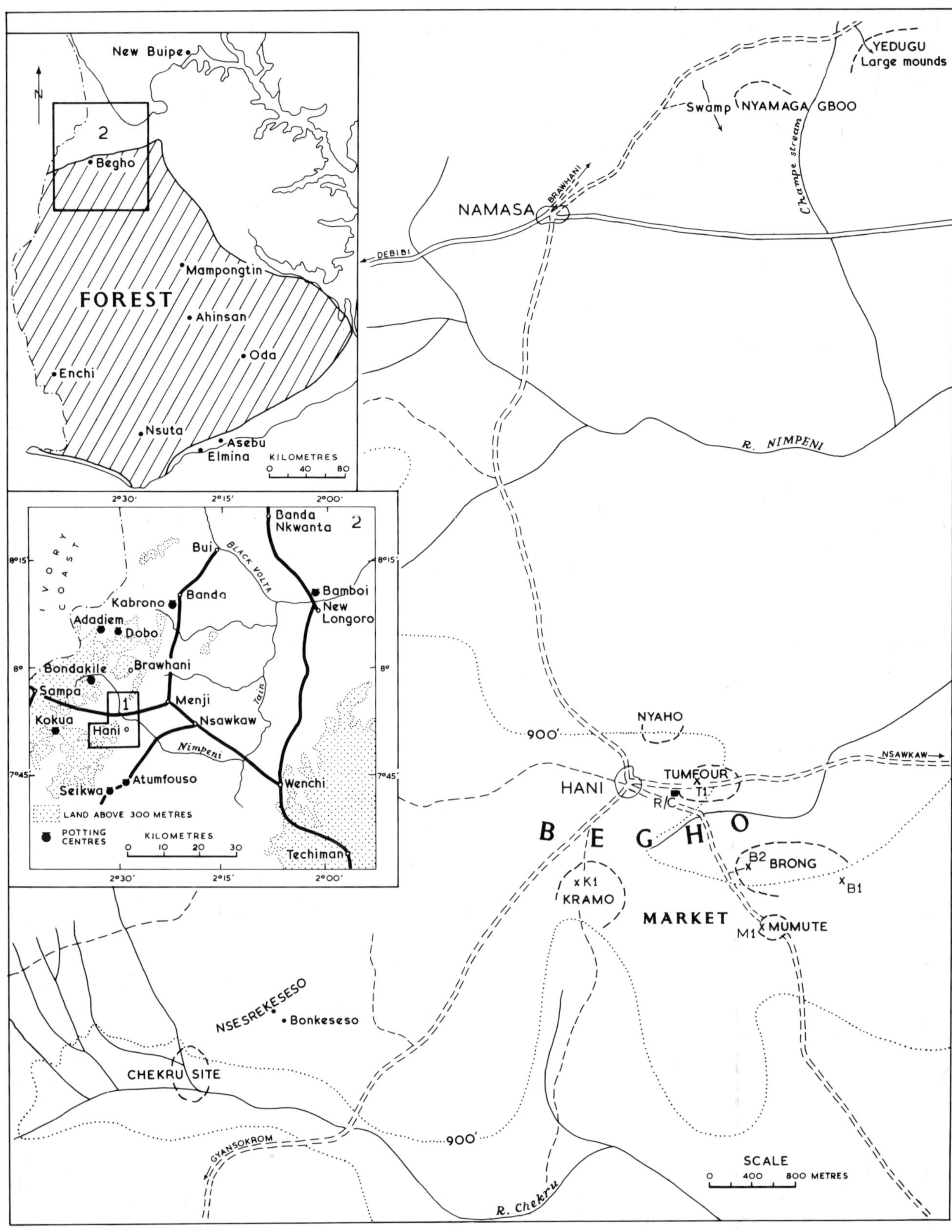

Figure 1. Archaeological sites in the Begho area and location of Begho area in Ghana. N.B. Since this paper was written, intensive botanical research has been undertaken at Begho which indicates that the Begho area is located in the true Savannah belt. The edge of the forest on inset 1 should, therefore, be marked several miles to the south of Begho.

theory. Though iron was smelted and in use by the first quarter of the first millennium A.D. in Nigeria and Senegal, the earliest radiocarbon dates for iron-using societies in Ghana are those from the eighth century A.D. at New Buipe (York 1973). It is, however, probable that further excavations will provide an earlier date. From around the fifteenth century A.D., there is evidence of the growth of settlements in the Brong Ahafo region on the northern boundaries of the forest and to the north of it, as well as in the confluence area of the Volta. These settlements owe much to the beginnings of the exploitation of Ghanaian gold and to the trade in that commodity and kola, to the large towns on the Niger, like Jenne and Timbuktu in the state of Mali. The development of such towns as Jenne also owed much, probably, to the southward expansion of Mande traders engaged in the gold trade. I have dealt elsewhere, in some detail (Posnansky 1972; 1973), with the importance of this trade. Unfortunately, except for the one site of New Buipe, there is no reliable data on the Iron Age between the time of the Kintampo sites and that of the Begho sites, in just the period that we have to look to for the origins of the Akan. The earliest Akan state, founded in the fifteenth century, was that of Bono Manso where archaeological work under the direction of Mr E. Effah-Gyamfi is presently being undertaken.

Though there is no Early Iron Age site in the area where the earliest Akan states arose, or dating to the period immediately prior to their presumed origin, nevertheless archaeology can provide useful viewpoints, as has been shown by research conducted at Begho from 1970 onwards. So far, four relatively small excavations have been carried out at Begho. The site is probably typical of many around the fringes of the forest in the area described as 'derived savannah', in which the predominant vegetation consists of three-metre-tall elephant grass and residual forest trees. Mounds, rarely more than a metre and a half high and up to thirty metres across, often L-shaped and very much disturbed by burrowing creatures that can be as large as aard-varks, occur in four groups, indicating the former quarters of a once large town. The quarters, which are one to two kilometres from one another, are reputed by the present Brong inhabitants of the area to belong, respectively, to the Akan-speaking Brong at present incumbent at Hani, a modern village within the area of the four quarters; to the Kramo, the Muslim merchants presumed to have spoken Mande dialects and to have come from Mali to the north-west; to the Tumfour or artisans and, finally, to the Nyaho, a mixed group.

The Brong quarter was the largest, with perhaps 200 or more habitation units. The houses here have solid mud walls built up in layers 60 cm. high and up to 25 cm. thick. The mud for their construction was obtained from shallow depressions around the houses. Observation of modern weathering indicates that many houses, built in a similar fashion at the present day, collapse because the splashing up of rain-water dripping from the grass roofs undercuts the wall at the base. As a result of this process of undercutting, it is very difficult to pick out walls, though fragments of floors can normally be distinguished. The evidence of oral tradition and six radiocarbon dates both confirm that the town was occupied between A.D. 1400 and 1725, and attained the peak of its prosperity towards the beginning of the seventeenth century. Imports consisted mainly of glass beads and copper in various forms, chiefly jewelry, while small pieces of late sixteenth-century Chinese porcelain and a piece of glass have also been found. Local manufactures consisted of iron, carved objects of ivory, beads, as well as ceramics and also textiles, which were probably both spun and dyed at Begho.

Detailed analysis of the house-structures and ceramics, as well as such indications as can be gleaned of the ritual life of the inhabitants, burials and offerings to ward off evil spirits, all indicate a continuity in practice between people of the Brong quarter of Begho and their modern descendants. At Begho B1 site in a corner of a room was a heap of over fifty small open bowls made of a peculiar light paste and largely undecorated. Similar bowls are still used by chiefs and fetish priests and left in houses when they are abandoned. A pot set into the floor and containing the whole skeleton of a chicken has been interpreted as an attempt to keep off malignant spirits. It is particularly surprising that the pottery from the Brong and the Kramo quarters does not differ significantly which suggests, either that the foreign trading element was not very large, or that those people who came from Mali or, more probably, the Brong and the Kramo, both obtained their pottery from the same potters. At present the potters are Mo peoples who do not speak Brong or Mande and probably represent a Mossi-speaking group (Goody 1966:18). The working hypothesis expressed by local historians and social anthropologists, based upon oral traditions, linguistic analysis and a study of the present-day social and ritual organization, is that towns like Begho developed as collecting centres for gold. These towns grew up in an area where movement was still by pack-animal in a zone south of the bend of the Black Volta where movement was easy and agriculture was relatively productive, and where iron, ivory and tree-cotton (kapok) was locally available. The towns probably developed in response to the Mande trade connection and some of the Brong groups may have moved from the south, if they are to be considered as Akan (Boahen 1966:8-9), in response to the collecting and trading opportunities provided by the Mande. The rise of developed political states amongst such towns would imply that the trade brought wealth, and the wealth political power; but the strength of the ritual foci, such as local shrines or fetishes, may have been the element determining where the centres of these early states were located. Were there elements in this process of state formation indicative of influence from distant and alien lands? This is a difficult question for an archaeologist to answer, but certain significant evidence in the archaeological record is worth emphasizing, as it suggests the existence of influences from the Sudan belt, and more particularly from the Mali empire, in the Akan hinterland.

Though the pottery at Begho was, in the main, made from local clays and, by inference, made by indigenous potters, the forms do reflect some northern influence. Pedestals, ring bases and elongated pedestals termed 'chalices' by some writers, all seem to be variations on designs that may have come down from North Africa to the Sudanic belt, where they are found in Mali in presumed early second millennium A.D. contexts. Other pots appear to copy metal prototypes such as those with sharp body-angles forming carinations between neck and body, rim and neck, or body and base, or others with wide flat horizontally-everted rims. It is conceivable that the popularity of polished red slips can also be related to the influence of imported brass-ware. Brass-ware was one of the main imports into this area from the north and some brass bowls, which can be dated to the fourteenth or fifteenth century from their overall Islamic style of decoration and ornamental Arabic script, have survived in Brong Ahafo and in Asante in the forest zone to the south, and are now regarded as fetishes. At least ten sites with such bowls are known. At some of the sites, such as Ejisu east of Kumasi, tradition records that the bowls were once in use in Brong Ahafo and that they were later brought down to Asante when Bono Manso and the other Brong commercial towns went into decline, after the emergence of the Asante in the eighteenth century. One of the objects which may also have been brought down by Asante soldiers as booty, or sent as tribute, is a large bronze ewer bearing the arms of Richard II of England. This ewer, in the British Museum, was found in one of the Asantehene's enclosures at the time of the British sack of Kumasi in 1896. Research is presently being conducted by John Hunwick to determine the date and provenance of the largest collection of exotic brass-ware, that at Nsawkaw. The designs on the bowls in this collection, as well as on isolated finds, such as a heavy bracelet from Begho, and particularly the intricate overall patterns and absence of figurative art, provide a link between Malian brass-ware and the later, better known, Asante brass-ware tradition. Recorded tradition suggests that, with the fall of Bono Manso, actual craftsmen were taken to the Asante court (Meyerowitz 1952:39) from the northern city.

The houses at Begho, from the admittedly small sample of five so far excavated, were of solid mud construction, even though wood must have been abundant. They were built on a rectilinear pattern with relatively narrow rooms two to three metres wide and up to four to five metres long. Platforms both inside and outside the walls were common. From the size and layout of the mounds, it may be deduced that most houses were built around a working compound. From the abundance of sherds in the collapsed wall material, it would appear that broken pottery was probably puddled and used during the construction of the *swish* walls. This method of mud architecture is common in the Sudanic belt, where the mosques at Jenne, Timbuktu, Mopti and other old centres on the Niger provide spectacular examples of this method of construction. Though there are insufficient sites to provide conclusive evidence, it is probable that this building method spread from the Mali area to Brong Ahafo at the time of the expansion of the gold trade to Ghana.

In the earlier 'Neolithic' period, a wattle-and-

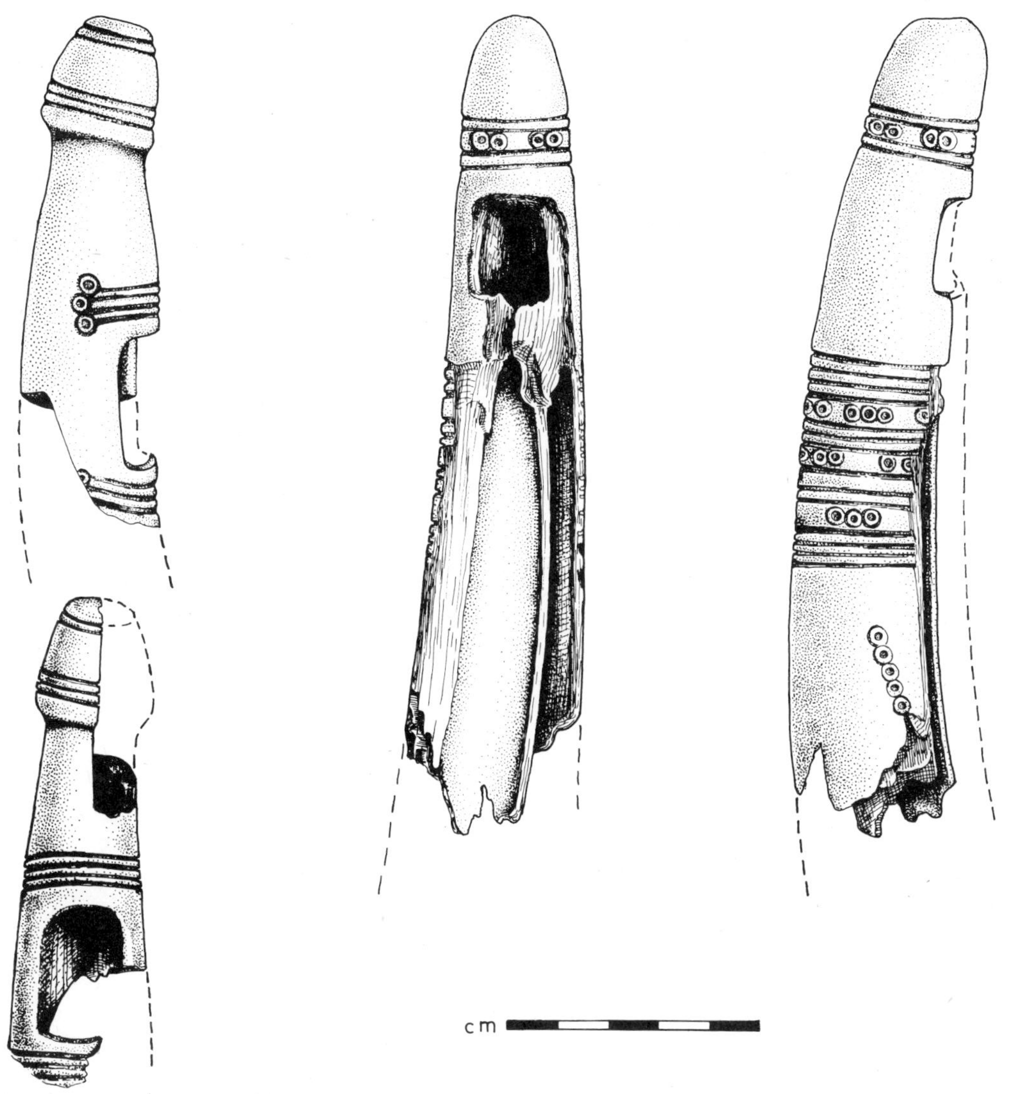

Figure 2. Ivory side-blown trumpets from Begho B2 site (Museum acc. nos. 73.68 and 73.69).

daub method of house construction (Davies 1967) was practised in Ghana. I have suggested elsewhere (Posnansky 1972) that, though the Mande were in a minority and therefore adopted local pottery wares with the addition of a few new forms, they may have been responsible for altering the local architecture, replacing the rather transitory wattle-and-daub structures that require renewal every five to ten years with the more substantial *swish* buildings having a life at least three times that of such wood-based houses, which are subject to continuous attack by termites.

It is quite a common practice in modern Brong villages, and was evidently so in the Begho community, to throw rubbish just outside house walls or leave useless items against compound walls. During excavations on the Brong quarter B2 site at Begho in 1972, the blowing ends of two ivory side-blown trumpets were found, in a sixteenth- or seventeenth-century context, outside what appeared to be the walls of an excavated house. The trumpets were cleaned and stabilized by the British Museum Research Laboratory. Both these trumpets, which measure 15.3 by 3.2 cm. (maximum diameter) and 9.1 by 2.3 cm. respectively, are decorated with incised lines and with circles and dots (Fig. 2). Similar, though undecorated, side-blown trumpets, made from ivory from the tusks of the last elephant killed in the Begho area, sometime in the last century, are still in the possession of the Hanihene and are used for ceremonial occasions.

The ivory side-blown trumpet is a particularly important instrument amongst the Akan and is used in royal and chieftainly ceremonial (Fig. 3). It is not an instrument of every-day use. Throughout a large belt of Africa ivory trumpets, or side-blown trumpets in other materials, are similarly associated with chiefs. Moreover, in many parts of Africa elephant ivory is the monopoly of chiefs, so that side-blown trumpets in ivory are of special significance. In Buganda a set of five trumpets, made from Calabash covered with thin hide, were traditionally blown as an ensemble to announce the arrival of the Kabaka. On the east African coast, similar proclamation horns (*mbiu*) of ivory or metal are associated with sultans. Though the Begho trumpets are the earliest yet found in an archaeological context in West Africa, a rather more ornate trumpet with a human figure on one end has been found at Sofala, on the Mozambique coast, and this is believed to date from the sixteenth century (Fagan & Kirkman 1967).

In West Africa, remains of these instruments have been found in a number of interesting contexts. Miniature side-blown trumpets of terracotta found at Ahinsan, in the forest region of Ghana, are of particular importance. This site is notable for its funerary terracottas, mainly consisting of terracotta portrait heads, but also including decorated pots and miniatures of regalia items in more general use. A particularly fine representation of someone blowing a side-blown trumpet was excavated by David Calvocoressi at Ahinsan in 1968 (Fig. 4) and was probably formerly part of a decorated pot; whilst others, also of terracotta, were found by Dr O. Davies in 1952 at the same site (Fig. 5). There is a fine brass figure of a trumpet blower, recovered from Benin, in the British Museum (B.M. No. 1949 Af 46.156), whilst Dark (1962:62) illustrates a brass plaque, also from Benin, which depicts what appears to be a similar ivory trumpet in the act of being blown. The art of Benin is intimately connected with the divine monarchy of the Obas and the two Benin pieces probably date from the

Figure 3. Chief's attendants with hornblower at ceremony in Abur, Ghana. (Photo by permission of the Ghana Ministry of Information).

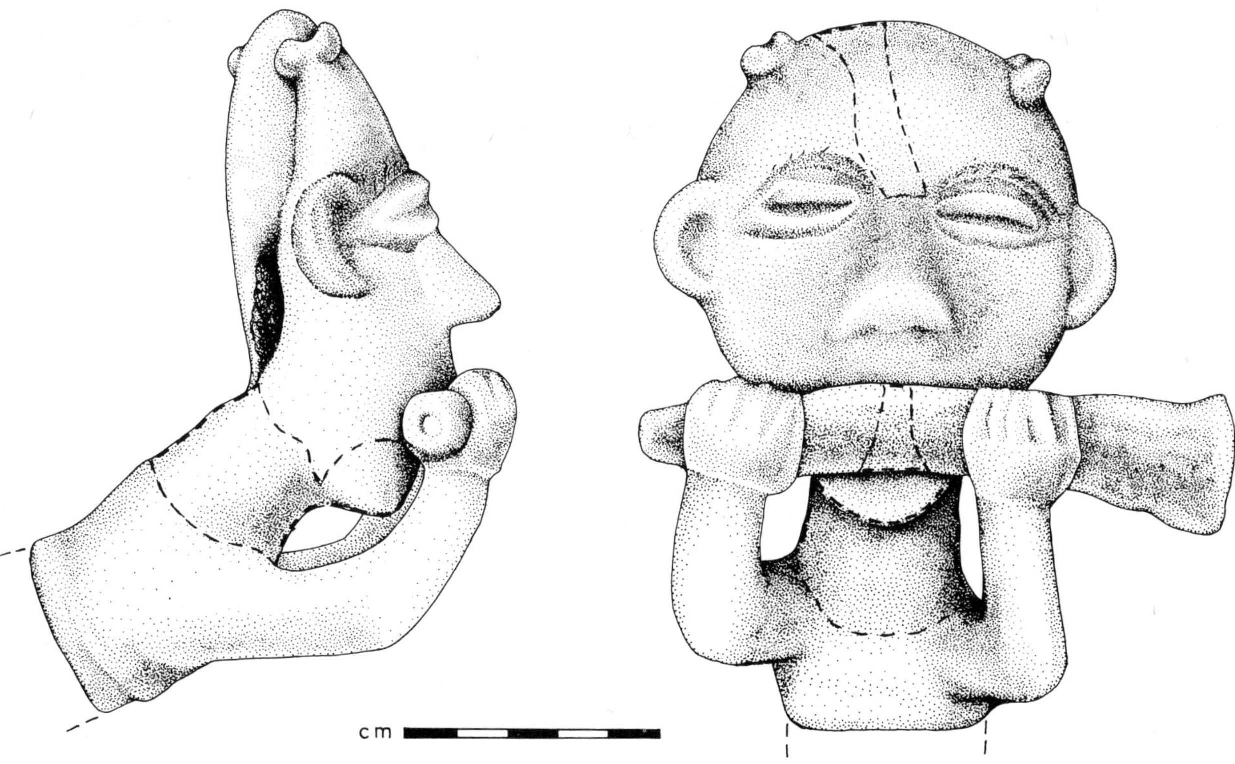

Figure 4. Terracotta figure from side of pot, Ahinsan (acc. no. 73.2.148).

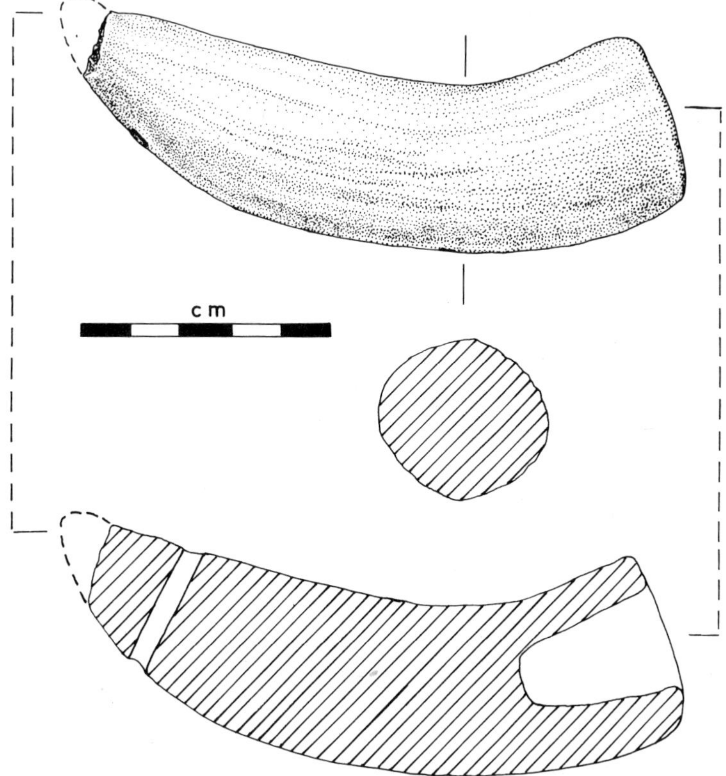

Figure 5. Miniature terracotta side-blown trumpet from Ahinsan (acc. no. 52.235).

seventeenth century, which is the date assigned to the Ahinsan pieces of Calvocoressi (1970).

It is interesting to note that the first illustration from a European source of a readily identifiable ivory side-blown trumpet is in Michael Praetorius's *Theatrum Instrumentorum* of 1620 (Wachsmann 1970:101), which also depicts a 'Ginny' (Guinea) drum, another West African piece. Both items probably formed part of the Tradescant Collection, purchased in London in the late sixteenth century, presumably from sailors who had voyaged to West Africa at the time, and so found a place in the collections of the Ashmolean Museum. Blades (1961:327) recognizes that ivory trumpets were probably played, together with drums, as part of the West African musical ensemble in the seventeenth century. The side-blown trumpet itself probably originated in the Sudan or North Africa. It is not found in Europe or in the Near East, where end-blown trumpets and horns were, and are, more common. Farmer (1939:570-2) provides various Arab references to what appear to be side-blown trumpets in the fourteenth century in Mali; Ibn Battuta is quoted as describing a royal band and military chiefs with what are probably side-blown trumpets; whilst at Mogadishu, on the Somali coast, Ibn Battuta also described a royal procession preceded by 'drums, horns and trumpets'. There are, surprisingly, no well-known traditions of origin about ivory trumpets amongst the Akan but, as they are associated with chiefs, there is a strong argument in favour of their relatively recent introduction. On the basis of the present information, it would seem that the side-blown trumpet spread south from Mali, together with a knowledge of brass-working, systems of weights, building methods and ceramic forms. These items, in turn, were transmitted from the forest fringe states like Bono Manso to Asante.

One of the most interesting results of the excavations at Begho has been the discovery of large numbers of potsherds chipped, and often ground, to a regular form that varies from between a circle and a square to an oblong with rounded corners. They were first thought of as counters or gaming pieces, following the normal interpretation of such finds on sites in many parts of the world. On the advice of Mr Tim Garrard, they have all been carefully weighed and are found to conform, often to within a few tenths of a gramme, to the Islamic system of weights used principally for weighing gold or silver, and based on the *mitkal* and *wakia* now current in Timbuktu and Jenne. The pieces for weighing gold and silver thus represented very specific weights; for example, four of the sherds in Fig. 6 (nos. 1, 4, 8, 9) are within the normal variation from 27 grammes, or half a *wakia*, whilst no. 2 approximates to 4.5 grammes, the normal weight of a *mitkal*. The close approximation of these weights to those of the Islamic system provides a strong argument for the actual transmission of the whole mechanism of the gold trade from Mali to Begho. This gold trade was eventually taken over by Asante and the earliest Asante gold weights were also based on the Islamic standard (Garrard 1972), though they later became very elaborate and comprised geometric forms and designs as well as figurative pieces of brass cast in the *cire perdue* method. In Mampong, just north of Kumasi, the capital of Asante, there is a song about Begho that specifically refers to the weighing of gold (Nketia 1973) and, perhaps, may be taken to confirm the transmission of gold-trade practices from Brong Ahafo to Asante in earlier times.

There are other minor indications of the same movement of ideas and practices from the Islamic Sudan to the forest fringe states and towns, and then to the forest states. The calendrical system of 42-day months, for example, possibly combines a Moslem 7-day system with an indigenous 6-day system, about which there are also traditions concerning Asante indebtedness to the Brong (Goody 1966:20). The region of Begho was known to the seventeenth-century coastal writers as 'Insoco' (1629 map – Daaku & van Dantzig 1966; Dapper 1670; Loyer 1714) and was also noted for its blue textiles. Similar textiles were noted by the earliest Portuguese visitors to the Gold Coast, more than a century and a quarter before, who commented on the presence of Wangara (Mande) traders. Present-day textiles such as *kente* are woven in narrow strips on looms that would seem to have a Sudanic ancestry. The evidence provided by spindle-whorls at Begho, which are similar to some found in archaeological horizons at Jenne, and the existence of strong oral traditions, backed by the seventeenth-century literary sources already referred to, suggest that Brong intermediary groups may have been responsible for the transmission of textile technology. Traditions speak of the survivors of the Bono Manso state teaching state-craft to the

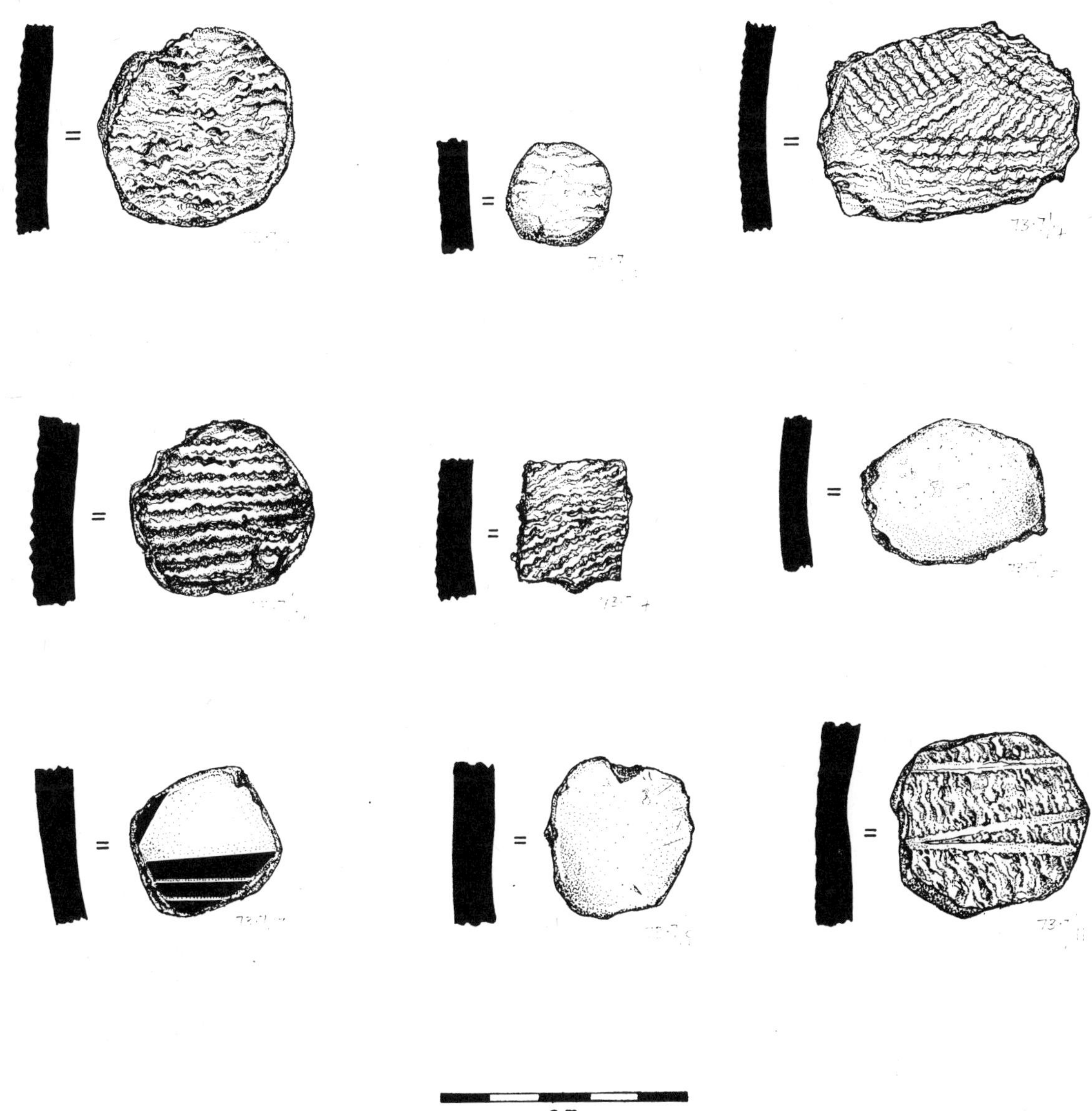

Figure 6. Pottery discs from Begho B2 site, probably used as gold weights.

Asante in the early seventeenth century, while other northern influences in Asante still exist in the use of ostrich feathers in processions (Nketia 1973) and Mande loan-words in the Twi language (Wilks 1962).

When we turn to the scanty archaeological evidence that we have in the forest region, we find that the most striking type of site consists of earthworks, such as those in the Oda area. These earthworks comprise trench systems, banks and interior ditches approximately six metres deep, normally of an irregular ovoid plan, sometimes with exterior lobate enclosures, and anything up to three kilometres in circumference. Numerous mounds are found within the trenched enclosures, indicating settlement. Altogether, ten such sites have been listed by Davies (1961). The only site to be extensively excavated is at Abodum, excavated by Junner in 1934-35 (Junner 1935; Braunholtz 1936), the first scientific excavation conducted in Ghana. Ozanne (1971) considers these sites to be pre-1640 and as labour camps for forced labour working the Birim River alluvial gold deposits. Other authorities have considered them to be defensive (Davies 1961:26). Similar sites to these also occur in the Ivory Coast. It is interesting to note that the pottery of the Ghanaian sites is distinctive, being characterized by heavy flanges and collars. However, there are elements in the pottery forms that appear to relate the irregular earthworks to the post-1600 forest sites of Ahinsan, Mampongtim and Asebu. The degree of continuity among these sites might well be determined by a careful examination of the Abodum pottery now in the British Museum.

Post-1600 sites in this region are characterized by a multiplicity of pottery types, applied decorative ornament on a wide range of pots and a distinctive black polish. These are all features that could be expected to develop, once a series of rich states grew up in the forest. The rest of the panoply of these states is well known and it seems that ceramic ostentation was just one feature of a remarkably rapid development of what may be termed the 'Akan civilization'. Crossland (1973) has indicated the lack of typological resemblance between the Begho/Brong Ahafo ceramics and those of the forest. This being so, we can infer that, if there is ceramic continuity within the forest area, there was probably ethnic continuity also.

Conclusions

The scanty archaeological evidence thus may be used to support historical reconstructions, such as those of Boahen (1966) which see a relatively dispersed, negro, iron-using, agricultural population of the Niger-Congo linguistic group, both in the forest and the forest fringe areas, before the fourteenth century. In the fourteenth century, or a little later, Mande traders moved south to exploit the gold resources of the forest; and a series of market towns, of which Begho is presently the best known, developed immediately north of the forest, in a favourable ecological zone. The growth of these towns probably caused certain Akan groups to move northward to take advantage of the commercial opportunities. The state of Bono Manso was formed at this period, or slightly later. With them the Mande brought certain architectural techniques and an Islamic system of weights based on that established in Jenne and Timbuktu, two of the principal Malian commercial centres. Though certain ceramic forms were introduced, there are strong grounds for believing that existing pottery traditions in the area were continued, while the strong influence of metal imports can be seen in the resultant Begho pot-forms. Contemporary with the development of the towns may have been the building of the forest earthworks by a people with a ceramic tradition different from that of Brong Ahafo. Deriving from the Mali area there were also certain elements associated with chieftaincy, of which the use of ivory side-blown trumpets is recognizable in the archaeological record. A brass-working tradition, textile technology, and possibly bead-working, were also established under the northern influence.

From the sixteenth century, there was a short-circuiting of the old trade network to the Niger towns with the establishment of the Portuguese trade forts on the Gold Coast, leading to a growth of wealth in the Akan hinterland and the development of the first recognizable forest states. The economic momentum was increased in the seventeenth century with the arrival on the coast of the Dutch and the English, coinciding with a temporary collapse of the wealth of Sudanic states around the Niger bend following the Moorish invasion of 1591. The seventeenth century was marked by an accelerated growth of Akan states where wealth is observed in the luxury of their material culture and the complexity of their chieftainly rituals. Aspects of their technology, *swish* building methods, and certain aspects of statecraft were evidently diffused from the Brong Ahafo area to the forest. The Asante state marked the apogee of Akan 'civilization', in which elements from the Mali area were evident, particularly in the material arts; basic crafts, such as pottery, continued in their old traditions though embellished with elaborate decoration.

The ultimate origins of the Akan still await discovery but, from the archaeological record, it is apparent that one cannot expect an answer in any theory of a simple migration from outside Ghana to account for the nature of Akan 'civilization', but we must look to the historical events between A.D. 1350 and 1700 for their explanation. The basic population of the Akan states was that which existed in the area prior to the second quarter of the second millennium A.D. There is, as yet, nothing in the archaeological record to link the Akan directly with ancient Ghana, the Sahara or the Nile valley.

Acknowledgments

The research at Begho is part of the West African Trade Project being conducted with the institutional and financial support of the University of Ghana, the Leverhulme Trust and the Wenner-Gren Foundation for Anthropological Research, to all of which I am deeply grateful. I particularly appreciate the help given to me by Mr L.B. Crossland, who has assisted me at Begho and whose research on ceramic analysis in Ghana has opened new insights into the archaeology of Ghana. Figs. 4 and 5 are published with appreciation to D. Calvocoressi and O. Davies, from whose excavations the objects were recovered. I am indebted to D. Agyei-Henaku, who drew Figs. 2, 4, 5 and 6, and M.A. Torgbor who drew Fig. 1. All the figured pieces are in the collections of the University of Ghana Museum of Archaeology. Professor K. Nketia most kindly discussed with me matters of musicological importance.

REFERENCES

Birmingham, D.B. (1966) The Akan of Ghana. *Ghana Notes and Queries*, 9, 1-3.

Blades, J. (1961) The orchestral instruments of percussion. In Baines, A.C. (ed.), *Musical Instruments through the Ages*, 327-49. Harmondsworth, Middlesex.

Boahen, A.A. (1966) The origins of the Akan. *Ghana Notes and Queries*, 9, 3-10.

Braunholtz, H.J. (1936) Archaeology in the Gold Coast. *Antiquity*, 10, 469-74.

Calvocoressi, D.S. (1970) A funerary site at Adansi Ahinsan. *W. African Arch. Newsletter*, 12, 82-3.

Calvocoressi, D.S. and York, R.N. (1971) The state of archaeological research in Ghana. *W. African Jour. Arch.*, 1, 87-103.

Crossland, L.B. (1973) *A Study of Begho Pottery in the light of Excavation conducted at the Begho B2 Site.* M.A. thesis, University of Ghana, Legon.

Daaku, K.Y. and van Dantzig, A. (1966) Map of the regions of the Gold Coast in Guinea. *Ghana Notes and Queries*, 9, 14-15.

Danquah, J.B. (1957) *The Quest for Ghana.* Accra.

Dapper, O. (1670) *Beschreiburg von Africa.* Amsterdam.

Dark, P.J.C. (1962) *The Art of Benin.* Chicago.

Davies, O. (1961) *Archaeology in Ghana*, 14-26. Edinburgh.

Davies, O. (1963) Neolithic hoe-cultures in West Africa. *Comptes Rendus VIe Cong. Int. des Sciences Anthropologiques et Ethnologiques, Paris 1960*, 2, 385.

Davies, O. (1967) Timber construction and wood-carving in West Africa in the second millennium B.C. *Man*, n.s., 2, 115-18.

Fagan, B.M. and Kirkman, J. (1967) An ivory trumpet from Sofala, Mozambique. *Ethno-musicology*, 11, 368-74.

Farmer, H.G. (1939) Early references to music in the Western Sudan. *Jour. Royal Asiatic Soc.* 1939, 569-79.

Flight, C. (1968) Kintampo. *W. African Arch. Newsletter*, 8, 15-20.

Gerrard, T.F. (1972) Studies in Akan gold weights: 1. The origins of the gold weight system. *Trans. Hist. Soc. of Ghana*, 13, 1-20.

Goody, J.R. (1966) The Akan and the north. *Ghana Notes and Queries*, 9, 18-24.

Greenberg, J.H. (1953) *Studies in African Linguistic Classification.* Bloomington.

Junner, N.R. (1935) Ancient trenches in the Birim district. *Ann. Rep. Geol. Survey Gold Coast, 1934-5*, 14.

Loyer, G. (1914) *Relation du voyage du Royaume d'Issyny.* Paris.

Meyerowitz, E.L.R. (1952) *Akan Traditions of Origin.* London.

Meyerowitz, E.L.R. (1960) *The Divine Kingship in Ghana and Ancient Egypt.* London.

Nketia, K. (1973) Personal communication.

Ozanne, P.C. (1971) Ghana. In Shinnic, P.L. (ed.), *The African Iron Age*, 36-65. Oxford.

Posnansky, M. (1970) Discovering Ghana's past. *Ghana Mus. Ann. Lectures*, 59-69. Accra.

Posnansky, M. (1972) The early development of trade in West Africa – some archaeological considerations. *Ghana Social Science Jour.*, 2 (2), 87-100.

Posnansky, M. (1973) Aspects of early West African trade. *World Arch.*, 5, 149-62.

Wachsmann, K.P. (1970) A drum from seventeenth-century Africa. *Galpin Soc. Jour.*, 23, 97-103.

Wilks, I. (1962) The Mande loan element in Twi. *Ghana Notes and Queries*, 4, 26-8.

York, R.N. (1973) Excavations at New Buipe. *W. African Jour. Arch.*, 3, 1-189.

DEREK ROE

Typology and the trouble with hand-axes

Introduction

In his long and distinguished career, Grahame Clark has seen many major shifts of emphasis in the study of prehistory and has himself, of course, been closely indentified with some of the most important of them. High on any list of productive changes of direction over the past two decades or so would, or should, come the general loss of interest in artefact typology for its own sake, and the compensating growth of concern to study artefacts for what they can tell us about the activities and abilities of their makers, rather than to arrange them in arbitrary patterns of supposed development through time.

This small revolution has been vital in many fields of prehistoric archaeology, but perhaps especially so in earlier Palaeolithic studies, where so many find-spots of material yield nothing but a quantity of stone artefacts far removed from their primary context – evidence which one is hesitant either to use or wholly to discard. Certainly a large majority of the world's hand-axes have been found in such circumstances: to take the example of Britain alone, the present writer in his doctoral research examined some 38,000 of these implements, and it would be hard to argue convincingly that more than a couple of hundred of them belonged to good groups found in primary context, while a few thousand more occurred in slightly disturbed contexts such as stream-channel situations (Roe 1967; 1968). If the rest are to be studied at all, it is likely that some kind of typological approach must play a part. But should they be studied at all, as opposed to merely being recorded? Disenchantment with traditional hand-axe typology was only beginning to be widespread when the present writer was an undergraduate at Cambridge. Most of his research work over the twelve years since then has been concerned with hand-axes, first in Britain and later in Africa. Is there really any place for such studies? Are they totally divorced from any insight into the lives of actual people in early prehistoric times? Can there still be a typological approach to hand-axes? To answer such questions, it is best to consider typology first and hand-axes second, and this is briefly done in the two sections following. In the section on typology, it will be clear that the writer has lithic industries primarily in mind, but the general remarks are not intended to apply to stone tools only and may be worth considering in regard to other kinds of prehistoric artefacts.

Some approaches to typology

It is easy enough, with hindsight, forgetting the recent nature of so many great advances in the techniques of both field and laboratory archaeology, to pour scorn on the old typological approach and on its leading exponents. Yet their work was of major and permanent importance as an initial sorting operation, carried out on what was already a formidable backlog of data. It permitted the formulation of many hypotheses that had a period of usefulness, even if they had in most cases later to be abandoned. The same kind of comment may very well be made in due course on some of the archaeological methods and approaches that look potentially most productive to us in the mid-1970s.

It might be thought good basic new archaeology to reject 'typology' wholesale, without wasting valuable time or space in defining or discussing exactly what is being cast aside; students do this every year as a matter of course to impress examiners. Yet all too often there is confusion over what 'typology' really is and how it differs from taxonomy, from morphology, from style, even from technology. The extreme result of such confusion may be a tendency to reject *any* form of classification of artefacts. It is true that such drastic views do not normally attain publication in the best manuals for the teaching of archaeological methods but, of the whole archaeological community in any country, professional and amateur, active participant and committed spectator, how many have been carefully taught only from the best manuals? For many, there is nothing so influential as a set of attractively radical opinions, persuasively put forward and concise through absence of documentation. Over-reaction against obviously out-dated views may indeed often contribute to a situation of mutual distrust and intolerance between professional and amateur archaeologists, which benefits neither group.

There is nothing wrong with classifying artefacts. The process, however arid on occasion, is indeed almost the life-blood of archaeology. In the natural order of things it comes second to discovery and excavation of sites, yet at its simplest level, identification, it is the link between the field archaeologist and the fulfilment of most of his intentions for the elucidation of his site. So, too, it is normally the first requirement by members of the public from the world of archaeological scholarship: 'what is it?' usually even precedes 'how much is it worth?'. Nor is there anything wrong in taking classification to a more detailed level by dividing a contemporary series of artefacts into classes and producing a break-down list of artefact *types*. No archaeologist has got far without the use of the word 'type', and perhaps none ever will, though the quality of individual definitions is highly variable. Even analytical archaeologists use and define the word (e.g. Clarke 1968: 669).

Such a classified breakdown of a set of artefacts is indeed an essential basis for the most sophisticated as well as the most simple statistical or mathematical methods of processing such data. Thus, for example, the factor-analysis experiments of L.R. Binford relied heavily on the artefact type-lists of F. Bordes (Binford 1972; Binford & Binford 1966). It is the archaeologist who must say to which particular class a given artefact belongs, and that is the same as saying that he must be capable of accurate classification. Consciously or unconsciously, he achieves it by considering the actual features (attributes or traits would be better technical terms) of the specimen and checking them against whatever set of features he considers essential to the artefact-type concerned. Setting aside matters concerning archaeological evidence of provenance and association, such features may be quantitative or qualitative; technological and morphological data will be included, any evidence for function must be considered, analysis of raw materials may be important and there may be decoration to be taken into account. This process of classification is essentially the same, whether long drawn out for a specialist report published after months of study or condensed into an unenthusiastic flash of recognition by a harassed provincial museum curator identifying his fourth clay-pipe stem or George III halfpenny of the day. But the more explicit and consciously objective the mechanical side of the exercise, the better the quality of the results: hence the detailed check-lists of attributes to be noted as present or absent and hence the importance of metrical analysis to define aspects of morphology, especially of size and shape. Hence, too, the care required in deciding upon the attributes to study or the measurements to take. There is no more comprehensive waste of time than measurements, taken to a high degree of accuracy, that have not been precisely defined or that do not give unambiguously the information the analyst supposes that they do.

All of this is concerned with typology, in the sense of defining artefact-types and sub-types and assigning individual artefacts to them. It is as coldly scientific a process as excavation ought to be and, though a certain range of gadgetry can be of assistance, there is no basic requirement of either mathematical wizardry or obscure language. If that were all there were to typological studies, it is doubtful whether newer or older archaeologists would have much to complain about, especially since it can hardly be denied that ancient artefacts constitute a large and important class of the evidence with which the archaeologist must deal. But there are at least three objections that could certainly be raised even at this stage. First, the process of classification can be badly carried out by analysts who make errors of observation or recording, leading to results that are just plain wrong. Secondly, the archaeologist who is a specialist in classifying artefacts may come to regard the establishment of his type-list for any set of artefacts as an end in itself, without going on to draw conclusions or test and compare results in the full context of the accumulated knowledge of a particular archaeological period or region. Thirdly, having made his typological classification and, perhaps, compared it rigorously with the results of other work by himself and his colleagues on several sets of artefacts of the same or of different ages, he may make the assumption that there is no other way in which those artefacts can profitably be studied.

Any of these criticisms may on occasion be justified, but they are really all of a general kind and could as readily be levelled at the exponents of other specialized aspects of archaeology – excavation, for example – which can also be badly done, treated as an end in itself or wrongly regarded as the only way of studying a site. Even the tireless codifiers and rationalizers of archaeological method and theory are sometimes correspondingly accused by some of their colleagues of getting it all wrong, losing interest in field or laboratory work or taking an inflexible view of the future of the discipline. It is therefore, perhaps, only when the whole typological process is taken yet a stage further, beyond the level of descriptive and comparative classification, that the weightier and more particular criticisms arise.

The situation at this next level is simple enough, and it shows what an integral part of archaeology classification is: in any local sequence, typological study of the artefacts collected from different sites, or from different levels of the same site, quickly shows that different types are present in each set, or else that, though the range of types is similar, the emphases fall on various occasions in fundamentally different areas of the range. Typological study encounters no difficulty in demonstrating this: the problems arise only when *interpretation* of the observed variation between artefact-sets is attempted. There are so many possible explanations and the archaeologist, lacking clear evidence of their relative importance, may fall into the trap of regarding them as mutually exclusive and selecting just one, settling perhaps for 'functional variation' or for 'tribal differences' or for 'arrival of new people'. Then the circling vultures begin to descend, the word 'model' is bandied around, and there is a real risk that the actual data from the various sites may be forgotten while much energy is expended in an inconclusive battle of principles – and of words, since one paradigm may be worth many paragraphs.

Yet not to attempt some explanation of observed variation, in human terms, is unthinkable: merely to record the differences of typology for artefact-sets over a long period of time in a given area is to seek the notoriety of a 'culture historian'. That particular term of abuse is perhaps ill-chosen, for history in the best sense involves a carefully documented social and economic study of a people through time, giving full play to cause and effect: this writer would certainly be more than happy to know the culture history of the Palaeolithic period. 'Chronicler of material culture' would perhaps be a more accurate phrase (quite apart from having twice as many words). Certainly, however, there was a long period, only recently ended, when many prehistorians were much occupied with the order of events in the long-term development of human material culture, especially in the Palaeolithic period. In a sense, this was only a continuation of the essential process of sorting out antiquities of unknown age, which in the early nineteenth century had contributed to the development of a Three Age system (Daniel 1943; 1950), but now there was a regular basis of stratigraphy. It is easy enough to understand the urge to fill and calibrate the immense time-span of the Palaeolithic by making particular well-known sets of artefacts into 'typical' patterns of typology and 'typical' levels of technology and finding the stratigraphic or geochronological evidence to place them in their correct order. The errors of supposition were merely that these arbitrarily selected levels and patterns were regular steps on a simple, predictable, ascending staircase of technological and typological evolution; that the sequence they formed was valid over a vast area, if not indeed world-wide; and that this evolutionary process continued more or less under its own power, while its direction was mainly dependent on Pleistocene climatic and ecological change – helped on perhaps by major events in the parallel process of human physical evolution, but only tenuously connected with the day-to-day affairs of ordinary or extraordinary men.

Such a simple typological sequence, of course, never existed in the Palaeolithic, but it appeared to exist, which was all that mattered. The principle of typological development through time, even divorced from its technological partner, the sequence of improving methods of manufacture, could stand as sufficient explanation of much of the observed variation. It could thus be used as a relative dating method –

perhaps, allied with Pleistocene geology, even as a rough chronometric method. Palaeolithic sites were especially responsive to such an approach in the days when most of them yielded nothing but the remains of a fairly simple stone tool kit and some evidence for assignment to one or another of the main phases of the Pleistocene sequence. If an elephant molar could be assigned at a glance to an early, middle or late stage of the Pleistocene by anyone who knew about elephant teeth, why could not a hand-axe be firmly attributed to a numbered stage of the Acheulian culture by anyone who knew about hand-axes, *for much the same reasons*? Thus, in the very first number of the *Proceedings of the Prehistoric Society of East Anglia* of Grahame Clark's editorship, R.A. Smith, giving an account of some hundreds of implements collected (without stratigraphic evidence) from the high-level Stour gravels at Fordwich, near Canterbury, Kent, could confidently write (1933:169):

> At Fordwich the pear-shaped hand-axe seems to be a good deal earlier than the fine St Acheul tools and therefore probably contemporary with the tortoise-cores and flakes of Clacton type. This classification is to some extent supported by the obvious resemblance of several hand-axes of the earlier facies to the rostro-carinate form from below the Crag; and Mr Reid Moir's theory that the hand-axe was derived from the leading pre-Crag type is so far confirmed.

It is in fact not really with 'typology' or with 'typological classification' that the opponents of 'the old typological approach' have their just quarrel, but with the antiquated doctrine of typological evolution as a major force in what is now called culture process. It was in Grahame Clark's Cambridge Archaeology Department of the late 1950s that the present writer, beginning his undergraduate studies, first heard (from Clark's successor in the Disney chair, as it has turned out) of the geological 'doctrine of uniformitarianism' preached by Charles Lyell in the 1830s: the then almost heretical view that there had never been a Great Universal Deluge, because there were no processes in the geological past essentially different from those that could be seen at work today; nor had deposits that could be seen forming extremely slowly ever been put together, complete with fossils, by one hard-working Creator over six days' worth of evenings and mornings. A similar doctrine of (biological) uniformity soon afterwards swept man into his proper place in the animal kingdom for the purposes of the theories of Darwin and others. Archaeology has been affected since then by many other uniformitarian theories, and yet we have had to wait (except for a few far-sighted individuals) until the mid-twentieth century for the application to artefacts of the principle of cultural uniformity: that people did things in the past for the very same reasons for which they do things today. Artefacts are certainly surviving material evidence for human activities. They were by definition never a mobile, intermarrying, breeding population, or capable of mutation, but even in earlier prehistory were objects made by men, not as an exercise in archaeological typology but on every single occasion for some specific human reason. Similarly, the way in which any artefact was made was determined, not by biological evolution but by its maker's considering such everyday factors as economy of effort, function, efficiency and urgency or otherwise of production; by his personal expertise and experience, or lack of them, and doubtless also his personality and inventiveness; by the tractability and suitability of the available raw material; and also, perhaps, by local traditions of style or technology.

If this view of artefacts is kept clearly in mind, and if it is accepted that there is a basic and continuing need for the classification of artefacts discovered by archaeologists, for purposes of description, comparison and interpretation, then no one ought to feel that artefact-typology is an arid field of study. Perhaps more emphasis should be placed on the fact that there are really two kinds of types: there are *archaeologists' types*, defined for the purposes of classification; and *makers' and users' types*, which are classes of functional objects, internally consistent as regards their manufacture and use. There may still of course be a range amongst the individual items falling into any one such class: not all knives, for example, are made and used identically, yet the class of knives retains its integrity. Thus, both archaeologist and artefact-maker allow for sub-types; and the functional differences between the sub-types may, of course, be very important. For mere analysis and comparison of artefact-sets at the simplest level, archaeologists might sometimes get away with using archaeologists' types, but when it comes to the vital matter of interpretation they certainly cannot do so.

Therefore, if we are not to lose the precious glimpses of the people who made the artefacts through concentrating only on the objects themselves, it is essential that the archaeologist should make his own list of types coincide as closely as possible with the types envisaged by the artefact-maker. He should hardly need reminding that the onus for this is wholly on him: the maker fulfilled his side of the bargain long ago.

Typological evolution is dead, then, but typological classification lives on. Industrial archaeology and kindred studies are bringing ever more recent periods within the scope of both new and traditional archaeological operations. In the report on a fascinating experiment in interpretation of an abandoned domestic site of extremely recent age, Millie's Camp, even evaporated-milk tins, plastic bags and egg-cartons are quite rightly listed and treated as archaeological finds (Bonnichsen 1973). The present writer has not yet read of an attempt by an archaeologist to classify and interpret a set of golf clubs, but the time may yet come. How will he account for the wooden clubs and especially the matched set of irons – so similar in style, yet with such vital differences in the size and shape of the head and angle of the face – morphological points, all precisely quantifiable if required? Dare we assume that the history of typological classification has already reached a stage where he could not finally decide to interpret them as a chronological series, with the irons developing through time from No. 1 iron to sand wedge, the woods as prototypes and the putter possibly an import of exotic origin?

Studying hand-axes

There can be no denying that the implements known as hand-axes comprise a sizable chunk of the surviving material culture of the Lower Palaeolithic period, though they are more important in some parts of the Old World than others. If we had available for study all the artefacts for which hand-axe makers were ever responsible, the numerical significance of the completed hand-axes themselves would, in fact, be minute since, apart from other shaped tools, very large quantities of waste flakes and debris may be produced in the fashioning of a single hand-axe: just how numerous is seldom realized (*cf.* Newcomer 1971). But, human nature and collectors being what they are, vast quantities of hand-axes and relatively small quantities of the lesser tools and debris have been accumulated in the world's museums. Apart from pure collecting preferences, this balance has been affected by the fact that comparatively few of the known Acheulian sites of the Old World seem to be pure factory sites: in other words, the manufacturing debris has not always been there for collectors even to consider. One way and another, vast hoards of hand-axes of almost nightmare abundance await the dedicated student, even without discovery of new sites. The sheer quantities should not be surprising when one considers that hand-axes were being made from at least as early as the date of the site EF-HR in Middle Bed II at Olduvai Gorge, probably around 1.2 to 1.4 million years ago (M.D. Leakey 1971: 124-36), until well into the final glaciation of the northern hemisphere series, to which period certain French and German Late Acheulian and Micoquian sites seem clearly to belong, quite apart from various well known Mousterian of Acheulian Tradition occurrences, some at least of which should be less than 50,000 years old (for a summary of all this material, mentioning most of the main sites, see Bordes 1968: Chs. 4, 7 and 8). This vast distribution in time is matched by a geographical range almost as impressive, covering the whole of Africa and also stretching from peninsular India through much of the Middle East and around almost the whole Mediterranean coastline to central, west and Atlantic Europe as far north-west as the English north Midlands and just into Wales.

What are hand-axes, and what is the element of unity that is reckoned to hold together an implement-class stretched over such monstrous distances of time and space? Definitions are rare in the literature, and even the name 'hand-axe' goes mainly unchallenged or by default: few of the implements themselves look at all like axes as they were known in the Mesolithic or Neolithic periods, or as we know them today; nor can we be sure that all of them were designed for holding in the hand. Indeed, those that most resemble an axe to be held in the hand are frequently classed separately as cleavers! Most of the rather small number of writers who have sought to explain hand-axes have concluded that they were 'all-purpose tools' and this alone might suggest a lack of typological integrity: the present writer does not believe that a concise form of words exists that would catch all the variants and yet define no more than a single artefact-type. In a recent study of certain tool-classes, including hand-axes, from several floors at a single locality, Kalambo Falls, Zambia, he wrote (Roe, forthcoming):

> *Hand-axes*. These are shaped tools, often large, characterized by the presence of a sharp edge which usually extends round all or most of the circumference and includes a flat tip, more or less pointed or rounded or occasionally squared. The butt may or may not be worked. Hand-axes are almost always flaked on both main faces . . . Hand-axes as a class include a considerable range of outline shapes (plan forms), which tend to show regularity and approximate bilateral symmetry, especially in the better made examples. The long and short sections of a hand-axe are often regularly biconvex or more or less lenticular, though an unworked butt will leave the long section irregular at one end.

All this is loosely descriptive rather than definitive, and the frequent qualifications, 'often', 'usually', 'almost always' are no accident. We may believe that any known hand-axe would fall somewhere in the area covered by the description, but that area is a large one and it is clear enough that the degree of variation catered for is far greater than that envisaged above as appropriate to the various sub-types within a maker's or user's artefact-type. Thus, we may be quite wrong to regard a large, rough-butted, thick-pointed, triangular hand-axe and a small, flat ovate, sharp-edged round its whole circumference, as variants within a single tool-type, and 'hand-axe' is seen to be no more than a misleading term used by archaeologists to group together implements of a broadly similar nature but different individual purposes; just as one might class knives, forks and spoons, all as 'cutlery'; or chairs, tables and cupboards, all as 'furniture'. As regards hand-axes being all-purpose tools, it would be nearer the mark to say that certain kinds of hand-axe seem to offer more than one functional aspect; a sharp point, good cutting edges and a heavy, hammer-like butt may all occur on one implement. Other kinds do not: the finest ovates may offer no more than a very sharp but rather delicate continuously curved cutting edge. Perhaps the truth is that no single hand-axe was ever really an 'all-purpose tool', but that all the main tasks envisaged by those who use the phrase could be accomplished with a small set of hand-axes.

This question of the function of hand-axes is entirely vital and quite unsolved. From what has just been said, it will be seen that there is no need to suppose a common function for all hand-axes; yet the writer, who has looked at perhaps 50,000 of these implements, cannot state as an absolute fact based on unimpeachable evidence the manner in which any single one of them was used. This is the greatest single barrier between the analyst of hand-axes and an appreciation of 'makers' and users' types' as advocated in the previous section, and it is hard to see in present circumstances just how it can be breached successfully. The leading methods by which the archaeologist usually attains understanding of the functions of artefacts either do not apply to hand-axes or else have so far given poor or ambiguous results. There are, for example, no clear ethnographic parallels from recent or present-day hunter-gatherer peoples for the use of stone implements that resemble hand-axes at all closely, whatever the popular archaeology books may suggest. Again, Lower Palaeolithic hand-axes survive in vast numbers but, as we have seen already, extremely few have been found in 'primary context' and, on these occasions, the primary context preserved no more than a fraction, if that, of the organic substances and fragile materials that must have been present when the sites were in use. There are certainly a number of associations known of stone artefacts, including hand-axes and cleavers, with partially articulated skeletal remains of large animals; a classic view, based on such 'kill' or 'butchery' sites, is that hand-axes and cleavers were weapons or implements used at some point between the final stages of a hunt and the consumption of the meat from the quarry – most probably as butchering implements. Yet it was precisely from a survey of such associations that J.D. Clark (Clark & Haynes 1969: 409) reached an opposite conclusion, 'that Palaeolithic meat-butchering equipment consisted predominantly of small numbers of light-duty tools and cutting flakes and small scraping tools with a few only of larger elements', the latter being 'supplementary rather than primary to the main purpose of the equipment'. Lastly, the study of microwear traces on stone implements (Semenov 1964; 1970; Keeley 1974), that great white hope of the interpretation of Palaeolithic material culture, seems as yet to have made no impact at all on the interpretation of hand-axes. A main reason for this may well be the scarcity or absence of Lower Palaeolithic hand-axes in the U.S.S.R. and U.S.A., where many of the microwear experiments have been carried out. This line of research, so far as hand-axes are concerned, is unexplored rather than shown to be unfruitful. We may certainly retain cautious hopes for the future in this direction, but there will often be grave difficulties in obtaining samples in the optimum condition for study and, even if consistent patterns of utilization traces can eventually be demonstrated for certain kinds of hand-axe, we cannot count on having a clear indication of what particular materials hand-axes were used to process (*cf.* Keeley 1974).

For the moment, then, the functional nature of hand-axes, both general and particular, remains obscure, which helps the typologist not at all. We do not even possess a formal demonstration that their inclusion in the category 'large cutting tools' (Kleindienst 1959; 1962 etc.) is in all cases correct, though what we take to be cutting edges are certainly the commonest feature. This lack of information on function, together with the great diversity of the implements grouped under the title 'hand-axes' as noted above, means that we should approach with caution any classification or study of Lower Palaeolithic artefact-sets in which all the hand-axes are lumped together as a single class. It might, for example, give misleading or incomplete results in a factor analysis study if, after classifying all the various implements and allowing for sub-divisions of some major classes like scrapers, the analyst decided to take hand-axes as a single unit (*cf.* Binford 1972).

What were hand-axes for? – that remains the crucial question. Some at least of our seventeenth-century predecessors (e.g. Tollius and Aldrovandus, quoted in Daniel 1950:25-6) were convinced that they were thunderbolts, and the present writer has on occasion when confronted with crates of unprovenanced British hand-axes, heavily abraded, deeply stained and mostly broken, felt that it might have been a good idea if a few of them were. Even a tiny fraction of the information we now possess regarding the technology, distribution, archaeological occurrence and dating of hand-axes would have profoundly enlightened John Frere (1800), considering his finds at Hoxne, Suffolk, in the closing years of the eighteenth century, yet what can we add now in cold scientific terms or put in place of his historic conclusion that they were 'weapons of war fabricated and used by a people who had not the use of metals'?

If then, as argued here, we do not know precisely the function or functions of hand-axes, and if we cannot be sure that all the implements so called belong to the same class, what is to be the approach to them of the typological classifier whose existence the previous section sought to justify? In the writer's view, the best approach at the present time is, in the first instance, not so much typological as *morphological* – that is, through analysis not so much of preferences of type as of preferences of form, where 'form' is a matter of dimensions, proportions and shape. Morphological study does not beg questions of typology, and permits analyses and comparisons of sets of hand-axes, which give factual results with no bias towards any particular interpretation of the observed and quantified differences and similarities. For one thing has long been observed and is beyond dispute: there certainly *are* morphological preferences in all the best and largest unmixed hand-axe industries of the world. Recurrent outline shapes (plan forms) usually afford the clearest evidence for this, but there may be strong concurrent preferences, too, for certain implement sizes or proportions (notably thickness in relation to length or breadth).

It was on the basis of such morphological evidence that the present writer (1967; 1968) proposed a division of 38 British hand-axe assemblages into various groups. If nothing else, the 'shape diagrams' he produced should convince any observer of the strong and very different morphological preferences in such assemblages as those from, say, Swanscombe Barnfield Pit Middle Gravels, Hoxne or Chadwell St Mary on the one hand, and Warren Hill (fresh series), High Lodge or Corfe Mullen on the other. On a broader basis, there seem to be major differences between the morphological range of British and African hand-axes, for which many explanations are possible, though within individual African sites shape preferences may be just as strong as in Britain, as shown by the studies of Glynn Isaac (1968; *cf.* 1972) on the various occurrences at Olorgesailie, Kenya, or of the present writer (forthcoming) on those at Kalambo Falls. A layman, given a glance at a large number of the hand-axes from Kalambo Falls Site B Floor 5, might well think they were objects that had been cast from a small number of similar moulds, rather than fashioned by flaking from unpromising quartzites. It is interesting to reflect that the attitude 'when you've seen one hand-axe, you've seen the lot', still quite frequently encountered, could well arise out of a single-site or strictly local study, but not out of long work involving several areas. Even in local circumstances it is a morphological comment rather than a typological one, and the typological unity of hand-axes in general is not to be assumed on a local basis.

It is now widely, if sometimes a little reluctantly, accepted that for purposes of description and comparison the morphological study of hand-axes and similar stone tools must be fully quantitative and based on a carefully worked out system of metrical analysis. Several such systems have been proposed (e.g. Bordes 1961; Roe 1964; 1968; Balout 1967; Isaac 1967; 1968; Cahen & Martin 1972). There is no virtue in reducing a stone hand-axe to a set of figures simply for the sake of the figures themselves, but it is only when precise metrical definitions and quantitative data exist, that useful objective descriptions and comparisons of different artefact-sets in morphological terms can be made.

No sooner does one enter the field of metrical analysis and comparison by mathematical or statistical methods than one encounters the whole set of problems relating to ensuring the validity, let alone the good quality, of the 'samples' studied. This is no place for a proper technical discussion of such problems, but it is worth pointing out that all hand-axe 'samples' are inherently uncertain and unreliable. In the older literature may be found various calls for good, undisturbed, primary context Acheulian sites; find them, and then we would really know about hand-axe industries. Now, a healthy number of large concentrations of Acheulian artefacts are known; one might, for instance, hope that the study of the best occurrences at Olduvai, Olorgesailie, Kalambo Falls, Isimila, Kariandusi, Melka Kontouré and other such sites would have told us most of what we wanted to know about the Acheulian of East and Central sub-Saharan Africa, and there are plenty of other good sites elsewhere in the Old World. Yet we find, first, that many of these occurrences are associated with stream-channels, and even if the artefacts were originally left by their users in dry stream-beds, as they may well have been, one cannot trust these as undisturbed or unmixed samples, thanks to the 'kinematic wave effect' (Isaac 1969: 9-10 & ref. quoted) and the general behaviour of stream-beds in semi-arid lands. It is true that some occurrences, like several at Kalambo, have clearly not been affected by stream action, and there are also now a good number of Acheulian occupation levels of various ages known in caves – Montagu Cave (Keller 1966; 1970; 1973), or the Cave of Hearths (Mason 1962) in South Africa, for example, or several in France described recently in some detail by Bordes (1972), de Lumley (1969a; 1969b; 1971) and others. But even these samples are open to doubt and uncertainty. The best modern archaeological methods cannot inform us how long the accumulations took to form on the open sites, or the layers to build up in the caves – whether they are the work of one group of people on one single day, or of many bands, not necessarily related, over centuries or more. Nor is there any prospect yet of such information becoming obtainable. Again, in many cases, Acheulian 'floors' are either incomplete because of later erosion, or else for one or another perfectly valid reason could not be completely excavated. One has only to imagine that different tool-types were made by specialist workmen on different parts of a 'manufacturing site' floor, or that different activities involving different tools were carried out on different areas of an 'occupation' floor, to realize that only total excavation of the original whole could ensure proper representation of the surviving assemblage – and even then, how should we ever know the relationship of the residue of tools left on the abandoned site (our 'sample') to the actual whole tool kit (the 'population') made, possessed or used by the original inhabitants? It is time to face the fact that there is not, and will not be, a site that gives a 'perfect' sample of hand-axe makers' artefacts from the analyst's point of view. Most samples indeed are downright poor, but that does not prevent us from studying them and making the best of them we can, remaining aware that all conclusions will be tentative.

Apart from morphology, *technology* may be

an important field for the classifier of hand-axes, though the writer does not propose to discuss it at length here. Quite simply, the way in which the preferred hand-axe forms were obtained often shows remarkable consistency within a given series and important variations when different assemblages are compared. In Britain, the writer (1968: 64-8) noted the occurrence of certain technological features like twisted profile, twisted tip and tranchet finish amongst the hand-axe assemblages he studied, and the distributions seemed to him to match up reasonably well with the groupings deduced from the morphological study, though he did not study in detail the selection or production of the blanks on which the hand-axes were made. In the case of Kalambo Falls, almost every hand-axe was made on a big specially-struck flake of one sort or another, as is appropriate to the obtaining of hand-axe blanks from quartzites in boulder form. A flake is by its nature inclined to flatness, and usually has an edge-angle of less than 90° round almost all of its circumference: that is, an angle that permits the removal from either face of secondary trimming flakes. The flat, regular and elegant Kalambo hand-axes simply could not have been made out of the local quartzites unless the blanks had been flakes. Indeed, the ability to obtain such blanks is the vital key to hand-axe refinement in the later Acheulian in many parts of Africa and elsewhere. As regards the large number of hand-axes and cleavers from Olduvai, which the writer is now studying, the blanks for the implements, which are made of several different rocks, seem likely to show greater variation. This kind of technological evidence, along with flake-scar counts and so forth, is perfectly susceptible to quantitative treatment, and is certainly important to typological classification in its best sense, being very much concerned with the recognition of 'makers' types'.

Conclusion

Ultimately it may be possible to link morphological and technological evidence with direct functional evidence, to construct a true and comprehensive typology of hand-axes, compatible with the view of typology suggested above. Meanwhile, it seems to the writer well worth pursuing any of these lines of evidence, morphology, technology and function, wherever there is suitable material to study. There is no need to feel qualms about separating off hand-axes and cleavers from all the small tools and other artefacts that may be associated with them, and giving them special treatment, so long as such other artefacts receive fair attention when a properly excavated 'complete' assemblage is described. On such occasions the hand-axes can also be seen in their true context and in perspective.

The writer takes the view that the hand-axes and other large tools were carefully made, with a considerable expenditure of effort, in a certain tradition; this may be true of some other Acheulian artefacts but not, for example, of *ad hoc* tools fabricated quickly on waste flakes which might be of any size or shape, or of any pieces used with a minimum of modification. It seems to him that the information potential of the more formal tools should therefore be correspondingly higher, and we have certainly not realized that potential yet. In studying hand-axes in detail without paying equal attention to the accompanying artefacts, one must do so with full awareness of aims and limitations, just as one might make a special study of the swords or spears of a later period without particularly concerning oneself with shields or helmets. No study of hand-axes is going to tell us everything about the life of Lower Palaeolithic man or even, of course, everything about his stone tool kit. The aim is altogether lower: to build up a pattern of likes and unlikes, based on a single important area of the tool kit, which ultimately, taken in conjunction with all the other archaeological evidence, one may hope to interpret in terms of human behaviour, both general and specific, at this fairly early stage of man's development.

It is very pleasing that this paper is to appear in a volume offered to Professor Grahame Clark, who has always taken great interest in the writer's research on hand-axes, and who gave him much kind encouragement during his time as undergraduate and graduate research student at Peterhouse, Cambridge.

REFERENCES

Balout, L. (1967) Procédés d'analyse et questions de terminologie dans l'étude des ensembles industriels du paléolithique inférieur en Afrique du nord. In Bishop, W.W. and Clark, J.D. (eds.), *Background to Evolution in Africa*, 701-36. Chicago and London.

Binford, L.R. (1972) Contemporary model building: paradigms and the current state of Palaeolithic research. In Clarke, D.L. (ed.), *Models in Archaeology*, 109-66. London.

Binford, L.R. and Binford, S.R. (1966) A preliminary analysis of functional variability in the Mousterian of Levallois facies. In Clark, J.D. and Howell, F.C. (eds.), *Amer. Anthrop.*, 68(2), Part 2, 238-95.

Bonnichsen, R. (1973) Millie's Camp: an experiment in archaeology. *World Arch.*, 4, 277-91.

Bordes, F. (1961) Typologie du paléolithique ancien et moyen. *Pubns Inst. préhist. Univ. Bordeaux* (Mémoire no. 1). Bordeaux.

Bordes, F. (1968) *The Old Stone Age*. London.

Bordes, F. (1972) *A Tale of Two Caves*. New York.

Cahen, D. and Martin, P. (1972) Classification formelle automatique et industries lithiques: interprétation des hachereaux de la Kamoa. *Mus. Royale Afrique Cent. Ann. – sér. In-8° – Sci. Hum.*, 76. Tervuren.

Clark, J.D. and Haynes, C.V. (1969) An elephant butchery site at Mwanganda's Village, Karonga, Malawi and its relevance for Palaeolithic archaeology. *World Arch.*, 1, 390-411.

Clarke, D.L. (1968) *Analytical Archaeology*. London.

Daniel, G.E. (1943) *The Three Ages*. London.

Daniel, G.E. (1950) *A Hundred Years of Archaeology*. London.

Frere, J. (1800) Account of flint weapons discovered at Hoxne in Suffolk. *Archaeologia*, 13, 204-5.

Isaac, G.Ll. (1967) Some experiments in quantitative methods for characterizing assemblages of Acheulian artefacts. *Cong. panafr. préhist. Actes 6e session, Dakar 1967*, 547-55. Chambéry.

Isaac, G.Ll. (1968) The Acheulian Site Complex at Olorgesaile, Kenya: a contribution to the interpretation of Middle Pleistocene culture in East Africa. Ph.D. thesis, Cambridge University.

Isaac, G.Ll. (1969) Studies of early culture in East Africa. *World Arch.*, 1, 1-28.

Isaac, G.Ll. (1972) Early phases of human behaviour: models in Lower Palaeolithic archaeology. In Clarke, D.L. (ed.), *Models in Archaeology*, 167-99. London.

Keeley, L.H. (1974) Technique and methodology in microwear studies: a critical review. *World Arch.*, 5, 323-36.

Keller, C.M. (1966) Archaeology of Montagu Cave. Ph.D. dissertation, University of California, Berkeley.

Keller, C.M. (1970) Montagu Cave: a preliminary report. *Quaternaria*, 13, 187-204.

Keller, C.M. (1973) *Montagu Cave in Prehistory: a descriptive analysis* (Anthropological records, 28). Univ. of California.

Kleindienst, M.R. (1959) Composition and significance of a Late Acheulian assemblage, based on an analysis of East African occupation sites. Ph.D. dissertation, University of Chicago.

Kleindienst, M.R. (1962) Components of the East African Acheulian assemblage: an analytical approach. *Actes IVe Cong. panafr. préhist. Sect. III (Mus. Royale Afrique Cent. Ann. – sér. In-8° – Sci. Hum., 40)*, 81-111. Tervuren.

Leakey, M.D. (1971) *Olduvai Gorge*. Vol. 3: Excavations *in Beds I and II, 1960-1963*. London.

Lumley-Woodyear, H. de (de Lumley, H.) (1969a) Une cabane Acheuléenne dans la Grotte du Lazaret (Nice). *Mémoires Soc. préhist. Française, 7.*

Lumley-Woodyear, H. de (1969b) *Le paléolithique inférieur et moyen du midi méditerranéen dans son cadre géologique (Ve supp. à Gallia-Préhist.) Tome 1: Ligurie-Provence*. Paris.

Lumley-Woodyear, H. de (1971) *Le paléolithique inférieur et moyen du midi méditerranéen dans son cadre géologique (Ve supp. à Gallia-Préhist.) Tome 2: Bas-Languedoc-Roussillon-Catalogne*. Paris.

Mason, R.J. (1962) *The Prehistory of the Transvaal*. Johannesburg.

Newcomer, M.H. (1971) Some quantitative experiments in hand-axe manufacture. *World Arch.*, 3, 85-94.

Roe, D.A. (1964) The British Lower and Middle Palaeolithic: some problems, methods of study and preliminary results. *P.P.S.*, 30, 245-67.

Roe, D.A. (1967) A study of hand-axe groups of the British Lower and Middle Palaeolithic periods, using methods of metrical and statistical analysis, with a gazetteer of British Lower and Middle Palaeolithic sites. Ph.D. thesis, Cambridge University.

Roe, D.A. (1968) British Lower and Middle Palaeolithic hand-axe groups. *P.P.S.*, 34, 1-82.

Roe, D.A. (forthcoming) The Kalambo Falls large cutting tools: a metrical analysis. In Clark, J.D. (ed.), *Kalambo Falls, vol. 3*. London.

Semenov, S.A. (1964) *Prehistoric Technology: an experimental study of the oldest tools and artefacts from traces of manufacture and wear* (trans. Thompson, M.W.). London.

Semenov, S.A. (1970) The forms and functions of the oldest tools (a reply to Prof. F. Bordes). *Quartär*, 21, 1-20.

Smith, R.A. (1933) Implements from High-level Gravel near Canterbury. *P.P.S. East Anglia*, 7, 165-70.

PART II

America and Asia

WARWICK BRAY

From predation to production: The nature of agricultural evolution in Mexico and Peru

It is a basic fact of archaeology (and one which Grahame Clark has always stressed) that man does not exist in isolation but as part of nature in general. In a previous paper (Bray 1973) I have argued that the distinction between biological and cultural evolution is an artificial one, since both serve the same purpose of maintaining equilibrium between man and his environment. The same paper attempted to demonstrate that the laws governing cultural evolution have their counterparts in biological evolution. If this general principle is accepted, it seems likely that some of the very precise models developed by geneticists and ecologists for the study of biological adaptation (e.g. Levins 1968; MacArthur 1972) will have applications in the field of culture change. Some of them, in fact, are already being applied to such archaeological problems as the spread of farming from its centres of origin (Ammerman & Cavalli-Sforza 1971; 1973). In the belief that the best way to prove a theory is to test it in a real situation, the present paper shows how analogies drawn from genetics and ecology can be useful in the study of one aspect of cultural evolution, the change-over from a hunting-and-gathering way of life to one based on agriculture.

Among human communities, as a sociologist has commented in a recent paper, 'adaptation, in all but a few physiological respects, is a collective phenomenon; it is achieved not by individuals acting independently, but by combining their abilities in an organization that operates as a unit of higher order' (Hawley 1973:1197). In studying the changing nature of the food quest we are therefore examining the evolution of an

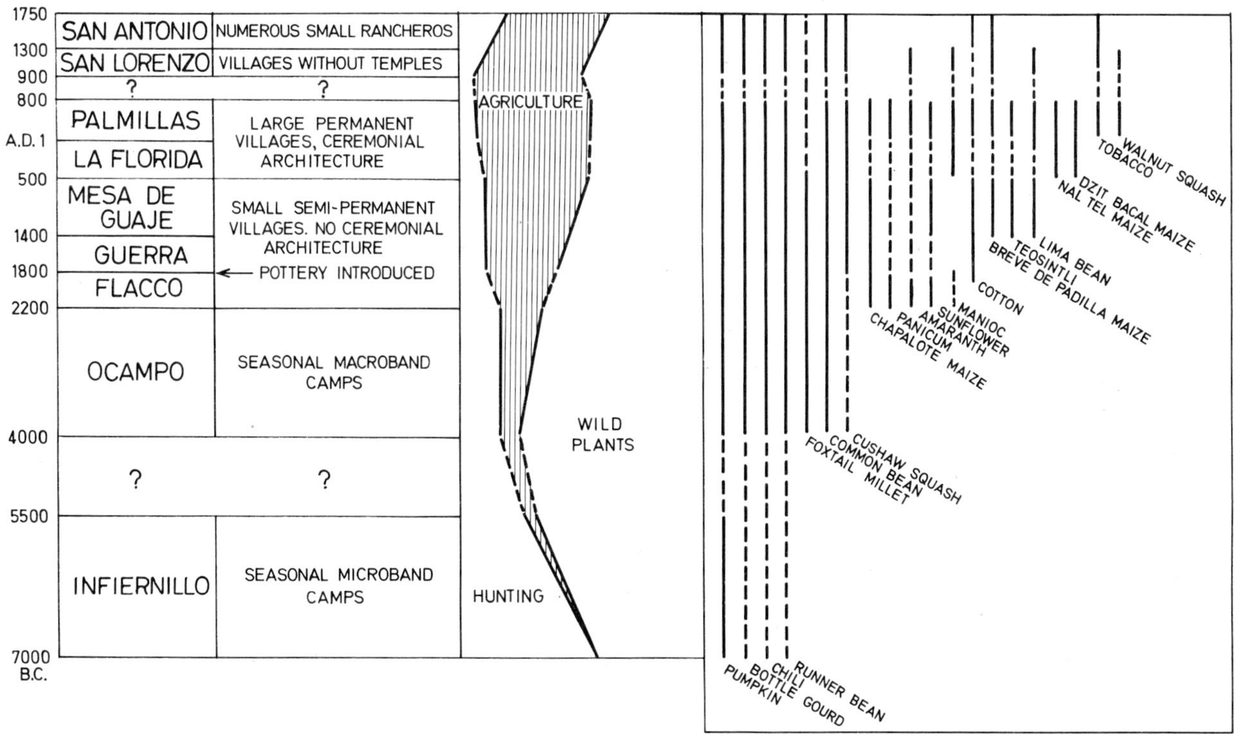

Figure 1. Agricultural development and settlement patterns in the Sierra Madre of south-west Tamaulipas, Mexico.

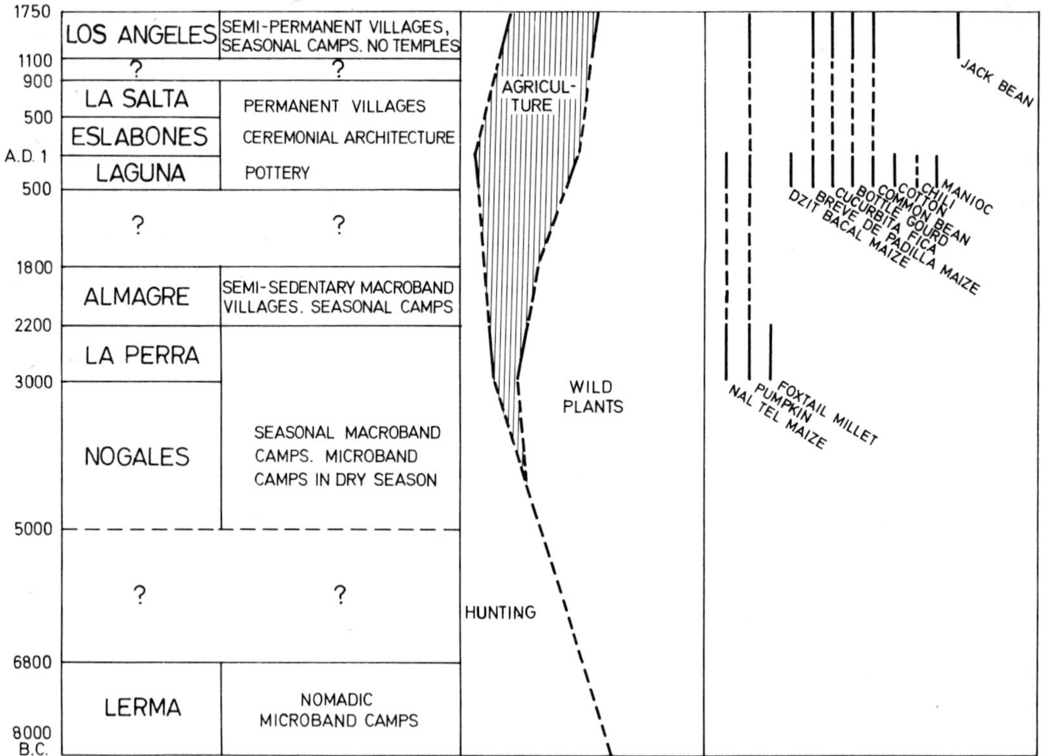

Figure 2. Agricultural development and settlement patterns in the Sierra de Tamaulipas, Mexico.

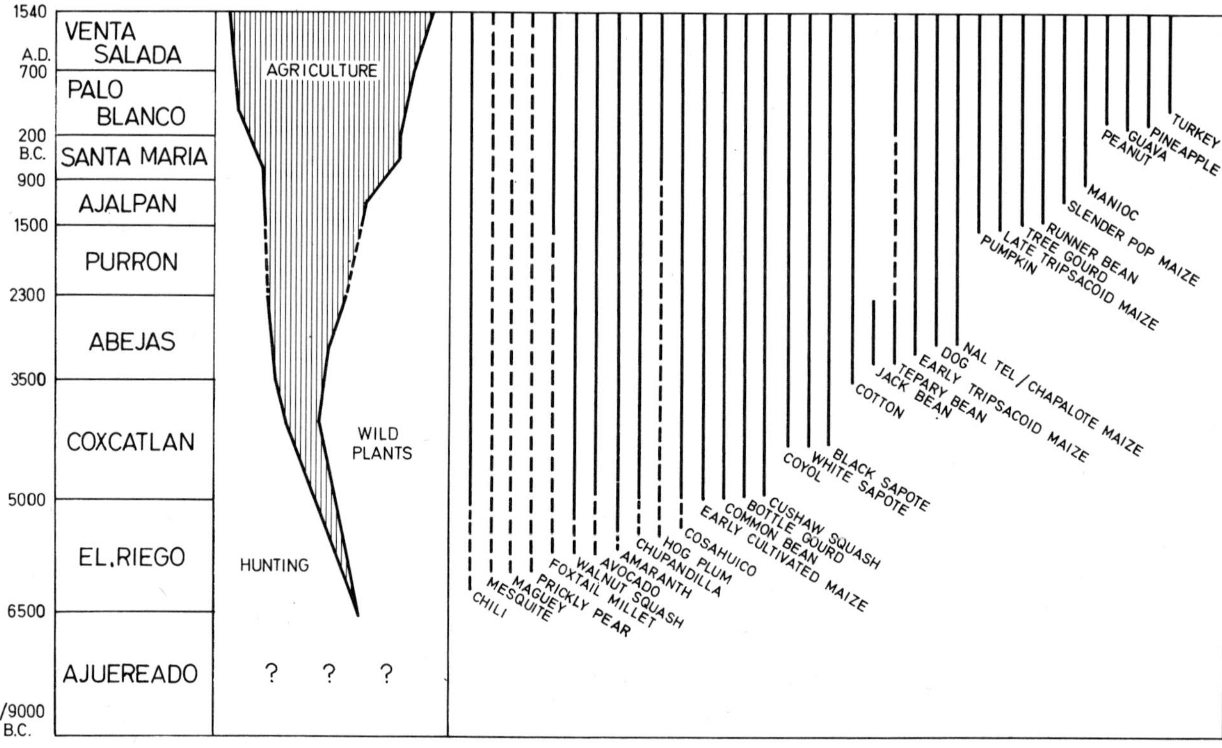

Figure 3. Agricultural evolution and plant domestication in the Tehuacan Valley, Mexico. Bottle gourd, perhaps cultivated, is now reported for the period 8000-6000 B.C. (Lathrap 1973C). The sieva bean (*Ph. lunatus*) was introduced during the Venta Salada phase, and the pumpkin may have been cultivated by the Abejas period.

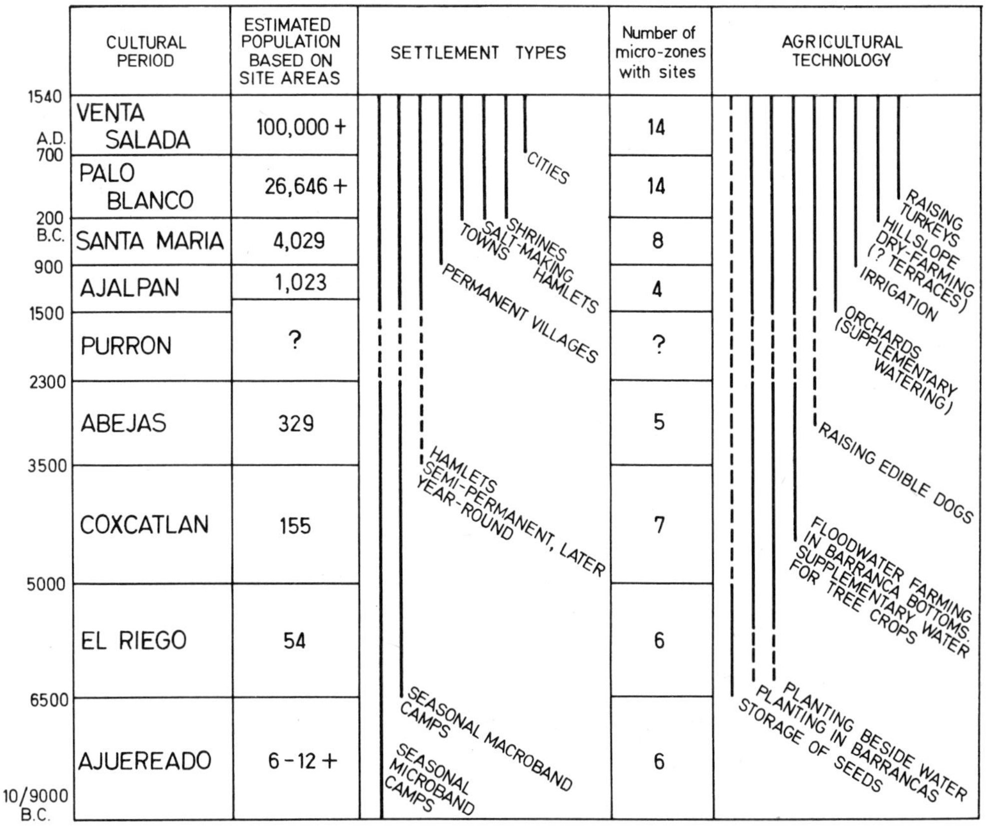

Dates	CULTURAL PERIOD	ESTIMATED POPULATION BASED ON SITE AREAS	SETTLEMENT TYPES	Number of micro-zones with sites	AGRICULTURAL TECHNOLOGY
1540 A.D. – 700	VENTA SALADA	100,000 +	CITIES	14	
700 – 200 B.C.	PALO BLANCO	26,646 +		14	RAISING TURKEYS; HILLSLOPE DRY-FARMING (? TERRACES)
200 B.C. – 900	SANTA MARIA	4,029	SHRINES; SALT-MAKING HAMLETS; TOWNS	8	IRRIGATION
900 – 1500	AJALPAN	1,023	PERMANENT VILLAGES	4	
1500 – 2300	PURRON	?		?	ORCHARDS (SUPPLEMENTARY WATERING)
2300 – 3500	ABEJAS	329		5	RAISING EDIBLE DOGS
3500 – 5000	COXCATLAN	155	HAMLETS SEMI-PERMANENT, LATER YEAR-ROUND	7	FLOODWATER FARMING IN BARRANCA BOTTOMS. SUPPLEMENTARY WATER FOR TREE CROPS
5000 – 6500	EL RIEGO	54		6	
6500 – 10/9000 B.C.	AJUEREADO	6 - 12 +	SEASONAL MACROBAND CAMPS; SEASONAL MICROBAND CAMPS	6	PLANTING BESIDE WATER; PLANTING IN BARRANCAS; STORAGE OF SEEDS

Figure 4. Changes in population, settlement pattern and farming technology in the Tehuacan Valley, Mexico. (Population figures are based on MacNeish 1970 and have not been corrected to incorporate new sites discovered by Sisson 1973. Where a small increase is needed, a + sign has been added to the original figure).

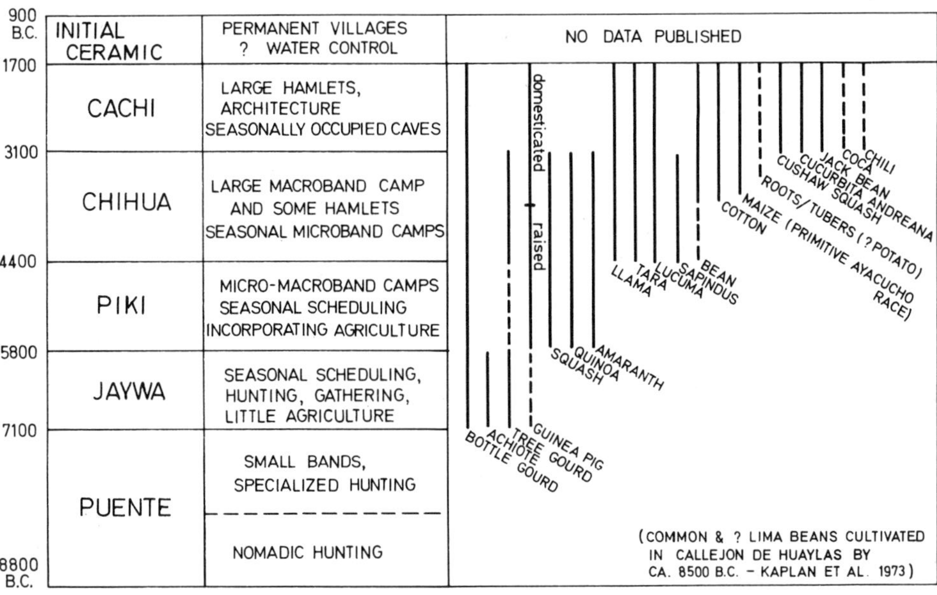

Figure 5. Agriculture and settlement pattern during the preceramic period in the Ayacucho Basin, Peru. Bottle gourd is now reported as early as 11,000 B.C. (Lathrap 1973c), but its status as a cultigen is ambiguous.

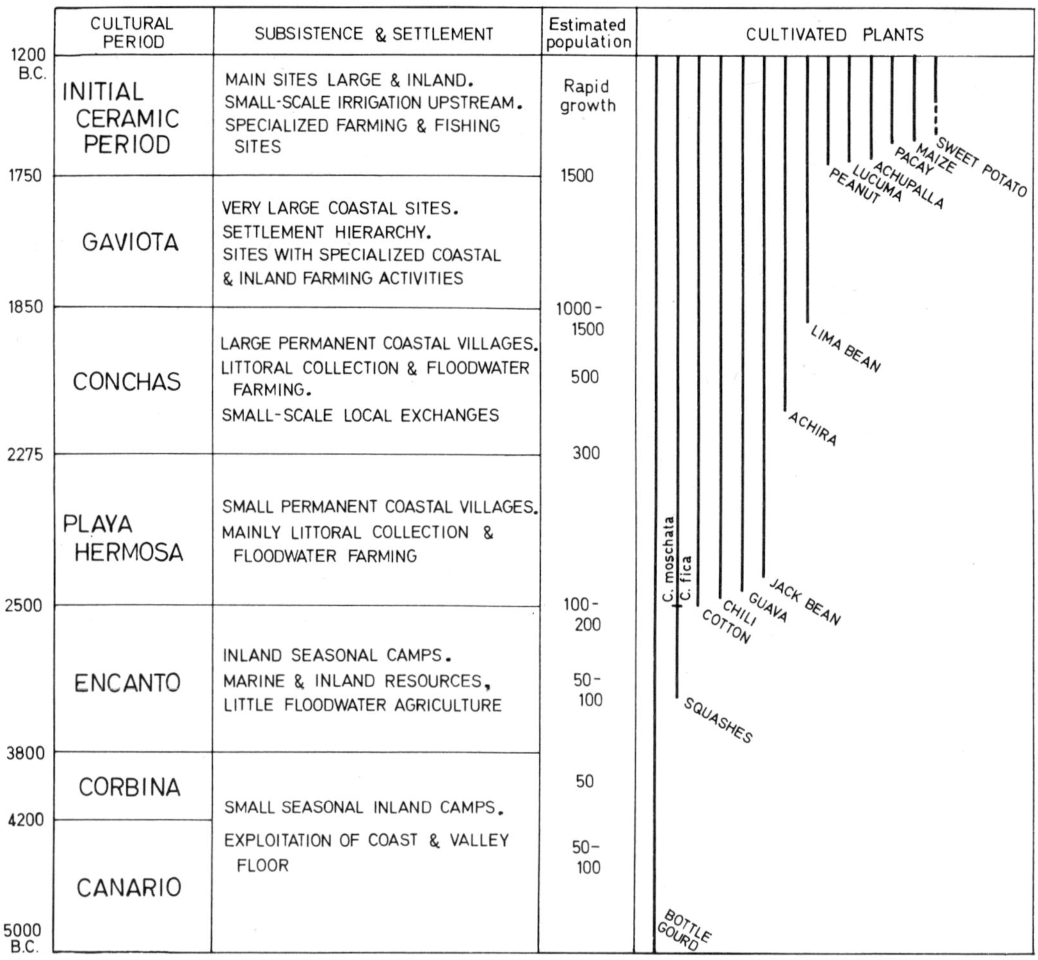

CULTURAL PERIOD
SUBSISTENCE & SETTLEMENT
Estimated population
CULTIVATED PLANTS
1200 B.C.
INITIAL CERAMIC PERIOD
MAIN SITES LARGE & INLAND.
SMALL-SCALE IRRIGATION UPSTREAM.
SPECIALIZED FARMING & FISHING SITES
Rapid growth
1750
1500
GAVIOTA
VERY LARGE COASTAL SITES.
SETTLEMENT HIERARCHY.
SITES WITH SPECIALIZED COASTAL & INLAND FARMING ACTIVITIES
1850
1000-1500
CONCHAS
LARGE PERMANENT COASTAL VILLAGES.
LITTORAL COLLECTION & FLOODWATER FARMING.
SMALL-SCALE LOCAL EXCHANGES
500
2275
300
PLAYA HERMOSA
SMALL PERMANENT COASTAL VILLAGES.
MAINLY LITTORAL COLLECTION & FLOODWATER FARMING
2500
100-200
ENCANTO
INLAND SEASONAL CAMPS.
MARINE & INLAND RESOURCES,
LITTLE FLOODWATER AGRICULTURE
50-100
3800
CORBINA
50
4200
SMALL SEASONAL INLAND CAMPS.
EXPLOITATION OF COAST & VALLEY FLOOR
CANARIO
50-100
5000 B.C.
SWEET POTATO
MAIZE
PACAY
ACHUPALLA
LUCUMA
PEANUT
LIMA BEAN
ACHIRA
C. moschata
C. fica
JACK BEAN
GUAVA
CHILI
COTTON
SQUASHES
BOTTLE GOURD

Figure 6. Settlement pattern, subsistence and population in the Ancón-Chillón region of the central Peruvian coast. Population figures are from Patterson (1971b); Cohen (1973) prefers a higher estimate. The common bean, avocado, ciruela, manioc and campomanesia were introduced soon after 900 B.C.; llama and guinea pig were domesticated from 200 B.C.; *Cucurbita maxima* first appears after A.D. 1000; quinoa, cherimoya and (?) oca were not introduced until the Inca period. All supplementary data are abstracted from Cohen (1973).

organization, the *food procurement system.*

Rather than attempt a world-wide comparative survey of this process (*cf.* Harris 1973b) I have preferred to concentrate on a limited number of regional sequences from Mexico and Peru. From these areas the information is unusually complete, and covers the entire period from the end of the Pleistocene to the Spanish conquest (Figs. 1-6). Comparison of these diverse local sequences leads to the recognition of a general model of agricultural evolution that has applications in other parts of the world.

The archaeological evidence and its limitations

Tamaulipas (in north-east Mexico), the Tehuacan Valley (in the central Mexican state of Puebla), and the Ayacucho Basin (in the Peruvian Andes), are inland areas of diverse topography and low rainfall, with a marked dry season. It was the policy of the excavators to test sites in as many different ecological zones as possible, and the plant material comes mainly from dry caves where preservation was good. Most of the crop plants were already available nearby and were exploited in the wild state before being brought into cultivation.

The Ancón sequence (Fig. 6), on the other hand, derives from excavations in open settlements on the central coast of Peru, an area with some of the world's richest marine resources (fish, molluscs, sea mammals and birds) but with virtually no rainfall. The lower slopes (*lomas*) directly behind the coast, at altitudes between 200 and 800 metres, bear vegetation in the months from May to November, although there is disagreement about what sustains this plant cover. The nature of prehistoric settlement in the *lomas* zone is also a subject of controversy (Lanning 1963; Craig & Psuty 1968; Parsons 1970; Moseley 1972; Engel 1973). Terrain fit for simple cultivation is limited to a few patches of bottom-land and flood-plain in the river valleys; elsewhere, agriculture is impossible without irrigation. None of the staple food crops is native to the coast, and agriculture was therefore based on introduced plants, some of them originating in the tropical forest east of the Andes but the majority coming from the sierra at altitudes between 1,000 and 3,500 metres. The Ancón situation offers a valuable opportunity to study what happens when a non-indigenous form of subsistence is introduced into a hunter-gatherer economy.[1]

The archaeological evidence from all four regions is set out in Figs. 1-6. Of necessity these diagrams are only schematic, and for full details the original reports must be consulted.[2] Since the figures are intended to be self-explanatory, it must be emphasized that they give a false air of precision and conceal a number of controversies. Before discussing the significance of the archaeological evidence it is therefore important to appreciate its limitations.

In the first place, botanical specialists have often been unable to agree among themselves about the status of particular plants. The problem is acute with the bottle gourd (usually the first domesticate to appear in the archaeological record), and with such species as maguey and prickly pear that are vegetatively propagated, and whose cultivated forms show few differences from their wild prototypes. The very earliest generations of any domesticate will, moreover, be unrecognizable as such, and there is always the possibility that, at a very early stage, plants and animals were being manipulated in ways that caused no visible change (Smith 1967; Higgs & Jarman 1972).

A further problem is created by differential preservation and its effects on archaeological recovery. In Tehuacan, manioc and (imported) pineapple were not recovered during excavation but were identified in some of the coprolites (Callen 1967b). The same was true of *Setaria* (foxtail millet) in the Sierra Madre de Tamaulipas, where the plant was not recovered from the living-floors within the caves but was common in the faeces after about 4,000 B.C. In the same Tamaulipas sequence, sunflower and (?) manioc appeared in coprolites at an earlier date than in the midden refuse – though, conversely, maize was absent from faeces at a time when it was well represented in the cave debris (Callen 1963; 1967a).

In attempting to quantify the information and to convert the excavated samples into percentage figures for total diet, all sorts of additional problems arise. Any conversion factor is bound to be arbitrary, and there remains the question of whether the sample is representative of the whole. The evidence from coprolites, for instance, is often incompatible with the information derived from excavated plant fragments (Callen 1963; 1967b). Most of the plant and animal material is from cave sites and may therefore over-emphasize cave-based activities at the expense of those carried out at open sites. This is especially so in later times, after the growth of town and city life, when the people who used the caves and rock shelters belonged to the lower strata of society and lived a very different life from that of the urban elite. Callen (1967b), on the basis of coprolite analysis, has postulated the existence of distinct 'cave' and 'town' diets in the Tehuacan Valley after 900 B.C. This would be quite consistent with the documentary sources, which indicate that wild foods were an important element of rural diet at the time of the Spanish conquest. With these provisos in mind, the information contained in the figures may be taken as the best available approximation, not completely reliable but probably of the right order of magnitude. Chronology of the early phases is based on uncalibrated radio-carbon dates and may need adjustment (Johnson & MacNeish 1972).

More important than local differences are the following general conclusions, which emerge from a comparison of all the sequences and which must be explained by any model of agricultural development:

1. The 'Neolithic revolution' in America was not a sudden breakthrough – the moment when natural man discovered progress. Agriculture was adopted only slowly, and there was a marked reluctance – or inability – to give up the hunting-and-gathering way of life and to make a commitment to farming.

2. The increasing importance of cultivated foods in the diet can be correlated with (a) the emergence of more productive races of certain

plants that eventually became staple foods and (b) the adoption, where practicable, of certain techniques of intensive agriculture.

3. These changes in subsistence pattern took place against a background of climatic fluctuations.

4. Increasing commitment to farming was accompanied by population growth.

5. Larger populations and more effective agriculture can be correlated with changes in social organization: larger and more stable communities, the development of political institutions, the growth of states and, ultimately, the emergence of civilization.

These generalizations seem also to hold good for other areas of the world where seed crop agriculture developed *in situ* in a fairly dry environment. Because of poor preservation, comparable information from the moist tropics of America is lacking until the introduction of pottery between 3,000 and 2,000 B.C. and, even after that, is very scanty, though there are good reasons for believing that root crop agriculture has an equally long history in lowland South America (Lathrap 1970; 1973b). It seems likely, therefore, that when we have information from these areas, it will confirm the general trends indicated above, though we can expect many differences of detail (*v.* Harris 1973b; Lathrap 1973c).

Alternative models of agricultural evolution

The list of generalizations given above also serves to define our terms of reference. Items (1) and (2) indicate the main changes that took place in the nature of (i.e. within) the food procurement system. Items (3) to (5) list the changes in the environment to which this system had to adapt. Hawley (1973:1197) has pointed out that the word environment has no fixed meaning and is best defined as 'a generic concept for whatever is external to, and potentially influential upon, a unit under study'. This definition is the one employed throughout the present paper.

Models of agricultural evolution can be divided into two categories: *cause-and-effect* models and *equilibrium* models. It is characteristic of the first group that one variable in the environment (usually climate or population) is chosen, often arbitrarily, as *the* prime mover, or 'cause', of change in the food procurement system. Population is allowed to increase, grasslands to dry up, sea levels to rise or fall, and the effects of these fluctuations are then traced throughout the ecosystem as a whole.

In the second category, *equilibrium* models are based on concepts derived from systems theory. Their application to the central problem of archaeology, the analysis of culture change, has been discussed at a theoretical level by David Clarke (1968). The approach is equally relevant to the examination of biological and genetic change. In an equilibrium model, evolution is seen as a continuously changing adaptation between the organism (or organization) and its environment, rather akin to a game of chess in which each move a player makes is conditioned by his opponent's previous move and by the entire past history of the game. In systems terminology, there is a 'feedback' relationship between the two.

Since the environment itself has many components, none of which is stable, the situation becomes enormously complex. Innovations arising in one component (food procurement, biophysical environment, technology, social organization etc.) give rise to correlated changes in all the other components. Not only is the point of balance *between* the components of the system in a constant state of motion; so, too, is the internal equilibrium *within* each sub-system. Since all parts of the system are in a perpetual state of flux, and all components are interdependent, there can be no single 'cause' of change. Within the framework of an equilibrium model, the question 'What caused agriculture?' is as meaningless as 'What caused elephants?'.

The rest of this paper is an attempt to test these kinds of model against the archaeological evidence and to demonstrate that:

(a) simple cause-and-effect models, which invoke either population pressure or fluctuations in the biophysical environment as the sole cause of change, are not adequate to explain the emergence of agriculture;
(b) some form of equilibrium model best fits the observed data;
(c) a similar equilibrium model also describes biological adaptation;
(d) the evolution of food production obeys many of the ecological rules that govern the changing relationship between an organism and its food supply.

Changes in the biophysical environment

There is no need to emphasize that the biophysical environment is in a continuous state of change. More to the point is that there are different kinds of change and that they originate in different parts of the environment.

Changes in climate

Climatic change (in temperature, precipitation etc.) is outside man's effective control, and for that reason is often treated as an independent variable. It is this that makes it so attractive to proponents of cause-and-effect models. The influence is apparently all one way (from climate to man), and the ultimate cause so remote that the archaeologist can avoid considering it – as if, somehow, the boot of God had delivered a series of kicks to the backside of mankind and thus impelled him into adopting agriculture.

Changes in resources

As far as the food procurement system is concerned, climate exerts its effect by causing changes in resources, i.e. in the kinds and/or numbers of plants and animals available for exploitation. Climate, however, is not the only factor that influences resources, for some changes originate with man himself. Into this category come the landscape changes that take place under agriculture, and also those alterations that result from practices such as the burning of vegetation (Harris 1973b) or selective hunting (Martin 1973; Martin & Wright 1967), both of which are archaeologically documented for pre-agricultural times. In these cases, environmental changes exist in a reciprocal type of relationship with the food procurement system, so that the influence goes both ways.

Changes in the size of the environment

Climate and resources figure in almost every model of agricultural development. Equally important, though often ignored, is the fact that the *size* of the environment is not constant; its boundaries are continuously changing and expanding. As Hawley (1973:1198) pointed out, 'Where the means of movement are crude and costly, where production techniques are primitive, and where marketing facilities are non-existent, a community lives in intimate association with its biophysical environment. The model of a closed ecosystem is nearly approximated under such conditions.' As population grows and more complex forms of social organization emerge, the constraints of a closed system are relaxed and the segment of the total environment accessible to the community increases. Eventually, the closed ecosystem model ceases to be applicable. Long before this stage is reached, social organization begins to mitigate the effects of changes in climate or resources and, at the same time, to influence directly both the food procurement system and the number of people an area can support.

The history of coastal Peru (Fig. 6) shows that here these factors came into play at a very early date. Lynch (1971) has argued that seasonal transhumance through the several altitude zones of the Andes may have been the general rule before effective agriculture was developed (for a contrary view, see Moseley 1972:36), and there is evidence to show that food-stuffs were exchanged between the coast and the highlands soon after the end of the Pleistocene. The Andean caves of Quiqché and Tres Ventanas in the upper reaches of the Rio Chilca, which drains westwards to the coast, have yielded wild forms of edible tubers from several different altitude-zones (*jíquima,* potato, manioc, *olluco*, sweet potato), as well as fish bones, sea shells and prickly pear fruits in strata dated to 8,000-6,000 B.C. (Engel 1970; 1973). In the reverse direction, vicuña skins first reached Paracas, on the south coast of Peru, during the early Preceramic period (Engel 1970).

By about 2,500 B.C., the pattern of community self-sufficiency had begun to break down in the Ancón-Chillón region, with the emergence of settlements of specialist cultivators and fishermen, who practised intensive exploitation of local resources, exchanging their surplus for the products of other specialist villages up to a day's walk away. By *c.* 1900 B.C., villages three or four days' walk apart were linked by exchange networks. Soon after that, we can probably talk of organized states and, by about 500 B.C., such trade networks embraced several coastal valleys (Patterson 1973:93-100). A similar process, ending with the states of the Formative period, has been recognized in parts of Mesoamerica in the second and first millennia B.C. (Flannery & Coe 1968). At each stage of development the size of the effective environment increases and the closed ecosystem model becomes less and less relevant.

Post-Pleistocene readaptation and the origins of agriculture

Reduced to its essentials, the cause-and-effect model argues that climatic changes at the end of the Pleistocene resulted in the extinction of big game and led to the emergence of new food procurement patterns based on smaller animals, aquatic resources and wild plants. This situation encouraged man to carry out further experiments with plants and, eventually, to invent agriculture, the advantages of which he appreciated at once.

In favour of this theory, the dates for the earliest agriculture in America coincide well enough with the onset of Post-Pleistocene conditions. At Guitarrero Cave, in the Peruvian Andes, beans were definitely cultivated by 6,000 B.C. and probably as early as 8,500 B.C. (Kaplan *et al.* 1973). Similar dates are attested for the Ayacucho Basin (Fig. 5). On the coast, cultivated plants are reported from a sedentary fishing village on the Pampa de Santo Domingo, near Paracas in southern Peru, at around 7,000 B.C. (Engel 1966:77), though the evidence for this has not yet been presented and the C14 date is some two thousand years older than any other figure for coastal agriculture. In north-east Mexico, farming of a sort had begun by about 7,000 B.C. (Fig. 1); in central Mexico, by 6,500 B.C. (Fig. 3); and in Oaxaca, by the seventh millennium (Flannery MS). This widespread agreement can hardly be coincidental; there must have been *something* in the early Post-Pleistocene situation that was conducive to experimentation. But was this 'something' climatic change?

Information on prehistoric climates in Middle and South America is scanty and ambiguous. It is therefore more profitable to approach this question from another angle and to examine the archaeological record to see whether, in fact, big changes did take place in food procurement systems at the close of the Pleistocene. Evidence is accumulating to suggest that they did not. The view that big game formed the basis of diet during the late Pleistocene is a persistent myth, but is becoming more and more difficult to sustain. The conspicuous and spectacular mammoth kill sites of central Mexico (Aveleyra 1964) have tended to dominate the archaeological picture to the exclusion of other activities, but the focus changes drastically in those areas where caves and rock shelters have been excavated.

As usual, some of the most complete information comes from the Tehuacan Valley. Tehuacan seems to have been cooler and drier during the Late Pleistocene than it is today (Byers 1967: Ch. 4, Ch. 8). The fauna from archaeological sites of the Early Ajuereado phase (which is older than 7,000 B.C. and must, therefore, be roughly contemporary with the mammoth kill sites elsewhere) included extinct species such as the horse, and also animals like the pronghorn antelope and the large jack rabbit, whose present range is limited to the cooler, and often drier, regions much further north. By 6,500 B.C. (the Late Ajuereado phase) the Tehuacan fauna was of completely modern type. This faunal and climatic change took place in the middle of a single archaeological phase and unmarked by any change in the stone tools.

The readaptation in the food procurement system was equally undramatic. Although mammoth bones have been found in the Valley (and kill sites may remain to be discovered), the animals brought back to the caves during the Late Pleistocene were mainly small, which is suggestive of broad-spectrum hunting rather than specialization on big game (Flannery 1967:171). Horse and antelope are rare in the Early Ajuereado fauna. About 55% of the individual animals are rabbits, and most of the others are of small size (fox, skunk, quail and other birds, coyote, turtle, lizard, ground squirrel, various rodents). Plant remains are too scarce for quantitative analysis, but there are traces of plant exploitation both in Early Ajuereado (mesquite, palm leaf, clumps of grass) and Late Ajuereado (foxtail, amaranth, prickly pear, avocado, chupandilla) (Smith 1967).

The end of the Pleistocene was also the end of the megafauna in the Valley. Flannery (1966; 1967) believes that the change in food animals may have caused some alteration in hunting practices, but points out that in many cases (e.g. turtle, rodents, fox, quail) the Pleistocene forms were merely replaced by their modern equivalents. Bones from the later archaeological stages show that the hunting of small game continued virtually unchanged.

The preliminary results from Oaxaca tend to confirm the belief that broad-range hunting and collecting were the general custom during the terminal Pleistocene, and that no major change took place with the onset of Recent conditions (Flannery MS). The lowest floors in the cave of Guilá Naquitz represent short seasonal occupations by small groups of people who hunted deer and rabbit, collected mud turtles and foraged for wild plants (acorns, pinyon, mesquite, fruit and berries, maguey and prickly pear, wild onions, runner beans and squashes). Radiocarbon dates for these deposits cluster between 8,750 ± 35 and 7,280 ± 120 B.C., though there are a few anomalous later ones. This pattern of life continued alongside the first cultivation, with C14 dates in the early seventh millennium B.C.

Tamaulipas, Ayacucho and the Peruvian coast have all produced some sort of evidence for climatic change at the end of the Pleistocene, but the corresponding data on subsistence are so meagre that no useful conclusions can be drawn.

The available information, then, is neither complete nor very detailed but, in sum, it tends to suggest that climatic change at the close of the Pleistocene was not so extreme as to provoke major readaptations in food procurement habits (at least in highland areas), still less to make agriculture inevitable. Broad-spectrum hunting and collecting, which were probably the rule during the Late Pleistocene, continued to form the basis of the economy under Post-Pleistocene conditions until long after the first attempts at cultivation.

Population growth and agriculture

In the words of an eminent geneticist and biologist, 'Some of the most radical changes in human environments arise from there being more and more humans' (Dobzhansky 1962:299). Ignoring short-term fluctuations, the overall trend of population change is unidirectional: the number of people is constantly growing. One of the oldest chicken-and-egg questions in archaeology is whether agriculture (by providing a more stable food supply or a better diet) *allowed* population to increase, or whether population growth *compelled* man to experiment with farming. The evidence presented below tends to show that neither of these simplistic propositions is true, and that the relationship between population and food procurement is a complex and reciprocal one.

Hunting versus plant collecting

The archaeological evidence from Tamaulipas and the Tehuacan Valley (Figs. 1-3) suggests that the importance of hunting decreased between 7,000 and 4,000 B.C. and that wild plants came to provide the bulk of the diet. If further research demonstrates that this is a general phenomenon, not confined to a few arid zones of America, it has significant implications. Whether or not the shift in emphasis was a conscious choice or was forced by climatic changes or by dwindling game resources,[3] its effect would be the same: it would, by itself and without the need for cultivation, allow a population increase (Deevey 1960:202; MacArthur & Connell 1966:172-81).

Each stage in the food chain (plant → herbivore → primary carnivore → secondary carnivore) can expect to harvest only about one-tenth of the energy accessible to the previous stage. Since the amount of available energy decreases rapidly as the food chain lengthens, the most efficient exploitation is the one that operates at the lowest trophic level. A band of foragers acting as herbivores (plant collectors) can, therefore, rely on about ten times as much food energy as they would obtain if they acted as pure carnivores or hunters (MacArthur & Connell 1966:179). This, of course, is a measure of energy alone; it ignores preferences for certain foods, the nutritional requirement for a balanced diet, and the fact that some foods can be obtained with less effort than others. It therefore remains a theoretical model, but one which predicts that increased exploitation of wild plants may be correlated with population growth – though it does not predict which of these is cause and which effect.

Stability or growth: ethnographic analogy

It has become clear, during the last decade or so, that many present-day hunter-gatherer groups lead a fairly comfortable life, spending as little as two to five hours per person per day in the search for food, and enjoying a varied and nutritious diet. Far from being on the increase, their populations remain stable at something between 20% and 50% of the ecological carrying capacity, and shortage of food is not a problem (Sahlins 1972:1-39; Lee & DeVore 1968). These groups are also nomadic.[4] Some authors (e.g. Hayden 1972:205; Harris 1973b) have assumed that past hunter-gatherers behaved in the same way as those of today, and normally stabilized their populations at well below the carrying capacity of the environment. If this is so, population pressure could hardly have been the force that drove man to take up agriculture.

However, the belief in a stable prehistoric population depends on faith rather than on proof. It can be objected that the sample of present-day groups is small, that they live in marginal areas that are not favourable to agriculture, and that they are not necessarily representative of those much earlier communities of foragers who evolved into farmers. Opinion among modern demographers seems to accept that population growth is the 'normal' condition of mankind, and there is another line of enquiry that suggests that there was, in fact, a slow build-up of population among the hunting-and-gathering groups of the early Post-Pleistocene.

A closer look at the ethnographic data on the stable hunter-gatherer communities of today shows that the biological controls on population growth are supplemented by other measures. Among the !Kung Bushmen (whose population appears to be stable, and who are so often quoted as the ethnographic counterparts of pre-agricultural man) natural fertility is unusually low, but is nevertheless inadequate by itself to hold numbers in check. The 'modest amount of excess fertility . . . is readily absorbed by infant mortality, occasional infanticide and out-migration' (Lee 1972a:337). Cultural controls – abortion, infanticide, long lactation, abstinence, delayed marriage, contraception etc. – are recorded among so many present-day hunter-gatherer groups (Hayden 1972:208) that this situation probably represents the general rule.

It seems, then, that the 'natural' condition is a low rate of increase, and that those populations that are stable have, in some way, made a deliberate choice to remain well below carrying capacity. We shall return to this point later on.

Although dietary changes may biologically affect fertility, as well as support more or less people (Katz 1972), the first real change in growth pattern seems to coincide not with the beginnings of agriculture but with the start of settled life. This is not unexpected. Small-scale cultivation of plants (which were already being eaten in the wild form) does not greatly alter the food intake; the crucial factor is not diet, but sedentism.

Sussman (1972) cites statistics to show that the average spacing of offspring among contemporary nomads is about four years, but is reduced to about two years among sedentary populations. In nomadic communities, where young children have to be carried, a woman is unable to nurture and bring up more than one small infant at a time. This agrees with first-hand observations on two segments of the same !Kung Bushman population, one of which has kept its nomadic hunting-and-gathering way of life, while the other settled down in the 1950s and 1960s to become sedentary cultivators (Lee 1972a). The mean birth-interval among the nomadic !Kung is one child every four years, and Lee's calculations demonstrate that, as one moves from a large to a shorter birth-interval, the mother's work-load increases progressively. Death of one offspring is inevitable when the interval drops below two years. After the introduction of agriculture and the consequent reduction of travel, selection pressures against closely spaced families were relaxed and the observed mean birth-interval among sedentary !Kung dropped from 48 to 33-36 months. A decrease in child-spacing from four to three years can increase the birth-rate by a factor of almost one-third and the net reproductive rate from nearly zero to a high value (Cavalli-Sforza 1973:22). As Weiss (1973:48-51) has already noted, skeletal evidence suggests that population growth during the Neolithic was achieved by allowing more people to live, rather than by increasing individual life expectancy.

That sedentism, rather than an agricultural diet, triggers off this population expansion is demonstrated by Binford's study of the Nunamiut Eskimos of Alaska, who doubled their population between 1950 and 1960 when they switched from long-distance caribou hunting to the exploitation of a wider variety of more local game, allowing the family to stay together longer (Binford 1971). In this case, agriculture is not a factor at all. Although direct proof is lacking, it seems probable that the same constraints applied to prehistoric nomads. Apart from coastal Peru (which is examined as a special case below) all the sequences discussed in this paper are from semi-arid regions with fluctuating seasonal resources. The evidence from plant remains, coprolites, and from the size and location of settlements, all goes to confirm that the adoption of small-scale agriculture did nothing to change the annual cycle, and that mobility was the rule for several millennia after the first experiments with crop plants.

The degree of mobility among prehistoric foragers and incipient cultivators is almost impossible to gauge by archaeological means. At one end of the scale, long-distance transhumance has been suggested for Peru (Lynch 1971); at the other extreme, the diagrams published by MacNeish (1971a) suggest very small home ranges for Tehuacan bands. Both these estimates are frankly speculative. Since the effort involved in child-carrying is proportional to the distance travelled (Lee 1972a), data from modern nomads should not be applied uncritically to prehistoric communities. Nevertheless, Flannery (1968) and MacNeish (1973) have convincingly suggested that, under a seasonal régime, settled life is not possible until a stage of reasonably effective agriculture has been reached, after which sedentism becomes inevitable. Flannery argues that between 5,000 and 2,000 B.C., during a long period of selection under cultivation, certain quite small genetic changes took place in maize and beans that rendered these species more productive. The botanical evidence from the Tehuacan excavations shows that beans became more permeable in water (improving their germinating properties and making the seeds more edible) and also developed limp pods, which prevent shattering and make harvesting easier (Kaplan 1967). Races of maize crossed with each other and with their wild relatives, resulting in loss of glumes, increase in the number of cobs, and more kernels per cob (Mangelsdorf, MacNeish & Galinat 1964; 1967). This process of improvement was slow: as late as 1500 B.C., when we have the first unambiguous evidence for permanent villages, domesticated maize was still only about one-fifth the size of today's races; even on the best land it would barely produce the 250 kg. per hectare that modern peasants regard as the minimum yield for reliance on maize as a staple food (Flannery 1972:27, 37).

As the food plants gradually became more productive, agriculture became increasingly profitable, so that the seasonal round was rescheduled and both hunting and collecting diminished in importance. In these conditions, sedentism arose as a by-product of change within the food procurement system. Wild plants have only to be harvested; cultivated plants must be sown and protected as well. An increase in agriculture thus has the effect of tying people to one place for a longer period of time. In areas like Oaxaca and the Pacific coast of Mesoamerica, where two harvests per year are possible, sedentary agriculture can quickly replace other forms of food procurement once this take-off point has been reached. This sequence of events is supported by archaeological evidence, which shows that, in arid areas, full sedentism came long after the first agriculture (Figs. 1, 2, 3, 5) and that, in Mesoamerica at least, the curve of population-growth steepened considerably during the first millennium B.C., when village life was well established (Sanders 1972).

Population-growth in areas with rich natural resources

Flannery's case study does not provide a universal explanation for the emergence of settled life. What it does show is that population-growth can be linked with sedentism, and sedentism with control over food supplies. In areas of sparse and/or seasonal resources that vary unpredictably, full control must wait for the development of efficient agriculture; in these regions cultivation precedes settled life. In areas with rich and predictable resources the converse should be true: sedentism will normally precede efficient agriculture. In extreme cases, where natural resources are more productive than primitive agriculture, farming may not be adopted at all and the line of development will culminate in sedentary communities of specialized hunter-gatherers with many of the socio-political characteristics of advanced farming societies. Stable non-agricultural life is possible in many coastal, lagoon and riverine localities that offer year-round supplies of fish, aquatic mammals, shell-fish and waterfowl, and also in areas with abundant seasonal resources in easily storable from — e.g. acorns and nuts in California (Harris 1973b) or the stands of wild wheat and barley in Anatolia and the Levant (Flannery 1972).

Binford (1968) has attempted to combine climatic change with population growth into a stress model for the emergence of agriculture.

His hypothesis is that the changes in sea level that accompanied the end of the Pleistocene made available new year-round littoral resources that allowed hunter-gatherer communities to stay in one place, resulting in population growth and ultimately in population pressure. Since favourable coastal localities are limited in number and circumscribed in extent, they would quickly fill to capacity. Some of the surplus population would be forced to migrate inland, thus transmitting the pressure to the nomadic hunter-gatherers of the interior. In these marginal 'tension zones' the reaction to the pressures caused by the immigrants would be an improvement in food procurement, i.e. the invention of agriculture. Binford conducts his discussion at a theoretical level, but animal ecology offers appropriate numerical models for this situation (MacArthur 1972:149-53; and see Carneiro 1970; 1972).

Binford's argument has a number of weaknesses (Meyers 1971), but it has the advantage of being testable and it draws attention to the need for more research on the coast. In Mesoamerica, many coastal shell-mounds are of recent or unknown age, but there are examples dating to the Late Preceramic period in Guerrero (Brush 1965), Veracruz (Lorenzo 1961:16) and Nayarit (Mountjoy, Taylor & Feldman 1972). Other more ancient settlements have been discovered around the lagoons of the Chiapas coast (Lorenzo 1955) and in the Palma Sola area of Veracruz, where the stone tools suggest a date in the fourth millennium B.C. (Benson 1968:115). Some coastal sites are therefore older than the first sedentary villages in the highlands, and were presumably occupied throughout the year. Veracruz, in particular, is said to have many large sites, with much denser and more settled populations than are known from any inland region at this time. The shell-middens do not usually contain milling stones, mortars or tools associated with plant-processing. Nor have plants been reported from them, but under humid tropical conditions such organic materials are unlikely to be preserved. Data from comparable shell-mounds along the desert coast of Peru indicate a mixed economy based on marine resources supplemented by both wild and cultivated plants (Fig. 6), and it would be naive to assume, at this stage, that all Mesoamerican coastal settlements were strictly non-agricultural.

Although the coast may have been a centre of early population growth, the evidence from inland regions offers no support whatsoever for the rest of the Binford hypothesis. There is no sign of large-scale immigration or of sudden population expansion. More importantly, there is no sign of urgency in the slow and almost imperceptible development of agriculture. Either the population pressure was so small that the existing system could absorb it, or else the response to the stress was completely ineffective. In neither of these cases is Binford's prediction fulfilled. The nearest that archaeology can offer to a test situation is provided by the long and uninterrupted sequence from the Ancón-Chillón region of Peru (Fig. 6) – though, as a coastal desert where none of the major crop plants was indigenous, this area is ecologically anomalous and does not offer a very reliable basis for generalization.

Although the published evidence from the central coast is ambiguous and can be interpreted in different ways, the broad outline of development is becoming fairly clear. Contrary to expectation, the earliest sites are not along the coast but are found a few kilometres inland, situated on or close to the *lomas*. *Lomas* seeds and wild game were important in the diet, but much of the protein was derived from shell-fish carried up from the coast. The existence of nearby (and dependable) littoral resources allowed some of these inland sites to grow into permanent settlements. Engel (1973) reports year-round villages in the Chilca Basin as early as 7,000 B.C., and Patterson (1971b) has described a permanent village in the lower Lurín Valley with a date around 5,000 B.C. Elsewhere (e.g. around the Bay of Ancón, where resources are more scattered) a seasonal pattern may have persisted until the end of the Encanto phase at about 2,500 B.C., by which time gourds and squash were already being cultivated (Moseley 1972; Patterson 1971b). *Lomas* resources gradually became less important, and from *c.* 2,500 B.C. settlements were relocated near to the coast. In all these sub-areas, and whatever the date of the first permanent village, sedentism preceded efficient agriculture. Patterson's figures for the central coast suggest a population expansion beginning around 3,000 B.C. and accelerating after about 2,300 (Patterson 1971b:319). It was not until *c.* 1900 B.C. that the bulk of the population was concentrated in areas suitable for farming rather than fishing.

The overall change in the food procurement system at Ancón has been summarized in the following words by Moseley (1972:33): 'Hunting and gathering was completely replaced by fishing. In turn, fishing was displaced to a secondary economic role when farming assumed primacy. Each of the major changes was preceded by a gradual build-up in reliance on products that were to assume primacy in the succeeding subsistence pattern.' This process of innovation followed by consolidation and, eventually, by commitment is characteristic of evolution rather than revolution.

The riverine areas of the Amazon and Orinoco basins must also be included as possible foci of early sedentism and population growth. The main food crops are starchy, but the rivers provide abundant year-round protein in the form of fish, reptiles and aquatic mammals. With the development of agriculture, the tendency towards large and settled populations would be reinforced. Cultivated manioc is vegetatively reproduced and differs in nearly all of its properties from the seed crops that form the staples in arid America (Bronson 1972; Harris 1973b; Lathrap 1973a). Unlike maize, it is not a seasonal resource. Both the bitter and the sweet varieties of manioc can be planted and harvested throughout the year, and are stored in the ground until needed. The alluvial soils of the active flood-plain, which are rejuvenated every year by silt-laden waters, permit continuous root crop cultivation for fifteen or twenty years and allow farming villages to stay permanently in one place. Since the amount of flood-plain is limited, these alluvial soils constitute a circumscribed environment of the kind that figures in the Binford model discussed above (see also Carneiro 1970). By 2000 B.C., when pottery made its appearance, there is archaeological evidence for large and permanent settlements along the lowland rivers of Amazonas, and Lathrap has argued that the subsistence pattern must have been established as early as 7,000/5,000 B.C. (Lathrap 1970:57).

These postulated early sites will lack pottery, will have little or no stone, and will consist almost entirely of perishable materials. Since the main South American root crops have been so modified under cultivation that they have virtually lost the power to set seed, they can be expected to leave little trace in the pollen record (Lathrap 1970:48). In the moist tropics, where even bones and teeth disappear within a couple of centuries, it is difficult to think of a more perfect formula for archaeological invisibility.

Population pressure

In Binford's model, as in all others which invoke population growth as the cause of agricultural change (e.g. Smith 1972; Boserup 1965), it is not population size *per se* but population *pressure* that compels readjustments in the food procurement system. In this section I shall indicate some of the difficulties in defining what constitutes 'pressure', and will argue that any simple deterministic model is inadequate to explain the development of early agriculture. One of the clearest statements on this subject comes from the economist and demographer Alfred Sauvy (1969) who has defined several types of population threshold that apply to all forms of human society from the hunter-gatherer level to modern industrial civilization. Two of these thresholds, the *optimum economic population* and the *maximum population*, are of particular relevance to our theme.

The *maximum population* can be equated with the ecologists' 'carrying capacity', i.e. the greatest number of people a given area can support when each individual enjoys only the minimum resources needed to keep him alive. Beyond this point the number of inhabitants cannot be increased. Sauvy's *optimum economic population* is defined as the number of people that an area will support in maximum comfort, and his optimum level occurs at the moment when the individual standard of living is at its highest. Sauvy argues that in the early stages of population growth, each extra individual will increase the efficiency with which the environment is exploited and will raise the standard of living of every member of the community. Standards continue to rise until an optimum population level is attained. Beyond this critical point, the law of diminishing returns begins to operate. Further people will slightly increase the community's total output, but the increase is no longer proportional to the excess man-power, and individual standards of living begin to fall.[5] The *optimum population* is, therefore, always well below the *maximum population* – though the absolute values of these are constantly changing and are a function of climate, technology, social organization etc.

Sauvy does not attempt to express the *optimum economic population* as a fixed percentage of the *maximum population*, since the figures will vary according to local circumstances. If one makes the assumption that present-day hunter-gatherers have chosen to stabilize close to the optimum population level, this would be somewhere around 20% to 50% of the theoretical maximum under a non-agricultural economy. Whether or not this guess is correct (and it is something that anthropologists could check), it is evident from Sauvy's discussion that population pressure, in the form of a deterioration in the quality of life, begins to make itself felt as soon as the optimum population figure is exceeded, and long before the crisis of carrying capacity is reached. The moment at which pressure is translated into action may come at any point between the optimum and maximum figures, and depends on how much of a fall in standards the community is prepared to tolerate. To this extent, population pressure is a subjective thing that exists primarily in the mind of the sufferer. One community may decide to take action as soon as standards begin to fall; its neighbour may prefer to put up with a progressively less comfortable existence, or even to sit out the crisis until carrying capacity is reached.

This 'tolerance factor' is illustrated by Birdsell's data on outmigration from a number of small islands. On Pitcairn, the first emigration took place when the population reached 34% of carrying capacity; on Tristan da Cunha, the figure was 50%; and on the islands of the Bass Strait, the first budding-off came at *c.* 60% (Birdsell 1957: 50-4). There is no reason to think that these figures exhaust the total range of variability. If the previous standard of comfort is to be maintained, then there are only two possible courses of action, once the optimum population level has been reached. One is to prevent further population growth, either by birth control or by migration: the other is to develop a more productive technology that will raise the carrying capacity of the land and, at the same time, will raise the optimum population threshold. Both courses are attempts to achieve the same end – to maintain the *status quo*, the 'good life', the 'optimum population' – in short, to maintain a favourable equilibrium with the environment. Phrased in that way, the relevance of the biological analogy becomes clear; the adaptive changes are not so much attempts to be progressive as to maintain an existing relationship with a fluctuating environment.

It must be emphasized that a genuine choice of action exists. There is abundant evidence that hunters and gatherers are capable of dealing with excess fertility by means of simple non-biological methods (see page 82). As pure speculation, I offer the suggestion that those modern hunter-gatherers with stable populations at very low densities are the end product of a tradition in which the good life has been preserved by a wilful refusal to increase and multiply – either because they preferred their own way of life (like those groups that are today exposed to agriculture but refuse to adopt it), or because a hostile physical environment did not permit farming under aboriginal conditions. The agriculturalists, by contrast, may be the descendants of those groups that followed the other path and accommodated increasing population (and other correlated changes) by adapting their food procurement systems and social organization.

Carrying capacity, optimum population and social organization

The relationship between food production, population size and the complexity of social institutions has been widely discussed in the anthropological and archaeological literature (e.g. Forge 1972; Carneiro 1967; 1970; Dumond 1965; Sanders & Price 1968; several papers in Spooner 1972). Rather than go over all this ground again, I shall concentrate on just one problem: the relationship between social organization and the concepts of optimum and maximum population. The purpose of the exercise is to demonstrate once again that no sub-system can be considered in isolation from the others.

Let us begin by referring back to those present-day nomadic hunters and gatherers who have stabilized their populations far below the carrying capacity of the areas they occupy. In many cases, it turns out that the reasons for these low population densities are not exclusively to do with ecology and food supply but also with socio-political factors. The Mbuti, for example, spread themselves thinly to avoid conflict with their neighbours (Turnbull 1968:132-7, 245). Hadza camps tend to break up as a result of conflict when the size of the community reaches about fifty adults, so that 'differences in camp size both in a given season and between seasons are a product of multiple causes and are not neatly co-ordinated with variations in the overall amount of food that is locally available' (Woodburn 1972:201). Similar forces come into play among !Kung Bushmen:

> This perception of the threat of conflict functions to maintain group size and population density at a much lower level than could be supported by the food resources, if the population could be organized to use these more efficiently. By stabilizing numbers at a lower level through a behavioural spacing mechanism, the population is buffered against a wide range of variations in the abundance of food resources [*cf.* page 89]. Thus conflict, far from being a causal factor that is opposed to an ecological explanation, may best be seen as an ecological variable, a usage that is consistent with contemporary thinking in animal behaviour and animal ecology. (Lee 1972b:183)

The biological equivalent to this argument is discussed by Wynne-Edwards (1962), MacArthur & Connell (1966:138-40) and MacArthur (1972:118-9).

At this point in the argument it becomes impossible to treat social organization, population size and food procurement systems as independent variables. A change to a more authoritarian and centralized form of social organization, with the power to resolve conflicts, could in itself lead to increased density of population without any corresponding change in food gathering techniques or in the availability of natural resources. The relationship between these phenomena is of feedback type, and it is impossible to isolate any one of them as the cause of change in the others.

Similarly, that deliberately vague phrase 'the good life' implies more than a full stomach. It also implies freedom from tension, from oppression and from over-work. Most of today's hunter-gatherer groups could produce more food by working harder, but the nature of their social organization offers little incentive to produce a surplus. As Carneiro (1970) has already noted, agriculture does not automatically create a food surplus, even when it is technically feasible to produce more than is consumed. Without the stimulus of over-population, taxation, trade or psychological needs (the 'Protestant ethic'), people simply prefer to take life easily. Once these social factors are introduced into the model, the whole concept of optimum and maximum population is altered.

Sauvy's *optimum economic population* is calculated on the basis of the greatest happiness of the greatest number, but – as history shows – this is not always the prime consideration of political systems. A trend towards increasingly centralized forms of government is one of the things that characterizes the growth of states. Under a hierarchical régime, with the means to enforce its authority, the needs of the state (or of the elite group that runs it) take precedence over the welfare of the individual. The optimum population is now the one that gives the greatest power to the organization, even if most individuals suffer a fall in their standard of living and are coerced into working harder so as to provide a surplus. At this point, the independent cultivator has been transformed into a peasant (Wolf 1966:9-10). For this situation Sauvy has coined the term *power optimum*, which is attained when a small ruling group enjoying a privileged position controls the largest possible number of producers, each of whom gives up most of his surplus to the state. In other words, the *power optimum* will fall somewhere above the *economic optimum* but below the maximum carrying capacity (Sauvy 1969:51-60). This change in the optimum figure may or may not be accompanied by a change in the technology of food procurement.

Other factors, for instance foreign trade, may also affect the optimum population figure (Sauvy 1969:157-68). Sauvy's approach is based ultimately on *productivity*, and it thus avoids the common archaeological pitfall of relating carrying capacity and optimum population exclusively to food supply. Herein lies the main difference between human and animal ecology. Once the era of isolated self-sufficient communities is over, the model of a closed universe no longer applies. Local shortages can be made good by purchase, exchange or extortion; the size of the community and the strength of the state depend in part on military power and purchasing power, both of which are ultimately linked to social organization.

Food exchange, as we have seen, is documented from earliest times. By 1500 B.C. (i.e. about the time when we can begin to talk of effective agriculture) there is archaeological evidence for state institutions and long-distance trade networks in both Mesoamerica and Peru. Eventually, with the emergence of tribute-extorting empires, certain ruler-states had more inhabitants than could be supported by local resources alone (Bray 1972:920-2). Since population pressure starts to be felt as soon as the optimum threshold is crossed, archaeologists who invoke such pressure as the cause of agricultural development must stop thinking solely in terms of food resources and must ask such social and political questions as 'Optimum for whom?', 'Optimum for what?' and 'Optimum under what conditions?'.

Biological models and the evolution of food procurement systems

For reasons of space it is impossible to consider every single innovation that took place within the food procurement system. In any case, such details will usually be of only local significance. This section concentrates on just one theme – the slowness of change – since this seems characteristic of all regions where agriculture developed *in situ*. Elsewhere (Bray 1973:83), it has been pointed out that Childe's 'Neolithic revolution' follows the rules of biological evolution in that it proceeds by means of small cumulative improvements until the stage of effective agriculture is reached, after which a sort of explosion seems to occur. What we are witnessing is the gradual evolution of one food producing system (hunting-and-gathering) into another (agriculture). In biological terms this is analogous to the process of anagenesis, or successional speciation, when change takes place in a single line of descent until eventually the product is so different from the original that it can be considered a new species. There is no sudden break or discontinuity; in fact, it is impossible to define the exact moment at which the transition occurred.

Another way of describing the evolution of farming is to see it as a gradual change-over from a broad-spectrum food procurement system to a more specialized one, with a reduction in the number of major food sources exploited and a concentration of effort on just a few of the available plants and animals that eventually come to provide the bulk of the diet. These dietary changes are accompanied by ecological changes. Harris (1969; 1973a) has made a distinction between 'palaeotechnic' and 'neotechnic' systems of agriculture. In the former (which usually incorporate a wide variety of crops) useful plants and animals are substituted for their wild equivalents, and the natural ecological diversity is maintained. A system of this kind is ecologically stable. At the other end of the range are 'neotechnic' systems which destroy the natural ecosystem and replace it by an artificial one that has quite different properties and that relies on man for its successful maintenance. The natural diversity is reduced, and the outcome in extreme cases is the kind of monoculture represented by the modern wheatlands of North America or the cash-crop plantations of the tropics. The more drastic the transformation, the more unstable the system, and the greater its vulnerability to climatic disaster or attack by species-specific pathogens.

Harris suggests that there is a temporal progression from one kind of system to the other, and that the period of incipient agriculture was characterized by manipulation of the environment and by species replacement rather than by transformation of the entire landscape. With improved technology, a 'palaeotechnic' system will normally evolve into a 'neotechnic' one characterized by landscape transformation. This marks the transition from incipient to effective agriculture.[6]

Harris's study provides just one example of a general rule that applies to evolution as a whole. I have already argued (Bray 1973) that changes, whether genetic or cultural, that involve increased specialization are achieved only at the cost of reduced flexibility and, in extreme cases, by a dangerous degree of dependence.[7] If this is so, a commitment to agricultural life is neither natural nor inevitable. Before extolling the advantages of an agricultural economy, it might be as well to examine what was given up as well as what was gained.

As the starting point for such a discussion we can begin with a general statement on the nature of biological adaptation:

> We should not expect visibly big mutations to be beneficial, although very small ones may often be. In essence, Fisher's (1958) argument is that, if an animal is poorly adapted, random mutations of visible size will sometimes improve the adaptation, but if an organism is nearly perfectly adapted, it will virtually never be improved by a big mutation. A microscopic analogy is useful here: a random change in the focus of an out-of-focus microscope stands about half a chance of improving the focus. A random change in a well focused microscope, however, cannot possibly improve the focus and will always be considered harmful. Thus we should expect only relatively small mutations to be beneficial; if

an organism is already well adapted, the mutation will have to be almost invisibly small to stand a chance of being beneficial; . . . only when there is a sharp change in the environment which causes new phenotypes to be better adapted, do we expect a visible mutation to be beneficial occasionally. (MacArthur & Connell 1966:80)

This biological argument can be expressed in two alternative ways: (a) If the degree of adaptation is good and the environment fairly stable, the organism will evolve very slowly and by gradual changes. (b) If the organism can be shown to evolve slowly and gradually, this implies a reasonably stable environment and effective adaptation.

Testing this model against the archaeological situation, the fit seems very close. Archaeological evidence demonstrates that the food procurement system evolved by an accumulation of small improvements (Figs. 1-6), and the data already presented on climate and population indicate that changes in the environment were neither sudden nor massive. In this case, the genetic model also predicts that the food procurement system was, *and remained*, well adapted to the gradually changing environment.

Broad-spectrum hunting and collecting

Before examining the evolution of farming, we must begin by emphasizing the virtues of the system that it replaced. In those cases for which we have evidence, the first experiments with agriculture took place within an economy based on broad-spectrum procurement of wild foods. Midden deposits of the early Post-Pleistocene contain bones of small and medium-sized animals, fish and molluscs where available, and also a great variety of plant foods. The oldest coprolites show that insects, grubs, mice, snails, lizards, snakes and birds' eggs were eaten (MacNeish 1964b; Callen 1963; 1967b), and the general impression is that virtually everything that was edible was consumed.

In a classic paper, Flannery (1968) analysed the changing subsistence patterns in prehistoric Mesoamerica by considering food procurement as itself a system with various sub-systems. Within the overall procurement system, he identified several activities (maguey and cactus fruit collection, wild grass collection, exploitation of tree legumes, deer-hunting, rabbit-trapping etc.) and suggested that the balance between them was governed by two mechanisms which he called seasonality and scheduling. The existence of these activities, and also their seasonal nature, is fully documented in the archaeological record.

Flannery noted that modern American hunting and gathering communities in arid environments are forced to split up into family units to exploit the few and scattered resources during the lean season of the year, but that during the season of plenty – when many alternative foodstuffs are available at the same time, and people can congregate in multi-family macrobands – the group has to schedule its activities and decide which resource to exploit. The choice is made on the basis of profitability; whichever source of food offers the highest yield for the least effort is the one selected. Since the wild resources fluctuate unpredictably and vary a good deal from one year to the next, the final decision is best left until the last minute and the choice will not be the same every year.

These individual variations . . . combined with the scheduling pattern to make it unlikely that specialization in any one resource would develop. This prevented over-utilization of key plants or animals, and maintained a more even balance between varied resources. Because scheduling is an opportunistic mechanism, it promoted survival in spite of annual variation, but at the same time it supported the *status quo*: unspecialized utilization of a whole range of plants and animals whose availability is erratic over the long run. (Flannery 1968:76)

In the jargon of systems theory, seasonality and scheduling are negative feedback mechanisms that serve to promote stability and to counteract deviation.

Flannery's conclusions are in conformity with a general principle that applies to man and animal alike, and for which mathematical models already exist in animal ecology. At a low level of technology, with little direct control over his food supply, man is in roughly the same position as any other predator and subject to the same ecological constraints. Ecologists (e.g. Slobodkin 1961:157; MacArthur 1955) have demonstrated that the stability (in the sense of stable population size) in a predator population is increased if the predator spreads its efforts over several alternative sources of food energy. If one of these fails, others will compensate. In contrast, a specialized predator that draws most of its sustenance from one or two prey species is vulnerable to every short-term fluctuation in the prey population and has nothing to fall back on in times of crisis. This, of course, is just one instance of the general argument on page 87.

All lines of argument lead to the same conclusion – that pre-agricultural food procurement systems, though differing in detail, shared the same quality of delicate adjustment to their respective environments. In these circumstances, and *provided that all the other variables remain constant*, there is little incentive to abandon a safe hunting-and-gathering life in favour of an agricultural existence, to give up predation in favour of production. What then brought about change?

It is essential to the concept of both biological and cultural evolution that the variables do *not* remain constant, that a state of static equilibrium is never attained, and that changes are continuously taking place in both the organism/organization and its environment. The main environmental changes have already been discussed, and we must now examine those changes that originated within the food procurement system itself.

The first steps towards agriculture

The biological analogy (pages 87-8) explains why a big mutation in an organism will be harmful rather than beneficial. For the same reasons, the sudden introduction of large-scale agriculture into a finely balanced hunter-gatherer economy will be traumatic rather than beneficial, and will disrupt almost every aspect of life. A sudden leap into agriculture is therefore a gamble that is doomed to failure. In practice (unless there is a sudden change in the environment) most of the small beneficial changes that form the substance of both biological and technological evolution consist of slightly improved ways of doing what is already being done. Their effect is to increase efficiency within the existing way of life, rather than to overthrow the system and to replace it with something entirely different. As a geneticist has expressed it, 'selection' (in most cases) 'acts so as to maintain, rather than to change, the adaptations of a population' (Maynard Smith 1966:40).

In the context of early farming, this implies that the first small-scale attempts at cultivation were not designed to pave the way for an agricultural economy but merely to increase the efficiency of the existing pattern of broad-spectrum hunting and collecting. The security of a broadly based economy was not given up, and changes were minimal. The plants that were cultivated were those already being exploited in the wild state, as they continued to be long after cultivation began. It was not until about 3,000 B.C. that domesticated maize achieved parity with its wild equivalent in the Tehuacan Valley (Mangelsdorf *et al.* 1967:199). Nor were the earliest cultigens much more productive than their wild prototypes. In these circumstances, a certain amount of planting and tending simply made the existing range of plant foods more accessible and, perhaps, ensured a more reliable yield, but as a contribution to the total economy it can virtually be ignored. One unforeseen effect of these minor innovations was the evolution under selection of new and improved races of plants, after which various reinforcing mechanisms came into play and strongly encouraged the transition to a fully agricultural economy.

This, of course, is a hypothetical reconstruction, but it is one that does no violence to the archaeological evidence and adheres strictly to the rules governing organic evolution. In both processes selection favours changes that offer immediate advantages in the conditions of the moment, without thinking ahead to the long-term consequences (Bray 1973). Paradoxically, a course of action begun as an attempt to preserve the adaptive advantages of broad-spectrum hunting-and-gathering ended in something quite different, a highly specialized farming economy.

In this, too, the evolution of the food procurement system duplicates a common feature of organic evolution. 'A new structure evolves at first because it confers advantage by performing one function, but in time it reaches a threshold beyond which it can effectively perform a different function' (Maynard Smith 1966: 278) – the words of a geneticist writing about organic evolution; they might equally well have been written about the evolution of a hunter-gatherer economy into one dependent on agriculture. It is not the planting of the first seed which constitutes the start of the 'Neolithic', but the crossing of the critical threshold between agriculture as a subsidiary activity and agriculture as the essential basis of life.

Stability versus efficiency

The evolution of a farming economy has already been characterized as the replacement of a generalized food procurement system by a specialized one. The argument from animal ecology can be pushed a stage further to show that this decision makes good strategic sense. It also allows agricultural technology to be built into the model. To survive under natural conditions a species needs stability (i.e. the ability to maintain its level of population) and also efficiency, but in practice these two requirements are in partial conflict with each other (MacArthur 1955). As we have already indicated, population stability can best be achieved by exploiting a wide range of food sources. On the other hand, efficiency is increased by restricting the diet so as to take advantage of specializations (biological or technological) that allow intensive exploitation of just one or two resources. The mathematical models developed by ecologists (e.g. MacArthur 1955) show that the most effective strategy is a compromise: first ensure the necessary minimum of stability (by retaining a broadly based economy) then go for increased efficiency (i.e. productivity) after that. Adding a little cultivation to a subsistence pattern based on hunting and collecting becomes explicable in the context of this kind of strategy.

The ecological model also suggests the course that this increase of efficiency through specialization will take. As Levins has demonstrated, in genetic evolution the fittest (i.e. most specialized) adaptation takes place when the environment is uniform (Levins 1968: Ch. 2). Other things being equal, where food is concerned efficiency is likewise increased by making the food procurement system more specialized, a process that is aided by making the environment more uniform. Looked at in this way, the development of agricultural technology (weeding, manuring, terracing, irrigation etc.) can be regarded as a device to make the environment more homogeneous – in the case of our example from arid America, to reduce as much of it as possible to agricultural land with good soil and enough water to grow maize, beans and squashes.

This transformation represents the conversion of an *unpredictable* environment into a *predictable* one. The general ecological-genetic model indicates that this change will be accompanied by a change in adaptive strategy: the fail-safe strategy that is most effective in a fluctuating environment will be replaced by a strategy based on specialization as the environmental conditions beome more and more predictable (MacArthur 1972:142). In the terminology of game theory, a satisficer (randomized or minimax) strategy is replaced by an optimizer (maximizing) strategy (Clarke 1968:94-5). The transition from one kind of environment (or strategy) to another is neither sudden nor complete. There is no sharp break, but at some point in this evolution a critical threshold is passed and a commitment to agriculture is made. Once this has happened, the situation is irreversible – as are all major changes in biological evolution (Dobzhansky 1962:170). The only possible course is the one that leads to increasingly more effective agriculture. It is this critical threshold – if only archaeologists could define it more precisely – that marks the end of the period of incipient cultivation and the start of the 'Neolithic' proper.

Fig. 4 illustrates these processes at work in the Tehuacan Valley. During the period of incipient cultivation, when agricultural technology was poorly developed and high-yield plants were not yet available, the subsistence strategy was of broad-range, satisficer, fail-safe type. Even though population was low, the earliest cultivator-collectors exploited between five and seven microzones on a seasonal basis. By the Ajalpan phase, in spite of a greatly increased population, agricultural specialization is indicated by a reduction in the number of occupied microzones and by the concentration of some 77% of the valley's inhabitants in just one environment, the bottom-lands where barranca cultivation could be practised (MacNeish 1970:221, 224). The rapid population expansion from the Santa Maria phase onwards is accompanied by an equally sharp rise in the number of microzones with settlements. This does not, however, represent an attempt to diversify the economy, but is a function of improved technology (irrigation and terracing) which allowed more and more econiches to be converted into farmland. This, in turn, is reflected by an increased commitment to cultivated foods (Fig. 3). A similar process has been recognized in Oaxaca, where technological improvements allowed farming to become established in regions previously unsuitable for cultivation (Flannery *et al.* 1967).

Conclusions

Writing as an ecologist rather than an archaeologist, Harris (1973a:392) has remarked that models of agricultural evolution fall into two classes:

> Explanation of the transition from food-collecting to plant and animal domestication can thus be approached with two different but complementary objectives in view: first, to seek to understand it as the transformation from one major stage to another in man's overall cultural progress, which implies a generalizing cultural-evolutionary approach, and second, to reconstruct the actual sequence of events that took place in specific locations at known times, which is the aim of the particularizing culture-historical approach.

In the present paper, I have attempted to argue from the particular to the general – from a few specific case-histories in Mexico and Peru to a model of agricultural evolution as a general process. Although many of the details remain to be filled in, the *nature* of the general model is clear. Simple cause-and-effect explanations do not account for the emergence of agricultural economies. Instead, we must think in terms of a dynamic equilibrium model in which food procurement technology is just one component of a larger system, and is in a state of constant and reciprocal interaction with all other components. Not surprisingly (since cultural and genetic evolution are parts of the same adaptive process by which man tries to keep himself in equilibrium with his environment) the same kind of model governs organic evolution. In these circumstances, where there is no prime mover, the search for the 'origins' of agriculture loses its point.

Within the context of the general evolutionary model, each organization (cultural or genetic) has its own individual history, and no two histories will be exactly alike. There are many possible circuits through a complex system (Clarke 1968:47), just as there are many genetic routes to the same biological end (Maynard Smith 1966:219) and many alternative pathways to agriculture (Harris 1973b).

And that is about as far as we can go. At the specific level, we do not fully understand the development of any single food procurement system. Although the general model is mathematical in origin, where human behaviour is concerned there are too many components that cannot be expressed in numerical terms. As I have indicated in this paper and elsewhere (Bray 1973:76), adaptation is psychological as well as material. The 'rational' decision (in purely economic terms) may be psychologically unacceptable in the prevailing climate of opinion. Until we can quantify and give proper weight to the crucial psycho-social factors of motivation, goals, ethics, tolerance to stress etc., we shall never achieve the degree of mathematical predictability demanded by those who see archaeology as a science governed by scientific 'laws' (see discussion in Sabloff *et al.* 1973:116-18).

This lack of rigorous numerical definition does not mean that the general model is invalid, any more than the original Darwinian model of adaptation was invalid because Mendel had not at the time worked out the statistical laws governing heredity. As Haggett and Chorley (1968:24-5) have pointed out, models must be judged by their usefulness rather than their truth. All laws are models, but not all models are laws.

Acknowledgments

I am grateful to Kent Flannery, Lewis Binford, Mark Cohen, Donald W. Lathrap and David Harris for allowing me access to unpublished information. Fig. 5 is based on data supplied by R.S. MacNeish and incorporates the most recent results of his Ayacucho project.

REFERENCES

Ammerman, A. and Cavalli-Sforza, L.L. (1971) Measuring the rate of spread of early farming in Europe. *Man*, n.s. 6, 674-88.

Ammerman, A. and Cavalli-Sforza, L.L. (1973) A population model for the diffusion of early farming in Europe. In Renfrew 1973, 343-57.

Aveleyra Arroyo de Anda, L. (1964) The primitive hunters. In Wauchope, R. (ed.), *Handbook of Middle American Indians*, I: 384-426. Austin, Texas.

Benson, E.P. (ed.) (1968) *Dumbarton Oaks Conference on the Olmec.* Washington.

Binford, L.R. (1968) Post-Pleistocene adaptations. In Binford, S.R. and L.R. (eds.), *New Perspectives in Archaeology*, 313-41. Chicago.

Binford, L.R. (1971) Personal communication, Sheffield.

Birdsell, J.B. (1957) Some population problems involving Pleistocene man. In *Population studies: animal ecology and demography* (Cold Spring Harbor Symposium in Quantitative Biology 22), 47-69.

Boserup, E. (1965) *The Conditions of Agricultural Growth: the Economics of Agrarian Change under Population Pressure.* London.

Bray, W. (1972) Land-use, settlement pattern and politics in prehispanic Middle America: a review. In Ucko, Tringham and Dimbleby 1972, 909-26.

Bray, W. (1973) The biological basis of culture. In Renfrew 1973, 73-92.

Bronson, B. (1972) Farm labor and the evolution of food production. In Spooner 1972, 190-218.

Brush, C.F. (1965) Pox pottery: earliest identified Mexican ceramic. *Science*, 149, 194-5.

Byers, D.S. (ed.) (1967) *The Prehistory of the Tehuacan Valley: I – Environment and Subsistence.* Austin and London.

Callen, E.O. (1963) Diet as revealed by coprolites. In Brothwell, D.R. and Higgs, E.S. (eds.), *Science in Archaeology*, 186-94. London.

Callen, E.O. (1967a) The first New World cereal. *American Antiquity*, 32, 531-7.

Callen, E.O. (1967b) Analysis of the Tehuacan coprolites. In Byers 1967, 261-89.

Carneiro, R.L. (1967) On the relationship between size of population and complexity of social organization. *Southwestern Jour. Anthro.*, 23, 234-43.

Carneiro, R.L. (1970) A theory of the origin of the state. *Science*, 169, 733-8.

Carneiro, R.L. (1972) From autonomous villages to the state: a numerical estimation. In Spooner 1972, 64-77.

Cavalli-Sforza, L.L. (1973) Origin and differentiation of human races. *Proc. Royal Anthro. Inst.*, 1972, 15-25.

Clarke, D.L. (1968) *Analytical Archaeology.* London.

✓Cohen, M.N. (1973) Population pressure and origins of agriculture. Paper presented to I.C.A.E.S. Symposium on *Origins of Agriculture.* Chicago, August 1973.

Craig, A.K. and Psuty, N.P. (1968) Marine desert ecology of southern Peru. *The Paracas Papers* 1(2). Boca Raton, Dept. Geography, Florida Atlantic Univ.

Deevey, E.S. (1960) The human population. *Scientific American*, 203, 195-204.

Dobzhansky, T. (1962) *Mankind Evolving: The Evolution of the Human Species.* New Haven and London.

Dumond, D.E. (1965) Population growth and cultural change. *Southwestern Jour. Anthro.*, 21, 302-24.

Engel, F. (1966) *Geografía humana prehistórica y agricultura precolombina de la Quebrada de Chilca: Tomo I, Informe preliminar.* Lima.

Engel, F. (1970) Exploration of the Chilca Canyon, Peru. *Current Anthropology*, 11, 55-8.

Engel, F. (1973) New facts about Pre-Columbian life in the Andean Lomas. *Current Anthropology*, 14, 271-80.

Fisher, R.A. (1958) *The Genetical Theory of Natural Selection.* New York.

Flannery, K.V. (1966) The postglacial 'readaptation' as viewed from Mesoamerica. *American Antiquity*, 31, 800-5.

Flannery, K.V. (1967) Vertebrate fauna and hunting patterns. In Byers 1967, 132-77.

Flannery, K.V. (1968) Archaeological systems theory and early Mesoamerica. In Meggers, B.J. (ed.), *Anthropological Archeology in the Americas*, 67-87. Washington.

Flannery, K.V. (1972) The origins of the village as a settlement type in Mesoamerica and the Near East: a comparative study. In Ucko, Tringham and Dimbleby 1972, 23-53.

Flannery, K.V. (ed.) MS. *Preliminary Archaeological Investigations in the Valley of Oaxaca, Mexico, 1966-9* (Report to Nat. Sci. Found. and Inst. Nacional de Antropología e Historia, Mexico).

Flannery, K.V. and Coe, M. (1968) Social and economic systems in Formative Mesoamerica. In Binford, S.R. and L.R. (eds.), *New Perspectives in Archaeology*, 267-83. Chicago.

Flannery, K.V., Kirkby, A.T.V., Kirkby, M.J. and Williams, A.W. (1967) Farming systems and political growth in ancient Oaxaca. *Science*, 158, 445-54.

Flannery, K.V. and Schoenwetter, J. (1970) Climate and man in Formative Oaxaca. *Archaeology*, 23, 144-52.

Forge, A. (1972) Normative factors in the settlement size of Neolithic cultivators (New Guinea). In Ucko, Tringham and Dimbleby 1972, 363-76.

Haggett, P. and Chorley, R.J. (1968) Models, paradigms and the new geography. In Chorley, R.J. and Haggett, P. (eds.), *Socio-Economic Models in Geography*, 19-41. London.

Harris, D.R. (1969) Agricultural systems, ecosystems and the origins of agriculture. In Ucko and Dimbleby 1969, 3-15.

Harris, D.R. (1973a) The prehistory of tropical agriculture: an ethnoecological model. In Renfrew 1973, 391-417.

Harris, D.R. (1973b) Alternative pathways towards agriculture. Paper presented to I.C.A.E.S. Symposium on *Origins of Agriculture*, Chicago, August 1973.

Hawley, A.H. (1973) Ecology and population. *Science*, 179, 1196-201.

Hayden, B. (1972) Population control among hunter/gatherers. *World Arch.*, 4, 205-21.

Higgs, E.S. and Jarman, M.R. (1972) The origins of animal and plant husbandry. In Higgs, E.S. (ed.), *Papers in Economic Prehistory*, 3-13. London.

Johnson, F. and MacNeish, R.S. (1972) Chronometric dating. In MacNeish, R.S. (ed.), *The Prehistory of the Tehuacan Valley*, IV:3-55. Austin, Texas and London.

Kaplan, L. (1967) Archaeological *Phaseolus* from Tehuacan. In Byers 1967, 201-11.

Kaplan, L., Lynch, T.F. and Smith, C.E. (1973) Early cultivated beans (*Phaseolus vulgaris*) from an intermontane Peruvian valley. *Science*, 179, 76-7.

Katz, S.H. (1972) Biological factors in population control. In Spooner 1972, 351-69.

Lanning, E.P. (1963) A pre-agricultural occupation on the central coast of Peru. *American Antiquity*, 28, 360-71.

Lathrap, D.W. (1970) *The Upper Amazon.* London.

Lathrap, D.W. (1973a) The antiquity and importance of long-distance trade relationships in the moist tropics of Pre-Columbian South America. *World Arch.*, 5, 170-86.

Lathrap, D.W. (1973b) Gifts of the Cayman: some thoughts on the subsistence basis of Chavín. In Lathrap, D.W. and Douglas, J. (eds.), *Variation in Anthropology*, 91-105. Illinois.

Lathrap, D.W. (1973c) Our father the cayman, our mother the gourd. Paper presented to I.C.A.E.S. Symposium on *Origins of Agriculture.* Chicago, August 1973.

Lee, R.B. (1968) What hunters do for a living, or, how to make out on scarce resources. In Lee and DeVore 1968, 30-48.

Lee, R.B. (1972a) Population growth and the beginnings of sedentary life among the !Kung Bushmen. In Spooner 1972, 329-42.

Lee, R.B. (1972b) Work effort, group structure and land-use in contemporary hunter-gatherers. In Ucko, Tringham and Dimbleby 1972, 177-85.

Lee, R.B. and DeVore, I. (eds.) (1968) *Man the Hunter.* Chicago.

Levins, R. (1968) *Evolution in Changing Environments: Some Theoretical Explorations.* Princeton.

Lorenzo, J.L. (1955) Los concheros de la costa de Chiapas. *Anales del Inst. Nacional de Antropología e Historia*, 7, 41-50.

Lorenzo, J.L. (1961) *La Revolución Neolítica en Mesoamérica.* Pubn. 11, Dept. de Prehistoria, Inst. Nacional de Antropología e Historia, Mexico.

Lynch, T.F. (1971) Preceramic transhumance in the Callejon de Huaylas, Peru. *American Antiquity*, 36, 139-48.

MacArthur, R.H. (1955) Fluctuations in animal populations, and a measure of community stability. *Ecology*, 36, 533-6.

MacArthur, R.H. (1972) *Geographical Ecology: Patterns in Distribution of Species.* New York.

MacArthur, R.H. and Connell, J.H. (1966) *The Biology of Populations.* New York.

MacNeish, R.S. (1958) Preliminary archaeological investigations in the Sierra de Tamaulipas, Mexico. *Trans. Amer. Phil. Soc.*, n.s. 48 (6), 1-206.

MacNeish, R.S. (1961) Recent finds concerned with the incipient agriculture stage in prehistoric Mesoamerica. In *Homenaje a Pablo Martínez del Río*, 91-101. Mexico.

MacNeish, R.S. (1962) *Second Annual Report of the Tehuacan Archaeological-Botanical Project.* Andover.

MacNeish, R.S. (1964a) Ancient Mesoamerican civilization. *Science*, 143, 531-7.

MacNeish, R.S. (1964b) The food-gathering and incipient agriculture stage of prehistoric Middle America. In Wauchope, R. (ed.), *Handbook of Middle American Indians*, I: 413-26. Austin, Texas.

MacNeish, R.S. (1969) *First Annual Report of the Ayacucho Archaeological-Botanical Project.* Andover.

MacNeish, R.S. (1970) Social implications of changes in population and settlement pattern of the 12,000 years of prehistory in the Tehuacan Valley of Mexico. In Deprez, P. (ed.), *Population and Economics*, 215-49. Manitoba.

MacNeish, R.S. (1971a) Speculation about how and why food production and village life developed in the Tehuacan Valley, Mexico. *Archaeology*, 24, 307-15.

MacNeish, R.S. (1971b) Archaeological synthesis of the Sierra. In Wauchope, R. (ed.), *Handbook of Middle American Indians*, XI: 573-81. Austin, Texas.

MacNeish, R.S. (1972) The evolution of community patterns in the Tehuacan Valley of Mexico, and speculations about cultural processes. In Ucko, Tringham and Dimbleby 1972, 67-93.

MacNeish, R.S. (1973) The scheduling factor in the development of effective food production in the Tehuacan Valley. In Lathrap, D.W. and Douglas, J. (eds.), *Variation in Anthropology*, 75-89. Illinois.

MacNeish, R.S., Nelken-Terner, A. and Garcia Cook, A. (1970) *Second Annual Report of the Ayacucho Archaeological-Botanical Project.* Andover.

Mangelsdorf, P.C., MacNeish, R.S. and Galinat, W.C. (1964) Domestication of corn. *Science*, 143, 538-45.

Mangelsdorf, P.C., MacNeish, R.S. and Galinat, W.C. (1967) Prehistoric wild and cultivated maize. In Byers 1967, 178-200.

Mangelsdorf, P.C., MacNeish, R.S. and Willey, G.R. (1964) Origins of agriculture in Middle America. In Wauchope, R. (ed.), *Handbook of Middle American Indians*, I: 427-45. Austin, Texas.

Martin, P.S. (1973) The discovery of America. *Science*, 179, 969-74.

Martin, P.S. and Wright, H.E. (eds.) (1967) *Pleistocene Extinctions, the Search for a Cause.* Yale.

Maynard Smith, J. (1966) *The Theory of Evolution* (2nd ed.). Harmondsworth, Middlesex.

Meyers, J.T. (1971) The origins of agriculture: an evaluation of three hypotheses. In Struever 1971, 101-21.

Moseley, M.E. (1972) Subsistence and demography: an example of interaction from prehistoric Peru. *Southwestern Jour. Anthro.*, 28, 25-49.

Mountjoy, J.B., Taylor, R.E. and Feldman, L.H. (1972) Matanchén complex: new radiocarbon dates on early coastal adaptation in west Mexico. *Science*, 175, 1242-3.

Nance, C.R. (1972) Cultural evidence for the Altithermal in Texas and Mexico. *Southwestern Jour. Anthro.*, 28, 169-91.

Parsons, M.H. (1970) Preceramic subsistence on the Peruvian coast. *American Antiquity*, 35, 292-304.

Patterson, T.C. (1971a) The emergence of food production in central Peru. In Struever 1971, 181-207.

Patterson, T.C. (1971b) Central Peru: its population and economy. *Archaeology*, 24, 316-21.

Patterson, T.C. (1973) *America's Past: A New World Archaeology*. Glenview.

Patterson, T.C. and Lanning, E.P. (1964) Changing settlement patterns on the central Peruvian coast. *Ñawpa Pacha*, 2, 113-23.

Patterson, T.C. and Moseley, M.E. (1968) Late preceramic and early ceramic cultures of the central coast of Peru. *Ñawpa Pacha*, 6, 115-33.

Renfrew, C. (ed.) (1973) *The Explanation of Culture Change: Models in Prehistory*. London.

Sabloff, J.A., Beale, T.W. and Kurland, A.M. (1973) Recent developments in archaeology. *Annals Amer. Acad. Pol. and Soc. Sci.*, 408, 103-18.

Sahlins, M.D. (1972) *Stone Age Economics.* Chicago.

Sanders, W.T. (1972) Population, agricultural history and societal evolution in Mesoamerica. In Spooner 1972, 101-53.

Sanders, W.T. and Price, B.J. (1968) *Mesoamerica: The Evolution of a Civilization.* New York

Sauer, J.D. (1969) Identity of archaeologic grain amaranths from the valley of Tehuacán, Mexico. *American Antiquity*, 34, 80-1.

Sauvy, A. (1969) *General Theory of Population.* London.

Sisson, E.B. (1973) *First Annual Report of the Coxcatlan Project.* Andover.

Slobodkin, L.B. (1961) *Growth and Regulation of Animal Populations.* New York.

Smith, C.E. (1967) Plant remains. In Byers 1967, 220-55.

Smith, C.E. (1968) Archaeological evidence for selection of chupandilla and cosahuico under cultivation in Mexico. *Economic Botany*, 22, 140-8.

Smith, P.E.L. (1972) Changes in population pressure in archaeological explanation. *World Arch.*, 4, 5-18.

Spooner, B. (ed.) (1972) *Population Growth: Anthropological Implications.* Cambridge, Mass.

Stephens, S.G. and Moseley, M.E. (1973) Cotton remains from archaeological sites in central coastal Peru. *Science*, 180, 186-8.

Struever, S. (ed.) (1971) *Prehistoric Agriculture.* Garden City, New York.

√Sussman, R.W. (1972) Child transport, family size and increase in human population during the Neolithic. *Current Anthropology*, 13, 258-9.

Turnbull, C.M. (1968) The importance of flux in two hunting societies. In Lee and DeVore 1968, 132-7; 245 for discussion.

Ucko, P.J. and Dimbleby, G.W. (eds.) (1969) *The Domestication and Exploitation of Plants and Animals.* London.

Ucko, P.J., Tringham, R. and Dimbleby, G.W. (eds.) (1972) *Man, Settlement and Urbanism.* London.

√Weiss, K.M. (1973) *Demographic Models for Anthropology.* Memoir 27 of the Soc. for Amer. Arch.

Whitaker, T.W. and Cutler, H.C. (1971) Prehistoric cucurbits from the Valley of Oaxaca. *Economic Botany*, 25, 123-7.

Wolf, E.R. (1966) *Peasants.* Englewood Cliffs., N.J.

Woodburn, J. (1972) Ecology, nomadic movement and the composition of the local group among hunters and gatherers: an East African example and its implications. In Ucko, Tringham and Dimbleby 1972, 193-206.

Wynne-Edwards, V.C. (1962) *Animal Dispersion in Relation to Social Behaviour.* Edinburgh.

NOTES

1. The full report on the Ancón excavations is not yet in print, and the preliminary reports are sometimes contradictory. Figure 6 is based primarily on Patterson (1971b:320) modified by information generously provided by Cohen (1973).

2. *Tamaulipas:* MacNeish 1958; 1961; 1964b; 1971b; Mangelsdorf, MacNeish & Willey 1964; Callen 1963; 1967a; 1967b. For discussion of the chronology, see also Nance 1972; Johnson & MacNeish 1972: Fig. 4.

Tehuacan: Byers 1967; MacNeish 1962; 1964a; 1964b; 1970; 1971a; 1972; 1973; Sauer 1969; Sisson 1973; Flannery 1972:37.

Ayacucho: MacNeish 1969; MacNeish *et al.* 1970.

Ancón: Moseley 1972; Patterson 1971a; 1971b; 1973:57-64; Patterson & Moseley 1968; Stephens & Moseley 1973; Engel 1973; Cohen 1973.

See also, preliminary reports on the Valley of Oaxaca, Mexico: Flannery *et al.* 1967; Flannery & Schoenwetter 1970; Flannery MS; Flannery 1972: 44-6; Whitaker & Cutler 1971.

3. See the discussion by Nance (1972) of the Altithermal period (a warm dry interlude lasting from 5,500 to 2,500 B.C.) and its possible effects on food procurement in Mexico and the U.S.A. If Nance's chronological arguments are correct, Tamaulipas may have been largely depopulated during that period.

4. Excluded from discussion are such 'advanced' hunter-gatherers as the tribes of the Pacific North-West and the aboriginal Californians. They had higher population densities, were sedentary or semi-sedentary, and had more complex forms of socio-political organization. They serve as a warning that generalizations are dangerous, but nothing remotely like them has yet appeared in the American archaeological record for the early Post-Pleistocene. Archaeological evidence shows that the cultures of California and the Pacific North-West are the end-product of a long evolution from simpler to more complex forms within the hunter-gatherer tradition.

5. The same argument underlies Boserup's contention that population growth eventually reduces agricultural efficiency to the point where, rather than accept further reduction of the standard of living, people are compelled to adopt more productive (i.e. intensive) techniques of cultivation (Boserup 1965).

6. Present-day Tropical Forest swidden cultivation in lowland South America has retained many of the characteristics of 'palaeotechnic' cultivation, though in a rather specialized form.

7. A pertinent example is given by Lee (1968:39) from the Kalahari region of Botswana. In conditions of severe drought, it was the cultivators and pastoralists who suffered. The Bushman hunter-gatherer economy felt no strain.

CHARLES BURNEY

Haftavan Tepe and early settlement patterns in north-west Iran

The problems connected with settlement patterns in north-west Iran are, at least indirectly, a subject of concern to several archaeological expeditions currently at work in this area, and to others who have completed excavations within the last fifteen years or so. Any new light that can be cast upon these problems must be of major interest to archaeologists, not only in Iran but also in Turkey, Iraq and the U.S.S.R. This is a subject of investigation that the writer hopes will be suitable for a volume dedicated to Professor Grahame Clark.

The thirty or more expeditions currently involved in excavations in different regions of Iran include more than one whose work is clarifying the changing patterns of settled life, transhumance and nomadism in successive periods.[1] The writer has deliberately limited the scope of this short article to north-west Iran, for to have attempted a wider geographical coverage would have been foolhardy, on account of the shortage of evidence. In order to gain any adequate understanding of the emergence of the very earliest village communities, however, it is essential to look further south, to the central Zagros highlands, the north of Luristan and the plain of Kermanshah. Here, the discoveries of Philip Smith (1972) at Ganj Dareh Tepe have put the earliest phases in the central Zagros in an entirely new perspective: small as this site is, it is culturally very advanced for its period and the attachment of animal skulls to the wall of a building at the very centre of the mound at this site gives a tantalizing hint of a relationship between the Zagros people of the eighth and the inhabitants of Çatal Hüyük of the seventh millennium B.C. So small a community as that of Ganj Dareh can scarcely have ranged far for food and, unless equally advanced sites existed in the neighbourhood, vast areas must surely have remained virtually unexploited. Neither Tepe Asiab nor Tepe Sarab, both close to Kermanshah, can be compared in terms of cultural advance with Ganj Dareh, although the latter shared with Tepe Asiab a considerable dependence on goat-herding (Braidwood 1961).

The small size of Ganj Dareh Tepe was brought home to the writer on a brief visit this summer (1973): any sedentary population was clearly small in size, perhaps little more than the local chieftain and his retainers, but some form of organized administration is strongly hinted at by the architectural remains. The economy of the Zagros highlands as a whole, including the Kermanshah plain, must have continued to be overwhelmingly semi-nomadic or transhumant; and this was probably the way of life of the majority of the population, at least until the third millennium B.C. In other words, the archaeological record with its emphasis on agriculture gives, and will no doubt continue to give, a distorted picture.

The work of Braidwood, Solecki, Mortensen and Smith has revealed data providing a reasonably continuous sequence of economies, with narrower gaps than existed a decade ago, from that of Shanidar and Zawi Chemi Shanidar to those of the upper levels of Jarmo and Tepe Guran, and also Tepe Sarab and sites further north (Mellaart 1967: for general discussion and references). But this is, of course, no straightforward progression, for there was clearly a wide disparity in importance between the settlements of different mountain valleys and plains; with Jarmo now, inevitably, having to be reckoned as being a relatively backward community, for the seventh millennium B.C. This is not to belittle the significance of the discoveries made at Jarmo, but merely to point out that the significance of such pioneering efforts has, all too often, to be reinterpreted in the light of later finds.

There is room for discussion on the subject of estimates of population in the earliest settlements of western Iran, Khuzistan and the hills of Iraqi Kurdistan. The suggested figure of not more than 100 per hectare (2½ acres) seems slightly cautious, judging by present-day villages in many parts of the Near East (Hole, Flannery & Neely 1969:370, Fig. 136). But even if we accept, for example, a figure of about 150 per hectare, this would still leave most of the reasonably fertile land available for the flocks and herds of nomadic or semi-nomadic groups; it would thus necessitate no radical reappraisal of the economy of the village settlements of the seventh and sixth millennia B.C. There can, of course, be no doubt that the introduction of irrigation in Khuzistan must have led to a marked rise in population, thus preparing the way for the growth of a semi-urban economy, itself still dependent on the barley and sheep and other food produced in the villages surrounding emergent towns (Hole, Flannery & Neely 1969:354-8 for summary of the Sabz phase). In the cooler climates of the highlands, however, salinization of the soil through excessive irrigation can hardly have been a relevant factor until far later times, if then.

There is evidence, both archaeological and botanical, for a significant increase in population in the central Zagros region during a period very roughly equivalent to the seventh millennium B.C. Indeed, the botanical evidence from the Deh Luran project suggests contact with the hills to the north-east as early as the Bus Mordeh phase. Archaeological evidence, especially that of pottery, also indicates a gradual northward movement from the Kermanshah region to the Solduz plain, immediately south of Lake Reza'iyeh (Urmia), at the village of Hajji Firuz, one of the three successive sites surrounding Hasanlu excavated by R.H. Dyson, probably attributable to the mid-sixth millennium B.C. (Dyson & Voigt 1969). Only a little later is the Neolithic site adjacent to the main site of Yanik Tepe, close to Tabriz (Burney 1964). Detailed attempts to distinguish connexions between these sites and the ceramic levels of Jarmo and Tepe Sarab are probably of only limited significance; for such indicators as painted pottery and stone bracelets demonstrate, beyond serious doubt, the wide geographical extent of the culture of this district which might, perhaps, suitably be termed the 'Zagros Late Neolithic'; parallels between Hajji Firuz and Tell Hassuna are quite insufficient grounds for calling this 'Early Chalcolithic'.

The available evidence from the Trans-Caucasian region of the U.S.S.R., summarized up to 1968-70 by the writer (Japaridze & Javakhishvili 1967), adds to the impression of a steady, if unspectacular, northward spread of a village farming economy, from the region of its possible origin, in and around the Kermanshah plain, to eastern Georgia, where the settlement of Shulaveri is distinguished by its round houses. Unfortunately, there is still not the evidence required to reconstruct, in any authoritative or detailed form, the settlement pattern of the Urmia region including the Salmas plain at the north-west corner of Lake Reza'iyeh, during the sixth millennium B.C. and in later periods. Such unpublished evidence as there is comes from surveys which, if carried out again on a much more intensive scale, would assuredly cause a modified picture to emerge. A recent (Mortensen 1973) survey in one small upland plain in Luristan serves as a salutary reminder of the limitations of these surveys, in that a vastly greater number of sites was found than in previous surveys in this area, carried out by the same person. Intensive investigations in the Urmia region would, very possibly, reveal that there were settlements of the seventh millennium B.C., antedating the 'Zagros Late Neolithic' of Hajji Firuz and Yanik Tepe; though the absence of such sites in the well investigated Solduz plain is against this suggestion. At least one settlement mound, of a period not later than the sixth millennium B.C., with its characteristic straw-tempered pottery, does exist close to Haftavan Tepe.

The excavations at Yanik Tepe suggest an almost continuous occupation, including the small Neolithic site, from the sixth to the late-fourth millennium B.C. Surveys suggest, too, that the number of settlements, a barometer of fluctuations in population even more important than their size, increased steadily down to *c.* 3,000 B.C. After this period Yanik Tepe was deserted, in the first phase of the Early Bronze Age (the Early Trans-Caucasian I period). Newcomers appeared, with distinctive architectural and ceramic traditions, at Yanik Tepe round about 2,600 B.C. or slightly earlier; and a swift-moving group of these Early Trans-Caucasian II people seems to have been responsible for the arrival of an intrusive culture in the fourth level at Godin, half-way between Hamadan and Kermanshah (Burney & Lang 1971: Ch. III for general discussion).

The four seasons of excavations so far carried out at Haftavan Tepe, in the Salmas plain, are relevant to questions of settlement patterns from the late-third millennium B.C. onwards. The results of the fourth (1973) season include the discovery of a round house of Period VIII, the same period as that of the similar houses at Yanik Tepe, thus demonstrating the movement of northerners down both sides of Lake Reza'iyeh, instead of only on the east side. (The excavations at Geoy Tepe did not provide evidence to this effect – see Burton-Brown 1951: period K).

A more extensive proportion of the town of Period VII at Haftavan Tepe, which probably came to an end about 2,000 B.C., was also exposed in 1971-3, chiefly on top of the citadel (Burney 1972a; 1973). As at the contemporary settlement of Yanik Tepe, following the earlier long succession of phases with round houses and distinctive incised ceramic decoration, this appears to have been a peaceful period at Haftavan Tepe, without traces of burning and with the usual minimum of finds *in situ* to be expected under such conditions. Although burning can possibly be too readily attributed to enemy attack, there can be little doubt that the preceding period (Early Trans-Caucasian II) had been marked by frequent fires at Yanik Tepe; and a disturbed period would be a stimulus to concentration of population in fewer but larger settlements, by the growth of towns at the expense of the surrounding villages. Such a development may well have occurred in Period VII at Haftavan Tepe.

More distant parallels are available when attention is turned to the next period (VIB) at Haftavan Tepe, for which a radiocarbon date with a mean value of 1772 B.C. is now available (Mahdavi 1973). To the south, the site of Dinkha Tepe has yielded painted pottery of which most, though not all, is comparable with that from Haftavan VIB, the different types including Khabur ware from upper Mesopotamia and north Syria (Dyson 1967; Muscarella 1966). The fertile Reza'iyeh plain, where Austrian excavations are now in progress at Kordlar Tepe (Kromer 1973), is sure to yield evidence that, as in the Salmas plain, the early-second millennium B.C. marked a high point in the history of settled life in the whole of north-west Iran. This was a period not undisturbed by conflict, if the repeated burnt layers are correctly interpreted, earthquakes being an improbable explanation. Moreover, whereas no written record can come to the aid of the archaeologist for the earlier periods, by this time there are historically attested movements, likely to have left some traces in the archaeological record. One need mention only the Hittites and the Kassites; and in connexion with the Kassites, skilled horsemen, it may be not inappropriate to mention the occurrence of a number of sherds, of the characteristic burnished and painted pottery of Haftavan VIB, depicting horses. One such sherd shows two horses drawing a vehicle, the pole of which is partly preserved – a tantalizing fragment.

Though continuing to expand in area during the following period (VIA), it seems that Haftavan Tepe may have entered upon a long, if very gradual, decline, probably eventually accelerated by the arrival of the first of the Iranians, though their impact was much more limited than, for example, at Hasanlu (period V at both sites).

Comparisons with Trans-Caucasia to the north and westwards with the Van region and other parts of eastern Anatolia, apart from the Elazığ plain (Altinova, part of the area to be flooded by the Keban Dam), would suggest a reversion to an economy dependent on pastoralism with very few settlements of any size, though with tribal cemeteries, from about the early second millennium B.C. The new pastoralism persisted, at least in the greater part of eastern Anatolia, until as late as the ninth century B.C., when the kingdom and civilization of Urartu became firmly established. The full results of the latest excavations in Trans-Caucasia not being available, the sequence is less certain in this region; but the general picture appears to be similar. The settlement pattern in the Urmia region of north-west Iran was, however, utterly different, since here urban life seems to have reached its apogee precisely at the time that even village life was disappearing in the lands lying to the north and west. Haftavan Tepe was more extensively occupied than ever before, even though the summit of the citadel had been abandoned, probably not to be reoccupied till the time of Urartu. Disruption came to the Urmia region only with the Iron I period, and then much less so at Haftavan than at Hasanlu, presumably because it was less close to the path of the incoming Iranian tribes, recognizable in the archaeological record by their distinctive grey ware.

This brief article should conclude by pointing out the limited extent and reliability of evidence on settlement patterns in north-west Iran, on which Urartian irrigation works had only a brief effect in the eighth and seventh centuries B.C. (Burney 1972b). Much remains to be discovered, and the writer hopes that his earlier field-work, owing so much to his training with Grahame Clark and others in Cambridge, will continue in the form of detailed, intensive surveys of north-western Iran, associated with future seasons of excavations at Haftavan Tepe.

REFERENCES

Braidwood, R.J. (1961) The Iranian prehistoric project, 1959-60. *Iranica Antiqua*, 1, 3-7.

Burney, C.A. (1964) Excavations at Yanik Tepe, Azerbaijan, 1962. *Iraq*, 26, 54-61.

Burney, C.A. (1972a) Excavations at Haftavan Tepe 1969: Second Preliminary Report. *Iran*, 10, 127-42.

Burney, C.A. (1972b) Urartian irrigation works. *Anatolian Studies*, 22, 179-86.

Burney, C.A. (1973) Excavations at Haftavan Tepe 1971: third preliminary report. *Iran*, 11, 153-72.

Burney, C.A. and Lang, D.M. (1971) *The Peoples of the Hills – Ancient Ararat and Caucasus*. London.

Burton-Brown, T. (1951) *Excavation in Azerbaijan 1948*. London.

Dyson, R.H. (1967) Brief report on excavations at Dinkha Tepe. *Iran*, 5, 136-7.

Dyson, R.H. and Voigt, M. (1969) Brief report on 1968 excavations at Hajji Firuz. *Iran*, 7, 179-80.

Hamlin, C. (1974) The early second millennium ceramic assemblage of Dinkha Tepe. *Iran*, 12, 125-53.

Hole, F., Flannery, K.V. and Neely, J.A. (1969) *Prehistory and Human Ecology of the Deh Luran Plain* (Memoirs Mus. Anthro., Univ. Michigan). Ann Arbor.

Japaridze, O.M. and Javakhishvili, A.I. (1967) Results of the work of the Kvemo-Kartlian archaeological expedition (1965-6). In Georgian with brief Russian summary. This deals with Shulaveri I only. *Proc. Acad. Sci. Georgian S.S.R.*, 3, 292-8.

Kromer, K. (1973) Brief report on excavations at Kordlar Tepe. *Iran*, 11, 197-9.

Mahdavi, Miss (1973) Personal communication from Nuclear Physics Laboratory, University of Teheran. (Further details are awaited.)

Mellaart, J. (1967) The earliest settlements in Western Asia. *Cambridge Ancient History* I (revised ed.), fasc. 59, 9-19. London.

Mortensen, P. (1973) Unpublished communication to Second Annual Symposium in Teheran, under the auspices of the Iranian Ministry of Culture.

Muscarella, O.W. (1966) Excavations at Dinkha Tepe, 1966. *Metropolitan Mus. of Art Bull.*, 25, 16 ff.

Smith, P.E.L. (1972) Brief report on 1971 excavations at Ganj Dareh Tepe. *Iran*, 10, 165-8.

NOTES

1. Communication between the directors of these expeditions is now greatly assisted by the institution of an annual symposium, meeting at the end of October in Teheran, under the auspices of the Iranian Ministry of Culture. Two such meetings have now taken place.

NORMAN HAMMOND

A Classic Maya ball-game vase

The ball game, *pok-ta-pok* to the Maya, *tlachtli* to the Aztec, was a salient and, in many ways, definitive feature of Precolumbian Mesoamerican culture. In its various forms it was played from northern Mexico and the southwestern United States to Central America, and from the early first millennium B.C. down to the Spanish conquest and beyond. The rules and equipment of the game must have varied considerably over this area and period (Borhegyi 1968), although certain features must also have remained constant. These latter included the form of competition, between two individuals or teams; the ball, of solid rubber; and the locale, a court comprising the open alley between two parallel structures, together with the surfaces of the structures facing on to the alley. The court itself might be large, as at Chichén Itzá, or small as at Tikal, but the form of its architecture was characteristic (Blom 1932; Quirarte 1970) and it was always located in, and often helped to define, a 'ceremonial centre', a concentration of public buildings, collectively constructed and often grandiose, that served as a local focus of religious, secular and commercial activity.

The iconography of the ball game is an important feature of Mesoamerican art, most commonly represented in sculptures associated with ball-courts or on commemorative monuments elsewhere in ceremonial centres; in the Maya area, figures identified as ball-game players by their dress, equipment and actions are portrayed on sculptured friezes and markerstones in ball-courts, and on stelae, while items of ball-game equipment are also reproduced in stone. Most of this sculpture was essentially public art in its location and potential audience and in the system of patronage that produced it, although participation has been suggested as being restricted to the élite in Maya society (Joyce 1933) and, in some cases, even watching the game may have been a carefully guarded privilege (Hammond 1972a:769).

The game was, however, also portrayed in private art such as figurines and painted vases, objects no less the result of a patronage system than the public sculptures but, from their small size and portability, intended for use in the home or tomb, directly comparable with the products of the Dipylon workshops of Classical Athens in both the skill of manufacture and in the complex intellectual substratum that rendered them meaningful. In this short paper I am concerned with an apparent portrayal of the Maya ball game, and perhaps of a specific match, on just such a piece of private art, and its implications for a long-held theory.

The work in question, the remains of a Late Classic Maya polychrome cylinder vessel, was discovered in 1970 during excavations at the small and geographically peripheral ceremonial centre of Lubaantún, Belize. A preliminary account of these excavations has been published and a final report is in press (Hammond 1970; n.d.) and here it will suffice to note that the vessel was found in the construction fill of one of the massive hill-platforms that were constructed to enlarge the area of the ceremonial centre in the latter part of the eighth century A.D. The fragments, together with those of a polychrome drum (Hammond 1972b:124), rested on the buried surface of an earlier terrace, also eighth century in date, and, from their relatively undamaged condition, may have been intentionally deposited rather than tipped in with the massive rubble fill, which contains blocks up to 60 cm. in diameter. The trench in which they were found was dug into the eastern slope of the ridge on which Lubaantún stands, immediately below the two major pyramids, Structures 10 and 12 (Hammond 1970:Fig. 2).

Two large fragments of the vessel survive, but do not join (Fig. 1); it is, however, clear from the paste and slip colours, the radius of curvature and the style of painting, that they are from the same vessel, a sub-cylindrical vase

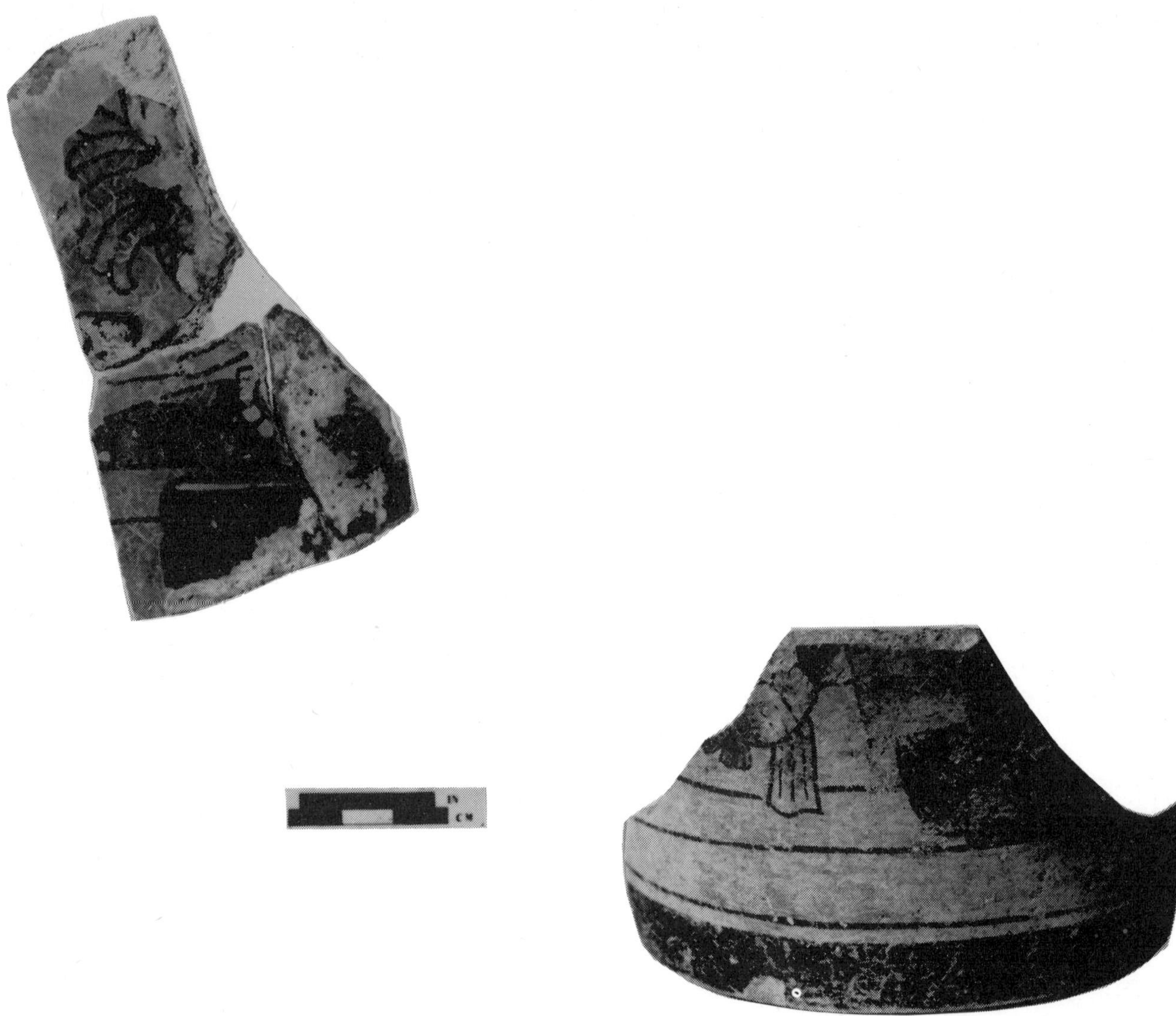

Figure 1. The two surviving fragments of the Lubaantún ball-game vase.

14-15 cm. in diameter, tapering slightly at the base and probably originally 20-25 cm. in height. The larger fragment includes half of the circumference at the base and is 7 cm. high. The paste is brick-red, with a cream-buff slip on which a figured polychrome design is outlined in black. A black band, 1.8 cm. high, encircles the base and above this are roughly parallel and horizontal thin black lines spaced irregularly 1-2 cm. apart. One of these acts as a baseline on which a human figure rests on one knee, while the others pass behind this figure, either suggesting a stepped or terraced architectural background or simply providing perspective to the action.

Of the figure, we have the right knee and right elbow, painted in a rich reddish-brown; the elbow is bound with material tied in a knot, the knee rests on a pad tied around the leg just below the joint. The pad bears a face-like design, of which one eye is visible, and has a circumferential fringe; a full-face version of such a pad is known from a figurine fragment found at the nearby site of Pusilhà, also in 1970 (Hammond 1971:Fig. 11). Both elbow- and knee-bindings are light in colour, tinted with a fugitive violet, and this coloration is also found on the loin-cloth that cuts across the thigh. Only the lower right-hand portion of the loin-cloth is present, but it is clear that the front of it was decorated with a circular solid black design, now partly broken off, with a light circle just inside its lower margin containing a small and delicately drawn open circle on black. I suggest that this design is a symbolic Ahau glyph (cf. Thompson 1960:Fig. 10, 46 ff.). The elbow- and knee-bindings are the normal accoutrements of a ball-game player, and the pose suggests that the player portrayed here is going down to his right (spectator's left) on to one knee to take a shot – in other words that the scene depicts a ball game in progress.

In parenthesis, I should like to advance a speculation: I have identified the circular black device on the loin-cloth as a symbolic Ahau glyph. This glyph means 'lord', but the present device could be indicate that the wearer is one of the Hunahpu. If so, we may perhaps identify the ball game portrayed on this vase as being not merely a genre scene, but specifically the game played by the Hero Twins in the Popol Vuh epic against the Lords of Hell. Coe (1973) has shown that many of the scenes on Maya figured polychrome vessels are susceptible of a particularistic, legendary and infernal interpretation, and this vase may be another such.

The other fragment, from the vessel wall, seems to depict his opponent. Against the cream-buff background with its quasi-parallel black lines passing behind the figure, and possibly terminating at head height, is a frontal figure with its head turned in profile to the left (spectator's right). The skin is again coloured reddish-brown, the area around the neck being darker and redder. The right arm is flung out horizontally, the left downwards. The face, except for the point of the chin, has been erased, an occurrence which, on this vessel as on others, appears to be intentional and which supports the notion of deliberate disposal of the vase. The figure wears a necklace of large spherical beads of a light colour, and on the head a high cap surmounted by a panache of what seem to be feathers; the face seems to have been bare, not covered by a helmet or mask. Across the chest below the armpits is a broad and thick ribbed object, chestnut-brown on the outer surface and white on the inner; the impression of solidity and curvature suggests that it is a stuffed or padded object, and from numerous other more complete depictions we may identify it as a ball-player's 'belt', although that term is scarcely appropriate for such a substantial protection as this. The colour of the covering suggests that it was made of deer-skin, the tougher back hide being used for the outer covering and the soft light skin of the belly being in contact with the player's flesh, and it may be that the ribbed effect derives from the use of the complete skins of several deer, stuffed and sewn together. Analysis of the faunal remains from Lubaantún by Elizabeth S. Wing (in Hammond n.d.) has shown that the white-tailed deer, *Odocoileus virginianus*, was heavily exploited at Lubaantún, as at other lowland Maya sites, as a protein source, and the manufacture of ball-game equipment would have been one of many obvious uses for the resulting skins.

The second fragment, therefore, also shows a human figure in action and with the trappings of a ball-game player, in a standing position consonant with opposing the figure seen on the first fragment; by combining the information from the two fragmentary figures, one present only in the upper part, the other only in the lower, we may propose that the equipment used in this game consisted of a loin-cloth as normal male attire, a thick padded deer-skin 'belt' across the lower chest and stomach, a tall cap with a feather panache worn on top of the head and leaving the face free, a sewn knee-pad with a fringe and a mask ornament, and an elbow-binding consisting of a long strip of material tied in a knot behind the elbow.

It could legitimately, if implausibly, be argued that the two figures did not, in fact, wear the same equipment on their missing halves, were it not for the fact that the three limestone ball-court markers from Lubaantún, found by R.E. Merwin in 1915 and now in the Peabody Museum at Harvard University (together with the vase described here), depict scenes very similar to that on the vase (Fig. 2; Morley 1937-8: Pl. 162). All three show two ball-game players wearing crested caps, ribbed 'belts' and knee- and elbow-pads, in action in front of a horizontally divided background that terminates at head height and which would seem to be the ball-court; they were found by Merwin set in the floor of the playing alley of the south ball-court at Lubaantún, an identification confirmed by excavation in 1970 (Hammond 1970:Fig. 2, structure 4). The parallels in design on two of the markers, with a standing figure to the spectator's left and a kneeling one to the right,

Figure 2. One of the Lubaantun ball-court markers found by R.E. Merwin in 1915.

are so striking as to suggest that the vase acted as exemplar for the sculptures or *vice versa*; the former is the more likely on two grounds: the quality of design and execution on the vase is much higher (although this is not conclusive, given the difference in material) and the sculptures are certainly of local material and, presumably, of local workmanship, while the vase is of a type and quality rare enough at Lubaantún to be a plausible import (a point that we hope to settle by neutron activation analysis in the near future).

The question of importation is less irrelevant than it might at first seem, since it raises an important point: is the range of ball-game equipment depicted on the vase and ball-court markers that normally in use at Lubaantún in the eighth century A.D.? That it is ball-game equipment is indisputable, but its use at Lubaantún has been disputed; or, more accurately, an entirely different set of equipment has been proposed, and for forty years tacitly accepted, as being the ball-game apparatus used at Lubaantún (Joyce 1933:xix-xxiii; Butler 1935:648; Thompson 1966:308, 317; Carmichael 1973:53; Corson 1973:63).

This equipment (Fig. 3) is depicted on numerous pottery whistle-figurines found at the site, principally by the British Museum in 1926-7 (Joyce 1926; 1933; also Joyce, Clark & Thompson 1927) and the Cambridge-Harvard project in 1970 (Hammond 1970; n.d.). They are undoubtedly of local origin, since many of the moulds used in making them have been found at the site and very few figurines have been found more than a few kilometres from the ceremonial centre. Among the multitudinous designs is one which, within a fairly narrow range of variation, consists of a standing male figure wearing a narrow loin-cloth or *maxtli* around the waist with the end falling between the legs to knee level or lower. This may be worn over a wider garment reaching from the waist down over the upper thighs (Fig. 3:19, 20, 22). Over the upper sternal region is a fringed or reeded ornament, possibly of cloth, rectangular and quite small – relative to a modern Maya it would be about 20 cm. in length and 10-15 cm. wide.

The most striking item of equipment is a helmet completely covering the head, with a rectangular horizontal slit at eye-level in which the nose is also seen.[1] From a number of frontal and profile depictions, it appears that the helmet was made of a piece of flexible material, perhaps hide as Joyce suggested, with the cheek-pieces fastened at the front. At the back, a flat stiff structure rises behind the head, possibly fastened to the shoulders, and sometimes the helmet itself is surmounted by a feather panache, apparently supported on a hidden framework (Carmichael 1973: Pl. 41). The general appearance is very similar to that of mediaeval European tilting-helmets of early type (Figs. 3, 4). The figures often wear wristlets or bracelets on both forearms and the other distinctive piece of equipment associated with the helmeted figures is a massive 'glove' on the right hand, varying in size and sometimes decorated.

Joyce (1933:xix-xxiii) noted the persistent concurrence of the helmet, glove and thigh-flaps worn beneath the *maxtli*, and matched these with items described as ball-game equipment in the Quiché epic, the *Popol Vuh*; he suggested that the helmeted figures were ball-game players, and that the helmet was the inspiration for the later beaked mask of Ehecatl, the Aztec wind-god, since the ball game was known to be connected with planetary and climatic deities. This identification of the figurines has remained unchallenged ever since; it is a well-argued case, but I think that it is wrong.

There are, in fact, two definite ball-game

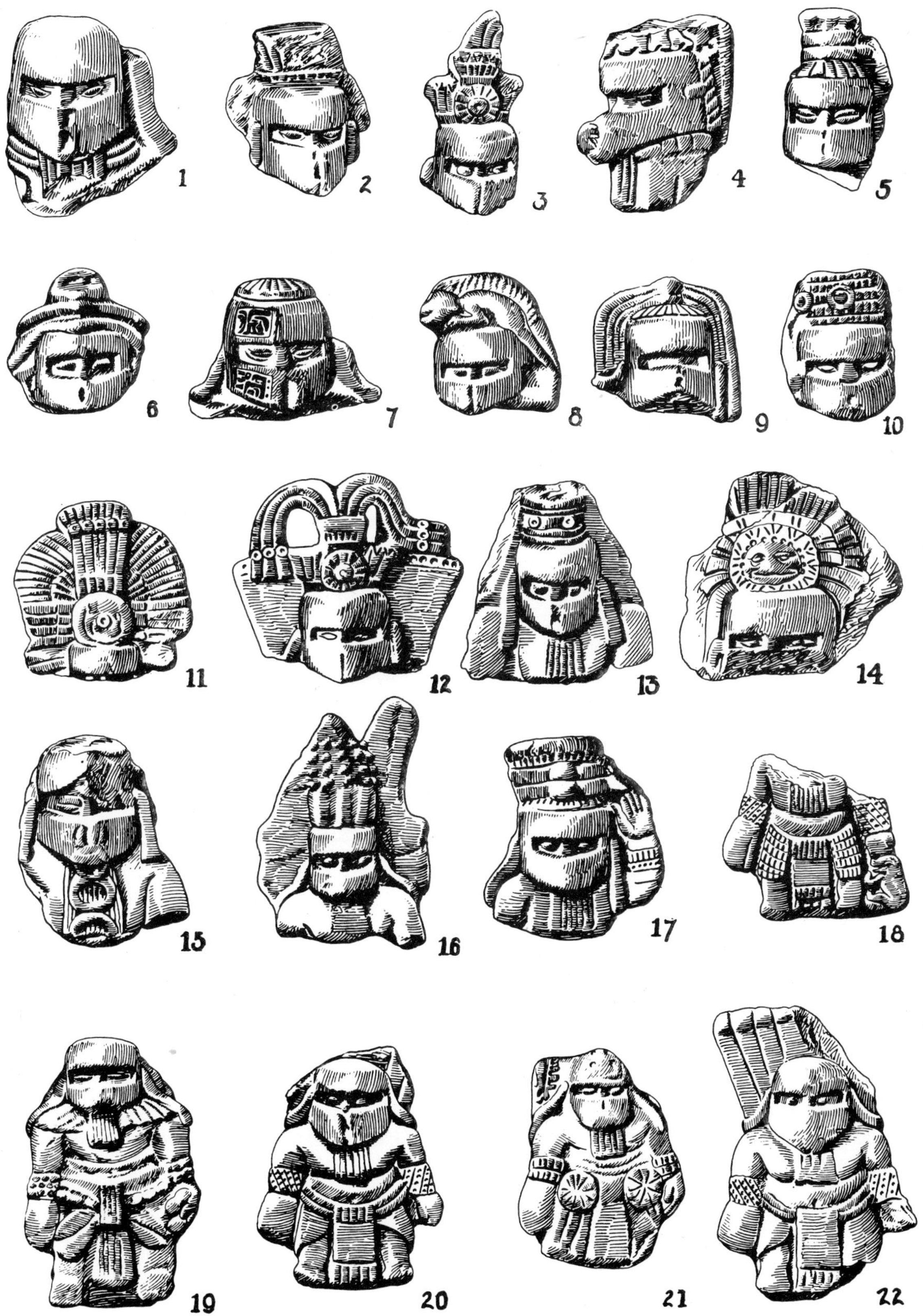

Figure 3. Helmeted figurines from Lubaantun [after Joyce, 1933, Plate VII].

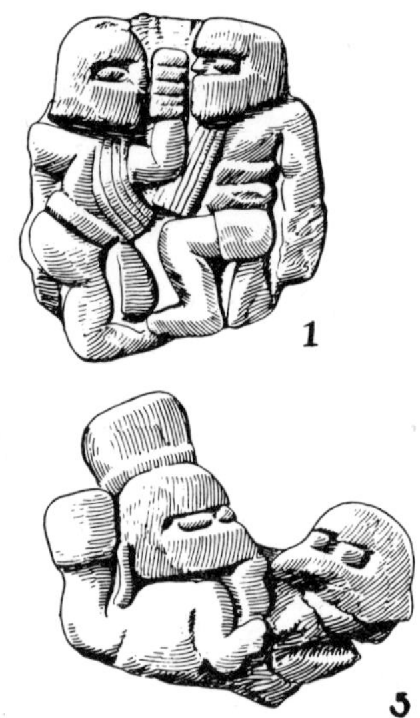

Figure 4. Pair of helmeted figures [after Joyce, 1933, Plate VIII].

player figurines from Lubaantún but Joyce does not comment upon them (Fig. 5, from Joyce 1933: Pl. V); both wear a broad belt held in place by a narrow decorated strip resembling a *maxtli*, and both wear a garment beneath resembling the under-garment (Joyce's 'thigh-flaps') of the helmeted figures. One wears a knee-pad on the right knee, with a mask decoration, and may have padding on the forearm, but does not wear a glove; the other is broken off at wrist and knee so that no evidence is available as to his equipment, but also lacks a glove. Both figurines have neck-pendants, completely different from the rectangular ornament worn by the helmeted figures; both are headless, so that the presence or absence of a helmet

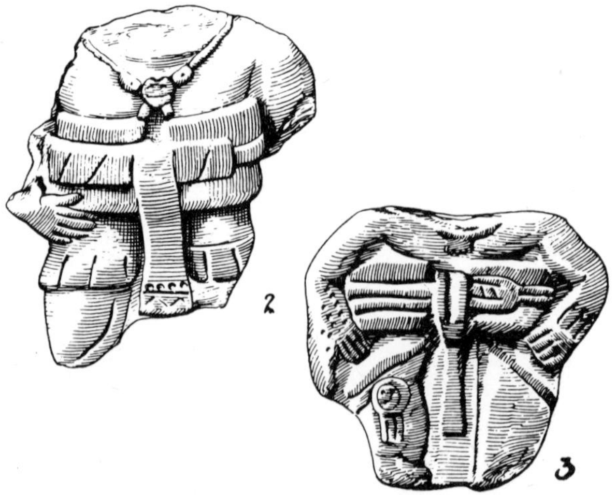

Figure 5. Two ball-game player figurines from Lubaantún [after Joyce, 1933, Plate V].

cannot be established. A figurine from Pusilhà, wearing a similar belt, wore a cap that left the face free (Hammond 1971:Fig. 13).

The only item of equipment common to these two ball-game player figurines and the helmeted figures is the 'thigh-flaps', but these are certainly not a diagnostic piece of the player's outfit, being seen on a number of figurines that lack both helmet-glove and pad-belt equipment (e.g. Joyce 1933: Pl. III, 1-2) and also occasionally lacking on helmeted-type figures (Joyce 1933: Pl. III, 6). The 'thigh-flaps', in fact, seem to be part of a normal male outfit, perhaps protective in function but certainly not confined to the equipment of a ball-game player. On the basis of comparison with the two player figurines and the unequivocal depictions of the ball game on the ball-court markers and the polychrome vessel under discussion, there is no evidence whatsoever that the helmeted figures are ball-game players.

Then what are they? Most of the figurines show them simply standing frontally, their arms by their sides or occasionally with one hand raised, and give no hint of their function. Three, however (Fig. 4, from Joyce 1933: Pl. VIII, 1, 5; Field Mus. Chicago: No. 188252), show two helmeted figures in profile, facing each other in close proximity and apparently involved in some kind of altercation involving the raising of heavily gloved hands: one might almost say that they were having a fight, and that is exactly what I think they are doing. Whether the fighting is serious combat or a ritualized combat where manhood is to be proven (as in German *Schlager* fencing) it is impossible to say, but another polychrome vessel recently restored by the British Museum, and probably from Lubaantún (otherwise from nearby Pusilhà), supports this interpretation (Fig. 6). Fig. 6a shows this vessel and the best-preserved figure on it: he is wearing a visored helmet, neck ornament and *maxtli*, but no belt or knee-pad; he is not a ball-game player. Fig. 6b shows two figures from the back of the vase, both again wearing helmets: they are standing facing each other, a short distance apart, with spread legs. The figure to our left seems to be striding forward over a bent knee and, at the same time, thrusting out an arm horizontally towards the face of the other figure who, in turn, has his right arm raised and thrust out towards the other. The arms are damaged, and what is actually being

a

b

Figure 6. A recently restored vase from Lubaantún or Pusilhá showing helmeted figures. (a) standing figure; (b) two figures in combat.

done is not clear, although the left-hand figure has some sort of binding or padding around his forearm and hand, but one thing is certain – none of the figures on this vase is playing the ball game, or is equipped to do so.

In the light of this evidence, the survival of Joyce's identification of the figurines as ball-game players would require a high acceptance of coincidence: that there were two distinct sets of equipment used in the ball game at Lubaantún, only one of which (the pad-belt set) has been found portrayed in an unequivocal ball-game context, on the vase and stone markers; while the other, lacking such portrayals, was not only unique to Lubaantún but also, in its lack of protective padding for the body and limbs, unique in the Maya area.

What the helmeted figures are, and what they are doing on the few representations of them in action, is a matter for conjecture. They are shown either just standing fully accoutred, or in a close active juxtaposition that might reasonably be called 'combat': whether this is the combat of warriors in battle, the controlled combat of a sport or the quasi-combat of a ritual, we have no way of telling, although the emphasis on protection of the head and perhaps the thighs, and the lack of recognizable weapons suggests that the first answer is the least likely. All that we can certainly say is that the activity for which the helmet-glove equipment was required was of fair importance in the iconography and way of life of Classic Lubaantún.[2]

Acknowledgments

The excavations at Lubaantún were supported by Cambridge and Harvard Universities, the British Museum and the British Academy, the Pitt-Rivers Museum at Oxford University and the Wenner-Gren Foundation for Anthropological Research Inc.

Fig. 1 is by L.P. Morley; Fig. 2 is by courtesy of the Peabody Museum, Harvard University; Figs. 3-5 are reproduced by courtesy of the Royal Anthropological Institute; Fig. 6 is by the author and was taken by permission of the Trustees of the British Museum.

REFERENCES

Bernal, I. (1973) Stone reliefs in the Dainzu area. In Bernal *et al.* (eds.), *The Iconography of Middle American Sculpture*, 13-23. New York.

Blom, F. (1932) The Maya ball-game *Pok-ta-Pok* (called *Tlachtli* by the Aztec). *Middle American Res. Pubn.*, 4, 485-530. New Orleans.

Borhegyi, S. de (1968) The pre-Columbian ball-game — a pan-Mesoamerican tradition. *Verhandlungen des XXXVIII Internationalen Amerikanistenkongresses*, I, 499-515.

Butler, M. (1935) A study of Maya mould-made figurines. *Amer. Anthro.*, 37, 636-72.

Carmichael, E. (1973) *The British and the Maya.* London.

Coe, M. (1973) *The Maya Scribe and His World.* New York.

Corson, C. (1973) Iconographic survey of some principal figurine subjects from the mortuary complex of Jaina, Campeche. *Contribns. Univ. Cal. Arch. Res. Facility*, 18, 51-75. Berkeley.

Hammond, N. (1970) Excavations at Lubaantún 1970. *Antiquity*, 44, 216-23.

Hammond, N. (1971) The arts and trade of Lubaantún. *Ill. London News*, 258, No. 6864, 28-9.

Hammond, N. (1972a) Locational models and the site of Lubaantún: a Classic Maya centre. In Clarke, D.L. (ed.), *Models in Archaeology*, 757-800. London.

Hammond, N. (1972b) Classic Maya music. *Archaeology*, 25, 124-31.

Hammond, N. (n.d.) Lubaantún: a Classic Maya realm. *Papers Peabody Mus., Harvard Univ.*, in press.

Joyce, T.A. (1926) Report on the investigations at Lubaantún, British Honduras, in 1926. *Jour. Royal Anthro. Inst.*, 56, 207-30.

Joyce, T.A. (1933) The pottery whistle-figurines of Lubaantún. *Jour. Royal Anthro. Inst.*, 63, xv-xxv.

Joyce, T.A., Clark, J. and Thompson, J.E. (1927) Report on the British Museum expedition to British Honduras, 1927. *Jour. Royal Anthro. Inst.*, 57, 295-323.

Morley, S.G. (1937-8) *The Inscriptions of Peten.* Carnegie Inst. Washington Pubn., 437.

Quirarte, J. (1970) El juego de pelota en Mesoamerica: su desarrollo arquitectónico. *Estudios de Cultura Maya*, 8, 83-96.

Thompson, J.E.S. (1960) *Maya Hieroglyphic Writing: An Introduction* (2nd. ed.). Norman, Oklahoma.

Thompson, J.E.S. (1966) *The Rise and Fall of Maya Civilization* (2nd. ed.). Norman, Oklahoma.

NOTES

1. Twenty-nine sculptured slabs recently excavated from Mound A, Dainzu, Oaxaca, Mexico, and dated to Monte Alban II (conventionally 400/300 B.C.-A.D. 0) have been identified by Bernal (1973) as ball-game players. They wear helmets with a cross-barred visor, knotted bands around both arms, and a loincloth; some of the helmets are decorated with jaguar ears, others have crests; none of the figures wears a knee-pad. Each clutches in the right hand a small round object which, identified as a ball, marks the figures as ball-players; most appear singly, in a variety of poses reminiscent of the Monte Alban *danzantes*, none of which are particularly suggestive of ball-game activity. I am indebted to Gordon R. Willey for this reference.

2. Three other, complete, ball-game vases are known to me in U.S. private collections, where the scenes portrayed essentially confirm the reconstruction of that on the Lubaantún vase. They are from looted sites and thus without acknowledged provenance, robbing them of much of their potential value; they are also unpublished.

DAVID and JOAN OATES

Early irrigation agriculture in Mesopotamia

Four types of evidence have been adduced for the use of at least simple irrigation techniques in Mesopotamia as early as the sixth millennium B.C. Palaeobotanical data have been used in two ways. Some authorities, notably Helbaek, postulate a direct relationship between seed size and water supply, and identify certain samples as evidence for irrigation conditions. Secondly, the discovery of evidence for certain crops in places where modern rainfall is insufficient to support them, but water for irrigation is available, has been taken to indicate some artificial manipulation of water supplies during the period from which the samples date. For this conclusion it is necessary to assume that there was not at that time a substantially different climate. We have as yet no direct evidence for climatic history, but the limit of modern rainfall agriculture in northern Mesopotamia coincides approximately with the boundary of ancient settlement outside the river valleys, suggesting that any difference in rainfall was at most marginal. The third argument is, again, topographical and depends on the same assumption. The distribution pattern of settlements in some areas outside the present rainfall zone incorporates alignments that appear to be at variance with the pattern of natural watercourses, and which may indicate the lines of artificial channels irrigating the land around the settlements. The fourth criterion, and perhaps the only one that can be accepted without further consideration, is the actual discovery of water channels that can be shown to be artificial, and that can have been used only for the purpose of diverting water on to agricultural land. Prehistoric evidence that can be categorized in any of these ways is minimal. In Mesopotamia proper, palaeobotanical evidence has been recovered from only two sites, Tell es-Sawwan and Choga Mami, that lie within the present-day irrigation zone (Helbaek 1964;1972a). To these data can be added information from Tepe Sabz and Chagha Sefid in Khuzistan (Helbaek 1969; Hole: personal communication).

It has been assumed, not unreasonably, that the economies of the earliest settled communities yet known from Sumer, *inter alia* Eridu, Ur and Warka, and Ras al 'Amiya to the north in what was later Akkad, were based on cereal agriculture together with a full range of domestic animals. In this arid zone such an assumption presupposes the knowledge of at least simple techniques of flow irrigation, in itself not surprising since, as we shall see later, these were apparently in contemporary use in middle Mesopotamia and Khuzistan. But direct evidence from these early 'Ubaid settlements is almost wholly absent, and our deductions are based almost entirely on the frequent occurrence of agricultural implements, together with the size and apparently settled nature of the communities. Helbaek (1960:195) has identified seven impressions of emmer, fourteen of barley and three of linseed on 'Ubaid sherds from Ur, but this constitutes the only botanical evidence for these crops. In general, surveys of sites within the present-day irrigation zone suggest that, in the earliest periods for which we have evidence, villages tended to be aligned along natural watercourses (Adams 1965; Adams & Nissen 1972); but from the beginning the villagers probably made small local modifications to flood-plain stream patterns. Later, more substantial manipulation of water resources is thought to be documented by major changes in settlement pattern including artificial alignments of sites (Adams 1962:112-3; Oates 1972:303).

With regard to actual traces of canals or smaller water-channels, only at Choga Mami, a prehistoric site east of Baghdad, can we with any certainty adduce physical evidence for their existence before 5000 B.C. (below, pp. 128ff.); no other site has yet yielded comparable evidence for this period.

The purpose of this paper is not so much to re-assess this existing evidence as to re-examine the assumptions on which it is based; to consider, in the light of this re-examination, how irrigation might have come to be practised in these

Table 1 Rainfall figures based on Republic of Iraq Meteorological Department and Development Board Statistics; approximate mean annual figures drawn from Guest and al-Rawi (1966), Fig. 6.

Station	*Years Recorded*	*Lat.*	*Long.*	*Elevation*	*Maximum water year (mm.)*	*Approx. mean*	*Minimum water year (mm.)*	*Month of May* Max.	*Month of May* Mean	*Month of May* Min.	*Month of October* Max.	*Month of October* Mean	*Month of October* Min.	*Nearby archaeological sites*
A. Mountain Region														
Amadiya	1936-58	37°05′	43°20′	1236m.	1375.4	870	540.4	175		—	84.6		0.0	
Chemchemal	1939-58	35°32′	44°51′	701m.	1110.5	556	187.1	118.4		0.0	29.9		0.0*	Jarmo, elevation *c.* 750m.
Halabja	1936-58	35°11′	45°59′	724m.	2301.0	815	353.9	120.6		0.0	423.0		0.0†	
Penjwin	1939-58	35°37′	45°58′	1311m.	1843.3	1220	200.6	223.0		—	99.0		0.0†	
B. Northern Plain and Steppe														
Mosul	1923-58	36°19′	43°09′	222m.	643.2	385	188.4	79.2	20.3	tr.	54.6	7.1	0.0†	Hassuna
Erbil	1935-58	36°11′	44°00′	414m.	1095.5	494	202.7	108.1		0.0	54.2		0.0†	
Tell Afar	1939-58	36°22′	42°28′	373m.	478.8	337	193.9	105.7		0.0†	34.3		0.0*	Yarim Tepe
Tuz Khurmatli	1935-58	34°53′	44°39′	220m.	404.4	280	178.0	30.0††		0.0	0.0		0.0	Matarrah
Mandali	1935-58	33°45′	45°33′	137m.	549.0	300	191.9	16.3		0.0†	14.7		0.0*	Choga Mami
Baiji	1936-58	34°56′	43°29′	115m.	218.4		—	51.8		0.0	16.3		0.0	
Samarra	1935-58	34°11′	43°50′	65m.	215.0	155	67.0	49.3		0.0†	43.5		0.0*	Tell es- Sawwan
Anah	1935-58	34°28′	41°57′	150m.	207.7	132	74.4	30.0		0.0†	26.0		0.0*	Baghouz
Rutba	1928-58	33°02′	40°17′	615.5m.	248.4	121	46.8	67.9	9.7	tr.†	65.3	5.0	0.0*	
C. Southern Alluvium														
Baghdad	1887-1958	33°20′	44°24′	34.1m.	483.2⊕	149	50.6	31.7	7.1	0.0†	21.2	3.0	0.0*	
Diwaniya	1929-58	31°39′	44°59′	20.4m.	195.3	116	42.9	113.6	9.0	0.0†	3.8	1.3	0.0*	Nippur
Nasiriya	1940-58	31°01′	46°14′	3m.	249.3	121	33.5	46.8	5.4	0.0†	10.8	1.3	0.0*	Ur, Eridu
Basra	1900-58	30°34′	47°47′	2.4m.	314.1	169	53.7	56.2	7.3	0.0	20.8	0.8	0.0*	
Fao	1935-58	29°59′	48°30′	2m.	339.0	190	54.5	20.5		0.0†	17.6		0.0*	

†† only recorded May rain.

⊕ in 1893-4; the maximum figure for a period comparable with the rest of the table is 255.6 in 1954-55.

† frequently no rain or very small amounts.

* frequently no rain in November as well as October.

prehistoric communities; and to assess the social and economic implications of its practice. Much that has been written about the development of irrigation agriculture in Mesopotamia is remarkably misinformed, both about the nature of the regimes of the two famous rivers that supplied the water and about farming practices in an environment such as that of ancient Sumer. It is therefore necessary to treat both these subjects in some detail, but as the question of climate is crucial to most of the conclusions that can be and have been drawn, it provides the most appropriate starting point for discussion.

Modern climate

Parts of Mesopotamia, together with the shores of the Arabian Gulf, form in summer one of the hottest and most oppressive areas of the world, though in winter the country is colder than is normal for this latitude. There are three climatic regions: the western and southern deserts, the northern steppe and plains, and the mountains. Throughout the country there are only two pronounced seasons, summer and winter. Summer begins in May and lasts until October; the heat is intense, the sky cloudless, the atmosphere dry and rain extremely rare.

Only in the northern plain and in the mountains is rain-fed agriculture possible. Rainfall is far from being the only factor that affects the growth of crops but it is the most readily measurable and, properly understood, rainfall figures provide the simplest guide to whether or not rain-fed agriculture is possible in any given area. It is generally agreed to be true that, in Iraq, 200 mm. of rain is the minimum required for the growth of wholly rain-fed cereals. This is not to say, however, that an annual average of 200 mm. is adequate for this purpose. It is the 200 mm. *reliable* annual aggregate that is relevant and for practical purposes this has been found to coincide roughly with the *300* mm. average rainfall isohyet (see Fig. 1).

It may be stated as a generalization that no significant rain falls in any agricultural area of Iraq from June to September. This includes cultivable mountain valleys at quite high elevations (Rayat, the highest recording station in Iraq, at an elevation of 1610 m., recorded rain twice in June for the years 1942-58, but at Penjwin, elevation 1311 m., which has the highest recorded average annual rainfall, no rain at all was recorded for these months during the period 1939-58). Table 1 shows clearly that a total lack of rain is common in October throughout the country. November also is often rainless, even occasionally in mountainous regions; in 1949 no rain was recorded in either month at Penjwin, while 1950 was almost as dry. Thus no summer crops can be grown anywhere without irrigation and, in dry years, winter planting of rain-fed land may have to be delayed as late as December.

In an essentially arid climate like that of Iraq the annual aggregate can vary greatly. This is clearly shown by the figures for maximum and minimum water years, and it is perhaps relevant in this respect that variability of world rainfall, measured as a percentage of some long-term average, is greatest in, and near, the fringes of the arid zone (Lamb 1968:107). In Iraq, beyond the true 'rainfall zone', in which rain-fed agriculture affords wholly reliable subsistence, there is an extensive marginal belt where cultivation is theoretically possible in some years and not in others. All the stations in the northern plain and steppe, and even on the higher Chemchemal plain, record years of low rainfall when crops would have been partial or total failures. But there is a significant difference between the plains of Mosul, Erbil and Kirkuk with an annual average rainfall of 350-500 mm. and, for instance, Tell Afar, 75 km. west of Mosul, where despite an average annual aggregate of 337 mm. there has been, in our experience, at least a partial crop failure in the land south-west of the town in two out of five years. Approaching the steppe, agricultural activity becomes even more precarious, although yields may be outstanding in a wet year. For the sake of brevity we may describe these as low, medium and high risk areas. In modern times, Tell Afar farmers insure against potential loss by cultivating both medium and low risk land, south-west and north-east of the town, while the high risk area on the border of the steppe, with potentially greater rewards, is normally sown only by entrepreneurs from Mosul backed by private or government capital. Before the emergence of urban economies with the capital resources, whether commercial or private, to insure against occasional disaster, the prehistoric farmer was presumably dependent on the yield of the land around his village and could not have tolerated for long even the incidence of crop failure that we have designated as a medium risk; it is well known that the effect of drought on subsistence-level cultivators is aggravated by the need to eat the

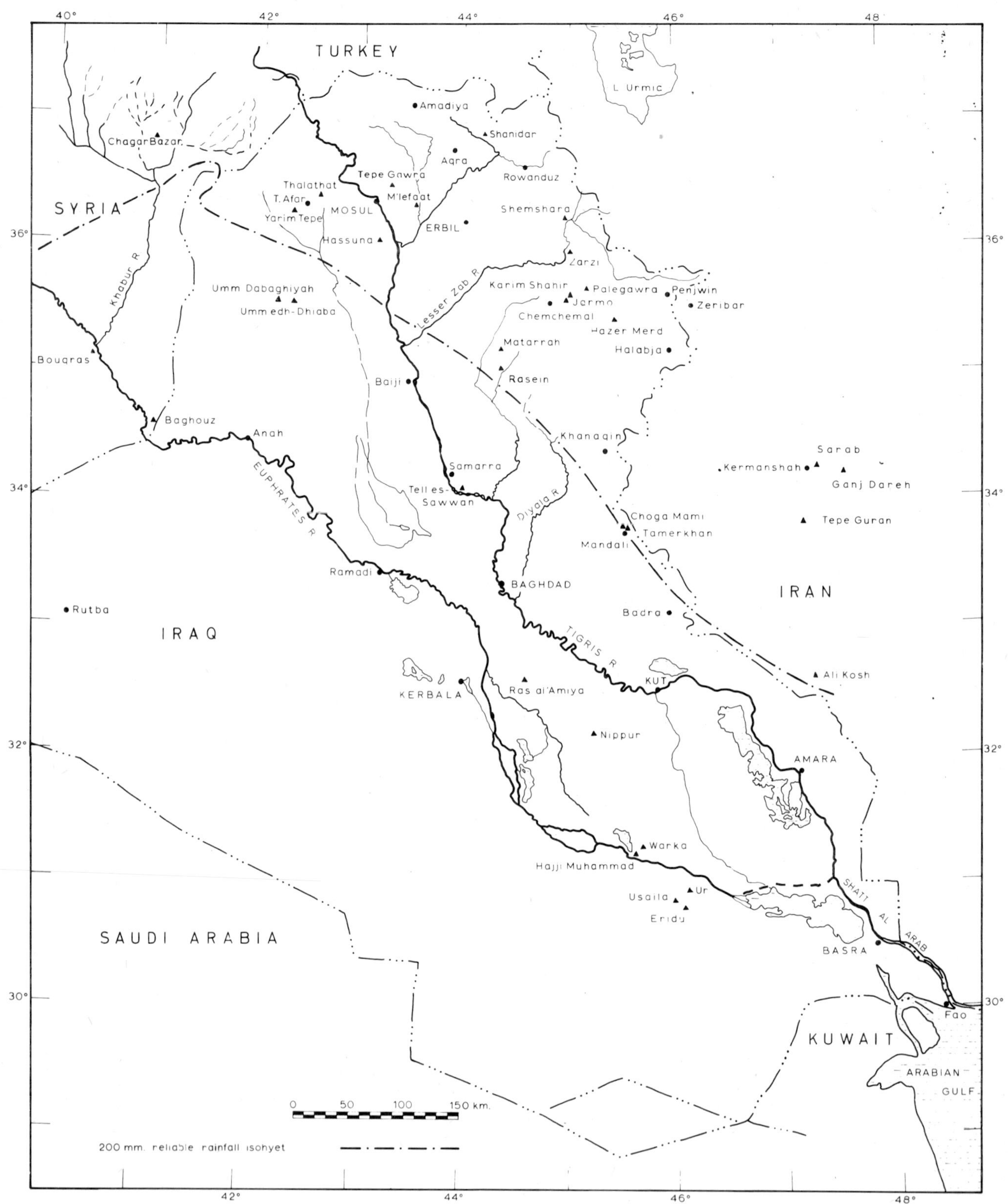
TURKEY
SYRIA
IRAQ
IRAN
SAUDI ARABIA
KUWAIT
ARABIAN GULF
L. Urmia
Amadiya
Shanidar
Chagar Bazar
Aqra
Rowanduz
Tepe Gawra
Thalathat
T. Afar
M'lefaat
Yarim Tepe
MOSUL
ERBIL
Shemshara
Hassuna
Zarzi
Khabur R.
Lesser Zab R.
Karim Shahir
Palegawra
Penjwin
Umm Dabaghiyah
Jarmo
Zeribar
Umm edh-Dhiaba
Chemchemal
Hazer Merd
Matarrah
Halabja
Bouqras
Baiji
Rasein
Baghouz
Anah
Khanaqin
Sarab
Kermanshah
Ganj Dareh
Samarra
Tell es-Sawwan
EUPHRATES R.
Diyala R.
Choga Mami
Tamerkhan
Tepe Guran
Mandali
Ramadi
BAGHDAD
Rutba
Badra
TIGRIS R.
KUT
Ali Kosh
KERBALA
Ras al'Amiya
Nippur
AMARA
Warka
Hajji Muhammad
Usaila
Ur
Eridu
SHATT AL ARAB
BASRA
Fao
0 50 100 150 km.
200 mm. reliable rainfall isohyet
40°
42°
44°
46°
48°
36°
34°
32°
30°

Figure 1.

reserves of seed that they have stored for the next season. It is therefore interesting, and perhaps relevant to the question of marginal climatic differences, to note that our incomplete surveys show both a relatively high frequency of sixth-millennium sites in the medium-risk zone and a considerable scatter of smaller settlements of the same date in the high-risk zone on the border of the steppe. We must apparently postulate either a more reliable rainfall pattern in these areas or a much more elaborate economic organization dependent on urban centres. We know from Çatal Hüyük and Jericho that such centres existed by 6000 B.C.; we know nothing of the status, extent or organization of contemporary Nineveh, because it is overlaid by the ruins of a much later metropolis, but the possible existence of an influential centre there cannot be discounted in any hypothesis.

The distribution of rainfall through the winter and spring season is no less important than the annual aggregate. Smaller quantities coming at the crucial periods of crop germination and growth will produce a greater yield than far larger amounts falling at the wrong time. In the northern plain, where barley normally ripens about the first week in May, rain in the preceding month is considered essential to 'fill out' the head, and without it the crop will be depleted however wet the winter may have been. Moreover, heavy downpours on land that is subject to accentuated erosion due to long-term deforestation on the nearby hills and the more recent dust-bowl effects of deep ploughing, are more destructive than beneficial. Their penetration is surprisingly small; we have often observed that, after hours of torrential rain that flooded excavations and turned the normally dry watercourses into torrents, the topsoil was wet to a depth of, at most, only fifteen to twenty centimetres. Tell Afar's highest annual aggregate, 478 mm. in 1945-46, included 105 mm. that fell in May, a month when most of the rainfall results from thunderstorms, and the result would have been to beat down the ripened grain and empty the heads; when this occurs the most that can be recovered is a poor, self-sown crop in the following year.

In 1971 there was no winter rain in the plains of Mosul or the northern steppe from the beginning of November. The crop was a complete failure, as were the spring pastures. Many villages on the border of cultivation were deserted, and thousands of sheep that normally grazed west of the Tigris were transported, with the shepherds and their households, to the valleys of Kurdistan. The expenses of this mass exodus were met by selling animals, and the price of a sheep dropped from £10 to little more than £2. In this year, abnormally heavy rains in April and early May served only to cause flooding and disrupt transport. The widespread nature of this catastrophe is reflected in the reports, during the following winter, of deaths in many parts of Iraq caused by eating imported seed grain that had been chemically treated against disease.

From Baiji (latitude 34° 56′) southwards, irrigation is now necessary to enable winter crops to be grown. This can be seen in the rainfall pattern but it must be remembered that other factors affect the amount of moisture available to plants. These include dewfall, cloud cover, temperature, wind and soil type. In the winter months, dew undoubtedly provides useful additional moisture in the southern plains but for long periods, some 5-6 months even in northern Iraq, dewfall is either virtually non-existent or so minimal as to be of little benefit (Guest 1966:59). Summer in the alluvial plain is a season of extremely high temperatures, almost total lack of cloud cover, relatively low humidity and drying winds. This results in rates of evaporation so high that water loss actually exceeds the annual rainfall, often by as much as twenty to forty times (Guest 1966:18). Summer gardens must be protected both from the withering sun and from desiccating winds, and the use of a belt of trees or a brush shelter for this purpose is recorded as early as the Sumerian period (third millennium B.C.) (Kramer 1956:66). It should be noted that humidity in places near the Gulf, like Basra and Fao, is significantly higher than in the more waterless areas of the alluvium and that in this southernmost area higher rainfall also contributes to a greater total moisture.

Over most of Iraq the short cool winter lasts only from December to February, but the January mean temperature for much of the area that constituted ancient Sumer falls to between 10° and 12°C. (Repub. Iraq *Climat. Atlas*, n.d.:32). This is considered to be near the critical point for plant growth in Iraq and where the mean January temperature is not materially above 10°C. the winter growing season is interrupted. Thus, in many areas of the alluvium some of the benefit of the winter rain is lost, in terms of plant growth.

Ecology

Geographers and botanists, not to mention archaeologists, vary in their use of terms to describe the physical environment of the northern and southern plains of Mesopotamia. The boundary between northern 'steppe' and southern 'desert' lies very approximately on the 35th parallel of latitude at an altitude of 150 m. But the use of such descriptive terms can be very misleading to anyone unacquainted with the real nature of the countryside. The distinction between 'steppe' and 'desert' is, in many respects, an arbitrary one, and a truer picture of the land surfaces and vegetation of southern Iraq would undoubtedly be conveyed by the term 'dry steppe'. Zohary (1950:9) defines steppes and deserts as 'open plant communities, both limited as to climatic conditions which do not allow the development of an arboreal vegetation', and argues that they are distinguished from one another mainly by the degree of vegetation coverage. In the true steppe, rainfall is sufficient to enable vegetation to form a close network of plant roots which survive the hot dry summers and play an important part in preventing soil erosion. The critical limit of atmospheric moisture below which plant life ceases to exist is, moreover, relative. For southern Jordan this limit has been found to be approximately 100 mm., while for northern Egypt and for the western Negev it lies far below this level, owing to the proximity of the Mediterranean. In Iraq the critical limit is considerably higher, and one finds 'deserts' even in areas receiving over 150 mm. of rainfall annually.

Guest and al-Rawi in *Flora of Iraq* (1966:69) distinguish between extreme or absolute desert and a less extreme category, sub- or semi-desert, which 'provides grazing, though often bad grazing, at all seasons'. They classify by far the greater part of the desert region of Iraq as sub-desert and go on to say that, taking the region as a whole, there are few natural areas of any size where plant cover is so scanty that, provided drinking water is available, it cannot support animal life. Broadly speaking, the factor that inhibits grazing throughout the year is not lack of vegetation, except locally in areas of edaphic or secondary desert, but lack of water-points at which animals may drink during the long dry summer season. Where well-water is available, flocks and herds can generally subsist in the 'desert' regions of Iraq throughout the year. Apart from perennial wells, water can often be found in rain-pools and depressions during the winter months and, except in abnormally dry seasons, there are few areas that cannot support an appreciable population of nomads. Regular cultivation is impossible even in the semi-desert areas without irrigation, however, although in wet years nomads raise catch-crops of grain in wadi-beds and natural hollows.

The irrigation potential of the different regions of the plain is discussed below, but at this point we must recall the existence of another feature of the southern landscape in both ancient and modern times. For thousands of years the rivers have discharged the bulk of their flood-waters, together with enormous quantities of silt, into vast areas of lagoon and marsh; R.C. Mitchell (1958) estimates an annual soil increment in the plains of 47.5 million tonnes from combined flood silt and wind-blown deposits. That the marshes have not long ago silted up is due to the periodic subsidence of the whole basin in response to recent and episodic tectonic movements in the adjacent mountain chains (Lees & Falcon 1952; Mitchell 1958). At the present time the marshes consist of some 6,000 sq. miles of lakes and waterways, interspersed with beds of reeds, bulrushes and sedges. Fish and wild-fowl are plentiful, and wild boar are found in large numbers; all are resources that could have been exploited by a prehistoric population, together with the giant reeds (*Phragmites communis*) from which the modern inhabitants still make their houses and rafts as well as matting for export to other areas.

These marsh areas offer not only additional resources in an otherwise 'desert' environment but would in the past have offered profitable niches for semi-settled but non-agricultural communities. Moreover, there is evidence to suggest that both seasonal and permanent swamps formed a much more conspicuous part of the ancient landscape. Their presence in now-desiccated regions east and north of the site of Warka in central Sumer is inferred from prehistoric settlement patterns (Adams & Nissen 1972:86) and there is similar evidence for the northern, Akkadian, part of the plain (Jacobsen 1958:83). Moreover, excavation reports for virtually every site in Sumer, with the exception of Eridu which clearly stood on a ridge or dune, mention the swamp or marsh-like nature of the soil on which prehistoric settlements were founded. There is evidence, too, that early settlers much further north, in areas where rainfall may have been marginal for agricultural purposes, also looked for sites in the neighbourhood of marshy areas. At Umm Dabaghiyah, in the northern steppe, palaeobotanical samples from the earliest settlement indicate the presence nearby of apparently saline swamps (Helbaek 1972b:17) and at Choga Mami the presence of the marsh plant *Salsola* is noted (Field 1969:141; Oates 1969:143). A point of interest is that sea-blite, a marsh plant reported both from Umm Dabaghiyah and Choga Mami, is still collected and sold as a salad-green in Kuwait today (Helbaek 1972b:19, Table 2).

Thus, the ancient environment in Sumer may have been far less hostile than might at first appear. In ancient times even the sub-desert vegetation was undoubtedly denser than it is today; even today, in depressions and other favourable habitats, the coverage of vegetation may exceed 70% while, after a wet winter, the herbage may become 'almost luxuriant' during its short-lived spring growing season (Guest & al-Rawi 1966:71). In the natural state, tamarisk and poplar were probably characteristic trees of the river embankments in association with oleander, acacia and thorny *Zizyphus*. But the seasonally inundated flats would be parched by early summer, permitting a vegetation of brush and grasses only, while beyond the floodplain, plant growth would generally have been limited to desert or semi-desert scrub. Dense thickets of tamarisk, poplar and *Zizyphus* persist even today in narrow intermittent strips along the rivers and on riverain islands, although such tree cover has been very greatly diminished by wood-cutters and fuel-gatherers. Much of this destruction has taken place within living memory: *Haloxylon ammodendron*, which is characteristically associated with sand-dune areas of the desert, has in recent years almost disappeared from the *jazirah* or northern steppe. In 1954 Guest and al-Rawi found only isolated shrubs in the Wadi Tharthar, some 50 km. north-east of Ramadi, where the guide remembered 'extensive thickets' only thirty years before. In modern times the process of destruction has been much speeded up by charcoal-burners who are brought by lorries and left for some days in the desert. The charcoal from *H. ammodendron* is of such a high grade that not only are the trees cut but the roots are dug out as well, thus totally destroying this useful resource.

Ancient climate

Most discussions of ancient settlement and agriculture in Mesopotamia assume a climate and environmental setting comparable with those of today, although noting the probability of much greater areas of natural vegetation in the sub-desert even in relatively recent times. Although we can be reasonably certain of the essentially arid nature of the alluvial plain throughout the periods with which we are concerned, the question of ancient climate undoubtedly affects assumptions about marginal areas in which are situated sites like Choga Mami that have produced much of our hard evidence. In considering the question of ancient climate one must insist emphatically that the evidence available to us is far too limited in its scope and quantity to support *any* generalizations or far-reaching conclusions. Nevertheless, the question is of such importance as to justify suitably cautious attempts to rationalize what evidence there is.

This evidence is of two sorts. One derives from a limited number of pollen cores, for the most part from the mountainous areas surrounding the Mesopotamian plains. The other is based on archaeological evidence for farming communities practising rain-fed agriculture in areas that would now be described as climatically marginal. In general the palynological evidence for the period between *c.* 35,000 and 14,000 B.P. would seem to indicate a period of relative dryness characterized by the absence of oak pollen in the Zagros mountains where the deciduous oak now constitutes an important element in the present summer-dry forests. After 14,000 B.P. trees began to spread from their refuge areas, and the occurrence of oak charcoal at the cave site of Palegawra (Braidwood & Howe 1960:59) confirms the presence of this tree. Between *c.* 10,000 and 8,000 B.P., the period in which the beginning and early spread of agriculture in the Near East appears to have taken place, 'steppe forest' is apparently found in areas where oak forest now constitutes the natural vegetation (Van Zeist 1969:43). This would imply that in the crucial period between 8,000 and 6,000 B.C. the climate had a 'drier' character than today, and the vegetation would generally have been more open than later in the Post-Glacial. This pollen evidence is contradicted to a certain extent by that of archaeology. The geographical position of sites like Ramad near Damascus, Beidha in western Jordan, Ali Kosh in Iranian Khuzistan, Abu Hureyra in north Syria, from which there is early evidence for cultivation of cereals and other crops, cannot be reconciled with an assumption of less rainfall. Moreover, early in the eighth millennium B.C. wild einkorn constituted a substantial part of the diet of early villagers at Mureybit, not far north of Abu Hureyra, where einkorn will not now grow. At Umm Dabaghiyah which lies in the northern Jazirah at the very edge of present possible, but unreliable, rain-fed cultivation, the evidence for agriculture is perhaps less conclusive (Helbaek 1972b), but there is proof of the existence of marshes nearby and it is clear that the area was undoubtedly wetter *c.* 6,000-5,000 B.C. than it is today. In the same area are a number of small Hassuna/Samarra sites that can only have been agricultural settlements.

Van Zeist attempts to reconcile this conflicting evidence by suggesting that during the period *c.* 8,000-6,000 B.C. annual precipitation was not less than it is today but that as a result of higher temperatures, or of a longer rainless period, the summers were drier. A glance at the rainfall figures (Table 1) will show that it would indeed be difficult for summers to be drier than they are now, even in the mountainous regions of Iraq where virtually no rain falls between May and October. We know that wild cereals grew and matured in the Zagros during this period. Their normal harvest now falls in May and June, the wild forms ripening slightly later than domestic varieties (Bor 1968). Any *longer* summer dryness must thus have been accompanied by higher temperatures to encourage earlier ripening as any shortening of the present rainy season would certainly have been detrimental to cereal crops, assuming that their growth cycle has not changed. Certain of the pollen evidence might also suggest higher temperatures for this period. The Lake Zeribar core shows a sharp increase in *Plantago c.* 9,000 B.C. Today plantain is more common in the pollen rain of the lower steppe than at higher elevations. Thus, this trend would seem to indicate a climate both warmer and drier than that of today at Lake Zeribar (Wright 1968:337). No pollen cores are available for Mesopotamia itself, so that it is difficult to say how far these apparent trends in the Zagros are relevant to what is, today, an environment of desert and steppe at lower elevations, although a pollen core from the Ghab valley in north-western Syria seems to show an approximately similar pattern (Niklewski & Van Zeist 1970).

The question of climate is crucial, not only to patterns of ancient settlement and their economies, but also to the assumed distribution of the wild cereals and other potentially cultivable crops. Wild emmer, which is the most demanding of the wild cereals in its requirements, is now found in oak forest and open grassy places in coppiced oak scrub, at an altitude of 700-1450 m. (Bor 1968:204). Wild einkorn also is common in the lower forest zone of Iraq, on grassland on lower limestone mountain slopes and in degraded oak forest and oak scrub, at 700-1300 m. (Bor 1968:200), although its major modern distribution is on interior plateaux and in the mountains as high as 2000 m., in particular on the basaltic slopes of volcanic mountains in south-eastern Turkey (Harlan & Zohary 1966:1078). In considering the palynological evidence for climate, one is driven to speculate that if oak woodlands did not occur in the Zagros region before *c.* 9,000 B.C., emmer may also have been absent at that time; it is conceivable also that wild einkorn may have been more common in the Zagros foothills and in the Mesopotamian piedmont than it is today (Wright 1968:338). Even more relevant to our present subject is the evidence for barley, which has a much lower distribution than the wild wheats and is more tolerant of arid conditions. There is indeed a special 'wadi' race of barley that thrives at elevations from *c.* 600 m. to 350 m. below sea level in the Jordan rift. 'It is a small, slender, very "grassy" type, easily distinguished from the more robust races of the lower, oak woodland belt. Intermediate types are often found about the edges of the plains and deserts, and when the Bedouin cultivate a little barley in the wadi bottoms in good years, hybrid-swarms between the wild wadi race and cultivated barley can be found' (Harlan & Zohary 1966:1076). The more common forms of wild barley may also have had a lower distribution than today in the period before 9,000 B.C.; and Wright goes so far as to suggest that at that time wild barley may even have been 'confined to the now-desert Arabian Peninsula' (1968:338). Should this prove to have been the case, there would be no need to assume that cultivated barley must have been introduced into

Sumer and the history of agriculture in the now arid regions of Mesopotamia and Khuzistan would present a significantly different aspect.

Unfortunately we do not know the climate of Sumer during this period or even *c.* 5,000 B.C. when we find evidence for the first agricultural settlements. One can safely assume its essential aridity, but a very marginal increase in precipitation, given the right distribution, might have made possible the cultivation of barley without irrigation. Even today, such cultivation is frequently, though not reliably, possible on suitably moist soils, e.g. in wadi bottoms. Emmer is a more sensitive crop, however, and its presence in late 'Ubaid times (p.109) almost certainly implies irrigation agriculture.

Although we have no direct evidence for the climate in Sumer, recent discoveries in Saudi Arabia lend credence to theories of a relatively wet phase sometime between 5,500-3,500 B.C. One must understand in this context that a 'relatively wet phase' does not imply any major change in the essentially arid, summer-dry nature of the climate, but would – and clearly did – allow settlements in areas that were at other times hostile. There is even some evidence to suggest a lacustrine environment along the now barren north-east coast of Saudi Arabia, comparable with that of southern Mesopotomia (*inter alia* McClure 1971). Recent soundings on 'Ubaid sites in this area suggest quite rapidly alternating moist and dry periods (Abdullah H. Masry, personal communication). In historical times there is undoubtedly evidence for periods of more dependable rain and of warmer temperatures. One rare example of documentary evidence, a diary or calendar written by Ptolemy (Claudius Ptolemaeus), probably at Alexandria in the second century A.D., certainly shows the normal occurrence of summer as well as winter rain (Lamb 1968:107). The distribution of the date palm in mediaeval times indicates an average temperature in northern Iraq at least marginally higher than today. Muqaddasi (tenth century) mentions this tree as flourishing in the districts of Sinjar and Tell Afar, (Le Strange 1905), whereas today dates fail to ripen north of Hit. No doubt the climate in prehistoric times also varied to a similar degree and one can only conclude that considerable caution is necessary in making sweeping assumptions at any period.

Farming practices

The growing season of cereals, and in fact all major Middle Eastern crops that are known in prehistoric times, is a winter one. Even as late as Sumerian times, in the third millennium B.C., there is no evidence for summer crops (Jacobsen 1958:81), and it seems virtually certain that large-scale summer irrigation is a very late phenomenon. Summer vegetables were undoubtedly grown on a small scale at the edges of drying river-beds, as they are today, and in small gardens, but the staple crops for which we have evidence in prehistoric times are not, in fact *cannot* be, grown in the conditions of a Mesopotamian summer even with irrigation. These winter crops, known today in Arabic as *shitwi*, include barley, wheat, linseed, lentils, vetch and chick peas. Present-day summer crops (*saifi*) include cotton, rice, sesame and millet, none of which appears to have been grown in Mesopotamia before historical times. A single impression of millet is known from the Jamdat Nasr period (*c.* 3,000 B.C.) but this cereal is not common even in later times. Cotton and rice do not appear to have been introduced until the first millennium B.C., while sesame, in spite of the similarity of the Babylonian name *šamšammu*, would seem to have arrived from India in early Islamic times (Helbaek 1966:616-18). Even in modern times winter cultivation remains the more important, and only about a fifth of the land under *shitwi* crops is used for *saifi* cultivation (al-Barazi 1961:71).

The normal pattern of farming before the advent of tractors, modern pump-fed irrigation, fertilizers and crop rotation with such recently introduced nitrogenous crops as alfalfa and berseem clover, must in many ways reflect practices of great antiquity. Fertilizers were never used and the land was restored through weed-fallow rotation. In any single year only about half the available land would be planted to *shitwi* crops, the rest lying fallow and at the same time providing winter pasture. In dry years, when the natural winter growth of annual grasses and legumes was insufficient for pasturage, sheep and goats were, and are, often grazed on young barley shoots, a practice that results, surprisingly, in less than a 10% crop loss (Adams 1965:169). Nowadays, land that is deliberately to be cropped in this way is normally oversown, and impoverished farmers often rent their fields of immature barley to shepherds in need of pasture. That this was an

Table 2 Choga Mami palaeobotanical specimens (*cf.* Helbaek 1972a, 35-47).

		Samarra							Post-Samarra	'Ubaid	E.D.
	Samples:	I	II	III	IV	V	VI	VII	VIII	IX	X
GRAMINEAE											
Aegilops crassa	Goat-face grass	—	11	—	—	—	—	—	—	—	—
Aegilops sp..	indet. Goat-face grass	—	—	—	1	1	—	—	—	—	—
Triticum boeoticum	Wild einkorn	—	—	—	1	1	—	—	1	1	—
T. dicoccum	Emmer	—	15	2	1	2	4	—	6	—	1
T. monococcum	Einkorn	—	5	—	5	3	1	—	1	—	1
(Spike parts of	Emmer and einkorn)	—	6	—	—	24	37	18	4	—	38
Triticum aestivum	Bread wheat	2	11	—	2	7	2	—	1	—	—
Hordeum spontaneum	Wild barley	—	14	—	—	—	—	1	—	—	—
H. distichum	(internodes) two-row barley	—	—	—	—	2	—	—	—	—	1
H. vulgare var. *nudum*	Naked six-row barley	2	28	1	1	5	1	—	1	—	—
H. vulgare	Hulled six-row barley	—	1	—	—	—	—	—	—	—	—
Hordeum sp.	indet. hulled barley	7	46	2	4	6	5	1	5	5	5
Avena ludoviciana	Wild, large-grain oat	—	8	—	—	1	—	—	—	—	—
Avena sp.	Wild, small-grain oat	—	—	—	5	—	—	—	1	—	—
(Small grasses:)											
Lolium temulentum *L. persicum* *L. rigidum* *Gramineae* spp.	Darnel Persian rye grass Swiss rye grass Other small grasses	24	†	21	97	†	†	49	126	8	33
Bromus spp.	Brome grasses	—	16	1	1	2	—	1	—	—	2
Phalaris paradoxa	Canary grass	43	4	—	3	—	—	—	—	—	—
CYPERACEAE											
Scirpus tuberosus (tuber)	Tuberous rush	1	2	—	—	—	6	—	1	1	—
Scirpus tuberosus (fruit).	Tuberous rush	—	7	—	—	1	1	—	—	—	—
LILIACEAE											
Muscari longipes	Grape hyacinth	—	17	—	2	11	—	1	—	—	—
CHENOPODIACEAE											
Suaeda maritima	Sea-blite	—	2	—	—	—	—	—	—	—	—
FUMARIACEAE											
Fumaria parviflora	Fumitory	—	1	—	—	—	—	—	—	—	—
CAPPARIDACEAE											
Capparis spinosa	Caper	—	4	—	1	—	—	—	—	—	—
MIMOSACEAE											
Lagonychium farctum	Prosopis (Ar.: Shōk)	—	7	—	—	5	3	—	4	—	2
PAPILIONACEAE											
Medicago (*hispida* type).	Medick	1	48	2	3	15	4	—	2	—	1
Small legumes et spp. al.	(mainly Clovers)	1	†	—	13	25	2	3	14	—	7
Astragalus sp.	Milk-vetch	—	—	—	—	—	—	—	—	—	2
Vicia spp./*Lathyrus* spp.	Vetch/vetchling spp.	—	26	—	6	21	18	1	4	—	—
Pisum sp.	Pea	—	3	—	1	1	—	—	—	—	—
Lens esculenta	Lentil	2	30	3	8	11	15	3	10	5	—
Lathyrus sativus	Blue vetchling	—	—	—	—	—	—	—	—	1	—
LINACEAE											
Linum usitatissimum	Flax or linseed	2	39	4	3	21	11	1	3	—	—
ANACARDIACEAE											
Pistacia atlantica	Pistachio	—	12	1	—	11	1	1	4	—	2
RUBIACEAE											
Galium tricornutum	Corn bedstraw	—	1	—	—	—	—	—	—	—	—
Galium ceratopodium	Swamp bedstraw	—	7	—	—	5	—	—	—	—	—
Rubia sp.?	Madder?	—	†	†	—	—	—	—	—	—	—
COMPOSITAE											
Compositae sp.	indet. flower head	—	—	—	—	1	—	—	—	—	—

† = Uncounted quantities from *c.* 500 to *c.* 1,200 specimens.

ancient practice can be seen from the Code of Hammurapi (57-8).

The normal time for sowing winter cereals is October to November and the crops ripen in April to May. With irrigation, barley can be sown as early as September, but in rain-fed areas planting must await the autumn rains and must, therefore, sometimes be delayed until December. Wheat and linseed are normally planted in late November or even December, and in abnormally dry years wheat can be planted as late as January. Earlier sown crops produce better yields than late plantings, as the ripening takes place in the early spring when crops are less likely to suffer from pests, plant diseases and dust storms. We know from Sumerian and Akkadian sources that sowing began as early as September, lasting till December, and that considerable attention was given during the late spring and summer months to the preparation of the recently flooded land (Landsberger 1949). Barley is grown more widely in the irrigated areas than wheat, as it has a shorter growing season, requires less water and can endure a greater degree of soil salinity.

Tillage practices, in the few areas where agriculture is not yet mechanized, are primitive but practical. Ploughing is still carried out with a wooden ard-type or 'breaking' plough, drawn by oxen. Modern mould-board ploughs are less suitable, as deep ploughing destroys the plant roots that hold the soil together and leads to heavy wind erosion and soil drift. Shallow tillage with an ard-type plough is generally recognized as particularly suitable in semi-arid regions where winter cereals are grown and conditions are generally warm and dry (White 1967). We do not know how early the Mesopotamian plough was invented, but there is evidence for domesticated cattle, capable of pulling ploughs, at the time of the earliest agricultural villages in the plains (Umm Dabaghiyah, Yarim Tepe). Certainly the increase in the number and size of 'Ubaid settlements must reflect some improvement both in agricultural methods and tools, and it is conceivable, indeed probable, that plough cultivation accompanies irrigation agriculture in the earlier Samarra period (Oates 1972:305).

The earliest pictographic tablets, some time before 3,000 B.C., illustrate the plough thus:

and several types of plough are referred to in texts of the Sumerian period. At the present day, seeds are usually broadcast by hand, often without furrowing or harrowing, but a seeder-plough was known in Sumerian times (Salonen 1968: Taf. VI). An instrument known as the *ḫarbu*-plough was apparently used to break up the soil while the *epinnu*-plough drew the furrow into which it dropped the seeds (CAD 6:98). Ploughshares, literally the 'tongue of the plough', when used, were of bronze until iron came into general use in the first millennium B.C. The ground was broken up several times by hand before ploughing, however, and a Sumerian 'Farmers' Almanac' (Kramer 1963:340-2; Salonen 1968:202-12) gives lengthy instructions concerning the preparation of land for planting. In this, the farmer is told to plough eight furrows to each strip of about six metres; this refers to planting, however, and takes place only after extensive hoeing, harrowing, raking and 'hammering'. The Almanac continues: 'Brook no interruptions. Do not distract your field workers. Since they must carry on by day and by heaven's stars for ten days, their strength should be spent on the field, and they are not to dance attendance on you.'

As we have seen, the time of autumn ploughing, and consequently the planting, is determined by the timing of the first rain or the availability of irrigation water. The Sumerian almanac instructs the farmer to irrigate his wheat or barley four times, a practice in line with modern usage; grazed barley would receive an additional irrigation. Fields might also be irrigated after the harvest, to encourage the growth of weeds for summer pasture.

Reaping was carried out by hand sickle. In the earliest periods the blades were of flint while in southern Mesopotamia, which lacks both stone and metal, surprisingly effective clay sickles were employed until metal came into more common use. Threshing was carried out immediately after the harvest and in Sumerian times, as now, was done by means of a sledge with flint or metal blades which is drawn over the heaped-up grain stalks. Pitchforks were used for winnowing. Threshing and winnowing, even now, are very slow operations and often last from July to October, leaving little time for other work (Admiralty Handbook:451).

It is very difficult to obtain reliable figures for average yields at the present day, partly because under the prevalent share-cropping system the peasant has an interest in under-estimating, the landlord in over-estimating the yield. Estimates for irrigated land go as high as 1,400 kg. of barley per hectare and 1,100 kg. of wheat (Adams 1965:17) while official government figures for barley give 800 kg./ha. for rain-fed and 1,000 kg./ha. for irrigated land. Other figures, both ancient and modern, suggest a range for irrigated barley between 300 and 1,200 kg./ha., the differences depending on such factors as soil salinity, fallow ratio, type of land tenure, amount of seed corn, etc. Poyck (1962) gives an average for small-holdings of 720 kg. of barley and 520 kg. of wheat per hectare.

At present, on irrigated land, a family of six needs six hectares for its support at subsistence level and without lowering the fertility of the soil. Half this land would lie fallow, while the other half should produce a minimum of 1,500 kg., of which the family need consume no more than 600 kg. A tonne of grain would easily supply an adequate diet for such a nuclear family and figures used by the International Bank for Reconstruction (1952) for the economic development of Iraq suggest this minimum requirement. The Iraq Development Board regarded the cultivation of 12.5 ha. as within the theoretical capacity of such a family, so six hectares would certainly not overtax its resources and, on fertile irrigated land, could well produce as much as 3,000 kg. of barley on a half-fallow system. It would follow that *maximum* population figures, assuming plough cultivation, can be calculated at the rate of six hectares of land per family of six and minimum figures on fully occupied agricultural land at about ten to twelve hectares per family.

The area that can be maintained with small axe and hand hoe is, of course, considerably smaller than with a plough. Allan (1972) estimates it as about one-half hectare per head. With a minimum acceptable cereal yield of 550 kg. per hectare on a simple fallow system of one to four years, and a diet supplemented by hunting, fishing and gathering such as the evidence from all early village farming sites attests, the land requirement would be about one and a half hectares of cultivable land per head of population. This is half as much again as the minimum requirement where the plough is used. Land varies greatly in cultivability, but in general the carrying capacity, in terms of population, of early agriculture in the Near East may have been as much as 200 times as great as that of earlier exploitive economies (Allan 1972:215).

Town populations today are about 50% agricultural but the unusually high figure of 75% at Tell Afar (D. Oates 1968:16) may come closer to later prehistoric town averages. A family size of approximately six remains surprisingly constant through modern town and country populations (al-Barazi 1961:228-30). A further factor that must be kept in mind in calculating ancient town or village populations is accessibility of land. There is a limit beyond which agricultural workers will not walk to their fields; in modern practice in northern Iraq we have found this limit to be roughly seven kilometres. On large holdings, farm workers camp on the land at crucial times such as the harvest but this does not, of course, affect the overall population supported by any given area, though it permits a greater number of households to be concentrated in individual settlements during most of the year. Direct evidence of such a practice in prehistoric times is unlikely to be forthcoming, owing to the very impermanent nature of the camps. Density of population is a variable factor but it may be noted that as settlements increase in size, houses tend to be constructed closer together and less land within the settlement area lies unoccupied (see also Oates 1972:301).

After the harvest, sheep and goats are grazed on the stubble. In the summer, pasturage can be found on irrigated fallow, in river beds and low-lying basins and near permanently flooded areas. Large flocks are taken into the desert with the first autumn rains, and returned in March and April to graze on fallow and waste land. This transhumant pattern allows the exploitation of immense areas. Cattle are herded today for the most part on riverine land with permanent pasture. They are rarely kept primarily for milk as they seldom yield for more than three to four months of the year. Milk products are consumed mainly in the form of yoghurt or cheese made of sheep or goat milk.

A wide variety of native plants grow wild on both cultivated and uncultivated land. Annuals comprise the greatest numbers of species but certain perennials are of great economic importance, the principal ones being *shok* (*Prosopis farcta* or *stephaniosa*), common thorn, and *agul* or camel-thorn (*Alhagi maurorum*). These persist even on cultivated land because the local ploughs penetrate only the surface soil, seldom disturbing their deep and tough roots. Their preservation creates a deep-lying dry zone that helps to prevent the rise of salts in the soil (p.124). Moreover, they constitute the most readily available form of fuel and in this respect are essential to Mesopotamian 'desert' economy. *Prosopis* pods are eaten by shepherds at the present day and clearly provided additional supplies of food in prehistoric times. Both *shok* and camel-thorn grow as weeds in cereal fields and can be found either scattered or in dense thickets over almost every part of the country. In some places along the Euphrates *shok* still forms thickets over two metres high, but elsewhere most of the stands have been trimmed by persistent fuel gatherers.

Another important fuel source is dung. Even today nearly all manure is mixed with straw, kneaded into flat cakes and dried in the sun to provide fuel, particularly for use in bread ovens. This very ancient practice of using dung for fuel, and not for fertilizer, is often criticized as wasteful but Buringh (1960) points out that in arid and hot regions organic manure disappears in a short time, owing to rapid oxidization. 'Therefore soils obtained no benefit from it' and it is more sensible and efficiently used as fuel.

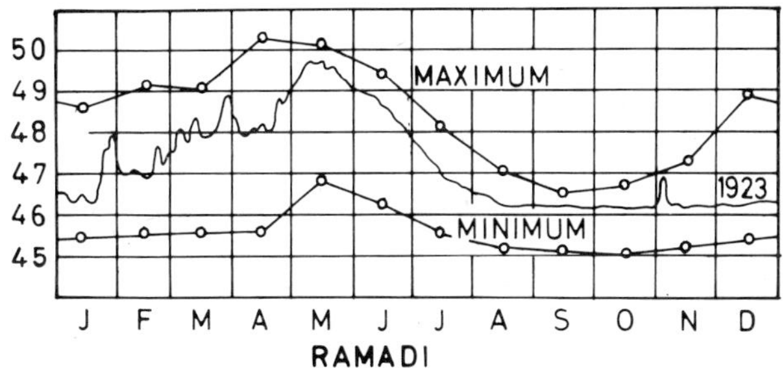

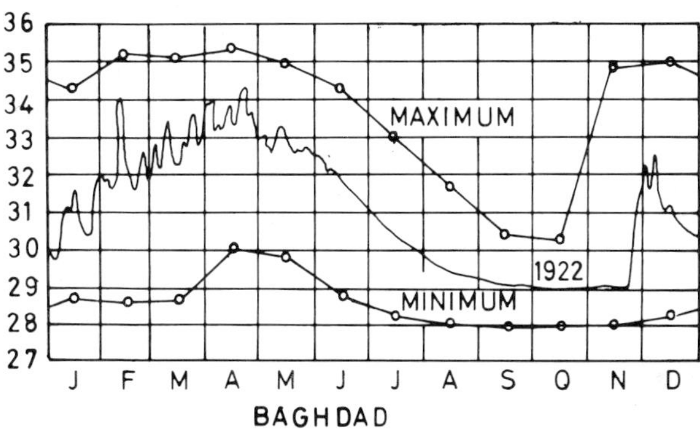

Figure 2. Hydrographs showing Euphrates at Ramadi (1911-32) and Tigris at Baghdad (1906-32), after Ionides (1937), p. 3.

River regimes

In Egypt the gods are truly kind: the Nile floods at the end of the summer: by the end of September the swollen river has inundated the whole of the alluvial plain and by the end of November has receded, leaving moist fields covered with a thin layer of fresh silt, ready and fertile for the annual planting. Thus, the timing of the Nile flood makes possible winter cereal cultivation without recourse to irrigation. A comparable late summer, early autumn flood pattern obtains also in the Indus valley; in both areas, even if winter rains are late, the fields are moist when the time for planting comes. At the same time, the idea of retaining flood-water deliberately and artificially would easily suggest itself as a means of ensuring greater and longer-lasting supplies at a time when they would be agriculturally beneficial. In the valleys of Mesopotamia's two great rivers the situation is quite different. Fig. 2 shows hydrographs of the Euphrates at Ramadi and the Tigris at Baghdad, that is, at approximately the same latitude. The general pattern is similar for both rivers. The first rains in late autumn herald an increase in water-level which continues to rise over the winter months, reaching a maximum in April or May when spring rains coincide with melting snow in the mountains of Turkey and Iran.

The regimes of the two rivers are, however, far from identical. Both rise in the mountains of eastern Turkey but the Euphrates takes a widely circling course to the west, and then flows on through northern Syria, and after its confluence with the Khabur runs through arid country for a distance of some 1,200 km., joined by no perennial tributaries and, at most, occasional spates from deep-cut wadis in the western desert. The Tigris, on the other hand, receives four main tributaries on its left bank within Iraq. The lower reaches of the Tigris are consequently subject to flash-floods resulting from heavy rain, a situation unknown on the Euphrates. Disastrous Tigris floods can occur at any time throughout the spring whereas those of the Euphrates occur more predictably in April or May. The last great Tigris flood, in 1954, occurred early in the spring in February and March: the roads were cut, Baghdad itself was threatened and when the waters finally receded they left a mud deposit some 30 cm. thick. Normally, the floods come later, however, and from June onwards both rivers shrink gradually until, unlike the Nile, they reach their lowest levels in September or October. In the summer there is a great shortage of water and with the rivers low, flow-irrigation becomes extremely difficult.

It can readily be seen that this distribution pattern of river water does *not* well fit the needs of agriculture as described in the previous section. Not only the first rains but the first rise of the rivers may be delayed until December. Once the sowing season is past, both river and rain water tend to increase towards the harvest, but the river then takes the other extreme and more often than not 'threatens with inundation the crops it was with difficulty persuaded to germinate' (Ionides 1937:4-5). For the more recent practice of summer irrigation, conditions are reversed, and water supply dwindles steadily as the season progresses, while the merciless sun shrivels anything that dares to grow.

A further Mesopotamian problem is related to the physical landscape. In Upper Mesopotamia the Tigris and its tributaries flow in deep-cut valleys well below plain level. Here, of course, irrigable land is entirely restricted to the flood-plains within these valleys. In the south both rivers meander over a vast alluvial plain. Their courses tend to be braided and irregular, with large areas of marsh between them and especially to the east of the Tigris. In this unstable situation both rivers are subject to violent floods, which can result not only in the total destruction of villages and ripening crops but also in changes of course that may leave previously prosperous areas of land wholly without water. From Baghdad to the Arabian Gulf, a distance by river of some 900 km., the drop in elevation is only 34 m. with a final fall of only some three metres over the last 160 km. beyond Qurna. This means not only that irrigation water must often be taken from its source well above the actual area to be irrigated, thus adding substantially to the cost in time and labour of canal construction, but that the drainage of water from the land becomes a problem of major import.

Both rivers carry vast quantities of silt which is deposited during flooding in such a way that natural levees are created (Fig. 3). Deposition also raises the river bed, so that the rivers flow substantially above plain level. This makes gravity irrigation simple but flood control difficult. The process is, moreover, self-accelerating, since the higher the levee system the more rapidly the water

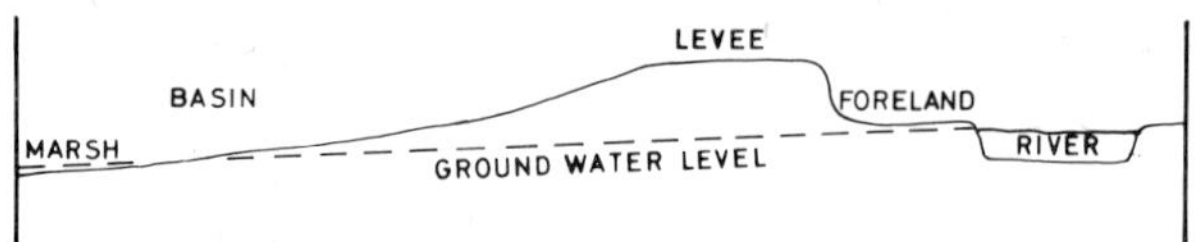

Figure 3. Cross-section of a typical river levee, after Buringh (1957) Fig. 3.

loses velocity when it overflows, thus depositing the greater part of its sediment on the back slopes of the levees. In this way considerable areas of readily drained and easily cultivated soils are created on back slopes and in the higher parts of basins; where flood-water collects in poorly drained depressions the land itself is useless for agriculture but can provide summer pasture, as well as useful drainage for adjacent cultivable areas.

The area of potential cultivation in the southern alluvium is limited both by the amount of river water available and by the quantity that can in practice be diverted on to the land. Surprisingly, in spite of the vast amounts of water that come down in the spate of spring floods, the whole annual flow of the rivers, even if it could be put to use, would prove insufficient to irrigate all the potentially cultivable land in the alluvium (Ionides 1937:5). Since much of the water comes at times when it cannot be of immediate use, and may indeed be destructive to agriculture, storage might provide a theoretical solution. But on a large scale the engineering problems are insuperable, and even if vast reservoirs could be created, evaporation in the great heat of a Mesopotamian summer would substantially reduce their potential. Even today, with a number of modern schemes in operation, large quantities of irrigation water are wasted through inadequate control and the evaporation of excess supplies. The evaporation of undrained excess water encourages salination, and over-irrigation does not contribute to crop growth; it may even impede it.

Crop responses to irrigation water

A great variety of experimental work has been carried out to determine the response of various crops to different conditions of soil moisture, but there are few areas of general agreement owing to the varying nature of experimental treatments and measurements, to a lack of information about the environmental conditions under which experiments have been carried out, and even to fundamental theoretical disagreements on plant development. A differential response to water at various stages of growth has been reported for many, but by no means all, plants and it is at least clear that in interpreting palaeobotanical materials, one cannot assume the beneficial effects of increases in water, even on crop-yield. In many cases, in fact, a slight water deficiency is less harmful to growing plants than an excess of water. In the case of cereals, Guest (1966:73) remarks: 'In the forest zone of Iraq, spring cereals (wheat and barley) suffer from excessive leaching of the soil in years of unusually high rainfall, but give better yields in years of normal or sub-normal rainfall except, perhaps, in the driest parts of the zone.' Moreover, the reaction of a perennial crop to its soil moisture supply depends very much on such other climatic factors as light quantity and temperature (Salter & Goode 1967:192). Undoubtedly for most *annual* crops there is an optimum water regime. The effects of deviations from the optimum are not the same at all times during growth. These crops are especially sensitive to shortage of water from the time of flower initiation, during flowering and, to a lesser extent, during fruit and seed developments. There are other relevant factors such as soil structure and texture, wind, humidity, and dewfall. Dew and atmospheric moisture may in fact increase growth beyond the same amount of water added to the soil because it results in direct rehydration of the plant tissues (Salter & Goode 1967:11).

Wheat, like other cereals, is particularly sensitive to water in the month before earing, but thrives in relatively drier conditions thereafter; irrigation and rain have generally been shown to have the maximum beneficial effects during shooting and earing (Salter & Goode 1967:5, 29). The higher figures for wheat-yields given for irrigated compared with rainfall land in Mesopotamia (see p.120), reflect for the most part an increased number of spikelets, resulting in an overall increase in the number of grains produced from each seed. Palaeobotanists, however, assume an increase also in actual grain-size, but here the experimental evidence is much less conclusive. Salter and Goode (1967:45) state that the length of the moisture-sensitive period has been shown to vary with different cereal crops and with different varieties of the same crop, 'but it usually ends when fertilization occurs', i.e. the later development of the seed or grain itself is unaffected, or certainly less affected, by soil moisture. They go on to say that the main effect of water supply during this critical period of plant development is to influence the *number of grains* formed in the ear, nevertheless adding that moisture conditions at other growth states can also affect grain-yields by their influence on one or other of the components of the yield. For example, tiller number, and hence ear number, is affected by water supply in the early stages of growth, while the *size of grain is affected by conditions after flowering* (Salter & Goode 1967:45). This observation is supported by the view of our Sharqati workmen in northern Iraq, who supplement their income as farmers in a marginal area by seasonal employment on excavations. Their belief, based on experience with locally established varieties of wheat and barley rather than scientific experiment, is that a rain in late March or April is necessary to 'fill out' the head. We have observed that in certain years when the winter rain was sufficient to ensure germination and the crop had grown to a considerable height by late March, a lack of spring rain was accompanied by very small grain size. At present this obviously beneficial late rain is unreliable in marginal areas. If palynologists are right in reconstructing a drier prehistoric climate – and this is not yet generally accepted (p.116) – the lack of late rains might help to account for observable differences in grain size between rain-fed and irrigated crops.

With very few exceptions, experimental results indicate that most of the economically important leguminous crops also have marked moisture-sensitive stages of growth, if seed-yield is taken as the criterion of plant response. Moreover, irrigation given during pod growth influences yield by increasing the 1,000-seed weight (Salter & Goode 1967:59), i.e. the seed-size is or can be affected by soil moisture. In the case of linseed, another crop grown by early farmers in Mesopotamia and elsewhere, one experiment showed that 'the effect of the treatments on the 1,000-seed weight was negligible', while in another 'early periods of drought before flowering *reduced* the 1,000-seed weight' (Salter & Goode 1967:79). Seed yield and oil content are clearly affected by water supply, but observations on seed size or weight are certainly less conclusive. In the Near East, Helbaek has observed a significantly larger size of linseed under irrigation than under rain-fed conditions among specimens of similar date (1960:193; 1972a:39), although it should be pointed out that the largest specimens of all come from Late Assyrian Nimrud, where supplies from both unirrigated and a small area of irrigated land might have been available.

We can only conclude that palaeobotanical evidence for irrigation on the basis of seed size must be interpreted with much caution, but that there are undoubtedly some experimental data to support such conclusions, particularly among annual crops such as wheat and barley, certain legumes and linseed. What there can be no doubt about is the beneficial effect of irrigation in terms of increased yield and this is clearly reflected in ancient figures for crop yields that can hold their own against yields in the best of modern Canadian wheatfields (Jacobsen 1958:81).

Side-effects of irrigation: salination

We have seen how irrigation was essential to the growing of staple crops in southern Mesopotamia and how the application of irrigation water to crops, winter cereals in particular, increased yields sometimes to almost double those on rain-fed land. But not all the consequences of irrigation were to prove beneficial.

The soils of southern Iraq are young alluvial soils, generally of low permeability. In a semi-arid climate, such soils are prone to dangerous accumulations of exchangeable sodium and of salt. For the most part the Mesopotamian salts come from irrigation or flood water and appear to originate in the sedimentary rocks of the northern mountains where both rivers rise. Exchangeable sodium tends to have a detrimental effect on soil texture and may collapse it to almost total impermeability, while excessive concentration of salt is harmful to crops and can eventually render agricultural land totally useless. Salts accumulate steadily in ground-water; hence it tends to be extremely saline and probably constitutes the immediate source of Mesopotamia's saline soils. The distribution over the land of irrigation water in excess of crop requirement leads to percolation to the water-table, which then shows a tendency to rise. In modern times, rises of as much as 60 m. have been recorded over a few decades in India and Pakistan (Hutchinson 1969:131). When the water-table reaches levels one to two metres below the surface, not only do drainage problems arise but with wet soils sodium and dissolved salts are brought by capillary action into the root zone or even to the surface. Concentrations of salts in the root zone and upper soil layers begin to be injurious to agricultural crops when they reach 0.1-0.2% and land becomes unusable for normal cultivation at concentrations of from 0.5-1.0% (Jacobsen 1958; Jacobsen & Adams 1958).

Ancient farming practices, in particular fallow rotation, were particularly well-suited to alleviating the problems of saline soils. The deep-rooted leguminous perennials *shok* and *agul* (p.120) mature relatively late. Thus not only do they not compete for water with crops in which they grow as weeds but they actually dry out the soil by using up water left in it, thereby lowering the water-table. As a result, at the end of an eighteen-month idle period the soil is usually dry to a depth of at least two to three metres. Moreover, the first subsequent applications of irrigation water dissolve surface salts and, particularly when extra water is applied, carry them back down to the subsoil. Thus over-irrigation, a practice often criticized, actually helps to leach the soil (Buringh 1960:250). Flood water can have a similar effect in helping to leach saline soils. Russel (1957) has calculated that the ancient fallow and idle land systems with the aid of *shok* and *agul* enable farmers to use land for about 450 to 500 years. Then salt concentrations reach a point where the land to be reclaimed must be abandoned for a very lengthy period, during which the ground-water tends to fall to a depth of five to seven metres and further, extensive leaching becomes possible. Thus the generally unusual feature of 'shifting cultivation' on irrigated land obtains in many areas of Mesopotamia. Modern agricultural studies in Iraq suggest that as much as 60% of cultivable land has gone out of cultivation through soil salination (Warriner 1969:84), while ancient records establish at least three major debilitating occurrences of salinity in Sumer (Jacobsen & Adams 1958:1252).

The type of weed-fallow cultivation that we have just described is applicable only in the more northerly parts of the alluvial plain. In the marshy regions of the river delta, where the land gradient is virtually nil and ground-water always high, a method of 'isolating' salt areas is now employed. Extra irrigation water is applied to cultivated *shitwi* crops in order to leach salt from the surface soil. As there is a hydraulic gradient, the resulting saline ground-water is 'pushed' to adjacent fields deliberately left 'idle' for the purpose of allowing salts to rise and accumulate on the surface.

Effective drainage is, of course, always an answer to salination but it would be difficult to think of a better method of coping with problems of salinity on virtually level land, as in the delta areas of Sumer, than in this clearly very ancient practice.

Irrigation presents another major problem in that not only do artificially constructed canals require regular cleaning but, often, the deposition of silt is such that even the natural river-bed must be treated in the same manner, to enable water to continue to flow in the desired direction. The very heavy silt content of the rivers tends not only to raise the levels of adjoining levees in flood but also to raise the actual level of the river bed. Processes of scouring in one place and deposition in another are in large part responsible for changes of course, either as a whole body of water or in multiple channels. A higher river or canal bed is, of course, desirable in terms of availability of water, especially in seasons of low water, but deliberate banking to encourage this, or simply as flood protection, ultimately creates a risk of greater flood disaster.

In the case of canals, regular cleaning is essential to maintain a reliable flow of water. When river water enters a canal, or when it overflows a levee, the drop in velocity from that of the river itself leads to an immediate deposition of silt. Thus the head of a canal silts up most rapidly, leading to a decline in its carrying capacity. As flood irrigation inundates only those fields nearest the river, so canal irrigation, unless careful maintenance is carried out, brings water only to those fields nearest the beginning of the canal.

Much has been written on the effects on the development of ancient society of the co-operative efforts required not only in the construction of canals but also in their maintenance, but modern studies have shown that relatively little manpower is required for either purpose, particularly on the scale of irrigation that would have been practicable among early farming communities. Canals must be cleaned before cultivation begins but even with today's sizeable canals the total amount of time devoted to this task is 'remarkably small'. When the work is to be done tribesmen and share-croppers from the area served by the canal are summoned, but each normally contributes his labour for a total of only one or two days. Each man is given a section from which to dig out the accumulated silt; the general expectation is that in a day each man will be able to clear about 4.5 cubic metres of silt (Fernea 1970:130). The work is more arduous than it might seem as the silt must be tossed to the top of banks already piled as much as five to eight metres high. When canal walls become too high, a new canal is dug parallel to the old one. Today on the alluvial plain one can see places where as many as five or six ancient canal beds lie closely beside one another. Small ditches on the scale of those of sixth-millennium Choga Mami (p.132) can be constructed relatively quickly and maintained at a more leisurely pace. The larger canals, up to ten metres wide, however, represent major public works whose excavation and maintenance imply a large labour force. Such construction can, and certainly does, occur gradually, and even in the modern situation existing canals of this scale are only gradually extended, year by year; cleaning must be done by a directed group, however, and is certainly not within the capabilities of a small work force between times of agricultural activity. At Choga Mami such prehistoric canals have been traced some four to five kilometres from the main river source and may have extended still further (see p.129).

Date palm

One aspect of the economy of the southern alluvium has not yet been discussed. Provided it is supplied with water the date palm is 'perfectly adapted to the ecologic conditions of the region' (Guest 1966:62). It matures its fruit only where there are long, hot, rain-free summers, since rain prevents the fertilization of the flowers and the ripening of the fruit. Palms need liberal supplies of water at the roots, but the quality of soil and water is relatively unimportant. In fact, the date palm is more tolerant of soil salinity than any other cultivated crop in Iraq and will even endure unfavourable moisture conditions for years.

The date palm has long been one of the most useful plants known to man; the Greek geographer Strabo refers to a Persian poem extolling 360 uses of this extraordinarily versatile tree. Apart from the fruit, the palm sprout is still a popular vegetable, while the sap can be made into a honey-like syrupy sweetener or a potent alcoholic beverage. Date stones are dried for fuel, particularly for smelting, or may be pounded for cattle fodder. The trunk, though notable for elasticity rather than strength, provides timber suitable for light building construction, boats, furniture and even small canal bridges, while the fibres may be extracted for rope-making. The fronds are widely used to build temporary shelters, and individual leaves for weaving baskets. Most important of all, the fruit, even today, is not a mere sweetmeat in the areas where it is grown, but a staple food. Harvested in late summer, it can then be dried and stored, and provides carbohydrate which eliminates the need for more common staples such as cereals. Together with wildfowl, and fish, that can also be dried and stored, it affords a completely adequate human diet of which all the components are available locally.

One of the most interesting aspects of date cultivation in southern Iraq, and one of particular relevance in an account of early irrigation, is that regular irrigation is provided by nature in the lower reaches of the two rivers. Owing to tides in the Gulf and also to the almost non-existent slope of the land below Basra, which has an elevation of only 2.5 m., the water in the numerous creeks that make up the estuary of the Shatt al Arab is driven inland naturally twice a day. This tidal section at the present day extends over 100 miles upstream and affects 112,000 acres through 70 major creeks (Admiralty Handbook:440). It is felt as far north as Qurna (elevation 3 m.), which was once the junction of the two rivers, 75 km. up river from Basra. The extreme difference today between high and low flood, as affected by the tide and the discharge of the river itself, is about three metres (Willcocks 1911:30). Within this natural tidal area lies the greatest concentration of date palms in the country where, at present, 50,000 ha. of dates are 'naturally' irrigated twice daily (Nelson 1962:71). At the present time, full advantage is taken of this natural irrigation in the growing of summer vegetables among the boles of the palms. Not only does this mean advantageous utilization of the natural irrigation water, but the palms themselves afford protection against the desiccating summer sun and damaging dust storms. It seems not unreasonable to suppose that in such an environment in prehistoric times, an appreciation of the beneficial effects of the artificial application of water to growing plants would easily have been observed and understood. Indeed, in later times, the Garden of Eden was thought to have been situated in this very area.

It should, perhaps, be added that although mature palms can tolerate standing water and can withstand flood-water, young trees must be protected against heavy flooding until they have become sufficiently deep-rooted to survive. Thus, although tidal irrigation provides an ideal environment for palm plantations, palm trees along reaches of the rivers subject to devastating floods must be protected against them.

Ancient irrigation

We have examined the practice of agriculture in Mesopotamia and in particular the techniques and effects, both beneficial and otherwise, of irrigation. It remains to consider how and when such techniques might have developed. It is more than likely that, in certain suitable areas, artificial manipulation or control of water supplies for agricultural purposes may actually have preceded the deliberate sowing of crops. Allan (1972:212) has pointed out that Jericho lies in a situation where irrigation would be technically simple, a matter merely of guiding the flow of water to extend the area of moist soils. Water-spreading of this sort may even have preceded the evolution of cultivars. In Mesopotamia certain localized areas would also have lent themselves to the easy control of irrigation water, for example the estuary of the Shatt al Arab and deltaic fans like those at Mandali and Badra, where river water is easily accessible and the problems of severe flooding on the destructive scale of the Tigris and Euphrates do not arise. There are ethnographic parallels for people who irrigate but do not cultivate, that is, food-collectors who deliberately direct water, often over considerable distances, on to naturally growing crops; this practice is to be found, for example, among certain North American Indians (Forde 1934:35). Thus it is not unreasonable to suppose that similar practices might have been followed in physically suitable areas of the Middle East at an early date.

What is absolutely clear is that the popular reconstruction of newly arrived settlers developing 'basin-flow irrigation' on the alluvial plains of the twin rivers is ill-conceived. In the first place, there is no archaeological evidence whatsoever to support such a movement of people (Oates 1973). We have already seen that there is substantial evidence to suggest that the environment was less hostile than at present, and even some evidence to suggest a marginally wetter phase at the time of the earliest agricultural settlements, in both the northern and southern plains. Resources were more than adequate for *non*-agricultural settlement in the marsh and estuary areas of the south, flocks could survive and catch-crop cultivation was possible without irrigation. Heavy deposits of silt seriously hamper attempts to investigate early archaeological horizons in Sumer, but this is no reason to assume that the area was uninhabited or uninhabitable prior to the time of the agricultural settlements for which we have direct evidence.

In the Nile valley the development of basin-flow irrigation was undoubtedly a simple matter but, as we have observed, in Mesopotamia the rivers flood at the wrong time of year, threatening the harvest, not assisting the planting. It is true that conditions in the higher parts of the natural basins that accompany a meandering, levee-forming river regime (Fig. 3), and on the backslopes of the levees themselves, were highly favourable for cultivation, but the techniques of irrigating winter crops with a spring flood regime are exceedingly complex, requiring far more planned intervention both to provide water when needed and to build embankments to protect ripening crops, than most writers have been willing to concede. Certainly by the time of the 'Ubaid settlements, these techniques must have been well developed, but they must also have been invented long before, not necessarily in Sumer. In Sumer in particular our investigations of these problems are handicapped not only by the inaccessibility of prehistoric evidence but also by the lack of any direct climatic evidence. Nevertheless, the size and extent of the 'Ubaid settlements, together with the evidence for the more demanding cereal, emmer, imply both a relatively complex society and advanced farming methods.

Water control in the tidal estuary and in the marshes would have been less complex, but prehistoric evidence is wholly lacking for these areas. A remark of Wilfred Thesiger's (1967:133) is perhaps of interest in this context. Speaking of a local sheikh in the marsh country, he wrote: 'He was also an efficient landlord, who knew every corner of his estate and had half a century's experience of judging the water-level on which its prosperity depended. He knew exactly when and where to build a dam, when to reduce its waters and by how much. I was always amazed to see the way that deep rivers, fifty yards wide and tearing along in flood, could be dammed with nothing more than brushwood, reeds and earth.' Thesiger also remarks that a great deal of labour was required not only to build such dams but also to clean out the canals and strengthen the banks. It is clear that even in such relatively primitive situations, irrigation and all its concomitant activities require forethought and the expenditure of considerable physical labour, imposing at least a low level of co-operation among farmers using the same water sources.

A further point that may be noted is that the size of settlement increases significantly during the period we are considering. Most farming villages of the Hassuna phase, at least on the plains west of Mosul, where we have examined a large number, are relatively small, often about a hectare in size, sometimes even less. The one early (Jarmo) site in the Mandali area, Tamerkhan, is of approximately the same size. But Samarran sites, which can now be shown to depend on irrigation agriculture, are significantly larger. Choga Mami is some five to six hectares in area, while in the south individual settlements could exceed five hectares by the Hajji Muhammad ('Ubaid 2) period and ten hectares by the end of the 'Ubaid period (Adams & Nissen 1972:11). In the Kish area of Akkad three of the eleven 'Ubaid sites exceeded four hectares in area (Gibson 1972). The best known of these is Tell 'Uqair, where the famous temple overlies what is obviously a large and complex 'Ubaid town. Total populations for these settlements are difficult, even impossible, to calculate as the density tends to increase in proportion to the size, and no site has been excavated over an area sufficient to give a reasonable estimate of density for any period. An average density of *c.* 200 people per hectare is often quoted but one modern population study provides figures ranging from 96 to 395 persons per hectare (Adams 1965:25), and it is more than likely that prehistoric settlements were equally variable. We know, in fact, that they were seldom occupied over their total area. Nevertheless, the general pattern is clear, that from the Samarran period onwards both the size of settlements and their frequency show a significant increase.

Archaeological surveys in Sumer and Akkad also indicate that, in the earliest periods for which we have evidence, villages tended to be aligned along essentially natural watercourses and present an isolated rather than a clustered distribution pattern. We shall see that this is not true of the Mandali area, where irrigation conditions are different and where there is evidence for a considerable concentration of population in the Samarran and 'Ubaid phases. This trend continued with the growth of cities in Sumer in the

Uruk period and an increasing concentration of population in urban centres. Mesopotamian economic potential was, of course, enormous. Once the basic techniques of water management had been learned, the highly fertile alluvial soils were capable of producing vast and, perhaps more important, reliable surpluses. Assuming a general yield of 1,200 kg. per ha. (Herodotus' figures indicate even higher yields) Allan (1972:223) calculates that the Mesopotamian plain could have supported densities of 300 or more people per sq. km., with less than half the population wholly engaged in agriculture, that is, three times the carrying capacity assumed for small-holdings. In the irrigation zone of Mesopotamia there are some twelve million acres of cultivable land, with about ten million in the rainfall zone (Admiralty Handbook:448).

One further aspect of Mesopotamian irrigation must be mentioned. The amount of land that can be irrigated by flow irrigation is limited by the very low land gradients. Thus techniques for lifting water had to be developed in order fully to exploit the land potential. How early this development took place we do not know; the earliest evidence for the *shaduf*, a water-lifting device still in use, is found in the early second millennium (Salonen 1968:230, taf. 4) but some sort of lift irrigation was certainly employed in Sumerian times and may date much earlier (*ziriqu,* CAD 21, 134; it is of interest that this is an Akkadian loan word in Sumerian). In modern times land irrigated by lift is reckoned as more valuable than that irrigated by flow. Where gravity irrigation is employed little actual control of the flow of water is obtained, primitive flooding being normally practised. Water flooded over the land is only partly directed by ditches in modern practice, resulting in much wastage of water and unequal distribution of water over the crop.

Evidence for prehistoric irrigation systems in the Mandali area

We have referred above to evidence of early irrigation that came to light during the excavation of Choga Mami, on the eastern rim of the Mesopotamian plain about 120 km. north-east of Baghdad and 4 km. north-west of the modern town of Mandali. We were drawn to investigate this area because it seemed likely that early prehistoric settlements here might not be completely concealed beneath alluvial deposits as they are in Babylonia and Sumer. A number of sites dating from the Samarra to the Early Dynastic periods were discovered, as well as one earlier site and much evidence of later occupation, and the topography of the area itself proved to be of considerable interest and relevance to the study of early irrigation systems. Our topographical observations were made in such time as could be spared from the excavations and were further hampered by the difficulties of travel, even by Land-Rover, in an area where agriculture and local transport are still almost entirely unmechanized, and any track may be cut at need by an irrigation channel, leaving only a palm-trunk bridge for pack-animals. Consequently, we do not claim to have recovered more than a selection of evidence, and its interpretation is hampered by the fact that modern contour maps, giving an accurate record of the relief, are not yet generally available. Nevertheless, the facts we were able to assemble present a coherent, if incomplete, picture and suggest a pattern of irrigation development that may well have wider relevance.

The dominant physical feature of the area is the outermost crest of the Zagros, known north of Mandali as the Jebel Kahnah Rig, the line of which here marks the frontier between Iraq and Iran. North-west of this ridge, the hills decrease rapidly in height towards the upper Diyala basin. The two perennial streams at either end of the ridge consequently emerge into the plain at markedly different levels (Fig. 4a). The Gangir, flowing past Mandali, debouches from a narrow gap, between Jebel Kahnah Rig and Jebel Komah Sang, at approximately 500 feet above sea-level, while the Ab-i-Naft meets the plains at less than 300 feet and flows southwards just below the 250-foot contour. The westerly slope of the ground at the foot of the hills is further accentuated by what appears to be an alluvial fan radiating from the Gangir gorge above Mandali; its limits cannot be precisely defined without detailed contour survey, but its existence is confirmed by the behaviour of the erosion gullies descending from Jebel Kahnah Rig, which near Mandali itself are diverted from their normal south-westerly course to run almost due west. This effect can be observed as far as the site of Gok Tepe, some 12 km. north-west of Mandali.

These gullies are dry except after rain, when they become swirling torrents fed not only from the hills, but conspicuously by run-off from the surface of the plain which, after a heavy

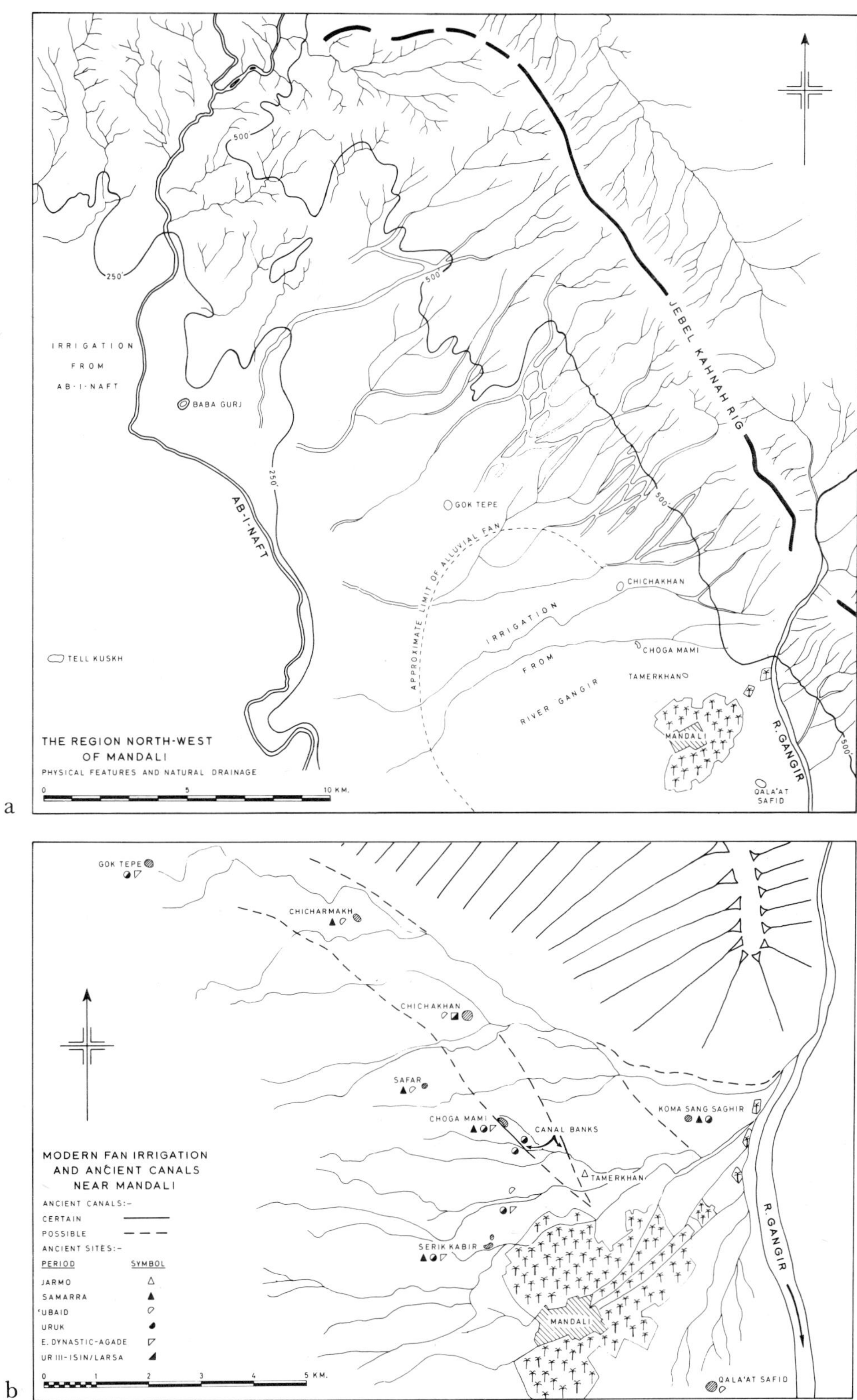

Figure 4. (a) The area north-west of Mandali, showing physical features and the natural drainage pattern; (b) Modern irrigation patterns near Mandali, with traces of ancient canals and selected sites 6,000-2,000 B.C.

downpour, is so impermeable as to present the appearance of a single sheet of water. We have no means of knowing how long the present erosion regime has been in force, but there is evidence to suggest that it has alternated with aggrading conditions on at least two occasions since 6,000 B.C. At the time when Choga Mami was occupied, in the sixth millennium, the land surface around the settlement was clearly rising, and continuing deposition during the Early Dynastic period, *c.* 3,000 B.C., can be demonstrated at the site of Chichakhan, some two kilometres to the north. Here, in the side of a modern gully just north-east of the site, we found pottery kilns with Early Dynastic sherds resting on, and covered by, alluvial deposits. On the other hand, the erosion channels beside the site of Choga Mami showed in their sides the profiles of an earlier gully system that had filled with silt before the current down-cutting regime came into force. Pottery from the beds of the earlier gullies does not, unfortunately, provide any significant dating evidence, since it was of the post-Samarra 'Transitional' type and points only to the erosion of the corresponding levels on the nearby mound, at some time after 5,000 B.C.

As a result of the differences in level noted above, nearly all the land between Jebel Kahnah Rig and the Ab-i-Naft can be irrigated only from the Gangir. The modern system is a fan of small channels, fed from the river at the mouth of the gorge, which water the palm groves of Mandali itself and an area of cereal cultivation to the north-west and west (Fig. 4b), where they follow the contours at the foot of Jebel Kahnah Rig or, in the plain, skirt the low ridges between erosion gullies. The extent of the irrigation fan, which is the simplest and most obvious system available during a down-cutting regime, has obviously varied even in recent times, presumably reflecting security in the region and the available water supply. British Army surveys in 1917 reported wet channels only in the immediate vicinity of Mandali, and after an intervening period of expansion the system is once again threatened with contraction by the cutting off of a large part of the Gangir water within Iran. It should be borne in mind, however, that the economy and the importance of the Mandali oasis was not, in ancient times, wholly dependent on local resources, as it was a staging post on the great highway – the Achaemenid Royal Road – that skirted the foothills of the Zagros from northern Mesopotamia to Khuzistan, and which seems to have been an important commercial route at least as early as the sixth millennium.

It is obvious from the configuration of the land that an improvement in the irrigation system, and an increase in the land available for cultivation, could be effected by replacing the fan of small channels with one or more larger canals running parallel with the line of Jebel Kahnah Rig, although their construction and maintenance would be feasible, without modern engineering methods, only in an aggrading phase when their course was not constantly interrupted by erosion gullies. One of the most interesting results of our work was the excavation of closely datable canals of this type at Choga Mami itself, and the discovery of what appeared to be superficial traces of them elsewhere in the vicinity. Fig. 5 shows a schematic north-south cross-section of the mound and of the slight depression to the south. The vertical scale on the section has been

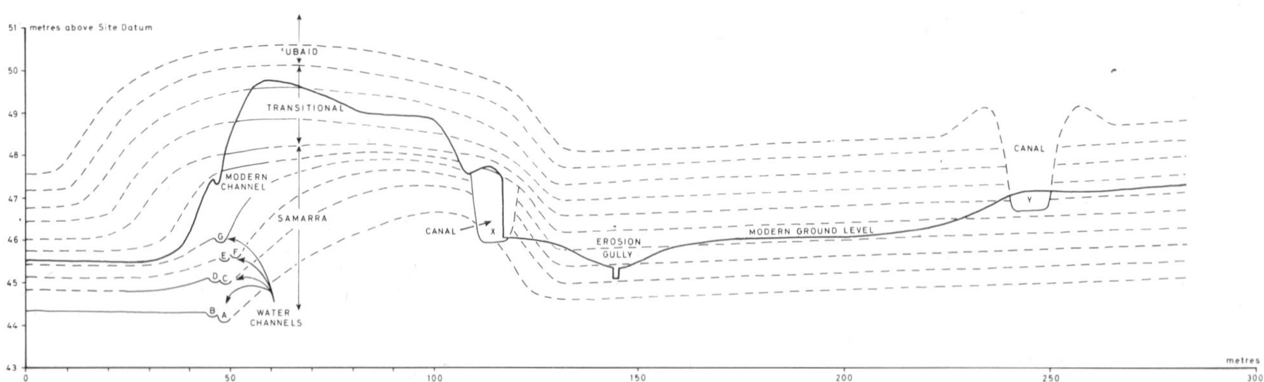

Figure 5. Schematic north-south section through the mound of Choga Mami, showing the relative heights of ancient water channels and canals. The vertical scale is exaggerated ten times.

a

b

Figure 6. (a) View looking south-east from Choga Mami towards Mandali showing spoil banks of an ancient canal and, in the foreground, a modern irrigation channel identical with those of the 6th millennium; (b) The plain north-east of Choga Mami, with Jebel Kahnah Rig in the background. In the foreground, the modern irrigation channel skirting the mound.

exaggerated by a factor of ten for the sake of clarity; this depression, in fact, is relatively insignificant and would probably have been obliterated during an aggrading regime. On the north side of the mound we found a series of small water-channels, some two metres in width (A-G on the section; for a fuller description see Oates 1969). Of these C-G were almost certainly above contemporary ground level outside the settlement, are clearly artificial and must have been used for irrigation. One of the minor channels of the modern fan system (Fig. 6a) now skirts the side of the mound immediately above them, neatly reflecting their location and function. This whole series is stratigraphically associated with occupation levels of the Samarra period within the settlement, but judging by the modern analogy the channels could have formed part of the simpler fan pattern of irrigation. On the south slope of the site, however, a sounding revealed part of the profile of a much larger channel (X on the section) that must have approached ten metres in width, with its bottom at approximately the same level as the small channel G on the north side. This was obviously a major canal, and the pottery recovered from its fill was, again, exclusively of the Samarra period. Although it was excavated only at this point, its course is clearly visible farther to the west, where erosion at the edge of the mound has produced a vertical face consisting of water-laid clay interrupted by thin horizontal bands of a fine-grained red deposit, of the sort we have observed elsewhere as the result of flash-floods in modern seasonal watercourses. Similar red bands were observed in channel A of the northern series, and again in another wide canal bed (Y on the section) revealed by a sounding some 120 m. south of the mound. This would appear to be a later version of canal X; its bottom lies at a slightly higher level, and the fill immediately above the bed yielded waterlogged sherds of 'Ubaid 3 date. The line of this canal is also visible where it cut through a slight elevation about half a kilometre east of Choga Mami (Fig. 6b). Here a site some 200. m. in diameter straddles the canal bed, which is bounded by spoil banks containing 'Ubaid 3 sherds; surface material from the site itself attests 'Ubaid 3-4 and Uruk, as well as some later occupation.

We thus have convincing evidence for small-channel, possibly fan, land irrigation during a considerable period of the Samarran occupation of Choga Mami and for the existence before the end of the Samarran period of a much larger lateral canal, which continued in use, with local realignments to compensate for silting and a rising land level, through 'Ubaid and probably Uruk times. Our observations elsewhere are less specific, but reveal a suggestive pattern. Between Choga Mami and Jebel Kahnah Rig we observed three possible alignments of ancient lateral canals (Fig. 4b). The first branches off the Choga Mami canal just south-east of the possibly seventh-millennium site of Tamerkhan, and then runs almost parallel with it to join the line of the modern watercourse north-east of Chichakhan. On this alignment, about 500 metres north-west of Tamerkhan, we found a group of small low mounds, obviously artificial but with a meagre scatter of pottery that did not suggest a settlement site. We believe that they may represent eroded spoil-banks; the only two identifiable sherds were 'Ubaid and late Uruk in date. The second possible alignment can be discerned crossing the modern road about two kilometres east of Tamerkhan and passing close to the site of Koma Sang Saghir, where there is evidence of Samarra, 'Ubaid 2-4 and Uruk occupation; it joins a modern watercourse at the foot of the hills and follows the contours north-westwards. The third alignment is perhaps a later version of this, taking water from the Gangir where it debouches into the plain, and skirting the foot of the hills to join the second alignment about three and a half kilometres north of Tamerkhan; again, much of its course is approximately followed by a modern channel. Although none of these has been positively identified as an ancient canal line, a series of canals establishing a progressively higher head of water would be a natural answer, either to a continuing rise in land level or to a desire to extend the area of cultivation farther to the north-west. We have already noted the evidence for a rising land level at Chichakhan, where the Early Dynastic ground surface lies 1.4 metres below the modern, presumably eroded, plain level, and the evidence of the successive water channels at Choga Mami leads us to postulate a substantial rate of deposition in the prehistoric period. Our survey is, as yet, too incomplete to define the extent of settlement at different periods, but it is noteworthy that the land around the two large tells that we have examined, Gok Tepe and Chichakhan, could be watered only by canals at a higher level than those at Choga Mami, and that their principal periods of occupation seem to fall respectively in the fourth millennium at Gok Tepe and the third and early second millennia at Chichakhan.

We do not yet know at what date irrigation was first practised in the Mandali region; despite its position on both ancient and modern water channels, there is no direct evidence to associate the Jarmo-period settlement at Tamerkhan with the system. But we have shown that the fan system was established in the Samarra period – in round terms not long after 6,000 B.C. – and that substantial lateral canals were in use before 5,000 B.C. It seems likely that there was then continuous development until the early second millennium; but we must note that, although the irrigated area may have been extended northwestwards along the hills during this time, there is little evidence of an extension to the south-west beyond the alluvial fan of the Gangir, where the majority of the sites examined were Sassanian or Early Islamic in date. Our present, admittedly fragmentary, data suggest a breakdown of the early system some time after 2,000 B.C., a hypothesis that is reinforced from the Diyala basin (Adams 1965), and this breakdown *may* be equated with the first phase of erosion and gully formation referred to above. There was certainly a widespread resettlement in the plain, possibly beginning in Parthian times and certainly flourishing in the Sassanian and Early Islamic periods, but the major irrigation works on which this expansion depended seem to have served the wider expanse from the Ab-i-Naft westwards. Outside the immediate environs of Mandali itself, with the Parthian-Sassanian site of Qalat Safid to the south and Islamic ruin-fields west of the town, there is little to suggest intensive settlement on the old prehistoric pattern.

To sum up, however controversial the general climatic and palaeobotanical data, there can be no doubt that the archaeological evidence from Choga Mami demonstrates conclusively that the sixth-millennium farmers in the Mandali area practised irrigation and that before 5,000 B.C. canals of substantial size were being dug, implying a degree of planning and labour organization that must, however temporarily, have transcended the limits of individual settlements. We do not claim that irrigation was invented here, only that this is a so far unique example of the type of evidence that may be found elsewhere in comparable environmental situations. We have no evidence for the background development of irrigation techniques in Sumer, but we have seen that the practice of irrigation in the alluvial plain requires skills far more complex than in the simpler situation of fan deltas like the Mandali oasis. At present, there is no evidence to suggest that the earliest 'Ubaid farmers in Sumer learned the techniques of irrigation from Samarran farmers in middle Mesopotamia, though it is clear that the practice of irrigation at Choga Mami, and presumably also, in some form, at sites like Sawwan and Baghouz, pre-dates the earliest known 'Ubaid settlements (Oates 1973:173). There is reason to believe that a knowledge of the techniques of irrigation was carried to Deh Luran from the Mandali area, or some intermediate point, as the earliest palaeobotanical evidence for irrigated crops at Chagha Sefid coincides with the occurrence of the distinctive Choga Mami 'Transitional' pottery (F. Hole: personal communication). But the occurrence of a few sherds of this pottery at two sites in Sumer (Adams & Nissen 1972: Site 298; Hout 1971: Fig. 2:221.2) does not constitute proof of a similar pattern, and the 'Ubaid 1 or 'Eridu' ceramic that is our most effective evidence for this phase certainly does not derive directly from that of Samarra. More archaeological evidence is our immediate need, but it should be clear that the history of agriculture in the alluvium is more complex than has usually been assumed.

Acknowledgments

We should like to express our gratitude to Professor Sir Joseph Hutchinson for much expert information on crop husbandry, in particular on water requirements, and to Mrs Heather Jarman for many helpful discussions.

REFERENCES

Adams, R.M. (1962) Agriculture and urban life in Early Southwestern Iran. *Science*, 136, 109-22.

Adams, R.M. (1965) *Land behind Baghdad*. Chicago.

Adams, R.M. and Nissen, H.J. (1972) *The Uruk Countryside*. Chicago.

Admiralty Handbook (1944) Admiralty Intelligence Division, *Iraq and the Persian Gulf*. London.

Al-Barazi, N. (1961) *The Geography of Agriculture in Irrigated Areas of the Middle Euphrates Valley*. Baghdad.

Allan, W. (1972) Ecology, techniques and settlement patterns. In Ucko, P.J., Tringham, R. and Dimbleby, G.W. (eds.), *Man, Settlement and Urbanism*, 211-26. London.

Bor, N.L. (1968) Gramineae. *Flora of Iraq* IX. Baghdad.

Braidwood, R.J. and Howe, B. (1960) *Prehistoric Investigations in Iraqi Kurdistan*, Studies in Ancient Oriental Civilizations No. 31. Chicago.

Buringh, P. (1957) Living conditions in the Lower Mesopotamian plain in ancient times. *Sumer*, 13, 30-46.

Buringh, P. (1960) *Soils and Soil Conditions in Iraq*. Baghdad.

C.A.D. (n.d.) *The Assyrian Dictionary*. Chicago.

Davies, D.H. (1957) Observations on land use in Iraq. *Economic Geography*, 33, 122-34.

Fernea, R.A. (1970) *Shaykh and Effendi*. Harvard.

Field, B.S. (1969) Preliminary report on botanical remains. In Oates 1969, 140-1.

Forde, C.D. (1934) *Habitat, Economy and Society*. London.

Gibson, M. (1972) *The City and Area of Kish*. Miami, Field Research Projects.

Guest, E. and al-Rawi, A. (1966) *Flora of Iraq* I. Baghdad.

Harlan, J.R. and Zohary, D. (1966) Distribution of wild wheats and barley. *Science*, 153, 1074-80.

Hayes, W.C. (1965) *Most Ancient Egypt*. Chicago.

Helbaek, H. (1960) Ecological effects of irrigation in ancient Mesopotamia. *Iraq*, 22, 186-96.

Helbaek, H. (1964) Early Hassunan vegetable food at Tell es-Sawwan, near Samarra. *Sumer*, 20, 45-8.

Helbaek, H. (1966) The plant remains from Nimrud. In Mallowan, M.E.L. (ed.), *Nimrud and its Remains*, 613-20. London.

Helbaek, H. (1969) Plant collecting, dry-farming and irrigation agriculture in prehistoric Deh Luran. In Hole, F.J., Flannery, K.V. and Neely, J.A. (eds.), *Prehistoric and Human Ecology of the Deh Luran Plain* (Univ. of Michigan Mus. of Anthrop. Memoir No. 1), 383-426, Ann Arbor.

Helbaek, H. (1972a) Samarran irrigation agriculture at Choga Mami in Iraq. *Iraq*, 34, 35-48.

Helbaek, H. (1972b) Traces of plants in the early ceramic site of Umm Dabaghiyah. *Iraq*, 34, 17-9.

Hout, J.-L. (1971) Tell El Oueili: surface exploration. *Sumer*, 27, 45-58.

Hutchinson, Sir J. (ed.) (1969) *Population and Food Supply*. London.

Ionides, M.G. (1937) *The Regime of the Rivers Euphrates and Tigris*. London.

International Bank for Reconstruction and Development (1952) *The Economic Development of Iraq*. Baltimore.

Jacobsen, T. (1958) The Diyala Basin archaeological project. *Sumer*, 14, 79-89.

Jacobsen T. and Adams, R.M. (1958) Salt and silt in ancient Mesopotamian agriculture. *Science*, 128, 1251-8.

Kramer, S.N. (1956) *From the Tablets of Sumer*. Colorado.

Kramer, S.N. (1963) *The Sumerians*. Chicago.

Lamb, H.H. (1968) The climatic background to the birth of civilization. *Advance of Science*, 25, 103-20.

Landsberger, B. (1949) Jahreszeiten im Sumerisch-Akkadischen. *Jour. Near Eastern Studies*, 8, 248-97.

Lees, G.M. and Falcon, N.L. (1952) The geographical history of the Mesopotamian plains. *Geog. Jour.*, 118, 24-39.

Le Strange, G. (1905) *Lands of the Eastern Caliphate*. London.

McClure, H.A. (1971) *The Arabian Peninsula and Prehistoric Populations*. Miami, Field Research Projects.

Mitchell, R.C. (1958) Instability of the Mesopotamian Plains. *Bull. Soc. Géog. d'Egypt*, 31, 127-40.

Nelson, H.S. (1962) An abandoned irrigation system in southern Iraq. *Sumer*, 18, 67-72.

Niklewski, J. and Zeist, W. van (1970) A Late Quaternary pollen diagram from north-western Syria. *Acta Botanica Neerlandica*, 19, 737-54.

Oates, D. (1968) *Studies in the Ancient History of Northern Iraq*. London.

Oates, J. (1968) Prehistoric investigations near Mandali. *Iraq*, 30, 1-20.

Oates, J. (1969) Choga Mami 1967-68: a preliminary report. *Iraq*, 31, 115-52.

Oates, J. (1972) Prehistoric settlement patterns in Mesopotamia. In Ucko, P.J., Tringham, R. and Dimbleby, G.W. (eds.), *Man, Settlement and Urbanism*, 299-310. London.

Oates, J. (1973) The background and development of early farming communities in Mesopotamia and the Zagros. *P.P.S.*, 39, 147-81.

Poyck, A.P.G. (1962) Farm studies in Iraq. *Med. van de Landbouwhogeschool te Wageningen*, 62 (1), 1-99.

Repub. Iraq, Min. Comns. Dir.-Gen. Civil Aviation, Met. Dept. Climat. Xn. (various years), *Monthly Climatological Data*. Baghdad.

Repub. Iraq, Min. Comns. Dir.-Gen. Civil Aviation, Met. Dept. Climat. Xn. n.d., *Climatological Atlas for Iraq*, Pubn. No. 13. Baghdad.

Repub. Iraq, Development Board (1959) *Summary of Monthly Precipitation at Stations in Iraq 1887-1958*. Baghdad.

Russell, J.C. (1957) *Tillage Practices in Iraq*. Abu Ghraib. (Mimeographed.)

Salonen, A. (1968) *Agricultura Mesopotamica nach Sumerisch-Akkadischen Quellen*. (Annales Academiae Scientiarum Fennicae, ser. B, tom. 149). Helsinki.

Salter, P.J. and Goode, J.E. (1967) *Crop Responses to Water at Different Stages of Growth*. Farnham Royal.

Thesiger, W. (1967) *The Marsh Arabs*. Harmondsworth, Middlesex.

Warriner, D. (1969) *Land Reform in Principle and Practice*. Oxford.

White, K.D. (1967) *Agricultural Implements of the Roman World*. London.

Willcocks, Sir W. (1911) *The Irrigation of Mesopotamia*. London.

Wright, H.E. (1968) Natural environment of early food production north of Mesopotamia. *Science*, 161, 334-9.

Wright, H.T. (1969) *The Administration of Rural Production in an Early Mesopotamian Town* (Anthropological Papers No. 38). University of Michigan.

Zeist, W. van (1969) Reflections on prehistoric environments in the Near East. In Ucko, P.J. and Dimbleby, G.W. (eds.), *The domestication and exploitation of plants and animals*, 35-46. London.

Zohary, M. (1950) *The Flora of Iraq and its Phytogeographical Subdivision* (Iraq Min. Econ. Dir.-Gen. Agric. Bull. No. 31). Baghdad.

COLIN RENFREW and JOHN DIXON

Obsidian in western Asia: a review

Trade has long been one of the traditional interests of the prehistorian, and the special interest of obsidian as an identifiable raw material was recognized early (Ordoñez 1892; Bosanquet 1904). The study of prehistoric trade as an economic process, however, rather than merely as an indication of contact between distant places, is a much more recent development. Like so many developments in current prehistoric research, this view of trade as economic activity can be traced back to the appropriate chapter of Grahame Clark's *Prehistoric Europe: The Economic Basis*, published in 1952. The study of trade seen instead as a social process, implying human interactions of more than purely economic significance, is well established in the field of cultural anthropology, but it is again to Grahame Clark that we owe a pioneering application of the ideas of Malinowski and Mauss to the material of prehistory. His 'Traffic in Stone Axe and Adze Blades' (1965) reminded us that non-urban communities have their own exchange mechanisms, working by principles not intuitively obvious to modern western man. The notion of reciprocity which, in the form of ritual gift-exchange, he applied to the British Neolithic axe trade, can be applied with equal force to the 'down-the-line' trade of obsidian in the early Near East (Renfrew, Dixon & Cann 1968; cf. Renfrew 1972:466). With the prestige element again prominent, it is relevant also to the east European *Spondylus* trade (Shackleton & Renfrew 1970), itself investigated in his pioneering study twenty years ago (Clark 1952:242-3).

The present paper owes more to Grahame Clark, however, than simply the example of his writings or the general encouragement offered to the study of economic prehistory during the authors' years in Cambridge. The programme of obsidian analyses, which we are here reviewing, had its beginning early in 1962 and the first results were reported, at Professor Clark's invitation, to a meeting of the Cambridge Prehistorians in his rooms in Peterhouse. His generous encouragement then, and the invitation to publish the work under his editorship in the *Proceedings of the Prehistoric Society* (Cann & Renfrew 1964), stimulated the further progress reported in later volumes of that journal (Renfrew, Dixon & Cann 1966; 1968) and elsewhere. In offering to Grahame Clark this progress paper, we are reporting upon work that he has influenced and encouraged from its very earliest stages.

The sources and the analyses

The obsidian sources of Europe and western Asia were listed, on the basis of current knowledge (Cann & Renfrew 1964). They were there assigned a numerical classification based on trace-element analyses obtained by optical emission spectrography, and this classification has been refined and extended on the basis of further analyses. The technique of neutron activation analysis has subsequently been applied by Wright, Gordus and their co-workers at the University of Michigan (Wright & Gordus 1969a; 1969b; Wright 1969), and samples of material, previously analysed by us using optical spectrography, have been re-analysed by them by neutron activation. They report a good correspondence between the groups determined by the two methods, and have continued to use our original group designations, where possible.

More recently, neutron activation analysis of Old World obsidian has been carried out at the University of Bradford, confirming and extending the conclusions obtained for the Aegean by means of optical spectrography (Aspinall, Feather & Renfrew 1972), and this work is now being extended to western Asia. Neutron activation analysis has also been undertaken in Teheran (Mahdavi & Bovington 1972). Fission track analysis has likewise been used upon the Aegean material (Durrani *et al.* 1971), again confirming the earlier results. There is good agreement,

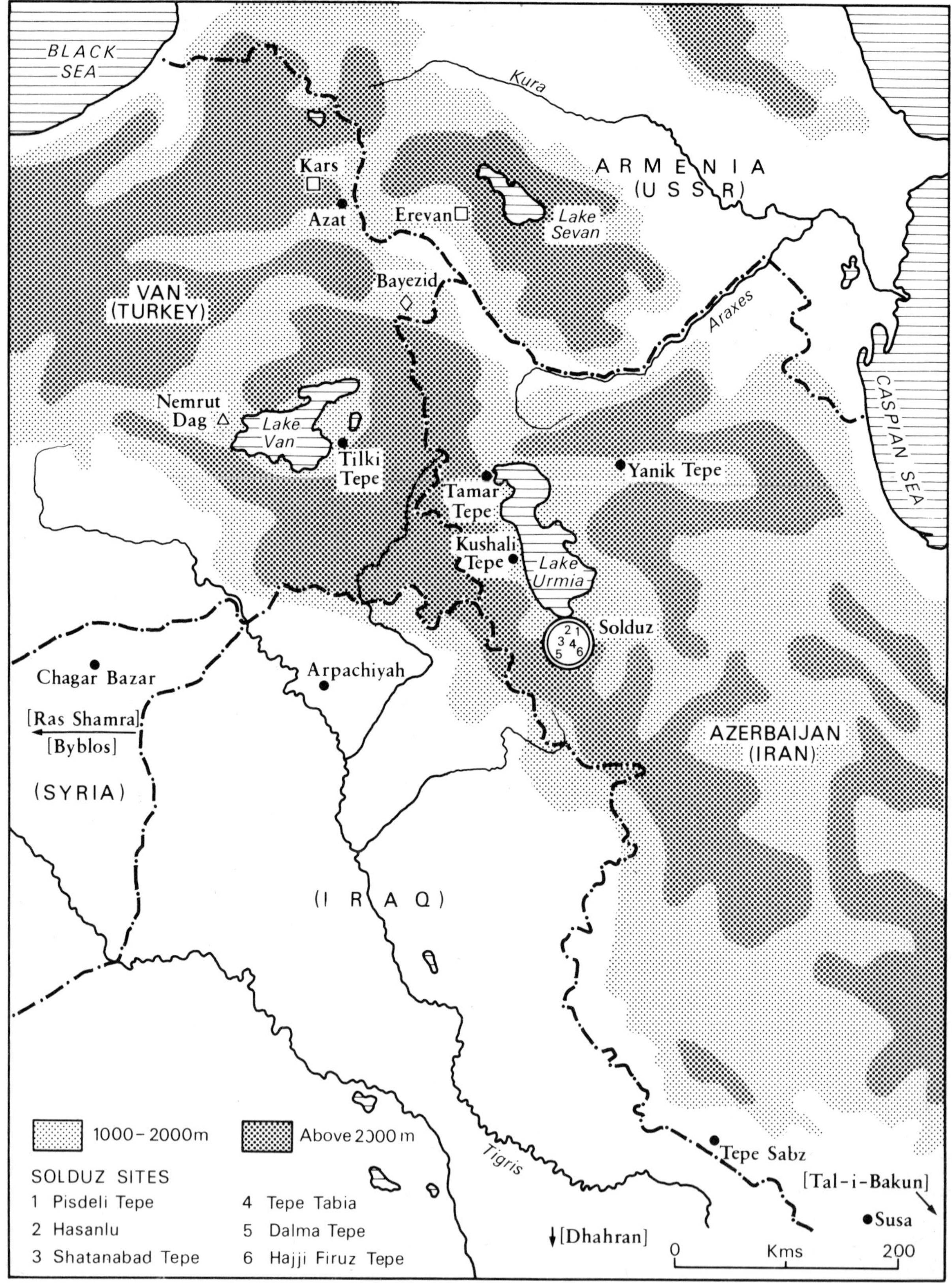

Figure 1.The Van-Azerbaijan-Armenian S.S.R. (VAA) region and the distribution of find-spots of group 3 obsidian (indicated by dots). Sources are shown by open symbols: only the source at Bayezid, of those so far studied, is of group 3.

therefore, that the analytical techniques in use do discriminate, effectively and reliably, between obsidian sources. The problems that remain arise, primarily, from the scarcity of reliable information and of provenanced samples from the east Anatolian sources, located within the boundaries of modern Turkey (principally in the Van and Kars vilayets), in the province of Azerbaijan in north-west Iran, and in the Armenian Soviet Socialist Republic within the territory of the U.S.S.R. These comprise the general area designated 'Armenia' in earlier articles, with the medieval state of that name in mind. But şince this term has not found favour with Soviet and Turkish colleagues, the term 'Van-Azerbaijan-Armenian S.S.R.' will be used to designate this general region, abbreviated to VAA. Undoubtedly, there must be sources in this area that have not yet been reported in the literature. The term 'Cappadocian' will again be used to designate the central Anatolian sources.

All subsequent work, so far, supports the earlier conclusion that there was no additional source of obsidian in western Asia, other than those of the Arabian peninsula. In making this statement, we should not exclude the possibility of minor outlying sources on the western side of the VAA region, for instance the source at Bingöl, 100 km. west of Lake Van (Renfrew, Dixon & Cann 1968:320), although this may not have been of great importance. Its obsidian was assigned by us, like that of Nemrut Dağ on Lake Van, to group 4c. Neutron activation analysis does, however, discriminate between the two sources (Wright & Gordus 1969b): so far the only artefact identified from this source is a single flake from the early site of Çayönü, where group lg and group 4c obsidian is none the less more common. There remains also the possibility of a natural source of obsidian near Trebizond, on the Black Sea coast, with chemical properties like those of group 2b obsidian (Renfrew, Dixon & Cann 1966: nos. 301-2).

We are inclined to discount the verbal reports of obsidian sources in southern Iran or Baluchistan cited by Beale (1973:136 & Fig. 1). It is, of course, impossible to *prove* the absence of a source in a given area without undue reliance upon negative evidence. At the same time, the very small quantities of obsidian found at sites within 200-300 km. of the proposed sources, such as Tepe Yahya and Tal-i-Iblis, are entirely consonant with the supply pattern already established for the obsidian of VAA origin, and much less than would be predicted on any existing model, were the sources so close at hand. Citations from the geological literature, and preferably hand specimens for examination and analysis, are required before such reports can be accepted.

As shown below, the obsidian sources so far known in Arabia are located at the south and south-west of the Arabian peninsula, and the small quantities of obsidian found at sites in the Persian Gulf are of Anatolian origin. The position remains, then, that there are two major source regions for western Asia: Cappadocia (central Turkey), with the group 2b source at Çiftlik and the group le sources at Acigöl; and VAA, with sources of groups 1f, 1g, 3 and 4c. It is known that there are several flows in the Acigöl region, and samples have not been tested from all of them. The distribution of analysed artefacts does suggest, however, that although their products may be distinguishable on the basis of neutron activation analysis, they will probably fall within the broad group le-f. The overall source-pattern is thus clear: problems concerning the precise location of sources in the VAA area are discussed below.

Obsidian in Arabia

Information on the obsidian sources of Arabia is now coming to hand, thanks to the kindness of Mr T.C. Barger of the Arabian American Oil Company, and of Mrs Bert Golding and Mrs Grace Burkholder. In an earlier article we reported analyses (Cann & Renfrew 1964: nos. 96-7) from Huraidha in the Hadhramaut area of what was then the Aden Protectorate and is now the Peoples Democratic Republic of Yemen (*c.* 16°N, 48°E). The quantities of material from this site made it likely that a source was not far distant. It was classified among the peralkaline obsidians of group 4d. Mr Barger subsequently supplied us with a geological hand specimen (no. 436) from the area of Khaibar in the Hejaz in Saudi Arabia, near the Jebel Abyadh (*c.* 26°N, 40°E). This has more zirconium, yttrium and niobium than other specimens of group 4c-d, but otherwise conforms to the peralkaline obsidians in general.

Samples from the Yemen (*c.* 15°N, 44°E), are at present undergoing neutron activation analysis at Bradford. Analyses are given below for three specimens (nos. 383-5) from the Dahlak Islands in the Red Sea (*c.* 16°N, 40°E), although these

Table 1 The provenances of the obsidian analysed

No.	*Group*	*District*	*Site*	*Cultural context*	*Object*	*Collected by*	*Received from*	*Reference*
435	lg	Arabia (Gulf)	Just S of Dhahran airport	Unstratified	Bead	Geoff. Bibby	Thos. C. Barger	
383	lj	Red Sea	Dahlak Is.	'Mesolithic Wilton type'	Flake	A. Carlo Blanc 1952	Daniel Evett	
385	lj	Red Sea	Dahlak Is.	'Mesolithic Wilton type'	Flake	A. Carlo Blanc 1952	Daniel Evett	
392	1	NW Iran	Tepe Tabia	Dalma phase	Flake	R.H. Dyson Jr.	Nan Shaw	
403	2b	W Iran	Tepe Sabz	Bayat phase	Blade	Frank Hole	Frank Hole	Hii/268
386	3a	S Iran	Tal-i-Bakun	Unstratified	Flake	Unknown	R.J. Braidwood	
388	3a	NW Iran	Kushali Tepe	Possibly Pisdeli period	Lump	R.H. Dyson Jr.	Nan Shaw	
389	3a	Arabia (Gulf)	70 km N of Dhahran	Unstratified ('Ubaid site)	Chip	Geoff. Bibby	Geoff. Bibby	390.F6
393	3a	NW Iran	Tepe Tabia	Dalma phase	Lump	R.H. Dyson Jr.	Nan Shaw	
394	3a	NW Iran	Tepe Tapia	Dalma phase	Lump	R.H. Dyson Jr.	Nan Shaw	
396	3a	NW Iran	Shatanabad Tepe	Dalma phase	Blade	R.H. Dyson Jr.	Nan Shaw	
398	3a	NW Iran	Dalma Tepe	Dalma phase	Flake	R.H. Dyson Jr.	Nan Shaw	
400	3a	SW Iran	Tepe Sabz	Sabz phase	Blade	Frank Hole	Frank Hole	
404	3a	SW Iran	Susa	Apadana – ?Achaemenid	Flake	Jean Perrot	Jean Perrot	
405	3a	SW Iran	Susa	Apadana – ?Achaemenid	Flake	Jean Perrot	Jean Perrot	
407	3a	SW Iran	Susa	Acropolis – Susa A	Blade	Jean Perrot	Jean Perrot	357.2
409	3a	SW Iran	Susa	Acropolis – Susa A	Blade	Jean Perrot	Jean Perrot	377.2
197	3a	E Turkey	Tilki Tepe	Unstratified ?Halafian	Flake	R.J. Braidwood	R.J. Braidwood	
198	3a	E Turkey	Tilki Tepe	Unstratified ?Halafian	Flake	R.J. Braidwood	R.J. Braidwood	
86	3a	NW Iran	Yanik Tepe	Late Chalcolithic	Flake	Chas. Burney	Chas Burney	MC 8 286
45	3a	NW Iran	Yanik Tepe	Uppermost Chalcolithic	Flake	Chas. Burney	Chas. Burney	MC 5 286
46	3a	Iraq	Arpachiyah	Halaf or 'Ubaid	Blade	M.E.L. Mallowan	M.E.L. Mallowan	
204	3a	NW Iran	Pisdeli Tepe	Hasanlu phase VIII	Chip	R.H. Dyson Jr.	R.H. Dyson Jr.	P2-C
317	3a'	Lebanon	Byblos	Middle Neolithic	Blade	Jacques Cauvin	Roger Saidah	A.19465
80	3a'	Iraq	Arpachiyah	Halaf or 'Ubaid	Blade	M.E.L. Mallowan	M.E.L. Mallowan	
85	3a'	Syria	Chagar Bazar	Halaf	Flake	Brit. Mus. excav.	M.A.A.C.	36.165
391	3a"	NW Iran	Tamar Tepe	Hajji Firuz phase	Lump	R.H. Dyson Jr.	Nan Shaw	
408	3a"	SW Iran	Susa	Acropolis – Susa A	Chip	Jean Perrot	Jean Perrot	400.1
30	3b	E Turkey	Bayezid (source)	–	G.H.S.	Not known	British Museum	BM 93035
326	3b	NW Iran	Pisdeli Tepe	Hasanlu phase VIII	Chip	R.H. Dyson Jr.	R.H. Dyson Jr.	P2 5B
329	3b	NW Iran	Hasanlu	Period V fill	Chip	R.H. Dyson Jr.	R.H. Dyson Jr.	
330	3b	NW Iran	Hasanlu	Period III	Chip	R.H. Dyson Jr.	R.H. Dyson Jr.	
395	3b	NW Iran	Shatanabad Tepe	Dalma phase	Lump	R.H. Dyson Jr.	Nan Shaw	
195	3c	NW Iran	Yanik Tepe	Late Chalcolithic	Flake	Chas. Burney	Chas. Burney	MC 5 286
196	3c	NW Iran	Yanik Tepe	Late Chalcolithic	Flake	Chas. Burney	Chas. Burney	M8/B 286
181	3c	NW Iran	Hajji Firuz Tepe	Hasanlu phase X	Chip	T. Cuyler Young Jr.	R.H. Dyson Jr.	
182	3c	NW Iran	Hajji Firuz Tepe	Hasanlu phase X	Chip	T. Cuyler Young Jr.	R.H. Dyson Jr.	

Table 1 (continued)

No.	*Group*	*District*	*Site*	*Cultural context*	*Object*	*Collected by*	*Received from*	*Reference*
183	3c	NW Iran	Hajji Firuz Tepe	Hasanlu phase X	Chip	T. Cuyler Young Jr.	R.H. Dyson Jr.	
387	3c	NW Iran	Kushali Tepe	Possibly Pisdeli period	Blade	R.H. Dyson Jr.	Nan Shaw	
87	3c'	NW Iran	Yanik Tepe	Early bronze II	Flake	Chas. Burney	Chas. Burney	L 3 A 286
171	3d	Syria	Ras Shamra	P.P. Neolithic Palace court 3	Blade	Claude Schaeffer	Claude Schaeffer	325
235	3d	Arabia (Gulf)	Dhahran	Unstratified	Blade	P.V. Gløb 1963	Peder Mortensen	
287	3	E Turkey	Azat Hüyük	Early Bronze Age	Chip	I. Kilic Kökten	I. Kilic Kökten	
281	?3	NW Iran	Yanik Tepe	Late Chalcolithic	Flake	Chas. Burney	Chas. Burney	MH1 286
282	?3	NW Iran	Yanik Tepe	Early Bronze II	Flake	Chas. Burney	Chas. Burney	L3/3 Rm.18
397	4c	NW Iran	Dalma Tepe	Dalma phase	Flake	R.H. Dyson Jr.	Nan Shaw	
399	4c	SW Iran	Tepe Sabz	Mehmeh phase	Blade	Frank Hole	Frank Hole	
401	4c	SW Iran	Tepe Sabz	Batat phase	Blade	Frank Hole	Frank Hole	
402	4c	SW Iran	Tepe Musiyan	Musiyan E (Early 'Ubaid)	Blade	Frank Hole	Frank Hole	E/483
406	4c	SW Iran	Susa	Acropolis – Susa A	Blade	Jean Perrot	Jean Perrot	357.1
433	4c	Arabia (Gulf)	100 km N of Dhahran	Unstratified with 'Ubaid pottery	Blade	Thos. C. Barger	Thos. C. Barger	
434	4c	Arabia (Gulf)	Just S of Dhahran airport	Unstratified	Bead	Geoff. Bibby	Thos. C. Barger	
384	4c-d	Red Sea	Dahlak Is.	'Mesolithic Wilton type'	Flake	A. Carlo Blanc 1952	Daniel Evett	
436	4c-d	Arabia, western	Khaybar in the Hejaz (source)	–	G.H.S.	French geological party	Glen F. Brown via Thos. C. Barger	

islands are, in fact, nearer to the Eritrean coast, and hence to the Ethiopian sources, than to those of the Arabian peninsula. No. 384 is a peralkaline obsidian, although with a low yttrium content, and may thus be classed with the other group 4c-d obsidians, including no. 436 from the Hejaz, although its zirconium content is also low. Nos. 383 and 385 are quite different, resembling rather the obsidians of group 1g although clearly distinguishable from them. Nos. 383 and 385 evidently represent a hitherto unrecorded obsidian source, whose location may yet prove to be to the east in the Arabian peninsula, or to the west in Ethiopia.

All these specimens, however, are from lands bordering on the Red Sea or the western Arabian Sea, and some 800 km. from the Persian Gulf or from any known find-spot of Anatolian obsidian, so that the two distributions are entirely separate. Within the latter category come the four specimens from sites near Dhahran, on the west coast of the Persian Gulf, near Bahrain (*c.* 26°N, 50°E), nos. 389 and 433-5. These belong to groups 3a, 4c, 4c and 1g respectively, and thus derive from the VAA source region. The Persian Gulf at this time may be regarded as an extension of the Tigris interaction zone, and perhaps of the Urmia/Plateau zone also. An earlier analysis of a specimen from Dhahran (Renfrew, Dixon & Cann 1966: no. 235) was likewise placed in group 3, and the analyses clearly suggest that all the obsidian in use in the Persian Gulf was of east Anatolian (VAA) origin. Dhahran is 1,500 km. from Lake Van, and this is the greatest distance from the original natural source recorded for any obsidian find in the Old World.

The new analyses

Trace-element analyses are given in Table 2 below for the specimens listed in Table 1. Included with them are all specimens formerly analysed that have proved to belong to group 3. It should be stressed that the subdivisions offered within

Table 2. The trace element concentration of the obsidian analysed

Analyses in parts per million are given for fifteen elements for each of the specimens analysed. An asterisk against the serial number indicates that the sample is not from an artefact but from a natural source.

Abbreviations Ba: Barium. Sr: Strontium. Zr: Zirconium. Y: Yttrium. Nb: Niobium. La: Lanthanum. Rb: Rubidium. Li: Lithium. Mo: Molybdenum. Ga: Gallium. V: Vanadium. Pb: Lead. Ca: Calcium. Fe: Iron. Mg: Magnesium. For convenience the analyses of calcium and iron have been divided by 100. The sign < signifies 'less than'.

The abbreviations used for the colour of the specimens in transmitted light are: E: Green or Brown. G: Grey or Smokey. W: Clear (White).

In the *Transparency/Translucency* column the scale used signifies: O: not transparent/opaque. 1: not transparent/almost opaque. 2: not transparent/fairly translucent. 3: fairly transparent/almost opaque. 4: fairly transparent/fairly translucent. 5: fairly transparent/translucent. 6: transparent/translucent.

In the *Remarks* column: C = opaque clouds and S = striations in transmitted light.

Serial No.	*Origin*	*Group*	*Ba*	*Sr*	*Zr*	*Y*	*Nb*	*La*	*Rb*	*Li*	*Mo*	*Ga*	*V*	*Pb*	*Ca* x 10^{-2}	*Fe* x 10^{-2}	*Mg*	*Colour*	*Transparency/ translucency*	*Remarks*
			(*Figures indicate parts per million*)																	
435	Dhahran	lg	880	100	220	13	30	190	200	47	3	17	3	67	42	100	450	—	0	
383	Dahlak Is	lj	1400	54	220	40	65	350	125	35	<3	17	<3	<5	42	120	250	E	4	
385	Dahlak Is	lj	1850	100	350	40	65	250	125	22	<3	17	<3	22	42	100	200	—	0	
392	Tepe Tabia	1	880	23	14	18	16	70	100	16	<3	5	<3	22	23	29	160	W	6	C
403	Tepe Sabz	2b	240	17	20	13	22	70	160	47	<3	11	<3	36	23	29	110	W	6	
386	Tal-i-Bakun	3a	70	30	160	32	30	70	200	63	<3	11	<3	36	23	70	160	G	5	
388	Kushali Tepe	3a	54	30	120	32	40	100	160	63	<3	11	<3	67	27	70	130	G	5	
389	Nr. Dhahran	3a	70	23	160	32	30	100	100	80	<3	11	<3	36	32	70	160	W	6	C
393	Tepe Tabia	3a	54	17	160	24	22	70	200	47	<3	11	<3	22	23	56	160	G	4	C
394	Tepe Tabia	3a	70	23	160	32	22	100	320	80	<3	11	<3	67	27	56	130	G	4	
396	Shatanabad Tepe	3a	90	30	160	32	30	100	320	63	<3	25	<3	36	32	56	200	G	4	C
398	Dalma Tepe	3a	54	17	160	24	30	130	160	47	<3	11	<3	36	32	47	130	G	0	
400	Tepe Sabz	3a	54	13	120	18	22	70	200	63	<3	11	<3	36	23	56	110	G	5	
404	Susa	3a	54	23	160	24	22	100	200	63	<3	17	<3	36	23	56	130	G	5	
405	Susa	3a	70	23	160	40	22	50	250	100	<3	11	<3	22	23	47	160	G	5	
407	Susa	3a	40	17	120	24	22	70	250	100	<3	11	<3	22	23	56	110	G	0	
409	Susa	3a	40	13	160	24	40	50	250	80	<3	11	<3	22	27	56	130	W	6	C
197	Tilki Tepe	3a	46	16	220	31	60	120	125	42	<3	29	<5	52	36	79	210	G	4	
198	Tilki Tepe	3a	68	16	220	31	40	80	125	56	<3	12	<5	52	31	79	170	G	4	
86	Yanik Tepe	3a	83	20	170	25	22	80	125	56	3	17	<5	52	31	79	210	G	5	
45	Yanik Tepe	3a	83	16	170	25	46	<50	100	42	<3	8	<5	33	31	45	110	G	0	
46	Arpachiyah	3a	100	29	220	22	37	<50	100	56	<3	17	5	38	27	55	110	G	1	
204	Pisdeli Tepe	3a	100	16	170	31	46	<50	160	56	<3	17	<5	38	27	29	130	G	4	

Table 2 (continued)

317	Byblos	3a’	160	50	160	40	50	70	125	47	<3	25	<5	100	42	100	300	G	4	
80	Arpachiya	3a’	83	16	220	25	30	50	160	130	<3	17	<5	38	41	120	210	G	5	
85	Chagar Bazar	3a’	120	43	170	31	30	80	160	75	<3	17	<5	44	35	93	240	G	2	
391	Tamar Tepe	3a”	70	15	160	32	22	70	100	80	<3	11	<3	36	32	47	450	G	5	
408	Susa	3a”	40	15	160	24	40	70	250	63	3	11	<3	22	27	47	370	G	4	C
30*	Bayezid	3b	83	<10	340	18	30	150	80	24	7	8	<5	29	35	65	240	G	0	
326	Pisdeli Tepe	3b	140	40	250	40	65	130	80	22	<4	17	<5	100	36	83	250	G	5	
329	Hasanlu	3b	70	15	160	32	30	50	80	22	<3	11	<5	22	32	83	130	G	5	
330	Hasanlu	3b	140	32	160	40	40	50	125	27	<3	1>	<5	36	42	83	200	G	4	
395	Shatanabad Tepe	3b	90	30	160	32	22	100	160	27	<3	17	<3	36	32	47	160	G	5	
195	Yanik Tepe	3c	46	24	56	<10	46	80	100	24	3	12	<5	44	31	45	130	W	6	
196	Yanik Tepe	3c	56	24	32	<10	46	80	125	24	4	8	<5	38	31	37	210	W	6	
181	Hajji Firuz Tepe	3c	46	24	56	<10	46	80	125	42	4	12	<5	44	36	37	170	W	6	
182	Hajji Firuz Tepe	3c	46	13	44	<10	37	<50	63	18	<3	12	<5	38	31	37	210	W	6	
183	Hajji Firuz Tepe	3c	56	20	56	<10	30	80	160	42	<3	12	<5	38	31	37	170	W	6	
387	Kushali Tepe	3c	54	15	30	8	40	100	125	35	<3	7	<3	22	32	20	110	W	6	S
87	Yanik Tepe	3c’	38	20	44	<10	37	100	80	24	4	8	5	33	41	55	1600	W	6	
171	Ras Shamra	3d	46	20	100	22	37	150	500	180	<3	29	<5	62	36	79	300	G	2	
235	Dhahran	3d	40	20	120	18	40	130	500	125	4	36	<5	100	42	100	130	G	1	
287	Azat	3	40	<10	90	32	40	50	125	35	4	17	<5	22	23	47	90	G	1	
281	Yanik Tepe	?3	95	50	50	10	50	130	80	13	4	17	<5	100	42	47	200	W	6	
282	Yanik Tepe	?3	10	<10	35	6	40	50	80	22	3	11	<5	100	32	32	110	W	6	
397	Dalma Tepe	4c	3	<10	920	50	50	190	200	47	3	36	<3	36	12	47	48	E	6	C
399	Tepe Sabz	4c	4	<10	800	50	65	190	250	47	3	36	<3	36	15	100	58	E	6	C
401	Tepe Sabz	4c	6	<10	920	63	50	190	320	100	5	25	<3	36	18	180	40	E	5	
402	Tepe Musiyan	4c	5	<10	920	63	65	130	160	63	3	17	<3	36	13	120	48	E	6	C
406	Susa	4c	4	<10	800	85	50	190	320	100	5	17	<3	22	15	83	33	E	6	C
433	Dhahran	4c	12	<10	1100	110	65	250	320	63	3	36	<3	67	20	150	40	E	6	
434	Dhahran	4c	9	<10	920	85	65	250	200	47	3	25	<3	67	18	120	40	E	6	
384	Dahlak Is.	4c-d	15	<10	350	32	85	250	250	22	3	25	<3	22	23	180	48	G	1	
436*	Hejaz	4c-d	7	<10	1400	140	220	250	400	100	3	50	<3	67	12	120	40	G	4	S

group 3 are both hypothetical and tentative, although the group itself is well defined. In addition, numerous analyses are now available from the sites of Ali Kosh and Chagha Sefid, excavated by Dr Frank Hole: these analyses will be given in full in the Chagha Sefid publication. All the specimens from these two sites fall within groups 1g and 4c, with the exception of no. 422 from Chagha Sefid, which has some claims to unique status, being low in zirconium (and gallium, lead, calcium and iron), and high in lanthanum and lithium, in comparison to members of group 1g.

Another problematic case is no. 392 from Tepe Tabia (listed here as group 1) which, with its high barium and low zirconium, conforms to no known source, when the other elements are taken into account. In such cases as these, the possibility must be contemplated that each is the first indicator of a hitherto unrecognized source. At the same time, undue weight should not be put upon a single anomalous specimen. The possibility exists that this is a 'joker' or 'sport'. The occurrence of such anomalies has already been clearly documented by a specimen from the Lipari Islands (Cann & Renfrew 1964:117, no. 7).

No such reservations apply to nos. 383 and 385 from the Dahlak Islands in the Red Sea, mentioned above. Two analyses such as these, in an area that from the present perspective is still uncharted, are sufficient to indicate a new group, here designated lj.

There is only one further analysis that occasions surprise, no. 403 from Tepe Sabz, which clearly falls within group 2b, although a little low in calcium and iron. The correspondence is such that the result must be accepted, although this is the first instance of group 2b material east of the Syrian desert. The beautiful obsidian bowl from Tepe Gawra previously analysed (Renfrew, Dixon & Cann 1968: Pl. XXVI) did, however, prove to be of group le-f obsidian, probably from Acigöl, so that here, too, we have Cappadocian material east of the desert.

In general, it should be stressed that the analyses fall neatly within the groups already identified, thus lending further support to the existing classification. Only the tentative subdivisions formerly proposed within group 3 are called into question. Indeed, the quantity of material now identifiable as belonging to group 3 makes a reconsideration of that group desirable.

Group 3 and its subdivisions

The obsidians of group 3 were first recognized (Cann & Renfrew 1964: Fig. 2) on the basis of their content of barium and zirconium, and ascribed to sources in what is now termed the VAA area. A tentative subdivision into groups 3a, 3c and 3d was later outlined (Renfrew, Dixon & Cann 1966:33), but this now needs some modification. Revised subdivisions of group 3 obsidians, including all specimens formerly analysed, are seen in Tables 1 and 2. The procedure adopted was the equivalent of a 'visual' examination of the whole group 3 cluster in 15-D space, with the object of identifying natural gaps in the range of values of any element and any outliers that scored particularly high or particularly low values for particular elements. In this way, sub-groups within group 3 can be characterized, each of which approaches the 'tightness' or homogeneity of known single-source populations such as group 4c.

Group 3 is defined as occupying the middle ground of barium – zirconium space or, more precisely, as lying below the line (Ba 50, Zr 10) to (Ba 300, Zr 200) and above the line (Ba 7, Zr 10) to (Ba 20, Zr 100). The group may then be divided into four subordinate groups: 3a, 3b, 3c and 3d, on the basis of zirconium, yttrium, lithium and rubidium content.

The characterization of group 3c as a distinct low-zirconium, low-yttrium (<10 p.p.m.) group within group 3 is particularly clear, and strongly suggests that at least two different sources exist for group 3 obsidians. Groups 3a, 3b and 3d all have higher zirconium and yttrium ($Y \geqslant 18$ p.p.m.). Group 3b is characterized by its low lithium content of $\leqslant 27$ p.p.m. compared to a lithium content of $\geqslant 47$ p.p.m. in 3a and 3d, and group 3d is characterized by its very high rubidium (500 p.p.m.) and moderately high lithium content. That these three groups also correspond to three separate sources is rather less certain.

Three specimens in Tables 1 and 2 remain outside this four-fold subdivision. No. 287, Azat, has claims to unique status, and is classed simply as group 3. Nos. 281 and 282, from Yanik Tepe, lie outside group 3 itself, as defined above, but do not clearly belong to any of the other established groups and are accordingly classed as ? group 3. Within groups 3a and 3c, further sub-groups: 3a′, 3a″, and 3c′, have been tentatively distinguished on the basis of particularly high values of one element. Thus, 3a′ consists of nos. 80 and 85, which have high iron; while 3a″ comprises nos. 391 and 408, which have high magnesium. No. 317 also has high iron, and is included in 3a′, but also has some claim to unique status as an outlier, from its barium, strontium, lead, calcium and magnesium content when compared with other values in group 3a. Sub-group 3c′ is a single specimen, no. 87, with exceptionally high magnesium, perhaps the result of contamination with a mineral fragment. Groups 3a, 3b and sub-groups together, and group 3c correspond approximately to the groups 3a and 3c, respectively, of Renfrew, Dixon and Cann (1966).

These subdivisions of group 3 must remain tentative, however, until more is known of the relevant sources. But there is no doubt that groups 3a and 3c, as here defined (and taken apart from sub-groups 3a′ and 3c′) are homogeneous, so that the samples in each are likely to have come from a single source. Just where these sources lie within the VAA region, and the changing pattern in their utilization, is reviewed in the next section.

Zones of interaction

Distribution as an indicator of source location within the VAA region

Following the group division on the basis of trace-element analysis, described above, it is possible to return now to the difficult question of the location of the various obsidian sources within the VAA region. The position of the Cappadocian sources, as outlined above, is clear enough, and the importance of the group 4c source at Nemrut Dağ on the north-west side of Lake Van, in the VAA region, has been fully documented. The rest, however, is less clear, and an examination of the find-spots of the artefacts analysed for the present study does offer useful information to supplement that already elucidated from the analyses themselves.

The position of the group le-f obsidian sources in the VAA area is less clear than that of the group 4c source, despite the identification of sources at Kars and Erivan described in previous studies; for, at present, insufficient source samples have been analysed to distinguish the obsidian from the flows at Acigöl in Cappadocia (notionally group le) from these sources in the VAA area (notionally group lf). As a result, the designation 'group le-f' has still to be used for obsidian from both areas. It appears, however, that group le-f obsidian was not much traded southwards from the sources in the northern part of the VAA area, so that this problem is more relevant to Anatolian prehistory than to that of the Near East in general.

The location of the sources for obsidian of groups lg and 3 is a more pressing problem, and fortunately the analyses now available do throw some light upon it (Fig. 1).

In earlier studies (Renfrew, Dixon & Cann 1966:40) it was suggested that the location of the lg source is likely to be not far from Nemrut Dağ on Lake Van, in view of the similarity of the lg and 4c distributions in the Early Neolithic. For groups 3a and 3b sources, a location in the VAA region was suggested, the sample from the source at Bayezid giving a useful indication. 'Group 3c obsidian has been found almost exclusively in the Lake Urmia region – at Yanik Tepe and in the Solduz valley. Its distribution is more limited than that of group 3a, and it seems reasonable to expect the source to lie in east Armenia' i.e. in the east VAA region, 'perhaps close to Lake Urmia itself'.

Inspection of Tables 1 and 2 shows that these remarks still hold good for obsidian of group 3c; it is found in the Solduz region from the Early Neolithic Hajji Firuz Tepe phase at the eponymous site and, so far, nowhere outside the Iranian province of Azerbaijan. The source must lie in, or near (possibly just to the north of) this region.

Obsidian of group 3a has a wider distribution, although this is again centred upon the Lake Urmia region. It extends south, however, to Khuzistan – to Susa and Tepe Sabz at a time contemporary with late 'Ubaid – and to Tal-i-Bakun just a little later. To the west, it is found at Tilki Tepe, on the east side of Lake Van, and south of Van at Arpachiyah, but not further west. Samples of groups 3c′ and 3d are found further afield.

The distributions of group lg and of the various groups within group 3, taken together, are seen in Figures 2 and 3. It is immediately noticeable that, in the early period, the distribution of group lg obsidian approximates to that of group 4c (Fig. 2 does not show a find of group 4c obsidian, in very small quantity, at Beidha). In the later period, it is the distribution of group 3 obsidian that approximates to that of group 4c (although 4c obsidian is also found at Byblos). It should be stressed, however, that only one piece of group 4c obsidian has been identified in the Solduz-

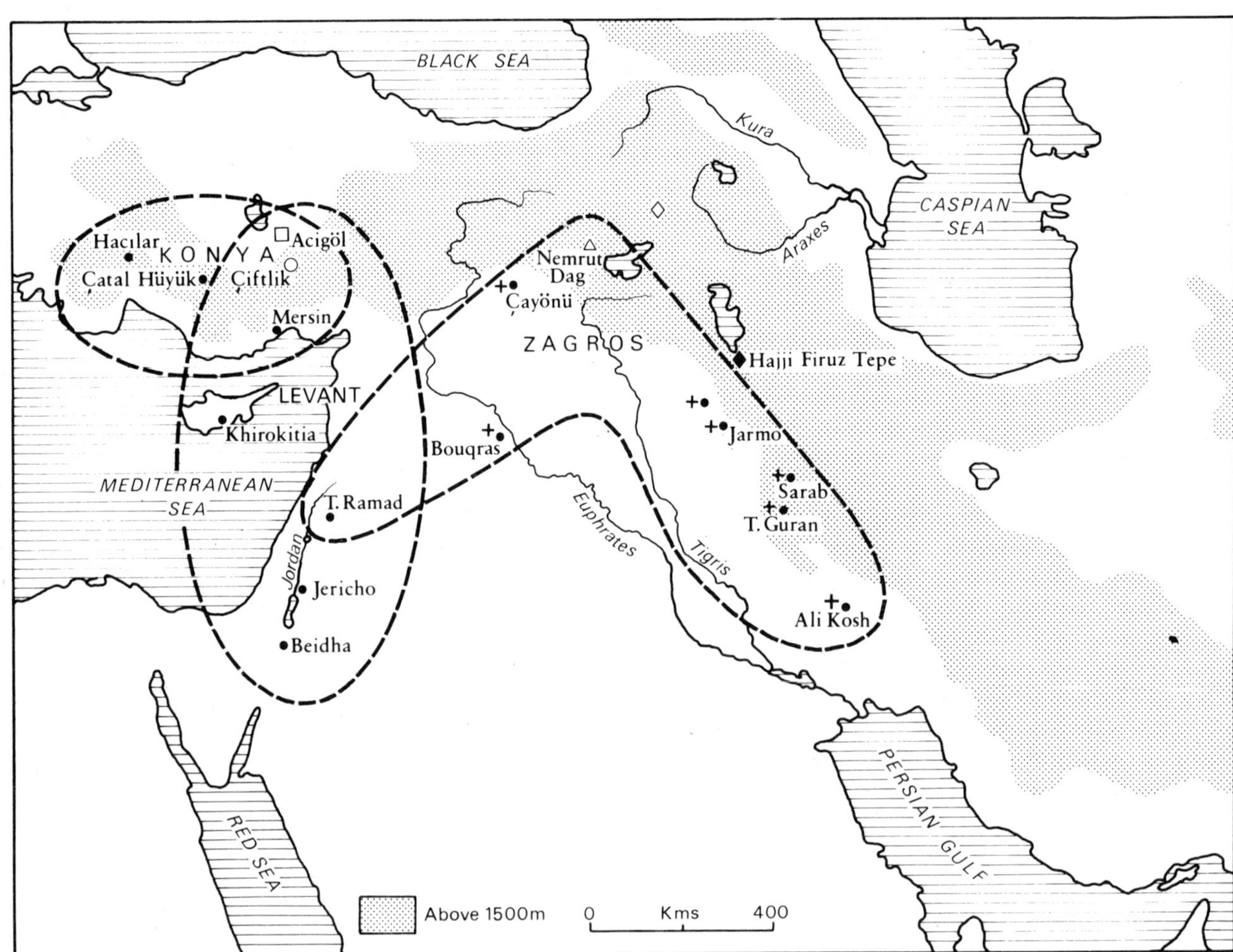

Figure 2. Obsidian interaction zones *c.* 7,500-5,500 B.C. In the Levant zone the obsidian is predominantly of group 2b (from Çiftlik); in the Konya zone, of group le-f (from the Acigöl region); in the Zagros zone, of group 4c (from the Nemrut Dağ area) and of group lg. Find-spots of group lg obsidian are indicated by a cross. The single known find-spot of group 3 obsidian of this period is indicated by a lozenge.

Urmia region (no. 397 from Dalma Tepe).

The most notable features in these distributions are the replacement of group lg obsidian by group 3 in the Zagros area and the shift in the distribution of group lg obsidian westwards to the Levant.

Our suggestion, on the basis of these observations, is that the group lg source lies some way to the west, perhaps to the south-west of Nemrut Dağ; and secondly, that the group 3 sources used, notably the 3a source, lie some way to the north-east of Lake Van. It may be that the developments at the site of Tilki Tepe, on the east of Lake Van, in Halafian times, were important. Our analyses document two specimens of group 3a from this site (nos. 197 and 198) and Wright 1969:22), although giving no detailed analysis, states in a synoptic table that a further four analysed specimens of group 3a and three of group 4c are documented for this site. It is clear that the group 3a source was located in a position accessible from Tilki Tepe as well as from the Solduz area, so that the indication offered by the single source-specimen analysed from Bayezid can tentatively be followed. It occurs to us that the development of transport on Lake Van at this time would introduce an appropriate factor making group 4c obsidian more accessible at Tilki Tepe and group lg obsidian, at least by comparison, less so. The opening up at this time of a route between Mesopotamia and Tilki Tepe, to the east of Van, would explain the conjunction of groups 4c and 3a obsidian in the Tigris/Plateau area, and the diminution in the importance of group 4c obsidian, at least in comparison to group lg, in the Levant.

At the moment these speculations are hypothetical, but they do give rise to three predictions open to testing:

(i) that the group lg source lies to the west, or south-west, of Nemrut Dağ;
(ii) that the principal group 3a source or sources lie, like Bayezid, to the north, or north-east, of Lake Van;
(iii) that the group 3c source was more accessible from the Urmia area than from Lake Van, and probably closer to Shahpur than to Tilki Tepe.

Changing patterns of interaction

On the basis of the analyses now available, it seems possible to delineate a number of interaction zones. They do give some indication of the locations in western Asia that were intercommunicating at different periods and those which, as far as the evidence of obsidian indicates, were not. At the same time, however, it should be remembered that any obsidian distribution must, inevitably, centre upon a natural source, and that the quantities of material found tend to decline as distance from the source increases.

An obsidian interaction zone may be defined as the area within which sites, within the time-range considered, derived 30% or more of their obsidian from the same specific source. This definition allows for the overlapping of zones (e.g. the Konya and Levant zones at Mersin) or for the regular association of obsidian from two different sources within a single zone (e.g. groups lg and 4c in the Zagros zone in the Early Neolithic).

Fig. 2 shows the situation in the Early Neolithic

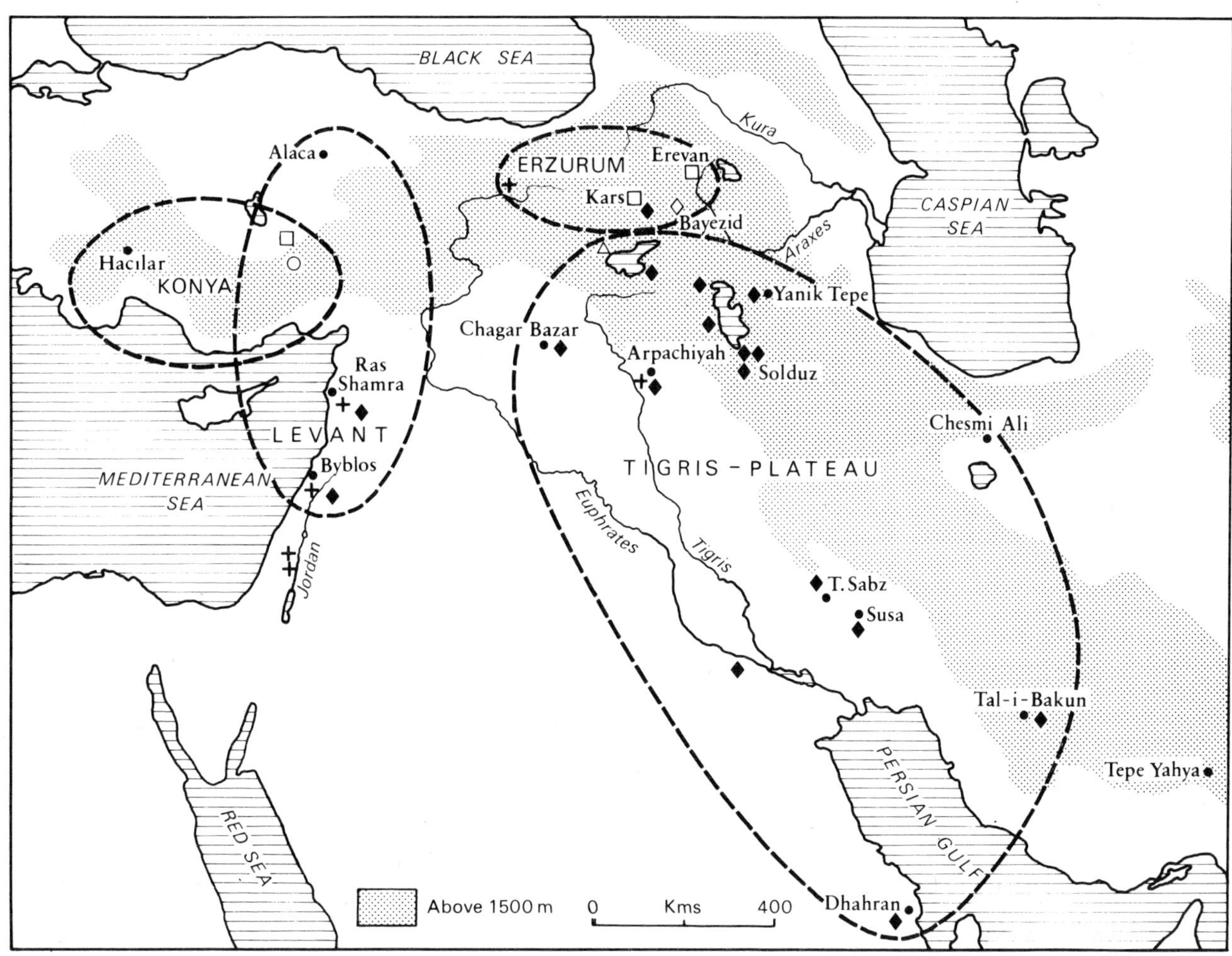

Figure 3. Obsidian interaction zones *c.* 5,000-3,000 B.C. In the Erzurum zone the obsidian is predominantly of group le-f (from sources in the VAA area); in the Tigris-Plateau zone, of group 4c and group 3. Find-spots of group lg obsidian are shown by crosses; of group 3 obsidian, by lozenges.

period, *c.* 7,500-5,500 B.C. Sites in the Levant are linked by the predominance of group 2b obsidian from the Çiftlik source, although quantities in the south are very small. Those in west-central Anatolia are linked by their dependence on group le-f obsidian from the Acigöl area. The two zones overlap in Cappadocia and at Mersin.

Further east, obsidian of groups 4c and lg is found along the western foothills of the Zagros mountains and, indeed, in the western horn of the fertile crescent also. We have called this the Zagros zone. Find-spots of group lg obsidian are shown by crosses in Fig. 2. The occurrence in small quantity of group 4c obsidian at Beidha, and of group le-f obsidian at Byblos, are the only instances documented by our analyses of obsidian finds lying outside the appropriate zones as they are shown here.

Fig. 3 shows the rather different situation in the Late Neolithic and Chalcolithic, from *c.* 5,000 to 3,000 B.C. The Konya zone is unchanged, but the Levant zone no longer extends so far south, although communication with the north is now established. In the northern part of the VAA region there is interaction with the relevant group le-f sources in what we have labelled the Erzurum zone. The great shift, however, is in Iran, where the Zagros zone is now replaced by the Tigris/Plateau zone. Group lg no longer has a significant role here, being replaced by group 3 (shown by lozenges). The most striking feature of the distribution is its extension southwards and eastwards. The Iranian plateau is now an integral part of this interaction zone: group 4c obsidian has been found at Chesmi Ali and, with obsidian of group 3a, at Tal-i-Bakun. Analyses are at present awaited for obsidian from Tepe Yahya. The southward extension is indicated by these sites and by a number of finds from the area of Dhahran, near Bahrain on the west coast of the Persian Gulf. The quantities of obsidian there are small, but they are not negligible. Once again this map shows individually the group 3 specimens analysed by us (lozenges), plus one from 'Ubaid reported by Wright, and all the lg specimens that we have studied (crosses), plus those reported by Wright from Munhata. All the specimens of other groups analysed by us fall within their appropriate zones, with the addition of a single group 2b find from Tepe Sabz and finds of group 4c from Byblos.

Settlement organization, exchange mode and supply

Finally, mention must be made of the changing mechanism of trade that the two maps represent. We have previously shown (Renfrew, Dixon & Cann 1968:328) that in the Early Neolithic period represented by Fig. 2, a regularity in the proportion of obsidian found in relation to other chipped stone may be observed. Outside a radius of some 300 km. from the sources, where finds are very abundant (the supply zone), the proportion of obsidian falls off exponentially with distance. We have suggested that this distribution is the result of down-the-line trade (cf. Renfrew 1972:465) working on a basis of reciprocity. It is a fundamental feature of such trade that the curve relating quantity of obsidian to distance may be described as monotonic decreasing.

Although quantitative data are not yet available on many sites for the later period represented in Fig. 3, it is clear that the same will not hold for this period, or at least not outside the limits of the supply zone for each source. The pattern appears to be one with *less* obsidian reaching minor sites, such as Tepe Sabz or Chagha Sefid or Tell Farukhabad in Khuzistan (Wright 1972:101). At the same time, obsidian is still found in some quantity at major sites like Susa, and over still greater distances than before, as the finds from Tepe Yahya and from the Persian Gulf document. This implies, of course, that the curve of quantity against distance is no longer monotonic decreasing (Fig. 4a) but shows local maxima (Fig. 4b). In other words, certain locations are obtaining a preferential supply by what we have termed 'directional trade' (Renfrew 1972:470).

Two things are happening here. In the first place, the old method of supply – reciprocal exchange by down-the-line trade – is no longer working as effectively as before. And secondly, those persons transporting the traded goods are undertaking longer journeys to specific locations. In other words, we are witnessing the effects in the archaeological record of the emergence of central places and perhaps of middleman traders.

The obvious first effect of the emergence of a hierarchy of places is that exchange can take place at different levels, and long-distance trade takes place primarily between the central places, ensuring them a supply of exotic goods. These then pass on down the spatial hierarchy only in

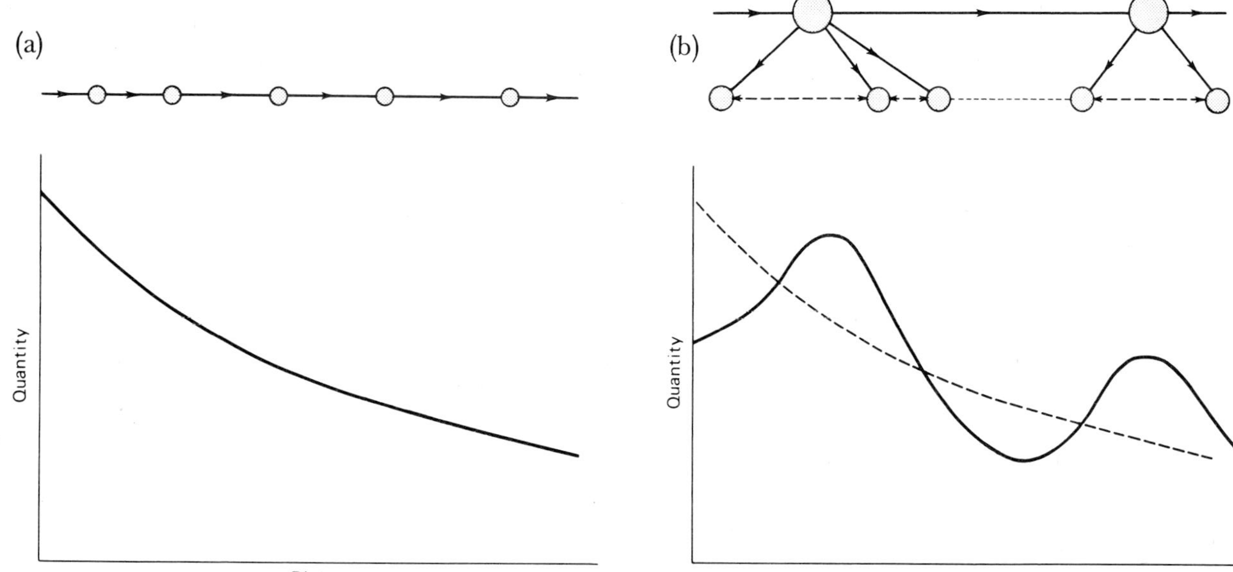

Figure 4. Relationship between settlement organization, exchange mode and supply, for a commodity traded on land.
(a) Simple village settlement served by down-the-line exchange (on a basis of reciprocity) leading, in the archaeological record, to a monotonic decreasing supply curve for a single-source commodity.
(b) Central place settlement with directional exchange between centres (and with either redistribution or central market exchange at local regional level) leading to a multi-modal supply curve. Note the tendency for lower-order settlements to exchange with the higher-order centre, even if the latter actually lies further from the commodity source than an accessible lower-order settlement.

reduced quantity (Fig. 4b).

The second, less obvious, effect is the reduction in the underlying down-the-line trade between lower-order places. For, whereas these were formerly symmetrically placed with respect to one another (Fig. 4a), this is no longer the case. Those within the sphere of influence of a given central place are now linked primarily *through* that place: those within the spheres of different central places are much *less* strongly linked than before, for the strengthened interaction with the central place is likely to be accompanied by a weakened interaction with peer settlements (of the same order in the hierarchy), and especially with those falling within the sphere of other central places. The rise of redistribution, or of market exchange, implies a diminution in reciprocity.

In the case of obsidian, of course, there is not merely a difference in exchange mechanism between the two periods but of function. For in the Late Neolithic/Chalcolithic, obsidian tools began to be replaced by metal ones, and obsidian was increasingly used for stone bowls and other special objects. At the beginning of this time period, however, early in the fourth millennium, the use of copper tools cannot have been universal, and the decrease of obsidian observed in Khuzistan must surely represent a real decline in the availability of a useful raw material.

For lower-order locations, directional trade through central places may well have implied a decrease in the standard of living, or at least of supply, compared with that formerly maintained by means of the surprisingly effective down-the-line exchange. No doubt the emergence of central places was accompanied by that of central persons of considerable prestige, able to secure a high proportion of the traded product for themselves. The hierarchy of places implies also a hierarchy of persons, and those at the lower end of this hierarchy are likely to have been the worse off through this shift to a less egalitarian society. The new supply pattern indicated in the archaeological record of the time is a reflexion of this disparity.

Acknowledgments

The analyses described above were carried out with the Hilger Littrow E 478 spectrograph of the Department of Mineralogy and Petrology, University of Cambridge, by the method outlined in our previous publications, and we are grateful to R.S. Allen for preparing the plates themselves and for much helpful co-operation. In addition to all those who have sent us obsidian, listed in Table 2, we are very grateful for the information and advice offered by Mr Thomas C. Barger, Mrs Grace Burkholder, Dr Charles Burney, Mr R.H. Dyson Jr., Mrs Bert Golding, Dr Frank Hole and Dr Joan Oates.

REFERENCES

Aspinall, A., Feather, S.W. and Renfrew, C. (1972) Neutron activation analysis of Aegean obsidians. *Nature*, 237, 333-4.

Beale, T.W. (1973) Early trade in highland Iran: a view from a source area. *World Arch.*, 5, 133-48.

Bosanquet, R.C. (1904) The obsidian trade. In Atkinson, T.D. *et al., Excavations at Phylakopi in Melos* (Society for the Promotion of Hellenic Studies, Occasional Paper No. 4), 216-33.

Cann, J.R. and Renfrew, C. (1964) The characterization of obsidian and its application to the Mediterranean region. *P.P.S.*, 30, 111-33.

Clark, J.G.D. (1952) *Prehistoric Europe: the Economic Basis.* London.

Clark, J.G.D. (1965) Traffic in stone axe and adze blades. *Economic Hist. Rev.*, 18, 1-28.

Dixon, J.E., Cann, J.R. and Renfrew, C. (1968) Obsidian and the origins of trade. *Scientific American*, 218(3), 38-46.

Durrani, S.A., Khan, H.A., Taj, M. and Renfrew, C. (1971) Obsidian source identification by fission track analysis. *Nature*, 233, 242-5.

Mahdavi, A. and Bovington, C. (1972) Neutron activation analysis of some obsidian samples from geological and archaeological sites. *Iran*, 10, 148-51.

Ordoñez E. (1892) Algunas obsidianas de Mexico. *Memorias de la Sociedad Cientifica 'Antonio Alzate'*, 6, 33-45.

Renfrew, C. (1972) *The Emergence of Civilization, the Cyclades and the Aegean in the Third Millennium B.C.* London.

Renfrew, C., Cann, J.R. and Dixon, J.E. (1965) Obsidian in the Aegean. *Ann. Brit. School Arch. Athens*, 60, 225-47.

Renfrew, C., Dixon, J.E. and Cann, J.R. (1966) Obsidian and early cultural contact in the Near East. *P.P.S.*, 32, 30-72.

Renfrew, C., Dixon, J.E. and Cann, J.R. (1968) Further analysis of Near Eastern obsidians. *P.P.S.*, 34, 319-31.

Shackleton, N. and Renfrew, C. (1970) Neolithic trade routes re-aligned by oxygen isotope analysis. *Nature*, 228, 1062-5.

Wright, G.A. (1969) *Obsidian Analysis and Prehistoric Near Eastern Trade: 7,500 to 3,500 B.C.* (Anthropological Papers, Museum of Anthropology, University of Michigan, no. 37.)

Wright, G.A. and Gordus, A.A. (1969a) Source areas for obsidian recovered at Munhata, Beisamoun, Hazorea and El-Khiam. *Israel Exploration Jour.*, 19, 79-88.

Wright, G.A. and Gordus, A.A. (1969b) Distribution and utilisation of obsidian from Lake Van sources between 7,500 and 3,500 B.C. *Amer. Jour. Arch.*, 73, 75-7.

Wright, H.T. (1972) A consideration of interregional exchange in Greater Mesopotamia: 4,000-3,000 B.C. In Wilmser, E.N. (ed.), *Social Exchange and Interaction* (Anthropological Papers, Museum of Anthropology, University of Michigan, no. 46), 95-105.

PART III

Australasia

PETER BELLWOOD

Prehistoric plant and animal domestication in Austronesia

The geographical area denoted by the term 'Austronesia' includes Indonesia (with Malaya), the Philippines, Taiwan, Micronesia, Melanesia and Polynesia; the latter three areas together constitute Oceania. Austronesia thus defined is the area where languages of the very widespread Austronesian family are spoken; a valid unit of study in archaeological and ethnological as well as in linguistic terms. Madagascar is excluded from consideration, despite its Austronesian language, but on the other hand New Guinea, predominantly a non-Austronesian speaking area, is included because its prehistory is closely interlocked with that of the other Pacific Islands.

The expansion of the Austronesians within the past 5,000 years is closely related to their economic development; it can hardly be coincidence that the settlement of most of the vast area of Oceania, excluding western Melanesia, began soon after the time that the first definite evidence appears for developing plant and animal domestication in south-east Asia. This essay is concerned specifically with these twin topics, which are of course only two aspects of the whole study of prehistoric economy. Professor Clark's outstanding contribution to this study needs no emphasis, but I would here acknowledge his long-standing interest in Australasian prehistory (e.g. Clark 1965). The subject matter of the essay is drawn from archaeology, and from recent societies that have not been transformed by the Indian, Islamic and European influences that have penetrated the area over the past 1,700 years. In general, the term 'cultivation' is used in preference to 'horticulture' and 'agriculture', which are difficult to separate in a prehistoric context, and the term 'domestication' is used in connexion with animals, although this does not necessarily imply breeding isolation imposed by man.

A small digression is necessary at this point to place the prehistory of Austronesia in perspective. Despite Pleistocene settlement extending back some two million years or more in western Indonesia, man does not appear, on present published evidence, to have crossed the water gaps to the Philippines, eastern Indonesia, Australia and New Guinea until about 30-40,000 years ago. However, the phase of settlement that encompassed New Guinea and Australia probably did not extend much further than the Bismarcks or the Solomons, if indeed it extended beyond New Guinea itself. The human settlement of Oceania beyond this south-western corner was entirely an Austronesian achievement, and was accomplished from about 3,500 years ago with the aid of a range of introduced plants and animals and, the *sine qua non*, an advanced voyaging technology.

The present Austronesian languages can be traced linguistically to a proto-language (proto-Austronesian), which may in reality have existed as a chain of related dialects somewhere in the area of the Philippines, eastern Indonesia and western Melanesia, very approximately around 5,000 years ago, if not before. Contrary to popular opinion, there is no archaeological or linguistic evidence to derive the Austronesians from mainland south-east Asia within the last 5,000 years. The expansion through Indonesia to Malaya and South Vietnam is poorly recorded archaeologically and linguistically, but seems to have come to an end 2,000 years ago. Between 3,000 and 4,000 years ago the major expansion into Micronesia and Melanesia commenced, and the first Polynesian group to be settled, the Tongan Islands, was peopled by about 1000 B.C. After this the settlement of the vast area of Polynesia took place fairly slowly, and New Zealand was probably not reached until later in the first millennium A.D. In world terms, the Austronesian expansion is fairly recent and quite striking, and ranks with the prehistoric expansion of the Indo-European languages. A review of the economic prehistory associated with this phenomenon will at least provide a context for it, although the immediate psychological motivation that took men to remote corners of the Austronesian domain may always remain unknown.

Turning now to the immediate subject matter, this essay is organized in four parts. These are, in succession: the food plants and their origins; the systems of cultivation and their origins; the domesticated animals; and, finally, a discussion of some major problems of culture history that might relate to economic and ecological variables.

In an area as large as Austronesia, it is to be expected that the patterns of animal and plant exploitation will be varied. Since the area is almost entirely within the tropics, there are environmental features held widely in common, but there is nevertheless a range of variation from equatorial rain forest, through tropical savannah, to the temperate land-mass of New Zealand with its unique prehistoric economy. The most important economic activities were, and still are in many areas: rice or tuber cultivation by swidden or irrigation techniques; tree-crop exploitation; pig husbandry; and hunting, gathering and fishing. The proportional importance of each of these activities varies across Austronesia, with wet rice cultivation being dominant today in the more densely settled parts of Indonesia and the Philippines, dry rice and millet cultivation in the remoter areas of island south-east Asia, tuber cultivation in Melanesia, and both tuber and tree-crop cultivation in Polynesia and Micronesia. Fishing is naturally mainly restricted to coastal areas, so that in inland areas such as the New Guinea Highlands, pigs and wild game provide the bulk of the meat supply. In Indonesia and the Philippines, the range of domesticated animals today includes goats, cattle and water-buffalo, but it is certainly significant that none of the gregarious herbivores, or cereal cultivation, entered Oceania in prehistoric times. Hunting and gathering on a small scale was undoubtedly universal in the pre-urban past, but only in southern New Zealand, the Chatham Islands, parts of inland Sumatra and Borneo, and amongst the Negritos of Malaya, the Philippines and the Andaman Islands does it appear that plant cultivation was entirely absent. Many peoples of coastal New Guinea depend to a large extent upon wild sago-palm exploitation, but in most reported cases there is some subsidiary cultivation. Indeed, there is an observable gradation in economies within the area from non-cultivation right through to intensive cultivation; and, if we exclude wet rice agriculture, there is no marked break in this gradation. This is an important point, to which I shall return.

Indigenous major food plants of Oceania

Firstly, there is a linguistic observation of great importance: words for taro, yam, bread-fruit, banana and coconut (but not rice) are all present in the Proto-Austronesian vocabulary (Pawley 1971; Chowning in Barrau 1963:39-44). This makes it highly likely that each of these vitally important plants was present in Austronesia by some 5,000 years ago, possibly in domesticated form. Let us look at these and others in turn, progressing from tree crops to tubers and cereals.

The coconut palm (*Cocos nucifera*) is a pan-Austronesian cultigen with an astounding range of uses. Prior to European contact it appears to have had a restricted distribution on the Pacific coast of central America from Panama to the Gulf of Guayaquil, and Heyerdahl (1968: ch. 7) has assembled a degree of botanical support for an American origin of the domesticated species. The question is an open one, because the coconut has no known ancestor. On the other hand, fossil members of the genus *Cocus* are known from New Zealand, fragments of charred coconut shell from Aitape in northern New Guinea are reliably carbon-dated to within the third millennium B.C. (Hossfeld 1964), and the Indo-Oceanic area supports a majority of insects specific on *Cocus*, together with the coconut crab (Child 1964: ch. 1). Interestingly enough, the evidence from insects might well suggest a Melanesian origin, and an origin within the Indo-Pacific area generally seems more likely than an origin in the Americas. The ability of the coconut to remain viable at sea for long periods might also have assisted its dispersal, although there is in fact no need to invoke this mechanism to explain its prehistoric distribution (Merrill 1954:241; Barrau 1965:70; Sauer in Riley *et al.* 1971:309-19).

The bread-fruit tree (*Artocarpus altilis*), symbol of a Pacific paradise and ultimate source of the mutiny on H.M.S. Bounty, occurs across Austronesia, but not in the Americas. Wild relatives of the tree are found in Indonesia, the Philippines, New Guinea and the Marianas Islands (Barrau 1963:4; 1965:67-8), and it attains great importance as a cultigen in parts of Micronesia and Polynesia.

The pre-European bananas of the Pacific area belonged to two species (excluding those restricted to south-east Asia) – *Musa troglodytarum* with a vertical fruit-stalk, and the more familiar *Musa sapientum.* Both these cultigens are indigenous to Austronesia, and the distribution of the former is shown in Fig. 1 (after the ethnobotanist Jacques Barrau). There is some evidence for cultivation of bananas in pre-Columbian South America, and prehistoric transportation from Polynesia is a possibility (Heyerdahl 1968:57-8; Merrill 1954:272-9).

A tree of great importance in the swampy areas of coastal New Guinea and the Moluccas is the sago palm (*Metrxylon* spp.), and this palm may once have been utilized as far east as Fiji. It is not a true cultigen and is generally exploited from wild stands, although some planting may be carried out. Between the eighth and fifteenth years of life, approximately, the tree flowers and dies, exhausting in the process a reserve of starch contained within its trunk. Therefore, the palms are felled before they flower, and the starch is washed out from the grated pith chopped out from the trunk. In some cases sterile palms may produce up to 900 lb. of starch, but the normal yield is between 250 and 350 lb. (Barrau 1958:38-9). The starch may be made into porridge or cakes, and was at one time traded for long distances by sea along the Papuan coast of New Guinea. The sago palm is a New Guinea native, as probably is the sugar cane (*Saccarum officinarum*) (Barrau 1965:71), although this plant does not appear to have had great economic importance in prehistoric times.

Two other cultivated trees merit mention, the first being the paper mulberry tree (*Broussonetia papyrifera*), the inner bark of which was at one time beaten into a felt used for clothing throughout the Pacific. Secondly, the betel-nut palm, *Areca catechu*, provides a nut that is chewed as a stimulant together with a pepper (*Piper betle*) and crushed lime. This tree is grown from India, through Austronesia, to as far east as western Micronesia and the Solomon Islands. East of the betel zone a different stimulant was prepared from the root of *Piper methysticum*, which was chewed and mixed with water to provide the Fijian *yaqona* and Polynesian *kava.* In Fiji, Tonga and Samoa, *kava* drinking was elevated into a ritual that accompanied many important events involving high-ranking personages (Williamson 1939: chs. 2 and 3). The *kava* and betel zones are approximately exclusive, although *kava* is used in parts of coastal New Guinea. The paper mulberry tree, the betel complex and *kava* are each almost certainly of Indo-Pacific origin, and there is evidence for the use of betel nuts in the lower layers of Spirit Cave in Thailand, between 10,000 and 6,000 B.C. (Gorman 1971:310-11).

The list of other Indo-Pacific trees (such as *Pandanus* spp.) in the category of semi-cultigens is very lengthy, and outside the scope of this paper. Before passing to the tubers, there is the puzzling matter of the gourd (*Lagenaria siceraria*) to be considered – the only true cultigen that was widespread in both hemispheres in prehistoric times, probably prior to 7,000 B.C. The gourd is the only important Oceanic cultigen that requires seed propagation, and is a monotypic species evidently of African origin, which may have spread naturally by sea (Whitaker in Riley *et al.* 1971:320-7; Merrill 1954:223; Gorman 1971:311). In Oceania it was used mainly for containers, but young gourds could also be eaten.

With the exception of the coconut and bread-fruit in localized areas, none of the tree crops listed could rank in importance with the two groups of edible tubers – the yams and the taro-like plants (aroids). The yams and the aroids are both Indo-Pacific cultigens of high antiquity, although both groups have largely given way to rice and recently introduced crops in island south-east Asia.

The yams (*Dioscorea* spp.), of which there are five main species in Austronesia, were probably first brought into cultivation in the areas of seasonal monsoon rainfall in northern south-east Asia, and secondarily perhaps in the Philippines and Sulawesi (Barrau 1965:65-6; Alexander & Coursey 1969; Coursey 1972). Today, yams have retained their importance mainly in Melanesia, and never seem to have attained much importance in comparison with the aroids in most parts of Micronesia and Polynesia. They do not thrive in areas of high all-year-round rainfall, and where necessary are grown on ridges

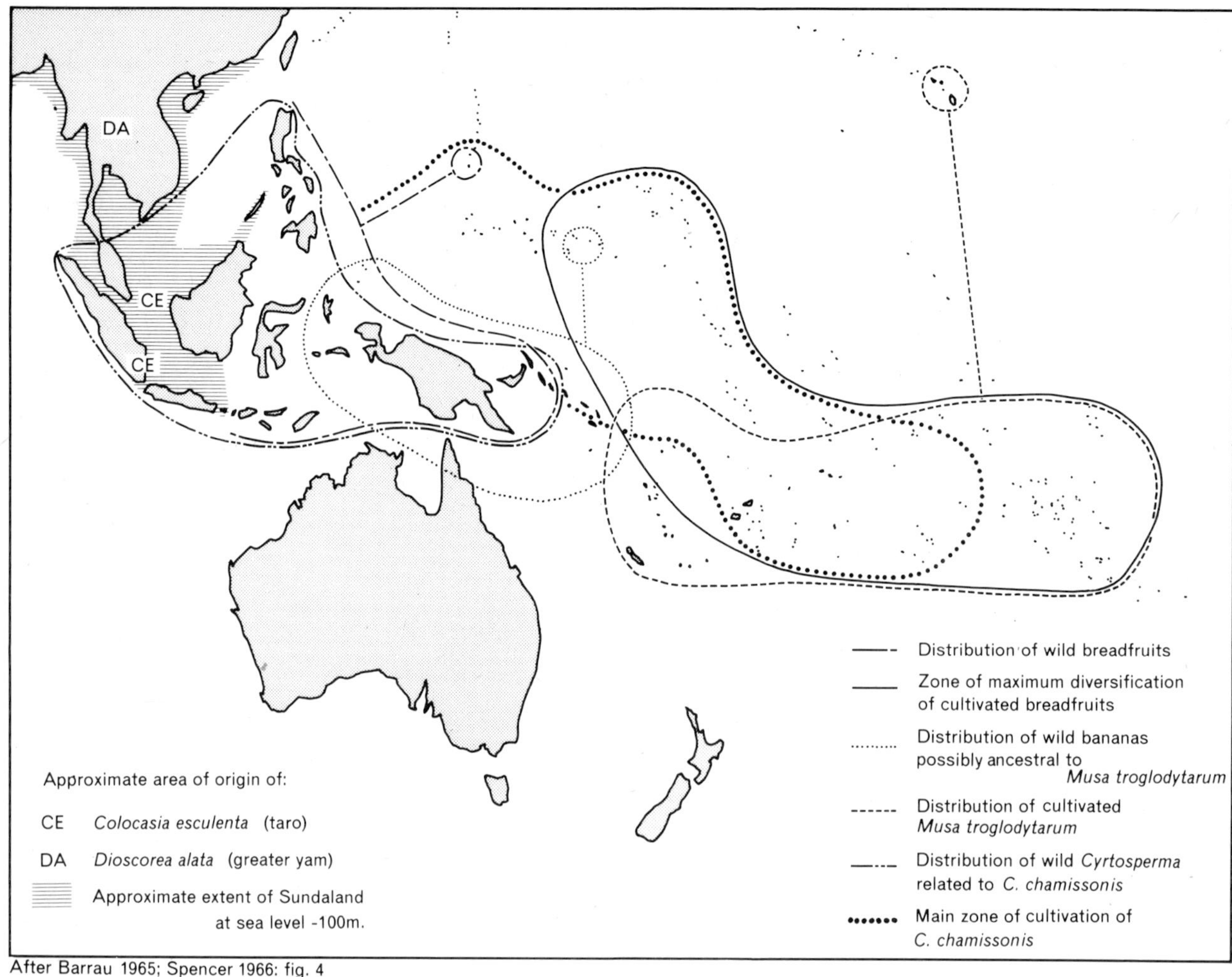

Figure 1. Map of Austronesia.

of friable drained soil. The aroids belong to the family *Araceae*, and the most important species, *Colocasia esculenta* (taro), is grown throughout Austronesia and may have originated as a cultigen in equatorial Indonesia. It thrives in conditions of constant dampness, and requires irrigation in many areas of Oceania where rainfall has a seasonal occurrence, for instance New Caledonia, Fiji, and the Cook, Hawaiian and Society Islands of Polynesia. Another aroid, *Cyrtosperma chamissonis*, is a major cultigen of the atolls of Micronesia and Polynesia to as far east as the southern Cook Islands, and is normally grown in deep pits excavated through the coral to the water-table and partially filled with decomposed organic materials (Barrau 1968:121). The labour involved in the construction of such pits was often immense. On the island of Pukapuka in the northern Cook Islands the taro excavations cover at least several acres, and the amount of soil moved may probably be measured in thousands of tons. Beaglehole (1938:40-1) is of the opinion that these pits are partly natural, but I feel that he minimizes excessively the human labour input. *Cyrtosperma* has wild relatives in Indonesia and New Guinea, but is mainly cultivated outside this zone (Fig. 1). As pointed out by Barrau (1965:68; 1970:498-9), a distinction between area of natural occurrence and area of cultivation applies to a number of Oceanic crops, including bread-fruit and the banana *Musa troglodytarum*, and the importance of such a distinction in crop-plant evolution is now well known to botanists and archaeologists alike. In these cases the domesticated forms probably arose owing to the removal by man of clones from the natural habitat into areas where new selective factors gave rise to different varieties, which are now used as cultigens.

Amongst the other plants with edible tubers in Austronesia the most controversial is undoubtedly the sweet potato, *Ipomoea batatas*. Botanists now seem to agree that the plant is American with a likely ancestor, *I. trifida*, found in tropical central America (Nishiyima in Barrau 1963:119-28; Brand in Riley *et al.* 1971:343-65; Yen in Riley *et al.* 1971:328-42). It has been recovered from eighth millennium B.C. archaeological contexts in Peru, and was certainly cultivated by the second millennium B.C. (Yen 1971:12). It is generally agreed that it could not have reached Polynesia without the aid of man, and Merrill (1954:212) suggested that it must have been transported as a living plant in a bed of soil, although the possibility of transporting seeds would seem to merit more attention (Yen 1960; Baker in Riley *et al.* 1971:433-5). The Polynesian word *kumara* (or close cognate) is paralleled by the word *cumar*, which is used for sweet potato in the highlands north-west of Cuzco by speakers of the Chinchasuyo dialect of Quechua (Brand in Riley *et al.* 1971:359-63). The word is not in use on the coast of Peru, and how it reached Polynesia, if indeed the two forms really are cognate, is a mystery. Claims for a European introduction of the plant into Polynesia after A.D. 1500 are unlikely, given the strange prehistoric distribution of the plant in peripheral areas of Polynesia that are not known to have been visited at an early date by Spaniards, *viz.* the Hawaiian Islands, New Zealand and Easter Island. It was also of minor importance in the Society and Marquesas Islands, but not certainly present anywhere else in Austronesia (Dixon 1932). Barrau (1965:66) has suggested that early reporters of sweet potatoes in New Caledonia and Tonga may have confused them with a species of yam, *Dioscorea nummularia*.

There is also a small amount of archaeological evidence that bears on the antiquity of the sweet potato in Polynesia. Field boundary walls and underground storage pits are known to date from the thirteenth century A.D. onwards in New Zealand (Leach & Leach 1971; Bellwood 1971a:67), and there is strong evidence for associating these with sweet potato cultivation. Actual remains of tubers are reported from archaeological sites in New Zealand, Easter Island and the Hawaiian Islands, but unfortunately the radiocarbon dates applicable to these situations do not make a date prior to A.D. 1500 for the plant a certainty (Rosendahl & Yen 1971). Because sweet potato so rarely flowers in Polynesia, future assistance from pollen analysis is not very likely. However, my own view is that the plant is a prehistoric introduction from America into central Polynesia, possibly about 1,500 years ago when the Polynesian peripheries were about to be settled (Yen 1971:12 states this view in more detail). Its later importance in New Zealand and Easter Island almost certainly arose because it was one of the few Polynesian crops that would thrive outside the tropics.

As for other possible American introductions into Polynesia, a lot of literature has given very few conclusive results, which do not require consideration here (Heyerdahl in Barrau 1963:23-36; Heyerdahl 1968:51-74; Merrill 1954; Carter 1950; Emory 1971). The prehistoric cultivation systems of Oceania were based on vegetative propagation of a range of Indo-Oceanic fruits and tubers, and they have been under development within Austronesia for at least 5,000 years. Seen in perspective, the sweet potato is a rather insignificant intruder from the east.

Of cereals grown in Austronesia, only two appear to have achieved prehistoric significance, namely millet and rice. The foxtail millet (*Setaria italica*) was probably domesticated by Yang-shao times in fifth millennium B.C. central China (Barnard 1972: for radiocarbon dates), and was cultivated in prehistoric times in south-east Asia, possibly to as far east as New Guinea. It retains economic importance today amongst some of the Austronesian peoples of Taiwan, and a probable seed of *Setaria* has been recovered archaeologically in Portuguese Timor in a context that may be as early as 1000 B.C. (Glover 1972:I, 320). However, whatever its prehistoric importance, it has now given way largely to rice cultivation in south-east Asia, and there is in fact little that may be said about prehistoric millet cultivation from present knowledge.

The cultivation of rice (*Oryza sativa*) in island south-east Asia may well have been restricted mainly to western Indonesia in prehistoric times. The plant was absent in Oceania, except for the Marianas Islands of western Micronesia (Yawata in Barrau 1963:91-2), and even in eastern Indonesia and the Philippines it may have attained much of its importance since European contact. Rice was perhaps first domesticated in the monsoonal areas between north-east India and northern Indo-China (Spencer in Barrau 1963:83-90; Bartlett 1962), and the earliest archaeological evidence for the plant comes from Chekiang Province in China, and from the site of Non Nok Tha in north-east Thailand, where rice husks were used for tempering pottery from about 3,500 B.C. (Bayard 1972:32). The dates for this site are at present controversial, and should be accepted with some caution. Rice husks from a Neolithic site in Chekiang Province, in central coastal China, have been dated to *c.* 3,300 B.C. (Barnard 1972, sample ZK 49). Non Nok Tha provides suggestive, but not definite, evidence that villages appeared in south-east Asia at about the same time, and excavations of settlements in this hitherto neglected area are undoubtedly a vital necessity. Because rice is absent in Oceania it is generally accepted that it was domesticated in south-east Asia later than the fruits and tubers, but there is no archaeological evidence to support this view, apart from its probable absence in the Yang-shao culture of central China where millet appears to precede rice. The absence of a word for rice in the proto-Austronesian vocabulary would also suggest that the plant could be a relatively late arrival in Austronesia. On the other hand, it is particularly sensitive to temperature, length of daylight, cloud cover and light intensity, and seems to prefer a monsoonal to an equatorial climate. Spencer (in Barrau 1963:83-90) has suggested that rice did not enter Oceania because of its slow rate of adaptation and its vulnerability, and that it was not able to compete with the dominant crops of the area. Therefore environmental factors, rather than a late date for domestication, may also be used to explain its distribution.

Cultivation systems and their development

The prehistoric cultivation systems of Austronesia ranged from the most simple forms of swidden gardening to intensive monocropping of irrigated fields. Between these extremes there is an even continuum, and many societies practise both swidden and irrigation in combination at the present time. In this section I propose to describe various economies along this continuum, beginning with hunter-gatherers and proceeding through swidden gardeners to irrigation farmers. The culmination will be a brief discussion of wet (as opposed to swidden) rice agriculture, which on present evidence may well be of recent introduction into western Austronesia and certainly not connected with the early expansion of the Austronesians themselves. To simplify presentation this section is in the present tense, although I am aware that some of the systems described are undergoing rapid transformation, and some are of course extinct.

To begin at the simplest end of the scale, the Senoi Semai of interior Malaya still tend patches of giant wild yams, the tubers of which may grow to a length of 6 ft. The tubers, fruits and seeds are harvested, and some seeds are dropped or excreted around settlements, where they germinate and grow (Dentan 1968:47; on wild yam harvesting in Africa: Coursey 1967:12). The Semai periodically move their settlement sites, but often find a supply of yams when they return to a previously settled locality. Although these people are now cultivators of rice and millet, it is possible that their use of yams reflects a hunting and gathering past. The Andamanese hunter-gatherers also harvest wild yams, and even provide them with ritual protection during the growing season; the theoretical implication of this was pointed out over twenty years ago by the botanist I.H. Burkill (1953:12). In addition, wild yams are widely exploited in northern Australia, and artefacts identified as seed-grinders are possibly up to 10,000 years old in the Western Desert of Australia (Gould 1971:171). In theory, such instances could indicate a context for early cultivation, although the mere fact that it never did begin with these peoples certainly weakens any analogy.

The most widespread form of crop production in Austronesia is shifting cultivation, which basically involves a short period of cropping on a cleared plot, after which the plot is abandoned to a long fallow period, when nutrients are replaced through a natural cycle of regeneration. The literature on shifting cultivation generally, and in Austronesia particularly, is so large that little would be gained by presenting a summary at this point, and as might be expected the degree of local variation is enormous (Freeman 1955; Barrau 1958; Blaut 1960; Watters 1960; Conklin 1961; Geertz 1963; Spencer 1966). In addition, the range of crops introduced since European contact has naturally blurred prehistoric cultivation patterns. Archaeologically, the evidence for shifting cultivation is expectably slight, but if forest clearance is any clue to its presence then the palynological evidence claimed for this at about 9,000 B.C. in central Taiwan (Tsukada 1966; Chang 1970), and about 3,000 B.C. in the New Guinea Highlands (Powell 1970), is of obvious significance. So too is the palynological evidence for possible agriculture in north-west India at about 7,500 B.C. (Singh 1971). The wide range of plant remains from levels dated to between 10,000 and 6,000 B.C. at Spirit Cave in north-west Thailand is also valuable evidence, which Gorman (1971:311) summarizes as follows: 'The presence of *Lagenaria, Cucumis, Trapa* and the legumes I feel suggests a stage of plant exploitation beyond simple gathering. Whether they are definitely early cultigens (see Yen 1971:4) remains to be established.'

The continuum between extensive and intensive cultivation is best illustrated at the present day from the New Guinea Highlands (Clarke 1966; Brookfield & Hart 1971: ch. 3-4; Brookfield 1962). In the case of the Bomagai and Angoiang of the Bismarck Ranges, recently described by Clarke (1971), plots are used for 18 to 22 months for yams, taro, and introduced sweet potatoes and *Xanthosoma* (an American aroid), after which they are left for a fallow period of up to 40 years. Bomagai-Angoiang population density is low, at about six persons per cultivated hectare; they are not short of land, and in fact are still able to extend their clearings into virgin forest. Technologically their cultivation techniques are very simple, and do not involve any modification of the ground-surface. From a case such as this, it is possible to proceed through societies with increasing levels of intensity and efficiency, achieved by means of such techniques as drainage, tillage (especially in grasslands), mounding and terracing. With the most complex systems, the intervals of cropping and fallow may be almost equal, and such systems in the New Guinea Highlands are interestingly confined to two distinct areas of high population density – the Wissel Lakes and Baliem Valley areas of West Irian, and the Chimbu and Wahgi valley areas of Papua New Guinea. In these areas sweet potatoes are grown on beds that are divided by drainage ditches of gridiron pattern in the Wissel Lakes, Chimbu and Wahgi valley areas, and of parallel pattern in the Baliem Valley. The soil from the ditches is thrown on top of the beds together with cleared grasses, and nutrients can be added at intervals by cleaning out the ditches and adding to the beds. This kind of system provides well-drained plots for sweet potato, while taro can be grown in the wet ditches. In the Chimbu District plots can be used for several years with secondary fallows before full fallow abandonment is necessary and, for the latter, casuarina trees are commonly planted to provide humus and to fix nitrogen (Brookfield & Brown 1963). The Enga of the Western Highlands construct drained plots also, and in addition they till the soil and pile it into composted mounds about 2 m. in diameter and 65 cm. high (Meggitt 1960).

Recent archaeological research in the Wahgi Valley by Golson and his colleagues from the Australian National University has yielded evidence of field drains dating from about 300 B.C. (Golson *et al.* 1967; Powell 1970), together with digging-sticks, a paddle-shaped spade and stone axes. These discoveries are a little enigmatic at present: first of all they render untenable Watson's hypothesis (1965a; 1965b) that cultivation in the Highlands is mainly a result of the introduction of the sweet potato in, or after, the sixteenth century. We now have to allow for intensive agriculture over 2,000 years or more, but there is still the problem of which crops were grown. Taro has been suggested, and since Golson is still actively continuing investigations, this problem may be solved by future botanical analyses.

Apart from the two Highland areas of intensive cultivation, there are also local pockets of intensification in coastal New Guinea. Artificial raised garden plots are built in swamps by the Kimam and Marinds of West Irian, and the former have managed a most remarkable adaptation to an extremely difficult semi-marine environment (Serpenti 1965; Barrau 1958). The localization of these intensive systems within New Guinea suggests that they are probably local independent developments. They are part of a continuum, which is also apparent in the varied importance of hunting and gathering, and an important question for the prehistorian is whether this continuum reflects the developmental trajectory of prehistoric agriculture in

New Guinea, or whether it is merely a present-day reflection of environmental and demographic variation with no historical significance at all. We have too little evidence to choose either way at present, but the future answer may lie between the two extremes.

In the Oceanic islands beyond New Guinea, agricultural intensification usually takes the form of wet-field cultivation of taro, which is found in the Palau and Marianas Islands, localized areas of eastern Melanesia, and on many of the Polynesian high islands (Damm 1951). The related technique of pit cultivation, already referred to above, is found on many atolls. In general, the importance of shifting cultivation fades from west to east, and the islands themselves decrease in size in an irregular fashion in the same direction. For reasons that may in some way be related to this factor, the islands of eastern Polynesia supported dense prehistoric populations that were dependent to a great extent on intensive taro cultivation and utilization of tree crops, particularly coconuts, bread-fruit, bananas and pandanus (Barrau 1961).

The most remarkable evidence for prehistoric wet-field taro cultivation in Melanesia comes from New Caledonia, where contour terraces were constructed along the sides of steep slopes, staircase terraces alongside stream-beds, and raised beds built up in swamps in which the plants were grown in holes sunk to the water-table (Barrau 1956). Yam cultivation was carried out on drained crescentic mounds up to 1.5 m. high, sometimes stone-faced. Wet-field cultivation of taro was also present in the Solomons, New Hebrides and Fiji, but is better known from the high Polynesian islands. In the Hawaiian Islands, recent excavation in the Makaha Valley on Oahu has indicated that some form of terracing has existed there since the fourteenth century A.D. (Yen *et al.* 1972), although whether this is true wet-field terracing or more simple dry-land terracing for soil and ground-water retention is not clear. The latter kind of terracing was dominant in the Marquesas Islands, and tree crops appear to have been more important than tubers there. In the southern Cook Islands, the wet-field terraces of Mangaia have been described by Allen (1971; Bellwood 1971b:157-9), and I have recently surveyed staircase terraces on Rarotonga. It seems from a fairly superficial examination that the wet-field terracing (as opposed to simple planting in swamps) is confined mainly to areas with seasonal variation in rainfall, as is the case for New Caledonia and many of the Polynesian islands. In areas of high all-year-round rainfall, such as Samoa and the Bismarck and northern Solomon Islands, this form of cultivation appears to be absent, and there is sufficient rain for simple cultivation of taro. Whether wet-field taro cultivation is an innovation of the first Austronesian-speaking settlers of eastern Melanesia and Polynesia about 1000 B.C. is not clear, for the technique does have a sporadic distribution in western Austronesia, particularly in northern Luzon and on Botel Tobago Island (Yen 1971:5). At a more general level, the totality of evidence makes it very likely that the first Austronesian settlers of Oceania were at least agriculturalists, although an ingenious and differing argument has been put forward recently by Groube (1971) for an initial settlement of eastern Melanesia and Tonga by non-agricultural peoples. Another interesting point has been noted by Yen (1971:7-10): the islands of eastern Oceania share a number of restricted innovations such as the storage of fermented bread-fruit in pits, and consumption of the root of *Cordyline terminalis* (a small tree), and to these we might also add the ritual consumption of *kava*. These innovations, while fairly minor, are at least evidence for a continuous adaptation of the cultivation system to newly-settled island groups.

This aspect of adaptation is of course most strongly marked in New Zealand. Of the tropical crops grown in Polynesia, only the sweet potato could flourish, but it had to be grown annually in a spring-to-autumn growing season. Of the other crops, only the gourd, paper mulberry, yam and taro were taken to New Zealand, and their cultivation remained extremely limited (Best 1925). However, the adaptation required for sweet potato cultivation was quite remarkable (Yen 1961), as it involved winter storage in sealed semi-subterranean storehouses in which the temperature needed to be kept above 42° F. Generally, the heat given off by metabolic activity within the tubers avoided the need for artificial heat, although quite a number of archaeologically excavated pits do contain small hearths. The plant was restricted to north of the Christchurch area of the South Island, and the inhabitants of the far south remained non-agriculturalists until the European introduction of the white potato. Even in the warmer parts of the North Island, sweet potato cultivation was difficult, and in parts of the inland Waikato district large amounts of gravel were added to alluvial soils to improve drainage and heat-retention. A recent analysis of aspects of Maori agriculture by K. Shawcross (1967) has shown that the indigenous fern rhizome (*Pteridium esculentum*) probably retained more importance than sweet potato as a food source.

Another interesting feature of cultivation in New Zealand and eastern Polynesia concerns the widespread survival of associated stone structures. In fertile but stony areas, loose stones were sometimes cleared from ground surfaces and built into a variety of boundary alignments, platforms, terraces and other structures which, of course, are of invaluable assistance to the archaeologist. Detailed surveys of such field remains have been undertaken in New Zealand (Leach & Leach 1971: for Wairarapa district; Mrs A. Sullivan for Auckland Province: current Ph.D. work), in the Hawaiian Islands (Yen 1971:11; Green 1969; Green 1970; Ladd & Yen 1971) and in the Marquesas Islands (Kellum-Ottino 1971; Bellwood 1972). Many of the Marquesan examples can be interpreted as orchard walls, while in New Zealand and Hawaii they are evidently associated with dry-land tuber cultivation.

Having reviewed some of the voluminous evidence for intensification and diversification of cultivation in the eastern part of Austronesia, I will finish this section with a reference to the most important form of intensification in the west – wet rice cultivation. Surprisingly, wet rice cultivation is totally without archaeological documentation at present. Prior to A.D. 1500 it seems to have been present only in the Indianized islands of Java, Bali and in a few other pockets in western and central Indonesia, and on the west coast of northern Luzon. Only unsupported theories are available concerning its origin: for instance, Spencer and Hale have suggested that it first evolved in northern Indo-China about 2000 B.C., as a result of diffusion of the terracing technique from the Middle East (1961); Otley Beyer (1955) was of the opinion that wet-field terracing was present in Luzon from the first millennium B.C., but while it was certainly recorded at Spanish contact in 1572, Keesing (1962) felt that most of the spectacular inland terracing on Luzon developed after Spanish contact. Whether wet-field rice cultivation is associated with wet-field taro cultivation in origin is unknown, but an expansion of the technique with Indianization in south-east Asia seems very likely, and prehistoric rice cultivation may have been mainly of swidden type, of the kind described by Freeman for Sarawak (1955), with the proviso that the Iban now use iron tools. However, Barrau (1968:128-9) supports an origin for rice as a wet-field crop, perhaps first utilized as a weed in wet-taro gardens. In Thailand, there is some evidence that wet rice cultivation developed, together with water-buffalo domestication and iron metallurgy, from about 500 B.C. (Higham 1972).

As far as conclusions about the prehistory of cultivation in Austronesia are concerned, there is now perhaps enough linguistic, botanical and archaeological evidence to suggest the presence of cultivation, at or before 3000 B.C. There is a great deal of synchronic evidence to suggest that localized adaptation and intensification has taken place right through the area, and there is the possibility that wet rice may be a later introduction into western areas. So far, the earliest evidence for intensification falls about 2,000 years ago in New Guinea, but the techniques of ditching, irrigation and mounding were probably present long before this. I am fully aware of claims for late Pleistocene agriculture in south-east Asia made by scholars working in the area, and of the productive influence of Carl Sauer (1953; Solheim 1972; cf. Higgs & Jarman 1972 on general arguments for Pleistocene cultivation and animal husbandry). There are in fact good logical and circumstantial grounds for suggesting that basic techniques of domestication do go back into late Pleistocene times, although I think it should be made clear that direct evidence of this is so far lacking in south-east Asia.

Domesticated animals in Austronesia

Only three domesticated animals were taken by man right across Austronesia, and these are the pig, dog and fowl. The rat was also transported, probably accidentally, to most island groups, and was frequently eaten. However, it was never to my knowledge kept in captivity, and as an extraordinarily aggressive and adaptable animal it may well have spread partly by natural means; rats were the only placental land mammals to reach Australia and New Guinea across the sea lanes of Wallacea in pre-human times (Darlington 1957:388-9, 573).

The pig, dog and fowl have no wild ancestors in the greater part of Austronesia, and this is of course a matter of great significance; wherever and whenever they are found in archaeological deposits beyond their wild habitats, the hand of man may be inferred. Of the three, the least is known about the fowl, which is a descendant of the wild jungle fowls of mainland south-east Asia and the Sunda Islands (Ball 1933; Carter in Riley *et al.* 1971:181-3; Darlington 1957:294). Domesticated fowls provided meat, but eggs seem rarely to have been eaten. In Oceania today fowls are generally allowed to scavenge freely around settlements, and there are many feral populations. Archaeologically there are few observations to make, except to note the occurrence of fowl in Chinese Lungshanoid cultures which may pre-date 1700 B.C. (Chang 1968:134), and to note also that the fowl was the only domesticated species to reach Easter Island, the uttermost limit of Austronesia.

The evidence for the dog in prehistory is slightly better than that for the fowl. No dogs are reported from the Pleistocene deposits of Indonesia, although they were present in the Upper Pleistocene of China (Movius 1944:53). Dogs are reported for the Chinese Yang-shao culture of the fifth millennium B.C., and from about the fourth millennium B.C. at Non Nok Tha in Thailand (Bayard 1972:15), although they are not so far reported from Hoabinhian sites. In the islands, dogs appear at about 2000 B.C. in Niah Cave, Sarawak, where they appear on osteological grounds to be domesticated (Clutton-Brock 1959), and they appear in cave deposits in Portuguese Timor at about the same time (Glover 1971:176). They are present in the Toalean sites of Sulawesi, and in the New Guinea Highlands there are feral populations of dogs that may be of considerable antiquity (Titcomb 1969:60-6). The most puzzling evidence is for their possible presence in Australia by about 6,000 B.C. (Mulvaney 1969:65). The date 5,000-7,000 B.C. for Mount Burr may not be absolutely reliable, and further investigation of this evidence is proposed. Otherwise the oldest evidence for dingoes in Australia is from *c.* 1,000 B.C. at Fromm's Landing in South Australia (Mulvaney: personal communication). In this case they were undoubtedly brought by man, and the logical route is through Indonesia.

The role of the dog in prehistory in Austronesia is now uncertain, but it was clearly more than a hunting companion in many areas. In the Hawaiian Islands, for instance, dogs were bred on a vegetable diet for meat, and up to 200 were killed for recorded feasts (Titcomb 1969:8). Others were kept as pets, and puppies occasionally suckled by women. The eating of dog meat is widely recorded throughout the Pacific, and the industrial uses of a dog carcase were quite numerous, particularly in New Zealand, where it was the only domesticated animal (Allo 1970).

The most important animal of the triad, and the one about which there is a wealth of archaeological and ethnographic information, is the pig. Wild populations of pig were present in western Indonesia to as far east as Sulawesi, while they were absent in many of the Philippines, the Lesser Sundas and Moluccas, and in Oceania. Pig bones in archaeological deposits beyond Sulawesi not only strongly indicate transport by man, but if there are grounds for considering them to be domesticated (and transport of wild pigs is always a possibility), then they may also indicate the existence of plant cultivation. Pigs in captivity need to be fed to some extent on food that is actually produced by man, and therefore would be a most uneconomic proposition for a society dependent upon hunting and gathering.

The archaeological evidence for pig domestication in south-east Asia is extensive, but all unfortunately of a partly circumstantial nature. No direct osteological evidence for domestication has been published, and if surviving patterns of pig husbandry in the New Guinea Highlands are any guide, detailed measurements on bones may be of little assistance. For instance, the Bomagai and Angoiang of the Bismarck Ranges in Papua New Guinea keep pigs, but castrate the males and allow the females to mate with feral boars. To complicate matters further, feral pigs are commonly hunted (Clarke 1971:84).

Turning to the archaeological evidence, we may begin with the Hoabinhian levels in the cave of Gua Cha, in Kelantan (Malaysia). Here, Sieveking (1954) reported 25 discrete heaps of pig bones, each 3 to 4 feet in diameter. Most of the bones are skulls and jaws, and most are from immature individuals. Theoretically, this evidence could indicate domestication at a date prior to 3,000 B.C., but it is also possible that herds of wild pig could have been ambushed at river crossings (Medway 1969:203). In addition, a high proportion of young may indicate selective hunting, as pointed out by Hooijer for the orang-utan bones in the Niah Cave deposits (1962:487). Elsewhere on mainland eastern Asia, pigs were present in the Yang-shao culture of central China, and pigs have been found as burial offerings in a fourth millennium B.C. context at Non Nok Tha in Thailand (Bayard 1972:15).

In the Ryukyu Islands, a deposit of juvenile pig bones from Ishigaki Island dated to *c.* 6,500 B.C. is possible, but not dependable, evidence for domestication (Whitmore 1960: not personally seen by me; Pearson 1967). From the Toalean sites of Sulawesi, Hooijer (1950) has demonstrated a general reduction in size of all mammals (including cuscus, macaque monkey, civet cat, rat, deer and the wild Babirussa pig) through the Holocene period, with the single and significant exception of *Sus*, which becomes larger. Hooijer does not bring the possibility of domestication into his discussion, but it would seem to be at least worthy of consideration. Unfortunately, this particular example of osteological change is undated, although recent work on Toalean sites has shown that the distinctive stone tools of this industry go back to at least 4,000 B.C. (Mulvaney & Soejone 1970).

In Portuguese Timor, the pig had been introduced by 2,500 B.C. (Glover 1971:76), and is known by at least this time, and perhaps earlier, in two sites in the Highlands of Papua New Guinea (White 1971a:50). It seems likely that it was taken by the first settlers into Oceania from about 1,500 B.C., although as Groube points out (1971:311) it has not yet been reported from the earliest sites in the area. In sum, this archaeological evidence suggests strongly that pigs were domesticated, i.e. tamed, and transported by man, by at least 3,000 B.C., and probably by several millennia earlier. (The factor of transport is very important here; none of the osteological evidence given can more than suggest domestication, if taken alone – *cf.* Jarman & Wilkinson 1972).

It is of course necessary to keep Pacific animal domestication in some perspective, for the above triad can hardly be considered in the same category as the herd grazing animals of Eurasia. They provided an occasional and often ceremonial meat supply, rather than a daily dinner, which more often took the form of fish in coastal areas. In inland areas, pigs might be the major meat supply, and the role of pigs in subsistence is best recorded in the New Guinea Highlands. Rappaport's unique survey (1967) of the socio-economic functions of pigs amongst the Tsembaga of the Bismarck Ranges, Papua New Guinea, presents some extremely interesting, if localized, information. Ninety-nine per cent of Tsembaga diet by weight comes from plant foods, cultivated and gathered, while the other 1% is mostly from pork. Yet pigs are obviously a very major factor of life among the Tsembaga; they are cared for individually by the women, and may consume up to 40% of Tsembaga cultivated foods. They are killed occasionally to provide food for the sick, for birth and marriage ceremonies, but the majority are killed in a veritable bonanza every 8-12 years, when special ritual cycles of great social importance take place. The Tsembaga case may be rather extreme, and many peoples probably ate pork more frequently than this in prehistoric times in Oceania (Vayda, Leeds & Smith 1961). Furthermore, the roles of domesticated animals in prehistoric Austronesia may have been very varied, and it is also of interest in this respect to note the very spotty distribution of the three members of the triad amongst the scattered islands of Oceania (Urban 1961: map 1).

The fowl, pig and dog were of course not the only domesticated animals present in prehistoric times in western Austronesia, and Indonesia at least seems to have received cattle and caprovines prior to Indianization. Indonesia is poorly known archaeologically, and so far the only reliable evidence comes from Glover's excavations in Portuguese Timor (1971). Here, it appears that caprovines and bovids of undetermined species were introduced around, perhaps before, 1,000 B.C. The presence of bovids so far east by this date may be surprising, but domesticated *Bos indicus* is reported from Thailand at or before 3,000 B.C. (Higham & Leach 1972). Caprovines are not reported archaeologically anywhere in south-east Asia, but were of course present in India and China by this time. The history of the water-buffalo is an open question, but recent evidence from Thailand suggests that here it makes an appearance, together with iron and wet rice cultivation, about 500 B.C. (Higham 1972).

There is one other rather salutory piece of evidence which arises from Glover's work; around 2,500 B.C. (very approximately) three wild species, the civet cat, the macaque monkey and the cuscus, were introduced to Timor, most probably by man. The moral here is that not every case of prehistoric transport by man can be assumed to involve domestication, if one takes this term to imply some degree of direct and conscious control by man over the breeding pattern of an animal population. However, the three introduced animals could have been tamed and fed by man, just as the Bomagai and Angoiang capture cassowary chicks from the wild and keep them in pens, but do not attempt to breed them (Clarke 1971:88). This kind of taming is a point along the continuum between hunting and animal domestication, and may be viewed as a kind of food storage similar to the storage of live fish in tanks and enclosed lagoons in Polynesia.

Two culture-historical problems

The first question is whether cultivation by vegetative reproduction is an independent development in Harlan's south-east Asian 'non-centre' (1971), and if so, why it might have taken place. I do not presume to be able to give anything like a conclusive answer to this question, but I have already shown that there is no *direct* evidence for cultivation or animal domestication prior to, at the earliest, 4,000 B.C. While there is a growing number of claims for this area as the first 'hearth' of cultivation, this view can really be assessed only in the light of future knowledge. At present, it is a little premature to ask whether south-east Asia is the first hearth, but there are at least indications that better evidence for Early Holocene plant and animal domestication could appear in the future. Should this turn out to be the case, reasons for the development might be sought in a major environmental change of the terminal Pleistocene period. Between approximately 14,000 and 7,000 years ago, the sea rose an estimated 110 m. or more (Milliman & Emery 1969; Haile 1971) and flooded perhaps half a million square miles of land on the Sunda Shelf. This land, low-lying and probably of high diversity in flora and fauna, may well have supported wild ancestors of many of the Pacific cultigens in quantity. There is no reason to doubt the presence of man, or to doubt that he would exploit wild aroids or yams wherever they were available. At first sight, a rise in sea-level spread over 7,000 years or more might seem too slow a transformation to have had any effect upon human economic systems, but there are three very important points to be considered. Firstly, the Sunda Shelf is well over 500 miles wide in some places and, even with regular eustatic rise, coast lines might have been receding locally at a rate of one mile every ten years. Secondly, the eustatic rise was probably irregular, and localized speeding-up is possible. Thirdly, some outer north-eastern parts of the shelf could have sunk 50 m. or so due to tectonic movement (Haile 1971: 338), although it is not known whether this movement would be contemporary with the eustatic rise.

However one assesses these three pieces of evidence, there can be little doubt that coastal populations on the Sunda Shelf were obliged to move, owing to an inexorable encroachment by the sea. The significance for man in Australasia of this drowning is discussed by Tindale (1967) but not in an agricultural context. Some groups may have moved several times during the course of a single generation; is it possible that local temporary land shortage may have induced demographic pressure, and perhaps systematic cultivation? The full answer to this question may never be known, since details of natural resources and population densities in an area now beneath the sea may always remain unknown. However, explanations of this general demographic kind have been put forward to explain agricultural intensification in the New Guinea Highlands (Brookfield & Hart 1971:92), as well as agricultural origins in western Asia (Binford 1968). The factors causing the demographic pressure of course vary from place to place, but the hypothesis given for south-east Asia at least deserves a brief statement.

The second question is of more restricted scope, but of great importance nevertheless. Today, Indonesian languages are totally within the Austronesian family. While the origins of the family may lie in eastern Indonesia and surrounding areas, there is strong linguistic and physical anthropological evidence to suggest that the large islands of western Indonesia, particularly Sumatra, Java and Borneo, were originally settled by non-Austronesian speakers with a physical type close to that of present Melanesians (Pawley 1971; Jacob 1967). There are in fact Melanesian populations in several areas of eastern Indonesia even today. It is clear that Austronesian-speaking populations with a degree of Mongoloid genetic heritage have at some time in prehistory absorbed all previous ethnic groups, even though genetic absorption may not be complete everywhere. The importance of this problem was first suggested to me by Dr A.K. Pawsey, with whom I have discussed it several times.

Now compare this situation with New Guinea, where Austronesians have but a few toeholds in coastal areas, but where most peoples speak non-Austronesian languages and, especially in the Highlands, are probably fairly directly descended from an ancient stock that settled the island at least 25-30,000 years ago. Again, I cannot suggest definite reasons for this situation, but the geographical isolation of highland and parts of central New Guinea may be one factor. In addition, it may be that early Austronesians bringing in cultivation techniques, pigs, dogs and perhaps even cattle, may have experienced a massive population growth after settling the outstandingly fertile islands of Java and Bali. The development of wet rice cultivation, whether contemporary with or later than initial Austronesian expansion, would of course intensify the process of population growth, so that today some 99.3% of the approximate total of 150 million Austronesian speakers live to the west of New Guinea. Whatever the reason for this, Indonesia does present an Austronesian success story that is unparalleled in western Melanesia, except of course in areas with no previous inhabitants.

These two problems are both worthy of attention by economic prehistorians. Likewise, there remains the question of the exact economic base of the first Austronesians to commence the settlement of Oceania; the evidence suggests that they were equipped with a full range of cultigens and domesticated animals by at least 1,500 B.C., and a better range of archaeological evidence should be available in the fairly near future.

Acknowledgments

I wish to thank Professors J. Golson and D.J. Mulvaney of the Australian National University for their comments on a draft of this paper.

REFERENCES

Alexander, J. and Coursey, D.G. (1969) The origins of yam cultivation. In Ucko, P.J. and Dimbleby, G.W. (eds.), *The Domestication and Exploitation of Plants and Animals*, 405-25. London.

Allen, B. (1971) Wet field taro terraces in Mangaia. *Jour. Polynesian Soc.*, 80, 371-8.

Allo, J. (1970) *The Maori Dog.* M.A. thesis, Auckland University.

Ball, S.C. (1933) *Jungle Fowls from the Pacific Islands* (*B.P. Bishop Mus. Bull.* No. 108). Honolulu.

Barnard, N. (1972) *The First Radiocarbon Dates from China* (*Monographs on Far Eastern History* No. 8). Canberra.

Barrau, J. (1956) *L'Agriculture Vivrière Autochthone de la Nouvelle-Calédonie.* Noumea.

Barrau, J. (1958) *Subsistence Agriculture in Melanesia* (*B.P. Bishop Mus Bull.* No. 219). Honolulu.

Barrau, J. (1961) *Subsistence Agriculture in Polynesia and Micronesia* (*B.P. Bishop Mus. Bull.* No. 223). Honolulu.

Barrau, J. (ed.) (1963) *Plants and the Migrations of Pacific Peoples.* Honolulu.

Barrau, J. (1965) Histoire et préhistoire horticoles de l'Océanie tropicale. *Jour. Soc. des Océanistes*, 21, 55-78.

Barrau, J. (1968) L'humide et le sec. In Vayda, A.P. (ed.), *Peoples and Cultures of the Pacific*, 113-32. New York.

Barrau, J. (1970) La région Indo-Pacifique comme centre de mise en culture et de domestication des végétaux. *Jour. d'Agriculture Tropicale et de Botanique Appliquée*, 17, 487-503.

Bartlett, H.H. (1962) Possible separate origin and evolution of the Ladang and Sawah types of tropical agriculture. *Proc. 9th Pacific Science Cong.*, 4, 270-3. Bangkok.

Bayard, D.T. (1972) *Non Nok Tha: The 1968 Excavation.* Dunedin, N.Z.

Beaglehole, E. and Beaglehole, P. (1938) *Ethnology of Pukapuka (B.P. Bishop Mus. Bull.* No. 150*).* Honolulu.

Bellwood, P. (1971a) Fortifications and economy in prehistoric New Zealand. *P.P.S.*, 37, 56-95.

Bellwood, P. (1971b) Varieties of ecological adaptation in the Southern Cook Islands. *Archaeology and Physical Anthropology in Oceania*, 6, 145-69.

Bellwood, P. (1972) *A Settlement Pattern Survey, Hanatekua Valley, Hiva Oa, Marquesas Islands* (Pacific Anthropological Records No. 17). Honolulu.

Best, E. (1925) *Maori Agriculture* (*Dominion Mus. Bull.* No. 9). Wellington, N.Z.

Beyer, H.O. (1955) The origin and history of the Philippine rice terraces. *Proc. 8th Pacific Science Cong.*, 1, 387-97. Manila.

Binford, L.R. (1968) Post-Pleistocene adaptations. In Binford, L.R. and S.R. (eds.), *New Perspectives in Archaeology*, 313-41. Chicago.

Blaut, J.M. (1960) The nature and effects of shifting agriculture. *Symposium on the Impact of Man on Humid Tropics Vegetation*, 185-202. Goroka.

Brookfield, H.C. (1962) Local study and comparative method. *Annals Assoc. American Geographers*, 52, 242-54.

Brookfield, H.C. and Brown, P. (1963) *Struggle for Land.* Melbourne.

Brookfield, H.C. and Hart, D. (1971) *Melanesia – A Geographical Interpretation of an Island World.* London.

Burkill, I.H. (1953) Habits of man and the history of cultivated plants in the Old World. *Proc. Linnaean Soc. London*, 164, 12-42.

Carter, G.F. (1950) Plant evidence for early contacts with America. *S.W. Jour. of Anthropology*, 6, 161-82.

Chang, K.C. (1968) *The Archaeology of Ancient China.* Yale.

Chang, K.C. (1970) The beginnings of agriculture in the Far East. *Antiquity*, 44, 175-85.

Child, R. (1964) *Coconuts.* London.

Clark, J.G.D. (1965) Traffic in stone axe and adze blades. *Economic History Review*, 18, 1-28.

Clarke, W.C. (1966) Extensive to intensive shifting cultivation – a succession from New Guinea. *Ethnology*, 5, 347-59.

Clarke, W.C. (1971) *Place and People.* Canberra.

Clutton-Brock, J. (1959) Niah's Neolithic dog. *Sarawak Mus. Jour.*, 9, 143-5.

Conklin, H.C. (1961) The study of shifting cultivation. *Current Anthropology*, 1, 27-61.

Coursey, D.G. (1967) *Yams.* London.

Coursey, D.G. (1972) The civilizations of the yam. *Archaeology and Physical Anthropology in Oceania*, 7, 215-33.

Damm, H. (1951) Methoden der feldbewässerung in Ozeanien. *Südseestudien*, 204-34. Basel.

Darlington, P.J. (1956) *Zoogeography.* New York.

Dentan, R.K. (1968) *The Semai.* New York.

Dixon, R.B. (1932) The problem of the sweet potato in Polynesia. *American Anthropologist*, 34, 40-66.

Emory, K.P. (1972) Easter Island's position in the prehistory of Polynesia. *Jour. Polynesian Soc.*, 81, 57-69.

Freeman, D. (1955) *Iban Agriculture.* London.

Geertz, C. (1970) *Agricultural Involution – the Process of Ecological Change in Indonesia.* Berkeley.

Glover, I.C. (1971) Prehistoric research in Timor. In Mulvaney and Golson (eds.), 1971, 158-181.

Glover, I.C. (1972) *Excavations in Timor.* 2 vol. Ph.D. thesis, Australian National University.

Golson, J., Lampert, R.J., Wheeler, J.M. and Ambrose, W.R. (1967) A note on radiocarbon dates for horticulture in the New Guinea Highlands. *Jour. Polynesian Soc.*, 76, 369-71.

Gorman, C. (1971) The Hoabinhian and after: subsistence patterns in south-east Asia during the Late Pleistocene and Early Recent periods. *World Archaeology*, 2, 300-20.

Gould, R.A. (1971) The archaeologist as ethnographer: a case from the Western Desert of Australia. *World Archaeology*, 3, 143-77.

Green, R.C. (ed.) (1969) *Makaha Valley Historical Project: Interim Report No. 1* (Pacific Anthropological Records No. 4). Honolulu.

Green, R.C. (ed.) (1970) *Makaha Valley Historical Project: Interim Report No. 2* (Pacific Anthropological Records No. 10). Honolulu..

Groube, L.M. (1971) Tonga, Lapita pottery and Polynesian origins. *Jour. Polynesian Soc.*, 80, 278-316.

Haile, N.S. (1971) Quaternary shore lines in West Malaysia and adjacent parts of the Sunda Shelf. *Quaternaria*, 15, 333-43.

Harlan, J.R. (1971) Agricultural origins: centres and noncentres. *Science*, 174, 468-74.

Heyerdahl, T. (1968) *Sea Routes to Polynesia.* London.

Higgs, E.S. (ed.) (1972) *Papers in Economic Prehistory.* London.

Higgs, E.S. and Jarman, M.R. (1972) The origins of animal and plant husbandry. In Higgs (ed.), 1972, 3-14.

Higham, C.F.W. (1972) Initial model formulation *in terra incognita.* In Clarke, D.L. (ed.) *Models in Archaeology*, 453-76. London.

Higham, C.F.W. and Leach, B.F. (1972) An early centre of bovine husbandry in south-east Asia. *Science*, 172, 54-6.

Hooijer, D.A. (1950) *Man and Other Mammals from Toalean sites in south-west Celebes.* Verhandelingen der Koninklijke Nederlandische Akademie van Wetenschappen, Afdeling Natuurkunde vol. 46, no. 2.

Hooijer, D.A. (1962) Pleistocene dating and man. *Advancement of Science*, 18, 485-9.

Hossfeld, P. (1964) The Aitape Calvarium. *Australian Jour. of Science*, 27, 179.

Jacob, T. (1967) *Some Problems Pertaining to the Racial History of the Indonesian Region.* Utrecht.

Jarman, M.R. and Wilkinson, P.F. (1972) Criteria of animal domestication. In Higgs (ed.), 1972, 83-96.

Keesing, F.M. (1962) *The Ethnohistory of Northern Luzon.* Stanford.

Kellum-Ottino, M. (1971) *Archéologie d'une vallée des îles Marquises* (Pubn. Soc. des Océanistes No. 26).

Ladd, E.J. and Yen, D.E. (eds.) (1972) *Makaha Valley Historical Project: Interim Report No. 3* (Pacific Anthropological Records No. 18). Honolulu.

Leach, B.F. and Leach, H.M. (1971) Radiocarbon dates for the Wairarapa – II. *N.Z. Archaeological Assoc. Newsletter*, 14, 201.

Medway, Lord (1969) Excavations at Gua Kechil, Pahang: III -- Animal remains. *Jour. Malaysian Branch, Royal Asiatic Soc.*, 42, 197-203.

Meggitt, M.J. (1960) Notes on the horticulture of the Enga people of New Guinea. *Symposium on the Impact of Man on Humid Tropics Vegetation*, 86-9. Goroka.

Merrill, E.D. (1954) *The Botany of Cook's Voyages and its Unexpected Significance in Relation to Anthro-*

pology, Biogeography and History (Chronica Botanica 14, no. 5-6). Waltham.

Milliman, J.D. and Emery, K.O. (1969) Sea levels during the past 35,000 years. *Science*, 162, 1121-3.

Movius, H.L. (1944) *Early Man and Pleistocene Stratigraphy in Southern and Eastern Asia* (Papers of the Peabody Museum, vol. 19, no. 3). Cambridge, Mass.

Mulvaney, D.J. (1969) *The Prehistory of Australia.* London.

Mulvaney, D.J. and Golson, J. (eds.) (1971) *Aboriginal man and Environment in Australia.* Canberra.

Mulvaney, D.J. and Soejono, R.P. (1970) Archaeology in Sulawesi, Indonesia. *Antiquity*, 45, 26-33.

Pawley, A. (1971) *Austronesian Languages.* Auckland.

Pearson, R. (1967) Recent radiocarbon dates from Ryukyu sites and their chronological significance. *Asian and Pacific Archaeology Series*, 1, 19-24. Honolulu.

Powell, J.M. (1970) The history of agriculture in the New Guinea Highlands. *Search*, 1, 199-200.

Rappaport, R.A. (1967) *Pigs for the Ancestors: Ritual in the Ecology of a New Guinea People.* New.Haven and London.

Riley, C.L., Kelley, J.C., Pennington, C.W. and Rands, R.L. (eds.) (1971) *Man Across the Sea.* Austin, Texas and London.

Rosendahl, P. and Yen, D.E. (1971) Fossil sweet potato remains from Hawaii. *Jour. Polynesian Soc.*, '80, 379-85.

Sauer, C. (1952) *Agricultural Origins and Dispersals.* New York.

Serpenti, L.M. (1965) *Cultivators in the Swamps.* Assen.

Shawcross, K. (1967) Fern root and 18th-century Maori food production in agricultural areas. *Jour. Polynesian Soc.*, 76, 330-52.

Sieveking, G. de G. (1954) Excavations at Gua Cha, Kelantan, 1954 . Part 1. *Federation Mus. Jour.*, n.s. I and II, 75-143.

Singh, G. (1971) The Indus Valley culture. *Archaeology and Physical Anthropology in Oceania*, 6, 177-89.

Solheim, W.G. II. (1972) An earlier agricultural evolution. *Scientific American*, 226, 34-41.

Spencer, J.E. (1966) *Shifting Cultivation in south-east Asia.* Berkeley.

Spencer, J.E. and Hale, C.A. (1961) The origin, nature and distribution of agricultural terracing. *Pacific Viewpoint*, 2, 1-40.

Tindale, N.B. (1967) Peopling of the lands south-east of Asia. *Colorado Quarterly*, 15, 339-53.

Titcomb, M. (1969) *Dog and Man in the Ancient Pacific* (B.P. Bishop Mus. Special Pubn. No. 59). Honolulu.

Tsukada, M. (1966) Late Pleistocene vegetation and climate in Taiwan (Formosa). *Proc. National Acad. Science*, 55, 543-8. Washington.

Urban, M. (1961) *Die Haustiere der Polynesier.* Ph.D. dissertation, Georg-August-Universität, Göttingen.

Vayda, A.P., Leeds A. and Smith, D.B. (1961) The place of pigs in Melanesian subsistence. In Garfield, V.E. (ed.), *Proc. 1961 Ann. Spring Meetg. American Ethnological Soc.*, 69-77. Seattle.

Watson, J.B. (1965a) From hunting to horticulture in the New Guinea Highlands. *Ethnology*, 4, 295-309.

Watson, J.B. (1965b) The significance of a recent ecological change in the Central Highlands of New Guinea. *Jour. Polynesian Soc.*, 74, 438-50.

Watters, R.F. (1960) The nature of shifting cultivation. *Pacific Viewpoint*, 1, 59-99.

White, J.P. (1971) New Guinea: the first place in Oceanic settlement. In Green, R.C. and Kelly, M. (eds.), *Studies in Oceanic Culture History,* vol. 2 (Pacific Anthropological Records No. 12), 45-52. Honolulu.

Whitmore, F.C. (1960) Fossil mammals from Ishigaki-shima, Ryukyu retto. *Geological Survey 1960: Short Papers in the Geological Sciences.* Washington.

Williamson, R.W. (1939) *Essays in Polynesian Ethnology* (Piddington, R.O. ed.). London.

Yen, D.E. (1960) The sweet potato in the Pacific: the propagation of the plant in relation to its distribution. *Jour. Polynesian Soc.*, 69, 368-75.

Yen, D.E. (1961) The adaptation of the kumara by the New Zealand Maori. *Jour. Polynesian Soc.*, 70, 338-48.

Yen, D.E. (1971) The development of agriculture in Oceania. In Green, R.C. and Kelly, M. (eds.), *Studies in Oceanic Culture History*, vol. 2, (Pacific Anthropological Records No. 12), 1-12. Honolulu.

Yen, D.E., Kirch, P.V., Rosendahl, P. and Riley, T. (1972) Prehistoric agriculture in the Upper Valley of Makaha, Oahu. In Ladd and Yen (eds.), 1972, 59-94.

RALPH BULMER

Selectivity in hunting and in disposal of animal bone by the Kalam of the New Guinea Highlands

New Guinea Highlanders keep mammal bones, mainly mandibles and crania, of the larger marsupials and rodents that they hunt, as trophies to decorate their houses. Wild mammals, unlike birds and certain other groups of creatures, are difficult to observe and identify on sight, and research-workers who need to draw up local faunal lists have to make collections. They can often purchase hunters' trophies relatively easily, and find this a much simpler and less time-consuming process than the acquisition of live or newly-killed animals, whether by purchase from local people or by their own efforts in trapping and hunting. Collecting of the regurgitated debris found at owl roosts can also produce large quantities of vertebrate material with relatively little effort, though in this case mainly of the smaller mammals.

Both men and owls are selective in their hunting, as can be demonstrated by comparing lists of specimens acquired by owls, by locally resident human beings, and by transient zoologists and other research workers in the same region (Bulmer & Menzies 1972-3:488-9). Further, men, if not also owls, are selective in their disposal of the animals they kill. Thus hunters' trophy collections, like any other assemblages of animal bone that have been deliberately or casually accumulated and deposited by men, reflect only indirectly the local incidence of animal populations, being the residue after two processes of selection have occurred. This paper attempts to describe the selective factors that operate, both in the slaughter of animals and in the disposal of animal bone, in one particular small human population in the New Guinea Highlands.

It will be shown that, although the people concerned kill, at least occasionally, all locally present mammal species, and eat all but two of them, they in fact pursue and obtain different species with very different degrees of intensity; and further, that the species they kill most frequently are not reflected in the same proportions in the trophy collections which they retain (see Tables 1 and 2). While, by and large, small animals are hunted or collected less systematically than larger ones, and their fragments are almost never retained in trophy collections, there are also significant differences in the treatment accorded to larger species of approximately similar sizes, both in hunting and in ultimate disposal.

The people whose practices are here described are the Kalam-speaking[1] communities of the Upper Kaironk Valley and adjacent areas of the Schrader and Bismarck Ranges in the Madang District of Papua New Guinea, among whom I undertook 17 months of field-work in the period 1960-73. In these studies I have had the collaboration of several vertebrate zoologists, who have identified my collections, and two of whom have worked with me in the field.

The Kalam are gardeners, growing sweet potato, taro and a wide range of other vegetables; mainly in garden areas which, between cultivation periods, are left to fallow under grass or plantations of casuarina trees; but in part in forest-edge swiddens. Pig husbandry is also very important in their economy. In the Upper Kaironk Valley, homesteads and most gardens lie between 1,500 and 2,200 m. The crests of the steep ridges that form the sides of the valley, rising to approximately 2,300 m. on the south side and 2,700 m. on the north side, are largely forest-covered from about 2,200 m. upwards. These forests continue to rather lower altitudes in the less densely populated adjacent valleys, where many Upper Kaironk people have hunting and collecting rights, and some have gardens and residential areas to which they periodically migrate.

The settlement pattern is one of dispersed homesteads and small straggling and temporary hamlets which often focus on a ceremonial house. A ceremonial house is built by a small

Table 1 Sources of mammal specimens and records, Upper Kaironk Valley, 1960-1973

	Specimens obtained by Kalam		Specimens obtained otherwise*	Totals
Larger mammals (adult weights above 400 g)	Whole animals recorded	Animals in trophy collections		
Marsupials				
Bandicoot, *Peroryctes longicauda*	8 (38%)	3 (14%)	10 (48%)	21 (100%)
Cuscus, *Phalanger gymnotis*	0 (0%)	49 (94%)	3 (6%)	52 (100%)
Cuscus, *Phalanger vestitus*	3 (9%)	31 (91%)	0 (0%)	34 (100%)
Ringtail, *Pseudocheirus forbesi*	5 (21%)	3 (12%)	16 (67%)	24 (100%)
Ringtail, *Pseudocheirus corinnae*	4 (24%)	13 (76%)	0 (0%)	17 (100%)
Ringtail, *Pseudocheirus cupreus*	6 (13%)	39 (87%)	0 (0%)	45 (100%)
7 other species	1 (9%)	9 (82%)	1 (9%)	11 (100%)
Rodents				
Giant rat, *Hyomys goliath*	1 (11%)	8 (89%)	0 (0%)	9 (100%)
Giant rat, *Mallomys rothschildi*	4 (9%)	37 (86%)	2 (5%)	43 (100%)
6 other species	4 (36%)	5 (46%)	2 (18%)	11 (100%)
Bat				
Fruit-bat, *Dobsonia moluccensis*	2 (50%)	2 (50%)	0 (0%)	4 (100%)
Smaller mammals (adult weights under 400 g)				
Marsupials				
Pygmy possum, *Cercartetus caudatus*	15 (68%)	0 (0%)	7 (32%)	22 (100%)
Sugar-glider, *Petaurus breviceps*	5 (36%)	0 (0%)	9 (64%)	14 (100%)
3 other species	2 (25%)	0 (0%)	6 (75%)	8 (100%)
Rodents				
Pogonomys sylvestris	26 (<74%)	0 (0%)	9 (>26%) } +13	35 (<100%) } +13
Pogonomys mollipilosus	4 (<27%)	0 (0%)	11 (>73%) }	15 (<100%) }
Rattus exulans	1 (< 1%)	0 (0%)	99 (>99%) }	100 (<100%) }
Rattus ruber	2 (< 7%)	0 (0%)	25 (>93%) } +78	27 (<100%) } +78
Rattus niobe	1 (< 2%)	0 (0%)	42 (>98%) }	43 (<100%) }
Rattus verecundus	2 (9%)	0 (0%)	21 (91%)	23 (100%)
Melomys lorentzi	1 (10%)	0 (0%)	9 (90%)	10 (100%)
Melomys platyops	0 (0%)	0 (0%)	16 (100%)	16 (100%)
5 other species	3 (13%)	0 (0%)	21 (87%)	24 (100%)
Bats				
3 species	5 (31%)	0 (0%)	11 (69%)	16 (100%)
Totals, larger mammals	38 (14%)	199 (73%)	34 (13%)	271 (100%)
Totals, smaller mammals	67 (15%)	0 (0%)	377 (85%)	444 (100%)
Totals, all mammals	105 (15%)	199 (28%)	411 (57%)	715 (100%)

* i.e. from debris left by owls and other birds of prey, by dogs in cases when remains not kept by Kalam for trophies, and from research workers' traps and shooting.

local kin-group, which acts as host for a major ceremony (*smy*) in the year in which their house is constructed and then uses it as an extended family residence for the following two or three years.[2]

Within the confines of the Upper Kaironk Valley, an area of some sixty square kilometres, 215 species of vertebrate animals have so far been recorded (43 mammals, 137 birds, 14 reptiles, 20 frogs, 1 fish), and it is doubtful if this list is more than 70% complete. There are many scores of additional species present within a few hours' walk of the Upper Kaironk settlements, at lower altitudes in the Kaironk Valley itself, and in adjacent valleys to the north and south. Nearly all these animals are, at least occasionally, killed and eaten. Of species present within the Upper Kaironk Valley the only exceptions are the dog (ritually prohibited as food), the common rat around the homesteads (*Rattus exulans*) and four very common small birds found in settlement areas (all of which are regarded as unclean because of their feeding habits), two small lizards (one regarded as mystically dangerous, the other merely as inedible), two snakes (mystically dangerous) and seven of the nine locally recorded microhylid frog species (believed, possibly in some cases correctly, to be poisonous). Of these animals that are not eaten, dogs are nevertheless killed occasionally, and rats, lizards and snakes more frequently. At least 80 species of invertebrate animals, mainly insects or their larvae, spiders and snails, are also eaten.

Factors affecting the number of animals of different species killed include their population densities; the extent and proximity of their habitats to homesteads, gardens and other regular scenes of human activity; the degree to which they are domesticated; their habits, which may make them difficult or easy to capture; the relevant skills, knowledge and technology possessed by the human population; the seasonality with which they are hunted or collected; the economic and ritual values attached to the categories in which the human population classifies them; and the time which humans are prepared to devote to hunting and collecting, which is itself largely determined by the other factors previously listed. Of these factors only domestication, economic and ritual values, and seasonality of hunting will be discussed in any detail.

Domestication

Prior to first effective contact with Australian administration, in 1956, the Kaironk Valley Kalam kept only two domestic animals, pig (*Sus scrofa*) and dog (*Canis familiaris*), both of which are also present as feral animals in adjacent valleys, though not normally crossing the ridges into the Upper Kaironk Valley itself. Although some other ethnic groups in the Bismarck Range kept domestic fowl (*Gallus gallus*), and also captured and reared cassowary chicks (at higher altitudes, the dwarf mountain cassowary, *Casuarius bennetti*), the Kalam did neither. The only semi-domesticated creature they kept was the white cockatoo (*Cacatua galerità*), chicks taken from nests in lower-altitude forests being occasionally reared for periodic plucking to provide plumes for dance regalia.

According to the oral traditions of the Kaironk people, pig husbandry is a recent development, within the time of the grandparents of older living men (i.e. perhaps 70-100 years ago), and the introduction and expansion of pig husbandry have coincided with an extension of gardening (particularly of sweet potato production) and forest clearing, a decline in the quantity of wild game killed, and a considerable increase in human population. Over the decade 1960-70 the number of domestic pigs present

Table 2 Incidence of eight commonest mammal species in trophy collections by order of size

	Maximum weight in kg.*	Specimens obtained by Kalam: Animals in trophy collections	Specimens obtained by Kalam: Whole animals recorded	Specimens obtained otherwise	Totals
Cuscus, *Phalanger gymnotis*	3.43	49 (25%)	0 (0%)	3 (9%)	52 (19%)
Ringtail, *Pseudocheirus cupreus*	2.44	39 (20%)	6 (16%)	0 (0%)	45 (17%)
Cuscus, *Phalanger vestitus*	?2.25	31 (15%)	3 (8%)	0 (0%)	34 (12%)
Giant rat, *Mallomys rothschildi*	1.81	37 (18%)	4 (11%)	2 (6%)	43 (16%)
Giant rat, *Hyomys goliath*	1.31	8 (4%)	1 (3%)	0 (0%)	9 (3%)
Ringtail, *Pseudocheirus corinnae*	1.13	13 (6%)	4 (10%)	0 (0%)	17 (6%)
Ringtail, *Pseudocheirus forbesi*	1.05	3 (2%)	5 (13%)	16 (47%)	24 (9%)
Bandicoot, *Peroryctes longicauda*	0.45	3 (2%)	8 (21%)	10 (29%)	21 (8%)
14 other species		16 (8%)	7 (18%)	3 (9%)	26 (10%)
Totals		199 (100%)	38 (100%)	34 (100%)	271 (100%)

*Weights are taken from Van Deusen (in White 1972: 152), with the exception of *Phalanger vestitus* which, perhaps through a printing error, is grossly underestimated in that source.

appeared, on average, to equal the number of humans, though still increasing. By 1973, the gross number of pigs present appeared to exceed considerably the number of humans, even though this also had doubled, through immigration as well as natural increase, over a thirteen-year period.[3]

All domestic pigs are intended for slaughter and consumption, and even those that die of disease are consumed. The occasions and locations of pig-slaughter and consumption are discussed later. Here, it may merely be noted that, whenever possible, pigs are kept until they are two to four years old, and are then slaughtered in groups at initiation ceremonies, which are also occasions of dancing (*smy*) and ceremonial exchange, held at the time of the taro harvest (August-November). However, many pigs are killed individually, often before reaching their desired maturity, to placate the dead, to ward off sickness, and for other ritual reasons of a personal or domestic nature. Some pigs are killed because they are ailing. A few are killed by angry garden-owners after they have broken into crops.

An aspect of Kalam pig husbandry that could be of interest to the archaeologist, as affecting the osteological record, is that all male pigs are gelded, either as piglets, or when they are eight to ten months old, after they have, for a brief spell, been available to impregnate the local sows.

Dogs, though domesticated, are never eaten by Kalam, and are only slaughtered if they become a persistent nuisance by killing poultry and young pigs. Wild dogs are said never to be killed, though their puppies are captured and tamed. Dogs are kept mainly for the valuable aid they give the forest hunter (Bulmer & Menzies 1972-73:486), though the flesh of animals that dogs kill on their own account, including that brought home by bitches hunting to feed their pups,[4] is also consumed by the dogs' owners, if they can find it in time. Two reasons are given by Kalam for their complete prohibition on the consumption of the dog (see also Bulmer 1967:19) – that it is an unclean feeder which eats refuse in and around homesteads, and sometimes breaks into graves; and that its blood and bones are very harmful to growing taro, so that anyone who has killed or buried a dog, let alone eaten one, should keep away from taro gardens for a month.

At present only about a dozen dogs are kept by a population of approximately 700 people in the census area of the Upper Valley with which I am most familiar, nearly all of these by men whose houses lie close to advanced bush-fallow and forest. While the number of dogs kept was considerably greater prior to the early 1960s, when poultry-keeping became general, there were still then many households, especially those in grassland areas well away from the forest, where there were no dogs.

Intensity of hunting of different species

One might reasonably assume that the main factors governing intensity of hunting and collecting of particular species, apart from their scarcity and accessibility in terms of habitat and habits, would be size, in the case of animals taken mainly for their meat, or exchange value, in the case of creatures taken mainly for plumes or pelts. While this is broadly true, two major additional factors that affect the intensity with which animals are hunted for food are the extent to which they are considered appropriate for consumption by men and adolescent boys, and the extent to which they are required or desired for ritual cooking and ceremonial distribution. Subsidiary factors of some significance include the value set on skins, teeth or bone of certain species for technological purposes, the prestige accruing to the successful hunter of certain species, and restrictions on killing and consumption based on 'totemic' association and on the antithesis that Kalem recognize between certain forest animals and the cultivation of taro.

Male dietary restrictions

Women and young children can eat any animals other than the few already listed as completely prohibited or regarded as totally inedible. Young teenage boys can eat no animal food, other than pork and cassowary, for a period of from one to three years between their first and second participation in initiation ritual. For older boys and adult men, animals are placed in a long and finely graded series, ranging from those that, apart from totemic and garden restrictions, can be freely eaten by all initiated males, to those that very few of any age are permitted, or prepared, to eat. In general, animals that are terrestrial or subterranean in habit are considered less edible than those that are arboreal; those found in the cultivation and grassland zone are less edible than those of the forest; those that are deemed to have soft or rapidly decomposing flesh are less edible than those that are deemed to have strong firm flesh; those that are 'cold', i.e. aquatic creatures such as eels and frogs, and the kinds of reptiles that do not warm themselves in the sun, are less edible than those that are 'warm'; those that eat clean food (i.e. the herbivorous and frugivorous species and the raptors that in turn eat these) are more edible than insectivores and especially the creatures that eat earthworms, terrestrial insects and carrion (and the raptors that, in turn, prey upon these unclean feeders); and those that are invoked in certain powerful magical spells have to be avoided by men who practise these forms of magic.

After pig and cassowary, the animals that can most freely be eaten by men are wallaby, most of the larger, mainly arboreal, marsupials and rodents of the forest (cuscuses, ringtail possums, striped possum, the giant rats *Mallomys* and *Uromys*); and one other giant rat, *Hyomys* which, though essentially terrestrial and often found in cane beds outside the forest, is treated as a sort of honorary arboreal mammal, possibly because of its morphological similarities to *Mallomys*. These were the only animals that could be eaten by unmarried young men who had been initiated but were growing their hair long to make their first ceremonial wigs. After they had cut their hair, they could also eat bats, most forest birds regardless of size, a limited number of birds of the open country that are either arboreal or aerial feeders, or raptors that eat other 'clean' creatures, and eels.[5]

Animals listed above that can be eaten by the majority of men, but are avoided by the relatively few who possess magical spells that invoke them, are the two local cuscus species, which are the largest arboreal mammals of the forest, and bats. Eels and all frogs have to be avoided as food by a larger number of magicians, and are also not normally eaten by young unmarried men who want to keep 'hot', i.e. in prime physical condition, as these creatures, like sexual contact with women, will cool them down. The smaller arboreal mammals of the forest, such as the sugar-glider (*Petaurus*), the dasyurid marsupials and arboreal mice (*Lorentzimys*) can be eaten by most men. A wider range still, eaten by few men other than the elderly, includes such large species as the bandicoots and some of the giant rats that are, or are classified as, terrestrial (e.g. *Anisomys, Parahydromys*); water-rats, the great majority of rat- and mouse-sized rodents of the forest and cultivation zones, which are either terrestrial or if arboreal haunt low vegetation and in many cases have their nests and burrows underground; certain common ground-feeding birds of the cultivation zone such as quail; certain frogs and lizards that are regarded as having 'firm' flesh, and pythons. Finally, creatures that are avoided as food by almost all men include the small rodents that are most similar in appearance, habits and habitat to the completely avoided *Rattus exulans* of the homesteads; the remaining birds of the open country, excluding only the four common species whose feeding habits make them totally prohibited; those frogs that are regarded as having 'soft' flesh, and the majority of small lizards.

Women freely eat these animals, and some that are readily accessible to them (e.g. frogs) they collect in large numbers. When new gardens are being cleared in bush-fallow and cane-grass they obtain fair numbers of small rodents which nest in low foliage or underground. However; women do not hunt with bow and arrow, do not climb trees, do not set traps and, in general, spend much less time in the forest than men do, so their opportunities for obtaining for themselves many kinds of animals that they alone are likely to be able to eat are strictly limited. To a variable extent men will kill animals they happen to encounter that they themselves cannot eat, so that their womenfolk and young children can have them. However, it would be most unusual for men to make any systematic effort to kill even the larger mammals that are considered to be women's food. In general, Kalam say, men hunt only the largest animals and those that live in trees. When a young man or adolescent boy kills terrestrial game such as bandicoot, he should not even handle it. Since a high proportion of the mammals men catch are taken by hand, this is a severe restriction. Thus, if a young man does kill a large bandicoot or terrestrial rodent with his bow, he will carefully lodge the animal in a convenient tree or bush to disengage his arrow, and leave it there for a female relative to recover.

There is only one animal that men avoid to any extent which is nevertheless highly valued and intensively hunted or trapped by them. This is the eel. The reason for this is partly that those who are permitted to eat eel recognize that it is excellent eating, and partly that it is appropriate for ritual cooking.

Ritual and ceremonial requirements for game

With the exception of the eel, the creatures for which there is heavy demand for ritual cooking in propitiation of ancestor spirits and of the recent dead, and for distribution as feast food on ceremonial occasions, are all included in the list of those that most men can freely eat. However, some animals in the freely eaten categories are not used for any ritual or ceremonial purpose. Thus, of the arboreal mammals, only the five largest locally present species are regarded by most men as appropriate for ritual and ceremonial occasions (the cuscuses *Phalanger gymnotis* and *P. vestitus*, the ringtail possums *Pseudocheirus cupreus* and *P. corinnae*, and the giant rat *Mallomys rothschildi*), and of the forest birds, only arboreal feeders are used. Further, of the animal and bird species that are ritually cooked or ceremonially distributed, not all are appropriate for all types of occasion. Thus, for ritual cooking at the graves of recent dead, which takes place each year at the harvest season, and on other occasions when sickness or misfortune are attributed to them, arboreal forest mammals are a necessity (if not available a pig has to be substituted), eels are much desired, and the arboreal forest birds are also appropriate. For ritual cooking in newly planted taro gardens, to propitiate the ancestors who formerly cultivated there, the same animals are used, except that the largest and in other respects most highly valued of the arboreal mammals, the cuscus *Phalanger gymnotis*, has to be excluded, because its influence is thought to be inimical to taro; and of the birds the mountain pigeon, *Gymnophaps*, is thought to be particularly appropriate, because its seasonal movements are seen as mystically related to the growth-cycle of the taro.

For cooking and distribution at the annual harvest-season *smy* festivals (which combine initiation ceremonies, delayed bridewealth distributions, and ceremonial exchange), cassowary, wallaby, the five large arboreal mammals (including in this case *Phalanger gymnotis*), and eels, are all in much demand, though birds are not used. It is said that before domestic pigs were available, wallabies and arboreal mammals were required in large numbers for these ceremonies, most being obtained and smoked over the previous three to four months, though some were newly killed and at least one animal, preferably a wallaby, had to be ritually killed at the ceremony. The cooked carcases of smoked arboreal mammals still are the proper gift on these occasions for kinsfolk in other local groups who have buried near relatives of the feast-holders.

While the build-up of pig-husbandry and concurrent decline in local wallaby populations have led to a virtually complete substitution of pig for wallaby in *smy* feasts, the demand for the larger arboreal mammals, both for these occasions and for propitation of ancestors and recent dead, is a prime factor in accounting for efforts made to hunt these animals.

Use of animal parts for ornaments and technological purposes

Plucked fur of the silky cuscus, *Phalanger vestitus*, is used to work into fibre for men's string-aprons. The tail of the striped possum, *Dactylonax*, is sometimes set on a cane as a minor head-dress ornament. Apart from these, Kalam do not use the pelts of any mammals present in the Upper Kaironk Valley, and are interested in those of only three species found at lower altitudes, only the least important of which is normally found within a day's walk. The white pelts of some male spotted cuscuses, *Phalanger maculatus*, are highly valued as necessary head-ornaments for boys emerging from initiation seclusion, and small pieces of white, golden or spotted fur of the same species also have some minor value as ornaments. Tail-skins of the tree kangaroo, *Dendrolagus goodfellowi*, are also occasionally used as ornaments, and tails of the larger lower-altitude striped possum, *Dactylopsila*, are used in the same way as those of the locally present species, *Dactylonax*.

Teeth of several mammal species are, or were until recently, used in necklaces. Canines and incisors of dog were most highly valued, but pig tusks, pig incisors, the lower incisors of wallaby and of the larger arboreal marsupials, and the canines of fruit-bats, were also used. The lower incisors of the largest giant rat, *Mallomys*, left in the half-mandible, were used as gravers to decorate arrow shafts and small bamboo containers, and occasionally the lower incisors of other large rodents were used for the same purpose. Pig tusks, ground down, were used as wood-scrapers, as an alternative to stone flakes. Pig scapulae were formerly fashioned into spoons, and the tibia of pig and of the larger wallaby, *Thylogale*, were made into spatulate taro-scrapers. Skins of several of the arboreal marsupials, but especially of the small ring-tail possum, *Pseudocheirus forbesi*, are used as drum-skins. Wing-bones of fruit-bats are used for needles. However, although these technological uses of mammal parts affect the disposal of carcases and bones (see below), their significance in creating additional demand for the species concerned, and thus the intensity with which they are hunted, is probably negligible.

In contrast, the intensity with which certain bird species are hunted directly reflects the value of their plumes as ornaments. There are eighteen locally occurring birds that are more highly valued for their plumes than for their meat, though all are regarded as edible: 2 large hawks, 7 parrots, 8 birds of paradise, 1 bower-bird. Of plumes acquired by trade or hunting in other areas, nine additional species are particularly highly valued. Prior to European contact the most highly valued of all, worth a shell ornament, a good stone axe-blade or a small pig, were the plumes of Pesquet's parrot, *Psittrichas fulgidus*, which was seldom obtained locally, and skins of the lesser bird of paradise, *Paradisaea minor*, common at lower altitudes within half a day's walk, and the Papuan lory, *Charmosyna papou*, which was found in local forests, though the plumage phases most highly regarded as headdress ornaments were normally found only at lower altitudes. The plumes of the New Guinea eagle, *Harpyopsis novaeguineae*, were almost equally highly valued, and this bird was occasionally killed locally, while four local birds of paradise (*Epimachus fastosus, E. meyeri, Astrapia stephaniae* and *Pteridophora alberti*) were sufficiently highly valued for personal ownership rights in forest tracts and display trees where they were taken to be jealously maintained, as was also the case with the lesser bird of paradise which, as already mentioned, was found in near-by lower-altitude regions.

Talons of the larger raptors and of other large birds are sometimes kept as personal ornaments, and as probes for extraction of thorns and splinters. Beaks are also sometimes kept, but the only one of value is the maxilla of the hornbill (*Aceros plicatus*), found at lower altitudes within half a day's walk, and also highly valued for its plumes.

Bird plumes were, and still are, a major item in trade both in and out of the Upper Kaironk Valley; and those of certain species, notably the lesser bird of paradise and the Papuan lory, are necessities, at *smy* festivals, for visiting dancers and newly initiated boys respectively. A high proportion of plumes used on these occasions is newly purchased, or borrowed from kinsfolk, the appropriate recompense for a loan being a share of the cooked pork received at the *smy* feasts.

The cassowary is in many respects in a class of its own (see Bulmer 1967). By far the largest bird present in New Guinea, it is very highly valued for its meat. However plumes were also used formerly for warriors' headdresses, long-bones for pandanus-fruit splitters, the claws of its inner toes as spear-points, and remaining claws and featherless wing-quills as personal ornaments. The fact that the cassowary was regarded as highly as the wild pig, even though a large wild pig might provide three times the weight of meat that the local small cassowary species would, may to some extent reflect the additional value of the creature's non-edible parts.

Prestige accruing to the hunter

The successful hunter of wild pig or cassowary enjoys respect and renown that may survive his death for a generation or longer. That men see the hunting of wallaby and of the five largest arboreal mammals as prestigious is shown by their retention of bones to decorate their houses, and by the oblique way they boast of their achievements in the long detailed narratives of hunting expeditions which are a regular feature of male conversation. While success in hunting smaller arboreal mammals, and also birds, generally correlates with success in hunting the larger species, only the killing of large birds of prey and large pigeons is a matter of pride or special comment.

Totemism

Apart from the restrictions on eating and killing certain species that are associated with sex and age and the possession of particular forms of magic, Kalam also recognize hereditary prohibitions associated with particular descent groups. These groups are mainly patrilineal, and are geographically dispersed, though with areas of local concentration caused in part by the fact that they are not exogamous, in part by descendants of women whose husbands have moved in from other areas accepting the prohibitions of their mothers' patrikin, as well as retaining, at least for a generation or so, those of their fathers' groups.

The prohibitions, some of which involve plants and others animals, are justified in each case by reference either to events at the putative origin of the group concerned, or at an ancestral shrine of the group, normally no longer in use but still visible as a rock outcrop or small clump of surviving tall trees in land otherwise under cultivation or grass.

Locally present animals which may not be killed or eaten by members of descent groups which are well represented in the Upper Kaironk Valley are the striped possum (*Dactylonax*), large fruit-bat (*Dobsonia*), sooty owl (*Tyto tenebricosa*), dragon-lizard (*Goniocephalus nigrigularis*), python (*Liasis boeleni*) and the largest local frog (*Rana grisea*). Of these, the frog is common, the owl rare, the python very rare, while the striped possum, fruit bat and dragon-lizard are all taken regularly but in small numbers. Though these particular totemic prohibitions probably hardly affect the overall intensity with which the animals concerned are hunted by the population at large, some of these species are totally avoided by residents of particular settlement areas, and would thus be very unlikely to be consumed at their homesteads, rock-shelters and other cooking sites.

There are descent groups mainly based in areas outside but adjacent to the Upper Kaironk Valley which are said to observe prohibitions either on certain of the above animals which are more common in their localities (e.g. the fruit-bat), or on other species which might otherwise be of considerable importance in the diet (e.g. large pigeons, *Ducula* spp.) or at least be highly prized game (e.g. cassowary and wild pig).

Restrictions associated with gardening

There are three creatures, other than dog, the killing or eating of which entails a period of restriction from entering gardens in which taro, the most important ceremonial crop, is being grown. These are cassowary; the largest local cuscus, *Phalanger gymnotis*; and the striped possum, *Dactylonax* (see Bulmer 1967:15, 23, n. 13; Bulmer & Menzies 1972-3:86-7, 495). The period of restriction following killing is only four to eight days, but that following eating is likely to be extended to up to a month, particularly in the case of cassowary. As taro cultivation is a very important activity for many Kalam from the months August-November (when new gardens are planted) to April-May, after which the crop can largely be left to look after itself until it is harvested from July to November, the garden prohibitions may somewhat restrict the hunting of these animals and, to a more significant extent, concentrate this activity in the dry-season months of May to July. As noted below, there is a range of social as well as environmental factors which tend to concentrate most forest hunting in this period.

Although Kalam exploit to some extent nearly all vertebrate species present in their domain, these preferences, requirements and proscriptions discussed above result, in combination, in a complex set of weightings affecting the intensity with which different animal species are hunted. One may state the overall consequences in the following somewhat over-simplified form:

(i) There is a concentration of male effort in hunting larger arboreal mammals, especially those of five particular species; plumed birds; and those arboreal forest birds which are either most highly valued for their flesh, i.e. pigeons, or most readily obtainable on account of their feeding habits, i.e. honey-eaters. In the course of systematic pursuit of these creatures, other smaller and less valued arboreal mammals, and other birds, are also frequently taken.

(ii) There is a concentration of female effort in capturing frogs and, seasonally when new gardens are being cleared, certain of the small rodents of the bush fallow and cane-grass.

(iii) The larger rare species of mammals and birds are certainly taken when opportunity offers, but because of their rarity cannot be said to be systematically hunted.

(iv) Creatures which are under-exploited, in terms of their numbers and accessibility, are the medium and small-sized terrestrial marsupials and rodents, which are largely left to women to kill, though women lack the time and the technology to pursue these systematically. A high proportion of the fairly readily available birds of the cultivation zone is also relatively neglected by Kalam.

(v) Cultural as well as environmental factors lead to a seasonal concentration of hunting both of the most valued arboreal mammals and of many of those birds which are taken primarily for their plumes. Dry weather in the months from May to August certainly makes it much easier to move about and hunt in the forest, especially at night; and these are also the months when the adult males of the most important birds of paradise are in full plumage and displaying (they moult in the wet months December-February). However, this is also the period immediately before that of the *smy* festivals (August-November), which is also the time when propitiatory offerings at the graves of the dead, and in new gardens, are most likely to be made. For all these occasions game is required, either fresh or smoked. Further, the dry months are also a time when garden work is relatively light, so that time can be readily spared for hunting, and restrictions on entering gardens, incurred through handling or eating certain animals, weigh least heavily. They are also the months when the high-altitude mountain pandanus nuts, the most highly valued vegetable product of the forest, are harvested, so that family parties camp up near their pandanus groves for this purpose, as well as to hunt.

While some individual men hunt arboreal mammals at other seasons, the main forest hunting during the wetter months is for those birds which can be most readily obtained either at the nest or at the seasonally blossoming and fruiting food trees which they visit.

We have no evidence that seasonal movements of animal populations significantly affect hunting practices, except in the case of one bird, the mountain pigeon (*Gymnophaps*), which, though present in all months in the local forest, gathers there in large numbers to breed in the wet season, when it is commonly taken at or near the nest. Most New Guinea montane mammals and birds appear to be very sedentary, though hunters say that some arboreal mammals (e.g. the ringtail, *Pseudocheirus cupreus*, and the giant rat, *Mallomys*) tend to move within the montane forest from the ridge-crest trees down to trees near water-courses in the dry months. However, the distances involved would not be more than a few hundred metres.

The disposal of bone

Vermin, notably *Rattus exulans* and other rats killed in or near homesteads, are thrown into grass or bushes where most would be consumed by pigs or other scavengers. The corpses of dogs are believed to be dangerous to crops and for this reason are never disposed of near to homesteads or gardens, or where they might contaminate humans or pigs who in turn would harm the gardens. They are therefore taken to forest or bush-fallow areas and either buried in a shallow grave, left on the ground surface covered over with cut foliage, or placed up in a cleft in a tree. I was told that a dog which has been a notably successful hunter might be buried like a warrior, placed on a platform above the ground, within a small fenced enclosure. Teeth for necklaces were extracted after the animal's flesh had completely decomposed. In the case of animals the Kalam eat, however, the location at which bone is finally destroyed or deposited is most often the location at which the animal is cooked.

Kalam roast or bake food in open fires, broil it in bamboo segments or tightly parcelled bundles of leaves, or cook it in ovens heated by stones which have been pre-heated in an adjacent fire and placed in the oven with wooden tongs. Prior to Australian contact they lacked pottery or metal cooking vessels. Vertebrates other than frogs and the smallest lizards and birds are almost always cooked in ovens.

Daily cooking of vegetable food is in pit ovens, and these are also often used for meat. However meat is also cooked in stone-heated ovens on the ground surface, often enclosed in a temporary circle of tree-bark, and in raised ovens shaped rather like flattened birds' nests supported about 50 to 90 cm. above the ground on a framework of sticks or, occasionally, by the fork of a convenient small tree-stump. Depending on how much food is to be cooked in them, these raised ovens range from 60 to 180 cm. in diameter. The use of a raised oven always implies that food is being cooked ritually, in propitiation of ancestors or of the recent dead, whereas pit and surface ovens are only occasionally used for ritual cooking. When a pig or cassowary is cooked, ovens are constructed at all three levels, the head, heart and upper thorax being cooked above the ground, the main joints in one or more pit-ovens, and the guts on the ground surface. Other mammals, birds and eels are cooked either in raised ovens (ritually) or in pits (normally, but not always, non-ritually), though when guts are removed prior to cooking these are not normally placed in the raised oven, but cooked on the ground-surface.

Domestic pigs are slaughtered and cooked outside ceremonial houses, outside ordinary homesteads, at graves and mortuary shrines (which are usually near homesteads though occasionally at the edge of the forest) and, though infrequently, in gardens. They were also formerly, until 1956, cooked in men's cult houses, one of which was associated with each well-established local kin group. At each of these locations certain wild animals can, or could, also appropriately be cooked, but some wild species are also often cooked in the forest, and in non-ritual open-air cooking sites in cultivation areas.

A forest cooking site is usually associated with a shelter containing a hearth for warmth, minor cooking and heating stones for oven-cooking, and sometimes for smoke-drying game. The shelter itself may be a small open-sided hut, the hollow under the trunk and roots of a large tree, or in a small minority of cases, a rock-shelter. Ovens are normally outside the shelter, though occasionally a pit-oven is dug within the sheltered area.

A special variant of the forest camp, which is often located at the edge of the forest or even within a settlement area if this is close to the forest, is the cassowary cooking site. This includes a larger than average sheltered area and at least three ovens, in, on and above the ground, for cooking different portions of the carcase. If in a settlement area, it is likely to be a rock-shelter which can be fenced off to keep pigs out.

A different range of animals is cooked at each of the main categories of cooking site:

Ceremonial houses: domestic pig; cassowary (formerly); wallaby (formerly); large arboreal forest mammals; eel.

Homesteads: domestic pig; wild pig (very rare); wallaby (very rare); all other edible wild mammals, with partial restriction on cuscus (*Phalanger gymnotis*), striped possum (*Dactylonax*), bandicoots and large terrestrial rodents; all edible reptiles; frogs; eel.

Men's cult houses: pigs; cassowary; large arboreal mammals; arboreal forest birds.

Graves and mortuary shrines: domestic pig; large arboreal mammals; arboreal forest birds; eel.

New gardens: domestic pig (unusual); large arboreal mammals except *Phalanger gymnotis*; arboreal forest birds; eel.

Open sites in cultivation areas: all edible wild mammals, birds, reptiles and frogs; eel.

Ordinary forest sites: all forest mammals except, normally, wallaby; all forest birds, reptiles and frogs.

Cassowary cooking site: cassowary; arboreal forest mammals; arboreal forest birds.

At ceremonial houses, men's cult houses, graves and mortuary shrines, in new gardens and at cassowary cooking sites, all animals are normally ritually cooked. At homesteads and at ordinary forest sites some animals are cooked ritually, others are not. At open sites in cultivation areas animals are not normally ritually cooked.

Whether or not an animal is cooked ritually considerably affects the treatment accorded its bones, provided only that the creature is consumed at the cooking site. Animals, especially pigs cooked at ceremonial houses and at homesteads, provide the only meat which is distributed in any quantity to be taken to eat elsewhere. All surviving bone of animals cooked at men's cult houses had to be most carefully retained within the house because, on account of the war rituals performed there, food remnants were thought to cause considerable damage to people and to pigs if cast about so that they came in contact with them.

Bone remnants of animals cooked ritually and consumed at cooking sites other than men's cult houses are placed in the branches of cordyline and other shrubs, only teeth which are wanted for necklaces and bone wanted for technological purposes being retained. Three reasons are given by Kalam for placing bone in shrubs: that it is part of the ritual, being a tangible indication to the spirits that they have been propitiated; that it prevents pigs from eating the remains of other pigs from the same family herds, and especially of cassowary, as the spirits of these could affect them adversely, and also from eating the remains of creatures which are believed to adversely affect gardens (the cuscus *Phalanger gymnotis*, the striped possum *Dactylonax* and, again, the cassowary), as pigs could by so doing contaminate either the gardens themselves or, more readily, the humans who need to work in them; and that it demonstrates to visitors the affluence, or hunting skill, of the site-owners.

Bone exposed to the elements by being placed in shrubs weathers rapidly, and much of it eventually falls to the ground. Though Kalam generally pick up and replace fallen bones when they notice them, the fact that much of it disappears in time does not worry them greatly. This is partly because bone is only contaminating as long as it still bears traces of flesh and blood, partly because more recent occasions of propitation of the spirits will have diminished the importance of the earlier performances. Bone which is placed in grave-side shrubs is most likely to remain *in situ* after it has fallen, as graves are initially fenced and later, when untended, become small thickets of vegetation which minimize disturbance by pigs and other agents of dispersal.

All surviving bones of animals cooked in men's cult houses were left permanently in the house or at the site. If the house itself was eventually abandoned, the site remained fenced for some years, until a dense thicket had grown over it which would still protect it from wandering pigs and children. Even enemies moving in to a settlement area to replace the former owners of a cult house would not interfere with it, for fear of the magic it contained.

No bones are removed from cassowary cooking sites, except for technological purposes.

Bone of animals not cooked ritually, or from meat (mainly pork) which is distributed for consumption away from the ritual cooking site, is treated quite casually, much of it either deliberately fed to pigs and dogs, or left around where these scavengers can readily find it for themselves. Eel bone from fish which have not been ritually cooked is kept to break into fragments and feed to pigs with their vegetable food, as it is believed to cause them to grow fat. Bone discarded at sites in the cultivation zone, where pigs are present, is the least likely to survive. The chances of bone surviving at forest cooking sites depend very much on whether or not dogs are accompanying the hunters, or roaming in the area.

The bone of animals which have not been ritually cooked can also, however, be kept as trophy material, to decorate hunters' houses. As Tables 1-3 indicate, the bones retained as trophies come almost exclusively from animal species which are appropriate for ritual cooking (the four largest arboreal marsupials and two largest rodents found in local forests, plus wallaby and other large arboreal marsupials which Upper Kaironk hunters occasionally capture in lower-lying areas); so a trophy collection represents a selection from the residue of a

Table 3 Numbers of bones in trophy collections obtained in Upper Kaironk Valley, September-December 1973

Species	Crania	Half mandibles	Whole mandibles	Half pelvises	Others	Totals
Cuscus, *Phalanger gymnotis*	11 (11)	46 (27)	2 (2)	5 (3)	5 (3)	69 (36)
Cuscus, *Phalanger vestitus*	4 (4)	20 (14)	1 (1)	0 (0)	0 (0)	25 (19)
Ringtail, *Pseudocheirus corinnae*	0 (0)	20 (11)	1 (1)	0 (0)	0 (0)	20 (11)
Ringtail, *Pseudocheirus cupreus*	12 (12)	35 (19)	4 (4)	2 (1)	5 (2)	58 (31)
Giant rat, *Hyomys goliath*	2 (2)	4 (3)	0 (0)	0 (0)	0 (0)	6 (5)
Giant rat, *Mallomys rothschildi*	6 (6)	24 (15)	0 (0)	0 (0)	0 (0)	30 (19)
10 other species	2 (2)	11 (7)	5 (5)	2 (1)	5 (2)	25 (12)
Species undetermined	0 (0)	0 (0)	0 (0)	9 (5)	0 (0)	9 (5)
Totals	37 (37)	160 (96)	13 (13)	18 (10)	15 (7)	242 (138)

Figures in brackets refer to numbers of individual animals. Minimum numbers of whole animals were inferred both by matching parts and from information provided by vendors.

hunter's total catch after animals which he has cooked ritually, animals which he has given away or traded as whole carcases, and animals which are not prestigious game, have been removed; to which may be added the remains of prestigious animals which his dog has captured. If a hunter owns a particularly good dog, he may hang up, in a separate line from the crania and mandibles of animals he himself has killed, those from beasts that his dog has brought down.

Additional factors affect the quantity and condition of bone of different species which may be deposited. These are the extent to which it is consumed by humans along with the meat; the slaughtering, butchering, smoke-drying and culinary techniques employed; and the ornamental and technological uses to which some of it may be put. Kalam usually consume most of the bone of small (rat- and mouse-sized) mammals, of birds up to the size of a pigeon or small hawk, and of frogs and small lizards. The parts of these animals that are likely not to be eaten by people – jaws of small mammals, reptiles and frogs, and beaks and feet of small birds – must often be picked up by pigs and dogs. The smaller and softer bones of larger animals are equally likely to be eaten. The extent to which bone is eaten reflects the amount of meat available at the time, and the hunger of those present. While most Kalam are, for example, quite capable of chewing up the wing- and leg-bones of a domestic fowl,[6] they do not bother to do so if food is plentiful and they are replete.

Domestic pigs are slaughtered by a series of blows with a heavy stake on the front of the skull, above the eyes, which considerably damages the cranium. The crania of cuscuses and other large arboreal mammals are often also extensively damaged by a slaughtering technique which consists of grasping the animal by its tail and swinging it so that the back of its head is dashed against a tree-trunk, root or rock. Many mammals of all sizes which are caught after a chase along the ground are killed by blows on the head with a stick, and this is particularly damaging in the case of smaller species with relatively fragile skulls.

The butchering of animals smaller than pig and cassowary does not involve further damage to the skeleton, as they are cooked whole. However, pig and cassowary are jointed prior to cooking and, in the case of pig, the pelvis is smashed with heavy stones, using a hammer-and-anvil technique, to enable the haunches to be separated from each other and from the trunk-joint by cutting with a bamboo knife.

After cooking, further damage is inflicted on the skeleton. In the case of pigs, skulls are smashed open with stones to extract the brain. The mandible is, however, normally left intact, or merely separated into its two halves; because of its convenient shape, and because pigs' heads are seldom distributed to be consumed away from the cooking site, it is the part most likely to survive for many years lodged in cordyline shrubs. Whether or not people bother to smash long bones in order to extract the marrow depends on how much meat is available. The host-group at a *smy* would often not do so, but guests who take meat home for consumption, and also family groups killing individual pigs, would almost always do so.

The crania of larger marsupials and rodents are likely to be broken after cooking only if women or boys are sharing in the animals' consumption. The brains of these animals are not normally eaten by men. However, since women and children are more likely to be present on non-ritual cooking occasions, especially when animals are cooked at homesteads, and in any case some crania have already been damaged in slaughtering, a relatively small number of whole crania is either kept as trophy material or likely to be deposited in locations where these will be preserved for long. Badly damaged crania are sometimes retained as

Table 4 Damage to bones in trophy collections obtained in Upper Kaironk Valley, September-December 1973

Bone category	*Extent of damage*			
	None or very minor	Noticeable	Very severe	Totals
Crania	19 (51%)	15 (41%)	3 (8%)	37 (100%)
Whole mandibles	12 (100%)	0 (0%)	0 (0%)	12 (100%)
Half-mandibles	133 (83%)	25 (16%)	2 (1%)	160 (100%)
Other	33 (100%)	0 (0%)	0 (0%)	33 (100%)
Totals	197 (82%)	40 (16%)	5 (2%)	242 (100%)

trophies (see Table 4), whereas relatively few other damaged bones are kept. Thus mandibles, and especially half-mandibles, outnumber crania very considerably in trophy collections (see Table 3), and one might expect that they would also survive in larger numbers than other bones in the debris of cooking sites, as indeed is the case in some of the first archaeological deposits to be reported from the New Guinea Highlands (White 1972:4, 59).

After mandibles and crania, the bones most often retained in trophy collections are half-pelvises of the larger marsupials. Long-bones, scapulae and vertebrae are relatively rarely kept.

Cassowary crania, which are very hard and contain proportionately very little brain, are only broken up if there are boys at the cooking site. Cassowary heads lack feather on top and sides, and men do not eat them, they say, because they would risk premature baldness if they did.

In contrast, crania of other birds, which are much more fragile than those of mammals, are almost always broken up for extraction of brain, and the fragments are as likely as not to be consumed. Though beaks and feet of many species are kept as trophies or personal ornaments, the only crania and other large bones of birds recorded in trophy collections were those of the largest local flying species, the New Guinea eagle, *Harpyopsis novaeguineae*, and one other particularly ferocious bird of prey, the sooty owl, *Tyto tenebricosa*. However, preserved skins of birds of paradise and lorikeets normally retain both beaks and crania, so that long-term survival of these might occur if the skins were eventually left in old house-sites or thrown away in some context favourable to their preservation.

As noted earlier, larger forest mammals and arboreal forest birds are often smoke-dried either for later domestic or private consumption (at forest sites, homesteads, and open-air cooking sites in cultivation areas) or, more often, for *smy* feasts and for propitiatory offerings at graves and shrines, or in gardens. Smoking starts in the forest camps near where the animals are killed, and is continued, if there is to be a long delay before they are required for consumption, in the homesteads. The tissue surrounding crania, mandibles and limb-extremities of animals which have been smoke-dried for some weeks becomes very hard and firmly attached to the bone, and traces of it are obvious in trophy collections and might be expected to survive for considerable periods in favourable contexts. Bone itself is also likely to show blackening. This is particularly the case with larger mammals such as wallaby and the cuscus, *Phalanger gymnotis*, which are initially placed on smoking racks nearer to the fire than those used for smaller creatures. Noticeable burning or fire-blackening of bone hardly ever occurs in the singeing process which precedes butchering and cooking of furred animals.

Eels are not smoked, even though they are most often trapped in the dry-season months some time before they are wanted for ceremonial and ritual occasions, but are kept alive in basketry or tree-bark containers left in the rivers, for periods of up to at least four months.

It is hard to estimate distances for which animals are carried before cooking, but it would appear that, eels and smoke-dried animals apart, it is unusual for beasts to be cooked at sites, either in the forest or the cultivation zone, which are further than half a day's walk from the point of capture. Smoke-dried carcases are not infrequently ultimately cooked and eaten at sites up to a full day's walk from places of capture, and occasionally at even greater distances.

While the overwhelming majority of bones in trophy collections also comes from animals killed within half a day's walk of the owner's homestead, a small proportion (approximately 2%), mainly bones of rarer animals, was reported as coming from distances of between half a day's and two days' walk.

The ornamental and technological uses of teeth and bone have already been described. Here it is merely necessary to note briefly the extent to which technological uses of pelts, skins and plumes affect the disposal of skeletal material, and the prospects of ultimate deposition of ornaments and utensils of tooth and bone.

Skins of birds, for ornament and trade, and skins of ring-tail possums and other marsupials wanted as drum skins, are normally removed in the forest as soon as possible after the animal is killed, and the remains are cooked non-ritually. Teeth, for necklaces, may be retained from forest mammals cooked either ritually or non-ritually. The half-mandibles of giant rats, for use as gravers, are normally kept from animals cooked non-ritually, and thus may equally form part of a trophy collection or be removed from this, or initially set aside, for technological use. The bone from pig, cassowary, wallaby and fruit-bat which is kept for fashioning into utensils may come from animals which have been cooked ritually or non-ritually, but in the former case the fashioning of the artefact concerned is likely to have been commenced, and perhaps even completed, at the cooking site.

Turning to the ultimate fate of ornaments and utensils: tooth necklaces of minor value and other minor ornaments such as necklaces or pendants or cassowary claws or hawk talons are sometimes, like shell ornaments of minor value, left hanging on cordyline shrubs at the grave of the owner. Bone utensils, when old and damaged, are just thrown away like other household refuse, or left in the walls of houses. In general the most likely final resting places of tooth-necklaces and all other ornaments and utensils of bone, as also of hunters' trophy collections, are old house-sites. I was told that, specifically, men were most unlikely to remove a trophy collection from an abandoned house, but would instead start a new collection to decorate their new residence. Similarly animal bone kept in a men's cult house was left in the old house when this was abandoned. There is normally nothing to prevent early disturbance by pigs or humans of old homesteads after they have either fallen down or been pulled down, whereas a former men's cult house site was kept fenced until either a thicket had grown over it or it was re-used for a new cult-house; so material located in a cult house might have the highest chance of any of survival *in situ*, except that accidentally deposited in rock-shelters.

It would be misleading to suggest that the Kalam practices here described are likely to correspond in detail with those of the majority of other present or prehistoric peoples of the New Guinea Highlands. My own limited observations of other contemporary groups indicate that some of these, which have generally higher population densities and less access to forest animals than Kalam have (Melpa of Mount Hagen, Kyaka Enga of Baiyer Valley, and the Minj-Wahgi peoples) trap both arboreal and terrestrial animals more intensively than Kalam do, and in particular exploit the smaller rodents and birds of cultivation areas to a much greater extent than do the Kalam. Unlike the Kalam, these groups, as also the Chimbu, regard the common domestic rat, *Rattus exulans*, as edible, at least for women and children. However, these groups appear to set much the same high value as the Kalam do on the larger arboreal mammals, and on wallaby.

In contrast, my impression from discussion with a number of colleagues who have done fieldwork in lower montane and lowland areas of New Guinea, where human population densities are lower than those in most of the Highlands, and wild game, particularly pig and cassowary, is in general more plentiful, is that these populations are generally more selective than Kalam in their concentration on larger, and neglect of smaller, mammals and in the very limited attention they pay to birds, except for a few large species, as a source of food. However, I have heard of no group which does not exploit the larger arboreal mammals fairly extensively, as also wallabies where these are available.

Within the Highlands region and its peripheries, Kalam are unusual in that they do not capture and rear cassowary chicks, and in that they had no domestic fowls prior to Australian contact. Some other Highlands groups, for example the Melpa of Mount Hagen, kept a much wider range of wild animals and birds than the Kalam, as pets, for plucking and for ultimate consumption (Vicedom & Tischner 1943-8: I, 177, 198, 201).

Turning to patterns of utilization of animals, as these may affect disposal of bone: it is known that dogs are eaten by some Highlands peoples (e.g. Enga, Melpa, Chimbu), though in these societies they are also in some cases prominent in lists of animals avoided as food by certain descent groups because of their totemic associations (Strauss & Tischner 1962:43-4). Restrictions on adult male consumption of particular animals, and additional restrictions observed by men who practise certain forms of magic or other ritual, probably occur in all Highlands societies, though the line or lines between permissible and prohibited categories may be expected to be differently drawn in different cultural groups. Similarly, regardless of prohibitions, consumption of larger forest mammals at cooking sites within the forest is likely to involve adult men more frequently than women and children in most Highlands societies (A. & M. Strathern 1968:197). The importance of activity-based and generally seasonal restrictions, and of totemic restrictions, on hunting and consumption of different species probably varies widely in different Highlands societies. Whereas, for example, these appear to be much less important among the Kyaka Enga than among the Kalam, one may infer from published accounts (Strauss & Tischner 1962; A. & M. Strathern 1968) that the Melpa people observe quite complex restrictions. Larger rodents and marsupials, like pig, dog and cassowary, are reported as being always ritually cooked by the Melpa (Vicedom & Tischner 1943-8; Strauss & Tischner 1962), though the unusually rich ethnographic reports on these people still do not make it clear how many different types and contexts of ritual cooking are involved, apart from noting that wild mammals as well as pigs are cooked in garden rituals (Vicedom & Tischner 1943-8:I, 191) as well as in domestic and communal cooking near houses and at ceremonial grounds. Like the Kalam, the Kyaka Enga cook most small animals and birds non-ritually, but unlike the Kalam they roast many of these on open fires, rather than cooking them in ovens, as also appears to have been the practice of the prehistoric occupants of Batari Cave in the Eastern Highlands (White 1972:17).

Three animals, dog, cassowary and the cuscus *Phalanger gymnotis*, appear to be the focus of special ritual attitudes in many Highlands societies, and one would expect that these attitudes would be reflected in their slaughter and cooking, and in the disposal of their bones. In the high value they attach to bird plumes, Kalam follow patterns that are general to much of the Highlands, but they make less use of mammal pelts than do some other groups (A. & M. Strathern 1971:188 n.34, and *passim*). As noted earlier, what may perhaps loosely be described as 'trophy collections' of animal bones appear to be kept by men in many Highlands societies, though it may be that in some cases these collections are retained primarily for ritual reasons. In one case known to me from personal collecting, that of the Kyaka Enga, a much higher proportion of post-cranial material is retained, together with crania and mandibles, than is the case among the Kalam.

While there is some local variation in technological and ornamental uses of mammal bone, the retention of half-mandibles of *Mallomys* and other giant rats for use as gravers appears to be quite general within the Highlands, as is also the use of flying-fox bones for needles and of cassowary long bones to fashion pandanus-fruit splitters.

It must also be constantly born in mind that contemporary Highlands peoples are essentially horticulturalists and pig-raisers, for whom hunting represents a small sector of the economy. While there is growing archaeological and palaeobotanical evidence for the considerable antiquity of horticulture in this region (Powell 1970) the extrapolation of ethnographic evidence in interpretation of the archaeological record must be undertaken with considerable caution. Many aspects of life in the Highlands must have been different before horticulture and pig-husbandry developed, or when they were of less importance than in recent times, and also when human population densities were substantially lower.

With these qualifications in mind it is still perhaps possible to offer some comments on the possible implications of the kinds of selectivity exercised by Kalam and other Highlanders both in hunting of wild animals and in disposing of their remains, for the interpretation of assemblages of bone from archaeological sites in New Guinea.[7]

Archaeologists in New Guinea, as elsewhere, are hopeful of inferring from animal bones information about ecological conditions pertaining in the vicinity of their sites, and about the economies of the groups who deposited the bone. Changes in the frequency with which different species or faunal groups are represented over time are seen as offering, in particular, evidence suggestive of environmental changes in the locality, human-induced or otherwise (White 1972:4, 16, 59). Ethnographic evidence suggests three main difficulties in making these inferences, at least while material from only a small number of sites, and all of them rock-shelters and caves, is available:

1. It may well be that different human groups with essentially the same technology and the same range of animal species available to them concentrate to a greater or lesser degree on the capture of certain of these animals. This could depend in part on the total amount of animal food available to them, but also in part on special value being set on certain species for ritual and ceremonial cooking and distribution.

2. Different categories of site utilized by the same human group are likely to preserve very different samples of the total range of fauna that

they capture. Thus J.P. White's working assumptions 'that prehistoric practices are similar to modern ones and that a random selection of animals is brought back to the site for butchering' (White 1972:4) are both questionable.

3. Presence or absence of scavenging pigs or dogs in the vicinity of cooking places is likely to affect the gross quantities of bone preserved, and could also affect the selection preserved if site owners made any deliberate effort to place certain bones out of reach of these animals.

Thus, to take White's best-documented sequence of faunal change, that at Aibura cave in the Eastern Highlands (1972:57-9), the increasing proportions of wallabies and small rodents and decreasing proportions of cuscuses over the last thousand years or so could, if the most recent level and period is excluded, be accounted for by changing frequencies of domestic versus ritual cooking as plausibly as they are by the increase in local areas of grassland and decrease in local populations of larger arboreal game,[8] though perhaps it is more plausible still that both sets of factors were involved.

Two additional points may be mentioned in conclusion. One is the continuing importance of smoke-drying of mammals and birds among the Kalam and some other New Guinea peoples, particularly when there is some seasonal concentration of hunting. If this was important in prehistoric times, it would be reflected in the location and perhaps the condition of bone remnants, and possibly also by small post-holes from smoking-frame supports surviving in rock-shelters and caves. The other point is that if prehistoric peoples retained, as present-day Highlanders do, crania, mandibles and certain other bones as trophy collections or for ritual reasons, it becomes crucial for the adequate analysis of archaeological deposits that post-cranial bones be identified and counted. This has so far proved impossible (White 1972:3-5). The lack of reference collections of post-cranial skeletal material for New Guinea mammals is, as White rightly emphasizes, a severe handicap to the archaeologist, and one which should not be too difficult to remedy.

In his interpretations of faunal remains from his sites, the archaeologist can only work within the limits of available zoological information on the anatomy and ecology of the species with which he is concerned. To this extent the archaeologist working in New Guinea is at a considerable disadvantage as against his colleagues in many other regions, for scientific knowledge of even the commonest vertebrate animals in that country is still at a rudimentary level, though happily there has been a rapid acceleration of research in this field within the last ten years. However, in partial compensation for this temporary disability, the New Guinea archaeologist can draw on a body of ethnographic research, potentially relevant to his interests, which is unusually extensive. And if certain matters of crucial interest to him are not adequately reported in the ethnographic literature, he can still, if he has time, supplement the record by making his own ethnographic observations; or he can encourage the professional ethnographer to pursue and present some of his enquiries in ways which may contribute to both disciplines, as has been my intention in this paper.

Acknowledgments

In my first year as an undergraduate at Cambridge I was fortunate enough to be allocated to Professor Clark for supervision in prehistoric archaeology. One of the many topics he discoursed upon in his inimitably provocative and stimulating manner was the use of ethnographic evidence in the interpretation of the archaeological record. At the end of my first year I then spent three months undertaking apprentice fieldwork in social anthropology among the northern Mountain Lapps. On my return I showed my photographs to Professor Clark, who scanned them with interest and asked a series of questions about the siting and construction of camps, and about the slaughtering of reindeer and the disposal of bone and antler. Perhaps it was no coincidence that this was in 1950, in the period of the Star Carr excavations. This paper is a small offering to Professor Clark, and to the many other archaeologists who, over the past twenty-three years, have asked me questions of ethnographic detail that might be relevant to their own research, all too few of which I have been able to answer adequately.

I owe much gratitude to my Kalam informants and assistants, most notably Saem Majnep (now of the Department of Anthropology and

Sociology, University of Papua New Guinea) and Councillor Simon Peter Gi; and also to the many biologists who have helped me with my studies, especially my collaborator J.I. Menzies, of the Department of Biology, University of Papua New Guinea. For financial support for those periods of field-work among the Kalam in which most of the data drawn upon in this paper were collected I must thank the University of Papua New Guinea Research Committee and the Wenner-Gren Foundation.

Appendix: Tables 1-4

Explanatory note

A full list of marsupials and rodents recorded in the Upper Kaironk Valley is presented in Bulmer & Menzies 1972-3, Table 2, pp. 481-3. Table 3, pp. 488-9, of the same publication enumerates, according to mode of capture, specimens of different species acquired up to 1972. Additional specimens were obtained in 1973, and are included in the present Tables, though identifications of some of this new material are only provisional. In particular, numbers of the larger ringtail possums *Pseudocheirus cupreus* and *P. corinnae* may require some minor adjustment when further work has been done on the collections, and some of the smaller rodent specimens from owl pellets have not yet been identified to species level.

While animals listed in Tables 1 and 2 as 'obtained by Kalam: whole animals recorded' include every creature seen newly killed or captured, they would not constitute a random sample of the products of Kalam hunting, for two main reasons. Firstly, research periods have not covered a calendar year, and have for the most part been in wet-season months, whereas larger arboreal mammals are hunted most intensively in the dry season (Bulmer & Menzies 1972-3:484). Secondly, hunters have, not unnaturally, shown the investigator animals which they did not wish to use for ritual cooking, but which they did anticipate, generally correctly, that he might purchase. Thus both the most highly valued animals (e.g. the cuscus *Phalanger gymnotis*), and the commonest small species of rodents, are under-represented.

On the other hand the skeletal material sold to us probably does fairly faithfully reflect the typical proportions of different species in trophy collections, though there may be a slight over-representation of rarities, either retained specifically to sell to us, or kept originally for their curiosity value but selected to sell to us because of our known interest in obtaining as full as possible a record of the local fauna.

The 'larger mammals' listed in Tables 1 and 2 include those marsupials and rodents classified by Kalam as *kmn*, while the 'smaller mammals' include those they classify as *as* and *kopyak* (Bulmer & Menzies 1972-3:487-91).

Tables 3 and 4 include only trophy material collected in 1973, as our earlier collections were not accessible for re-analysis. There may be some under-representation of post-cranial bones in this collection, not because these were refused when offered to us for sale, but because the field-worker's attention to dentition as a means of species identification may have suggested, correctly, to some vendors that he was more interested in crania and mandibles than in other bones.

REFERENCES

Aufenanger, H. (1964) Aus der Kultur der Simbai-Pygmäen im Schradergebirge Neuguineas. *Ethnos*, 29, 141-74.

Bulmer, R.N.H. (1967) Why is the cassowary not a bird? *Man*, 2, 5-25.

Bulmer, R.N.H. (1968) The strategies of hunting in New Guinea. *Oceania*, 38, 302-18.

Bulmer, R.N.H. and Menzies, J.I. (1972-3) Karam classification of marsupials and rodents. *Jour. Polynesian Soc.*, 81, 472-99; 82, 86-107.

Bulmer, R.N.H. and Tyler, M.J. (1968) Karam classification of frogs, *Jour. Polynesian Soc.*, 77, 333-85.

Bulmer, S.E. (1966) The prehistory of the Australian New Guinea Highlands. Unpublished M.A. thesis, University of Auckland.

Bulmer, S.E. and Bulmer, R.N.H. (1964) The prehistory of the Australian New Guinea Highlands. *Amer. Anth.*, 66, 4 (part 2), 39-76.

Gusinde, M. (1958) Die Ayom-Pygmäen auf Neu-Guinea. *Anthropos*, 53, 497-574, 817-63.

Powell, J.M. (1970) The history of agriculture in the New Guinea Highlands. *Search*, 1, 199-200.

Strathern, A.J. and Strathern, A.M. (1968) Marsupials and magic. *Cambridge Papers in Social Anthrop.*, 5, 179-202.

Strathern, A.J. and Strathern, A.M. (1971) *Self-*

decoration in Mount Hagen. London.

Strauss, H. and Tischner, H. (1962) *Die Mi-Kultur der Hagenberg-Stämme im östlichen Zentral-Neuguinea.* Hamburg.

Vicedom, G.F. and Tischner, H. (1943-48) *Die Mbowamb* (3 vols). Hamburg.

White, J.P. (1972) Ol Tumbuna: Archaeological excavations in the Eastern Central Highlands, Papua New Guinea. *Terra Australis*, 2. Canberra.

NOTES

1. Spelt 'Karam' in previous publications, e.g. Bulmer 1967; Bulmer & Tyler 1968; Bulmer & Menzies 1972-73.

2. More detailed accounts of Upper Kaironk Valley society, economy and ecology may be found in Bulmer 1967 and Bulmer & Tyler 1968:337-9; a description of houses is given by Aufenanger 1964; for an account of the Kalam-speakers in the neighbouring Asai Valley see Gusinde 1958.

3. There were in 1973 probably 2,900 Kalam-speakers resident in the Upper Kaironk Valley, though many of these were also using garden land and houses in nearby areas outside the Upper Valley.

4. I have not observed this myself, and was provoked to ask questions on this topic through reading an unpublished ethnographic report on the Miyanmin of the West Sepik District by George Morren, to whom I am very grateful.

5. Kalam abandoned these practices in 1961-63, the majority giving them up at the time of a cargo-cult connected with an eclipse of the sun in December 1962. Today most wigs are stuffed with coconut fibre brought back from plantations, and not with human hair.

6. A capacity not unique to Kalam. A well-known New Zealand archaeologist has been known to enliven dinner-parties by demonstrating how easily this can be done, though it is understood that in this case the fragments are discreetly concealed in a napkin and not swallowed.

7. Three archaeologists have so far reported finding considerable quantities of faunal remains in cave and rock-shelter sites in the New Guinea Highlands, S.E. Bulmer (1964:62, 65; 1966:94), J.P. White (1972) and M.J. Mountain (pers. comm.), but of these only White has so far reported his finds in any detail.

8. White was unable to get species identifications for the smaller rodents in this site, or for nearly half of the macropods (wallabies & tree-kangaroos). This also weakens his interpretation. The majority of small rodents in the genera he lists are probably species found in forest and well developed garden-fallow, while only some of them would also be found in grassland, and few if any exclusively in grassland (*cf.* Bulmer & Menzies 1972-3:482-3, 92-7). While *Dorcopsulus*, *Dendrolagus* and the unidentified specimens might be forest species, *Thylogale bruijni*, which constitutes only just over half of his macropods, frequents garden and bush-fallow areas and the forest edge, as well as grasslands.

PETER GATHERCOLE

A Maori shell trumpet at Cambridge

In the University Museum of Archaeology and Ethnology, Cambridge, is a Maori shell trumpet (*pu tatara*)[1] that is part of the Pennant collection, obtained by the Museum in 1912.[2] Thomas Pennant (*b.*1726, *d.*1798), a notable naturalist, traveller and dilettante, was a friend of Cook, Banks, J.R. Forster and others connected with Cook's three great voyages of discovery to the South Seas between 1768 and 1780 (Pennant 1793). Pennant's collection at Cambridge includes in its Pacific section objects from the Society Islands, New Zealand, Tonga, the New Hebrides, Hawaii and the American North West Coast.[3] These must have been collected, therefore, at various times during the course of all three voyages for, while the Society Islands and New Zealand were visited on each voyage and Tonga on the second and third, there was only one visit to the New Hebrides (on the second voyage) and to Hawaii and North America (on the third). The documentation of the collection is poor. The accessions register, besides giving the island of origin, merely records: 'Cook Collection given by Banks to Pennant'. This information must have come from the eighth Earl of Denbigh, who inherited the collection, to the then Curator, Baron Anatole von Hügel, in 1912. The objects are therefore unprovenanced as to place and date of acquisition, and their value as specific reflections of early contact between Europeans and Pacific peoples is correspondingly limited. It is important to stress this point because Shawcross has recently discussed the five Maori objects included in this collection and assumed that, owing to Pennant's friendship with Banks, they were obtained by Banks on Cook's first voyage, i.e. in 1769-70 (Shawcross 1970:305). As Banks was only on this voyage, however, he could not have collected the objects in Pennant's collection from the second and third voyages himself, although some of them may have passed through his hands afterwards in England. Thus, the association of the collection with Banks may be only a Pennant family tradition, acquired because some of the pieces, as yet unidentified, were thought to have come directly from him. In any case, as New Zealand was visited by Cook in 1769-70, 1773, 1774 and 1777, Pennant's Maori objects could have been obtained on any of these occasions from a number of possible locations. I argue in this paper that one of the objects, the shell trumpet, was actually collected on 4 June 1773, on the second voyage, in circumstances that throw a good deal of light on its role in Maori society. Four other objects in the Pennant collection, a whalebone *patu* (hand club), a wooden *patu*, a lure hook and a doghair plume, are more mundane and more commonly represented in museum collections attributed to the 1770s and might have come from any of the three Cook voyages.

The shell trumpet (Fig. 1) can be very closely matched with the specimen that was one of three Maori artefacts illustrated (no. 4 on Pl. XIX, reproduced here as Fig. 2) in Cook's account of his second voyage, first published in 1777. This correlation was noticed, I think for the first time, in 1917 by Skinner, who assumed that the trumpet was obtained by Cook himself at Queen Charlotte Sound. Skinner (1923:101) did not attempt to tie down its date, or circumstances of acquisition, but merely assumed that this collecting point demonstrated that a similar type of mouthpiece was then being used in both Islands. The purpose of this paper is to test these assumptions against the available documentary evidence from the voyage and, further, to suggest that this evidence, with reference to the appropriate ethnographic and archaeological data, can help to clarify the functions and meaning of shell trumpets, as a 'class' of artefact, in Maori society in prehistoric and early historical times.

The Pennant trumpet is a remarkably fine object. It consists of a trumpet shell, *Charonia*

Figure 1. Maori shell trumpet (*pu tatara*) in the Pennant Collection, University Museum of Archaeology and Ethnology, Cambridge (25.374).

capax (Powell 1966:III, 456), that has been worked smooth over much of its surface. A wooden mouthpiece is attached by a binding of flax, *Phormium tenax*. The overall length is 25.8 cm. and the length of the mouthpiece about 5 cm. The latter has been carved to form two human faces or masks that are counterposed, Janus-like, on opposite sides, with a common 'mouth' at the blow-hole, and the flax has been dextrously and neatly bound in a series of overlapping strands. In these respects, the specimen is similar to others examined in museum collections, though its craftsmanship is superior to most of those seen. The distal end of the mouthpiece is, of course, hidden by the flax binding but is probably attached to the sawn-off apex of the shell in the usual way, i.e. by flax strings that pass through small holes drilled in the shell walls at this point (Fisher 1937:116). The natural lip' at the distal end of the shell has a notch cut into it on one side, and has been shaped on the other, to form a projection round which can be tied one end of the flax carrying-cord which, at its other end, is bound to the mouthpiece. On one side of the bowl, the shell is cracked and broken, a roughly rectangular piece 1.9 cm. by 1.4 cm. being missing.

In at least two respects however, this specimen is very unusual. Firstly, the base of the bowl has been deliberately and evenly sliced off and replaced by a piece of wood carefully shaped to conform to its contours and firmly joined to it by ten flax bindings. In addition, a single string of flax runs along the line of the join. The latter has been caulked by an application of gum which, in at least two places, has traces of an impressed crescentic (finger-nail?) decoration; there are also slight traces of finger impressions on the gum. I know of only two other shell trumpets with comparable features. One, previously in the Oldman Collection (no. 636) and now in the Otago Museum, Dunedin, New Zealand, has a small oval of wood, 3.8 cm. by 2.9 cm., inserted in its bowl, held by

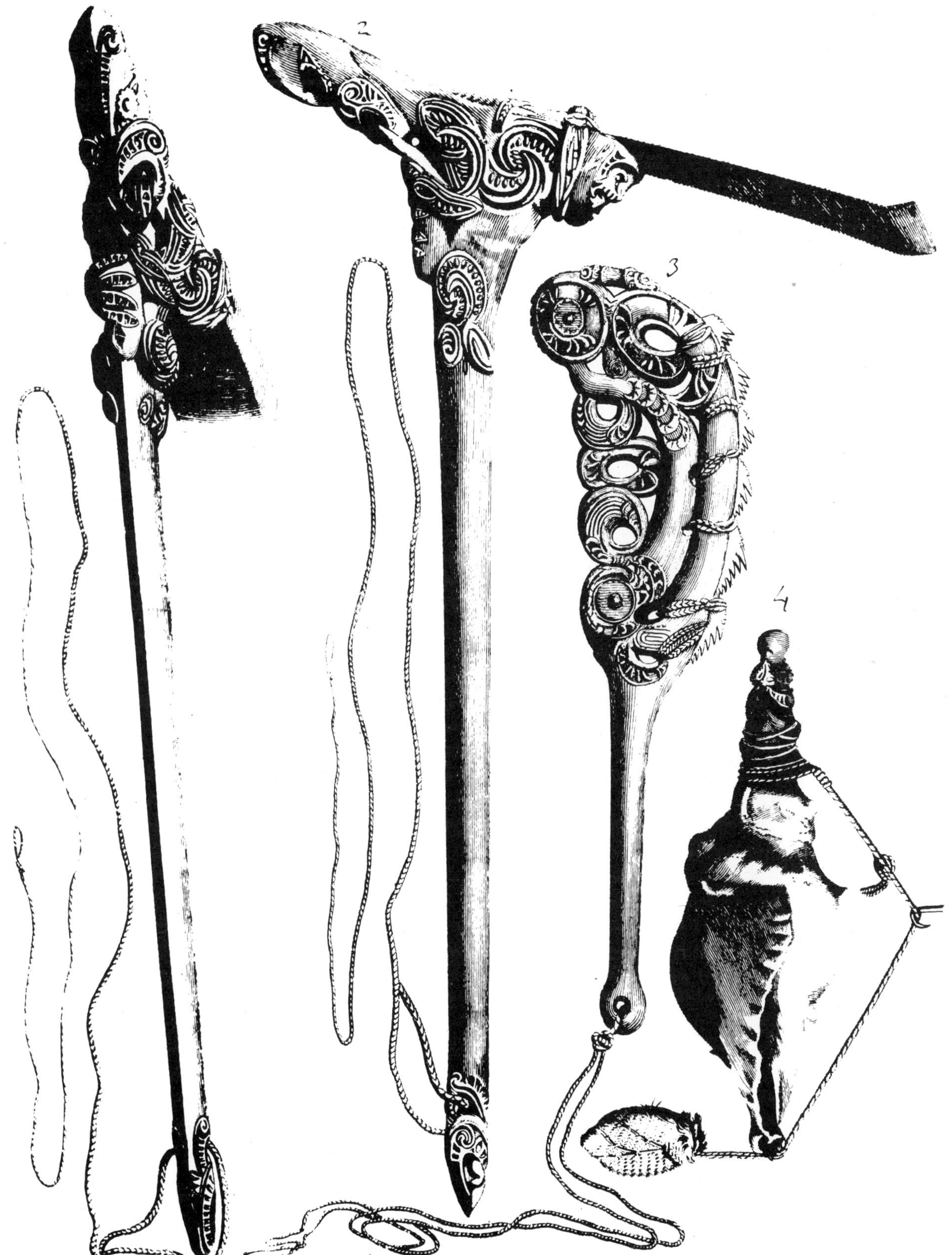

Figure 2. 'Specimens of New Zealand workmanship, etc' from *A Voyage towards the South Pole, and Round the World . . .* (I), by James Cook, Plate XIX (opp. p. 245).

four flax bindings (Oldman 1946:21, Pl. 58). The present location of the other specimen is unknown, but it was described in some detail by Colenso (1880:79), in terms that make clear that it was very similar to the Pennant trumpet: 'An ancient trumpet of this kind (formerly belonging to the old patriotic chief of Table Cape, Ihaka Whanga, but now the property of Mr. Samuel Locke, of Napier,) has a thin piece of dark hard wood, of a broadly elliptic form, and measuring 5 x 3 inches, most dexterously fitted in to fill up a hole in the upper part of the body or large whorl of the shell; which piece of wood is also curved, and ribbed, or scraped to resemble and closely match the transverse ridges of the shell; and additionally carved, of course, with one of their national devices'.[4] Colenso then cited as a parallel the illustration in Cook's account, referred to above.

The second unusual feature of the Pennant trumpet is that an oval ball, 8 cm. by 4 cm., is attached to the carrying-cord by a short flax string. It comprises a piece of woven flax carefully folded and sewn into the required shape, a technique reminiscent of that used in the manufacture of some *poi* dancing balls. This ball has traces of ochrous stain on its surface, and it is noted briefly and without explanation in the Museum register as 'the original modulator'.[5] As the same object also appears in Cook's illustration, there is no reason to doubt either its association with the trumpet at the time of acquisition, or that this description, whatever its accuracy, was obtained on that occasion. The ball fits snugly into, and so effectively blocks, the aperture of the shell. It is too large, and its own cord too short, to be used to block the wooden mouthpiece.

There are a few more surviving examples of flax or other objects attached to shell trumpets, though they have been noted by ethnologists only in passing and their significance has never been discussed in detail. The only close parallel to this flax ball is one attached to a shell trumpet, no. 36 in the Oldman Collection (Oldman 1946:10, Pl. 33). From an examination of Oldman's photograph, it appears to be very similar in character, though differing in shape because, naturally, it conforms to the shape of its own shell. Oldman noted only that 'a flax cloth pad is attached to fit in [the] mouth of [the] shell', without discussing its possible function. Another specimen, superficially similar, is in the Auckland Institute and Museum (no. 81.E), and has been illustrated, but not discussed, by Best (1925a:162, Fig. 100 *left*), Andersen (1934:285-6, Fig. 64a) and Buck (1950: Fig. 70b).[6] Contrary to the impression one gets from these illustrations, however, it is clear from inspection that this attachment is different from the Pennant ball in at least two respects. It is made of flax wound round a piece of cloth, and it was obviously shaped to fit into the wooden mouthpiece of the trumpet to which it is attached, not into the bowl. It was also less carefully made than either the Oldman or Pennant pieces. It would seem, then, that these attachments could have been used to block one or other of the apertures of shell trumpets. But they were not always made of flax, nor was there always only one per specimen. A shell trumpet bequeathed by Mrs E. Hunter Blair of Edinburgh to the National Museum, Wellington (no. ME 3725), has two pieces of cloth attached to it by flax cords. One, as large as a handkerchief, is fixed in such a way that it can be stuffed into the shell's aperture. The other, bound to the correct size by leather strips, fits into the mouthpiece. In the same Museum is a shell trumpet with an attachment of bird feathers (Best 1925a:162, Fig. 101b), while at Canterbury Museum, Christchurch, is another example which has affixed feathers of the *kakapo* or ground parrot, *Strigops habroptilus* (Best 1925a:162, Fig. 101a). Colenso said of the trumpet described by him above that it was 'ornamented with strips of birds' skin and feathers; – the plumage of the *kaakaapo*' (Colenso 1880:79). Polack (1840: II, 173), writing of the period 1831-37, reported that 'a strip of dog's skin is attached to shells or conches for portability'. Buck mentioned that 'a loop was sometimes attached through a hole in the outer rim of the shell and this sometimes carried tufts of dog's hair or feathers as ornamentation' (Buck 1950:257).

It seems then, that particular specimens of shell trumpet could have possessed a number of attachments of various materials, for which there may have been a purpose, either pragmatic or ornamental. To seek an explanation, by reference to the relevant ethnological literature, on the functions of the trumpet itself is not particularly helpful. Its uses are rarely stated with precision, backed by specific ethnographic evidence. Best (1927:115), followed by Vayda

(1960:54-5, with ref.) and others, referred to its use, along with alternative devices, by night watchmen at occupied *pa* to warn the enemy that the defenders were alert. To Oldman (1946:10, 11, 21), it was also a war trumpet. Polack (1840: II, 173) said that 'they are *sometimes*' (my emphasis) 'used in war to collect a scattered party, but as they do not admit of modulation the name of musical instrument can scarcely be applied to them'. On the other hand, ability to modulate the sound was claimed, as we have seen, by Colenso and by the registration note for the Pennant piece. Neither Colenso nor Buck, however, made specific reference to its use in war. Buck (1950:258, 345) said only that it 'was used to assemble the people, to announce visitors, and in some chiefly families to announce the birth of a first-born son'. Of course shell trumpets could have had numerous uses in Maori society over time and space. The ethnological literature probably reflects a telescoping of information, in most instances casually collected and consequently difficult to assess. Let us now return to the Pennant specimen to see if it can be set more precisely into a Maori context by examining its circumstances of acquisition.

Both Cook (Beaglehole 1955:285) and Banks (Beaglehole 1962:II, 30) mentioned the existence of shell trumpets among the Maori in their first voyage journals, but neither said that examples were obtained. For the second voyage, the only reference (Forster 1777:194-231) is in an account of the first visit of H.M.S. *Resolution* to Queen Charlotte Sound, between 18 May and 7 June 1773, by George, the son of J.R. Forster, one of the official scientists on the expedition, who acted as assistant to his father. He published a detailed and lively record of the relations between Cook's men and the Maoris over this period, which can be used to indicate the *milieu* in which trading for artefacts took place.

The crew of the *Resolution* had previously encountered a few Maoris in Dusky Sound, to whom Europeans had been previously unknown. Relations had been hedged to some extent by fear and ritual observance on the Maori side, and only a few artefacts were obtained (Forster 1777:131-74; Beaglehole 1961:121-6, 134). In Queen Charlotte Sound the atmosphere was more relaxed. There were many more Maoris and the exchange of artefacts for the medals specially struck by Boulton at Soho, Birmingham, for red cloth, iron and other items proceeded apace. This was particularly so on 29 May, when prostitution and stealing began. This prompted George Forster to comment adversely on the character of the Maoris who, he stressed, were all from the local area. Contact and trade continued intermittently for several days. On 1 June nephrite objects and dogs were acquired, and some Maoris went aboard the *Resolution*, for the first time. Prices rose. They 'demanded the best price for every little trifle which they offered for sale', and in the evening 'returned to the upper part of the Sound from whence they came' (Forster 1777:207-21). The situation changed dramatically, however, on the morning of 4 June, when a large number of Maoris under two chiefs appeared in canoes from outside the Sound. One chief was called 'Teiratu' (Te Ratu or Tairatu, according to Beaglehole 1967:67) and 'he came from the opposite shore of the northern island, called Teera Whittee' or Terawhiti (Forster 1777:223-31, esp. 225). Some local Maoris were aboard the *Resolution* at the time who regarded these strangers as enemies, but 'Teiratu' pronounced an oration and Cook invited him and his men abroad. These Maoris impressed Forster as different:

> Teiratu and all his companions were a taller race of people than we had hitherto seen in New Zealand, none of them being below the middle size, and many above it. Their dress, ornaments, and arms were richer than any we had observed among the inhabitants of Queen Charlotte's Sound, and seemed to speak a kind of affluence, which was entirely new to us. (Forster 1777:225)

Forster described their clothing and personal appearance in some detail, and then commented on the artefacts which they traded:

> All their tools were very elegantly carved, and made with great attention. They sold us a hatchet, of which the blade was of the finest green jadde, and the handle curiously ornamented with fretwork. They also brought some musical instruments, among which was a trumpet, or tube of wood, about four feet long, and pretty strait; its small mouth was not above two inches, and the other not above five in diameter; it made a very uncouth kind of braying, for they always sounded the same note, though a performer on the French horn might perhaps be able to bring some better music out of it. Another trumpet was made of a large whelk (*murex tritonis*), mounted with wood, curiously carved, and pierced at the point where the mouth was applied; a hideous bellowing was all the sound that could be procured out

of this instrument. The third went by the name of a flute among our people, and was a hollow tube, widest about the middle, where it had a large opening, as well as another at each end. (Forster 1777:227)

After leaving the ship, the visitors set up temporary shelters on Motuara Island nearby, together with their women and children. Here, later the same day, they were visited by Cook and others, where 'the captain distributed many presents to them' including medals. At the same time, 'in exchange for iron, cloth, and beads, our people collected a great number of arms, tools, dresses, and ornaments, as curiosities among them, they having greater quantities of these things than any New Zealanders we had seen' (Forster 1777:229).

This contact developed into a trading spree for the crews, who probably thought that South Seas artefacts would have a sellers' market in England. The interest of collectors had certainly been kindled following the return of the *Endeavour* from the first voyage in 1771. For the first time on this second voyage, many valuable objects were readily available for exchange.[7] But it seems that this occasion had an even greater significance. These were not local Maoris but visitors from the North Island who were eager for trade, and had objects of quality to exchange. They would return to their own area and talk about Cook's visit. Cook, on the other hand, did not intend to have much direct contact with Maoris outside the Sound, which he intended to use as one of his bases for Antarctic exploration. It would seem that both sides wished that relations should remain peaceful and that the correct courtesies should be observed. Moreover, Forster said that 'Teiratu seemed to be the principal or chief among them, by a certain degree of regard which the rest paid to him' (Forster 1777:229). He should be treated with proper attention. Guided by his previous experiences of Polynesian etiquette, Cook visited the northerners' camp and accorded 'Teiratu' and his companions due respect, as they had treated him and his crews since their arrival from Cape Terawhiti. An example of this is the oration made by 'Teiratu' before boarding the *Resolution*. He 'pronounced a long speech well articulated, loud, and very solemn, and gave his voice great variety of falls and elevations' (Forster 1777:224).

It was in this social and ceremonial context (on a day, incidentally, when Cook's crews also celebrated George III's official birthday) that took place, in Forster's words (1777:227), the sale of 'a hatchet, of which the blade was of the finest green jadde, and the handle curiously ornamented with fretwork' and when the Maoris 'also brought some musical instruments'. One was a large wooden war trumpet, *pu kaea* (Best 1925a:153-60); another, 'made of a large whelk' was a *pu tatara*, and a third was 'a hollow tube, widest about the middle, where it had a large opening, as well as another at each end' (Forster 1777:227) i.e. another type of trumpet, *pu torino* (Best 1925a:128-34). There is apparently no *pu kaea* among surviving Forster collections, but it is possible to match Forster's 'hatchet' (*toki pou tangata*, a ceremonial adze) and *pu torino* obtained on this day with specimens now in the Pitt Rivers Museum at Oxford, which were given by J.R. Forster to the Ashmolean Museum in 1775-6.[8] Alongside the Pennant trumpet illustrated on Cook's Plate XIX (Fig. 2) are two other specimens: the *toki pou tangata* just mentioned, and a shark-tooth knife, *mira tuatini*, no. 110 in the Forster Collection at Oxford (Gathercole n.d.: 18). These are two fine objects which were not often available for exchange to Europeans in the 1770s, yet the Forsters obtained both of them, the 'hatchet' certainly on the morning of 4 June 1773. There would seem little doubt therefore that they also acquired the Pennant trumpet on this occasion, as well as the other two trumpets. Two further pieces of evidence link this trumpet directly with the Forsters. Firstly, J.R. Forster had been on close terms with Thomas Pennant since about 1768, a relationship which lasted at least until 1786 (Hoare 1972:12-3). Pennant, 'who perhaps did most to introduce Forster to a scientific career in Britain' (Hoare 1972:12), thought highly of his friend's abilities as a zoologist and ornithologist, and they had much in common. A gift from Forster of a rare worked shell artefact, which was thus both a 'natural' and an 'artificial curiosity' (in the eighteenth-century parlance), would have surely been very acceptable to Pennant. He was, after all, the author of *The British Zoology* (1776), *A Tour in Scotland* (1771) and other works reflecting his scientific and topographical interests. An artefact derived from such an auspicious occasion of Maori-European contact would have enhanced significance. It can be suggested that Pennant received it soon after the *Resolution* returned to England in July 1775, when the Forsters were also preparing to send part of their collection to Oxford (Gathercole n.d. 2-4). That Pennant valued the specimen is clear from the fact that a drawing of it survives, executed by his personal artist, 'that treasure', as Pennant (1793:10) called him, Moses Griffith (B.M. Add. MS. 15508: f. 32).

The second piece of evidence to relate the trumpet and the Forsters comes from Cook's Plate XIX itself. This is one of five plates used by Cook to portray a selection of the objects obtained during the voyage. With the exception of the New Zealand specimens, they came from islands not previously visited by the British. Cook's intention was to show his readers something new. To include a New Zealand plate at all when, for example, there was not one of Tahitian material, therefore implied that these particular Maori objects, which had not been illustrated in previous voyage accounts, were considered to be of particular rarity and importance. It also suggests that they were probably associated together in some way, as has been argued above concerning their place and date of acquisition. Some of the objects shown on the other artefact plates can be traced to collections made by the Forsters.[9] J.R. Forster must have had some say in the selection of the objects to be drawn and in the composition of the plates.[10] As the New Zealand plate was clearly of such importance, it is likely that he chose for it special objects obtained by either himself or his son.[11]

So much for the particular historical circumstances surrounding the acquisition of the shell trumpet. This indicates that Skinner was correct in his assumption that it came from Queen Charlotte Sound. It was, however, obtained by the Forsters, not Cook as Skinner thought. He also suggested that a similar form of mouthpiece was found in both the North and the South Islands. Although this assumption may still be correct, the Cambridge specimen can no longer be used to support it. The object certainly is from the North Island and had, by mid-1773, a specific association with a group of Maoris under a known chief possessing a wide range of objects of high quality. The fact that George Forster, always alive to cultural differences between groups of Maoris that he met, commented on the superiority of this group's artefacts to those found among the inhabitants of the Sound at that time, could mean that trumpets of this form were found only in the North Island. But it is clear from other comments by Cook that the population of the Sound was very mobile in the 1770s (e.g. Beaglehole 1961:172). This suggests that for the time of initial European contact, and probably for earlier times too, it is rather unproductive to look for regional distributions of types of mouthpieces or, for that matter, of shell trumpets or artefacts of like quality.

The circumstances in which the Pennant trumpet was obtained make clear that it was regarded as a valuable object by the Maoris but that it could, none the less, be exchanged for European goods. Why was this so, when the unusual features of the trumpet suggest that it had particular value, and when there was no shortage of objects to quench the European thirst for 'curiosities'? If it can be shown that this specimen *once* had a high value in Maori society but had lost it by mid-1773, both the rarity of *pu tatara* in early collections and the exchange of this particular example might be explained. What had been its meaning to the Terawhiti Maoris?

Colenso said that the purpose of the wooden base of the trumpet he described referred to 'a most curious plan which the old Maoris seem to have had for increasing, or altering, the power of the sound of their conch shell'. He concluded that, in the cases both of this specimen and of the one illustrated by Cook, the wooden insert was not a repair, but 'was done purposely. The old Maoris informed Mr Locke that only one sort of wood was used by them for such purposes, it being very sonorous, *viz. kaiwhiria* (also *'koporokaiwhiri'* and *porokaiwhiri*) = *Hedycarya dentata.* Of this wood they anciently made their best loud-sounding drums, or gongs (*pahu*), which were suspended in their principal forts. They also manufactured several other musical instruments from this wood, for the producing of delicate sounds to accompany their singing' (Colenso 1880:79).

Oldman (1946:21) said of the specimen no. 636 in his collection, which has a small piece of wood let into the bowl: 'this is apparently filled to increase the volume of the sound'. The wooden inset to the Pennant piece could have had a similar function. If so, the statement in the museum register that the flax ball is a 'modulator' is likely to be correct. The efficacy of the wooden bowl as a sounding-board would be enhanced by using such a muffler to help to vary the amount and quality of the sound. It is worth remembering that, on the second voyage, a high level of interest was shown in Polynesian music by the Forsters, Cook and Midshipman James Burney, a son of Dr Charles Burney, the well-known musicologist.[12] It is likely on these grounds alone that the information concerning the modulator was correctly passed to Pennant. But did Maoris actually modulate the sound by these means and, if so, why? According to Banks (Beaglehole 1962: II, 30), the sound made by shell trumpets was 'not much differing from that made by boys with a cow horn', while George Forster (1777:227) said that 'a hideous bellowing was all the sound that could be procured out of this instrument'. I believe this to be an accurate description of the sound made by this particular specimen because the shell is broken. But there is some evidence to support Colenso's statement that the power of the sound could be altered, which must now be assessed.

George Forster knew more about this specimen than appeared in the English edition of his book. In the German editions, in which were published some of Cook's plates including Plate XIX, the modulator was described in the relevant caption as a stopper to keep out the dust.[13] This may have been, of course, an inspired guess by Forster, but in view of his close observation of the Cape Terawhiti Maoris it was probably more than this. I suggest that he obtained from the Maoris a notion that the modulator had more than a pragmatic function.

Let us assume, for the moment, that Forster was correct. Why should the dust be excluded? The obvious explanation is that whatever was within the trumpet had to be kept free from dust or dirt, i.e. unpolluted. Unfortunately, there is no satisfactory evidence that Maoris regarded dust as a polluting agent,[14] and in any case the modulator is neither shaped nor attached in a way that could keep the interior of the shell literally dust-free. On the other hand, if we regard Forster's statement as his interpretation of a *metaphorical* explanation given to him by the Maoris, then it might be explicable. Let us now assume that the modulator could affect not only the actual quality of the sound produced, but also its symbolic quality, i.e. it did not keep out the dust, but it helped to keep certain symbolic attributes of sound safe within the trumpet, especially when not in use. This could explain its oval shape and the care lavished on its manufacture. After all, simple muffling could have been done just as effectively with the hand, as it was at times elsewhere in Oceania.[15] If we also accept that the attention devoted to making the trumpet air-tight – even to the extent of decorating the caulking gum – was for symbolic as well as practical purposes, then the complete artefact begins to acquire a possible meaning. When the trumpet was blown, the blower could control the sound produced in three ways: by the volume of his breath or the shape of his lips, by the presence of the wooden base, and by using the modulator. These were the means used 'for increasing, or altering, the power of the sound of their conch shell', as Colenso put it. When not in use, the modulator could seal both the aperture and the latent sound within it.

It might be argued that this interpretation is at variance with the remarks by Banks that the noise of the trumpet was like that 'made by boys with a cow's horn' and by Forster that its sound was 'a hideous bellowing', i.e. that the sound was not controlled. Actually, Banks and Forster were commenting that the sound did not appear to them to be musical, which is not necessarily the same thing. That the sound could be controlled (and varied) is indicated by the remarks of two other European observers, Monneron (1769) and Tasman (1642). The former, who was with De Surville in Doubtless Bay, compared the sound 'to those of the bagpipes' and said that it was 'without doubt the instrument of which Abel Tasman speaks'.[16] Tasman himself likened the sound to that of 'the moor's trumpets', and 'had one of our sailors (who could play somewhat on the trumpet) blow back to' (the Maoris) 'in answer' (Sharp 1968:121) i.e. the Maori sounds were sufficiently varied and noteworthy to Tasman to be copied in reply.

Tasman's contact at Golden Bay in December 1642 was, of course, the first known between Maoris and Europeans. It is relevant to notice from the Tasman and Haalbos-Montanus accounts that not only were the Maoris extremely hostile, but they also indulged in much noise, both shouting and blowing trumpets. The latter may have been of the long wooden variety (*pu kaea*), though these are not elsewhere described by ethnologists as making the 'shrill sound' recorded in the Haalbos-Montanus account (Sharp 1968:41). If Monneron is correct, it was the shell trumpet that was used in the Maori canoes, in which case its function was similar to that described later with regard to *pa*: to ward off the enemy.[17] The Maoris were faced with a completely new, dangerous and frightening situation. To employ shell trumpets at this juncture implies, I suggest, that they were thereby symbolically summoning outside assistance at a time of stress.

What could have been the nature of this assistance? To answer by saying that it was to call on Tu, the god of war and of man, is not, unfortunately, very satisfactory. Tu (or Tumatauenga), though of great importance, according to Buck (1950:460-1), 'was a remote classical god . . . closer and more active gods were needed for the frequent field campaigns in New Zealand . . . hence most of the tribal gods in New Zealand were war gods who protected their tribes in defensive measures and assisted them in offensive operations'. Now, Best said (1925a:160) that 'in Maori myth the first shell trumpets are said to have been made by Tupai, a younger brother of Tane' (the eldest son of the primal parents, Rangi and Papa). The trumpets figure in at least one myth where they were blown to mark a relatively minor phase in the creation process (Best 1924:104). Tupai himself appears to be a rather sinister figure, described by Best (1925b:872) from data collected among the Tuhoe people, as 'the name, or personified form, of lightning, or of a thunderstorm accompanied by lightning. Any thing struck by lightning is said to have been so stricken by Tupai'. One of Best's informants said that his wife's mother 'was burnt up by Tupai. The act for which that woman was destroyed was a desecration of *tapu* connected with her daughter, my wife, Te Whakahoro. Her father was a human medium of the demon Tupai . . . On that same day, another woman was burnt by Tupai, her breast was scorched. Her sin was food, meddling with sacred food. She was not killed outright, because her sin was a mild one. Had she sinned deeply, she would not have escaped Tupai'. (Best 1925b:873-4). Tupai personified a capricious force, a 'demon' which could suddenly strike against wrong-doers but as Best (1925b:873) made clear, it could be controlled: 'But should a person of sacred, esoteric knowledge be present, he may succeed in diverting that man-burning demon, or render it harmless by a certain rite, and reciting a "warding-off" charm'. Tupai, the thunder god, the mythical maker of the first shell trumpets, therefore, could be controlled, but only by a man of appropriate status.

It is now appropriate to refer to the other objects that are sometimes found attached to shell trumpets. Those noted in this paper are dog skin, dog hair and *kakapo* feathers (page 190). Most writers have regarded these objects as mere 'ornamentation' (e.g. Buck 1950:257; Colenso 1880:79) but this is no explanation at all. It is more logical to regard them as metaphorical expressions of the functional meaning of the actual trumpets. Thus it may be significant that, according to Williams' Maori Dictionary (1957:300), the term *whakapu* means to 'make a long continuous wail or sound, howl as a dog'. More convincing, no doubt, is Best's data, also from the Tuhoe, concerning their lore about the *kakapo*. For example, Best refers to Buller's remark (1877:202) that the proverb *Ka puru a putaihinu* 'is used to denote the rumbling of distant thunder', a reference to the fact that the noise of the birds, which were once abundant, could be heard at night 'to a considerable distance.'[18] Moreover, the Tuhoe Maoris maintained that every flock of *kakapo* had its leader (*tiaka*) who acted as a sentry at a 'playground' where the birds did at night 'a strange kind of performance, each beating its wings on the ground and making a hole therein with its beak, at the same time uttering deep-toned cries. As dawn approached, the leader of the flock led it back to the common home, generally situated at some steep or rough place' (Best 1942:213). This is a striking analogy to the role of a night sentry at a *pa*, equipped with a trumpet to show that the defenders were alert. One must be careful, of course, not to generalize too readily from information derived from one Maori source. On the other hand, it is now possible to argue that the shell trumpet had a sacred function, hallowed in myth and associated with Tupai, a thunder-demon who could strike down offenders against *tapu*. But he was capricious, and therefore he had to be controlled. To invoke his aid, by sounding the trumpet, could be dangerous. Therefore the sound had to be regulated by modulation in the ways suggested above for the Pennant specimen. The fact that man-made, regulated, sound had sacred associations in numerous other situations in Maori society is consistent with this interpretation.[19]

It is now possible to look at the Pennant trumpet in a new way. If the act of modulated blowing invoked the latent power of a capricious god, that power was, for the time of blowing at least, controlled by the blower: he was in direct contact with the god. Indeed, the physical actions of the blower mirrored this. His lips were the point of contact between his own *moko* (tattoo), the symbol of his completeness as a man, and the stylized Janus mask carved on the mouthpiece.[20] The identity of the two was very close. Each possessed a split representational design which was temporarily joined. Moreover, the Pennant modulator was originally painted red, of which traces remain (*cf.* Jackson 1972: 20-1 and ref.). Thus, it can be seen as the symbolic extension of the blower's lips. The shell, then, was the extension of his mouth, joined to him by the mouthpiece, which he blew in a very precise way. The asymmetrical surface wear on the lip of the mouthpiece and the differential staining on the outside of the wooden bowl, which are apparent from close inspection, show that the trumpet was held slightly askew against the lips, so that each side of the Janus head was visible in profile as a split representational design directly opposite that of the blower's *moko*. The bowl was supported by the cup of one hand, and so, over time, became stained by use. The other hand was free to manipulate the modulator, which was hanging from the projection at the distal end of the shell.

In this connexion, it is instructive to note that this trumpet has certain material features and, I suggest, certain functions, in common with godsticks. The latter were ably described by Richard Taylor from objects and information collected by him before 1855:

> These images were only thought to possess virtue or peculiar sanctity from the presence of the god they represented when dressed up for worship; at other times they were regarded only as bits of ordinary wood. This dressing consisted in the first place of the *pahau*, or beard, which was made by a fringe of the bright red feathers of the *kaka*, parrot – next of the peculiar cincture of sacred cord with which it was bound; this mystic bandage was not only tied on in a peculiar way by the priest, who uttered his most powerful spells all the time he was doing it, but also whilst he was twisting the cord itself and lastly, painting the entire figure with the sacred *kura*; this completed the preparation for the reception of the god who was by these means constrained to come and take up his abode in it when invoked. But the presence of the *atua* was not supposed to be confined to these images, he more frequently took up his abode in the priest himself. (Taylor 1870:212, quoted in Barrow 1959:186)

This discussion is consistent with, and helps to explain, certain other information mentioned in this paper. For example, the rarity of specimens in Cook collections, even allowing for the limited 'sampling' conditioned by coastal contact and restricted social intercourse, must reflect also their continuing importance in the 1770s and the reluctance of Maoris to part with them.[21] The disposal of this specimen in Queen Charlotte Sound was probably due to the fact that it was broken, for the break is an old one, and this would have rendered it useless by destroying its power to make suitable sounds.[22] In addition, this specimen has no attachment for blocking the mouthpiece, such as is found on the Auckland and Wellington (ME 3725) examples. Whether it ever had one or not cannot be proved; but it is possible that at some time a small flax stopper for insertion into the mouthpiece was attached by a string to the loop that is knotted into the suspension cord, in the same way as on the Auckland specimen. In any case, it seems that to be properly effective a shell trumpet should have had two flax attachments: one to be used in the bowl as a modulator and the other as a much smaller stopper at the mouthpiece. A Europeanized version of the complete artefact surviving today is the Wellington specimen with two cloth stoppers, which is quite inexplicable without reference to the Pennant, Auckland and Oldman (no. 636) pieces. By June 1773, therefore, the Pennant trumpet was, in Maori eyes, fit only to be discarded. It was exchanged for novel British artefacts, notably the medals personally bestowed by Cook himself, an occasion that heralded more far-reaching changes in Maori values. The consequent significance of Cook medals to the Maori, incidentally, can be demonstrated indirectly by the fact that they have been found at six locations, at least, in the South Island, some of them protohistoric sites far removed from Cook's stopping points (Begg & Begg (1969:121). The two most southerly sites are Murdering Beach (Skinner 1959:221) and Katiki (Trotter 1970: 469, Pl. 2), both in Otago.

The argument advanced in this paper has been deliberately focused on one object in order to describe and to seek to explain its material features in an integrated way. Parts of the explanation are inferred from hypotheses concerning the possible meaning of the object in the context of Maori systems of belief. Without this approach certain features of the object could have been regarded as anomalous and discreetly ignored, as indeed they have been hitherto by earlier writers. This is not to say that the Pennant trumpet should be regarded as a 'type-specimen' against which other examples might be measured by means of formal typological analysis. The approach has been to attempt to understand all its material attributes. The absence of these, in other specimens of trumpet, might then be explained by means of comparative historical and ethnographical analysis similar to that undertaken here. Other Maori ethnological specimens, which often lie undisturbed and ignored in museums throughout the world, might well be examined by such methods and related to the wider context of Maori anthropological studies.

It would be a naive procedure to look elsewhere in the South Pacific for ethnographic parallels in order to 'explain' this specimen. On the other hand, it is relevant to note at this point, that the role of Maori shell trumpets suggested here is not generally at variance with that recorded for many other parts of Polynesia and Melanesia (Fischer 1958:66-72, Taf. xxviii, xxix). To that degree, therefore, the *pu tatara* can be viewed as an artefact as old as Maori society itself, embodying certain values derived from that society's tropical Polynesian heritage, but given specific form by the Maori physical and ideological environment. Unfortunately, it is not possible to be more precise than this, since the archaeological evidence for the existence of the form in prehistoric times is ambiguous. A single specimen recorded by von Haast from Moa-bone Point Cave is now lost, and his surviving notes do not make clear where precisely it was found (Skinner 1923:101). The six specimens found at Oruarangi *pa* could have come from either prehistoric or early historic layers (Shawcross & Terrell 1966, with ref.). However, if shell trumpets were as rare and treasured as I have suggested, their absence on investigated prehistoric archaeological sites is not surprising. It is a reasonable assumption that, as reflexions of status, their survival was ensured, even when they had been repaired or given fresh mouthpieces. Here, as elsewhere, archaeological criteria, taken by themselves, can be misleading indicators of social values. However, I have tried, in this paper, to indicate some of the other methods available for the study of objects derived from Cook's voyages and those of his contemporaries, when a range of evidence from a number of disciplines can be brought together to answer specific questions prompted, but not always explicitly posed, by the artefacts themselves. An archaeologist may no longer regard artefacts as central to his discipline but, unfortunately perhaps, they are still *there*, and have to be explained. Empiricism is not usually enough.

Acknowledgments

An early version of part of this paper was included in an open lecture given at the University of Otago in March 1973 on 'Eighteenth-century Polynesia and the European Imagination', also given later at the University of Hawaii. For access to museum specimens and information, I am grateful to Mrs B. McFadgen (National Museum, Wellington), Miss J. Davidson and Mr D.R. Simmons (Auckland Institute and Museum), Dr R.S. Duff and Mr M.M. Trotter (Canterbury Museum, Christchurch), Mr G.S. Park (Otago Museum, Dunedin), and Dr E.S. Dodge (Peabody Museum, Salem, Mass.). The following made critical comments and suggestions: Mr E.C. Chamberlain, Dr R. Dawson, Dr M. Jackson, Dr A.L. Kaeppler, Dr M. McLean, Mr and Mrs G.S. Park, Mr E.L. Phelan, Dr H.D. Skinner, Mrs J. Smith and Dr M. Urban. The photographs were prepared by the University Library, Cambridge, and Mr L.E. Morley, Mr J. Osbourn made certain repairs to the Pennant trumpet and assisted in its detailed examination. The opportunity to study specimens in New Zealand occurred during a term's leave of absence granted by the University of Cambridge.

REFERENCES

Andersen, J.C. (1934) *Maori Music with its Polynesian Background* (Mem. Polynesian Soc. No. 10). New Plymouth, N.Z.

Barrow, T. (1959) Maori Godsticks collected by the Rev. Richard Taylor. *Dominion Mus. Records in Ethnology*, 1, 183-211. Wellington, N.Z.

Beaglehole, J.C. (ed.) (1955-67) *The Journals of Captain James Cook on his Voyages of Discovery* (3 vols.). London:

Beaglehole, J.C. (1955) *I – The Voyage of the* Endeavour *1768-1771.*

Beaglehole, J.C. (1961) *II – The Voyage of the* Resolution *and* Adventure *1772-1775.*

Beaglehole, J.C. (1967) *III – The Voyage of the* Resolution *and* Discovery *1776-1780.*

Beaglehole, J.C. (ed.) (1962) *The* Endeavour *Journal of Joseph Banks 1768-1771.* Sydney.

Begg, A.C. and Begg, N.C. (1969) *James Cook and New Zealand.* Wellington, N.Z.

Best, E. (1924) *The Maori.* Mem. Polynesian Soc. No. 5, Wellington, N.Z.

Best, E. (1925a) *Games and Pastimes of the Maori.* Dominion Mus. Bull. No. 8. Wellington, N.Z.

Best, E. (1925b) *Tuhoe: The Children of the Mist.* Mem. Polynesian Soc. No. 6. New Plymouth, N.Z.

Best, E. (1927) *The Pa Maori.* Dominion Mus. Bull. No. 6. Wellington, N.Z.

Best, E. (1942) *Forest Lore of the Maori.* Dominion Mus. Bull. No. 14. Wellington, N.Z.

Buck, Sir P. (1950) *The Coming of the Maori* (2nd ed.). Wellington, N.Z.

Buller, W.L. (1877) Further notes on the ornithology of New Zealand. *Trans. N.Z. Inst.*, 10, 201-9.

Colenso, W. (1880) Contributions towards a better knowledge of the Maori race. *Trans. N.Z. Inst.*, 13, 57-84.

Falla, R.A., Sibson, R.B. and Turbott, E.G. (1966) *A Field Guide to the Birds of N.Z.* London and Auckland.

Fischer, H. (1958) *Schallgeräte in Ozeanien: Bau und Spieltechnik, Verbreitung und Funktion.* Sammlung Musikwissenschaftlicher Abhandlungen 36. Baden Baden.

Fisher, V.F. (1937) The material culture of Oruarangi, Matatoki, Thames. IV: Musical instruments. *Records Auckland Inst. and Mus.*, 2, 111-18.

Forster, G. (1777) *A Voyage round the World, in His Britannic Majesty's Sloop* Resolution *commanded by Capt. James Cook, during the Years 1772-3-4-5.* London.

Gathercole, P. (n.d.) *From the Islands of the South Seas 1773-4: An Exhibition of a Collection made on Capt. Cook's Second Voyage of Discovery by J.R. Forster.* Oxford.

Hoare, M.E. (1972) 'A strange and eventful history': the scientific correspondents of J.R. Forster (1729-98). *Records Aust. Acad. Sci.*, 2 (3), 7-17.

Jackson, M. (1972) Aspects of symbolism and composition in Maori art. *Bijdragen tot de Taal-, Land- en Volkenkunde*, 128, 33-80.

Larsson, K.E. (1960) *Fijian Studies*, Etnologiska Studier 25.

Oldman, W.O. (1946) *Skilled Handwork of the Maori: Being the Oldman Collection of Maori Artifacts* (2nd ed.) Mem. Polynesian Soc. No. 14. Wellington, N.Z.

Pennant, T. (1793) *The Literary Life of the Late T. Pennant, Esq. By Himself.* London.

Polack, J.S. (1840) *Manners and Customs of the New Zealanders.* London.

Powell, A.W.B. (1966) Trumpet, Large (*Charonia capax*). In McLintock, A.H. (ed.), *An Encyclopaedia of New Zealand.* Wellington, N.Z.

Sharp, A. (1968) *The Voyages of Abel Janszoon Tasman.* Oxford.

Shawcross, F.W. (1970) The Cambridge University collection of Maori artefacts, made on Captain Cook's first voyage. *Jour. Polynesian Soc.*, 79, 305-48.

Shawcross, F.W. and Terrell, J.E. (1966) Paterangi and Oruarangi Swamp Pas. *Jour. Polynesian Soc.*, 75, 404-29.

Skinner, H.D. (1923) Archaeology of Canterbury, I: Moa-bone point cave. *Records Canterbury Mus.*, II (3), 93-104.

Skinner, H.D. (1959) Murdering Beach: collecting and excavating. The first phase 1850-1950. *Jour. Polynesian Soc.*, 68, 219-38.

Taylor, R. (1870) *Te Ika a Maui; or New Zealand and its Inhabitants* (2nd ed.). London.

Trotter, M. (1970) Excavations at Shag Point, North Otago. *Records Canterbury Mus.*, 8, 469-85.

Vayda, A.P. (1960) *Maori Warfare* (Maori Monograph No. 2). Wellington, N.Z.

Williams, H.W. (1957) *A Dictionary of the Maori Language* (6th ed.). Wellington, N.Z.

NOTES

1. One of ten names noted by Best (1925a:160). The commonest synonym appears to be *pu moana*.

2. Originally a loan from the 8th Earl of Denbigh, the collection was eventually donated by the 9th Earl in 1925 (letters from the latter to A. von Hügel, 19 and 30 March 1925). The accession numbers of the Maori objects mentioned in this paper are: 25.374 shell trumpet; 25.372, whalebone *patu*; 25.373, wooden *patu*; 25.382, lure hook; 25.375, plume of dog hair. Thomas Pennant lived at Downing Hall, Flintshire. According to the 9th Earl (30 March), 'the 8th Earl of Denbigh came into possession of the Downing property on the death of his first wife who was the great granddaughter of Mrs Pennant and heiress of the property, which was sold and' (the rest of) 'the collection and library dispersed in 1920'. After Pennant's death in 1798 the collection appears to have remained at Downing until 1912, not moved elsewhere as implied by Shawcross (1970:305).

3. Accession numbers 25.365-89; 25.401-10; 25.418-24; 25.426.

4. William Colenso F.R.S. (*b.*1811, *d.*1899) was a missionary, printer, botanist and politician, who also became one of the leading authorities of his day on Maori culture. For much of his life he lived in Napier, where he must have met Mr Locke and seen his trumpet.

5. Sometime before Shawcross examined the Pennant trumpet in 1968 the modulator had become detached, and he did not include it in his discussion (Shawcross 1970:337-8, Fig. 36).

6. According to Andersen, this specimen, called *Te Awa a te atua*, once belonged to the Heuheu family of Taupo and 'used to be sounded only on the birth of a first-born male child'.

7. The evidence for the growing appreciation of Polynesian artefacts as an aspect of European taste, notably after the second and third voyages, is still largely unpublished and is too complex to review here. The relative lack of interest among collectors immediately after the first voyage, compared to that shown later, is indicated by the fact that few surviving collections or individual specimens can be definitely assigned to the first voyage. The Sandwich (or Trinity College) Collection at the University Museum of Archaeology and Ethnology, Cambridge, is a rare exception (Shawcross 1970).

8. In the *Catalogue of Curiosities sent to Oxford*, written in George Forster's hand, the *toki pou tangata* is No. 109 and the *pu torino* No. 116 (Gathercole n.d.; 17, 19).

9. E.g. at least three of the Marquesan objects illustrated on Plate XVII are in the Forster Collection in the Pitt Rivers Museum: No. 129, headdress of coconut fibre; No. 133, breast ornament; No. 134, feathered headdress. The large Tongan basket shown on Plate XXI is No. 87 (Gathercole n.d.: 16, 20).

10. Hence, I think, Forster's remarks in his preface (1777: viii): 'That account' (i.e. Cook's) 'will be ornamented with a great variety of plates, representing views of the countries which we visited, portraits of the natives, figures of their boats, arms, and utensils, together with a number of particular charts of the new discoveries; and all these plates, engraved at the expence of the Board of Admiralty, are the joint property of captain Cook and my father'. Reinhold Forster was initially permitted to use some of the plates for his projected contributions to the official account. This permission was withdrawn after his breach with the Admiralty in 1776 over his rights and responsibilities in matters of publication (Beaglehole 1961: cxlviii-ix).

11. Plate XIX, unlike the other artefact plates, has no artist's name given. In view of the close association of the three specimens illustrated with the Forsters, it is not impossible that the draughtsman was George himself. If this was the case, his father's behaviour would have made it embarrassing for George to appear publicly as a contributor to the official account of the voyage. The English edition of his own version had no illustrations except for one map.

12. For example, George Forster gave a spirited description of a Maori dance (Forster 1777:220-1) and Burney provided the first notation of Maori and Tongan music (Beaglehole 1961: cxxxix).

13. Forster's *Reise um Die Welt*... first appeared in two volumes in 1778 and 1780. The caption reads 'No. 4. Kriegstrompete aus einer Muschel gemacht, mit einem höltzernen Mundstück und einem Stöpsel von Matten versehn, damit kein Staub hinein falle' ('... so that no dust should fall inside'). I am indebted to Dr Ruth Dawson for this reference and translation.

14. Best (1924:432-4) said that 'in times of great scarcity a kind of clay, called *uku*, was eaten'. Although this seems to have been an unusual occurrence, it need not suggest that clay was normally polluting.

15. e.g. in Fiji (Larsson 1960:121-3) and New Hebrides (personal communication from Mr K. Huffman).

16. Quoted in Best (1925a:161). The journal of P. de l'Horne (first lieutenant) has a similar statement: 'with this instrument they produce a sound like that of the bagpipes, which little resembles that of the common trumpet, as Tasman said when he heard it' (quoted in Andersen 1934:26).

17. The long war trumpet would surely have been a cumbersome thing to use in a crowded war canoe. There is a drawing in the British Museum of a 'New Zealand canoe the crew peaceable' where a man is blowing a shell trumpet and a child holds a *pu torino* (Add. MS. 23920: f. 51). It probably dates from the first voyage.

18. Cf. 'The most characteristic call' (of the *kakapo*) 'is a series of bittern-like booms heard during the breeding season; other calls are hisses, croaks, screams and mewings' (Falla, Sibson and Turbott 1966:170).

19. There are examples given by Best, e.g. a priest spoke in a distinctive 'whistling tone of voice' when communicating a sacred message (1924:248); flutes made of human bone were sometimes blown to assist a difficult parturition, the sound representing ancestral spirits (1924:298); sacred chants (*karakia*) had to be recited correctly 'in a measured, rhythmic manner', and if one chanter ran out of breath mid-way, another took over at once (1924:265). In any case, a use of aerophones implied efficient breath control.

20. Jackson (1972:69-72) has recently discussed the symbolism of *moko* in relation to that of Maori wood carving, on which these remarks are based.

21. For example, there is no record of Maori shell trumpets in the ethnological collections at the Leverian Museum (personal communication from Dr A. Kaeppler). This was a large and famous museum, with some emphasis on its ethnological exhibits, especially after the death of Cook in 1779. It was founded by Sir Ashton Lever (*b.*1729, *d.*1788) at his home near Manchester, and was transferred to London in 1775. The contents were sold by auction in 1806. A guide (*A Companion to the Museum* 1790) and the sale catalogue provide detailed knowledge of its contents.

22. The artist who drew the trumpet on Plate XIX was careful to show the intact side. The published engraving has been 'reversed' and appears to have been put together hurriedly without much attention to the niceties of balanced composition. The trumpet is squashed into one side of the Plate – almost as an afterthought. If the original drawings were done, as suggested in note 11, by George Forster, the Plate may have been completed only after his influence had been removed, when he could not supervise its production.

JACK GOLSON

Archaeology and agricultural history in the New Guinea Highlands

For the ecosystems approach which he pioneered in archaeology and developed particularly to understand and interpret the economic life of prehistoric societies, Grahame Clark integrated evidence derived from the nature and properties of the raw materials used by prehistoric man, a fuller exploitation of the potential of the biological concomitants of prehistoric human activity and a judicious use of appropriate historical and ethnographic observations on the economic operations of pre-industrial societies. Of recent years, with increasing ecological emphases over a range of disciplines, the Clark approach in archaeology has been considerably strengthened and developed, conceptually and methodologically. Archaeologists are now looking at the large persisting problems in human prehistory within a theoretical framework designed to synthesize a whole range of cultural, biological and physical variables and shared with biologists, ethnographers and geographers.

A series of recent studies by anthropologists and geographers centring on the agricultural systems of the inhabitants of nuclear and marginal areas of the Central Highlands of New Guinea falls within this developing tradition (Brookfield & Brown 1963; Rappaport 1967; Bowers 1968; Clarke 1971; Waddell 1972). Some of the issues they raise are the subject of archaeological and allied research now being carried out in the swamps of Kuk Tea Research Station in the upper Wahgi Valley, near Mount Hagen township, in the western Highlands District of Papua New Guinea.[1]

A first report of preliminary results from these investigations into the agricultural history of the New Guinea Highlands is offered in this volume honouring Grahame Clark, because its subject matter is appropriate to his archaeological interests and in recognition of his stimulus to archaeological research throughout the world and his continuous interest in his former students' contributions.

The Central Highlands: agricultural systems (Fig. 1)

The Central Highlands of New Guinea consist of a series of massive mountain ranges, 3°-7° south of the equator, which trend W.N.W. and E.S.E. 700 miles along the length of the island, from the western bird's head to the eastern tail. Reaching heights of 12,000-16,000 feet, they form the largest cordillera between the Himalayas and the Andes. Their falls to north and south are steep and their rivers drain to the lowlands by way of gorges and rapids through few eventual outlets. Physical and ecological obstacles en route have probably always kept them somewhat isolated from the lowlands. Until the '30s of this century the outside world thought of them as a single continuous and uninhabited mountain chain. Exploration during that decade and subsequently has made known the existence of about a million people – perhaps a third of New Guinea's population overall – four-fifths of whom inhabit a series of intermontane valleys between 4,500 and 6,500 feet above sea level, some of them up to 60 miles long and 5-15 miles wide.

To the incoming Europeans everything they saw contrasted with the New Guinea that they knew: the numbers of people and of pigs, the vast managed landscapes comprising grasslands, planted groves of *Casuarina* and bamboo and large, orderly plantations, and particularly the nature and elaboration of agricultural practices. These features have been a particular focus for academic interest in more recent years, though it is now clear that the contrast between Highlands and Lowlands New Guinea agricultural systems has been overdrawn (Yen 1971:6; Waddell 1972:8; *cf.* Brookfield & White 1968:49-50).

The characteristic and surprising feature of New Guinea Highlands agriculture is the dominance of the sweet potato (*Ipomoea batatas*), a plant of undoubted South American ancestry

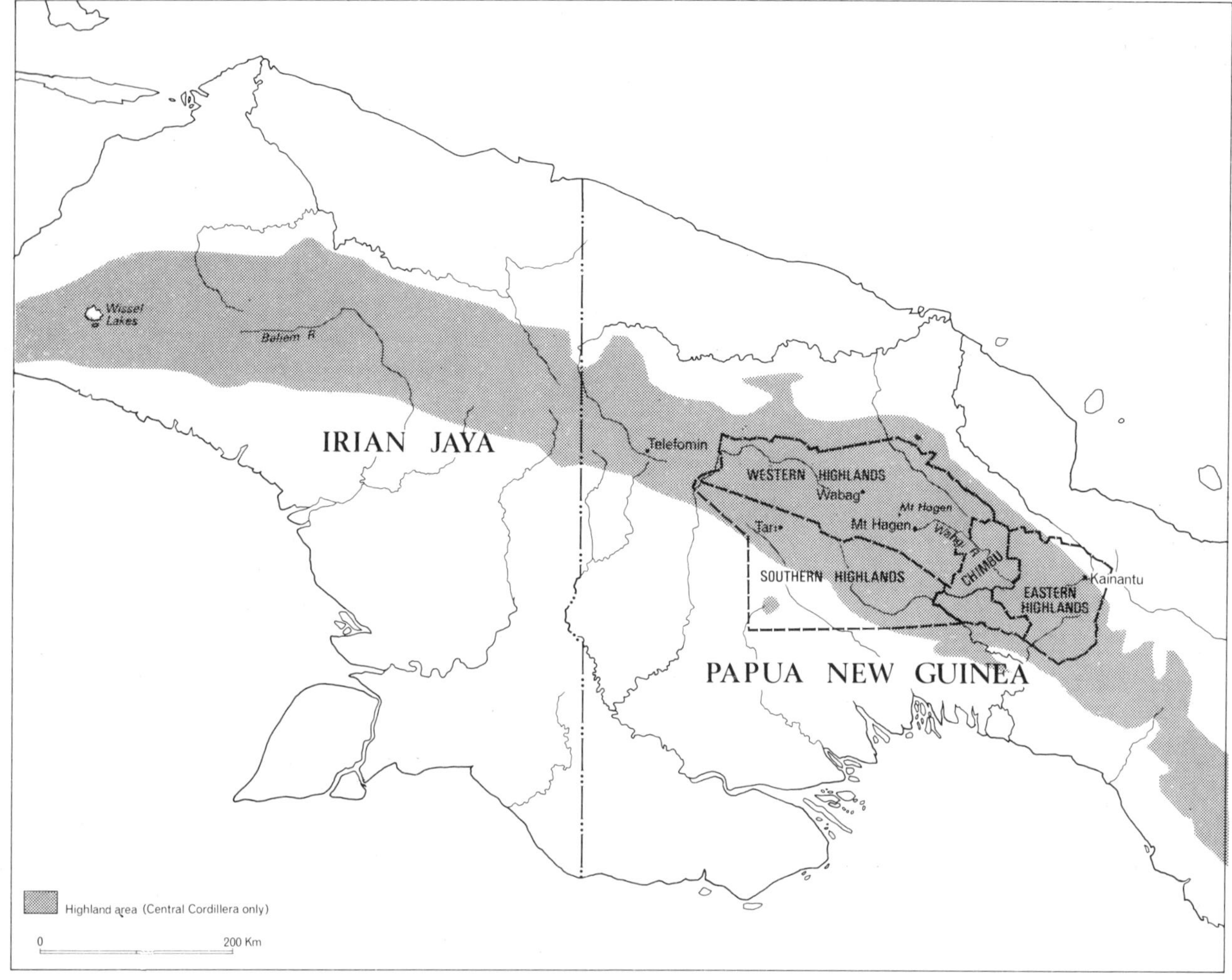

Figure 1. New Guinea, showing central highlands.

(Nishiyama 1963; Yen 1963; 1968), which supplies the vast bulk of Highlands diet and is a main support – at times and in places amounting to two-thirds of the crop (Waddell 1972:118-20) – of the fluctuating populations of pigs which play a basic role in Highlands social, political and ritual life. Because of the equableness of the climate generally and the lack of marked seasonality overall, planting takes place at different times throughout the year, harvesting is a daily occurrence and no storage facilities are necessary.

With the sweet potato is associated a range of secondary crops indigenous to the Indo-Malaysian plant world, some of which, like taro (*Colocasia esculenta*), yam (*Dioscorea* spp.) and, more locally, banana (*Musa* spp.) are staple foods elsewhere in New Guinea. A few of the plants involved, like sugar cane (*Saccharum officinarum*) and bananas of the Australimusa type, may well have been domesticated in New Guinea or the New Guinea region (e.g. Bulmer & Bulmer 1964:46). Different crops achieve regional importance in Highlands subsistence within the secondary register for reasons that seem to be environmental ones of soil, rainfall or altitude, but the four plants specified above are likely, in marked contrast to the sweet potato, to be significant in male-dominated ritual (e.g. Watson 1965a:300; 1967:90-3).

With the aid of the sweet potato the Highlanders have pushed tropical settlement to its altitudinal limits (Brookfield 1961:437). Brookfield (1964) has suggested the factors that define their habitat in this context. The upper limit varies between 6,000 and 9,000 feet and seems to be governed by the level of cloud formation and by rain, and, where these are not restrictions to upward expansion, by frost. By 4,000 feet settlement has fallen off due to a complex of factors amongst which the incidence of malaria is probably significant (see also Brookfield 1971:72-3). The performance of the various food plants varies over this altitudinal range (Bulmer & Bulmer 1964:46). With the exception of the semi-cultivated nut pandanus, the sweet potato is the only crop to flourish over 6,500 feet, although small quantities of taro, banana and sugar cane are grown up to 7,000 feet in some areas. The now unimportant legume, *Pueraria lobata*, with a large tuber that may have been an important food in former times, is known up to at least 6,500 feet. It is below 6,000 feet, however, that these plants do 'reasonably well', while yams come into prominence only below 5,500 feet. Everywhere taro, yam and *Pueraria* take longer to mature than the sweet potato and the yields of the first two at least are much smaller. Sweet potato has a significant further advantage in its tolerance of poor soils (Clarke 1971:98 n.; *cf.* Brookfield 1971:84, 124 n.). Yen (1968:389) also characterizes it as one of the easiest of plants to propagate. The tools of cultivation are very simple and traditionally consisted of the stone axe or adze and the digging-stick, including varieties with expanded blades for earth working, the so-called paddle-shaped spade, which has been widely recorded throughout the Highlands (e.g. Watson 1967:95-6; Lampert 1967:308; Heider 1970:40).

There are, however, within the Highlands marked differences in agricultural techniques and population densities, which through a number of publications Brookfield (1961; 1962; 1964; 1971:94-124) has been concerned to characterize and assess in relation to each other and to a range of environmental and agronomic variables. He defines two areas of high intensity agriculture, making comprehensive use of labour-intensive cultivation techniques and corresponding tolerably well with highest population densities (Brookfield 1971:116). These are the Wissel Lakes-Baliem Valley region of former Dutch New Guinea (now Irian Jaya) and the central valleys of Papua New Guinea (formerly Australian New Guinea) from Tari in the west to Kainantu in the east. The techniques concerned comprise complete tillage involving the arrangement of the turned-over soil in beds with groove-drains or in small mounds (Chimbu and east); grid-iron ditching, where the spoil from the close-spaced grid is thrown up to form the garden surface (Chimbu and Wahgi and Wissel Lakes); and the more elaborate large mounding with mulching practised west of Wahgi. While the particular techniques adopted may be regarded as meeting the physiological requirements of the staple crop under different environmental conditions (Brookfield 1962:248, 250; Yen 1968:405), they are all seen as being designed 'to sustain deforested areas in frequent or continuous use at altitudes where slower soil processes and weed growth facilitate use of such practices' (Brookfield 1971:112). Cultivation is extended to areas of less favourable terrain by techniques of slope retention as in Chimbu and of drainage as at the Wissel Lakes. The highest development of such techniques occurs amongst the Dani of the Baliem Valley who operate systems of regional drainage of the valley bottom with control of water level at all seasons by the use of dams and practise soil retention on the slopes with the aid of dry stone walls (Brookfield 1971:114). Dense populations of 300 to 500 per square mile are locally maintained by the most intensive agricultural systems (e.g. Brookfield 1962:245).

Within the two areas of agricultural intensification, it is obvious that agronomic elaboration varies. Between and away from them, often at high altitudes, are systems of lower intensity, where the characteristics of Highlands agriculture are less developed (Brookfield 1971:109, 111). In one intermediate area, Telefomin, taro is the major crop (Brookfield 1962:244).

At the same time the low intensity practices of swidden cultivation, characterized by dependence on prolonged natural regeneration between short periods of cultivation and by simple cultivation techniques not involving tillage, form part of some of the high intensity systems. We owe the fullest characterization of the association to Waddell (1972:202-6), who links it with the possession by some groups of deep, naturally fertile soils on river terraces or in swampy plains. On these soils 'effective permanency' (Waddell 1972:204) is often achieved in the cultivation of the staple in 'open fields', with 'casual, extensive cultivation' of subsidiary crops on adjacent thinner-soiled hill slopes. This type of agricultural system he contrasts with one of lower but more generalized intensity, characteristic of parts of Chimbu and other areas of dissected landscape and thinner soils; here all agricultural land is fallowed, but the fallow is controlled, and its length reduced, by deliberate planting of *Casuarina* and protection of the seedlings of this and other quickly growing trees (Waddell 1972:143-4). Both types of system involve the segregation of the sweet potato staple from the mixed plantings of subsidiary crops and are regarded as responses in different terrain to cultivation in a predominantly grassland environment. Local circumstance fosters variation within the two broad types of agricultural regime, as amongst the Kapauku of the Wissel Lakes (e.g. Waddell 1972:202-3).

Waddell (1972:210-2) points to a general tendency for the less intensive of these two agricultural types to be associated with comparatively low densities of human and pig populations, a high degree of cooperation in establishing new gardens after fallow, and nucleated settlement. Where on the other hand the open field/mixed garden distinction exists, both people and pigs are numerous and the stability of open field cultivation reduces the need for cooperation in clearing and fencing. The possibility this offers of locating residence close to garden is seen as creating a dispersed pattern of settlement, which is further recommended by the need to provide for the adequate pasturing of the large pig populations. Exceptions within this system, such as the nucleated settlements of the Baliem Dani, are to be explained by the necessity for cooperative work, such as the upkeep of the drainage systems. Thus the distinction between the village settlement of the Eastern Highlands and the homestead pattern of the Western Highlands noted by the first explorers of Australian New Guinea and repeatedly since then would have an explanation, as should be expected, in man-land relationships.

The Central Highlands: agricultural evolution

Comparative work on Highlands agriculture and studies of the organization and dynamics of individual systems have led inevitably to a consideration of the course and causes of agricultural evolution. Attention has been focussed on the question of intensification and increasing reference made to Boserup's (1965) propositions about the relationship between population growth and agrarian change (Clarke 1966; Brookfield 1971:80-124; Waddell 1972:206-20).

The starting point for discussion has been acceptance of Robbins' (1963a; 1963b:51-8) proposition that agricultural Highlanders created the grasslands in which they live out of a natural vegetation of lower montane rain forest, though his attempt to explain the character these grasslands have assumed in terms of human impact overriding environmental variables, and his historical conclusions based on this, have not won acceptance (e.g. Brookfield 1964:32-3; 1971:51-3). The process is seen as the deflection of the natural vegetation succession under a system of simple shifting cultivation, where in conditions of slow natural regrowth expansion of population led to shortening of the fallow. Clarke (1971:192-3) describes how the conversion to grassland makes the techniques of shifting cultivation inadequate for its cultivation and requires an input by man in the form of tillage, with or without fertilization, to secure output (see also Clarke 1966:358-9 n.; Clarke & Street 1967). By this argument intensive agricultural practices emerged from within a system of simple shifting cultivation in response to population pressures and an associated initial degradation of the environment (Clarke 1966; Brookfield 1962:252-3; Waddell 1972:209; Yen 1973:78). The process of intensification is self-perpetuating (Waddell 1972:213), since the conversion to grass increases dependence on agriculture by the loss of forest foods (Bulmer & Bulmer 1964:72), while the grasslands themselves are in part maintained by the use of fire in hunting the animals for which man has created a habitat there (Bulmer 1968:312, 314). Intensive practices vary in type and in degree of intensity. Type may be related to the environment in which they are found (e.g. Brookfield 1962:250; Waddell 1972:204). Degree is to be explained by the need to have as permanent use as possible of the soil under the continuing pressure of human and pig population increase (Waddell 1972:209; *cf.* Brookfield 1971:92-3). This development is marked by what both Brookfield (Brookfield & White 1968:50) and Waddell (1972:209) have called the substitution of labour for land as the major factor in production.

Yet the sweet potato, in whose cultivation the intensive practices of Highlands agriculture are employed, is thought to be a plant of relatively recent introduction in New Guinea. Because of the lack of historical record of its presence in island Melanesia overall before the nineteenth century (Dixon 1932) and linguistic evidence for its European introduction into island and mainland south-east Asia (Conklin 1963), an antiquity for it in New Guinea of more than 350 or 400 years is considered unlikely (e.g. Barrau 1957). Given the evidence for the slower maturation and lesser productivity of the other Highlands crops at altitude, the question is what type of agriculture and settlement they sustained before the sweet potato arrived. In an early review of Highlands prehistory Bulmer & Bulmer (1964:47) proposed that much lower densities of population than at present then existed between 5,000 and 6,000 feet and only sparse populations higher up, and that major redistributions of population followed the introduction of the new crop. The importance of the sweet potato in allowing the upward spread of close settlement is a matter on which all authorities are agreed (e.g. Brookfield & White 1968:50; Waddell 1972:208) but a series of papers by Watson (1965a, 1965b, 1967) has developed the general theme along rather different and more controversial lines.

Watson considers four hypotheses about the situation into which the sweet potato entered and the effects its introduction had and opts for the most radical of these (Watson 1965a:301-3; *cf.* Watson 1967:83). This is the now well-known thesis of an Ipomoean Revolution which converted small populations of perhaps semi-nomadic horticulturalists and bands of hunters into large populations of settled agriculturalists and spread them into higher areas previously beyond the range of cultivation or even habitation (see also Watson 1965b:443-8). Watson justifies his choice, amongst other reasons that do not concern us here, because the characteristic features of Highlands culture depend on a plentiful food source and the intensive methods of cultivation which ensure this are everywhere primarily associated with sweet potato, while the older plants of cultivation like taro, even where dominant, are accorded in comparison only 'casual' planting status (Watson 1965a: 297-8; 1967:94-5).

To Clarke, however, implicitly (1966) and explicitly (1971:98-9 n.), the advent of the sweet potato is of no great significance for the processes of intensification in Highlands agriculture, since the root cause lies in the growth of population and its effect on the environment, not in the nature of the crop itself. In this view taro and yam, together with a variety of minor crops, could have provided a substantial enough subsistence base for the effects of population on environment to have resulted in a drift from extensive to intensive agriculture in some places, over a long period of time. In support of Clarke's position one might indeed quote evidence provided, and appreciated, by Watson himself (1967:91, 95) for the elaborate and segregated cultivation of yams and beans in the Kainantu area.

This evolutionary hypothesis was developed by Brookfield & White (1968) in a paper critically reviewing the entire range of evidence presented by Watson in support of an Ipomoean Revolution. Of particular relevance here are their conclusion (pp. 44-5) that all inferential demographic evidence suggests that the present large Highlands populations were built up through an irregular growth over a very long period of time, their claim (p. 50) that it is the emergence of such population concentrations, not the arrival of the sweet potato, that explains the evolution of intensive methods of agriculture, and their hypothesis (p. 49) that the sweet potato was adopted simply because it offered a higher return for comparable inputs of land and labour. The most compelling arguments in support of this position they found in the first diachronic evidence to become available. Data of this character were obviously essential if the debate was to advance at all.

The Hagen district: archaeology and palynology (Fig. 2)

The excavations in 1966 which provided these data formed part of a small salvage operation conducted over 300 square metres of an 850 acre plantation, as tea beds were being prepared for planting. The Warrewau Tea Estate comprises a large area of swampland just south of the Wahgi River 6 miles east of Mount Hagen township and 5,200 feet above sea level. Reports of numbers of wooden paddle-shaped spades, digging-sticks and fence posts, stone axes and axe-sharpening stones being found on the estate during drainage operations prompted an effort to recover some of them *in situ.* The investigated site is known as *Manton's* in recognition of the cooperation of Mr I.V. Manton of Mount Hagen Tea Growers. It has been briefly reported by Golson *et al.* (1967) and Lampert (1967), with supplementary information in Powell (1970b).

Excavation revealed a series of superimposed barets,[2] interpreted as water-control ditches, cut at different levels in a black, structureless, well humified peat, interpreted as a garden soil. From this peat and the barets associated with it came a small collection of artefacts, indicative of gardening activities and like those whose previous discovery had drawn attention to the site. The agricultural horizon lay on top of peat and wood detritus, accumulating on alluvium after about 5,000 B.P., and below felted peat and was broadly dated from included wooden artefacts from 2,300 ± 120 B.P. (A.N.U.-43) to 470 ± 75 B.P. (A.N.U.-289), though this latter date was unavailable until Powell (1970b). The excavators noted the occurrence of barets sealed in by felted peat in drain sections throughout the Manton plantation and elsewhere in the upper Wahgi Valley, and also the appearance of old drainage lines on aerial photographs throughout the area. They therefore inferred the widespread existence of agricultural systems in drained swamp antedating the arrival of the sweet potato but employing techniques of grid-iron ditching and types of tool directly related to those of the sweet potato agriculture described for the area by European pioneers. The evidence thus interpreted was seen as fatal to Watson's hypothesis of an Ipomoean Revolution and suggestive on the contrary of the acceptance of the new crop into an already stabilized agricultural economy without its radical alteration (Lampert 1967:308-9).

These indications from the archaeological evidence were taken up, as we have noted, by Brookfield and White (1968) and developed in ways already discussed. They are seen (pp. 47, 50) as signifying the early existence of a labour and skill intensive system, demanding a stable and concentrated population and in all likelihood based on taro. Subsequently Brookfield (1971:81) has suggested that the swamp system was the intensive part of an intensive/extensive agricultural complex like those described for a number of modern Highlands societies, thus giving a respectable time depth for this adaptation.

Waddell (1972:219), on the other hand, notes the existence of evidence in the Highlands for the development of agricultural intensification in response to environment, irrespective of population, citing mound cultivation at high altitudes as a protection against frosts as an example. He sees the prehistoric Wahgi systems as a response to the edaphic needs and altitudinal limitations, of the pre-ipomoean crops employed, which restricted populations to areas where these requirements could be satisfied. The intensification involved in the Wahgi systems would, by this interpretation, have taken place at low population densities (Waddell 1972:218). Brookfield also has some recent qualifications to make on the relationship between population and intensification, both in general (1971:120) and in respect of the possible effect of the soil intolerances of the taro on the nature of pre-ipomoean Highlands agriculture (1971:124 n.). Both he and Waddell (1972:219) suggest that the first effect of the sweet potato might have been the dispersal of people and cultivation and the abandonment of intensive for extensive methods of agriculture, with later re-intensification on the basis of the new crop. The same issues are raised by Yen (1971:7; 1973:80) in papers discussing New Guinea agriculture in the context of south-east Asian and Oceanic agriculture as a whole.

Further important diachronic data have been provided by Powell's (1970a) investigations into the impact of man on the vegetation of the Hagen region, so far only briefly reported in print (1970b). Powell did pollen analytical work at two sites: the Manton site already described and Draepi, which is a modest swamp-filled depression and small pond at a height of 6,200 feet on the Wahgi-Baiyer River Divide at the base of Mount Hagen and 8 miles N.N.W. of Mount Hagen township. In the course of Powell's research the northern end of the swamp was drained for development as part of Minjigina Tea Estate and archaeological evidence discovered, of which R.J. Lampert made a small investigation at the Minjigina archaeological site.

As interpreted by Powell, the six pollen diagrams for the two sites, four of them for Draepi-Minjigina, are more favourable to the Brookfield than to the Waddell view of upper Wahgi agriculture in pre-ipomean times. By about 5,000 B.P. at both sites, forest clearance was already extensive on surrounding slopes; this clearance was maintained, as a result, it is presumed, of agriculture of the simple shifting type. By 2,300 B.P. at both sites, there is direct evidence for agricultural use of the swamp itself in the form of barets and associated agricultural tools. The pollen diagrams suggest that at this stage pressure was removed from the forest, which recovered and to some extent stabilized, though use and clearance of it continued. This is precisely the situation that could be predicted (e.g. Waddell 1972:209) as the result of the introduction and operation of a system under which agricultural production was segregated into intensive and extensive categories, as Brookfield (1971:81) has suggested for the Wahgi systems.

Qualitative evaluation of the vegetation evidence overall does not lend support to Waddell's picture (1972:218-19) of low-density populations restricted to intensive cultivation of the Wahgi swampland because of the altitudinal and ecological intolerances of pre-ipomoean crops.

Powell lists the useful trees and shrubs, herbaceous domesticates and garden weeds which the record shows to be present at this stage. Though there is no evidence of the main crops grown, not a surprising circumstance in the light of the breeding system and phenology of the likely plants and native practices in their cultivation, she considers taro to be the most probable crop of the swampland systems, used either pure or in mixed plantings.

At a maximum date of 470 ± 75 B.P. (provided by a fence post in the top of the agricultural soil at Manton's) at least the immediate vicinity of the excavated site reverted to swamp. The date is suggestively close to that postulated for the entry of the sweet potato into Highlands agriculture. The zone of unhumified peat that now formed at Manton's contains evidence in its included pollen for renewed pressure on the forest land. A similar picture is provided by the upper levels of Draepi/Minjigina where, however, the final stages of site history are so far undated. This latest phase of clearance of forest and/or of secondary regrowth, exhibits a controlled character, with indications of the conservation or planting of trees; rising values for *Casuarina* are indeed in evidence from about 1,200 B.P. in the Draepi-Minjigina pollen diagrams.

This character of the pollen diagrams during the last few hundred years could be used to

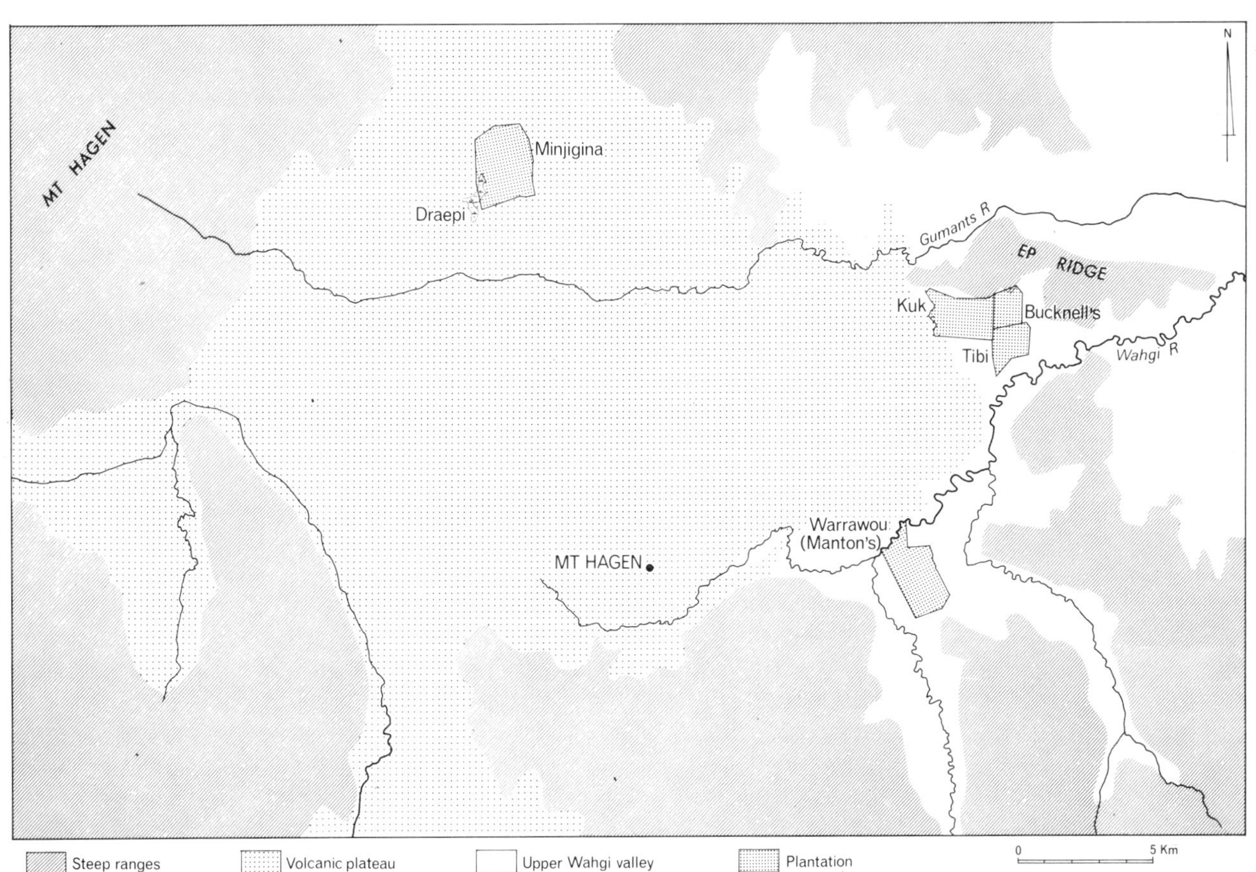

Figure 2. Mount Hagen district.

Figure 3. Area of 1972 investigations.

support a thesis that the adoption of the sweet potato with its greater productivity at high altitudes and its wider ecological tolerances led to the abandonment of swamp cultivation. Such an interpretation would tend to support the independently formed opinions of Waddell (1972:219) and Brookfield (1971:124 n.) that the first effect of the sweet potato might have been the abandonment of intensive for extensive methods of agriculture, and Yen (1973:80) has explicitly proposed it. The first season of the current project centring on Kuk Tea Research Station has provided some pertinent information on this.

The Hagen district: the Kuk project (Figs. 2, 3)

Planning for a major attack on Highlands agricultural history began as soon as both the implications of the Manton evidence and the potential of the Wahgi swamplands were appreciated. The envisaged project had amongst its aims combined archaeological, palynological and geomorphological work to confirm and extend the indications of previous investigations as to the antiquity of agriculture in the New Guinea Highlands; the age and circumstances of the move of cultivation into the swamplands; the nature and organization of agricultural activities there and of associated settlement; and the date, causes and extent of their abandonment. Particular attention was to be focussed on this last question in view of the successful adaptation of the sweet potato to swamp cultivation elsewhere in the Highlands and a few indications in the literature of early contact for some agricultural use of swamp in the upper Wahgi Valley (e.g. Vicedom & Tischner 1943-8, vol. 1:185). This necessitated planning for ethnographic enquiries into traditional land use in the area, with particular reference to the role of swampland. On all points indeed there would be need for close attention to cultural and ecological aspects of the ethnographic situation from which local prehistory is at a bare 40 years' remove.

Though as yet no systematic study of upper Wahgi agriculture has appeared, the Hagen tribes are ethnographically well served. Besides the shorter reports and observations of early explorers and visitors, resident German Lutheran missionaries in the '30s collected data which have formed the basis for published ethnographies of fundamental importance (esp. Vicedom & Tischner 1943-8). More importantly the Hageners have been for some years the subject of continuing ethnographic study by A. and M. Strathern, major monographs by whom are now appearing (A. Strathern 1971, 1972; M. Strathern 1972; Strathern & Strathern 1971).

Typical features of Hagen agricultural practice are conveniently summarized by Gitlow (1947:61-7) and A. Strathern (1972:46-7). Gardens are of two types: those for sweet potato are characterized by the digging of shallow, flat-bottomed barets in a grid-iron pattern, others for mixed plantings are less systematically trenched. This is the dichotomy with which we have now become familiar. On wet ground the shallow field barets are combined with bigger drainage barets (e.g. Vicedom & Tischner 1943-8, vol. 1:185). The sizes of the barets of the sweet potato fields and of the square or rectangular plots they enclose vary but dimensions of 10 in. wide and deep for the former and 9 feet by 9 feet for the latter are typical (Gitlow 1947:62). Though, as all authorities mention, the field barets, and indeed barets of all types, are convenient markers of garden ownership, their primary purpose is agronomic. The spoil thrown up from them provides the earth for the garden beds, there being no other form of tillage, while the barets themselves lower the soil water table from the proximity of growing roots (Brookfield 1962:250; Yen 1968:405). Powell (1970a:99-104) notes how these practices, combined with intensive weeding and periodic burning, allow for the fairly continuous use of gardens with a short-term (4-5 years) mixed-grass fallow, as opposed to the mixed rotation gardens where one or two years' cultivation is followed by lengthy fallowing under a woody regrowth, permitted by less intensive operations and including the conservation and planting of trees.

A. Strathern (1972:54-60) describes the dispersed settlement pattern that is associated with this gardening system, the requirements of pig husbandry and the characteristic separation of men's from women's houses. Since women have responsibility for the daily harvesting and pig care, it is convenient for them to live near gardening and grazing areas, which they do in long, low, apsidal-ended houses divided internally to allow individual stalling of pigs. The round men's houses are not normally widely separated from the women's houses but form part of the same settlement complex, which may range from a single house or unit of man's house plus woman's house up to a hamlet cluster. These settlement-places are scattered over clan territories, which in the past were defended by clansmen as a whole against enemies. Gross population densities are moderate compared with those of the Chimbu and Wabag, averaging around 100 per square mile (A. Strathern 1972:33-4).

The opportunity for systematic archaeological work in this field occurred in connection with major drainage operations on the new Tea Research Station established at Kuk in 1969 by the Department of Agriculture, Stock and Fisheries. Recognition of the site and its importance is due to Jim Allen, who carried out investigations soon after drainage was begun, reported a system of barets and a range of finds comparable to the Manton evidence (Allen 1970) and recommended it to the writer as worthy of large-scale investigation.

Kuk is a 700 acre property about 9 miles north-east of Mount Hagen township, excised from one of the areas of extensive swampland which are characteristic of the upper Waghi and its tributaries at the eastern margin of the Mount Hagen volcanic plateau. It occupies perhaps 70 square miles of territory (Haantjens *et al.* 1970:64-5). Aerial photographs show old baret systems over virtually the entirety of the swamp of which Kuk forms a part. This swamp is bounded to the north by the steep slopes of Ep Ridge, rising 500-1,200 feet above the swamp basin at 5,200 feet, and to the south by rolling ash-mantled hills of very low relief. At Kuk itself, where the swamp is somewhat over 1,000 metres wide and falls 4 or 5 metres from south to north, there is a barely perceptible divide, with drainage west into the Gumants and east into the Wahgi. The watershed falls within the at present undeveloped eastern half of the station, all 350 acres of which were available for investigation. Here, the only substantial creek enters through a narrow gap in the southern hills and immediately divides in the vicinity of an isolated volcanic knob on the southern boundary; one branch going northwest, a second north and eventually west, the third in somewhat anastomosed form northeast and eventually east. The increasingly divergent courses of creeks 2 and 3 leaves a vast intervening area of uncoordinated drainage in the eastern quarter of Kuk and beyond in the Bucknell lease north of Tibi Plantation. Investigations so far have focussed around creek 2.

Before drainage started in 1969, Kuk was everywhere under water. Even in June 1972 when the present project started, most of the eastern half was very wet; its drainage required the organization of 11,000 metres of major ditch digging by the station management. This incidentally provided cross sections throughout the entire area for stratigraphic investigations of every kind. The archaeological work has so far involved the digging of around 2,000 metres of close-spaced drains (22.5 metres apart) to the specifications of the station drainage plan and the detailed stratigraphic record there and elsewhere of 4,000 metres of drain wall; the clearance by bush knife of close on 100,000 square metres of swamp grasses, to expose surface features of houses and artificial and natural drainage channels; hand probing at close intervals of a 28,000 square metre block, in the area of close drainage, to enable accurate plotting of the pattern of the most recent baret system, which proved impossible to map from the slight surface indications; and total or partial excavation of five of the forty or so house sites, visible at the surface as the result of clearance and the effects of an abnormally long and rainless dry season.

Investigations at Kuk (Figs. 4-11)

The Kuk swamp is shown to have a long and complex history going back into the Late Pleistocene and contains, in mainly thin and scattered lenses of ash, the record of up to a dozen volcanic eruptions. The upper part of the sequence, below the felted peat of recent swamp vegetation, comprises largely inorganic sediments made up of clay-size particles of old volcanic ash. This is thought to be derived from the ash-mantled catchment immediately to the south and to be deposited by shallow, slowly moving, distributary floods of the type actually observed after an overnight downpour of 1.8 inches, early in the dry season of 1972.

As reported by Allen (1970:177) for the western half of Kuk swamp, old barets were everywhere exposed in the walls of drains dug in the eastern half of the station, though aerial photographs record no baret systems in the south-eastern quarter of that half. All barets

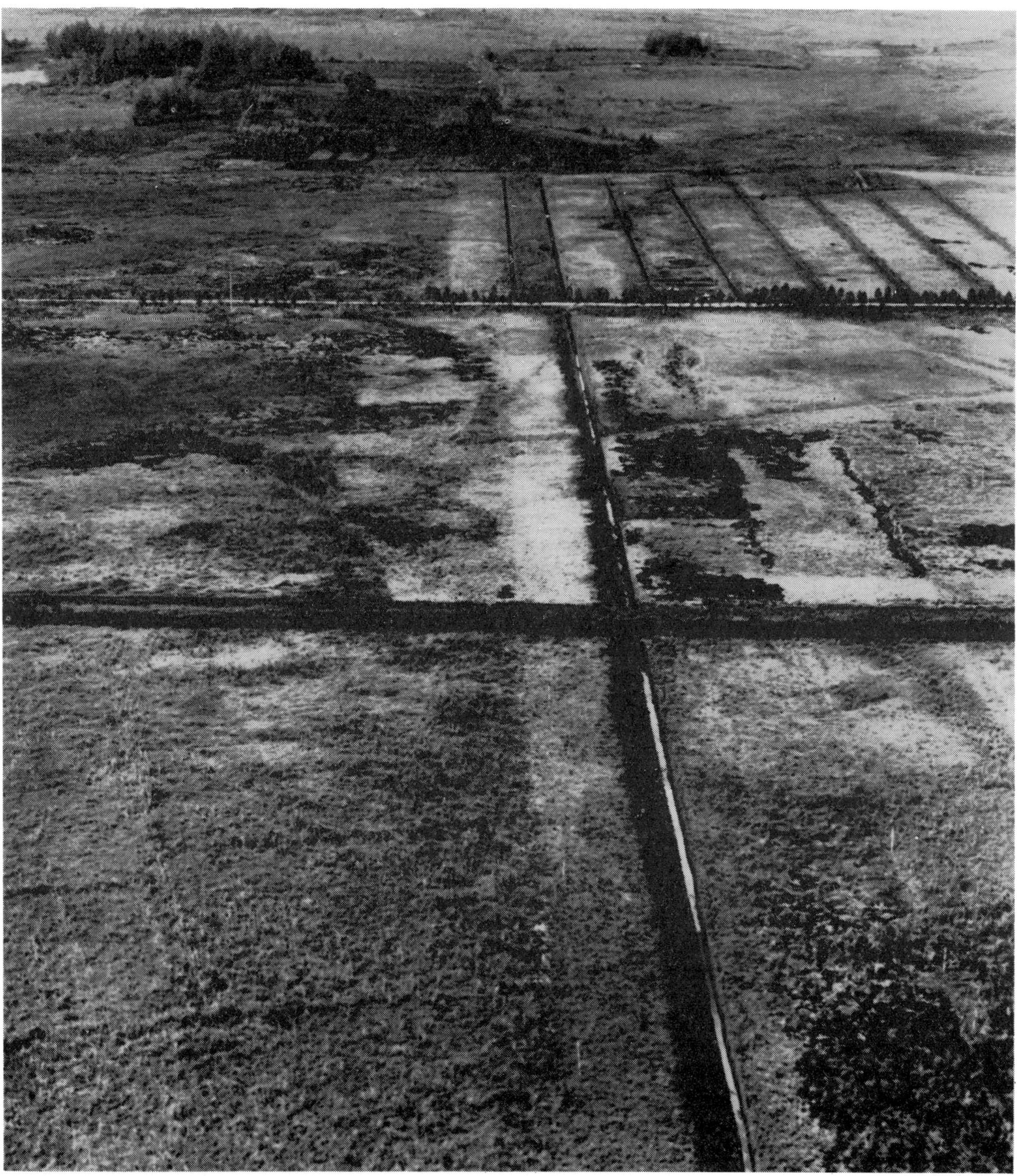

Figure 4. Aerial view of the area of the 1972 investigations at Kuk, looking south. One drain of no.4 N-S road has been completed; the other drain has been dug from the southern boundary of the station, beyond which is native land, to no.1 E-W road. To the right of this sector of no.4 N-S road is the area of intensive drainage and our own main work; the site of house excavations can be seen in the second block right of the N-S road and of test excavations of field systems in the sixth block. The course of creek no.2 as drawn in Fig. 3 is visible. In the foreground, north of no.2 E-W road, are the large barets of the elaborate drainage system described in the text, with, just north of no.2 E-W road and west of no.4 N-S road, the U-shaped baret, base WSW, of a house site. (Photo: W.R. Ambrose.)

Figure 5. Part of the area of intensive drainage and investigation at Kuk, looking NNW from the low volcanic hill on the southern boundary towards Ep Ridge. The grass has been cut to expose surface evidence of the latest prehistoric drainage system. (Photo: W.R. Ambrose.)

belong to the upper part of the sequence and are later than a grey clay which is its most conspicuous member in the southern part of the site. This grey clay rests on and is overlain by a clay of the same character, but black in colour as a result it is presumed of organic staining. The overlying black clay, which varies in thickness from 8-20 cm., is evidently of slow deposition for its history spans a time range from before 5,970 B.P. ± 80 (A.N.U.-1057) up to at least 1,190 B.P. ± 60 (A.N.U.-1206). This latter is a reasonably precise date for the youngest of three ash showers which fell during the formation of the clay. Each of these ashes has been found in association with systems of rather widely spaced barets, so that the black clay was for a long time a gardening horizon. The nature and organization of these baret systems is a matter for future investigation, but the latest of them appears in the investigated areas to be based on an open grid of slot-like barets averaging 20-30 cm. wide at the top and 30-40 cm. deep. With these are associated a few large barets 75-100 cm. wide and 50-75 cm. deep.

Above the black clay and below the swamp deposits that close the sequence is a layer which stands in marked contrast to them, by virtue of its earthy character and crumby structure and its greater thickness with less time available for formation. This is associated with a baret system which contrasts equally strongly with those that had gone before. This comprises a grid of barets somewhat wider and deeper and much more closely spaced than the big barets of the previous system, subdivided by a close grid of small, shallow, flat-bottomed barets generally wider than they are deep. The big barets and sometimes the small ones of this system are those that are visible on the aerial photographs, for their unconsolidated infilling provokes a vegetation response. This unconsolidated fill is also responsible for some slight surface expression and was sufficiently responsive to probing to permit detailed mapping in one area. The

Figure 6. Stratigraphy at Kuk. The slot-type baret penetrates grey clay but is dug through overlying upper black clay, as shown by the layer of volcanic ash, the second youngest of the Kuk series, which dips into the fill of the baret; the two upper pegs mark its upper margins. Above the black clay into which the baret is dug is a layer of dark crumby earth, sealed in by the deposits formed when the area reverted to swamp, which are characterized by vertical slash-like cracks on drying. Just below the level of the peg at the base of the baret is the top of lower black clay underlying grey clay. The three pegs are data for baret and stratigraphic record. The staff is graduated in 20 cm. intervals. (Photo: J.W. Rhoads.)

large barets were by this method shown to enclose square or rectangular blocks of 100-200 square metres, subdivided by the smaller barets into plots of 20-30 sq. m. The spoil from the digging of these barets, disposed of in the intervening enclosures, accounts for the formation of the earthy layer above the upper black clay and functioned as a raised garden bed in the agricultural system. The much more widely spaced barets of previous systems did not produce enough spoil to register stratigraphically in the same way and consequently the cultivated plots associated with them were not of this raised bed kind.

The evidence of the types and disposition of the latest barets and of the size and character of the raised garden plots points to sweet potato cultivation on the Wahgi grid-iron pattern. The system was established shortly before the youngest ashfall at the site, securely dated between 240 ± 60 B.P. (A.N.U.-1053) and 290 ± 60 B.P. (A.N.U.-1054), which agrees well with the presumed late date of the sweet potato's arrival in New Guinea. The features of intensive drainage reflect the need to take adequate measures to protect a moisture-sensitive plant. The water was carried to existing natural drainage channels. In the area between creeks 1 and 2, which is nowhere more than 400 metres wide, this was simply done by digging a framework of major barets between the two and constructing a network of subsidiary barets around them. The large area without coordinated natural drainage which lies between the rapidly diverging courses of creeks 2 and 3 has posed problems of a different order. Though these have not yet been investigated in detail, in the field, it is obvious from the aerial photo-

Figure 7. Two barets exposed in the wall of a modern drainage ditch at Kuk and pegged for recording. To the right a slot baret; to the left a baret of the youngest system. The complex profile represents an original deeper, narrower baret and a phase of recutting, wider and shallower. The staff is graduated in 20 cm. intervals. (Photo: J. Golson.)

graphs that very large and very long barets had to be dug, to collect and transport water to the nearest natural outfall.

The fortunes of sweet potato cultivation in the drained swamp can be reçonstructed from the history of the major barets on which the agricultural system rested. In the area of simple drainage between creeks 1 and 2 the barets were periodically cleaned out and recut as the loose soil of the raised gardens was continually washed back into the channels from which it had been dug. The evidence of this process is to be found in their complex profiles and remnant fills. A 'modern' radiocarbon date (A.N.U.-1035) for a digging-stick from the last phase of recutting in one such baret shows that these activities continued into recent times; i.e. within the last 100 years (personal communication, H.A. Polach, A.N.U. Radiocarbon Laboratory).

Where the stratigraphic evidence is clear, a baret in its final recut phase is normally shallower and wider than at any previous phase and deepest and narrowest in the form in which it was first dug. This suggests that a rising base-level made deep digging increasingly more difficult and compelled the digging of wide barets as a method of providing adequate drainage channels and enough soil for a sufficiently raised garden-bed. It seems reasonable to suppose that this hydrologic deterioration resulted from the fact that in being washed back down again from the raised beds formed from it, the loose soil from baret digging clogged up not only the man-made barets themselves but increasingly, as well, the natural stream courses on which the whole artificial drainage system depended. Preliminary sediment analysis of stream channel infill lends some support to this supposition. The barets, which were of limited extent, could be, and were, cleaned out. There is no evidence that the stream channels, some miles in length, ever were. The task may have been beyond the organizational capabilities of the communities involved.

It is clear that this process created additional problems, for as their channels became clogged, the creeks showed a tendency to depart from their old courses and find new ones. Sometimes these new courses were former baret lines: the latest course of creek 2, for example, which turns four unnatural right-angled corners in its middle reaches, appears to flow along stretches of four such former barets. Besides being immediately destructive, a change of stream course required the rearticulation of the artificial with the natural drainage and there is good archaeological evidence of such remodelling.

As we have seen, the latest phase of baret use at Kuk Swamp falls within the last 100 years. The suggestion is that after this stage the system

Figure 8. A slot baret, partly recut on a different line. The baret is sealed in by a mounded house floor, the southern half of which is unexcavated in the background. One of the centre posts of the house has cut through the slot baret in the centre of the picture; another is visible in profile above the right hand wall of the baret behind the scale (10 cm. graduations). The base of a cooking pit in the house appears middle right. (Photo: M.J. Woods.)

became inoperative: a number of scattered raised areas of small extent, recorded in the area of the detailed survey, may well mark the final efforts to cultivate land inexorably reverting to swamp.

The barets that comprise the sweet potato system in the area of complex drainage between creeks 2 and 3 appear on the present restricted evidence to have a totally different history from those in the area of simple drainage just discussed. They show no evidence of recleaning or recutting: their profiles are regular and the youngest volcanic ash, which fell soon after they were dug, lies undisturbed low down in their fill. It seems that this complex drainage network was

Figure 9. One of the larger barets of the youngest agricultural system at Kuk, showing complex profile reflecting phases of recutting and thickening of recent swamp deposits over the unconsolidated fill. The scale is graduated in 10 cm. intervals. (Photo: W.R. Ambrose.)

Figure 10. One of the minor barets of the latest agricultural system at Kuk, subdividing the blocks formed by larger barets of the type shown in Fig. 9. These wide, shallow, flat-bottomed barets are like those that form the grid-iron pattern of modern dry-land cultivation of sweet potato in the upper Wahgi, shown in Fig. 11. The staff is graduated in 20 cm. intervals. (Photo: W.R. Ambrose.)

Figure 11. Sweet potato gardens in grassland in the upper Wahgi, with scattered women's houses of long apsidal form, a round men's house, and groves of planted trees. The grid-iron pattern of the gardens is formed by shallow, flat-bottomed barets of the type shown in Fig. 10. The gardens centre right are actually of the large mounded form more typical of the region to the west. (Photo: R.J. Lampert.)

abandoned soon after it was established and it may be that the size and length of the major barets of which it consisted hastened the crisis of silting that affected other areas at a later stage. The possibility thus exists that blocks of swampland went out of productive use at different times after the arrival of the sweet potato, whose requirements for close drainage upset the previous balance between artificial and natural drainage in the swamp.

The abandonment of swamp cultivation was not restricted to Kuk or to the Kuk basin, as we know. Oral testimony systematically collected from old people throughout the Hagen area during the 1972 season supports the evidence from early European sources, both documentary (e.g. Leahy 1936:248 referring directly to Gumants and Kuk in 1933) and oral (e.g. J. Fox referring directly to Manton's in 1933, see Golson *et al.* 1967), that there was no systematic agricultural use of the valley bottom swamps of the upper Wahgi and its tributaries at contact. A measure of their unimportance in the recent subsistence economy of the Hagen region is the vast areas that have been alienated over the past twenty years to the New Guinea administration, which has leased them to Europeans for plantation development or drained them for the resettlement, on smallholder blocks, of people from more densely populated parts of the New Guinea Highlands outside the Wahgi, particularly Wabag and Chimbu.

What the data suggest is the recency of this process of abandonment. The baret systems that are visible on the aerial photographs of Kuk are those of the sweet potato regime; they show up because their fill, derived by inwash from surrounding garden beds, is earthy and unconsolidated, allows freer movement of water and evokes a differential vegetation response. The older systems do not appear on the aerial photographs at all; their fill is almost as clayey and consolidated as the sediments into which they are dug. The evidence of aerial photographs of the former widespread use of upper Wahgi swampland for agriculture is thus most likely to relate to the post-ipomoean situation, not to the pre-ipomoean one, as claimed by the excavators of the Manton site (Golson *et al.* 1967; Lampert 1967) and assumed by subsequent authorities, who have built on their conclusions.

By this argument the drainage systems which are visible from the air would have been established for, and gone out of use under, sweet potato cultivation. It seems likely therefore that the same factors which destroyed the system at Kuk were widely operative through the upper Wahgi swamplands as a whole, all of which are typically developed on flood plains with meandering streams and oxbows and on tributary plains with ill-defined stream patterns (Haantjens *et al.* 1970:65; Haantjens 1970:22).

The contrast between this area and the apparently successful exploitation of swampland for sweet potato cultivation in other Highlands localities cannot be explored because of the general shortage of information on the hydrology of the sites and on the hydraulics of the systems involved. At one large drained block at the Haibuga Swamp near Tari, however, the deep perimeter barets were seen merely to feed into a slightly lower part of the swamp. In the Baliem Valley, where cultivation of the swampy valley floor seems likely to be prone to problems of the type which the Wahgi systems incurred, Brookfield's description (1962:248; 1971:114) suggest that any such difficulties are overcome at the level of organization, something the Hageners never achieved. Baliem swamp agriculture involves systems of regional drainage whereby the outflow of whole drainage districts is carried out to the river at controlled points. Though the relation of these drainage districts to territorial groupings and social organization has not been described, Heider (1970:79-81) identifies one such territorial unit, the confederation, which, as the most important territorial, social and political grouping of Dani society, would seem likely to possess the necessary attributes of power and authority. Interestingly enough, Brookfield (1971:115) says that the Dani drainage system is not presently used to capacity and that some discordance apparently exists between drainage districts and present political groups.

Discussion

From about 300 years ago Hageners made widespread use of drained swampland in their system of sweet potato agriculture. The baret pattern found at Kuk suggests that the swamp was the focus for intensive cultivation of the staple crop, perhaps with some taro planted along the sides and edges of the barets, as is reported for similar systems elsewhere (e.g. Powell 1970b:200). More extensively worked mixed-gardens presumably occupied adjacent drier land. Settlement in the Kuk swamplands was of the homestead and hamlet type found with the intensive sweet potato field/extensive mixed garden organization of present-day Hagen agriculture, suggested by Waddell (1972:210) to be functionally adapted to such dual systems. By the 1930s systematic swamp cultivation had ceased in the upper Wahgi. The circumstances of the incorporation of the sweet potato into swamp-based agriculture and the consequences of its abandonment can only be understood in the light of pre-ipomoean swamp use and the type of settlement which it sustained. This question has not, so far, received detailed attention.

Strictly speaking, the archaeological stratigraphy at Kuk, as it is interpreted here, records only the period when the sweet potato began to be cultivated in the swamp. Though the date for this is close to the maximum age accepted for its presence in New Guinea, the plant could conceivably have been used previously in dryland systems of cultivation, whether as the result of an earlier than expected introduction into New Guinea or not. If this were so, it might have led to the situation envisaged by Brookfield (1971:124 n.), Waddell (1972:219) and Yen (1971:7; 1973:80), that is, to the initial abandonment of intensive cultivation of pre-ipomoean crops with later reintensification in terms of the new plant.

The available evidence, I think, weighs sufficiently against the proposal for a significant hiatus between the entry of the sweet potato into the Hagen region and its cultivation in swamp-based agricultural systems for it to be discounted. At Kuk there is a dramatic change in the organization of the baret systems, which is interpreted as the beginning of such swamp-based sweet potato cultivation, shortly before 290 ± 60 B.P. At Manton's the phase of swamp cultivation, which comes to its close at 470 ± 75 B.P. or shortly after, does not, on the limited evidence available, exhibit this change: it appears to be organized to the end on the pattern of pre-Ipomoean swamp use. The date from Manton's for the end of this phase is so close to that from Kuk for the beginning of the later one that there appears to be no possibility of a third phase in between. The case, however, is not as unchallengeable as could be wished and particular attention will have to be paid, in further work at Kuk, to the critical question of how the latest of the pre-ipomoean baret systems approximates in time to the first sweet potato cultivations in the swamp.

As we now see from the Kuk evidence, pre-ipomoean swamp cultivation in the upper Wahgi is not likely to register on aerial photographs. Accumulating field evidence, however, shows it to have been widespread, extending from Manton's and Kuk in the Wahgi bottoms to Minjigina, 1,000 feet higher up, on the Baiyer Divide. The associated pollen diagrams show long-lived and sustained regional interference with forest growth in both these localities, which is interpreted as the result of agriculture. Agricultural impact on the forest was already significant by 5,000 B.P. The two and a half millennia that elapse between this date and the first indications of swamp cultivation allow ample time for the building up of population and of the associated impact on the environment that have been suggested as root causes for agricultural intensification. The pollen diagrams from Manton's (Powell 1970a:148-64) show considerable further inroads into forest during the later period; those from Draepi-Minjigina (Powell 1970a:174-86) show rather the attainment and maintenance of a balance between forest and non-forest vegetation. This ecological balance at Draepi-Minjigina continues over most of the period when swamp cultivation was practised at the Manton site. Here, in contrast, the beginning of cultivation of the swamp is accompanied by recovery of the forest and its maintenance thereafter until the period of the sweet potato.

These differing vegetation histories illustrate the significance of altitudinal differences on the pre-ipomoean crop regime, when the Draepi-Minjigina site lay near the upper limit of effective cultivation. By this interpretation the Manton site on the Wahgi flats would represent a real process of agricultural intensification, with environmental deterioration halted by the institution of the intensive techniques by way of the cultivation of a new type of land; the wide distribution of pre-ipomoean baret digging at Kuk would be consistent with this view. At Draepi-Minjigina an unknown extent of cultivation at the small swamp (880 yards long and 110 yards wide), and even at similar ones in the neighbourhood, need not denote a process of the same type.

The suggestion now made is that, with the potential afforded by the upper Wahgi Valley, large areas of swamp could be opened up to productive agriculture through drainage, which could lead to differentiation between populations with clan territories restricted to the valley bottom at the one extreme (e.g. Kuk) and to plateau and upland country at the other (e.g. Draepi-Minjigina). The scale of the Hagen district landscapes renders such differentiation entirely possible. Of the Chimbu, whose sub-groups occupy strip-like territories running up and down slopes over belted terrain and have scattered access to different types of land for different purposes (Brookfield & Brown 1963:157), it is noted (Brown & Brookfield 1967:148) that the extreme range of holdings operated from any house lies within 5,000 yards. A circle of this radius drawn from the middle of the Kuk swamp is within the main valley system of the Wahgi and its tributaries, here diversified only by tongues of higher land of at most moderate relief.

If indeed group territories became stabilized in this way, the valley bottom communities at the one pole would under pre-ipomoean conditions be economically advantaged by their continuous access to swamp gardens at lower elevation as against the hill dwellers at the other pole, suffering the acknowledged altitudinal and other limitations on their crops. To each of these archetypal groups, who both accepted it, the sweet potato must have made a different appeal. It liberated the hill dwellers from previous environmental constraints and allowed their upward expansion. Its speedier rise to maturity and greater productivity, even at lower elevations, will have recommended it to increasingly populous valley communities, whose growing numbers were perhaps straining the capacities of their defined territories, but could be mobilized for the much more labour-demanding pattern of swamp drainage which the new plant required. The wide distribution through the upper Wahgi of systems adapted to these requirements is a measure of the need for them; though some areas, like the south-eastern part of Kuk and the vicinity of at least the excavation site at Manton's, apparently proved too wet to be incorporated.

We have looked in detail at the progressive decay of the new systems at Kuk and suggested that similar factors were at work throughout the upper Wahgi. The consequences for valley-based communities of the continuing loss of their most intensively worked and productive land must have been severe and inevitably have involved them in a series of adjustments by way of fragmentation, alliance, migration and war. The migration of the Kawelka (A. Strathern 1972:36-40) from their traditional territories at and around Kuk, to their present location above 5,300-7,000 feet, on the steep hillsides of the Wahgi-Sepik Divide, in the vicinity of Buk, 15 miles to the north, could exemplify the situation. Taking place in the lifetime of the informant's father, the move dates from the period when swamp cultivation at Kuk was in its dying stages, though the traditional story is couched in terms of a forced evacuation due to defeat in fighting.

Certainly the decay of swampland agriculture must in the upper Wahgi Valley be numbered amongst the diachronic processes which Strathern and others have found it necessary to invoke in considering the structures of Highlands social groups (A. Strathern 1971:16-19). A particular feature of this amongst the Hageners, the vast range, from 68 to 6,749, in the populations of recognized 'big name' tribes (A. Strathern 1971:17), might find an explanation in the distinctive history of upper Wahgi agriculture.

It has been said (Watson 1967:83) that in parts of the Highlands the consequences of the introduction of the sweet potato have not yet been fully realized. This can be nowhere truer than in the upper Wahgi Valley, where communities must still be adjusting to unexpected consequences in the form of the reversion to swamp of large areas of agriculturally once productive land and for the future face adjustment to a situation where most of that land has now passed into other ownership.

REFERENCES

Allen, J. (1970) Prehistoric agricultural systems in the Wahgi valley – a further note. *Mankind*, 7(3), 177-83.

Barrau, J. (1957) L'énigme de la patate douce en Océanie. *Études d'outre-mer*, 40, 83-7.

Boserup, E. (1965) *The Conditions of Agricultural Growth.* London.

Bowers, N. (1968) The ascending grasslands: an anthropological study of ecological succession in a high mountain valley of New Guinea. Unpublished Ph.D. thesis, Columbia University, New York.

Brookfield, H.C. (1961) The highlands peoples of New Guinea: a study of distribution and localization. *Geog. Journ.*, 127, 436-48.

Brookfield, H.C. (1962) Local study and comparative method: an example from central New Guinea. *Annals Assoc. of Amer. Geographers*, 52, 242-54.

Brookfield, H.C. (1964) The ecology of highland settlement: some suggestions. In Watson, J.B. (ed.), *New Guinea: the Central Highlands. Amer. Anthrop.*, 66 (4 part 2), Special Publication, 20-38.

Brookfield, H.C. (with Hart, D.) (1971) *Melanesia: a Geographical Interpretation of an Island World.* London.

Brookfield, H.C. and Brown, P. (1963) *Struggle for Land: Agriculture and Group Territories among the Chimbu of the New Guinea Highlands.* Melbourne.

Brookfield, H.C. and White, J.P. (1968) Revolution or evolution in the prehistory of the New Guinea Highlands: a seminar report. *Ethnology*, 7, 43-52.

Brown, P. and Brookfield, H.C. (1967) Chimbu settlement and residence: a study of patterns, trends and idiosyncrasy. *Pacific Viewpoint*, 8, 119-51.

Bulmer, R. (1968) The strategies of hunting in New Guinea. *Oceania*, 38(4), 302-18.

Bulmer, S. and R. (1964) The prehistory of the Australian New Guinea Highlands. In Watson, J.B. (ed.), *New Guinea: the Central Highlands. Amer. Anthrop.*, 66 (4) part 2, Special Publication, 39-76.

Clarke, W.C. (1966) From extensive to intensive shifting cultivation: a succession from New Guinea. *Ethnology*, 5, 347-59.

Clarke, W.C. (1971) *Place and People: an Ecology of a New Guinea Community.* Berkeley, Los Angeles and Canberra.

Clarke, W.C. and Street, J.M. (1967) Soil fertility and cultivation practices in New Guinea. *Journ. Tropical Geog.*, 24, 7-11.

Conklin, H.C. (1963) The Oceanian-African hypotheses and the sweet potato. In Barrau, J. (ed.), *Plants and the Migrations of Pacific Peoples: A symposium*, 129-36. Honolulu.

Dixon, R.B. (1932) The problem of the sweet potato in Polynesia. *Amer. Anthrop.*, 34, 40-66.

Gitlow, A.L. (1947) *Economics of the Mount Hagen Tribes, New Guinea.* Monographs of the American Ethnological Society, no. 12. Seattle.

Golson, J., Lampert, R.J., Wheeler, J.M. and Ambrose, W.R. (1967) A note on carbon dates for horticulture in the New Guinea Highlands. *Journ. Polynesian Soc.*, 76, 369-71.

Haantjens, H.A. (1970) Geologic and geomorphic history of the Goroka-Mount Hagen area. In *Lands of the Goroka-Mount Hagen Area, Territory of Papua and New Guinea*, 19-23. C.S.I.R.O. Canberra (Land Research Series no. 27).

Haantjens, H.A., Reiner, E. and Robbins, R.G. (1970) Land systems of the Goroka-Mount Hagen area. In *Lands of the Goroka-Mount Hagen Area, Territory of Papua and New Guinea*, 24-65. C.S.I.R.O. Canberra (Land Research Series no. 27).

Heider, K.G. (1970) *The Dugum Dani: A Papuan culture in the Highlands of West New Guinea.* Viking Fund Publication in Anthropology no. 49. New York.

Lampert, R.J. (1967) Horticulture in the New Guinea Highlands – C14 dating. *Antiquity*, 41, 307-9.

Leahy, M. (1936) The central highlands of New Guinea. *Geog. Journ.*, 87, 229-62.

Nishiyama, I. (1963) The origin of the sweet potato plant. In Barrau, J. (ed.), *Plants and the Migrations of Pacific peoples: a symposium*, 119-28. Honolulu.

Powell, J.M. (1970a) The impact of man on the vegetation of the Mount Hagen region, New Guinea. Unpublished Ph.D. thesis, Australian National University, Canberra.

Powell, J.M. (1970b) The history of agriculture in the New Guinea Highlands. *Search*, 1, 199-200.

Rappaport, R.A. (1967) *Pigs for the Ancestors: Ritual in the Ecology of a New Guinea People.* New Haven and London.

Robbins, R.G. (1963a) The anthropogenic grasslands of New Guinea. In *Proceedings of the UNESCO Symposium on Humid Tropics Vegetation, Goroka 1960*, 313-29. Canberra.

Robbins, R.G. (1963b) Correlations of plant patterns and population migration into the Australian New Guinea Highlands. In Barrau, J. (ed.), *Plants and the Migrations of Pacific Peoples: a Symposium*, 45-59. Honolulu.

Strathern, A. (1971) *The Rope of Moka: Big-men and Ceremonial Exchange in Mount Hagen, New Guinea.* Studies in Social Anthropology 4. London.

Strathern, A. (1972) *One Father, One Blood: Descent and Group Structure Among the Melpa People.* Canberra.

Strathern, A. and M. (1971) *Self-Decoration in Mount Hagen.* London.

Strathern, M. (1972) *Women in Between: Female Roles in a Male World: Mount Hagen, New Guinea.* London and New York.

Vicedom, G.F. and Tischner, H. (1943-8) *Die Mbowamb: die Kultur der Hagenberg-Stämme im östlichen Zentral-Neuguinea*, 3 vols. Hamburg.

Waddell, E. (1972) *The Mound Builders: Agricultural Practices, Environment, and Society in the Central Highlands of New Guinea.* Seattle and London.

Watson, J.B. (1965a) From hunting to horticulture in the New Guinea Highlands. *Ethnology*, 4, 295-309.

Watson, J.B. (1965b) The significance of a recent ecological change in the Central Highlands of New Guinea. *Journ. Polynesian Soc.*, 74, 438-50.

Watson, J.B. (1967) Horticultural traditions in the eastern New Guinea Highlands. *Oceania*, 38(2), 81-98.

Yen, D.E. (1963) Sweet-potato variation and its relation to human migration in the Pacific. In Barrau, J. (ed.), *Plants and the Migrations of Pacific Peoples: a Symposium*, 93-117. Honolulu.

Yen, D.E. (1968) Natural and human selection in the Pacific sweet potato. In Drake, E.T. (ed.), *Evolution and Environment: a Symposium Presented on the Occasion of the One Hundredth Anniversary of the Foundation of Peabody Museum of Natural History at Yale University*, 387-412. New Haven and London.

Yen, D.E. (1971) The development of agriculture in Oceania. In Green, R.C. and Kelly, M. (eds.), *Studies in Oceanic culture history*, vol. 2, 1-12. Honolulu.

Yen, D.E. (1973) The origins of Oceanic agriculture. *Arch. and Physical Anthrop. in Oceania*, 8, 68-85.

NOTES

1. The project is almost entirely funded by the Research School of Pacific Studies, The Australian National University, Canberra; and the archaeologists principally involved, W.R. Ambrose, J. Golson, R.J. Lampert and W.I. Mumford, are members of the Department of Prehistory in that School. Other principal investigators are R.J. Blong, School of Earth Sciences, Macquarie University, Sydney (geomorphology, ash and swamp stratigraphy), J.M. Powell, now with the New Guinea Research Unit of The Australian National University, Port Moresby (palaeo- and ethno-botany, swamp stratigraphy) and I.M. Hughes of the same Unit (traditional land use and settlement). The project has been aided by the work, cooperation and goodwill of many individuals and institutions, to whom full acknowledgment will be made in the final report. I take this opportunity, however, of making known our very great debt of gratitude to John Morgan, Manager of the Kuk Tea Research Station, without whom nothing could have been done. Thanks are also due to the Papua New Guinea authorities for permission to carry out the investigations.

I should like to express my own personal debt to my colleagues in the project, whose work I have drawn upon where necessary for the elucidation of the history of the agricultural systems, my primary concern in the field and in this article. Their contributions will appear in due course under their own names. Any weaknesses in present interpretation are incontrovertibly my own.

2. I shall use the Pidgin (Pidgin English, Neo-Melanesian) term *baret* for ditch or drain to distinguish the prehistoric and ethnographic features from the modern plantation drains.

CHARLES HIGHAM

The economic basis of the Foveaux Straits Maori in prehistory

Few would dispute that *Star Carr* is one of the most widely read and influential excavation reports to have appeared. The inhabitants of Star Carr did not, as far as is known, contribute to such cultural innovations as the development of agriculture or metallurgy which have recently been the subjects of concentrated research. Nor were they in possession of an appealing art style or of artefacts likely to attract widespread attention. The importance of Star Carr lies rather in the completeness of the excavations and the wide range of organic material to have survived (Clark 1954). These permit an unusually complete reconstruction of the way of life of the site's prehistoric inhabitants. If a clear case of adaptation to a changing environment is to be presented to an undergraduate audience, then there is no better vehicle to portray such change than the excavations at Star Carr. Having heard such a series of lectures from the excavator, and having in due course presented lectures on the same subject, it is not long before one faces the question which the original report left unanswered – 'Where did the inhabitants go in the summer?'

This is an important issue not simply for our consideration of the proto-Maglemosan culture in north-east Britain but more generally in prehistory. The question of a group's annual territory has been a basic theme in recent research undertaken in Cambridge (Higgs 1971) and has encouraged consideration of the resources available during a site's prehistoric occupation period. The problem of changing activities with changing seasons has been squarely before the prehistorian at least since Thomson's (1939) publication on the Wik Monkan. In what must be one of the most widely cited articles by adherents of the economic 'paradigm' in prehistory, Thomson made the now famous remark that the casual observer would not recognize the same group in the dry, as that he had earlier observed during the wet season. In advancing our knowledge of the occupants of Star Carr, therefore, it must be asked what activities they undertook when they deserted their lakeside. This question has now been answered, at least partially, by a recent reconsideration of Star Carr in which Clark (1972) has convincingly argued that they followed the herds of red deer on to the high moorland as the animals migrated with the improving summer climate. Thus the annual territory of the proto-Maglemosan hunters and gatherers is beginning to emerge, and a much clearer idea of their way of life is available.

This extension of our knowledge into the summer activities stresses a variable that has received, perhaps, insufficient attention in recent considerations of the relationship between the culture and the environment: the variable of seasonality. It might be that the importance of the seasonal factor is such that writers on the environmental constraints on culture take it for granted. Yet in many areas, prehistoric societies, just like their modern counterparts, have to cope with more than one environment. Animals migrate, plants mature, rains come and go, a place is hospitable at one time of the year but at other times rendered uninhabitable by the presence of mosquitos or floods or dearth of food. Certainly, the disparate activities undertaken at different times of the year by the Wik Monkan would leave archaeological remains which the archaeologist might find extremely difficult to interpret. Nor are the Wik Monkan an isolated case: even today, typical lowland wet rice farmers in south-east Asia spend large parts of the dry season occupying upland caves on hunting expeditions. The potential importance of transhumance in prehistory is stressed by ethnographic studies. Some Eskimo combine caribou hunting with fishing, and others do not. The Kwakiutl are reported to have moved the heavy timbers of their houses with them when they migrated up and down the sounds to exploit the seasonal availability of fish.

It would be an over-simplification to stress simply the mobility of groups between resource areas in considering the dynamics of hunter-gatherer societies. One of the most recently discovered hunter-gatherer groups, the Tasaday, have sanctions against moving away from their home cave. Perhaps this stability of settlement is linked with the absence of seasonal change in their environment.

Clark has noted that a proper understanding of the relationship between man and environment is an essential prerequisite to fruitful research in prehistory. Such a precept necessitates a knowledge of the variations in the environment on a seasonal basis. It also necessitates the development of techniques for assessing the time of the year at which individual settlements were occupied. The former is not a difficult exercise if the habits of the animals and plants that make up the principal proportion of the food quest are known from a study of their modern counterparts. The latter is at times straightforward, as in the case of the analysis of red-deer antler from Star Carr, but in other cases it can be extremely difficult and may necessitate the development of new analytical techniques.

Economics and New Zealand prehistory

This review will consider the aspect of seasonal variation in the environment in an interesting area from the point of view of the prehistorian: the southern part of the South Island of New Zealand. This area experiences considerable variations in climate and the availability of food, both regionally and seasonally. It was occupied during the greater part of the known prehistoric period by a recently intrusive society whose economy evolved from one incorporating tropical horticulture and stock raising to one in which hunting and gathering was the basis for survival.

As one proceeds south in New Zealand, progressive changes to a more extreme climate rule out in turn each of the food crops which the inhabitants were able to cultivate in the far north. These included the taro, yam and kumera. Thus, whereas the inhabitants of the exposed coastal strip of the southern Wairarapa evidently cultivated the kumera from at least the twelfth century A.D., this possibility was ruled out in most of the South Island and certainly in all parts of the South Island south of the Waitaki River. Although there is an increasing body of evidence documenting a sharp climatic deterioration from the fifteenth century A.D. onwards, there is no evidence in southern New Zealand that the economy was at any time based upon any resource other than those acquired by hunting and gathering until early whalers and sealers brought the pig and potato. It would be extremely difficult to pin down the precise point of departure in tropical Polynesia of the original inhabitants of New Zealand, but it would be most surprising if they did not possess knowledge of the domestic pig and a range of root crops, some of which they brought with them to New Zealand. They did, in fact, introduce the domestic dog.

The technology of the inhabitants of prehistoric New Zealand displayed from the earliest date a marked expertise in stone-working, including adze manufacture. The variations in the shape and type of adze manufacture has, in association with other groups of artefacts, formed for some time the foundation for syntheses of the prehistoric culture history in New Zealand. Thus, Duff (1958) sub-divided the thousand years of New Zealand prehistory into two principal periods, the earlier called Moa Hunter because of the early date of sites yielding evidence for the exploitation of the extinct species of this struthious bird, and the latter called Classic. It was the classic Maori that Cook encountered when he first navigated the seas off New Zealand. In a later review of New Zealand prehistory, Golson (1959) reaffirmed the technological dichotomy of the sequence by sub-dividing it into an Archaic phase of New Zealand East Polynesian culture followed by a Classic Maori phase.

There has been a notable rejection, by more recent workers in the field, of such attempts to present an overall synthesis of the prehistoric occupation of New Zealand. They have concentrated rather on documenting local culture sequences in which full justice can be given to the extreme environmental diversity of New Zealand as a whole. The fruits of such research can be seen in the reports on the prehistoric sequence in the Wairarapa shortly to be published (Leach & Leach, in press), the research into the occupation in the Waikato by Bellwood (1969) and Cassels (1972) and the environmental and cultural studies of Hamel in the Catlins district of South Otago. Each of the three areas mentioned displays distinct settlement patterns and economic bases that can be fully appreciated only in terms of their local environments. This is an important phase of the history of the research into New Zealand's prehistoric period, and one in which seasonal variation of environments and activities plays a considerable part.

The protohistoric period

The brevity of human occupation in New Zealand and the comparatively recent date of European colonization add to the importance of the early descriptions of the indigenous inhabitants, as a source of information relevant to understanding the prehistoric period as a whole. Such studies must, of course, be undertaken with circumspection; much of what the early observers saw was aberrant or unusual, due to their very presence. Nevertheless, some of the extensive literature has been reviewed recently, with particular reference to the Bay of Islands as observed by the crew of Marion Du Fresne's expedition (Kennedy 1969), and to the Wairarapa Valley (Mair 1972). In the South Island, studies have been undertaken for Fjordland (Coutts 1972), the west coast and east coast between Lake Ellesmere and the Taeri Plain (Leach 1969), and the Foveaux Straits region (Bathgate 1969).

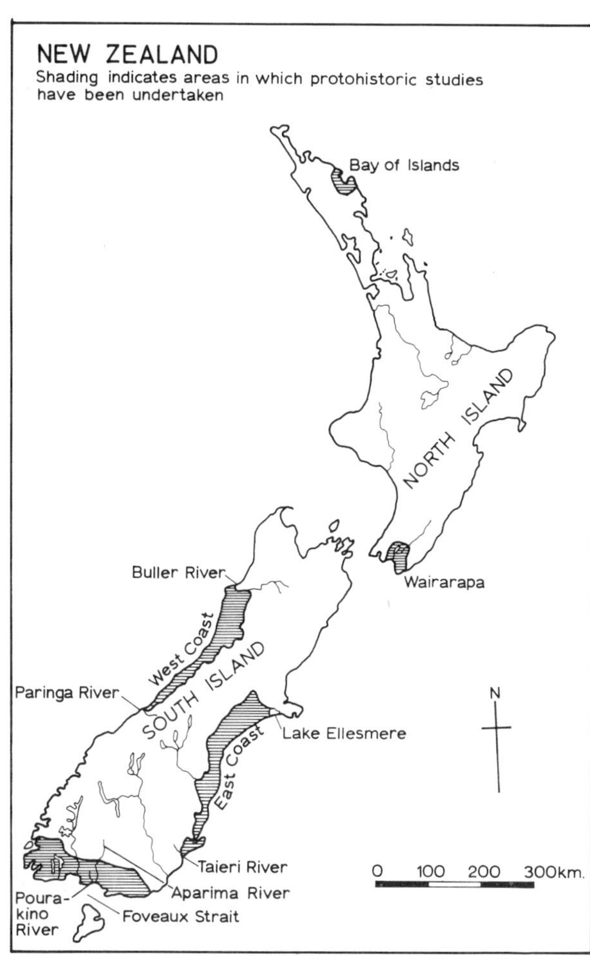

Figure 1. Map of New Zealand showing areas in which studies in Protohistory have been undertaken.

These studies indicate the considerable degree to which early nineteenth-century Maori culture varied with the nature of the local environmental conditions (Fig. 1). The climatic limitations imposed on the cultivation of kumera meant that only certain coastal tracts in the North Island and a few similar enclaves in the South could support the higher population densities normally encountered under conditions of food production rather than plant and animal collection. Where such valued land lay close to good fishing grounds, the maintenance of the relatively dense population was possible, provided that techniques for food preservation were developed. That such techniques were present in the late eighteenth-century is clearly indicated by Crozet's description of defended settlements in the Bay of Islands:

> In the second storehouse where the savages keep their communal food, we found sacks of sweet potatoes, bundles of fern root hung up, various shell-fish, cooked, shelled, threaded on rushes and hung up in the air; a quantity of pieces of large fish of all kinds, cooked, wrapped and tied in packages of fern leaves. (Translation by J. Kennedy)

The dense distribution of pits, presumably intended for food storage, in areas suited to root cultivation, indicates that this technique was practised during the greater part of the prehistoric period in New Zealand. The cold climate associated with even coastal regions of the South Island, ruled out effective root crop cultivation and favoured an economy based on the exploitation of widely distributed, seasonally abundant foodstuffs. Although the absence of archaeological fieldwork in the west coast of the South Island makes it impossible to explore the prehistoric economic pattern, the historic records, particularly those of Heaphy and Brunner, provide a clear insight into the mobility necessary to survive there. Reviewing their diaries, H. Leach (1969) has reconstructed the subsistence techniques of the indigenous inhabitants during the mid-nineteenth century.

They disclose that the winter and summer economic activities were quite different. During the former, the Maori occupied winter bases situated near greenstone sources. Greenstone artefacts were made for local use and for exchange. Such industrial activity was permitted by the availability of food accumulated on foraging expeditions to widely scattered, seasonally productive resource zones. Leach (1969) has stressed the importance of tapping eel runs and the subsequent preservation of eel meat for winter use. Fern root was transported thirty miles to base camps from the few areas where it could flourish. The west coast podocarp forest was a rich source of fruits, berries and birds. Estuaries were visited for flounder (*Rhombosolea* sp.), and favourable beaches for shellfish and seals.

A similar pattern of distinct economic activities was observed by early European visitors in the areas bordering the Foveaux Straits. Although, by the mid-nineteenth century, the European potato was grown in favourable coastal areas, base villages were still abandoned for part of the year during fishing, fowling or collecting activities elsewhere. The occupants of Ruapuke Island, for example, left for the offshore islands to obtain mutton birds (*Puffinus griseus*) in March and April. Their subsistence activities involved visits to the mainland to obtain eels (*Anguilla* sp.), lampreys (*Geotria australis*) and bush birds. The occupants of permanent villages in the Colac Bay area visited the western sounds to obtain seal, fish and crayfish (*Jasus edwardsi*) and bush birds, such visits being expedited by boat and being particularly rewarding during the late summer and autumn.

The relevance of season

Each study of the protohistoric period in New Zealand, irrespective of the region involved, stresses the importance of seasonal variations in subsistence activities. Because it would be illogical to view the protohistoric period as characteristic of the millennium preceding it, it is necessary to devise seasonal dating techniques in order to reconstruct prehistoric activity patterns. Moreover, in a country where the cultivation of the root crops was marginal, slight climatic fluctuation could well be of critical importance in determining the viability of cultivation as opposed to collecting.

Perhaps the most easily applied technique for seasonal dating of prehistoric sites, relies on the recognition of species whose very presence in New Zealand is seasonally restricted. Thus the muttonbird is found only between the months of November and May. The white-faced storm petrel (*Pelagodroma marina*), while not totally absent from New Zealand waters, is easily obtained only during the summer months. To a lesser extent, some fish are only available seasonally. The habits of the barracouta (*Thyrsites atun*), a prolific visitor in South Island coastal waters during the summer, take it to deeper waters during the winter months. The presence of young seal bones indicates January to February exploitation.

The discovery of such bones in prehistoric sites, however, may not indicate the season or even the place where they were obtained. As has already been observed, much of the summer was spent, at least during the protohistoric period, preserving the flesh of seasonally abundant species for subsequent consumption elsewhere. Without a detailed knowledge of the treatment of individual species during the process of preservation, it is not easy to say whether the differential survival of individual anatomical bones indicates either that the stored food was consumed at a given site, or that the site was the scene of a summer food processing.

Where sufficient bones have survived, however, it is possible to attempt such an important task of differentiation of site function. Coutts & Jurisich (1972) have approached this problem for sites on Ruapuke Island. Thus, if the preservation of birds was undertaken at the site, most vertebrae would be absent, in contrast to the relative abundance of the jettisoned bones of the extremities and the cranium. Such a distribution would, it is assumed, be reversed at the site where the preserved meat was consumed.

A more certain procedure for determining seasonal occupation is to consider the growth dynamics of species whose very abundance, wide distribution and all-year availability ruled out transport from one area to another. One such species is the cockle (*Chione stutchburyi*). Shells of this species are common in many prehistoric coastal middens, and an analysis of their structure has revealed the presence of clearly defined growth increments, which not only vary in size seasonally, but also occur at short, perhaps bi-tidal, time intervals. In applying this technique to the study of prehistoric shells, it is necessary to obtain specimens with an undamaged edge, and to analyse enough individuals to rule out statistical fluctuations and to ensure that the time span of the occupation period is adequately covered. Analysis of even a single shell, however, is so intricate that this technique has not been applied as widely as it deserves (Coutts & Higham 1971).

A similar study of the growth dynamics of the sea egg (*Evechinus chloroticus*) has indicated that, at least in southern New Zealand, this species too is relevant for determining seasonality. On viewing X-ray photographs of the coronal plates taken from specimens collected in June and September, Coutts and Jones (in press) detected marked bands. Dix (1969) has correlated such bands with seasonal growth.

By combining, wherever possible, the results of such determinations based on significant species from prehistoric sites, a consideration of seasonal activities may be undertaken. This approach is designed to elucidate the nature and variation of the prehistoric economy in New Zealand. As has been noted above, the diversity of the economic base, particularly between groups solely reliant on hunting and gathering and those for whom horticulture was a major preoccupation, promoted different social adjustments and distinct regional artefact assemblages. It is unfortunate, however, that research priorities in the study of New Zealand prehistory before the sixties did not incorporate the collection of stratigraphically secure biological material necessary to approach the definition of economic patterning (Green 1972).

The Foveaux Straits: a test case

Sufficient research has been undertaken in the margins of the Foveaux Straits to be able to delineate some features of its prehistoric economy. Even granted a warmer climate between initial settlement and the fifteenth century A.D., archaeological evidence shows that this region would have been outside the limits for horticulture. The degree of adaptability on the part of the prehistoric Maori, however, is clearly demonstrated by the early occupation of this region. The first settlers would have encountered a wide range of resource zones, many corresponding closely to those described by early European observers. The local shore line may be subdivided into rocky beach, open or sheltered sandy beach and estuarine zones, each being distinguished by the relative abundance of different assemblages of shellfish (Morton & Miller 1968). Their relative value for the prehistoric hunter and gatherer varied with the nature of the adjacent vegetation, the local geology, the configuration of the submarine environment and with the season of the year. Thus, podocarp forest not only provided edible foods and berries, but also supported a wide range of bird species. Beech forest, on the other hand, is low in plant and animal resources. A beach platform as at Sandhill Point attracts shellfish, and the presence, as at Riverton and Tiwai Points, of outcrops of fine-grained argillite attracts settlement and local exploitation.

As one proceeds into the hinterland of the Foveaux Straits region, the contrast between the Western mountain range with its high rainfall and beech forests on the one hand, and the eastern plains of Southland and Otago on the other, becomes clearly apparent. The interior is bisected by swift rivers, such as the Waiau, Mataura and Clutha, and has such valued industrial resources as fine-grained ortho-quartzite. Compared with the coast, however, food is scarce. It is true that the rivers provide eels regularly, but due to the rain-shadow effect of the western mountain ranges, podocarp forest gives way to large tracts of tussock grassland.

Modern archaeological research demands data formerly overlooked or ignored. Indeed, in order to be of use in reconstructing the nature and development of economic activities in New Zealand, a site should yield biological material permitting the quantification of all subsistence activities and an estimation of the season of occupation. Its full extent at any given occupation period should be known, as should evidence for activity patterns within the site. The contemporary environment should be known sufficiently well to allow site-catchment analyses to be made (Vita-Finzi & Higgs 1970). It should be adequately dated, and the industrial activities, together with all finished artefacts, should be available.

Very few sites anywhere, and none in southern New Zealand, fulfil all these requirements. Perhaps the best documented site in the Foveaux Straits area is Wakapatu, a coastal occupation site on Kawakaputa Bay, Western Southland (Higham 1968). Most foreshore sites in New Zealand are partially destroyed through natural erosion, or so covered with sand that to map their areal extent would be extremely arduous. Again, the possibility that such sites were reoccupied from time to time would make necessary careful consideration of horizontal as well as vertical stratigraphy. At Wakapatu, however, a small extent of *in situ* cultural deposit, protected by an overburden of sand, lies in the centre of a recently exposed horizon covering an area of 1,350 sq. yds. Of course, it is impossible to be sure that both the eroded and undisturbed material belong to the same occupation phase, but this does seem likely since they are contiguous and the undisturbed material has been ascribed to a single phase of occupation. The radiocarbon dates suggest an occupation in the thirteenth century A.D. (Leach & Higham 1971).

During the early years of this century, the podocarp/beech forest in the Wakapatu area came down to the back coastal dunes. There is no reason to doubt that Wakapatu was situated near a forest even more favourable for food collection than the podocarp/beech association which is found today on the nearby Longwood Range, since the site was occupied prior to the sharp climatic deterioration of the fifteenth century. The foreshore at Wakapatu is exposed and sandy, with an occasional rock outcrop supporting the main local shellfish populations. It is still regarded as a good area for sea fishing. The headlands of Oraka Point and Howell's, respectively 1.5 and 13 km. away, comprise green argillite of sufficiently high quality for the manufacture of adzes.

If one were to adopt Vita-Finzi and Higgs's (1970) effective radius of 10 km. as demarcating the area likely to have been exploited from a hunter-gatherer occupation site, then the catchment of Wakapatu would have incorporated an extensive tract of shore, including a major rock resource, and podocarp forest. The site is 13 km. from the mouth of the Aparima and Purakino rivers, the nearest major source of eels. It is held to be unlikely that eeling would have been a major activity at Wakapatu, despite the fact that rapid sea transport would, under good weather conditions, have made the 10 km. restriction academic in the coastal New Zealand context.

Excavations revealed a midden layer of between 3 inches and 3 feet thick in association with a series of ovens. There were substantial quantities of green argillite flakes and food remains. The mussel (*Mytilis edulis*) comprises 65% of all shellfish obtained, followed by *Lunella smaragda* and *Lepsiella scobina.* The species associated with sheltered sandy beaches, such as cockle and pipi (*Amphidesma australe*), are either very rare or absent.

The avifauna is characteristic of podocarp forest, except that moa, so common in the analagous if more sheltered habitats at such east coast sites as Papatowai and Pounawea, are absent. The most abundant species is the red-fronted parakeet (*Cyanoramphus novaeseelandiae*) comprising 60% of the total number of bird individuals represented. The pigeon (*Hemiphaga novaeseelandiae*), white-faced storm petrel and tui (*Prosthemadera novaeseelandiae*) are relatively common, but the mutton bird is notable for its rarity. The parakeet, pigeon and tui are forest birds and the petrel is a marine species. By far the greatest effort appears to have been expended in obtaining birds from the podocarp forest, particularly since nearly all the 14 specimens of storm petrel were recovered in one concentrated group of articulating skeletons. With the exception of the pigeon, the birds represented could not have supplied very much meat. Indeed, the petrel and parakeet may well have been valued for feathers rather than for food.

The spotty (*Pseudolabrus* sp.) was the commonest fish, but its numbers are not significantly greater than either the red cod (*Physiculus bachus*) or the barracouta (*Thyrsites atun*). One-piece bone fishhooks were locally manufactured.

In keeping with the number of microenvironments within the site's catchment area, the food resources are diverse. The absence, however, of *Evechinus* and the rarity of cockle shells make it difficult to obtain an estimate for seasonality which is not biased by factors such as the consumption of stored foodstuffs referred to above.

Nevertheless, three sources of evidence suggest a summer occupation period. Perhaps the most compelling is the presence of a cache of storm petrel skeletons. This bird is only available when it commences nesting on islets in the Foveaux Straits during October. It departs from the Foveaux Straits area between late February and early March. These specimens are most unlikely to represent stored food in view of the completeness of the skeletal remains. Supporting evidence for a summer occupation is derived from the presence of bones of the barracouta, a species which is absent from coastal waters in winter. The few seal bones recovered represent young animals. Finally, a surface examination of *Protothaca crassicosta* specimens, a species of shellfish resembling the cockle, suggests summer collection.

Apart from a few complete adzes with triangular and quadrangular cross-sections and some one-piece and two-piece fishhooks, the material cultural assemblage from Wakapatu comprises argillite flakes. Some of these bear signs of polishing and pecking characteristic of the surface of finished adzes. A close examination of the flakes reveals an absence of large specimens with cortex characteristic of the initial stage of manufacture, a finding which suggests that adze rough-outs were brought to the site for completion. It is by no means easy to explain why so many flakes with a pecked dorsal surface should be found at this site. A dispassionate review of the material would suggest that complete adzes were destroyed there (Leach 1969). On the other hand, it might be that some uncompleted adzes were regarded as unsatisfactory and converted into alternative tools. At least one adze rough-out had been converted into an awl.

Just as it was appropriate to ask where the inhabitants of Star Carr went in summer, so is it necessary to question the activities of the Wakapatu inhabitants during winter. In contrast with the situation at Star Carr, however, there is no gregarious and important food resource, such as the red deer (*Cervus elaphus*) whose seasonal movements are sufficiently predictable to permit hypotheses concerning human mobility to be framed and tested (Clark 1972). Before proceeding with this question, however, a brief review of other sites in the Foveaux Straits region is necessary.

The Tiwai Peninsula is a low-lying, sandy tongue of land which protects Awarua Bay and Bluff Harbour from the Foveaux Strait. In her study of the area's ecological characteristics, Hamel (1969) has pointed out that Bluff Hill, which lies just over 2 km. to the east of the prehistoric settlement at Tiwai Point, was under podocarp forest during the mid-nineteenth century, and that even today, despite the effects of fire, sheep and rabbit, the peninsula itself supports a few regenerating Hall's totara (*Podocarpus hallii*).

There is a wide range of beach habitats in the vicinity of the site, with complex shellfish associations. At present, cockles occur in moderate densities in the sheltered waters of adjacent Awarua Bay. The mussel (*Mytilis edulis*) may be obtained on boulder beaches inside Awarua Bay or on the reefs facing the open straits. *Alcithoe* prefers an open sandy beach such as that on the seaward side of the peninsula. The open sea remains a rich source of the cod and barracouta, while flounder are available in the sheltered bay itself. One of the most important resources of the peninsula is the large outcrop of green and black argillite at its eastern extremity. Since the Tiwai Peninsula provided food and stone likely to have been exploited during the prehistoric period, it has long attracted the interest of archaeologists. It was during 1968 that plans to construct an aluminium-smelter there provided the impetus to excavate in the threatened area (Park 1969, 1971). Two occupation areas, one of 115 and the other 50 square metres, were discovered. The former evidenced argillite working, and the latter comprised a series of working floors together with concentrated food refuse. The occupants of the site would, granted a similar rainfall to that experienced in the area today, have lived in the vicinity of extensive podocarp woodland, a wide variety of shore habitats and both the open sea and a sheltered harbour. The only available radiocarbon date is A.D. 1508 ± 53. The fishhooks and adzes discovered belonged to the same tradition as those recovered from Wakapatu.

The material from the midden differs from that from Wakapatu in a number of respects. While the parakeet remains the most common bird represented, the mutton bird is also abundant, followed by the broad-billed prion (*Pachyptila vittata*), spotted shag and Stewart Island shag (*Stictocarbo punctatus* and *Phalacrocorax carunculatus*). Although later in date than Wakapatu, the Tiwai Point midden also includes at least four genera of moa (*Emeus, Euryapteryx,*

Anomalapteryx and *Megalapteryx*). The presence of the native pigeon and parakeet indicates the exploitation of local stands of podocarp forest. Hamel (1969) has suggested that the shags and mutton birds could have been obtained from their most likely nesting grounds on the slopes of Bluff Hill, and the prions on the end of the Tiwai Peninsula itself. Little is known of the ecology of the moa species except that in Otago, the area of tolerance certainly included podocarp forest. Fish remains from Tiwai Point were dominated numerically by the barracouta. The cockle was the most abundant shellfish recovered and immature seal bones were relatively common. With the exception of the slender extremities of the parakeet, all bird bones were present in anatomically consistent numbers. Taken in conjunction with the presence of young seal, mutton birds and barracouta, an occupation between October and April is indicated. When the micro-rings on the cockle shell (n = 7) are taken into account, the occupation period can be confined to the months of November to February.

Together with Pounawea, Papatowai is one of the classic, early South Otago moa hunter sites (Lockerbie 1959). It is situated by the estuary of the Tahakopa River and is backed by the extensive podocarp forest of the Catlins ranges. Faunal remains from Lockerbie's excavations have been used to support the hypothesis that an early period of moa hunting gave way, with their progressive extinction, to a more widely-based economy similar to those described for Wakapatu and Tiwai Point. During 1971, Hamel excavated an undisturbed portion of the site and recovered four occupation layers, the latest of which was disturbed. The lowest layer has a radiocarbon date of A.D. 1039 ± 76. This excavation, limited as it was, has provided important information to supplement that obtained during Lockerbie's research in the 1950s. The number of moa species and the actual number of birds represented declined from the lowest layer (No.4) to layer 2. The same pattern is true of the sea mammals. Layer 4 contained the remains of a southern sea-lion (*Phocarctos hookeri*), southern fur-seal (*Arctocephalus for-*

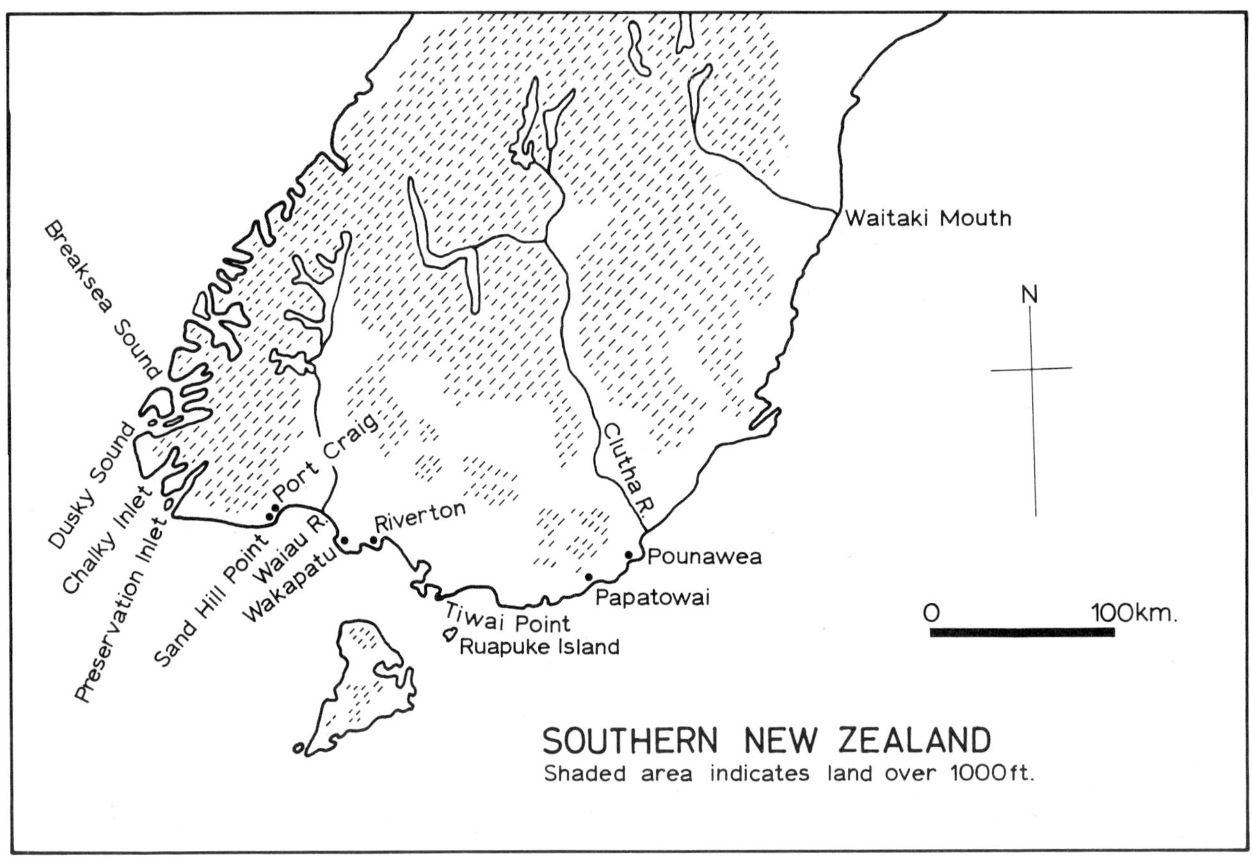

Figure 2. The location of the principal sites discussed in the text.

steri) and sea-leopard (*Hydrurgia leptonyx*) including bones from immature specimens of the first two and a fur-seal pup, but layer 3 is devoid of any of these species and layer 2 contains bones of only the southern fur-seal. There were no fish bones from the lowest layer, but barracouta are present in layers 2 and 3. The incidence of shellfish, particularly pipi and cockle, increased progressively with time.

Seasonal indicators from Papatowai included seal pups, barracouta and mutton bird. All point to summer occupation. Further refinement of this broad estimate awaits the analysis of the cockle shells from each layer.

As one proceeds westwards from the Waiau Estuary (Fig. 2), one encounters a distinct environmental change. Mean annual rainfall at Milford Sound is 253.3 compared with 43.4 at Riverton. The lowland podocarp forest gives way increasingly to beech, and the coastal plain narrows with the presence of extensive fiords.

It is only during the last five years that extensive archaeological research has been undertaken in this remote and forbidding area. Coutts (1972) has examined sites from Port Craig, Sandhill Point, Preservation Inlet, Chalky Inlet, Dusky Sound and Breaksea Sound (Coutts 1969a, 1969b, 1969c, 1970, 1972). The chronology of the Fiordland sites is difficult to define due to the inconsistency of the available radiocarbon dates and the rarity of diagnostic forms of artefact. Coutts (1972) has subdivided them into three major chronological groups of which one is ascribed to a period after European contact, the second to a late and the third to an early prehistoric period (A.D. 1000-1400).

It is perhaps significant that of all the sites discovered, only two levels were ascribed to the early period on artefactual evidence; these being layers 2 and 3 at the site of Port Craig. The Port Craig area is the most easterly of those examined and is, in fact, more akin environmentally to the sites discussed above rather than the Fiordland Caves. It is situated on the extreme western margin of Te Waewae Bay on a shore backed by mixed podocarp/beech forest. The contents of the small midden include shellfish characteristic of the rocky shore, two specimens of the southern blue penguin and five individuals of fish. Intensive field-work undertaken by Coutts, for Fiordland, failed to produce any other unequivocal early prehistoric sites, even in naturally protected cave localities. The majority of layers excavated belong either to the late prehistoric or protohistoric periods. The former group have general characteristics in common. Sites tend to be small and often include the occupation of caves. The available data indicate an orientation towards a marine economy. The evidence for seasonality points overwhelmingly to occupation during the summer, with particular emphasis on the months September to January inclusive. Apart from the Southport sites, there is no convincing evidence for food preservation in the prehistoric Fiordland settlements.

All sites so far considered are coastal. This situation reflects the relative ease with which they are located, the abundance of biological material which has survived and probably the concentration of prehistoric occupation in such areas. It is worth reflecting that only a small rise in sea level would destroy this aspect of the prehistoric settlement of New Zealand. Occupation in the interior is documented archaeologically and ethnographically, although very few sites have been adequately examined. It is evident that the exploitation of the favoured rock resources was an important aspect of the prehistoric settlement pattern from an early date (Leach 1969). There are a number of inland sites yielding evidence of hunting the moa (Lockerbie 1959), and although riverine camps for eel fishing are hardly known, due presumably to the destructive effects of flooding, such activities are likely to have been important during the prehistoric period.

The bias in favour of summer occupation sites is precisely what one might expect in a situation where most durable remains of collected food were only available during summer. It is true that there are some species which can be used as indicators of winter occupation, such as the frost-fish (*Lepidotus caudatus*), sea egg and cockle. It is easy to demonstrate summer presence but difficult to disprove winter absence. The midden layers at Wakapatu and Tiwai Point are thin and are not likely to represent a lengthy occupation. Moreover, they would be exposed to extremely cold, gale-force winds during winter, when local food resources would have been minimal. If it is conceded that such coastal sites were at least in part occupied to amass seasonal surpluses, then consideration must be given to the likely location of the winter settlements.

It has been mentioned earlier that, unlike

the situation at Star Carr, there is no major animal resource with predictable seasonal movements to lead us to the most likely locality. Moreover, the over-wintering problem may well have varied during the course of the prehistoric period. It would not be difficult to follow in the path of the New Archaeologists and propose hypothetico-deductive models to assist in the resolution of this problem. One such model would suggest that during the early prehistoric period, the non-agricultural parts of the South Island were visited during the summer to take advantage of the seasonal abundance, before hunters returned to the warmer North Island in the winter. Such visits could have been extended as population pressure built up in the agriculturally attractive territory. The sea passage between the north and southern areas would not, presumably, have daunted the descendants of those who were able to reach New Zealand in the first place.

An alternative model is that the initial settlers of Southland over-wintered within the confines of their summer territory. In the absence of southern varieties of stone or distinctively southern artefact types in the North Island agricultural zone, the latter hypothesis appears the more acceptable. In formulating a deductive hypothesis for the location of winter settlements, it is necessary to review where they might be located and what archaeological remains would be characteristic of them. This problem is, of course, not encountered in much of the North Island, where winter settlement would probably have concentrated near subterranean kumera stores.

Among basic requirements of a South Island winter camp would be a central, defensive, sheltered location within the annual territory. Archaeologically, it would incorporate structural evidence in the form of post-holes representing both domestic dwellings and storehouses. Since most food consumed locally would be processed during summer, there would be little accumulated midden material, although access to year-round food resources would be an advantage. If near a stone source, then there may be evidence of tool manufacture, but it is possible that imported adze blanks would have been pecked and polished at the site. Nucleated inhumation burials with associated artefacts could be more characteristic of a winter base than a transient summer camp. The range of complete artefact types would be greater than in specialized sites, and the distribution of bird and fish bones should be restricted.

It seems reasonable initially to examine the known movements of the indigenous inhabitants during the nineteenth century. On the west coast, for example, they withdrew to winter camps adjacent to greenstone sources. In the Foveaux Straits it is known that the island of Ruapuke was occupied during the winter months. It is only recently that the Maori owners of the island have permitted archaeological field-work to be undertaken, a very reasonable policy in view of the destruction of mainland sites by *pakeha* curio-hunters (Leach 1972). At present, only a 2-week reconnaissance has been undertaken, but with intriguing results (Coutts & Jurisich 1972). Despite the island's small size (3,200 acres), it is environmentally diverse. It incorporates lagoons which not only support duck populations, but also permit eels to breed. The more sheltered eastern side supports a mixed podocarp forest. The rocky shore has substantial reserves of shellfish and there are a number of off-shore islets well known as the breeding grounds for both seals and mutton-birds. Fish and crayfish are abundant and the amount of whalebone on the beaches today suggests that stranded whales were not an uncommon phenomenon. While not a major source of stone, pebbles of argillite, greywacke and quartzite are common on the beaches. The climate of Ruapuke is unusual in its absence of frosts, and its relative difficulty of access makes it the easier to defend. One of the sites discovered, Parangiaio Point, lies on an isthmus of a small promontory. Coutts discovered an extensive occupation soil which included ovens and midden deposits, and obtained a small sample of organic material from one of the latter.

Compared with mainland middens, the pattern of remains is familiar although, as one might expect, relative proportions of the major species differ in line with the different extent of the local resource zones. Parakeets and pigeons are very scarce (less than 2% of all birds recovered), but the mutton bird is abundant (77%).

Five individual southern fur-seals are represented, two of which come from very young individuals. Barracouta, spotty and blue cod are the predominant fish species represented. There are, however, two variables which differ from those discussed from mainland midden assemblages. The first is that, compared with the minimum number of individual mutton birds represented by bones as a whole, ninety percent of the wing bones are missing. This suggests the possibility that stored specimens were being consumed. Secondly, the shellfish data indicate winter collection. These factors stress the importance of undertaking major excavations at Parangiaio Point to determine its extent and date of occupation within the prehistoric period, to obtain evidence of structures and attempt to falsify the hypothesis that the site was occupied during the winter as well as the warmer seasons of the year.

If Parangiaio Point is indeed a winter base, the putative characteristics of such sites as set out above must be altered. There is, of course, no reason why the site should not have been occupied by some members of the social group during the summer months, a situation which would result in the accumulation in the middens of fish and shellfish equivalent to the normal summer activities. However, this situation only serves to emphasize the importance of a minute examination of the faunal and floral material.

Conclusion

Polarization into an early and a later prehistoric period in New Zealand has been a characteristic of some well known syntheses of New Zealand prehistory (Duff 1956; Golson 1959). Such a distinction has been broadly based on artefactual typology, although Duff named his early phase the 'Moa-Hunter' period. This bimodality has been stressed on economic grounds for Southland by Bathgate, when he recognized an early (A.D. 1000-1400) and a late period, the latter being characterized as a 'recessional fowling economy'.

It is not disputed that aspects of the material culture did change; the range of adzes made was reduced. The quartzite-blade knife was first developed, and then neglected. Fishhook morphology was subject to gradual stylistic variation (Hjarno 1967). These are not the principal concern of this paper, which has concentrated on the economic and social basis of prehistoric Maori culture in the Foveaux Straits area. The basis of the culture was a broad-spectrum hunting and gathering economy, the resources exploited being remarkably similar from the earliest known sites until the advent of Europeans. Indeed, many continue to be important. The mutton bird islands are still visited in season, shellfish are still consumed although some are protected, the waters are still fished and eeling is a major industry. The fur-seal and most forest birds, however, are now protected. Of the principal food resources, only the moa failed to survive the prehistoric period.

In his important study of South Island forest associations, Holloway (1954) suggested that intrusions of beech into podocarp stands was compatible with a climatic deterioration. This hypothesis has recently been confirmed by Hendy and Wilson's (1968) study of speleothems, which discloses that the mean temperature in New Zealand between A.D. 1200 and 1400 was significantly warmer than that from A.D. 1400 to 1700. This change would have been critical for kumera cultivation in the more marginal coastal areas, but may not have been so germane to South Island culture history. It is possible, however, that there was an increase in storminess associated with the climatic deterioration (Wilson & Hendy 1971). This would have been significant for the Foveaux Straits region for two reasons. It may well have affected the viability of the moa species accustomed to nesting in coastal areas, and would have impeded marine transport in an area still noted for its storm hazards.

It is true that settlement based on a wide-spectrum hunting and gathering continued despite the climatic deterioration, but it is quite possible that the extinction of the moa and difficulties in transport to productive off-shore islands encouraged the expansion of settlement into such marginal areas as Fiordland, where the excavated caves indicate initial occupation late in the prehistoric period.

The social adjustments to such an economic base appear to have involved the dispersal of small, mobile groups over a large annual territory and their coalescing during the difficult winter months. There are, at present, insufficient published data to compare such a strategy with that of other regions of New Zealand. Relevant research is, however, being undertaken in the Wairarapa and the Waikato, and it is already possible to distinguish a radically distinct culture sequence in the former, where an initial period of hunting and gathering allied with kumera agriculture on the narrow coastal strip, was followed by the abandonment of the area. The abandonment is correlated with a period of climatic deterioration which would have ruled out local agriculture and restricted it in more favoured areas further north. The advent of land scarcity is a possible motivating factor in social friction, but that is another problem in economic and social prehistory.

Acknowledgments

I have pleasure in recording the assistance, stimulation and advice of many of my colleagues in the field of New Zealand prehistory, and in particular Helen and Foss Leach, Jill Hamel, Peter Coutts, Gaela Mair, Murray Bathgate, Jean Kennedy and Stuart Park. Professor Grahame Clark was William Evans visiting Professor in Prehistory, University of Otago, in 1964 and came to New Zealand again in 1968. Many of the archaeologists mentioned above remember the value of his presence, and all are indebted to his influence.

REFERENCES

Bathgate, M.A. (1969) *The Maori Occupancy of Murihiku 1000-1900 A.D.: A geographic study of change.* M.A. thesis, University of Otago.

Bellwood, P. (1969) Pa excavations at Otakanini, South Kaipara and Lake Mangakaware, Waikato, *N.Z. Arch. Assoc. Newsletter*, 12(1), 38-49.

Cassels, R.J.S. (1972) Prehistoric man and his environment. In Goodall, D.H. (ed.), *The Waikato, Man and His environment.* Waikato.

Clark, J.G.D. (1954) *Excavations at Star Carr.* London.

Clark, J.G.D. (1972) *Star Carr: a Case Study in Bioarchaeology.* Reading, Mass.

Coutts, P.J.F. (1969a) Merger or takeover: a survey of the effects of contact between European and Maori in the Foveaux Strait region. *Journ. Polynesian Soc.*, 78(4), 495-516.

Coutts, P.J.F. (1969b) The Maori of Dusky Sound: a review of the historical sources. *Journ. Polynesian Soc.*, 78(2), 178-211.

Coutts, P.J.F. (1969c) Archaeology in Fiordland, New Zealand, *N.Z. Arch. Assoc. Newsletter*, 12(3), 117-23.

Coutts, P.J.F. (1970) Port Craig/Sandhill Point regions of Southland: a preliminary archaeological report. *Arch. & Physical Anthrop. in Oceania*, 5(1), 53-9.

Coutts, P.J.F. (1972) The Emergence of the Fiordland Maori from Prehistory. Unpublished Ph.D. Thesis, University of Otago, N.Z.

Coutts, P.J.F. and Higham, C.F.W. (1971) The seasonal factor in Prehistoric New Zealand. *World Arch.*, 2, 266-7.

Coutts, P.J.F. and Jones, K.L. (in preparation) Seasonal dating on the basis of growth bands in *Evechinus chloroticus.*

Coutts, P.J.F. and Jurisich, M. (1972) An Archaeological Survey of Ruapuke Island, N.Z. *Anthrop. Dept. Univ. Otago Studies in Prehist. Anthrop. No. 5.*

Dix, P.G. (1969) The Biology of the Echnoid *Evechinus chloroticus* (Val) in different habitats. Unpublished Ph.D. Thesis, University of Canterbury, Christchurch, N.Z.

Duff, R. (1956) *The Moa Hunter Period of Maori Culture.* Wellington.

Golson, J. (1959) Culture change in prehistoric New Zealand. In Freeman, J.D. and Geddes, W. (eds.), *Anthropology in the South Seas*, 29-74. New Plymouth.

Green, R.C. (1972) Moa-hunters, agriculture and changing analogies in New Zealand prehistory. *N.Z. Arch. Assoc. Newsletter*, 15(1), 16-39.

Hamel, G. (1969) Ecological method and theory: Tiwai Peninsula. *N.Z. Arch. Assoc. Newsletter*, 12(3), 147-63.

Hendy, C.H. and Wilson, A.T. (1968) Palaeoclimatic data from speleothems. *Nature*, 219, 48-51.

Higgs, E.S. (1972) (ed.) *Papers in Economic Prehistory.* London.

Higham, C.F.W. (1968) Prehistoric research in Western Southland. *N.Z. Arch. Assoc. Newsletter*, 11(4), 155-64.

Hjarno, J. (1967) Maori fishhooks in southern New Zealand. *Records of Otago Mus. in Anthrop.*, No. 3.

Holloway, J.T. (1954) Forests and climates in the South Island of New Zealand. *Trans., Royal Soc. New Zealand*, 82, 329-410.

Kennedy, J. (1969) Settlement in the Bay of Islands 1772. *Anthrop. Dept. Univ. Otago Studies in Prehist. Anthrop. No. 3.*

Leach, B.F. (1969) The Concept of Similarity in Prehistoric Studies. *Anthrop. Dept. Univ. Otago Studies in Prehist. Anthrop. No. 1.*

Leach, H.M. (1969) Subsistence Patterns in Prehistoric New Zealand. *Anthrop. Dept. Univ. Otago Studies in Prehist. Anthrop. No. 2.*

Leach, H.M. (1972) One hundred years of Otago anthropology: a critical review. *Records of the Otago Museum*, No. 6.

Leach, B.F. and Higham, C.F.W. (1971) Radiocarbon dates from Southland. *N.Z. Arch. Assoc. Newsletter*, 14(4), 202-3.

Leach, B.F. and Leach, H.M. (in press) *Archaeology in the Wairarapa.*

Lockerbie, L. (1959) From Moa-Hunter to Classic Maori in southern New Zealand. In Freeman, J.D. and Geddes, W. (eds.), *Anthropology in the South Seas*, 75-110. New Plymouth.

Mair, G.M. (1972) The protohistoric period of Wairarapa Culture History. Unpublished M.A. thesis, University of Otago.

Morton, J. and Miller, M. (1968) *The New Zealand Seashore.* London.

Park, G.S. (1969) Tiwai Point: a preliminary report. *N.Z. Arch. Assoc. Newsletter*, 12(3), 143-6.

Park, G.S. (1971) Chemical analysis in archaeology. *N.Z. Arch. Assoc. Newsletter*, 14(4), 173-8.

Thomson, D.F. (1939) The seasonal factor in human culture, illustrated from the life of a contemporary nomadic group. *P.P.S.*, 5, 209-21.

Vita-Finzi, C. and Higgs, E.S. (1970) Prehistoric economy in the Mount Carmel area of Palestine: site catchment analysis. *P.P.S.*, 36, 1-37.

Wilson, A.T. and Hendy, C.H. (1971) Past windstrength from isotope studies. *Nature*, 234, 344-5.

RHYS JONES

Tasmania: aquatic machines and off-shore islands

> Precisely at what stage of prehistory boats were first brought into use is still an open question, but at the moment there is no evidence that this happened during Palaeolithic times. (Clark 1952:282)

Matthew Flinders saw the problem clearly enough. For weeks, he and a volunteer crew in the schooner *Francis* had been systematically and gingerly pushing southwards through the chain of large islands named after their 'discoverer' Captain Furneaux, and which seemed to straddle the eastern portals of a great bay or inlet lying to the south of the coast of New South Wales (Fig. 1). These islands were totally devoid of any native inhabitants. There was no sign of huts, hearths, middens, marked trees, smoke, burnt bush, or any of the other tell-tale signs which had been ubiquitous on the continental shore to the north. Even wombats foraged amongst the sea weed in broad daylight on some of these islands, whereas in the secluded forested hills behind Sydney, they were shy nocturnal animals, skulking deep within their setts away from prying human eyes during daylight. Now, having reached latitude 40° 50′ south on 25 February 1798, the explorers were standing off a great mass of land, the coast of which came up to them from the south and then turned abruptly westwards and stretched away out of sight in that direction. There was no doubt that this was Van Diemen's Land, which previous navigators had shown to be part of the domain of man.

There was, however, a strange combination of facts which puzzled Flinders. On the one hand,

> The smokes which had constantly been seen rising from it showed that there were inhabitants; and this, combined with the circumstances of there being none upon the islands, seemed to argue a junction of Van Diemen's Land with New South Wales; for it was difficult to suppose, that men should have reached the more distant land, and not have attained the islands intermediately situated; nor was it admissible that, having reached them, they had perished for want of food. On the other hand, the great strength of the tides setting westwards, past the islands, could only be caused by some exceedingly deep inlet, or by a passage through to the southern Indian Ocean. These contradictory circumstances were very embarrassing; and . . . I was obliged, to my great regret, to leave this important geographical question undecided. (1814:cxxxvi-cxxxvii)

But not for long, because nine months later, in the sloop *Norfolk*, Flinders and George Bass pushed through 200 miles to the west until, rounding the tip of Three Hummock Island, they suddenly perceived a long swell 'to come from the south west, such as we had not been accustomed to for some time . . . Mr Bass and myself hailed it with joy and mutual congratulation, as announcing the completion of our long-wished-for discovery of a passage into the Southern Indian Ocean' (1814:clxxi).

So Van Diemen's Land, or Tasmania as it is now called, was an island, and the major problem solved; yet there still remained the second half of Flinders' conundrum. Indeed their further discoveries had added to it. In their traverse of the eastern half of the north coast of Tasmania, they had inspected several islands only two miles or less off the coast, and had found them all empty of man and his remains. Moreover, the islands supported large colonies of sea birds and seals which seemed to be unafraid of man. By the time they had reached the sheltered estuary of Port Dalrymple (Tamar River), they had concluded that 'the natives of this part of Van Diemen's Land have not the means of transporting themselves across the water' (1814:cliv).

Yet on the western edge of the strait, an hour or so before feeling that south-westerly swell, they had established that the hilly promontory which they had named Three Hummock Land was in fact an island, and that it had on it considerable evidence of native occupation. As Flinders argued:

> The channel which separates it from the land to the west, is, at least, two miles in width, and is deep; so that it was difficult to conjecture how the indians were able to get over to the island. It was almost certain that they had no canoes at Port Dalrymple, nor any means of reaching islands lying not more than two cables length from the shore; and it therefore seemed improbable that they should possess canoes here. The small size of Three-hummock Island rendered the idea of fixed inhabitants inadmissable; and whichever way it was considered, the presence of men there was a problem difficult to be resolved. (1814:clxxi)

It is to the three questions raised by Flinders that I wish to address myself in this paper, namely:

1. Why was it that the islands off north-west Tasmania had been occupied by Aboriginal man, whereas those of equal or less distance off the north-east, had not been?
2. How could men have reached the 'more distant land', viz. Tasmania, and not the 'islands intermediately situated' viz. the Furneaux Group and King Island in Bass Strait?
3. Was it completely *in*admissible that having reached the large Bass Strait islands, 'they had perished for want of food'?

Tasmania and its Aborigines

Tasmania is a mountainous island of some 26,000 square miles, lying 150 or so miles to the south of the continent of Australia, and separated from it by the waters of Bass Strait. On this island lived people whose simplicity of economy and material culture has fascinated students of the human condition ever since the Tasmanians were first brought to the notice of civilized man late in the eighteenth century. Unfortunately, both for civilized values and for the science of civilization, these savages did not long survive their elevation into the known world, a condition accelerated somewhat by a surfeit of hot lead and the common cold early in the nineteenth century, so that the last official survivor died, surrounded by eager scholars, in 1876. Their epitaph was written both by themselves in what they did to the land during the many millennia of their sojourn on the island, and by a few travellers who saw them briefly during their death throes. The first systematic ethnography of the Tasmanians was written by H. Ling Roth in 1890 (first edition), but almost thirty years before that, scholars were beginning to grapple with the problem of where to place the Tasmanian Aborigines within their evolutionary schemes (for instance Huxley 1869; also Tylor 1865, 1893). The last ten years have seen a resurgence of interest in the Tasmanians, and in the old problems raised, but not satisfactorily answered, seventy and more years ago. In 1961, Grahame Clark recognized the importance of the Tasmanians by devoting a sub-chapter of his *World Prehistory* to them (240-2). He saw that any meaningful attack on the problem would have to be archaeological, and it was largely due to his influence and encouragement that this happened when it did, not only on the island itself but also on a continent-wide scale (for instance, see Mulvaney 1971:228-9). Coincident with the deployment of this new discipline was the re-discovery of a vast corpus of ethnographic data buried in the Tasmanian field journals of G.A. Robinson, 1829-1834, and published in 1966 by N.J.B. Plomley.

The modern Tasmanian State consists of more than one hundred islands, and in fact ought to be seen as an archipelago extending southwards from the main spine of the Great Dividing Range (Fig. 1). These islands are however dominated by one whose area is 17 times as great as all the others combined (Lakin 1972:40). The 'off-shore' islands range in distance from a few score yards to more than 50 miles from the main island of Tasmania (Davies 1965). The coastline is indented with numerous estuaries, harbours and peninsulas, especially along the southern half of the island. An annual rainfall of over 100 inches on the western mountains feeds strong fast rivers which flow into the northern, western and southern coasts. It is only in the north-east and in the Midland Valley that the streams are sluggish and braided and the coast tends to be smoother with accumulation of sand (Davies 1965:22; 1967). The south-west, however, is exposed to the fury of the Roaring Forties, and its climate echoes to the maelstroms a thousand miles to the south. It is a world of gales and of rain; of wind and water. It is the maritime province of Australia.

The coast with its rich food resources formed part of the habitat of every Tasmanian band at some stage of its seasonal peregrination (Jones 1971a, 1971b; Appendix A, 1974). The reason

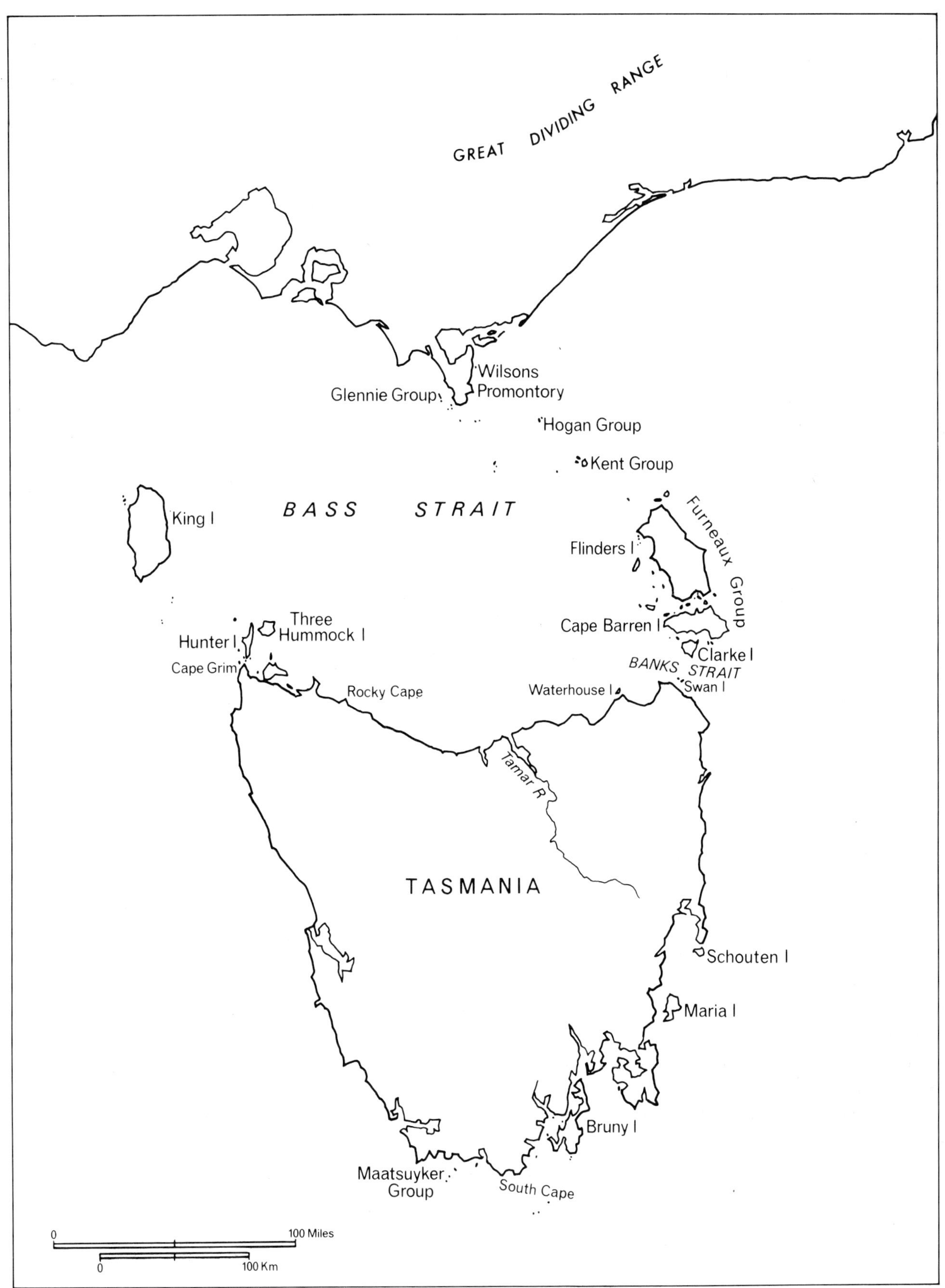

Figure 1. The Tasmanian Archipelago.

for this may be gauged by the fact that, even excluding all offshore islands, Tasmania consists of only 29 square miles of land for every mile of coast, compared with 260 square miles per mile of coast for the Australian mainland (Lakin 1972:42). The ability to cross river mouths and bays, to reach islands and to forage in the sea offered immense advantages to the Aborigines, both in terms of increasing the sum of exploitable resources and in reducing the effort involved in getting them. On the other hand, the sea does not forget such transgressions and exacts its penalty for incompetence or foolhardiness. It is the interplay between the possibilities and the problems inherent in various water crossings that forms the theme of this paper.

Aquatic locomotion: swimming

Some Tasmanian women were excellent divers and swimmers. Labillardière (1800:309-10) has described a group of women and their daughters from the d'Entrecasteaux channel, South Tasmania, repeatedly diving off rocks into the sea to get abalone shell-fish (*Notohaliotis ruber*) and cray-fish, which they put into little baskets hung around their necks or shoulders. To get these foods they must have dived to depths of at least ten feet and stayed under water long enough to prise the abalone off the rocks with wooden spatulae. They dived repeatedly until their baskets were full, took them on shore to cook, then returned until they had obtained enough for their families' meals. In between dives they warmed themselves by the cooking fires, which their husbands never left during the whole operation. Robinson several times described similar procedures from Bruny Island and the southeast coast (9 June 1829:63; 28 September 1829:79; 24 March 1830:135). Piron's drawing (1800, Atlas no. 4; see also Jones 1971a: Pl. VII), shows that the women swam, facing the water, with an action similar to a breast stroke or dog paddle, and Robinson's sketch of women towing him across a river also suggests a breast stroke action (10 June 1830:171; Plomley 1966:Pl. 3b). Before diving into the water south-western women used to stand on the rocks in what Robinson thought was 'rather an obscene position' and chanted a song – perhaps an incantation against the dangers of their vocation (24 March 1830:135). Girls were trained from childhood so that by the time they were women 'water becomes their own element' (Robinson 28 September 1839:79). (All page references for Robinson's diary are to Plomley's edition of 1966).

This method of food getting was one of the major economic activities of the coastal groups, especially along the western and southern shores, as witnessed by both the ethnographic accounts and the archaeological remains. At the Rocky Cape caves, north-west Tasmania, I estimated that approximately half of the flesh intake of the prehistoric inhabitants there came from shell-fish, every species of which had to be collected from below low-tide mark and is typically found near deep crevices and ledges. This situation pertained throughout the archaeological sequence, down to the lowest levels dated to 8,000 years ago, implying that advanced skills of diving, swimming and foraging under water were possessed by the ancestors of the Tasmanians even at that antiquity (Jones 1968:199; 1971b).

Women also could swim long distances or in hard conditions, as indicated by the following examples. Two European men belonging to a 'conciliatory' expedition were trying to cross the Pieman River on the west coast on a raft and were being carried by the powerful current to the raging surf at the bar. Two Tasmanian women dived into the water and swam to them trying to tow the raft to safety, but in vain, for it was smashed to bits and the Europeans drowned, the women reaching safety when the danger seemed to overwhelm them (Report by Cottrell 19 January 1833 in Plomley 1966:804, note 7; Robinson 31 August 1833:786).

Women belonging to some north-west coast bands used regularly to swim to a pair of great stacks called The Doughboys, lying about a half mile off Cape Grim, in order to catch and then tow back mutton birds (*Puffinus tenuirostris*) (Robinson 24 June 1830:183). They only did this in fine weather, but even on such rare benign moments the swell surges and sucks past glistening black walls, so that one wonders how boats, let alone human swimmers, could survive in it.

Sometimes, women even swam from Cape Grim to Trefoil Island, a distance of a mile and a half, and to Hunter Island (Robinson 24 June 1830:183, 19 October 1832:672). This latter crossing is about three and a half miles wide, with several islets and reefs on which to rest. Nevertheless it is also characterized by vicious tidal rips, as great masses of water, swinging against the north-western shoulder of Tasmania, pour through the narrow channels between rocks and islands (e.g. Robinson 18 June 1830:176; Meston 1936:157). To swim these straits must have required great stamina and courage, backed by a meticulous knowledge of the local conditions. In addition to the danger of being carried away by currents, women were sometimes drowned by being entangled in skeins of under-water kelp, and there are stories of shark attacks (Robinson in Plomley 1966:1004, note k).

Most descriptions of swimming come from the west and south coasts, and it is from here that we get our spectacular feats. However, some eastern women could swim, as shown by Kelly's account of a group of them stalking seals on wave-covered rocks off north-eastern Tasmania (Bowden 1964:40-3). Note that the women had to be taken to these rocks in an European boat, though they were situated only about a mile and a half off shore. The matter was well summed up by a woman who told Robinson that whereas the western women prided themselves on their ability to dive for shell-fish, those from the east and inland districts could climb trees for possums. These contrasting physical skills were developed to take advantage of the different food resources of the two regions.

Some men could also swim (e.g. Robinson 28 September 1829:79; 26 March 1830:139), but less well than the women. On one occasion while crossing the Arthur River, a woman swam to the aid of her husband who, though seated on a raft, was in danger of being carried away by the current. The woman herself had already swum across (Robinson 9 April 1834:878). This difference in skill between the sexes may have both cultural and physiological explanations. Shell-fish gathering was woman's work (Hiatt 1968; 1970), and there were no male activities that necessitated much swimming skill. Women with their higher percentage of subcutaneous fat seem to be better adapted to enduring exposure in cold water, such as is found around Tasmania (and also Tierra del Fuego). To protect themselves from cold and wet, Tasmanians of both sexes anointed their skins with a paste of seal or mutton-bird fat mixed with red ochre, which they burnished by rubbing to a high gloss. This not only acted as an insulating layer, but also kept the natural oils within the skin.

There is good evidence that some north-eastern men could not swim at all. Mannalargenna, an old warrior from the east coast just north of Oyster Bay, could not swim, and had to be carried across streams in craft specially constructed for him by Robinson's people (e.g. 15 August 1831:402). Eumarrah, a midlands man of great courage in his fight against his white oppressors, 'was exceedingly afraid of water and it was some time ere he could be prevailed upon to venture himself upon the catamaran' (Robinson 26 March 1930:139). This was a river crossing which the western men negotiated easily 'holding up their kangaroo mantles with one hand whilst they swam across with the other'.

Watanabe (1971:2) has reminded us that swimming is an art that humans have had to learn, they being apparently the only apes to possess it. The Tasmanian evidence supports such a 'cultural' view of swimming ability; not only could women swim much better than men, but some men could not even swim at all. This contrast between the north-east on the one hand and the west and south on the other is reinforced by other evidence presented below.

Aquatic machines

There are severe limitations on human swimming ability, so that for systematic, safe journeys to be made across open bodies of water, a maritime technology of some sort has to be developed. The Tasmanians, simple though their material culture was, proved to be no exception. Tasmanian watercraft have previously been ably discussed by Ling Roth (1899:154-9), Meston (1936), Macintosh (1949), Hiatt (1968:213-14) and Völger (1972:167-71).

Simple rafts

A variety of *ad hoc* floats were sometimes used either to sit on, or more commonly as an aid in swimming. For this purpose logs, driftwood, or bundles of bark were used (e.g. Meredith 1852 in Ling Roth 1899). Slightly more sophisticated rafts were also constructed by lashing two logs side by side with strips of grass, the navigator sitting on top (Robinson 9 April 1834:876-8). Obviously such a craft would break apart if any significant torque was applied to the bonding as in a choppy sea or bad weather (e.g. Robinson 11 May 1830:160) and they were only intended for such purposes as river crossings when the materials happened to be handy and when there was not enough time or need to build a more sophisticated craft.

Simple though they were, there would have been a severe shortage of raw materials from which to build these rafts, because most common Tasmanian timbers are in fact denser than water when green, e.g. *E. obliqua.* On the west coast, only the relatively uncommon Huon Pine and allied trees, or perhaps heavily leached and dried driftwood, would have been effective as floats. All logs would have to be close to the water's edge and although these can be found at the mouths of some rivers, having been swept down stream after fires or land subsidence, the Tasmanians, with only hand-held stone tools, would have had negligible capacity for trimming tree trunks or large logs. There is no hint that they ever used fire or any other means either to fell trees or to hollow out logs to increase their bouyancy. To solve the problems presented by the environment and by the limitations of their own technology, the Tasmanians invented, or perhaps retained, a type of water craft which is unknown on the Australian mainland.[1]

Canoe rafts[2]

1. Construction and description

These rafts were made out of pieces of bark or sometimes of dry reeds. For the bark craft, the trees chosen were either Eucalyptus 'stringy barks', e.g. *E. obliqua* or 'paper bark' tea trees, especially *Melaleuca* spp. Tea trees are common on the west coast and in swampy areas generally. In regions such as Bruny Island, which is within the *Eucalyptus*-dominated, dry sclerophyll woodland zone (Jackson 1965), 'stringy barks' were used. The reeds included an edible variety (Robinson 27 June 1831:366), possibly bull-rushes, e.g. *Typha* or related plants. There are no accounts of Tasmanian Aborigines actually cutting sheets of bark off trees, nor of scars of such operations being seen on living trees; rather, loose pieces of bark were pulled off the trunk or picked up from the ground; both the 'stringy' and the 'paper' bark trees are particularly suitable for this, as their old bark is constantly curling away from, the trunk and hanging down in strips. Prior to construction of the raft, all hands were required to gather together the raw materials (Robinson 25 July 1831:389; 15 August 1831:400). The pieces of bark thus collected were short, 'some not above a foot in length which, when collected in a mass, are tied together with long grass' (Robinson 15 February 1830:119; see also 4 September 1832:653). These bundles of bark were made into long cylindrical sausage-shaped objects, tied together at both ends with a string made from inner bark or a long broad tough-leafed grass. The wall of the cylinder was held in place by a loose polygonal network of interlaced and knotted string.

Each vessel consisted of three such bundles laid parallel to each other; the longest one in the middle and the two side ones tied to it at both ends, forming a bulbous boat-shaped structure with a slightly hollow centre and upwardly curving stem and stern. Freycinet's excellent description (1816) of one of these craft from the d'Entrecasteaux channel, south-eastern Tasmania has been quoted before (e.g. Ling Roth 1899:155; Meston 1936:158-9), but it is worth repeating here;

> Three rolls of Eucalyptus bark formed the body. The principal roll or piece was 4 m. 55 cm. (14ft. 11in.) long by 1 m. (3ft. 3in.) broad, the two other pieces being only 3 m. 90 cm. (12ft. 9in.) long by 32 cm. (12½ in.) broad. These three bundles, which bore a fair resemblance to a ship's yards, were fastened together at their ends; this made them taper and formed the whole of the canoe. The scarfing was made fairly compact by means of a sort of grass or reed. So completed, the craft had the following dimensions: length inside, 2 m. 95 cm. (9ft. 8in.); outside breadth, 89 cm. (2ft. 11 in.); height, 65 cm. (1ft. 3½in.); depth inside, 22 cm. (8½in.); thickness at the ends, 27 cm. (10½in.).

Rossel's (1808 in Ling Roth 1899:155) vessel was slightly shorter but broader than Freycinet's, being 7 to 9 feet (2 m. 13 cm. to 2 m. 74 cm.) long and some 3 to 4 feet (91 cm. to 1 m. 22 cm.) wide in the middle; and one of the ones that Robinson saw was 10 feet long (3 m. 5 cm.) (24 March 1830:136). These descriptions are confirmed by other maritime explorers such as Labillardière and Péron, and from early colonial observers such as Collins (in Knopwood 21 June 1804), Kelly (Bowden 1964) Gunn (in West 1852: Vol. 2:76-7), Backhouse (1843:58), McKay (in Calder 1874:22-3), Meredith (1852:139) and Roberts (in Bonwick 1870:51).

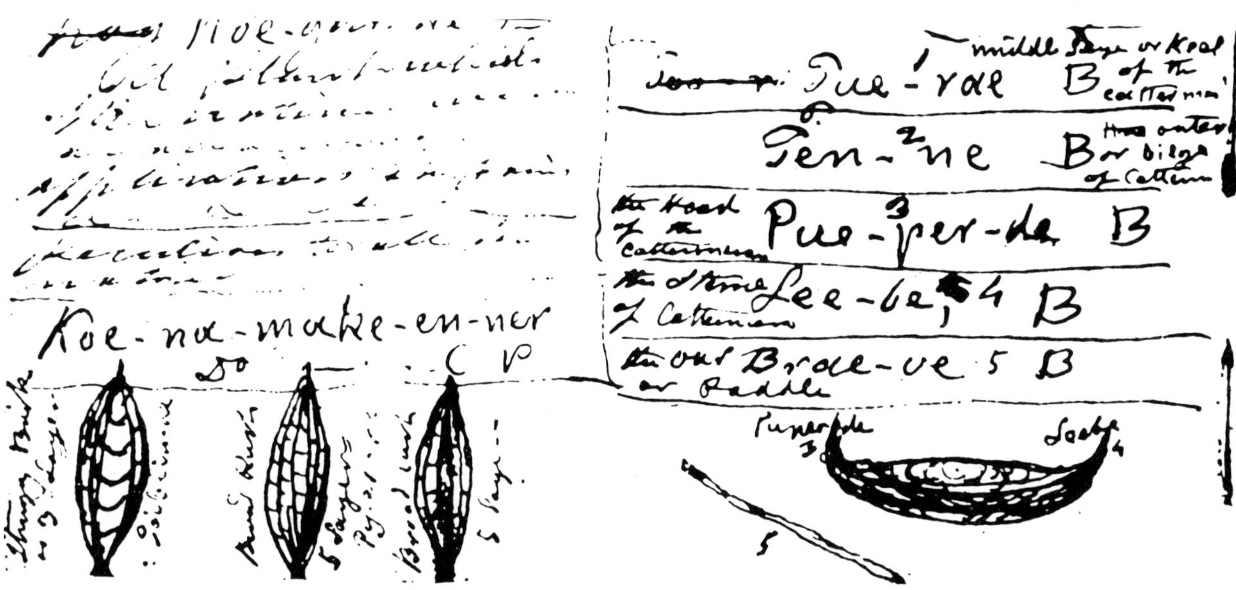

Figure 2. Robinson's sketches of various types of canoe-rafts; and Aboriginal nomenclature (by permission of the Mitchell Library, Sydney, and N.J.B. Plomley).

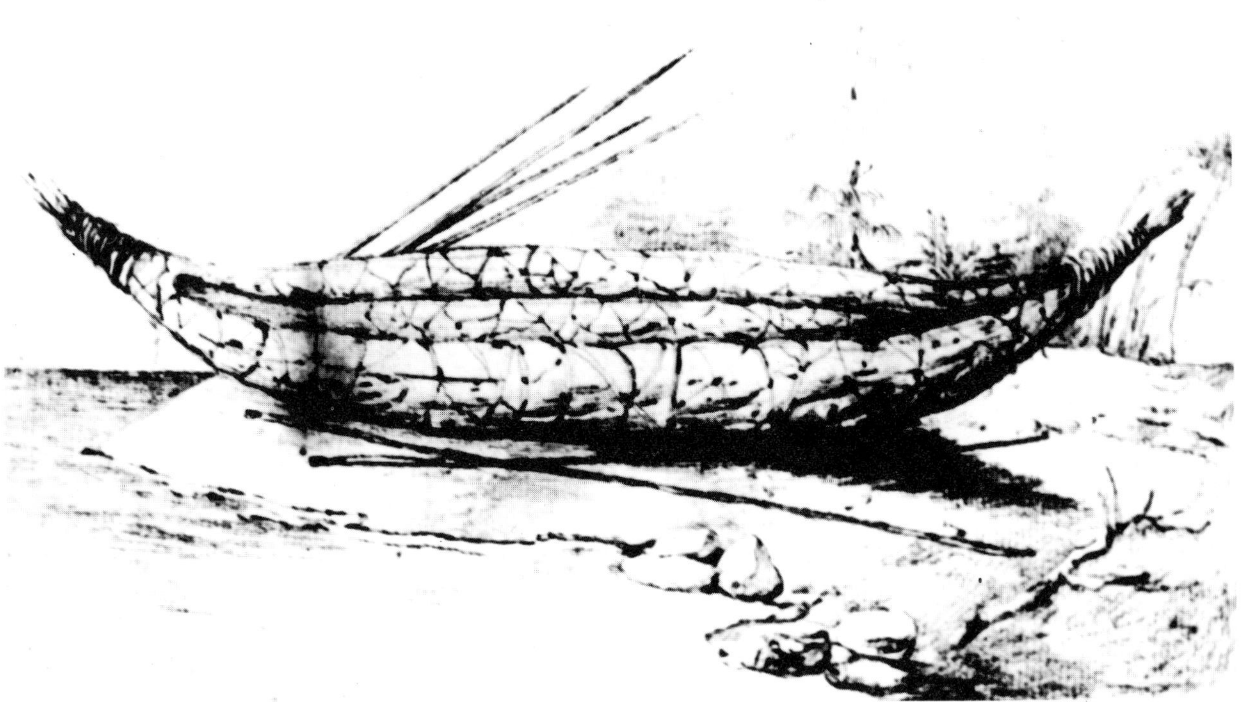

Figure 3. Field sketch, probably by N.M. Petit, of a Tasmanian canoe-raft, 1802. Redrawn by C.A. Lesueur (Lesueur & Petit 1807/11: PC.10) and reproduced by permission of M.A. Maury, Director, Museum d'Histoire Naturelle, Le Havre.

Figure 4. Tasmanian canoe-raft, drawn by Piron (Labillardiere 1800: Pl. 46, opp. p.81 in English edition).

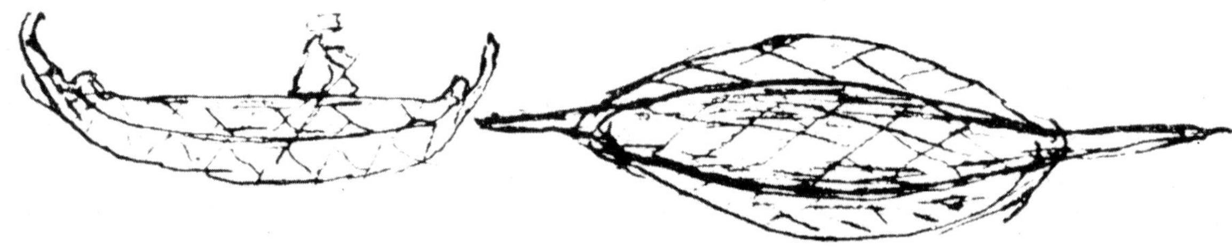

Figure 5. Robinson's sketch of a Tasmanian canoe-raft, 15 Feb. 1830 (see Plomley 1966:199 and Pl. 2A) by permission of the Mitchell Library, Sydney, and N.J.B. Plomley.

This evidence is discussed by Ling Roth (1899:154-9) and Meston (1936) and additional evidence from Robinson has recently been made available.

Bundles of dry reeds or rushes were also used for the cylindrical floats (Freycinet 1816; Robinson 25-27 June 1831:366). Robinson, describing one being built, comments that reed vessels consisted of five bundles tied together instead of the three for bark ones, and he illustrates his point with a tiny sketch reproduced here (Fig. 2) after Plomley (1966:367). The total time taken to manufacture these craft, either from bark or from reeds, ranged from a little over a day, to two or 'several' in one day, the average, according to Robinson's notes, being a large proportion of one day. Woorrady, the Bruny Islander, was particularly skilled at making them and once the raw materials had been gathered together, he usually worked on his own. On one occasion, he was aided by his wife and another woman (Robinson 15 August 1831:400).

In addition to the published descriptions, we are also fortunate in having several illustrations of canoe-rafts, which are totally consistent with the other evidence. The most detailed drawing, by the scientific artists N.M. Petit and C.A. Lesueur, who accompanied Péron on the Baudin expedition, is probably a representation of the same vessel described by Freycinet. This superb engraving (Lesueur & Petit, 1807-11; Atlas no. XIV) shows two canoes, one on shore in the foreground and the other afloat with two men in it. It is a composite picture, made up of several separate scenic and ethnographic elements, but inspection of photographs in the Mitchell Library, Sydney, of drafting sketches and alternative compositions held by the Museum of Natural History in Le Havre, shows the structural details of the canoe-raft unaltered. One of Petit's pencil drawings is reproduced here as Fig. 3 (Hamy 1891:610; sketch no.17; Le Havre no.17H; Mitchell Library Mss. 760/1 17H. Other relevant sketches are 18H; 19H; 20H; 129H; 130H; in the same file, see also Hamy 1891:610, 619; Mander-Jones n.d.; and Marchant, 1969). Labillardière's artist Piron (1800: Plate 46, opposite p. 81) has a less elegant but still detailed picture of a canoe (reproduced here as Fig. 4), and Robinson's simple but clear field sketches again confirm the shape and construction of these craft (reproduced here as Figs. 2 and 5, after Plomley 1966: Pl. 2A facing page 131; 367).

To complete the evidence, several models were made of Tasmanian water craft, some of which still survive. Three, now in the Pitt Rivers

Museum, Oxford, were obtained in 1843 by Sir John Franklin when he was Governor of Tasmania, and three others are in the Tasmanian Museum, Hobart (Ling Roth 1899: 153, 156-7; Plomley 1962:11). Another model now in the British Museum (Reg. no. 51. 11-22.5), was taken to the Great Exhibition of 1851 by J. Milligan, Secretary of the Royal Society of Tasmania (Ling Roth 1899:157; Plomley 1962:11). This latter,[3] 75 cms. long and 14.5 broad, consists of three bundles of paper bark pieces (probably *Melaleuca* sp.), each bundle being bound with a polygonal network of split and rolled tough grass string. The inner bundle seems to have been bound first, then its network used as the base for the attachment of the others. Each 'horn' where the three bundles meet, is covered by a cap, consisting of tapered sheets of bark, bound with string in a tight helical or tubular fashion. It is likely that these models were manufactured by, or with the aid of, surviving Tasmanians, and are fairly accurate representations. In details of construction they correspond well with the written descriptions and drawings of full-sized craft.

Fires were often carried on raised beds of clay in the body of the craft (Freycinet 1816; see Meston 1936:159). This was essential for long journeys, as the Tasmanians seemed not to have been able to make fire (see Plomley 1962:11-12; 1966:225, n. 5; Hiatt 1968:211), and during their travels they transported it in smouldering fire-sticks or in beds of glowing cinders in their canoe-rafts.

2. *Aboriginal nomenclature*

From Robinson we have some Aboriginal words from the 'Bruny Island' or another south-eastern language for these craft and for various parts of them. His transcriptions were linguistically naive and must be treated with caution, yet they do give us an insight into how the Aborigines themselves saw their own artefacts (15 February 1830:119; 25 March 1830:136; 14 October 1830:249; 27 June 1831, see figure reproduced Plomley 1966:367).

Of interest here is that the Aborigines clearly distinguished between the different types of craft and between the various components that went into their making. *Ning.her* is also recorded as being the southern Tasmanian word for the swamp or paperbark tea tree (Robinson 15 February 1830:119) and it could be that the same term was used both for the artefact and for the raw material or plant supplying it. In Roberts' vocabulary (Ling Roth 1899:XVI), the word for stringy bark is *toilena*, and there may have been a similar relationship between the words for a stringy bark canoe raft and its raw material. So also Milligan's south-eastern Bruny word *poi.erinna* for *Typha* bullrush (1866) and the term for the reed bundle craft. A parallel example comes from the Gidjingali of northern Arnhem Land who have the same word *ngumula* for a rigid walled bark canoe and for the tree *E. tetradonta* which usually provided the raw material for it (B. Meehan and R. Jones pers. obs. 1973); as for instance in the English language, we also talk of a *tin* of jam or a *glass* of beer.

Canoe Raft

General term, or one made from paperbark	Three-bundled stringy bark type	Five-bundled reed type
NING.HER	TOIL.LIN.NE	PY.ER.RE
Bark bundles		Long grass for tying bundles
Middle or keel	Outer or bilge	
TUE.RAE	TEN.NE	LEM.MEN.NE
Bow	Stern	Propelling stick
PUE.PER.DE	LEE.BE	BRAE.VE

Separate words for bow and stern implies that the craft were built so as to move through the water in one direction. This is not obvious from the ethnographic descriptions, yet there may have been subtle features of design or positioning of the crew or fireplace to facilitate this.

3. *Performance*

Basically these craft were rafts, their buoyancy depending on the displacement of water by an equal volume of lighter material. The careful caulking and packing of the outer surface of the bundles would have helped to trap small air bubbles within the fabric, but I doubt if this could have been done tight enough to make the central well of the craft waterproof. I think that the main function of the side bundles was to give it stability. With a crew sitting or standing upright, the centre of gravity would have been high above the centre of buoyancy, and a single cylindrical float would have been extremely unstable. Robinson is explicit on this point, saying the craft 'cannot sink from the buoyancy of the material; and the way in which they are constructed prevents them from upsetting' (15 February 1830:119). Throughout his travels, Robinson recorded only one occasion when an upset occurred, and only luggage was being carried at the time.

The speed and manoeuvrability of these craft, however, depended on their streamlined canoe-like shape. The high upturned stem and stern facilitated riding in surf or rough water, and seems to have been an essential design feature of all small rough-water craft.

For propulsion, long poles were sometimes used. According to Freycinet (1816 in Ling Roth 1899:155) these poles ranged in length from 2.5 m. (8 feet) to 4 or 5 m. (13-16 feet) and were about 2 to 5 cm. (3/4 to 2 inches) thick, with no suggestion of any flattening or other paddle-like features. Sometimes, in shallow water, these poles were used as punt poles to push against the river or sea bottom (Freycinet 1816. in Ling Roth 1899:155). More commonly, they were used in the way described by Robinson (9 April 1834:878) where Woorrady 'having seated himself cross-legged . . . plied himself across by means of a stick which he grasped with both hands in the centre and made alternate strokes first on one and then on the other side. This is the general mode adopted by all of them, sitting with their face to the object they are making for' (see also Lesueur and Petit 1807/11 Atlas no. XIV). Freycinet says that small bundles of grass were used to sit on, though sometimes people stood up. Although nowhere explicitly stated in the literature, the long poles would also have been useful in maintaining the balance of the canoeist.

On other occasions, people swam, holding on to the craft with one hand and paddling with the other. This method was used for short trips, especially in crossing heads of bays or rivers (Backhouse 1843:58). The swimmers were usually women, whereas on the rafts were 'their husbands, children and raiment and things' (Robinson 9 April 1834:878). Four women helped Robinson across the mouth of the Giblin River on the west coast. The water was rough and they were careful not to allow the craft to overturn 'if a surge came on one side, they would bear on the other side to keep it steady' (26 March 1830:138). On another occasion, Robinson has a sketch of his being ferried over the Arthur River on a clumsy, European built wooden raft by two Tasmanian women (see Plomley 1966:Pl.3B; 10 June 1830:171). On board were three men, a dog and six knapsacks. It is interesting that the Tasmanian man Woorrady '*paddled*' (my italics) this raft back to the other side and brought the rest of the party over. In a later Arthur River crossing alluded to above, when a party of twenty Aborigines were crossing, Woorrady and the other men either paddled themselves across, or were ferried by women, the women themselves swimming in the water holding on to the floats (9 April 1834:878).

In the literature, it is almost always the women who propelled the craft by swimming and the men who paddled or punted. This sexual division of labour was consistent with other economic activities, the long poles, like spears, being manly artefacts, and swimming, either for food collecting or for transport, being a female speciality.

4. Carrying capacity

Often, the canoe-rafts were made for one person only (see Table 1). This was especially so for river crossings, for example the Arthur and Pieman Rivers on the west coast (Robinson 4 September 1832:652, 1 September 1833:788). A craft made for Robinson's use was so small that he had to dangle his legs over the edge (26 March 1830:138). For some sea voyages also, one-man craft were used, for example by Mangerner, Woorrady's father-in-law, when he sailed from Bruny Island to Oyster Cove on the adjacent mainland in south-eastern Tasmania (28 September 1829:78).

Other craft however, were big enough to carry several people, and the data have been presented in Table 1. Freycinet said that the craft described by him was capable of holding 5 or 6 people, though the usual number was 3 or 4. This range from a normal 3 up to about 7 passengers is confirmed by Knopwood, Gunn, Roberts, Backhouse and Robinson (see Table 1). One day, Woorrady described to Robinson the exploits of his own and neighbouring peoples in going to the islands off southern Tasmania in search of seal. He said that the canoe-rafts were large enough to carry 'seven or eight people,

Table 1 Pay Loads: ethnographic evidence

Pay Load		Reference
No. of People	*Approx. weight in lbs.*	
A. *One person*		
1	130	Robinson 28 September 1829:78
1		15 February 1830:119
1		4 September 1832:652
1		1 September 1833:788
B. *Several people*		
3-4	400-500	Backhouse 1843:58
4	500	Robinson 18 July 1831:381
4-6	500-800	Roberts (in Bonwick) 1870
4-7	500-900	Gunn (in West 1852, 2:76-7)
{5-6 / 3-4} usual number	650-800	Freycinet (1816; see Ling Roth 1899:155)
6	800	Collins in Knopwood 21 June 1804
7-8 plus dogs and spears	900-1000	Woorrady in Robinson 15 July 1831:379
C. *Baggage*		
European clothes		Robinson 1 September 1833:788
3 hundredweight of luggage	350	15 September 1831:400

their dogs and spears. The men sit in front and the women behind' (15 July 1831:379). Records of baggage carried in canoe-rafts range from a Tasmanian woman's European clothes placed on a raft to keep dry, to 3 cwt. of Robinson's expedition equipment (15 August 1831:400, 1 September 1833:788).

Translating these loads into weights, let us assume that an average Tasmanian man weighed about 9 to 10 stone (approx. 130 lb.) (Ling Roth 1899:8-9); then the loads carried by the larger craft ranged from about 400 lb. up to 800 or 1000 lb. as shown in Table 1.

These are impressive loads – are they in fact possible? Assuming flat oval cross-sections for the bundles and taking into account the pronounced tapers at the end, I have calculated that the volume of the craft described by Freycinet was of the order of 30 cubic feet and that of Rossel's 20 cubic feet (Table 2). Mr C. Turner of Burnie very kindly carried out some experiments on the density and 'seepage rates' of small bundles of stringy bark (*E. obliqua*) and of paperbark (*Melaleuca ericifolia*) under laboratory conditions, the results of which are shown in Table 3. Obviously, while care must be exercised in extrapolating from these to a full-sized craft, the data allow us to make an educated guess as to the weight and carrying capacity of the latter.[4] Had Freycinet's craft been made of shredded *E. obliqua* bark with a packing density of 26 lb. per cubic foot, it would have weighed about 800 lb., and Rossel's 500 lb. Using the lighter paperbark at 17.5 lb. per cubic foot, they would have weighed 550 and 350 lb. respectively (Table 2). This must have been the correct order of weight of these craft, because a small, poorly constructed one sufficient for only one person, built near Port Davey, had to be carried a distance of a mile to the water and required four men, one at each corner to do so (Robinson 15 February 1830:119).

When a craft floated, there would have been some seepage of water into the fabric of the bundles but, conversely, small air pockets would also have been trapped for a while. Taking Freycinet's craft first, assuming under a 'light' load that it settled so that half its volume was submerged, a stringy-bark one would have carried only one man (Table 2), but a paperbark one could have carried about three. Under a 'heavy' load where two-thirds of the volume was submerged, a paperbark craft could have carried up to five or six men. Equivalent calculations for Rossel's craft are also shown in Table 2, showing a maximum load of about four men. Crude though they are, these calculations accord extre-

Table 2 Pay load calculations

Craft	Volume (cu. ft.)	Weight: Stringy bark (lb.)	Weight: Paperbark (lb.)	Light Load x ½ Submerged: Weight of displaced water (lb.)	Light Load x ½ Submerged: Pay load (lb.) Stringy bark	Light Load x ½ Submerged: Pay load (lb.) Paperbark	Heavy Load x 2/3 submerged: Weight of displaced water (lb.)	Heavy Load x 2/3 submerged: Pay load (lb.) Stringy bark	Heavy Load x 2/3 submerged: Pay load (lb.) Paperbark
Freycinet's	30	780	530	940	160	410	1250	470	720
Rossel's	20	520	350	630	110	280	840	320	490

merly well with the eye-witness accounts (Table 1), and give us confidence that we have a reasonable understanding of the structure and carrying capacity of these craft.

5. Range

The major limitation of these bark-bundle craft is that sooner or later, water seeps into the structure of the fibre, so that it becomes waterlogged and so no longer boyant. Again, Turner's experiments are most illuminating (see Table 3). He found that his standard bundle made from *E. obliqua* bark sank after only 30 minutes floating on fresh water, and that the addition of a load equivalent to two-thirds of its weight (10g.) caused it to sink after only three minutes, hardly propitious facts for a would-be mariner! A bigger bundle would probably take longer to sink simply because of its geometry, having a smaller surface area and hence diffusion rate per unit volume. Nevertheless, it is obvious that *Eucalyptus* bark craft would have been limited to river crossings or only the shortest island jumps – a journey of anything over a mile might have been inviting trouble.

The performance of the paperbark was distinctly better, the bundle itself being almost awash but still afloat after 50 hours, and even with the addition of the equivalent of its own weight, was just buoyant after 48 hours. Clearly a craft made from this material might be expected to remain afloat for two days or so, even with a load. However, another factor that must be considered is that as water is absorbed into the bark fibre, the latter becomes soggy and loses its rigidity. Insertion of longitudinal wooden formers inside the bundles would reinforce against this tendency, but there is no record of the Tasmanians ever doing this. Taking these factors into consideration, I would guess that a well constructed paperbark craft under a medium load could retain its sea-going characteristics without significant impairment for a period of several, say up to six, hours. After that the craft would steadily become less manoeuvrable and more waterlogged, although it might be expected to float as a semi-submerged mass of wet bark for a period of up to two days or more if the seas did not break it up. Naturally, during the second phase, any passenger would be at the mercy of currents, incapable of making significant headway againt the water. Gunn's assessment (West 1852:II, 76-7) that the canoe-raft seen by him on Maria Island would have been sufficiently strong 'to drift for 16 or 20 miles' is consistent with this conclusion. There are no data on Tasmanian reed craft.

As to the question of a speed, there are almost no worthwhile ethnographic data. Bonwick (1870:51) quotes the reminiscences of an European settler that the bigger craft holding four to six paddlers could travel 'as quickly as an English whaleboat. At each stroke, the rowers utter(ing) a loud "Ugh" like a London pavior'. However this account was given several decades after the event, and also mentions the use of bark paddles, which may have been an embellishment of the informant's memory as they are mentioned by no other author. A crude calculation based on the Principle of Conservation of Momentum and using the parameters of the craft and paddle-pole described by Freycinet, shows that two men, paddling at two strokes per second, could hardly do better than propel their craft forward one foot per second, or approximately half a knot, even ignoring the factors of friction and turbulence. This is likely to have been the upper limit of the speed of these craft in windless conditions. Standing high out of the water, they would of course be susceptible to being blown along by the wind. The experienced sailors, Labillardière and Freycinet, both thought that the craft which they saw would have been highly vulnerable in rough seas and most accounts state that the Aborigines carried

Table 3 Turner's experiments on the density and seepage of bark bundles

Bark	*Eucalyptus obliqua*	*Melaleuca ericifolia*
Common names	*Brown top stringy bark (Mesmate)*	*Swamp paperbark*
Basic density[1]		
(lb o.d./ft^3 wet volume)	31	Ca. 20
(g/cc wet volume)	0.5	0.32 (of cork – 0.22-0.26)
Bark bundle[2]		
Air dried wt. (g)	14.7	14.7
Equiv. oven dried wt. (g)	12.8	12.7
Packing density[3] (lb o.d./ft^3 bundle volume)	Ca. 26.5	Ca. 17.5
Time to sink[4]		
Bundle only	30 min	70% submerged after 50 hrs.
Bundle + 2.5g wt.	13 min	–
Bundle + 5g wt.	7 min	–
Bundle + 10g wt.	3 min	90% submerged after 48 hrs.
Bundle + 15g wt.	–	Just buoyant after 48 hrs.
Bundle + 20g wt.	–	Sank – 3 hrs. 20 min.
Bundle + 22g wt.	–	Just buoyant at 0 hr.

1. *Basic Density*

This is a measurement usually applied to wood in which its significance is more readily seen. It is often quoted as airdried cut/unit volume. It assumes that the wood is in the fully swollen state but devoid of water. It has all sorts of uses in pulping technology.

Our bark measurements were made in the same way as for wood but some slight error may be involved in measurement of wet volume, since the surface area is relatively great compared with wood, so that surface water not removed by centrifuging or blotting may inflate the volume measurement. The results were surprisingly reproducible and the estimate is reliable to ±5%. The true values may be somewhat higher in the case of *E. obliqua* because of its more fibrous nature.

2. *Bundle measurements*

Apart from weight measurements, the rest of the data can be only approximate.

3. *Packing density*

This depends on the way you pack, obviously. The value for paperbark is fairly reproducible. *E. obliqua* is much higher when care is taken not to fiberize.

4. *Times to sink*

These experiments were carried out in fresh water. (cf. sea-water at S.G. about 1.026). The bundles were loaded with weights hanging from fine wire.

No account is taken of the air held between the layers of bark – except that the bundles were pushed under occasionally, and some air escaped.

Sinking time for *E. obliqua* was not lengthened very much for bundles not teased out.

(Data supplied by C.H. Turner, Associated Pulp and Paper Manufacturers, Burnie, Tasmania) out their open-water crossings in fine weather, with suitable combinations of wind and tide (Robinson 24 March 1830:136).

To sum up this section on range, it is clear that canoe-rafts made purely from *Eucalyptus* bark would have had a severely limited range, say less than a mile. The *Melaleuca* paperbark, and probably also the reed ones, would have had much better performances, being capable of open-sea voyages of several hours' duration in reasonable conditions, giving them perhaps a range of 5 to 10 miles or even more, before they became seriously waterlogged. However the factors of tide, wind and waves would have been crucial. The penalty for error or bad luck would have been severe, as the crafts had limited or nil capability of making headway against adverse wind or tide conditions, and progressively after a few hours, their fabric would start to disintergrate. There are several stories of Aborigines drowned or lost at sea during their various expeditions especially in southern Tasmania (Robinson 21 September 1829:76, 15 July 1831:379). Obviously, experiment with full-sized craft would be most illuminating.

Distribution of Tasmanian watercraft

The distribution of Tasmanian canoe-rafts is shown on Fig. 6, from ethnographic observations tabulated in Table 4. As can be seen, there was a marked disconformity of distribution. Canoe-rafts were made and used all along the west coast from the Hunter Island Group to South Cape, along the shores and islands of Storm Bay in the south, and up to Oyster Bay on the mid-east coast.

In contrast to this, there were no observations of watercraft of any description made by the indigenous inhabitants of the north-east and northern coasts, nor those of the river and lagoon systems in the Midland Valley. This

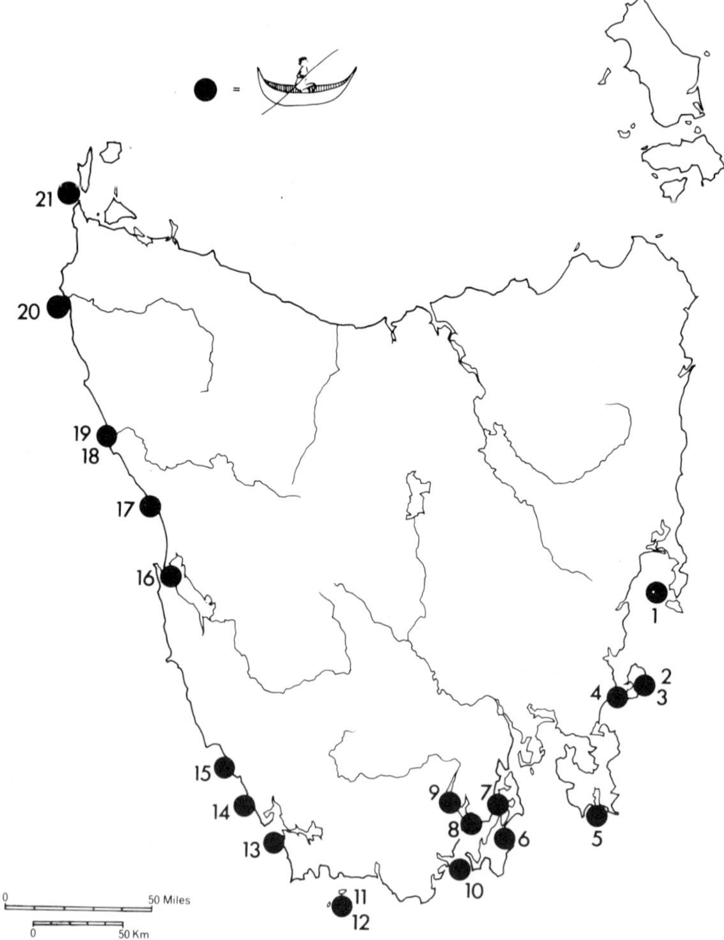

Figure 6. Distribution of canoe-rafts

Table 4 Distribution of canoe-rafts. I have excluded those occasions when Aborigines made canoe-rafts outside their own country at Robinson's special request or command during one of his expeditions

Number on map Fig. 6	*Location*	*Reference*
1	Schouten Island	Cotton in Walker (see Ling Roth 1899:158)
2	Maria Island	Freycinet 1816 (see Ling Roth 1899:155)
3	Maria Island	Gunn in West 1852, *2*:76-7
4	Maria Island/Oyster Bay	Meredith 1852:139
5	Tasman Peninsula	Robinson in Plomley 1966:1004 nt. k.
6	Adventure Bay, Bruny Island	Labillardière 1800, *2*:80
7	Bruny Island	Robinson 28 September 1829:78
8	Huon River/Recherche Bay	Robinson 21 September 1829:76
9	Huon River	Collins in Knopwood 21 June 1804
10	D'Entrecasteaux Channel	Freycinet 1816 (See Ling Roth 1899:155)
11	De Witt Island	Roberts in Bonwick 1870
12	De Witt/Maatsuyker Island	Robinson 15 July 1831:379
13	Port Davey	Robinson 15 February 1830:119
14	Green Island	Robinson 24 March 1830:136
15	Giblin River	Robinson 26 March 1830:138
16	Macquarie Harbour Heads	Backhouse 1843:58
17	Little Henty River	Robinson 11 May 1830:160
18	Pieman River	Jorgenson and Lorymer (in Meston 1936)
19	Pieman River	Robinson 1 September 1833:788
20	Arthur River	e.g. Robinson 4 September 1832:652; 9 April 1834:878
21	Hunter/Trefoil Island	Robinson 13 August 1832:641

absence is explicitly stressed by Robinson who stated that, in north-eastern Tasmania, 'none of the natives on this side of the island know how to construct a catamaran' (25 July 1831:389), thus confirming the earlier suppositions and experience of Flinders, Bass and Kelly.

There is no ecological reason for this, there being both the raw materials for the manufacture of craft, and a potential need for their use in northern Tasmania (e.g. Robinson 14 October 1830:249; 27 June 1831:366; 8 July 1834:897). We must look for a cultural explanation, and one is suggested by comparing the distribution of watercraft (Fig. 6) with the location of tribal territories, the data for the latter being taken from Jones (1971a, 1971b, 1974). Of the maritime tribes, the Western, South-eastern and Oyster Bay tribes used watercraft, whereas the North-eastern, North Midlands and Northern tribes did not. Small though the Tasmanian population was, consisting of only 3,000 to 5,000 people (Jones 1971a:281), there was considerable cultural diversity across the island in terms of language, artefacts and the programming and location of economic activities. Watercraft was only one of several artefacts whose distribution or type seems to have been associated with tribes, or groups of related tribes, the others being houses, mortuary artefacts, rock art, personal decorations, stone tools and, in a prehistoric phase, bone tools (Hiatt 1968, 1970; Lourandos 1970; Jones 1971b; Völger 1972:244-6). There was no clear-cut division of tribes, rather for each trait there was a slightly different configuration, so that the total picture can only be built up by superimposing each distribution to form a complex mosaic. Robinson was surely being naïve in ordering the destruction of all watercraft made by his southern Tasmanian companions in the north-east, so as to deny the inhabitants of the latter region 'the opportunity of learning' (25 July 1831:389). Although the north-east and midlands peoples were generally hostile to their southern and western neighbours, there were many occasions during an annual cycle when members of the two sets of groups would have met, or observed each other either by accident or by design. In addition there was some intermarriage and temporary affiliation of people with neighbouring groups to facilitate the process of cultural diffusion (e.g. see Jones 1974). That this did not happen in the case of watercraft or with swimming ability, must be ascribed to the positive forces of *cultural prohibition* rather than to the negative factors of ignorance or lack of opportunity. Here lies the explanation for the first part of Flinders' conundrum.

The use of watercraft

The southern and western tribes used their watercraft for two main purposes, firstly to cross rivers and secondly to get to offshore islands.

Rivers

Along the west coast, the habitable zone was narrow and had partly to be maintained open by fire (Hiatt 1968:194; Jones 1968:205-10). Inland, the topography is rugged with dense rain forests, so that the main, or in some places the only, practicable route for travel lay close to the sea shore. The major Aboriginal 'road' of the island ran along this coast for 250 miles from Recherche Bay in the south up to West Point or Cape Grim in the north, and Robinson travelled up and down it several times. The large rivers were major obstacles, especially as they had to be crossed at their mouths, and were usually not fordable. It was here that watercraft were systematically built and used, some of the major crossings being shown on Fig. 7. Large inlets

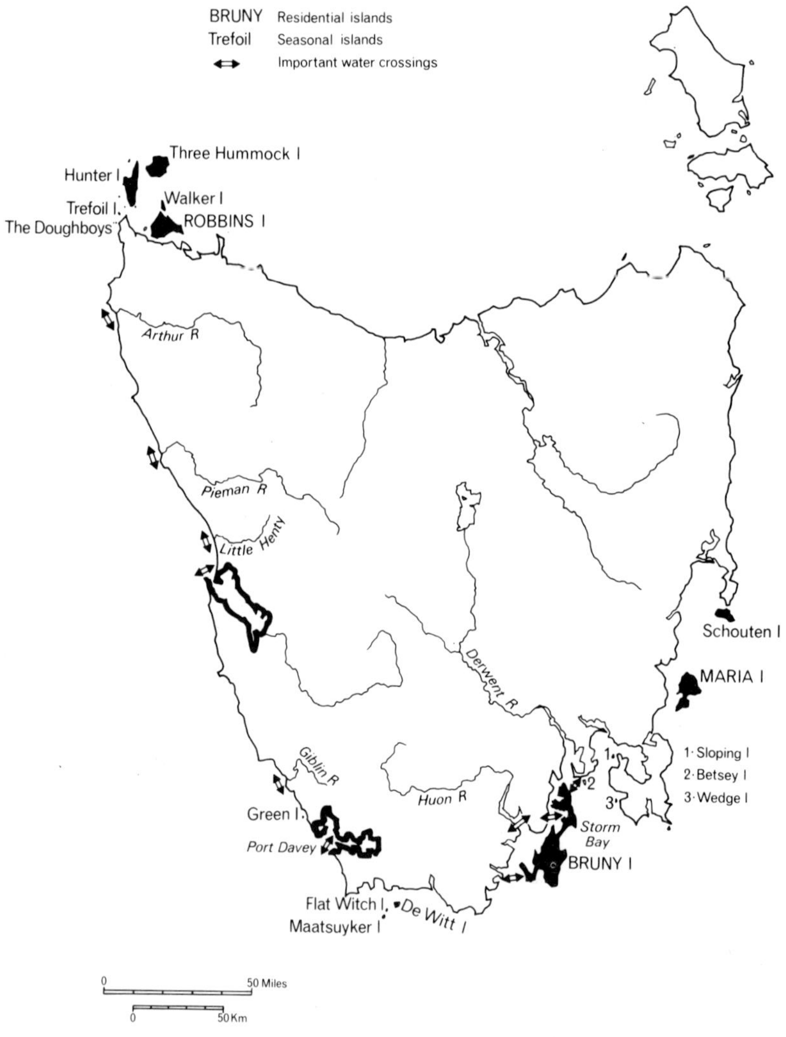

Figure 7. Occupied islands; ethnographic data.

presented similar problems, and watercraft were again used to cross the heads or various arms of Macquarie Harbour and Port Davey (Fig. 7). Each west coast band travelled along substantial proportions of this coastal 'road' in its seasonal cycle, and might be expected to have made at least ten to twenty major crossings per year. There were about ten of these bands, and remembering that several craft would have been used per crossing, we can see that several hundred tons of suitable raw materials would have been used every year to support the system. Carried out year after year, this would seriously have depleted the conveniently available resources, so it was common practice to beach the crafts at the landings for re-use or 'cannibalization' on some future occasion (e.g. Robinson 24 March 1830:136, 9 April 1834:876).

In the more sheltered south-east coast, canoe-rafts were used to travel along and across the Huon and probably the Derwent estuaries and to cross various arms of the greatly indented Storm Bay (Knopwood 21 June 1804; Robinson 25 March 1833:710).

Offshore islands

The Aborigines also visited many of the offshore islands around the Tasmanian coast, the evidence being presented in Table 5 and Figs. 7 and 8. No systematic archaeological work has yet been done on them,[5] but despite this, on every island reported ethnographically to have been visited, numerous archaeological remains have also been found. These consist of shell middens, occupied caves, rock shelters, stone tools, art sites and burials, for which many references can

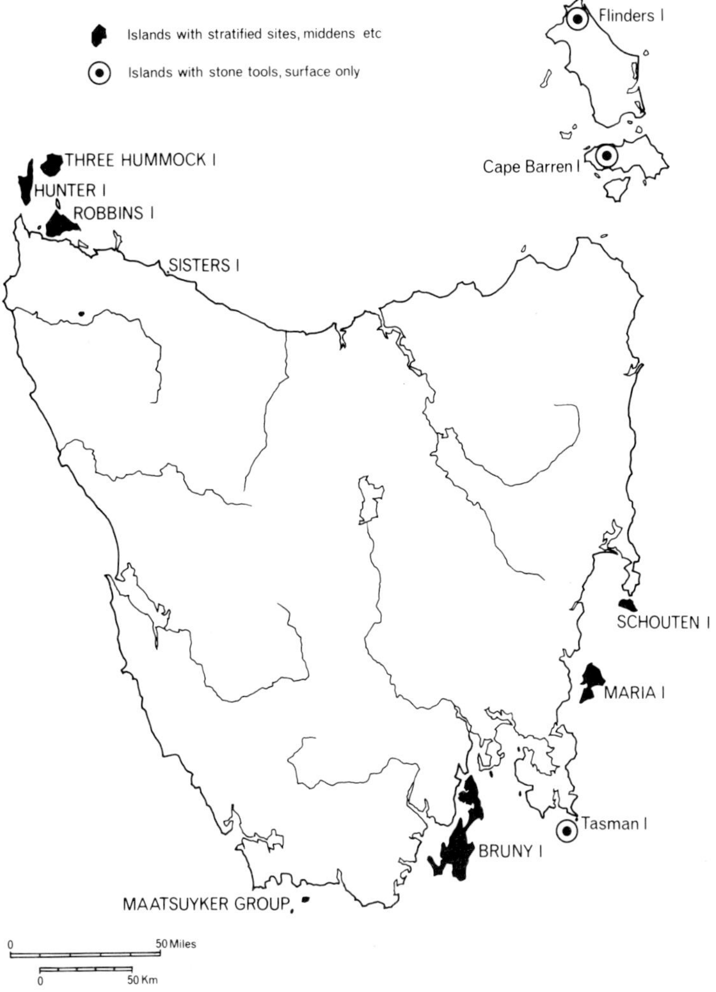

Figure 8. Occupied islands; archaeological data.

Table 5 Close offshore islands

Island	*Group*	*Region*	*Ethnographic accounts of visits*	*Archaeological evidence*	*Minimum sea crossing miles*	*Nature of crossings*	*Special reasons for visits*	*Approximate area square miles*	*Approximate length of coastline miles*
Hunter		N.W.	Yes	Middens, cave	3½	Strong tidal rips etc.	Mutton birds, seals	28	35
Three Hummocks		N.W.	Yes	Middens, rock carving	2½ (from Hunter) 7 (from Walker)	Tides	Mutton birds	25	28
Robbins	HUNTER	N.W.	Yes	Middens, rock shelters	1	Mud flats etc. Sheltered	*Residential Island*	40 } 43	35 } 40
Walker		N.W.	Yes	?	⅛ from Robbins	Sheltered, can wade		3	5
Trefoil		N.W.	Yes	?	1½	Exposed to ocean swell	Mutton birds	<½	3
The Doughboys		N.W.	Yes	?	¼ to ½	Exposed to ocean swell and tides	Mutton birds	<¼	–
Sisters'		N/N.W.	No	Middens	½	Sheltered	?	<¼	–
Green		S.W.	Yes	?	½	Exposed to swell	–	<¼	–
Maatsuyker		S.W.	Yes	Middens	6½ (from mainland Red Point). 8 (from mainland Cox Bluff). 4½ (from De Witt Isle). 1 (from Flat Witch Isle)	Exposed to ocean swells and storms: dangerous	Seals	¾	3
De Witt	MAATSUYKER	S.W.	Yes	Middens	4 from mainland	Exposed to ocean swells and storms: dangerous	Seals	2½	7
Flat Witch		S.W.	?	?	5 from mainland, 3½ from De Witt	Exposed to ocean swells and storms: dangerous	?	½	2
Bruny		S.E.	Yes	Numerous middens. C14 date 6,000 BP (Reber 1965)	1 from Dennes Pt. 1½ from Ninepin Pt. 3½ from Burnett Pt. 3 from South Arm.	Sheltered	*Residential Island*	140	175
Small islands in Storm Bay e.g. Betsey; Sloping and Wedge	STORM BAY	S.E.	Yes	Middens	Approx. 1	Sheltered	?	<½ each	–
Tasman		S.E.	No	Stone tools, skull	½; but nearest practical landing; 6 miles.	Exposed to ocean swell	?	<¼	–
Maria	OYSTER BAY	E.	Yes	Numerous middens	2½	Sheltered	*Residential Island*	36	50
Schouten		E.	Yes	Middens, stone tools	1	Fairly sheltered	Part of estate of a band	10	18
Swan		N.E.	No	Nil	2	Sheltered, strong tides	–	1	4
Waterhouse	N.E.	N.E.	No	Nil	2	Sheltered, tides	–	1½	5
Small island in Tamar mouth		N.E.	No	?	½	Sheltered	–	<½	–
Total approximately								290	370

be supplied: Robinson (e.g. 19 October 1832:671), Meston (1936), Crowther (1950), Clarke (1898, see Plomley 1969:54), Reber (1965 and pers. comm.), Lourandos (1968 and pers. comm.), Sutherland (1972), F. Ellis (pers. comm.), C. Turner and P. Sims (pers. comm.), J. Thwaites (pers. comm.), Tasmanian Museum archives and my own field files.

Conversely, where the ethnography suggests or explicitly states that the islands were not occupied, there is an absence of archaeological sites, the only finds being a few surface stone tools on some, the significance of which will be discussed later. Thus the ethnographic and archaeological evidences are in excellent accord, and both support the picture given by the distribution of watercraft, that where suitable islands are located in the north-west, the south and the south-east, they were regularly visited, whereas those in the north-east were not, despite the fact that some of the latter, for example Waterhouse and Swan, are only two miles from the shore.

Confining the discussion to the occupied

islands, it can be seen from Table 4 that the minimum sea distances to be travelled ranged from a few hundred yards up to about five miles, with most of the larger islands requiring a voyage of between two and three miles. These figures do not give the entire picture, for to get to Maatsuyker one could choose a route via De Witt and Flat Witch Islands, which would involve a minimum single sea voyage of only four and a half miles, yet the total distance would add up to eight miles, the minimum direct voyage from the mainland being six and a half miles. A similar situation would have pertained in getting to Three Hummock Island via either Hunter or Walker and Robbins Islands. Conversely, Tasman Island is only half a mile from Cape Pillar, yet the cliffs are so precipitous that the closest feasible embarkation point is some six miles from it (Meston 1936:157).

Variable also are conditions such as currents, swell and exposure to weather. The water between the mainland and Bruny or Maria Islands is sheltered and usually calm; on the other hand there are the dangers of the crossings to the islands of the Hunter Group, which have already been alluded to above. The seas around the Maatsuyker Group take the full brunt of the southerly gales and are dangerous even for modern craft. The voyages to these islands must rank high in the maritime achievements of any hunting and gathering society, and they mark the most southerly penetration of prehistoric man in Australia.

The motives for going to all these islands varied. Some islands are small, often being little larger than rocks (Table 5), but they supported

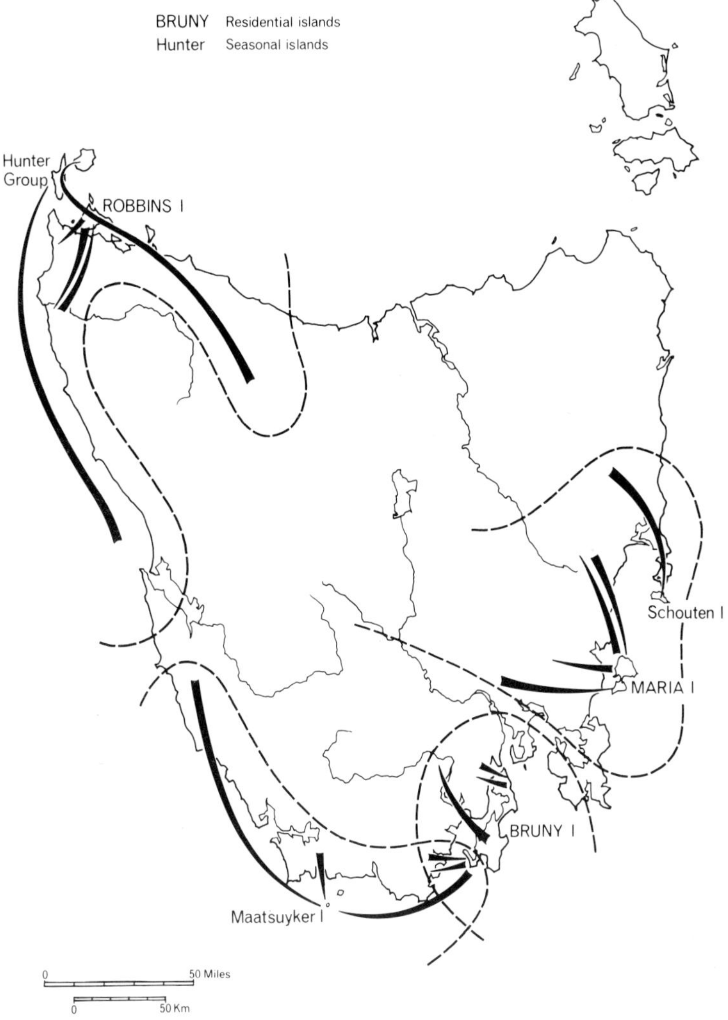

Figure 9. Regional role of offshore islands.

extremely rich food resources, usually seasonally abundant. The most important were mutton birds (*Puffinus tenuirostris*) which nested in vast numbers during summer; fur-seals and southern elephant seals which formed breeding colonies on various islands again during summer; sea birds of various species including gulls, cormorants, penguins and perhaps albatrosses which foraged and nested on rocks and islets; together with the other rocky-coast sea foods such as shellfish and crayfish. It was for mutton bird chicks and shells for necklaces that the Aborigines went to the Hunter Group, as some of their descendants still do today; and the southern bands braved the dangers of Maatsuyker and Eddystone for seal, a prize worth the penalty which many paid (Robinson 19 June 1830:178; 14 October 1832:669; 15 July 1831:379; 15 December 1831:554). Although food on some of these islands was abundant during certain times of the year, the seasons were limited, and there is no record that they were inhabited by man for prolonged periods, nor that they were the permanent homes for anyone. These I shall call *seasonal islands.*

In three cases however, namely Robbins, Bruny and Maria, each island itself formed the territory of a named land-owning local group or band (Plomley 1966:968-76; Jones 1971a). These I shall call *residential islands* and they are shown in Table 5 and Fig. 9. It is possible that Schouten was also part of the territory of a band together with the adjacent Freycinet Peninsula (Plomley 1966:975; Jones 1972). In these cases, the islands are providing not merely seasonally abundant delicacies, but the core of the subsistence, involving land as well as sea resources, vegetable food as well as meat and fat. These residential islands have many features in common. They are relatively big,[6] with Robbins at 40 square miles, Maria at 36 square miles, Bruny at 140 square miles, and they are close to the mainland with easy sheltered crossings. Indeed at very low tides it is possible to wade from Robbins to the mainland (Robinson in Plomley 1966:233, n. 117). It may be that the minimum area to support an autonomous land-owning band under Tasmanian conditions lay close to 30 to 35 square miles (see Table 5). Such bands usually numbered of the order of 35 to 60 members or about seven to fifteen families (Jones 1971a:278-9). Like the estates of Tasmanian mainland bands, these islands did not provide all of the subsistence throughout the year. Bruny islanders often crossed the d'Entrecasteaux Channel and went south-west as far as Maatsuyker. Robbins islanders foraged on the west coast as far as the Arthur River at least, and also visited the other islands of the Hunter Group (Jones 1974). Equally, mainland groups visited Robbins for special resources.

We may look upon the economic role of the islands in the total Tasmanian economy in another way. The combined area of the occupied islands comes to some 290 square miles, which is an insignificant one per cent of the area of Tasmania. However, when we add up the actual coast line of these offshore islands, we find that it totals some 350 to 400 miles even excluding islets and rocks. Since the Tasmanian coastline itself is about 1000 miles in length, we can see that by the use of their simple maritime technology, the Tasmanians increased the potential seashore available to them by an extraordinary 30% to 40%, this factor being even more pronounced for the western and southern tribes who used watercraft.

The effect of these island resources, seasonal though most of them may have been, on the economies and seasonal movements of the bands neighbouring them is shown on Fig. 9. Here I have indicated the ethnographically documented movements of named bands who utilized the resources of the various islands at some stage of their annual cycles, the evidence taken from Jones 1974. I have enclosed these various movements with dotted envelopes, producing for each island something analagous to Vita-Finzi and Higgs' 'catchment area' (1970). It can be seen that the handful of utilized islands listed in Table 4 affected the economic life of bands from most areas of western and south-eastern Tasmania, underscoring the importance of the special resources available on them and of the technology that enabled them to be exploited. The absence of watercraft among the north-eastern tribes becomes even more extraordinary and it is to the uninhabited islands that I now wish to turn.

Islands with no people on them

Recent archaeological work has shown that man was firmly established in Australia by at least 30,000 years ago, and that he was occupying a variety of ecological zones along what is now the south-eastern coast of the mainland by 17,000 to 20,000 years B.P. (Jones 1968; Bowler *et al.* 1970; Barbetti & Allen 1972; Lampert 1971; Gallus 1971; Flood pers. comm.). From that time until about 12,000 years ago, there was a broad land bridge extending southwards from Wilson's Promontory, past what were then the mountains of the Furneaux Group to north-eastern Tasmania. Another peninsula (and perhaps land bridge to Victoria) extended from north-western Tasmania past the Hunter Hills to King Plateau. It was along these land bridges that man almost certainly walked to Tasmania, and though full Pleistocene dates for human occupation have not yet been found there, I am sure that they will be, probably in lunette or sand-sheet deposits in eastern Tasmania. It is an explanation that Flinders might have found hard to believe. The Post-Glacial sea level rise cut off Tasmania about 12,000 years ago, and continued to rise, reaching its present coastline about 8,000 years ago in some places. From this time onwards we get ample evidence of men living in Tasmania and utilizing its rich coastal resources (Jones 1968, 1971b; Reber 1965; Lourandos 1970). The archaeological sequences on the island show the continuity and internal evolution of a single cultural tradition, which proceeded from at least 8,000 years ago up to the 'ethnographic present'. It was a culture which sprang from a Late Pleistocene Australian context, and it was protected by the waters of Bass Strait from all further external influences (Jones 1971b).

That is how man got to Tasmania: what about the islands in between? The ethnographic evi-

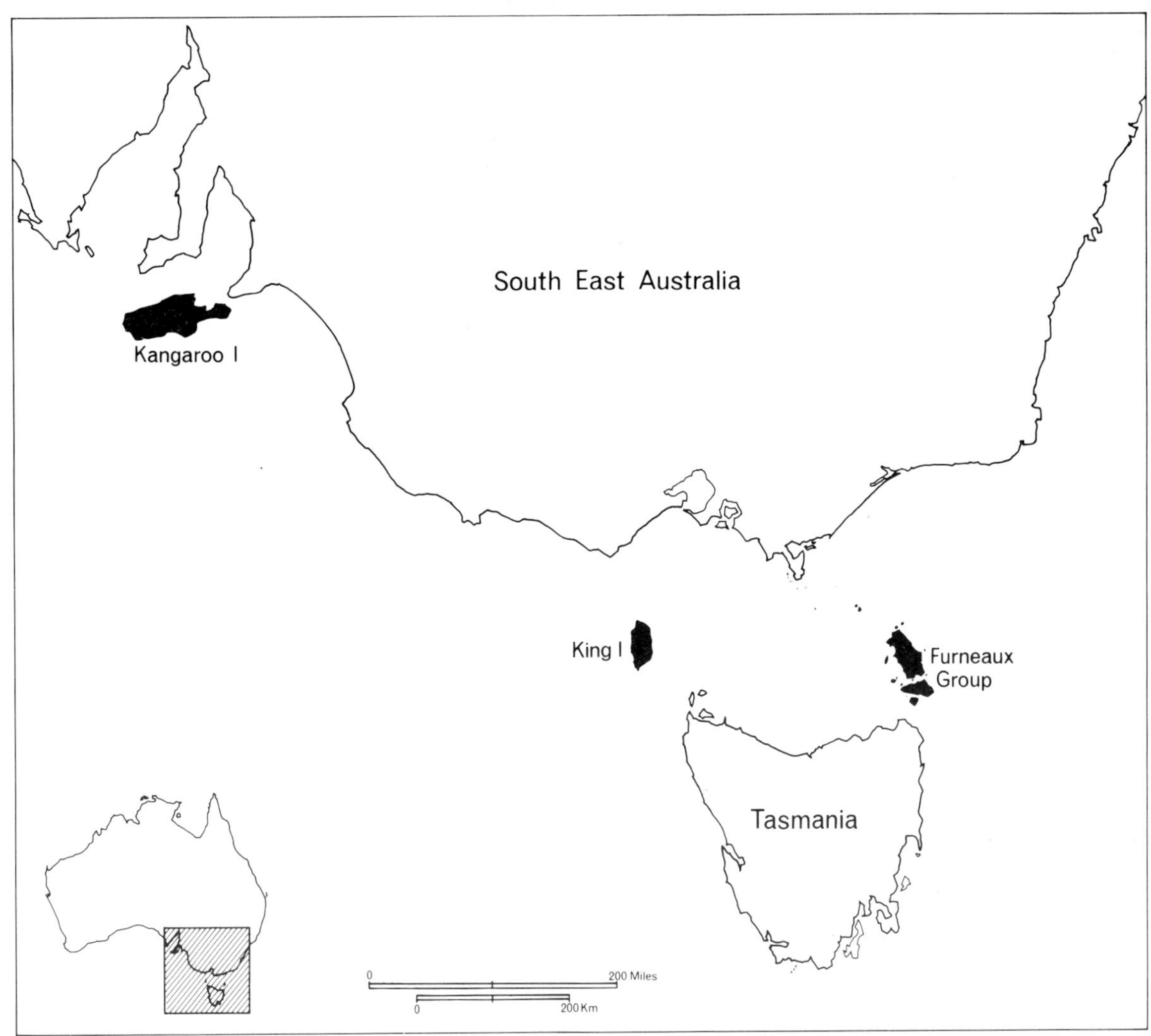

Figure 10. Islands with no people on them.

dence is unanimous that at the time of European contact there were no native inhabitants on the large Bass Strait islands of the Furneaux group and King Island nor on the smaller Kent and Hogan groups (Fig. 10). There has been considerable scientific exploration done on all of these islands (e.g. Hope 1973:170) but no shell middens nor other stratified sites have ever been found on them, in stark contrast to the situation along the coasts of Tasmania, the Victorian mainland and the close offshore islands discussed above. On Flinders Island, Hope (1973:167-70) excavated Ranga Cave, but found no evidence for human occupation in the fauna-rich deposits, though she was especially on the look out for it. The top of the deposit is dated to about 8,000 years ago and it probably extends back in time hundreds, if not thousands, of years prior to that. It was thus coeval with the later stages of the sea level rise, and with the formation of Flinders Island itself, the bridge to Tasmania being drowned about 8,500 to 10,000 years ago (Jennings 1971:9). The abundant charcoal in the top layers may indicate the occasional presence of man and his fire sticks somewhere in the neighbourhood at that time. The evidence available to us at present is unequivocal that for many thousands of years, probably at least since the sea reached its present level, the large islands of Bass Strait did not support any human populations, and were not visited casually nor seasonally by mainlanders from either side of the strait. The north-east Tasmanians even believed that 'when black men die they go to the islands' (Robinson 14 August 1831:400) – a place of the dead and not of the living.

The distance from Cape Portland to Clarke Island, the nearest one of the Furneaux group, is fourteen miles across Banks Strait, with a few islets a mile or two from the Tasmanian shore. Once on Clarke, the other major islands of the group are easily accessible, so it is the width of Banks Strait that is decisive. According to Wyrtki (1960:4, 14) there is generally a steady current moving east through eastern Bass Strait at a rate of nine to twelve miles a day, and the hydrographic charts show particularly strong tides in Banks Strait (Macintosh 1949). To get to Clarke Island in a Tasmanian canoe-raft one would leave the Tasmanian shore about fifteen or twenty miles to the west of Cape Portland and allow the current to carry one east while one made headway to the north. The trouble arises when one tries to get back, for in fact Clarke Island is north-east of Cape Portland, and the prevailing current and winds would tend to carry one inexorably eastwards. Perhaps only in unusual conditions of current, tide and wind would one have a chance of making the return trip, and this does not take into consideration the limitations of the craft discussed above. The distance from the Hunter Group to King Island is about 45 miles, and the problems inherent in that crossing need not be further elaborated.

On the northern side of Bass Strait, a similar situation obtained, despite the use of rigid-walled tied or sewed bark canoes (e.g. Davidson 1935). There is a thick shell midden in a cave on Glennie Island five miles off the south-west coast of Wilson's Promontory (Fig. 1) (Jones: field notes, site inspected by D. Dorward, J. Allen and R. Jones 1969). Stone tools have been found on Lady Julia Island five miles off Port Fairy in Western Victoria (R. Hill and R. Warneke, *T.V. Times*, 30 September 1970). Further offshore however, islands such as the Curtis and Hogan Groups were not visited, nor have archaeological remains been found there, and the Furneaux and King Island evidence shows that these islands were also beyond the technological capacity of the recent mainlanders to reach. Further west, we have the famous example of Kangaroo Island which was also uninhabited by Aborigines, the shortest water crossing to the adjacent mainland areas – Backstairs Passage – being only eight miles wide.

We are now in a position to summarize these data on sea distance in the south-eastern Australian context. For those societies which possessed watercraft, distances of a mile or two were no real problem in normal travels, even including family groups and entire bands. Distances of three and even up to five miles were covered regularly when rewards such as seasonal delicacies were available, and possibly slightly longer voyages might have been attempted by the foolhardly or the brave for a special reason. On the other hand this was the *limiting distance*, for the field evidence suggests that open-sea distances of somewhere between 6 and 14 miles were beyond the capabilities of Tasmanian and south-eastern Aboriginal man even over a period of thousands of years.

I do not wish it thought that I consider such journeys *impossible*, since the splendid adven-

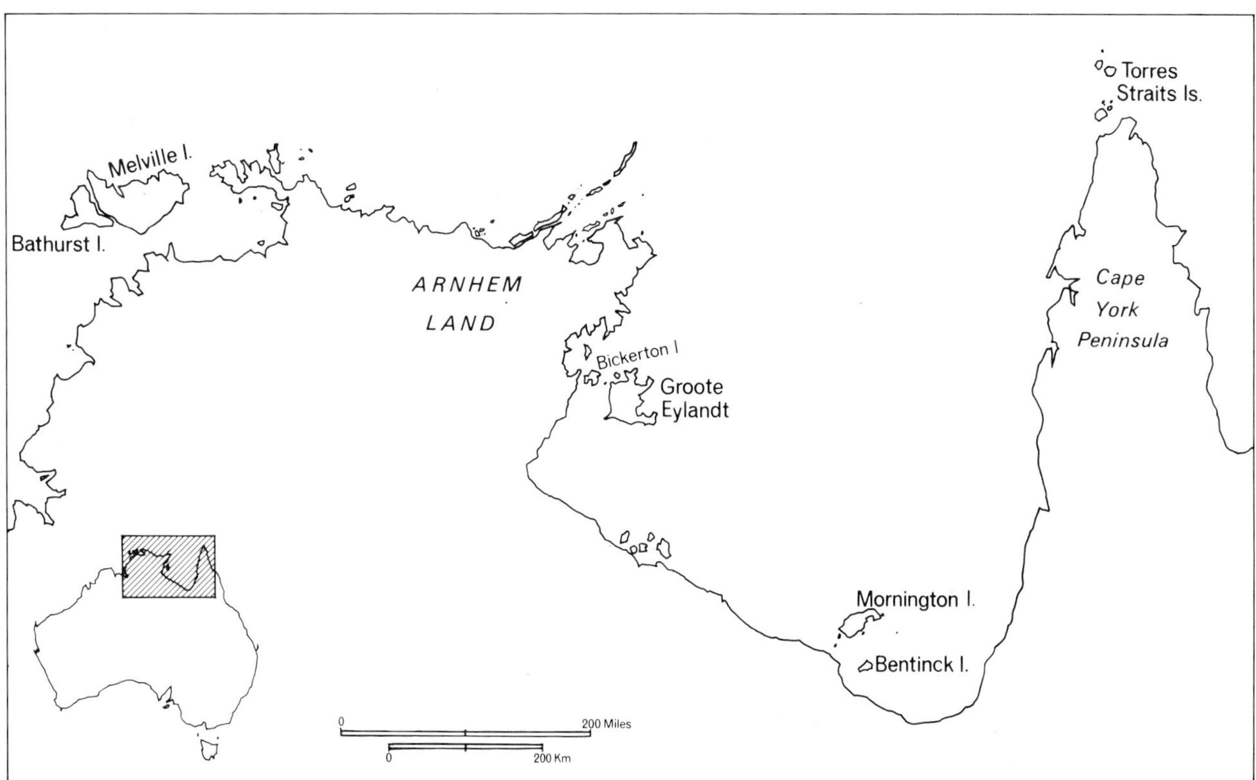

Figure 11. Islands north of Australia.

tures of people such as Heyerdahl have shown the foolishness of such dogmatism, simply that the dangers and the risk of disaster rise exponentially as the distance increases, so that at some stage the cost totally outweighs the gain. An example of such a situation is given by Tindale (1962:310) for the Kaiadilt of Bentinck Island, Gulf of Carpentaria (Fig. 11). Due to stress of warfare or starvation, groups of people on two separate occasions used their rafts of dry mangrove branches to cross eight miles of open sea to neighbouring Allen Island. The death tolls were staggering, for out of 15 people embarking in 1940, three were drowned, and on the second occasion seven years later, no less than 14 people were drowned out of the 19 who started the voyage. No return journeys from Allen Island were ever recorded, despite the fact that it was almost devoid of water and subject to massacre raids from the adjacent mainland.

Conjectural history is not science, but I wonder if such a series of disasters in attempting the widening sea passages to the old traditional lands of the Furneaux Group might have caused the neighbouring north-east Tasmanian societies to proscribe all water transport, a decision that persisted until last century. If such a cultural decision was ever taken, it would have been the most important one in Tasmanian prehistory, as it would finally have defined the size of the envelope insulating the Tasmanian universe.

Insulation of man and the limiting size of human population

We are left with the last problem. As the chain of mountains was gradually transformed into an island chain, the human population would have been slowly driven back until the coast reached its present configuration. Some of these people would have been located on what are now the large islands. Why did they and their descendants not survive on them in isolation?

A handful of stone tools have in fact been found on several occasions on both Flinders and Cape Barren Islands, in all cases either on the surface of ploughed land or eroding from sand dunes (Tindale 1941; Casey n.d.; Jones and Littlewood n.d. and A. Bickford and J. Birmingham pers. comm.). The implements that I have seen, collected by Tindale and Littlewood, are large core-scrapers or concave and nosed steep-

Table 6 Population

Island	*Area square miles*	*Coastline approximate length miles*	*Distance from adjacent mainland miles*	*Estimate of potential or actual Aboriginal population*			*Number of potential or actual local groups*	*Aboriginal population in 1800 AD*	*Contact with mainland*	*Reference*
				Based on land area	*Based on coastline*	*Average*				
A. Islands south of the Australian mainland										
Tasmania	26,000	1000 (1400 incl. close offshore islands)	150	—	—	4000	75	Yes	No	Plomley 1966; Jones 1971a, 1974
Kangaroo	1,700	250	8	300	750	500*	10*	No	—	—
Furneaux Group (3 largest islands only)	770	250	14 from Tas.	150	700	400*	10*	No	—	—
King	420	100	40 from Tas.	70	300	200*	5*	No	—	—
B. Islands north of the Australian mainland										
Bathurst and Melville	3,000	400	25m Island chain. Max. single sea crossing is 8 m.	—	—	1,000	9	Yes	No	Hart and Pilling 1962
Groote Eylandt and Bickerton	1,300	350	26m Island chain. Max. single sea crossing is 5 m.	—	—	400 Approx.	12	Yes	Yes	Rose 1960; Turner 1973
Bentinck	60	60 incl. Sweers Isle.	17m Max. single sea crossing via Allen Isle is 8 m.	—	—	125 Max.	8	Yes	Probably No	Tindale 1962
Mornington	380	130 (170 incl. close offshore islands)	17m. Island chain. Max. single sea crossing is 4 m.	—	—	350	?	Yes	Yes	Cawte 1972; Tindale pers. comm.

* Estimate of potential population only.

edged scrapers characteristic of old Australian and Tasmanian industries. Their typology and weathered surfaces, together with the absence of any recent archaeological sites, strongly support Tindale's view that at least some of them are Pleistocene in age and were dropped by people foraging over what were then inland hills (1941).

A totally analogous situation occurred on Kangaroo Island. Here numerous stone tools have been collected from the surfaces of eroding deposits or ploughed fields. Typologically, they form a distinctive industry, called the Kartan by Tindale and his co-workers (1937; Cooper 1960; Bauer 1970), and are characterized by large horse-hoof core-scrapers and abruptly flaked pebble 'choppers'. On typological and geological grounds, Tindale has always given them a Pleistocene age (1937) and Lampert's recent work (1972) seems to confirm this. Lampert discovered the first stratified archaeological deposit on the island in a small aeolianite rock shelter, and the very topmost layer was dated to 11,000 years B.P. The industry throughout the deposit consisted of small scrapers similar to contemporary assemblages in south-eastern Australia and was manufactured from flint and quartz as opposed to the quartzite of the massive Kartan tools. Lampert argues convincingly that the Kartan is a different industry and is older, perhaps much older, than his excavated one. No prehistoric shell middens have ever been found on the island, and when it was discovered by Europeans it was devoid of any human inhabitants (see Bauer 1970:199). Kangaroo Island was cut off from the mainland about 10,000 years ago, and thus we have a neat picture of its being occupied by man over a long period, while it was part of the continent, and yet at the very point of its insulation, occupation ceased (see Lampert 1972:223).

We must look at this problem in the broader context of the biogeography of islands and of the pauperization that seems inevitably to occur to the fauna of a continental region when it gets split up into island units by a rise in sea level (e.g. Darlington 1957; Main 1961). Such a study has been done by Hope (1973) for the archipelago of Bass Strait. She found that the number of species of herbivorous marsupials on an island was directly related to its size. The smaller the island, the less species it could support, so that whereas Tasmania with 26,000 square miles had ten species, King with an area of 400 square miles had only six and so on down to Kangaroo (Furneaux Group) which at 0.5 square mile was the smallest island capable of supporting a single species (Hope 1973:187). A similar process was observed with related species of different sizes, for example the macropods. Tasmania was the only island big enough to support the grey kangaroo (*M. giganteus*); islands down to 3.5 square miles could support the smaller red-necked wallaby (*M. rufrogriseus*), whereas on the smallest islets only the thylogale (*T. billardierii*) could survive. For each species there was a minimum area and thus number of individuals below which long-term survival of a local population could not be maintained.

Man is also subject to these same forces, and the islands south of the Australian continent allow us to calculate the limiting parameters of habitat dimension and of population in a hunting context. The approximate areas and lengths of coastlines of the four largest islands (Tasmania, the Furneaux Group, King and Kangaroo) are shown on Table 6. From analyses of ethnographic sources, I think that Tasmania supported between three and five thousand Aborigines, divided into about nine tribes and approximately seventy-five named local groups or bands (Jones 1971a, 1972, 1974; Plomley 1966:968-76). The resources of both land and sea contributed to supporting this population, and so the carrying capacity can be calculated as some combination of land area and length of coastline per person. Doing this, we find that, on average, it required between five and eight square miles to support one person, or alternatively, there were between two and four people per mile of coast (including close offshore islands). Internal analysis of the various tribal groups shows some variation due to ecological and other differences such as whether a particular tribe had predominantly a maritime or an inland economy, but the overall impression is one of consistency within the general range indicated above (Jones 1972, 1974). A similar order of population density has also been calculated for various coastal regions of mainland south-eastern Australia (e.g. Radcliffe-Brown 1930; Megitt 1964; Lawrence 1968; Allen 1972; J. Flood pers. comm.), giving us confidence that these were the fundamental parameters of the carrying capacity of this environment, under a hunting and gathering regime. Taking the figures of five square miles of land and 0.3 miles of coastline per person and then averaging the two results I have calculated the hypothetical populations that the three large uninhabited islands could have supported (Table 6).

It can be seen that about 400 or 500 hunting and gathering people could have lived on both Kangaroo and the Furneaux Group, while 200 might have lived on King. The implication of this study is that human populations of this size are not large enough for long-term viability when their period of isolation from other men is to be measured in terms of thousands of years. Quite clearly, the 4,000 people on Tasmania were able to survive ten millennia on their own whereas the presumed 500 on Kangaroo or Furneaux were not.

We can refine the range of this limiting population by looking at a parallel situation along the northern coast of Australia. Four large islands, Bathurst/Melville, Groote Eylandt, Bentinck and Mornington (Fig. 11) were also formed by the Post-Glacial rising sea, and in area they range from 3,000 square miles down to 60 square miles (Table 6) and in minimum distance from the mainland from 25 miles to 17 miles. However, in all cases, there are some small islands in the straits, reducing the maximum single sea crossings to between four and eight miles (Table 6). All of these islands supported Aboriginal populations which were to a significant extent isolated culturally and genetically from the mainland (Hart & Pilling 1961; Rose 1960; Tindale 1962; Simmons *et al.* 1962; Moore 1967; Cawte 1972; Turner 1973). In two cases, Bathurst/Melville and Bentinck, this isolation was total, the Tiwi Aborigines of the former believing that the distant mainland was the home of the dead (Hart & Pilling 1961:9). In the other two cases, there was some sporadic or trading contact with the mainland. It is interesting that an eight mile water gap (via intermediary islands) was as effective in culturally isolating Bathurst/Melville and Bentinck islands as it was with Kangaroo Island on the other side of the continent. However, gaps of four or five miles were capable of being systematically negotiated at Mornington as they were at Maatsuyker. It does seem that in Australia, the limiting distance beyond which regular open sea voyages were not attempted, can be narrowed down to the range of between four and eight miles, at least with technologies limited to canoe-rafts or bark canoes.[7]

No stratigraphic archaeology has yet been done on these northern islands so that we cannot assess the antiquity and degree of the isolation, but material culture and genetic studies indicate that it may have lasted substantially or totally for perhaps several thousand years at least. Professional anthropological censuses have been made on the living populations of each of these islands, with results shown in Table 6. It can be seen that isolated or semi-isolated populations of between 1,000 people down to 350 people seem to be stable in these areas. Bentinck Island may in fact have been too small in the long run, as Tindale's fascinating data indicate (1962; Cawte 1972:140-1). In 1948, this island was swept by a tidal wave which flooded over half its area, destroying the vegetation there and fouling almost all of the waterholes. This was, moreover, only the last of several disasters including bad seasons, internecine warfare, and drownings, so that the population dropped to 60% of its former size in nine years, with a death rate of 250 per 1,000 in the year 1947/8. It is a possibility that the remaining inhabitants, down to 70 in number, could not have survived, had they not been removed from their island by Europeans.

My conclusion from these data is that totally isolated populations of between 1,000 and 4,000 people are perfectly viable over extremely lengthy periods, but that ones of under about 350 or 400 are vulnerable in the long run. In hunter-gatherer conditions, the limiting viable population may be somewhere in the range of 400 to 600 depending on local circumstances and the vagaries of chance. In looking for the mechanisms for local extinction, we must stress social as well as possible genetic factors. A population of 500 people in Aboriginal Australia would almost certainly have been divided into semi-autonomous land-owning bands each of about 30 to 60 people, giving say 10 bands. It is probable that complex rules of marriage would have obtained, including band exogamy and other prohibitions, thus greatly reducing any individual's choice of potential partners. Random catastrophes might have occurred such as natural disasters, hunting or watercraft accidents involving most of the adult women of a band, the over-exploitation and local extinction of a major food source such as seals, warfare, a decision to leave the island *en masse* and so on. Another possibility to consider is that the seasonal movements of the bands of the island took them outside its confines to the adjacent mainland, as was the case with the 'residential islands' of the ethnographic Tasmanians, and that as the waters rose and water barriers widened, a decision was made one year not to return. I am certainly inclined to a 'catastrophist' view rather than one of slow population decline, but only future archaeological work will solve this problem and the allied one of possible multiple re-colonizations. It is interesting to note that the limiting population size I have argued for is the same as that which constitutes a 'tribe' in Australia and Tasmania (Birdsell 1971:354; Tindale 1974; Jones 1971a). This is the major genetic, linguistic and social unit of Australian society, and it may also be the minimum unit for long term survival. It was not from a lack of food that the ancient inhabitants of Furneaux, King and Kangaroo had 'perished' but from a lack of people. Areas once occupied by man, and full or rich unused resources, were abandoned, an extraordinary event which locally reversed the whole trend of human history.

The very presence of man on the Australian continent more than 30,000 years ago (Bowler *et al.* 1970), to say nothing of probable Middle Pleistocene stone tools on Timor and the Philippines (Glover & Glover 1970; R. Fox pers. comm.), implies that even then he possessed watercraft capable of crossing the 40 to 60 mile barrier separating the continent from Asia, even during a period of low sea level. The Tasmanian and other evidence outlined here shows what a formidable barrier this must have been, even for a people possessing and using quite serviceable aquatic machines. The limitations of such watercraft and the whole rhythm of Australian prehistory imply that contacts across the 'Wallace Line' were sporadic and rare, the result of accident rather than of design. Taking a world view, islands with high Pleistocene occupations such as Japan, Java, Ceylon and Britain are all continental ones with past land bridges connecting them to the mainland; even the road to the Americas need not have had extensive water crossings during winter or in an ice age. It is likely that the Straits of Gibraltar and the Bosphorus were crossed at least several times by ancient hunters, but we seem to have to wait for a different economic system to colonize the more isolated islands such as Cyprus, Crete, Majorca, Ireland, New Ireland, Fiji, Madagascar and so on (see also Clark 1936, 1952:282-92). The eastern flank of the Malayo-Melanesian archipelago became the springboard for some of the greatest maritime feats of non-industrial man (Lewis 1972). Perhaps it will be here, at the junction of the world's greatest ocean and the worlds greatest archipelago, that we will eventually find man's oldest watercraft.

Acknowledgments

It is a great pleasure to be able to offer this paper in a volume dedicated to Grahame Clark, as a token acknowledgment of my immense debt to him as mentor and teacher.

For various conversations while preparing the paper, I should like to thank Harry Allen, Sandra Bowdler, Jack Golson, Jeannette Hope, Ronald Lampert, Betty Meehan, Nicolas Peterson, Norman Tindale and Charles Turner. An early version was given to a seminar in the Department of Prehistory, A.N.U., Canberra, in 1970, and the present one has benefited from that exposure.

Winifred Mumford drew the figures, Dragi Markovic took the photographs and the text and tables have been typed by Beverley Fox.

REFERENCES

Allen, H.R. (1972) '*Land where the Crow Flies Backwards . . .*'. Unpublished Ph.D. thesis, Aust. National University, Canberra.

Backhouse, J. (1843) *A Narrative of a Visit to the Australian Colonies.* London.

Barbetti, M. and Allen, H. (1972) Prehistoric man at Lake Mungo, Australia, by 32,000 years B.P. *Nature*, 240, 46-8.

Bauer, F.M. (1970) The Kartans of Kangaroo Island, South Australia: a puzzle in extinction. In Pilling, A.R. and Waterman, A.R. (eds.), *Diprotodon to Detribalization*, 198-216. Lansing.

Birdsell, J.B. (1971) Ecology, spacing mechanisms and adaptive behaviour in Aboriginal land tenure. In Crocombe, R. (ed.), *Land Tenure in the Pacific*, 334-61. Melbourne.

Bonwick, J. (1870) *Daily Life and Origin of the Tasmanians.* London.

Bowden, K.M. (1964) *Captain James Kelly of Hobart Town.* Melbourne.

Bowler, J.M., Jones, R., Allen, H., and Thorne, A.G. (1970) Pleistocene human remains from Australia: a living site and human cremation from Lake Mungo, western New South Wales, *World Arch.*, 2, 39-60.

Calder, J.E. (1874) Some account of the wars of extirpation and habits of the native tribes of Tasmania. *J. Anthrop. Inst.*, 3, 7-28.

Casey, D.A. (n.d. = 1968) Prehistory of Flinders Island. Unpublished ms.

Cawte, J. (1972) *Cruel, Poor and Brutal Nations.* Honolulu.

Clark, J.G.D. (1936) Early navigation in north western Europe. *Proc. Prehist. Soc.*, n.s. 1, 146.

Clark, J.G.D. (1952) *Prehistoric Europe; the Economic Basis.* London.

Clark, J.G.D. (1961) *World Prehistory, an Outline.* Cambridge.

Cooper, H.M. (1960) The archaeology of Kangaroo Island, South Australia. *Rec. S. Aust. Mus.*, 13, 481-503.

Crowther, W.L. (1950) On the formation and disposal of a collection. *Pap. and Proc. Roy. Soc. Tasmania,* 1949, 83-92.

Darlington, P.J. (1957) *Zoogeography: The Geographical Distribution of Animals.* New York.

Davidson, D.S. (1935) The chronology of Australian watercraft. *J. Polyn. Soc.*, 44, 1-16; 69-84; 137-52; 193-207.

Davies, J.L. (ed.) (1965) *Atlas of Tasmania.* Hobart.

Davies, J.L. (1967) Tasmanian landforms and quaternary climates. In Jennings, J. and Mabbutt, J. (eds.), *Landform Studies from Australia and New Guinea,* 1-25. Canberra.

Edwards, R. Clinton (1965) Aboriginal watercraft on the Pacific coast of South America. *Ibero-Americana,* 47.

Flinders, Matthew (1814) *A Voyage to Terra Australis.* London.

Freycinet, L. (1816) See Péron and Freycinet 1807/1816.

Gallus, A. (1971) Excavations at Keilor. Report no. 1. *Artefact,* Newsletter No. 24, 1-12.

Glover, I.C. and Glover, E.A. (1970) Pleistocene flaked stone tools from Timor and Flores. *Mankind,* 7, 188-90.

Golson, J. (1972) Land connections, sea barriers and the relationship of Australian and New Guinea Prehistory. In Walker, D. (ed.), *Bridge and Barrier: The Natural and Cultural History of Torres Strait,* 375-97. Canberra.

Hamy, E.-T. (1891) L'oeuvre ethnographique de Nicolas-Martin Petit dessinateur à bord du 'Géographe', 1801-1804. *L'Anthropologie,* 2, 601-22.

Hart, C.W.M. and Pilling, A.R. (1961) *The Tiwi of North Australia.* New York.

Hiatt, Betty (1967/68) The food quest and the economy of the Tasmanian Aborigines. *Oceania,* 38, 99-133, 190-219.

Hiatt, Betty (1970) Woman the gatherer. In Gale, F. (ed.), *Woman's Role in Aboriginal Society,* 2-8. Aust. Abor. Studs., No. 26, Canberra.

Hope, J.H. (1973) Mammals of the Bass Strait Islands. *Proc. Roy. Soc. Victoria.* 85, 163-96.

Huxley, T.M. (1869) On the distribution of the races of mankind and its bearing on the antiquity of man. *Internat. Congr. Prehist. Archaeol.* (1868), 3, 92-105.

Jackson, W.D. (1965) Vegetation. In Davies, J.L. (ed.), *Atlas of Tasmania,* 30-7, Hobart.

Jennings, J.N. (1971) Sea level changes and land links. In Mulvaney, D.J. and Golson, J. (eds.), *Aboriginal Man and Environment in Australia,* 1-13, Canberra.

Jones, Rhys (1968) The geographical background to the arrival of man in Australia and Tasmania. *Arch. and Phys. Anthrop. in Oceania,* 3, 186-215.

Jones, Rhys (1971a) The demography of hunters and farmers in Tasmania. In Mulvaney, D.J. and Golson, J. (eds.), *Aboriginal Man and Environment in Australia,* 271-87. Canberra.

Jones, Rhys (1971b) *Rocky Cape and the Problem of the Tasmanians.* Unpublished Ph.D. thesis, University of Sydney, Sydney.

Jones, Rhys (1972) A hunting landscape. Paper delivered to the Australian Association of Social Anthropologists, annual conference 1972, Monash University, Melbourne (unpublished ms.).

Jones, Rhys (1973) Emerging picture of Pleistocene Australians. *Nature,* 246, 278-81.

Jones, Rhys (1974) Tasmanian Tribes. Appendix to *Aboriginal Tribes of Australia,* by N.B. Tindale. San Francisco.

Jones, Rhys and Littlewood, R.A. (n.d.) Stone implements from Cape Barren and Flinders Islands, Bass Strait. Unpublished ms.

Knopwood, R. (1947-8) The diary of the Rev. Robert Knopwood, 1805-8 (eds. W.H. Hudspeth and S. Angel). *Paps. and Procs. Roy. Soc. Tasmania* for 1947, 69-126.

Labillardière, J.J.H. de (1800) *Rélation du Voyage à la Recherche de La Pérouse . . .* (English translation by J. Stockdale, London, 1800). Paris.

Lakin, R. (1972) *Tasmanian Year Book, No. 6.* Hobart.

Lampert, R.J. (1971) *Burrill Lake and Currarong: Coastal sites in southern New South Wales. Terra Australis* No. 1, Canberra.

Lampert, R.J. (1972) A carbon date for the Aboriginal occupation of Kangaroo Island, South Australia. *Mankind,* 8, 223-9.

Lawrence, R. (1968) *Aboriginal Habitat and Economy.* Occ. Paper No. 6, Dept. Geography, School of General Studies, Austr. National Univ., Canberra.

Lesueur, C.A. and Petit, N. (1807/1811) Atlas with *Voyage de Découvertes aux Terres Australes . . .* by F. Péron and L. Freycinet. Paris.

Lewis, D.H. (1972) *We the Navigators.* Canberra.

Ling Roth, H. (1899) *The aborigines of Tasmania,* 2nd ed. Halifax.

Lourandos, Harry (1968) Dispersal of activities; the east Tasmanian Aboriginal sites. *Paps. and Procs. Roy. Soc. Tasmania,* 102, 41-6.

Lourandos, Harry (1970) *Coast and Hinterland: The Archaeological Sites of Eastern Tasmania.* Unpublished M.A. thesis, Austr. National Univ., Canberra.

Macintosh, N.W.G. (1949) A survey of possible sea routes available to the Tasmanian Aborigines. *Rec. Q. Vict.*

Mus. Launceston, Tasmania, 2, 123-44.

Main, A.R. (1961) The occurrence of Macropodidae on islands and its climatic and ecological implications. *J. Roy. Soc. W. Aust.*, 44, 84-9.

Mander-Jones, P. (n.d.) *Ethnographical drawings, Van Diemen's Land and New Holland.* Unpublished ms., Mitchell Library, Sydney.

Marchant, L.R. (1969) *A List of French Naval Records and Illustrations relating to Australian and Tasmanian Aborigines.* Aust. Abor. Studs. No. 21, Canberra.

Meggitt, M.J. (1964) Indigenous forms of government among the Australian Aborigines. *Bijdragen tot de taal ...* . 120, 163-80.

Meredith, L.A. (1852) *My Home in Tasmania.* London.

Meston, A.L. (1936) Observations on visits of the Tasmanian Aborigines to the Hunter Islands. *Paps. and Procs. Roy. Soc. Tasmania* for 1935, 155-62.

Milligan, J. (1866) *Vocabulary of the Dialects of some of the Aboriginal Tribes of Tasmania.* Hobart.

Moore, D.R. (1967) Island clues to Aboriginal prehistory. *Aust. Natural History*, Dec., 418-22.

Mulvaney, D.J. (1971) Prehistory from antipodean perspectives. *Proc. Prehist. Soc.*, 37(2), 228-52.

Péron, F. and Freycinet, L. (1807-1816) *Voyage de découvertes aux Terres Australes* . . . Paris.

Plomley, N.J.B. (1962) A list of Tasmanian Aboriginal material in collections in Europe. *Rec. Q. Vict. Mus. Launceston*, Tasmania, 15 n.s.

Plomley, N.J.B. (1966) *Friendly Mission: The Tasmanian Journals and Papers of George Augustus Robinson, 1829-1834.* Hobart.

Plomley, N.J.B. (1969) *An Annotated Bibliography of the Tasmanian Aborigines.* Roy. Anthrop. Inst. Occ. Pap. No. 28, London.

Radcliffe-Brown, A.R. (1930) Former numbers and distribution of the Australian Aborigines. *Official Yearbook of the Commonwealth of Australia*, 23, 687-96. Canberra.

Reber, G. (1965) Aboriginal carbon dates from Tasmania. *Mankind*, 6, 264-8.

Robinson, G.A. (1829-34) *Tasmanian Journals and Papers.* ms. in Mitchell Library, Sydney. See Plomley 1966.

Rose, F.G.G. (1960) *Classification of Kin, Age Structure and Marriage amongst the Groote Eylandt Aborigines.* Berlin.

Rossel, E.P.E. de (1808) *Voyage de D'Entrecasteaux, envoyé à la recherche de la Pérouse.* Paris.

Simmons, R.T., Tindale, N.B. and Birdsell, J.B. (1962) A blood group genetical survey in Australian Aborigines of Bentinck, Mornington and Forsyth Islands, Gulf of Carpentaria. *Amer. J. Phys. Anthrop.* 20:3, 303-20.

Sutherland, F.L. (1972) The classification, distribution analysis and sources of material in flaked stone implements of Tasmania Aborigines. *Rec. Q. Vict. Mus. Launceston*, Tasmania, No. 42, n.s.

Tindale, N.B. (1937) Relationship of extinct Kangaroo Island culture with cultures of Australia, Tasmania and Malaya. *Rec. S. Aust. Mus.*, 6, 39-60.

Tindale, N.B. (1941) The antiquity of man in Australia. *Aust. J. of Science*, 3, 144-7.

Tindale, N.B. (1962) Some population changes among the Kaiadilt people of Bentinck Island, Queensland. *Rec. S. Aust. Mus.*, 14, 297-318.

Tindale, N.B. (1974) *Aboriginal Tribes of Australia.* San Francisco.

Turner, D.M. (1973) The rock art of Bickerton Island in comparative perspective. *Oceania*, 43, 286-325.

Tylor, E.G. (1865) *Researches into the Early History of Mankind and the Development of Civilisation.* London.

Tylor, E.G. (1893) On the Tasmanians as representatives of Palaeolithic man. *J. Anthrop. Inst.*, 23:141-52.

Vita-Finzi, C. and Higgs, E.S. (1970) Prehistoric economy in the Mount Carmel area of Palestine. *Proc. Prehist. Soc.*, 36, 1-37.

Völger, Gisela (1972) *Die Tasmanier: versuch einer ethnographisch-historischen rekonstruktion.* Wiesbaden.

Watanabe, Hitoshi (1971) Running, creeping and climbing: a new ecological and evolutionary perspective on human locomotion. *Mankind*, 8, 1-13.

West, John (1852) *The History of Tasmania*, 2 vols. Launceston.

Wyrtki, K. (1960) The surface circulation in the Coral and Tasman Seas. *Tech. Pap. Div. Fish. Oceanogr. CSIRO*, Pap. No. 8.

NOTES

1. Like several authors before me (e.g. Meston 1936:159; Edwards 1965:1-16, 85-9), I am aware of the similarity of these craft to other types made variously on the west coast of South America, Egypt, Lake Tchad, east Iran, New Zealand etc. Rather than invoke any specific diffusionist influence, for which there is no evidence in Tasmania, I agree with Edwards that these bundle craft could have been independently invented many times, or that they belong to an extremely ancient type, or both (Edwards 1965:89).

2. In the early colonial accounts, the most common term used was 'catamaran'. This is not such an inappropriate name as might be thought from its modern usage, for according to the O.E.D., the word comes from the Tamil and one definition of it is a 'raft or float of logs tied side by side, longest in the middle, used for communication with shore or short voyage'. Australian colonial society had strong links with British India and many Indian words entered the language at that time. An alternative name is suggested by Rossel (see Ling Roth 1899:155) where he described the water craft as being 'small rafts to which had been given the form of a canoe'. Plomley has coined the word 'canoe-raft' for them (1962:11 ; 1966:36, no. 21) and since this is both descriptive and unambiguous, I shall use it here.

3. Which I was able to inspect in February 1972 through the courtesy of Mr B.A.L. Cranston.

4. These 'calculations' are my own responsibility entirely.

5. S. Bowdler of the Department of Prehistory, R.S.Pac.S., A.N.U. has recently begun such a study.

6. All calculations are approximate, based on measurements from standard maps.

7. Golson (1972:381-7) has also found the Tasmania/Bass Strait evidence of value in understanding the prehistory of the various island groups of the Torres Strait (Fig. 11).

NICOLAS PETERSON

Ethno-archaeology in the Australian Iron Age

Modern ethno-archaeological work in Australia began when Grahame Clark stimulated Thomson (1939) into writing his now classic paper on the seasonal factor in human culture before European influences disrupted the Aboriginal way of life.

Thomson's paper was based on observations of a nomadic group, still in the 'Stone Age', winning its living from the bush and the sea in Cape York. The message for the prehistorians was clearly spelt out: adjacent but different archaeological assemblages did not necessarily reflect different groups, but could be left by a single group responding to seasonal variations in climate. There was no specific message for social anthropologists as such, but there was clear evidence, if they wished to see it, that detailed ethnography on economic life and land-use could still be gathered. Australianists ignored the message, however, so that in 1951 Clark's comment (1951:52) that there was a rift between archaeology and ethnography in Britain, was equally true of Australia. The anthropologists were more active in the 1950s but, despite the opportunities, no ethnographic work was carried out on the economy and ecology of bush groups. Yet, as late as 1969, a handful of Aborigines who had not seen white men were living in the Western Desert, and today there are still Arnhem Landers living in, and off, the bush, although they have had substantial contact with Europeans.

The years between those of Thomson's field-work and today saw the end of the Stone Age in Australia: everywhere stone tools have been replaced by those of iron, although a number of men retain stone-working skills. If ethnographic analogies are to be used in the interpretation of archaeological evidence, therefore, the choice now lies between relying only on published ethnographies that sparsely document the earlier subsistence economies and fail to provide the kind of information that prehistorians require, or collecting new data on Iron Age Australians to illuminate the Stone Age remains.

Ethnographic analogies constructed from observations made in situations of culture change are likely only to compound the objections of those prehistorians who feel that the most serious failings in the present models for interpretation of archaeological evidence relate directly to the fact that they incorporate numerous analogies with modern groups, and that models based on ethnographic analogy force the prehistorian to adopt the frames of reference of the social anthropologist (Freeman 1968:262).

Here, I shall state the case for the relevance of contemporary ethnography in spite of the changes. Drawing mainly from data on Arnhem Land, I shall argue that the sense in which the Australian Aborigines are conservative places much archaeologically relevant ethnography beyond most of the effects of cultural change. As an example of such conservatism, I will discuss a feature of the Arnhem Land settlement pattern and the reasons why a band from that area postponed the adoption of horticulture until 1971.

The contemporary situation in Arnhem Land

Today, there are at least twenty groups living in, and off, the Arnhem Land bush. Although distant from missions and settlements, they are in regular contact with them, and receive visits by aeroplane, truck or boat every second or third week. These visits bring foodstuffs such as flour, tea, sugar, jam and tobacco, as well as other non-edible supplies including ammunition for .22 rifles and shot-guns, fishing lines and hooks. The bulk of the imported food is usually consumed within three or four days, when the people return to traditional food sources until the next visit.

The impedimenta of European culture are

Figure 1. A typical aboriginal camp. A blanket has been draped over bedding left inside the hut.

immediately noticeable on entering one of these camps (see Fig. 1). Blankets, tent-flies, suit-cases, mosquito-nets, clothing, guns, billy-cans and discarded tins are the most obvious. Besides these additions, there are other items that fit more naturally into the scene as substitutes. Hunting spears, once armed with wooden or stone points, now have blades fashioned from car springs; the bone or wooden prongs of the fish-spears are replaced by fence wire; digging-sticks, formerly of ironwood, are now made from iron rods and all axes are of steel. Indeed, the only unchanged traditional tools sure of a place are the pestle and mortar. The material culture is irrevocably of the Iron Age, but the economy is still based on hunting, fishing and gathering, as it has been for 30,000 years.

Aboriginal conservatism

Despite the success and persistence of their adaptation to the Australian environment, the Aborigines' long period of conservative history has often been used as a reproach. Why have the people changed so little and why, in particular, did they never take up horticulture, even when they were in regular contact with traders from Indonesia and Papua?

The least sympathetic views on this question are those of Lommel (1970:232), who concludes an essay on rock-art with the statement that the typical Australian characteristic seems to be the 'incapability to change and to assimilate'. More sympathetic is the view of Meggit (1964:35), who attributes the failure to change to a conservative philosophy that enjoins magical and ritual means to control the environment and discountenances technological change in general; or the view of the Berndts (1964:419), who speak of an emphasis on an essentially unchanging panoramic view of life. The two most recent considerations of the failure to take up horticulture (White 1971; Golson 1972:387-91) also favour a view that sees cultural factors as the main inhibitors.

Although characterized as unchanging, there is ample evidence for the ready adoption of cultural and technological innovations in the past. Without accepting all of Davidson's geographical distribution theory, one can point to his numerous papers on the distribution and diffusion of ideas and objects over much of the continent (e.g. Davidson 1937). In a number of cases, the source of origin of these innovations appears to be within the continent itself, but the ready adoption of elements from overseas is well documented on the north coast, where for hundreds of years the Aborigines came in contact with the Macassan trepangers and people from Papua. Among other things readily adopted in Arnhem Land (see Macknight 1972) were several dozen words, including those for the winds, some place and personal names, and references to the Macassans in songs and mythology. The technology and material culture adopted included some iron, dug-out canoes, and probably the use of detachable harpoon-heads for turtle and dugong hunting as well as fishing lines and hooks. Cloth was obtained and became, as it still is today, an item of wealth exchanged and stored for display at mortuary ceremonies. Smoking was taken up as a result of contact, as was alcohol. Other things were rejected, however: notably eating of trepang, use of pottery and horticulture, in spite of the fact that a number of Aborigines had been substantially exposed to life in Indonesia, through travel to Macassar. In 1876, for instance, there were said to be at least seventeen Aborigines, mainly from Port Essington, living in Macassar (see Macknight 1972:286). This was not unusual, for 29 years earlier Jukes (1847, I:359) reported the practice and both the Berndts (1954:54-8) and Tindale (1925) describe these travellers and indicate that men from all parts of Arnhem Land were involved.

It is clear, therefore, that if the Aborigines are to be called conservative, it must be in a special sense. Both before and after European arrival, the people readily accepted changes to the cultural and technological sphere, but not to the subsistence base. Though culturally adaptable, they remained economically resistant to change. The roots of this resistance, and of the continuities between past and present, lie not in a philosophical outlook but in the nature of their economy itself.

The nature of Aboriginal economies

Sahlins (1972) has pointed out that, in an economy geared to subsistence, productive *intensity* is inversely related to household productive capacity and that, in consequence, this domestic mode of production is inherently an anti-surplus system. Details of two central north-east Arnhem Land bands illustrate this point.

Columns 2 and 3 of Table 1 indicate the ratio, in fourteen households, of regular male and female food-collectors to dependants. It can be seen that when a male collector is present in a household, he supports from 1 to 8 people, but that half the households have no active male collector. In the same households a woman supports from 1 to 4.5 dependants, with only one household in which there is no regular female contributor.

The band itself is not an economic unit. Food is collected on a non-competitive and largely non-co-operative basis by each person, for their own household and for specific dependants in other households; any surplus beyond this is distributed through gift-giving which is sanctioned by an ethic of generosity. Adult dependants are nearly always parents of the providers. Households where this sharing relationship exists usually live adjacent to each other in a band-camp, and when away from it camp together to exploit special resources; thus they form an economic unit.

Columns 4 and 5 of Table 1 indicate the alteration in the ratio of providers to dependants in the only regular associations of households seen during visits to the same band over a period of three years. It can be seen that, in this situation, a male supports between 4.6 and 17 persons, only one group of households being without an active male provider. The result of two or more households forming a unit is to increase the average number of dependants on an active man. The numbers of such men are few, because men contribute food for only a limited period of their life, approximately from 18 to 45 years of age. Women, on the other hand, provide food from about 12 until, in their fifties, they become too old and frail to gather.

Co-operation between households makes only a marginal difference to the ratio of female collectors to dependants; slightly increasing the minimum number supported and reducing the maximum. The overall effect, therefore, is to

Table 1 The ratio of regular contributor males and females to dependants in individual households, compared with groups of households that regularly camp together

Household Number	*Individual households* Male	Female	*Co-operating households* Male	Female
1	1 : 4.5	1 : 4.5	1 : 7.5	1 : 3.25
2	0 : 6	1 : 2		
1	1 : 4.5	1 : 4.5	1 : 4.6	1 : 2.4
3	1 : 5	1 : 1		
4	1 : 8	1 : 3.5	1 : 17	1 : 3.5
5	0 : 9	1 : 3.5		
6	0 : 2	1 : 1		
9	0 : 10	1 : 2.3	0 : 15	1 : 2
14	0 : 3	1 : 2		
11	1 : 1	1 : 1	1 : 5	1 : 2
12	0 : 4	1 : 3		
8	0 : 5	1 : 4		
10	1 : 3	1 : 1	1 : 10	1 : 1.7
6	0 : 2	1 : 1		
8	0 : 5	1 : 4	1 : 9	1 : 4
13	1 : 4	1 : 4		
7	1 : 3	0 : 4		
8	0 : 5	1 : 4	1 : 5.5	1 : 3.3
10	1 : 3	1 : 1		

prevent those households with a potentially high productive capacity from using it for their benefit alone. The figures also reinforce the evidence for the importance of women in Aboriginal economic life. It is not just that they collect the dependable and immobile foods but that, in contrast to men, who may kill a large animal and thus have meat much beyond their own immediate household requirements and obligations, they have to accumulate their contribution through the massing of a large number of individual seeds, roots, fruits or shell-fish. Consequently, women have to make a conscious decision about the amount of food that they need to collect to meet their obligations every time they start work.

Another feature of Aboriginal economies, given a particular level of subsistence, is an inherent pressure towards reduction of work-effort. Assumptions about work-effort reduction that have been implicit in much archaeological and anthropological thinking are now being made explicit through such methods as input-output (Lee 1969) and site-catchment analysis (Vita-Finzi & Higgs 1970). What is not always sufficiently emphasized, however, is the contrast in the results of maximizing return on energy expended between western industrial and agricultural economies, on the one hand, and hunter-gatherer economies on the other. In the former, energy-saving in one process is usually reinvested in increasing production or in another material productive process. This is not true of most hunter-gatherer societies. By and large, these societies are characterized by long-term stability of population numbers and no substantial attempt is made to accumulate food or increase production of it. Food requirements, therefore, remain more or less constant from year to year. Under these conditions, and given a stable environment, the forces of selection are directed more consistently than in other economies in a single direction, making a strong case for a simple optimizing model, not as the basis for understanding self-conscious decision-making, but for analysing the effects on the economy and settlement pattern of selection-pressure over long periods of time.

The effects of such selection-pressure show themselves in a number of ways. The most striking is, perhaps, the amount of leisure time many hunter-gatherers enjoy (see Sahlins 1972).

Physically, there are indications in the small size and body-weight of the people and the small changes that have taken place since contact, and new diets. Warner measured north-east Arnhem Land males between 1927 and 1929 and found that their mean weight was 55.8 kilogrammes and mean height 1.67 metres. For women from Arnhem Land generally, the figures were 43.5 kilogrammes and 1.58 metres (Howells & Warner 1937).

Interestingly, these figures are very similar to those for people in the same period in Central Australia. Changes in stature between the 1930s and the 1960s show that present-day heights of young adults there exceed earlier ones by 5.5 cm. for men and by 5.7 cm. for women (Barrett & Brown 1971:1170). More subjective, although in theory susceptible of measurement, is the marked contrast in levels of energy-expenditure put into daily life by Aborigines as compared with New Guinea horticulturalists. Such subjective comparison is most easily made by viewing films of the two peoples in action.

Given the Aborigines' style of life and lack of materialism, there is a good *prima facie* case for saying that their economies have evolved to a point where they are as close to a purely work/energy reduction situation as any economy has ever been. It is this feature that maintains the continuity in Aboriginal subsistence strategies and ensures that much contemporary ethnography is archaeologically relevant. Thus, while there is dependence on traditional food sources that remain distributed as they were in the past, women, whose extractive technology has changed only in that it needs less maintenance, will expend the same work/energy in extracting specific quantities of traditional foods as they always have done. Men, aided by guns, spend less time and energy than formerly, although the reduction is not as great as might have been expected. Generally the people are poor shots and consequently have a preference for shot-guns, which tend to frighten game away. The limited savings in input are absorbed in a more leisurely time-table (McCarthy & McArthur 1960 describes an Aboriginal group where, during 14 days at Fish Creek, the men left camp before 9 a.m. on only two days), in ritual activity, in substantial rests throughout the day (McCarthy & McArthur 1960:190-1; Sharp 1952:20) and in the manufacture and maintenance of material equipment. One result of the use of guns may be a slight increase in the amount of meat eaten by inland groups. However, a high value is placed on a mixed diet. The people, of the two bands referred to, complain that their minds become sluggish when they have had too much meat and no vegetable food; they use the term *bukumuktun*, literally 'forehead to stop'. If the diet is lacking in meat, the men will be heard to complain that they want something to relieve their tongues (*matayal*). There are thus strong biocultural restraints on the composition of the diet.

Under the foregoing conditions and as long as movement is by traditional means, the same pressures will be at work on the settlement pattern, ensuring similarity with the past. The similarity extends beyond the exploitation of the same kind of spatial area, however, to the fact that all the groups in the bush are living on lands with which they have traditional associations. Not everybody would accept this view of continuity. Birdsell (1970) has recently argued that studies of local organization, made since 1930, do not accurately reflect the traditional settlement pattern; Sharp's study (1952) of the results of introducing steel axes in Cape York suggests that changes in technology have created an absolute discontinuity with the past. I shall now consider these alternative views, beginning with evidence derived from settlement pattern.

On the basis of recent field-work, a number of anthropologists (Hiatt 1962; Lee & DeVore 1968; Woodburn 1968) reject the rigid patrilineal/patrilocal model of Aboriginal local organization in particular and that of hunter-gatherers in general, as formulated by Radcliffe-Brown (1930) and Service (1962), which encapsulated each group within its own territory. Plausibly, they have argued that such a rigid organization is not as adaptive as a fluid and variable group, which provides an efficient mechanism for adjusting to both seasonal and yearly variations in abundance of resources, and to demographic changes and opportunities to avoid open conflict. As Lee puts it (1972:128), contemporary field-work emphasizes that people may live wherever and with whomever they please.

Birdsell (1970) has levelled criticism against this recent emphasis on fluidity of organization, on the grounds that it is the product of what he calls *degenerative change.* Degenerative change results from depopulation, displacement, dependency on European foods and from competition with introduced pastoral animals. These factors, he argues, lead to the disappearance of the local group, the dissolution of the constant state of tension associated with territoriality, the opening of previously closed ecological systems (1970:117) and the reduction of extractive pressure on the environment (1970:118).

The adaptive arguments for a fluid and flexible traditional pattern of hunter-gatherer land use are persuasive and hard to reject, even though the pattern is formed in conditions of change. Nevertheless, the proponents of permissiveness are in danger of overlooking the equally important adaptive fact that there are groups, and that they exist through time. The position is illustrated by the current writings on !Kung Bushmen. Lee (1972:129) states that rarely does a !Kung Bushman group's association with a water-hole go back as far as the grandparents' generation of the oldest person living. The implication, here, is that particular groups are associated with particular water-holes, but that over time the group either fades away through loss of members or actually leaves as a unit. The thought of a life-supporting water-hole, that has maintained a group for half a century or more, remaining unused seems so unlikely that Lee must mean either that another group becomes associated with the water-hole, or that the kinship composition of the original group changes through fluidity of movement. Archaeologically, of course, this would appear as a continuous occupation, provided that the people had the same technology.

In the same paper, Lee reconstructs the local groups in the area for the 1920s, together with their movements under varying conditions of drought, implying that there are ongoing groups, even if their composition was changing from day to day. Yellen and Harpending (1972), in their report on the same people, suggest that the classic notion of the band is more aptly applied to primitive agriculturalists and to people with a relatively more stable resource-base than hunter-gatherers, and that in a continuum of degrees of nucleation the hunter-gatherer is close to the anucleation end (1972:244). Confusingly, but perhaps revealingly, they remark in conclusion that bands *do* exist among the !Kung.

Yellen and Harpending might seem to have fallen into the trap feared by Freeman (1968). In over-reacting to the Radcliffe-Brown model of Aboriginal organization, attention has become focused on what is primarily a social anthropological issue, the short-term composition of groups, to the neglect of the long-term adaptational aspects. Birdsell's preoccupation with model-construction may have attracted him to the neat ideology of land ownership that divides up the countryside in Australia into self-contained units and which, he would like to think, reflected the pattern on the ground. In neither case have the authors advanced any cogent reason for supposing that energy-expenditure in the food quest has been increased. If anything, such points as reduction of extractive pressure, raised by Birdsell, would tend to strengthen the traditional pattern. It is doubtful, however, if reduction of extractive pressure has had much effect, particularly on the vegetable foods, as most people are living in places where there has been continuous, or almost continuous, occupation for the last twenty years. While change has led to depopulation of much of Arnhem Land, thus reducing inter-group tension, it has not led to displacement of those people still living in the bush. Only in Central Australia has the possibility of competition with pastoralism been a problem; today, those Aborigines still living off the bush are well beyond cattle-supporting country, and any small introduced mammals are now part of the Aboriginal diet.

Sharp's study indicates that discontinuities in one sphere of life need not necessarily affect others. In a well-known paper (1952), he has described several dramatic changes to the life of the Yir Yoront people of Cape York associated with the introduction of the steel axe. There was a decline in the prestige of masculinity and age, a shift from self-reliance in trading partnerships to dependence on the mission, a weakening of the totemic ideology and of kinship relations generally. Mulvaney (1971:377) has quoted this as a case-study of the effects of cultural change precipitated by technological innovation, as Sharp clearly intended him to do. The paper is, however, better described as an allegory, since Sharp writes: 'The introduction of the steel axe indiscriminately and in large numbers into the Yir Yoront technology occurred simultaneously with many other changes. It is therefore impossible to separate all the results of this single innovation . . . [the] axe may be used as an epitome of the increasing quantity of European goods and implements received by the aboriginals and of their general influence on the native culture' (1952:20). However, more significantly for the argument here, he also states that any leisure time that the Yir Yoront may have gained was invested in sleep, 'an art they had mastered thoroughly' (1952:20), and the practical effect on their standard of living was 'negligible' (1952:20). The change with the most economic significance, in this region, must have been the introduction of the outrigger canoe, which would have allowed people to travel over greater distances in safety and to hunt turtles and dugong more effectively. Although undated, this change almost certainly took place several centuries before the arrival of Europeans, since such canoes have been in use by the neighbouring Papuans for a considerable time.

Although the changes that *have* taken place with the arrival of Europeans have created discontinuities in the social and cultural life of all Aborigines, the nature of their subsistence economy has ensured that where Aborigines are still living in, and off, the bush there is a strong continuity between past and present in the exploitation of resources.

Localized adaptation

The major disadvantage of the hunter-gatherer mode of subsistence is, as Sahlins points out, the imminence of diminishing returns: an initial success develops the probability that further efforts will yield lower returns (1972:33). It is this fact that makes movement fundamental to the hunter-gatherer adaptation.

In all but the desert cultures, there are factors that mitigate the imminence of diminishing returns to a substantial degree; principal among these are seasonality and scheduling (see Flannery 1968:74-6). The necessity to move on was countered by the superabundance of particular foods for brief seasons and, in all but the desert environments, by the wide range of foods available at most times of the year; indeed, so numerous were the food plants that, in Arnhem Land for example, such a fundamental desert and riverine staple as *Panicum decompositum* is not even harvested (see Golson 1968:255). In areas rich in resources such as swamps, permanent rivers, estuaries and sections of coast, the movement of base-camps during a year tends to be greatly restricted; for example, one of the two bands in Table 1 kept its base-camp within an area of 3.2 km. radius from November 1966 to November 1967 (see Peterson 1973).

Under these conditions, highly localized adaptations in the subsistence economy and settlement pattern are likely to develop, provided there is some long-term continuity of occupation in an area. A striking example of this is found in the Castlereagh Bay area and immediately to the south in the freshwater Arafura swamp. In this district huge mounds, composed entirely of shell and up to 27 m. long and 6 m. high, are found along thirty kilometres of coastal plains and the adjacent islands. More widely spread around the inland swamps are earth mounds, usually smaller than 12 m. in diameter and 1.2 m. high. The impressive size, and the restricted distribution, of the shell mounds have puzzled a number of investigators (e.g. McCarthy & Setzler 1960:248-50) who have felt that some special non-economic factors, and conscious effort in building, must be invoked in explanation. Ethnographic analogy was of no help, since the people do not use the mounds today. However, present-day observations of the two Arnhem Land bands mentioned above, who live to the east of the Arafura swamp in an area where there are earth mounds, suggest by analogy that the mounds are an extreme reflection of localized adaptation to work/effort reduction.

The earth mounds, which usually occur in clusters of up to twenty, are all located in areas that flood at the end of the wet season, but where it is desirable to camp from a locational point of view (see Peterson 1973). Flooding in these places is often no more than five to seven centimetres deep, so that even a slight elevation provides freedom from dampness several weeks before the surrounding ground dries out.

Significantly, the people do not consider the mounds to be man-made. Their genesis is not problematic, however. It seems that at some time in the past (no carbon-dates have yet been obtained), men out fishing in the swamp areas would have used naturally high spots (often decayed termite mounds) on which to cook their catch and quickly noted the advantages of living in such a place. Oven-making on such spots would have led to the growth of the mounds, since cooking takes place in termite-nest ovens that usually contain from thirty to fifty pieces of broken nest, averaging five to seven centimetres in diameter. Such pieces of nest last for only two or three uses before becoming too brittle and then being discarded for new pieces, thus contributing to mound accumulation. The flood-water would ensure that ovens were built on the mounds. Once the flood-water had returned to the river courses, the mounds were abandoned and camps built along their banks, or beside the ponds and lakes. The coastal shell-mounds appear to have had a similar history, although used earlier in the wet season. Flood-water, wind and the high tides of the wet season led to the inundation of the coastal plains, which lay midway between the fruits of the more forested inland tracts and the sea resources of the inter-tidal zone. Mounds on the coastal plain were not only locationally in the right place but gave protection from the mosquitoes and sand-flies, through being open to the winds. The large size of the mounds reflects their long period of use, at least 1,300 to 2,500 years (see Mulvaney 1969:182), as well as the high proportion of waste in shell-fish food.

This interpretation is strengthened when the Australian distribution of such mounds (which are quite distinct from large but scattered middens) is considered. So far, they have been reported from only two other places: a stretch of one or two kilometres of coast, 16 km. to the west of Castlereagh Bay, and a small area around the Hey and Embley rivers, 700 km. to the east on Cape York. The earth mounds are more widely found around swampy areas in Arnhem Land, and in south-eastern Australia. Such widely discontinuous distribution discounts regional cultural idiosyncrasy and points to the economics of food collecting as the cause of the mounds.

The development of such localized adaptations in settlement pattern has its counterpart in technology. Thus, for example, in Arnhem Land, three mutually exclusive styles of fish-trap are found along a hundred miles of coast. South of Goulburn Island, on the mainland, stone fish-traps are found. Eighty miles to the west, on the Blyth River, long cylindrical wicker traps are used (McCarthy [1957:95] believes that they were introduced by the Macassans); again, twenty miles further east, a complex dam and 'water-sieving' system is found that is unknown outside three small rivers (see Thomson 1938). Such localized adaptations as these have, to some extent, been obscured by the continent-wide existence of a basic Australian tool-kit of spear, throwing club, brush-fence trap, digging-stick and knapped and core implements (McCarthy 1957:93) that has been taken as evidence for the Aborigines having 'imposed their way of life on the Australian habitat' (McCarthy 1957: 95) and contributed to the impression of an unchanging people. These views have only been able to prevail in the absence of ethnographies of living economies, with their evidence of the degree to which particular groups have shaped their subsistence pattern to exploit fully minute variations in the patterns of distribution and abundance of food resources.

The reality of these localizing forces has recently been dramatically brought home with the discovery of the isolated and remanent Kow Swamp population (see Thorne & Macumber 1972). Archaeological remains rarely provide such striking evidence for localized subsistence adaptations, however, not only because most technology was made from organic materials, but also because skill and knowledge were integral to the elegant Aboriginal adaptation, further reducing the range of material objects required to win a living. The history of the development of such adaptations will not be found in the stone technology of the Australian core-tool and scraper tradition (Bowler *et al.* 1970:52), since this was a generalized maintenance kit for the working of wood and bone, but will be distilled from the combination of organic food remains, site variation and settlement pattern with the aid of the template of contemporary ethnography.

An Arnhem Land garden

From the preceding discussion, the highly restricted food-quest movement in many parts of Arnhem Land, combined with the widespread practice of conservation of *Dioscorea sativa* vars. *rotunda* and *elongata*[1] might have been expected to lead to horticulture. We shall see how this was undertaken in one case. The bands mentioned in Table I have been subjected to mission pressure to take up gardening for a number of years. Occasionally their co-operation went as far as accepting a banana sucker or two and planting them at the end of the wet season, but if these survived the burning-off of the country, they never survived the summer. Melon

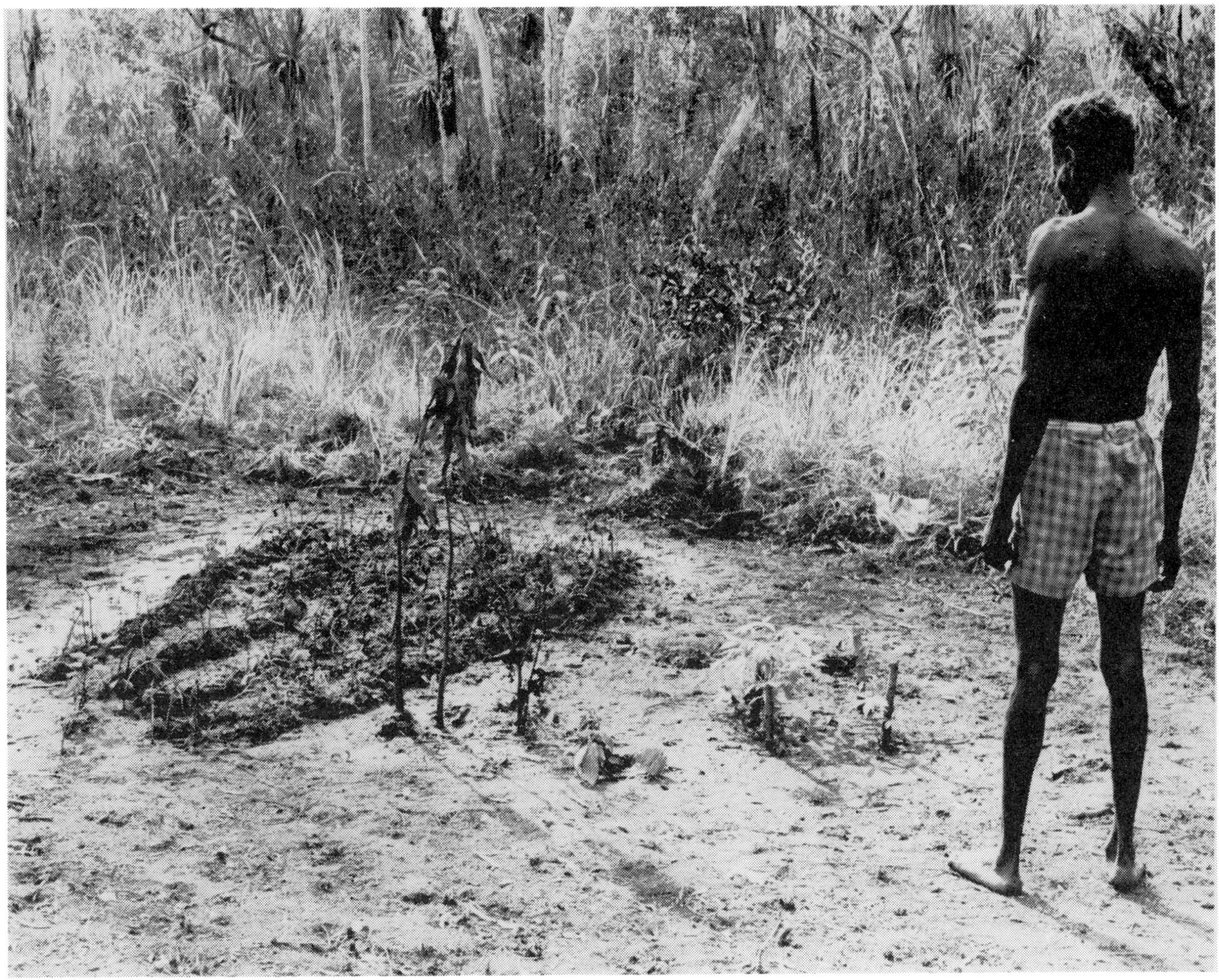

Figure 2. An Arnhem Land garden.

seeds were sought after since, once planted, they could be left and, nearly always, produced a good crop of melons at the beginning of the dry season; but they were never more than a tasty snack at the time of the year when food was naturally at its most abundant. In 1971, however, one band suddenly decided to take up gardening and approached the mission for plants. The plants arrived at a remote air-strip and were then carried 43 km. to the band base-camp. An area 5.5 m. in diameter was cleared, 18 m. from a small stream, and 100 potato plants, several small mango saplings, a lime tree and four cassava plants set in the ground (see Fig. 2). The women and young men in the group watered the garden daily with the aid of a tin can. Two weeks after the planting in early April, it was decided to move camp about 1.5 km. away. Watering the garden posed a problem, since it meant that somebody had to walk past it each day. The solution was quickly found: shifting cultivation! On the second day after the move, the garden was uprooted and re-planted beside the new camp. Not surprisingly, it failed to survive. At about the same time, this band also built a stock-yard near the original garden, although the closest cattle were 80 km. away and the area clearly unsuitable for grazing.

The motivation for both garden and stock-yard was political. In the preceding six years, the people had seen their land increasingly encroached upon by whites and had found that mining surveyors were damaging stones of significance. They understood that there was a threat of expropriation on the grounds that the country was not in use. The garden and stock-yard were an attempt to utilize the land in ways that they believed Europeans would identify with effective land-use.

It is significant that it was defence of territory, not economic pressure, that persuaded the people to try horticulture. In those parts of Arnhem Land where horticulture is possible, famine is unknown and population pressure was traditionally controlled ultimately by infanticide. Infanticide was not practised through awareness of population problems, but through pressure on individual women in the food quest. This lack of environmental stress plus the lack of materialism in the Aboriginal outlook, which may be ascribed in part to the need for portability and to the ethic of generosity, removed any economic motivation for the development of labour-intensive subsistence patterns. If there were no economic motive for taking up horticulture, the question of the failure to do so becomes decidedly ethnocentric. To attribute the absence of horticulture to other than economic factors is to ignore the ancient and enthusiastic history of borrowing from the north, and the fact that Aboriginal people throughout the continent have many husbanding and conservationist practices. Everywhere their aim appears to have been the protection of the efficiency of their subsistence adaptation and avoidance of the drudgery of horticulture.

Conclusion

Aboriginal conservatism is not the product of isolation, lack of inventiveness or lack of enthusiasm for change. It derives from the fact that hunting, gathering and fishing was the most efficient adaptation that Aboriginal man could have made from the time of his arrival to the coming of Europeans and of mechanized agriculture. The effectiveness of the adaptation ensures that, while there is dependence on traditional food sources that are distributed as they were in the past, and while movement is still by traditional means, Iron Age ethnography will continue to illuminate Stone Age remains.

REFERENCES

Barrett, M.J. and Brown, T. (1971) Increase in average height of Australian Aborigines. *Medical Jour. Australia*, 2, 1169-71.

Berndt, R.M. and Berndt, C.H. (1954) *Arnhem Land: its history and its people.* Melbourne.

Berndt, R.M. and Berndt, C.H. (1964) *The world of the first Australians: an introduction to the traditional life of the Australian Aborigines.* Sydney.

Birdsell, J.B. (1970) Local group composition among the Australian Aborigines: a critique of the evidence from field-work conducted since 1930. *Current Anthropology*, 11, 115-41.

Bowler, J.M., Jones, R., Allen, H. and Thorne, A.G. (1970) Pleistocene human remains from Australia: a living site and human cremation from Lake Mungo, Western New South Wales. *World Arch.*, 2, 39-60.

Clark, J.G.D. (1951) Folk-culture and the study of European prehistory. In Grimes, W.F. (ed.), *Aspects of Archaeology in Britain and Beyond*, 49-65. London.

Davidson, D.S. (1937) A preliminary consideration of Aboriginal Australian decorative art. *Mem. Amer. Phil. Soc.*, 9, 1-147.

Flannery, K.V. (1968) Archaeological systems theory and early Mesoamerica. In Meggers, B.J. (ed.), *Anthropological Archaeology in the Americas*, 67-87. Washington.

Freeman, L.G. (1968) A theoretical framework for interpreting archaeological materials. In Lee, R.B. and DeVore, I. (eds.), *Man the Hunter*, 262-7. Chicago.

Golson, J. (1971) Australian Aboriginal food plants. In Mulvaney, D.J. and Golson, J. (eds.), *Aboriginal Man and Environment in Australia*, 196-232. Canberra.

Golson, J. (1972) Land connections, sea barriers and the relationship of Australian and New Guinea prehistory. In Walker, D. (ed.), *Bridge and Barrier: the natural and cultural history of Torres Strait*, 375-97. Canberra.

Gregory, A.C. (1887) Memoranda on the Aborigines of Australia. *Jour. Anthrop. Inst.*, 16, 131-3.

Hiatt, L.R. (1962) Local organisation among the Australian Aborigines. *Oceania*, 32, 267-85.

Howells, W.W. and Warner, W.L. (1937) Anthropometry of the natives of Arnhem Land and the Australian race problem. *Pprs. Peabody Mus. Amer. Arch. and Ethnol.*, 16, 1-97.

Jukes, J.B. (1847) *Narrative of the Surveying Voyage of H.M.S. Fly . . . During the Years 1842-1846.* London.

Lee, R.B. (1969) !Kung Bushman subsistence: an input-output analysis. In Vayda, A.P. (ed.), *Environmental and Cultural Behaviour: Ecological Studies in Cultural Anthropology*, 47-79. New York.

Lee, R.B. (1972) !Kung spatial organization: an ecological and historical perspective. *Human Ecology*, 1, 125-47.

Lee, R.B. and DeVore, I. (1968) Problems in the study of hunters and gatherers. In Lee, R.B. and DeVore, I. (eds.), *Man the Hunter*, 3-12. Chicago.

Lommel, A. (1973) Changes in Australian art. In Pilling, A. and Waterman, R.A. (eds.), *Diprotodon to detribalization: studies of change among Australian Aborigines*, 217-36. East Lansing, Michigan.

Macknight, C.C. (1972) Macassans and Aborigines. *Oceania*, 42, 283-321.

McCarthy, F.D. (1957) Habitat, economy and equipment of the Australian Aborigines. *Australian Jour. Sci.*, 19, 88-97.

McCarthy, F.D. and McArthur, M. (1960). The food quest and the time factor in Aboriginal economic life. In Mountford, C.P. (ed.), *Records of the American-Australian scientific expedition to Arnhem Land,* II, 1450194. Melbourne.

McCarthy, F.D. and Setzler, F.M. (1960) The archaeology of Arnhem Land. In Mountford, C.P. (ed.), *Records of the American-Australian scientific expedition to Arnhem Land*, II, 215-95. Melbourne.

Meggitt, M.J. (1964) Aboriginal food-gatherers of tropical Australia. In. *The ecology of man in the tropical environment (I.U.C.N. Publ. Ser. 4)*, 30-7, Morges.

Mulvaney, D.J. (1969) *The Prehistory of Australia.* London.

Mulvaney, D.J. (1971) Aboriginal social evolution: a retrospective view. In Mulvaney, D.J. and Golson, J. (eds.), *Aboriginal man and environment in Australia*, 368-80. Canberra.

Peterson, N. (1973) Camp site location among Australian hunter-gatherers: archaeological and ethnographic evidence for a key determinant. *Arch. and physical anthrop. in Oceania,* 8, 173-93.

Radcliffe-Brown, A.R. (1930) The social organisation of Australian tribes. *Oceania*, 1, 34-63.

Sahlins, M. (1972) *Stone Age Economics.* Chicago.

Service, E.R. (1962) *Primitive Social Organisation: An Evolutionary Perspective.* New York.

Sharp, L. (1952) Steel axes for Stone Age Australians. *Human Organisation*, 11, 17-22.

Thomson, D.F. (1938) A new type of fish trap from Arnhem Land, Northern Territory of Australia. *Man*, 38, 193-8.

Thomson, D.F. (1939) The seasonal factor in human culture: illustrated from the life of a contemporary nomadic group. *P.P.S.*, 5, 209-21.

Thorne, A.G. and Macumber, P.G. (1972) Discoveries of Late Pleistocene man at Kow Swamp, Australia. *Nature*, 238, 316-9.

Tindale, N.B. (1925) Natives of Groote Eylandt and of the west coast of the Gulf of Carpentaria. *Records S. Australian Mus.*, 3, 61-134.

Vita-Finzi, C. and Higgs, E.S. (1970) Prehistoric Economy in the Mount Carmel Area of Palestine: Site Catchment Analysis. *P.P.S.*, 36, 1-37.

White, J.P. (1971) New Guinea and Australian prehistory: the 'neolithic problem'. In Mulvaney, D.J. and Golson, J. (eds.), *Aboriginal Man and Environment in Australia*, 182-95. Canberra.

Woodburn, J. (1968) An introduction to Hadza ecology. In Lee, R.B. and DeVore, I. (eds.), *Man the Hunter*, 49-55. Chicago.

Yellen, J. and Harpending, H. (1972) Hunter-gatherer populations and archaeological inference. *World Arch.*, 4, 244-53.

NOTES

1. Conservationist practices with various root staples are well known from various parts of Australia. A.C. Gregory reported the replacing of yam heads as widespread in Western Australia (1887:131). The practice probably derives from the method by which the yams are excavated. In Arnhem Land, the aerial part of the yam is followed down to where it enters the ground. The collector starts digging a hole in front of the vine, which is embedded in the back wall of the hole, with only the front surface exposed. When the tuber is reached, the hole is enlarged, but the vine still remains half embedded in the back wall after the tuber is broken free. This sometimes leaves a small piece of the top of the tuber attached to the plant, and adult women gatherers are careful to see that this happens, although young men, who sometimes dig to feed themselves when travelling cross-country, are not always so careful. Since the yams grow only in the small stands of monsoon forest that have escaped destruction by burning, mainly because of their location on the escarpments, or as strand vegetation along the rivers, ponds and lakes, a person returning to the same area can easily find the same hole again and notice the root re-growth. If a yam is harvested immediately after the end of the wet season and left to regenerate, it is possible to harvest it again three months or so later. Such young roots are soft and sweet, and are reserved for old people; a taboo that must have a conservationist effect, too.

WILFRED SHAWCROSS

Kauri Point Swamp: the ethnographic interpretation of a prehistoric site

Introduction

In some geographical respects New Zealand is a Southern Hemisphere counterpart of western Europe and Scandinavia, where so much of Grahame Clark's work has been done. Even so, I believe it is a tribute to the worth and practicability of his approaches that they should transplant so successfully, for by no means all archaeological formulae have travelled so well. Much of my own work, commencing in 1965 with the excavation of the Galatea Bay midden, which I carried out jointly with John Terrell, has been a development of the economic analysis embodied in the Star Carr report. However, my first investigation in New Zealand, hitherto incompletely reported, and the subject of this contribution, also took *Star Carr* as a model, but has moved in an entirely different direction. I am sure no other single piece of archaeological research has served so fruitfully as a guide to my work.

I can see several reasons why *Star Carr* has influenced me so deeply. When I was a student, I found great difficulty in discovering how archaeologists divined prehistory out of the material in the ground, but *Star Carr* was an exception, for in it one was led to an explicit view of the evidence by a structured argument. The evidence of human behaviour, long dead, in a society alien to one's own, does not organize itself into a self-evident pattern, but can only be articulated into a complex chain of reasoning, which seems to twist back and forth, and should be open to inspection. This pattern of evidence was set forth in *Star Carr*.

A second reason for my appreciation of the Star Carr report was the emphasis laid on the ethnographical evidence. Long before the current revival, Grahame Clark made his students conscious of the importance of modern ethnographic parallels. This explains the readiness with which so many of them turned to ethnographical evidence when working in Africa, America and Australasia. But it is not as obvious as it might appear, nor as straightforward, to combine archaeology with ethnography, as the present study will show.

Finally, *Star Carr* is a site report that reviews the state of the subject and re-synthesizes it. By comparison, most other reports fall short intellectually, as they are simply catalogues prepared under an assumption of objectivity, which miss the point that the archaeologist must actively interpret his evidence. Though Grahame Clark published many other significant works on European and World Prehistory, it is the Star Carr report, above all, whose influence will be detected here.

Background: New Zealand prehistory

The prehistory of New Zealand has been approached through Maori tradition, ethnology and archaeological field-work. Accounts reveal that as long ago as the 1840s buried sites were being excavated (Taylor 1870:414) and certain earthworks, middens, quarries and other sites are sufficiently striking features of the landscape to remind the thoughtful observer of ancient settlement. Systematic excavations, carried out in Otago in the earlier years of the present century (Skinner 1933:102; Leach 1972), revived the archaeological discoveries of von Haast in the 1870s. But the capacity of archaeology to establish an objective basis for prehistory was only established with Roger Duff's excavation and description of the site of Wairau Bar, on the basis of which he defined a 'Moa Hunter period of Maori culture' (1956), later called 'Archaic' by Golson (1959:36), the chronology of which was established by Lockerbie (1959:81) by means of radiocarbon dating. The bulk of earlier archaeological work had been undertaken in the South Island, which has rich coastal sites but a relatively restricted Late Prehistoric (eighteenth-century) population. In the 1950s, archaeological research developed rapidly in the North Island, the area within which Maori culture evidently reached its fullest development and, probably, the homeland where the culture evolved (Duff 1956:7). When, in 1959, Jack Golson reviewed New Zealand prehistory and presented the first strictly archaeological synthesis, including a definition of the later period, or 'Classic Maori', assemblage, he was unable to use evidence from controlled archaeological excavations comparable to that obtained for the Archaic in the South Island or from his own excavations in the north. For the later period, he was forced to rely on assemblages from a number of sites that had been excavated to supply ethnological collections, the best of these being that obtained from the North Island site of Oruarangi (Fisher 1934:275; Shawcross & Terrell 1966:404). In addition, he used non-excavated ethnographic material such as the collections of artefacts made by early explorers, and also that illustrated in published ethnologies such as *The Coming of the Maori* (Buck 1958). The result was a comprehensive review of the material culture of the early and late Classic assemblages, but one that inevitably showed little definition of the order in which changes took place within these periods, especially the later one.

Golson's 1959 survey focused attention on two issues; first, the problem of the relation of Archaic to Classic, whether the former was ancestral to, or submerged by, the latter. It also brought to light the need for archaeological research in the Classic Maori period which had, up to that time, probably seemed to be adequately accounted for from ethnological sources. Golson set out to investigate these questions and chose the Kauri Point *pa* site for excavation (1961:13). This choice was governed by the preservation of earthwork features at the site and by its position in an area where, since there are overlapping concentrations of both the Archaic and Classic forms of adze (1959:68), it was reasonable to expect evidence for their association, and perhaps even for their evolution, on a single site. Preliminary reports have already been published on these excavations (Ambrose 1962:56). It will be necessary to draw attention here only to a few general points arising from the excavation of the *pa*.

The results of the second and later seasons' work at Kauri Point have shown that there is not sufficient evidence that certain forms of earthwork were associated exclusively with one culture or period (see Groube 1968:141). The excavations revealed a complex of surface and semi-subterranean earthworks, including extensive scatters of post-holes, evidently the remains of timber-framed structures, and also groups of pits, usually rectangular, of various sizes. This range of material culture is now seen to be common to a substantial part of New Zealand archaeology. Unexpectedly, however, the site possessed only a limited quantity of portable artefacts, including very few classified as adzes. The relative poverty of artefactual materials on such sites has recently been confirmed by an excavation at the Ongari *pa* site, one and a half miles distant from Kauri Point (Shawcross 1966). The problems of developing a refined archaeological definition of the Classic assemblage and of finding evidence for the evolution of Classic culture remained unsolved by the excavation of the dry-land site occupied by the *pa* at Kauri Point. It therefore seemed reasonable to search for this missing evidence round the edges of the *pa*, where occupation debris may have been spilled over, especially where it may have accumulated in the adjoining gully. A further reason for investigating the gully is that a considerable part of Maori and Polynesian material culture was made of relatively perishable organic materials. For example, pottery, the dominant archaeological relic in many parts of the world, is absent from the Maori assemblage where it has been replaced by vessels of wood, gourds and matting. Swamps had long been known in New Zealand as a source of such ancient Maori woodwork, but almost always the discoveries had been made in the course of drainage and, with the exception of Duff's investigation of Waitara Swamp in North Island in 1960, very little attempt had been made to excavate them archaeologically. Waitara was the first large-scale and deliberate excavation of an archaeological swamp site and involved the digging of some 1,000 sq. yds. of swamp, with the objective of finding carved woodwork, whose presence had been indicated by the chance discovery of two carved panels. Although no further carving was found, eight separate groups of digging-sticks were recovered, as well as a number of individual specimens of this type (Duff 1961:303). Though not entirely success-

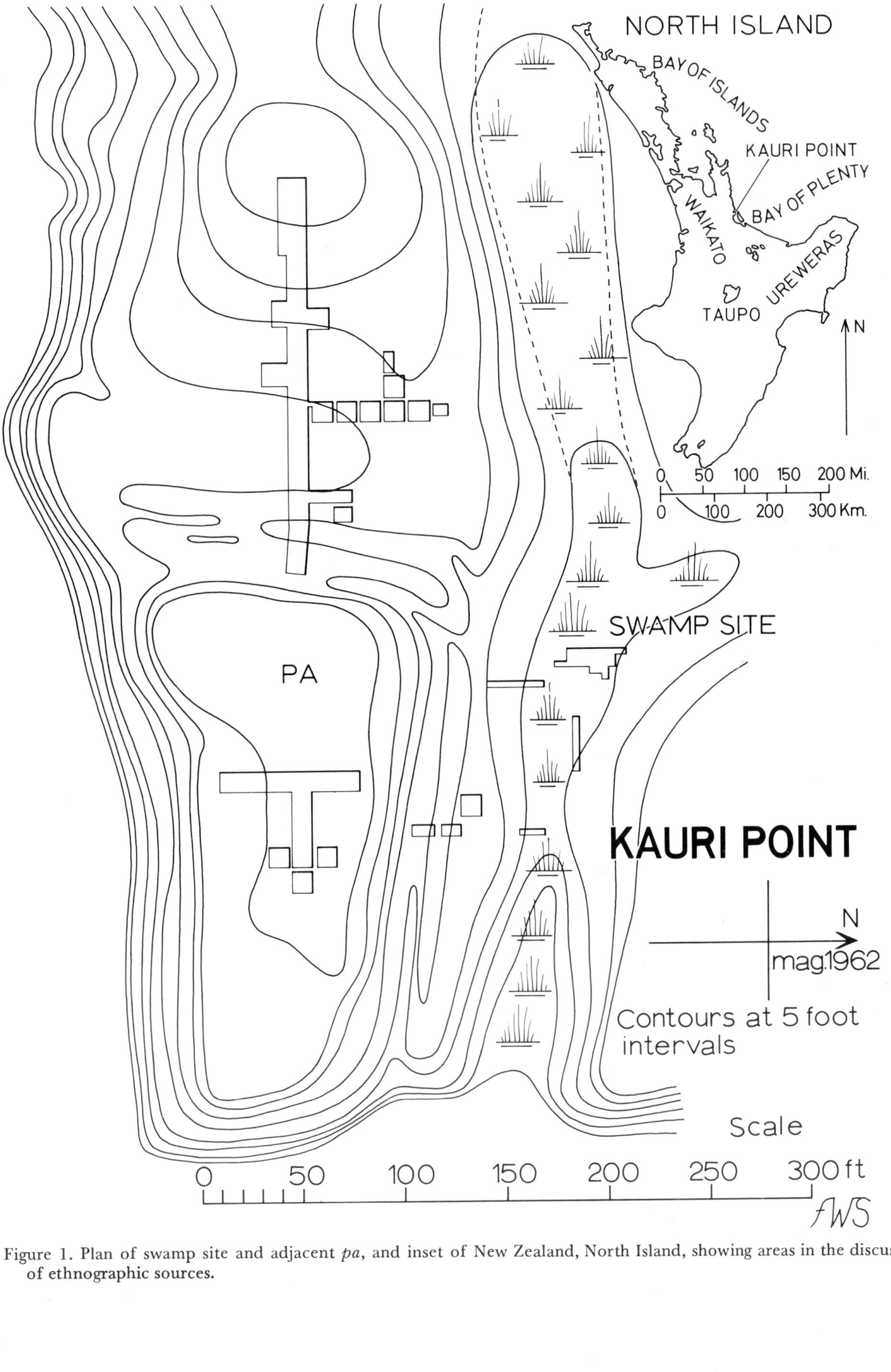

Figure 1. Plan of swamp site and adjacent *pa*, and inset of New Zealand, North Island, showing areas in the discussion of ethnographic sources.

ful, the Waitara Swamp excavations indicate the potential of such investigations, and the Kauri Point swamp site seemed a promising locality to pursue such an approach. The first season's excavation started in January 1962, and was followed by a longer season in 1963 and several short spells of work in subsequent years.

Kauri Point Swamp: physical description of the locality

The Kauri Point Swamp lies adjacent to the fortified earthwork of Kauri Point *pa* (N.Z. A.A. site no. N 53-54/5) which was the scene of the intensive excavation programme described above. The *pa* itself is one of a group of five located on the peninsula of Kauri Point, a consolidated sandstone plateau jutting out into the northern end of the sheltered waters of the Tauranga Harbour (see plan, Fig. 1). The swamp lies in the bottom of a narrow steep-sided gully, fed by two springs 200-300 yards inland, which empties by a low and picturesque waterfall into the sea. The gully forms a natural defence along one side of the *pa*, which is protected on two other sides by cliffs.

Swamp investigation

There were two immediate problems about investigating the swamp for possible archaeological evidence. In the first place, there was the difficulty of locating remains in a relatively large and featureless swamp. It was not considered justifiable to excavate completely so large an area, nor was there adequate labour. A second problem was the height of the water-table, which supported a great body of water and waterlogged vegetation in the form of a quaking morass. Archaeological finds were likely to be discovered at some depth below the level of the water and there was no knowing how this spongy deposit would sustain either vertical archaeological sections or even the archaeologists themselves.

The method of location employed was to survey two parallel rows of pegs at one-yard intervals running on either side of the swamp. A tape-measure was then drawn between the pegs on opposite sides and one worker would traverse the swamp along the tape, driving a steel probe or 'gum spear' down into the deposits at yard intervals. The probe is a five-foot length of 3/8 in. diameter mild-steel reinforcing rod with a handle at one end and the other end slightly expanded to form a button. Such implements are known as gum spears as they have long been employed in New Zealand to search the swamps for buried kauri gum, the solidified blocks of resin formed by kauri pine. It is possible to discriminate between soft and hard deposits by this simple device, both by feel and by sound, and in this survey the worker who used the spear called out the nature and depth of the materials encountered to another worker on the shore, who plotted the information on a scale-drawing of the yard grid.

After a traverse had been completed, the tape-measure was advanced another yard upstream and the process repeated. Although this may appear to be laborious, the whole survey was completed in two days. The resulting plan showed a number of isolated obstructions caused by pieces of wood and stones and one area, stretching out about six yards into the swamp by about three yards wide, opposite to the *pa*. The distinctive feature of this area was its consistency and the ringing note given out by the obstructions, which were thought to be shells but turned out to be flakes of obsidian. This area was selected for excavation, and was at first thought to be a midden spilling out into the swamp.

The second problem, that of drainage, was tackled by digging a channel 4-5 ft. deep, up from the waterfall, surrounding the proposed excavation area, so that all surface-water was diverted; sufficient gravity drainage was established for the first season. In the second season, a small motor-pump was obtained and these methods were sufficient to enable excavations to be carried out to a final depth of nearly six feet.

Swamp excavation

The tools used in the swamp excavation were the small pointing trowel, sharpened to a knife-edge along one side, and the plasterer's small tool with a triangular blade about 2 in. by 1 in. These tools were well adapted to the slow rate of excavation, averaging about 1.5 cu. ft. per worker per day. Footboards of various sizes were found to be necessary for walking across the site and for standing or kneeling upon, and wooden boxes or 'horses' also used here were imitated from the equipment of the fenmen used at Peacock's Farm by Clark (1936). These 'horses' had a variety of uses, such as steps and building blocks to support planks. The excavating tools could not be used in the normal dry-land manner, for scraping or digging, because these methods produced an uncontrolled mess. Instead, the deposit had to be cut out, like blocks of cake, usually about an inch deep and the same wide, by about six inches long. The trowel was used like a knife and, with experience, it was sensitive enough to allow the change in texture between the deposit and other materials to be detected. If nothing was encountered, the block was lifted and crumbled in the hands to avoid overlooking small pieces. This was effective because the blocks would break away easily from any smooth-walled substance, and the success and delicacy of the excavation methods is shown by the small number of objects that were damaged.

The level of water in the site controlled the method of excavation, making it impossible to operate in isolated squares or at different levels. Excavating would commence at the end of the trench closest to the centre of the swamp, that is, to the lowest point of drainage, and proceed towards the landward end, following a slight slope parallel to the original surface. If the excavator went below this common level of drainage, his part of the deposit was immediately flooded with muddy water and became impossible to excavate. Owing to the limited equipment, the water-levelled excavation surface was used in measuring the depth of the finds, relative to the top of the section closest to the find.

The method of excavation aimed to leave artefacts and structural evidence standing until their positions had been three-dimensionally recorded. Most of the small objects were left standing on pedestals of deposit until recorded and were then placed in sealed plastic bags. The larger structural timbers were left for as long as possible, until their presence began to interfere seriously with excavation. However, if this had been applied to the obsidian flakes, of which there were some 14,000, progress would have been far too slow, so they were normally excavated and recorded in grid squares (1 yd. square), with no effort to record the exact position of every piece, except where the flakes were identified as being in clusters, and then these were treated in the same way as the other artefacts.

Swamp deposits and stratigraphy

'Swamp' as used here is a precise term. Swamps are fed by mineral-rich water, are eutrophic and moderately acid, whereas 'bogs' are considered to be fed by rain-water only, are oligotrophic and much more acid than swamps (Newbould 1958:88). In New Zealand, the flora characteristic of the eutrophic swamp includes *raupo*, flax, *toetoe, carex* and *scirpus* sedges, swamp *coprosma*, cabbage-trees and willows; whereas bogs would include *Manuka* and *Epacris paniflora,* (*Utricularia* spp., *Drosera binata, Drosera*

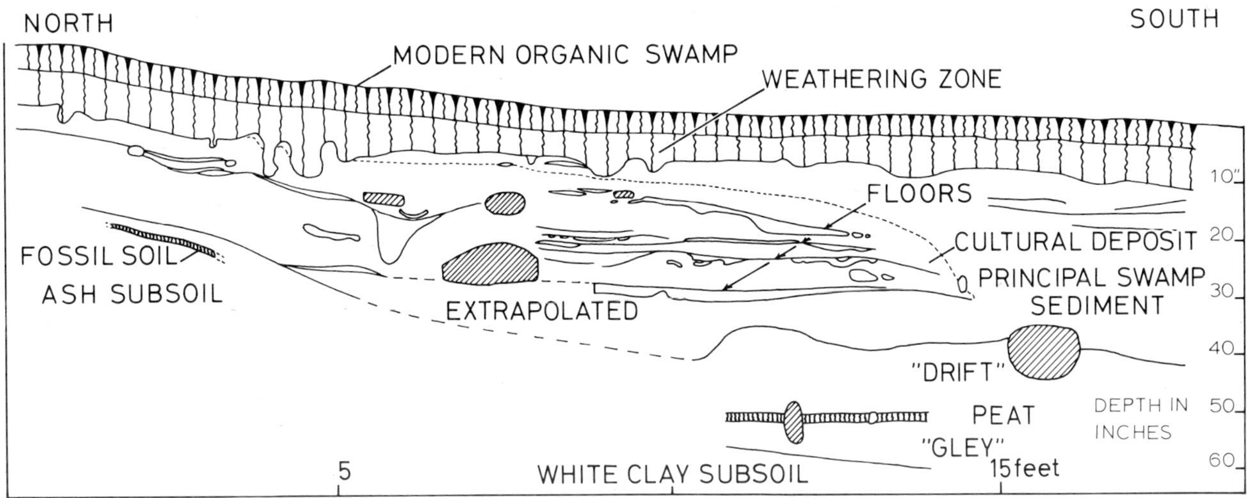

Figure 2. Section of swamp site.

spathulata – all species of insectivorous plants), *Schoenus brevifolius* and *Cladium teretifolium* sedges, lycopods, the umbrella and comb ferns, sphagnum mosses and liverworts (Butcher 1965:55, 61). The flora of the swamp before excavation and partial drainage is judged to correspond to Butcher's swamp plant assemblage, and certainly the hydrology of the site is that of a swamp, while the most acid parts of the deposits, having a pH value of 5.8, correspond to an apparently normally acid turf loam and are considerably less acid than the values of 4.0-3.8 pH given for bogs (Butcher 1965:60).

The stratum through which the swamp-filled gully is cut is a consolidated sandstone, capped by volcanic ashes of the Waihi formation of Pleistocene age, which is of considerably greater antiquity than man in New Zealand. The sediments (see section, Fig. 2) that form the swamp deposit consist of re-deposited sand, derived in part from the sandstone, mixed with a considerable proportion of organic material, macroscopic, microscopic and amorphous. These organic sandy sediments, which will be called the principal swamp sediments, are a dark reddish brown, with a Munsell soil-colour of 2.5 YR N3 and a pH of 5.8. They are homogeneous, showing virtually no sorting throughout the full depth of over five feet of examined sections. There are, however, some almost horizontal laminations in the cultural deposits which are referred to as 'floors', some of which are clearly man-made, from local ash-soil, and there are thin dense organic 'floors', presumably made from crushed plants. There are also several small lenses of cleaner silt that are thought to have been deposited in running water, probably due to small-scale flooding.

The principal swamp sediments, containing the archaeological deposits, do not directly overlie the consolidated sandstone, but are separated by a distinct dark-grey zone with a pH of 6.6, generally about six inches deep. This soil is found at the base of all sections and overlies a plastic light-coloured sandy deposit, 10 YR 3/2, pH 6.7, thought to be a weathering product of the consolidated sandstone. It was surprising that, in two of the separate cut sections, small flecks of charcoal occurred below the lower soil-zone. The charcoal is certainly not a recent intrusion and certainly there is no evidence for cultural deposits underlying the soil.

The upper part of the principal swamp deposit is marked by a zone of severe weathering and by irregular disturbances of the surface, caused by root systems of water-plants. This upper oxidized zone was, clearly, subsequent to the formation of the main deposit, because it contained obsidian and, in its lower parts, the badly-damaged remains of combs and other woodwork. There is no reason to suppose that oxidation took place at the time of excavation, or immediately before, as the deposits were protected by waterlogged vegetation that acted as a reservoir throughout the summer, not normally an extended dry period in this part of New Zealand. It is suggested that there must have been a period, at the end of the formation of the main sediments, when the water-level of the swamp was seriously lowered, presumably due to a decline in activity of the local springs allowing the swamp surface to dry and initiating oxidation of the upper sediment zone. These springs must be fed by water falling in the Kaimai hills about five miles inland, and a tentative explanation would be that their activity was reduced as a result of deforestation from milling during the late-nineteenth and early-twentieth centuries.

A further feature of the swamp sediments may be noticed here. Above the old buried soil-zone there is a deposit of tangled timbers and branches of the type described as 'drift' in Danish archaeological usage (I thank Jan Hjarno for advice on this point). The 'drift' does not appear to have been wood growing on the spot where it is now found, so it may represent timber washed into the gully shortly after the commencement of the formation of the principal sediments and can be taken to mark the initial forest clearance of the area, accompanied by accelerated erosion.

The cultural deposits are formed within the principal sediments and combine artificial with natural elements. The obvious artificial introductions are artefacts, timber structures and concentrations of sticks. Additionally, there is a distinct reddening of the deposits immediately surrounding the archaeological materials, caused by small particles of red ochre.

Structural evidence (Fig. 3)

The archaeological evidence for structure on the site may be divided into four types. The first indication of a structure that is encountered is a

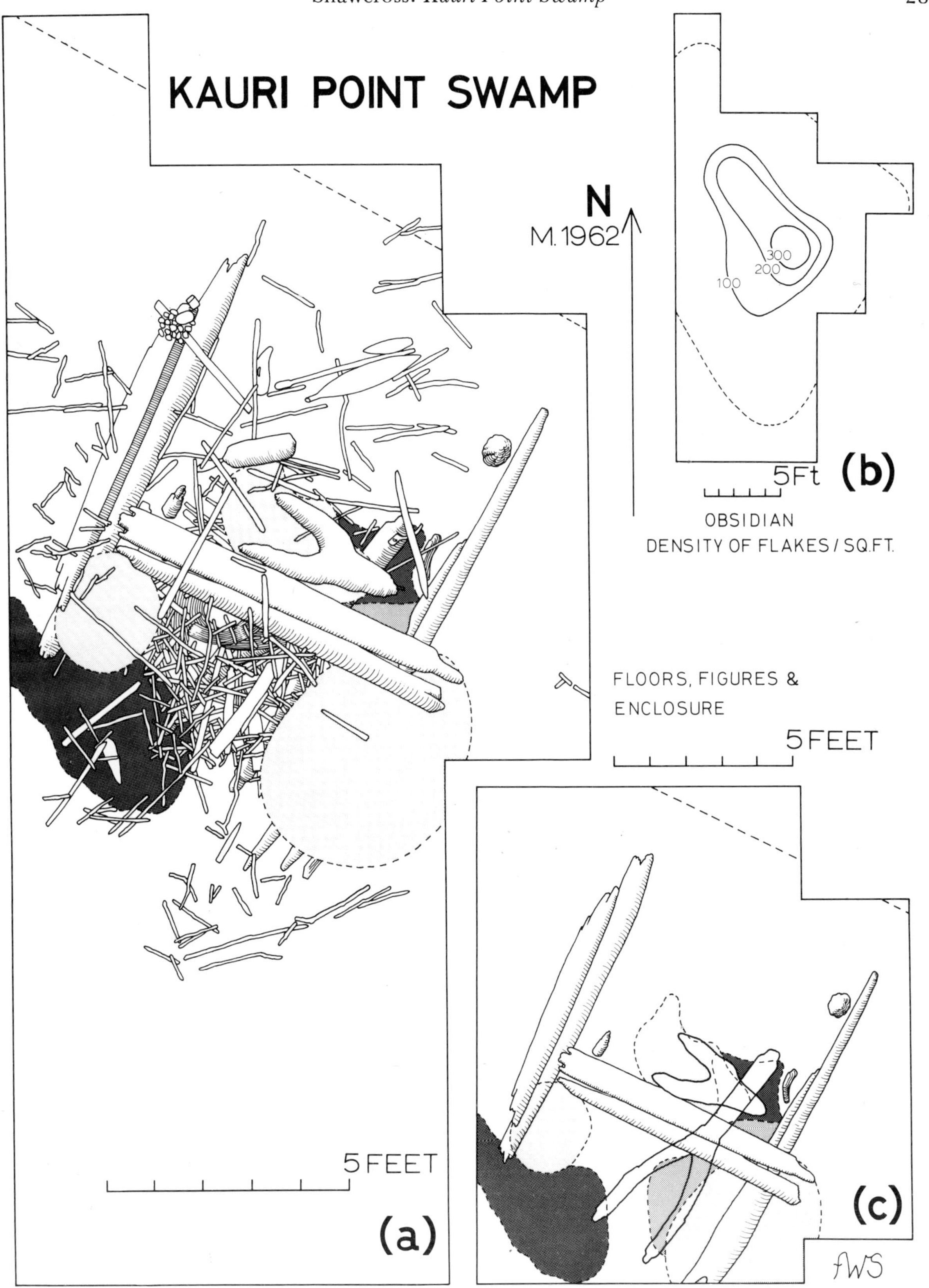

Figure 3. (a) Composite plan of finds and structures within the site. (b) Plan of density of obsidian flakes with contours at intervals of 100 flakes/sq. foot. (c) Main timber structure, wooden figures and floors.

scatter of sticks and twigs, the uppermost being considerably decomposed. Some of these sticks appear to have been worked and had sharpened ends, and with these may be included a number of, usually broken, shafted artefacts such as spears, digging-sticks and at least one paddle. When this scattered material was first found it was not immediately obvious that it was structural, as many of the unworked pieces might have been light driftwood such as one would expect to find in a swamp. Fortunately, most of these objects were planned, and the deeper the excavation continued the more clear it became that these sticks were concentrated in a single area, not randomly scattered. The majority of this group of objects were placed horizontally, as if piled on one another, but some had been driven roughly vertically into the deposits. Several of these must have stood above the former water-level, for their upper parts were badly decayed, yet they were otherwise too deep to have been recently affected. With these should be included six more substantial vertical pieces that seem to have been intended to pin part of the structure together. They were not obviously made for the job and do not give the appearance of careful planning and, like some of the smaller sticks, are decayed at the top as if they, too, had stood proud of the swamp surface.

The second distinctive structural feature is a rectangular construction (Fig. 3c), formed on three sides by pairs of worked timbers about eight feet long apiece. Some of these had clearly been carefully worked but, equally clearly, they had originally been intended for some other function – judging by the tenon joints found on one specimen, they may have been house-timbers (Bellwood 1971:83) and their incorporation in the present structure was a re-use. The fourth side of the rectangle was formed by the shelving shore of the swamp. The horizontal timbers were pinned in place by the six vertical posts previously mentioned. The scatter of twigs and sticks coincides with the rectangular structure and spills out beyond it into the swamp.

The third structural feature is a group of small horizontal lenses or floors, of which seven are recorded (Fig. 3c). They are irregular patches, roughly 3 to 10 sq. ft. in area, superimposed within the stratigraphic sequence at the off-shore end of the rectangular structure. Several of the floors are extremely obvious, having been formed of bright yellowish volcanic ash or sandy subsoil found in the neighbourhood of the swamp. They were tightly compressed, no more than an inch thick, and stood out sharply in colour and texture from the surrounding deposit. These soil-floors showed no sign of exposure, being neither weathered nor penetrated by roots. Two of them were formed out of chips of wood, presumably waste from the adze-dressing of timbers. With so much woodwork, stone and these chips, the first impression of the site was a bit like a workshop, but anyone who has any experience of woodworking will know that a real workshop produces vast quantities of wood-waste, far more than is represented here. Finally, there appear to have been several surfaces of organic material of the type already discussed in the section on stratigraphy. The plants in these deposits were perhaps reeds that had been compressed, but they had not been woven and may merely have been deformed by trampling. These surfaces were very difficult to follow in plan, although they showed up quite well in section.

The final structural feature is the dense concentration of artefacts, including obsidian flakes, wooden combs, gourd sherds and numerous less common items, such as broken muscial instruments and wooden vessels. The concentration of these finds is very high by any archaeological standards. Within a single area of 150 sq. ft. were deposited 200 originally complete combs (Shawcross 1964b:385), and about 14,000 obsidian flakes (Shawcross 1964a:15), see Fig. 3b. Furthermore, about 95% of each artefact-class was concentrated within a much smaller area of 50 sq. ft., within the rectangular structure defined by the timber frame. It is clear that the association of these different features, the timber frame, scatter of sticks, floors and artefacts was not accidental, but was deliberately contrived. It should be stressed that the concentration of objects and structural features coincide, so that there is no possibility of the excavated area being merely part of a random distribution of material throughout the swamp.

It may be asked whether the evidence suggests a deliberate pile of objects in a structure erected over a short time; or an enclosure left open over a period of time, into which objects were occasionally placed. The stratigraphic, typological and other evidence points to the latter conclusion. It is certain that the concentration was not built from a reinforced deposit of earth and artefacts, constructed in a short time. There is no sharp stratigraphical break between the principal swamp-sediment and the sediments within the structure, indeed they are homogeneous. Nor is there evidence for the disturbance of the deposits within the structure, such as one would expect if they had been formed as an earthwork fill. The 'floors' that are integral with the structure also extend outside into the swamp sediments and show no sign of disturbance; indeed they effectively seal artefacts, lessening the risk of the order of artefactual deposition being inverted or otherwise disturbed. Admittedly, it may be argued that if the structure was a receptacle for artefacts, why should some of them be outside its formal limits? This could be explained by water-action for the smaller wooden objects, though it would not explain the dispersal of the obsidian. However, when one looks at the plan of the frequency distribution of the flakes in Fig. 3b, one is struck by the resemblance of the diagram to that of a pattern of shots fired at a target. This suggests that many of the objects may have been thrown at the marked rectangular area from the shore of the swamp. Clearly, at this range, very few would have fallen short, but a proportion must have overshot the mark, as will be seen in comparing the distribution of flakes with the structure.

The typological argument against deposition at a single instant rests on the evidence, discussed below, that there was a formal change in the wooden combs, which correlates with the depth of their deposition and that, in the period of immediate contact with Europeans, only one of these forms or types was encountered, suggesting that the other forms were truly prehistoric.

A further sedimentological line of argument for the gradual formation of the deposit is the way the archaeological relics remained at approximately the same distance from the shore at whatever depth they are found in the deposits. Thus, the upper timbers of the rectangle are definitely offset from those beneath.

These observations combine to suggest that the framed structure was a rectangular enclosure, into which objects were intentionally and occasionally, though not always accurately, placed. This interpretation is accepted in preference to the suggestion that the site may have been a platform within the swamp, and that the deposit might have been formed as the result of one event.

Artefacts (Figs. 4 and 5)

The following is a brief catalogue of the artefact assemblage, whose purpose is to illustrate the range of material so that the function of the site may be more fully assessed. References are given to previously published discussions on parts of the assemblage, with a few additions, principally those suggesting the fluctuating intensity in the use of the site.

Stone flakes

The most frequent items found in the Kauri Point Swamp site are obsidian flakes (Shawcross 1964a:15). These were originally estimated at a little over 13,000 pieces, but subsequent investigations have now increased their numbers to close on 14,000. It was recognized during excavation that the flakes were technologically simple and that they were unlikely to reveal significant typological variation over time, which led to the decision not to measure their position as closely as that of other artefacts. It also became apparent that quite a number of the flakes occurred together in clusters and, wherever possible, these were isolated and excavated as a group, of which twelve were recorded. The size of the clusters ranged between five and sixty specimens, the latter being the number of flakes recorded in an exceptionally perfect group, found with a hammer-stone inside a gourd (Shawcross 1963:50). Probably more, if not all, of the flakes were also originally in clusters, though this was very difficult to recognize during excavation, and a proportion of the observed groups were placed in containers, either gourds or rough 'wallets' made out of fine matting.

The discovery of this assemblage prompted an investigation of other flakes in Oceania and an analysis was developed from first principles. The term 'flake' is used here in preference to 'lithic', which is now gaining acceptance, because the term 'lithic' must also include stone adzes on which there is now a massive literature in Oceania. Apart from Australia and New Zealand, little of significance has been reported on the flake industries, where even now excavators have

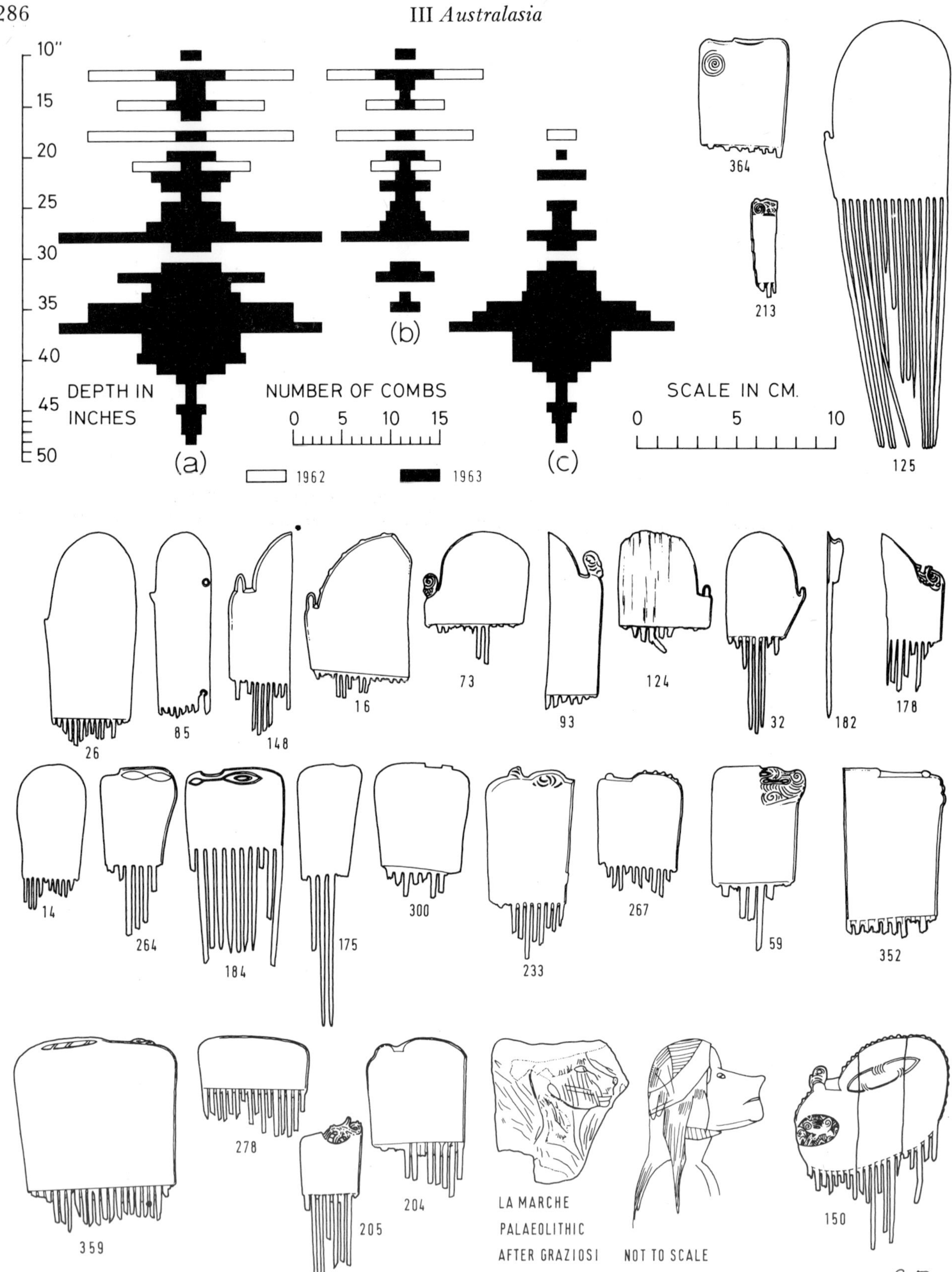

Figure 4. (a) Bar diagram of all combs excavated at depth intervals of 1 in. (b) Frequencies of all round-topped and side-knobbed combs. (c) Frequencies of all square-topped and notched combs. All combs drawn to scale. Lower row, Palaeolothic engravings of 'muzzled' men (not to scale).

either found only relatively small assemblages, as in Samoa (see Peters 1969:210), or may still be ignoring the material.

In New Zealand there have been a number of flake studies, notably a classification published by Skinner and Teviotdale on South Island material, based on an assemblage from the Shag River site (1927:180). This and other analyses were a combination of three different concepts: technique of manufacture, form and function. Some of the formal types distinguished in these studies have been borrowed, without adequate definition, from Palaeolithic and American studies, which results in miscellaneous groups of objects being squeezed into formal classes. Generally, also, functions of flake tools have been little better than guessed. In spite of optimism in the 1960s, progress in the study of the function of flake-tools has not been particularly noteworthy. Two directions seemed open for further work in this field: the first based on a study of the techniques of manufacture, and the second was on a supposedly objective study of traits.

The analysis of the Kauri Point assemblage supported the original opinion that it possessed no formal types. Indeed, this was among the earliest departures from the rigid application of typology in the local stone industries, which has not yet led to a more positive understanding. At the same time, the assemblage was compared with others in New Zealand, and a group of experimental obsidian industries were manufactured to assist in evaluating the comparisons. These led to the conclusion that the Kauri Point and certain South Island assemblages, particularly in the area of the Waitaki and Shag rivers, are less closely related than might be expected from the otherwise apparent homogeneity of Archaic Maori culture. Indeed, these South Island industries, which have been further studied by B.F. Leach (1970), look thoroughly out of place in Polynesia. The analysis also suggested that the Kauri Point assemblage could be distinguished from flake assemblages that were the waste products of adze manufacture. A discussion of its possible function will be left to a later section.

Combs (Fig. 4)

The group of wooden combs found at Kauri Point is a remarkable one, and approximately doubles the number of authentic Maori combs known to exist. It is of exceptional value because of the information it gives on the interpretation and antiquity of various motifs in Maori art, and Classic Maori culture, of which the art is a defining trait. Indeed, the assemblage offers insights into the character of the ancient Maori artist himself, which conflict with the conventional view of the 'primitive artist', but fall in with opinions recently expressed by Gerbrand's (1967) ethnographic study. Finally, the assemblage offers a rare opportunity to study the processes of formal change in an artefact-class under archaeologically controlled conditions.

Some 334 large fragments and almost complete combs were recovered. The majority had been broken along the grain and across the teeth, resulting in over 1,000 separate teeth being collected from the deposits. It is possible to estimate how many combs must originally have been represented from the pattern of breakages. The closest estimate for complete combs would be 187. The frequencies and distributions of the measured dimensions are given in Shawcross (1964b). The average length of the frames of these combs is 6.3 cm. and ranges between 3 and 13 cm. The average width of the frames is 4.4 cm. with a range between 2 and 7 cm. The thickness of the wood is far less variable, with a mean of 4 mm. and a range of 3 to 6 mm. In general, these wooden combs are considerably smaller than the better-known whale-bone specimens, though larger wooden ones appeared in the upper levels, and there were also a few large examples from the lower levels.

The evidence for the evolution of the comb design can be shown much more specifically, through the recognition of two basic formal types, round and square-topped respectively. The frequencies of these two types are plotted against their depths (see Figs. 4b, 4c), which discloses that only square-topped combs are found at the greatest depths (up to 48 in. below datum) and it is only above 35 in. that round-topped specimens appear, finally replacing their predecessors entirely above 18 in. The accompanying figure is a more precise description of the frequency and depths of the combs than that of the previously published report. A certain amount of inaccuracy is introduced in the uppermost 21 in., owing to imprecise

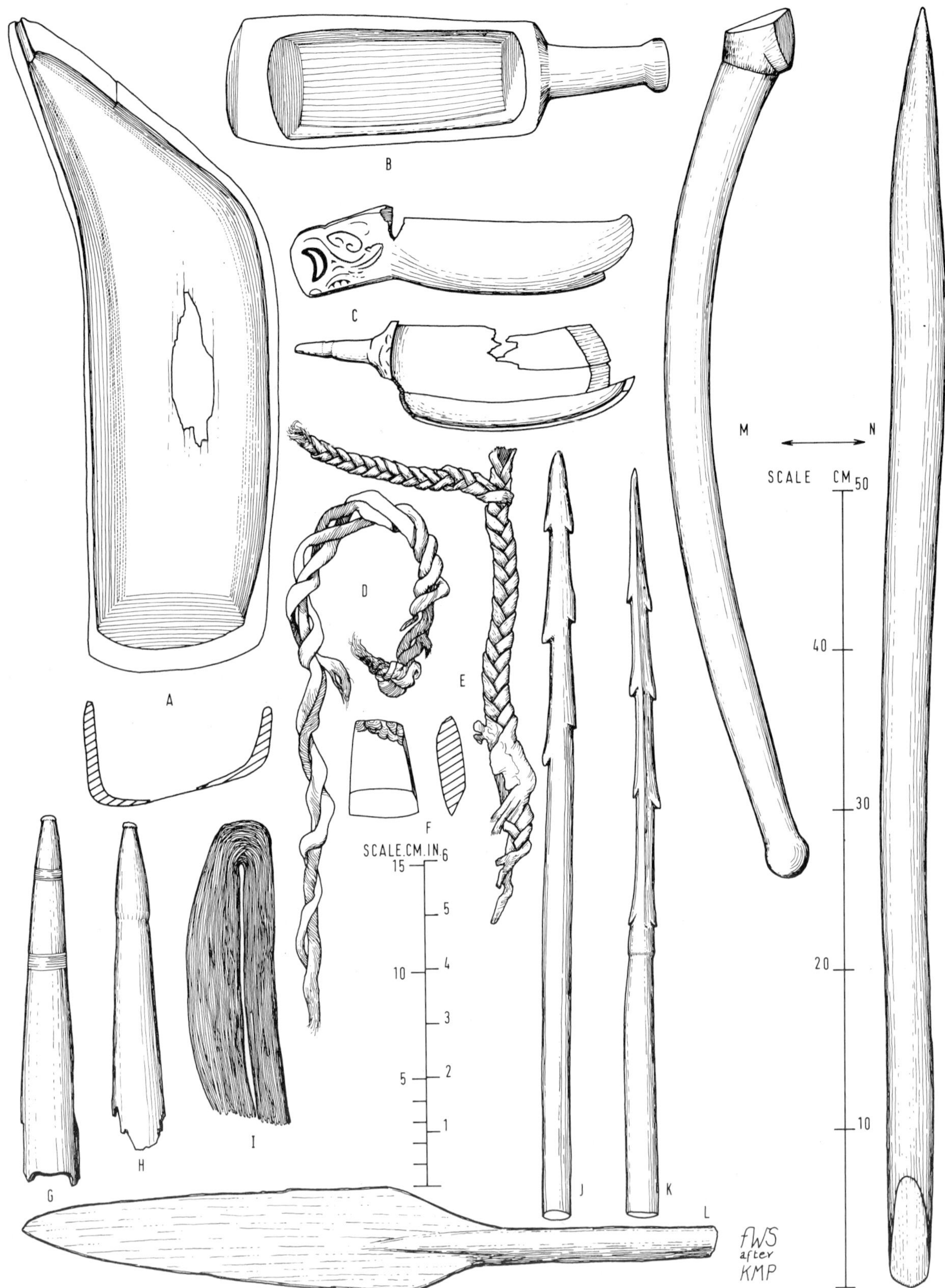

Figure 5. A-C, vessels; D, E, cordage; F, adze-blade; G, H, flutes; I 'brush'; J, K, spears; L, gardening tool. M, N, adze-handle and digging-stick, at different scale. Drawings after originals by K.M. Peters.

recording that occurred during the first season in some squares. The first bar-diagram, (a) in the figure, represents totals of all combs according to depth and it will be seen that the frequencies are not constant. To some extent the sharp decrease in numbers below 41 in. can be explained by a reduction in the volume of excavated deposit and it should be possible to make corrections for this factor, but these could not explain the fluctuations in the higher levels, due to altering rates of sediment formation, or of comb deposition, the latter seeming to be the more probable.

The earliest definite increase in comb deposition appears at a depth of 41 in. and reaches a peak at 37 in. and subsequently declines before a second smaller peak which is followed by a break. There is a third major peak followed by a rapid decline to a low figure, then a fourth increase. The upper part of the sequence cannot be so certainly interpreted, but may represent as many as three increases of deposition, giving a maximum of seven peaks of deposition and three or four possible breaks.

Maori decorative motifs

Many of the combs in the upper levels of the site compare closely with specimens collected on Captain Cook's voyages and illustrated by the expedition artists, notably a series by Sydney Parkinson (1784: Pl. XVI, XVII). The combs themselves are a trait of Classic Maori culture, with the qualification that they were probably not worn in certain important areas, particularly the Waikato Basin, and generally in the west of the North Island. However, a number of the combs carry 'ornamental' motifs that form an important part of the repertoire of Maori art. Therefore, the assemblage provides a rare instance of material evidence for the antiquity both of these motifs and of characteristic elements of Classic Maori culture.

The two most important motifs are the spiral and the *manaia*, often identified as a bird's head or bird-headed man. The *manaia* may be further subdivided into a naturalistic profile head, resembling a small profile human face, and a stylized form, recognizable by its eye, spurred nose and elongated mouth or beak. Combs with naturalistic and stylized *manaia* are found in the upper levels of the site and, indeed, a comb with a *manaia* motif was collected on Captain Cook's first voyage (Shawcross 1970:305). Examples of both motifs are found down to two-thirds of the depth of the deposit, the deepest example of the naturalistic form at 32 in. and of the stylized type at the 36 in. level. Combs with spiral designs are more rare, but two rather crude specimens, nos. 213 and 364 (see Fig. 4), are found at 35 in. and 36 in. respectively. On the evidence for age of the site, these specimens would have been deposited between the mid-sixteenth and the late eighteenth century, and it makes them the oldest stratified examples of Classic Maori motifs. If the traits have this age, then the art-style itself has at least an equal antiquity. It might seem obvious that such a distinctive art-style would have a recognizable ancestry, but forceful arguments have been made to reduce the antiquity of the Classic Maori culture (Groube 1967:453). It seems more probable, judging from the restrained use of decoration throughout the Kauri Point material and its absence from some items such as flutes, which were so highly decorated in the late eighteenth century, that the extensive use of rich decoration developed only in late prehistoric times. This may have been a process of secularization of formerly powerful images, just as in modern times the semaphore symbol of the Campaign for Nuclear Disarmament has become temporarily a motif in popular jewelry.

When the assemblage was originally excavated, the forms and decorations of the combs appeared wholly obscure, indeed wilfully strange. No explanation could be given for asymmetrically placed knobs or notches cut into the comb profiles, or for small zones of fretted or engraved decoration. It has since become apparent that the knobbed round-topped (Fig. 4, upper row) and notched square-topped ones are the same design adapted to two different frame shapes. Later, one comb, no. 150 (Fig. 4), was found that combined the motifs of both frame shapes, with additional designs that clearly demonstrated the anthropomorphism of the combs. Here the eye is obvious, as is the mouth, with its three triangular teeth and small inexplicable figure between the teeth. The nose consists of a bridge, represented by a horizontal notch, and bulbous nose-tip, which is a naturalistic *manaia*, not unlike a miniature of the face on the comb itself. This practice of identifying parts of the body and features by means of small anthropomorphic designs seems to be a rare but distinctive feature of Polynesian art from a number of islands. The best known and most dramatic example of the convention is the wooden figure, identified from the Austral group, now in the British Museum, in which the eyes, nose and mouth, as well as other parts of the body, are represented by small human figures (Ellis 1829, II:220; Barrow 1972:112). There are several other examples of this convention illustrated by Barrow, and one must conclude that it was a feature of early Polynesian art, before the dispersal of the Polynesians to distant island-groups such as New Zealand.

Comb no. 150 at Kauri Point Swamp is especially relevant to the debate among Polynesian art historians over the derivation and identification of the *manaia* design. Barrow is with Skinner in believing that the motif is that of the head and beak of a bird (1972:54). In its more conventional versions the design closely resembles the frigate-bird motif found in works of art of the distant, and culturally unrelated, Admiralty Islands (Haddon 1895). Barrow also points to the significance of bird heads and bird-headed men in the art of Easter Island, which is culturally much closer to New Zealand (Barrow 1972:134). In contrast, Archey (1933:209) has developed an interesting argument showing how the *manaia* design could be derived by intermediate examples from one or other side of the frontal mask that is a common element of Maori anthropomorphic carving, concluding that the *manaia* was a conventionalized human face. Indeed, he went further and showed how reorganization of the *manaia* would even transform it into the double spiral. The awkward aspects of Archey's argument were that they had an evolutionary basis that required ancestral and derived forms, whereas the examples were all drawn from that ungainly division of time, the 'ethnographic present'. In a study of 'anthropomorphic forms' in Palaeolithic art, Andrée Rosenfeld suggests (Ucko & Rosenfeld 1972) that there is an apparently high level of ambiguity among supposedly human forms and that figures that would be identified as human on their specifically human characteristics may also possess features taken from other, equally specific, animals. The relevance of this to the problem of human or bird derivation of a motif in Maori art is obvious: from the point of view of European categories or objective classification, it may not be feasible to force an exclusive interpretation on the evidence. However, there is continuity of Maori art from prehistoric times to the present and the carved figures with frontal masks are found on the vertical panels of meeting-houses, where they are identified with human ancestors. Thus, one can say that certain possibly ambiguous forms are identified as human in the culture itself.

Returning to comb no. 150, it is suggested that the elliptical eye, toothed mouth, nose with bridge and tip, and knobbed profile that may represent hair, all converge to make the design anthropomorphic. In no other comb are all elements so complete or so obviously related, but the location or combination of these motifs is always consistent with the explicit arrangement of this comb. In the illustration (Fig. 4, lower row), this comb has been juxtaposed with some Palaeolithic anthropomorphic engravings from the site of La Marche (Graziosi 1960:85), which have been chosen to illustrate how the, presumably human, face was distorted in a similar, almost animal-snouted, manner within the artistic conventions of a cultural tradition that could scarcely be more separated from the Maori.

The apparently regular manner in which the earlier square type of comb and decoration became replaced by the later round-topped form is an unusually well-documented and stratigraphically controlled example, and has been used by D.L. Clarke for teaching purposes as an illustration of what he calls 'double lenticular ontogeny' (1968:204). The more frequent examples of such ontogeny are arrangements of isolated assemblages or grave-goods into a seriation. In the past few years, such seriations have achieved a high level of perfection of ordering through computer application of consistent rules of what might be called artefactual genetics. In a sense, however, the results of such analyses may be almost too perfect. At Kauri Point the time element, which is normally predicted in such seriations, is under a rigid stratigraphic control. It is almost as close as archaeological conditions are ever likely to approximate to a sensitive relative chronology. The rate of swamp-deposition was fairly rapid, of the order of 1 cm. per annum, as against 0.1 cm. per annum in Palaeolithic caves. At this point it can only be said that the assemblage does not 'behave' in as straightforward a manner as might be expected of the birth of new forms and the extinction of old ones. Admittedly, the apparently lenticular replacement of square by round-topped forms holds good. But, when one looks at the relationships of the motifs in greater detail, there are inconsistencies; for example, one would expect the most explicit and naturalistic piece, such as comb no. 150, to be the prototype, from which others were abstracted. But it appears at a depth of 32 in. below datum, whereas the deposits commence at 48 in. and it cannot, therefore, be a candidate for the prototype. In the same manner, the earliest round-topped comb, no. 182, is found at 35 in. and is decorated with a restrained side-knob (known to be a stylized *manaia* from other examples), but it is several inches deeper, and therefore 'older' than any example of round-topped side-knobbed combs with explicit *manaia*, such as no. 178. In other words, the apparently rational rules of chronology for deriving abstractions from prototypes are not consistent with the stratigraphy. One might suspect that it would be easier to organize the assemblage if it was not stratified! The obvious solution is to conclude that the order of deposition does not exactly correspond to the order of manufacture. This is hardly unexpected, but it exposes a potential source of error that must exist both in the interpretation of stratified finds and in the rigid application of seriation to dating sites or deposits. For artefacts, the order of manufacture (the time when formal design takes place) and the order of deposition are not necessarily either coincidental, nor need they take place in the same staggered sequence.

In studying the art of the combs we have to take into account the position of the ancient Maori artist. In the past there has been a general, if not very explicit, view that the 'primitive artist' was an almost mechanical and standardized translator of the art-style of his culture. In an extreme formulation, it seemed as if any individual in a society could produce the standard forms of that people's art, almost genetically. This assumption must have arisen out of a failure to observe artists and the processes of creativity in society. It is interesting to learn from Adrian Gerbrands's observations among the Wow Ipits that, in a society that holds wood-carving in high esteem, there is a hierarchy of artists and one can readily distinguish the individuality of each artist, his level of competence and also the capacity he may have as an initiator of variation and new forms (Gerbrands 1967). The result of such a view is to bring the primitive artist far closer to the artist in our own societies.

Inspection of the Kauri Point combs makes it unthinkable that they were manufactured by more than a few, related craftsmen. The technical skill required for the manufacture and decoration of these small and delicate objects is exceptional. It is against all technical probability that the combs were made by their individual wearers. To this argument can be added evidence from another line of investigation into the motifs. Judging from the lenticular distribution of the combs, they must have been made over a period of time, perhaps 200 to 250 years. During this period the images of the designs and motifs remained remarkably consistent, in spite of variation. In his studies of memory, Sir Frederic Bartlett (1932:95) adopted the simple party game of transferring an image or passage of language, by drawing or memory, through a series of people, and observing the transformation of the exchanged pattern. In general, this process produced a rapid degeneration of the original with serious losses and distortions, such as changes of sex or of the entire nature of the original. At least one major reason for such transformation was the loss of meaning in the passage of the object between individuals, accelerated by an ambiguity in the copied or memorized examples. This would suggest that the knowledge of the motifs and meanings of the Kauri Point combs was confined within a very small and closely related group of craftsmen, who were able to transmit the meanings to their successors. The combs are therefore not mechanical copies, and their variation must be explained by supposing that their makers were deliberately exploring the variability of an almost formal language of motifs. It seems likely that, at some point after European contact, the continuity must have been broken. Firstly, the motifs are found to degenerate in design in museum collections. Secondly, under the influence of Christian missionaries, long hair became associated with ungodliness, so that the need for combs had ceased by the 1840s. Warfare and cannibalism continued for a time to be practised under the more wholesome guise of a 'short back and sides' haircut. Thirdly, there seems to have been a local revival of decorative comb-making in the later nineteenth century, but by this time the motifs and meanings had probably been forgotten, and the decorations that were applied were not only gross, but apparently selected from a now virtually meaningless vocabulary of motifs.

Wooden figures

Two heavy forked timbers are identified as anthropomorphic statues. They were found, one in the uppermost and the other close to the base, of the deposits: the upper is too decayed for a confident identification and can be thought of only as analogous to the lower one. The more complete specimen consisted of a forked tree-trunk, originally a little over two metres high, with peg-shaped feet, knees and waist marked by a reduction in diameter, and the head or neck by a further, badly rotted, peg-like projection. No arms were indicated, but a large vertical hollowed groove at the fork may be the vulva. The figure is very simple, otherwise undecorated, and does not possess parallels in museum collections; indeed, there is nothing stylistically Maori about it at all, and its elementary form can be paralleled by figures from many parts of the world such as, for example, the figures from the Foerlev Nymølle, Rebild Skovhuse and Broddenbjerg bogs in Denmark (Glob 1969:190; Grigson 1968:968). Judging from the decayed head of this figure, it must have stood vertically in the open for some time before being deposited in the swamp. The upper figure is too far decayed to be certainly identified or to give useful measurements, but the surviving forked part suggests that it was similar in dimensions to the lower one and that the two would have had the same purpose, though there is no evidence to explain what this could have been (see Ellis 1829:203).

Horticultural tools

In this class are included one complete short digging-stick (N) and several broken longer ones, and also some small pointed spatulate objects (Fig. 5, L) that resemble pieces illustrated by Elsdon Best as hand cultivating tools (1924b:183). Such tools would be useful as trowels, dibbers and grubbers, and the identifications made by Best seem sufficiently plausible to require no critical discussion. The short digging-stick is pointed at one end, chisel-shaped at the other, and 80 cm. long. In the 1950s, Jack Golson and the Auckland University Archaeological Society excavated a re-used bell-shaped underground store-pit on Great Mercury Island that supplied experimental evidence for a short digging-stick of exactly these dimensions (Golson: personal communication).

Woodworking tools

Woodworking tools are represented by a small stone adze-blade of quadrangular section with unmodified unhafted butt (Fig. 5, F), and also a wooden adze-handle (Fig. 5, M), 55 cm. long, without a fitted blade. These were found well apart and there is no reason to suppose that they belonged to each other, for the handle is suitable for a fairly heavy blade, much larger than the one we found. The blade is perhaps only formally an adze, for it is quite small and no hafted specimen of this size is known. It closely resembles a piece obtained on Captain Cook's first voyage (Shawcross 1970:308, 6a) and it has been suggested that these blades may have been hammered, rather than hafted (e.g. Barrow 1972:39). Alternatively, there is increasing evidence that stone blades were mounted in wooden sleeves (Shawcross 1970:311; Keyes 1971:83). The handle is a well-shaped functional piece of wood, formed from the junction of a branch with the trunk. It has no elaborate carving, such as is found on some of the adze-handles collected from New Zealand in the time of Captain Cook and later, but the proximal end is slightly swollen, rounded and detailed so that the whole object becomes an unmistakable and impressive penis. There is nothing surprising in this, for the Maori made extensive use of the parts of the body in metaphor and although saws and chisels were vigorously applied in the nineteenth century in order to subdue parts of Maori carvings (Barrow 1959:114), the human form remains paramount in Maori art.

Spears

Broken parts of three wooden barbed spears have been found (Fig. 5, J,K). These were all carefully made, with their shafts accurately rounded, and about 1.5 cm. in diameter. It is not possible to determine the length of the originals, but they look a little lightly made for the spears up to twenty feet in length that were used on the fighting stages in the defence of hill-forts. On the other hand, these specimens seem too big, and too heavily barbed, to have been throwing-spears (Buck 1958:272; Ryden 1963:87), of the type vaguely reported in ethnographies, though the use of missile weapons in Maori warfare was played down in nineteenth-century evidence. The size of the barbs shows that these were weapons for use against men, and not birds or fish. They must have been weapons of warfare. In view of the importance of warfare in Maori culture and the range of weapons employed, it is, if anything, a little unexpected that so few obvious weapons have been found in the swamp.

Flutes

Badly broken fragments of at least two specimens of a characteristic Maori wind-instrument, the *putorino* or flute, are in the assemblage (Fig. 5, G,H). The reconstructed fragments are the distal ends of two separate instruments which have been broken at their widest point, where it is weakened by a large wind-hole. These instruments are known from many ethnographic collections (see Oldman 1946:8) and examples were observed on Captain Cook's first voyage (Parkinson 1784: Pl. 26). This form of instrument is, as far as we know, unique to New Zealand and is most ingeniously manufactured. Curiously, however, in spite of its elaborate construction and the names given to it by ethnologists, it is relatively limited as a musical instrument (Dodge & Brewster 1945:39) and has far less range than the simple *koauau* (McLean 1968:213). The Kauri Point specimens are entirely undecorated, although all the ethnographic specimens and those illustrated by the explorers were carved, and the wind-hole is usually incorporated in a human mask, of which it is the open mouth, and both ends usually carved with masks. This lack of ornament on the Kauri Point flutes supports the inference drawn from the comb assemblage, that extensive ornamental decoration was a relatively late development accompanying increasing secularization of motifs.

Gourds

Numerous fragments or sherds of small gourds were excavated. Their sizes varied, roughly, between that of a large orange, about 7 cm. diameter, and that of a small melon, about 15 cm. diameter. Although no specimen is complete, it is possible to estimate the numbers from the surviving ends and to determine that their form was globular at the end with the sepal scars and pointed at the stalk end. The stalk ends were evidently pierced with a hole at the side, though some were probably cut in halves and cup-shaped. Inspection of the sherds revealed only one certainly decorated piece, which had a rough double-spiral design about 1.5 cm. in diameter scratched on to the skin. These gourds were both considerably smaller and far less highly decorated than specimens known from nineteenth-century ethnographic collections and the gourds now obtainable in New Zealand, decorated with Maori motifs in the recently revived decorative craft. No obvious function can be ascribed to the Kauri Point gourds, but several contained obsidian flakes or red ochre.

Wooden vessels

Three different forms of wooden container were excavated (Fig. 5, A,B,C). The first of these is an elongated asymmetrical funnel-shaped bowl with a hole now pushed through the bottom. It would have held the best part of 250 ml. of liquid; the only hint of what it might have been intended to contain lies in traces of red ochre. No example of a similar form is known from ethnographic collections or documentary sources, but the spout resembles that of a so-called 'chief's feeding funnel', of which some elaborately carved examples were to be found in the Oldman collection (Oldman 1946:7). Such objects are described as having been used for feeding *tapu* persons, who were not themselves allowed to handle food directly.

The second (Fig. 5, B), is a perfectly preserved mallet-shaped vessel, made of a dense wood, also stained with red ochre. Its trough-shaped bowl and end handle seem typical of Maori woodwork, such as water-troughs or feather-boxes although, once more, no exact parallel is known. It would make a moderately satisfactory drinking vessel, holding about half a cupful of liquid (150 ml.), although it would not have been particularly easy for the lips.

The third (Fig. 5, C), has been reconstructed from three pieces. It is well made, with an offset decorated handle. Although it also is not closely paralleled in museum collections, it does not look out of place and would serve as a drinking-cup.

Textiles and cordage

Examples of textile work recovered from the swamp (Fig. 5, D,E) include ten pieces of matting, six pieces of cordage and four other items consisting of long fibres with knotted ends. The raw materials are assumed to be the New Zealand flax, *Phormium tenax*, though no botanical identification has so far been made.

Most of the pieces of matting are in poor condition. They appear to have been strips about 8-10 cm. wide and 30 cm. long, probably of simple shapes, folded over several times into 'wallets'. The method of manufacture employed was a fairly fine twilling of between 2 and 4 wefts to the centimetre, with some variation in pattern; though it is no longer possible to tell if this was accompanied by the use of different-coloured fibres. Their workmanship is good, but finer examples of the same kind are known from ethnographic collections in New Zealand (Shawcross 1970:326). Some of these 'wallets' were found to contain pieces of red ochre and obsidian flakes; on the whole, the 'wallets' would seem to have been containers casually converted from other uses.

The specimens of fibres with knotting are too incomplete for discussion, but may have been decorative fringes from garments.

The cordage is also fragmentary and in poor condition. The collection includes 3-stranded ropes, of which the longest piece is about 30 cm. long, and also several knotted pieces, as well as two interesting objects that appear to be medium-weight cords to which have been joined lighter ones at right-angles. These joints seem to be deliberate and are fixed, not running, knots. One explanation from ethnography is that, when complete, they could have been what Elsdon Best (1924b:122) calls 'pack straps'; that is, straps bound round bundles so that they could be slung on the back.

Kauri gum spindles

Four small pieces of worked kauri gum were found, three of which were roughly cylindrical or slightly conical, 2.5-3.0 cm. long and about 1.0 cm. in diameter. Two of them had been carefully finished with dull abrasion; one was very rough; and the fourth was pitted as if it had been heavily chewed (a few of the combs also show tooth-marks). Fresh kauri gum is tacky and aromatic like the resins from other pines, but the common form is in hard lumps that have lain in the ground, often for thousands of years. The resin is translucent, sometimes transparent, and usually an orange or yellow colour, but when found in the ground will have a pale opaque cortex. All of the archaeological pieces belong to this sub-fossil form. These objects are so forcibly reminiscent of barley-sugar sweets that it is difficult to think of any other explanation than that they were sucked or chewed in a similar way. The tooth-marks on one, and remarks of ethnographers on the Maori habit of chewing kauri gum (probably the tacky form), support such an explanation, though scarcely giving any very obvious idea of why they should be in the swamp.

Brushes

At least four unidentified fibrous objects were recovered (Fig. 5, I). They consisted of hanks of stiff plant-fibres, originally between 25 and 35 cm. long, bent double to form what were named, for convenience, 'brushes' although no sign of pigment was found on them. As with so many other objects in the assemblage, there are no comparable specimens in modern collections or ethnographic illustrations, and a possible, if obscure, functional explanation will be left until later when the generalized ethnographic interpretation of the site is discussed.

Age of the site

Three lines of enquiry have been followed for determining the age of the site: direct dating of the deposits by radiocarbon; cross-dating by stratigraphic linkage with the radiocarbon-dated excavations on the fortified site; and cross-dating by means of cultural evidence.

There are seven radiocarbon determinations for the swamp site, carried out by the New

Zealand laboratory, three from charcoal and four from wood. Each sample was in a well-controlled stratigraphic situation so that, although the initial estimates of absolute age were floating, their relative ages should have behaved predictably. When all the determinations were available some inconsistencies become apparent (Shawcross 1969:184).

The strategy used in selecting the Kauri Point radiocarbon samples was to bracket the formation of the deposit with samples from the latest and the earliest cultural deposits, and from earlier deposits in the swamp sequence. In addition, several of the samples were in stratigraphic pairs, to check on variation within a common level. The dating of the end of the occupation can be correlated with cultural evidence (see below), but while for one sample, R 1950/1, 279 ± 53 years B.P. is acceptable, if a little old; for the other, R 1418/2, 684 ± 57 seems excessively aged. The beginning of the occupation is fairly well bracketed by three dates: R 1418/1, 398 ± 56 and R 1950/4, 430 ± 54, which agree well and R 1950/5, 547 ± 71, which is stratigraphically later but about 150 years too old. Two wood samples, R 1950/2, 594 ± 45 and R 1950/3, 410 ± 54, from earlier in the swamp-formation sequence, disagree with each other and give only a rather general confirmation for the antiquity of the swamp.

A rough calibration was carried out on several of the most realistic-looking dates, using Suess' bristlecone-pine calibration curve (1970:303). Thus, R 1950/1 assumes three possible mean dates of A.D. 1518, 1550 and 1638 ± 53; R 1418/1 gives a date of A.D. 1481 ±53; R 1950/4 becomes A.D. 1462 ± 54 and R 1950/5 becomes A.D. 1400 ± 71. From the archaeological point of view, these dates are not improvements and, specifically, the end of the sequence now becomes too early on typological grounds. As there is no independent cross-reference on the dates for the beginning of the sequence on the site, the earlier dates are not necessarily astray. Indeed, Duff (1956:17) originally proposed that the stimuli for the development of a distinctive Maori culture came in the mid-fourteenth century with the arrival of the so-called 'fleet' of migrating canoes. However, subsequent research on the sources of the supposed traditional evidence for this date has largely demolished the dating evidence for the 'fleet', and with it the chronology based upon it.

Cross-dating with the occupation-sequence on the *pa* is made possible by a stratigraphic link through a shell-midden 80 feet downstream of the main excavation, between the formation of the principal swamp-deposit and an early period of fortification. The shell-midden was formed before the excavation of a small outer defensive ditch of the *pa* (Golson 1961:25; Ambrose 1962:62), which cuts through the midden. The same midden spills into the swamp, where it is inter-bedded within the upper part of the main swamp-sediment. The combination of acid swamp and alkaline midden has produced abnormal local chemical conditions, but it is quite clear that the midden was not formed prior to the principal swamp deposits, and neither can the midden have been formed after this deposit had ceased to form, nor could it have been secondarily deposited. Radiocarbon dates for early structural features in the *pa* site are ANU-25, 495 ± 100 B.P., for a platform preceding the defences; and ANU-16, 230 ± 100 B.P., for the earliest-dated pit (Polach *et al.* 1967:15); which effectively bracket the swamp site and the earlier of which may be close to the original settlement date for the locality. However, none of these methods provides a very satisfactory estimate for the end of the occupation sequence. But, at this point, the cultural evidence offers an independent method of determining age.

The material culture of the site resembles the Classic Maori as defined from ethnographic sources. The most specific indicators are the wooden combs, of which the later round-topped form corresponds closely to specimens observed on Captain Cook's first voyage. There is a wooden comb in the Cambridge University Museum collection that is round-topped with a side knob and *manaia*, which is technically close in design to some of the later specimens from Kauri Point (Shawcross 1970:308). Likewise, a group of whalebone combs, collected on Cook's second voyage (Moschner 1955:138) and now in the Vienna *Museum für Völkerkunde* approximate to the more common plainer side-knobbed form in the swamp assemblage. The difficulty with this, as with any other, method of cross-dating is to reduce the latitude in the bracket of age on either side of the pairs of similar objects. Even were it possible to determine the age of manufacture to within a few years, through style, there would be the lag between manufacture and deposition or ethnographic collection. There is one hint that the comb assemblage ends somewhat prior to the close of the third quarter of the eighteenth century. This is the relative lack of ornamentation in contrast to that found on the earliest ethnographically-collected specimens. The assumption behind this is that there was a progressive increase of decorative ornamentation, in which the Kauri Point assemblage is prior to the more highly decorated assemblage of the late eighteenth century which is, in turn, less heavily decorated than nineteenth-century material. In summary, the three approaches to dating all point to a period of occupation commencing about the middle of the sixteenth century or earlier and ending during the mid-eighteenth century.

Interpretation

The function of most archaeological sites is taken as self-evident, or ignored in favour of the formal interest of their assemblages. However, the Kauri Point Swamp site demands an explanation for which no immediate answer is forthcoming, as nothing comparable has ever been archaeologically reported in Oceania. Two paths of inductive reasoning are open in the search for interpretation: the first derives directly from the excavated evidence and the second relies on the study of ethnographic sources. These have been separated in order to increase their independence and therefore improve their value as mutual cross-checks.

Archaeology

If one is to interpret a site purely from its intrinsic evidence, it is necessary to purge the mind of all subsidiary sources of information, specifically a knowledge of Maori culture. But a little thought suggests that this is unrealistic, for the archaeologist will be interpreting only on the basis of his own cultural experience. It is a characteristic assumption of certain scholars that the archaeologist's mind can be supposed to be objective, presumably because, by analogy, this same mind operates objectively and effectively when dealing with the phenomena of physics and chemistry. Yet it seems clear that, when dealing with cultural phenomena, the mind is incapable of objectivity; so, in the present circumstances, a more modest approach would be to assume that the site was very much older, in a totally different cultural context and without any cultural continuity with the present, to view the site as a Palaeolithic archaeologist might.

Several possible interpretations may be considered: the site could represent a haphazard accumulation of material lost or thrown out from the adjacent inhabited area; it might be a workshop where combs were manufactured, and those found could be considered wasters (this could explain the obsidian, adzes and woodchips); finally, the site might be a place for the deposition of specific items, that is, an intentional as opposed to accidental deposit. These three hypotheses seem to exhaust the possibilities at this level of generalization.

The first explanation can be dismissed on the grounds that the assemblage is neither haphazard nor a random sample of normal occupation debris. It has already been established that an enclosing structure originally existed, into which material was concentrated over a period of time. It is very difficult to construct a true sample of prehistoric (Maori) material culture; indeed, one of the more obvious conclusions from the assemblage is that it shows how greatly the preservation of organic material in a swamp extends the rather attenuated assemblages normally found on dry land. However, if one assumes that a comb represents an individual and ignores the factor of time, one would expect the combs to represent a community of two to three hundred people, who might possess a similar number of digging-sticks, baskets, gourds, gardening tools and garments, and about a hundred weapons plus fishing gear and small numbers of woodworking tools, musical instruments, food-pounders, tattooing gear and toys (this estimate is based on a knowledge of excavated Maori assemblages). According to this simple reasoning, most of these items which one might expect to find are under-represented on the site, or not represented at all; the only artefacts that look at all in proportion to the combs are the obsidian flakes. There are too few weapons and clothing, and no fishing gear or greenstone ornaments, and it must be concluded that the assemblage is not the product of randomly discarded worn-out objects from the settlement.

The second hypothesis, that the site was a

workshop of a comb-maker, may be quickly discarded. The combs have been deliberately broken and a proportion of them show re-working, sometimes crudely done, or repairs by drilling and binding. There is very little real woodworking waste, the chipping-floors being small, and there is too little other waste, which would certainly have been accumulated from so specialized a manufacture. The obsidian flakes are unsuitable for more than the most simple woodworking. Volcanic glass is too brittle and the edges of the flakes are too irregular for the finish achieved on the combs. Nor is the range of other artefacts appropriate for a workshop. Finally, it is difficult to imagine why a craftsman should work in a swamp, for there is no possibility of the site having started as dry land, to be subsequently inundated by the growth of the swamp.

The third hypothesis, of deliberate deposition, is thus arrived at, both by reduction and by the findings of the discussion on the first hypothesis. However, it may be extended as follows: the combs and many other artefacts were carefully made and must have been comparatively valuable objects; one may therefore ask what happens to valuables in a simple society? Obviously attrition, decay, loss and social obsolescence are factors, but beyond these there are several possible destinations. An object may be handed on to descendants as an heirloom, or transferred as a gift to others, and in this way survive until disintegration; or its social value declines to a point where it will be casually lost; or a valued object may be destroyed in an act of conspicuous waste, such as that practised by the Kwakiutl with their coppers. Presumably, such destruction removes the value from the surviving fragments, if any, so that they would be abandoned or, if still useful, re-cycled. Alternatively, valuables might be destroyed or disposed of, at crucial times such as on the death of their owner. These last two destinations have been distinguished because the former is in a sense a medium of exchange, whereas the latter involves personal identity.

Almost all of the assemblage has been deliberately slighted. The teeth are broken off the combs and the frames split in halves; two of the bowls are broken, as are the spears and all but one of the digging-sticks; the gourds are all shattered and the flutes savagely smashed. Deliberate and final destruction, rather than mere obsolescence, was thus the characteristic pattern of deposition of organic objects on the site. Admittedly, the obsidian flakes are not damaged, but their being put out of the way in the swamp precluded their re-use and wasted a valuable raw material. Therefore, the consequences of this site were to withdraw from use valuable or useful objects, yet not physically to destroy their substance, and, lastly, it concentrated the objects. These conclusions suggest that haphazard abandonment or total destruction, as by fire, were somehow improper and that deposition in the swamp formally marked the end of the everyday lives of the objects. This seems about as far as one could legitimately extend interpretation without recourse to ethnographic information.

Ethnography

In turning to ethnography one enters a fiercely debated field for, while Grahame Clark (1951:49) was demonstrating the enriching value of ethnography to archaeology, at a time when archaeologists generally ignored such opportunities, the 1960s have seen a vigorous revival of its application. Inevitably, the revival has taken on a momentum in which many of the qualifications made by earlier archaeologists have been forgotten. Recently, Nicolas Peterson (1971:241) has drawn attention to several sources of trouble. He remarks that archaeologists have had a tendency to 'raid the ethnographic literature for the odd fact and generalize on the strength of it'. The subjects have different theoretical approaches, which means that phenomena interesting to one discipline may be irrelevant to the other. The ethnologist is necessarily working in societies that are altered through culture contact, including his own presence, and finally, any extrapolation into the past must recognize the continuous nature of the process of culture change.

These considerations apply with particular force in the case of New Zealand, where European settlement began in 1815 and rapidly accelerated after 1840. In many respects Maori culture changed quickly and radically and, although the inner core remains in a vigorous sense of Maori identity, all attempts at ethnography are partial reconstructions. This raises a very serious point concerning the work of Elsdon Best who, because of his valuable and prolific writing at the beginning of the present century, is generally taken as the official authority on New Zealand, especially by unwitting outsiders. There is no denying that the wealth of Maori ethnography owes much of its substance to Best's field-work in the isolated Urewera country between 1895 and 1910 (Craig 1964:55). However, scholarship is not static, and the aims and methods of infant anthropology at the end of the nineteenth century cannot always be expected to stand up to modern requirements. In particular, the following reservations must be put forward. When one reads Elsdon Best's published work, one is frequently baulked by what might be called the 'Best barrier': when some phenomenon is described but the reader has no way of knowing whether the information came from direct observation in the Ureweras, or was supplied as historical evidence by a Maori informant, or came from less definite hearsay, or was derived from earlier documentary sources. The very desperation with which Best recorded his knowledge of vanishing Maori culture diminished his provenancing of information. It must also be admitted that in certain matters Best was undiscriminating, so that he became the unconscious vehicle for some very dubious information later in his life. The two most serious errors as yet recognized concern a supposed monotheistic cult of Io and a travesty of traditional history derived from the elderly priest Te Whatahoro (Simmons 1969:14). Best almost invariably describes a Maori culture apparently uninfluenced by European culture, yet this cannot have been the case, even in the Ureweras, by the time he was active and, indeed, it seems likely that he adjusted evidence to conform with what he judged to be the pure state. Consequently, while the modern worker is still likely to find what he wants somewhere in Best's work, he will be insecure if he does not look also for earlier, and more direct, evidence.

There are two distinct lines of investigation open to such a search, the first and easier being the accounts of European travellers and explorers, from the voyages of Captain Cook up to the mid-nineteenth century, and the second lies in the records of the Maori themselves, including their traditional history and poetry, and also the records of Land Court cases. There are problems in the use of all these documents, whether European or Maori. In using nineteenth-century accounts one must recognize what J.L. Bradley (1965: xxiii) has called 'an infrequently considered but not uncommon aspect of Victorian literary activity: the persistent "borrowing" of material by one author of another'. Published sources in New Zealand cannot all be treated as independent observations. Maori records are relatively more inaccessible and, not being presented as observations, that is, from outside, many objects and institutions are discussed only indirectly.

The evidence will now be outlined: as the literature does not specifically record any site where combs, obsidian and other objects were deposited in an enclosure within a swamp, the study will commence with the artefacts themselves, beginning where possible with Elsdon Best as a source and then tracing earlier sources. This leads on to certain institutional explanations for the site; once more Best provides useful evidence.

Elsdon Best states that it was men who wore their hair tied in a knob, into which feathers or combs of bone or wood were placed, and illustrates this with an engraving by Parkinson (1924b:224). This is confirmed by Captain Cook (Beaglehole 1955:278) and Sir Joseph Banks (Morrell 1958:49). However, Edward Shortland (1856:96), who was the first New Zealand Protector of Aborigines in the 1840s, has stated that combs that were in contact with a chief's head became desecrated when left in a cook-house, a place entered only by inferior persons such as women and slaves; and G.F. Angas (1846:39) explained that chiefs used combs to confine their hair before going into battle, a particularly sacred event for the Maori. The Rev. Richard Taylor (1870:140) and Sir George Grey (1855a:185) supply information based on Maori poetry; the former, though obscure, appears to agree with Grey that a long white comb of whalebone was a symbol of rank. Combs, then, are clearly connected with men of high rank in Maori society and embody some degree of sacredness that centres particularly in the head and hair.

In his monograph on *Maori Religion and Mythology*, Best (1924a:207) explained that human hair was peculiarly *tapu* (sacred), because the head was the most sacred part of a man. It is evident that this was still believed by the Tuhoe people of the Ureweras when he was doing his field-work. The earliest account of the head and hair being sacred, though he did not use the word *tapu*, is given by John Savage (1807:23) who was in the Bay of Islands in 1805. The Rev. William Yate, an early missionary, also recorded (1835:87) that the head of a chief was sacred and that hair-cutting involved *tapus.* There are much fuller accounts given by two early traders: Joel Polack (1840:38) whose book has a slightly questionable reputation as a historical source, but who seems quite reliable in the present instances; and Judge Maning (1863:20) the anonymous author of *Old New Zealand*, who shows how the sacredness of the head extended to the back, stopping men of rank from carrying loads (see also Shortland 1856:107). Taylor describes how, if a chief accidentally touched his head, he had to snuff up the *tapu* from his hands (1870:164), and how the backbone symbolized *tapu* (1870:168). Finally, from Grey's transcription of Maori poetry comes evidence for the cursing of a chief's head and topknot (1885a:158).

There is a considerable body of sources on the sacred rites connected with hair-cutting. Best mentions (1925:1075) the existence of intensely *tapu* secluded places where the hair of important people was cut. The importance of hair-cutting to the Maori is first recorded by Savage (1807:23), but Cruise (1820:27) gives a description of a hair-cutting ceremony performed on a chief aboard a British vessel, which made *tapu* both the chief and equipment connected with the head and hair-cutting, and generalized that after hair-cutting the person cannot approach others, cannot handle food and has to be fed by another. This state would wear off after several days (Cruise 1820:184). Polack adds (1840:38) that the hair-cutter also became *tapu* and had to be purified afterwards. An example of how this might be achieved, in which the hands are rubbed on fern-root cooked over a sacred fire, is described by Shortland (1856:110), while the cutting was later stated to be done with an 'obsidian flint' (1882:32). Taylor adds that offerings of locks of hair of those slain in battle were made in a sacred grove or *wahi tapu* (1870:190), and that hair was also cut as a mark of grief at the death of a chief (1870:217).

It is evident from Taylor's observations that hair-cutting is related to scarification as a visible gesture of distress. An example of this was seen by Captain Cook in Queen Charlotte Sound in January 1770 (Beaglehole 1955:24) when several women slashed themselves with 'shells and jasper'. Even such relatively trivial causes, such as separation for a journey, justified scarification with shells or broken glass (Earle 1827:91); and Yate adds that the piece of flint used for mourning scarification became sacred (1835:136), and this is confirmed by Taylor (1870:207, 217).

There is far less evidence available on the use of gourds and matting, but Polack (1840:278) makes the interesting observation that portions of food were often placed in baskets and hung on a tree or a notched stick to propitiate spirits, or were placed in small gourds, and then pierced with a stick and placed in the nearest *wai tapu*, or sacred spring. Maning mentions that drinking vessels became *tapu*, and that in a ceremony for the removal of *tapu*, household utensils were smashed and clothes deposited in a distant thicket (1863:115, 133). Taylor also notes that food baskets and sacred uneaten food were deposited in a sacred place, along with old garments and the hair of chiefs (1870:174).

A behaviour pattern in which the objects found in the swamp can seem to have a sacred character is now beginning to be documented. The combs are definitely connected with high status and sacredness; the obsidian flakes might be, if used either for hair-cutting or scarification (and they do not seem to have had any obvious industrial use); the gourds, basketry and wooden vessels could also have been hallowed. This pattern appears to continue, though more tenuously, among the other artefacts. Taylor (1870:187) gives an account of a war ceremony in which the weapons used by young warriors who had made their first kills are broken, which might explain the broken spears. Augustus Earle (1827:129) makes a unique reference to the chips formed from making a canoe becoming sacred; and, while there seems to be no direct evidence for the sacred quality of musical instruments, they certainly were considered to be sacred in the Society Islands (Ellis 1829:281).

Two much more obscure identifications are the previously described 'brushes' and the scatter of sticks. Shortland (1882:56) describes a traditional account of a sacred ceremony in which a wisp of weeds or grass, called a *ueta* and used to wipe the anus of a corpse, became a talisman. The swamp 'brushes' look rather abrasive by modern standards if this was their function, but the subjects were scarcely in a position to complain. The great scatter of sticks in the site is puzzling, particularly as they look too regular to be natural flotsam. It is therefore interesting to find, in Yate's (1835:91) description of the consultation of an oracle before battle, that rows of sticks were set up, within a 6-ft. square, which were either blown or randomly knocked over. This use of sticks is supported by Shortland (Shortland 1856 :117), who recounts another kind of divination in which sticks were thrown in the direction of a path of death (1882:64), called *niu* (Taylor 1870:178).

A final element of the site, which fits the pattern of sacredness, is the presence of red ochre on artefacts and as an independent feature of the sediments. Banks observed a man who was rubbed all over with dry red ochre (Morrell 1958:60), which Savage said was applied with oil on particular occasions (1807:52). Cruise adds that the painting of a post with red ochre marked a sacred place (1820:218), while Taylor refers to sacred trees daubed with ochre and having rags tied to them. Furthermore, smearing with red ochre was used to mark places made *tapu* by the presence of great chiefs (Taylor 1870:171, 209), as seems to be indicated in the account of the story of *The Patupairehe and Pirongia* in which red ochre was smeared on a house in order to protect it from the fairies (1870:268).

Maori ethnographic literature will now be reviewed for evidence of sacred sites, but at the outset it may be stated that they are not monumental features of the landscapes as are the stone courtyards or *marae* of the Marquesas (Suggs 1961:161) and *ahu* of Easter Island (Heyerdahl 1961:53). However, the physical absence from the modern landscape is more than compensated for by frequent allusions to sacred places in the literature. Indeed, at least seventeen different terms have so far been encountered, though some of these are, admittedly, synonyms, while others are enigmatic and do not translate easily.

The most frequently occurring term for a sacred place is *tuahu*, clearly related to the *ahu* of other parts of Polynesia. Elsdon Best gives fairly full accounts of the nature of these *tuahu*; they were sometimes marked by one or several rough stones or, occasionally, had a small platform of sticks, called a *tiepa*, on which offerings were placed, but might also be unmarked (1924a:170). Best later cites Maori informants for the *tuahu* being occasionally identified by one or two wooden staves, sometimes carved, which might temporarily represent spirits (*atua*), and says that in certain rites the priest would construct two earthen mounds that were male and female, the latter of which was supposed to contain all things evil and would be destroyed (1925:1072-3). Every settlement of any importance was supposed to have its *tuahu*, which was normally set outside in some secluded place, such as forest, shrubs or flax, and was always *tapu* and to be avoided (1925:1074). Rites of active magic were evidently carried out at these places and the only other ritual described in this context is hair-cutting and the casting away, or giving as offerings, of *tapu* food (1924a:170). Lastly, Best comments that the *tuahu* was simply a *wahi tapu*, literally sacred or prohibited place (1925:1072), and that its purpose was sometimes served by the village latrine (*turuma* or *turumatanga*) or, for special ceremonies, by the *ahurewa* which was an indoors *tuahu* (Williams 1971:444), or *rua iti* which can be translated as a small hole or small grave (1971:349). It seems possible that, as Best gives no obviously eye-witness description of such a place, he either never saw one or saw only unimpressive examples.

From the time of the first contact, Banks gives two descriptions of sacred places. He notes that there are few signs of religion and no places of public worship, but observed one place close to a sweet-potato cultivation, consisting of a small square bounded by stones, in the middle of which stood a spade from which hung a basket of fern-root. His other, earlier, observation refers to Lieutenant Monkhouse finding objects, including locks of men's hair, tied up in the branches of trees, which he supposed to be a consecrated place (Morrell 1958:149, 102). Cruise (1820:147) recounts how an English pea plant was *tapued* by being fenced round with little sticks. Later, he states that places where people died, or where their remains were deposited, became sacred and were marked with a carved and ochred post (1820:218). The *tapu* area described by Earle (1827:63) has the corpse of a chief hanging among the branches of a tree. Shortland (1882:69) recounts an interesting traditional story in which a chief was cheated of his land-right by the falsification of an ancient-looking *tuahu* of old posts and rotting fish (an early record of archaeological forgery). He describes a *tuahu* as a place where food offerings and first-fruits were deposited for the spirits, but his other descriptions seem to refer to the posts, *rahui* or *ri*, which were sacred markers of land boundaries (1882:78, 80). Taylor describes a *tuahu* as marked by a short slanting stone pillar or by fern-stalks stuck into the ground (1870:183); he also states that hair was deposited at the *tuahu* (1870:208) and that the first victims of a battle were offered there (1870:213). He cites traditional stories for *tuahu* being stages of stone and places where omens for war were sought (1870:250, 273). Finally, the *tuahu* that appear in Grey's translations resemble in appearance that described in Shortland's account of the trick over the land-ownership mark (1885a:89, 95, 134, 144). All of these sites appear to have been on dry land and were used for the disposal of the dead or of objects that became sacred, or were places where offerings were made to spirits, or served as sanctified boundary-markers in land ownership. The swamp site could possess some of the same characteristics, by its reception of sacred objects and possible offerings, and the presence of sticks and posts in the swamp also seems highly suggestive, but there was no sign of human remains or hair.

As the site is located in water, it is logical to turn next to the *wai tapu* or sacred spring. Best cites a traditional story in which a man had his excessive *tapu* removed in a ceremony at such a sacred spring (1925:295). He also describes a specific place, a small pond, which he calls a *wai karakia* but which seems to be synonymous with a *wai tapu* (1925:148). The early missionaries are very poor sources on Maori religion. However, Yate (1835:82) refers to 'baptism' in a stream with a small stick placed on the ground, which surely cannot mean a Christian baptism. Taylor remarks that there was a baptismal ceremony in the north carried out in running water, and that on declaration of war people resorted to a sacred stream (1870:185, 224). Polack records that food offerings in gourds pierced by sticks, as already noted, were placed in the *wai tapu* (1840:278). The information is disappointingly limited but there is no reason to suppose that the concept of the religious properties of water was a Christian introduction to the Maori, as the magical analogy that water can wash away spiritual pollution must be universal.

The term *wahi tapu* or sacred place, ought to be the general name for these different sites; at least, this is what Best implies (1925:1072). Maning, the earliest writer to use the word, applies it explicitly to a burial place (1863:72). The most frequent references to *wahi tapu* are made by Taylor, who equates them with Polynesian *marae* (1870:98), saying that they were fenced enclosures (1870:216) and, most important, that the *tuahu* was the altar found within the enclosure (1870:208). The functions of the *wahi tapu* were to be the burial place of chiefs and a dump for their goods, or clothing tainted with their blood, and for offerings of the locks of hair of slain enemies (1870:174, 164, 190). Grey's reference, in the story of *The Magical Wooden Head*, is a little confusing in its implication that the *wahi tapu* was within a *pa* or fortified settlement (1885a:176). It only remains to add that Taylor uses the term *whare kura*, or sacred house, which seems to have been a large house, equivalent to the open-air *wahi tapu* (1870:175). It is tempting to see this as a Maori adaptation of the missionary-introduced church and it would be interesting to have the idea investigated further.

The last important site is known as the *wai kotikoti, tuahu kotikotinga uru* or *wai whakakaika*, which all refer to the place of (hair-) cutting (Williams 1971:148). Curiously, Best is the only authority for these terms, though this may be due to the local usage of the *Tuhoe* people (1924a:207, 1925:1074). It is clear that water was desirable for this ceremony, but it is not so certain that a sacred place was uniquely set aside for the function.

The remaining terms are: *wai taua*, on which Best cites a Maori informant for its being a separate place concerned with war ceremonies (1925:1074); *wai whakaika* is once referred to as a sacred place near to which the two small earth-mounds, or *tuahu*, were erected (1925:1073). The word *ika* can mean either a warrior, corpse, fish or heap (Williams 1971:76), which suggests synonymy with *wahi tapu*. Taylor once refers to *te rahau tapu*, which seems to be a sacred tree (1870:175), while Williams translates *hau* as sacred food used in the ceremony to remove *tapu* (1971:39). Shortland (1882:56) makes an obscure reference to a *koari*, or sacred place, where the talismanic objects possibly identified with the 'brushes' were deposited: Williams (1971:122) translates this word as 'abashed', which is little help. Finally Grey, in one of his transcriptions of traditional stories, refers to a *rua o te ngana*, which he translates as a 'pit of wrath', used in a particularly powerful curse (1885b:87).

Discussion

In answer to criticism of this use of ethnography, it may be pointed out that, although none of the sources refers specifically to Kauri Point, Best's Urewera country is not far distant, while Shortland was originally stationed in the Bay of Plenty and worked with the Ngaiterangi, whose disputed tribal boundary lay at Kauri Point itself. Taylor travelled extensively in the North Island, but his main missionary area was in the Taupo district of the interior, while most of the other observations must have been made in the Bay of Islands in the north. The separation in time of the archaeological material from the ethnographic observations is not very great although, after the period of the earliest explorers, a fair amount of acculturation must have taken place. But, overall, the continuity between the two fields is impressive.

However, the ethnographic evidence itself needs further investigation, for in its present form it is awkwardly inconsistent. Are all of these different kinds of religious site distinct, that is, did different terms apply to the same site according to function, or could they be explained by regional variation, or confusion among the ethnographers? Is it possible that the nineteenth-century observers were recording a disintegration into separate sites of what had formerly been carried out in a single centralized place? Or was it the European intellectual habit of discriminating and classifying that created a confusion that would not occur to the Maori mind?

Prytz Johansen, probably the most authoritative of recent scholars to have studied Maori religion, has clearly recognized the disturbing fluidity with which these different kinds of site merge (1958:64). The weight of numbers seems to have led him to identify the *tuahu* as the most general term. This would be convenient, but there are three arguments against it: semantically, *wahi tapu* is more general; next, and most important, Taylor distinguishes the *tuahu* as an altar, whereas the *wahi tapu* was the entire enclosure; lastly, the term *wahi tapu* is first used by Maning, who settled in the 1820s, whereas it is not clear when *tuahu* was first recorded as a word, except that it is used, as *tua ahu*, by Grey. There remains an outside possibility that the word was introduced by other Polynesians, who arrived aboard European boats and settled among the Maori very early. The strongest argument is that of Taylor, and the remainder of this discussion will proceed on the assumption that the broadest term for a formal sacred place was *wahi tapu*, and that *tuahu* applies to a structural feature, often one or more mounds of earth, or stones, set within the enclosure. This conforms well enough with the evidence, in other parts of Polynesia, for a courtyard, often stone-lined, and *ahu* of stone set within, and it is easy to see why the name for this feature might come to be applied to the whole structure. Furthermore, it appears that there were also informal sacred places, areas made *tapu* by the passing presence of an especially sacred person, or by a death, or where sacred food was disposed of during a journey. It is such an adventitious site that is probably shown in one of the very few known illustrations (Angas 1846: Pl. XIX).

It is also clear that the conventional *wahi tapu* could itself take several forms. It might be situated in water, in which case the structural evidence would probably be of upright posts and a wooden platform, or *tiepa*, which might in this case be synonymous with *tuahu*. Or it might be on dry land, in which case the *tuahu* could be of stone, if this was at hand, or in the form of earthen mounds which, again, may merely reflect local geography, rather than cultural difference. A final alternative variety of *wahi tapu* that must not be ignored is the latrine, or *turuma*, one of which has recently been archaeologically excavated by Peter Bellwood (1972:259). It is clear from Best (1924a:171; 1925:1075) that such places were sacred and were resorted to for ceremonial or magical purposes. An elementary understanding of magic will be sufficient to explain why this should be. At the same time it is clear that some of the terms, such as *wai kotikoti, wai taua* and *wai karakia*, do not refer to separate places but to a specific activity held in a sacred place of a type used for many purposes.

Conclusion

It is now possible to juxtapose the archaeological evidence with the ethnography. A knowledge of Polynesian culture establishes that the combs would be intensely sacred and that the other material would, under certain conditions, also become sacred. The evidence for their being broken or slighted, and that associating them with the combs and red ochre, increases the probability of the entire assemblage being sacrosanct. The obsidian flakes are not necessarily sacred, but they are known to have been used in ritual such as mourning scarification and, indeed, were used for this after the introduction of metal tools for industrial purposes. Here, again, the association would emphasize a sacred reason for the presence of the obsidian. The structural elements of the site conform with descriptions of sacred places. There are upright posts, wooden figures and a scatter of light woodwork, which might be either the *tiepa* stages or divination with sticks, or both. The rectangular enclosure agrees with the descriptions by Sir Joseph Banks and the Rev. William Yate, in the latter case even to exact dimensions. Lastly, the site is located in permanent water, which was important for certain ceremonies, particularly those for the removal of *tapu*. Therefore, in as far as proof may be taken in this branch of archaeology, it has been demonstrated that the Kauri Point swamp site was a sacred spring (*wai tapu*), which was itself one of several forms of sacred place (*wahi tapu*).

The investigation does not end here, for the discovery of such a site introduces new evidence on the Maori institutions of *tapu* and *pure*, the act of removal of the former. The exercise contains a number of lessons for those archaeologists who are re-discovering the uses of ethnography.

Acknowledgments

In ten years of work I have relied on the help and ideas of many people and it would be difficult to acknowledge them all fairly. Here, I would like to thank those who helped me on the excavation, chiefly my wife Kathleen, my sister-in-law Eleanor Bassett, Lala Frazer and members of the Auckland University Archaeological Society. The Kauri Point Swamp assemblage is now preserved in the Waikato Museum, Hamilton, New Zealand, under controlled conditions and in an important centre of Maori culture.

REFERENCES

Ambrose, W. (1962) Further investigations at Kauri Point, Katikati. *N.Z. Arch. Assoc. Newsletter*, 5, 56-67.

Angas, G.F. (1846) *The New Zealanders Illustrated.* London.

Archey, G. (1933) Wood carving in the north Auckland area. *Records Auckland Inst. & Mus.*, 1, 209-18.

Barrow, T.T. (1959) Free standing Maori images. In Freeman, J.D. and Geddes, W.R. (eds.), *Anthropology in the South Seas*, 111-20. NewPlymouth,N.Z.

Barrow, T.T. (1972) *Art and Life in Polynesia.* London, and Wellington, N.Z.

Bartlett, Sir F.C. (1932) *Remembering.* London.

Beaglehole, J.C. (ed.) (1955) *The Journals of Captain James Cook on his Voyages of Discovery.* Vol. 1. *The Voyage of the* Endeavour *1768-1771.* London.

Bellwood, P. (1971) Fortifications and economy in prehistoric New Zealand. *P.P.S.*, 37, Part 1, 56-95.

Bellwood, P. (1972) Excavations at Otakanini Pa, South Kaipara harbour. *Jour. Royal Soc. New Zealand*, 2, 259-91.

Best, E. (1924a) *Maori Religion and Mythology* (Dominion Mus. Bull. No. 10). Wellington, N.Z.

Best, E. (1924b) *The Maori As He Was.* Wellington, N.Z.

Best, E. (1925) *Tuhoe: The Children of the Mist* (Memoirs Polynesian Soc. No. 6). New Plymouth, N.Z.

Bradley, J.L. (ed.) (1965) Selections from *London Labour and the London Poor* by Henry Mayhew. London.

Buck, Sir P.H. (1958) *The Coming of the Maori.* Wellington, N.Z.

Butcher, E.W.E. (1965) Some remarkable plants of the Waikato bogs. *Jour. Royal N.Z. Inst. Horticulture*, 6 (2), 54-64.

Clark, J.G.D. (1951) Folk-culture and the study of European prehistory. In Grimes, W.F. (ed.), *Aspects of Archaeology in Britain and Beyond*, 49-65. London.

Clarke, D.L. (1968) *Analytical Archaeology.* London.

Craig, E.W.G. (1964) *Man of the Mist.* Wellington, N.Z.

Cruise, R.A. (1823) *Journal of a Ten Months' Residence in New Zealand 1820.* London.

Dodge, E.S. and Brewster, E.T. (1945) The acoustics of three Maori flutes. *Jour. Polynesian Soc.*, 54, 39-61.

Downes, T.W. (1928) A 'Tuahu' on the Wanganui river. *Jour. Polynesian Soc.*, 37, 165-8.

Duff, R. (1956) *The Moa-Hunter Period of Maori Culture* (Canterbury Mus. Bull. No. 1). Wellington, N.Z.

Duff, R. (1961) The Waitara Swamp search. *Records Canterbury Mus.*, 7, 303-26.

Earle, A. (1838) *Sketches Illustrative of the Native Inhabitants and Islands of New Zealand.* London.

Ellis, W. (1829) *Polynesian Researches, during a residence of nearly six years in the South Sea Islands.* London.

Field, H.C. (1876) Notes on some ancient Aboriginal caches near Wanganui. *Trans. N.Z. Inst.*, 9, 220-9.

Fisher, V.F. (1934) The material culture of Oruarangi, Matatoki, Thames. 1. Bone ornaments and implements. *Records Auckland Inst. & Mus.*, 1, 275-86.

Gerbrands, A.A. (1967) *Wow-Ipits: Eight Asmat Woodcarvers of New Guinea.* The Hague.

Gløb, P.V. (1969) *The Bog People: Iron Age Man Preserved* (trans. R.L.S. Bruce-Mitford). London.

Golson, J. (1959) Culture change in prehistoric New Zealand. In Freeman, J.D. and Geddes, W.R. (eds.), *Anthropology in the South Seas*, 29-74. New Plymouth, N.Z.

Golson, J. (1961) Investigations at Kauri Point, Katikati, Western Bay of Plenty. *N.Z. Arch. Assoc. Newsletter*, 4 (2), 13-41.

Graziosi, P. (1960) *Palaeolithic Art.* London.

Grey, Sir G. (1885a) *Polynesian Mythology and Ancient Traditional History of the New Zealand Race* (2nd ed.) Auckland, N.Z.

Grey, Sir G. (1885b) *Ko Nga Mahinga a Nga Tupuna Maori* (2nd ed.) Auckland, N.Z.

Grigson, G. (1968) The land of the fishhook. *Country Life*, 143, 966-8.

Groube, L.M. (1967) A note on the Hei-Tiki. *Jour. Polynesian Soc.*, 76, 453-7.

Groube, L.M. (1968) Research in New Zealand prehistory since 1956. In Yawata, I. and Sinoto, Y.H. (eds.), *Prehistoric Culture in Oceania*, 141-9. Honolulu.

Haddon, A.C. (1895) *Evolution in Art.* London.

Heyerdahl, T. *et al.* (1961) *Archaeology of Easter Island.* London.

Johansen, J.P. (1958) Studies in Maori rites and myths. *Historisk-filosofiske Meddelelser Danske Videnskabernes Selskab*, 37, no. 4.

Keyes, I.W. (1970) A possible *tuahu* at Lake Kohanga-te-Ra, south-eastern Wellington. *N.Z. Arch. Assoc. Newsletter*, 13, 147-55.

Keyes, I.W. (1971) Composite adze hafts in New Zealand prehistory. *Dominion Mus. Records in Ethnology*, 2 (8), 83-96.

Leach, B.F. (1969) *The Concept of Similarity in Prehistoric Studies* (Studies in Prehistoric Anthropology No. 1). Dunedin, N.Z.

Leach, H.M. (1972) A hundred years of Otago archaeology: a critical review. *Records of the Otago Museum*, Anthropology 6: 1-19.

Lockerbie, L. (1959) From Moa-Hunter to Classic Maori in southern New Zealand. In Freeman, J.D. and Geddes, W.R. (eds.), *Anthropology in the South Seas*, 75-110. New Plymouth, N.Z.

McLean, M. (1968) An investigation of the open tube Maori flute or *kooauau*. *Jour. Polynesian Soc.*, 77, 213-41.

[Maning, F.E.] A Pakeka Maori (1863) *Old New Zealand.* Auckland, N.Z. and London.

Morrell, W.P. (ed.) (1958) *Sir Joseph Banks in New Zealand, from his Journal.* Wellington, N.Z.

Moschner, I. (1955) Die Wiener Cook-Sammlung, Sudsee-Teil. *Archiv für Völkerkunde*, 10.

Newbould, P.J. (1958) Peat bogs. *New Biology*, 26, 88-105.

Oldman, W.O. (1946) *Skilled Handwork of the Maori* (Memoirs Polynesian Soc. No. 14). New Plymouth, N.Z.

Parkinson, S. (1784) *A Journal of a Voyage to the South Seas, in His Majesty's Ship The Endeavour.* London.

Peters, K.M. (1969) Excavation of a Star Mound and Earthen Terrace at Su-Lu-53. *Bull. Auckland Inst. & Mus.*, 6, 210-21.

Peterson, N. (1971) Open sites and the ethnographic approach to the archaeology of hunter-gatherers. In Mulvaney, D.J. and Golson, J. (eds.), *Aboriginal Man and Environment in Australia*, 239-48. Canberra.

Polach, H.A., Stipp, J.J., Golson, J. and Lovering, J.F. (1967) ANU Radiocarbon Date List I. *Radiocarbon*, 9, 15-27.

Polack, J.S. (1840) *Manners and Customs of the New Zealanders.* London.

Ryden, S. (1963) *The Banks Collection, an Episode in 18th Century Anglo-Swedish Relations* (Ethno. Mus. Sweden Monograph Series No. 8). Stockholm.

Savage, J. (1807) *Some Account of New Zealand, particularly the Bay of Islands.* London and Edinburgh.

Shawcross, F.W. (1963) Kauri Point Swamp. *N.Z. Arch. Assoc. Newsletter*, 6, 50-6.

Shawcross, F.W. (1964a) Stone flake industries in New Zealand. *Jour. Polynesian Soc.*, 73, 7-25.

Shawcross, F.W. (1964b) An archaeological assemblage of Maori combs. *Jour. Polynesian Soc.*, 73, 382-98.

Shawcross, F.W. (1966) Ongari Point – second season. *N.Z. Arch. Assoc. Newsletter*, 9, 53-71.

Shawcross, F.W. (1969) Archaeology with a short, isolated time-scale: New Zealand. *World Arch.*, 1, 184-99.

Shawcross, F.W. (1970) The Cambridge University collection of Maori artefacts, made on Captain Cook's first voyage. *Jour. Polynesian Soc.*, 79, 305-48.

Shawcross, F.W. and Terrell, J.E. (1966) Paterangi and Oruarangi swamp *pas*. *Jour. Polynesian Soc.*, 75, 404-29.

Shortland, E. (1856) *Traditions and Superstitions of the New Zealanders* (2nd ed.). London.

Shortland, E. (1882) *Maori Religion and Mythology.* London.

Simmons, D.R.(1969) A New Zealand myth, Kupe, Toi and the 'Fleet'. *N.Z. Jour. History*, 3, 14-31.

Skinner, H.D. (1933) Archaeology in New Zealand. *Jour. Polynesian Soc.*, 42, 102-5.

Skinner, H.D. and Teviotdale, D. (1927) A classification of implements of quartzite and similar materials from the Moa-Hunter camp at Shag River Mouth. *Jour. Polynesian Soc.*, 36, 180-93.

Suess, H.E. (1970) Bristlecone-pine calibration of the radiocarbon time-scale 5200 B.C. to the present. In Olsson, I.U. (ed.), *Radiocarbon Variations and Absolute Chronology*, 303-11.

Suggs, R.C. (1961) The archaeology of Nuku Hiva,

Marquesas Islands, French Polynesia. *Anthro. Papers Amer. Mus. Natural Hist.* 49 (1). New York.

Taylor, R. (1870) *Te Ika a Maui; or New Zealand and its inhabitants* (2nd ed.). Wanganui, N.Z.

Ucko, P.J. and Rosenfeld, A.J.D. (1972) Anthropomorphic representations in palaeolithic art. In Almagro Basch, M. and García Guinea, M.A. (eds.) *Santander Symposium*, 149-215. Santander, Madrid, U.I.S.P.P.

Williams, H.W. (1971) *A Dictionary of the Maori Language* (7th ed.). Wellington, N.Z.

Yate, W. (1835) *An Account of New Zealand* (2nd ed.). London.

PART IV

The British Isles

PETER ADDYMAN

Archaeology and Anglo-Saxon society

Grahame Clark has only rarely strayed into the paths of mediaeval archaeology, and probably never by choice. It is a paradox, therefore, that the discipline in its modern form in Britain will be one of the enduring monuments to his Disney professorship. Many of those who helped to formalize the subject in the 1950s and 1960s passed through his hands, or came under his influence, at Cambridge. The discipline owes much to their sound training in the basics of prehistory, and to Clark's own brand of social and economic archaeology. If practice is better than precept, then it is no surprise that mediaevalists-to-be were to be found on the excavation teams at Star Carr and at Peacock's Farm. Furthermore, the convictions that have avowedly governed the course of Clark's own research could well be adopted by mediaeval archaeologists at the present expanding stage of their discipline. As it passes from its youth, its periodical literature already has enough of what Clark has described as self-validating routines in which we watch 'archaeologists going through the familiar motions and committees voting resources to excavators to go on finding the same categories of object, the same kind of information' (Clark 1972:4). This paper concerns itself with some aspects of Anglo-Saxon archaeology for which it can be said, in hindsight, that Grahame Clark has provided the stimulus, and where it is time to break out in new directions.

There is still a lingering dichotomy in Anglo-Saxon studies among those whose approach is, in the main, through written sources and those whose primary concern is with the material evidence. There are few people who are at home in more than one of the many disciplines through which the history of the period may be reconstructed; and co-operative ventures are rare. Encouragingly, the mature works of the present generation of scholars (Loyn 1962; Alcock 1971; Finberg 1972; Morris 1973) show a conscious desire, on the part of historians and archaeologists alike, to make use of the full range of evidence. Also a new journal, *Anglo-Saxon England*, promotes communication, if not mutual comprehension, between archaeologists, philologists and historians. The problem is only partly, however, one of misapprehension. There is also mistrust of evidence through an inability to criticize it. Archaeological field reports vary in their reliability, and historians rightly doubt their ability to distinguish the good from the bad, when archaeologists themselves are often manifestly unable or unwilling to do so. The archaeologists' own interpretative works are even more suspect. This is probably the reason why archaeology has made so little impact on Anglo-Saxon historical studies; a valuable opportunity lost for, in early Saxon studies at least, archaeology is potentially the best source of dependable data. The period (A.D. 450-650) is to all intents and purposes prehistoric. There is no documentation at all for large tracts of the countryside, and such history as there is peoples the land with eponymous heroes or ghostly kings whose real and imagined exploits are inextricably interwoven. At best it gives a general impression of the character of life at the time; a collective folk memory of what Middle Saxon descendants felt had happened in the early days of England. Even if the historicity of many events or persons can be proved it will hardly provide illuminating history and can never give the essential facts of social, economic, cultural and environmental conditions. A biography of Aethelbert of Kent, for instance, would be brief, unrevealing and open to doubt at almost every point. In the circumstances, the methods and aims of prehistoric archaeology seem entirely appropriate: but they have not been widely adopted, nor have the essential problems been stated. The process might be of benefit to both disciplines.

As field-work, excavation and corpus-production begin to provide the essential data for an archaeology of Anglo-Saxon England, it is clear that the period shows a remarkable parallelism with later prehistoric times and, in particular, with the British Early Iron Age. The bases of economy and society; the general intensity and location of settlements; the relative technological levels and the exploitation and sources of raw materials are all similar. Incipient urbanization occurs in both periods. Hill-forts in the Early Iron Age developed from ancient origins into settlements that provided refuge in times of strife for the inhabitants of dispersed rural estates. Latterly, they developed almost into towns, and many were re-founded on economically more suitable sites in Late Iron Age or Roman times. A similar story can be read in the Anglo-Saxon period. Towns and fortifications were used from the start. Under Alfred and Edward the Elder they multiplied and acquired a function as refuges serving a hinterland of villages. They were ultimately crucial for the survival of England against Scandinavian attack. Most provided the nuclei for mediaeval towns and many were re-founded in economically more propitious valley positions. Such parallels are worth-while, since they deal with very similar situations in the same areas and, more importantly, because they suggest ways in which the theoretical bases of later British prehistory and protohistory may be tested. It seems increasingly unlikely, for example, that archaeological cultures will ever be effectively defined within Anglo-Saxon England. Professor Jope long ago showed how difficult it was to identify mediaeval cultures, as distinct from various regional traditions (Jope 1963). This may point to the reason why the cultural approach to the British Iron Age, so optimistically propounded by Hodson (1962:152-3; 1964), has not provided a complete understanding of the period, any more than did the rigid regional and chronological frameworks of earlier interpretative devices (Hodson 1960). As soon as it is possible to judge, that is in late Saxon times, it becomes clear that the culture model is too simple a device to describe, at one and the same time, the broad underlying unity of England and also the intense regional variations capable of expression in modes of architecture for one geographical reason, or in dialect for another; in terms of ceramic types, because of certain economic factors; in terms perhaps of dress, for reasons to be found in the ancestry and kinship of people themselves; or in terms of politics for immediate, unrecorded, ever-changing and irrecoverable reasons. Late Anglo-Saxon society was complex and varied, sharing a certain general unity by which its traditions might be recognized as a 'culture' in archaeological terms; defying any attempt to sub-divide it into sub-cultures; but readily understandable, in all its diversity, with help from historical sources.

If history cannot be so helpful in earlier Anglo-Saxon times, it at least provides a clear record of invasion and population replacement. Invasion also occurred in the ninth century, in the early eleventh century and in 1066. Each invasion had a different character and a different effect, demonstrable archaeologically and historically, on indigenous material, social and economic conditions. This criterion for the concepts of invasion and diffusion as means of culture spread could have exposed the mythology of British prehistory long before Clark (1966) found it necessary to do so. The concepts that replace them could, however, similarly be tested. It is difficult for any Anglo-Saxon archaeologist, for instance, to countenance the widespread and uncritical use of geographical techniques of locational analysis in prehistoric and Roman studies, when misleading results come from their application in historically documented contexts.

For all its potential as a test-bed where archaeological conclusions may be compared with recorded facts, Anglo-Saxon archaeology is still in a formative period. The mere recovery of material has hardly started. There are only a few adequately excavated settlements in the whole of England over the 600-year period. Except for the narrow, and perhaps untypical, range of artefacts normally found in early Anglo-Saxon graves, there is a dearth of knowledge about Anglo-Saxon cultural material and its accompanying technology. With the notable exception of Anglo-Saxon coinage and, in recent years, the pottery of eastern England in late Saxon times, no range of artefacts has a firmly dated typology; yet these exceptions have shown what potential dividends are available for economic history.

Even in the Early Anglo-Saxon period there is much to be done. Many thousand early Anglo-Saxon graves have been excavated, but there are still few complete cemeteries and fewer still have been described in print. Thousands of skeletons have been recovered, but few populations have been studied. It is not yet possible, therefore, to set anthropological data against the typological studies that have consumed so much scholarly energy, nor for sociological or demographic interpretation of cemeteries to be attempted. If we are to avoid work on Anglo-Saxon cemeteries becoming a self-validating routine, then new questions must be posed and new procedures adopted. Future excavations should be directed to specific problems; they should at once be selective and comprehensive; and they must be co-operative ventures in which various specialists are brought together in one team to give an integrated approach related to the realities of the field situation. Typological studies will still be important, but many other factors demand equal attention. Cemetery lay-out and maintenance are not yet understood. Potential grave sequences can be formulated for complete cemeteries by consideration of vertical and lateral stratification. Social and kin groups within the cemetery are potentially identifiable, as continental excavations have shown. Anthropological study of burials is still often done as if by rote, without much thought for its general potential. The study of environmental evidence in cemetery excavation is in its infancy, though it could well be informative about funerary practice and the contemporary environment and post-burial conditions (for the study of insects, Stafford 1971). Artefacts that are social indicators (such as swords, weaving battens, gold braid fillets), or burials of special rites, are slowly being recognized and studied for what they mean (Chadwick 1958:30-5; Crowfoot & Hawkes 1967). The incidence of poorly equipped graves is being recognized as a positive factor in understanding the date, social stratification or rite of a cemetery. Excavations in the inhumation cemetery at Cannington, Somerset (Rahtz, forthcoming) show what can be done with a really large sample. The Norfolk Archaeological Unit plans to excavate a complete urn-field of several thousand cremations at Spong Hill, North Elmham: a lead that must be followed if Anglo-Saxon cemeteries are ever to provide social history as well as archaeological typology. The recent excavations at Helgö, a contemporary manufacturing site in Sweden, have shown how fallible are arguments from type-sequence and distribution of grave-goods; they suggest that much recent work of this sort may be invalid (Holmqvist 1972). Perhaps cemetery artefacts are best thought of as potential data for economic and technological history, more appropriate subjects for students of material culture than ethnic influences or optimistic brooch-defined invasions, peddling routes, or the politics of pottery.

Archaeological facts, because they are usually unconscious evidence not created with communication in mind, are often thought less prone to misinterpretation than written evidence with its possible conscious or unconscious bias. There are, however, very firm limits to inference in Anglo-Saxon archaeology, in particular those imposed by the methods employed by the excavator, his skill and experience, and the quality of his recording. There has been an extraordinary increase in the amount of excavation undertaken in Britain in the last few years. More and more people of limited experience are being faced with the task of 'rescuing' archaeological facts, the recovery of which would tax the most skilled practitioner. Speed is often the only essential. There is always a very real danger, particularly in the present rescue situation, that apparent archaeological facts are not always what they seem, or are claimed, to be. Worse still, they may be positively wrong. When it comes to interpreting their significance, the problems are compounded. A simple review of the history of the study of Anglo-Saxon houses may be used to illustrate the difficulties. Until 1920, our knowledge of the Anglo-Saxon house came from literary sources and pictorial representations alone. Sensible ideas derived from these sources (Brown 1903:101-5) were shattered by Leeds' revelation of the archaeological realities. Leeds' excavations at Sutton Courtenay led a generation of scholars to believe that the Anglo-Saxon peasant lived in a hovel (Leeds 1936:21). Structures such as those found at Sutton Courtenay were soon revealed across the face of England. Their interpretation remained unchallenged for so long that some historians still accept it (Finberg 1972:428). Excavations are increasingly demonstrating, however, that such structures are normally ancillary to much larger buildings: they are only the sheds to be found around the farm buildings (Addyman 1972). If Leeds could have used modern methods of open-area excavation at Sutton Courtenay, he would have found larger buildings, as recent excavations on a nearby settlement have shown. How many excavation reports must therefore be rejected as unacceptable interpretations of incompletely observed facts? Those at Wykeham, Yorkshire, certainly (Moore 1966), where excavation was necessarily limited. Is it special pleading to say that either deep ploughing or deep mechanical topsoil stripping at Mucking, Essex (Jones & Jones 1974), accounts for the almost total absence of large buildings amongst a huge number of sunken-floored huts there? Certainly such stripping would have removed all traces of houses on some sites, such as Maxey (Addyman 1964). Who is to warn historians that these things may be so? The remainder of this paper seeks to show something of the range of interpretative detail that can be derived for three archaeological sites with very different strengths and weaknesses; and to examine documentary sources which show that all these have considerable shortcomings.

At Chalton, near Petersfield in Hampshire (Addyman & Leigh 1973), the ground traces of an Anglo-Saxon settlement are strikingly clear. Techniques borrowed directly from prehistoric archaeology enabled us to record the position and lay-out of every building whose foundations penetrated the subsoil (Fig. 1). With careful excavation it is sometimes possible to show that several buildings succeeded one another on the same site; artefacts give some indication of the period at which the buildings were occupied; scientific dating techniques may be able to refine the dates. Even if this can be done, however, the interpretation of the settlement will still be difficult.

Problems begin immediately one asks the question: What did the buildings look like? The ground-plan of each one is different. Together, they seem to embody a host of constructional methods and, although certain themes are recurrent, there are several possible reconstructions for each building (Warmington 1972:24-8). Simple questions, such as whether any or all had a second storey, seem impossible to resolve: even the number of rooms is in doubt. Suggested reconstructions always attract a hail of criticism, though the carefully-argued hypothesis, doubtless later to be replaced by a succession of others, would seem to be the soundest way to progress. Experimental archaeology can plainly be of some help here. Some of the buildings should be reconstructed and it would, doubtless, be salutory and instructive if the latest hypothesis were to collapse in a gale.

If the design of the buildings cannot be restored with certainty, can we at least identify what went on in them? This might be possible on other sites, but at Chalton ploughing has removed all the house floors and all traces of activity within. Even so, the very lay-out and conjunction of the Chalton buildings invites an interpretation. The buildings AZ, erected in the last period of reconstruction, seem to belong together as a group (Fig. 2). They include a large rectangular structure AZ 1, which has both a large and a small room, doors at the mid-point of the sides, and a door in one end-wall. The gable-door (if such an interpretation be permitted) leads into an enclosure some 22.6m. by 45m. (*c.* 1017sq.m.), defined by a stout fence of horizontal planks held by alternate-set split posts buttressed outside at 3.80m. intervals. Within the enclosure were three smaller buildings, one facing the main building and two flanking the space in front of it. From their alignment, lay-out and stratigraphic position it seems most likely that the buildings were conceived as parts of a single unit.

This is the extent of the archaeological fact. All beyond it is to touch the ark: but to touch it is, in this case, a temptation impossible to resist. Few would argue with an interpretation of the large building as the main dwelling house of what is doubtless an economic unit, and the smaller ones as dependent buildings, perhaps byres, barns, servants' quarters or workers' quarters or separate sleeping accommodation. There is an inevitable temptation to see the unit as a farm with farmyard and service buildings, but one factor demands caution; there seems to be no way into the fenced enclosure except from the house. This makes it unlikely that the enclosure or the dependent buildings within can ever have accommodated stock.

The AZ group is just a formalization of an arrangement found elsewhere in the Chalton settlement, and all elements were already present in the preceding periods A and B (Fig. 1). The group A1 + A9, B6 and B7 are also set within a fenced enclosure, precisely one-half the size of its successor. Elsewhere there seem to be groups that contain some, but not all, of the elements. Sometimes the buildings seem to have been fenced, and sometimes not. Nevertheless the Chalton occupation unit, or economic unit,

Figure 1. Chalton, Hampshire. Anglo-Saxon village (6th-7th centuries A.D.) as excavated in 1973.

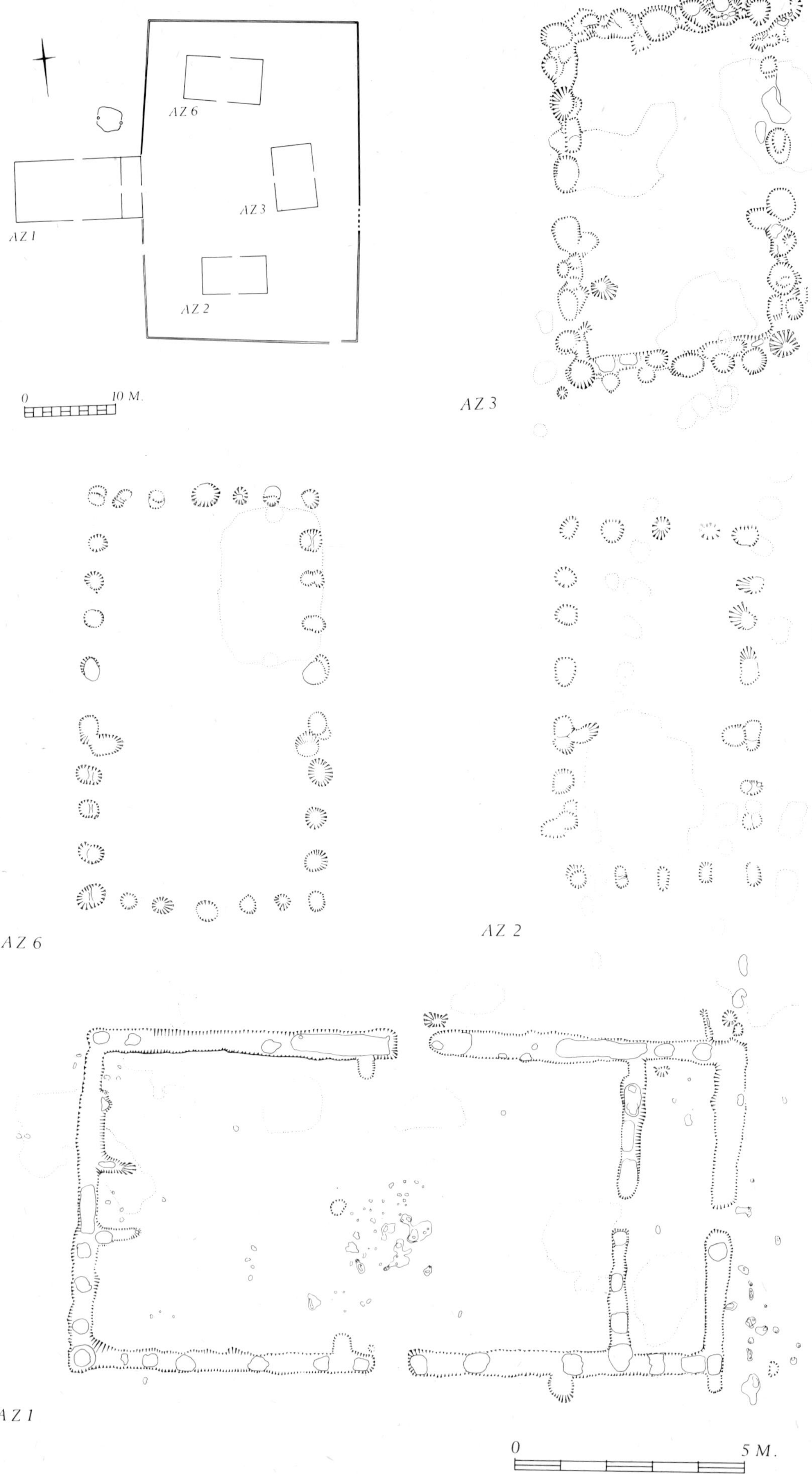

AZ 6
AZ 3
AZ 1
AZ 2
0
10 M.
AZ 3
AZ 6
AZ 2
AZ 1
0
5 M.

or social unit, whichever way one choses to characterize it, seems clearly to have been a house and yard with ancillary buildings, or a farm with farm buildings, or a peasant family with an individual holding. The settlement is clearly a nucleated one, as there are many such units. In period A there are at least six, set in rows some 25 m. apart across the axis of the hill (Fig. 1).

It is interesting to speculate how many of these deductions would have been made had the excavators not been well aware, from the historical sources, that the late-seventh-century Wessex village was regarded by contemporaries as a nucleated settlement of individual homesteads held by free peasant farmers, *ceorls*, each farming a hide which, it might be thought, was some 60 acres in Wessex at this time. Would the excavator have been so ready to identify the AZ complex as a peasant homestead had he not been aware of the fortieth clause of the laws of Wessex (datable to A.D. 688-694): 'A ceorl's homestead must be fenced in winter and summer. If it is not fenced, and his neighbour's cattle get in through his own gap, he has no right to anything from that cattle; he is to drive it out and suffer the damage' (Whitelock 1955:368)?

When a site is as completely preserved and as coherent as that at Chalton, the question immediately arises of its relation to its fields, its cemetery and the countryside around. Is it typical or could it be unique? At Chalton, it seems likely that a fairly complete picture of local land-use will be revealed as a result of Professor Cunliffe's thorough and continuing field survey. Cunliffe (1972, 1973) uses techniques of geographical analysis to suggest that contemporary local settlements not only existed but are now all known. Here, if anywhere in Anglo-Saxon England, it is possible to proceed from hypothetical deduction to field tests. The results of these tests and of the final survey should be of great value.

While Chalton has provided new hope of understanding the structure of rural Anglo-Saxon society and its expression in terms of buildings and settlement lay-out, the site tells us little about technology, economy or contemporary environment. There are few work-places, very few artefacts and hardly any animal bones; the chalkland conditions have inevitably limited the range of environmental evidence. A nearby Hampshire site, Hamwih or Hamwich, in part at least probably contemporary with Chalton, has provided a more or less complementary set of data, albeit for a different type of site (Addyman & Hill 1968-9). Hamwich was an Anglo-Saxon port serving a broad south English hinterland. In its heyday it covered more than 30 hectares. Though many excavations have taken place there, very few buildings have been located. The evidence for settlement lay-out (Addyman & Hill 1968-9:81) comes, in fact, from scraps of evidence fortuitously preserved between areas of contiguous rubbish pits, wells, latrines and other intrusions. These intrusions, however, are the source of quantities of pottery and other artefacts, animal bones, prēserved botanical and entomological and other organic materials. From them it is possible to build up a most detailed picture of local industry, infinite in variety and remarkable in intensity, of local and international trade on a vast scale and also to gain some idea of standards of contemporary everyday life. The latest excavations are on a scale large enough to confirm general impressions gained from over a century or more of discoveries. Such a site, threatened with destruction by development, is one where massive resources should be deployed to recover an adequate sample, and scientific techniques employed in the fields of dating, analysis, characterization of artefacts, as well as the extraction and identification of environmental evidence and study of food remains. It is equally important that large-scale excavations should continue at this site until the chances of survival provide us with actual buildings to add to the other excellent evidence. The dividends of such an approach can be seen in the transformation in recent years of our understanding of the comparable town of Dorestad on the continent (Es 1969).

Grahame Clark's work at Star Carr was the result of a conscious search for an early Mesolithic site immediately contiguous to waterlogged deposits that offered the possibility of recovering the organic materials that have so generally vanished (Clark 1972:4). He hoped thereby to obtain:

(a) a much more complete range of material equipment, including objects of antler, bone and hopefully also of wood;
(b) food refuse, animal bones and plant remains;
(c) evidence for the environmental conditions

← Figure 2. Chalton, Hampshire. The structures of an Anglo-Saxon homestead.

prevailing in the immediate locality at the time it was occupied;

(d) clues to the scale of the social unit represented.

Such a site of Anglo-Saxon date would provide us with very similar opportunities and, in fact, these conditions obtain in much of Anglian and Anglo-Danish York, as has been well known from the early years of this century (Benson 1903:64). It is surprising, therefore, that evidence from a multitude of commercial excavations in the area has only recently been drawn together (Radley 1971), and archaeological investigations have only lately begun at modern standards. The preliminary results show that the area is deeply stratified, and contains in places up to ten metres of archaeological deposits of which some five metres belong to the Anglo-Saxon period. Timber buildings are well preserved and thus explain the real significance of certain arrays of post-holes found in previous investigations. In one place, ten successive structures have been investigated (Addyman 1974). A full range of artefacts of organic materials has been recovered, including structural fittings from buildings, wooden vessels and tools, birch-bark rolls perhaps used for writing messages, textiles, and leatherwork and leather off-cuts. As well as these, the laminated floors of the buildings contained botanical and faunal remains that have allowed detailed reconstructions of the immediate environments and of the range of human activities on the premises. This study of mediaeval York (Buckland *et al.* 1974) highlights the squalor of life in an Anglo-Danish town and illustrates the practice of both an early mediaeval tannery and cobbler's shop and the contrasts and contacts of the city at the time. It also shows what lacunae there are in our understanding of those sites where conditions of preservation are not so good as at York, and demonstrates the future possibilities of environmental archaeology (Dimbleby 1967:11-13).

Even on a site such as York, where evidence is so abundant and fruitful, there are still problems. So much material exists that only limited excavation is practicable. Even small excavations are so complex that resources are unlikely to suffice for a proper series of such investigations that might provide samples from different areas of the town. Each project of this sort requires the attention of a team of natural scientists for months, if the information is to be extracted. There are also the usual problems of excavation in the heart of a flourishing modern city. Nevertheless, if research priorities are to be established, propitious sites such as Anglo-Danish York must inevitably claim especial attention on this sort of scale.

Chalton, Hamwich and York have in their own ways, and with their respective limitations, added much to the historical information available for the area and period. It would be wise to end on a note of caution, however, as none of these approaches a complete picture of everyday life for the period, or even hints at the complexity of contemporary practice. Domesday Book records thousands of *vills* of which no complete contemporary example has yet been investigated. We are only now beginning to recognize and excavate late Saxon estates, so often alluded to in charters in a way that assumes in the reader an utter familiarity with the economic unit. Sulgrave (Davison 1967) or North Elmham (Wade-Martins 1972) may well be such estates but, if they are, we still have to recognize and document the practices of their everyday life. The well-known *Rectitudines Singularum Personarum*, a tract on estate procedures, apparently of the eleventh century, is at present a much better source of information. The tract *Gerefa* (Appendix I), which is an adjunct to this manuscript, shows how far archaeology still has to go (Cunningham 1915:571-6). It purports to tell a reeve how to run an estate. The first eight paragraphs are sound and universal advice on general management. Paragraphs 9 to 13 form an instructive list, season by season, of tasks around the estate, with a final paragraph on such duties as are always present. Many of these activities should be recognizable archaeologically. It cannot be long before the fish-weir becomes a known Anglo-Saxon archaeological type. A near-contemporary mill at Old Windsor (Hurst & Wilson 1958:183-5) has already been excavated, though not yet published, and an earlier version of the same kind has recently been found at Tamworth (Rahtz & Sheridan 1972). It is clear, also, that when an estate is found where appropriate conditions have existed since Anglo-Saxon times, it is possible to establish, through pollen analysis and the examination of macroscopic plant remains, the local agricultural regime and consequent changes in the environment. This has, apparently, proved to be possible at Old Windsor.

Examination of this document should also stimulate the excavator to a more imaginative interpretation of excavated settlement structures. Hedges, for instance, seem to be assumed to exist along the ditches of the estate, if a Latin gloss for the Anglo-Saxon term is to be believed, and excavated settlements of the period often seem to be a maze of ditches (Addyman 1969:67-71, 76). Planks should be laid between the houses: this is both an interesting comment on farmyard conditions and also a warning that not every timber assemblage excavated on a settlement need be a building. Ovens and kilns, presumably for domestic drying, are clearly envisaged in the manuscript as indoor structures.

Paragraphs 14 to 18, however, provide the greatest challenge to archaeologists. They enumerate tools that ought to be provided on an estate. An archaeological identification of some of these is attempted in Appendix II. In paragraph 15, the axe, adze, bill, awl, plane, saw, tie-hook and auger are apparently thought of as everyday estate equipment, a comment on the status of the carpenter. This corroborates the impression that many late Saxon structures were of wood and that carpentry must have been a common skill. It is the millwright who is singled out in the next paragraph as a skilled workman. No doubt, examples of all the woodworking tools enumerated in paragraph 15 exist now in museums and groups of excavated finds. Wilson's recent review of the Anglo-Saxon woodworkers' tool-kit makes possible some identifications (Wilson 1968:143-50). It is less clear that mattocks and prises have been identified. The nature of the late Saxon ploughshare and coulter continues to give rise to discussion, crucial as these are for the origin of the strip-field. At least, they were present by the eleventh century in a form capable of achieving the long furrow. The goad-iron may never be recognized, but eventually most of the cultivation equipment should become apparent. Some of the tools should have been of wood, but these may well be revealed when sites with good conditions of preservation are found and systematically excavated. It is likely that there will be considerable regional variations in such tool-types. The enormous variety achieved by the Irish spade in recent times (Gailey & Fenton 1970) shows what may be expected and there were also, doubtless, different spades suited to the immensely varied soil-types of Anglo-Saxon England. In this period the normal estate was clearly expected to produce textiles. The equipment listed was largely of non-durable materials, mainly wood. Spinning was clearly still undertaken with a spindle, usually of wood. Stone or pottery whorls are ubiquitous in late Saxon sites, though they disappear from the archaeological record soon thereafter. Is the stoddle to be identified as the equally ubiquitous pin-beater? The slay can be exemplified by one found recently at Wallingford. It is interesting that no mention is made of loom-weights. This may be an omission, or it may imply that another device was used. Alternatively, an horizontal loom may be envisaged, as loom-weights also begin to disappear from the archaeological record at about this time. This subject has been studied in a recent paper on the inferences derived from textiles themselves, which shows the dividends that are to be gained from a multi-disciplinary approach (Carus-Wilson 1969).

The archaeologist should compare the paucity of finds on a normal late Saxon settlement (e.g. St. Neots – Addyman 1973:45-99) with the wealth of vessels, tools and other equipment the sagacious reeve was expected to provide (see para. 17). It is cheering to recognize a few old friends, such as awls, dishes, bowls with handles, combs and lamps, and even a few of the less familiar artefacts: tubs, buckets and perhaps butts, vessels and cups. Clearly, excavated evidence represents but little of what was there. Perhaps the most revealing artefacts, being non-durable, are now gone. We may never recognize the mouse-trap. What is more, we have no hope at all of finding the peg for the hasp, though one is known from an illustration.

Documents as archaeologically revealing as the *Gerefa* are rare in Anglo-Saxon literature, but there is still much scope for the perceptive archaeologist in correlating textual detail or illustration with archaeological fact. The process will become the more productive as excavated material begins to accumulate from rescue excavations. With such a combination of evidence, many customs and practices of Anglo-Saxon society previously thought unknowable may become apparent. Place-name scholars have hopefully suggested environmental conclusions from early names, albeit often with a very uncertain chronology. Environmental scientists, who are able now to provide a detailed history of land-use from pollen analysis (Oldfield 1969), should find a profitable field for collaboration here and, perhaps, also significant leads to follow. Population at Domesday is a contentious problem but, with co-operative work, new dimensions can be added to the bare fiscal statistics through the excavation of cemeteries. Mortality rates, physical types, levels of general health, and even blood-groups may be established for selected groups of burials, to make Domesday into a true document of social history. These results will only be achieved, however, if there is a determined policy on the part of archaeologists to excavate the relevant material: and on the part of historians and anthropologists and natural scientists alike to come together to study it. If they do, then the golden age of Anglo-Saxon archaeology, too, will be in the future.

Appendix I: 'The Sagacious Reeve'

The document, Corpus Christi Library MS. CCCLXXXIII of 102, has been printed by Liebermann (1903-16: I,453-5) and, with translation by Skeat, by Cunningham (1915:571-5). A new translation is at present being prepared, together with a detailed consideration of its implications. In the meantime, the Skeat translation is reproduced here in the hope that its more general availability will provide a stimulus to archaeologists.

1. The sagacious reeve ought to know both the lord's landright and the folk-rights, even as the counsellors of olden days have determined; and the season of every crop that pertains to a homestead; since, in many districts, the farm-work is earlier than in others; that is, ploughing-time is earlier, the season for mowing is earlier, and so likewise is the winter-pasturing and every other kind of husbandry.

2. Let him who holds such office take heed that he guard and further every work according as is best for it; and he must act with regard to it as the weather directs him. He ought prudently to consider and diligently to look into all the things that may be for his lord's advantage.

3. If he wants to begin well, he must not be too lax nor too overweening, but he must know both the less and the more, both the greater and the less important matters that concern a homestead, both in the farm-yard and on the down, both in wood and in water, both in field and fold, both indoors and out. For I tell you of a truth, if he be too proud or negligent to undertake and attend to the things which belong to cattle-stall or threshing floor, the result, in so far as it depends on such matters, will soon shew itself in the barn.

4. But I advise that he do as I said before. Let him pay attention to things great and small, so that neither go wrong as far as he can control it; neither corn nor sheaf, nor flesh nor cream, nor cheese nor rennet, nor any of the things that can ever be of use.

5. So should a good reeve keep his lord's goods; let him do what he will with his own. Ever, as he becomes more diligent, will he be more valued, if he observes a course like that of a wise man.

6. He should ever stimulate his servants by an admonition (to observe) their lord's desire; and moreover should pay them according to what they deserve.

7. He should never let his servants get the upper hand of him, but let him wish (to direct) each one, with a lord's authority and according to folk-right. Far better were it for him to be always out of office rather than in it, if they whom he should rule come to rule him. It will not be prudent for his lord to permit this.

8. He can ever be finding out something to be useful in, and be thinking of useful things to assist him. However, it is most desirable for him to search out how he may promote the estate by farming, when the right time for it comes round.

9. In May and June and July, in summer, one may harrow, carry out manure, set up sheep-hurdles, shear sheep, build up, repair, hedge, build with timber, cut wood, weed, make folds, and construct a fish-weir and a mill.

10. In harvest one may reap, in August and September and October one may mow, set woad with a dibble, gather home many crops, thatch them and cover them over, and cleanse the folds, prepare cattle-sheds and also shelters, ere too severe a winter come to the farm; and also diligently prepare the soil.

11. In winter, one should plough, and in severe frosts cleave timber, make an orchard, and do many affairs indoors; thresh, cleave wood, put the cattle in stalls and the swine in pig-sties, set up a stove on the threshing floor – for an oven and a kiln and many things are necessary on a farm – and moreover (provide) a hen-roost.

12. In spring one should plough and graft, sow beans, and set a vine-yard, make ditches, hew wood for a wild-deer-fence; and soon after that, if the weather permit, set madder, sow linseed (i.e. flaxseed) and also woad-seed, plant a garden, and (do) many things which I cannot fully enumerate, that a good steward ought to provide.

13. He can always find something on the manor to improve; he need not be idle, when he is in it; he can keep the house in order, set it to rights and clean it; and set hedges along the drains, mend the breaches in the dikes, repair the hedges, root up weeds, lay planks between the houses, make tables and benches, provide horse-stalls, scour the floor, or let him think of something that may be useful.

14. He should provide many tools for the homestead, and get many implements for the buildings: (as, for instance) –

15. An axe, adze, bill, awl, plane, saw, chimbe-iron, tie-hook, auger, mattock, prise, share, coulter; and also a goad iron, scythe, sickle, weed-hook, spade, shovel, woad-dibble, barrow, besom, beetle, rake, fork, ladder, horse-comb and shears, fire-tongs, weighing scales and many spinning-implements, (such as): flax-threads, spindle, reel, yarn-winder, stoddle, weaver's beams, press, comb, carding-tool, weft, woof, wool-comb, roller, slay (?), winder with a bent handle, shuttle, seam-pegs, shears, needle, slick-stone.

16. And if he has skilled workmen, he should provide them with tools. As for the mill-wright, shoe-maker, plumber, and other artisans, each work itself shews what is necessary for each; there is no man that can enumerate all the tools that one ought to have.

17. One ought to have coverings for wains, ploughing gear, harrowing tackle, and many things that I cannot now name; as well as a measure, an awl, and a flail for the threshing floor, and many implements besides; as a caldron, leaden vessel, kettle, ladle, pan, crock, fire-dog, dishes, bowls with handles, tubs, buckets, a churn, cheese-vat, bags, baskets, crates, bushels, sieves, seed-basket, wire-sieve, hair-sieve, winnowing-fans, troughs, ash-wood-pails, hives, honey-bins, beer-barrels, bathing-tub, bowls, butts, dishes, vessels, cups, strainers, candle-sticks, salt-cellar, spoon-case, pepper-horn, chest, money-box, yeast-box, seats (?), foot-stools, chairs, basins, lamp, lantern, leathern bottles, box for resin (or soap), comb, iron bin, rack for fodder, fire-guard, meal-ark, oil flask, oven-rake, dung-shovel.

18. It is toilsome to recount all that he who holds this office ought to think of; he ought never to neglect anything that may prove useful, not even a mouse-trap, nor even, what is less, a peg for a hasp. Many things are needful for a faithful reeve of a household and for a temperate guardian of men.

19. I have declared all as well as I could; let him who knows better declare more than this.

Appendix II: Some archaeological evidence for the Sagacious Reeve's provisions

(a) Iron tools (by Ian H. Goodall)

In an attempt to find examples of at least some of the day-to-day tools, fittings and other artefacts that are listed in the document as a normal provision on just a single estate, it is necessary to turn to the whole spectrum of archaeological sites – to urban and rural settlements, hoards and chance finds. Furthermore, unless there are special ground conditions, only the metal part of the tool survives: handles and associated fittings are lost.

Excavation of several late Saxon settlements in the St. Neots, Huntingdonshire, area in all instances produced knives (Lethbridge & Tebbutt 1935:97, Fig. 2, *5-7*; Addyman 1965:65, Fig. 11, *5-7*; 1969:86, Fig. 16, *1-4*; 1973:91, 93, Fig. 19, *2-6*); only St. Neots provided more significant tools in the form of a reaping hook, a T-shaped carpenter's axe and a ploughshare (Addyman 1973:93-4, Fig. 19, *26, 29, 30*). Tools from the Saxon palace at Cheddar, Somerset (Rahtz 1962-3:53-66, for their context) comprised several knives, a pair of shears, a steel and a chisel; but of these only the shears are specifically mentioned in the *Gerefa.* A greater range of objects is known from the late Saxon town of Thetford, Norfolk, where excavations by the late Group Captain G.M. Knocker took place in a peripheral area near the town defences (Davison 1967, for their context in the town as a whole). Tools and fittings include knives, shears, a reaping hook, scythe blade, hoe, hammers, saw, adze, file, spoon-bits, chisels, punch, probable flesh-forks, steels, a ploughshare, ferrules and spade irons. Other towns have also produced objects of this date, including axes and knives from York (Waterman 1959:71-3, Fig. 5, *5-8*, Fig. 7, *1-13*; Richardson 1959:83, Fig. 18, *5-12*). York has also recently produced several tools, including awls and a needle, probably associated with leather-working (Addyman *et al.* 1975, forthcoming). There is a similar range of tools from London (Wheeler 1927:18-26), and the tongs from the group of objects found near Old London Bridge (Wheeler 1927:18-23, Fig. 1, *15*) may well resemble the fire-tongs listed in the *Gerefa*.

A number of objects, some in the list, including scythe blades, axes, adzes, a spoon-bit and a double-ended pick were found in the Hurbuck, Co. Durham, hoard of tools (*V.C.H.* 1905:214; Wilson 1971:77, Fig. 11). A carpenter's T-shaped axe, a chisel, two punches and a socketed gouge are among the objects in a hoard from Crayke, Yorkshire (Sheppard 1939:273-81) and a ploughshare and a punch were found with a bill, spearhead and other fragments in the Westley Waterless, Cambridgeshire, hoard (Fox 1923:300). Carpenters' tools from Anglo-Saxon England have been discussed in detail by Wilson (1968) but other types await a general survey; the very many manuscript illustrations and documentary references await correlation with the archaeological material.

(b) Objects of materials other than iron (by Peter Addyman)

Of the artefacts mentioned in the *Gerefa*, some 75 were probably wholly or largely made of wood or other botanical materials. Some 33 may have been of iron, and perhaps 12 of metals other than iron. At very most, only 18 were of pottery or fired clay, and probably far less. Eleven could have been of bone; five may have been of textile; one or two may have been of stone. More than half, therefore, and probably far more than half, were of organic materials. All were quite humble objects and none seems to have survived to the present except in archaeological contexts. As yet, in England, very few archaeological contexts of the period have been excavated in which conditions of preservation – waterlogging or desiccation – obtained, such as would ensure the survival of organic materials. The archaeologist is normally restricted to metal, bone, stone, and pottery objects. In most reports the pottery looms largest, whet-stones are frequent, metals other than iron are rare, and bone tools are very limited in range. Where pottery is not present and bone does not survive, as on some sites in western England (e.g. Lydford, or Hound Tor on Dartmoor), there is hardly anything. Yet it is hard to believe that citizens of the *burh* of Lydford were not familiar with most of the everyday objects enumerated.

In southern, eastern and northern England, where pottery was in common use in late Saxon times, it is possible that ladles, pans, crocks, dishes and bowls with handles might have been of pottery, as might bowls, vessels, cups, strainers, candlesticks and salt-cellars, the money-box and the lamp. The oil flask may have been of pottery or glass. Amongst these, however, it is extremely difficult to exemplify types except for the distinctive ones. In eastern England, bowls with handles are surely the common St. Neots ware type with socketed handle (Kennett 1966) or its counterpart in other wares (Barley 1964:184-6). The round-based handled type (Dunning *et al.* 1959:56-60) might also have been so described, though it might equally have been a ladle. Candlesticks are rare but known, and lamps occur in pottery at least in the eleventh century and later (Jope *et al.* 1950). Clearly bowls, dishes, vessels, cups, crocks and pans could all be identified amongst the very varied ceramics of late Saxon England, but there is no certainty that the identifications would be correct. Equally clearly, certain ceramic types are not enumerated for the reeve; and certain of his types must have been of wood, as is evident when organic materials survive.

Mediaeval archaeologists seem prone to postulate the former existence and widespread use of metal vessels though they rarely find them. The reeve's 'caldron' must have been one such, as may have been the kettle. Leaden vessels are a more common find: the Westley Waterless hoard was contained in one, and another of the tenth century from Willingdon, Sussex (Lower 1848), is preserved in Lewes Museum. Scales are likely to have been common, if their frequent appearance in Scandinavian graves in Britain and abroad is an indicator. It is possible that the horse-comb, carding-tool and wool-comb may have been of metal (Brown 1973), of wood or of bone. Though the bone combs found in late Saxon times in a variety of types are normally interpreted as for personal use, there is no reason why some of them should not have been used in weaving. The identification of the ubiquitous pin-beater is not clear.

There are a few dozen objects of organic materials from York, a handful from other sites in England, and some rare survivals in tombs or as relics. It is not surprising, therefore, that to find examples of even part of the range of objects in the *Gerefa*, it is necessary to resort to comparative material from elsewhere. Various Irish sites supply some types: there are bowls, a stave-built churn and perhaps a stool from Lissue (Bersu 1947:53-4); from Lagore (Hencken 1950:151-70) there are stave-built buckets, tubs and mugs, lathe-turned wooden bowls; scoops, boxes, pins, spindles, mallets, handles and pegs, though not all are contemporary. From the tenth- and eleventh-century deposits at Ballinderry Crannog No. 1 (Hencken 1936) there are tubs, tankards, bowls, mallets, a pile-driver, a straddle, scoops, ladles, the well-known gaming board and a variety of objects of unknown use. The excavations currently in progress in Viking and mediaeval Dublin, where waterlogged conditions similarly obtain, have produced a wealth of artefacts in organic materials, including a wooden weaving-sword (O'Ríordáin 1971:80).

The objects from York are enough to indicate that a similar range of wooden objects would have been used in contemporary English settlements. There is a variety of lathe-turned bowls, staves from various stave-built vessels and parts of tools of unknown use; wooden combs and wooden spoons have also been found (Waterman 1959; Richardson 1959; Radley 1971; Addyman *et al.* 1975). It will be fortuitous, indeed, if any of the larger tools of the list are found, but what is apparently a ladder has been recognized at Pevensey Castle, together with a large wooden barrel and two spades (Dunning 1958, with *comparanda*). Even if the strict chronological limits of this superficial review were relaxed, it is doubtful whether even near-contemporary examples could be found of most of the other objects listed in our document.

REFERENCES

Addyman, P.V. (1964) A Dark-Age settlement at Maxey, Northants. *Medieval Arch.*, 8, 20-73.

Addyman, P.V. (1965-69-73) Late Saxon settlements in the St. Neots Area: Parts I, II and III. *Proc. Cambridge Antiq. Soc.* 58, 38-73; 62, 59-93: 64, 45-99.

Addyman, P.V. (1972) The Anglo-Saxon house: a new review. *Anglo-Saxon England*, 1, 273-307.

Addyman, P.V. (1974) Excavations at York: first interim report. *Ant. Jour.*, 54, 200-31.

Addyman, P.V., Harrison, M. and MacGregor, A. (1975) An Anglo-Scandinavian site at Pavement. In Addyman, P.V. (ed.), *The Archaeology of York*, forthcoming. York.

Addyman, P.V. and Hill, D.H. (1968-9) Saxon Southampton: a review of the evidence. *Proc. Hants. Field Club*, 25, 61-93; 26, 61-96.

Addyman, P.V. and Leigh, D. (1973) An Anglo-Saxon village at Chalton, Hampshire: second interim report. *Medieval Arch.*, 17, 1-25.

Addyman, P.V., Leigh, D. and Hughes, M.J. (1972) Anglo-Saxon houses at Chalton, Hampshire. *Medieval Arch.*, 16, 13-31.

Alcock, L. (1971) *Arthur's Britain.* London.

Barley, M.W. (1964) The Mediaeval borough of Torksey, Lincolnshire: Excavations 1960-2. *Ant. Jour.*, 44, 165-87.

Benson, G. (1903) Excavations at 25-7 High Ousegate. *Yorks. Phil. Soc. Ann. Rep.*, 1902, 64-7.

Bersu, G. (1947) Excavations at Lissue. *Ulster Jour. Arch.*, 10, 30-58.

Brown, G.B. (1903) *The Arts in Early England: The Life of Saxon England in its relation to the Arts.* London.

Brown, P.D.C. (1973) Linen heckles. In Brodribb, A.C.C., Hands, A.R. and Walker, D.R. (eds.), *Excavations at Shakenoak IV*, 134-6. Oxford; privately printed.

Buckland, P.C., Greig, J.R.A. and Kenward, H.K. (1974) York: an Early Mediaeval site. *Antiquity*, 48, 25-33.

Carus-Wilson, E. (1969) Haberget: a Mediaeval textile conundrum. *Medieval Arch.*, 13, 148-66.

Chadwick, S.E. (1958) The Anglo-Saxon cemetery at Finglesham, Kent: a reconsideration. *Medieval Arch.*, 2, 1-71.

Clark, J.G.D. (1966) The invasion hypothesis in British archaeology. *Antiquity*, 40, 172-89.

Clark, J.G.D. (1972) The archaeology of Stone Age settlement. *Ulster Jour. Arch.*, 35, 3-16.

Crowfoot, E. and Hawkes, S.C. (1967) Early Anglo-Saxon gold braids. *Medieval Arch.*, 11, 42-86.

Cunliffe, B. (1972) Saxon and Mediaeval settlement-pattern in the region of Chalton, Hampshire. *Medieval Arch.*, 16, 1-12.

Cunliffe, B. (1973) Chalton, Hants: The evolution of a landscape. *Ant. Jour.*, 53, 173-90.

Cunningham, W. (1915) *The Growth of English Industry and Commerce* (5th ed.). London.

Davison, B.K. (1967) The Late Saxon town of Thetford: an interim report on the 1964-6 excavations. *Medieval Arch.*, 11, 189-208.

Davison, B.K. (1968) Excavations at Sulgrave, Northamptonshire, 1968. *Arch. Jour.*, 125, 305-7.

Dimbleby, G. (1967) *Plants and Archaeology*. London.

Dunning, G.C. (1958) A Norman pit at Pevensey Castle and its contents. *Ant. Jour.*, 38, 205-17.

Dunning, G.C., Hurst, J.G., Myres, J.N.L. and Tischler, F. (1959) Anglo-Saxon pottery: a symposium. *Medieval Arch.*, 3, 1-78.

Es, W.A. van (1969) Excavations at Dorestad: a pre-preliminary report, 1967-1968. *Berichten van de Rijksdienst voor het OudheidkundigBodemonderzoek*, 19, 183-207.

Finberg, H.P.R. (ed.) (1972) *The Agrarian History of England and Wales I & II*, A.D. *43-1042*. London.

Fox, C.F.(1923) *The Archaeology of the Cambridge Region*. London.

Gailey, A. and Fenton, A. (1970) *The Spade in Northern and Atlantic Europe*. Belfast.

Hencken, H. O'N. (1936) Ballinderry Crannog No. 1. *Proc. Royal Irish Acad.*, 43 (Sect. C), 103-239.

Hencken, H. O'N. (1950) Lagore Crannog: an Irish royal residence of the 7th to 10th centuries A.D. *Proc. Royal Irish Acad.*, 53 (Sect. C), 1-247.

Hodson, F.R. (1960) Reflections on 'The ABC of the British Iron Age'. *Antiquity*, 34, 318.

Hodson, F.R. (1962) Pottery from Eastbourne, the 'Marnians' and the Pre-Roman Iron Age in Southern England. *P.P.S.* 28, 140-55.

Hodson, F.R. (1964) Cultural grouping within the British Pre-Roman Iron Age. *P.P.S.* 30, 99-110.

Holmqvist, W. (1972) *Helgö IV*. Stockholm.

Hurst, J.G. and Wilson, D.M. (1958) Mediaeval Britain in 1957. *Medieval Arch.*, 2, 183-213.

Jones, M.V. and Jones, W. (1974) Excavations at Mucking, Essex. In Rowley, T. (ed.), *Anglo-Saxon Settlement and Landscape*, Oxford, forthcoming.

Jope, E.M. (1963) The Regional Cultures of Mediaeval Britain. In Foster, I.L. and Alcock, L. (eds.), *Culture and Environment*, 327-50. London.

Jope, E.M., Jope, H.M. and Rigold, S.E. (1950) Pottery from a late 12th-century well-filling and other Mediaeval finds from St. John's College, Oxford, 1947. *Oxoniensia*, 15, 44-62.

Kennett, D. (1966) Some St. Neots Ware socketed bowls in Bedford. *Beds. Arch. Jour.*, 3, 19-21.

Leeds, E.T. (1936) *Early Anglo-Saxon Art and Archaeology*. Oxford.

Lethbridge, T.C. and Tebbutt, C.F. (1935) Ancient Lime-kilns at Great Paxton, Hunts. *Proc. Cambridge Antiq. Soc.*, 35, 97-105.

Liebermann, F. (1903-16) Die Gesetze der Angelsachsen. Halle.

Lower, M.A. (1848) An ancient leaden coffer found at Willingdon. *Sussex Arch. Coll.*, I, 160.

Loyn, H.R. (1962) *Anglo-Saxon England and the Norman Conquest*. London.

Moore, J.W. (1966) An Anglo-Saxon settlement at Wykeham, North Yorkshire. *Yorks. Arch. Jour.*, 51, 403-44.

Morris, J. (1973) *The Age of Arthur*. London.

Oldfield, F. (1969) Pollen analysis and the history of land use. *Advancement of Science*, 25, 298-311.

O'Ríordáin, B. (1971) Excavations at High Street and Winetavern Street, Dublin. *Medieval Arch.*, 15, 73-85.

Radley, J. (1971) Economic aspects of Anglo-Danish York. *Medieval Arch.*, 15, 37-57.

Rahtz, P. (1962-3) The Saxon and Mediaeval palaces at Cheddar, Somerset – an interim report of excavations in 1960-62. *Medieval Arch.*, 6-7, 53-66.

Rahtz, P. (forthcoming) *Cannington Cemetery, 1962-3.*

Rahtz, P. and Sheridan, K. (1972) Fifth report of excavations at Tamworth. *Trans. S. Staffs. Arch. & Hist. Soc.*, 13, 9-16.

Richardson, K.M.(1959) Excavations in Hungate, York. *Arch. Jour.*, 116, 51-114.

Robertson, A.J. (1956) *Anglo-Saxon Charters* (2nd ed.). London.

Sheppard, T. (1939) Viking and other relics at Crayke, Yorkshire. *Yorks. Arch. Jour.*, 34, 273-81.

Stafford, F. (1971) Insects of a Mediaeval burial. *Science and Arch.*, 7, 6-10.

V.C.H. (1905) *The Victoria History of the County of Durham* I. London.

Wade-Martins, P. (1972) Excavations at North Elmham. *Norfolk Arch.*, 35, 416-28.

Warmington, R. (1972) Reconstruction of the buildings. In Addyman *et al.* (1972), 24-8.

Waterman, D.M. (1959) Late Saxon, Viking, and Early Mediaeval finds from York. *Arch.*, 97, 59-105.

Wheeler, Sir R.E.M. (1927) *London and the Vikings*. London.

Whitelock, D. (1955) *English Historical Documents c. 500-1042*. London.

Wilson, D.M. (1968) Anglo-Saxon carpenters' tools. In Claus, M., Haarnagel, W. and Raddatz, K. (eds.), *Studien zur Europäischen Vor- und Fruhgeschichte*, 143-50. Neumünster.

Wilson, D.M. (1971) *The Anglo-Saxons*. Harmondsworth, Middlesex.

MARTIN BIDDLE

Hampshire and the origins of Wessex

The transition from Roman Britain to Anglo-Saxon England was marked by the earliest large-scale migration into these islands of which we have more than the slightest mention in the written record. And among all the problems of the English settlements none is more difficult, or has been the subject of more debate, than the question of the origins of Wessex, 'the thorniest of all political problems in this period' (Myres 1937: 393). It is not simply that this debate concerns the origins of the kingdom out of which a unified England finally emerged, although that would be 'something better than a topic of antiquarian speculation' (Young 1934: 4). Difficulties arising from the apparent impossibility of reconciling the historical, archaeological and place-name evidence have 'seemed to involve a direct attack upon the established literary tradition' (Myres 1937: 396).

It is now twenty years since the problem was last discussed at length (Copley 1954; Leeds 1954). There have been important contributions in the meantime, notably by J.N.L. Myres (1964, 1969), but since the early sixties and especially in the last five or six years new discoveries have been made, and new views put forward, in all the disciplines involved. The time has come perhaps to draw some of these threads together. And if particular attention has usually been given to the part played in the formation of Wessex by the Anglo-Saxons of the upper Thames valley, it may provide a contrast to examine the role of the peoples to the south, in the former *civitates* of the Belgae and the Atrebates. In offering this review to the author of 'The invasion hypothesis in British Archaeology', I hope to indicate that even in this, the best evidenced of early invasions, more may have been due to forms of culture contact other than large-scale immigration than has usually been perceived (Clark 1966).

The principal written evidence for the origin of the kingdom of Wessex is contained in a small group of annals in the *Anglo-Saxon Chronicle* (ed. Plummer 1892) and in a few references in Bede (ed. Plummer 1896). By the late nineteenth century these had been elaborated to the extent that J.R. Green (1881) could write 'as if he had been present at the landing of the Saxons, and had watched every step of their subsequent progress' (Plummer 1896: ii, 28). The outline sketched by the annals indicated that the West Saxons made a landing or landings on the coast of Hampshire about A.D. 500 and fought their way slowly north-west, succeeding to the kingdom (whatever that may mean) in 519, and reaching Salisbury by 552. The sources give no indication of a Saxon presence in southern Wessex before 500, and provide no hint of penetration from any other quarter.

Historians had long subjected the annals to critical comment on internal evidence (Wheeler 1921), but it was a growing appreciation of the archaeological and subsequently of the place-name evidence which eventually raised the most serious doubts as to their reliability. The case for their dismissal was elaborated by E.T. Leeds in a series of papers over the twenty years from 1913 to 1933. Basing his position principally on the absence of pagan Saxon cemeteries in southern Wiltshire and Hampshire (outside the so-called Jutish areas of the Meon valley and the Isle of Wight), and on their relative abundance and early date in the upper Thames valley, in the northern part of what later became Wessex, he first proposed to explain this pattern by suggesting a line of Anglo-Saxon penetration along the Thames valley (Leeds 1913: 49-55). Leeds later modified this view, on evidence that seemed to indicate that Saxon settlers had reached the upper Thames mainly from the north-east, along the line of the Icknield Way (Leeds 1925). In 1933 he re-emphasized the importance of this route, denying any role to Hampshire or the lower Thames in the early settlement of Wessex. 'It is a question', he concluded, 'whether [the early entries of the Chronicle] are worth the vellum on which they were first written' (Leeds 1933: 251). In a posthumous paper he reiterated this position, but allowed the possibility of 'a band of adventurers apparently mixed Juto-Saxons advancing from the south coast but only in sufficient strength to make slow headway with a very moderate area of actual settlement' (Leeds 1954: 59).

Other workers had meanwhile been seeking a rapprochement between the various strands of evidence. Characteristically, Crawford attempted to follow on the ground the route of Cerdic's advance indicated by the annals. He concluded from this comparison that their account was 'a trustworthy historical description of events which actually took place' (Crawford 1931: 456). In 1934 the historian and essayist G.M. Young published a lecture in which he made striking use of place-names, archaeology, and a sensible approach to the annals ('Archaeology', he averred, 'is a science which I approach with diffidence anywhere, and in Wiltshire [he was speaking at Wilton] with trepidation. Archaeologists are such savage creatures'. Young 1934: 12-13). But the first full-dress effort on these lines was the work of R.H. Hodgkin, originally published in 1935 (third edition, Hodgkin 1952). The relative absence of pagan cemeteries in Hampshire and Wiltshire was still the greatest difficulty in approaching the problem through the Chronicle. To avoid it Hodgkin had to suppose that cremation and the deposition of grave goods were abandoned by the invaders, under the influence of the Christian fashions of the Britons. 'One need only suppose that Cerdic and his chiefs were clever and adaptable men who saw that the depositing of weapons and jewellery with the corpses was an unnecessary extravagance' (Hodgkin 1952: 131).

This Gordian solution did not entirely satisfy reviewers (e.g. Wilson 1936) or subsequent commentators (e.g. Myres 1937: 401), for Hodgkin had not in his first edition taken sufficient account of the weakness of the place-name evidence. This difficulty was emphasized by Myres in his review of the first edition of the Ordnance Survey *Map of Britain in the Dark Ages* in 1935 (Myres 1935: 464). He pointed out that Wessex was poor not only in pagan cemeteries, but also in the *-ing*, *-ingas* place-names which were then believed to belong to the oldest stratum of Teutonic nomenclature in England.

It was Myres who in 1936 produced the standard account of the English settlements in the first volume of the Oxford *History of England*. It went quickly to a second edition and remained for more than thirty years the textbook statement; it is still not superseded. His review of the Wessex question (Myres 1937: 393-405) accepted a northern, upper Thames origin for the bulk of the West Saxon population who in the later sixth and early seventh century occupied the area between the Thames and the Hampshire coast and 'accepted in return little but the political dominance of a southern royal family' (Myres 1937: 405). For the original penetration of the upper Thames by Anglo-Saxon settlers he allowed the use of both the Thames and Icknield routes, a modified and more moderate statement of Leeds's various proposals.

The evidence for the southern element in the settlement of Wessex was given full weight, but in the comparative absence of pagan cemeteries and early place-names, there was little on which to build. The few Hampshire cemeteries suggested Kentish (Juto-Frankish) connections rather than a Saxon origin. The best that could be said was that the annals represented 'a general body of tradition recording in the main the exploits of one family' (Myres 1937: 397). These traditions were preserved, Myres implied, precisely because this family laid, or was believed to have laid, the foundations of the royal house of Wessex. There was the 'stubborn tradition of a southern origin' for this royal house, linked to southern Hampshire and especially to Winchester, and their association with the *Gewissae*, a name apparently applied broadly to the people of Hampshire, and perhaps 'primarily applicable to the kingly family and its immediate dependents' (Myres 1937: 403-4; but see below, p.336). Faced with the lack of place-name and archaeological evidence, the nature of the original settlement associated with this family could not be defined, but it has remained impossible to believe that 'the main mass of the West Saxon people followed the traditional founders of their dynasty at the traditional date into their homes in Hampshire and Wiltshire' (Myres 1937: 402). Of the many further problems, the most striking was perhaps the Celtic element in the place-names of Hampshire (Myres 1937: 401; Jackson 1953: 237) and in the personal names of the royal house, among which Cerdic himself, it is generally agreed, bore the Old Welsh name *Ceretic* (Chadwick 1907: 28-9; Ekwall 1928: lxviii-ix; Myres 1937: 401, 446; Jackson 1953: 613-4; Sisam 1953: 305; Stenton 1971: 25). A further difficulty was provided by the geographical contrast between the area in south-east Hampshire which showed at least some archaeological evidence of Anglo-Saxon activity in the first half of the sixth century and the barren area west of the Test in which the Chronicle account placed the activities of the invaders. This contrast was pointed by the Kentish character of discoveries in the south-east, and the presumptively Saxon origin of the invaders as they appeared in the Chronicle and in their royal genealogy. When the evidence for a Jutish presence on the Isle of Wight and in southern Hampshire was added, whether from Bede, from place-names, or from archaeology, it was clear that substantial uncertainties remained, and that several strands might have been involved in the settlement of even the southern part of Wessex.

Myres's analysis of 1936 stood for some thirty years virtually unchallenged by new discoveries or radical re-interpretation. Sir Frank Stenton followed it in 1943 in the first and subsequent editions of his *Anglo-Saxon England* (Stenton 1971: 19-31), and so did G.J. Copley in his lengthy, detailed and somewhat uncritical survey of 1954 (Copley 1954: esp. 159-68). For Copley there was no 'real conflict' between the Chronicle record of the origins of Wessex and the archaeology of Hampshire and Wiltshire (Copley 1954: 159). Since the early sixties, however, there has been a steady flow of new discoveries and substantial revision of existing theories in all the main fields involved in this 'thorniest of all political problems' of the English settlements. It will be convenient to take them in turn, beginning with the archaeological evidence, and continuing with place-names, topography, and the written materials.

Archaeology

As recently as 1960 the comparative absence of pagan Saxon cemeteries in mainland Hampshire was equalled only by the lack of Anglo-Saxon material that could be dated earlier than the middle of the sixth century. For the period before 500 there was a complete blank. The apparent gap in the fifth century has now been approached from both directions, by study of late Roman materials, and by a fresh consideration of pagan Saxon sites and finds, extended by new discoveries.

Late Roman

There can be no doubt that the identification of late Roman military equipment in the towns and some of the lesser settlements of Roman Britain has marked a major advance in our understanding of the fourth and early fifth centuries (Hawkes & Dunning 1961; 1964). This is not the place to enter on a detailed discussion of a now famous thesis. It will suffice to list the points crucial for the present argument. The materials in question are the bronze mounts from official belts of 'Sam Browne' type. They can be divided into two classes, the one closely comparable to Continental examples of this equipment from northern Gaul, the Rhine and Danube frontiers, the other of similar character but restricted in its distribution to Britain. When present in any quantity both classes can be taken to indicate the presence of military detachments, and thus something of the deployment of late and sub-Roman troops. The class with continental affinities is perhaps the earlier, belonging essentially to the second half of the fourth century. It should thus represent arrangements made under imperial authority. The question is whether it represents simply the issue of standard equipment to local forces, or whether it can be taken to suggest the actual presence in towns and elsewhere of foreign troops, whether *laeti* or units of the regular field army (*cf.* Frere 1971: 18-19). The latter view has been generally accepted and is now supported by the finding of examples of this equipment in graves of alien character at Winchester (Clarke 1970: 295-8, Fig. 4, no. 92 shows a naturalistic Type IIA buckle more comparable to the continental than to the insular material; 1972: 97-8; 1975, two Type III buckles). The class of insular distribution is perhaps rather later in date and may represent either a localization of manufacture for the same forces, or the emergence of a native militia with its own and now restricted sources of supply. In summary, sites (especially towns and other fortified places) producing either or both classes of this material may be regarded as military centres in late and sub-Roman times, with all that this may imply for their continued existence into the fifth century (Frere 1966; 1967). In addition, those places producing material of the continental type may reasonably be supposed to have had an alien element in their population during the latter part of the fourth century. Whether this alien element should be regarded as Germanic is not so clear, although there are reasonable grounds for arguing that this may have been so at least in some cases.

Since the publication of the original statements in 1961 and 1964 there have been widespread further discoveries of this equipment, whether in unsorted collections, older publications, or on new excavations. Of importance here is the situation at Winchester, from which material of both classes was absent in the original publication, strikingly so because of the number of insular examples from Silchester and the countryside west and north of Winchester. Examples of both classes are now known from the walled area of Winchester and from the eastern and northern cemeteries, notably from Lankhills (Biddle 1970: 311-14; Clarke 1970; 1972). Taken in conjunction with the discovery of a bastion added to the town defences in the fourth century (Biddle 1975a), an addition which implies the reorganization of Winchester's defences at this date on lines well recognized elsewhere (Corder 1955; Frere 1967: 255-7, 357-9), we may now be certain that the city was equipped to defend itself with some confidence well into the fifth century.

Other sites in Hampshire, including Rockbourne and Portchester, have produced further examples of this late Roman equipment, particularly of the insular class, or related material, and we must therefore beware of supposing that the local population was unable to defend itself after 407-10, whether from internal or external aggression. The actual situation was perhaps quite the reverse. In this context the recent suggestion that Honorius's rescript of 410 may have been less an abdication of Roman authority than a directive in the exercise of that authority takes on an added meaning (Ward 1973: 255).

Anglo-Saxon

In Anglo-Saxon archaeology, there have also been important advances. Pagan Saxon pottery has been found on Roman sites, new cemeteries have been discovered, and older finds have been reconsidered, whether cemeteries, individual objects or categories of object. Of particular interest have been the discoveries of early pagan Saxon pottery at Winchester and Portchester.

(*a*) *Early Anglo-Saxon pottery on Roman sites.* At Winchester pottery of this kind was first identified in 1970 on the Lower Brook Street site (Biddle 1972: 101-2). The sherds included fragments of several faceted carinated bowls of early fifth-century date, as well as other pieces belonging to the latter part of the century. Continuity of occupation on or near this site into the sixth century is suggested by some of the Anglo-Saxon sherds (e.g. Biddle 1972: Fig. 3, no. 6), as well as by the discovery on the same site in 1971 of several stamped sherds of Frankish type and a sherd of a Frankish biconical urn of the same date.[1] Pagan Saxon pottery was also found at South Gate, Winchester during 1971 (Biddle 1975a). The distribution of pagan Saxon pottery within the walls of Winchester can be greatly extended if the grass-tempered pottery found in small quantities in the latest Roman levels on all major excavations in the lower part of the city can also be accepted as Anglo-Saxon rather than sub-Roman. This now seems probable, and for several reasons. At Lower Brook Street pagan Saxon gritted and burnished sherds and grass-tempered sherds were found together, and on some vessels (e.g. Biddle 1972: Fig. 3, no. 6) the two fabrics seem to merge almost imperceptibly one into the other. Further, grass-tempered fabrics would be entirely at home in the fourth and fifth-century coastal sites of Holland and northern Germany, where they occur in normal association with vessels of native and Anglo-Saxon type.[2] By contrast, grass-tempered pottery is alien to the Romano-British tradition (but *cf.* Cunliffe 1970: 70; and see also Avery & Brown 1972: 78-81).[3] In summary, the Winchester evidence now suggests an Anglo-Saxon presence inside the walled city from the earliest years of the fifth century, continuing through that century and into the sixth, when its contacts were sufficiently extensive to include the importation, by whatever means, of contemporary Frankish pottery from the continent. A handful of sherds do not make a major settlement, but there are perhaps sufficient, over a sufficiently long period of time, and their find-spots are perhaps widely enough distributed, for a significant and continuous Anglo-Saxon presence to be indicated. As I have argued elsewhere such a presence is suggested and even required by the group of sixth-century cemeteries clustering around the city walls (Biddle 1973: 237-41). For our present purposes, the fact of the greatest importance is that this Germanic element must have been established in the city well before the collapse of Romano-British town life, protected as it was by refurbished defences and garrison troops, the evidence for which has been outlined above. The presence of this Germanic element within the city walls at so early a date suggests that it was as mercenaries, whether *laeti* or *foederati*, that the newcomers first arrived in Winchester.

Portchester has produced early Anglo-Saxon pottery and grass-tempered fabrics in similar association and in similar contexts to those from Winchester, and Cunliffe has tentatively suggested 'the presence of Germanic settlers, possibly mercenaries, in Portchester in the first half of the fifth century' (Cunliffe 1970: 68-70). At Portchester too, the sequence is apparently continuous through into the sixth and later centuries, but *unbroken* continuity is difficult to establish without long structural sequences and both there and at Winchester further evidence is clearly required. Nevertheless, the continuing focus required by the cemetery distribution at Winchester (Biddle 1973: 237-41), and the growing evidence at Portchester for early Saxon structures and a general topographical continuity within the walls (Cunliffe 1972a: 74-6, Figs. 3-6), seem to argue in favour of unbroken settlement, perhaps varying in intensity from period to period. It is certain that in both places the density of occupation was uneven within the relatively large areas enclosed by the Roman walls.

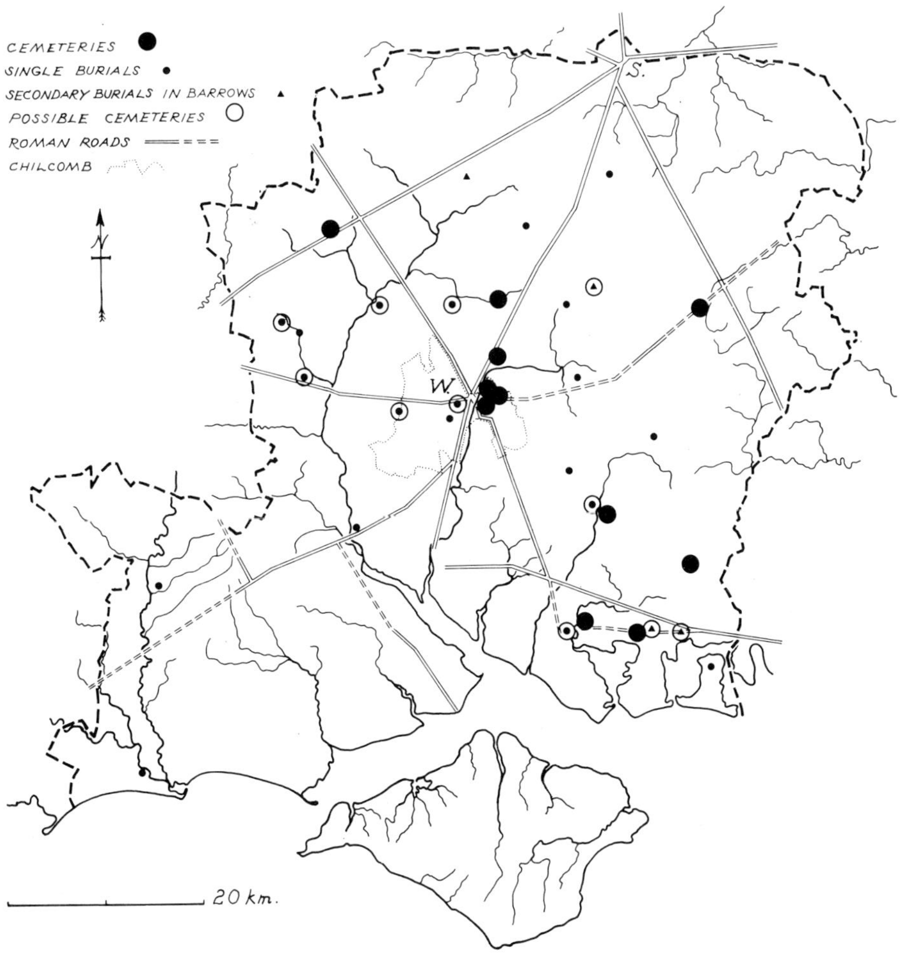

Figure 1. Early Anglo-Saxon burial-sites in Hampshire

(*b*) *Anglo-Saxon cemeteries* (Fig. 1). New discoveries and the reconsideration or first appreciation of older finds means also that the relative paucity of Anglo-Saxon cemeteries in Hampshire is no longer so stark a factor in the discussion as it has been previously. The new discoveries are still mostly unpublished and one is very recent, but they must be considered. The most important is undoubtedly the cemetery at King's Worthy (Worthy Park), three km. north of Winchester, excavated in 1961-2 (Meaney 1964: 102-3; Wilson 1962-3: 307; 1964: 233; Swanton 1973: 207, 209, Figs. 83 & 85). Some forty cremations, mainly of the mid and later sixth century were found, together with about ninety-five inhumations ranging in date from the late fifth to the seventh centuries. Another cemetery was excavated at Alton in 1959-60, with some twenty-nine cremations and perhaps twenty inhumations of the sixth (or even late fifth) and seventh centuries A.D. (Meaney 1964: 94; Wilson 1960: 134; 1961: 309; Evison 1963: 43, Figs. 19-20). A third new cemetery was found in 1974 at Portway, Andover, in the course of the rescue excavation of prehistoric ring-ditches and linear features. So far, some sixty-two inhumantions of sixth-century date and eighty-three cremations have been examined and there are certainly more burials to come (pers. comm. from Miss Alison Cooke and Mr Max Dacre).

The new discoveries bring with them new problems. First, there is the gap of half a century, and perhaps much longer, between the earliest Anglo-Saxon presence now recognizable in walled places like Winchester and Portchester and the earliest cemeteries in the surrounding countryside. This problem needs further discussion later on (p.332-3). Second, there is the obvious importance of cremation. At both Worthy Park and Alton, cremations account for about half the known burials. This new perspective contrasts strongly with the absence of Anglo-Saxon cremation in the county as it appeared only twenty years ago (Leeds 1954: Fig. 13). The importance of this rite in Hampshire has since been confirmed by the publication of older and lost or half-forgotten finds from several sites (Hawkes 1968). Difficult and premature as any interpretation must still be, it seems clear at least that the cremations and the urns containing them point to yet another element in the make-up of Anglo-Saxon Hampshire, an arrival around the middle of the sixth century A.D. of fashions of upper Thames or even Middle Anglian origin.

Reconsideration of the known cemeteries and their distribution has also provided new insights into the problems they pose. It seems certain, for example, that many of the single Anglo-Saxon burials known from the county represent cemeteries, as may some of the secondary burials in barrows (Aldsworth 1974: 23-8). These isolated chance discoveries have rarely been followed up by further investigation, but their siting may sometimes suggest that they derive from otherwise unlocated cemeteries (Fig. 1).[4] To the known and suggested cemeteries there must also be added at least some of the 'heathen burials' recorded in Anglo-Saxon charter bounds and now generally recognized as likely to refer to pagan Anglo-Saxon rather than to prehistoric burials (Bonney 1966; 1972: 172). The term occurs eleven times in the bounds of Hampshire charters. There is also evidence that the term *hlaew*, as opposed to *beorg*, was reserved for pagan Saxon barrows, or barrows into which pagan Saxon burials had been inserted. There are five Hampshire occurrences of this term in the bounds of Anglo-Saxon charters (Bonney 1972: 172-3). Because most of the evidence comes from charter bounds, it is inevitable that virtually all the places mentioned lay on boundaries. This too obvious fact needs always to be remembered in evaluating discussions of the relationship between pagan Saxon burial sites and boundaries, for the written evidence by its very nature must tend to support the reality of this relationship. More striking is the fact that in Hampshire as in Wiltshire over 40% of archaeologically-attested pagan Saxon burial sites do actually occur on or near boundaries. Even so, over 50% show no such relationship in terms of surviving or recoverable boundaries. Like the shapes between Picasso's figures, the places enclosed by Anglo-Saxon bounds were perhaps more interesting than the bounds themselves, and would certainly have been more informative.

To summarize, there are eleven known pagan Anglo-Saxon cemeteries in Hampshire. Some eight single burials and three secondary burials in barrows may represent the sites of as many as another eleven cemeteries. To these should be added some of the eleven sites of 'heathen burials' (at least one of these seems to refer to the known cemetery at Droxford), and possibly the five *hlaew*, although these latter may as well refer to individual graves. There is evidence then, of various sorts, for perhaps thirty pagan Anglo-Saxon cemeteries in Hampshire. It is not a great number and it covers more than two centuries, but it is far from the comparative absence of such cemeteries which so troubled earlier commentators.

(*c*) *The Winchester cemetery cluster* (Fig. 1). Topographical study of the location of cemeteries and their relation to settlements has so far made little progress, if only because the settlements remain archaeologically elusive – Chalton being the notable exception (Addyman *et al.* 1972; Cunliffe 1972b: 1973). However, recognition of the exceptional cluster of Anglo-Saxon cemeteries close to the walls of Roman Winchester has provided an observation of the first importance (Meaney & Hawkes 1970: 1-4) on which it has been possible to construct a model for the continued settlement of the city during this difficult period (Biddle 1973: 237-41; 1974). Three km. north of the city lies the King's Worthy cemetery already discussed. Close outside the eastern walls are the cemeteries of Winnall I and St. Giles Hill, both in use in the sixth century. To the west is the West Hill cemetery, possibly of the same date. Seventh-century burials, of secondary importance here, come from Winnall II and Oliver's Battery and from within the walls at Lower Brook Street (Biddle 1975a). These cemeteries form a group without parallel in Hampshire and testify to a continuing focus of interest in and around the former Roman city in the sixth century and possibly before. The nature of this focus will be discussed further on, but it is relevant to remark here on the contrast between the occurrence of early fifth-century Anglo-Saxon pottery on two or more sites within the walls and the apparent lack of material of this date in the surrounding cemeteries.

(*d*) *Early Anglo-Saxon objects other than pottery*. A sustained attempt has been made to identify fifth-century Anglo-Saxon objects among the cemetery finds from the area south of the Thames (Evison 1965). The enquiry made a valuable contribution to our knowledge of two categories of object in particular, metal-inlaid work and objects decorated in the so-called Quoit Brooch Style. It was less successful in isolating material that was buried in the fifth rather than the sixth century A.D., even if it had actually been manufactured in the earlier period, as reviewers were quick to point out (e.g. Hawkes 1966; Myres 1966). Controversy apart, this study underlined the extreme rarity of the material in question in mainland Hampshire, by contrast with the Salisbury region and the Isle of Wight, a situation which provides further evidence, whether the date be later fifth or sixth century, for the reality of the distinctions between these areas discernible in both the written evidence and in aspects of the archaeological record.

(*e*) *Anglo-Saxon pottery*. The most important single contribution to the study of the English settlements in recent years has undoubtedly come from the maturing results of J.N.L. Myres's analysis of the pottery (Myres 1969). Its significance goes far beyond the material itself, for Myres has succeeded in replacing the overtly simplistic explanation of the change from Roman Britain to Anglo-Saxon England, in terms of invasion and annihilation, by mechanisms of much greater sophistication, inherently more likely to explain the extent and complexity of the cultural changes which took place. Yet in outline his scheme is simple. It envisages three successive stages in a process covering the later fourth, fifth and sixth centuries: a phase of overlap and controlled settlement, a phase of transition, and a phase of uncontrolled settlement leading eventually to the consolidation of the Anglo-Saxon presence in Britain. In the first phase, which is seen as beginning in the mid-fourth century[5] and ending with the *de facto* cessation of imperial administration in the province around A.D. 410, Germanic groups were settled in Britain as part of the arrangements made under central government control for purposes of defence. In some cases the newcomers may have received grants of land in return for defence service; in other cases they may have formed part or the whole of more regular military units. This phase would thus have seen the controlled intrusion of Germanic people into the functioning framework of Romano-British life and their establishment side by side with existing communities. The second phase, beginning about A.D. 410 and lasting until around the middle of the fifth century, is seen by Myres as a phase of transition in which the policy of controlled settlement was continued by the sub-Roman rulers of Britain for the same purpose of defence, but perhaps on an increasingly localized basis. These more formal arrangements were now accompanied by less controlled or even uncontrolled settlement, as new groups joined the established Germanic communities, or entered of their own will into areas not previously available. As the pressure mounted and the power of the British communities to sustain the cost, whether in cash or in kind, of the previous mercenary arrangements waned, this phase degenerated into outright conflict of the kind recorded in the Kentish annals of the Chronicle under the years 449, 455, 457, 465, 473. Transition from the rule of the individual successor states of Roman Britain to the ascendancy of the emerging Anglo-Saxon groups took place in different areas at different dates, but there is sufficient evidence to indicate a major change in the balance of power around A.D. 450, the moment formerly characterized as the *adventus Saxonum*, but which must now be seen rather as the culmination of contact and overlap during the whole of the preceding century. The breakdown of old compacts and the increase in the rate of immigration usher in the stage of uncontrolled settlement, the third of Myres's proposed phases, and take us into the history and archaeology of the English settlements of the later fifth and sixth centuries.

This wholly revised view of the possible stages by which the culture of Roman Britain was first modified and then replaced by that of the English settlers is capable of almost infinite variation as to the rate, extent and character of the cultural change involved in any one area. It allows us to move away at last from the concept – influenced surely by the battle maps of European wars, if not by the westward movement of nineteenth-century America – of advancing frontiers, fixed bounds and territory fully and firmly held. If in some areas Anglo-Saxon rule of a mainly Anglo-Saxon population was established early, in other areas native British control of a mainly British people lasted long. Frontiers were perhaps rarely permanent, more often fluid. Nor must it be imagined that relations were never friendly. It is inconceivable that farming communities could have maintained a hostile stance for a century and more on a permanent footing. It is in the light of this new and inherently more likely approach – some might say model – that we must now return to the problems of Hampshire in the fifth century A.D.

In 1968 and before, when Myres was writing, evidence for the phase of overlap and controlled settlement was almost wholly wanting in Hampshire. To the north, at Dorchester-on-Thames, to the north-east at Mitcham, it was present, but Hampshire itself was a blank. This situation has changed with the discoveries of the last few years at Portchester and Winchester. In neither place, nor elsewhere in the county, does the evidence yet include the early Anglo-Saxon cremation cemeteries that are so distinctive a feature close to the Roman towns of the eastern part of the island. But at Winchester there is now good evidence for the presence of an alien and probably South German element from the mid-fourth century onwards, while both there and at Portchester early Anglo-Saxon pottery testifies to the presence of north German people from the earliest part of the fifth century. Their evident association at Winchester with the latest aspect of the Roman town suggests that the policy of controlled settlement of barbarian people for defence service was continued there into the sub-Roman period.

The pottery takes us into the second of Myres's phases, the phase of transition. For this phase too, there was no Hampshire evidence in 1968. But along the upper Thames a line of Anglo-Saxon cemeteries were in use by the early fifth century – Frilford, Abingdon, Long Wittenham, Wallingford and sites in the Reading area, on the south bank, and Dorchester itself, Cassington and Brighthampton on the northern side. 'We seem,' Myres wrote (1969: 89), 'to be in the presence of something that looks uncommonly like a political frontier along the Berkshire bank of the upper Thames.' A frontier implies an authority with interests to define and guard. Myres pointed to Silchester, a few kilometres south of this line, as the possible focus 'for this period of transition at any rate . . . [of] some sub-Roman power . . . that was in a position to hold hostile barbarians at arm's length, and perhaps to employ more friendly ones to defend its northern frontiers in the Thames valley'. I shall deal below with some new evidence for the importance of Silchester in the earlier Anglo-Saxon period (p.334). For the present, it is enough to observe that Myres's pregnant suggestion may be relevant to a much larger area south of the Thames than the Silchester region alone.

For the third of Myres's phases, that of uncontrolled settlement, British recovery and Anglo-Saxon consolidation, there is now substantially more evidence than was available even five years ago. It is still apparently the case that there was only a very limited Anglo-Saxon presence in Hampshire before A.D. 500, and even after that date the settlement pattern as revealed by the cemeteries was relatively sparse by comparison with counties to the east and north. Even such settlement as the cemeteries do indicate is almost entirely restricted to the chalk, leaving large areas of south-central and south-western Hampshire without much trace of Anglo-Saxon occupation in the pagan period. Moreover the evidence suggests that even such settlement as the cemeteries show was of very composite origin: a Kentish (Juto-Frankish) component in the Isle of Wight and the Meon valley (reviewed in Evison 1965: 18-30, 37-40), a cremating element derived from the upper Thames or further afield (Hawkes 1968), and a mixed Frankish-Saxon group in the Salisbury region, possibly the result of the traditional incursion of Cerdic and his followers (Leeds & Shortt 1953: 3-5; Musty & Stratton 1964: 103-4; Evison 1965: 18-30, 37-40). There were other elements, some conceivably derived from the long-established 'town' Saxons, others more probably representing new arrivals, but until the cemeteries around Winchester and elsewhere in Hampshire have been fully published, their affinities will remain uncertain. So sparse and so mixed a population as the cemeteries indicate seems an insubstantial foundation for the role played by the south, by 'chalk' Wessex, in the origins of the kingdom. Archaeology is, perhaps, still telling a good deal less that even the main outlines of the story. A major, possibly the major, component of the settlement pattern may be missing.

To summarize the archaeological position: it is now clear that by shortly after A.D. 400 there were Anglo-Saxon people in the major Romano-British settlements of Hampshire and that other Germanic elements had been present from as early as the middle of the fourth century. There is also now rather more evidence for Anglo-Saxon settlement from around A.D. 500 onwards than has previously seemed likely, but it still suggests a settlement very sparse both by comparison with other areas, and in relation to the subsequent importance of the Wessex kingdom. There is a notable contrast between the presence of the earliest Anglo-Saxon elements in walled Romano-British places, and the absence of burials earlier than the late fifth century in the known Anglo-Saxon cemeteries.

Place-names

If the archaeological evidence for the English settlement of Hampshire is still thin, difficult to interpret, and conceivably so unrepresentative of the actual situation in the fifth to sixth centuries in the area as to be positively misleading, other kinds of evidence may be able to give some assistance. The relative absence of *-ing*, *-ingas* names in Hampshire has been seen as an argument against early Anglo-Saxon settlement in the county (see above, p.324). The infrequency of these names seemed to match the fewness of the cemeteries. As early as 1935, however, Myres had raised some of the difficulties in accepting *-ing*, *-ingas* names as evidence of the earliest phase of Anglo-Saxon settlement (Myres 1935). Thirty years later J. McN. Dodgson showed that these difficulties were conclusive evidence against the accepted relationship (Dodgson 1966). *-ingas*, *-inga-* names are evidence, it seems, of a later phase of Anglo-Saxon settlement, of a phase of onward colonization following immigration and settlement, rather than of the phase of immigration and settlement itself (the current state of the problem is reviewed in Fellows Jensen 1973: 11-12). Dodgson's work removed at a stroke one major obstacle in understanding the English settlement of Hampshire. But the difficulty had been based on negative evidence and, since nothing was proposed to replace the *-ingas*, *-inga-* names, the difficulty remained.

New evidence was not, however, long in appearing. In 1967 Margaret Gelling identified a group of at least twenty-eight place-names derived from the Old English compound *wīchām*, of which Wickham in Hampshire is one example (Gelling 1967). The conclusion of her careful analysis suggested that in the earliest period of English place-name formation 'there was a type of settlement called a *wīchām*, which occurred close to Roman roads and usually near small Romano-British settlements, and which derived its name from a connexion with the *vici* of Roman Britain' (Gelling 1967: 97). This suggestion, which could imply direct contact between surviving Romano-British settlements and immigrant English-speakers, introduces into the discussion the place-name element *hām*, 'a village, a collection of dwellings'. The early date of this element has been accepted for some time, but it is only in the last two years that it has been subjected to detailed topographical analysis over a wide area (Cox 1973; Dodgson 1973). The results of this work are of fundamental importance, for it appears that *hām* may now replace the *-ingas, -inga-* names as the most readily identifiable element characteristic of the pagan Anglo-Saxon period. Furthermore, since a close relationship appears to exist between names in *-hām* and Roman roads, and major and minor Romano-British settlements and villas, names of this class provide evidence for a degree of contact between the Romano-British and Anglo-Saxon settlement patterns that was not evident from names of the *-ingas*, *-inga-* type. This is not the place to summarize the detailed and lengthy analyses of names in *-hām* already available for thirteen counties in the Midlands and East Anglia (Cox 1973) and also for Kent, Surrey and Sussex (Dodgson 1973). However, it should be stressed that there are serious problems in distinguishing *hām* names from the quite different names in *-hamm* (Gelling 1960). Also, the interpretation of the pattern revealed by *hām* is highly complex (Dodgson 1973: 18-20). It appears to differ to some degree from area to area, and will certainly be subject to intensive further investigation.

Nevertheless, in Dodgson's view, *hām* names in Kent, Surrey and Sussex 'record a process which took place in the fifth and sixth centuries' (1973: 20). In some areas, such as the Darenth valley in Kent, the distribution of *hām* names close to Roman villa sites suggests 'continuous occupation of territory and use of land, whereas the habitations changed, the Roman *villa* being succeeded by the neighbouring *hām*'. Elsewhere, 'since *hām* names occur on the edges of the Romano-British settlement pattern, and in a distribution which extends out from that pattern, the users of this type of name recognized the Romano-British pattern and settled around it and beyond it'. Further, 'since the *hām* names occur in districts where there are *no* Anglo-Saxon burial sites, the type was in use after the pagan burial fashion had become obsolete; but, since the type also appears in districts where there *are* pagan burial-sites, some *hām* names were contemporary with the pagan burial custom' (Dodgson 1973: 18-19).

No analysis of *hām* names in Hampshire has yet been published by a place-name scholar, but the importance of this element for the early settlement of the county is not in doubt in the light of these results from neighbouring areas. The absence of a published study of the place-names of Hampshire is a serious drawback, but a provisional list of *hām* names has been compiled for the purposes of the present paper (see Appendix), using published sources and drawing on Mr. J.E.B. Gover's unpublished typescript account of Hampshire place-names.[6] There seem to be as many as nineteen names that can with probability or reasonable probability be derived from *hām*, and another fourteen that derive from *hām*, or *hamm*; the remaining names of this kind are probably or certainly from *hamm*. The distribution of the names probably in *-hām* shows a marked relationship to the Roman road system (Fig. 2). The exceptions to this pattern lie close to known Roman sites, or on valley or hill-top sites that correspond with those *hām* names seen on the fringes or beyond the limits of Romano-British settlement in the south-eastern counties. The distribution shows little obvious relationship to the known pagan Anglo-Saxon burial sites. If this really points to the formation of these *hām* names after the conversion to Christianity in the mid-seventh century, it would be difficult to account for their close relationship to the Roman settlement pattern.

The place-names in *-hām* provide positive evidence for the early Anglo-Saxon settlement of Hampshire, reversing the previous situation in which the absence of *-ing*, *-ingas* names was used as an argument against such settlement. Yet the new evidence brings us face to face once again with the problem of the absence of fifth-century cemetery evidence, and the still relatively small number of later cemeteries. The problem is underlined by the discrepancy between the distribution of the *hām* names and that of the known cemeteries. If we were to take the view that the *hām* names were mainly of fifth-century origin, in view of their marked relationship to the Roman settlement pattern (*cf.* the tentative remarks on *wīchām* names and settlements of *laeti*, Gelling 1967: 97-8), the contrast between

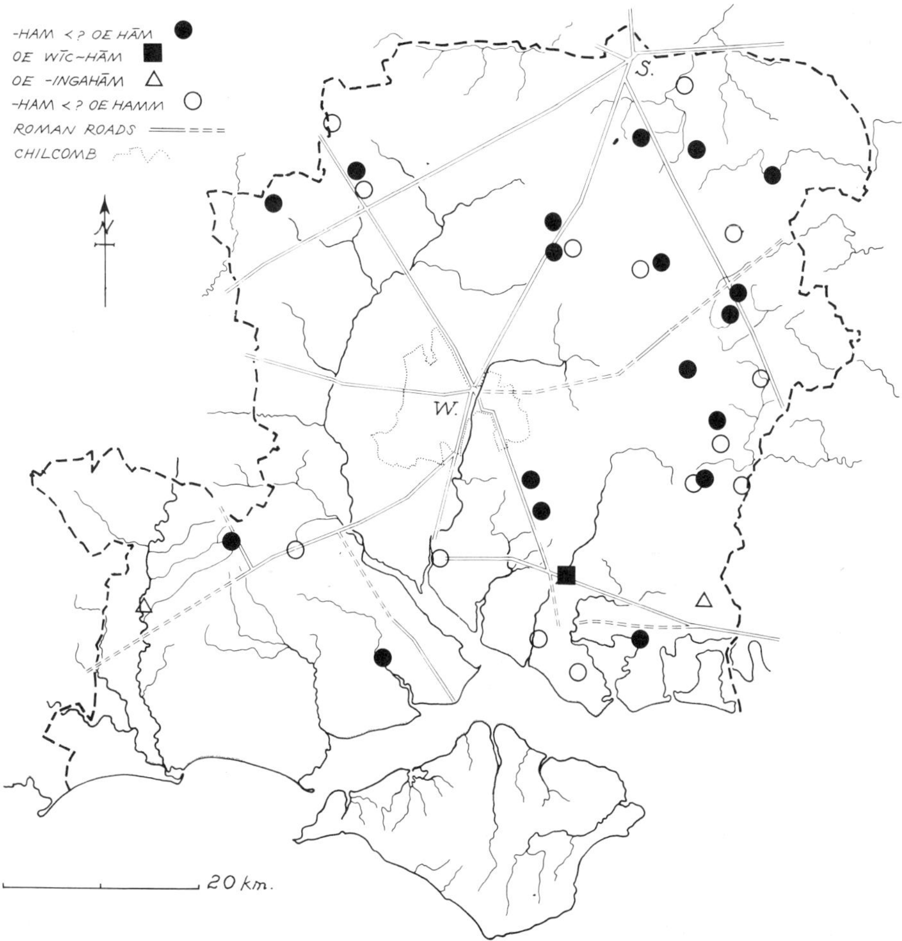

Figure 2. Hampshire place-names in *-ham*

the presence of *hām* names and the absence of early cemeteries would parallel the contrast between the discovery of early Anglo-Saxon pottery in the walled Romano-British settlements and the failure to identify the corresponding cemeteries (see above, p.323).

Topography

Attention has already been drawn to the central role that Winchester appears to have played in the sixth-century settlement of the county (p.329). This role may have survived unbroken from the Roman period and certainly formed the basis for the subsequent importance of the city, in which a church was founded by Cenwalh of Wessex about A.D. 648, perhaps to serve an already existing royal establishment (Biddle 1973: 237-41). A noteworthy feature of the topography of the Winchester area was the great monastic estate of Chilcomb which surrounded the city on all sides. Its bounds, partly recorded in the tenth century, can still be traced delimiting an area some 12 km. across (Figs. 1 and 2). The early history of this estate is obscure, but in the traditions of the Old Minster to which it belonged it had been granted to the church by Cenwalh at the time of its foundation in the mid-seventh century (Maitland 1960: 570-2; Finberg 1964: 214-48).

In the debate over the date of the original grant, comparative evidence of similar areas around other towns of Roman origin has not so far been critically assembled. A recent French study has shown the existence of such areas (*oppida*) around Paris, Lyon, Cambrai, Tours and Rheims, to name only some examples, from as early as the mid-fifth century (Lombard-Jourdan 1972). The methods of delimiting these areas by markers on the approach roads and their social and ecclesiastical significance in early mediaeval Gaul correspond to the little we know

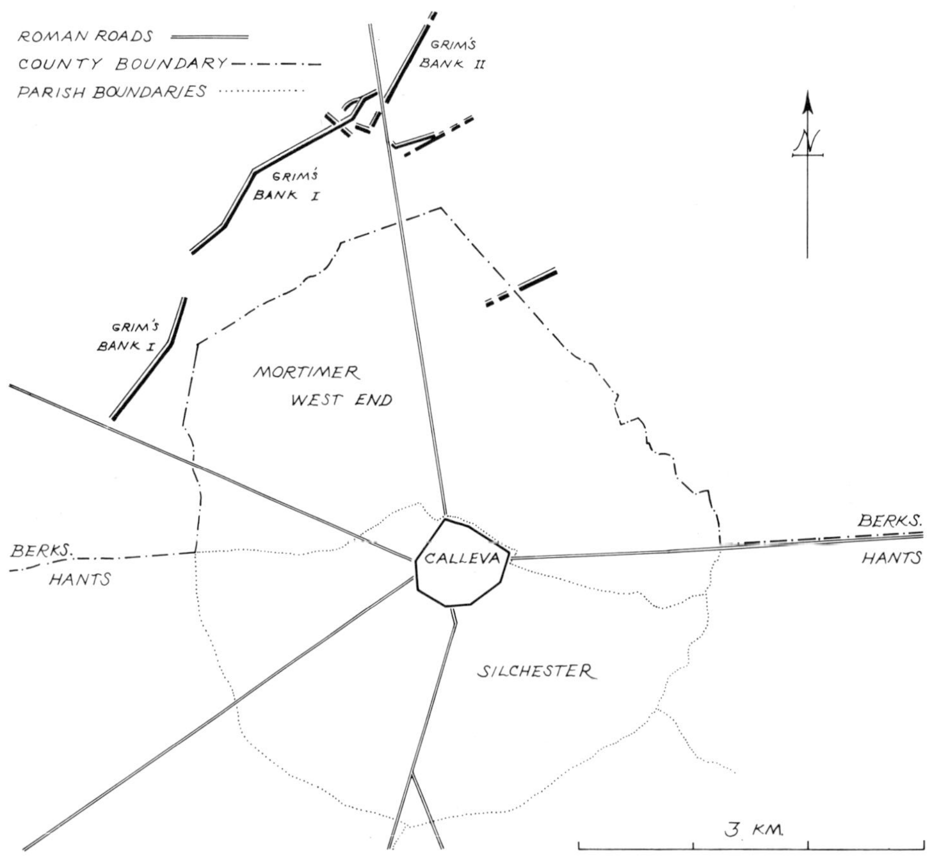

Figure 3. The parishes of Mortimer West End and Silchester

of the Chilcomb estate from late Saxon sources (Biddle 1975b: 256-7).

The date by which a territory dependent upon Winchester had been defined is possibly indicated by the situation at Silchester. The linear earthworks controlling the approaches to that town were first studied some thirty years ago by B.H. St. J. O'Neil who argued that they suggested the continuance of the town's authority into the sixth century (O'Neil 1944). Subsequent study of the latest finds from Silchester has shown that occupation of some sort continued well into the fifth century and that there are a few finds that must be dated as late as the seventh century (Boon 1959). These include the famous Ogham stone, the form of whose lettering 'probably precludes a date significantly earlier than the seventh century although the linguistic forms could suit rather better a somewhat earlier date' (Boon 1959: 97).

The parish boundaries around Silchester do not seem to have been brought into the debate since Williams-Freeman called attention to their singular character some sixty years ago (1915: 324, Fig. 22). They define an almost circular area 4.5 km. in diameter centred upon the Roman walled town and shared today by the parishes of Mortimer West End and Silchester (Fig. 3; *cf.* Figs. 1 and 2). The age of these boundaries cannot yet be established by any direct evidence, but two features argue for their early date. First, they form a conspicuous anomaly in the pattern of the surrounding parishes, an anomaly that can relate only to the walled area with which the boundaries are concentric. Second, the northern half of the circuit is followed by the county boundary, which here makes a wholly exceptional detour from its otherwise straight alignment. The shires of Wessex were probably in existence by the end of the eighth century (Chadwick 1905: 282-90; Stenton 1971: 292-3, 336-7). Their boundaries, except where altered, could be as old, and there is no reason to suspect that the Hampshire boundary has been altered at this point. The territorial unit around which the county boundary makes so marked a divergence should therefore be even older. Recent work has shown the possibility that some boundaries in Wessex may have had a continuous existence from Roman or even pre-Roman times (Bonney 1972). The survival into the late nineteenth century, and even down to the present, of bounds recorded in late Saxon charters has been demonstrated so frequently as to be almost commonplace. There is nothing therefore inherently improbable in the survival in the parish boundaries around Silchester of an early boundary defining a territory related to the walled area. There seems indeed to be nothing else to which such a territory could be related. If this is so, the boundary must be referred to a period when some authority still existed within the walls, and on the available archaeological evidence this cannot be placed later than about A.D. 600.

This review of the situation at Silchester provides some grounds for believing that the perhaps comparable territory around Winchester could be of early Anglo-Saxon or even sub-Roman date. Such a conclusion would accord with the evidence from Gaul which has already been mentioned. At Silchester the territory remained of importance long enough to influence the emerging pattern of the early mediaeval landscape. It indicates the possible survival into the post-Roman period of some authority based on the former town, a situation for which some other evidence has already been mentioned (p.330). Silchester did not of course survive as a focus of settlement, later to re-emerge as a populous centre like Winchester. Except as a land unit perpetuating its earlier boundaries, the place seems to have disappeared in the seventh century. By contrast, Winchester survived, although the archaeological evidence for the occupation of the walled area in the fifth and sixth centuries is almost as sparse as that from Silchester. But the focal role of Winchester in the evolution of the Anglo-Saxon settlement pattern of its area was already clear by the sixth century. If the implications of the present discussion are accepted, the territory around the walls of Winchester was already defined and probably in royal possession before the mid-seventh century when it was granted to the newly founded minster by the king of Wessex.

Written evidence

The written sources for the settlement of Hampshire in the early Anglo-Saxon period are few and it cannot be expected that they will now be substantially augmented, although the British sources may have more to tell us when their relevance and reliability can be more fully assessed (Morris 1973: 103-6, 225-7, 293-4). As fresh evidence accumulates from other disciplines, the written materials will need to be reconsidered in this light from time to time, but this is a task which should not perhaps be undertaken too frequently. The relationships between the various kinds of evidence are obscure and the implications of the now rapidly increasing quantity of archaeological evidence will need some time to mature. Meanwhile, internal criticism of the written sources may still have much to reveal.

A potentially interesting development has been provided by Kenneth Harrison's recent work on the dating of the early Wessex annals in relation to the reckoning likely to have been used (Harrison 1971; *cf.* Harrison 1973a and 1973b). He suggests that the well-known duplications and discrepancies in these annals can be reconciled on the assumption that the events were originally recorded – whether orally or with the help of some *aide mémoire* such as marked sticks – within the nineteen-year cycles of the lunar or Metonic calendar. Events that actually occurred in the nineteen-year cycle running from 513 to 531 may on this view have been attributed to the previous cycle running from 494 to 512 and thus duplicated. The simplicity (in one sense) and economy of this solution supports Harrison's view that 'our opinion of the reliability of this material [i.e. the annals] may well come to rest on a wider and firmer foundation than saga or folk-memory' (Harrison 1971: 533). The possible use of the Metonic calendar may also carry with it the implication that there was some influence from British sources on Anglo-Saxon reckoning in sixth-century Hampshire. As Harrison says, this must remain imponderable, but the possibility is of considerable interest in the light of the evidence now accumulating for long-continued contact between Briton and Saxon in precisely this area.

Of great interest also has been D.P. Kirby's work on the early West Saxon royal genealogy

(1965). This has defined the dual tradition in early Wessex history to which G.M. Young (1934) called attention so eloquently in his lecture at Wilton thirty years before. In setting out the contribution made to this tradition by the so-called Wiltshire Saxons on the one hand and the Saxons of the upper Thames on the other Kirby takes us beyond the limits of the present paper which has been concerned with the role played by Hampshire in the emergence of the former group. The difficulties in defining this role are precisely reflected in the adoption by both Young and Kirby of the term 'Wiltshire Saxons' to describe the southern element in the origins of Wessex.

The dual tradition in Wessex history has also been examined by Myres (1964) in a study of Wansdyke, a paper written in response to the detailed field-survey of that monument undertaken by Sir Cyril and Lady Fox (1958; see also Clark 1958). The archaeological evidence for the dual tradition was set out by Myres as fully as was possible in 1964, but at that time the Hampshire element in the southern tradition was still obscure, while the importance of the Salisbury region was by contrast archaeologically dominant (1964: 13-14).

Myres's views of the importance of Hampshire, and Winchester in particular, in the early history of Wessex and his interpretation of the role and location of the *Gewissae* (1937: 397, 403-4; see also above, p.324) have been questioned by H.E. Walker (1956). The argument is too complex to set out here in detail and suffers from a degree of polemic best avoided. In essence Walker argued that the *Gewissae* cannot and should not be restricted to one particular geographical location in Wessex, and certainly not to the Winchester region. The term, and here he follows Bede, was simply the older name for the West Saxons. The crucial part of his case (1956: 181) turns on a nice point of Bede's Latinity which he argues should be emended to suit an *a priori* interpretation of the historical situation. For Walker 'what happened in Winchester between 400 and 660 is anybody's guess' and 'for early settlement in mid-Hampshire the Chronicle is as negative as archaeology or the evidence of place-names' (1956: 182, n. 32). Archaeological negatives are notoriously unreliable and the weight of the present paper has been to demonstrate how both these statements must be revised in the light of increasing knowledge. With this prop removed, we may perhaps allow that the usage of the term *Gewissae* was complex and changing. It may be both an early term and a locational description. The vagaries of Bede's usage can be fully explained if the limited area to which the name was originally applied extended its authority, perhaps dynastically, first to the whole of southern Wessex and later, after Ceawlin, as far as the Thames, before the term began to give way, as Walker argues convincingly (1956: 183-4), to the new name West Saxon in the later seventh century. An explanation in the complexities of events may be more acceptable than the view that the straightforward rendering of Bede's language 'makes no *historical* sense'.

Conclusion

Our view of the nature and course of the Anglo-Saxon settlements, and of what used to be known as the *adventus Saxonum*, has changed out of all recognition over the last twenty years and is still changing (White 1971: esp. 592-3). The purpose of the present paper has been to examine an area whose importance in the origins of Anglo-Saxon England has been accompanied by a remarkable lack of observed fact, and to try to establish what might be the reason behind this discordance in the evidence.

The result has been to show that there is evidence for an Anglo-Saxon presence in Hampshire from at least the beginning of the fifth century, that it was established in contact with Romano-British society, and that it existed and ultimately grew within the functioning patterns of a landscape it inherited from the past rather than one of its own making. Each strand of evidence has contributed to the same broad picture. From archaeology we have evidence for early Germanic settlement in Roman walled places and the continuing significance of Winchester in the settlement pattern of the sixth century as reflected in the distribution of cemeteries. Place-name studies can now show a degree of topographical contact between the pattern of the Romano-British landscape and the communities who provided the oldest recognizable stratum of English place-names. The importance of the major centres of Romano-British authority survived to affect the boundaries of Anglo-Saxon land-holding and administration. In the written evidence, derived as it all is from

English sources, the name of an individual such as Cerdic, whether a figment or not (Hogg 1972), the survival of British place-names in central Hampshire, and possibly even the use of a certain reckoning of time, all hint at the existence of widespread contact between the native Celts and the Germanic arrivals.

Yet when all has been taken into account, there still remains a stubborn incongruity between the relatively small amount of evidence for Anglo-Saxon settlement in Hampshire in the sixth, let alone the fifth, century and the abundance of such evidence in areas to the west, north and east. If this relative paucity of evidence for Germanic settlement is contrasted with the increasing evidence for continuity of settlement, of landscape, even of nomenclature, above all with the subsequent importance of the role of Hampshire in the history of the kingdom of Wessex, a possible solution may suggest itself. Rather than invasion, and the annihilation or withering away of existing communities, there may have taken place a fusion of peoples upon a basis of contact and comprehension that originated under imperial edict and was continued under British rule while the forms of Romano-British society were still in being. The new Germanic elements, for which in the fifth century the evidence is so fleeting, may have been absorbed and assimilated into a society that was itself in a state of rapid change through its own economic and administrative collapse, as well as through the impact of the new arrivals themselves. It would have been a two-way process, but in an area where the newcomers were few in number, it may be they who were most changed. This is not to say that political power did not pass from hand to hand, but in a situation where the two elements were being fused together, it may not have been obvious and may not have mattered whether the ruler was an anglicized Briton or romanized Saxon.

It is clear of course that there was ultimately a gross change in the material culture of the community, but the relative lack of archaeological evidence for the fifth and even the sixth centuries in Hampshire may reflect not so much the absence of settlement as the notorious difficulty of recognizing sub-Roman material. In seeking specifically Anglo-Saxon evidence for the occupation of Hampshire in the fifth and sixth centuries we may be looking entirely, or almost entirely, for the wrong thing.

Hampshire in these centuries was not, on this view, a vacuum but rather a surviving, if greatly mutated, British community in which Saxon and Briton were being fused together. In the fringes of this area in the later fifth and sixth century other elements settled. Groups of Kentish (Juto-Frankish) origin entered the Meon valley, and perhaps other areas of the south, as well as the Isle of Wight. Another group, whose traditions are recorded, probably with some accuracy, in the Chronicle, entered the south-west of the county and moved north towards Salisbury. It is possibly significant that they avoided the approach to Winchester and the richer soils of the county, which were perhaps precisely those areas inhabited by the Britons they fought after *Cerdicesora*, at *Cerdicesford* and at *Cerdicesleag*. When these newcomers fought the Britons in 519, the battle took place within the limits of the Belgic *civitas*, and the kingdom to which they succeeded may have been that which had emerged from the former *civitates* of the Belgae and the Atrebates in the period of the gradual breakdown of centralized provincial and diocesan control in the fifth century. It would be this kingdom with its surviving centres at Silchester and Winchester which would at one time have controlled the frontier on the Thames for which the early Anglo-Saxon cemeteries along the river may provide evidence (see above, p.330). It would be this kingdom which would have provided the basis for the continuance of life in the Hampshire region during the fifth and earlier sixth centuries, and it would be within this kingdom that the fusion of Briton and Saxon would have taken place. Following the battle of 519 this kingdom would have formed the eastern element in 'chalk' Wessex, with its centre at Winchester, while the western element, the 'Wiltshire' Saxons, established an important centre in the Salisbury area. The contrast between the two areas, between Wilton and Winchester, was perceptively drawn by G.M. Young in 1934. Today it might have to be framed in rather different terms, but it still cannot be decided which area was the centre of southern Wessex, of 'chalk' Wessex, in the sixth century, if centre it had. By the mid-seventeenth century, after the adventure on the Thames, Wessex decided emphatically in favour of Winchester, where its Christian kings were so often to be buried (Krüger 1971: 256-8).

If our current approach to the archaeology of southern Wessex in the fifth and sixth centuries is positively misleading, as seems possible, and conceals from us the material culture of an essentially sub-Roman, native British community, is there anything that can be done to correct the situation? The answers are, in a sense, too obvious. The investigation of late Roman cemeteries, specially outside the walled places, Portchester, Clausentum, Silchester and Winchester, is of special importance. Those at Silchester, which must still lie essentially undisturbed, should be protected against damage from all forms of development. If unavoidably threatened, they should be extensively excavated. Work inside Portchester and Winchester is now producing relevant evidence. Inside Silchester an attempt should be made to isolate areas not trenched in 1890-1909, and to secure excavation before they are entirely disturbed by ploughing and treasure-hunters with metal detectors. Anglo-Saxon cemeteries must be investigated whenever possible. A careful watch should be kept when development is undertaken near known burials, for these may indicate the sites of undiscovered cemeteries. Previous finds and excavations must be published. But in the last resort it is settlements that must be found and excavated, and the developing land patterns around them studied in detail. Their discovery can only be a matter of time and their potential is illustrated by the excavation at Chalton (Addyman *et al.* 1972). If these things can be done, Hampshire in the early Anglo-Saxon period may yet show us, by way of paradox, that 'invasions and minor intrusions have undoubtedly occurred, even if far less often than other forms of culture contact, but their existence has to be demonstrated, not assumed' (Clark 1966: 188).

Appendix: Hampshire place-names in *-hām*: A provisional list

This list makes no pretence at originality. It has been compiled from the available place-name and other studies listed below to demonstrate the relative frequency of *-hām* names in the county and to provide the basis for a provisional study of their distribution (Fig. 2; see above, p.332). Because there is still no published account of the place-names of Hampshire, and in view of the problems of distinguishing *-hām* from *-hamm*, the list can do no more than indicate names probably in *-hām*. Names in *-hām* or *-hamm* are indicated by *?hamm* in the right-hand margin, but no attempt has been made to list names probably or certainly in *-hamm*. Names in *-ingahām* are given at the end.

The arrangement of these lists follows that used in Cox 1973: 50-61. For names that are no longer those of major settlements, the name of the parish in which they are situated is given in brackets. After each place-name, the nature of the basic element is cited. National Grid references for lost settlements are approximated to their supposed sites. For each place-name a bibliography is given for further reference.

Abbreviations used in the lists are as follows:

BCS — W. de Gray Birch (1885-99) *Cartularium Saxonicum.* London.

DEPN — E. Ekwall (1960) *Concise Oxford Dictionary of English Place-Names* (4th edn.). Oxford.

Gelling — See Gelling 1967.

Grundy — G.B. Grundy (1921-7) The Saxon Land Charters of Hampshire with notes on Place and Field Names. *Arch. Jour.*, 78: 53-173; 81: 31-126; 83: 91-253; 84: 160-340. References are given by the number Grundy allocated to each group of bounds, followed by the number on the boundary of the point in question, e.g. Grundy 212*a*/23.

PNBrk — Margaret Gelling (1973) *The Place-Names of Berkshire*. London.

PNHa — J.E.B. Gover (1961) *The Place-Names of Hampshire* (Unpublished typescript). Copies deposited at the Archaeology Branch, Ordnance Survey, Maybush, Southampton; at Southampton University Library; and elsewhere.

I am greatly indebted to Mr Alexander Rumble (English Place-Name Society) for his comments on names in this list, but the selection and any errors that remain are my responsibility. We intend to make a joint survey of *-hām* and *-hamm* in Hampshire, with particular reference to the archaeology and topography of the sites concerned.

Names probably in -*hām*

BEDENHAM pers. n.[1]	SU/5903	PNHa, 27; *cf.* DEPN, *s.n.* Biddenham	?*hamm*
BURKHAM el.	SU/6542	PNHa, 130	?*hamm*
CADNAM pers. n.[1] (pers. n.[2] possible)	SU/2913	PNHa, 193; DEPN	?*hamm*
CHINEHAM el.	SU/6554	PNHa, 141; DEPN	
COSHAM pers. n.[1]	SU/6505	PNHa, 19; DEPN	
CROOKHAM el.	SU/7952	PNHa, 109; DEPN; *cf.* PNBrk, 189	
DITCHAM el.	SU/7620 (*cf.* SU/7418)	PNHa, 55	?*hamm*
ENHAM el.	SU/3649	PNHa, 166; DEPN	?*hamm*
FRITHAM el.	SU/2314	PNHa, 206; DEPN	
GREATHAM el.	SU/7731	PNHa, 91-2; DEPN	?*hamm*
HIGHNAM el.	SU/7445	PNHa, 101	?*hamm*
HOLLAM (Fareham) el.	SU/5405	PNHa, 28	?*hamm*
HOLTHAM (lost, East Tisted) el.	SU/7032	PNHa, 95	
LASHAM pers. n.[1] or el. (pers. n.[2] possible)	SU/6742	PNHa, 133; DEPN, *s.n.* Lasborough	
MAPLEDURHAM (lost, Buriton) el.	SU/7221	PNHa, 55; DEPN	
MEARCHAM (lost, Buriton) el.	SU/7221	BCS 982; Grundy 212*b*/22, *cf.* 212*a*/31; *cf.* DEPN, *s.n.* Markham	?*hamm*
NEATHAM el.	SU/7440	PNHa, 105; DEPN	
NEWNHAM el.	SU/7054	PNHa, 128; DEPN	
PERHAM el.	SU/2549	PNHa, 169	
PITHAM el.	SU/7060	PNHa, 123	?*hamm*
POPHAM el.	SU/5543	PNHa, 83; DEPN	
STONEHAM (North and South) el.	SU/4416	PNHa, 41-2; DEPN	?*hamm*
THROUGHAM (lost, Beaulieu) el.	SU/3500	PNHa, 201, *cf.* DEPN, *s.n.* Fritham	
TICCESHAM (lost, Dummer ?) el. (pers. n. possible ?)	SU/5844	BCS 596; Grundy 216/18	?*hamm*
UPHAM el.	SU/5320	PNHa, 48; DEPN	
VERNHAM'S DEAN el.	SU/3456	PNHa, 161; DEPN	?*hamm*
WACCANHAM (lost, Steep?) pers. n.[1]	SU/7424	BCS 1319; Grundy 212*a*/23; cf. DEPN, s.n. Wacton	?*hamm*
WALTHAM (Bishops) el.	SU/5517	PNHa , 48-9; DEPN	
WALTHAM (North) el.	SU/5646	PNHa, 139; DEPN	
WESANHAM (lost, Hurstbourne Tarrant) pers. n.[1]	SU/3651	BCS 1080; Grundy 178/18	
WHEATHAM el.	SU/7427	PNHa, 59	
WICKHAM el.	SU/5711	PNHa., 34; DEPN; Gelling, 90	*wīc-hām*
WORLDHAM (East and West) pers. n.[3] (el. possible)	SU/7437	PNHa, 106; DEPN	

Names in *-ingahām*

ELLINGHAM pers. n.[2]	SU/1408	PNHa, 213; DEPN
MENGHAM pers. n.[1] (pers. n.[2] possible)	SZ/7299	PNHa, 16

REFERENCES

Addyman, P.V., Leigh, D. and Hughes, M.J. (1972) Anglo-Saxon houses at Chalton, Hampshire. *Medieval Arch.*, 16, 13-31.

Aldsworth, F.G. (1974) *Towards a Pre-Domesday Geography of Hampshire – A Review of the Evidence.* Unpublished B.A. dissertation, University of Southampton.

Avery, M. and Brown, D. (1972) Saxon features at Abingdon. *Oxoniensia*, 37, 66-81.

Biddle, M. (1970) Excavations at Winchester, 1969; Eighth interim report. *Ant. Jour.*, 50, 277-326.

Biddle, M. (1972) Excavations at Winchester, 1970: Ninth interim report. *Ant. Jour.*, 52, 93-131.

Biddle, M. (1973) Winchester: the development of an early capital. In Jankuhn, H., Schlesinger, W. and Steuer, H. (eds.), *Vor- und Frühformen der europäischen Stadt im Mittelalter*, Abhandlungen der Akademie der Wissenschaften, 3 Folge, No. 83, 229-61. Göttingen.

Biddle, M. (1974) The archaeology of Winchester. *Scientific American*, 230 (5), 32-43.

Biddle, M. (1975a) Excavations at Winchester, 1971: Tenth and final interim report. *Ant. Jour.*, 55 (forthcoming).

Biddle, M. (ed.) (1975b) Barlow, F., Biddle, M., Feilitzen, O. von and Keene, D.J., *Winchester in the early Middle Ages: an edition and discussion of the Winton Domesday*. Oxford (forthcoming).

Bonney, D.J. (1966) Pagan Saxon burials and boundaries in Wiltshire. *Wilts. Arch. & Nat. Hist. Mag.*, 61, 25-30.

Bonney, D.J. (1972) Early boundaries in Wessex. In Fowler, P.J. (ed.), *Archaeology and the Landscape*, 168-86. London.

Boon, G. (1959) The latest objects from Silchester, Hampshire. *Medieval Arch.*, 3, 79-88

Cam, H.M. (1944) *Liberties and Communities in Mediaeval England*, 64-105. London.

Chadwick, H.M. (1905) *Studies on Anglo-Saxon Institutions.* London.

Chadwick, H.M. (1907) *The Origin of the English Nation*. London.

Clark, A. (1958) The nature of Wansdyke. *Antiquity*, 32, 89-96.

Clark, J.G.D. (1966) The invasion hypothesis in British archaeology. *Antiquity*, 40, 172-89.

Clarke, G.N. (1970) Lankhills School. In Biddle, 1970, 292-8.

Clarke, G.N. (1972) Lankhills School. In Biddle, 1972, 94-8.

Clarke, G.N. (1975) Lankhills School. In Biddle, 1975a.

Copley, G.J. (1954) *The Conquest of Wessex in the Sixth Century*. London.

Corder, P. (1955) The reorganisation of the defences of Romano-British towns in the fourth century. *Arch. Jour.*, 112, 20-42.

Cox, B.H. (1973) The significance of the distribution of English place-names in *-hām* in the Midlands and East Anglia. *Jour. English Place-Name Soc.*, 5, 15-73.

Crawford, O.G.S. (1931) Cerdic and the Cloven Way. *Antiquity*, 5, 441-58.

Cunliffe, B.W. (1970) The Saxon culture-sequence at Portchester Castle. *Ant. Jour.*, 50, 67-85.

Cunliffe, B.W. (1972a) Excavations at Portchester Castle, Hants. 1969-71: Fourth interim report. *Ant. Jour.*, 52, 70-83.

Cunliffe, B.W. (1972b) Saxon and Medieval settlement-pattern in the region of Chalton, Hampshire. *Medieval Arch.*, 16, 1-12.

Cunliffe, B.W. (1973) Chalton, Hants: the evolution of a landscape. *Ant. Jour.*, 53, 173-90.

Dodgson, J.McN. (1966) The significance of the distribution of the English place-name in *-ingas*, *-inga* in south-east England. *Medieval Arch.*, 10, 1-29.

Dodgson, J. McN. (1973) Place-names from *hām*, distinguished from *hamm* names, in relation to the settlement of Kent, Surrey and Sussex. *Anglo-Saxon England*, 2, 1-50.

Ekwall, E. (1928) *English River Names*. London.

Evison, V.I. (1963) Sugar-loaf shield-bosses. *Ant. Jour.*, 43, 38-96.

Evison, V.I. (1965) *The Fifth-Century Invasions South of the Thames*. London.

Fellows Jensen, G. (1973) Place-name research and northern history: a survey. *Northern History*, 8, 1-23.

Finberg, H.P.R. (1964) *The Early Charters of Wessex*. Leicester.

Fox, (A. & C.), Sir Cyril & Lady (1958) Wansdyke reconsidered. *Arch. Jour.*, 115, 1-48.

Frere, S.S. (1966) The end of towns in Roman Britain. In Wacher, J.S. (ed.), *The Civitas Capitals of Roman Britain*, 87-100. Leicester.

Frere, S.S. (1967) *Britannia*. London.

Frere, S.S. (1971) Introduction to Butler, R.M. (ed.), *Soldier and Civilian in Roman Yorkshire*, 15-19. Leicester.

Gelling, M. (1960) The element *hamm* in English place-names: a topographical investigation. *Namn och Bygd*, 48, 140-62.

Gelling, M. (1967) English place-names derived from the compound *wīchām*. *Medieval Arch.*, 11, 87-104.

Green, J.R. (1881) *The Making of England*. London.

Harrison, K. (1971) Early Wessex annals in the Anglo-Saxon Chronicle. *English Hist. Review*, 86, 527-33.

Harrison, K. (1973a) The beginning of the year in

England, *c.* 500-900. *Anglo-Saxon England*, 2, 51-70.

Harrison, K. (1973b) The primitive Anglo-Saxon calendar. *Antiquity*, 47, 284-7.

Hawkes, S.C. (1966) Review of Evison 1965 in *Antiquity*, 40, 322-3.

Hawkes, S.C. (1968) Anglo-Saxon urns from Fareham. *Proc. Hants. Field Club & Arch. Soc.*, 25, 51-9.

Hawkes, S.C. and Dunning, G.C. (1961) Soldiers and settlers in Britain, fourth to fifth century. *Medieval Arch.*, 5, 1-70.

Hawkes, S.C. and Dunning, G.C. (1964) Krieger und Siedler in Britannien während des 4. und 5. Jahrhunderts. *Bericht der Römisch-Germanischen Kommission 1962-1963*, 43. 44., 155-231.

Hodgkin, R.H. (1952) *A History of the Anglo-Saxons* (3rd. edn.). Oxford.

Hogg, A.H.A. (1972) Cerdic and the Cloven Way again. *Antiquity*, 46, 222-3.

Jackson, K.H. (1953) *Language and History in Early Britain*. Edinburgh.

Kirby, D.P. (1965) Problems of early West Saxon history. *English Hist. Review*, 80, 10-29.

Krüger, K.H. (1971) *Königsgrabkirchen der Franken, Angelsachsen und Langobarden bis zur Mitte des 8. Jahrhunderts*. München.

Leeds, E.T. (1913) *The Archaeology of the Anglo-Saxon Settlements*. London.

Leeds, E.T. (1925) The West Saxon invasion and the Icknield Way. *History*, 10, 97-109.

Leeds, E.T. (1933) The early Saxon penetration of the upper Thames area. *Ant. Jour.*, 13, 229-51.

Leeds, E.T. (1954) The growth of Wessex. *Oxoniensia*, 19, 45-60.

Leeds, E.T. and Shortt, H. de S. (1953) *An Anglo-Saxon Cemetery at Petersfinger, near Salisbury, Wilts*. Salisbury.

Lombard-Jourdan, A. (1972) Oppidum et banlieue. Sur l'origine et les dimensions du territoire urbain *Annales: économies, sociétées, civilisations*, 27, 373-95.

Maitland, F.W. (1960) *Domesday Book and Beyond*. London. (1st edn. 1897.)

Meaney, A.L.S. (1964) *A Gazetteer of Early Anglo-Saxon Burial Sites*. London.

Meaney, A.L.S. and Hawkes, S.C. (1970) *Two Anglo-Saxon Cemeteries at Winnall* (Soc. Medieval Arch. Monograph series no. 4). London.

Morris, J. (1973) *The Age of Arthur*. London.

Musty, J. and Stratton, J.E.D. (1964) A Saxon cemetery at Winterbourne Gunner, near Salisbury. *Wilts. Arch. & Nat. Hist. Mag.*, 59, 86-109.

Myres, J.N.L. (1935) Britain in the Dark Ages (review of *Map of Britain in the Dark Ages, S. sheet*, 1935). *Antiquity*, 9, 455-64.

Myres, J.N.L. (1937) *Roman Britain and the English Settlements* (with Collingwood, R.G.) (2nd. edn.). London.

Myres, J.N.L. (1954) The Anglo-Saxon period. In Martin, A.F. and Steel, R.W. (eds.), *The Oxford Region: a scientific and historical survey*, 96-102. London.

Myres, J.N.L. (1964) Wansdyke and the origin of Wessex. In Trevor-Roper, H.R. (ed.), *Essays in British History*, 1-27, London.

Myres, J.N.L. (1966) Review of Evison 1965. *English Hist. Review*, 81, 340-5.

Myres, J.N.L. (1969) *Anglo-Saxon Pottery and the Settlement of England*. London.

Myres, J.N.L. and Green, B. (1973) *The Anglo-Saxon Cemeteries of Caistor-by-Norwich and Markhall, Norfolk* (Soc. Ant. Res. Cttee. Report no. 30). London.

O'Neil, B.H.St.J. (1944) The Silchester region in the 5th and 6th centuries A.D. *Antiquity*, 18, 113-22.

Plummer, C. (ed.) (1892) *Two of the Saxon Chronicles Parallel*. London.

Plummer, C. (ed.) (1896) *Venerabilis Baedae Historia Ecclesiastica*. London.

Sisam, K. (1953) Anglo-Saxon royal genealogies. *Proc. British Acad.*, 39, 287-348.

Stenton, F.M. (1971) *Anglo-Saxon England* (3rd. edn.). Oxford.

Swanton, M.J. (1973) *The Spearheads of the Anglo-Saxon settlements*. London.

Walker, H.E. (1956) Bede and the Gewissae: the political evolution of the Heptarchy and its nomenclature. *Cambridge Hist. Jour.*, 12, 174-86.

Ward, J.H. (1973) The British sections of the *Notitia Dignitatum*: an alternative interpretation. *Britannia*, 4, 253-63.

Welch, M.G. (1971) Late Romans and Saxons in Sussex. *Britannia*, 2, 232-7.

Wheeler, G.H. (1921) The genealogy of the early West Saxon kings. *English Hist. Review*, 36, 161-71.

White, D.A. (1971) Changing views of the *Adventus Saxonum* in nineteenth and twentieth century English scholarship. *Jour. Hist. of Ideas*, 32, 585-94.

Williams-Freeman, J.P. (1915) *An Introduction to Field Archaeology as illustrated by Hampshire*. London.

Wilson, D.M. (1960) Medieval Britain in 1959: I. Pre-conquest. *Medieval Arch.*, 4, 134-9.

Wilson, D.M. (1961) Medieval Britain in 1960: I. Pre-conquest. *Medieval Arch.*, 5, 309-12.

Wilson, D.M. (1962-3) Medieval Britain in 1961: I. Pre-conquest. *Medieval Arch.*, 6/7, 306-13.

Wilson, D.M. (1964) Medieval Britain in 1962 and 1963: I. Pre-conquest. *Medieval Arch.*, 8, 231-41.

Wilson, R.M. (1936) Review of Hodgkin, R.H., *A History of the Anglo-Saxons* (1st. edn. 1935). *Antiquity*, 10, 234-7.

Young, G.M. (1934) *The origin of the West-Saxon Kingdom*. London. Reprinted in 1950, without the important appendices, in Young, G.M., *Last Essays*, 112-29, London.

NOTES

1. I am indebted to Professor W.A. van Es and Dr J.N.L. Myres for their comments on this material.
2. I am grateful to Professor W.A. van Es for this information.
3. Mr P.D.C. Brown kindly informs me that he now accepts a continental origin for these grass-tempered wares.
4. I have benefited from discussions on this matter with Mr F.G. Aldsworth and I am grateful to him for information used in Fig. 1. His excavations at the Droxford cemetery in 1974 have shown how much can still be learnt from further investigation of known sites, even when these are supposed to have been destroyed. Thirty-four inhumations were discovered, most of them accompanied by grave-goods (*Hants. Chronicle*, 6 Sept. 1974).
5. For the possibility of an even earlier date, see Myres & Green 1973: 12-13.
6. I am greatly indebted to Mr Gover for allowing me to consult his typescript.

BARRY CUNLIFFE

Hill-forts and oppida in Britain

The last millennium B.C. in Britain was a period of dramatic social and economic change. At the end of the second millennium communities were largely dispersed, living in family or extended family sized groups, yet by the time of the Roman conquest in A.D. 43 the south-east of the country had developed a decidedly urban character, sufficiently advanced to be absorbed, almost unaltered, by the Roman administration. The raw material for studying the processes involved in this change consists almost entirely of the archaeology of settlements. In the following pages an attempt is made to examine the data for south-eastern Britain, where the record is the fullest and most accurately calibrated, in the hope of arriving at a series of generalized models that can be tested by planned excavation and systematic field-work.

In offering this paper[1] in homage to Grahame Clark, I find it difficult to over-emphasize my debt of gratitude to him. It will be immediately evident to the reader how much of this work has been directly inspired by his writing and teaching. To have been a member of his Cambridge school is a source of great personal pride and satisfaction.

The situation at the end of the second millennium

The basic settlement unit of the late second millennium was the homestead. Several examples have been extensively excavated, including Sheareplace Hill, Dorset (Rhatz & ApSimon 1962); Chalton, Hampshire (Cunliffe 1970); New Barn Down, Sussex (Curwen 1934); Cock Hill, Sussex (Radcliff-Densham 1961); in all of which the available accommodation was appropriate to a social group no larger than a single family. A few sites are known in which larger groupings are implied. At Plumpton Plain, site A, Sussex (Holleyman & Curwen 1935), four enclosures each of homestead size straggle along a track, superficially suggesting a loosely nucleated hamlet; while at Itford Hill, Sussex (Burstow & Holleyman 1957), a denser packing of such units gives the impression of being a village. Although it could be argued that the observed situation, both at Plumpton Plain and at Itford, was caused by the periodic replacement of a single homestead each time on a new site, the physical interdependence of the adjacent enclosures at Itford suggests that here a number of units existed together. We may be reasonably sure, therefore, that by 1000 B.C. the bulk of the population was still living in isolated family groups, allowing for the possibility of a few larger settlements representing extended families.

A second category of broadly contemporary sites includes the rectangular enclosures excavated by Pitt-Rivers (1898) on Cranborne Chase at Martin Down and Handly Down, together with a group of similar sites in Wiltshire, later described by Mrs C.M. Piggott (1942). Those examples that have been excavated contrast with the homesteads in that they were not, apparently, permanently occupied; an observation that has led to the assumption that many of them served a pastoral function. It should of course be stressed that until a reasonable sample has been examined by total excavation under modern conditions this generalization, while possible, remains unproven.

Early rectangular enclosures of this kind are more widespread than was once realized. In Sussex, for example, they are represented by Harrow Hill (which is usually referred to as a hill-fort), a site sampled by test excavation in 1936 (Holleyman 1937). Insufficient pottery was discovered to allow dating except to within the bracket *c.* 1600-1500 B.C. Several aspects of Harrow Hill are of considerable interest, not the least being its position high on a hill-top, in relation to the broadly contemporary homesteads that occupy the lower slopes of the surrounding hills (Fig. 1). One explanation for this pattern is that the enclosure served as a communal stock

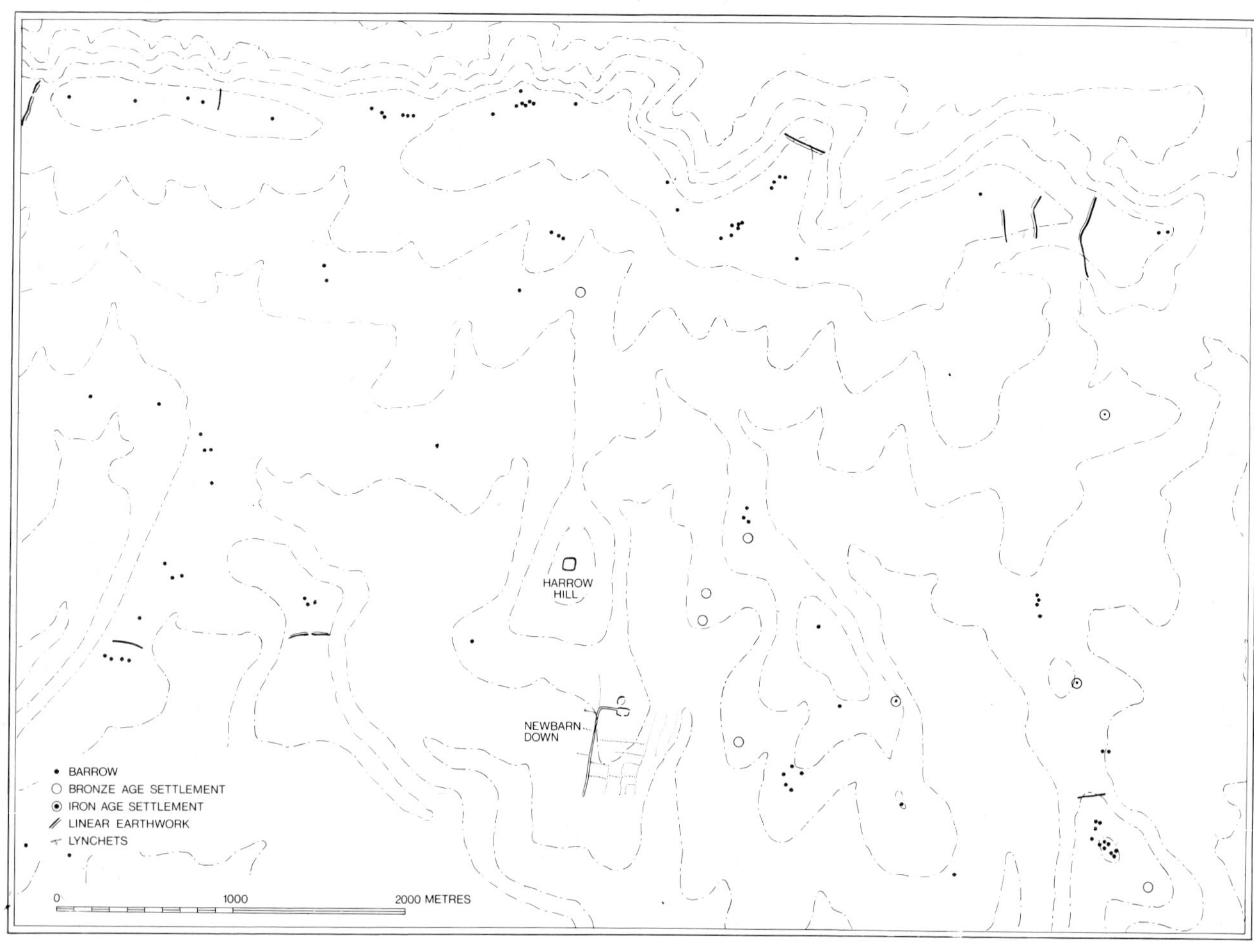

Figure 1. Early first millennium settlement on the South Downs. (The contours are at intervals of 100 feet; north is at the top.)

kraal. Such a facility would be necessary to a society whose economy was based on mixed farming and whose settlements were dispersed. During the farming year there would have been several occasions when livestock, ranging free on unenclosed pasture, had to be rounded up for culling, castration and redistribution; Harrow Hill would have been admirably suited to serve the neighbouring farms in this way. The discovery there of a surprisingly large number of cows' skulls might reflect the annual slaughter and attendant feasting which, it is reasonable to suppose, accompanied activities of this kind. If these arguments are correct, 'pastoral enclosures' represent the communal labour of a group of families and might, therefore, be thought of as the archaeological manifestation of a social unit approximating to the clan.

A third group of earthworks deserves discussion in this context. These can be called 'plateau enclosures', which may tentatively be defined as upland territories partially enclosed by stretches of bank and ditch running across spurs and cols. Usually, but not invariably, the ditches are on the inside of the banks. A classic example of a plateau enclosure is provided by the earthworks on Butser Hill, Hampshire, discussed by Piggott (1930:187-200). Little attention has since been paid to this type of site except for a brief reference by the author (Cunliffe 1971a). A detailed consideration of plateau enclosures would be out of place here; it suffices to say that they are widespread in southern England, often show signs of continued use into the Iron Age and Roman period and, where evidence is available, appear to belong to the third or second millennium B.C.[2]

One example, Hambledon Hill, in Dorset, may be briefly described, since it combines all the principal characteristics of the type. Earthworks

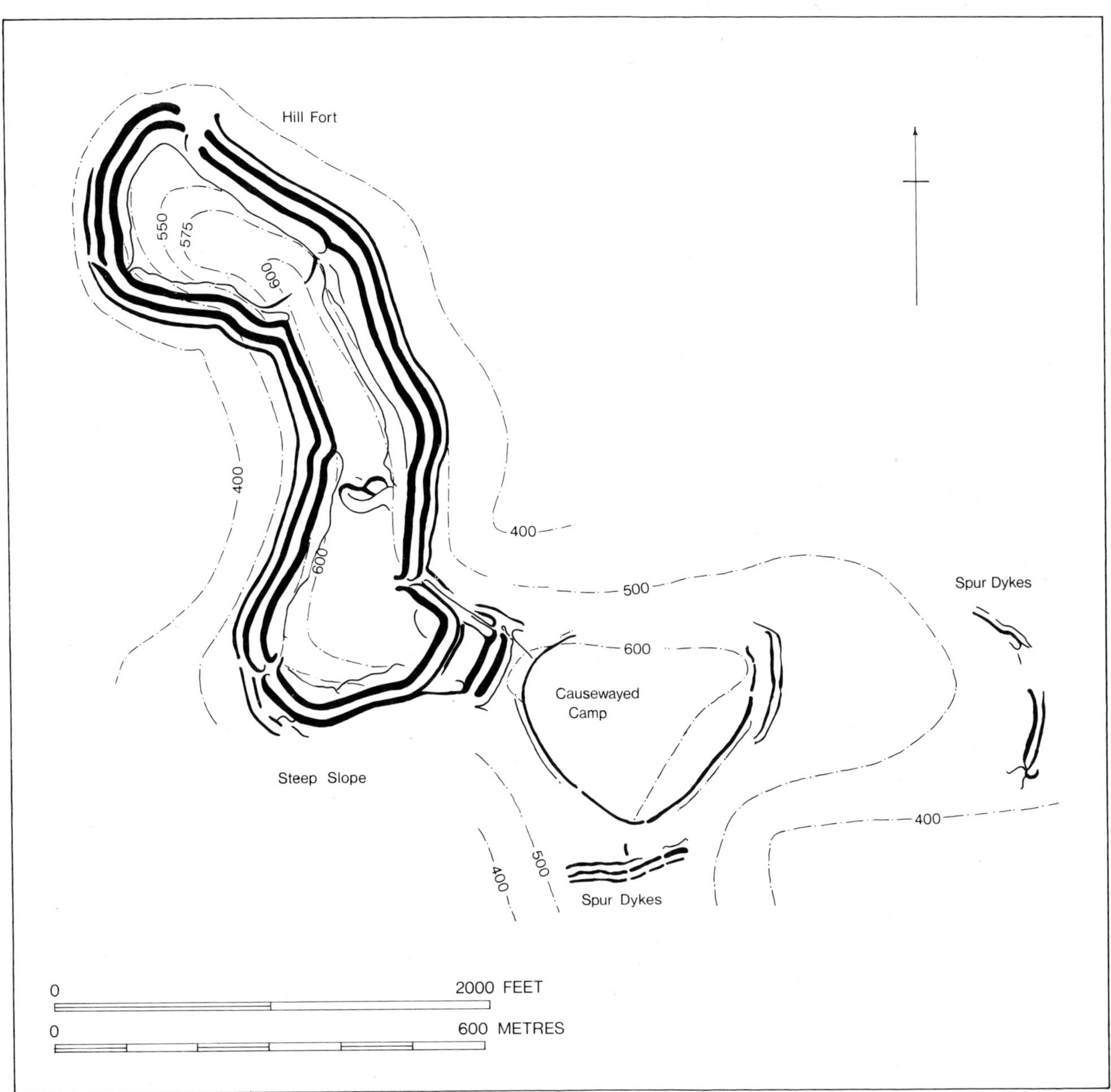

Figure 2. Earthwork enclosures on Hambledon Hill, Dorset (simplified after R.C.H.M. 1970).

of three distinct periods are represented (Fig. 2); a Neolithic causewayed camp, a group of spur dykes constituting the plateau enclosure, and a hill-fort, itself exhibiting at least three phases of development. Trial excavation showed that the causewayed camp was structurally similar to others of its type and produced early Neolithic pottery in the primary ditch silt. The spur dykes on the other hand were composed of continuous lengths of bank and ditch, the primary silt of one yielding sufficient charcoal for a radiocarbon determination of 2790 ± 90 B.C. (R.C.H.M. 1970:131). While too much emphasis must not be placed on such insubstantial evidence[3] it seems likely that the construction of the camp preceded the spur dykes. The site, on the evidence of pottery in the secondary filling of the ditches, was used at least into Late Neolithic times and it remains a possibility that its use continued into the first millennium, when the hill-fort represents renewed structural activity. Thus Hambledon Hill served as a significant location throughout the third millennium and into the second millennium and again during the first, the plateau enclosure phase filling at least part of the chronological gap between the causewayed camp and the hill-fort. This would appear to be generally true of similar sites where relationships of this kind are suspected.

While it is evident that much work remains to be done on the problem of plateau enclosures, particularly on the matter of their dating, it is tempting to see them as locations for tribal meetings, continuing the tradition which, it has been suggested, grew up with the development of causewayed camps and the larger henge monuments. Once such assemblies had become an integral part of life, towards the end of the fourth millennium, it is reasonable to suppose that they continued. The recognition of the class of monuments that we have called plateau enclosures and the recently published second-millennium radiocarbon dates from the larger henges (Burleigh, Longworth & Wainwright 1972) strongly suggest that different types of communal monuments were in use throughout the third and second millennia. How late the tradition continued is uncertain, but the erection of hill-forts at a number of these locations is suggestive of a thread of continuity, even if direct evidence of absolute continuity is at present wanting.

The evidence briefly laid out above allows us to suggest that by the latter half of the second millennium three different categories of 'settlements' existed: homesteads, pastoral enclosures and plateau enclosures, each representing a different level of social organization. The

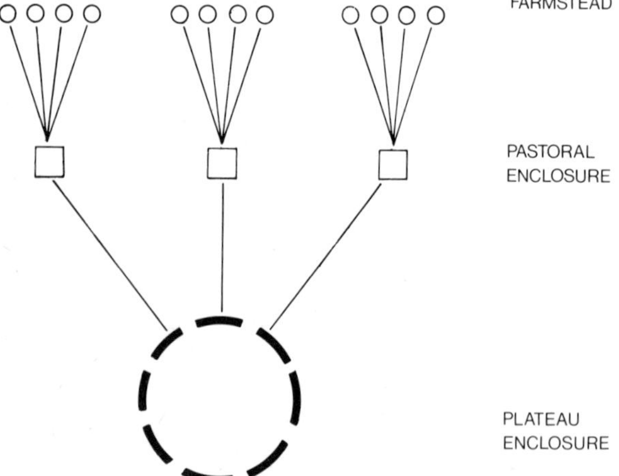

Figure 3. Settlement hierarchy: late second millennium.

diagram (Fig. 3) summarizes their relationship in a simplified form. The picture that emerges is of a simple egalitarian society in a state of equilibrium. It is against this background that the dramatic innovations of the first millennium must be seen.

The development of hill-forts

Large enclosures of the type usually classed under the general-purpose heading of 'hill-forts' began to appear in Britain soon after 1000 B.C. and by the end of the seventh century were being erected in most parts of the British Isles (for details of the evidence, see Cunliffe 1974). Some of the locations then chosen for defended enclosures had already been occupied by farms or small villages, e.g. Kaimes Hillfort, Midlothian (Simpson 1969); Mam Tor, Derbyshire (Jones & Thompson 1965; Coombs 1967; 1971); Highdown, Sussex (Wilson 1940; 1950); others were close to or superimposed upon earlier tribal foci, notably Hambledon Hill, Dorset; White Sheet Hill, Wiltshire; Danebury, Hampshire; Trundle, Sussex; while some seem to have been built on virgin land. But what is now clear, from a large sample of partially excavated sites, is that a very high percentage of our hill-forts were already established by the end of the fifth century: thereafter the number in use rapidly declined (Cunliffe 1971a).

The construction of several thousand enclosures in a restricted period of a few hundred years throws an interesting sidelight, both on availability of surplus labour and on the motivation of society. Tempting though it is to speculate as to possible causes, the present scarcity of evidence relevant to the use of the early enclosures demands a measure of restraint. It should be remembered, however, that the act of enclosure does not necessarily imply defence: aggressive connotations derive entirely from our use of the word 'hill-fort'.

The few early sites that have been examined on an adequate scale all conform to a remarkably consistent pattern. At Grimthorpe, Yorkshire (Stead 1965); Ivinghoe, Buckinghamshire (Cotton & Frere 1968); Balksbury, Hampshire (Wainwright 1970) and during the early phase at Danebury, Hampshire, the principal surviving structures consisted of approximately square settings of four posts, conventionally interpreted as granaries, together with pairs of posts of the kind that Bersu referred to as drying-racks. At Grimthorpe, Balksbury and Danebury, there is a marked tendency for the four-post structures to be arranged in rows. The extreme scarcity of pits is also a noteworthy feature. Given the proviso that lightly constructed buildings of turf or wattle would stand little chance of survival, the present evidence is suggestive of use but not necessarily occupation. An interesting, but so far undated, variant of this early type of arrangement is represented at Crickley Hill, Gloucestershire (Dixon 1972) and Ffridd Faldwyn, Montgomeryshire (O'Neil 1942), where regular linear arrangements of four-post or six-post units have been found flanking the roadways leading from the entrances. The extreme regularity of the plans recovered from Crickley Hill have suggested to the excavator their interpretation as continuously roofed structures of long-house appearance.

The evidence at present available for the use of these early-first-millennium hill-top enclosures is open to a variety of interpretations, ranging from enclosed communal grain stores, perhaps reflecting organized distribution, to villages of long-houses. Such a range of use may, indeed, eventually prove to be correct when a larger sample is available for comparison.

From the middle of the first millennium a significant change is discernible. It was at this stage that some hill-top enclosures ceased to be used, while in others internal activity intensified. At Danebury,[4] for example, storage pits were dug in considerable numbers (an estimated 5,500 in the period from the fifth to the end of the second century) while close to the rampart on one side of the enclosure, parallel rows of large four- and six-post structures were erected fronting on to streets, the spaces between the rows being reserved for contemporary pits. Even more remarkable is the fact that all of the structures were frequently rebuilt on the same sites, some of them up to four or five times. The overall impression given is one of rigorous order imposed over a considerable period of time. Danebury is not alone: a closely similar situation has been demonstrated at Credenhill Camp, Herefordshire (Stanford 1966-71) and at Croft Ambrey, Shropshire (Stanford 1967). Isolated large four- and six-post structures are known in other well excavated forts, e.g. Maiden Castle, Dorset (Wheeler 1943) and South Cadbury Camp, Somerset (Alcock 1972:83).

An initial assessment of the Danebury data strongly suggests that the site was now occupied, if not continuously, at least for long periods. Moreover, while the contemporary pits near the buildings contained occupation rubbish of all kinds, those nearer the centre of the fort produced very little, implying a differential intensity in domestic activity related to the presence or absence of timber structures. The function of the buildings is problematical; they were more substantially constructed than the early four-post structures, but whether they were used for storage or occupation must remain undecided until much larger areas have been excavated (Danebury, now one of the most extensively excavated forts, is at present only one-tenth examined). Nevertheless, the overall impression is clear enough – from about the middle of the first millennium some hill-top enclosures were subjected to continuous and controlled use by society, the internal organization giving the impression both of sustained order and of division into areas of specialized activity. In parallel with this, many enclosures show evidence for the continued maintenance of their enclosing earthworks and gates.

If the first half of the first millennium saw a rapid increase in the number of hill-top enclosures constructed, the second half of the millennium was characterized by an equally rapid decrease in the number maintained. But those that continued in use seem to have been subjected at this time to far more defensive care, including the strengthening of gates, the heightening of ramparts and, sometimes, the addition of secondary lines of defence. In other words, the term 'hill-fort' would from then on appear to be justified.

The rise to dominance of a few hill-forts in selected sample regions has been briefly discussed elsewhere (Cunliffe 1971a); one further example serves to emphasize the point. On the block of chalk downland between the rivers Test and Bourne, spanning the Hampshire and Wiltshire border, there are five hill-top enclosures (Fig. 4). Of these, Balksbury was no longer in use after the fifth century;[5] the remaining four, Figsbury, Quarley, Bury Hill and Danebury were all enclosed by earthworks in the fifth or early fourth century B.C. Assuming the major rivers to have formed significant boundaries, the theoretical territory of each location has been plotted (Fig. 4). It will be immediately apparent

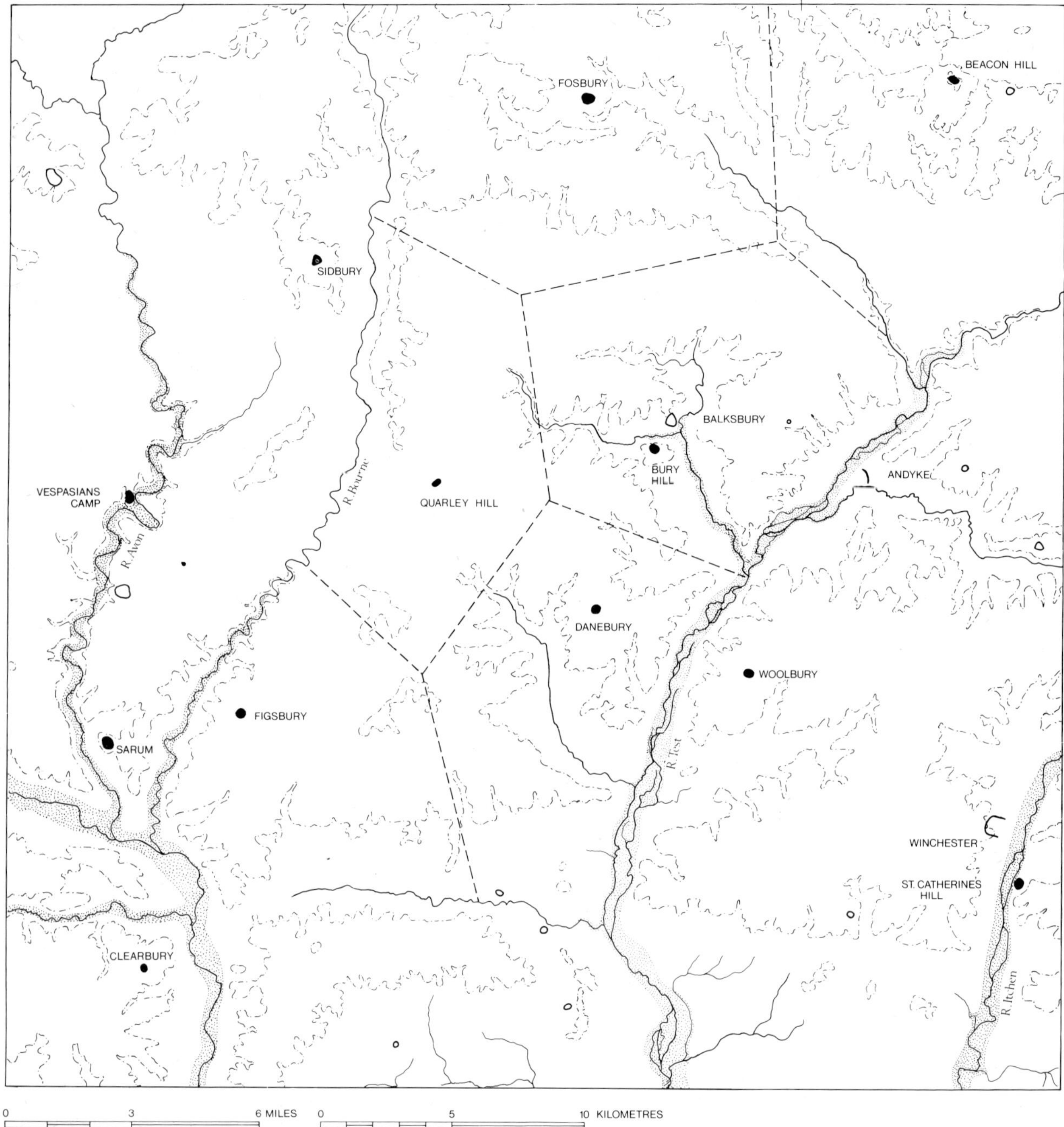

Figure 4. Hill-forts and their theoretical territories on the chalk downs between the rivers Test and Bourne. (Contours at 250 feet and 500 feet; north is at the top.)

that all four territories are closely comparable in size (30-40 square miles), a correspondence only to be expected in view of the equality in size of the enclosures themselves in this early period. By the third century B.C., Figsbury, Quarley and, probably, Bury Hill had been abandoned; while at Danebury, on the other hand, there is evidence both of continued use and of a considerable strengthening of the defences. It is difficult, therefore, to resist the conclusion that during the second half of the first millennium Danebury rose to a position of dominance, 'capturing' the territories of its neighbours and increasing its hinterland four-fold. This is precisely the process that can be traced with different degrees of clarity in many parts of southern England.

In the example just outlined, the reasons for

the rise of Danebury are more likely to be political or religious than purely economic, since all four enclosures were situated in equally favourable locations, but theoretical locational analysis should not be allowed to run riot at the expense of economic considerations. A glance at the hill-forts of the Salisbury Plain region is sufficient to show that their distribution is weighted in favour of river valleys. If we plot the forts in relation to ease of access to a permanent water supply (Fig. 5), the striking fact emerges that most of them lie on, or close to, a contour that represents one mile distance from the nearest permanent stream or river. In other words, the forts are so sited as to be at the interface between well watered meadows suitable for cattle and pastures more appropriate to sheep-rearing. Thus, *one* factor affecting choice of location for a successful hill-fort is optimal siting in relation to the different environments exploited by the subsistence economy of its community.

So far, we have made no attempt to assess the functions of late first-millennium hill-forts, and indeed it might be argued that the present state of knowledge precludes meaningful discussion, but already certain interesting points, worthy of consideration, are beginning to emerge. In socio-political terms, hill-forts can be seen to be central places within defined territories, maintaining a dynamic relationship one with another such that one fort might eclipse one or more of its neighbours, 'capturing' their territories. The relationship of the rural community to its fort is far more difficult to define; but there are several degrees of interdependency. The following propositions are, in theory, possible:

(a) forts were communal meeting places used

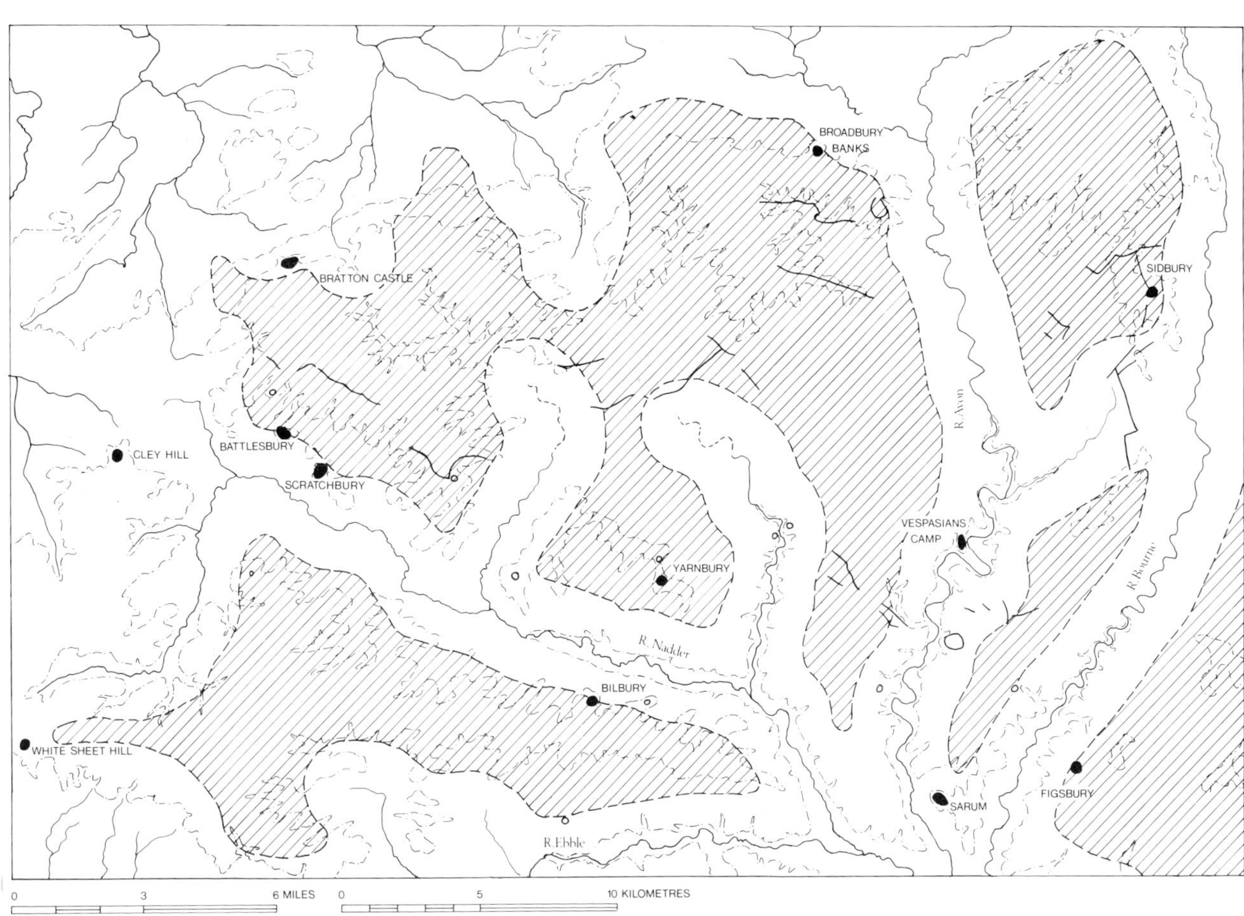

Figure 5. Wiltshire hill-forts in the third to second century B.C. The unshaded area represents potential pastureland within one mile of permanent water. The shaded areas are more than one mile from permanent water. (The contours are at 250 feet intervals; north is at the top.)

by a totally dispersed population only on certain occasions during the year;

(b) they were the permanent seats of a political and/or theocratic hierarchy served by the rural population;

(c) they were the permanent seats of a proportion of the population, partially maintained by providing services for the dispersed populace.

Clearly, to distinguish between these three states requires a meticulously documented record from at least one totally excavated site and this is not yet available. The distinct possibility remains, however, that the three propositions are, in fact, stages in the development of hill-forts. The first reflects a situation closely similar to that suggested for the second millennium plateau enclosures and, even before them, the henge monuments and causewayed camps; the second requires only the physical establishment of some aspect of the tribal hierarchy, such as the construction of a temple or a chieftain's house; while the third is a natural corollary of the first two. Similar developments are frequently to be found in pre-industrial society. In the Roman world, for example, many ancient religious locations were eventually equipped with stone-built temples, and later still acquired the trappings of trade and entertainment in the form of markets and theatres. Some remained at this level, serving as essentially rural markets and shrines, while others developed into towns with a stable residential population and were recognized as such by the Roman administration. Thus, for some places the process was continuous; for others, it was arrested.

A model of this kind may well prove to be correct for the development of hill-forts. Pre-Roman temples within hill-forts are now gradually being recognized. Some of them even continued to be rebuilt on the same sites in the Roman period long after the settlement was abandoned, but so far no firm evidence of a resident secular hierarchy has been defined within a hill-fort, except indirectly in the form of luxury goods. Nevertheless, the coercive power implicit both in the ordered lay-out of buildings and in the monumentally planned and executed defences of many of the late forts is strongly suggestive of the centralized power of a chiefdom, quite possibly based on the fort itself. If anything, the evidence tends to support, but not prove, the contention that some forts had reached the second stage of development.

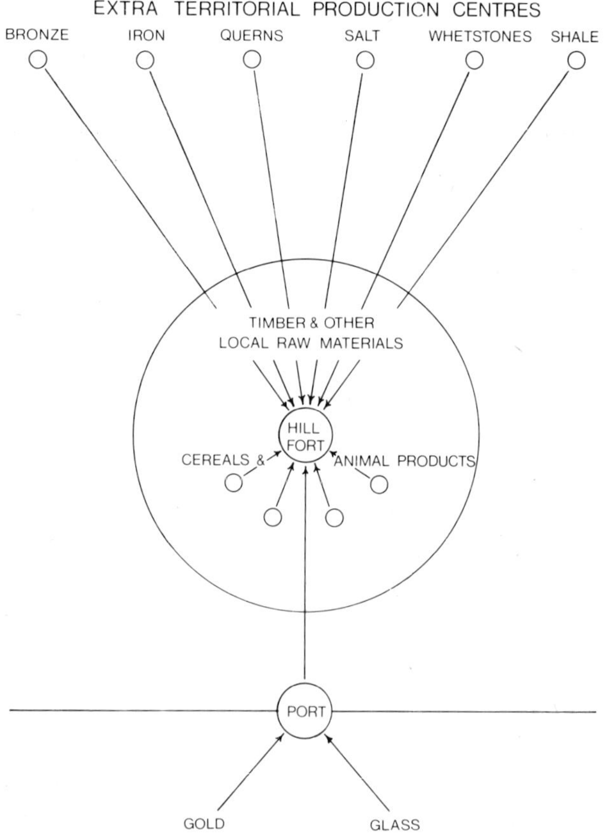

Figure 6. Diagram to illustrate Danebury in relation to the raw materials and manufactured goods found during the excavation: suggested spheres of exploitation.

The third theoretical stage hinges largely upon the services that a fort might provide for the occupants of its hinterland. Fig. 6 is a diagrammatic summary designed to show the relationship of Danebury to the productive capacity of its territory and to extra-territorial contacts. It is based on artefacts discovered during the excavation of 1969-72. Much depends on the way in which the diagram is interpreted but, if it is accepted that for each territory the hill-fort served as a redistribution centre where surplus farm products were exchanged for exotic commodities, e.g. salt or manufactured goods, then the fort must be providing a service to the community. The alternative view, that non-local goods passed direct from source to the consumers, seems hardly tenable at this stage. Whether or not raw materials were converted to manufactured goods within the hill-forts on a commercial scale, it is impossible to assess:

spinning, weaving, leather-working, carpentry, bronze-smithing and blacksmithing, are all attested; but the intensity of these activities in relation to home production remains undefined.

On present evidence, then, we may sum up the functions of late hill-forts in the south by saying that they were centre-places within well-defined territories; they were maintained by coercive control, able on occasions to order reserves of manpower, and they provided for their hinterlands such services as a religious focus, market facilities, allowing the redistribution of produce and, possibly, even the production of specialized manufactured goods. If, in the light of future work, we can add to this the presence of a resident population substantially engaged in providing these services, then we shall be forced to accept that the southern British hill-forts of the third and second centuries B.C. possessed the major characteristics of a proto-urbanized society.

Change in the first century B.C.

The first half of the first century B.C. was a period of rapid social and economic change in southern Britain, stimulated by folk movements from adjacent parts of northern Gaul. It is hardly surprising that hill-forts should reflect these developments. One facet of the changing scene was the intensification of trading contact between Britain and the continent, leading inevitably to the growth of specialized centres referred to as ports-of-trade. A very clear example is to be found on Hengistbury Head, Hampshire (Bushe-Fox 1915), where a promontory partially closing the southern side of Poole Harbour was defended by multiple banks and ditches. Excavations by Bushe-Fox in 1911-12, and more recently by Dr D.P.S. Peacock, have produced a wealth of material demonstrating the direct importation of pottery from northern France (the so-called Hengistbury Class B wares and graphite-coated vessels), the arrival of Mediterranean wine in amphorae of Dressel type 1A, and such complex manufacturing processes as the desilverization of lead. There can be little reasonable doubt that it was through Hengistbury that a wide range of imports reached sites in southern Britain.

The situation of Hengistbury is particularly interesting, lying as it does close to the

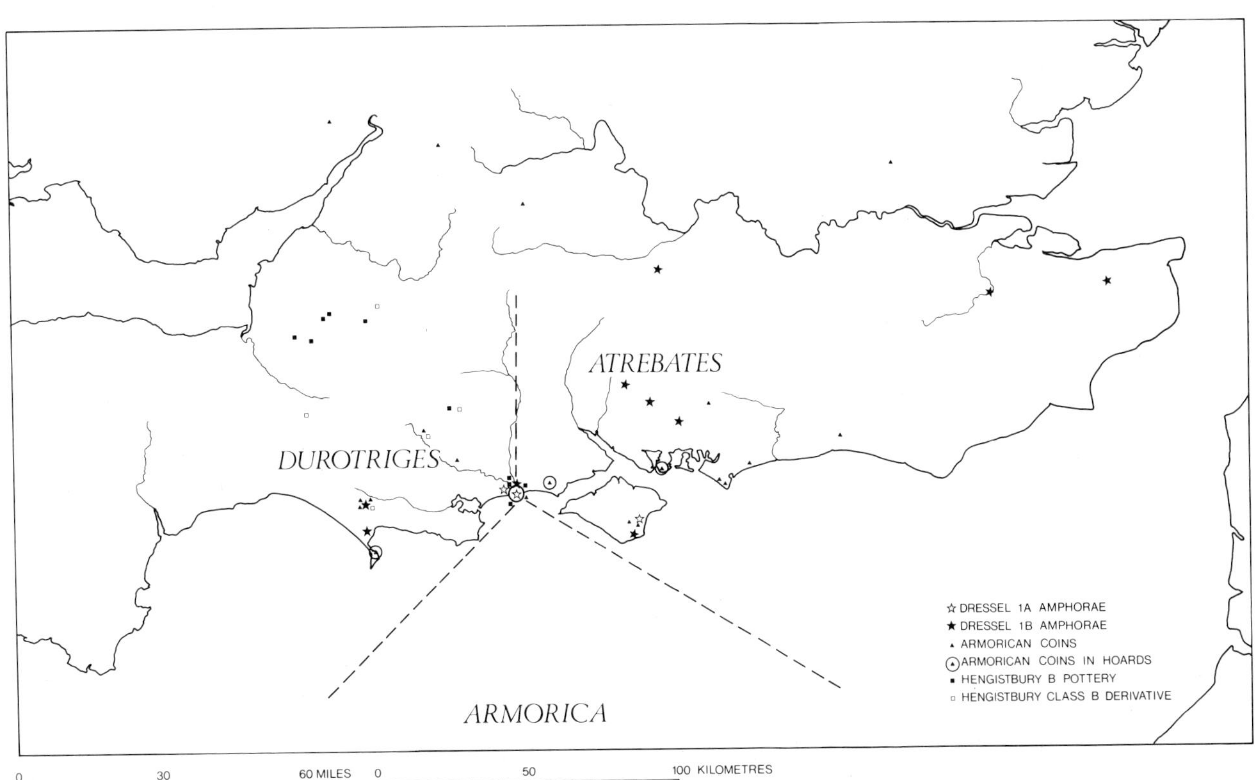

Figure 7. Hengistbury as a port of trade.

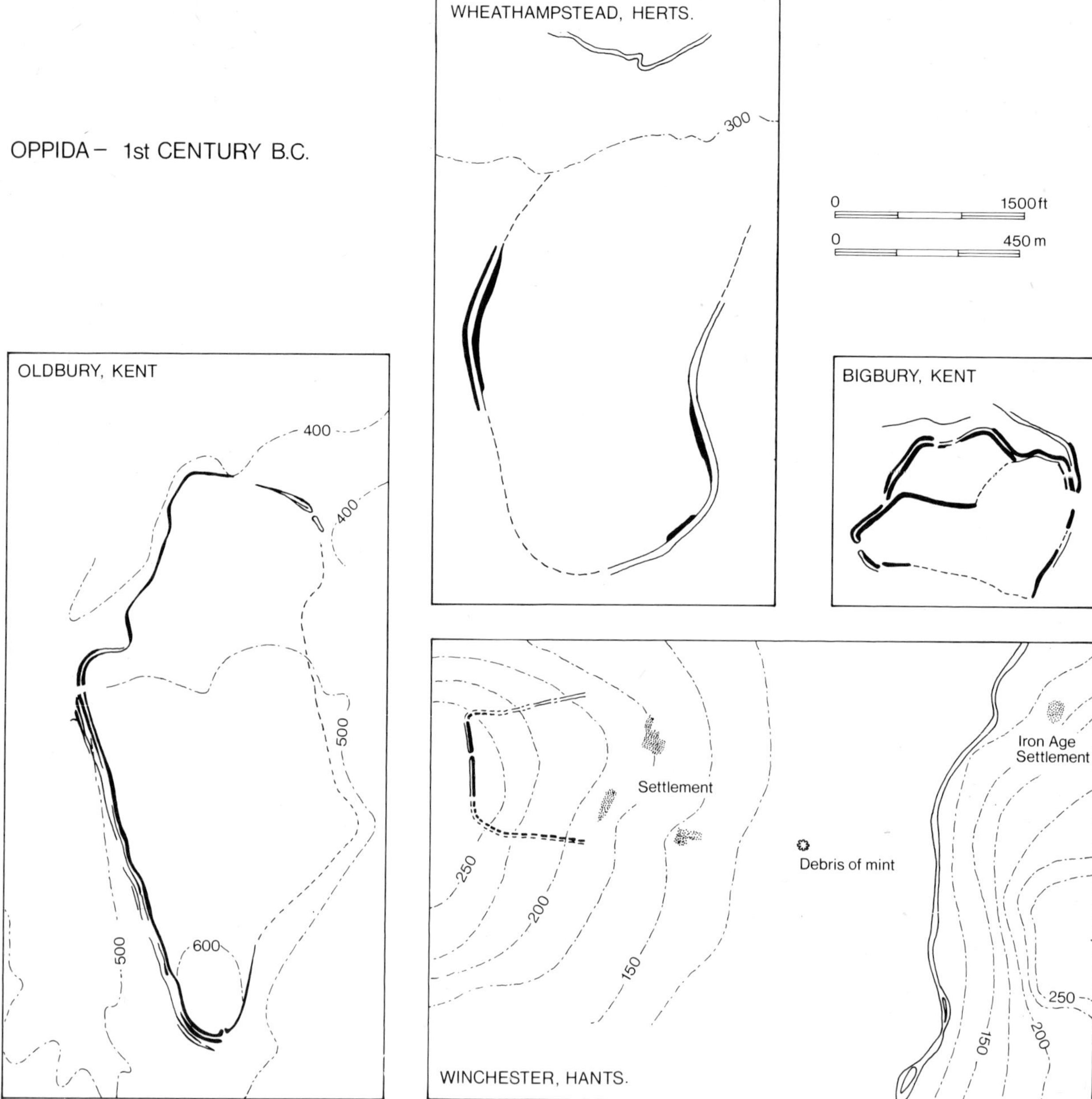

Figure 8. Enclosed oppida. (Contours marked in feet; north is at the top.)

boundary between the tribal territories of the Durotriges and the Atrebates, while at the same time marking a point of contact between the sphere of Armorican influence and the British Isles (Fig. 7). It is not a centre-place in the sense that hill-forts are centre-places, but it is strictly extra-tribal and presumably without a territory, thus conforming remarkably well to the theoretical characteristics of a port-of-trade (Polányi 1957).

Many, if not most, of the hill-forts excavated in Hampshire and Sussex were abandoned during the first century B.C., probably before the campaigns of Julius Caesar, and in their stead a new kind of fortification appeared, which tended to favour valley-side situations or promontories between rivers (Fig. 8). With a few exceptions, e.g. Bigbury and Oldbury in Kent, hill-top locations seem to have been avoided. Dating is notoriously difficult but, where evi-

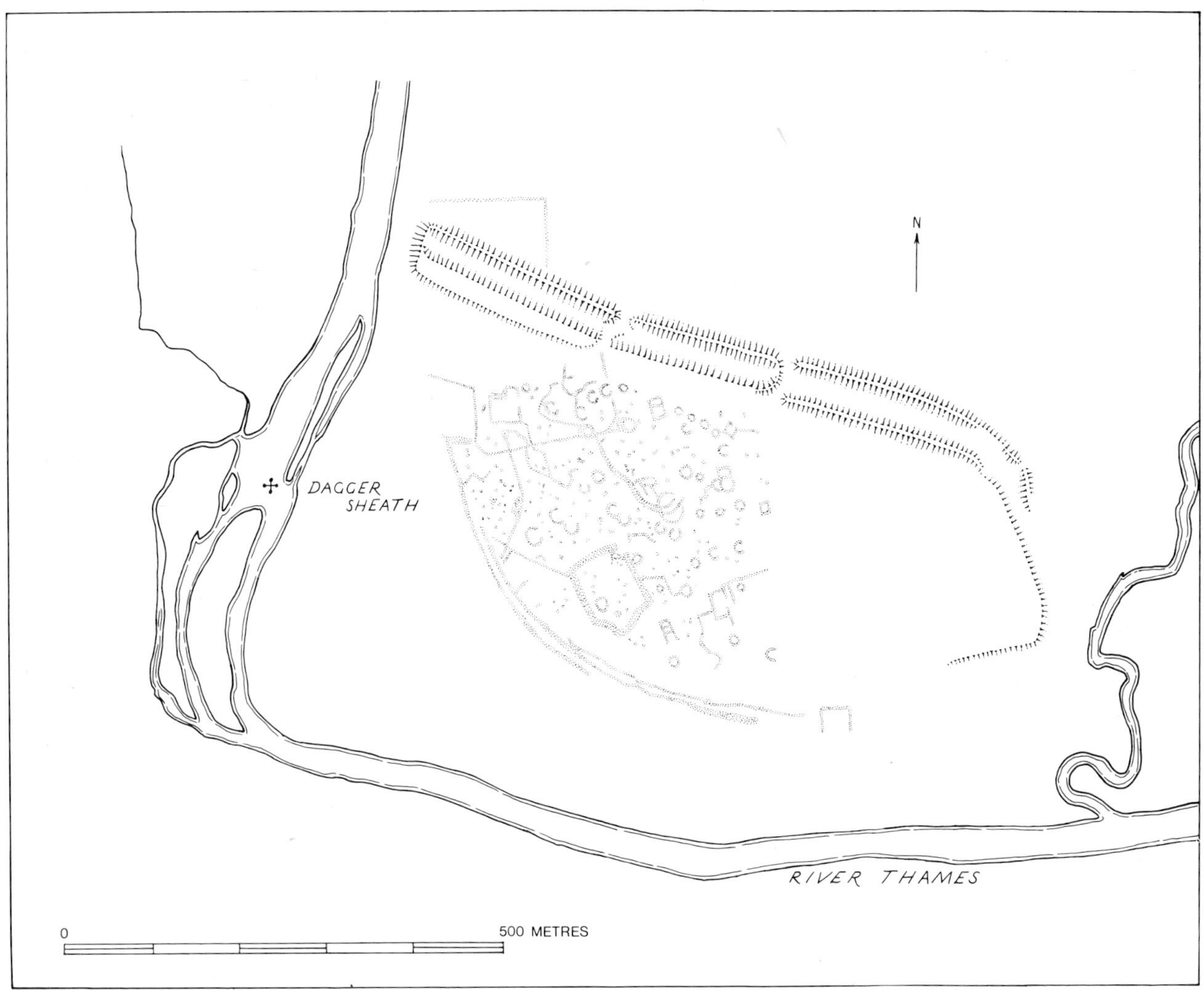

Figure 9. Dyke Hills, Dorchester, Oxon: Earthworks and crop marks visible on air photographs taken by Major Allen.

dence is available, a first-century B.C. date is indicated, although occupation may have originated on some sites a little earlier. It is presumably to this type of fortification that Caesar was referring when he said of Cassivellaunus' stronghold that it was 'protected by forests and marshes' and 'was of great natural strength and excellently fortified' (*Gallic Wars*). Little is known of the interior arrangements of any of these sites, but a remarkable air photograph of Dyke Hills, in Oxfordshire, leaves little doubt that, here at least, settlement was densely packed within the defences (Fig. 9).

A preliminary attempt is made in Fig. 10 to map the more obvious earthworks belonging to this category, which we may tentatively call 'enclosed oppida'. More may well exist, particularly among the lesser-known structures in Sussex and the Weald, but without extensive field-work the map will have to remain incomplete. It does, however, demonstrate the marked difference between the settlement pattern of the south-east, with its enclosed oppida, and the south-west, principally the territory of the Durotriges, where old hill-forts continued in occupation. Such a difference reflects a startling divergence in development between the two areas, the first of any significance that can be recognized for more than a thousand years.

The primary cause of the developments in the south-east must ultimately lie in strengthened ties with northern Gaul, which may well have started as early as 120 B.C. and were certainly evident in Caesar's time. A folk movement with the attendant disruptions consequent upon it seems to be the most likely stimulus, but

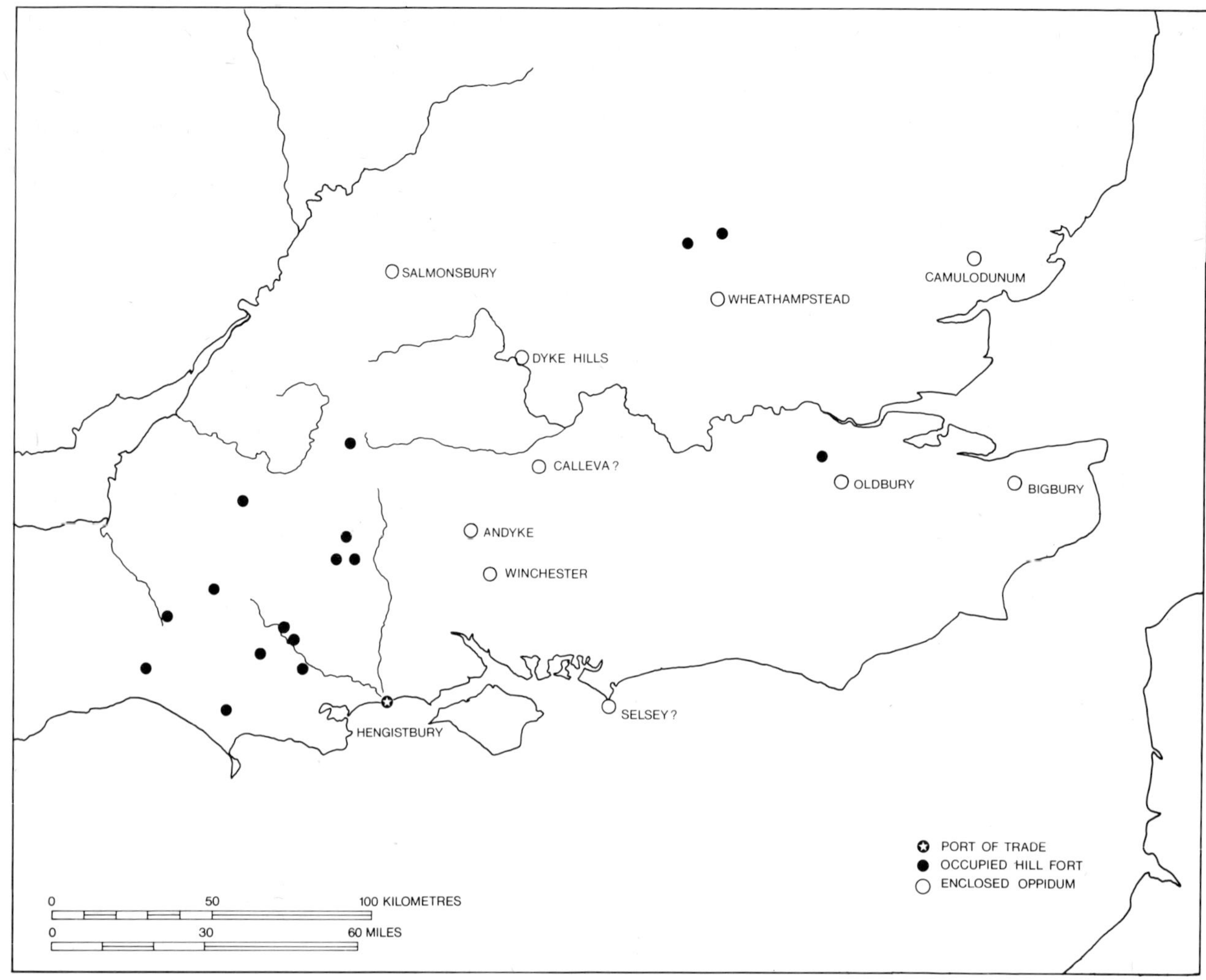

Figure 10. Nucleated settlement *c.* 100-50 B.C.

contributary factors such as expanding trading patterns must also have had an effect. Whatever the complex causes, the question that immediately arises is how, if at all, do the differences in settlement type reflect different social systems? Taken at its simplest level, the enclosed oppida are both fewer in number than the hill-forts and generally substantially larger, facts that could hint at the break-down of the old system of small independent units and its replacement with larger political configurations. Caesar's description of the south-east in the middle of the first century tends to bear this out. Named dynastic rulers appear to have wielded considerable power, the people acting in concert under elected war leaders. Even so, there was conflict and treachery among the ruling families. This does not, however, imply a state of civil war. The countryside was by now studded with thousands of farmsteads, as both Caesar and archaeology attest. Moreover, the preliminary results of area surveys around Danebury and in the parish of Chalton, Hampshire (Cunliffe 1973), suggests a marked increase in the number of farmsteads during this period and many of the contemporary sites that have been examined were less substantially defended than those of the preceding centuries. These scattered observations cannot claim to form a coherent picture but, as a broad generalization, we might suggest that in the south-east the hill-fort dominated landscape, with its overtones of local chieftains and the need for defence, had given way to a system in which dynastic kingships exercised control over larger areas – in terms of social organization, the end of chiefdoms and the emergence of the state. Until we know much more of the settlement archaeology of the first century B.C., a more detailed assessment of this vitally important period of change will be difficult to offer.

From Caesar to Claudius

The conquest of Gaul by Caesar in the middle of the first century B.C. was a significant factor in the subsequent developments in south-eastern Britain for, in one sweep, it removed the possibility of free movement between the communities on either side of the Channel; it restricted and controlled trade; and it introduced the constant threat of invasion, which could be used as a bargaining counter between rival British factions. In short, from 54 B.C. to A.D. 43, British society developed in relative isolation.

The differences between the south-east and the south-west remained evident, the communities who became collectively known as the Durotriges maintaining their old way of life up to the time of the Claudian conquest. In the south-east, on the other hand, the enclosed oppida of the earlier period gradually gave way to fewer, even larger, establishments, some of which, e.g. Calleva and Camulodunum, developed directly out of existing settlements. The principal feature that links the sites together and distinguishes them from the enclosed oppida, is that all (with the possible exception of Durovernum) were defined by, or associated with, extensive systems of earthworks that demarcate substantial territories of many square miles, within which lie one or more settlement areas. To distinguish them from the enclosed oppida the term 'territorial oppida' is used here. Where dating evidence is available, all were in use in the

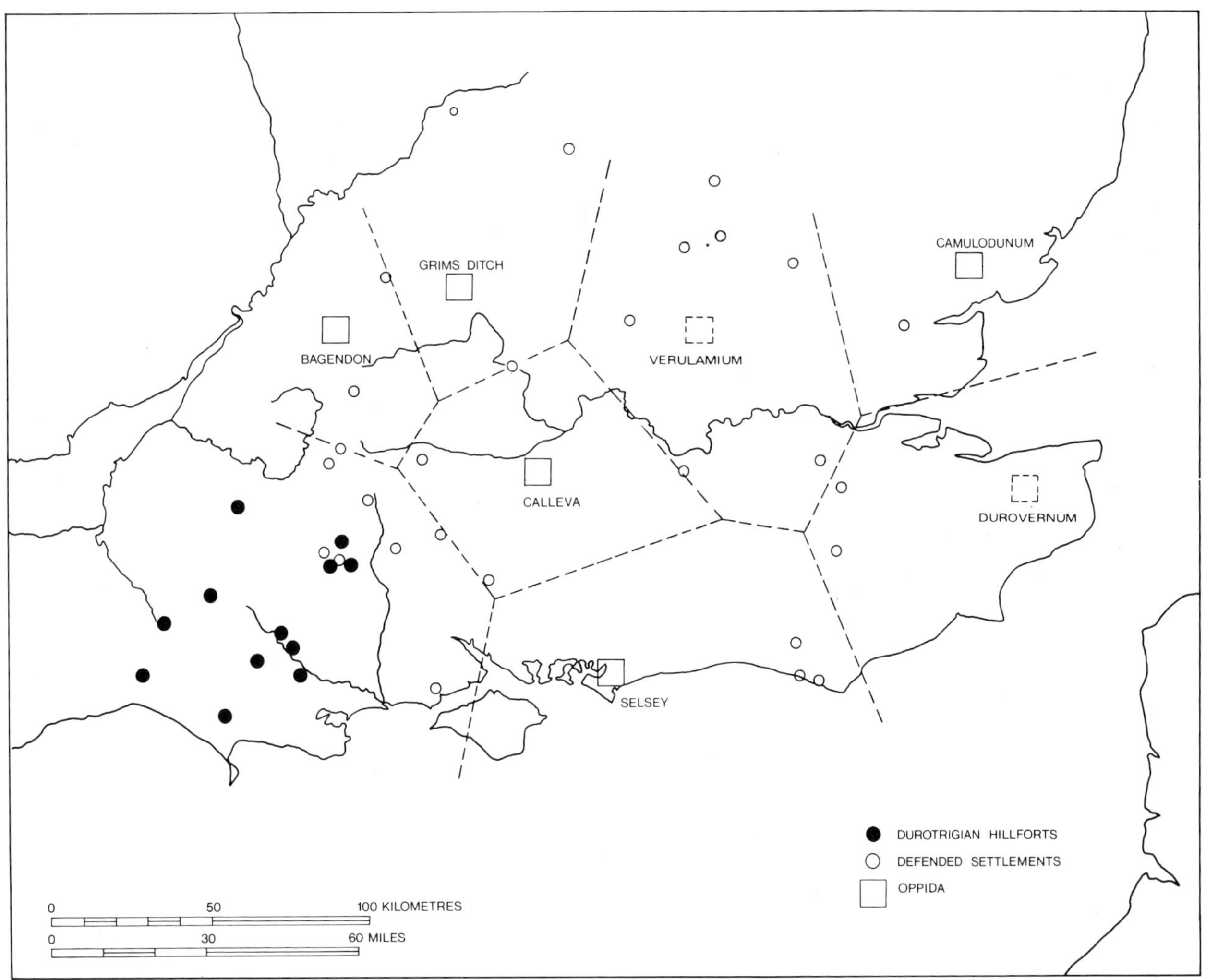

Figure 11. Nucleated settlement 0-40 A.D.

early first century A.D. and continued to be occupied after the Roman invasion. Of the seven oppida shown on Fig. 11, the form, though not the existence, of Durovernum (Canterbury) is unknown; the earthworks surrounding Selsey are well recorded, but its urban nucleus has not been discovered; Calleva, Camulodunum, Verulamium and Bagendon are known from surviving earthworks and limited trial excavation; while the inclusion of Grims Ditch (north Oxfordshire) rests entirely on its system of earthworks of the correct date, which have characteristics closely similar to those of the large oppida. It need hardly be stressed that our knowledge of this important category of sites is very sadly limited.

Fig. 11 shows the seven territorial oppida in relation to their theoretical territories. It will be evident that their distribution is such that they could not have provided market services sufficient to cover the entire south-east: such a spacing would, in theory, have required the support of satellite market centres close to the boundaries between one territory and another. When, however, other defended sites that show evidence of occupation during this period are plotted on the same map, it will be seen that they conform remarkably well with the pattern that would be expected of the satellite markets. In other words, the picture that is beginning to emerge suggests the existence of large territories served by single market-capitals supported by settlements of lower rank. The complexity of the organization implied strongly suggests that by this time the south-east was fully urbanized.

In such a system, some conformity would be expected between the theoretical territory and the distribution of artefacts reflecting the services specific to its centre. While the matter cannot be discussed in detail here, it may be said that certain types of coins show a close correlation, while the distribution of pottery styles is in good agreement.[6]

This simple model, involving the emergence of discrete economic territories in the first century A.D., in no sense conflicts with the more conventional approach based on a partial history of the ruling dynasties constructed from numismatic and historical sources. It merely offers an alternative method of studying the period, free from the uncertainties that must necessarily accompany historical models. The two approaches are, in fact, in very good agreement, if the vicissitudes of the period implied by the current interpretation of the coins are seen simply in terms of the dynastic rulers vying for control of the principal market centres.

In the south-west, the traditional organization of society based on individual hill-forts continued, although some growing element of centralization might be suggested by the increasing strength and dominance of Maiden Castle. The contrast between the two social systems is dramatically highlighted by the course of the Roman invasion in A.D. 43-4. The south-east offered unified resistance under elected war leaders which, once smashed in set-piece battles, allowed the rapid occupation of the entire territory. In the south-west, on the other hand, Vespasian and the second legion had to fight their way, one hill-fort at a time, across the land, eventually claiming to have subdued two tribes and to have taken more than twenty fortified positions.

The stability of the pre-Roman economic organization is demonstrated by the use that the Roman administration made of it. Civitas capitals were created in, or close to, six of the seven centres (the exception being Grims Ditch), while among the Durotriges the town of Dorchester (Dorset) soon took over the function of local government in the south-west. The system did not, however, remain static; the port-of-trade established at London grew rapidly to dominate the south-east and some satellite settlements of the pre-Roman era, such as Winchester, soon rose to the status of civitas centres while others, e.g. Dorchester in Oxfordshire, remained of secondary significance. Thus urban development in Britain under Roman rule should, strictly, be viewed as simply a continuation of a process already long established in the south-east.

In the above discussion, an attempt has been made to draw together some of the principal threads of evidence relating to the development of nucleated settlement in south-eastern Britain in the thousand years before the Roman conquest, and to offer some comment on its interpretation, in particular its relevance to the study of social change. What emerges is a tolerably cohesive picture, beginning with a simple egalitarian organization *c.* 1000 B.C. that developed rapidly into a complex of chiefdoms, some of which were to rise to positions of dominance by the fourth and third centuries. Many of the focal points of these chiefdoms, the hill-forts, grew out of tribal meeting places and soon acquired the additional functions of redistribution centres. By the first century B.C., a number of them were complex enough to be classed as proto-urban. The stimulus of overseas contact intensified the pace of change until, by the middle of the first century B.C., social organization had become sufficiently advanced to suggest the emergence of primitive states. This trend developed still further in the decades leading up to the Roman invasion of A.D. 43, by which time the economic systems had become focused on urban centres, each serving a well-defined territory, supported by a network of satellite markets. The system continued to develop until the early fifth century A.D., the only change being that the British hierarchy was gradually replaced by the Roman state system in the period following *c.* A.D. 43-75.

Ordering the material and constructing a model of this kind is both amusing and, I believe, worth while, so long as it helps to refocus attention and suggest areas in which further study will be rewarding. Our knowledge of first-millennium B.C. society is now at a stage when a series of plausible and attractive models can be offered but, unless they are tested by systematic excavation on an unprecedented scale, supported by intensive field-work of comparable standard, the archaeology of the period will rapidly degenerate into a purely theoretical game, enlivened only by an occasional new typological insight.

REFERENCES

Alcock, L. (1972) *'By South Cadbury is that Camelot . . .'*. London.

Burleigh, R., Longworth, I.H. and Wainwright, G.J. (1972) Relative and absolute dating of four late Neolithic enclosures: an exercise in the interpretation of radiocarbon determinations. *P.P.S.*, 38, 389-407.

Burstow, G.P. and Holleyman, G.A. (1957) Late Bronze Age settlement on Itford Hill, Sussex. *P.P.S.*, 23, 167-212.

Bushe-Fox, J.P. (1915) *Excavations at Hengistbury Head, Hampshire, in 1911-12* (Soc. Ant. Res. Cttee. Report No. 3). Oxford.

Coombs, D. (1967) Mam Tor. *Derbyshire Arch. Jour.*, 87, 158-9.

Coombs, D. (1971) Mam Tor, a Bronze Age hill-fort? *Current Arch.*, 27, 100-2.

Cotton, M.A., Frere, S.S. *et al.* (1968) Ivinghoe Beacon excavations, 1963-65. *Records of Buckinghamshire*, 18, Part 3.

Cunliffe, B.W. (1970) A Bronze Age settlement at Chalton, Hants (site 78). *Ant. Jour.*, 50, 1-13.

Cunliffe, B.W. (1971a) Some aspects of hill-forts and their cultural environments. In Hill, D. and Jesson, M. (eds.), *The Iron Age and its Hill-forts*, 53-70. Southampton.

Cunliffe, B.W. (1971b) Danebury, Hampshire: first interim report on the excavations, 1969-70. *Ant. Jour.*, 51, 240-52.

Cunliffe, B.W. (1973) Chalton, Hants: the evolution of a landscape. *Ant. Jour.*, 53, 173-90.

Cunliffe, B.W. (1974) *Iron Age Communities in Britain.* London and Boston.

Curwen, E.C. (1934) A Late Bronze Age farm and a Neolithic pit-dwelling on New Barn Down, Clapham, Nr. Worthing. *Sussex Arch. Coll.*, 75, 137-70.

Dixon, P. (1972) Crickley Hill 1969-71. *Antiquity*, 46, 49-52.

Holleyman, G.A. (1937) Harrow Hill Excavations, 1936. *Sussex Arch. Coll.*, 78, 230-51.

Holleyman, G.A. and Curwen, E.C. (1935) Late Bronze Age lynchet-settlements on Plumpton Plain, Sussex. *P.P.S.*, 1, 16-38.

Jones, G.D.B. and Thompson, F.H. (1965) Excavations at Mam Tor, 1965. *Derbyshire Arch. Jour.*, 85, 123-5.

O'Neil, B.H.St.J. (1942) Excavations at Ffridd Faldwyn camp, Montgomery, 1937-39. *Arch. Camb.*, 97, 1-57.

Piggott, C.M. (1942) Five Late Bronze Age enclosures in north Wiltshire. *P.P.S.*, 8, 48-61.

Piggott, S. (1930) Butser Hill. *Antiquity*, 4, 187-200.

Pitt-Rivers, A.H.L.F. (1898) *Excavations in Cranborne Chase, near Rushmore, 1893-1896.* Vol. 4. London; privately printed.

Polányi, K., Arensberg, C.M. and Pearson, H.W. (eds.) (1957) *Trade and Market in the Early Empires: Economics in History and Theory.* Glencoe, Illinois.

Ratcliffe-Densham, H.B.A. and Ratcliffe-Densham, M.M. (1961) An anomalous earthwork of the Late Bronze Age, on Cock Hill. *Sussex Arch. Coll.*, 99, 78-101.

R.C.H.M. (1970) *Royal Commission on Historical Monuments (England) Inventory of the Historical Monuments in the County of Dorset. III. Central Dorset.* London.

Rahtz, P.A. and ApSimon, A.M. (1962) Excavations at Shearplace Hill, Sydling St. Nicholas, Dorset, England. *P.P.S.*, 28, 289-328.

Simpson, D.D.A. (1969) Excavations at Kaimes Hill-fort, Midlothian, 1964-68. *Glasgow Arch. Jour.*, n.s. 1, 7-28.

Stanford, S.C. (1966-71) *Interim reports on the annual excavations on Midsummer Hill Camp, Eastnor, Herefordshire.* Duplicated.

Stanford, S.C. (1967) Croft Ambrey hill-fort. *Trans. Woolhope Naturalists' Field Club*, 39, 31-9.

Stanford, S.C. (1971a) Credenhill Camp, Herefordshire:

an Iron Age hill-fort capital. *Arch. Jour.*, 127, 82-129.

Stanford, S.C. (1971b) Invention, adoption and imposition – the evidence of the hill-forts. In Hill, D. and Jessop, M. (eds.), *The Iron Age and its Hill-forts*, 41-52. Southampton.

Stead, I.M. (1965) *The La Tène Cultures of Eastern Yorkshire.* York.

Wainwright, G.J. (1970) The excavations of Balksbury Camp, Andover, Hants. *Proc. Hants. Field Club*, 26, 21-55.

Wheeler, Sir R.E.M. (1943) *Maiden Castle, Dorset* (Soc. Ant. Res. Cttee. Report No. 12). Oxford.

Wilson, A.E. (1940) Report on the excavations on Highdown Hill, Sussex, August 1939. *Sussex Arch. Coll.*, 81, 173-203.

Wilson, A.E. (1950) Excavations on Highdown Hill, 1947. *Sussex Arch. Coll.*, 89, 163-78.

NOTES

1. This paper is an expanded and modified version of a lecture given at the Spring Conference of the Prehistoric Society in 1972.

2. It is hoped to offer a full survey and discussion elsewhere.

3. The material is not yet published in full, but for a note on the excavation of the Causewayed Camp see *Proc. Dorset Nat. Hist. & Arch. Soc.*, 73 (1951), 105-6.

4. Excavations have been in progress at Danebury since 1969. An interim report on the first two seasons' work has been published (Cunliffe 1971b).

5. Excavations in 1973, directed by Dr G. Wainwright, have shown that the old enclosure was later reused as a farmstead in the middle pre-Roman Iron Age and in the Roman period. This in no way invalidates the point made here.

6. Publication in preparation by the author.

ANDREW FLEMING

Early settlement and the landscape in west Yorkshire

And I have oft observed, on such grounds in many places of this island, and in other countries, clusters of little round and oval foundations, whose very irregularities speak their antiquity. (Henry Rowlands, *Mona Antiqua Restaurata* 1766)

One of the most interesting topics in British archaeology is that of the nature and chronology of man's settlement in the regions of mountain and moorland that constitute about 35 per cent of Britain's surface area. Ecologists and palaeobotanists working in these areas have reaped rich rewards. Yet, too often, the archaeologist, in his concern with dating and taxonomy, does not take account of local environmental considerations, preferring to write a short tentative postscript after the routine descriptive work has been completed. Ecologists, by contrast, usually consider man only as an agent of environmental change. In such a situation, it is no wonder that there is seldom any sense of dialogue between man and his environment. This paper attempts to redress the balance for one area, by discussing the high-altitude fields and settlement sites of the West Yorkshire Dales; if nothing else, it should highlight the need for more work at the interface between archaeology and ecology, a field of study pioneered by Grahame Clark in this country.

The sites

In the Carboniferous limestone country around Malham, Ingleborough, Ribblesdale and Upper Wharfedale, it is difficult to walk very far without encountering traces of early agricultural activity in the form of fields and enclosures with their associated hut sites. These sites have been described by Raistrick (1939; 1964), Raistrick & Holmes (1962) and later by King (1970). Figure 1 shows the situation of the sites in relation to drainage and altitude; it is based on information from the previous publications and the records of the Ordnance Survey, and on the results of field-work carried out by the author. It will be seen that most of the sites are to be found at 800-1,600 feet (*c.* 250-500 m.) above sea level. This is probably a fair representation of their original distribution. The upper limit can be treated with confidence, since it is at about 1,600 feet (500 m.) that the limestone is capped by millstone grit, usually covered in peat, that forms a very different vegetational cover and thus a much more severe environment. The millstone grit zone rises to summits of between 2,000 and 2,400 feet (*c.* 610-750 m.) and itself contains very little of archaeological interest, the outstanding exception being the hill-fort on the summit of Ingleborough, at 2,373 feet (723 m.).

It is hard to quantify the sites in relation to altitude, because they are difficult to count, their component parts being scattered and somewhat uncertainly related to one another. One has the impression that sites conform to a bell-shaped curve; the bulk of them occur between 1,000 and 1,400 feet (305-425 m.) and almost all would fall within the broader 800-1,600 feet (250-500 m.) range.

This material appears very variable at first, but distinct patterns occur. The walls of huts, normally circular but sometimes rectangular, are found in varying numbers and degrees of association with those of 'fields' and enclosures. Most of the walls are apparently of stone construction, but they vary in the extent to which they have been grassed over. In general, heavily weathered, exposed stones with little vegetation cover are found at high altitudes. Lower down, the stone banks are usually grass-covered. At some of the higher sites the heavily weathered stone walls, grassed over many years ago, are now being re-exposed; while in other places similar walls, in areas of what is presumably relaxed grazing pressure, are gradually being sealed by vegetation and humus. Much the same processes, incidentally, can be observed

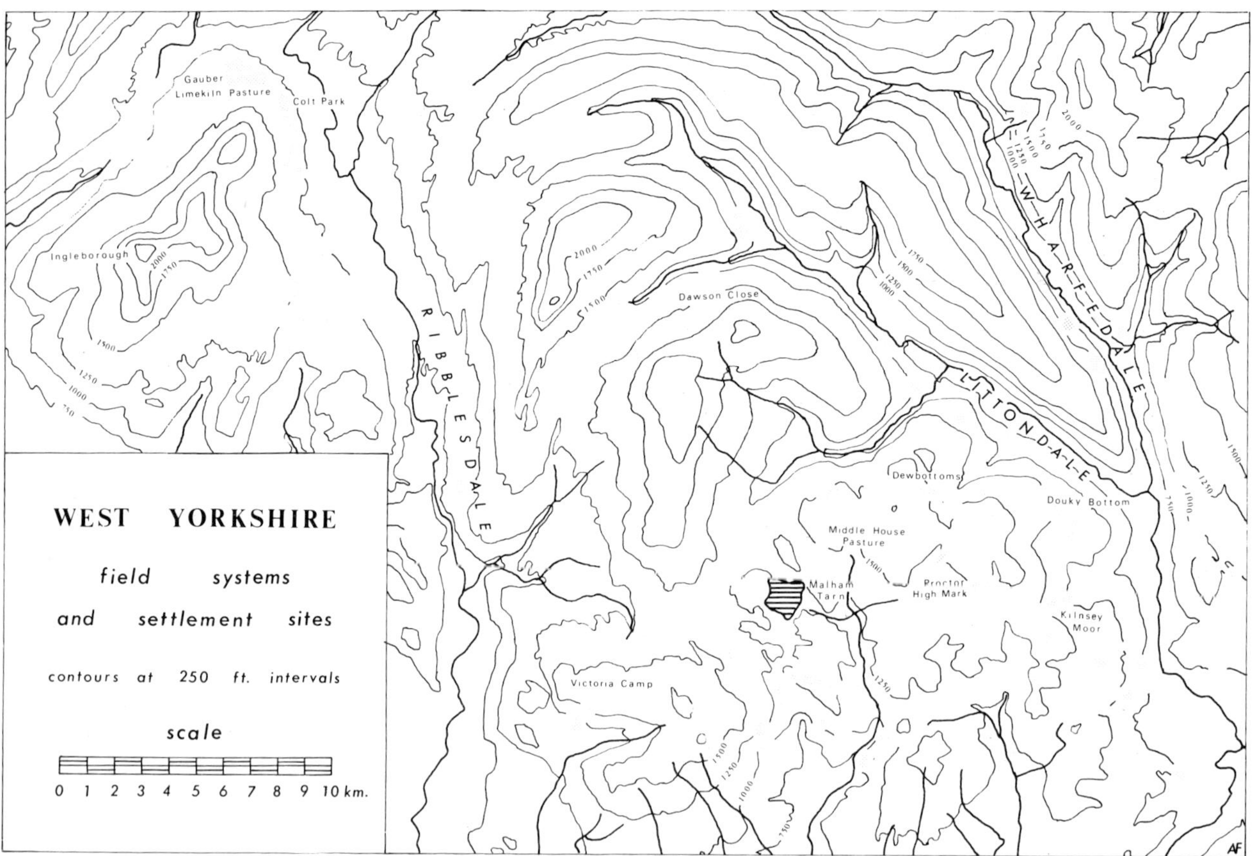

Figure 1. Map of the main sites of settlement and cultivation in west Yorkshire, in relation to altitude and drainage.

also on the natural limestone pavements themselves, whose occurrence has made the region a classic one for students of karst landforms; some of these are gradually being stripped, others have recently been covered.

The settlements and field systems in this area may be divided into two overall classes. The first class is composed of relatively large typologically well-defined settlements, frequently found in association with extensive field systems, which normally occur at lower altitudes. These can be divided into two groups. The first group is best exemplified by the sites at Helwith Bridge (SD 816694) Colt Park (SD 777775) Whit-a-Green (SD 776747) and Smearsett (SD 807680). These sites are laid out in a very characteristic manner, with large round or sometimes rectangular huts, and well-defined sub-rectangular enclosures bounded by relatively high banks. These seem to be 'domestic enclosures' or gardens; they cluster together at the centre of areas of extensive fields and are served by well-defined trackways which sometimes lead up to possible grazing areas at a higher level on the hillside. The fields themselves have been carefully planned and laid out; the well-known examples from Grassington (Raistrick 1938) are associated with similar settlements. In Ribblesdale, the sites mentioned form a closely-knit group between 900 and 1,100 feet (275-335 m.). They are dated to the Romano-British period (King 1970) and may be related to similar sites in Westmorland.

The second group, within the first class, includes Middle House Pasture (SD 901681; Raistrick & Holmes 1962), Victoria Camp (SD 842652) and Attermire East (SD 846641). These sites, in contrast to those of group 1, lie at high altitude (about 1,500 feet or 455 m.). They have between ten and twenty large, well-defined huts, normally found in one large enclosure. A few of these huts are in positions that give them commanding views or where they appear to guard the entrance of the compound. The huts are found incorporated in the main wall or spaced individually within the compound area. Victoria Camp, which has produced Romano-British material, has several large linked

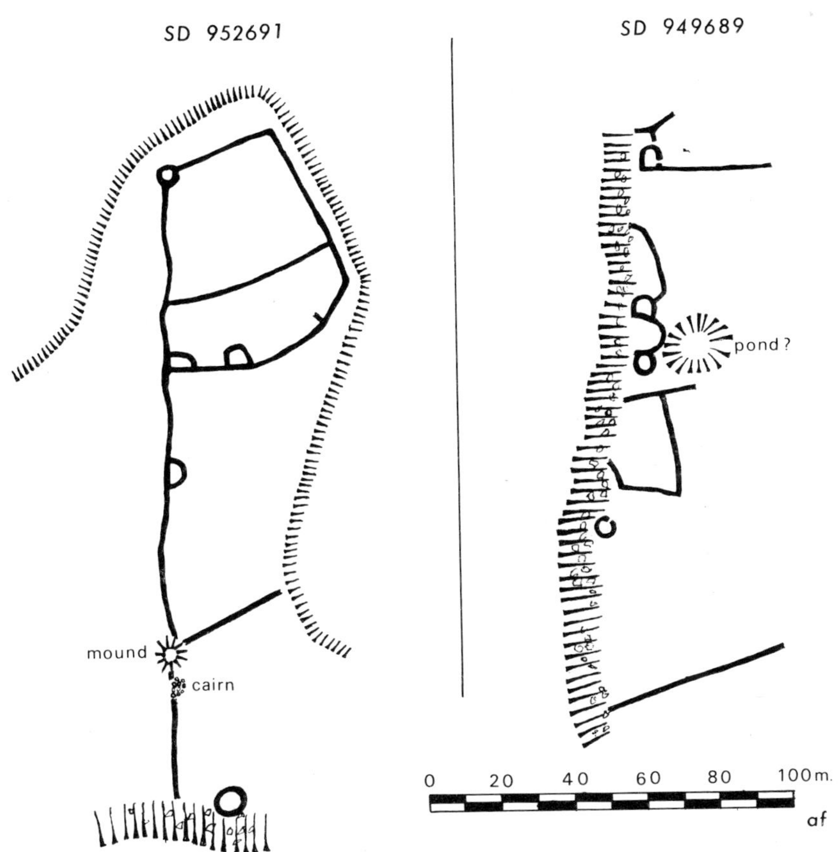

Figure 2. Typical plateau fields (left) and apron enclosure (right) at Douky Bottom.

compounds. The sites in this group give the impression that they are for upland grazing in the summer months, and the apparent pre-occupation with defence suggests that they are the Romano-British successors of the upland hill-forts.

In this paper I intend to concentrate on the less organized, more fragmentary remains that are found, in general, at higher altitudes than sites of the Helwith Bridge and Victoria Camp class. These are easily distinguished from the typological point of view, although their classification can usually be based only on their relationships with natural features. They are apparently undated. A tentative classification would produce the following groups:

Apron enclosures. A typical apron enclosure is D-shaped, the flat side of the D being formed by a vertical cliff (or 'scar') or by a steep, often scree-covered slope. The enclosure lies at the foot of the scar or slope. Sometimes it contains a hut, set in one corner. It is normally about twenty to thirty metres long (in a direction parallel to the scar) and five to ten metres wide, and an entrance is not normally apparent. Commonly, these apron enclosures are arranged in a row along a scar base, where they may be joined together or detached. Sometimes, if there is a substantial area of flat ground in front of the scar, other field-walls lead outwards from the base of the scar (Fig. 2).

Plateau fields. Plateau fields are in exposed situations, on high flattish ground where they sometimes coincide with areas of limestone pavement. Raistrick & Holmes (1962:Fig. 3) have recorded a good example of this type at Dewbottoms (SD 913694), though their survey is not strictly accurate. These fields, being up to about forty metres by forty metres in size, are larger than the apron enclosures. There are normally no more than five or six of them, and they are usually roughly rectilinear in plan.

Incorporated in the walls, either along the sides or at the junctions, are up to half a dozen small huts, which normally appear to have no 'domestic enclosures' of their own. These huts are usually round, although rectangular examples occur. Sometimes the small size of the huts, coupled with the tendency for the walls to collapse inwards, makes them difficult to distinguish from small cairns, but in one or two cases genuine cairns are incorporated. There are cases, such as Kilnsey Moor (SD 954665), where this type of field complex is found in a sheltered valley, but the same typological features, comprising a small number of small, squarish, linked enclosures accompanied by integrated huts, are found (Fig. 2).

Edge fields. Sometimes field-walls are confined to the tops of scars, but run along, or close to, the edges without occurring very far back. The fields may be long and narrow, running parallel to the edge, or they may be of irregular shape. One or two huts are sometimes found, and the whole grouping may be associated with areas of exposed pavement. The fields are rarely very large, and often take the form of narrow strips bounded by the edge on one side and walls on the others.

Ledge fields. These are found only in areas such as the east side of upper Wharfedale, where the limestone forms a series of natural ledges running along the hillside. The walls are short and run across the ledges; huts are also found.

Hollow fields or enclosures. In areas of exposed limestone there are often grassy hollows, either roughly circular or ovoid in form or else long and narrow. The circular hollows are surrounded by irregular walls, while the long narrow hollows tend to have several transverse walls that subdivide them into series of squarish fields. There are also larger hollows, which may have apron fields and huts disposed around the edges, or have entrances 'guarded' by one or two huts.

Environmental history

This is a region where environmental factors must play an important role in decision-making about the location of agricultural activities and settlement sites. In this section I propose to discuss what is known of the environmental history of the region in so far as it affects this study.

The soils of the Malham region have been treated recently by Bullock (1971). Almost all of them are derived from glacial drift, and only the very thin soils on gritstone pavement are residual. The Carboniferous limestone is being lowered chemically by only about 2 cm. every 500 years, so that any soil that is more than a few centimetres thick must be derived from drift, except on receiving sites. Thus only a few soils are directly related to the underlying geology, although most of the drift originates fairly locally, and this statement does not seriously affect the fundamental distinction between the limestone soils and the peats and gleys commonly found at the higher levels on the gritstone. On the limestone it is the thickness of the drift cover which governs the status of the soil and the character of the associated vegetation (Sinker 1960). At the present time rainfall exceeds evaporation, and leaching and decalcification are occurring, so that many soils are slightly acid even where the limestone is fairly near the surface. Fig. 3 shows an average profile; it is clear that the character of the soil can change markedly over short distances. The tops of the scars often carry bare limestone pavement, associated with clint rendzinas. Further back from the edge are brownearths, which become progressively more impoverished as one retreats from the edge, as they increase in depth. Near the edge are found eutrophic brownearths, and the nutrient cycling of the roots ensures a reasonable pH value in spite of the intense leaching. Further back, the brownearths become mesotrophic and then oligotrophic, and *Nardus stricta* associations replace those of *Festuca-Agrostis.*

Below the scars, or at the foot of slopes carrying scree rendzinas, there are usually receiving zones, where nutrient-rich drift accumulates from higher up, and *Festuca-Agrostis* associations are normally found.

The exposed pavements are a classic feature of the region. The pavements themselves are supposed to have been created by the action of ice during the last glaciation, but it may be presumed that most of them were subsequently covered by drift-based soils and their associated vegetation cover, and that they have been re-exposed in the last few thousand years. Nowadays, if a pavement is isolated from grazing activity, it soon develops a *Fraxinus*-dominated wood with a fairly rich associated flora. This has

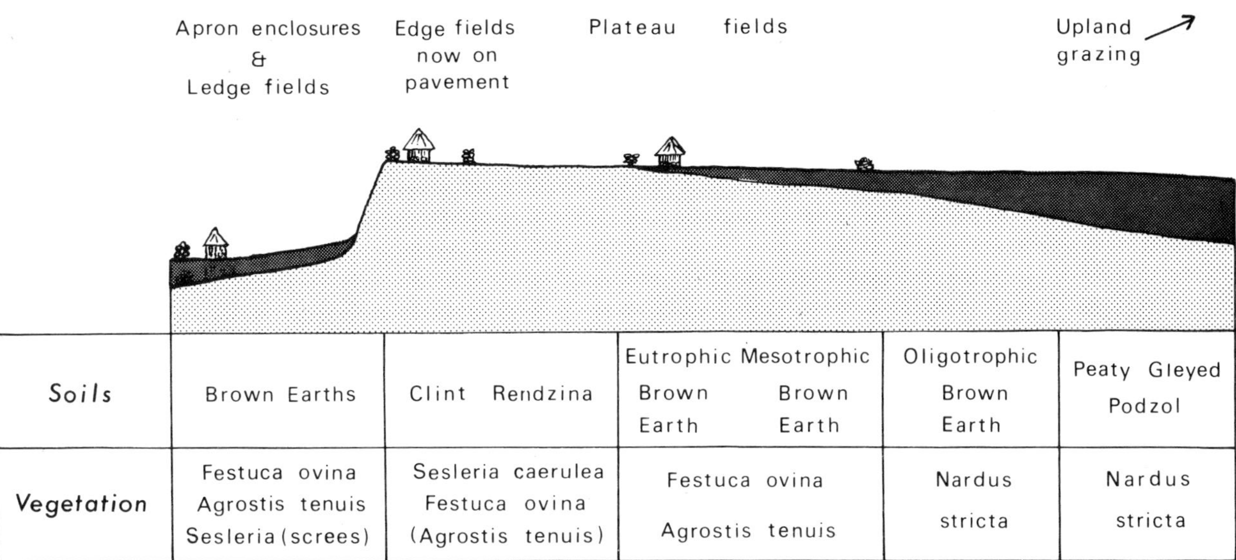

Soils	Brown Earths	Clint Rendzina	Eutrophic Brown Earth	Mesotrophic Brown Earth	Oligotrophic Brown Earth	Peaty Gleyed Podzol
Vegetation	Festuca ovina Agrostis tenuis Sesleria (screes)	Sesleria caerulea Festuca ovina (Agrostis tenuis)	Festuca ovina Agrostis tenuis		Nardus stricta	Nardus stricta

Figure 3. Relationships between soil types, vegetation associations and typical field and hut sites (adapted from Bullock 1971).

occurred at such places as Colt Park (SD 7777) or Scar Close (SD 7577) within the last few decades. Here the pavements have been fenced off because of the danger to sheep. It can also be seen that differential grazing pressure is responsible for a number of local effects in the region. On the limestone ledges, where the near-vertical cliffs and high modern walls have severely restricted access by sheep and cattle, some tree growth may be observed.

A study of pavement stripping and weathering has been made by Clayton (1966). He has pointed out that the pavements have been exposed gradually, and that those sections nearest to the tops of the scars have been exposed for the longest period. It is possible to demonstrate that the most heavily weathered pavement, therefore, is the one nearest to the edge; and that most recently exposed, and showing only slight traces of weathering, is that furthest from the edge. Old pavements are heavily fragmented by physical weathering processes, as are some of the field walls found in the area. Observation suggests that at the present time some pavements are being exposed, while some heavily weathered examples are gradually being covered.

Pollen samples from Malham (Piggott & Piggott 1959) have shown that zone VIIa was characterized by high alder frequencies, and there was oak, elm, ash, lime and yew. In zone VIIb occurred a rise in herbaceous pollen and that of *Plantago*. The pollen of herbaceous species and of *Fraxinus* increased in frequency in zone VIIb, a trend that continued into zone VIII. The authors suggested that a late Neolithic phase of deforestation has been succeeded by more extensive Iron Age clearances.

Prehistoric and later settlement

In general, the pollen evidence confirms what is known of the artefactual sequence of the area. There is plenty of evidence for the presence of man in the area from Mesolithic times onward, though the area has few burial mounds or ceremonial sites. It is possible that factors like climate, altitude and soils inhibited large-scale settlement in the Neolithic period. But some Neolithic settlement undoubtedly took place: there is the evidence of the leaf-shaped arrowheads; also of a site near Grassington (SD 99626722), which produced flints and broken stone-axe fragments (Raistrick 1938); a large mound containing possibly megalithic cists, at Giant's Grave, Penyghent Gill (SD 856732); and a henge monument near Grassington (SE 013654). Settlement continued to be fairly sparse in the Bronze Age, which is represented by barbed-and-tanged arrowheads and a number of barrows that have produced conventional Bronze Age material, plus a supposed stone circle at Bordley (SD 949653). There is also a trickle of metal artefacts belonging to the period

(King 1970). After this, a few metal objects and one or two hill-forts hint at a pre-Roman Iron Age population; but by far the bulk of the artefactual evidence points to extensive Romano-British activity. In addition, a few caves and rock fissures have produced material stretching from the Neolithic to Romano-British times. However, the bulk of the evidence for early settlement in the area is provided by the fields and field systems with their associated huts. Very few of these have been satisfactorily dated. Some, especially the more organized examples, have produced Romano-British material, but this does not allow us to generalize about all of them, especially those that are at higher altitudes and less formally organized.

Early economic strategies: grazing

There seems little doubt that any early economies in the area would have included a livestock-farming component, even in times when there was substantial cereal cultivation. Livestock would be essential to utilize the many areas unsuitable for cereal growing, to provide manure to compensate for depletion of soil nutrients by leaching and cropping, and as an insurance in bad arable years. Livestock farming is normal in the area at the moment, and some of the factors that are important now would have also been influential in pre- and proto-historic periods.

Williams (1963) and Holliday and Townsend (1967) point out that present-day patterns of exploitation make use of three different grassland associations. The *Festuca-Agrostis* associations, found on shallower limestone drift soils, form the main summer grazing, and are in any case preferred by sheep (Hunter 1962). But these deciduous grasses have a low wintering capacity, and it is the *Calluna-Erica-Nardus* associations of the upper, gritstone slopes which provide the main winter diet, the supply of which tends to determine the stocking rate nowadays (Hunter 1962). A third category is *Sesleria*, the blue moor-grass, which is restricted to very lime-rich soils, and starts its growth earlier than other grasses. This is often found on

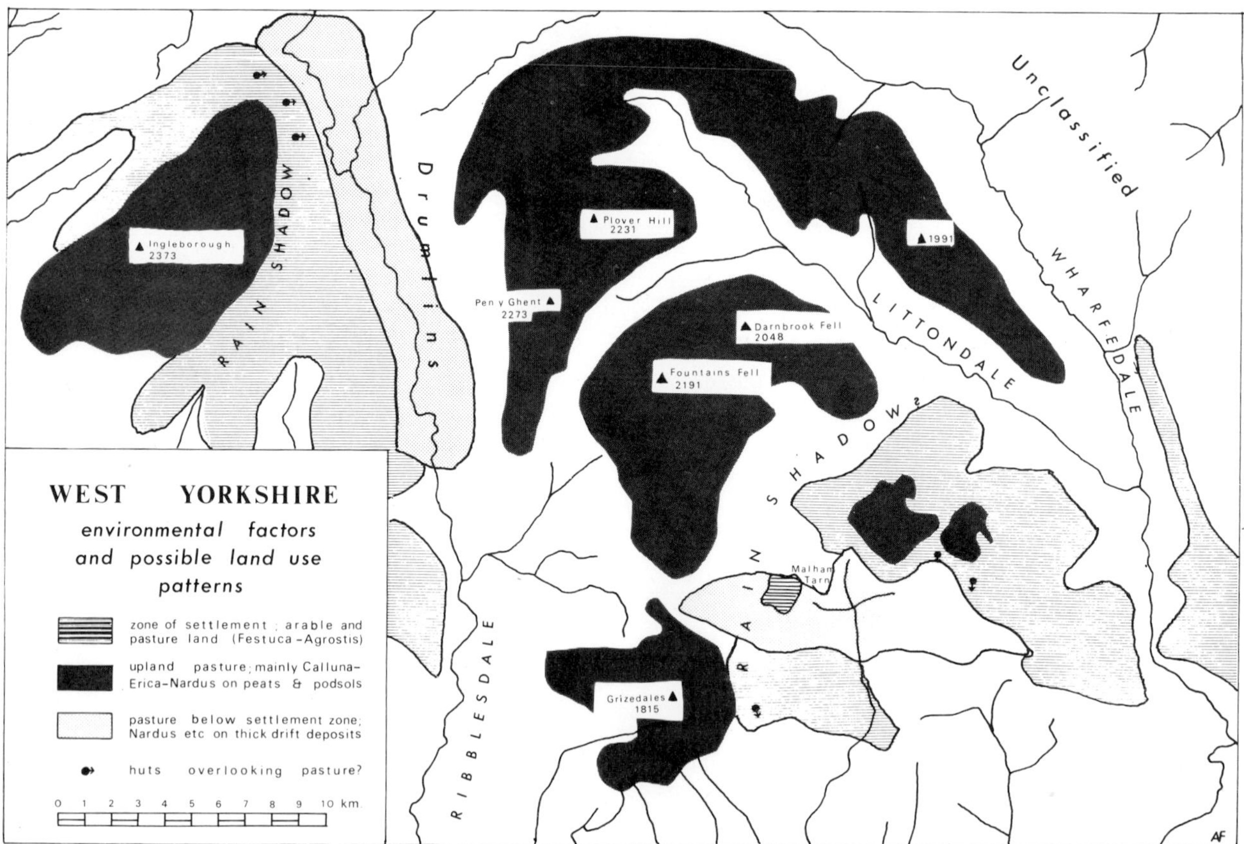

Figure 4. Summary map of settlement zones, possible grazing areas, and other environmental features.

thinner soils – for instance, those on tops of scars where the soils are in any case quick to warm up in spring; it provides an important grazing source for the February-April period.

It might be assumed that these relationships between different grassland associations would have some influence on pre- and proto-historic site locations. It might be further predicted that some settlements, as nowadays, would have been sited at the junction between these two main types of grassland, in other words at the limestone/gritstone junction. However, there are few signs that this kind of siting was important to early settlers. The settlements around Ingleborough would never have been very far from the gritstone 'black lands' anyway. But the lack of association between settlement and zone junction here argues either that hardy livestock were not available at this time, or that the settlers were more preoccupied with mixed farming. There is a small amount of evidence to suggest that some grazing may have been on land which was *lower* than the arable. For instance, the area to the north of Horton-in-Ribblesdale, to the east of the Ribble, is a badly drained zone of drumlins and glacial drift, where cultivation would have been very difficult; it may be significant that across the valley, in the Colt Park area, several huts, instead of being set in the shelter of a north-south limestone scar, are pushed out some 40-50 m. to the east, where they would be in an ideal position to overlook stock grazing across the valley. Much the same pattern occurs to the north-east of Malham, where a number of sites overlook an area of badly drained drift. These sites include: Middle House Pasture itself (SD 901681) where the southernmost hut and the group of three to the north (Raistrick & Holmes 1962:Fig. 5) are situated in positions commanding superb views of the land below; High Mark (SD 929676) where, despite good local shelter, at least one hut is set in a position giving excellent visibility, on an exposed natural terrace; and a site near Tattersal Pasture (SD 938670) where the view, both over the pasture to the south and over the countryside in general, is magnificent and extensive.

There are a number of reasons why herdsmen would need huts with good visibility over the pastures below them. It would be necessary to keep a check on the position of their animals, on the occurrence of possible dangers, and on the vigilance of those delegated to keep a closer watch on them. This would be especially true if the more able-bodied members of the group normally concerned themselves with agricultural work, leaving the task of looking after animals to the young or old, who might need assistance in certain circumstances. This sort of pattern is quite common in the ethnographic literature. As Samuel Johnson (1775) recorded, on the isle of Coll: 'In a district, such as the eye can command, there is a general herdsman, who knows all the cattle of the neighbourhood, and whose station is upon a hill, from which he surveys the lower grounds; and if one man's cattle invade another's grass, drives them back to their own borders.'

In practice, it is difficult to identify stock enclosures with any certainty; they are too easily confused with domestic enclosures or isolated fields. One may summarize the situation by saying that it is likely that stock-raising would have been important everywhere in the region in the past, that it was perhaps the badly drained drift *below* the arable fields which was most commonly exploited in this way, and that it is huts that command extensive views, particularly over such areas, which give the best clue to pastoral preoccupations.

Early economic strategies: problems of cereal growing

A difficult problem is posed by the evidence which exists for the growing of cereals at high altitudes, in a region that is considered climatically unsuitable today. This evidence consists of sickles, querns, and even plough-shares in the Romano-British period (Raistrick 1939; King 1970), even if these finds relate only to the lower part of the altitudinal range considered. Even if the apron enclosures are considered as stock compounds or domestic enclosures, the same interpretation cannot be applied to the plateau fields or some of those in the other groups defined above – they must, surely, be fields in the conventional sense and, as will be argued presently, their siting reinforces this view.

Not very much work has been published on the problems of cultivating cereals in such threshold conditions. In general, however, these are roughly understood. It is possible to grow crops at such altitudes, but climatic factors make both their yield and the possibility of their ripening very uncertain. At Malham the growing season is almost two months shorter than it is at York; it lasts from about the 15th of April to the 1st of November (Williams 1963; Manley 1956). This may mean that a harvest of some sort can be gathered, but the grain may not have time to ripen, so that it is unfit for seed corn, and may not even be edible. Persistent bad weather in the autumn may make harvesting very difficult. Wind or violent storms may knock the corn down, so that the birds are able to get to the grain before the harvesters. However, the corn may have been short-strawed, like some observed in Scotland by Dr Johnson, and as suggested by King (1970) for this region. The high rainfall of the region, normally over 50 inches (127 cm.) per annum at the moment, means that after clearance has taken place, the leaching process, always present to some degree even under grass cover, will be greatly intensified. At Malham the recorded totals of sunshine add up to about 1,130 hours per year (Manley 1956), which is 10-15% less than the totals for lower, inland stations. Cloud cover, which is more prevalent here than at lower altitudes, means that the crops depend more on diffuse than on direct radiation, at any rate in comparison with lowland sites. The relatively damp, overcast climate at Malham may account for the fact that here there is little difference between the land snails found in woodland and on grassland – in marked contrast to the situation in the chalk regions of lowland England (Cameron & Redfern 1972). According to Manley (1956) the upland wind-speed is approximately 150% of that for lowland regions, so shelter problems become correspondingly more important.

In general, cereals need at least 1,500 day degrees above 6° C (42.8° F) and for wheat 1,900 day degrees is a more realistic threshold (Symons 1963). Gregory's maps (1954) for accumulated temperatures, which are admittedly very generalized and based on a lapse-rate of 1° F for every 300 feet, show that this region is now within the 1,500-2,000 day-degree zone, making it in general difficult for oats and virtually impossible for wheat.

There is also the question of tolerance of neutral or acid soils. In Sweden, it has been shown (Russell 1961) that barley needs a soil pH of above 6. Some of the soils in the region under discussion would be inadequate, or only barely adequate, as far as pH levels are concerned.

Of course, there are differences in tolerance between cereals. Oats, which can be best harvested in an unripe state (Sanders 1958) and which tolerates pH levels down to 4.7 (Russell 1961:523), seems more appropriate for this region than barley, which seems to need a pH of over 6, and should be harvested when it is dead ripe; wheat seems to occupy an intermediate position with respect to these two factors.

The question of whether cereals will grow and ripen is one matter, that of whether the yield will be worth the effort is another. According to Thorne (1966:89), the yield is closely related to the leaf area after the ears emerge; the grain/leaf ratio is a measure of the photo-synthetic efficiency of the leaves in producing dry matter for the grain. Most of the variation within seasons, it is explained, relate to variations in radiation and temperature. It is these two factors, plus those of soil status and shelter, which are critical. It is known that dry-matter production of *Festuca-Agrostis* in Snowdonia falls off rapidly with increasing altitude, as the following figures (Perkins 1967) demonstrate:

1,200 ft (365 m.)	391 g. per square metre
1,600 ft (500 m.)	199 g. per square metre
3,000 ft (915 m.)	78 g. per square metre

Evidence from parallel situations in the past

It is known that cereals have been cultivated at high altitudes in the past, and that the height-range of human activities has fluctuated. Jones (1965) has pointed out that in north-west Wales during the period 1070-1300 the land was cropped at heights of up to 1,000 feet (305 m.) and the relatively warm conditions of the 1930s also witnessed an upward trend. Jones (1965) saw the Welsh data as evidence for a response to a similar favourable climatic phase in the period 1150-1300 (Lamb 1966:174). One Welsh site, Bwlch-y-Fign (Taylor 1973) has produced cereal pollen at 2,000 ft (610 m.), albeit in a sheltered natural amphitheatre, at a time during the mediaeval period. Graziers, too, seem to have been using the higher lands for both summer and winter grazing in the pre-1300 period, but afterwards only for summer grazing (Jones 1965:51).

Archaeological evidence provides some interesting, if inconclusive, data. It can be shown, for instance, that in north-east Yorkshire the barrows are distributed at a density of about 1 per square km. when they are on an 800-900 feet plateau, but are considerably less dense in an area of higher altitudes and steeper relief (Fleming 1971). It is hard to avoid the conclusion that the relationship between altitude and density of barrows here is not coincidental; the lower, flatter plateau perhaps permitted a greater occupation density, or alternatively such processes as leaching and iron-pan formation were slower here, allowing a longer duration of occupation.

A potentially even more interesting situation is that in Caernarvonshire (RCHM 1964:lix) where the barrows become increasingly frequent as one proceeds up the hillside, so that one-third of all the cairns in the county are found between 1,250 and 1,500 feet (380-455 m.). Above this level there is a sharp decline. These figures are to a large extent to be explained by the fact that many cairns are to be found in a restricted area, the hinterland plateau to the south of Penmaenmawr and Llanfairfechan, where steeply sloping land restricts the settlement areas to the narrow coastal strip or the 1,200 feet (365 m.) plateau. There is very little land on this particular coastal strip. It is highly probable that the upland plateau was a major area of economic activity, not simply a zone of transhumance in which burials were made. There is, as far as I know, no direct evidence of Bronze Age cereal farming here; but the same Royal Commission volume does record that settlement sites of their class IIa are also located in this altitudinal range, both on the northern coastal strip and further south where lower land was available. The Commissioners' description of them, and their illustrations, shows them to be very reminiscent of the informally-organized, high-altitude class of west Yorkshire:

> Characteristically, the settlements occur at a high level, almost invariably over 1,000 feet and often nearer 1,500 feet. They comprise an agglomeration of irregular enclosures of very variable size, bounded by walls of loose stones roughly heaped up. Small round huts, seldom more than 15 ft. in diameter, are scattered throughout the enclosures, generally though not invariably on the lines of the enclosure walls; sometimes they cluster in small groups. Small heaps of stone resembling cairns exist at some sites. (RCHM 1964:xcii)

The illustration of Cwm Ffrydlas shows a site that could easily be paralleled in west Yorkshire (RCHM 1964:xciii, Fig. 19). The Commissioners pointed out the absence of dating evidence for class IIa sites. They also referred to the unsuitability of the sites for arable cultivation under present-day conditions, and the possibility that they would have been exploited under better climatic conditions.

So it appears that both in west Yorkshire and Caernarvonshire there is evidence for past cultivation at altitudes of up to 1,600 feet (500 m.). In both areas, the typological distinctiveness of the sites diminishes as one climbs (this distinction, in Caernarvonshire, corresponds to the dichotomy between Gresham's (1963) Enclosed and Unenclosed Hut-groups). Leaving aside dating questions for the moment, it looks as if on the acid, podzolizing soils of the southern Pennines and north-east Yorkshire, early farmers were in difficulties above about 1,000 feet (305 m.), while in west Yorkshire and Caernarvonshire they could farm up to about 1,500 feet. This is probably a measure of the higher base-status of the soils in the latter areas and, in the case of Caernarvonshire, the effect of a maritime climatic régime, giving a less steep temperature-lapse rate.

Choice of field and settlement locations

As has been described above, the fields and settlements found at higher altitudes can best be classified on a topographic basis, rather than by morphology alone. This is because many of the sites have been placed, presumably deliberately, in locations where environmental difficulties are minimized.

The apron enclosures take advantage of geomorphic shelter. When the enclosures all lie close together along one linear scar, they are protected from only about 180° of the compass, but in some cases, where the scars form a more complex pattern and the enclosures are arranged sporadically among them, shelter from several different directions is provided. This would be important for stock, and if cereals were cultivated in these small enclosures it would ensure that, even in a bad summer, some of the crop would probably survive the effects of gales or freak storms.

Secondly, the fact that these enclosures are below scars and slopes would tend to make them receiving zones for lime-enriched colluvial soils;

this is a more important factor than chemical weathering in determining pH levels even in thin soils, since Carboniferous limestone weathers relatively slowly. Presumably the walls would help to concentrate this enrichment zone. If stock were periodically penned here, the enclosures would also be rich in phosphates. As Miller (1967) has pointed out, research shows that best results are obtained by fertilizing small areas intensively, since it is only in this situation that soil-status, earthworm populations and so on, can reach a critical threshold, above which fertility can be almost self-perpetuating.

Some apron enclosures slope in various directions and at various angles, allowing them to benefit from increased insolation in sunny seasons and probably, to some extent, counter-acting the general lateness of the onset of the growing season in this area. It is also possible that those apron fields where the scars are high would benefit from higher night-time temperatures as a result of re-radiation from the rock walls, an effect that is important, for example, in walled gardens (Manley 1952). The light-coloured cliffs would reflect light, as would the typical *Festuca-Agrostis* vegetation relative to other types (Manley 1952), so that conditions for crops grown here would be good. Sinker (1960) says specifically that, in the regions of the cliffs and screes, the south and south-west faces seem to enjoy a higher sunlight intensity, with plants above their normal altitudinal range.

The exposed fields on plateaux and edges would seem to have been laid out with regard to certain local advantages too. Many of them, today, lie on exposed pavements or include substantial areas of bare limestone; clearly this pavement-stripping must have occurred after the period of field use. The suggestion is that these fields were used when the soil cover was thin, and the cultivators were taking advantage of the eutrophic brownearths and brown rendzinas on the tops of the scars. These fields would not benefit from increased direct insolation in the early part of the season, as sloping sites would, but they would receive more direct radiation in mid-season, and – a factor which is very important here – the diffuse radiation which they would receive in cloudy conditions would be greater than that received in sheltered fields exposed to only half of the sky (Garnett 1939; Geiger 1966). However, these soils would warm up quickly in the spring, and in the average season this would be of more significance than their tendency to freeze for long periods in winter or their increased susceptibility to drought. Presumably, one disadvantage of these fields would be their exposed situation.

In seasons without extremes of weather these fields would probably prosper. However, in the long run, erosion might be expected to take its toll, especially if a plough was being used, which one might predict in view of the shallowness of the soils and the possibilities for maintaining the lime content by disturbing the B horizon. One would expect pavement to develop as a result of this erosion, and to creep back gradually from the edge, ultimately forcing the abandonment of the fields. Having inspected many of the sites, I am convinced that a major cause of pavement exposure has been early agriculture. This is an inescapable conclusion, given the number of cases where field walls and pavements occur together (see Appendix). It may be that some stripping occurred before field walls were developed; this is certainly the implication on a few sites where very short isolated lengths of walling are preserved.

On some of these sites the huts, too, are in exposed positions. This may be related partly to the need of commanding views (see above) but, in any case, the huts may have been for use in summer by those looking after the fields and keeping watch on the animals. In size, some of these compare very well with the small, single-person huts of the Scottish shielings.

Some fields are sited in hollows; in some cases, these partake of the walled-garden insolation effect; and others have impeded drainage, protecting crops from the worst effects of drought. Some of these field situations may be compared with those found on the Causses of southern France, where corn is grown nowadays in isolated patches, usually sited within natural hollows and depressions on the high, dry, limestone plateaux.

Thus, many of the west Yorkshire fields are sited with particular local advantages in mind. This is especially true at the higher altitudes; lower down, the fields cover large areas and run across varied terrain. The environment, as one would expect, seems to have been relatively restrictive at higher altitudes and relatively permissive at lower altitudes; early man reacted to this in a fairly sensitive manner.

In general, the strategy of growing cereals in

small patches, each possessing different natural advantages and vulnerabilities, would be a sound one, especially in situations where it was more important to avoid total crop-failure than to gamble in an attempt to maximize yield. This was certainly the strategy adopted in the eighteenth century in the Scottish outfields, another case where conditions for cropping were not good. Scottish farmers took advantage of small patches with local advantages, as Dr Johnson (1775:178-9) records of Skye: 'Some grass, however, grows here and there, and some happier spots of earth are capable of tillage . . . their corn grounds often lie in such intricacies among the craggs, that there is no room for the action of a team and plow.'

Near Inverness the outfield was cropped very sporadically, with oats and barley. 'Some cropped portions were small and scattered among the woods . . . the quantities sown at a time were extremely small, sometimes even less than a bushel . . . in 1774, 19 bolls of grain and peas were sown in 17 separate lots' (Symon 1959:126-7).

Problems of strategy, dating and explanation

I have discussed above the nature of the evidence for early cultivation in the region, and how the site locations were chosen to make the best of local difficulties. It may be helpful to consider one or two general points about high-altitude land use, if only in order to isolate suitable ways of approaching the problems of strategy and explanation. In the first place, the evidence cited above suggests that there are certain favoured situations for agriculture at high altitudes in this region, and that there is no reason to assume that early man saw the upper parts of his habitat as undifferentiated, or uniformly unsuitable for colonization. How far these sites are especially useful can be tested in the field with suitable techniques and instruments, and it is hoped to do this in the future. In any case, it may well be that, as in parts of Norway today (Utaaker 1968), the best zone for crop growth is one of intermediate altitude. Early man's concept of land utility may have centred on a core zone of land of medium altitude, whose limits may have varied from time to time and place to place; and land above and below this zone, which had various disadvantages, may have been used and settled in a more piecemeal manner, at any rate at first. Obviously the upper levels would have problems with climatic extremes; the lower ones might be badly drained and suffer from katabatic downflows of cold air, and so on. In places, of course, steep hillsides would impose a stark choice between the high plateaux and the valleys or coastal strips – or the choice of a form of land use including both zones. This may have been an important and rather deterministic factor in Caernarvonshire, and to a lesser extent in west Yorkshire. So, considerations of absolute altitude may be considered of less importance than the existence of favoured niches, in otherwise unpromising terrain, or the possibility that there are well-defined 'settlement zones', chosen for their environmental suitability or imposed by the local land-forms.

There are three general explanations that may be given for high-altitude cultivation of the sort discussed here: those involving climate; those involving demographic factors, such as population pressure; and those postulating some socio-economic factor such as, for instance, the demands of the Roman tax-gatherer. The situation is more complicated than this, partly because these variables are not necessarily independent and partly because there is also the perception or point of view of the farmers themselves to be taken into consideration.

Expansion to higher altitudes may have related to a phase or phases of better climate than that of today. It is possible to cite a number of occasions within the last millennium when man's response to short-term improvements was swift and sensitive (Lamb 1966), although unfortunately there are among them cases of circular argument where man's alleged response is used directly as evidence for the amelioration.

A Bronze Age, or more accurately a sub-Boreal, date has sometimes been suggested for upland field systems on climatic grounds. Manley (1952:232), specifically discussing sub-Boreal climate, says this:

> We have . . . seen that if in our uplands summer weather is predominantly anticyclonic the mean temperature deviates above the normal to a greater extent than in the lowlands. For example, if in a dry sunny summer month the mean in the lowland is, say 2° above normal, that on the high Pennines may be 3° above normal. Such an excess of temperature relative to the plains below would be just enough to raise the climatic tree line by five hundred feet or so compared with the present.

Unfortunately there is at the moment no easy way of deciding whether the high-altitude fields here relate to the generally better climate of the Bronze Age, or even the Neolithic period, or to a phase within the Iron Age or Romano-British period. There is inadequate excavational evidence on the dating question, so any dating must be provisional and speculative. The idea that population pressure led to colonization of marginal lands, including lands at high altitudes, has quite often been canvassed, and of course this process is not necessarily independent of climatic factors, since a better climate may have led to a higher survival rate and increased population numbers. At the moment, it seems pointless to speculate on whether the upland fields of west Yorkshire are evidence for population expansion in any given period. The data in this region are really not adequate; there is little pollen evidence and few of the kind of field monuments on which such tentative statements as those about population pressure are usually based.

It is also possible that some social system, either a Bronze Age or Iron Age chiefdom or the Roman state itself, may have been extracting a surplus, putting pressure on local agricultural systems. Once again, no conclusive argument can be adduced here on this point. Social considerations may have been, in some circumstances, more important than economic ones. One recalls the New Guinea farmers described by Clark (1971), who thought it important to re-use their ancestors' fields, which were at high altitudes, even though they knew the yields were less there. In this region the hill-fort of Ingleborough, built at 2,373 ft. (723 m.) on a very exposed hill-top and sited most inconveniently for either arable or pastoral purposes, is a reminder that, by the end of the prehistoric period, social factors were becoming increasingly important.

Future work

This study has shown that there is a need for more excavation on selected sites where dating evidence is likely to be obtained. There is a clear distinction between the extensive, well-organized sites at lower altitudes and the more fragmentary, less formal higher-altitude sites, but it is not clear whether the distinction is between the climatic regimes of the sub-Atlantic and sub-Boreal respectively, or how far the higher sites were carefully chosen under socio-economic pressures of some sort in, say, late Iron Age or Romano-British times. It may be that one or two sites were occupied more than once; at Dewbottoms (SD 913694) the rectangular huts clearly belong to a later period, while at Dawson Close (SD 865738) a round hut has been partially demolished to make a rectangular one. This latter site is similar, typologically and topographically, to Dewbottoms. It is possible, too, that the different degrees of weathering remarked on by Clayton (1966) may correlate with different types of settlement or field system. There are one or two clear cases (e.g. Gauber Limekiln Pasture, SD 765785) where the most 'primitive-looking' fields and huts are associated with heavily fragmented pavement though, in a situation when re-growth of vegetation may occur, a lightly weathered pavement is not necessarily evidence of a relatively recent field system. Clearly, the assistance of a karst geomorphologist would be needed to confirm these indications.

Other specialists in the field of topoclimatology and soil science could easily assess the relative advantage of some of the field sites. The advantages and disadvantages of certain fields and enclosures in terms of shelter, temperature, insolation and so on could be determined instrumentally and, although the soil status would be a more complex matter, some relative indications could be expected to emerge on analysis. Techniques of this sort, applied in specific locations of known agricultural activity, could be expected to by-pass the cruder and more problematical site-catchment analysis method which, in my opinion, is a very limited approach to early agriculture.

Finally, we need the co-operation of ecologists. Recent field-work, especially in this region, has convinced me that it is no longer adequate for the archaeologist to wander around on these sites armed with little more than knowledge of past excavation work, pollen analyses and the conviction that classification *via* site morphology is his main objective. One wonders, for instance, whether certain flora and fauna are sensitive at the present day to the same conditions as those required by man and his crops and animals. A number of the apron enclosures, for instance, are liberally sprinkled with mole-hills; the mole, at any rate in Snowdonia (Milner & Ball 1970) is significantly associated with freely drained mineral soils of pH greater than 4.0-4.5, usually more than one foot deep, and without a very stony matrix. In modern times they are attracted, perhaps by the arthropod populations, to sites giving a high return of sheep-dung. It is possible that if some of the apron enclosures were for stock, similar factors may have led to the original establishment of these colonies. In general one might expect, in a region where the soils are slightly acid in many places, that moles would pin-point the more lime-rich areas; Mellanby (1971:104) points out that mole activity tends, in upland regions, to follow the lines of roads laid with limestone chippings even when these run over peat.

Sometimes ancient field areas are favourite grazing spots even today. At SD 928676 the fields, visited in July 1973, were in a sheltered valley, and it was obvious that, perhaps because of the slightly warmer situation, sheep had been grazing more heavily here than elsewhere. Also the daisies here were extremely numerous, suggesting the possibility of increased lime in the soil (unless, of course, they represented a side effect of the grazing pressure). Above the site, where one or two huts were visible on a higher terrace, it was even possible to see where the cows had been recently lying, perhaps choosing a slightly warmer spot! Perhaps some of these effects are coincidental and it would, in any case, be presumptuous of an archaeologist to do more than note them and pass on. But it would be most interesting to have a list of animals and plants whose preferences might be similar to those of man at this altitude. After all, early man himself must have used ecological indicators, and it would be no bad thing for an archaeologist to develop a few similar indicators of his own that might, after experience, supersede instrumental measurements of a site's suitability for settlement. It is time, in fact, to do as Grahame Clark did at Star Carr and, with the help of ecologists, to develop a more balanced view of the place of man in ancient landscapes.

Summary

This paper considers the environmental context of the high-altitude fields and hut settlements of west Yorkshire, and the possible strategies of those responsible for their development. The main conclusions are as follows:

1. The well-organized, extensive field systems of the lower part of the range 800-1,600 feet (250-500 m.) above sea level should be distinguished from the more fragmentary remains of the upper part of that range from the points of view of typology, of relation to terrain and of cultivation difficulties.
2. The former group has produced evidence from Romano-British dating, while the date of the latter is strictly unknown. A similar situation obtains in north Wales.
3. It is impossible at the moment to arbitrate between macro-climatic factors, demographic factors and socio-economic pressures as possible causes of an upward expansion in cultivated land.
4. The upper fields can be divided in sub-groups based largely on specific types of location chosen for them; most of these sites possess characteristics which would modify the effects of altitude.
5. The correlation between fields and exposed pavements is high enough to allow the conclusion that agriculture was a principal agent in the uncovering of pavements.
6. Further work must involve environmental scientists in the elucidation of all these relationships.

Acknowledgments

I should like to thank the administrators of the Sheffield University Research Fund for financial assistance towards the cost of field-work; also Messrs A. King, K. Koolkin, J.A. Taylor and M. Zvelebil.

Appendix: Cases of association between field walls or huts and exposed limestone pavements (provisional list)

Grid Reference	*Site-name*	*Altitude (feet)*	*Comments*
SD 764786	Gauber Limekiln Pasture	1100	Several irregular huts and enclosures all near the north (front) edge of pavement
SD 791740-792733	Ringle Mill	1000	Many irregular enclosures stretching over ¾ km correlating very highly with pavement
SD 776729	Thieves Moss	1200	Most enclosures are of apron type, on grass; but a few walls overlie pavement
SD 728752	Raven Scar	1300	One possible hut and some heavily weathered fragmentary walls
SD 719766	Scales Moor	1200	One long isolated wall; large hut on grass
SD 775764	Selside Shaw	1200	Fragmentary walls, including one fairly complete field, amid scattered pavement
SD 776769	Bent Hill Rigg	1100	Hut group mostly on grass, but adjacent to pavement with hut and enclosure wall
SD 892647	Ing Scar Crag	1100	Isolated hut circle at rear of pavement
SD 898648	Malham Lings	1300	Fragments of walling on and off pavement; huts commonly just off rear edge
SD 865738	Dawson Close	1200	Several huts and fairly large fields, also in association with apron enclosures on grass
SD 902681	Middle House Pasture	1600	Various fields and enclosures occur to the south of the well known settlement. Most on grass, but some walls run across the pavement, along its edge, and between isolated sections of pavement
SD 903691	Cowside	1500	Fields with some exposed pavement within
SD 913694	Dewbottoms	1500	The 'B.A. farm' defined by Raistrick & Holmes (1962) has a few patches of pavement within the field area. Above the farm, to the south, is an extensive area of pavement, on which are two large fields. The back wall corresponds to the rear edge of the pavement
SD 933687	Lineseed Head	1500	Pavement bounded by an irregular wall, with other enclosures and one or two huts; the pavement/wall correlation is very striking
SD 938670	Tattersal Pasture	1500	A few small enclosures on front edge of pavement
SD 952691	Douky Bottom	1300	A group of plateau fields, apparently overlying an overgrown pavement
SD 993682	—	1100	Small enclosures on front edge, larger ones covering pavement at its southern end. Suggestions of two periods here
SD 990684	Hill Castles	1100	Very irregular small enclosures, frequently on pavement
SD 984693	Swineber Scar	1100	Small field walls and the fields themselves are being overgrown under low grazing pressure. They are associated with a heavily weathered pavement
SD 953649	Bordley	1300	Small enclosures and long walls in strong association with pavements
SD 906649	Abbott Hills	1300	A few small enclosures, edge fields and larger fields. Much of the area is now pavement

REFERENCES

Bullock, P. (1971) The soils of the Malham Tarn area. *Field Studies*, 3, 381-408.

Cameron, R.A.D. and Redfern, M. (1972) The terrestrial mollusca of the Malham area. *Field Studies*, 3, 589-601.

Clarke, W.C. (1971) *Place and People: an ecology of a New Guinean community*. London.

Clayton, K.M. (1966) The origins of the landforms of the Malham district. *Field Studies*, 2, 359-83.

Fleming, A. (1971) Bronze Age agriculture on the marginal lands of north-east Yorkshire. *Agricultural Hist. Review*, 19, 1-24.

Garnett, A. (1939) Diffused light and sunlight in relation to relief and settlement in high latitudes. *Scottish Geog. Mag.*, 55, 271-84.

Geiger, R. (1966) *The Climate near the Ground*. Cambridge, Mass.

Gregory, S. (1954) Accumulated temperature maps of the British Isles. *Trans. & Papers Inst. Brit. Geographers*, 20, 59-73.

Gresham, C.A. (1963) The interpretation of settlement patterns in north-west Wales. In Foster, I.L. and Alcock, L. (eds.), *Culture and Environment*, 263-79. London.

Holliday, R. and Townsend, W.N. (1967) Agriculture and soils. In Beresford, M.W. and Jones, G.R.J. (eds.), *Leeds and its Region*, 62-88. Leeds.

Hunter, R.F. (1962) Hill sheep and their pasture. *Jour. Ecology*, 50, 651-80.

Johnson, S. (1775) *A Journey to the Western Islands of Scotland*. London.

Jones, G. (1965) Agriculture in north-west Wales during the later Middle Ages. *Aberystwyth Symposia in Agricultural Meteorology*, Memo. 8, 47-51.

King, A. (1970) *Early Pennine Settlement*. Clapham, Yorks.

Lamb, H.H. (1966) *The Changing Climate*. London.

Manley, G. (1952) *Climate and the British Scene*. London.

Manley, G. (1956) The climate at Malham Tarn. *Ann. Rep. Field Studies Council*, 1955-6, 43-56.

Mellanby, K. (1971) *The Mole*. London.

Miller, R. (1967) Land use by summer shielings. *Scottish Studies*, 11, 193-219.

Milner, C. and Ball, D.F. (1970) Factors affecting the distribution of the mole (*Talpa europea*) in Snowdonia (north Wales). *Jour. Zoology*, 162, 61-9.

Perkins, D.F. (1967) The growth of plants in an upland environment. *Welsh Soils Discussion Group*, Report no. 8, 79-85.

Pigott, M.E. and Pigott, C.D. (1959) Stratigraphy and pollen analysis of Malham Tarn and Tarn Moss. *Field Studies*, 1, 84-101.

Raistrick, A. (1938) Prehistoric cultivations at Grassington, West Yorkshire. *Yorks. Arch. Jour.*, 33, 166-74.

Raistrick, A. (1939) Iron-Age settlements in West Yorkshire. *Yorks. Arch. Jour.*, 34, 115-49.

Raistrick, A. (1964) *Prehistoric Yorkshire*. Clapham, Yorks.

Raistrick, A. and Holmes, P.F. (1962) Archaeology of Malham Moor. *Field Studies*, 1, 73-100.

R.C.H.M. (1964) *An Inventory of the Ancient Monuments in Caernarvonshire III: West*. London.

Russell, E.W. (1961) *Soil Conditions and Plant Growth*. London.

Sanders, H.G. (1958) *An Outline of British Crop Husbandry*. London.

Sinker, C.A. (1960) The vegetation of the Malham Tarn area. *Proc. Leeds. Phil. & Lit. Soc., Sci. sect.*, 8, 139-75.

Symon, J.A. (1959) *Scottish Farming Past and Present*. Edinburgh.

Symons, L. (ed.) (1963) *Land Use in Northern Ireland* (Land utilization survey of Northern Ireland Cttee.). London.

Taylor, J.A. (1973) Chronometers and chronicles. *Progress in Geog.*, 5, 247-321.

Thorne, G.N. (1966) Physiological aspects of grain yield in cereals. In Milthorpe, F.L. and Ivins, J.D. (eds.), *The Growth of Cereals and Grasses*, 88-105. London.

Utaaker, K. (1968) A temperature-growth index – the respiration equivalent – used in climatic studies on the meso-scale in Norway. *Agricultural Meteorology*, 5, 351-9.

Williams, D.S.F. (1963) Farming patterns in Craven. *Field Studies*, 1, 117-34.

PAUL MELLARS

Settlement patterns and industrial variability in the British Mesolithic

Over the past seven or eight years considerable attention has been paid to the question of 'functional' patterning in prehistoric stone-tool assemblages. The best known of these studies are perhaps those of L.R. and S.R. Binford on the Middle Palaeolithic assemblages of Europe and the Near East (Binford & Binford 1966;1968) and those of F.C. Howell, J.D. Clark and others on the Acheulian industries of Southern Africa (Howell *et al.* 1962; Howell & Clark 1963; Isaac 1972). Even if the specific interpretations placed on the archaeological evidence have sometimes proved controversial, few prehistorians would nowadays deny the fundamental importance of this theoretical approach.

The aim of the present paper, therefore, is to look at British Mesolithic assemblages not from the view-point of 'cultural' or chronological variations but rather in terms of the varying activities undertaken at the different sites. No claim is made for priority in this direction. Important leads in this field have already been given by Professor Clark in his recent reassessment of the Star Carr investigations (Clark 1972) and also, in a more general way, in a series of stimulating papers published by the late W.F. Rankine on the Mesolithic industries of the Wealden area (Rankine 1949a; 1949b; Rankine & Dimbleby 1960). However, the large body of information which is now available on Mesolithic sites in Britain seemed to justify a consideration of this question in more general terms than has been attempted hitherto. The primary objective of the paper is in fact an empirical one: to collect together the scattered information available in the current literature on Mesolithic sites and to present this in such a way that the essential differences and similarities between the different assemblages can be readily assessed. The second objective is to put forward a number of tentative explanations for some of the more conspicuous patterns which emerge from this presentation. At the risk of offering simplistic solutions for inherently complex problems, these suggestions will at least provide a series of explicit 'models' which can be systematically tested – and modified – as further evidence comes to light.

1. Subsistence basis

While considerable attention has been paid to the role of hunting in the Mesolithic economy, rather less consideration has been given to other sources of food. The present remarks will be confined to the potential importance of (a) plant, and (b) coastal, resources in the Mesolithic food supply.

In the course of the *Man the Hunter* symposium several participants were at pains to point out that many of the present-day societies who are traditionally regarded as 'hunters' – and who indeed often regard themselves in this light – in reality obtain the greater portion of their food supplies from plants (Lee & DeVore 1968). Thus R.B. Lee (1968:33) has calculated that between 60 and 80 percent (by weight) of the food consumed by the !Kung Bushmen of South Africa is obtained from vegetable sources, while Woodburn (1968a:51) quotes a similar figure of 80 percent for the East African Hadza. Of particular interest in this context is Lee's observation that when the diet of non-agricultural communities is examined on a global scale the contribution of plant foods can be seen to increase in a more or less regular fashion as one moves from the poles towards the equator (Lee 1968:42-3). It is in fact only amongst groups occupying extreme arctic and sub-arctic environments that the hunting of mammals emerges as the dominant mode of subsistence activity. The obvious inference to be drawn from these observations would seem to be that amongst Mesolithic communities occupying the densely-forested regions of temperate Europe the collection of plant foods is likely to have made a substantial – if not dominant – contribution to the overall food supply.

Any attempt to assess the actual range of plant foods exploited by Mesolithic communities in Britain must inevitably rest more on speculation than on direct archaeological evidence. Useful lists of the wide range of edible plants potentially available in the Postglacial forests of Europe have been given both by Clark (1952:59-61; 1954:14; 1972:25-6) and by Dimbleby (1967:26-42). It will suffice here to point out that these lists include not only such obvious items as hazel nuts, blackberries, edible mushrooms etc., but also an extensive range of less obvious resources such as the inner bark of birch and pine trees, seeds of the yellow and white water lily, leaves of many species of herbs and grasses, and the roots, bulbs and rhizomes of a variety of both dry-land and aquatic plants. The idea that Mesolithic groups may have utilized a wide variety of plant foods is certainly in keeping with ethnographic observations; thus Lee (1968:34) records that a single group of Bushmen were observed to exploit at least 68 different species of plants on either a regular or casual basis, while Driver (1969:88-9) quotes a similar list of no less than 1,500 species for the various aboriginal Indian groups of North America.

Archaeological evidence for the consumption of plant foods by British Mesolithic groups is largely confined to a single resource – namely hazel nuts. While this fact undoubtedly reflects to a large extent the exceptional ability of hazel nut shells to survive in archaeological deposits (especially when burnt), there are grounds for thinking that this food resource did in fact play an important role in the economies of Mesolithic populations over large areas of north-west Europe. In Britain, identifiable remains of hazel nut shells have been found in association with Mesolithic artefacts in at least 20 different sites.[1] At most of the sites the remains occurred in small quantities (probably representing nuts which were accidentally burnt) but in at least three sites the remains occurred in quantities which appear to reflect exploitation on an extensive scale. Thus at the site of 'The Beacon', close to the Durham coast, a Mesolithic industry was recovered from a black deposit which was said to consist 'mostly of broken hazel nut shells' (Coupland 1948:2): Similarly Mercer (1970:181) has reported remains of approximately 1,000 hazel nut shells in his excavations at Lussa River on the Island of Jura (Argyll). Again, at the site Oakhanger VII in Hampshire, burnt and broken hazel nut shells were said to be scattered 'continuously' over the whole of the occupation floor (Rankine 1961:63).

The seasonal implications of hazel nuts on Mesolithic sites should perhaps be treated with caution. As Dimbleby has emphasized, the durability of hazel nut shells enables them to survive for long periods – possibly up to a year or more – after they have fallen to the ground (Dimbleby 1967:38). Thus in many areas Mesolithic groups may have been able to gather hazel nuts from the forest floor throughout the winter season. A more likely contingency, however, is that large stocks of nuts were built up during the autumn and deliberately stored for use during the winter months. Indeed, the major economic importance of hazel nuts to Mesolithic groups may well have been as a critical stand-by food resource for use during the winter season when food supplies in general were not only scarce but also subject to unpredictable fluctuations. (The latter would be especially true in the case of groups who subsisted throughout the winter primarily by the hunting of land mammals: Lee 1968:40.) Whether or not this is the case, the probability remains that hazel nuts were consumed at least to some extent throughout the winter season. Hence the mere presence of hazel nut shells on Mesolithic sites should not automatically be taken as an index of autumnal occupation.

The importance of coastal food resources in the Mesolithic economy is much more fully documented than that of plant foods (see Clark 1952:62-90). In addition to the direct evidence available from the Scottish shell-middens (Lacaille 1954:199-245; Mellars & Payne 1971; Coles 1971) the comparatively dense distribution of Mesolithic settlements along the whole of the western seaboard of Britain provides ample testimony to the economic potential of these coastal habitats. (The combined effects of the eustatic rise in sea level and crustal down-warping have of course removed traces of Mesolithic occupation from the greater part of the southern and eastern coasts of Britain.) As several writers have recognized, the overall concentration of food resources in these coastal situations may have been appreciably greater than that offered in almost any type of inland environment. Perhaps the most significant aspect of coastal economic resources, however, is their availability on a year-round basis. Even if the accessibility of sea fish and marine birds is influenced to some extent by seasonal factors, supplies of several species of molluscs (and perhaps seaweed?) remain readily available at all times of the year. In addition, any reduction in these resources as a result of winter weather conditions is likely to have been compensated for in many areas by the well-documented habit observed amongst present-day populations of red deer of congregating along stretches of coastline during the colder months of the year (Lowe 1966). All in all, therefore, coastal environments are likely to have offered exceptionally attractive economic prospects to Mesolithic communities during all seasons of the year.

2. The character and social implications of Mesolithic settlements

At the outset it should be pointed out that the concept of 'settlement' will be employed here with rather looser connotations than those usually implied by the use of this term in anthropological and archaeological literature. The term will be used here in the broad sense defined by Campbell (1968:15): 'a settlement is any place occupied by one or more individuals for one or more nights, for any purpose that falls within the ordinary, expected and predictable round of activities of the society in question'.

In view of the total absence of organic remains from all except a small handful of British Mesolithic sites, attempts to define the areas of settlements must rely on two kinds of evidence: (1) traces of structural features such as pits, post-holes, stone arrangements etc.; and, (2) the distribution of stone implements and the debris of stone tool manufacture. In theory other kinds of evidence could be employed – for example the analysis of phosphate content of soils – but in practice no attempt to apply such methods to Mesolithic sites in Britain has yet been made.

Where remains of living structures can be identified on occupation sites the definition of the limits of these structures is usually a straightforward procedure and calls for no special comment. The interpretation of artefact distributions, on the other hand, presents more difficult problems: social inferences based on this kind of evidence must proceed with more caution. In practice, however, the problems encountered in using the latter type of evidence are perhaps less serious than might be anticipated on theoretical grounds. In the cases where the distribution of stone tools and flaking debris have been accurately recorded (e.g. Star Carr, Flixton, Deepcar, Downton, Oakhanger Sites V and VII) it can often be seen that the artefacts exhibit a more or less uniform density over a fairly well defined area, and then decrease rather sharply beyond the limits of this area. Moreover, in the relatively few instances in which the distribution of retouched tools has been plotted separately from that of the flaking debris (Deepcar, Oakhanger Site VIII, Wawcott Site IV, Frensham Pond North Site) it is usual to find that the distribution of the finished tools corresponds closely with that of the general flint scatter. In cases such as these, therefore, the overall distribution of the artefacts does seem to allow a fairly accurate definition of the area in which the day-to-day 'domestic' activities of the community were carried out.

How far the areas of settlements defined on the basis of artefact distributions can be compared with those based on the dimensions of living structures is clearly a separate issue on which no general rules can be laid down. However it is interesting to observe that in the cases in which the dimensions of artefact distributions and structural features can be directly compared (notably at Star Carr, Deepcar, Low Clone and Broomhead Site 5) a surprisingly close measure of agreement can be discerned. Beyond the immediate confines of the British Mesolithic similar correlations have been observed at such sites as Pincevent in northern France and the cave site of Lazaret on the French Rivera (Leroi-Gourhan & Brézillon 1966; Lumley 1969). In view of these observations, therefore, there are perhaps grounds for hoping that settlement areas calculated on the basis of artefact scatters may not conflict too seriously with those based on the direct evidence of structural remains.

Of course the major problem encountered in attempting to make sociological inferences on the basis of artefact distributions arises from the difficulty of demonstrating that the whole of an area over which occupation debris is distributed was occupied at a single point in time. Evidence obtained from such sites as Oakhanger Site VII, Wawcott Site III and Thorpe Common demonstrates conclusively – if demonstration is needed – that certain favoured localities were visited on more than one occasion by Mesolithic groups.[2]

Thus the possibility must be allowed for that some of the larger Mesolithic sites represent not settlements of a large social group but simply palimpsests of repeated visits to the same locality by comparatively small social units. In the absence of living structures the only guidance on this point is provided by the detailed character of the artefact distributions themselves. Clearly, distributions which exhibit a sharply defined, concentrated and more or less circular pattern are more suggestive of a single episode of occupation than those which show a more diffuse and irregular form. Nevertheless it is apparent that any conclusions concerning the sizes of social groupings which rest entirely on the evidence of artefact distributions must be approached with some degree of caution.

Table 1 Approximate dimensions of some British Mesolithic sites, based on the observed distribution of stone implements and flaking debris

	Dimensions		*Estimated*		
	Length	*Breadth*	*Total area*	*Structural features*	*References*
TYPE I SETTLEMENTS					
Blubberhouses Moor	2.1 m	2.1m	3.3 m^2		Davies 1963
Dunford 'A'	2.4 m	2.4 m	4.5 m^2	? Roughly paved area	Radley *et al.* 1974
Dunford 'B'	2.4 m	2.1 m	3.9 m^2		Radley *et al.* 1974
Broomhead '5'	4.5 m	4.0 m	14.9 m^2	Linear setting of five stake holes	Radley *et al.* 1974
Sheldon	3.6 m	3.0 m	8.5 m^2	Rock crevice with stone 'wall'	Radley 1968
Thorpe Common	5.6 m	1.8 m	8.4 m^2	Rock-shelter with limestone wall	Mellars - unpublished
Kettlebury I	3.6 m	3.6 m	8.5 m^2		Rankine 1949a
Oakhanger VIII	4.2 m	2.1 m	8.8 m^2		Rankine & Dimbleby 1961
TYPE II SETTLEMENTS					
Deepcar	7.5 m	7.5 m(?)	44.0 m^2	Sub-circular stone structure	Radley & Mellars 1964
Mickleden '3'	7.5 m	7.5 m(?)	44.0 m^2		Radley & Marshall 1965
Iping Common	7.5 m(?)	7.5 m(?)	44.0 m^2	Roughly circular area of stained sand	Keef *et al.* 1965
Flixton I	8.0 m(?)	8.0 m	50.0 m^2		Moore 1950
Low Clone	13.6 m	5.5-2.4 m	54.5 m^2	Boomerang-shaped depression	Cormack & Coles 1968
Downton	8.5 m	8.5 m	60.0 m^2	Scattered stake-holes possibly associated	Higgs 1959
Oakhanger V	12.0 m	11.0 m	100.0 m^2		Rankine 1952
Thatcham I	13.5 m	12.0 m	116.0 m^2		Wymer 1962
Star Carr	16.5 m	14.5 m	185.0 m^2	Birchwood platform	Clark 1954
Oakhanger VII	16.5 m	16.5 m	210.0 m^2		Rankine & Dimbleby 1960
TYPE III SETTLEMENTS					
Morton	15.0 m	>10.0 m	>150.0 m^2	Multiple stake-hole arrangements	Coles 1971
Selmeston	>100.0 m	?	>2,000 m^2	Multiple 'pit-dwellings'	Clark 1934
Farnham	?	?	?20,000 m^2	Multiple 'pit-dwellings'	Clark & Rankine 1939

Typology of settlements

Reasonably full information bearing on the size and character of Mesolithic settlements is currently available from not more than 20-25 sites in Britain. Despite the limitations of the evidence it is nevertheless possible to observe a striking range of variation in the basic form and dimensions of the different sites. In a very provisional way, the settlements might perhaps be divided into three major types (Table 1).

Type I. This is represented by settlements which can be shown to occupy a very restricted area, not amounting to more than 10-15 square metres in total extent. Sites which can be assigned with reasonable confidence to this group include Dunford Bridge Sites A and B, Broomhead Site 5 and Blubberhouses Moor in the southern Pennines; Oakhanger Site VIII in Hampshire; Kettlebury Site I in Surrey; and the rock-shelter settlement of Thorpe Common in south Yorkshire. The definition of these sites rests largely on the evidence of artefact distributions although at two of the sites (Broomhead 5 and Thorpe Common) clear traces of structural features were also recorded. From the data summarized in Table I it will be seen that the largest of the Type I settlements (Broomhead 5) covers a total area of only 14.9 square metres, while three of the sites (Blubberhouses Moor and Dunford Sites A and B) amount to only 3-5 square metres. In the case of all these settlements, therefore, one seems justified in postulating residential groups of extremely limited size. It should perhaps be added that the numbers of artefacts recovered from the sites suggest that the occupations were in most cases comparatively short-lived.

Type II. These settlements are much larger than those described above – ranging between 44 and 210 square metres – and are defined on the basis of concentrated artefact distributions which exhibit a more or less uniform density over a well defined, regular area. Sites which appear to fall into this category include Downton, Oakhanger Sites V and VII, Deepcar, Star Carr, Flixton Site I, Thatcham, and Low Clone. In shape, the artefact scatters are usually more or less circular, although the elongated form recorded at Low Clone is clearly an exception to this general rule. Unambiguous evidence that these distributions provide an accurate reflection of the sizes of the social groups who occupied the sites is of course available only at the sites where well defined structural features are apparent (i.e. Deepcar, Low Clone and Star Carr). Nevertheless the rather sharply-defined, regular outlines exhibited by the majority of the sites would seem to provide some justification for this interpretation. Taking into account the evidence of both structural features and artefact patterns, residential groups substantially larger than those suggested by the Type I settlements may therefore be postulated for the majority, if not all, of the sites in question.

Type III. To this final group may be assigned sites characterized by artefact scatters which cover an extensive area but which show a marked tendency to concentrate at several localized points. The clearest examples of this pattern are provided by the multiple 'pit-dwelling' sites of Farnham and Selmeston in the Wealden area and by the recently-excavated coastal settlement of Morton in Fifeshire (Clark & Rankine 1939; Clark 1934; Coles 1971). The number of separate concentrations on these sites may be considerable. The total number of pits at Farnham has been estimated in the region of 40 (Rankine 1949a:44) and a similar number might well have existed at Selmeston (Clark 1934). No pits were identified at Morton, but the detailed distribution plans plotted by Coles (1971:321-41) suggest the existence of at least 10-20 localized occupation areas on this site. The well preserved traces of living structures identified at all three of the sites provide some insight into the character of the individual social units who occupied the settlements. The dimensions of the individual pits excavated at Farnham and Selmeston are comparable to those of the Type I settlements described above, and are likewise indicative of very small human groups. Even smaller areas are indicated by the individual artefact concentrations and stake-hole arrangements recorded at Morton. Evidently, the overriding problem at all of these sites is to know how many of the individual occupation areas were occupied at one and the same time. As Clark has emphasized, it would plainly be wrong to assume that all of the 40 or so pits represented at Farnham were occupied simultaneously (Clark & Rankine 1939:107). At the same time it seems unlikely that a site of this nature represents merely a succession of occupations by a single family group. Of the three types of Mesolithic settlement described here, therefore, these 'multiple-focus' sites would seem to present the most serious difficulties from the view-point of sociological interpretation.

Social implications

Ethnographic observations bearing on the relationships between the areas of settlements and the numbers of occupants seem too variable to provide any firm basis for calculating the absolute sizes of Mesolithic social groupings. Naroll's general estimate of 10 square metres of 'roofed living space' per individual would plainly make nonsense of the smaller Mesolithic settlements with total areas in the region of 3-5 square metres (Naroll 1962). Cook and Heizer (1968) have suggested a more plausible relationship which allows approximately 9-10 square metres for the first six or seven individuals, with a further 10 square metres for *each additional person*, although the social mechanisms which underlie this relationship are rather difficult to envisage. In any event, whether one proceeds on the basis of ethnographic observations or on the basis of more commonsense criteria it is evident that the smaller Mesolithic settlements belonging to the Type I form as defined above are unlikely to represent social units of more than five or six individuals; whether or not these groupings consisted of nuclear families or of more specialized 'task groups' – for example, male hunting parties – is clearly a separate issue which must be assessed on the basis of independent criteria. The larger settlements belonging to the Type II and Type III categories, on the other hand, are likely to represent social units equivalent to at least two or three nuclear families, and in some cases substantially larger groupings must be envisaged. Even Naroll's estimate of 10 square metres per person would predict group sizes of around 18-20 individuals for such sites as Star Carr and Oakhanger Site VII, while Cook and Heizer's formula would yield estimates in the region of 23-25 individuals for these occupations. These figures are in fact very close to those originally suggested for the Star Carr settlement in Clark's publication of 1954 (Clark 1954:12-16).

3. The influence of seasonal factors on economic activities and settlement patterns

In attempting to isolate some of the factors responsible for the observed variations in Mesolithic assemblages the influence of seasonally-patterned changes in food supplies, vegetation cover and, of course, climate deserve particularly close attention. The problem is evidently a complicated one, and the present attempt to examine the activities of Mesolithic groups under the broad headings of 'winter' and 'summer' settlements must inevitably represent an over-simplification. Nevertheless it is hoped that the observations which follow will provide a useful framework in which some of the more obvious functional patterning apparent in the tool assemblages can be assessed.

Factors influencing the location and character of winter settlements

In all societies inhabiting arctic and temperate regions of the world the winter season is likely to represent the period of greatest hardship from several points of view. In addition to the problem of coping with adverse climatic conditions, the winter season is generally characterized by a marked reduction in both the variety and the overall abundance of the food supplies available for exploitation. It would seem to follow from this that the winter months are likely to represent the period of the year in which the influence of environmental factors over the patterns of human behaviour is most effective – in the sense of allowing the minimum degree of freedom in the choice of alternative subsistence and settlement strategies. Consequently, relationships between human activities and environmental features at this time of the year should – at least in theory – be easier to discern.

Climatic factors. Climate exercises the most obvious and direct control over the patterns of winter settlement. The principal elements to be avoided were presumably low temperatures, high winds and heavy snowfall. The maximum protection in all of these respects would have been provided by locating settlements at the lowest possible altitude, and with the maximum natural protection from prevailing winds. For obvious reasons settlements at high altitudes would tend to be avoided, and the same is probably true of sites located on the exposed summits of hills and ridges. In many areas of Britain river valleys are likely to have provided the most congenial environments for winter settlements, especially if sites were chosen on the south-facing slopes of the valleys so as to obtain the maximum benefit from the low winter sun. Apart from the protection offered by the natural topography of the valleys, the existence of comparatively dense vegetation may have provided an additional element of shelter in these environments. As will be shown below, economic considerations may also have favoured the occupation of river valley environments during the winter season.

Food supplies. One of the most critical factors affecting the subsistence strategies of Mesolithic populations during the winter season must have been the marked scarcity of exploitable vegetable food resources. Virtually the only plant foods available for collection at this time of year were the roots and rhizomes of certain plants (especially aquatic species), together with a diminishing supply of fallen hazel nuts (and possibly acorns?) which could still be collected from the forest floor (Dimbleby 1967:37-8).

The virtual absence of vegetable foods meant that the overall food supplies accessible to Mesolithic populations during the winter season were sharply reduced – both in terms of variety and in terms of absolute abundance. Confronted by this situation the human groups were obliged to rely on the following sources to meet their subsistence requirements:

1. *Hunting.* The larger herbivorous mammals (red deer, roe deer, wild boar, aurochs etc.) can be regarded as an essentially constant food resource, more or less equally available for exploitation at all seasons of the year. In fact, reasons will be given below for thinking that the hunting of at least some of these animals may have been appreciably easier and more productive during the winter months than at other times of the year. Striking empirical support for the importance of hunting in the winter activities of at least one Mesolithic community is of course available from the site of Star Carr (Clark 1954).

2. *Fishing* in inland rivers and lakes can be regarded as another potentially year-round activity. In addition to the populations of strictly resident species, the economic potential of certain inland waters during the winter and early spring seasons may have been enhanced by the presence of migratory populations of trout and salmon which congregate in the upper reaches of certain rivers in order to spawn. The higher reaches of the Thames and its tributaries, for example, may well have served as the spawning grounds for these species.

3. *Coastal resources.* The importance of several coastal resources (molluscs, crustaceae, seaweed etc.) as perennial sources of food has already been stressed. The particular value of these resources lies not only in their relative abundance, but also in their predictability on a day-to-day basis. Attention has also been drawn to the behaviour observed amongst present-day populations of red deer of congregating along stretches of coastline during the winter months. All things considered, coastal habitats may have provided richer, and above all more dependable, supplies of food than those available in any of the other environments accessible to Mesolithic groups during the winter season.

4. *Stored foods.* The obvious reaction of human populations faced with seasonal fluctuations in food supplies is to build up a surplus of resources during the seasons of abundance and to preserve these in some way for consumption during periods of scarcity. Unfortunately, unequivocal evidence for the storage of foods is almost impossible to obtain from archaeological sources, but it has been pointed out that the rich harvests of hazel nuts which were available to Mesolithic groups during the early autumn season were particularly suitable for this treatment. The importance of food storage was probably greatest amongst inland communities who subsisted largely on meat throughout the winter season, since the hunting of large mammals is a notoriously unreliable subsistence activity, subject to large and unpredictable fluctuations in supply (Lee 1968:40; Woodburn 1968a:53). Storage of plant foods may also have served a more general need in ensuring an adequate supply of certain essential vitamins throughout the winter season.

Distribution of animal populations. From the preceding remarks it will be apparent that in many inland areas of Britain the bulk of the food supply throughout the winter season is likely to have been provided by the hunting of large mammals. The distribution and behaviour of these animals must therefore have played an important role in determining the patterns of human settlement at this time of year.

Whereas information on several of the animals exploited by Mesolithic groups is relatively sparse, we are fortunate in having a substantial body of data on the one species which is known to have been of particular importance to the Mesolithic economy – i.e. red deer (see Clark 1972; Jarman 1972). Systematic studies of present day populations of red deer in a variety of environments point to two general features of seasonally-regulated behaviour:

1. The existence of well-defined patterns of

movement between upland areas in the summer months and lowland areas in the winter (Flerov 1952:136-7; Ingebrigsten 1924; Schloeth & Burckhardt 1961; Lowe 1966; Darling 1937). The occurrence of these migrations evidently depends on the existence of fairly pronounced contrasts in relief, but as Clark (1972:31-2) has pointed out, such movements can reasonably be predicted amongst Mesolithic red deer populations in at least the major upland regions of the British Isles. Among the complex range of factors responsible for these seasonal migrations, depth of snowfall, disturbance by insects and, above all, distribution of food resources, seem to be the most important.

2. A general tendency for the red deer herds to disperse over extensive territories during the summer months and to congregate into much smaller areas during the winter season. Precise quantitative information on this point is difficult to obtain for European populations of red deer but studies of the closely-related American species (*Cervus canadensis*) suggest that the summer territories may be up to ten times as extensive as those utilized during the winter months (see Mellars 1975: Table 3). More general confirmation of the same pattern amongst European deer populations is provided by Ingebrigsten's (1924) study of red deer migrations in Norway, and by the recent studies of experimental red deer populations on the island of Rhum in the Inner Hebrides (Lowe 1966). The areas which are most frequently sought out by the deer for use as winter 'yards' appear to be stretches of low-lying river valleys which combine the maximum protection from adverse weather conditions with the maximum concentration of accessible food supplies. The effect of winter conditions is therefore to induce a much greater degree of stability and predictability in the distribution of the deer populations than that exhibited by the herds during the warmer months of the year.

Social groupings. Two aspects of winter food supplies have been stressed in the foregoing paragraphs: on the one hand the relatively *restricted range* of resources available for exploitation; and on the other hand the *concentrated distribution* of these resources in geographical terms. These two factors are of course to some extent interrelated, since a reduction in the variety of subsistence resources almost inevitably reduces the area over which the resources are found.

The combination of these two factors must have exerted a significant influence on the distribution and social groupings of the human populations themselves. This is certainly suggested by ethnographic studies on recent hunter-gatherer societies. Thus Birdsell (1968:234) writes:

> The type of food resourçe is perhaps the most important single determinant of local group size and composition. Where plant and animal resources are largely raised locally and comprise wide variety of forms, the size of the exploitive groups will be small, and figures tend to oscillate around an equilibrium value of 25 persons. . . . Where food resources are more concentrated, the dietary becomes more specialized and local group structure frequently changes. It should be stressed that this is not a consequence of increasing density, but rather a function of concentration. In such circumstances the average size of local groups may range between 50 and 100 individuals, and in some exceptional cases may reach several hundred persons.

Birdsell's remarks relate specifically to overall variations in food resources between different geographical areas, but there seems no reason why the same factors should not apply equally to seasonal fluctuations in food supplies. The mechanism linking group size and the distribution of food resources is of course a fairly obvious one. As Clark has recently emphasized (1972:24-8), the maximum size of social group supportable in any settlement is directly dependent on the quantity of food which can be obtained within a specific area of movement – what Higgs and Vita-Finzi (1972) have termed the 'catchment area' of the site in question. Hence concentration of food resources inevitably *facilitates* even if it does not *determine* the formation of comparatively large social aggregations.

It remains to point out that the formation of enlarged social units during the winter season may have been stimulated in a more positive fashion by two additional factors. In the first place it is likely that the need for *sharing* food resources was an important consideration amongst many Mesolithic communities during the winter months. For reasons already explained, this factor must have assumed its greatest importance amongst groups who depended for the greater part of their winter food supplies on the highly irregular and unpredictable products of hunting. The ability to 'average out' the individual successes and failures of a relatively large number of hunters may have had a critical bearing on the ability of such groups to survive over the winter season. Secondly, the threat of attacks from wolves and perhaps other predators may have provided a further inducement to the formation of large social groupings at this time of the year. It is well known from historical sources that the danger of such attacks is particularly acute during the winter months when the food resources of the predators themselves are in short supply. Evidently large social groupings would be in a stronger position to defend themselves from this source of danger than those divided into smaller, isolated units.

Factors influencing summer settlements

From what has been said so far it will be apparent that environmental factors are likely to have exerted much less control over the activities of Mesolithic communities during the summer half on the year than during the winter months. Faced with more abundant food supplies and more congenial climatic conditions the human groups were clearly in a position to exercise a much greater degree of choice with regard to such questions as the location and size of settlements, selection of different food resources, frequency of movement from one camp to another, and so on. Even at this season, however, it is likely that the behaviour of Mesolithic populations was guided by some general principles, of which the most important would appear to be as follows:

Climate. The most obvious consequence of summer weather conditions was to encourage the occupation of many areas and locations from which settlement had effectively been excluded by climatic factors during the winter months. This applies not only to settlements at high altitudes but also to sites located on the exposed summits of hills and escarpments. Indeed, there are grounds for thinking that the latter locations may have been deliberately chosen for settlement during the warmer months of the year because of their evident advantages as look-out points for observing the movements of game.

The inclination of Mesolithic groups to occupy high-altitude environments during the summer season may have been influenced in a more direct way by two additional factors. In the first place the character of the post-glacial 'climax' vegetation in many lowland areas may have acted as a powerful deterrent to human exploitation of these areas during the summer months. In this context one should think not only in terms of density of tree growth, but also in terms of heavy development of understorey vegetation (shrubs, immature trees, brambles etc.) which characterizes the forests developed on the richer clay soils of lowland Britain (see Tansley 1968:86-106). These factors are likely to have imposed significant limitations on the mobility of human populations at all seasons of the year, but the impact of vegetational conditions must have been especially severe during the summer season when the foliage of all forms of plant life was at the peak of its development. The obvious reaction on the part of human groups confronted by these conditions would have been to seek out areas where the natural vegetation was most open in character; in this respect the gritstone upland areas of northern and western Britain, and perhaps also the sandy heathland areas of south-east England, would have offered obvious attractions (Tansley 1968:106-7). A further deterrent to the occupation of low-lying habitats may have been provided by the attentions of mosquitos, midges and other biting insects in these areas. This is known to be one of the major factors which stimulates red deer and other animals to migrate into upland environments during the summer months (Darling 1937:131-46) and there is no reason to doubt that the same considerations proved equally persuasive to the human populations as well.

Food resources. The food supplies available to Mesolithic populations during the summer season are likely to have been characterized on the one hand by their abundance and on the other hand by their variety. The most significant factor in this connection, of course, was the appearance during the late spring, summer and early autumn months of a wide variety of plant foods. From a quantitative point of view, the richest supplies of vegetable foods are likely to have been available during the late summer and autumn, when the harvests of many varieties of fruits, nuts and berries come into season. The late spring and earlier part of the summer would have had rather less to offer in this direction (Dimbleby 1967:29-38).

Most of the other (i.e. non-plant) food resources exploited by Mesolithic groups during the winter season remained available in equal if not increased quantities throughout the summer months. The collection of birds' eggs may have made a significant contribution to the Mesolithic diet during the late spring, and at this time too the practice of capturing birds while they were on the nest may have proved an easy and profitable activity (Clark 1952:40-1). As already emphasized, the exploitation of both coastal and inland water resources should probably be regarded as an essentially year-round pursuit, capable of yielding substantial and dependable supplies of food at all seasons of the year. An obvious target for fishing activities along many rivers must have been provided by the regular migrations of salmon and trout to and from their winter spawning grounds. The timing of these runs varies a good deal according to local conditions but the principal migrations are usually in the months of May-June and August-September (Smythe 1964:52-62). As Clark has pointed out (1952:47), fishing for pike may also have assumed considerable importance during the spring and early summer months when the fish congregate in shallow inland waters in order to spawn.

The hunting of land mammals was presumably controlled not so much by variations in *abundance* as by variations in the *distribution* of the animals throughout the year. In many cases the greatly enlarged food supplies available to herbivorous species during the summer season leads to a dispersion of the animals over much larger territories than those occupied during the winter months. In the case of red deer, for example, it has been shown that the extent of summer territories may be up to ten times greater than the territories occupied during the winter season (*cf.* Mellars 1974). At the same time the animals tend to be more mobile in their habits – less 'hefted to the ground' – and frequently disperse into smaller herds. These behavioural characteristics must have influenced the ease with which the animals could be hunted, and perhaps also – as will be argued below – the social organization of the human groups themselves.

Settlement patterns. It remains to consider how far the comparatively relaxed economic and climatic circumstances experienced during the summer months are likely to have affected the social organization and overall settlement strategies of Mesolithic populations at this time of the year. Despite the obvious difficulties involved in such an attempt, two general suggestions may reasonably be made.

In the first place several factors are likely to have encouraged the formation of relatively small social groupings during at least part of each summer season. The most obvious factor in this connection was of course the variety and widespread distribution of the food supplies available at this time of the year. The ethnographic observations bearing on this issue have already been discussed in relation to the organization of winter settlements. The point emphasized by Birdsell (1968:234) is that the principal factor controlling the sizes of social groupings appears to be not so much the overall *abundance* of food supplies as the relative *concentration* of these supplies in geographical terms. By matching the distribution of human population as closely as possible to the actual distribution of food resources on the ground the human groups are able to reduce to a minimum the expenditure of time and effort involved in harvesting the resources. At the same time they are able to exercise the maximum degree of selectivity over the particular foods exploited. Thus the occurrence of widely distributed food resources can reasonably be said to 'encourage' the dispersion of hunter-gatherer populations into relatively small social units.

In the same context it should be recalled that two of the mechanisms which are thought to have favoured the formation of large social groups during the winter season would not operate – at least to the same degree – during the summer months. On the one hand the need for co-operative defence against predators was presumably less marked during the summer than during the winter season; and on the other hand the more abundant and predictable food resources available throughout the summer months probably obviated the need for extensive sharing of food. In both respects it would appear that summer conditions would have enhanced the viability of small social units.

Similar considerations to those discussed above may have encouraged more frequent movements on the part of human groups during the summer season. The variety of food resources exploited, the widespread distribution of these resources, and above all the increased mobility of the animal populations, would all seem to encourage this pattern of settlement strategy. A point which is relevant both to this issue and to the sizes of individual social units concerns the extent of the 'catchment areas' which could be exploited from particular sites. It could be argued, for example, that the development of exceptionally dense vegetation during the summer months would tend to reduce the areas which could be exploited economically from any settlement. Moreover, if it is assumed that most of the essential collecting of plant foods at this time of the year would be undertaken by women and children, this might have the effect of further reducing the overall areas which could be covered in the course of regular, day-to-day subsistence activities. (The mobility of women in hunter-gatherer societies is generally inhibited by the need to carry and look after young children.) Both of these factors would have had the effect either of reducing the size of the social unit which could be supported in any settlement or, alternatively, of increasing the frequency with which the groups were obliged to move from one settlement to another.

Finally, the point is worth recalling that the inclination of human groups to shift camp must have been influenced to a significant degree by the amount of time, energy and raw materials [illegible] tion of dwellings. [illegible] types of shelters [illegible] groups during the [illegible] ave imposed appreci- [illegible] nst frequent move- [illegible] required during the [illegible]

Ethnographic observations

The purely speculative nature of the foregoing discussion hardly requires emphasis. While there are grounds for hoping that many of the suggestions concerning the patterns of summer and winter settlement are valid in a broad sense, it is evident that the specific range of activities undertaken at any site, and the size of the social group involved in these activities, must depend to a large extent on purely local factors. This is especially true of settlements occupied during the summer season when the influence of environmental factors on the behaviour of human groups is likely to have been least effective. Thus it is possible to envisage that temporary concentrations of economic resources during the summer season might lead to the formation of social groupings much larger than those normally encountered at this time of year. Equally, localized conditions could no doubt lead on occasions to a division of the larger, winter-season settlements into more isolated, single-family groups. Thus the generalizations which have been offered can represent no more than general *tendencies* in the patterns of human behaviour which must inevitably have been subject to exceptions in response to purely localized circumstances.

Nevertheless it is encouraging to observe that many of the patterns which have been suggested here on the basis of theoretical considerations correspond fairly closely with those which have been observed by ethnographers amongst hunter-gatherer communities at the present day. In particular, the tendency for social groupings to fluctuate at different times of the year between large, multi-family aggregations and much smaller (usually single-family) units seems to be an almost universal feature of communities practising a nomadic, food-collecting way of life. Social as well as economic factors seem to contribute to this pattern. Thus the formation of large social units during some part of each annual cycle is usually essential not only to achieve the optimum exploitation of the available food resources but also to provide the social integration necessary for the organization of ceremonial activities, exchange of marriage partners and so on. Similarly, regular episodes of fission into smaller groups provide an important mechanism for the resolution of personal conflicts between individuals which might otherwise threaten the stability of the community as a whole (Woodburn 1968b:106; Turnbull 1968:135-7). In practice, however, the particular seasons of the year in which these episodes of fusion and fission occur appear to be controlled fairly closely by environmental factors. Thus several ethnographers have noted the tendency for large social aggregates to form during the periods of greatest scarcity of economic resources. In the case of groups occupying arid environments (for example the Bushmen and the Hadza) these large groupings generally coincide with the dry season when the food resources of both human and animal populations are in short supply (Lee 1968:31; Woodburn 1968b:104-6). In more northerly latitudes, on the other hand, the tendency to form extended, multiple-family settlements usually coincides with the winter season (Watanabe 1968:69-70). How far this kind of model can be applied to the documented settlements of Mesolithic communities in Britain will be examined further in the sections which follow.

4. Presentation of typological data

In compiling the data summarized in Table 2 the aim has been to focus attention on those features of British Mesolithic assemblages which are of most obvious significance from a 'functional' point of view. Before proceeding further, a few comments on the procedures adopted in tabulating the data should perhaps be made. In the first place it should be noted that the 'essential' tool percentages quoted in the table are based on a comparatively limited range of rather broad tool categories: microliths, scrapers, burins, 'saws' and transversely-sharpened axes or adzes. The criterion for excluding from this list such forms as 'awls', 'truncated flakes', 'notches' and 'miscellaneous retouched pieces' is essentially that of consistency. Even a casual acquaintance with the literature on Mesolithic sites suggests that the criteria adopted by different workers for identifying these forms varies within rather broad limits; examination of the illustrations which accompany excavation reports reveals that some workers are much more generous in allocating pieces to the 'awl' or 'truncated flake' category than others. To have included these forms in the calculation of the basic tool percentages would therefore have introduced unnecessary distortions into the frequencies of the better-defined types.

Similar considerations of internal consistency seemed to call for the use of equally strict definitions in identifying such forms as scrapers and burins. In both cases – so far as the published data permit – only 'typical' specimens manufactured on flakes and blades have been included in the totals used here. In some ways of course these strictures are unfortunate. No one would deny that irregularly retouched pieces, or even totally unretouched flakes, may have played an important part in the activities of Palaeolithic and Mesolithic societies (see Gould 1968). But the point hardly needs justifying that if comparative studies of this kind are to have any ultimate value, consistency in the presentation of the basic data must be the primary consideration.

The table includes information on two categories of 'waste-products' – cores and microburins. Frequencies of cores are expressed in terms of the numbers of cores per 100 'essential' tools, whilst frequencies of micro-burins (including 'mishit' and 'unfinished' forms) are similarly expressed in relation to the numbers of microliths. An obvious quantity to have included would have been the overall abundance of waste flakes in each assemblage; in practice, however, variations in the methods of excavation and recovery employed at different sites (for example, arbitrary decisions as to the minimum size of the waste flakes worth collecting in excavations) would appear to rob this parameter of much value. Data on the relative abundance of core-rejuvenating products might also have been included, but reliable information on this point is again available for only a limited number of the sites considered.

Leaving aside these methodological considerations, an examination of the data presented in Table 2 reveals a striking degree of variation in the relative proportions of different tool forms and waste products encountered at different sites. Perhaps the most conspicuous variations are apparent in the relative frequencies of microliths and scrapers. These variations in fact suggest an obvious division of the assemblages into three groups: (a) assemblages showing a strong dominance of microliths; (b) assemblages with more or less 'balanced' percentages of microliths and scrapers; and (c) assemblages with a clear dominance of scrapers. The possible significance of these and certain other variations in the assemblages are discussed in the sections below.

5. Type A: Microlith-dominated assemblages

A particularly well defined industrial pattern within the British Mesolithic appears to be represented by the assemblages listed in Table 3. The distinctive features of these assemblages are as follows:

1. Exceptionally high percentages of microliths among the retouched tools. In terms of the 'essential' tool frequencies defined above microliths account consistently for between 88 and 97 percent of the total tool inventory;
2. Correspondingly low proportions of all other tool forms; and
3. Perhaps most significant, extremely low percentages of typical flake and blade end-scrapers. Indeed, in several of the best documented assemblages (e.g. Dunford Site A, Oakhanger Site VIII and Thorpe Common) fully typical specimens of scrapers appear to be totally absent.

Other features of the assemblages call for less comment. Small blade-cores and micro-burins are in most cases well represented and presumably reflect the manufacture of microliths on the spot. Burins are usually present in small numbers. The only evidence for the use of axes on the sites is

Table 2 **Frequencies of principal tool forms and waste products in British Mesolithic assemblages. Frequencies of tool types are expressed as percentages of the 'essential' tool inventory, comprising microliths, scrapers, burins, 'saws' and transversely-sharpened axes. Frequencies of cores are calculated as numbers of cores per 100 'essential' tools. Micro-burin frequencies are expressed as numbers of micro-burins per 100 microliths. (N.B.: totals of scrapers and burins include only 'typical' specimens manufactured on flakes and blades; 'concave' and 'atypical' scraper forms are not included.) The assemblages marked* derive mainly from surface collecting; the remaining assemblages were obtained from excavations.**[3]

Site	*County*	*Source*	*Microliths*		*Scrapers*		*Burins*		*Axes/Adzes*		*'Saws'*		*Cores*		*Microburins*	
			No.	*%*	*No.*	*%*	*No.*	*%*	*No.*	*%*	*No.*	*%*	*No.*	*%*	*No.*	*%*
Abinger Common	Surrey	Leakey 1951	97	76.4	27	21.2	2	1.6	1	0.8	—	—	34	26.8	17	17.5
Barsalloch	Wigtownshire	Cormack 1970	8	42.0	9	47.4	2	10.5	—	—	—	—	85	447.0	—	—
The Beacon	Durham	Coupland 1939	73	82.0	15(?)	16.9	1	1.1	—	—	—	—	28	31.5	1	1.4
Blubberhouses Moor	W. Yorkshire	Davies	5	7.9	57	90.5	1	1.6	—	—	—	—	10	15.9	8	160.0
*Brigham	E. Yorkshire	Manby 1966	69	48.9	53	37.6	14	9.9	—	—	5	3.5	97	68.8	?	?
Broomhead 5	W. Yorkshire	Radley *et al.* 1974	37	90.0	4	10.0	—	—	—	—	—	—	14	31.2	8	21.6
Broxbourne	Hertfordshire	Warren *et al.* 1934	25	43.9	28	49.2	2	3.5	2	3.5	—	—	73	128.0	22	88.0
Dean Clough C	W. Yorkshire	Radley 1965	53	89.9	5	8.5	1	1.7	—	—	—	—	?5	?8.5	2	3.8
Deepcar	W. Yorkshire	Radley & Mellars 1964	68	59.6	37	32.5	8	7.0	—	—	1	0.9	17	14.9	102	150.0
Downton	Wiltshire	Higgs 1959	136	47.4	95	33.1	3	1.0	10	3.5	43	15.0	416	145.0	73	53.7
Dunford A	W. Yorkshire	Radley *et al.* 1974	41	93.2	—	—	3	6.8	—	—	—	—	7	15.9	13	31.8
Dunford B	W. Yorkshire	Radley *et al.* 1974	19	90.5	?	?	2	9.5	—	—	—	—	5	23.8	2	10.5
*Farndale Moor	N. Yorkshire	Radley 1969	58	88.0	2	3.0	3	4.5	—	—	3	4.5	25	37.9	3	5.2
Farnham	Surrey	Clark & Rankine 1939	690	75.5	181	19.8	26	2.8	15	1.6	1	0.1	1137	124.3	446	64.7
Flixton I	E. Yorkshire	Moore 1950	78	29.5	165	62.5	19	7.2	2	0.8	—	—	131	49.6	32	41.0
Freshwater West	Pembrokeshire	Wainwright 1959	—	—	219	90.1	24	9.9	—	—	—	—	704	289.0	4	?
Iping Common	Sussex	Keef *et al.* 1965	108	90.8	10	8.4	1	0.8	—	—	—	—	55	46.2	26	24.1
*Iwerne Minster	Dorset	Higgs 1959	165	39.2	210	50.0	2	0.5	37	7.6	12	2.9	963	229.0	15	9.1
Kettlebury I	Surrey	Rankine 1949a	4	18.2	18	81.8	—	—	—	—	—	—	8	36.4	2	50.0
Kettlebury II	Surrey	Rankine 1949a	41	93.2	3	6.8	—	—	—	—	—	—	13	29.5	37	90.2
Lealt Bay, Jura	Argyll	Mercer 1968	1283	84.5	217	14.3	18	1.2	—	—	—	—	129	8.5	250	19.5
Lominot I & II	W. Yorkshire	Radley & Mellars 1964	44	57.2	31	40.2	2	2.6	—	—	—	—	20	26.0	22	50.0
Low Clone South	Wigtownshire	Cormack & Coles 1968	30	46.1	21	32.4	14	21.6	—	—	—	—	47	72.3	—	—
*Lyne Hill	Northumberland	Raistrick 1933	45	42.0	56	52.4	6	5.6	—	—	—	—	34	31.8	?	?
*Mauley Cross	N. Yorkshire	Radley 1969	229	95.0	8	3.3	2	0.8	—	—	2	0.8	49	20.3	?	?
Mickleden 1-4	W. Yorkshire	Radley & Marshall 1965	28	66.7	12	28.6	1	2.4	—	—	1	2.4	9	21.4	15	53.6
*Misterton Carr	Nottinghamshire	Buckland & Dolby 1973	44	48.4	36	39.6	7	7.7	2	2.2	2	2.2	72	79.1	?	?
Morton	Fife	Coles 1971	226	26.8	518	61.3	101	11.9	?	?	—	—	280	33.2	49	21.7
Oakhanger V	Hampshire	Rankine 1952	1281	46.1	1052	37.9	1	0.04	1	0.04	444	16.0	705	25.4	346	27.0
Oakhanger VII	Hampshire	Rankine & Dimbleby 1960	1458	37.4	1927	49.4	—	—	2	0.05	512	13.1	1047	26.8	?	?
Oakhanger VIII	Hampshire	Rankine & Dimbleby 1961	28	93.3	—	—	2	6.7	—	—	—	—	19	63.4	—	—
Peacehaven	Sussex	Higgs 1959, Calkin 1924	69	39.4	88	50.3	—	—	10	5.7	8	4.6	83	47.4	8	11.6
Pike Low I	W. Yorkshire	Radley & Marshall 1965	31	50.9	29	47.5	1	1.6	—	—	—	—	8	13.1	11	35.5
Prestatyn	Flintshire	Clark 1938	65	81.3	15	18.7	—	—	—	—	—	—	26	32.5	10	15.4
Rocher Moss I	W. Yorkshire	Radley 1965	30	91.0	2	6.1	1	3.0	—	—	—	—	?5	?15.2	2	6.7
*Sandbeds	W. Yorkshire	Cowling & Mellars 1973	47	27.5	79	46.2	45	26.3	—	—	—	—	214	125.0	14	29.8
Selmeston	Sussex	Clark 1934	130	71.0	40	21.8	2	1.1	?	?	11	6.0	165	90.1	27	20.8
Star Carr	E. Yorkshire	Clark 1954	248	27.0	326	35.4	334	36.3	7	0.8	5	0.4	292	31.8	27	10.9
Thatcham I-III	Berkshire	Wymer 1962	285	57.0	129	25.8	57	11.4	10	2.0	19	3.8	265	53.0	72	25.3
Thorpe Common	S. Yorkshire	Mellars-unpublished	63	94.0	—	—	4	6.0	—	—	—	—	16	23.9	7	11.1
*Upleatham I	N. Yorkshire	Brown *et al.* 1974	29	50.9	24	42.1	4	7.0	—	—	—	—	174	306.0	7	24.1
Warcock Hill N.	W. Yorkshire	Radley & Mellars 1964	60	60.6	32	32.3	5	5.1	—	—	2	2.0	20	20.2	23	38.4
Warcock Hill S.	W. Yorkshire	Radley & Mellars 1964	21	61.9	12	35.3	1	2.9	—	—	—	—	9	26.5	17	81.0
Wawcott IV	Berkshire	Froom 1963	18	64.3	10	35.7	—	—	—	—	—	—	20	71.5	3	16.7
*White Gill	N. Yorkshire	Radley 1969	837	96.7	18	2.1	6	0.7	—	—	4	0.5	117	13.5	53	6.3
White Hill North	W. Yorkshire	Radley 1965	71	92.2	6	7.8	—	—	—	—	—	—	?7	?9.1	16	22.5
*Windy Hill 5	Lancashire	Radley 1965	61	88.4	5	7.2	2	2.9	—	—	1	1.4	?	?	5	8.2
Windy Hill 3	Lancashire	Radley & Mellars 1964	33	50.7	24	37.0	8	12.3	—	—	—	—	18	27.7	27	82.0

Table 3 **Type A assemblages. Frequencies of tools and waste products are calculated as in Table 2. Assemblages obtained by surface collecting are marked with an asterisk. References as in Table 2.**

Site	*Estimated area of site in square metres*	*Micro-liths %*	*Scrapers %*	*Burins %*	*Saws %*	*Axes/adzes %*	*Cores %*	*Micro-burins %*	*Total 'essent-ial' tools*
UPLAND									
Broomhead 5	14.9	90.0	10.0	–	–	–	31.2	21.6	41
Dunford A	4.5	93.2	–	6.8	–	–	15.9	31.8	44
Dunford B	3.9	90.5	?	9.5	–	–	23.8	10.5	21
Rocher Moss	? 8.0	91.0	6.1	3.0	–	–	?15.2	6.7	33
Dean Clough C	?	89.9	8.5	1.7	–	–	?8.5	3.8	59
* Windy Hill 5	?	88.4	7.2	2.9	1.4	–	?	8.2	69
White Hill	?12.0	92.2	7.8	–	–	–	? 9.1	22.5	77
* White Gill	?	96.7	2.1	0.7	0.5	–	13.5	6.3	865
* Mauley Cross	?	95.0	3.3	0.8	0.8	–	20.3	?	241
* Farndale	?	88.0	3.0	4.5	4.5	–	37.9	5.2	66
LOWLAND									
Thorpe Common	8.4	94.0	–	6.0	–	–	23.9	11.1	67
Oakhanger VIII	8.8	93.3	–	6.7	–	–	63.4	–	30
Kettlebury II	?	93.2	6.8	–	–	–	29.5	90.2	44
Iping Common	?44.0	90.8	8.4	0.8	–	–	46.2	24.1	119

provided by a number of characteristic axe-sharpening flakes from the site of Iping Common (Keef *et al.* 1965).

The greatest element of variety in the composition of the assemblages is apparent in the shapes of the microliths from the different sites. A particularly striking feature recorded at many of the sites is a pronounced bias in favour of one particular microlithic form. Thus the assemblages from such sites as Broomhead 5, Oakhanger VIII and Thorpe Common show a strong emphasis on small scalene triangles; while the assemblages from Dunford Bridge Site B, Rocher Moss I and Farndale Moor show an equally marked bias in favour of narrow rod-like forms. Again, at the site of White Hill small trapezoidal forms are dominant. Iping Common appears to be the only site belonging to this 'microlith-dominated' group in which 'non-geometric' microliths (chiefly obliquely blunted points) predominate.

Thus the overall impression created by the tool assemblages is one of marked industrial specialization. This appears to be indicated on the one hand by a heavy dependence on a single tool category (i.e. microliths), and on the other hand by the limited variety apparent in the shapes of the microliths themselves. Viewed in functional terms the assemblages appear to reflect a strong bias in favour of primary subsistence activities (presumably hunting) and against the usual range of 'maintenance' or 'domestic' activities (e.g. skin preparation, bone working etc.).

Site locations. The majority of the assemblages under consideration derive from settlements on the present-day moorland areas of the Pennines and north-east Yorkshire. In both areas the sites generally occur above the 1,000 foot (305 metre) contour, and frequently occupy prominent, exposed positions which command extensive views over the surrounding country. That assemblages of this type are not restricted to high altitude environments, however, is indicated by the sites of Thorpe Common, Oakhanger VIII, Iping Common and Kettlebury II. Thorpe Common is a rock shelter cut into the Magnesian Limestone formation in south Yorkshire; the remaining sites of Oakhanger, Kettlebury and Iping Common lie at heights ranging from 70 to 100 metres on the Lower Greensand belt in the counties of Hampshire, Surrey and Sussex respectively. Thus the sites can be seen to occur in at least two or three contrasting types of environmental location.

Size and character of settlements. Information on the dimensions of the settlement sites which have yielded Type A assemblages is limited but appears to form a consistent pattern. The striking feature is the very small size recorded for the majority of the sites. The sites of Dunford A, Dunford B, Broomhead 5, Oakhanger VIII and Thorpe Common can be shown to occupy total areas ranging from 3.9 to 14.9 square metres, and belong clearly to the category of 'Type I' settlements as defined in Section 2 above. The more tentative dimensions quoted for the sites of Rocher Moss I, White Hill and Kettlebury II would appear to place them in the same group. For all of these settlements social units approximating in size to that of a single nuclear family can therefore be postulated.

Clear traces of living structures are recorded from only three of the sites. At Thorpe Common a continuous setting of limestone blocks placed parallel to the back wall of the rock-shelter can presumably be interpreted as the foundation of some kind of tent or hut-like structure. An elongated arrangement of five stake holes at Broomhead Site 5 might similarly have supported a skin tent, or alternatively some form of wind-break. And at Dunford Bridge Site B the floor of some kind of living structure appears to be represented by a roughly oval area of stone paving. The remainder of the sites appear to have yielded no definite traces of structures although, of course, certain kinds of tents or lightly constructed huts might well have existed without leaving any enduring archaeological traces. Most of the sites showed evidence of hearths located either within or immediately adjacent to the main areas of flint distribution.

Seasonal indications. Unfortunately, any form of direct evidence bearing on the season of occupation of the various sites under discussion is entirely lacking. Nevertheless a case can be made out for thinking that at least some, and most probably the majority, of the sites were occupied primarily during the summer months. It has already been argued, on both climatic and economic grounds, that sites located above the 1,000-foot contour on the Pennines and north Yorkshire moors are more likely to represent summer than winter-season settlements, and the general lack of evidence for substantial living structures on these sites would appear to add further weight to this impression. A point of more general significance is the conspicuous scarcity of flint scrapers in the assemblages from both the upland and lowland sites. If one accepts the conventional interpretation of these implements as skin-working tools, their variable occurrence on Mesolithic sites might well be of seasonal significance. The need for animal skins – both for use as clothing and as coverings for dwellings – was presumably much greater during the winter than during the summer half of the year, and it is reasonable to assume that this fact would be reflected in the amount of skin working undertaken at different times of the year. Thus the scarcity of conventional scrapers on the sites under discussion might well be seen as a direct reflection of summer-season occupation.

Lastly, it is worth recalling that the overall impression created by the sites, of comparatively short-lived settlements occupied by very small social groups, would accord well with the theoretical model of summer-season settlements outlined in section 3 above.

Whether or not all the sites can be explained in these terms it is clearly impossible to say. The naturally sheltered location of the Thorpe Common site, coupled with the evidence of a substantial living structure, might seem more in keeping with a winter than a summer settlement, and in this context the occurrence of at least one fragmentary hazel nut shell on the site might also be significant. For the remainder of the sites, however, the bulk of the available evidence would seem to point rather strongly in favour of occupation during the warmer months of the year.

6. Type B: 'Balanced' assemblages

The assemblages assigned to this grouping contrast with those discussed in the preceding section in two major respects:

1. The occurrence of consistently lower proportions of microliths amongst the retouched tools – invariably lower than 85 percent and usually within the range 30-60 percent; and

2. The occurrence of higher percentages of typical flake and blade scrapers – consistently

Table 4 Type B assemblages. Frequencies of tools and waste products are calculated as in Table 2. Assemblages obtained by surface collecting are marked with an asterisk. References as in Table 2.

Site	*Estimated area of site in square metres*	*Micro-liths* %	*Scrapers* %	*Burins* %	*Saws* %	*Axes/adzes* %	*Cores* %	*Micro-burins* %	*Total 'essential' tools*
UPLAND									
Deepcar	44	59.6	32.5	7.0	0.9	–	14.9	150.0	114
Warcock North	?>100	60.6	32.3	5.1	2.0	–	20.2	38.4	99
Warcock South	?>40	61.9	35.3	2.9	–	–	26.5	81.0	34
Lominot	?	57 2	40.2	2.6	–	–	26.0	50.0	77
Windy Hill 3	?>42	50.7	37.0	12.3	–	–	27.7	82.0	65
Pike Low	?	50.9	47.5	1.6	–	–	13.1	35.5	61
Mickleden	44	66.7	28.6	2.4	2.4	–	21.4	53.6	42
LOWLAND									
Star Carr	185	27.0	35.4	36.3	0.4	0.8	31.8	10.9	920
Flixton I	50	29.5	62.5	7.2	–	0.8	49.6	41.0	264
*Brigham	?	48.9	37.6	9.9	3.5	–	68.8	?	141
*Misterton	?	48.4	39.6	7.7	2.2	2.2	79.1	?	91
*Sandbeds	?	27.5	46.2	26.3	–	–	125.0	29.8	171
*Upleatham	?	50.9	42.1	7.0	–	–	306.0	24.1	57
Broxbourne	?50	43.9	49.2	3.5	–	3.5	128.0	88.0	57
Thatcham	116	57.0	25.8	11.4	3.8	2.0	53.0	25.3	500
Wawcott IV	?	64.3	35.7	–	–	–	71.5	16.7	28
Oakhanger V	100	46.1	37.9	0.04	16.0	0.04	25.4	27.0	2779
Oakhanger VII	210	37.4	49.4	–	13.1	0.05	26.8	?	3899
Downton	60	47.4	33.1	1.0	15.0	3.5	145.0	53.7	287
Peacehaven	?>100	39.4	50.3	–	4.6	5.7	47.4	11.6	175
*Iwerne Minster	?	39.2	50.0	0.5	2.9	7.6	229.0	9.1	421
Morton	>150	26.8	61.3	11.9	–	?	33.2	21.7	845
Low Clone	54.5	46.1	32.4	21.6	–	–	72.3	–	65
Barsalloch	>50	42.0	47.4	10.5	–	–	447.0	–	19
*Lyne Hill	?150	42.0	52.4	5.6	–	–	31.8	?	107
TYPE 'B1'									
Farnham	?20,000	75.5	19.8	2.8	0.1	1.6	124.3	64.7	913
Selmeston	>2,000	71.0	21.8	1.1	6.0	x	90.1	20.8	183
Abinger	?	76.4	21.2	1.6	–	0.8	26.8	17.5	127
Prestatyn	?	81.3	18.7	–	–	–	32.5	15.4	80
The Beacon	?	82.0	16.9	1.1	–	–	31.5	1.4	89
Lealt Bay	>30	84.5	14.3	1.2	–	–	8.5	19.5	1518

higher than 14 percent and usually between 25 and 50 percent.

Within this rather broad grouping the assemblages listed in the lower part of Table 4 should perhaps be recognized as a separate sub-group. The characteristics of these assemblages (Type 'B1') are essentially intermediate between those of the Type B assemblages proper and those of Type A discussed above; microlith frequencies are found within the range 70-85 percent, while scraper frequencies are between 14 and 22 percent. This sub-group comprises two interesting groups of sites: on the one hand the well-known 'pit-dwelling' settlements of Farnham, Abinger Common and Selmeston in the Wealden area; and on the other hand the coastally-oriented settlements of Prestatyn in Flintshire, Lealt Bay on the Island of Jura and 'The Beacon' in Durham. Despite the clear predominance of microliths in the tool inventories from these sites, the assemblages contrast with those assigned to the 'A' grouping in the occurrence of a definite and numerically significant end-scraper element. As will be seen shortly, certain other features of the sites suggest that the overall affinities of these assemblages lie closer to the Type B than to the Type A grouping.

Other features of the Type B assemblages may be noted briefly. Percentages of flake and blade burins are for the most part comparable with those recorded in the Type A assemblages, although it may be significant that at three of the sites (Star Carr, Low Clone and Sandbeds) burin percentages rise appreciably higher than those encountered in any of the assemblages belonging to the latter grouping. Frequencies of cores show a wide range of variation, although it may again be significant that at seven of the sites (Farnham, Downton, Iwerne Minster, Broxbourne, Sandbeds, Barsalloch and Upleatham) percentages rise much higher than those recorded in any of the Type A assemblages. Transversely-sharpened axes are undoubtedly better represented in the assemblages under review than in the Type A grouping; typical axes and/or axe-sharpening flakes are represented in 14 of the 31 Type B assemblages, as compared with only one of the 14 assemblages assigned to the former group. The unusually high frequencies of flint saws recorded at Downton and Oakhanger Sites V and VII may also be referred to in this context.

Variations in the shapes of microliths encountered in different assemblages must clearly be explained to some extent in chronological terms (Mellars 1973; Jacobi 1973). Sites belonging to the earlier stages of the British Mesolithic appear to be characterized by a comparatively limited range of microlithic shapes from which the smaller 'Geometric' or 'Narrow Blade' forms are entirely lacking. The assemblages from such sites as Star Carr, Flixton, Broxbourne and Thatcham clearly fall into this category, and the same is probably true of the 'Broad Blade' assemblages from Deepcar, Warcock Hill, Pike Low and other sites in the southern Pennines. If attention is focused on the later, 'Geometric' industries, however, it would appear to be a valid generalization that the assemblages which have been assigned to the Type B grouping show a greater degree of variety in the shapes of the microliths than is encountered in the Type A assemblages. Whereas the assemblages belonging to the latter group generally show a heavy bias in favour of one particular microlithic form (usually scalene triangles, micro-rods or trapezoids), the Type B assemblages almost invariably exhibit a comparatively wide range of microlithic shapes comprising both geometric and non-geometric forms. This variability can be observed most strikingly in the assemblages from such sites as Farnham, Selmeston, Downton, Peacehaven and Iwerne Minster in southern England, but the same diversity can be seen on a more limited scale at Prestatyn, Lealt Bay, Upleatham and Lyne Hill.

In general, therefore, the composition of the microlithic forms seems to reinforce the rather 'generalized' impression conveyed by the assemblages under consideration. Viewed in functional terms the assemblages suggest an emphasis not only on hunting activities but also on a variety of more 'domestically' oriented tasks.

Location of settlements

The environmental locations from which the Type B assemblages derive may be grouped broadly under three headings:

1. *Lowland habitats in southern and eastern England.* This group includes the sites of Star Carr, Flixton, Brigham, Misterton Carr, Sandbeds, Broxbourne, Thatcham, Wawcott IV, Farnham, Selmeston, Abinger, Downton, Iwerne Minster, Peacehaven and Oakhanger. A striking feature is the number of sites which occur either in river valleys (Thatcham, Waw-

cott, Sandbeds) in or proximity to lakes (Star Carr, Flixton, Oakhanger, and possibly Brigham and Misterton). All of the sites are located below the 200-metre contour.

2. *Coastal habitats in northern and western Britain.* These include the sites of Prestatyn, Low Clone, Barsalloch, Lealt Bay, Morton, Lyne Hill and The Beacon.

3. *Upland habitats in the central and southern Pennines.* In this group must be included the sites of Warcock Hill ('North' and 'South' sites), Windy Hill Site 3, Lominot, Pike Low and Mickleden, all of which lie well above the 1,000-ft. (305m) contour. On balance the site of Deepcar (situated at 500 ft. O.D. on the eastern margin of the Pennines) should probably be included in this group rather than in the group of lowland settlements (Radley and Mellars 1964).

Thus it can be seen that the Type B assemblages occur in a range of environments which is rather wider than that represented by the Type A assemblages. Perhaps the most interesting feature which emerges is the strong representation of Type B assemblages at coastal sites; it is worth recalling that this type of settlement location does not appear to be represented – at least to judge by the published evidence – among the assemblages belonging to the Type A grouping.

Size and character of settlements

The available information relating to the dimensions of the settlements which have yielded Type B assemblages is summarized in Table 4 and the social implications of this evidence have been discussed in an earlier section. The main point to be noted here concerns the relatively large sizes attained by many of the settlements in question. The majority of the sites for which adequate information is available can be shown to cover areas of at least 50 square metres and in several cases (e.g. Farnham, Star Carr, Morton, Oakhanger sites V and VII) occupation areas appreciably larger than this figure have been recorded. In social terms these sites are likely to represent settlements of at least two or three family groups; whether or not the more extensive sites represent social groupings much larger than this is, for reasons already explained, difficult to ascertain.

The contrast between these settlement dimensions and those recorded for the sites yielding Type A assemblages is impressive. As already noted the latter sites rarely exceed ten square metres in total area and appear to represent settlements of much more limited social groupings – probably of the order of single families in most cases. The largest of the Type A settlements (Iping Common) appears to be roughly comparable in size to the smaller of the Type B sites (e.g. Deepcar and Mickleden) but the overall contrast between the two groups of sites is nevertheless sufficiently marked to merit attention.

Clearly defined traces of living structures are recorded from six of the sites under consideration. The well known 'pit-dwellings' excavated at Farnham, Selmeston and Abinger Common consist of roughly oval or sub-rectangular depressions ranging in length from 4.3 to 8.2 metres and generally excavated to a depth of between 0.6 and 1.2 metres below ground level; two post-holes were found in association with the Abinger pit dwelling, while a single post-hole was associated with one of the Farnham pits (Clark & Rankine 1939; Clark 1934; Leakey 1951). A very different kind of structure seems to be implied by the elongated 'boomerang-shaped' hollow identified at Low Clone South in Wigtownshire (Cormack & Coles 1968). This showed a maximum length of 13.6 metres, a maximum width of 5.5 metres and an average depth of 0.6 metres; traces of stake holes were detected at three points inside the hollow, but whether or not the whole of the scooped area is likely to have been covered by a single structure is clearly open to speculation. Evidence for a hut or tent structure at Deepcar took the form of a roughly circular arrangement of stones approximately 7.5 metres in diameter, with traces of a smaller setting of stones in the interior (Radley & Mellars 1964). Finally, excavations at Morton in Fifeshire revealed a series of rather small arrangements of stake holes (2.0-3.0 metres in diameter) interpreted by the excavator as supports for either windbreaks or lightly-constructed huts (Coles 1971).

Seasonal indications

The seasonal status of several of the sites under consideration has been discussed recently by Clark (1972:33-7) in connection with his reappraisal of the Star Carr investigations. Clark suggested that the 'Broad Blade' assemblages from such sites as Deepcar, Warcock Hill and Pike Low in the southern Pennines might well represent the summer encampments of early Mesolithic communities who spent the colder months of each year in the adjacent areas of the lowlands. The arguments advanced by Clark for this interpretation concerned on the one hand the elevated and exposed position of the majority of the sites, and on the other hand the well-documented behaviour exhibited by present-day populations of red deer of migrating between lowland areas in the winter and upland areas in the summer. Although there is at present no means of verifying this explanation of the Pennine assemblages, the climatic and ecological arguments in favour of the interpretation are evidently persuasive.

For the remainder of the sites which have yielded Type B assemblages, however, much of the current evidence would seem to point in the direction of winter, rather than summer, occupation. The relevant considerations may be summarized as follows:

1. In the first place, the location of the majority of the sites seems in keeping with the idea of winter occupation. In the case of inland sites it has already been suggested that settlements located along the edges of rivers and lakes would have offered the best available protection from winter weather conditions and – possibly more important – that these areas are likely to have served as the refuge areas in which herds of red deer and other animals congregated during the colder months of the year. Winter fishing may also have played an important part in the economic functions of these settlements.

In the case of coastal settlements it is likely that the year-round availability of maritime food resources was the major consideration. In addition to the obvious supplies of molluscs, crustaceae etc., it has been pointed out that these areas are again likely to have provided the winter feeding areas for substantial populations of red deer – at least along the margins of the upland zone of Britain. From the view-point of climatic conditions settlements located on the western coastline (Prestatyn, Low Clone, Barsalloch, Lealt Bay) would presumably have enjoyed a more congenial environment than those situated along the eastern sea-board (Morton, Lyne Hill, The Beacon).

2. More direct evidence of seasonal occupation is provided by the widespread occurrence of hazel nut shells at the sites under review. Remains of hazel nuts have in fact been found in association with Type B assemblages in at least nine separate sites (Star Carr, Thatcham, Farnham, Selmeston, Oakhanger, Morton, Lealt, The Beacon and Prestatyn) and at three of these sites (The Beacon, Oakhanger and Thatcham) the remains appear to have occurred in substantial quantities. The seasonal implications of this evidence are debatable, but reasons have been given for thinking that in many cases hazel nuts may have served as a major source of stored food for use throughout the winter period. In any event, judged on a more empirical level, the frequent occurrence of hazel nuts in association with Type B assemblages, as compared with their virtual absence from sites yielding Type A assemblages, must be seen as a significant point of contrast between the two groups of settlements.

3. Attempts to interpret living structures in seasonal terms present obvious difficulties, and it is salutary to recall that at the one Mesolithic settlement in Britain where winter occupation can be conclusively demonstrated (i.e. Star Carr) no trace of any kind of artificially-constructed shelter could be detected (Clark 1954). In the case of the semi-subterranean dwellings identified at Farnham, Selmeston and Abinger, however, a fairly strong case can be constructed on the basis of cross-cultural ethnographic observations in favour of specifically cold-season occupation (Clark & Rankine 1939:101-6). In the light of the evidence from Star Carr it would clearly be wrong to assume that sites with less substantial traces of living structures (e.g. Low Clone or Morton) *cannot* represent winter-season settlements.

4. The possibility of making seasonal inferences from the composition of the flint assemblages themselves has already been touched on in the discussion of Type A assemblages. It has been pointed out that the Type B assemblages contrast with those of Type A in suggesting a broader and less specialized range of economic activities. Perhaps the most important point to be recalled in this connection is the strong representation of scrapers in the Type B assemblages, which might well be seen as a response to the increased need for animal skins – for use as clothing, blankets and tent-coverings – during the winter season. The relatively high frequencies of burins recorded at the sites of Star Carr, Sandbeds and Low Clone might also be of some significance in this context; thus Clark has recently put forward the suggestion that the

primary function of burins lay in the working of red deer antler, and therefore that the highest percentages of these tools are to be expected on sites occupied during the late autumn and winter months when the antlers of red deer stags are in the best condition for tool manufacture (Clark 1972:34-5).

5. Finally, it is pertinent to refer again to the theoretical considerations relating to the patterns of winter versus summer-season settlements outlined in section 3 of this paper. It will be recalled that several factors – social as well as economic – appear to favour the formation of relatively large social aggregates during the winter season, followed by a division of these larger groupings into smaller units during the summer months. Assessed in these terms, the comparatively large areas exhibited by the majority of the sites which have yielded Type B assemblages would seem to accord better with the hypothetical model for winter-season settlements than with that postulated for sites occupied during the summer portion of the year.

7. Type C: Scraper-dominated assemblages

This grouping is represented by a small but interesting series of three assemblages from the sites of Blubberhouses Moor in west Yorkshire, Kettlebury Site I in Surrey and Freshwater West in Pembrokeshire. The striking feature which characterizes the tool assemblages from all three of the sites is the occurrence of exceptionally high proportions of flake and blade scrapers – ranging between 90 percent at Freshwater West and 82 percent at Kettlebury I (although it must be remembered that the latter percentage is based on a collection of only 22 'essential' tools). The three sites can best be described individually (Table 5).

The Blubberhouses Moor site lies at a height of 1,050 feet (320 metres) in the central Pennines. Excavations by J. Davies (1963) revealed that the entire site was confined to an area of only 36 square feet (3.3 square metres), with no traces of either hearths or obvious structural features. In addition to scrapers the assemblage comprises five microliths, a single flake-burin, four 'core-burins', eight micro-burins and seven cores. According to Davies, the large quantities of fine chipping debris recovered from the site suggest that the scrapers were probably manufactured on the spot. Approximately 6 g. of broken and charred hazel nut shells were found in association with the artefacts.

The site of Kettlebury I is located on the Lower Greensand formation of west Surrey at a height of approximately 300 feet (91 metres) O.D. The excavations carried out by W.F. Rankine (1949a: 31-3) suggest that this site again occupies a fairly restricted area, probably amounting to no more than 8-9 square metres. Groups of Carstone blocks found around the periphery of the flint scatter might represent either anvils for flint working, or conceivably traces of some kind of living structure. The total assemblage recovered from the site is a very small one, comprising 18 scrapers, four microliths, two micro-burins and eight cores. The small quantity of flaking debris represented on the site (approximately 350 pieces) reinforces the impression of a very brief occupation.

The site excavated by G.J. Wainwright at Freshwater West on the Pembrokeshire coast represents a third contrasting type of settlement location (Wainwright 1959). The site at present lies only a few metres above sea level, and the occurrence of substantial numbers of mussel, limpet and whelk shells in apparent association

Table 5 **Type C assemblages. Frequencies of tools and waste products are calculated as in Table 2. All of the assemblages derive from excavations. References as in Table 2.**

Site	*Estimated area of site in square metres*	*Microliths %*	*Scrapers %*	*Burins %*	*Saws %*	*Axes/ adzes %*	*Cores %*	*Micro-burins %*	*Total 'essential' tools*
Blubberhouses Moor	3.5	7.9	90.5	1.6	–	–	15.9	160.0	63
Kettlebury I	8.5	18.2	81.8	–	–	–	36.3	50.0	22
Freshwater West	20.0	?	90.1	9.9	–	–	289.0	?	243

with the flints suggests that the occupation cannot have been far removed from the Mesolithic coastline. The site in this case appears to be more scattered, possibly representing repeated visits over a period of time. The comparatively large assemblage includes over 200 scrapers, 24 burins, four micro-burins, and no less than 704 discarded cores. The occurrence of 11 stone 'limpet scoops' on the site represents an element encountered sporadically on Mesolithic sites along the whole of the western coastline of Britain. Despite the absence of typical microliths, the Mesolithic age of this assemblage seems well documented.

The tool assemblages from these three sites appear to reflect the performance of a rather limited and specialized range of activities in which the preparation of animal skins played an important – and possibly dominating – role. The manufacture of microliths evidently played some part at all of the sites, although this activity was apparently much less important than at any of the sites discussed hitherto. In the case of two of the sites (Blubberhouses Moor and Kettlebury) there is evidence that the social groups responsible for these activities were very small, and the occupations appear to have been of short duration.

The only evidence which bears directly on the seasonal occupation of the sites is provided by the fragmentary hazel nut shells from Blubberhouses Moor. If one accepts that sites located above the 1,000-foot contour are unlikely to have been occupied during the peak of the winter, this evidence might well be taken as a true indication of occupation during the autumn season. Such an interpretation would also accord well with the overall character of the tool assemblage. Thus the heavy predominance of scrapers in the tool inventory could be seen as a direct reflection of the intensive working of animal skins in anticipation of the increased need for skin clothing, tent covers etc. during the approaching winter months.

Whether or not the same explanation can also be applied to the sites of Kettlebury and Freshwater West must remain open to speculation, but there is nothing in either the location or the character of the settlements which conflicts with the idea of autumn or early winter occupation. The relatively strong element of burins in the Freshwater West assemblage (9.9 percent) might provide some further support for this view (Clark 1972:34-5). In any event, whatever the true seasonal status of the sites, the assemblages in question provide evidence for an interesting and distinctive variant of the British Mesolithic which appears to stand clearly apart from those represented by the assemblages discussed in the preceding sections of this paper.

8. Functional contrasts between the earlier and later phases of the Mesolithic

A detailed discussion of chronologically-patterned changes in the British Mesolithic is outside the scope of the present paper, and would in any case be hampered by the relatively limited number of accurately dated sites. The present remarks will be confined to a number of rather general observations which bear specifically on the 'functional' aspects of the assemblages.

With regard to the earlier stages of the Mesolithic one is struck primarily by the essential uniformity of the assemblages recovered from the different sites. The majority of the assemblages fall into the category of 'balanced' (Type B) assemblages as defined above. This is true not only of the assemblages from lowland sites such as Star Carr, Flixton, Broxbourne and Thatcham, but also of those from the Pennine localities of Warcock Hill, Windy Hill, Lominot, Pike Low etc. In this case, as already pointed out, it would appear that the uniformity in the composition of the assemblages embraces settlements occupied during both the winter and summer months. The only clear exception to this pattern is provided by the assemblage from Iping Common which can be attributed to the earlier phase of the Mesolithic on both typological and palynological grounds and which belongs clearly to the category of 'microlith dominated' (Type A) assemblages (Keef *et al.* 1965).

The later Mesolithic assemblages on the other hand exhibit a much greater degree of variability. The majority of the Type A assemblages can be attributed with some confidence to the second half of the Mesolithic, while Type B assemblages are represented at such sites as Lyne Hill, Barsalloch, Downton and Farnham. Clear examples of Type C ('scraper-dominated') assemblages appear to be represented by the finds from Blubberhouses Moor and Freshwater West. The impression of typological variability is reinforced further by the striking diversity apparent in the shapes of the microliths recovered from the different sites (see Section 5 above). Some possible explanations for this industrial complexity in seasonal and environmental terms have already been suggested, but the reasons why this complexity should be more marked in the later than in the earlier phases of the Mesolithic are by no means easy to discern.[4]

One final point which calls for comment concerns the well documented changes in the shapes of microliths which separate the later from the earlier Mesolithic developments in Britain. As already pointed out, the later phase of the British Mesolithic (from perhaps 6,500 B.C. onwards) is marked by the appearance of a range of small 'Geometric' or 'Narrow-Blade' microlithic forms which contrast sharply with the earlier 'Broad-blade'/'Non-Geometric' types (Mellars 1973; Jacobi 1973). A significant point in considering the functional implications of this change is the fact that at several sites (e.g. Farnham, Selmeston, Prestatyn) these new forms can be seen to occur *alongside* the earlier types in contexts which leave no doubt that both the 'Broad-Blade' and 'Narrow-Blade' forms were manufactured simultaneously by a single human group.

Functional interpretation of specific microlith shapes is a notoriously difficult issue for which hardly any direct evidence is available. There are however fairly strong grounds for thinking that the comparatively large, simple forms which characterize the earlier Mesolithic assemblages represent primarily the tips and barbs of wooden arrows. The fortunate discovery of a complete arrow-shaft at Lilla-Loshult in southern Sweden, with two microliths (an elongated triangular form and an obliquely blunted point) still in position provides unambiguous support for this view (Clark 1954:103). Interpretation of the smaller geometric types which characterize the later stages of the Mesolithic poses more difficult problems. However, the fact that these smaller forms occur *in addition to* the earlier types in several contexts may provide some grounds for thinking that they relate to projectile heads of a basically different form. Perhaps the most plausible explanation of these pieces, therefore, is that they represent the insets for elongated, multiple-barbed spear-heads analogous to – and most probably replacing – those manufactured from bone and antler during the earlier stages of the Mesolithic. Three observations would seem to provide some support for this interpretation:

1. The majority if not all of the barbed bone and antler projectile heads so far recovered from *inland* localities in Britain appear to date from the first half of the Mesolithic. They have so far been discovered in datable contexts at only three British sites (Star Carr, Skipsea and Leman and Ower banks), but typological analogies – particularly with dated examples on the continent – suggest strongly that the stray finds from such localities as Brandesburton, Catfoss, Royston, Battersea and Wandsworth can be assigned to either the Pre-Boreal or Early Boreal stages of the Post-Glacial (Clark & Godwin 1956, Louwe Kooijmans 1971). The only examples of bone and antler missile heads which can at present be assigned to the later stages of the Mesolithic are the biserially-barbed, 'Azilian'-like forms from the west Scottish shell-middens, but the overall distribution of these pieces suggests that they are associated with specifically coastal activities (Mellars 1970:345). Apart from these coastal discoveries, therefore, evidence for the manufacture of projectile heads from bone and antler materials during the second half of the British Mesolithic would appear to be lacking.

2. The shape and size of many of the Narrow-Blade microlithic forms would seem to accord well with the view that they represent the functional equivalents of the small pointed barbs encountered on the earlier Mesolithic bone points. Without entering into speculative discussions concerning the possible methods of hafting different microlithic types, it might be suggested that the small scalene triangles, sub-triangles and trapezoidal forms would be particularly suitable for use in this context. It is therefore interesting to note that these types appear to represent the numerically dominant element in a large proportion, if not the majority, of the later Mesolithic industries of Britain.

3. Lastly, some empirical support for these suggestions is provided by a number of discoveries of localized clusters – or in some cases linear arrangements – of the microlith forms in question in circumstances which suggest that they formed part of a single weapon. The best-known discovery of this type is the one recorded by Francis Buckley at White Hill in the central Pennines (Petch 1924:29), but similar discoveries have been reported from at least two further sites in the Pennines (Warcock Hill North Site and Green Crag Slack), from Beeley Moor in north Derbyshire and from Broxbourne in Hertfordshire.[5] All of these discoveries appear to relate to microliths of either triangular or trapezoidal form. Similar evidence involving a different Narrow-

Blade type is perhaps provided by Buckley's discovery of a localized concentration of 70 rod-like microliths on his Site 4 on Warcock Hill.[6]

The advantages to be gained from constructing multiple-barbed spear-heads in the manner suggested above are fairly easy to visualize. On the assumption that the microliths were set chiefly into wooden shafts, adoption of this method of production would allow not only a greater economy in the use of bone and antler materials, but also – in all probability – a considerable saving in the time and effort involved in the manufacturing process. In view of the inevitable high rate of loss of hunting projectiles, both of these considerations are likely to have assumed some importance.

Whether or not all of the smaller microlithic forms can be explained in these terms is clearly impossible to say. The wide range of variation in the shapes of microliths is one of the most striking features of the later part of the Mesolithic, and the possibility should certainly be kept in mind that some of the Narrow-Blade types were mounted either singly or in small numbers as the heads of light arrows or darts. The observations made by Woodburn (1970:17-31) on the wide variety of arrow-types employed by the present day Hadza of East Africa provide a clear warning against the dangers of over-simplified interpretations in dealing with evidence of this kind.

9. Conclusions

It is necessary to conclude this study by drawing attention to certain inherent limitations in the evidence considered. The fact that stone tool assemblages represent only a small fraction of the total material equipment of any hunter-gatherer society is a commonplace of prehistoric research and requires no further emphasis here. Two further features which are likely to introduce a significant element of distortion into the archaeological record, however, are perhaps less widely recognized. In the first place it is pertinent in this context to recall the observations made by J.M. Campbell in connection with a study of recently-abandoned settlements of Alaskan Eskimo groups. To quote Campbell (1968:18):

> We must recognize that the archaeological record is likely to be selective not only in respect to the kinds of artefacts that survive, but also in respect to the kinds of sites that can be recognized. Tuluaqmiut settlements of Type II, III, IV and VI are fundamental components of the way of life, and information derived from Type I and V alone gives a biased picture. However, only the latter types normally possess sufficient cultural debris to permit discovery by archaeologists centuries or millennia after their abandonment. This fact is not always fully recognized by specialists in Palaeo-Indian or Palaeolithic cultures; on the contrary, known sites are likely to be taken as representative of settlement patterns of these early hunting groups.

Applying Campbell's observations to the British Mesolithic we must therefore allow for the possibility that only sites which were occupied for a fairly substantial period – possibly amounting to several weeks – are likely to have found their way into the archaeological literature. Sites occupied on a more ephemeral basis may remain largely if not entirely invisible from the prehistorian's point of view.

The second element of distortion is likely to result from an over-representation of hunting equipment in the surviving archaeological material. The bulk of the distinctive artefact types which are normally recognized on Mesolithic sites – microliths, scrapers, burins, micro-burins – appear to be related directly either to the hunting of land animals, or to the processing of raw materials derived from animal carcases. The implements employed in other activities – for example the collection and processing of vegetable foods – may be either unrecognizable as intentional tools amongst the material recovered from occupation sites, or alternatively not specifically identifiable as Mesolithic forms. In either case we must recognize that settlements devoted largely or entirely to the pursuit of non-hunting activities are likely to be significantly under-represented in the current store of published information on Mesolithic sites.

REFERENCES

Binford, L.R. and Binford, S.R. (1966) A preliminary analysis of functional variability in the Mousterian of Levallois facies. *Amer. Anthro.*, 68, Pt. 2, 238-95.

Binford, S.R. and Binford, L.R. (1968) Stone tools and human behaviour. *Scientific American*, 220 (4), 70-84.

Birdsell, J.B. (1968) Some predictions for the Pleistocene based on equilibrium systems among recent hunter-gatherers. In Lee and DeVore (eds.), 1968, 229-40.

Brown, D.R., Goddard, R.E. and Spratt, D.A. (1975)

Mesolithic settlement sites at Upleatham, N.R. *Yorks. Arch. Jour.* (forthcoming).

Buckland, P.C. and Dolby, M.J. (1973) Mesolithic and later material from Misterton Carr, Notts. *Trans. Thoroton Soc.*, 77, 5-33.

Calkin, J.B. (1924) Pygmy and other flint implements found at Peacehaven. *Sussex Arch. Coll.*, 65, 224-41.

Campbell, J.M. (1968) Territoriality among ancient hunters: interpretations from ethnography and nature. In Meggers, B.J. (ed.), *Anthropological Archaeology in the Americas*, 1-21. Washington.

Clark, J.G.D. (1934) A late Mesolithic settlement site at Selmeston, Sussex. *Ant. Jour.*, 14, 134-58.

Clark, J.G.D. (1938) Mesolithic industries from tufa deposits at Prestatyn, Flintshire, and Blashenwell, Dorset. *P.P.S.*, 4, 330-4.

Clark, J.G.D. (1952) *Prehistoric Europe – the Economic Basis.* London.

Clark, J.G.D. (1954) *Excavations at Star Carr.* London.

Clark, J.G.D. (1972) *Star Carr: a case study in bio-archaeology*. Addison-Wesley Modular Publications No. 10, Reading, Mass.

Clark, J.G.D. and Godwin, H. (1956) A Maglemosian site at Brandesburton, Holderness, Yorkshire. *P.P.S.*, 22, 6-22.

Clark, J.G.D. and Rankine, W.F. (1939) Excavations at Farnham, Surrey (1937-38). *P.P.S.*, 5, 61-118.

Cook, S.F. and Heizer, R.F. (1968) Relationships among houses, settlement areas, and population in aboriginal California. In Chang, K.C. (ed.), *Settlement Archaeology*, 79-116. Palo Alto, California.

Coles, J.M. (1971) The early settlement of Scotland: excavations at Morton, Fife. *P.P.S.*, 37, 284-366.

Cormack, W.F. (1970) A Mesolithic site at Barsalloch, Wigtownshire. *Trans. Dumfries & Galloway Nat. Hist. & Antiq. Soc.*, 47, 64-80.

Cormack, W.F. and Coles, J.M. (1968) A Mesolithic site at Low Clone, Wigtownshire. *Trans. Dumfries & Galloway Nat. Hist. & Antiq. Soc.*, 45, 44-72.

Coupland, G. (1948) *A Mesolithic industry at 'The Beacon', S.E. Durham.* Privately printed.

Cowling, E.T. and Mellars, P.A. (1973) A Mesolithic flint site: the Sandbeds, Otley, Yorkshire. *Yorks. Arch. Jour.*, 45, 1-18.

Darling, F.F. (1937) *A Herd of Red Deer.* London.

Davies, J. (1963) A Mesolithic site on Blubberhouses Moor, Wharfedale, West Riding of Yorkshire. *Yorks. Arch. Jour.*, 41, 61-70.

Dimbleby, G.W. (1967) *Plants and Archaeology.* London.

Driver, H.E. (1969) *Indians of North America.* Chicago and London.

Flerov, K.K. (1952) *Fauna of the U.S.S.R.: Musk-deer and Deer.* Moscow and London.

Froom, F.R. (1963) The Mesolithic around Hungerford: Parts I & II. *Trans. Newbury & Dist. Field Club,* 11 (2), 62-87.

Gould, R.A. (1968) Chipping stones in the Outback. *Natural History,* 77 (2), 42-8.

Higgs, E.S. (1959) Excavations at a Mesolithic site at Downton, near Salisbury, Wilts. *P.P.S.*, 25, 209-32.

Higgs, E.S. and Vita-Finzi, C. (1972) Prehistoric economies: a territorial approach. In Higgs, E.S. (ed.), *Papers in Economic Prehistory*, 27-36. London.

Howell, F.C. and Clark, J.D. (1963) Acheulian hunter-gatherers of Sub-Saharan Africa. In Howell, F.C. and Bourlière, F. (eds.), *African Ecology and Human Evolution*, 458-533. Chicago.

Howell, F.C., Cole, G.H. and Kleindienst, M.R. (1962) Isimila, an Acheulian occupation site in the Iringa highlands, Southern Highlands province, Tanganyika. *Actes du IVe Congrès Panafricain de Préhistoire et de l'Etude du Quaternaire,* 2, 43-80.

Ingebrigsten, O. (1924) Hjorten utbredelse i Norge. (*Naturvidenskabelige rekke 6*). Bergen.

Isaac, G.L. (1972) Early phases of human behaviour: models in Lower Palaeolithic archaeology. In Clarke D.L. (ed.), *Models in Archaeology*, 167-99. London.

Jacobi, R.M. (1973) Aspects of the 'Mesolithic Age' in Great Britain. In Kozłowski, S.K. (ed.), *The Mesolithic in Europe*, 237-65. Warsaw.

Jarman, M.R. (1972) European deer economies and the advent of the Neolithic. In Higgs, E.S. (ed.), *Papers in Economic Prehistory*, 125-47. London.

Keef, P.A.M., Wymer, J.J. and Dimbleby, G.W. (1965) A Mesolithic site on Iping Common, Sussex, England. *P.P.S.*, 31, 85-92.

Lacaille, A.D. (1954) *The Stone Age in Scotland.* London.

Leakey, L.S.B. (1951) *Preliminary excavations of a Mesolithic site at Abinger Common, Surrey* (Research Papers of the Surrey Arch. Soc. No. 3).

Lee, R.B. (1968) What hunters do for a living, or, how to make out on scarce resources. In Lee and DeVore (eds.) 1968, 30-48.

Lee, R.B. and DeVore, I. (eds) (1968). *Man the Hunter.* Chicago.

Leroi-Gourhan, A. and Brézillon, M. (1966) L'habitation Magdalénienne No. 1 de Pincevent, près Montereau (Seine-et-Marne). *Gallia Préhistoire,* 263-385.

Louwe Kooijmans, L.P. (1972) Mesolithic bone and antler implements from the North Sea and from the Netherlands. *Ber. Rijksdienst Oudheidkundig Bodemonderzoek*, 20-2, 27-73.

Lowe, V.P.W. (1966) Observations on the dispersal of red deer on Rhum. In Jewell, P.A. and Loizos, C. (eds.), *Play, Exploration and Territory in Mammals,* 211-28. London.

Lumley, H. de (1969) *Une cabane Acheuléenne dans la Grotte du Lazaret (Nice).* Mémoires Soc. Préhist. Française No. 7.

Manby, T.G. (1966) A Creswellian site at Brigham, East Yorkshire. *Ant. Jour.*, 46, 211-28.

Mellars, P.A. (1970) An antler harpoon-head of 'Obanian' affinities from Whitburn, Co. Durham. *Arch. Aeliana*, 48, 337-46.

Mellars, P.A. (1973) The Palaeolithic and Mesolithic of Britain. In Renfrew, A.C. (ed.), *British Prehistory: a New Outline*, 41-99. London.

Mellars, P.A. (1975) Ungulate populations, economic patterns and the Mesolithic landscape. In Evans, J. and Limbrey, S. (eds.), *The Effect of Man on the Landscape: The Highland Zone.* London (in press).

Mellars, P.A., and Payne, S. (1971) Excavation of two Mesolithic shell middens on the island of Oronsay (Inner Hebrides). *Nature*, 231, 397-8.

Mercer, J. (1968) Stone tools from a washing-limit deposit of the highest post-glacial transgression, Lealt

Bay, Isle of Jura. *Proc. Soc. Ant. Scot.*, 100, 1-46.
Mercer, J. (1970) The Mesolithic succession in N. Jura, Argyll, W. Scotland. *Quaternaria*, 13, 177-85.
Moore, J.W. (1950) Mesolithic sites in the neighbourhood of Flixton, north-east Yorkshire. *P.P.S.*, 16, 101-8.
Naroll, R. (1962) Floor area and settlement population. *Amer. Antiquity*, 27, 587-9.
Newell, R.R. (1973) The post-glacial adaptations of the indigenous population of the northwest European plain. In Kozłowski, S.K. (ed.), *The Mesolithic in Europe*, 399-440. Warsaw.
Petch, J.A. (1924) *Early Man in the District of Huddersfield.* Huddersfield.
Radley, J. (1965) Regional developments in the Mesolithic of the Yorkshire river system. (Unpublished ms.)
Radley, J. (1968) A Mesolithic structure at Sheldon. *Derby. Arch. Jour.*, 88, 26-36.
Radley, J. (1969) The Mesolithic period in north-east Yorkshire. *Yorks. Arch. Jour.*, 43, 314-27.
Radley, J. and Marsall, G. (1965) Maglemosian sites in the Pennines. *Yorks. Arch. Jour.*, 41, 394-402.
Radley, J. and Mellars, P.A. (1964) A Mesolithic structure at Deepcar, Yorkshire, England, and the affinities of its associated flint industry. *P.P.S.*, 30, 1-24.
Radley, J., Tallis, J.H. and Switsur, V.R. (1974) Excavation of three 'Narrow Blade' Mesolithic sites the southern Pennines. *P.P.S.*, 40, 1-19.
Raistrick, A. (1933) Mesolithic sites of the north-east coast of England. *P.P.S. East Anglia*, 7, 188-98.
Rankine, W.F. (1936) A Mesolithic site at Farnham. *Surrey Arch. Coll.*, 44, 24-46.
Rankine, W.F. (1949a) *Mesolithic survey of the west Surrey Greensand.* (Research Papers of the Surrey Arch. Soc. No. 2).
Rankine, W.F. (1949b) Mesolithic chipping floors in the wind-blown deposits of west Surrey. *Surrey Arch. Coll.*, 50, 1-8.
Rankine, W.F. (1952) A Mesolithic chipping floor at the Warren, Oakhanger, Selborne, Hants. *P.P.S.*, 18, 21-35.
Rankine, W.F. (1961) Mesolithic folk movements in southern England: further evidence from Oakhanger, Hants. Phase II. *Arch. Newsletter*, 7, 63-5.
Rankine, W.F. and Dimbleby, G.W. (1960) Further investigations at a Mesolithic site at Oakhanger, Selborne, Hants. *P.P.S.*, 26, 246-62.
Rankine, W.F. (1961) Further excavations at Oakhanger, Selborne, Hants. Site VIII. *Wealden Mesolithic Research Bull.*
Schloeth, R. and Burckhardt, D. (1961) Die Wanderungen des Rotwildes *Cervus elaphus* L. im Gebiet des Schweizerischen nationalparkes. *Revue Suisse de Zoologie*, 68, 145-56.
Smythe, R.H. (1964) *The Haunts and Habits of Fishes: how to catch more fish.* Foulsham.
Tansley, A.G. (1968) *Britain's Green Mantle.* London.
Turnbull, C.M. (1968) The importance of flux in two hunting societies. In Lee and DeVore (eds.), 1968, 132-7.
Wainwright, G.J. (1959) The excavation of a Mesolithic site at Freshwater West, Pembrokeshire. *Bull. Board of Celtic Studies*, 18, 196-205.
Warren, S.H., Clark, J.G.D., Godwin, M.E. and MacFadyen, W.A. (1934) An early Mesolithic site at Broxbourne sealed under Boreal peat. *Jour. Royal Anthro. Inst.*, 64, 101-28.
Watanabe, H. (1968) Subsistence and ecology of northern food gatherers with special reference to the Ainu. In Lee and DeVore (eds.) 1968, 69-77.
Woodburn, J. (1968a) An introduction to Hadza ecology. In Lee and DeVore (eds.) 1968, 49-55.
Woodburn, J. (1968b) Stability and flexibility in Hadza residential groupings. In Lee and DeVore (eds.) 1968, 103-10.
Woodburn, J. (1970) *Hunters and Gatherers: the Material Culture of the Nomadic Hadza.* London.
Wymer, J.J. (1962) Excavations at the Maglemosian sites at Thatcham, Berkshire, England. *P.P.S.*, 28, 329-61.

NOTES

1. Aberfraw (Anglesey), Ascott-under-Wychwood (Oxfordshire), Blubberhouses Moor (Yorkshire), The Beacon (Durham), Cnoc Coig (Oronsay, Argyll), Farnham (Surrey), Greenham Dairy Farm (Berkshire), Ickornshaw Moor (Yorkshire), Lealt Bay (Jura, Argyll), Lussa River (Jura, Argyll), Morton (Fife), Oakhanger VII (Hampshire), Prestatyn (Flintshire), Salter's Brook (Yorkshire), Selmeston (Sussex), Star Carr (Yorkshire), Stump Cross (Yorkshire), Thatcham (Berkshire), Wawcott III (Berkshire) and Westward Ho! (Devon).

2. Details of the site of Oakhanger VII are given in Rankine and Dimbleby 1960). Information on the unpublished site of Wawcott III was kindly supplied by F.R. Froom. The rock-shelter site of Thorpe Common is currently being excavated by the writer.

3. Details of Francis Buckley's sites of Dean Clough, Rocher Moss, Windy Hill and White Hill are taken from an unpublished manuscript prepared by the late J. Radley entitled 'Regional developments in the Mesolithic of the Yorkshire river system' (1965). Radley's analyses were based on the excavation records and collections of Francis Buckley kept in the Tolson Memorial Museum, Huddersfield.

4. A further late-Mesolithic variant of a particularly idiosyncratic kind is represented by the assemblages from the 'Obanian' shell-middens of western Scotland. Although flint artefacts are by no means scarce in these sites, recent excavations have confirmed that the industries are almost entirely lacking in the usual Mesolithic tool types (Mellars & Payne 1971). Microliths, scrapers and burins appear to be absent and the only distinctive tool forms recovered so far are a series of heavily worked (or utilized) scaled pieces (*lames écaillés*). Analysis of the assemblages from these sites would therefore yield overall percentages of these scaled pieces approaching 100 per-cent. The obvious conclusion is that the assemblages reflect the performance of a highly specialized range of activities directed almost exclusively to the exploitation of marine food resources and from which the usual component of hunting and skin-working implements is therefore lacking. The chronological position of the Obanian assemblages has been fixed by radiocarbon at around 3,500-4,000 B.C. ('uncorrected' figures), but the cultural affinities of the sites remain as enigmatic as ever.

5. Most of these finds are unfortunately unpublished. Information on the discoveries at Green Crag Slack and Broxbourne was provided respectively by E.T. Cowling and R.M. Jacobi. Details of the Beeley Moor find are contained in the manuscript by J. Radley: 'Regional developments in the Mesolithic of the Yorkshire river system' (1965). The Warcock Hill find is referred to in Radley & Mellars 1964:18.

6. Information from the excavation records of F. Buckley in the Tolson Memorial Museum, Huddersfield.

IAN STEAD

The earliest burials of the Aylesford culture

One of the greatest obstacles to the study of the La Tène III period in southern England is that scholars still insist on using the word *Belgic*, a label which allows historical, numismatic and archaeological facts to be thoroughly confused. The material culture should be given a type-site name, and the word 'Belgic' should be banned from archaeological literature. This paper is concerned with one aspect of La Tène III in south-eastern England, an aspect that has been clearly defined (Hodson 1964:101-2) in archaeological terms – the burials of the Aylesford culture. There is no need to add Swarling to the title (see Birchall 1965:241), because the features from Swarling merely duplicate those from Aylesford. In particular, we are concerned with an attempt to define the earliest burials of this culture and to discover when they started.

A relative chronology for the Aylesford culture has been suggested on the basis of grave-groups from the cemeteries at Aylesford and Swarling, which have been divided into *early, middle* and *late* groups, possibly preceded by an *earliest* category represented by ungrouped vessels from Aylesford (Birchall 1965:247-9). This classification may be compared and correlated with that of the rich *Welwyn-type* burials (Stead 1967:46-8), which have been divided into phase I (cf. middle) and phase II (cf. late) – and would be much improved if the numbered phases were replaced by type-site labels.

Thus, the final phase may be named the *Lexden phase.* This can be defined by the presence of imported *Gallo-Belgic* wares, and is represented by the cemetery at Lexden, Colchester, whose burials have been found by chance, mainly during building works, in the course of the last 150 years.[1] Associated with the Gallo-Belgic wares elsewhere are Colchester, thistle and Langton Down brooches – the main types found, both in the large cemetery (463 burials) at King Harry Lane, St. Albans, (Stead 1969:49) and in the pre-conquest levels of the settlement at Camulodunum (Hawkes & Hull 1947: 308-28). The majority of Aylesford culture burials belong to the Lexden phase, and both Aylesford and Swarling cemeteries were in use at this time, as is shown by the butt beakers from Aylesford (Evans 1890:330, no. 13, Pl. ix, no. 1) and from Swarling (Bushe-Fox 1925:15, Pl. ix, no. 34).

Very few Aylesford culture burials are clearly earlier than the Lexden phase. The absence of Gallo-Belgic wares is insufficient to assign an individual burial to an earlier phase because, even in the Lexden phase, most of the pottery was manufactured locally. A more reliable criterion is the presence of imported metal vessels, which has been used to define phase I of the Welwyn-type burials (Stead 1967:46-8), in particular the bronze jug, patella and silver cups found in the Welwyn B burial, which can be dated to the second half of the first century B.C. These metal types are never associated with Gallo-Belgic wares, so they may be used to define the *Welwyn phase* of the Aylesford culture.

Metal-work has not been used to define a phase earlier than the Welwyn phase, although a case for this has been proposed, on the basis of a typological classification of seven pedestal urns from Swarling (Birchall 1965:243). This classification distinguishes between two short undecorated urns (Type Ib) and four tall grooved/cordoned urns (Type Ia) – with a fifth tall cordoned urn (38) which is dismissed as 'probably a degenerate version' of Type Ia. As the Type Ia urns are associated neither with other pots nor with brooches, a fragmentary grooved vessel, whose base alone survives, is used to link these urns with a fragmentary iron brooch described as 'probably the earliest typological form of fibula from Swarling'; and this 'homogeneous group' is then classified as the sole evidence for an early phase, which would be a phase earlier than our Welwyn phase (Birchall

1965:248). As it is based on such a small sample, the argument can carry little weight – but it is worth considering the position of the 'degenerate' urn no. 38. In form, this is very similar to no. 28 (Type Ia): it differs slightly in the details of base and decoration, but might well have been made by the same potter. This is important, because urn no. 38 was associated (Bushe-Fox 1925:8, 10) 'with another urn of the same type' (unfortunately this was never illustrated, and apparently it has not survived) and two fragmentary bronze brooches. One of these is a Colchester brooch and the other is a related piece whose external chord is attached by a hook to the head of a broad bow (see page 411). The pottery evidence alone provides no clear evidence for Aylesford culture burials earlier than the Welwyn phase.

The material that can be attributed to the Welwyn phase itself is scanty. The bronze jugs have been found in three graves (Welwyn A, Welwyn B and Aylesford Y); the patellae in two (Welwyn B and Aylesford Y); and the silver cups in two (Welwyn B and Welwyn Garden City). So the nucleus of the phase comprises four burials (for Aylesford Y, see Birchall 1964:26; and for the others, Stead 1967:57-9).

Dressel I amphorae were found in three of these graves, but at both Mount Bures and King Harry Lane, St. Albans, this type has been found with Gallo-Belgic pottery (Stead 1967:53 for Mt. Bures; K. Harry Lane as yet unpublished), so its use can be shown to extend into the Lexden phase. At Baldock (Stead 1968:306) and at Hertford Heath (Stead 1967:52), some Dressel I amphorae were found in graves without Gallo-Belgic pottery, and without other closely datable artefacts, so these burials might belong to the Welwyn phase. Other complete Dressel I amphorae from sites north of the Thames may well have come from burials, but no other grave-group has been recorded (Stead 1967: 44-60; Peacock 1971:173-7, 182-5).

Each of the four basic graves also contained a collection of native pottery. This is of limited value, because only two vessels apiece survive from Welwyn A and Welwyn B; because the pottery from Aylesford Y has been muddled (Stead 1971:260); and because the large group from Welwyn Garden City, which includes flagons and platters, belongs to the end of the phase.

The Aylesford Y burial lacks amphorae, and indeed no Dressel I amphora has ever been found with a burial in Kent (Peacock 1971:171, 182), but it is alone among these graves in having associated bronze brooches, and these have proved much more useful than pottery for extending the list of Welwyn phase burials. The original publication of the Aylesford Y burial records only two brooches found with calcined bones inside the well known bronze-plated wooden bucket (Evans 1890:317, 380-2), but three brooches were registered in the British Museum as coming from the site. As the additional brooch is the pair to one of the published examples, there can be no doubt that all three were found together. The three brooches are incomplete (all lack the foot) but sufficient survives to classify them:

1. Fig. 1, no. 1. (B.M. 86, 11-12, 9) Incomplete bronze brooch, with a boss on the bow and a trumpet-like expansion at the head covering a 4-coil spring, with internal chord (Evans 1890:380-2, Fig. 18; Birchall 1964:26, Pl. ix b, *left*; *B.M. Early Iron Age Guide 1925*:126, Fig. 138 – which suggests that the 'hook' on the bow moulding has been broken).
2. (B.M. 86, 11-12, 10) Similar, the pair to no. 1, but even less of the bow survives (Birchall 1964:26, Pl. ix b, *top*).
3. Fig. 4, no. 1. (B.M. 86, 11-12, 8) Incomplete bronze brooch, whose rounded bow has a slight rib along the top. Two projections at the head retain the internal chord; 4-coil spring. There are the remains of a disc near the foot of the bow: above, the bow is circular in section; below the disc, it is squared. The catch-plate is missing (Evans 1890:380, Fig. 17: Birchall 1964:26, Pl. ix b, *right*).

These are the only brooches recorded from the Aylesford cemetery.

The pair of brooches with a boss on the bow is particularly interesting, because similar examples have been found with other Aylesford culture burials. The type is absent from the collection of 222 brooches in the King Harry Lane cemetery, and from all other Lexden phase contexts (but see Hawkes & Hull 1947:308, Pl. lxxxix, no. 3, for a curious hybrid brooch related to this type). It would seem to be a useful type-fossil for the Welwyn phase, and its occurrence with Aylesford culture cremations is therefore examined in detail below. For the purposes of this enquiry, all La Tène III brooches with a boss on the bow

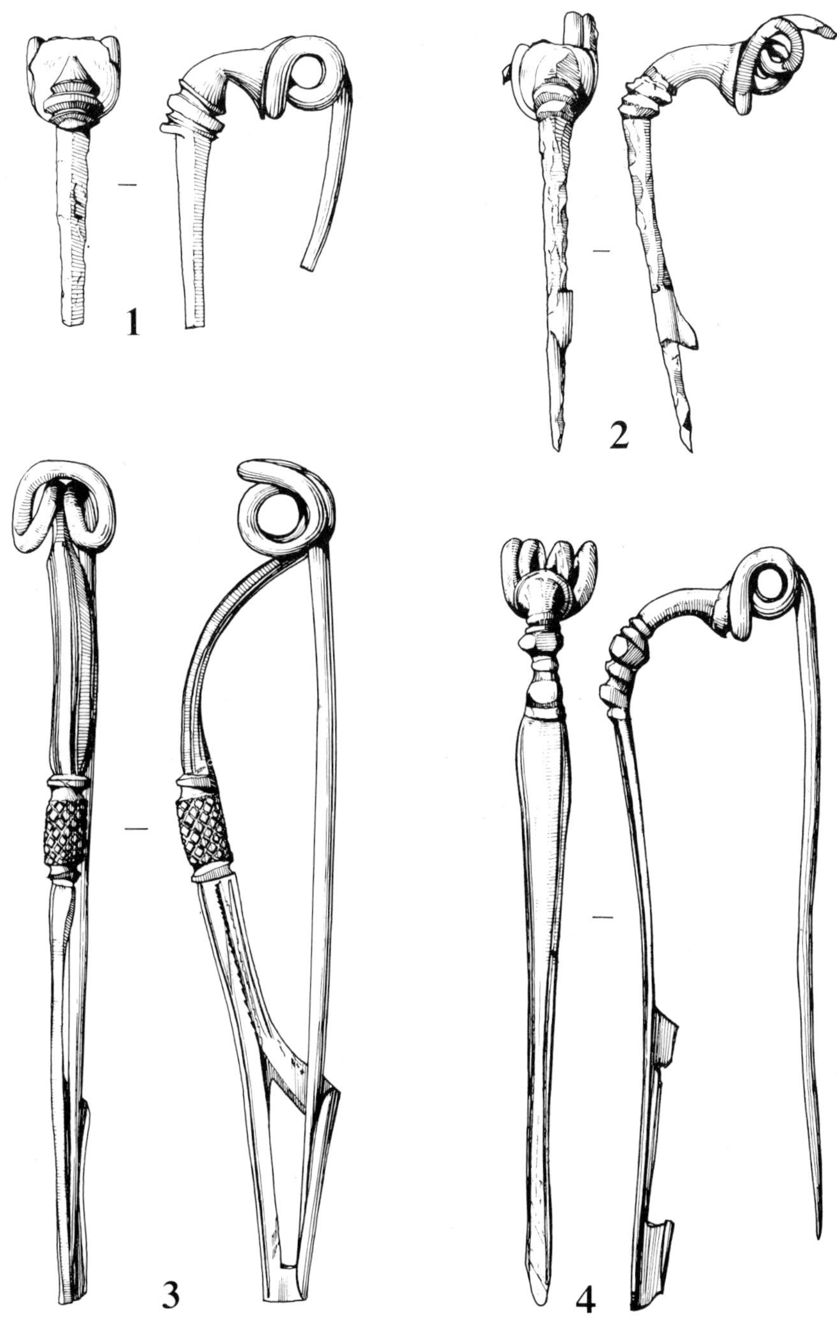

Figure 1. Bronze brooches: 1, Aylesford; 2, Swarling; 3 and 4, Deal. (Full size)

are treated as one type (but see below, page 409).

Swarling

A pair of bronze brooches very similar to the Aylesford pair was found in Grave 13 of the 1921 excavations at Swarling. They are in the British Museum, but they lack registration numbers:

1. Fig. 1, no. 2. Incomplete bronze brooch with a boss on the bow. Four-coil spring, distorted, with a thin bronze wire through it; internal chord (Bushe-Fox 1925: 41, Pl. xii, no. 3).

2. Similar, the pair to no. 1, but even less survives.

Six other brooches were found at Swarling, in four different graves (see page 410).

Deal

The important Aylesford culture cemetery at Deal was disturbed by quarrying, as were both Aylesford and Swarling. The site is at Mill Hill, which rises to just over 100 feet and is about a mile from the coast. At the highest point is an old chalk-pit and from there, and from other excavations in the vicinity, a rich collection of archaeological material has been gathered. A late prehistoric settlement to the north-east of the chalk-pit was uncovered during the construction of a housing estate in 1928 and 1934, and it is now commemorated by the street names 'Hallstatt Road', 'Quern Road' and 'Celtic Road' (*B.M. Later Prehistoric Antiquities 1953*:40, Fig. 16). There are other references to pre-Roman settlement material being found on the hill, but the site is best known for its burials – La Tène III, Roman and Anglo-Saxon – discovered on various occasions between 1885 and 1915. Six bronze brooches of the type under discussion have been found in the chalk-pit:

1. Fig. 1, no. 3. (B.M. 1900, 7-25, 1) Fine bronze brooch, with a cross-hatched boss on the bow; 2-coil spring with external chord (Woodruff 1904: 12-3, Pl. iv, no. 2; *B.M. Iron Age Guide 1925*:95, Fig. 100). The original publication is rather vague about the provenance of this brooch: 'found in the same locality as' the Roman burials. But the British Museum register is precise: it was 'found in a chalk-pit near the reservoir on the hill at the back of Walmer, in the parish of Deal'. This is the chalk-pit (TR 363508) that produced the other finds.

The following brooches, numbered 2 to 6, were from 'the same urn-field' as two burials with Colchester brooches which, in turn, were found in the chalk-pit at Upper Deal (Bushe-Fox 1925:18-9, 44; Birchall 1965:304-5 records as the discovery dates 1908 and 1909 for the two Lexden phase burials and a chalk-pit provenance for one of them – apparently this information was obtained from old museum labels at the Deal Castle Museum; the Ordnance Survey records confirm that all these finds came from the same chalk-pit). The brooches have been published in a small photograph in the Swarling report (Bushe-Fox 1925:44, Pl. xv, no. 16; no. 1 is also illustrated in the local H.M.S.O. guide, *Deal Castle* 1966: Pl. vi, no. 1) and they are housed in the Castle Museum, where they have not been given accession numbers.

2. Fig. 1, no. 4. Bronze brooch, with 4-coil spring and internal chord; slight trumpet-like expansion at the head of the bow. Boss on the bow, and below it the bow is flattened; open catch-plate.
3. Fig. 2, no. 1. Similar, but slightly smaller, bronze brooch.
4. Fig. 2, no. 2. Bronze brooch, with 4-coil spring and internal chord. A boss on the bow, and a step below it; from the boss to the foot, the bow is decorated with a series of slight incisions. Open catch-plate.
5. Fig. 2, no. 3. Rather similar, but with rounded bow and deep incisions adjoining the boss.
6. Fig. 2, no. 4. Small bronze brooch, with 4-coil spring and internal chord. The boss on the bow includes a slight hook. A line of four circular perforations in the catch-plate.

These six brooches came from the same site, but their associations are unknown. It is probable, but not certain, that they were found with burials. A fine bronze brooch of La Tène I construction came from the vicinity but, again, its associations are not recorded (Hawkes 1940a: 276-8); in southern England, a brooch of this type is more likely to have been found with domestic material than with a burial. In the La Tène III period, burials are clearly attested at Deal; these include the two Lexden phase groups with Colchester brooches found in 1908 and 1909 (Bushe-Fox 1925:18-9, 43, Pl. iv, xiii; Birchall 1965:304-5, Figs. 11-12, nos. 88-101); while amongst the finds in the Roman cremation cemetery excavated in the chalk-pit in 1903, there was a triangular knife of a type usually associated with La Tène III burials (Woodruff 1904:16, find no. 21; Stead 1967:38, Fig. 23, no. 3), and another grave found at the same time, an inhumation, contained a pair of pre-Roman bronze spoons (Woodruff 1904:11-12, Pl. iv, no. 1; Crow 1925:148). There is also a collection of Aylesford culture pottery from the Mill Hill site in the Deal Castle Museum (Ogilvie & Dunning 1967:224-6).

Folkestone

Aylesford culture cremation burials have been found in two places at Folkestone. One site, discovered in 1918 near Radnor Park, consists of three burials of the Lexden phase, with finds including a Colchester brooch, two butt beakers,

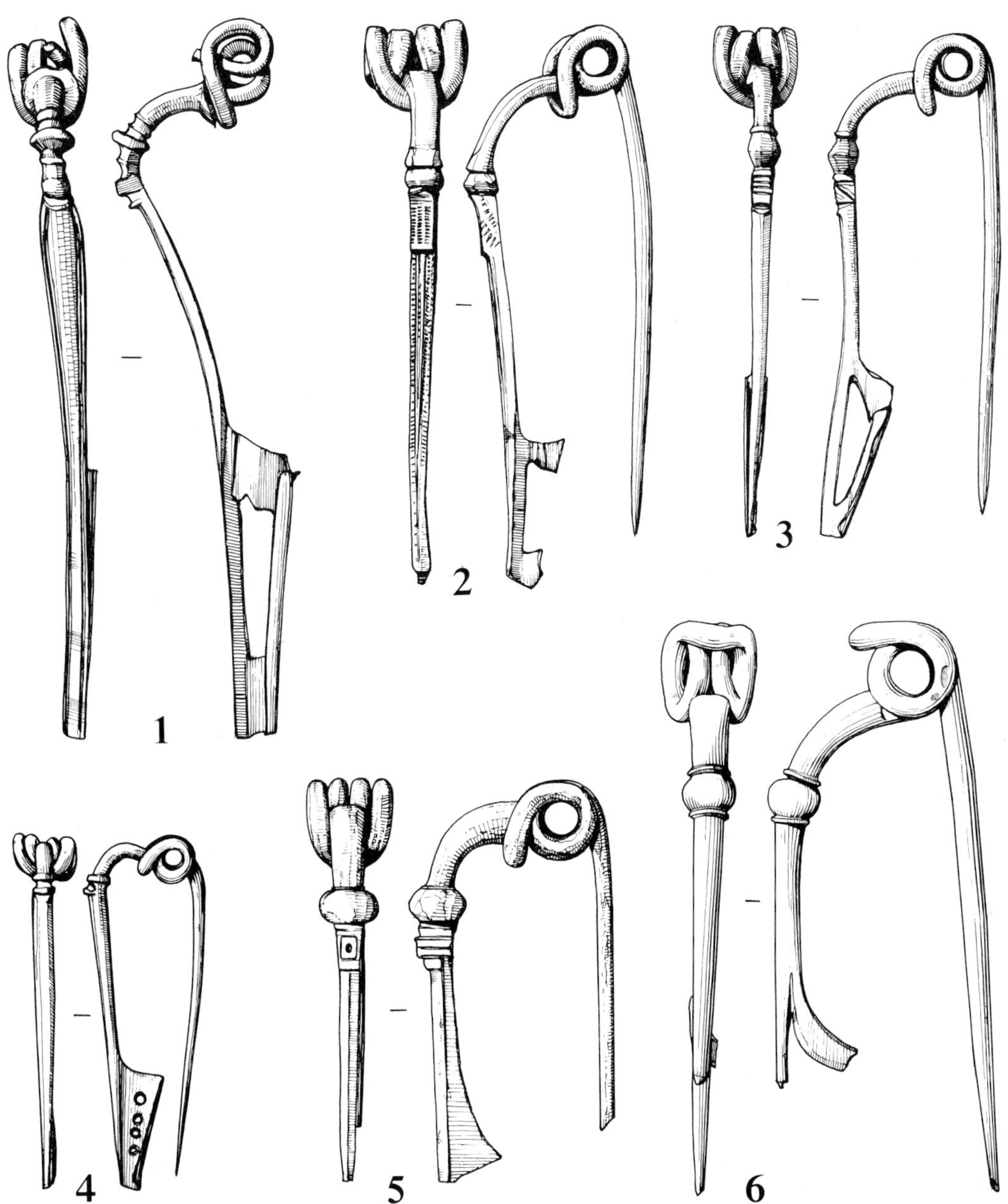

Figure 2. 1-4, Bronze brooches from Deal (nos. 3 to 6 in the text); 5 and 6, Silver brooches from Folkestone. (Full size)

a flagon and even a samian cup (Davis 1920:156-7; Bushe-Fox 1925:20-1, Pls. v, xi, xiv; Winbolt 1925b:63-4). At the other site, East Wear Bay, 1½ miles away, a cemetery was found during the excavation of a Roman villa in 1924. The published accounts claim variously that 5, 6, 7, 8 and 9 urns were found, and that two of these each contained a fragmentary brooch (Winbolt 1925a:112 n.l. – 9 urns, 93 – 8 urns; 1925b:65-6 – 6 urns; 1926:49 – 5 urns; Taylor 1932:114 – 7 urns). The precise location of the urns is not shown on any plan, but one was found (Winbolt 1925a:115-6) in Room 37 (Block A), one in Room 15 (Block B) and two in Room 18 (Block B). Rooms 15 and 18 are only 25 feet apart, but Room 37 is 200 feet away (Winbolt 1925a: frontispiece). The urns that held the brooches were found 'in S. corridor close to (S.W.) arch' on Wednesday, April 23rd, 1924 (Winbolt 1925a:16). This information cannot readily be correlated with the plan, but it seems likely that the 'S corridor' may be the feature numbered 13 on the plan, adjoining Rooms 15 and 18, where the other urns were recorded. If so, these brooches were found only 40 feet away from the cliff edge. This is interesting, because in the British Museum there is a brooch 'found on the shore, the Warren, Folkestone' before 1891. The Roman villa had, in part, been destroyed by cliff falls on to the shore at the Warren. It seems extremely likely that the two brooches found with cremations during the excavation of the villa, and the isolated brooch found on the shore, came from one and the same cemetery. The brooch in the British Museum and one of those from the Roman villa excavations belong to the type under discussion:

1. Fig. 2, no. 5. (Folkestone Museum) Part of a silver brooch, lacking most of the catch-plate. It is rather corroded and the details of the boss are not too clear; 4-coil spring with internal chord. (Winbolt 1925b:65, Fig. 3a).
2. Fig. 2, no. 6. (B.M. 91, 3-20, 18) Silver brooch with broken catch-plate; 2-coil spring, external chord and simple boss on the bow.

Faversham

Romano-British and Anglo-Saxon burials were discovered at Faversham between 1846 and 1869 (Bedo 1872-3:141). No grave-group was recorded, but the finds were collected by W. Gibbs and were bequeathed, in 1870, to the South Kensington Museum (later the Victoria and Albert Museum) and subsequently transferred to the British Museum. Among the material in the Gibbs collection, there are three brooches of the type under discussion:

1. Fig. 3, no. 1. (1090. 70) Incomplete silver brooch, lacking the foot. It has a boss on the bow and a 4-coil spring with internal chord.
2. (1090A. 70) Another, possibly the pair to no. 1, but only the head and spring survive.
3. (1091. 70) Bronze brooch, with open catch-plate. It has an indistinct, worn, boss on the bow and it lacks a spring.

There are no other details about these brooches. It is not certain that they were found with burials, nor that they came from Faversham – the only information available is that the objects in the Gibbs collection were 'for the most part found in graves in a locality adjacent to Faversham in Kent, known as the King's Field' (Roach Smith 1871:7).

Borough Green

A cremation burial was disturbed during quarrying carried out at Godden's Quarry, Borough Green, Wrotham, Kent, in 1953 (Warhurst 1953:157-60). It consisted of a large, but incomplete, jar that had held calcined bones, four bronze bracelets and a pair of bronze brooches. The group is in Maidstone Museum (49. 1953) and the brooches belong to the type under discussion:

1. Fig. 3, no. 2. Bronze brooch, with 4-coil spring, internal chord and a boss on the bow. The catch-plate is incomplete. (Warhurst 1953: Fig. 5, no. 1).
2. Similar, but the boss and the head of the bow are slightly narrower; also has an incomplete catch-plate.

The bracelets all have overlapping terminals: one (Warhurst 1953: Fig. 5, no. 2; Fox 1958: Pl. 26, d) is flat in section and has three bands of punched ornament; the others (Warhurst 1953: Fig. 5, no. 3) are more rounded in section and undecorated.

Great Chesterford

Although calcined bones were not recorded, the discovery of two cordoned shale bowls, two broken pots and two pairs of silver brooches sounds very like the remains of a cremation burial (Neville 1857:84-7; Krämer 1971:49, 124-7, Taf. 24-6). At the same time, in December 1856, a large urn containing 'burnt bones of animals' was found some twenty feet away. The two shale vessels, one of the associated pots and the four brooches are now in the University Museum of Archaeology and Ethnology at Cambridge.

1. Fig. 3, no. 3. Silver brooch, with a boss on the bow, 2-coil spring with external chord, and the open foot crossed by an elaborate bridge.
2. The pair to no. 1.
3. Very similar brooch, with only slight differences – head slightly narrower and the line from the foot along the side of the bow does not extend as far as the boss.
4. The pair to no. 3.

Only no. 1 is complete; the others lack all, or most, of the foot. The two pairs were linked by silver chain, some of which survives.

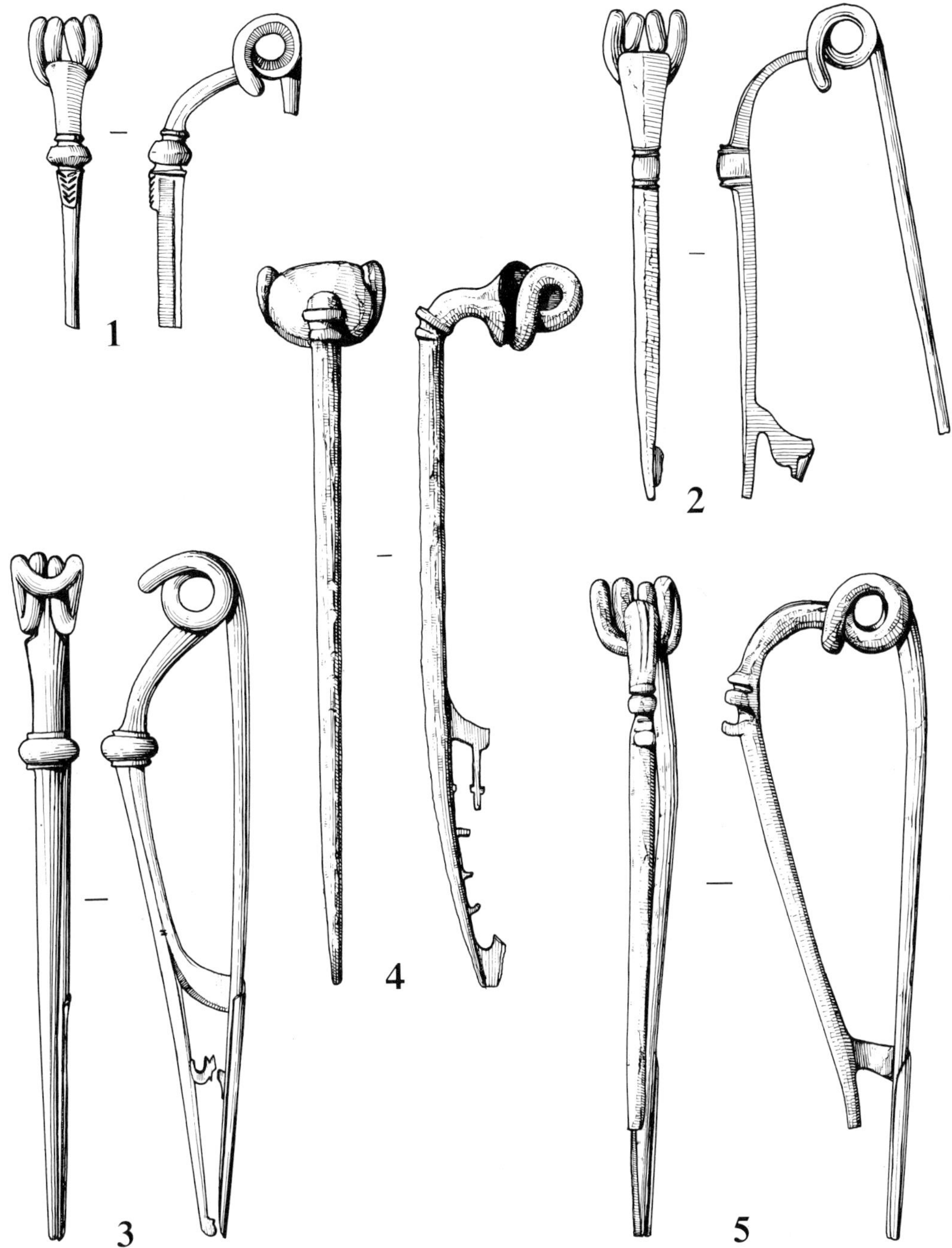

Figure 3. Silver, bronze and iron brooches: 1, Faversham (silver); 2, Borough Green (bronze); 3, Great Chesterford (silver); 4, Hitchin (iron); 5, Guilden Morden (iron). (Full size)

Hitchin

A cremation and inhumation cemetery in the grounds of *Foxholes*, a large house to the west of Hitchin, was excavated by the owner, W. Tindall Lucas, about 1880. No grave-group was recorded, and the finds were kept at Barclays Bank, Hitchin, until 1924, when they were given to Letchworth Museum (Westell 1928:22-5). Subsequently they were transferred to their present home in Hitchin Museum. In a list of finds there are nine brooches, two of which were represented only by a spring and pin. There are three bronze Colchester brooches (nos. 3691-3),[2] one developed Colchester (Colchester

B) brooch (no. 3685), and three iron brooches, one of which (no. 3687) cannot be located. One of the iron brooches is 68 mm. long and has a fairly high bow, rounded in profile but rectangular in section, with a 4-coil spring, internal chord and solid catch-plate. The other one belongs to the type under discussion:

1. Fig. 3, no. 4. Iron brooch, with 6-coil spring and internal chord. It has a trumpet-head, a simple boss near the head of the bow, and an elaborately perforated catch-plate. The brooch is in good condition, with patches of purplish colour indicating that it has been burnt – very probably with a cremation.

Most of the surviving pottery from this cemetery is Romano-British, but at least one vessel (no. 3658), a large beaker, is likely to be pre-Roman.

Guilden Morden

An inhumation and cremation cemetery, which had been disturbed by a chalk-pit, was excavated by Fox & Lethbridge in 1924 (1924-5:49-63). The finds are in the University Museum of Archaeology and Ethnology at Cambridge. Most of the burials were Romano-British, but certainly one was La Tène III. It consisted of a large pottery tazza containing calcined bones and, by the side of it, among calcined bones scattered from the pot, was found an iron brooch of the type under discussion:

1. Fig. 3, no. 5. Iron brooch, with 4-coil spring and internal chord. The boss on the bow includes a hook and the catch-plate, though incomplete, appears to have been open. (Fox & Lethbridge 1924-5:52-3, Fig. 5a – but the illustration is inaccurate in the details of the moulding.)

Four other cremations at Guilden Morden, all simple heaps of calcined bones, were assigned by the excavators to the same period, but the only associated object, the foot of a similar iron brooch, has apparently not survived.

The examples listed above appear to be the only Aylesford culture burials with brooches of this type. A brooch of this type is displayed with the Stanfordbury B finds, but the association is unrealiable (see page 414). In all, there are 23 brooches, including six pairs (13 bronze, including three pairs; eight silver, including three pairs; and two iron) and they come from nine different cemeteries: Aylesford, Borough Green, Deal, Faversham, Folkestone and Swarling, in Kent; Great Chesterford, in Essex; Hitchin, in Hertfordshire; and Guilden Morden, in Cambridgeshire. The three sites north of the Thames are not as scattered as their county attributions might suggest – they are all within four miles of a 25-mile length of the Icknield Way.

Only three of the graves were properly excavated and recorded: Swarling, Guilden Morden and Folkestone. At Swarling, the brooches were found with six pots and the remains of a wooden and iron bucket, but in the other two graves they were associated only with a single urn. The Borough Green group (a pair of these brooches with a pot and four bracelets) had been disturbed by quarrying, but may well have survived intact. The grave-groups at Great Chesterford and Aylesford are incomplete, but Aylesford is specially valuable because of the presence, in the associated group, of metal vessels. For the rest, there are no recorded associations. Although this evidence is very scrappy, not one of these brooches has been found with Gallo-Belgic pottery, nor with any Lexden phase brooch.

The La Tène III brooch with a boss on the bow has occurred in south-eastern England in contexts other than funerary, and also in the south-west (e.g. Wheeler 1943:258, Fig. 83, no. 9). There is a loose find from Arundel, Sussex (Hawkes 1940b:492-5); also an elaborate example from the River Thames (*B.M. Later Prehistoric Antiquities 1953*:64, Fig. 24, no. 4) and a fine fragment from a settlement at Welwyn Garden City, Hertfordshire. The last is particularly interesting, for the site is only two miles west of the rich Welwyn Garden City grave and two miles south of the Welwyn A and B graves discovered in 1906. The brooch was found in a ditch, with a small collection of domestic pottery that lacked Gallo-Belgic wares, at the site of Brickwell Hill (TL 223137), (Rook 1970:25, Fig. iii; associated pottery, Fig. ii, nos. 1-12).

Although not in England, there is one further useful context for these brooches in the British Isles, for three examples were found in the Le Catillon hoard, on Jersey (Krämer 1971:127, Abb. 4, 3-5). Not all scholars are satisfied with the Caesarian date proposed for this hoard (Krämer 1971:128), but a date before the start

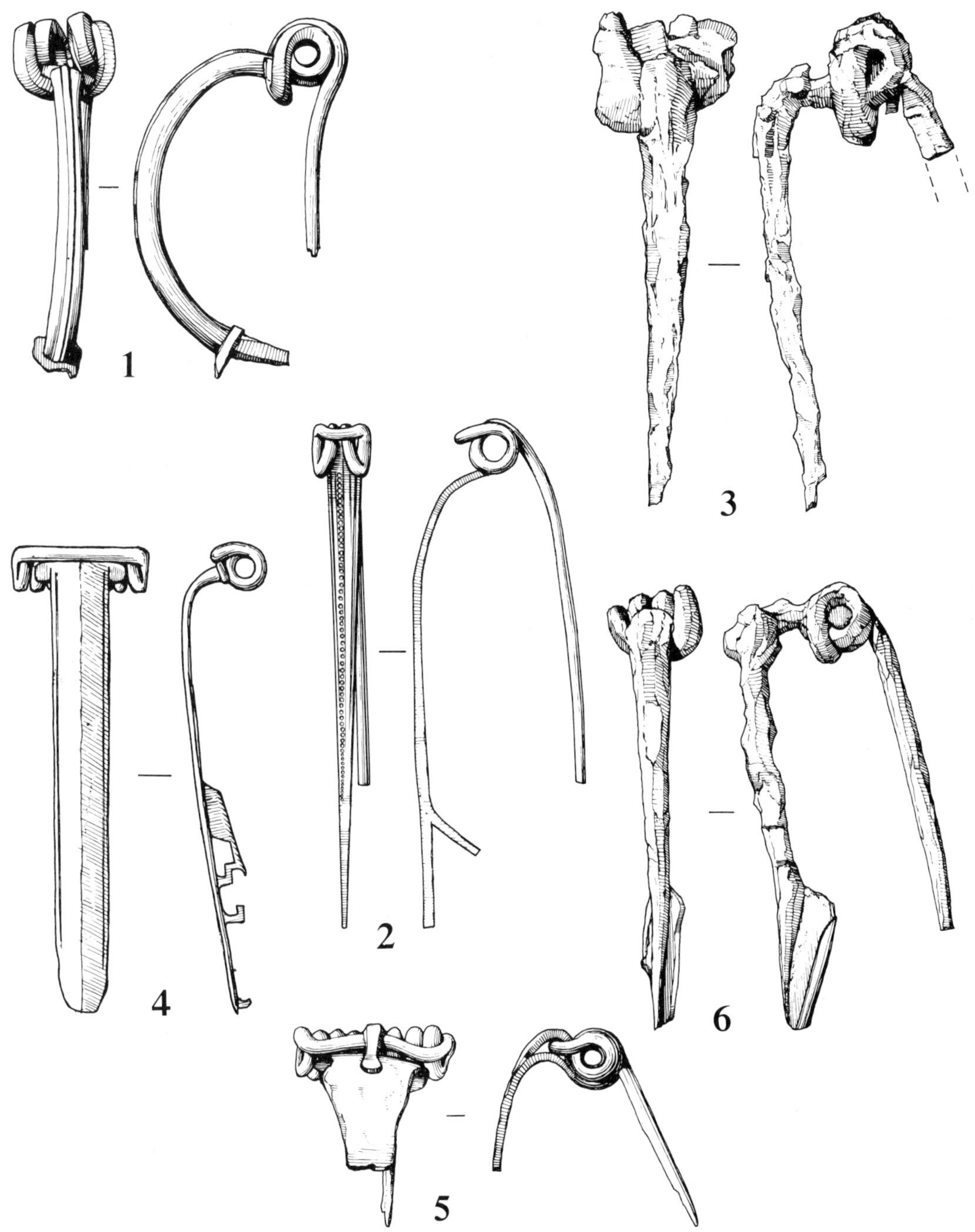

Figure 4. Bronze and iron brooches: 1, Aylesford (bronze), 2, Folkestone (bronze); 3, Swarling (iron); 4 and 5, Swarling (bronze); 6, Berkhamsted (iron). (Full size)

of the Lexden phase is certain.

The case for assigning this type of brooch to the Welwyn phase is founded on the lack of association with Lexden phase material. It is strengthened by the association at Aylesford with imported metal-work of the Welwyn phase, and at Le Catillon with a hoard of Gallic coins; and it is sealed by the absence of the type from the King Harry Lane cemetery at St. Albans.

Typologically, the brooches discussed above may be divided into three groups on the basis of the spring and the shape of the head. The simplest form, as at Great Chesterford, has a two-coil spring, external chord and simple head (Deal 1, Folkestone 2 and Great Chesterford). More elborate is the form whose spring has been given an extra turn, with internal chord, as at Folkestone (Deal 4-6, Folkestone 1, Faversham 1 and 2, Borough Green, Guilden Morden). And the final development comes when the head of the bow is expanded into a trumpet-like shape to hold down the internal chord, as at Aylesford (Aylesford, Swarling, Deal 2 and 3, Hitchin which has a 6-coil spring). There is little to suggest that this typological sequence has any chronological significance in Britain, although the three Le Catillon brooches do belong to the first group, with the possible exception of the one whose spring is absent. The developed form, as at Aylesford, is a well known continental brooch (Almgren 65) with an origin perhaps in Italy (see page 412) so there is no question of the sequence developing independently in Britain. It is interesting that the three typological forms are represented by the three examples found north of the Thames. These forms could, perhaps, themselves be sub-divided on the basis of the catch-plate – perforated, open-work or completely open – but the available material is too slight for the purpose, for of the 23 brooches considered no fewer than twelve have been broken and in these the foot does not survive.

Having dealt with the La Tène III brooches with a boss on the bow, it remains to examine other brooches which have been found with burials that might belong to the Welwyn phase or earlier. This can be approached by considering first, brooches found in the graves discussed above; second, brooches found in the same cemeteries; and third, brooches from other sites.

There is only one brooch in the first category, for only at Aylesford was there an association between a La Tène III brooch with a boss on the bow and one of another type. The other brooch here, described above (see page 402) is very interesting, but unfortunately incomplete (Fig. 4, no. 1). The foot is lacking and the disc that ornamented the bow is damaged. It belongs to the general class of disc-ornamented brooches that gave rise to the thistle brooch. The Aylesford example is particularly interesting because, judging from the form of the spring, it is typologically early – earlier than one from Goeblingen-Nospelt, for example, which was also associated with an Aylesford-type bronze jug and patella (from Grave B, Thill 1967a:94, Taf. ii, no. 10, B.24; bronze vessels, 89-90, Taf. i, nos. 1, 4, B.19, B.49); and earlier, too, than the examples from Pommiers, where a very similar brooch is also depicted on coins (Allen 1972:122-32).

Of the eight Welwyn phase cemeteries defined by brooches, five produced brooches of other types (a possible brooch fragment from the Welwyn Garden City cemetery is too small to classify: Stead 1967:42, Fig. 26, no. 6), but three of these were of the Lexden phase or later. Only at Folkestone and Swarling were there other brooches that might be earlier than the Lexden phase:

1. Fig. 4, no. 2. Folkestone. Simple bronze La Tène III brooch, with 2-coil spring, external chord, flat bow with simple punched ornament and an open catch-plate (Winbolt 1925b:65, Fig. 3b). It was found inside a jar (*ibid.* Fig. 2, no. 1) and is now in Folkestone Museum.

All the Swarling brooches are in the British Museum, but only one (no. 7, below) has a registration number.

2. Fig. 4, no. 3. (Grave 4) Fragmentary iron brooch. Two fragments join to form the piece illustrated: it has a 4-coil apring with internal chord and the foot is broken at the corner of the catch-plate. There are other iron fragments in the grave-group, apparently all from brooch pins: (i) one piece 49 mm. long; (ii) two pieces joining, 46 mm. long; (iii) three pieces joining, 52 mm. long (Bushe-Fox 1925: 40, Pl. xii, no. 1).

3-4. Fig. 4, no. 4. (Grave 18) Pair of bronze brooches, badly corroded and broken. The illustration previously published (Bushe-Fox 1925:40, Pl. xii, no. 2) is inaccurate – it has the head of the bow too low, omits the side-wings, and shows the spring too short (Fig. 4, no. 4, is idealized, as was the original illustration, because the brooches are in very poor condition). The brooches had either 6- or 8-coil springs, and there must have been a hook for the external chord, but nothing of it survives.

5. (Grave 19) Small and broken Colchester brooch – it appears to be a smaller version of nos. 3 and 4, although the bow is relatively higher, narrower and thicker. It has an 8-coil spring with external chord and hook, and the side-wings are ridged. The flat bow has been damaged and distorted, so much so that elsewhere it has been classified as a P-shaped brooch (Hawkes & Hull 1947:320); there are now two

bends in the bow, one near the catch-plate, which could have been done in antiquity, and the other higher up the bow, which is more recent and was presumably done at the time of discovery (Bushe-Fox 1925:42-3, Pl. xii, no. 6).

6. Fig. 4, no. 5. (Grave 19) Head of a bronze brooch, with broad bow, 8-coil spring, external chord and hook. There are no side-wings. (Bushe-Fox 1925:42, Pl. xii, no. 5).

7. (Grave 1) (B.M. 1923, 11-8, 4) Bronze Colchester brooch, with open catch-plate. (Bushe-Fox 1925:41-2, Pl. xii, no. 4).

The Folkestone example is interesting in being the nearest approach to a Nauheim brooch found with an Aylesford culture burial; but it is not a Nauheim brooch – it has an external chord. The Nauheim brooch is commonly found with La Tène III burials, particularly in Germany, whereas in northern France its counterpart is a brooch with a wire bow, instead of a flat bow (e.g. Birchall 1965:352, Fig. 29, nos. 239-42; 355, Fig. 32, nos. 277-9). Several examples of this type have been found during the recent excavations of La Tène cemeteries at Juniville, Ménil-Annelles and Ville-sur-Retourne, Ardennes. The iron brooch from Swarling, no. 2 above, appears to have been very similar to these French brooches. The Swarling and Folkestone brooches may be contemporary with the Nauheim brooch, but they need be no earlier than our Welwyn phase.[3]

The pair of brooches, nos. 3 and 4 above, from Swarling Grave 18, have a broad flat bow that does not taper, and can be matched exactly at Deal in a grave-group without Gallo-Belgic wares (Bushe-Fox 1925:43, Pl. xiii, no. 7; 18-9, Pl. iv, Fig. 1). The type is absent from Camulodunum, and from the King Harry Lane cemetery, so it is likely to be an early form of Colchester brooch. At Deal, in the same grave-group, was a Colchester brooch with straight bow, sharply angled at the head (Bushe-Fox 1925: 43, Pl. xiii, no. 8). This brooch is very similar in profile to no. 7 above, from Grave 1 at Swarling; the type is rare at King Harry Lane (three examples) and absent from Camulodunum. At King Harry Lane these brooches are associated with a normal Colchester brooch, a thistle brooch and a butt beaker. Both these are early Colchester forms which could belong to the end of the Welwyn phase, but clearly they cannot be much earlier than the introduction of Gallo-Belgic pottery. It is interesting that the probable predecessor of the flat-bow type of brooch, which lacks the side-wings, occurs at Pommiers, Aisne (Vauvillé 1907:9-10, Fig. 3, no. 5), and it may be that no. 6 above, from Grave 19 at Swarling, belongs to this type. The other early Colchester type, with a straight bow sharply angled at the head, was also found at Pommiers (Vauvillé 1907:9, Fig. 3, no. 2).

The third category of evidence to be examined consists of brooches found with burials on sites other than those considered so far. The material studied is listed in the Appendix, and nearly all of it belongs to the Lexden phase. One brooch that might add another site to the list of Welwyn phase burials is made of iron and has a 4-coil spring, internal chord and solid catch-plate (Fig. 4, no. 6). It was found with one of three cremations discovered during the construction of a school at Berkhamsted, Hertfordshire; no Gallo-Belgic wares were found on the site.[4] Although this brooch is simple enough, resembling a type found throughout the first century A.D. (e.g. Kenyon 1948:249, Fig. 80, nos. 1-2; Hawkes & Hull 1947:308, Pl. lxxxix, no. 4), the shape of the bow can be closely matched at Pommiers, Aisne, where it was a common form, and where it must be dated earlier than the Lexden phase (Vauvillé 1907:9, Fig. 3, no. 1).

To conclude this enquiry, one can refer to other metal-work found with burials, of types that might be of the Welwyn phase or earlier. In this category one can place the inhumation grave with two bronze spoons in the Deal cemetery, which was certainly in use during both the Welwyn and the Lexden phases (see page 404); Hawkes (1968:14) suggests that the Deal spoons are La Tène II. There is also a cremation from Letchworth, Hertfordshire, where a fine bronze strap-link was found in a pedestal urn (Smith 1914:238-40). The urn is in Letchworth Museum, but the writer has failed to locate the strap-link. These bronze objects from Deal and Letchworth, however, cannot be dated closely.

The evidence considered above enables the list of Welwyn phase funerary sites to be extended from four basic graves with imported metal-work to a maximum of fourteen sites;[5] most of this extension is due to the use of the La Tène III brooch, with a boss on the bow, as a type-fossil. Among the metal-work there is no type-fossil for an earlier phase of Aylesford culture burials, and it has been argued that, as yet, no earlier phase can be recognized on the grounds of pottery typology.

Werner (1954:43-73) dates the Aylesford type of patella and jug from 50 to 15 B.C., with an emphasis on the end of that period, and this has been supported recently by the discovery of the important group of graves at Goeblingen-Nospelt, in Luxemburg. In Grave B at this site, a similar patella and jug was associated with an Aco beaker and samian ware, suggesting a date in the final quarter of the first century B.C. for the group (Thill 1966:483-91; 1967a:87-98; 1967b:199-213). The silver cups found with these bronze types in Welwyn Grave B, and at Welwyn Garden City, were made in the second half of the first century B.C. (Stead 1967:22). The amphorae from the Welwyn-type graves belong to a type first produced *c.* 70 B.C. (Peacock 1971:165), but this continued in use and is associated with some Lexden phase graves (see page 402). As for the La Tène III brooch with a boss on the bow, at Aylesford this was associated with the imported metal-work (50 to 15 B.C.) and at Le Catillon it was perhaps Caesarian, but there is no evidence to suggest that it might be any earlier (Krämer 1971:111-32). It would be unrealistic to date these two phases of Aylesford culture burials more closely than within the general terms of half a century: the Welwyn phase occupying the second half of the first century B.C., and the Lexden phase the first half of the first century A.D.

Undoubtedly some of the Welwyn phase artefacts have close links with northern Gaul, in particular the pottery and some of the brooches: the disc-ornamented brooch from Aylesford, the ancestors of the Colchester brooch at Swarling, and perhaps some of the iron brooches. But this study has emphasized another interesting point: the importance of a direct link between Britain and Italy. The most striking external influences, as displayed by the Welwyn phase burials, are not from northern Gaul but from Italy. The amphorae were imported from Italy as containers of Italian wine; the bronze patellae and jugs, and the silver cups, are all of Italian manufacture. And the most popular form of brooch, the La Tène III brooch with a boss on the bow, might also owe something to Italian inspiration. Simple examples of this brooch are found in northern Gaul, but they are not common (Hawkes & Dunning 1930:201, Fig. 11, no. 4 and 206, Fig. 11, no. 7, for Normandy; Mahr 1967: Taf. 14, no. 9, for the Trier district). The more elaborate British brooches, including some made of silver, may well have had a more exotic source. In the original publication of the Aylesford grave it was suggested that the brooch was 'probably of Italian fabric' (Evans 1890:381) and subsequent work (Fischer 1966:307-8; Krämer 1971:120) has emphasized an Italian origin for that particular form (Almgren 65). It has also been suggested that the Great Chesterford brooches were of north Italian origin (Krämer 1971:127).

No Aylesford culture burial can be securely dated earlier than Caesar's expeditions to Britain. It could be argued that this is because the dating evidence is provided by the contact with Italy, but this does not affect the relative chronology. No cemetery, not even a single burial, can be shown to be earlier than the Welwyn phase. So it seems that the cremation rite was adopted little, if at all, before the time of Caesar. There can be no question of associating the introduction of cremation with the arrival of Gallo-Belgic coins towards the end of the second century B.C. (Allen 1958). However, this does not invalidate Allen's hypothesis that the coins were brought into Britain by invaders, for we are ignorant of the La Tène II burial rite in Artois and Picardy, the homeland of these Gallo-Belgic coins; it could even have been that mysterious rite practised in southern England for most of the Early Iron Age (Hawkes 1972: 110-11).

Appendix: Brooches found with Aylesford culture burials

1. Aldbury, Hertfordshire. (SP 967132) Three Colchester brooches found with cremations in 1943. Letchworth Museum.
2. Allington, Kent. a (TQ 746573) b (TQ 730562)
   a. Two Colchester brooches — one published in Bushe-Fox 1925: Pl. xv, no. 14 — and a Langton Down brooch. Probably from the cemetery at Tassel's Quarry (Bushe-Fox 1925:19-20, 44; Kelly 1971: 73). Maidstone Museum.
   b. Colchester brooch found with a crem-

ation in a short cordoned jar, accompanied by a platter; Hermitage Farm, 1923 (Bushe-Fox 1925:20, 44 and Pl. xv, no. 15; Pl. xi, nos. 7 and 8 for the pottery). Maidstone Museum.

3. Aylesford, Kent. (TQ 731593) See page 402.
4. Baldock, Hertfordshire. (TL 246336)
Rosette brooch, found with 'cremated remains' (Westell 1935:350). Letchworth Museum.
5. Berkhamsted, Hertfordshire. (SP 985089) See page 411.
6. Billericay, Essex. (TQ 680954)
Three brooches found in 1865, when a cemetery in Norsey Wood was disturbed by quarrying (Cutts 1873:212-4; Bayly 1879:73). ? Lost.
7. Borough Green, Wrotham, Kent. (TQ 603563) See page 406.
8. Boxford, Suffolk. a (TL 977391) b (TL 974395)
a. Pair of Colchester brooches and the catch-plate of another brooch, found in 1926 (Clarke 1939:52-4, Pl. x, no. 3; Owles 1967:88-107, Fig. 14, *g, i* and *j*). Ipswich Museum and private collection.
b. Colchester brooch, part of another, and two fragmentary iron brooches, found in 1966 (Owles 1967:88-107, Fig. 14, *a, b, d* and *e*). Ipswich Museum.
9. Cheriton, Kent. (TR 196370)
Colchester brooches in two burials (Tester & Bing 1949:21-36). Folkestone Museum.
10. Deal, Kent. a (TR 363508) b (TR 361526)
a. Mill Hill cemetery: six brooches, see page 404; also three Colchester brooches (Bushe-Fox 1925:18-19, 43, Pl. xiii). Deal Castle Museum.
b. Court Lodge Farm: two Colchester brooches found with a burial in 1962. (Ogilvie & Dunning 1967:221-4). Deal Castle Museum.
11. Dumpton Gap, Broadstairs, Kent. (TR 397665) See Birchall 1965:257.
12. Duston, Northamptonshire. (SP 730605)
Cremation and inhumation cemetery disturbed by ironstone working in the nineteenth century. No grave-group was recorded, but finds include ten Colchester brooches, four Langton Down brooches and a rosette – so the cemetery started in the Lexden phase (Sharp 1871:118-30). Northampton Museum.
13. Faversham, Kent. (TR 012609) See page 406.
14. Folkestone, Kent. Radnor Park (TR 218365) and East Wear Bay (TR 241370) See pp. 404-6.
15. Great Chesterford, Essex. (TL 520432) See page 406.
16. Great Wakering, Essex. (TQ 945882)
Head of a Langton Down brooch, with ornament on the spring-cover, found in an urn in one of three grave-groups (4006. 20, found in 4005. 20). (Wright 1922:9-10; and for the pottery, Birchall 1965: Fig. 18, 157-60). Colchester and Essex Museum.
17. Guilden Morden, Cambridgeshire. (TL 285401) See page 408.
18. Hatfield Peverel, Essex. (TL 794098)
Iron fragment, found in a pedestal urn, possibly part of a brooch (419. 28). (Hull 1929:10). Colchester and Essex Museum.
19. Hauxton, Cambridgeshire. (TL 435519)
Thistle brooch with a burial (Fox 1923:91, 101, Pl. xiii, Ia *upper*). University Museum of Archaeology and Ethnology, Cambridge.
20. Hitchin, Hertfordshire. a (TL 172290) b (TL 190304)
a. See pages 407-8.
b. Bronze brooch found with a burial (Ransom 1889:16-18; Clarke 1926:177, Pl. xxx, Fig. 2; Birchall 1965:306-7, Fig. 13-14, nos. 114-24). These references show the pottery from the site, now in the British Museum and in the University Museum of Archaeology and Ethnology, Cambridge, but the brooch has never been illustrated and it seems that it has not survived.
21. Kelvedon, Essex. (TL 864189)
Colchester brooch found with a burial (Bushe-Fox 1925:44, Pl. xiv, no. 13; the drawing is inaccurate, because the brooch has side-wings). British Museum.
22. Lexden, Colchester, Essex. (TL 975250)
The only brooches from the cemetery were in Claudian graves: (i) six thistle brooches in the Joslin Collection (Grave 9), found before 1893 (May 1930:255; two brooches are illustrated in Hawkes & Hull 1947:315, Pl. xciii, nos. 70-1); (ii) ten brooches, found in 1940 (Hull 1942:59-65). Colchester and Essex Museum.
23. Maidstone, Kent. (TQ 768558)
The spring of an iron brooch, having a 4-coil spring with internal chord, found with a

pedestal urn and a jar, in a burial discovered in 1963 (Kelly 1963:194-6). Maidstone Museum.

24. St. Albans, Hertfordshire. a (TL 133065) b (TL 140066)
 a. 222 brooches found in the King Harry Lane cemetery (Stead 1969:45-52).
 b. Three brooches (Colchester and two Nauheim derivatives) were found in the Lexden phase cemetery of 21 cremations, excavated at Verulam Hills Field in 1963-64 (Anthony 1968:14-17). Verulamium Museum.

25. Stanfordbury, Bedfordshire. (*c.* TL 148412) Bronze brooch, found in the rich Stanfordbury B grave (Dryden 1845:20). In the University Museum of Archaeology and Ethnology at Cambridge, there are two brooches displayed with the grave-group: one is a Langton Down brooch with decorated spring-cover; the other is a La Tène III brooch with moulding on the bow. The latter has a 4-coil spring and internal chord, and the moulding is a simple one consisting of five adjoining bands. The foot is broken but, judging from the remaining part, it could have been solid. As samian ware was found in this grave, and it may well be Claudian in date (Stead 1967:47), the Langton Down brooch is the more likely one to have been associated — but one can attach little weight to this, for it is known that the pottery was muddled with vessels from the Shefford cemetery and it is quite possible that the brooch was confused at the same time.

26. Stone, Kent. (TQ 562748)
 Four brooches (Colchester, Hod Hill, thistle and a simple flat-bow type with external chord and hook) in the cemetery discovered in 1939 (Cotton & Richardson 1941:141, Fig. 5). Dartford Borough Museum.

27. Swarling, Kent. (TR 128527) See page 403.

28. Welwyn Garden City, Hertfordshire. a (TL 226124) b (TL 254131)
 a. Four brooches found in four cremation groups at Attimore Road. They have not been illustrated, and it seems that they have not survived. The pottery includes a Roman jug and a platter (Hughes 1938:144). ?Lost.
 b. Two iron fragments, possibly from a brooch, in an urn in the cemetery near the rich Welwyn Garden City burial (Stead 1967:42, Fig. 26, no. 6). British Museum.

Acknowledgments

The writer is grateful to the following for their help in the study of the brooches published in this paper: Miss C. Johns and Dr I.H. Longworth (Department of Prehistoric and Romano-British Antiquities, British Museum); Miss M.D. Cra'ster (University Museum of Archaeology and Ethnology, Cambridge); G.M.R. Davies (Colchester and Essex Museum); Miss D.J. Hooker (Deal Public Library); K.C. Sussams (Folkestone Public Library, Museum and Art Gallery); Miss F.M. Gadd (Hitchin Museum and Art Gallery); Miss E.J. Owles (Ipswich Museum); A.B. Havercroft (Letchworth Museum and Art Gallery); D.B. Kelly (Maidstone Museum and Art Gallery). The illustrations are the work of F.J.H. Gardiner.

REFERENCES

Allen, D.F. (1958) The origins of coinage in Britain: a reappraisal. In Frere, S.S. (ed.), *Problems of the Iron Age in Southern Britain*, 97-308. London.

Allen, D.F. (1972) The Fibula of Cricirv. *Germania*, 50, 122-32.

Anthony, I.E. (1968) Excavations in Verulam Hills Field, St. Albans, 1963-4. *Herts. Arch.*, 1, 9-50.

Bayly, J.A.S. (1879) Roman Billericay. *Arch. Jour.*, 36, 70-77.

Bedo, G. (1872-3) Roman remains discovered around Faversham, Co. Kent. *Reliquary*, 13, 141-7.

Birchall, A. (1964) The Belgic Problem: Aylesford revisited. *B.M. Quarterly*, 28, 21-9.

Birchall, A. (1965) The Aylesford – Swarling Culture: the problem of the Belgae reconsidered. *P.P.S.*, 21, 241-367.

Bushe-Fox, J.P. (1925) *Excavation of the Late-Celtic Urn-field at Swarling, Kent.* (Soc. Ant. Res. Cttee. Report No. V). London.

Clarke, L.C.G. (1926) Prehistoric and Romano-British objects from England in the University Museum of Archaeology and Ethnology, Cambridge. *Ant. Jour.*, 6, 175-80.

Clarke, R.R. (1939) The Iron Age in Norfolk and Suffolk. *Arch. Jour.*, 96, 1-113.

Cotton, M.A. and Richardson, K.M. (1941) A Belgic cremation site at Stone, Kent. *P.P.S.*, 7, 134-41.

Crow, J.H. (1925) On two bronze spoons from an Early Iron Age grave near Burnmouth, Berwickshire. *P.S.A.S.*, 58, 143-60.

Cutts, J.E.K. (1873) Notes on Roman and British Remains found at Billericay in 1865 . . . *Trans. Essex*

Arch. Soc., 5, 208-18.

Davis, A.R. (1920) Researches and discoveries in Kent: Folkestone. *Arch. Cant.*, 34, 156-7.

Dryden, Sir H. (1845) Roman and Roman-British Remains, at and near Shefford, Co. Beds. *Cambridge Ant. Soc. Publications*, 1, 8.

Evans, A.J. (1890) On a Late-Celtic urn-field at Aylesford, Kent. *Arch.*, 52, 315-88.

Fischer, F. (1966) Das Oppidum von Altenburg-Rheinau. *Germania*, 44, 286-312.

Fox, Sir C. (1923) *Archaeology of the Cambridge Region.* London.

Fox, Sir C. (1958) *Pattern and Purpose.* Cardiff.

Fox, Sir C. and Lethbridge, T.C. (1924-5) The La Tène and Romano-British Cemetery, Guilden Morden, Cambs. *Proc. & Comns. Cambs. Ant. Soc.*, 27, 49-63.

Hawkes, C.F.C. (1940a) La Tène I brooches from Deal, Preston Candover, and East Dean. *Ant. Jour.*, 20, 276.

Hawkes, C.F.C. (1940b) An 'Aylesford' La Tène III brooch from Arundel Park, and the dating of the type. *Ant. Jour.*, 20, 492.

Hawkes, C.F.C. (1968) New thoughts on the Belgae. *Antiquity*, 42, 6-19.

Hawkes, C.F.C. (1972) Europe and England: fact and fog. *Helinium*, 12, 105-16.

Hawkes, C.F.C. and Dunning, G.C. (1930) The Belgae of Gaul and Britain. *Arch. Jour.*, 87, 150-335.

Hawkes, C.F.C. and Hull, M.R. (1947) *Camulodunum* (Soc. Ant. Res. Cttee. Report No. XIV). London.

Hodson, F.R. (1964) Cultural grouping within the British pre-Roman Iron Age. *P.P.S.*, 30, 99-110.

Hughes, W.R. (1938) The Belgo-Roman Occupation of the Welwyn Area. *East Herts. Arch. Soc.*, 10, 141-9.

Hull, M.R. (1929) *Colchester and Essex Museum Annual Report 1929.* Borough of Colchester.

Hull, M.R. (1942) An Early Claudian burial found at Colchester. *Ant. Jour.*, 22, 59-65.

Kelly, D.B. (1963) Researches and discoveries in Kent: Maidstone. *Arch. Cant.*, 78, 194-6.

Kelly, D.B. (1971) Quarry Wood Camp, Loose: a Belgic oppidum. *Arch. Cant.*, 86, 55-84.

Kenyon, K.M. (1948) *Excavations at the Jewry Wall Site, Leicester* (Soc. Ant. Res. Cttee. Rep. No. XV). Oxford.

Krämer, W. (1962) Manching II. *Germania*, 40, 293-317.

Krämer, W. (1971) Silberne Fibelpaare aus dem letzten vorchristlichen Jahrhundert. *Germania*, 49, 111-32.

Mahr, G. (1967) *Die Jüngere Latènekultur des Trierer Landes.* Berlin.

May, T. (1930) *Catalogue of the Roman Pottery in the Colchester and Essex Museum.* London.

Navarro, J.M. de (1972) *The Finds from the Site of La Tène.* London.

Neville, – (1857) Roman reliques in Essex. *Arch. Jour.*, 14, 84-7.

Ogilvie, J.D. and Dunning, G.C. (1967) A Belgic burial-group at Sholden, near Deal; and a Belgic tazza from Mill Hill, Upper Deal. *Arch. Cant.*, 82, 221-6.

Owles, E.J. (1967) Two Belgic cemeteries at Boxford. *Proc. Suffolk Inst. Arch.*, 31, 88-107.

Peacock, D.P.S. (1971) Roman amphorae in pre-Roman Britain. In Hill, D and Jesson, M. (eds.), *The Iron Age and its Hill-Forts*, 161-88. Southampton.

Ransom, W. (1889) Late-Celtic pottery . . . found near Hitchin. *Proc. Soc. Ant.*, 13, 16-18.

Roach Smith, C. (1871) *A Catalogue of Anglo-Saxon and other Antiquities.* London.

Rook, A.G. (1970) A Belgic and Roman site at Brickwall Hill. *Herts. Arch.*, 2, 23-30.

Sharp, S. (1871) An account of Roman remains found at Duston in Northamptonshire. *Arch.*, 43, 118-30.

Smith, R. (1914) A Late-Celtic cinerary urn found at Letchworth. *Proc. Soc. Ant.*, 26, 238-40.

Stead, I.M. (1967) A La Tène III Burial at Welwyn Garden City. *Arch.*, 101, 1-62.

Stead, I.M. (1968) A La Tène III Burial at The Tene, Baldock, Hertfordshire. *Ant. Jour.*, 48, 306.

Stead, I.M. (1969) Verulamium, 1966-8. *Antiquity*, 43, 45-52.

Stead, I.M. (1971) The reconstruction of Iron Age buckets from Aylesford and Baldock. *B.M. Quarterly*, 35, 250-82.

Taylor, M.V (1932) Romano-British remains: country houses and other buildings. *Victoria County History, Kent*, 3, 102-25.

Tester, P.J. and Bing, H.F. (1949) A first century urn-field at Cheriton, near Folkestone. *Arch. Cant.*, 62, 21-36.

Thill, G. (1966) Ausgrabungen bei Goeblingen-Nospelt. *Hémecht*, 1966, 483-91.

Thill, G. (1967a) Die Metallgegenstande aus vier spätlatènezeitlichen Brandgräbern bei Goeblingen-Nospelt. *Hémecht, 1967,* 87-98.

Thill, G. (1967b) Die Keramik aus vier spätlatènezeitlichen Bradgräbern von Goeblingen-Nospelt. *Hémecht*, 1967, 199-213.

Vauvillé, O. (1906) Découvertes faites dans l'oppidum de Pommiers (Aisne). *Mémoires de la Soc. Nat. des Ant. de France*, 66, 1-26.

Warhurst, A. (1953) A Belgic burial from Borough Green. *Arch. Cant.*, 66, 157-60.

Werner, J. (1954) Die Bronzekanne von Kelheim. *Bayerische Vorgeschichtsblatter*, 20, 43-73.

Westell, W.P. (1928) Romano-British objects from Foxholes, near Hitchin. *Trans. East. Herts. Arch. Soc.*, 8, 22-5.

Westell, W.P. (1935) Bronze objects found in Hertfordshire. *Ant. Jour.*, 15, 349-51.

Wheeler, Sir R.E.M. (1943) *Maiden Castle* (Soc. Ant. Res. Cttee. Report No. XII). London.

Winbolt, S.E. (1925a) *Roman Folkestone.* London.

Winbolt, S.E. (1925b) Pre-Roman finds at Folkestone. *Ant. Jour.*, 5, 63-7.

Winbolt, S.E. (1926) The Roman villa at Folkestone. *Arch. Cant.*, 38, 45-50.

Woodruff, C.H. (1904) Further discoveries of Late Celtic and Romano-British interments at Walmer. *Arch. Cant.*, 26, 9-16.

Wright, A.G. (1922) *Colchester Museum of Local Antiquities – Report.* Borough of Colchester.

NOTES

1. Although this cemetery has most of the distinctive elements of the phase, curiously it has yet to produce a Colchester brooch. At least twenty flat graves have been excavated, apart from the well-known tumulus, though the cemetery has never been published as a whole. For the most important groups, see Hawkes & Hull 1947:13, n.5.

2. The numbers given here are from the Letchworth Museum register; they are recorded in the publication, but are not on the objects.

3. See e.g. Krämer's chronological scheme, which puts The Nauheim brooch, the Aylesford type of brooch (Almgren 65), and the Aylesford jug in the same phase, La Tène D1 (Krämer 1962:306, Abb. 1). Navarro 1972 (I, Part I:317-19) provides a recent survey of the dating of the Nauheim brooch.

4. The writer is grateful to E.J. Holland, Field Officer of the Berkhamsted Archaeological Society, for information about this discovery.

5. Aylesford, Borough Green, Deal, Faversham, Folkestone and Swarling in Kent; Great Chesterford in Essex; Hitchin, Letchworth, Baldock, Hertford Heath, Welwyn and Welwyn Garden City in Hertfordshire; Guilden Morden in Cambridgeshire.

MICHAEL THOMPSON

The construction of the Manor at South Wingfield, Derbyshire

. . . edificavit manerium pulcherrimum de Wynfeld prope Derbye de lapidibus et cemento.
William of Worcester (*c.* 1480) referring to Ralph, Lord Cromwell

Winfeld, or Wenfeld, in Derbyshire is but a maner place but yt far passith Sheffield Castle.
Leland's *Itinerary* (*c.* 1540)

Winfield, a very rich mannour, where Ralph Lord Cromwel, in the reign of Henry the sixth, built a very stately house, considering that age. Camden's *Britannia* (1695)

The writer of this article, though by origin an historian, studied for his doctorate on a Mesolithic subject under Professor Clark. Circumstances caused him to return to his interest in the historical period, and this paper, which tries to relate a detailed written source to visible remains, lies in a frontier zone between archaeology and history. The interplay of the two sources of evidence, material and documentary, may help to a better understanding of this frontier and how it may be transcended.

The bold silhouette of the Manor at South Wingfield with its chimneys and turrets (Fig. 3), standing on the hill south of the village, has caught the attention of many antiquaries since Leland. After its abandonment as a residence in the latter part of the eighteenth century, Romantic interest stirred an antiquary to write a volume on its history (Blore 1793); later, during the Gothic revival, an architect was prompted to make a thorough survey of the ruins (Ferrey 1870), which has not been surpassed to this day and upon which the figures used here are based. It might be thought that nothing more could be said about the Manor but, unknown to the earlier writers, some of the papers of its builder had survived in the library of Viscount De Lisle, at Penshurst Place in Kent, and were listed and partly calendared by the Historical Manuscripts Commission in 1925 (Kingsford 1925). Among other papers are some building accounts for the college and castle at Tattershall (Simpson 1960), as well as two manorial accounts for Wingfield. To one of these is attached a very detailed record of expenditure during the construction of the Manor House, which sheds a good deal of light on the matter. This account, which is transcribed in an appendix, is the subject of this paper. We give a very brief history and description of the ruins before discussing this in detail, and conclude by trying to fit the manor at Wingfield into Lord Cromwell's other building activities.

I must thank the owner of the manuscript, Viscount De Lisle V.C., for so kindly allowing its use, and the Historical Manuscripts Commission for providing the photostat from which the transcript was made.

History

During most of the Middle Ages, South Wingfield was not the seat of an important family. In the thirteenth and fourteenth centuries, however, a set of fortunate marriages produced a concentration of estates right across the Midlands in the hands of one family, the Cromwells of Nottinghamshire origin, whose main seat was at Tattershall in Lincolnshire. Ralph Cromwell, the third baron (born *c.* 1394), who held high political office, transformed the position by erecting, south of the village, the great house that is the subject of this paper. Lord Cromwell died without heir in 1456, when the manor was sold to John Talbot, second earl of Shrewsbury. It remained a Shrewsbury seat until the seventeenth century and then began to decline. In the Civil War it suffered damage during a successful Parliamentary assault, subsequently compounded by deliberate slighting. Partial occupation was resumed at the Restoration, when the buildings were acquired by Immanuel Halton who probably mutilated the hall by inserting a first floor. His grandson abandoned the manor in the 1770s and erected the house known as Wingfield Hall in the valley below. The ruins of the older house remained

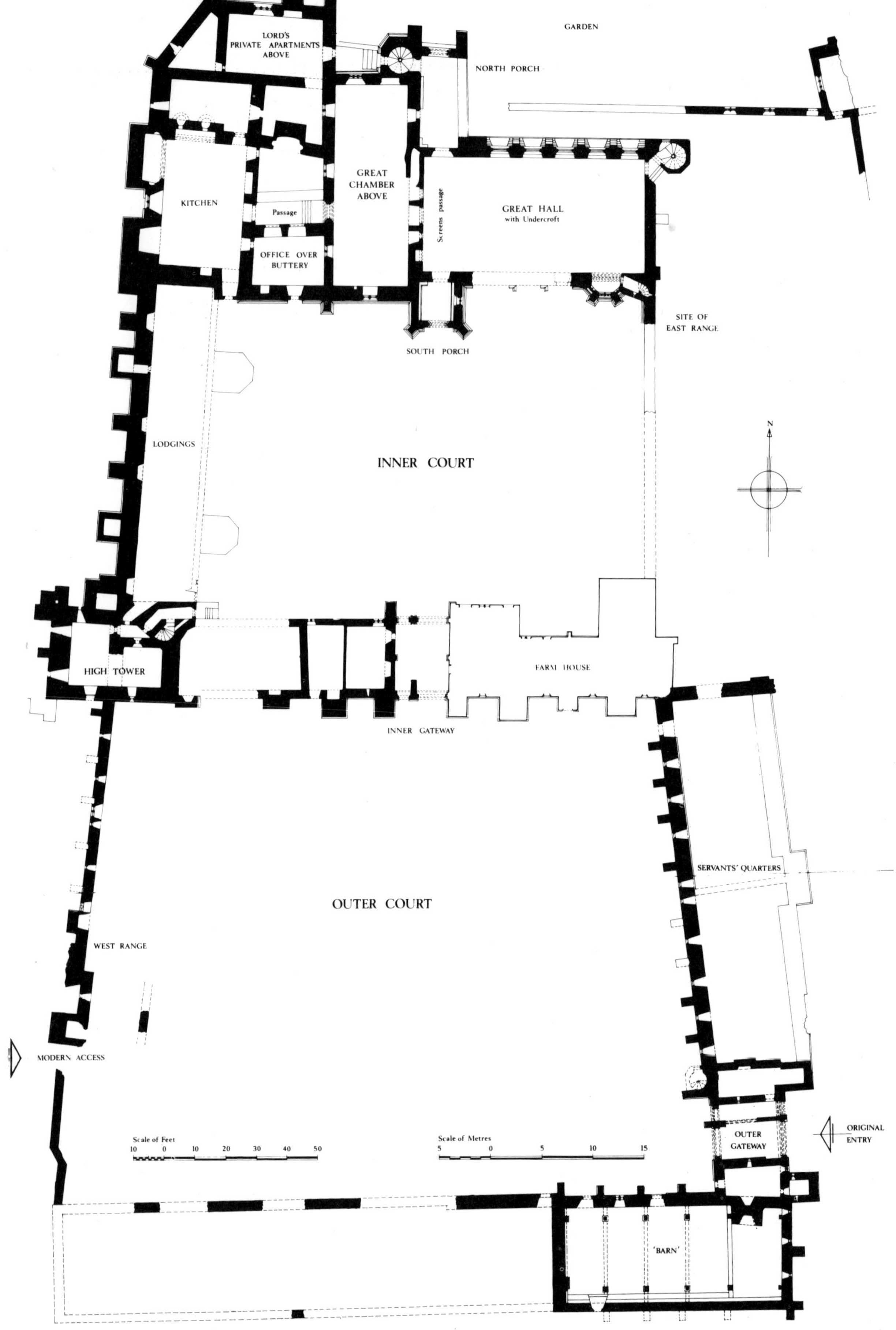
GARDEN
LORD'S PRIVATE APARTMENTS ABOVE
NORTH PORCH
GREAT CHAMBER ABOVE
KITCHEN
Passage
OFFICE OVER BUTTERY
Screens passage
GREAT HALL
with Undercroft
SITE OF EAST RANGE
SOUTH PORCH
LODGINGS
INNER COURT
N
HIGH TOWER
FARM HOUSE
INNER GATEWAY
SERVANTS' QUARTERS
OUTER COURT
WEST RANGE
MODERN ACCESS
Scale of Feet
10 0 10 20 30 40 50
Scale of Metres
5 0 5 10 15
OUTER GATEWAY
ORIGINAL ENTRY
'BARN'

Figure 1. Plan of the Manor (after E.B. Ferrey).

uninhabited until a farm-house was inserted into the east side of the cross range, in the last century. In 1960, the Department of the Environment (then the Ministry of Works) took the ruins into its care to arrest serious deterioration and undertake consolidation of the fabric.

Description of the Manor

The Manor has been designed to fit the shape of a northward-pointing spur of high ground, so that the hill-side slopes steeply down on the east and west but gently upwards from the southern base of the triangle (Figs. 1, 4). The converging east and west sides are linked transversely in the middle by a cross range, creating a larger, outer, court on the south and a smaller, inner, court on the north. The descriptions 'outer' and 'inner' are used here because, originally, access was up the valley southwards on the east side of the house, through the outer gate on its south-east corner (Fig. 4) into the outer court, from which a gate in the middle of the cross range led into the inner court (Fig. 5). The principal buildings of the Manor – hall, great chamber, kitchen – lie on the north side of this court, facing inwards on the south but commanding a fine view over the valley to the north. The triangular area in front of them, the tip of the spur, was enclosed by a ditch with its inner face revetted and buttressed in stone to produce a kind of ha-ha, and we may fairly assume that in the fifteenth century the area was a garden or pleasance. The ground level on the garden side is much lower than that of the court-yard, so that the south porch of the hall is at ground level and the north porch at first floor

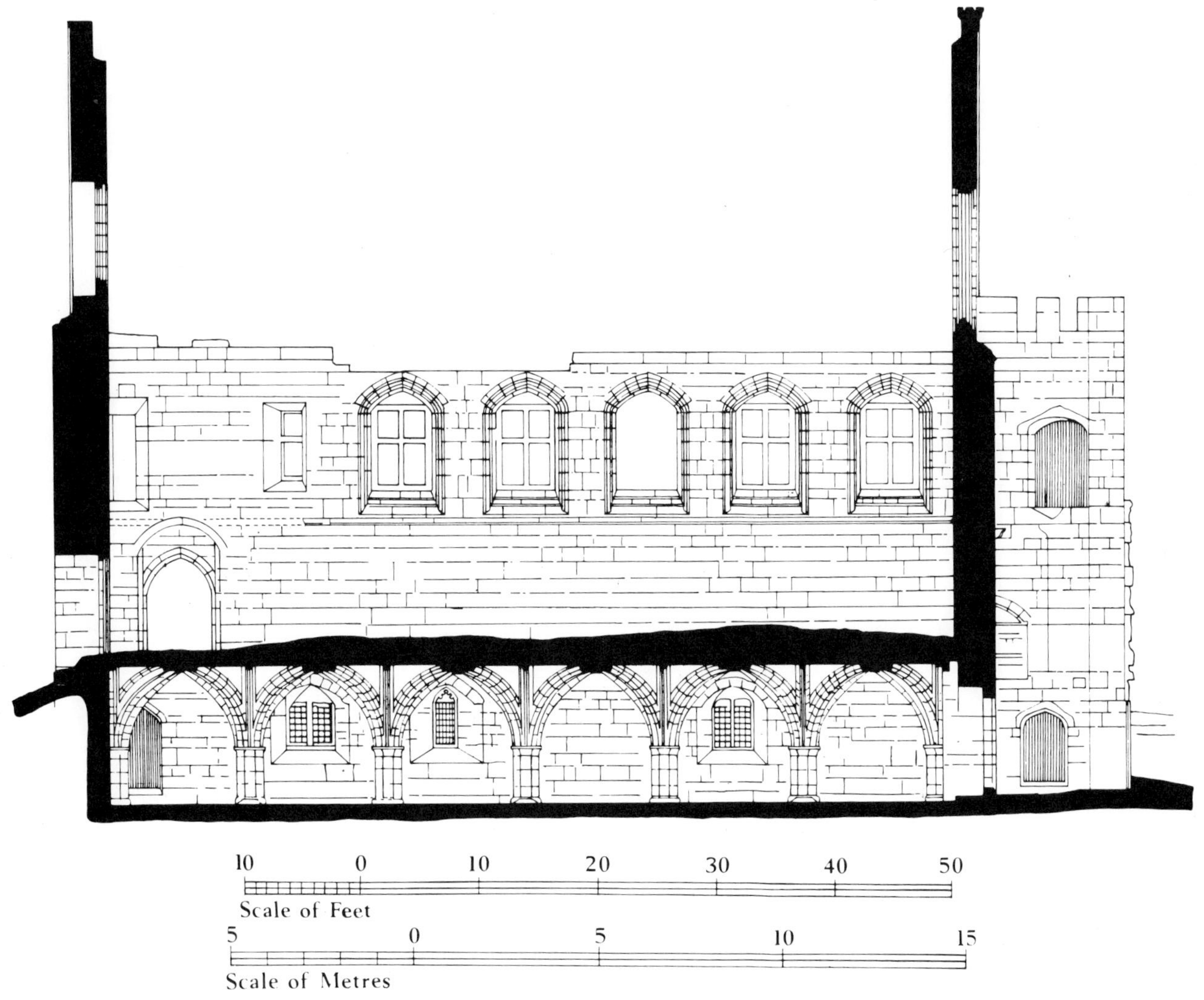

Figure 2. Longitudinal section of the Hall (after E.B. Ferrey).

Figure 3. View of the ruins from the west.

Figure 4. Aerial view from the east (Cambridge University collection: copyright reserved).

level, while the undercroft is buried on the south side but at ground level on the north (Fig. 2). The ha-ha wall terminates at the corner of the buildings on the west side, but on the east it sweeps round the site of the east range, as if to terminate at some eastward projection, which it is tempting to think was the chancel end of a chapel. The whole design suggests planning on a virgin site without regard having to be paid to pre-existing buildings.

The inner and outer gatehouses are very similar, with through pedestrian passages and no trace of portcullis or drawbridge: there are neither wall-walks nor towers, and it is clear that we are dealing with a house where defence, while not wholly ignored, was not a prime consideration. Fragments of the west range of the outer court survive, as does quite a lot of the east range, a two-storied dormitory-style building, perhaps intended as *bâtiments de servitude.* Most of the south range has vanished under the modern farm but, at its east end, adjoining the gate, is the only roofed building of the Manor, a two-storied aisled building with massive timbers, now called 'The Barn' but which probably originally comprised offices below and servants' quarters above. A modern farm-house has been inserted into the east side of the cross range, but the west side retains some fine chimneys. At its junction with the west range, at the angles of both courts, stands the high tower, with two of its sides missing, no doubt pulled down in the Parliamentary slighting (Fig. 5).

In the inner court no remains of the east range survive, although the door-ways and corbels at the east end of the hall indicate that it was three-storied, if it was ever built. The hall itself is of much finer work than the rest of the Manor: ashlar inside and out, carved merlons and frieze, a south porch originally fan-vaulted, an oriel with fine tracery, all set over a six-bay undercroft with octagonal columns and moulded

Figure 5. Aerial view from the south-west, with high tower in the foreground (Cambridge University collection: copyright reserved).

Figure 6. View of hall from the south.

ribs intersecting in wheel-bosses (Figs, 6, 7, 8, 9). The screens passage, beneath a wooden gallery entered from the first floor of the south porch, led to the north porch; at its north-west corner was a newel staircase and there was another one in the north-east corner of the hall. West of the hall, and at right angles to it, lies the great chamber block: basement, service floor, and above this the large audience chamber, with an impressive window facing into the court (Fig. 7). At the north end was an inner chamber and in the north-west angle a door that led to a suite of private chambers, accessible only from there and extending westwards to link up with the north end of the kitchen. At the south end of the audience chamber, a door on one side opened into a room over the porch, and on the other what appears to be an office over the buttery. Between these two projections was a small open court with a covered alley on the south side, which had hatches for serving the hall from kitchen and buttery. The kitchen closes the west end of the range and is abutted, on the south side, by the west range of the court. Only the outside wall of this remains but the groups of fire-places, latrines and windows in it show that it must have been divided into two groups of lodgings, set in pairs on two floor-levels over a basement (Fig. 10) served by two staircases in octagonal turrets, the bases of which can just be discerned in the ground.

This brief description, combined with the plan and photographs, may allow some appreciation of the ruin as it now exists. We can now turn to the documents.

The building account

The account, three membranes long and 11½ inches wide, is stitched to the back of the manorial accounts for the same year, the two forming one small roll. It bears the marginal heading: 'Wyndfeld – office of Supervisor of Works' and covers the period 1 November 1442 to Christmas 1443, i.e. just under fourteen months. The responsible officer, John Ulker-

Figure 7. Hall porch and great chamber gable, from the south.

Figure 8. Doors in screens passage of the hall.

thorp, bears the title 'Supervisor and Clerk of Works' on this account and 'Bailiff and Supervisor of the Whole Farm' (*totius husbandri*) on the manorial account. After the arrears and the Receiver's statement we are plunged straight into the building expenditure.

Following the heading in the margin, 'Costs of the Buildings of the Manor of Wingfield', the outlay is arranged methodically according to nature of work:

Winning of rubble freestone and carriage	£ 8 8 3
Purchase and manufacture of quicklime with the digging of gravel	£ 5 6 11
Wages of masons and their labourers	£ 83 3 11½
Carpenters' wages with plank sawing	£ 32 3 11½
Purchase of tiles and their laying	£ 6 4 0½
Purchase of lead and its use	£ 41 5 0
Purchase of ironwork, its use and other items	£ 7 11 2¾
Purchase of plaster and its application	£ 1 12 9
Servants' fees and purchase of hay	£ 21 5 0
Removing soil and other necessary costs	£ 15 15 10½

The total sum was £ 222 16 11¾ but this has been entered, crossed out and reduced to £ 216 3 7¾: lines 153-4 disclose that the mason, Richard North, was £ 6 13 4 in excess of the contract on the undercroft of the hall and this was not to be paid until Lord Cromwell had been consulted.

The account is extraordinarily full – verbose, one might say – and allows us to draw a number of conclusions about the state of the building at the time it was written. It is important to remember that *manerium* refers to the group of buildings (it is used only twice in the sense of the estate), so that the west lodgings of the inner court are located *ad finem occidentalem curie interioris manerii.* Practically every entry can be located fairly confidently. I have numbered the lines of the original account 1-154 for reference, and these are the numbers shown below in brackets.

The park is referred to frequently in the account and charges for renewing its fences, and so on, have their own special entries (140-50). We do not know where it lay, but it belonged to

Figure 9. Undercroft of hall, looking west.

Figure 10. Internal face of outer wall of west lodging range.

the earlier manorial seat in the village (Blore 1793:21, 28). This seat probably served as temporary accommodation for Lord Cromwell until the new buildings were habitable, since we are told of repairs to the kitchen of the lord's *hospicium* situated within the village of Wingfield (126). Apart from a reference (102) to an old stable (not necessarily on the site of the Manor), the account never hints at any other earlier building.

There can be no doubt that work had been going on for several years prior to this account, and we can make a fairly shrewd guess as to how long this period had been. Lines 51-2 and 76-7 refer to previous payments: in the fourth third and second year preceding, in the former case; and in the third, second and next last, in the latter. In line 76 the clerk has written 'third' and crossed it out to put 'second'. He was evidently a little confused as to whether to start counting in the present or previous year; I think it fair to assume that, in both cases, the three years immediately preceding that of the account are intended. Counting back from 1 November 1442, this takes us to 1 November 1439. As the payments in the first case refer to the original contract for the hall, presumably the first building to be erected, the work may have begun in the autumn of 1439 or the spring of 1440, or at all events not later.

It is apparent at first glance that we are dealing with buildings that were on the point of completion: the louver (115-16) and screens (67, 84) are being erected in the hall, doors and windows inserted in the chambers (35-7, 111-15), the west lodging range being roofed (95) and so on. Among the duties of Thomas Smyth and the 23 labourers was that of 'cleaning the inner court against the Lord's arrival' (63), from which it is reasonable to suppose that Lord Cromwell actually came into residence during the period of the account. Possibly, indeed, the reason that it ended at Christmas (the attached manorial accounts run to Michaelmas and none of the five Tattershall accounts finishes so late in the year) was because there was something of a rush to get the building ready, not an uncommon event in the building trade.

Apart from a single reference (102) to repairs to chambers in the south part of the Manor, perhaps workmen's quarters erected at the beginning of the operation, work was being carried on exclusively on the hall, to chambers to the west of it, to the kitchen and to the west lodging range in the inner court. In a verbose account like this it is highly unlikely that there would not be mention of at least minor work on the high tower, the gates and other ranges, had they existed at this time. The references to an inner court (but none to an outer court) lead to the interesting conclusion that, at the time this account was drawn up, the general design of the two courts had been marked out, or perhaps even foundations of the ranges laid, but that, with the exception of the north and west ranges of the inner court built for immediate use and a possible workmen's range in the outer court, the rest of the buildings of the Manor had not yet been erected.

One of the most remarkable features of the document is that the original contract between Lord Cromwell and John Enterpas for the construction of the hall is summarized (49-51): 'containing in length 72 feet, in breadth 36 feet, in height 12 feet with one vault of the same length and breadth within the walls and with one ring halfway down the middle and at the same time two vices and doors and windows as contained in the indenture . . .'. The existing ruined hall is at once recognizable in this description, its horizontal measurements being just these, although there is a discrepancy in the height, which is nearer 22 feet (could the scribe inadvertently have omitted an 'x' ?). The identification of the ring may perhaps be made from other entries referring to a louver, since its position in the middle of the hall corresponds to that of the central hearth: might the ring be an iron plate on top of the vault to protect it, or perhaps a circular hood or roof-opening below the louver? The vices are the two spiral staircases shown on the plan (Fig. 1).

The louver, *lodium* or *femoralis*, is mentioned several times (86-7, 104-5, 115). The great standard (*magna vexilla*) surmounting the louver and the sixteen vanes had been bought from John Ducheman (evidently a foreigner) and paid for separately by Lord Cromwell (87), who perhaps took some personal part in the choice. As the entry occurs in the carpentry section it is likely that the objects in question were of painted wood but it may merely mean that it was the carpenters' responsibility to put them up. The vanes may have rotated independently, or in clusters, or – if this is not being over-ingenious – the word might mean horizontal slats, pivoted on spindles, serving as adjustable vents on the four sides of the louver. Heraldically, a standard was a 'long and narrow flag, with the lower edge horizontal, and the upper aslant from the staff to the end, which was slit for a little way. An upright panel next the staff always contained the arms of St George, and the rest of the field was parted fessewise, or into three or four bars, and powdered with badges. It was also divided into three parts by two bends with the owner's word, reason or motto, and the first section then contained the crest or principal badge. The whole was fringed of livery colours. Standards varied in size with dignity of the owner, that of the King being twice as long as a knight's, while those of peers were of intermediate length according to their rank. Standards were used only for parade purposes . . .' (Hope 1913:45-6).

The reference (84-5) to the large door leading to 'le parler' from the hall is of interest. The hall has two porch doors and three service doors at its west end, so this can refer only to the door at the north-east corner; in other words, the adjoining room in the absent east range was intended to be the parlour. This is what we should expect and had there been a chapel at its south end in the centre of the range (see page 421), the arrangement would recall that of Haddon Hall in the same county. A further valuable piece of information in the records is that the chambers north of the kitchen (36), mentioned more than once, were called *Wythdragth* (withdrawing) which confirms the view that these rooms, entered from the north-west corner of the great chamber, were Cromwell's private retiring rooms (page 422). I take it that the work of timber over the west lodgings (38) merely refers to the continuous trusses and rafters over the range before they were slated as recorded elsewhere (95).

The original contract for the hall had been made with John Enterpas (51) or Entrepath (154), a mason whose name seems to imply that he was concerned with breaking-in the site (*cf.* 'enterprise'). By the time this account was made,

Enterpas had disappeared and the leading mason throughout, to whom the supervision of the erection of the undercroft vault is specifically attributed (153-4), was Richard North. He had exceeded the price of the original contract with Enterpas and the excess was not to be paid until he had spoken with Lord Cromwell. If, therefore, we wish to elevate the leading mason to the rank of architect, then North is clearly the man who deserves the title, unless we prefer to attribute the ground-plan to Enterpas and the elevations to North! Whether Ulkerthorp played some part in the design or was just an administrator it is impossible to say. It comes as no surprise to find that, four years later in 1447, a Richard North, presumably the same man, appears as Collector in the other surviving manorial account for Wingfield (Kingsford 1925:216) which, it may be fairly assumed, was a step up the ladder of manorial promotion.

The work was carried out by agreement or minor contract, *conuencio* (e.g. 57), as piecework (36, 55, 56) or by direct wages. Senior craftsmen, carpenters (67, 81) or masons were paid 6d. a day. Lines 41 to 47 are very revealing about the hierarchy of masons: North (3/4 a week); John fforman, presumably the foreman, and Nicholas Smart (3/- a week); and then various gradations: 2/10, 2/8, 2/4, 2/- and 1/10 a week. It is fair to assume that the lowest-paid masons were still apprentices, since the masons' labourers were paid 4d. a day (63) (Brown & Hopkins 1955). The lowest of the low were Cromwell's servants, 66/8 a year (125), but they had security of employment and may have received free board and lodging. On occasions there must have been 50 to 75 men at work on the site. It is fairly clear from the repetitive surnames that we are dealing with family groups, father and son, brothers and cousins.

921 cart-loads or waggon-loads of building materials are recorded in this account as having been brought to the Manor, and this may not be complete. Lord Cromwell's chief direct contribution to the work was to supply the waggons and three waggoners; their wages and the feed of the draught oxen (122-6) constituted almost ten per cent of the total cost of work (there were also minor items, like greasing and repairing the wheels, in other parts of the account). Three words are used: *plaustrum, plaustratum* and *carecta*, each being applied either to the load or to the vehicle, although the last word normally means the load (23-4, 26). The lord's vehicles – presumably there were three – are always called *plaustra* or *plaustrata*, a term that is normally regarded as meaning a four-wheeled waggon, not a two-wheeled cart (Salzman 1952:352; Jenkins 1961:6-8). That this is inherently likely is revealed, in the account, by the fact that they were also used to bring in the hay and corn harvests (124). There is a puzzling reference to repairs on pairs of wheels (92), as if they were attached to a rotating axle, but such a primitive design (even in a fore-carriage) is surely most improbable. The oxen were presumably attached to a draught-pole. The beasts ate 82 waggon-loads of hay, about 1½ waggon-loads a week, so it is fair to assume that three fairly large teams of four, six or, possibly, even eight animals were being employed. The steep hill at Wingfield must have made heavy demands on them.

One has the distinct impression, both from the use of oxen, rather than horses, for draught and the rather low level of craftsmen's wages, that we are in a backward or isolated area. When studying the fairly coarse workmanship of the masonry in the ruins, this is probably a factor to be borne in mind.

A great deal of information about the sources of raw materials can be culled from the document, although not much calls for special mention. The forty cart-loads of sea coal (23-5) brought from Swanwick, three miles away, presumably had been mined locally and not brought by sea. (For the use of coal at Tattershall, see Simpson 1960: 17, 35). Most raw materials were local, from the park or from only a mile or two away, and even with carriage their cost was considerably outweighed by that of labour. The only really dear raw material was lead, which was being used on the louver lantern (104-5) or being put in store, a fair indication that further work was proposed.

It is not so much the content of the account as its thoroughness that is its unusual feature. In stone country no doubt most of the work described was normal, but it may of course be contrasted with the five surviving accounts for Lord Cromwell's work at Tattershall Castle, each covering about a year in the period 1434-46 (Simpson 1960:1-37). Unfortunately these are far less informative about the buildings than that for Wingfield (Kingsford 1925:xxi), while the surviving remains to which they should be related are far less complete. The famous tower, for instance, is not identifiable until the last account in 1445-6

(Simpson 1960:36). But there are three striking differences: the scale of expenditure at Tattershall was about twice as great as at Wingfield: a good deal of expenditure at Tattershall was on brick-making and, arising from this, the leading craftsman at Tattershall was a foreign brick-maker, Baldwin (although perhaps Simpson exaggerated his status). A John Ducheman supplied the standard and vanes at Wingfield but the craftsmen, from Richard North downwards, were emphatically English. No doubt this was at least one reason for the marked contrast between the buildings erected for Lord Cromwell at the two different places.

Lord Cromwell and Wingfield Manor

Born in about 1394, Ralph Cromwell as a young man served in France and was at Agincourt. He succeeded to the title in 1417, was called to Parliament in 1422 and was a Chamberlain of the Exchequer from 1423-6. The high-water mark of his career was the post of Lord Treasurer that he held from 1433 to 1443. The family was not one that had an ancient seat, for its wealth had been acquired recently by a series of fortunate marriages; Cromwell's appointment on the one hand provided the motive to enhance his new dignity with appropriate buildings, while on the other the perquisites of office may have provided some of the means. It comes as no surprise, therefore, to find that the first surviving building account for Tattershall belongs to 1434, the first year after his appointment, and work probably went on for another dozen or so years. If the suggested date for the beginning of the work at Wingfield is right, 1439 or 1440, then it was started five or six years later than the castle, prompted by the same motive no doubt, except that Tattershall was his main seat and this a rural mansion.

As with a number of late mediaeval noblemen, Cromwell had turned his mind to the foundation of a college and issued a charter to this effect in 1440 (Kingsford 1925:172-3). The scheme was an ambitious one, requiring not only the erection of residential courts at Tattershall but the entire rebuilding of the adjoining church, and this was in fact largely carried out by his executors, after his death in 1456. He had no children and with increasing age his concern to see that the college should be completed after his death seems to have much occupied his mind, as can be seen in the copy of his will dated 30 September 1454 (Kingsford 1925:210). All his unentailed estates, including the manors of Collyweston, Northamptonshire, and Wingfield, were to be sold and the proceeds applied to charity and this end (Kingsford 1925:219; Smith 1906-10:I, 22). It would be interesting to know how long before this date the decision to dispose of Wingfield after his death had been taken, since it is unlikely that he would have continued building there after reaching such a decision. Work must have been pursued for some years after Christmas 1443, the termination of our account, in order to complete those parts that stand now but had not been erected then, but it may be that the task was never fully completed. If, for example, it turns out that the east range of the inner court was never built, this may be offered as a possible explanation.

Appendix: Transcript of account

The account transcribed here is listed under Cromwell Family Papers and Estate Accounts, No. 57, page 215 of Volume I of the Historical Manuscripts Commission Report on the Manuscripts of Lord De L'Isle and Dudley. It is attached to the back of the manorial accounts and this transcription, starting from the top, goes through the building works and park maintenance to the main *Summa* and includes the first note beyond, but the other entries below were not sufficiently relevant to include in what was becoming unmanageably long.

The reference numbers refer to the lines in the manuscript. The building works occupy several paragraphs, with marginal headings attached by calipers to the relevant parts. In the original the beginning of each paragraph is marked, but continues on the same line as the preceding sentence. The transcription starts a fresh line for each new paragraph, without re-numbering. The division into sentences is as in the original, but commas have been added to assist the reader.

Wyndfeld — officium Superuisoris operum]

Compotus Johannis Ulkerthorp Superuisoris et Clerici operum Radulphi domini Cromwell ibidem a primo die Novembris anno xxj^{mo}. Regis Henrici vj^{ti}. usque ffestum Natalis domini anno eiusdem Regis xxij^{do}. per unum annum integrum et liij dies.

Arreragia

Idem reddidit compotum de-xiiij li. xiij d. ob. de arreragiis ultimi compoti.

Summa — xiiij li. xiij d. ob.

Recepta denariorum de Johanne Sawcheuerell Receptore domini

Et de — Ciiij.^{xx} x.^{li} xiij.^{s} vij.^{d} ob. receptis de Johanne Sawcheuerell, Receptore domini in Comitatibus Not., derb. et leyc. ac Stafford tam de exitibus dominiorum domini ibidem quam in parcellis prout patet in compoto ipsius Receptoris huius anni in titulo liberacionis denariorum ultra, xv.^{li} vij.^{s} xj.^{d} ob. superato in compoto Ballivi Iconomie de Wyndfeld in titulo Recepta ffirmariorum

Summa — Ciiij.^{xx} x li. xiij s. vij d. ob.

Summa Recepte cum Arreragiis — CCiiij.li. xiiij.s. ix.^{d}

Custos edificiorum manerii de Wynfeld

Lucracio petrarum liberarum rugidarum cum cariacione viij li viij s. iij d.

In stipendiis Thome Waller fossantis et adquirentis C^{ma} asselars in parco ibidem ex certa conuencione in grosso — iij s. iiij d. Et in denariis concessis Edwardo Wylde pro fossacione et adquisicione tam petrarum liberarum vocatarum moldestones et asselars quam petrarum rugidarum pro omni opere cementariorum fiendo infra manerium de Wynfeld inter ij diem Decembris anno xxj^{mo} et idem diem proximam sequentem ex conuencione una cum adquisicione$^{xiij\ s.\ iiij\ d.}$ CCCC petrarum adquirend. pro operibus predictis in anno futuro cariand. eodem anno — vij li. xvj s. viij d. Et in denariis solutis pro cariacione xvij carectarum petrarum liberarum de diuersis locis tam parci quam Cruchmore, videlicet Willemo Colman, Thome Rawlynson, Roberto Wodhouse, Willemo Rawlynson et Johanni Wodehouse, pro singula carecta iij d., ad tascham — iiij s. iij d. Et in denariis solutis pro cariacione xxiiij$^{ij\ s.}$ plaustratorum petrarum rugidarum de ffischepoledamhed usque in manerium, pro plaustro j d., xij$^{ij\ s.}$ plaustra huius cariage, cariat. de quodam loco infra parcum vocato lytelhege, pro singula carecta ij d., ad tascham iiij s. De cariacione residuum nichil quia per seruientes et plaustra domini.

Set in denariis solutis pro cariacione x plaustratorum petrarum de lymeston de Cruchclyff videlicet per Willemum Colman, Thomam Rawlynson, Johannes Wodhousse, Willemum Rawlynson et Robertum Pryll, pro singula carecta iij d., ad tascham — ij s. vj d. Et in stipendiis Edwardi Wylde fossantis et adquirentis C^{ma}ij plaustrata petrarum de lymeston, Thome Samme lix. plaustrata pro calce inde cremenda, pro qualibet Centena viij s., ad tascham — xij.^{s} De fossacione et adquisicione xl plaustratorum dictarum petrarum nichil quia per seruientes domini conductos per annum. Nec de cariacione CC^{m} x carectarum Set in xl plaustratis carbonum maritinorum emptis apud Swanwyk de Johanne Holte et

Empcio et factura calcis viue cum fossacione zabuli Cvj s.xj d.

Johanne Skynnar, precio carecte ix d. cum stipendiis Thome
vj d.
Rawlynson cariant. j plaustrum dictorum carbonum de ibidem usque Wynfeld — xxx s. vj d.
De cariacione xxxix carectarum dictorum carbonum
ma
nichil hic in denariis quia per seruientes et plaustra domini. Nec de cariacione Cxl carectarum
meremii pro cremacione dictarum petrarum nichil quia
per seruientes domini. Set in stipendiis Miloms Mersdayn pro fraccione lx plaustratorum,
Willemi Crowford pro xl plaustratorum dictarum petrarum, pro carecta j d.
ma
ad tascham viij s. iiij d. De fraccione C dictarum petrarum nichil hic quia inter stipendia
iiij d. ij d.
laborariorum per dietam. Set in iij baskettez, ij bollez
vi d.
emptis pro portacione dictarum petrarum usque in ustrinam calcinam et in diuersis expensis
factis in cremacione dicte ustrine — xiij d. De
aliquibus denariis solutis pro cremacione dictarum petrarum nichil hic quia inter stipendia
laborariorum ad omnia per dietam. Set in lxvj quartariis
lx vj
calcis viue emptis apud Cruch videlicet de Johannis Strete et Johanne Idersay precio quartar
iij d. — xvj s. vj d. Et in stipendiis Johannis
ma
Moke et Thome Samme senior fossantium et adquirentium inter se CCxlviij plaustratorum
zabuli, pro carecta j d. ob., ad tascham — xxxvj s. De
ma
cariacione dictorum CCxlviij plaustrorum zabuli nichil hic quia per seruientes et plaustra
domini.

Et in denariis solutis Thome Cobyn in partem
solucionis de xxiiij li. pro opere cementariorum liberorum magni muri in fine occidentali
interioris curie ut in annis precedentibus ultra iiij li. solut.
anno secundo precedenti et viij li. v s. x d. anno proximo precedenti — vij li. viij s. De iiij li.
vj s. ij d. aretro de eadem nichil quia non solut.
xxiiij s.
Set in denariis solutis Ricardo North pro opere cement. iiij hostiorum in muro ex parte
occidentali manerii pro introitu habenda in cameris inferioribus
xxiiij s. vj s.
ibidem, pro pecia vj s., iiij hostiorum in muris coquine, pecia ad vj s., ij hostiorum in muris
nove camere ad finem borialem coquine vocate
v s. iiij s.
wythdragth, ij hostiorum paruorum pro latrinis ibidem, iiij fenestrarum pro lumine habenda
ma
ad dictas cameras — lxiij s. Et in CCC petris vocatis
xxxiijs.
asselars emptis de Richardo North pro longo muro ex parte occidentali manerii ibidem
faciend. subtus opus ligneum nouarum camerarum ibidem,
iiij s. iiij s.
pro Centena xj s., stipendia eiusdem Ricardi per viij dies, Willemi Clerk per viij dies, utroque
ij s. iiij d.
ad vj d. per diem, Johannis Kynston per viij dies,
v d. x d.
Thome Lowth per j diem, Nicholi Didesbery per ij dies, ad v d. per diem laborant. circa
cubacionem dictarum petrarum in dicto muro,

ultra fenestras in eodem muro inpositas, operat inter stipendia cementariorum per dietam — xliiij s. vij d. Et in denariis solutis Ricardo North

xxiij s. iiij d. lxx s. ij d.

pro vij septimanis et ij dies, ad iij s. iiij d. in septimana, Johannis fforman pro xxiij

ij s. viij d.

septimanis ij dies et di. ante ffestum omnium sanctorum, Nicholi Smarte pro j septimana

viij s. vj d. xj s. iiij d.

ad iij s.[1] in septimana, Johannis Lowth per iij septimanas, Willemi Byggyng per iiij

xxv s. x d.

septimanas ad ij s. x d. in septimana, Johannis Williamson per ix

xxij s. v d. xxxj s. jd.

septimanas et iiij dies, Johannis Demby per viij septimanas ij dies et di., Johannis Halys per xj septimanas et iiij dies, Nicholi Smarte per iiij septimanas

xvj s. iiij d. x s. viij d.

Johannis fforman per vj septimanas, Willemi Byggyng per iiij septimanas, Johannis Lowthe

viij s. xvj s. iiij d.

per iij septimanas ad ij s. viij d. in septimana, Johannis Kynston

xiij s. x d.

per vij septimanas iij dies et di. ad ij s. iiij d. in septimana, Thome Lowthe per vij septimanas et ad xxij d., Johannis Smyth per ij septimanas et iij

Stipendia cementariorum cum eorum operariis iiij^{xx} iij li. iij s. xj d. ob.

dies ad ij s. in septimana (operant. diuersis operibus infra manerium ibidem prout plenius annotant. in uno quatro papir penes ipsum computantem remanentem)[2] — xiij li. xv s. v d. Et in denariis solutis Ricardo North cementario in persolucionem de . . .[3] pro opere cementr. murorum lapidis fundi aule, ibidem continentis in longitudine lxxij pedum et in latitudine xxxvj pedum, altitudine xij pedum, cum j vawt per longitudinem et latitudinem predictas infra dictos muros, ac cum j rynge in medio per longitudinem, simul cum ij vicez ac ostiis et fenestris prout continetur in indentura facta inter Johannem Enterpas et dominum, de eadem conuencione ultra xxxviij li. xvj s. iij d. solut. anno quatro precedenti, et xvj li. ix s. iiij d. anno tercio precedenti, et xiij li. v s. iiij d. anno secundo precedenti — xx li. xiij s. iiij d.[4]

Et in denariis solutis Willemo Rasyn pro euacuacione et ffossacione fundi murorum coquine et ij parietum ex utraque parte introitus inter aulam et coquinam ex certa conuencione secum facta in grosso — ij s. ix d. Et in denariis solutis Johanni Arosmyth pro replecione dicti fundi cum petris rugidis ex certa conuencione in grosso — iij s. iiij d. Et in denariis solutis Johanni Arosmyth pro factura vij rodarum muri rugidi de le wythdragth nove camere ad finem occidentalem aule, pro singula roda xviij s. ex conuencione — vj li. xiiij s. Et in denariis solutis pro fraccione et dolacione CCC^{ma}xx virgatarum de asselars, pro centena xx s., ex conuencione lxiij s. iiij d. Et in stipendiis Ricardi Lee per C^{ma}xlvj dies, Willemi Lee per v^{xx}xij dies, Johannis Wilson per xxj diem,[5] Johannis Machon per xliiij dies et di., Ricardi Stabull per xxiiij dies et di., Henrici Coke per vij dies, Johannis Arosmyth per xxiiij dies et di. et Willemi Bochar per xviij dies operantium in factura murorum coquine operis rugidi longi muri subtus opus ligneum nouarum camerarum ad finem occidentalem manerii, parcelle muri rugidi in fine boriali magne camere ad finem occidentalem aule, inter se per CCClvij dies et di. ad v d. per diem, ad tascham – viij li. xiij s. xj d. ob. Et in stipendiis Thome Smyth et xxiij sociorum suorum laborantium in seruitura dictorum cementariorum in mixtur. calcis et zabuli et in mundacione curie interioris erga adventum domini, quo per CCC^{ma}iiij^{xx} xviij dies quolibet ad iiij d. per diem, ad tascham – vij li. xij s. ix d. Et in stipendiis Thome Lee per C^{ma}xlvj dies, Roberti Lee per v^{xx} xij dies operantium in dictis operibus et in cremacione calcis per vicez utroque, ad iij d. per diem – lxix s. vj d.

Et in stipendiis Ricardi Sawer sarrantis iij rodarum et di. j quart. vocatarum slytwarke, pro qualibet roda ij s. x d., pro edificiis ibidem hoc anno – x s. vij d. ob. Et in stipendiis eiusdem et seruientis sui sarrantium lez waynscottez et vetus meremium pro speres aule[6] per iiij dies ad xij d. per diem inter se – iiij s. Et in denariis solutis Ricardo Cokker Carpentario in persolucionem de vj li. pro opere carpentr. domatis coquine ultra lxvj s. viij d. solut. anno proximo precedenti – liij s. iiij d. Et in denariis solutis Willemo Wrigth et Ricardo Cokker pro exaltacione domatis coquine per vj[7] pedes ex precepto domini – xl s. De vij li. vj s. viij d. eidem Ricardo aretro de parte x li. xiij s. iiij d. de integra conuencione sua pro opere carpentr. ij baiarum edificand. ad finem borialem magne camere in fine occidentali aule nichil hic eo quod opus non dum perficitur neque sibi inde aliquid solut. Set in denariis solutis eidem Ricardo in partem solucionis de viij li. pro opere carpentr. unius camere vocate Wythdragth ut in compotis precedentibus ultra liij s. iiij d. sibi solut. anno proximo precedenti – lij s. vj d. De liiij s. ij d. eidem aretro de eadem conuencione nichil quia non dum opus perficitur neque sibi inde aliquid solut. Set in denariis solutis Johannis Masele et Willemo Masele carpentariis in partem solucionis de xxvj li. xiij s. iiij d. pro opere carpentr. nouarum camerarum edificand. ex parte occidentali interioris curie ultra iiij li. sibi solut. anno iij precedenti, vj li. xiij s. iiij d. anno secundo[8] precedenti, xx s. iiij d. anno proximo precedenti — xij li. ij s. xj d. De lvj s. ix d. eidem aretro de eadem conuencione nichil quia non dum solut. Set in denariis solutis Willemo Wrigth et seruienti suo existentibus cum Johanne Masele per xj dies circa exaltacionem et eleuacionem dictarum camerarum prout dictus Johannes asserit dominum sibi inuenire per conuencionem suam ut patet per indenturam inter

Stipendia Carpentariorum cum sarracione tabularum xxxij li. iij s. xj d. ob.

xlj s.
dominum et ipsum factam, ad xj d. per diem inter se — x s. j d. Et in stipendiis Willemi
vj d. xx xxxvj s.
Wrighth per iiij iij dies, Rogeri Alsebrok
xxvij s. vj d.
per lxxij dies ad vj d. per diem, Ricardi Cokker, Jacobi Cokker et Johannis Cortenall per lxvj dies inter se, Roberti Cortenall, Johannis
viij s. iiij d. xv d. xxxij s.
Melcham et Johannis Masele per xx dies inter se, Radulphi Alsebrok per iij dies, Johannis
vj d.
Tongge per lxviij dies ad v d. per diem, Petri
xxiiij s.
Radford per lxxij dies ad iiij d. per diem, operantium in opere Carpentr. de le syntrez et skaffoldez pro le vawt et planncheryn aule et facientium sperez pro eadem, emendantium plaustra, et facientium hostia, et facientium magnum hostium pro introitu inter aulam
xv s. xx
et le parler — viij li. xj s. j d. Et in stipendiis Johannis Kyghley et socii sui operantium per iiij dies inter se in factura angulorum aule, ad xij d. per diem, iij libris
vj d. viij d.
de glew, ij libris de wyre emptis pro le lovar aule — xlj s. ij d. De precio j magne vexille et xvj fanez emptarum de Johanne Ducheman pro le lovar aule nichil hic in allocacione quia soluuntur per dominum. Nec de quercis siue arboribus hoc anno prostratis pro edificiis infra manerium predictum nichil hic in allocacione in denariis quia succiduntur per Carpentarios ex conuencione operum suorum. Sine de cariacione huius meremii quia cariant. per plaustra et seruientes domini ad hoc conductos pro toto hoc anno. Et in stipendiis Rogeri
vj s. viij d. l
Stykland findulantis v m. stonlat de meremii domini, pro millena
ij s. xj d. xxj d.
xvj d., CClx tabulos vocatos Thakborde, pro C xiiij d., vij ganggez spokes pro le gangge[9] iij d. de meremio domini — xj s. iiij d. Et in denariis solutis Rogero Stykland pro emendacione et nova factura de lez baroes et trogez per tempus compoti ex conuencione in grosso iij s. iiij d.

De factura iiij parum rotarum de meremii domini nichil hic in allocacione in denariis quia facte fiunt per Willemum Grabar seruientem domini ad
iij s. iiij d.
quecumque opera conducta per annum in grosso. Set in unguento et pinguedine emptis pro
iij d.
rotis plaustratorum[10] domini, ij libris candelarum emptarum pro custodia boum tempore yemali — iij s. vij d.

Et in denariis solutis Johanni Moke et Henrico

ml
Lyndall pro cariacione xij petrarum vocatarum sclatston
de Northege infra campum de Wynfeld usque in manerium pro tegulacione camerarum ad
l
finem occidentalem manerii, pro m. xij d., ad tascham – xij s.
Et in denariis solutis eidem Johanni Moke pro cariacione omnium tegularum de dicto campo
pro tectura domatis coquine ex conuencione in grosso – vj s. viij d.

Empcio tegularum cum operacione earundem vj li. iiij s. ob.

Et in denariis solutis Johanni Sclater de Schirland et socio suo pro adquisicione et fossacione
tegularum et coperient. cum dictis tegulis viij rodarum et di.
super cameras ad finem occidentalem manerii, pro roda ix s., ex conuencione – lxxvj s. vj d.
Et in denariis solutis eidem Johanni Sclater pro
adquisicione tegularum et coperient. cum dictis tegulis[11] rodas super nouam coquinam ut in
partem solucionis de [12], pro roda ix s., ex
iiij s. iij s. iiij d.
conuencione – xviij s. Et in stipendiis Johannis Sclater per xij dies, Roberti Sclater per x dies
tempore yemali, ad iiij d. per diem, Johannis
ij s. vj d. xij d. ob.
Sclater per vj dies, Roberti Sclater per ij dies et di. ad v d. per diem, tegulantium super
nouam cameram ad finem occidentalem aule et emendant.
diuersos defectus diuersis locis tam camerarum ex parte australi manerii quam super vetus
stabulum – x s. x d. ob.

Empcio plumbi cum operacione eiusdem xlj li. v s.

xj li. x s.
Et in iij foders plumbi
xiij li. vj s. viij d.
emptis, precio foder. lxxvj s. viij d., iij foders viij petris j petra plumbi, precio foder iiij li.
xx d. emptis pro copertura lodii siue
femoralis aule – xxiiij li. xvj s. viij d. Et in denariis solutis Johanni Plumar de Worsop pro
fusione iiij foders dicti plumbi
vj s. viij d.
et coperienti cum dicto plumbo lodium siue femorale aule, una cum duabus duodecem
d.
soder. emptis pro eodem – lxxiij s. iiij d.
Et in consimilibus denariis solutis dicto Johanni pro fusione ij foders de remanentibus dictis
vj foders ex conuencione in grosso – x s. Et in
denariis solutis pro iij foders consimilis plumbi emptis per Receptorem pro stauro manerii
predicti, precio foder iiij li. xx d. – xij li. v s.

Et in
l l x s. l l l l l x s.
mmD clavis vocatis spykyngges, m ad iiij s., mmmm clavis vocatis bordenayle millena ad ij s.
ml xxxvj s. l
vj d., xxiiij stonlatnell m ad xviij d.,
xxj d. xx d.
DCC clowtnayle centena ad iij d. emptis de Roberto Huchynson, hoc anno, iiij seris vocatis
xx d.
stoklokez iiij seris pendentibus vocatis
henglokez emptis pro hostiis et portis ibidem hoc anno – lxj s. j d. Et in cordulis emptis
apud Derb. tam pro operibus quam pro lectis
ma
pendend.[13] – xij d. Et in denariis solutis Rogero Smyth pro C xxvij libris et di. ferri

Empcio ferrementorum cum operacione eorundem et aliis vij li. xj s. ij d. ob. q.[a]

fabricati in magnis clavis pro femorale aule
et pykeford graynez in Waynclowtez[14] et lynpynnez in hokez pro hostiis camerarum ad
finem occidentalem manerii et aule, in standerdez et
lokettez[15] pro fenestris magnarum camerarum, pro CCClx libris ferri fabricati in ferrementis
ij fenestrarum coquine, iiij fenestrarum in wythdraght,
iiij fenestrarum in cameris ex parte australi coquine, j fenestre in heronchambr., j fenestre in
camera Johannis Baker, in plates gogionez[16]
xx
et aliis ferrementis pro le lovar, pro v xvij libris ferri fabricati in stapuls, ryngez et hobez pro
carectis et hultuls[17] et emendacione lez
spyndull ferri pro lovar, et bandez pro hostiis camerarum ad finem occidentalem manerii, et
in ligatura v pannez maselyn,[18] pro singula
a
libra j d. ob. ex conuencione — iiij li. v s. vj d. ob. q. Et in stipendiis eiusdem facientis de
xij d.
nouo j wymbulbytt[19] pro tertcione lez
viij d. vij d. viij d. iiij d.
spynduls de le lovar, j adsse, j stonaxe, j trowell, j crow, ij pully pynnez, clavis emptis — iij s.
vij d.

Empcio plastri cum operacione eiusdem xxxij s. ix d[20]

Et in stipendiis Willemi
Plastrer comburantis x carectas plastri paris de remanenti anni precedentis super arias et
paruet. camerarum ad finem occidentalem manerii, pro
carecta ij s. ad tascham, cum ix d. sibi datis in regardum pro diligenti labore suo — xx s. ix d.
iiij
Et in denariis solutis Thome
iiij
Whytle et Thome Cobell pro cariacione viij carectarum plastre paris de Derb. usque
Wynfeld, pro carecta xviij d. ad tascham — xij s.

ffeoda seruientium cum empcione feni xxj li. v s.

Et in
feodo ipsius computantis pro superuiso operis edificiorum manerii ibidem prout allocatum
est in compotis precedentibus — xx s. Et in stipendiis Johannis
Blake, Willemi Grabar et Johannis Underwode conductorum ad seruiendum plaustra domini
super cariacione petrarum, meremii et aliorum pro edificiis predictis, necnon
super cariacione feni et bladorum tempore autumpnali a ffesto sancti martini in yeme anno
mo
xxj usque idem ffestum sancti martini anno eiusdem
do xx
Regis xxij quolibet carient. per annum lxvj s. viij d. — x li. Et in iiij ij plaustris feni emptis de
stauro manerii sui
ibidem super sustenacione boum pro plaustris attendentibus super opera infra manerium
ibidem, precio plaustri ij s. vj d. — x li. v s.

Et in
denariis concessis Thome Colwell per Senescallum et Receptorem in auxiliant. reparaciones
operis carpentr. j domus coquine infra hospicium domini infra villam de Wynfeld

scituand., ex certa conuencione – xiij s. iiij d. Et in denariis solutis Thome Samme junior in partem solucionis de xxj li. pro euacuacione parcell.
terre ad ffischepoledamhed ut patet in indenturis suis ultra xx s. sibi solut. anno proximo precedenti – ix li. xiiij s. iij d. De
x li. v s. viij d. de eadem conuencione aretro nichil quia non dum solut. Set in denariis solutis Thome Antylop pro emendacione
parcelle de le cawse apud ffischepole damehed per inuiam habundanciam aque dissolut., ex certa conuencione in grosso – vj s. viij d.
Et in denariis solutis Willemo Bardall pro stipendio suo causa scriptura parcellis tam operum domini apud Wynfeld quam Lamley
per tempus huius compoti ac super eadem opera attendent. de parte xxvj s. viij d. de integra conuencione secum facta videlicet ultra
xiij s. iiij d. allocat. inter parcellas reparacionis apud Lamley[21] – xiij s. iiij d. Et in expensis Johannis Sawcheuerell Receptoris domini ibidem existentis
per diursas vicez per tempus predictum circa superuisum et attencionem istorum operum domini per parcellas inde super hunc compotum examinat. et penes
mercedes eiusdem remanentes – lxij s. iiij d. Et in expensis tempore audit. compotorum domini in Comitatu derb., mense Novembris, anno Regis nunc xxij[do] apud
Wynfeld per parcellas inter mercedes huius anni remanentes – xxv s. x d. ob.

(Margin: Euacuacio terre cum aliis custibus necessariis — xv li. xv s. x d. ob.)

Summa – CCxvj li. iij s. vij d. ob. q.[a] [22]

Et in stipendiis Ricardi fflechar pro factura xlij [xiiij s.] rodarum noui palacii inter le hassekar et hayle, pro roda iiij d., eiusdem remouentis [vij s. iiij d.]
xliiij rodas palacii per circuitum inter dicta loca, pro roda ij d., ad tascham – xxj s. iiij d. Et in stipendiis eiusdem emendantis
palacium diuersis locis per circuitum parci ubi maxima necessitas requiret per xij dies, ad iiij d. per diem, ad tascham – iiij s.
Et in denariis solutis Thome Aston pro succiso et prosternacione subbosci et lez holez diuersis locis infra parcum pro saluacione ferarum[23] ibidem
tempore yemali ex certa conuencione in grosso – x s. Et in stipendiis Henrici Smyth facientis de nouo unam portam super aquam
de sluibur[24] pro saluacione pasture vocate lez holmez ex conuencione – viij d.

(Margin: Custus parci cum aliis)

Summa – xxxvj s.

Et in denariis solutis Thome Anteley dykar in partem solucionis de ix li. xvj s.[25] pro fossacione et plantacione xix [xx] xij rodarum souee[26] continentium

ffactura fossati pro elargacione parci

viij pedes in latitudine et iiij pedes in profunditate in oriente in campo Johannis Ulkerthorp ex opposito fossato ex parte boriali de Cachill

et extendent. usque Edefeld Cornar pro elargacione parci ex ordinacione domini, pro singula roda vj d., ad tascham – iiij li. xiij s. iiij d.

Summa – iiij li. xiij s. iiij d.

Summa omnium allocacionum predictarum – CCxxij li. xij s. xj d. ob.

Et habet superplusagium[27] – xvij li. xviij s. ij d. ob.

Et ulterius petit allocari de – vj li. xiij s. iiij d. de tot denariis solutis Ricardo North cementario pro factura de le waut subtus aulam superuis.

cancellat. de quod excedit conuencionem factam cum Johanne Entrepath per indenturam suam. hic in respectu ponitur quousque loquetur cum domino.

Notes to transcript

1. viij d. erased, but clearly the figure ought to be ij s. viij d.
2. The whole line in brackets is interlineated to be inserted here; an extra line has been counted in the numbering.
3. Blank in manuscript: a sum of money not entered.
4. xxvj li. erased; and possibly the erasure was meant to apply to the shillings and pence.
5. *sic.*
6. d erased.
7. d erased.
8. tercio erased.
9. Could this be a capstan for hoisting?
10. Here plaustrata means clearly the vehicles and not the load; the oxen in the next line (94) were for pulling them.
11. Space left blank in manuscript.
12. Space left blank in manuscript.
13. Presumably hammocks. The identification of the terms used for iron parts of doors and windows, as well as the varieties of nails, presents many difficulties and the reader is advised to consult Salzman 1952: ch.ix.
14. The meaning of this phrase is obscure.
15. Standards and lockets are vertical and horizontal window-bars.
16. Gudgeon plates.
17. Probably handcarts.
18. Maslin, meaning brass.
19. Wimble-bit, for operating spindles.
20. d. omitted in manuscript.
21. Lord Cromwell's parents were buried at Lambley, Nottinghamshire, and he made provision in his will for the rebuilding of the church, with the erection of a new tomb, but this refers to works on the manor, where new buildings were recorded a year later (Kingsford 1925: 210, 217).
22. CCxxij l. xvj s. xj d. ob. q. (which was line 139) erased; this figure is the true sum of the costs in the margin but £6 13 4 has been deducted for money due to Richard North for supervising the erection of the vault of the hall undercroft because this exceeded the original contract estimate with Entrepas (see lines 153-4).
23. ferarum = deer.
24. Presumably 'sluice'.
25. xix xij rod erased. (xx written above)
26. souee = sewer; O.E.D. gives sough (1440) = drain, sewer, trench.
27. superplusagium was the excess of expenditure over the total of receipts (£204 14 9) in the Receiver's statement (line 10).

REFERENCES

Blore, T. (1793) *An History of the Manor, and Manor House, of South Winfield, in Derbyshire.* London. (Reprinted by J. Nichols, printer to the Society of Antiquaries, in *Miscellaneous Antiquities*, No. 3, in continuation of the *Bibliotheca Topographia Britannica* 1793.) Pp. 21, 28 refer to the park in 1299 and again in 1392 when there was a capital messuage, a hall, many chambers, a dovecote and other buildings at Wingfield.

Brown, E.H.P. and Hopkins, S.V. (1955) Seven centuries of building wages. *Economica*, n.s. 22, 195-206 (reprinted in 1962 in Carus-Wilson, E.M. (ed.), *Essays in Economic History*, Vol. 2, 168-78). 6d. for a craftsman and 4d. for a labourer were the standard daily wages of the period.

Ferrey, E.B. (1870) *South Winfield Manor, Derbyshire.* London.

Hope, W.H.St.J. (1913) *A Grammar of English Heraldry*, 45-6. London.

Jenkins, J.G. (1961) *The English Farm Wagon*, 6-8. Reading.

Kingsford, C.L. (ed.) (1925) *Report on the Manuscripts of Lord De L'Isle and Dudley preserved at Penshurst Place*, Vol. 1, 171-218, esp. 215-6. London. A considerable number of college records have survived in this collection, dating from both before and after Cromwell's death. For works at Collyweston in 1445-6, see p. 219.

Salzman, L.F. (1952) *Building in England down to 1540*, 352. London.

Simpson, W.D. (ed.) (1955) *The Building Accounts of Tattershall Castle, 1434-1472* (Vol. 55 of the Publications of the Lincoln Record Society), Lincoln; contains the five building accounts from Cromwell's lifetime.

Smith, L.T. (ed.) (1906-10) *The Itinerary of John Leland*, Vol. 1, 22. 'Coly Weston for the most parte is of a new building by the Lady Margaret, mother to Henry vii. The Lord Cromwel had afore begunne a house ther. Bagges of purses yet remayne yn the chapele and other places.' Unfortunately nothing now remains above ground of the manor site.

DAVID WILSON

Defence in the Viking age

The evidence of war has long fascinated the archaeologist. The material available is vast and the study of this material has been basic to an understanding of much of the discipline. It is, however, difficult to re-create the actual processes of war from archaeological evidence. Occasionally, as at Maiden Castle (Wheeler 1943), deposits of ammunition or war cemeteries are found, but the remains of great battles are rare – a find like the graves left after the battle of Visby in 1361 (Thordeman 1941) is unparalleled. A combination of literary and archaeological evidence does, however, enable us to theorize concerning some uses of arms and fortification in Viking Age Europe. In this paper I shall confine myself to a consideration of the problems of defence.

Public defence

During the first century of the Scandinavian incursions into western Europe, one of the striking factors of the warlike activity of the invaders was their mobility. Even during the Alfredian wars, Scandinavian armies struck hard and often, in various directions. Towns were taken by surprise and their inhabitants put to the sword: Canterbury, York, Winchester, London, Cambridge, Exeter and Gloucester all succumbed to the attackers. It was not until 885, as Stenton (1971:264n.) pointed out, that according to the *Anglo-Saxon Chronicle* the English held a town – Rochester – against a siege. A similar picture emerges in France, where there were few sieges before the tenth century and towns fell easily to the Scandinavians (the French sieges are conveniently listed by Rocolle 1973). It was against this background that the English kings Alfred the Great (for references to earlier sieges, see Colvin 1963:8) and Edward the Elder and the French king Charles the Bald started to fortify towns; as, at a slightly later date, did Henry the Fowler in his struggle against the Hungarians (Lot 1946:109). The Spaniards were apparently aware of the problem at a slightly earlier stage. Oviedo was already fortified by Alfonso II (*d.* 842), apparently against Scandinavian attack, but this is an isolated instance. In England the system revealed in the *Burghal Hidage* was the result.

Alfred and his contemporaries may have taken a hint, as to the use of fortresses, from the Scandinavians themselves; perhaps basing their ideas on such forts as that built at Reading in 870, which featured in a number of Scandinavian campaigns. The first mention of an English fortification during these wars, other than Alfred's fortress at Athelney, occurs in the *Anglo-Saxon Chronicle, sub anno* 892, when the Danish army in Kent 'stormed a fortress in a fen. Inside were a few peasants and it was only half made' (A text: ond þær abræcon an geweorc inne on þæm fenne; sæton feawe cirlisce men on ond þæs samworht). From this date onward fortresses are frequently mentioned on either side and, as in France, sieges become the order of the day. The re-conquest of the Danelaw after the battle of Tettenhall was based on the construction of a series of fortifications (summarized by Colvin 1963: 9ff.), including the re-fortification of such prehistoric camps as Eddisbury (*Mercian Register, sub anno* 914).

There were, then, three systems of fortification extant in England by the time the Danelaw had been re-conquered. Firstly, the defensive *burhs* of the *Burghal Hidage*, either created *de novo* or consisting of re-fortified Roman fortresses; secondly, the fortresses established by Edward the Elder and the Lady Æthelflæd at strategic points in relation to their control of the Scandinavians; and thirdly, the towns fortified by the Scandinavians themselves. The thirty-one *burhs* listed in the *Burghal Hidage* extend across Wessex and do not appear to include towns in Kent or Cornwall, although Davison (1972) has suggested an identification of Eorpeburnan at Newenden, Kent. The *Burghal Hidage* is really a document of Wessex and is appropriate to the Wessex of the last years of Alfred's reign or the first years of Edward the Elder (the best commentary is Hill 1969). It does not include the fortresses erected in and after 912, but it does include one Mercian *burh*. The established view of the *Burghal Hidage* is undoubtedly best expressed by Stenton (1971: 264):

> The defence of southern England against earlier invaders had always been hampered by the absence or rarity of fortifications within which the inhabitants of a threatened district could take refuge. By the early part of the tenth century no village in Sussex, Essex, Surrey and Wessex east of the Tamar was distant more than twenty miles from a fortress which formed a unit in a planned scheme of national defence.

It has recently been pointed out, however, and quite rightly, that the rectilinear street-plan of these *burhs* represents part of a deliberate policy of urban foundation in response to a military situation. This is not to deny that these places had ample space within their defences to provide 'refuge for the population of the surrounding countryside . . . and represent more a change of emphasis . . . toward the concept of a fortified town, in which the rectilinear street-plan is a deliberate expression of the organization and apportionment of the land for permanent settlement' (Biddle & Hill 1971; for a summary of archaeological research on defence sites, see Radford 1970). That this dual policy sometimes failed is demonstrated by the fact that even some of the sites of the listed fortresses have been almost totally lost (Brooks 1964), and others, like the village of Lyng, in Somerset (Hill 1967), have sunk into insignificance. The primary function of such *burhs* was the defence of the population of a region. Once these expensive fortifications had been created they had to be administered. A senior royal official was allowed to farm them for taxes, and lesser men – thegns and the like – were allowed to settle there. Courts were erected and minting rights were granted. Some towns, those that survived, developed markets. The formula for a successful town – fortification plus administration plus market – may have been in the minds of Alfred and his successor, but the first element was paramount.

It was, presumably, also an element paramount in the minds of the Scandinavians who established themselves in the Five Boroughs. The very name of this undefined organization signifies fortification. Of the five fortified towns, four have surviving traces of their defences: at Lincoln and Leicester, the Roman walls were presumably used; at Stamford (Mahany 1969: Fig. 1) and Nottingham (Lobel 1969: Nottingham, 1), new fortifications were erected; but no trace of defences has yet been discovered at Derby (Radford 1970:102). These towns, like the towns of the *Burghal Hidage*, served as places of refuge – strongholds in time of trouble – for the surrounding population. Like some of the Alfredian *burhs*, they became successful administrative and mercantile centres. The only other major town of the Scandinavians was York, a town that was a major trading centre of the Scandinavian world. In this town, the Scandinavians repaired the defences of the Roman legionary fortress (Radley 1970: Fig. 6), but their main settlement seems to have lain outside these walls in the area of Ousegate: it is reasonable to suppose that the refurbished defences of the Roman fort served as a place of refuge in time of trouble, an idea familiar in the Scandinavian homeland at Birka (Arbman 1939) and Hedeby (Jankuhn 1963), where forts are associated with the towns themselves (although the connexion of fort and town at Hedeby is often questioned).

Although the Great Army threw up fortifications during its ninth-century campaigns in England, convincing traces of these camps have not yet been found. The same is true of the post-treaty period: no fortifications are recorded, or have been found, directly related to the Scandinavians outside York and the Five Boroughs, although we may assume that they would not ignore existing defences. (Dyer's (1972) identification of Scandinavian forts in the southern Danelaw must be treated with caution until their chronological position is proved.) The idea of the Alfredian *burh* did not die out when England was re-conquered. Similar steps were taken when Scandinavian pressure again built up in England. The re-fortification of the Iron Age and Arthurian hill-fort at South Cadbury by Æthelred about 1010 is an illustration of this (Alcock 1972:195ff.). The local mint was transferred to the new camp for a short period, and one may assume that with the mint went the local administration. The function of an important town as a refuge is clearly seen in this period in 1006 when, according to the *Anglo-Saxon Chronicle*, the Scandinavian army marched past the walls of Winchester (in the same year, one of the forts failed when Wallingford was sacked).

In Scandinavia, traces of Viking Age fortifications are sporadic. The towns of Birka and Hedeby have already been mentioned: to them can be added Aarhus (Andersen *et al.* 1971) and possibly Västergarn in Gotland (Lundstrom 1967-8: Fig. 3; or the same Fig. in 1968: Fig. 1); the semicircular *enceinte* of these towns presumably enclosed trading and administrative areas. Direct evidence of fortification at this period is otherwise confined to a handful of sites, mostly in Sweden, which may have been permanent settlements, like Eketorp (Näsman *et al.* 1971), or forts of refuge used only in times of trouble, like the strange sites of Ismantorp and Gråborg (Stenberger 1964:540 ff.) set in the infertile interior of Öland. The Tingstäde site (Zetterling 1934), with its vast Viking Age platform set in a lake, may well have functioned in a similar manner. Its attribution to the Viking Age has now been confirmed by radiocarbon dating.

Most of the hill-forts of Sweden are accepted as earlier than the Viking Age (Ambrosiani 1959) but some, like Gråborg (which has a surviving mediaeval gateway), were almost certainly used by the Vikings: Eketorp, for example, was re-fortified in the late Viking period. The most extraordinary fortified site in Scandinavia – a site that may well date back to the Viking Age – is undoubtedly Borgarvirki, in the desolate north of Iceland – a camp surrounded by marshy country, serving an obscure purpose (Ólsen 1880-1).

The most striking Viking fortifications are, however, undoubtedly the great circular earthworks of Denmark – at Trelleborg on Sjalland, at Odense (the site is known as Nonnebakken) on Fyn, and at Aggersborg and Fyrkat in Jutland. In 1970, I felt confident enough to write a fairly standard interpretation of them (Foote & Wilson 1970: 271):

> That they were military barracks seems unquestionable, despite the fact that they are without adequate parallel. They were useless as strong points for the defence of the Danish kingdom, but are well situated for the gathering of troops by means of the main lines of communication and must therefore have served some aggressive military purpose. The fact that, at the rate of fifty men per house, accommodation was provided in them for some 5,500 men at the beginning of the eleventh century suggests that they were the bases from which Sven Forkbeard and Knut the Great operated in their invasion and conquest of England and in their expeditions against the rest of Scandinavia. Only at this period could such an immense project as the building of these camps be undertaken – a period when money was flowing into the Danish kings' coffers.

Such a view was standard until a few years ago and is presented in its most classic form by Olaf Olsen (1969) and Tage E. Christiansen (1970). Since then it has been questioned in two papers, one by Ole Klindt-Jensen (1973) and the other by Else Roesdahl (1974), and I am grateful to both these scholars and to Olaf Olsen for their patience in many long discussions.

Roesdahl's short article (1969) triggered a reaction against the commonly accepted arguments concerning the Trelleborg series of fortifications. In her analysis of the finds from the excavated portions of Fyrkat, she showed that different buildings had different uses and that, in effect, only three out of the twelve excavated houses could be identified as normal dwelling houses with fire-places and, in two cases, benches. The other buildings may be interpreted as workshops and storage houses. The finds include spindle-whorls, loom-weights and beads, as well as evidence of metal-working; showing that both men and women lived on the site, a factor also revealed by the mixed character of the cemeteries at Fyrkat (Roesdahl & Nordqvist 1971) and at Trelleborg (Nørlund 1948). It is difficult to get at the evidence for the distribution of finds in the houses at Trelleborg, but Roesdahl postulates, on the evidence of the generality of the finds, a situation similar to that found at Fyrkat.

The idea that these fortifications were barracks was inspired by two factors: firstly, by the parallels with the community described in *Jómsvikinga Saga* (first written down *c.* 1200) that have since been questioned, as the source is corrupt, late and irrelevant to an enormous undertaking like that of the Danish fortifications; and secondly, by the subjective view that the accurate discipline of the lay-out could have been organized only by a central authority – presumably a king.

Such forts, if they were barracks, could function only in relation to a standing army – a type of organization unknown in western

Europe at this period. Warfare was primitive and little training would be necessary. The expense of keeping such an establishment would be beyond the competence of early mediaeval kings, even Sven Forkbeard or Knut the Great. Nørlund's interpretation of the fortresses as training camps and winter quarters for the youth of the region hardly accords with the finds or with the internal arrangements of such barracks. That they were laid down under central control is reasonably clear: only royal authority could order the construction of such works. It might, therefore, be suggested that there is a parallel here with the forts of the *Burghal Hidage* and, further, that these great forts were erected to fulfil a defensive function at a time of trouble for Denmark. There is a number of periods that fulfil such conditions, but a likely time is the period of the wars between Sven Forkbeard and the Swedish king Eirik in the 990s, which included the siege and battle at Hedeby, although there were always threats from neighbouring kings and chiefs. It seems possible that the effectiveness of the English *burhs* as places of refuge had been noted by the Danish kings who, in defending their own kingdom, erected a series of fortifications for use as refuges in time of trouble – refuges that attracted a caretaking and possibly administrative community and may even, as possibly at Odense, have turned into a major town.

By means of the forts and the fortified towns the country would be well covered by a defensive system in the late tenth century. Our knowledge of Danish towns *c.* 1000 is somewhat obscure, but Aalborg and Halsingborg, which are mentioned in roughly contemporary sources, could well have been fortified, as the place-name element *borg* (fortification) appears in their names. Aarhus and Hedeby (and its successor Schleswig) we know to have been fortified at this period, on the basis of archaeological evidence. Ribe, Ringsted and Roskilde, also, may well have been fortified at this period. Roskilde was described by Adam of Bremen as a great city, the seat of the Danish king, and the proposition that it was fortified at this period is vastly strengthened by the fact that the channel that led to it along the fjord was blocked *c.* 1000 by scuttled ships (Olsen & Crumlin-Pedersen 1969:125 ff.). Ribe was an extremely important town, but we know very little about its topography at this period, and practically nothing is known of Ringsted. This explanation of the forts – that they constituted a defence or refuge system – seems more reasonable than the thesis of Nørlund, or that of Aksel E. Christensen (1969) that they were used as a means of political control over the various regions or as training forts. As in England, one at least of the forts, Nonnebakken, may have developed into the present town of Odense; the others, like certain English examples, fell into disuse. The form of some towns may have been similar to that now lost, as in Nonnebakken, beneath urban sprawl. Hedeby (Jankuhn 1963) and Aarhus (Andersen, Crabb & Madsen 1971) had semi-circular walls, but the circular plan may have been immediately inspired by the fortifications of the Slav areas of Europe (Herrmann 1968:151-64; 1970: Figs. 31-2; Hensel 1967: Figs. 105-6), some of which certainly served as forts of refuge. Indeed, only a few miles from the Danish border, there are a number of such fortifications (e.g. Herrmann 1971: Fig. 28), mostly built in the ninth and tenth century in a period of consolidation of the Slav states, faced by a series of non-Slav (Saxon/north Frisian) forts to the west (Hinz 1972: Fig. 9). At the same time the form of the refuge fortifications of the Baltic islands or in Holland (Braat 1971:113), may have been in the minds of these Danish builders. There were, then, plenty of models for the Danish king to turn to in search of plans for forts of refuge – but it would seem possible that the idea of forts of refuge was imported from England where the Danish kings would have seen them functioning.

Else Roesdahl has pointed out to me that underwater fortification was also of some importance for public defence in the Viking Age. Unfortunately, little material of this sort has been investigated, apart from the series of sunken ships that barred the main channel into Roskilde at Skuldelev (Olsen & Crumlin-Pedersen 1969). Underwater palisades are known outside the harbours at Hedeby (Jankuhn 1963: Fig. 20) and possibly Birka (Arbman 1965:22). In the shallow waters of the Baltic, such underwater palisades would be of major importance in the defence against raiders who came from the sea, as important certainly as the great public linear earthwork of the period – the Danevirke (recently re-investigated by a Danish team; Jankuhn's 1958 summary is now out-dated) – which defended the southern approaches of Denmark by land. Little can be said generally about underwater palisades because of dating problems, although Ole Crumlin-Pedersen is investigating certain promising sites which should have important implications in the study of national defence (see, however, Schultz 1936 and Andersen 1964).

Private defence

The great public works of the *Burghal Hidage* and similar defensive systems would not be available to everybody, and in times of immediate danger local refuges would also be needed. An Anglo-Saxon village or house surrounded by a palisade or cattle fence (a *tun*) might make a poor defensive position in the face of attack. In the early Anglo-Saxon period we have some slight evidence of local fortification (there is some evidence in non-Anglo-Saxon areas of England of early Dark Age hill-forts, some of which are merely single residences; Fowler 1971): at Yeavering, where the enclosure might merely be a cattle pound; at Bamburgh, a royal seat where, if we believe Bede (731:III, ch. 16), a miraculous event raised a siege; and possibly at Meretun, where the rather equivocal reference to a *byrig* in the Cyneheard episode in the *Anglo-Saxon Chronicle, sub anno* 757, might imply in context a local fortification. Apart from the few 'strong-points' ('morfæstenum', ASC (A) *sub anno* 878) in Wessex and one or two other uncertainly phrased references, we hear little of local or private fortification. (The *deorhege to cyniges hame*, which appears in the *Rectitudes Singularum Personarum* as one of the thegn's major duties, may refer to the fortification of a king's residence or to a hedge against wild beasts; see Loyn 1962). In Germany, private fortifications are familiar both in archaeology and in history (e.g. Binding 1972; Fehring 1972), as they are in Ireland, where the small ring-fort has a long history (e.g. de Paor 1958: 79 ff.).

It is interesting that little trace of private fortifications has been found during the excavation of more important houses of the late Anglo-Saxon period. At Cheddar, for example, which is a royal manor, extensive excavation produced merely a storm-water ditch (Rahtz 1962-3). The Norman ring-work at Sulgrave, Northamptonshire, (Davison 1967) replaced an apparently unfortified residence of a man who might have been a thegn (although it should perhaps be noted that excavations have not yet been completed on this site). This latter site has, however, produced some evidence of fortification, in the form of a stone-built tower, a feature also seen in what might be a similar context – the ninth- to eleventh-century levels at Portchester, Hampshire (Cunliffe 1969).

Such stone towers presumably had a defensive function and it is tempting to compare them with the massive stone towers of such late Anglo-Saxon churches as Barton-on-Humber and Earl's Barton. Davison (1967: Fig. 2) has surveyed this latter site and shown that the church there may be an integral part of the defensive fortifications. The tower was the most important part of the church at this site. The nave was narrower than the tower and the tower was very solid (see Radford 1953:196 for plan). It is perhaps a wild flight of fancy to suggest that church towers like this were the origin of the stone keep of the Conquest period, but their very solidity and their similarity to the primitive *donjon* makes such a relationship attractive. This is especially so since, at Barnack, a later motte runs up against the tower of the Anglo-Saxon church, demonstrating the continuous defensive nature of the site. One must see Earl's Barton, like Barton-on-Humber, as a private church built by a major landowner, perhaps with an idea of defence against Scandinavian attack in his mind.

The idea of building the church in a defensive position was familiar in earlier times. A church – a strong stone building strengthened by spiritual taboos – would be an obvious point of refuge for the local population in any part of western Europe. The church tower of Bradford was the scene of a famous military action in the civil wars (James 1841: 130 ff.), while the churches of the Meuse region in the early Romanesque period were almost certainly built with the possibility of fortification in mind (Génicot 1972:283ff.). In Denmark, as in much of continental Europe, mediaeval churchyards were sometimes fortified (Schultz 1945), and the churches, as the most solid buildings in a region, were certainly sometimes used as refuges in troubled times. The round towers of Ireland, usually sited in churchyards, must have had a similar function (de Paor 1958: 151 ff.). It is in Ireland, also, that we have documentation of churches being attacked. A.T. Lucas (1967) has listed references of occasions when churches were attacked and sees them as centres of refuge for people and valuables in times of trouble. In spite of criticism by Kathleen Hughes (1972:148-59), the thesis he advances seems to be valid, in particular for the late Viking period, where Dr Hughes agrees with him. However, despite literary references, like those in the *Irish Annals*, traces of these refuges are rarely found in the archaeological record; a possible example of a church functioning as a strong-room for secular treasure occurs at St Ninian's Isle, in Shetland (Small, Thomas & Wilson 1973:146).

Conclusions

It seems clear that, from the end of the ninth century, in the face of the Viking incursion, the idea of temporary defence began to alter in western Europe. Strong-points were constructed, both on a public and a private basis, to which the local population could turn in times of attack. Public fortifications became incipient towns: some, like *Sceaftesege* and possibly Trelleborg, failed as economic or administrative centres and were abandoned; others became towns or major settlements. Private defence depended on the rich, or the church, providing a palisade, earth wall or stone building.

REFERENCES

Alcock, L. (1972) '*By South Cadbury is that Camelot . . .*' London.

Ambrosiani, B. (1959) Fornborgar. *Kulturhistorisk Leksikon for Nordisk middelalder*, 4, 508-12.

Andersen, A.W. (1964) Skuldelev Skibene i perspektiv. *Skalk*, 1964 (4), 10-15.

Andersen, H.H., Crabb, P.J. and Madsen, H.J. (1971) *Århus Søndervold* (Jysk Arkæologisk Selskabs skrifter, IX). København.

Arbman, H. (1939) *Birka, Sveriges äldsta handelsstad.* Stockholm.

Arbman, H. (1965) Birka handelsstaden. In Arrhenius, B. (ed.), *Ansgars Birka*, 19-26. Stockholm.

Bede, the Venerable (731) *Historia Ecclesiastica.*

Biddle, M. and Hill, D. (1971) Late Saxon planned towns. *Ant. Jour.*, 51, 70-85.

Binding, G. (1972) Spätkarolingisch-ottonische Pfalzen und Burgen am Niederhein. *Chateau Gaillard*, 5, 23-36.

Braat, W.C. (1971) Early mediaeval glazed pottery in Holland. *Medieval Arch.*, 15, 112-4.

Brooks, N. (1964) The unidentified forts of the Burghal Hidage. *Medieval Arch.*, 8, 74-90.

Christensen, A.E. (1969) *Vikingetidens Danmark.* København.

Christiansen, T.E. (1970) Træningslejr eller tvangsborg. *Kuml*, 1970, 43-64.

Colvin, H.M. (ed.), (1963) *The History of the King's Works*, Vol. 1. London.

Cunliffe, B. (1969) Excavations at Portchester Castle, Hampshire, 1966-68. *Ant. Jour.*, 49, 67-9.

Davison, B.K. (1967) The origins of the castle in England. *Arch. Jour.*, 124, 202-11.

Davison, B.K. (1968) Excavations at Sulgrave, Northamptonshire, 1968. *Arch. Jour.*, 125, 305-7.

Davison, B.K. (1972) The Burghal Hidage fort of Eorpeburnan: a suggested identification. *Medieval Arch.*, 16, 123-7.

Dyer, J. (1972) Earthworks of the Danelaw Frontier. In Fowler, P.J. (ed.), *Archaeology and the Landscape*, 222-36. London.

Fehring, G. (1972) Frümittelalterliche Wehranlagan in Südwestdeutschland. *Chateau Gaillard*, 5, 37-54.

Foote, P.G. and Wilson, D.M. (1970) *The Viking Achievement.* London.

Fowler, P.J. (1971) Hill-forts A.D. 400-700. In Hill, D. and Jesson, M. (eds.), *The Iron Age and its hill-forts*, 203-13. Southampton.

Génicot, L.F. (1972) *Les églises mosanes du XIe siècle.* Louvain.

Hensel, W. (1967) *Anfänge der Städte bei den Ost- und Westslawen.* Bautzen.

Herrmann, J. (1968) *Siedlung, Wirtschaft und Gesellschaftliche verhältnisse der slawische Stämme zwischen Elbe und Oder.* Berlin.

Herrmann, J. (1970) *Die Slawen in Deutschland.* Berlin.

Herrmann, J. (1971) *Zwischen Hradschin und Vineta.* Leipzig.

Hill, D. (1967) The Burghal Hidage – Lyng. *Proc. Somerset Arch. and Nat. Hist. Soc.*, 111, 64-6.

Hill, D. (1969) The Burghal Hidage: the establishment of a text. *Medieval Arch.*, 13, 84-92.

Hinz, H. (1972) Burgenlandschaften und Siedlungskunde. *Chateau Gaillard*, 5, 65-84.

Hughes, K. (1972) *Early Christian Ireland: Introduction to the Sources.* London.

James, J. (1841) *The History and Topography of Bradford.* London.

Jankuhn, H. (1963) *Haithabu, ein Handelsplatz der Winkingerzeit*, 4 Aufl. Neumünster.

Klindt-Jensen, O. (1973) The problem of evaluating archaeological sources in early historical times. *Actes du VIII Cong. Int. des Sci. Préh. et Prot., Beograd 1971*, 3.

Lobel, M.D. (ed.) (1969) *Historic Towns*, Vol. I. London.

Lot, F. (1946) *L'art militaire et les armées au moyen age en Europe et dans le Proche Orient*, Vol. I. Paris.

Loyn, H.R. (1962) *Anglo-Saxon England and the Norman Conquest.* London.

Lucas, A.T. (1967) The plundering and burning of churches in Ireland, 7th to 16th century. In Rynne, E. (ed.), *North Munster Studies*, 172-229. Limerick.

Lundström, P. (1967-8) Västergarn vid den gotländska

kusten, en topografisk studie. *Sjöhistorisk Årsbok*, 1967-8, 9-26.

Lundström, P. (1968) Ett vikingatida varv på Gotland. *Gotlandskt Archiv.*, 1968, 99-114.

Mahany, C.M. (1969) *The Story of Stamford.* Vol. 2, *The Archaeology of Stamford.* Stamford.

Näsman, U. *et al.* (1971) Undersökningen av Eketorps borg på södra Öland. *Fornuännen*, 1971, 186-201.

Norlund, P. (1948) *Trelleborg.* København.

Ólsen, B.M. (1880-1) Borgarvirki. *Árbók hins íslenzka fornleifafélags*, 1880-1, 99-113.

Olsen, O. (1969) The geometrical Viking fortresses. *Chateau Gaillard*, 4.

Olsen, O. and Crumlin-Pedersen, O. (1969) *Fem Vikingeskibe fra Roskilde Fjord.* Roskilde.

Paor, M. de and Paor, L. de (1958) *Early Christian Ireland.* London.

Radford, C.A.R. (1953) Earl's Barton church. *Arch. Jour.*, 110, 196-7.

Radford, C.A.R. (1970) The later Pre-Conquest boroughs and their defences. *Medieval Arch.*, 14, 83-103.

Radley, J. (1970) Economic aspects of Anglo-Danish York. *Medieval Arch.*, 15, 37-56.

Rahtz, P. (1962-3) The Saxon and mediaeval palaces at Cheddar, Somerset – an interim report of excavation in 1960-62. *Medieval Arch.*, 6-7, 53-66.

Roesdahl, E. (1969) Livet på Fyrkat. *Skalk*, 1969 (2), 3-9.

Roesdahl, E. (1974) The Viking fortress of Fyrkat in the light of the objects found. *Chateau Gaillard*, 6, 195-202.

Roesdahl, E. and Nordqvist, J. (1971) De døde fra Fyrkat. *Nationalmuseets Arbejdsmark*, 1971, 15-32.

Rocolle, P. (1973) *2000 ans de fortification français.* Limoges.

Schultz, C.G. (1936) Hominide og Pælværket i Vestre Skarholmsrende. *Lolland-Falsters Historiske Samfunds Årbog*, 1936, 95-113.

Schultz, C.G. (1945) En befæstet kirkegård. *Nationalmuseets Arbejdsmark*, 1945, 85-100.

Small, A., Thomas, A.C. and Wilson, D.M. (1973) *St. Ninian's Isle and its Treasure.* Oxford.

Stenberger, M. (1964) *Det forntida Sverige.* Stockholm.

Stenton, F. (1971) *Anglo-Saxon England* (3rd ed.). Oxford.

Thordeman, B. (1941) *Armour from the Battle of Wisby.* Stockholm.

Wheeler, Sir R.E.M. (1943) *Maiden Castle, Dorset* (Soc. Ant. Res. Cttee. Rep. no. 12). Oxford.

Zetterling, A. (1934) *Bulverket i Tingstäde träsk.* Stockholm.

PART V

Continental Europe

DAVID CLARKE

Mesolithic Europe: the economic basis

Archaeologists usually base their interpretations on particular sets of data – pots, flints, bones, seeds, sites – or on observations based on those data; the interpretations are, in a sense, the pendent consequences of the chosen data. Widely accepted interpretations then become the conventional framework for further discussion and research, and the conventional interpretation becomes traditional. Now, although in such a rapidly changing discipline all interpretations must remain transient conventions, there are nevertheless dangers that arise from working only within a set of data towards dependent conventional interpretations. These limitations arise from the observation that the analyses and interpretations of any data are constrained and distorted by missing information, inherent biases, sampling aberrations and persistent stereotypes (traditional misinterpretations) and by the fundamental difficulty that the results of any analyses will usually fit a very large number of different interpretative models. Inevitably, the concern with the explicit formation and testing of alternative hypotheses and their models emerges; in particular, there is the need to compare the interpretative models that arise as a consequence of the analysis of data, with models of expectation derived from other sources and which take account of the sampling problems of the data under analysis.

√The conventional interpretation that depicts the displacement of the European meat-eating Mesolithic hunter-fishers by Neolithic cereal farmers has indeed become traditional; a satisfactory evolutionary picture of the displacement of lower cultures and economies by higher ones – what one might call Social Darwinism in action. Satisfactory as this model may once have been in terms of the philosophy and ideology then prevalent, this conventional picture begins to look less likely in the light of more recent thought and work (Wilkinson, R.G. 1973; Higgs 1972; Lee & DeVore 1968). Characteristically, the traditional picture largely emerged from the typological analysis and interpretation of artefacts and site-data with little or no consideration for the technical and sampling difficulties of that data and but scant attention to organic, social and ecological considerations, before the pioneer work of Professor Clark at Star Carr. A particular interpretative model, based on one interpretation of a limited set of data, became at first conventional and then traditional, and still remains deeply entrenched, without due consideration for alternative interpretations of the same data and a proper evaluation in comparison with the expectations on ecological, environmental, ethnographic, economic and theoretical grounds.

A first step in any such study should at least attempt to assess and allow for the range of inherent assumptions, limitations, biases and sampling problems that will constrain and orientate both the set of data under analysis and the interpretations that seem to arise inexorably and conclusively from that analysis. Although this essay makes no pretence of being a formal study of the European Mesolithic, it is perhaps worth summarizing what seem to be the major biasing factors in the traditional interpretation in order to foresee their interpretative consequences.

The objective in this essay is, first, to outline the biases, sampling problems and stereotypes that currently seem to distort the interpretation of European Mesolithic material (Part I). Then, an attempt is made to put the artefact and site data on one side, so that a sketch model of the general ecological background of Europe *c.* 10,000-5,000 B.C. may independently suggest expectations about the nature and distribution of the Mesolithic subsistence systems (Part II). Finally, the data, observations and the ecological predictions are brought together, in an effort to throw some light on the many different interpretations of the 'transition' from regional Mesolithic economies to the Neolithic pattern of food production in Europe (Part III).

I. Bias, sampling problems and stereotypes

Meat fixation: a cultural bias

It is a culturally induced assumption that hunted mammals were the main source of Mesolithic food supply and meat quantitatively the most important food-stuff. Modern North Europeans and North Americans come from cultures that especially esteem meat, partly because meat protein has always provided an important source of immediate body heat in cold wet northern climates. However, even in these extreme modern diets, meat *rarely* contributes one-third of the diet by weight and *rarely* more than half of the daily protein intake. The partly illusory and partly modern emphasis on a meat diet and the animals that supply it has been compounded by the correlation between the area where this preference at present prevails, the area where archaeology as a modern discipline developed, and the area of local Late Glacial cultures in which, under tundra and steppe conditions, meat certainly did for a while constitute a major and visibly impressive part of the diet – the reindeer of the Magdalenian, the mammoth of the Gravettian and the buffalo of the Palaeo-Indian.

However, the hominids and primates are predominantly vegetarian omnivores, and this dietary flexibility has been one of the unspecialized characteristics that led to the great expansion of this mammalian order. The middle-latitude distribution of the earliest hominids was no accident: the middle latitudes of the globe are the richest in plant life, the prime regions for sunshine and photosynthesis. The dentition and skeletal structure of the early hominids clearly reflect the pursuit of an omnivorous diet with the emphasis on vegetable matter – basically leaves, shoots, roots, fruits, seeds, flowers, buds, nuts supplemented by insects and small animals. It is only in the photosynthetic deserts of near-arctic or antarctic conditions that man must rely predominantly on animal and marine foods, and substitute the moss from reindeer stomachs and the algae from fish gullets for missing vegetal elements. Man therefore makes the best of incident solar energy by cropping the trophic pyramid at the primary, plant level; as an omnivore he advantageously avoids the limiting consequences of a specialized herbivorous or carnivorous diet (Jolly 1970).

Certainly, one of the special characteristics that distinguished the early hominids from the other primates was the development of big herbivore hunting, but the quantitative significance of this activity for the diet is probably much over-emphasized. In any event, scarcely less important than the Pleistocene 'meat revolution' must have been the 'plant revolution' that followed the use of fire to roast plant foods, bursting the starch grains, making them more digestible and breaking down the cellulose cell-walls so that the gastric juices could reach the cell contents, thus greatly increasing the food value of plants and early focusing especial attention on the starchy roots, tubers, rhizomes and bulbs, with their simple vegetative reproductive system.

In short, modern studies and our vestigial soft anatomy confirm that man is a vegetarian omnivore whose diet and subsistence patterns are tightly correlated with latitudinal variations in sunlight and abundance of his primary plant foods. Since the abundance and species variety of plants decrease as one moves out of the tropical and temperate zones, and approach zero in the arctic, the incidence of hunting, gathering and fishing is inevitably related to latitudinal ecology. However, the trend is not a simple linear one, since *edible* plant species form an irregular proportion of the total plant cover, and this proves to be an important feature in European ecology, where the edible plant species of the Temperate Forest zone, taken as a whole, were quantitatively as rich as or richer than the Mediterranean zone, for reasons relating to soils, rainfall, plant community density and structure. In the end, it is the nature and juxtaposition of local micro-variations in ecological structure which add crucial positive and negative residuals to the overall trend in food potential (Lee & DeVore 1968:7, 42).

The so-called 'hunters' of Temperate and Mediterranean Europe probably depended for most of their subsistence on sources other than hunted mammal meat, namely gathered wild plant foods, fungi, algae, shell-fish and fish. It is probable that in these latitudes (35°-55°N), gathered vegetable foods would have provided 60-80% of the diet by weight, and meat from all sources – hunted mammals and gathered land, sea and riverine molluscs, crustacea, insects, fish, amphibians and small reptiles – only 30-40% by weight, *in toto*. With the important exception of the northern coniferous and birch forest zone and the arctic beyond, the European Mesolithic aboriginals were neither predominantly hunters nor mammal meat consumers but largely gatherers, with a substantially vegetal diet whose abundant sources are difficult to appreciate in the *degraded* ecology of modern Europe. They certainly hunted game and fished assiduously but these activities, however impressive in artefact equipment, however prestigious and time consuming, did not provide the greater part of the diet or protein by weight. The traditional misinterpretation rests on a series of biases which we should now examine critically.

Sampling aberrations – technical biases

The unbalancing effects of numerous cumulative unvoiced positive and negative sampling biases, over-representing some aspects and under-representing others, are for example:

1. *Faunal bias.* The artefacts aside, the archaeological record is dominated by the bone evidence. Meat inefficiently leaves much inedible bone waste that preserves relatively well under many conditions; plant-foods are much less wasteful and their small unconsumed residue preserves badly and survives, if at all, transformed into unrecognizable and often microscopic forms (decomposed faeces, plant fibres, seed spikelets etc.). This disproportionate representation can suggest that mammalian fauna with large robust bones provided the bulk of the diet. Thus, in a series of unargued steps, we may slip from '80% of the bones were red deer' (how many individuals, 4 or 400, how many got away, how many hunters, how many man-hours?) to '80% of the diet was red deer' (on what basis?) to 'deer formed 80% of the subsistence basis' (by weight, man-hours?) and, ultimately, to 'red-deer economies' in which anything from salmon to acorns may have provided the staple food.

2. *Northern and Alpine bias.* The great majority of wet Mesolithic sites with good organic preservation are in northern Europe or, more broadly, from the zone which at the time of occupation was within the northern edge of the northern forests and less than 500 miles from the contemporary Norwegian ice-cap. Star Carr, for example, was a winter site set in the sheltered fringes of the Northern pre-Boreal birch forest, facing the Norwegian ice-cap only 400 miles away across an exposed, ice-locked North Sea bay. In these settings and these contexts we would expect meat to be quantitatively well represented and vegetal foods difficult to substantiate; in fact, the evidence from the plant-remains and root-mattocks used at Star Carr shows how remarkably crucial were the lakeside and marsh plants in the northern subsistence pattern (Clark 1972:10-26). The only other significant group of wet Mesolithic sites are the equally unrepresentative Alpine lake sites. We lack investigated sites with good organic preservation from lowland Temperate Forest and Mediterranean zones. However, it is clear that such sites exist and that we should be concentrating on the wet Mesolithic sites of Southern Britain, France, South Germany and Central Europe and on the vast potential of the arid desert sites of Almerian Spain with their basketry and wooden equipment (Clark 1952: Pl. XIII). The Mesolithic sites from which we have organic and vegetal material are confined to extremely limited peripheral areas that happen to be locationally atypical of the Temperate and Mediterranean ecology as a whole.

3. *Artefact bias.* The asymmetric bias effects, which operate cumulatively on artefact production, use, preservation and interpretation, inevitably lead to an interpretative sump in which all surviving artefacts are assumed to be related to hunting and meat-processing.

(a) Asymmetric production and correlation with activities: large numbers of artefacts may be produced for particular tasks that are of short duration and little significance for subsistence whilst, conversely, major activities of staple subsistence-value may be represented by few or unspecialized artefacts. There is no one-to-one correlation between numbers of artefacts and the extent or value of the associated activity pattern. Vegetable and other gathered foods often need little more than dextrous hands and specialized teeth with the addition of a few wooden sticks and points, whereas a variety of specialized stone artefacts is necessary for the particular tasks of killing, skinning, gutting, butchering and otherwise processing animal carcases – especially those of large mammals. Vegetal and gathered food requires little artefact equipment and that largely in perishable materials.

(b) Asymmetric preservation: much of the organic equipment associated with vegetal and gathered foods will fail to survive whilst, conversely, a much greater proportion of the stone equipment associated with hunting and butchering will readily survive.

(c) Asymmetric interpretation: the final barrier – the little equipment associated with vegetal food gathering and processing that does survive may often be blindly misinterpreted in terms of hunting and butchering: the throwing-stick for nuts becomes a boomerang for small game; the Clacton digging-stick(?) becomes a spear-point; the antler mattock, a dispatching weapon; and the microlithic sickle armature, a projectile barb. There is a presumption that because some flint artefacts are associated with hunting and butchering, then others must be similarly associated, thus extending a weak probability to the status of an untested and sweeping general proposition (Clarke 1968:18); whereas a significant and possibly, in certain cases, a major proportion of flakes, blades, bladelets and microliths may have been associated with vegetal and other food-gathering and processing, as recent evidence suggests (Fig. 1; see below).

4. *Method and technique bias.* Archaeological techniques of excavation and methods of analysis partly decide what information will or will not be recovered. There has been insufficient large-scale excavation of Mesolithic open and cave sites and too few of these have been accompanied by the fine sieving, flotation, coprolite analysis, centrifuging and horizontal pollen studies that are necessary to discover the subsistence pattern in general and the role of plant foods in particular. Strangely, these techniques have been used on later open sites and mounds so that, paradoxically, wild plant-foods often first 'appear' in Neolithic to Iron Age contexts. However, the first appearance of a wild plant-food in a Late Neolithic deposit is more likely to represent the statistically sporadic discovery of an erratically preserved and, by Neolithic times, marginally present constituent, rather than the first use of the plant in the area. Much indirect evidence for the wild plant potential of Mesolithic Europe comes, therefore, from Neolithic and even later sites. In addition, many of the existing flotation techniques discriminate in favour of carbonized seed material and against microscopic fibres from roots, tubers and foliage; this bias for seed-recovery and against root-data may turn out to be of crucial importance in our interpretation of the development of food-production in Temperate Europe. Finally, some compensation for the lack of suitably processed sites, and the lack of sites with good preservation, may yet be achieved by the locational analysis of Mesolithic sites in relation to the vegetal and other resources of their catchment area (Fig. 6) (Cassels 1972).

Stereotypes: traditional misinterpretations

Strictly speaking stereotypes are fixed mental impressions, but we are here concerned with those that are supported more by convention than by evidence.

1. *Mesolithic = Microlithic = Bow-and-Arrow hunting; therefore Mesolithic equipment equates with a meat diet.* This stereotype is one of the most entrenched and most misleading of all conventional assumptions. Microlithic flints are rarely the most numerous flint artefact class in European post-glacial industries *c.* 10,000-4,000 B.C.: some industries have none at all and many have merely a few snapped trapezes. Even where they do appear, microliths were used in many different ways and there is growing evidence that a high proportion of these elements was employed in composite tools for plant-gathering, harvesting, slicing, grating, plant-fibre processing for lines, snares, nets and traps, shell openers, bow-drill points and awls; where they were employed as barbs in any number was most probably in a small amount of equipment not associated with hunting mammal meat (fish hooks, bird arrows, fish arrows and leisters). The evidence suggests that with the light Mesolithic bow the arrows used were also light, with a small penetration capacity and therefore encumbered with, at most, one or two armatures on mammal-hunting points; for example, the widely standardized single-point and cutting-side-barb Loshult type known from Scandinavia, Switzerland and Spanish Levantine art, or the narrow trapeze transverse arrow (Fig. 2).

The survival of microlithic-armatured knife-hafts at Shanidar (Iraq), Columnata (N. Africa), Murcielagos (Spain) and Bienne (Switzerland) opens up a rather different picture (Solecki 1963; Camps-Fabrer 1966; Vayson 1918). It is now clear that the ancestry of the Neolithic sickles lies in a wide variety of contemporary Mesolithic/Upper Palaeolithic composite cutting and harvesting knives in wood, bone and antler, either set with blades or microblades in line to give a straight cutting edge (Fig. 2) or set with slanting blades, microblades, broad trapezes, notched and serrated blades in line, or lunates or triangles set vertically, to give varieties of saw-edge (Fig. 1). It would appear that the ancestry of these types is very ancient, possibly extending into the Middle Palaeolithic, and that they are on the whole contemporary and associated functional variants with different duties, rather than a simple typological sequence. What those functions were we can only guess, but those from the Mediterranean zone are often accompanied by seed-grinding stones and the lighter, pointed-toothed varieties would be very suitable for comb-cutting light edible herbage, shoots, buds, small fruits, fragile legumes and grass seeds. The straight-edged or denticulate forms would be more suitable for sawing through thicker edible stems, roots and fruit-stalks, while the heavy oblique-edged settings of blades and trapezes could hack bunches of tough-stemmed grasses and plants with firmly attached seeds.

These implements would answer a pressing requirement for efficient 'mechanization' of laborious hand-plucking procedures, since small vegetal elements must commonly be gathered in vast numbers, thousands of seeds and hundreds of leaves, if they are to be of subsistence value. Such equipment would greatly increase the yield per unit of time and energy-expenditure, thus decisively raising highly abundant, nutritious but small-unit vegetal foods to more-than-marginal economic value by technological means; one more vital step in the increasingly intensive

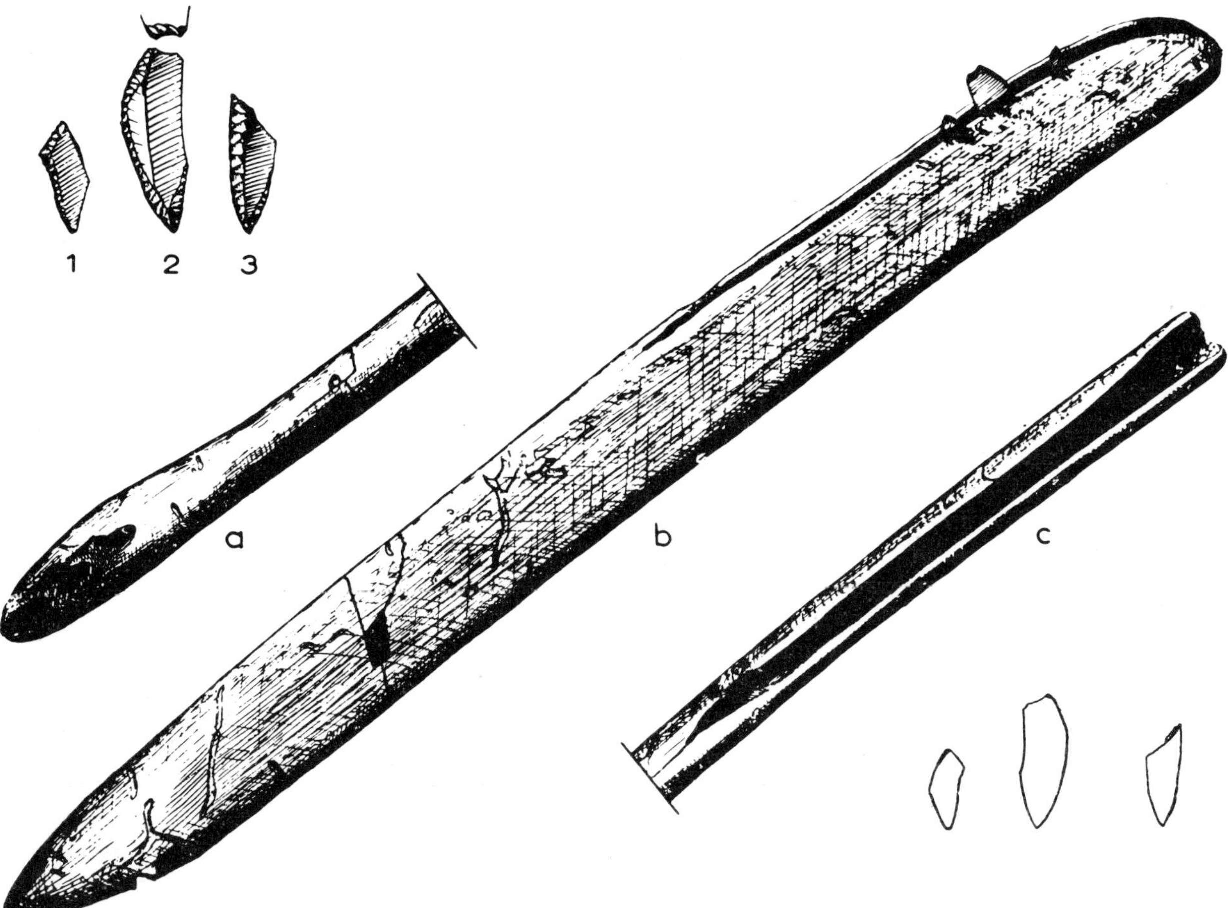

Figure 1. The harvesting knife from Columnata (North Africa), after J. Tixier. (Apart from the microliths 1, 2, 3, the scale is one third.)

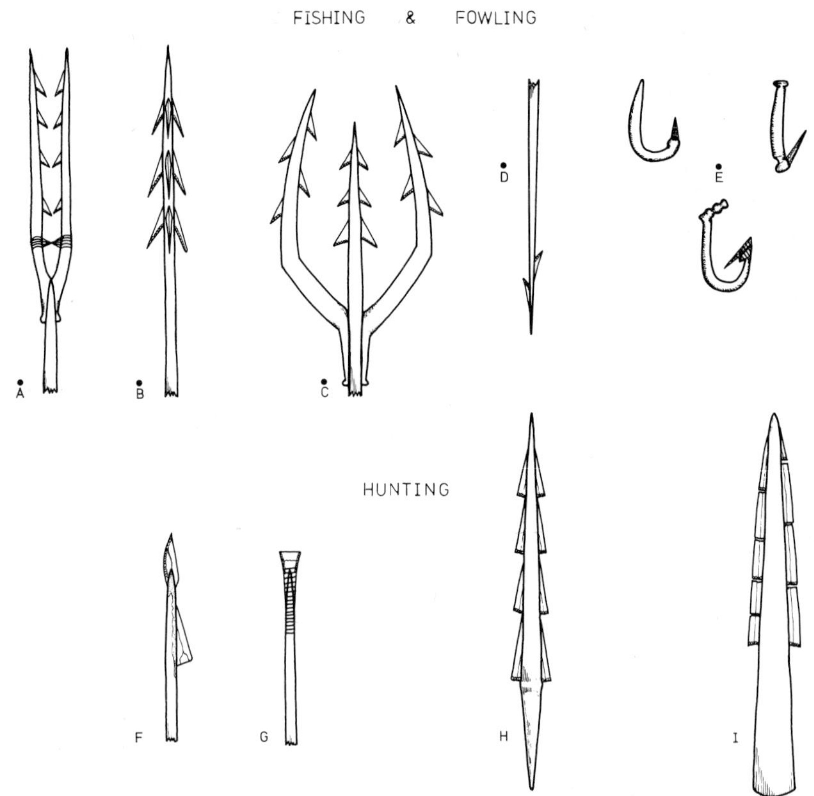

Figure 2. Hafted composite artefacts set with microliths and microblades. A, B, C, D, E, J, K are based on ethnographic models.

A — bident leister
B — fishing arrow
C — trident
D — razor shellfish dart
E — barbed fishhooks

F — Løshult type barbed arrowhead
G — Eising type narrow trapeze arrowhead
H — Trørød type projectile point
I — Tarvastu type thrusting spear

exploitation of vegetal foods.

The short harvesting knife from the Capsian levels at Columnata *c.* 6,000 B.C. is particularly informative (Camps-Fabrer 1966:147-8). In its present short form, with a total haft-length of 21 cm. and slotted section of 9 cm., it once held five microliths of which three broken stubs survive — two broken lunates and one triangle (Fig. 1). This single artefact raises in a particularly trenchant way a number of fundamental and interesting points. Here we have microlithic elements, of the forms conventionally interpreted as projectile barbs, patently hafted in a cutting-tool. Since the broken triangle is virtually the same as the Løshult arrow side-barb, we have visible proof that homogeneous morphological types may have more than one use. Conversely, the triangle was hafted in line with lunates, showing that different morphological types may have been used together for identical purposes and that the makers did not necessarily distinguish in their own ethno-classification between triangles and lunates; maybe they saw a single spectrum of 'micro-units' in which spurred triangles merged into triangles into lunates as, indeed, they visibly do. An archaeological classification based on total morphology provides only one taxonomy — a classification based only on the functional edges and points would produce another (White 1969). Many basic problems of Palaeolithic flint-artefact classification emerge here, but perhaps the immediate lessons are that microliths are not exclusively projectile barbs, that one artefact-

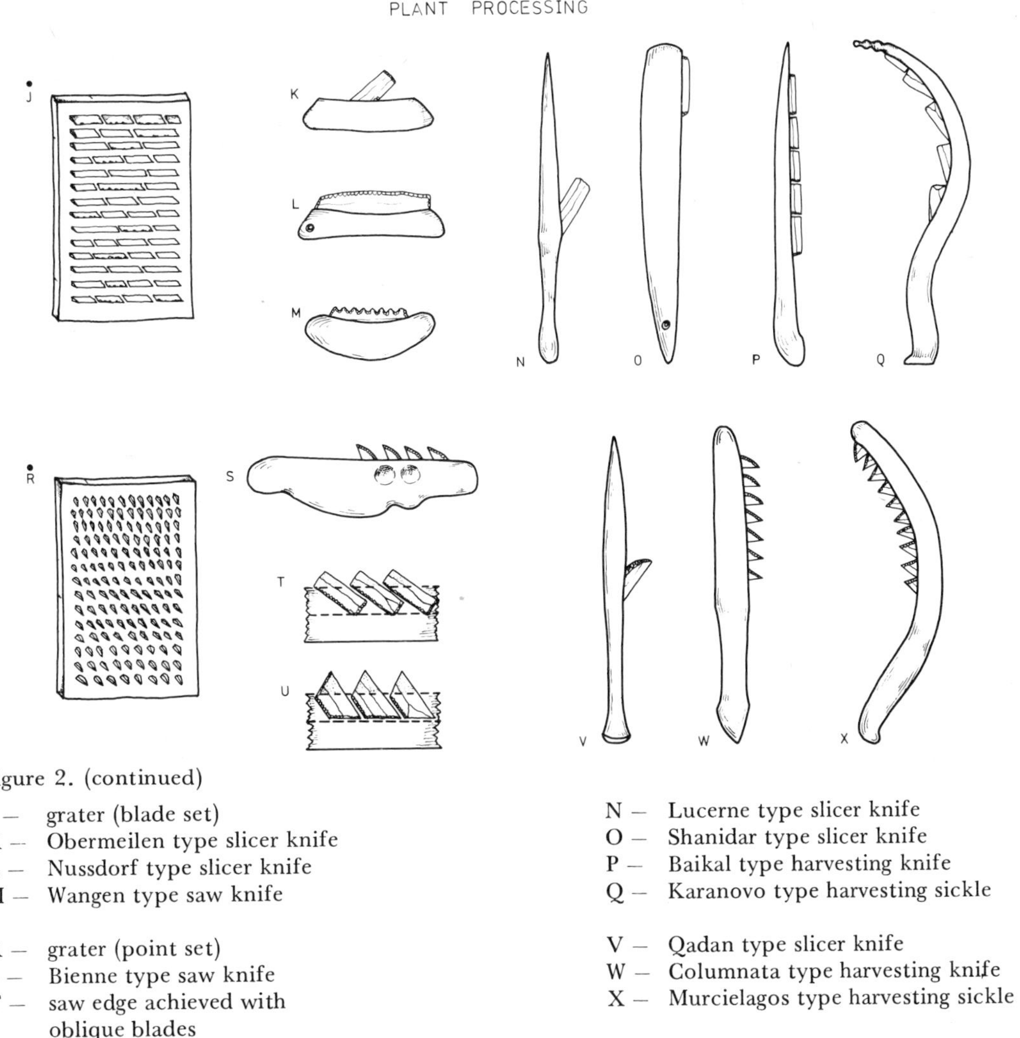

Figure 2. (continued)

J – grater (blade set)
K – Obermeilen type slicer knife
L – Nussdorf type slicer knife
M – Wangen type saw knife

R – grater (point set)
S – Bienne type saw knife
T – saw edge achieved with oblique blades
U – saw edge achieved with broad trapezes

N – Lucerne type slicer knife
O – Shanidar type slicer knife
P – Baikal type harvesting knife
Q – Karanovo type harvesting sickle

V – Qadan type slicer knife
W – Columnata type harvesting knife
X – Murcielagos type harvesting sickle

type may have many different haftings and uses, and *vice versa.*

The Shanidar hafts, and others from Europe, confirm the implications of the Columnata knife. The slotted length of these harvesting-knives averages 20-40 cm. with provision for some 5-30 microliths. Besides this diverse class of artefact for gathering vegetal foods, there were probably others for processing them – many of them equipped with blades, micro-blades and microliths. Some probably fall into the 'bean-slicer' class – one or more sharp flint units set in a small hand-grasped haft over which stems, roots and fruits could be quickly drawn in one motion to produce sliced or shredded elements suitable for cooking and digestion. Artefacts of precisely this type have been recovered from Switzerland, North Africa and Nubia, set with single blades, lunates or triangles (Clark 1971:45).

A most important related class of artefacts with microlithic units, of which we have at the moment only ethnographic evidence, is the composite grater board – a rectangular wooden board into which large numbers of microlithic flint points, microflakes, or transverse rows of straight, notched or serrated blades have been fitted (Fig. 2). Varieties of this implement are used throughout the surviving forest zones of South America, Africa and south-east Asia as the chief means of preparing many different species of roots, nuts and fruits; the grater is usually held face upwards like a washboard and the peeled or processed root or vegetable is rubbed up and down the surface to produce a coarse meal or mash. The universality of this simple and obvious instrument and its correlation with processing forest produce, especially roots, nuts and coarse fruits, suggests that one might well expect it to appear in any subsistence pattern similarly based on comparable forest foods. If such an artefact was in prehistoric use, then we might note that the number of flint or stone elements in just *one* such board ranges from 100-2,700 micro-points, or from 6 to 40 rows of flakes, blades, flakelets or microblades (Yde 1965:35).

At this juncture we might pause to make a brief mental simulation, not of any particular Mesolithic industry but of an elementary range of possibilities. As a start, we can visualize an industry in which, within a family unit, each hunter possesses half a dozen Løshult-type arrows (12 microliths in all), three or four bird and fish arrows (12-30 microliths) and a leister (6-30 microliths); he and four other family members carry varieties of harvesting knives (40-60 microliths) and two women hold slicing knives (2-6 microliths) and a grater board (100-2,700 microliths). At the other extreme, we can remove the grater board and increase the number of microlithic projectile barbs. However, even in the crude range that we have established, the industries still vary only from those in which the dominant proportion of vegetal to hunting microliths moves from approximately 2 to 1 at the lowest, to 40 to 1 and beyond, if any kind of composite grating board was in use, such as we might expect in a wet-forest environment. The figures establish little except the extreme position of the stereotype: microliths = mammal hunting.

The extended discussion of this aspect may be tiresome but it has wide repercussions. In Australia, microlithic industries are associated with the extensive exploitation of vegetal foods on a continent in which there is no evidence at all for the use of the bow in the aboriginal present, the extensive rock art, or the archaeological deposits. In the Wilton and other 'microlithic' industries of Southern Africa, modern evidence suggests a correlation between the increased production of microlithic elements and the more intensive exploitation of vegetal foods, particularly seeds, roots and bulbs (Deacon 1972). India and south-east Asia similarly possess microlithic industries associated with environments in which wet-forest and riverine vegetal foods were exploited. Perhaps then, it is not too outrageous to invert the old stereotype: not microliths = hunting but microliths = vegetal foods. Both statements are, of course, extreme forms, but it now seems perfectly reasonable to see the wider variety and use of microlithic elements in Post-Glacial woodland and forest situations as partly correlated with an increasingly mechanized interest in, and more efficient gathering and processing of, vegetal foods. This would form a suitable prelude to the rise of more intensive man/plant relationships.

Microlithic flintwork was a technical exten-

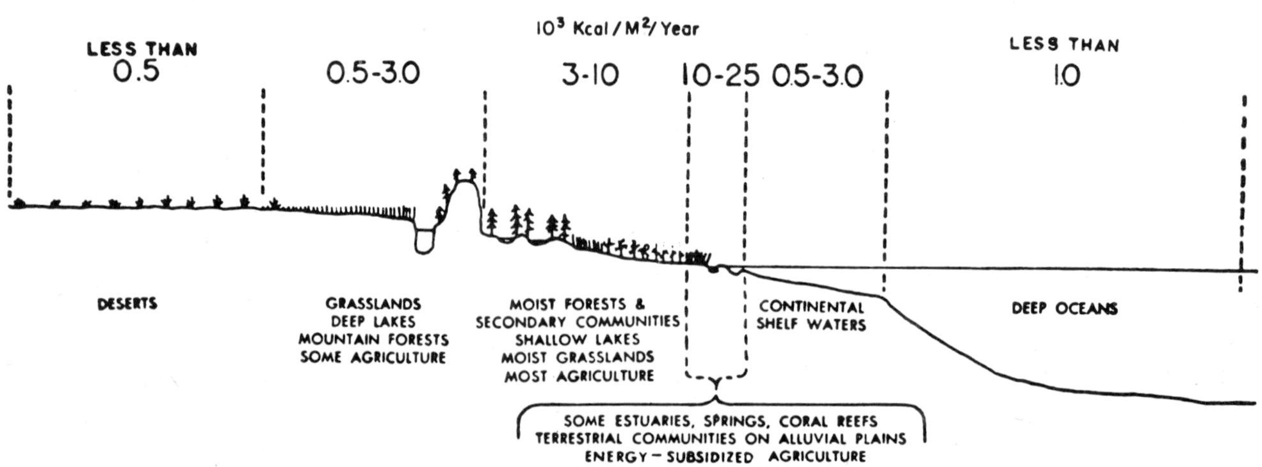

Figure 3. World distribution of primary ecological production in various sectors (after Odum).

sion of the Middle and Upper Palaeolithic development of hafted and composite tools, served by the flake and blade techniques. The microlithic technique enables the maximum length of edge and number of points to be extracted from a minimal volume of flint, so that even a large leaf-shaped thrusting-spear blade can be quickly, easily and more robustly made out of wood, bone or antler with only the working edges sheathed in flint (Fig. 2). Thus, the technique allows the regular exploitation of small, nodular pebbles for even large artefacts and this, in turn, allows the permanent occupation of territories without any other stone source. The procedure incidentally allows the more effective exploitation of small sources of extremely hard, or extremely sharp, materials for special purposes – obsidian, chalcedony, agate or cornelian. However, not the least economy of the technique was its construction of composite tools in terms of small, rapidly replaceable and interchangeable, standardized and mass-produced units, manufactured in advance and kept in readiness for inevitable wear-and-tear – a pull-out and plug-in construction. A broken Solutrean spearhead or splintered Magdalenian harpoon required a complete, specially designed replacement. In most composite tools the breakage would be localized to one or two elements and, in many cases, a standard bladelet or triangle could equally replace a reaping knife tooth or an arrowhead barb (see Columnata and Løshult: Figs. 1, 2).

If this microlithic technique is so efficient, possibly the ultimate in flint technology, how did it die out? Given the many different advantages of the technique and given the extremely diverse and interchangeable functions of microlithic elements, clearly no single, simple answer is universally applicable; the question is none the less a legitimate one and not to be shirked. Part of the answer is that in many areas, for many purposes, the microlithic stone technique was *not* displaced until cheap and satisfactory metal technology prevailed locally: flint microliths were produced in quantity even in some European Early Bronze Age contexts, and in India, Africa and south-east Asia they survive, not surprisingly, into historic contexts and recent times. However, it seems that an earlier factor was the gradual development of more powerful bows that could give a large heavy arrowhead very deep penetration, so that light composite points for maiming and poisoning were replaced by large leaf-shaped, tranchet, or barbed-and-tanged projectile points for killing. At the same time, domestic plant and animal foods increasingly displaced the need for the great variety of composite tools for gathering and harvesting many different kinds of vegetal foods on one hand, or the need for numerous specialized bird and fish arrows, leister barbs and shell-fish equipment on the other; the increasingly standardized heavy hacking-sickle and grinding-quern replaced the variety of specialized harvesting-knives, slicers, cutters, graters and, probably, wooden food-mortars. A highly specialized and diversified composite tool-kit, based on small replaceable units variously hafted, gave way to a less diversified tool-kit based on a few, standardized and specially-designed shapes, with a broad capability over a much more limited and focused range of faunal and floral tasks. In Europe, the steady development of farming and metallurgy between 4,000 and 3,000 B.C. quickly completed the transition, although microlithic flint drill-bits and lathe-tools continued to be made.

2. *Man-the-Hunter.* This stereotype partly relates to the northern meat fixation and partly to the more widespread cultural emphasis on meat, animal magic, hunting prowess and stock numbers, all of which bear either an inverse or no relationship to the dietary importance of meat in the cultures concerned. Until the work of Lee and DeVore (1968) there was a general archaeological failure to grasp the dietary actualities of man the omnivore, a failure to comprehend the quantity, quality, stability and variety of highly nutritional plant-foods widely available throughout most of the year in the forests of Temperate Europe and scarcely less abundant in the undegraded Mediterranean woodlands. Figures are misleading and to emphasize one particular plant species is to miss the very significance of the composite abundance and interlocking seasonality of large groups of plant food-species, which meant that there was hardly a month in which a new combination of edible gums, saps, barks, shoots, stems, buds, flowers, fruits, nuts, roots, tubers, rhizomes, corms, bulbs, mosses, seaweeds, water-plants or fungi was not available, waiting immobile, predictable, for the plucking, even signalling their presence with coloured flowers and distinctive foliage; insignificant perhaps species by species but,

gathered in diversified bulk, they provided an impressive and stable subsistence basis.

At most seasons in the year, any child over four could gather sufficient to feed itself and others, and in the lean seasons there were always the efficient and nutritious natural storage organs – the roots, seeds and nuts designed to over-winter without further treatment. It is easy to forget that the steady plucking of four Temperate-forest gatherers could at will pick the edible carcase weight of an adult red deer in less than four hours; whilst, in the Mediterranean park-lands, one worker with a harvesting-knife could gather enough wild grass seed to produce one kilogram of clean grain with twice the protein value of domestic strains. In three weeks of such work a family unit could gather more grain than it could consume in a year. The same Mediterranean woodlands in Italy alone yield some 400 tonnes of Stone Pine nuts in an average year with the protein equivalent of more than 600 tonnes of lean round steak, making these pine kernels the most nutritious of all European nuts, richer even than the mongongo nuts of the !Kung (Howes 1948: mongongo 27% protein; *Pinus pinea* nut 33.9% protein, 48.2% fat). Cooler Mediterranean woods will also yield a tonne of hazel nuts to the hectare, 3 tonnes of chestnuts a hectare and 10-20 tonnes of edible bulbs for each square kilometre of fertile woodland (Howes 1948; Hill 1952).

The temperate oak/hazel forests are no less productive and commonly yield 700-1,000 litres of edible acorns for each mature oak tree, half a tonne of hazel nuts a hectare, 20-50 tonnes of edible bracken root per square kilometre, 5,000-10,000 kilograms of fungi and 13-15 kilograms of blackberries a day in season. These figures are themselves dwarfed by the huge quantity of protein directly available in a wide range of edible herbaceous leaves and plants, consumed as cress, salad, spinach and asparagus meals. Even the less rich northern Boreal forests will regularly yield 137,000-273,000 litres of edible berries rich in sugars and vitamins (Howes 1948; Hill 1952).

To restore perspective, man-the-vegetarian will have been almost as rare as man-the-carnivore. What we have to compare and contrast is the complementary, but competitive, balance of energy-expenditure and energy-return from plant-gathering and meat-hunting, integrated as they always were within omnivorous seasonal schedules and skilful combinations – the high-risk, high-yield, high-energy-expenditure and dangerous pursuit of hunting against the low-risk, moderate yield, low-energy-expenditure and reliability of gathering. There are, after all, few plants that can escape the determined gatherer, but even the archaeological record widely documents the escaped aurochs, elk, reindeer, seal and pike; the mute testimony to the many wasted man-hours of patient travelling, waiting and stalking by one or more hunters – hours and equipment lost with no return.

Amongst the !Kung Bushmen, for example, Lee (1968:40) records that seven active men spent 78 man-days hunting but achieved only one successful kill for every four man-days' effort. Even in this rather moderate area for vegetal foods on the fringes of the Kalahari desert (85 edible plant species), one man-hour of hunting produced only 100 edible calories, whilst equivalent gathering produced 240 calories return; gathering was thus 2.4 times more productive than hunting. But even this must surely have been a low ratio in favour of vegetable foods for the warm wet Temperate European deciduous forest (*c.* 250-450 edible plant species), or the warm dry grassy Mediterranean woodlands (*c.* 200-350 edible plant species), around 7,000-5,000 B.C. If the stereotype 'man-the-hunter' has any basis, then it would appear to be that the less predictable, more expensive, food-source has gathered a greater accretion of cultural interest, myth and ritual than the routine staples of life, which rarely if ever fail (Lee 1968:40).

3. *Gathering-Hunting-Fishing – the primitive and marginal economy.* The traditional stereotype of the hand-to-mouth existence and continuous, leisureless food-quest, once thought to characterize gatherer-hunter-fishers, has been completely demolished (Lee & DeVore 1968: Wilkinson, R.G. 1973). Indeed, the collapse has been so complete that the revelation that the average gatherer-hunter-fisher works fewer hours for his food than the average peasant or factory-worker has combined with the pressing contemporary interest in ecological pollution to threaten a nostalgic renewal of the convention of the 'affluent innocent exploiting his everfruitful undegraded environment with infinite ingenuity', the 'noble savage' no less; a model which makes it even more awkward to account

for the adaptive development and successful spread of plant and animal domestication.

It is difficult to establish a fresh conventional position on this topic; so much depends on different cultural scales of values and our own ignorance of long-term cultural and environmental process. However, perhaps we can say that it is unlikely that Mesolithic man was less intelligent or ingenious than ourselves; that he was technologically restricted but not primitive, and that his subsistence patterns were probably productive, fragile and inelastic but rarely marginal. Gathering-hunting-fishing subsistence strategies have clearly existed in a great variety of varying patterns, in a great variety of environments of varying productivity and hazard. Clearly, there will have been a range of subsistence effort, diet adequacy, population stress, leisure time, health, security and stability and this range will have fluctuated over time, even in given environments, to varying degrees. The 'fragility' of these subsistence strategies will also have varied, but this inherent fragility rests upon the relatively direct effect of environmental oscillations upon these intricate and delicately scheduled economies, with their relatively short and simple food chains and their restricted capacity for environmental control. Food-producing communities are no less subject to environmental changes and periodic disasters but, by and large, their reciprocally specialized and more elastic economies, with longer and more complex food chains, give them a better chance of stability and control of at least the smaller peaks and troughs of environmental fluctuations, without decreasing their local populations.

In the artificially polarized discussions of gathering-hunting-fishing and food-producing subsistence economies, the most neglected point is perhaps the most important: that food-production with maintained, controlled and stored domestic plant and animal species *supplemented* revised gathering-hunting-fishing in the new economies. The change was an additive one with a net increase in social and economic variety, diversity, complexity and stability.

4. *Gathering-Hunting-Fishing into Food-Production: the artificial dichotomy.* The work of Higgs and Jarman has emphasized the artificiality of this over-simple economic division and clearly demonstrates that many of the problems surrounding this 'transition' circularly arise from the stereotyped division itself (Higgs & Jarman 1969; Higgs 1972). Man, plant and animal relationships are seen as complex and adaptively flexible so that patterns of exploitation will have varied recurrently in space, time and structure over the last two million years. Even the fluctuating trend towards increasingly complex and close relationships between man and certain species is seen as essentially analogous to comparable trends involving species associations other than man over similar time spans. The evidence shows that gatherer-hunter-fishers exist in complicated interrelationships with their plant and animal resources, amongst which some practices of herd and crop control and management and resource storage were seldom unknown, and patterns of exploitation resulting in the husbanding of plant and animal resources were a not uncommon feature. Hardly any Post-Glacial group will have been unaware of the potential of the simple control of vegetation by fire-setting, the elementary consequences of seed planting or root reproduction, animal taming and herd culling, or food storage by drying, freezing, or pickling in vinegars or honey. This latent knowledge, like the knowledge of converting clay into fired ceramics, was not seriously exploited until circumstances demanded it.

These views emphasize the artificiality of the simple bipolar division into gathering-hunting-fishing and food-producing economies and they underline the great dimensional variety and complexity of their development and interrelationships. Although no single criterion may, therefore, be usefully employed to differentiate these states one from another it is perhaps useful to have some basic gauge of the level at which the husbandry of nutritional resources begins to constitute food production. All economies expend energy in the maintenance and control of food supplies on the one hand and the detection and pursuit of food supplies on the other. Perhaps it might be said that husbandry moves into food production when the energy expended in the maintenance and control of food supplies first expands beyond that expended in the detection and pursuit of plant and animal food sources. Such an energy cost threshold might then provide a useful quantitative basis for our conventional division between gathering-hunting-fishing and food-producing systems (Lawton 1973).

Gathering, hunting and fishing easily satisfied

the demands for fresh food under normal conditions and food is rarely accumulated beyond possible need – a need which arises amongst hunting and gathering societies only if there is a part of the year not covered by the successive ripening of fresh wild crops as, for example, in winter in the deciduous forest zone. The lack of storage reflects conditions of plenty rather than scarcity and, in many ways, resource husbandry and food production may be seen as possible economic responses amongst several alternatives to poorer conditions and population stress, a response that would recur stochastically wherever and whenever such conditions might develop, but a response that would prevail and spread only when such conditions became permanent and widespread and where technology would allow; food production is perhaps the economy of a degraded environment (Wilkinson, R.G. 1973:47).

For Europe, the upshot of the dissolution of the extreme Mesolithic-man-the-hunter and Neolithic-man-the-food-producer stereotype has yet to be fully explored and tested by carefully designed research and excavation projects. However, it would appear that many areas of the European Temperate forests *c.* 7,000-4,000 B.C. were areas of very high edible productivity, as rich in wild foods as any areas in the world at that latitude: areas in which it was not so much a matter of the late arrival of advanced food production, diffused from distant sources, as of local continuance of rich wild-food resources and stable population pressure. Here, Temperate-forest husbandry had probably developed over the millennia in a rather different direction, of which we are only now beginning to catch glimpses. The northward spread of the productive species of hazel-nut, apple, pear and other food species in the oak/hazel forest, although part of an ecological and climatic succession, may well have been extensively and deliberately assisted by fire-clearance and even planting (Waterbolk 1968). The nut-bearing beech trees and some edible-root species seem to have made a similarly suspicious preliminary advance into north-western Europe.

There is also growing evidence of forest fire-setting in European pollen-sequences – a practice that opens up the forest canopy, fertilizes the forest floor and directly stimulates the growth and yield of out-shaded trees like hazel: this multiplies the proportion of edible herbaceous plants and especially develops the root and tuber growth of vegetatively reproducing forest-floor species like the edible bracken root. The artificial forest glades so created, directly open to the limited northern sunlight, then become important grazing and browsing resources for wild deer, cattle and boar, a hunters' trap until the forest succession reasserts itself. The food potential of fire-controlled oak/hazel/bracken associations is particularly large and a forest husbandry based on this elementary technique and a basic knowledge of vegetatively reproducing forest root-staples would be difficult to improve upon, until population pressure, climatic or ecological changes, or all three together, might combine with the availability of alternative forest swidden régimes to supplant it.

Summary

This discussion has tried to highlight the major biasing factors and the main conventional stereotypes that have channelled the analysis of European Mesolithic data. If one takes the more recent and carefully gathered information and combines it with the older sources of information, bearing in mind the inherent sampling biases and reinforcing stereotypes, then it would seem that several alternative interpretations of the same data are possible. At one extreme, it is still possible to accept the traditional model and assimilate the new evidence to it. At the other extreme, the evidence will allow the inversion of almost every step in the traditional argument: hunting was the main European Mesolithic food source (plants . . .); mammal hunting was the main role of microlithic equipment (plant gathering . . .); advanced food-producing societies and economies displaced hunter-fisher-gatherers (productive gathering-hunting-fishing societies and economies were increasingly forced, in adverse circumstances, to develop intensively food-productive techniques that they had long practised marginally). In between these positions are others that have no inherently greater probability by virtue of their median position alone.

There would seem to be, in the study of European Mesolithic industries between *c.* 7,000-4,000 B.C. and latitudes 35°-55°N:

(i) A current over-emphasis of the quantitative and general subsistence significance of mammal meat in the diet and the role of land-mammal hunting in the subsistence pattern.
(ii) A corresponding under-emphasis of the quantitative significance of gathered and vegetal foods in the diet of the gatherer-hunter-fishers of the ecologically rich European coastline, Temperate forest, Mediterranean wood and grasslands, and a neglect of the consequences of this for the social and economic organization and territorial sizes and schedules of the Mesolithic groups.
(iii) A general under-estimation of the overall productivity and probable sophistication of the diverse and subtly integrated gatherer-hunter-fisher societies and economies of this area and period.

The contemporary archaeological development of the ecological paradigm has been an important factor in redressing the biased conclusions that emerged from earlier studies restricted to artefact data (Clarke 1972:47). However, there has been a disconcerting tendency for essays in this new field to repeat the worst sins of the artefact typologist in a new dimension, merely substituting the differential minutiae of bone or seed measurements and statistics for those of typology and substituting doubtful generalizations, based on eccentric faunal and floral samples, for those once committed upon artefact assemblages. Perhaps the outstanding example of this has been the emphasis on single species studied in isolation from subsistence assemblages; clearly, this practice is in part a consequence, as was its artefact counterpart, of a misguided attempt to understand complex, inter-related systems by allocating research to one dismembered element at a time, by one man at a time – the reindeer man, the red-deer man, the cereal girl and so forth. It was on this basis that we long ago developed the specialized halberd man, the dagger man and the beaker man, which bring us no nearer understanding Early Bronze Age assemblages, and their social and economic correlations.

Specialized study of components is, to some extent, necessary but cultural assemblage systems or economic subsistence systems cannot be reconstituted merely as a list of their miscellaneous parts, in which certain elements are declared 'staple' or 'key' elements *ab initio.* Indeed, the whole emphasis on single elements – vegetal as opposed to meat foods, this species as opposed to that – is almost certainly yet another anachronistic, mono-focal, mono-cultural extrapolation of the present into the past. There is considerable evidence that plant species, at least, not only grew together but were also gathered together, planted together, cooked together, eaten together and perhaps classified together in complex associations and not in pure, single Linnaean species crops and meals (Renfrew 1973). Obviously, meat and vegetables are complementary resources for the omnivore and the specification of any subsistence system must deal with the relative balance of energy-expenditure in their intake and the relative values of their output at a particular time and place.

Real economies are integrated: only a fraction of their structure is represented by the list of resources exploited; indeed, only a small fraction if such a study is restricted to vegetal or animal sources alone, and less still if restricted to a single species, however dominant. The vital missing half of the systemic structure is contained in the specification of the *relationships* of the elements in the structure: their relative seasonal fluctuations, their relative energy-input/output, their relative contributions to the whole economy. Man/resource relationships are not simply the sum of the resource attributes but depend upon the competitive yields and demands – in time and labour – of other activities, both economic and non-economic, of different cultural priorities; the relationships depend not only on the 'mix' and the 'weighting' but also are relative to particular environmental and cultural states. Thus, the archaeologist's construction of an 'expected model' of subsistence behaviour in a given environment cannot treat each resource independently but must reconcile the hypothesized pattern of exploitation with the presence and abundance of other resources (organic and inorganic) and technologies at the same site and at complementary sites within the annual site system or network; an integrated approach is necessary (Wilkinson, P.F. 1973).

The second part of this essay will therefore

attempt to sketch, in a schematic form, a series of very general 'models of expectation' for European Mesolithic subsistence patterns derived from the ecological, biological, behavioural and economic attributes of the food resources of Mesolithic Europe. These gross expectations can then be compared with the direct archaeological observations, and areas of good fit or deviation from expectation can be highlighted. Finally, these 'sketch models' allow some further speculations to be made about the local nature of the transition from the Mesolithic to the Neolithic in Europe.

The framework for these speculations and hypotheses is provided by the conclusions of the preceding analysis of the biases, stereotypes and assumptions prevailing in European Mesolithic studies; those tentative conclusions provide our new conventions. It follows that special emphasis will be placed on the basic role of 'wild' vegetal foods within integrated subsistence patterns. Although the passing references to faunal food resources is a deliberate part of this attempt to redress a former unbalance, nevertheless it will be clear, from what has already been said, that in detailed studies the animal food sources must be properly balanced within the integrated patterns.

In conclusion, the grand synthesis attempted here is conjectural; in our own terms of reference the simulation of regional Mesolithic economies could be carried out realistically only at a far more restricted scale and in reference to regional and environmental factors tightly specified in time and space. The gathering-hunting-fishing potential of the Rhône delta, or in the English weald, *c.* 7,000-4,000 B.C., would indicate a more useful scale of unit for detailed studies, comparable to that of Yarnell's 'aboriginal relationships between culture and plant life in the Upper Great Lakes region' (1964). A more generalized study can only be justified by its value as a stimulus and focus for further research.

II. Europe: The general ecological background

According to our model, Mesolithic man in Temperate and Mediterranean Europe probably derived the greatest proportion of his food supply directly from plant sources, supplemented by wider gathering and by hunting herbivorous mammals who themselves relied upon, and competed for, many of the same plant resources; conveniently, where the edible roots, grasses, seeds, foliage, nuts and fruits were in season there, too, would be the wild pig, ovicaprids, cattle and deer. Wherever the productivity of a wide variety of plant foods was exceptionally high, there we would expect to find gatherer-hunter-fishers harvesting the vegetal abundance both directly and indirectly by culling the more efficient herbivores. Although man could directly utilize only a proportion of the plant resources, nevertheless that proportion was also certainly the favoured food of some other herbivorous animal. In short, if we wish to arrive at some expectation of where and when Mesolithic communities might be expected in Europe, then we must discover where the productivity and variety of edible plant foods was highest within European ecology. We need an elementary grasp of prehistoric European ecological energetics and food cycles, from the gross trends of the ecological and climatic zones to the productivity of particular catchment-areas, and ultimately the net edible yield, nutritional and utility value of key associations and their individual species.

In food cycles, non-living and living elements are bound together in a pyramidal system through which energy cascades and matter re-cycles – the ecosystem. Plants, the primary producers, use incident solar energy, minerals and water to make living tissue, later eaten by herbivores, which in turn are eaten by carnivores – the trophic levels of the trophic pyramid (*trophikos* = nourishment). As living tissue dies at each stage, it is decomposed and re-cycled, and in many productive food chains the decomposers form an important part of the system. The fungi in the deciduous forest are one example of nutritional importance.

The limitations of ecological efficiency predict that for every 1,000 plant calories consumed by herbivores only 100 are passed to carnivores and only 10 calories to top carnivores; the energy pyramid thus produces the related pyramids of biomass and numbers. Man, however, escapes some of these limitations by means of his omnivorous diet, feeding at all levels but roughly in proportion to their abundance. Thus, man makes the best use of solar energy by cropping the trophic pyramid directly at the plant level. Above this, the aims of converting as much solar energy as possible into protein for human use may be served best by cropping first those cold-blooded molluscs, crustacea and fish that waste no growth energy in maintaining body temperature, and then by cropping those herbivores with the highest growth efficiencies. In this way a gathering-hunting-fishing diet, omnivorously consuming conveniently gathered and gregarious plant foods, fungi, molluscs, crustacea, fish and herbivores best approaches a high subsistence efficiency (Phillipson 1966).

The direct connection between solar energy and primary productivity introduces a number of latitudinal constraints. Roughly speaking, the solar energy entering the atmosphere in the Mediterranean zone is about 6 x 10^8 cal./sq.m./yr.; in the Middle Temperate zone, about 4.7 x 10^8 cal./sq.m./yr.; and in the cloudy Northern Temperate zone around Britain, only about 2.5 x 10^8 cal./sq.m./yr. Under natural conditions the Mediterranean zone therefore has a greater *potential* productivity, a greater variety of species and a heavier standing crop than the Temperate forests, and the Temperate forests a similar potential advantage over the northern coniferous forests and tundra; it is this latitudinal variation that is behind the tightly correlated proportion of vegetal foods in gatherer-hunter-fisher diets (Lee & DeVore 1968:43).

However, although the gross trend of this latitudinal variation in potential productivity does directly influence human dietary variability, it is seriously modulated by a number of more localized factors. First of all, it is only a *potential* level of productivity and local productivity will be extensively modified by local-sector conditions in terms of regional water supply, altitude, location, geomorphology, soil fertility and ecological structure; thus a stand of hazel trees on good soils in southern Britain will produce more than some comparable stands on thin, dry, poor Mediterranean soils, although the *average* productivity would be half a tonne of hazel-nuts in Kent, as opposed to one tonne per hectare in Catalonia. It follows that, other things being equal, plant and animal species distributed widely in Europe will usually be significantly more productive at the southern margins of their distribution; a skewed productivity pattern. This turns out to have been an important factor in the super-productivity of deciduous forest species on the Mediterranean margins of their distributions and of the mixed deciduous/coniferous forests on the southern margins of the northern climatic zones, just as the Late Glacial tundra and steppe of Upper Palaeolithic France will have been much more productive than under present northern conditions.

The second modifying factor is that, from the human point of view, what is important is not the gross productivity of the environment but the edible productivity. Only a proportion of the biomass is directly edible and we therefore need to know where high primary productivity coincides with a high proportion of edible yield. For example, the coral animals that produce reefs are amongst the world's greatest primary producers but their productivity has not been directly tapped by man for food, although the indirect consequences of this colossal productivity are culturally important (Fig. 3).

Bringing these factors together, we see that even in crude terms the dietary potential of an area relates to its latitudinal position, the attributes of each catchment sector, the edible proportion of the total productivity and its seasonality, the output return for energy-expenditure in harvesting the sector produce and the location of that sector in relation to other productive sectors. These factors must coalesce to make up a viable catchment-area productivity for a site and to ensure its ease of access to reciprocally productive site sectors and catchment areas within an economic annual schedule.

In the European context, the zones with the highest directly edible productivity are shown in descending order in Table 1 overleaf (Whittaker 1970).

The warm damp Temperate deciduous forests and glades best combine a high nett productivity with a very high proportion of edible output, spread over a wide variety of plant and fungal species, exploited by a similarly wide range of productive herbivorous mammals and birds. The Mediterranean mixed woodland with sclerophyllous and xerophytic evergreens, stands of grassland and some interpenetrating deciduous communities produces a quantitatively high yield of edible plant foods and dependent fauna but, despite the latitudinal advantage, the average yield is lower than from much of the deciduous forest because of the long dry season, the high proportion of coarse and evergreen foliage, the simple wide-spaced forest structure and the large areas of poor soils. Nevertheless, in this zone in particular, exceptional sectors with unusually rich alluvial soils, plentiful local water

Table 1 Edible productivity in the European zones

	Relative edible proportion of nett productivity	*Number of edible species*	*Nett primary productivity dry g./sq.m./yr.*
Temperate deciduous forest	very high	*c.* 250-450	600-3,000
Mediterranean mixed woodland	high	*c.* 200-350	200-2,000
Boreal mixed deciduous and coniferous forest	high	*c.* 200-350	400-2,000
Boreal coniferous forest	low	*c.* 100-200	400-2,000
Tundra and Alpine	low	*c.* 50-150	10-400

supplies and suitable locations would produce edible yields greater than those of most of the deciduous zone.

The mixed deciduous and coniferous Boreal forest of the northern zone centred on the Baltic ranks next to the Mediterranean in edible productivity because of the advantageous mixture of species, the reliable rainfall and the rich glacial soils. The pure Boreal coniferous forests further to the north also show a surprisingly good nett primary productivity based on the adaptive efficiency of the evergreen coniferous species; however, very little of this productivity is directly edible by man and the edible elements are few and scattered in different communities. Naturally, these trends (few edible species and a low productivity) are continued in the northern tundra and, to some extent, in true Alpine peak areas to the south. Here we must be careful to distinguish cold-restricted true Alpine heights over 1500 metres, from the rich, highly productive sub-Alpine damp forested slopes and high alluvial valleys that flank and intersect the Pyrenean, Alpine, Carpathian and Balkan mountain systems.

Within and across these latitudinal trends, we have the additive effects of particularly productive geomorphological and ecological sectors — the swamps, marshes, deltas, estuaries, lagoons, littoral zones, lakes, river and stream valleys, alluvial plains, and marine shallows (Fig. 3). The productivity of individual sectors will vary with latitude and ecology but, by the very nature of their general structure, these sectors normally introduce limited areas of unusually high productivity combined with an unusually high edible portion (see Table 2).

The great fresh-water marshes and swamps of Europe (British Fens, the Hungarian Marshes, Pripet Marshes, and the extinct Mediterranean and Balkan lake marshes) and the deltas, estuaries and lagoons of the major rivers (Danube, Po, Rhône, Guadalquivir, Tagus, Rhine-Thames, Vistula deltas) have a nett primary and edible productivity probably greater than any other sector or zone. This is due to the extremely high productivity overall and because whole plant-communities, from the shore marginals to the floating flora, are directly edible by man, whilst incidentally supporting a wealth of mollusc, crustacean, fish, mammal and wildfowl life. In general, all the water-related sectors have the especial advantage of stealing water and nutrients from vast land-drainage surfaces — often crucial in dry Mediterranean or sparse northern conditions (Birdsell 1957).

Some inkling of the prodigious potential output of these waterlogged environments can be suggested by the 21.56 g./sq.m./day productivity measured for a temperate European grass swamp, of which a substantial proportion was the nutritious and easily gathered *Glyceria*

Table 2 Productivity of individual sectors, in descending order of edible output (Phillipson 1966, Whittaker 1970)

	Edible proportion of nett productivity	*Nett primary productivity g./sq.m./yr.*
Swamps, marshes, deltas estuaries, lagoons	high	800-4,000+
Littoral zones, alluvial plains, eutrophic lakes, river and stream valleys	high	500-2,000
Marine shallows, continental shelves, forested mountain slopes and high valleys, oligotrophic lakes, grasslands	moderate	200-1,500

fluitans, a wild rice-like plant (Hedrick 1972). Perhaps of equal importance is the extraordinary productivity, in the same temperate marsh environment, of the club-rush (*Scirpus lacustris*) which has the remarkable capacity to produce 46 tonnes/ha./yr. (dry weight) outstripping the most productive cereals including maize (*Zea mays*, 34 tonnes/ha./yr.) (Phillipson 1966:37). This rush has a high edible yield, including large tubers, the lower stems and seeds; traces of *Scirpus* have been recovered from several archaeological sites (Renfrew 1973). Only slightly less productive are the totally edible watercresses that, together with the other water-plants, provide valuable green food-stuffs long after northern land species have been cut back by late-autumn and early-winter frosts.

Altogether, the edible productivity of the water-related plant communities is remarkable, ranging from the reed, water-lily, watercress, and water-chestnut communities (*Scirpus, Typha, Phragmites, Nuphar, Trapa* etc.) to the long list of edible waterside grass, clover and herb associations (water-plantain, water-gladiolus, water-parsnip, water-speedwell, etc., marsh mallow, marsh samphire, marsh marigold, marsh cress, bog moss, swamp potato etc.). This abundance is partly accounted for by the constant supply of water, alluvium and rich nutrients, and partly by the important role of meandering and flooding streams, rivers, lakes and swamps in creating openings in the forest cover (Fig. 4). Similar factors account for the equally productive littoral communities of important edible plants, together with their preference for somewhat open, saline conditions and the frost-repelling winter warmth of the sea (sea holly, sea rocket, sea bindweed, sea fennel, sea parsnip, sea kale etc.).

A survey of the list of the highly productive edible-plant sectors stresses the underlying importance of damp montane, waterside and waterborne habitats. This correlation, in turn, introduces a number of consequences for Mesolithic Europe.

(i) The waterside effect: the connexion between Mesolithic sites and the flanks of freshwater swamps, marshes, rivers, streams and lakes has long been noted. The conventional explanation has been to stress the seasonal importance of the shell-fish, crustacea, fish, wildfowl and mammal sources of meat in these abundant environments. However, significant as those secondary food sources must always have been, we can now see that they themselves relate to the much greater primary edible-plant productivity of these sectors, covering an abundance of roots, rhizomes, tubers, stems, leaves and fruits that can hardly have been of lesser importance. A secondary sampling consequence of this effect has certainly been the constant destruction of waterside sites by erosion, dredging, flooding and meandering watercourses, or their burial under the accumulated alluvium of 6,000-10,000 years. The Mesolithic levels in the lower Po delta, for example, are now buried at a depth of more than 10 metres and the comparable deposits of the other major delta systems must lie at a similar depth, where they have survived at all. However, sporadic but invaluable sites are occasionally preserved in these situations, when set on hard hilly deposits that extrude above the accumulating alluvium, or when set at the hilly margins of the delta environment (e.g. Châteauneuf-les-Martigues) providing residual fragments of once extensive site systems.

(ii) The coastal effect: the correlation of Mesolithic sites and middens with deltas, estuaries, lagoons, salt marsh and littoral sectors has led to a similar tendency to stress the visible contribution of the fish, shell-fish and mammals, and to forget the much greater primary productivity of the wide variety of directly edible maritime plant-species and communities. The *Brassica, Beta, Crambe* and *Echinophora*, edible root ancestors of the beets, kales, turnips, cabbages and parsnips are all extremely important natives of these coastal areas, along with many other productive species and all the edible seaweeds (*Zostera, Atriplex, Lathyrus maritimus, Scirpus maritimus* etc.).

In terms of the productivity of the marine coastal zone itself then, once again, we must emphasize the greatly superior edible productivity of the Atlantic-shelf littoral, as opposed to the Mediterranean shallows, although both were certainly major resource zones. The tidal Atlantic littoral has the advantage of a higher oceanic and tidal energy system, a range of inter-tidal habitats, more complex estuarine and deltaic ecology, the productive intermixture of cold arctic and warm gulf streams and the upwelling of the nutrient-laden deep ocean waters against the shelf. These factors combine to make the Atlantic coastal zone prodigiously productive in seaweeds, shell-fish, crustacea, fish, seals and other marine mammals. The tideless, enclosed Mediterranean has a poorer ecology although its southern latitudinal advantage does once again produce larger yields of particular species in limited locations. The one European area that has the unique combination of a Mediterranean latitude and an Atlantic coastline is Portugal, where shell-fish gathered by hand and rake annually exceed 10,000 tonnes and the coastal interests of the local Mesolithic are widely evident; although, once again, one must also remember the abundant vegetal resources of the same highly productive alluvial littoral in this southern latitude.

The Galician and Tagus middens remind us of another major sampling consequence of this coastal correlation – the destruction of littoral sites by complex marine and land fluctuations. Most of the Mesolithic coastline and most of its littoral and associated sites are irretrievably lost. The only exceptions are the fragmentary Baltic areas of isostatic coastal recovery (Ertebølle phase), the uplifted patches of western Britain and Galicia and the coastal sites accidentally preserved where located high on the point or island remnant of a coastal hill range, well above the local inundation level. It is now apparent that, throughout the Atlantic and Mediterranean, we have only the 'stubs' of once extensive Mesolithic littoral systems, fortuitously preserved for us only in these few fragments – the Ertebølle, Obanian, Portland Bill, Teviec and Hoedic, the Galician and Asturian, and the Tagus middens. The strikingly similar location, dietary evidence, bone harpoons, shell-fish picks, scoops and Mesolithic flint-work that once led to speculation about Azilian movements from Iberia to Scotland can now be, more reasonably, associated with the common exploitation pattern of the same once widespread rich resource zone. In the Mediterranean, isolated sites like the Franchthi cave on the tip of the Argolid peninsula have been preserved only sporadically and for the same reasons; they serve to remind us of the gross sampling distortion imposed by the lost littoral sites and provide us with the limited means to reconstitute the probable forms of the missing evidence.

The general rise in Post-Glacial sea levels after *c.* 10,000 B.C. was certainly important as a contemporary environmental factor as well as for its present sampling consequences. In the Mediterranean in particular, the structural morphology of the northern Mediterranean coastline is such that for most of its length the mountainous or hilly interior rises abruptly behind the narrow littoral. This has nearly always been the case but the rapid Post-Glacial rise in Mediterranean sea-level between *c.* 10,000-5,000 B.C. reduced an already attenuated littoral band to some half or two-thirds of its total area, simultaneously removing two-thirds of the most productive coastal alluvium sector and its directly edible plant resources, and cutting to a critically low level the already restricted winter and spring browsing and grazing of the herbivorous mammals.

In the one or two extensive low-lying Mediterranean littoral plains such as the Rhône and Po deltas, the small rise in sea-level resulted in dramatic losses of fertile and very productive Mediterranean areas of alluvium, marsh and swamp. The Danube delta also lost about 10,000 square miles of highly productive land surface in 5,000 years, a scale broadly equivalent to the losses in the northern Adriatic. On the Atlantic coast an even more dramatic process took out some 20,000 square miles of comparably productive North Sea Basin alluvium and marsh, drowning one of the biggest estuaries in Europe – the joint estuary of the united Rhine, Thames, Meuse and Scheldt. British and Dutch studies have recently suggested that widespread Mesolithic territorial adjustments and other consequences followed the creeping inundation of the North Sea Basin and one might anticipate similar results for the circum-Adriatic/Ionian Sea complexes of the Mediterranean and the Danube/Dnestr/Crimean complexes of the Black Sea (Jacobi 1973; Kooijmans 1972).

The drowning of extensive shallow shelf-areas of the Mediterranean and North Sea between *c.* 10,000-5,000 B.C. and the breaching of the fresh-water Baltic Ancylus Lake in the north *c.* 7,000-6,500 B.C. were not entirely negative in their results. In all three cases productive littoral lost to land-plants and mammals became new, rapidly colonized coastal shallows even more richly productive in edible molluscs, crustacea and fish than the earlier marine zone. Thus, in the Mesolithic sites of the Adriatic, Portugal and probably in those of the Maglemose/Ertebølle transition in the north, we have some stratigraphic evidence for the growing importance of mollusc against red-deer meat in the period *c.* 8,000-3,000 B.C. Naturally, the development of the new marine habitats to a productive climax took many centuries after the initial drowning but, since the drowning was a semi-continuous process, high-productivity shallows were developed continuously, successive bands coming into and going out of peak productivity until marine conditions stabilized somewhat *c.* 5,000 B.C.

This 'climax effect', in which a new resource took many centuries after its initiation before it reached an ecologically productive peak, is also found in the development of the Post-Glacial rivers and lakes left behind by the glacier melt waters and multiplied by the havoc imposed by glaciers on ancient drainage systems. In the early centuries these fresh, primitive cold lakes – oligotrophic lakes, poor in nutrition, with little organic matter and low productivity – were gradually colonized by water-plants, fish and waterfowl. After several more centuries, and as cold conditions receded, animal and plant species diversified and multiplied, as the pioneer *Salmonidae* were joined by the numerous and very productive eel, carp and perch families (carp, roach, bream, pike, perch). The rivers and lakes slowly matured into a mesotrophic or eutrophic ecology, rich in nutrition, until both nett and edible productivity reached a maximum. Subsequent silting and organic accumulation downgraded productivity until ultimately only peat bogs were left. This process was most pronounced behind the retreating skirts of the northern glaciers, on a wide front from Yorkshire to the Polish Masovian Lakes, but it was also going forward on a smaller, but locally important, scale in the glaciated high valleys of the Pyrenees, Alps, Carpathians, and the Balkan-Pindus chain. As they were released, myriads of now-vanished lakes were successively colonized and successively grew to peak edible productivity some centuries or millennia after their initiation; so a sequential pattern, from south to north, of high lake-productivity was released *c.* 8,000-5,000 B.C. as continental climate improved. The Maglemose, Kunda, Ladoga and Onega sites eloquently testify to the speed with which the northern Mesolithic kept pace with the expanded plant, fish and wildfowl resources of the maturing northern lakes, and the large Alpine Mesolithic lakeside sites offer a similar testimony. In the Mediterranean, there is comparable, although less well-documented, evidence for the Mesolithic exploitation of Post-Glacial lake and swamp margins from Bulgaria, Albania, Epirus, Macedonia, Thessaly, at Lake Ohrid in Yugoslavia and on Lakes Fucino, Bolsena and Trasimeno in Italy. Significantly, in these damp plant-rich alluvial Mediterranean lake-basins, plant and animal husbandry were already well advanced by the seventh and sixth millennia B.C. and the preceding industries are either typologically indistinguishable or buried under earlier alluvium.

Summary

The distribution, territories and annual site systems of the Mesolithic communities of Europe must have been closely related to the edible productivity of their particular sectors and to the efficiency with which successively productive sectors could be linked within a continuous and convenient annual circuit. Under most European conditions, plant productivity provided the most abundant and most stable primary food supply for man and the herbivores. As the figures indicate, there are many natural ecosystems that have a greater edible productivity than many agricultural systems. This is because under natural conditions there is a full photosynthetically active plant-cover throughout most of the year, which traps the maximum amount of sunlight, water and nutrients in the complex layers of mutually adjusted foliage and roots; conditions rarely achieved with widely-spaced, single-layer, single-species crops (Fig. 5) (Phillipson 1966:45-7). The gatherer-hunter-fishers of Europe were not incompetent agriculturalists but employed different subsistence systems exploiting different, and sometimes richer, food resources in a different environment.

The ecological considerations discussed earlier identify the general areas in which we would expect to find relatively high concentrations of gatherer-hunter-fishers and their sites, together with some of the sampling problems that seriously modify those expectations. Thus, the close juxtaposition of the productive Mediterranean littoral wood and grasslands, with marsh and sea resources on one hand, and cooler higher foothills on the other, would lead one to expect a discontinuous, but relatively high, density of territorial occupation in the littoral band some 50 miles deep from the Black Sea to Iberia. The especially advantageous ecology of the Crimea/Danube delta, Adriatic/Po delta and Provence/Rhône delta sectors should have carried unusually high levels of occupation. On the Atlantic coast, the unique Portuguese combination of a Mediterranean climate, a mixed ecology and a tidal Atlantic littoral with major estuaries has already been stressed. Further north, the combination of the superior edible productivity of the southern margins of the Temperate deciduous forests with the rich Atlantic littoral and riverine resources more than compensated for the cooler climate. The great North Sea/Baltic plain, freshly colonized by the productive Temperate and Mixed forests, united a prodigiously productive littoral ecology with a recently-glaciated zone, speckled with countless productive lakes and rivers and floored with a variety of glacial soils. This productive band sweeps round through lower Poland, losing its coastline but picking up the Vistula and Dnepr river-systems, the Pripet Marshes, and the variegated and glaciated north flanks of the Carpathians, running east to the Danube delta again.

The expected-density model of European gatherer-hunter-fishers and their sites then takes on a roughly saucer-like distribution with a relatively high-density annular coastal and glaciated 'rim', probably of small, rich, closely-packed orthogonal territories and a low-level, less-populated interior of larger, less-productive territories, with the exception of certain major montane and riverine inliers – principally the Alpine system, the Carpathian/Bohemian system, and the Danube drainage system.

Not surprisingly, our expected model of Mesolithic site-distribution matches the actual distribution quite well, with certain important negative residuals. It should be remembered that we have offered a different ecological explanation of this distribution from the conventional correlation with meat food exploitation. The negative residuals are no less significant. The coastal Mesolithic sites are rich but extremely sparse, with the Ertebølle excepted. The Mesolithic sites expected from the rich-ecology area of the inland Danube/Tisza system are largely missing, as they are from the area of the Danube delta and the Bulgarian lowlands, even richer in natural resources. In all of these cases I would suggest, unless some special local circumstances prevail, that mainly sampling factors are intervening e.g. lack of research, deep alluviation, heavy erosion, extensive coastal inundation.

In all of these cases we have some few, usually peripheral, sites that represent, once again, the mere 'stubs' of the former Mesolithic territorial systems once centred in the lower riverine, deltaic or littoral sectors. In this light, we should perhaps see the Danube gorge sites of the Lepenski Vir complex as not so much a unique local adaptation but a restricted sample of the once extensive lower Danube riverine Mesolithic, preserved for us by its unusual location, where the deeply-channelled and constrained Danube cuts high ground. In the Black Sea littoral and the Danube estuary we have already noted that the original delta and littoral covered 10,000 square miles now lost to the sea. Nevertheless, there is still the significant juxtaposition of the Crimean/Dnestr sites, which were probably a seasonal part of these littoral-deltaic systems from the time when the rivers Dnepr, Bug, Dnestr, Prut and Danube shared a united outflow of potential comparable to or greater than the contemporary Thames-Rhine-Meuse confluence. The enigmatic early development of the coastal Neolithic Hamangija culture may then represent merely the 'ceramicization' and first visible traces of such a population. The situation would thus be analogous to the circum-Adriatic adoption of Impressed Ware by the divided but related gatherer-hunter-fishers of the drowned Adriatic basin and Po delta.

III. The regional Mesolithic economies and the Neolithic transition

Naturally, no detailed exposition is intended here, but merely an extension of the implications of the general ecological model to the different resources available to regional Mesolithic subsistence systems and the possible consequences of such regional differences for different developments in the ensuing Neolithic. We now wish to identify some of the regional plant communities that concentrated an unusually high yield and a high proportion of edible constituents and, in particular, the species that yielded an exceptionally abundant and nutritious resource whose subsistence value could hardly have been ignored. With what seasonal schedules, exploitation strategies and existing husbandry practices would these food associations be linked, and in what way can they be related to the food-producing practices developed between *c.* 6,000-4,000 B.C.?

The gatherer-hunter-fisher subsistence system is usually a seasonal circuit or alternation of successive sites and their catchment-areas, which exploit varied combinations of productive ecological sectors. The annual length of the circuit is normally the minimum necessary to produce an adequate level of nutrition for the group, season by season, but especially in the season of greatest scarcity. In the lean season site location is critical and must ensure a catchment-area of the greatest and most reliable food productivity possible in the circumstances (Fig. 3). These critical sites are the weakest links in the circuit, the annual bottle-neck through which the population must pass successfully, reduce its numbers, or change its strategy. We have already emphasized that, in Temperate and Mediterranean European conditions, the most abundant, most diversified and most reliable food source will normally come from vegetal sources. It therefore follows that the catchment-areas of most critical sites will often have to combine the most highly productive sectors of edible plant productivity – springs, deltas, estuaries, marshes, swamps, lagoons, sea coasts, lake and river margins or montane valleys (Fig. 3).

In a theoretically optimal situation, the annual circuit length would be zero and the annual subsistence strategy be accomplished by short expeditions from a permanent base site. Many advantages and some disadvantages accrue from a sedentary base but, in general, a successive range and variety of fresh food gained by periodic movement would take precedence over the mere advantage of a static residence – except in those unusual circumstances where a successive range of abundant fresh food *could* be gathered throughout the year from one site. Were there any such locations in Mesolithic Europe? We are not certain but, on ecological grounds, one can begin to point out where they might be and what their subsistence spectrum might embrace. However, even for the 'average' group there was no mobile/static dichotomy – if local conditions were exceptionally fruitful and exceptionally attractive then a static base might exist for a number of years until more variable conditions returned, and then a seasonal circuit might once again become the sounder strategy (Thomas 1972).

The annual schedules and territorial schemes that we might expect in Mesolithic Europe are likely to have covered a very wide range of flexible arrangements, altered sensitively from one year to another, oscillating back and forth around short- and long-term social and environmental trends. Higgs (1966) and Flannery (1969) have stressed the generality of vertical, transhumant economies, especially in mountainous zones in dry climates. When the lowland vegetal and animal resources are restricted by summer drought, then movement by men and game to higher altitudes allows the exploitation of the differing seasonal developments and the higher rainfall: an extended yield of spring vegetation and earlier autumn seeds, fruits and nuts can then be obtained by moving at a carefully judged speed through the ecological zones and communities. The tightly packed and variegated montane communities will also usually return a high and diverse yield for short-distance movements. Combined with a littoral or lacustrine winter base, such systems were ideally suited to Mediterranean and Alpine conditions and are frequently indicated by the transportation of mountain resources to lowland sites and *vice versa*. We have this kind of evidence, for example, linking the Peloponnesian mountains and littoral; the Pindus with the Thessalian lakes and Epirote coast; the Dalmatian Alps and the Adriatic coast; the Apennines with the Tyrrhenian and Adriatic littoral; the Ligurian Alps and the Ligurian coast; the Meseta rim and the Spanish Levantine coast; the Pyrenean and Cantabrian mountains with the Bay of Biscay and Golfe du Lion. Comparable inland régimes probably prevailed in the Swiss Alps, and very possibly in the Balkan and Carpathian systems and wherever productive lakes, marshes or littoral were closely adjacent to productive mountain foot-hills and uplands.

However, there is growing evidence that there were other and more complex movements, where differences in altitude and rainfall were insignificant or, where there was a scheduling conflict between the seasonal requirements of several productive resources, or special local, ecological or climatic conditions offered better alternatives. Such annual territories would probably include lateral coastal, orthogonal coastal, upper/lower riverine, deltaic and estuarine territories as well as forest/swamp, forest/delta, forest/lake and even alkaline/acid soil-combinations, all of which offer the possibility of reciprocal seasonal yields. In the deltaic marshes for example, winter flooding forces man, deer, pig and cattle into the upper delta or foot-hills but, in the summer, the greatly extended area of freshly productive lower delta is once more available to man and beast. It may be suggested that the subsistence relationship between the Dnestr/Crimea sites and the old Danube delta, the Alpine/Istria sites and the Po delta and between the Provence/Languedoc sites and the Rhône delta were, for some period, of this latter type. Across the flat Great North European Plain vertical economies could not be practised except at the extreme Pennine margin, in the form documented by Professor Clark (1972) at Star Carr, or at the extreme Bohemian and Carpathian margin. Over the great plain the territorial systems must have oscillated instead between varying combinations of coastal, deltaic, estuarine, riverine, swamp and lake-focused site networks.

What these speculations suggest is that if a sector is too homogeneous ecologically, too extensive or of low 'edible productivity', it will either be taken up only marginally or be virtually unoccupied. Thus, parts of the deep interior of the Spanish Meseta, and even the core of the larger loess areas of Central Europe, seem to have carried a sufficiently low-density Mesolithic population for their presence to be currently undetectable. In contrast, we may note the special importance of the so-called 'marginal' dissected mountains, deltas, swamps, marshes, estuaries and abundant forests for the gatherer-hunter-fisher economies. Marginal is a relative term and the distribution of Mesolithic sites may be marginal to the preferred terrain of modern agriculture but it was never marginal in terms of its own subsistence patterns.

Mediterranean Mesolithic

The Mediterranean is a climatic and ecological buffer-zone in which proximity to the Equator is set against distance from the ice-cap and reinforced by the ameliorating influences of the sea itself, so that development within the zone is marked by a continuity of species and associations, with fluctuations mainly in distribution and density. The same continuity is witnessed in many of the flint industries and it is a matter of preference whether we label the regional complexes of *c.* 10,000-5,000 B.C. Mesolithic, Epipalaeolithic or Protoneolithic. They are all of these things taxonomically, but about their subsistence status we are less clear. On ecological and flint-taxonomic grounds, divisions can be made between the characteristics of the Eastern Basin, the Western Basin and the North African littoral, but for our purposes we will concentrate on the European shores of the twin basins; although the great significance of Northern and Atlantic African interconnections for Iberia, and Anatolian and Steppe interconnections for the Balkans, should not be underestimated.

The regional pollen sequences for the Mediterranean countries will, in due course, provide the only sound basis for the detailed local studies that must ultimately frame the mosaic of Mesolithic developments. However, it would seem, in general, that between *c.* 10,000-7,000 B.C. the cool and temperate zone at the head of the Adriatic and the Franco-Ligurian seas was gradually colonized by warmer species from the south. Birch and pine gave way to juniper, pines and oaks, as the residual Mediterranean evergreen and drought-resisting flora gradually expanded from major pockets in southern Iberia, southern Italy, southern Greece and the South Balkans (although many deciduous tree species, such as hazel, survived inland at higher altitudes). In consequence, part of the ecological difference between the east and west Mediterranean basins, at this period, arose from the differing communities of local mixed deciduous woodland displaced from the littoral bands – pine/oak/hazel in the west and oak/elm in the east basin; and part from the differing remnants of Late Pleistocene flora left in the residual southern reservoirs to recolonize the north.

In this first complex phase, *c.* 10,000-7,000 B.C., the northern half of the Mediterranean was partly occupied by a mixed Temperate woodland, distributed well to the south of its present area above the Pyrenees and Alps. It has already been noted that the Temperate deciduous forest had an extremely high 'edible productivity' and that this would have been greatly multiplied by the increased productivity of this southern climate and the variety provided by intermixed

Mediterranean flora. The abundant deciduous browsing and grazing seems to have supported a prolific range of deer, aurochs, horse and boar, and both resources supported a flourishing Mesolithic population such as we see in the Spanish Levantine art – sufficiently numerous to give rise, perhaps, to the territorial skirmishes of the paintings. Further south, in the southern Iberian, Italian and Greek peninsulas the lower 'edible productivity' of the entrenched Mediterranean evergreen flora supported rather different régimes, in which coastal resources were critically important from an early phase.

Between *c.* 7,000-5,000 B.C. the Mediterranean vegetation gradually established itself throughout the peninsulas at least in the warm, dry littoral band. Perhaps in Iberia, and possibly in Italy, it now seems probable that this relict vegetation already included stands of some wild cereal grasses, legumes and the important wild olive, wild grape-vine, strawberry tree association with its high edible rating (*Olea oleaster, Vitis silvestris, Arbutus unedo*); the grass and legume seeds, such as *Secale dalmaticum*, were summer staples and the fruits of the trees and their associated creepers were important autumn and early-winter staples. Other commonly associated plants with edible elements included the cistus, myrtle, juniper and evergreen oaks with edible acorns (*Cistus* spp., *Myrtus communis, Juniperus phoenicea, Quercus suber, Quercus ilex*). High-yielding hazel-nut trees were also available at cooler altitudes, but more important than any other winter staple must have been the highly nutritious and very abundant 'pignolias' – the pine-kernels of the ubiquitous Stone Pine (*Pinus pinea*) with one of the highest protein yields of any known nut (Howes 1948:17).

The characteristics of the expanding Mediterranean climatic régime established the remainder of the ecological pattern. A moderate annual rainfall and a late summer drought of severe proportions at sea-level limited coastal woodlands to mainly xerophytic and evergreen tree species growing in widely spaced communities, interspersed with stands of flowers, grasses, legumes and herbs. Much of this predominantly annual herbaceous vegetation was directly edible as salads, and could be harvested throughout the year, thanks to the warm, wet, frostless littoral winters, or provided seeds that could be gathered in April and May before pursuing the same harvest slightly later at higher altitudes inland. Many of the herbaceous plants are drought-adapted, including the extremely important and numerous range of Mediterranean bulbs that remain dormant for long periods, commencing growth as soon as rain falls again. This 'bulb flora' includes many edible species, some famous for their easily recognizable flowers – *Iris sisyrinchium*, Grape Hyacinth (*Muscuri racemosum*), Orchids (*Orchis* spp.), Star of Bethlehem (*Ornithogalum umbellatum*), Lilies (*Liliaceae*), Crocuses (*Irideae*) and, above all, the important wild leek, shallot, garlic, onion family (*Allium* spp.). These edible bulbs and a number of comparably adapted edible-root plants (*Apium, Asphodel, Arum, Carum* spp., *Cyperus esculentus, Peucedanum graveolens* etc.) were widely distributed, but especially abundant in damper montane valleys, coastal clearings, marsh and swamp edges.

The early mixed Temperate and Mediterranean woodlands were very productive with a high quantitative yield and probably some 350-450 edible species, of which perhaps 100-150 would have been important locally. The later, more extensive, development of the full Mediterranean xerophytic ecology along the coastal strip substantially reduced the overall quantitative edible yield and reduced the range and density of edible plants to some 200-350 species. It is at this stage that an increased exploitation of productive rabbit, ovicaprid, shell-fish and marine foods seems to have augmented the decreasing abundance of red deer and other herbivores and, to some extent, the decreasing variety of vegetal foods. It is also against this context that a more intensive exploitation of the restricted food-species associated with the spreading southern flora may have led to more careful husbandry of the long-exploited wild olive, wild vine and many species of grasses and legumes over a wide area embracing southern Iberia, Italy and the Balkans.

Early Mediterranean ecology makes it likely that the vegetal basis of many of the Mesolithic subsistence systems on the European littoral will have been a pulses/bulbs/grass-seeds and nuts combination, balanced by coastal gathering, fishing and fowling, and inland hunting of ovicaprids, deer, aurochs and equids. The pulses provided protein, oil and carbohydrate; the bulbs and fruits produced water, carbohydrate and some protein and vitamins; whilst the nuts and grass-seeds contained a good supply of proteins, fats and carbohydrates. The very high water-content provided by bulbs, roots, leaves, shoots, buds, flowers, fruits and berries will have been a useful feature in the Mediterranean summer drought, with most of the concentrated nutrition coming from the seeds, fruits, nuts, fish and meat sources. The Mediterranean nuts were of particular importance as storable winter sources of calories and protein, at a season when game would have been more widely scattered. In general, over-wintering should have been little problem in the Mediterranean mild wet winters with a fairly constant basic supply of edible green salad plants, bulbs, roots and nuts. The critical period will have been late summer, when drought scorched the withered vegetation and game animals moved to fresher pastures at higher altitudes. Apart from the special alternatives based on marine, delta or marsh ecologies, many of the Mediterranean Mesolithic schedules seem to have followed the vegetal and faunal harvest into the hills.

This model suggests the basic and early importance of the pulse/bulb/grass-seed and nuts combination throughout the Mediterranean; probably acorns, hazel nuts and pine nuts were univerally important with perhaps walnuts, almond or pistachio in the Balkans and sweet chestnuts in the western Mediterranean. The traditional nutritional Mediterranean 'salep' meal of ground bulbs of many species may have supplemented the pounded mash of pulse and grass seeds reaped with composite harvesting-knives (Hedrick 1972:264, 560). The early familiarity with the edible seeds of a very large range of legumes and grasses will certainly have included some ancestors, or at least close relations, of the later Neolithic range of fully domesticated legumes and cereals and the possibility of an indigenous Southern Mediterranean and Balkan pre-Asiatic pulse and grass husbandry from at least the eighth millennium looks not implausible (Clark 1971). As we shall see, from about that time the northward spread of the limited Mediterranean xerophytic vegetation correlated with other changes that, perhaps, intensified the increasing exploitation of the olive/vine/arbutus, grass/legume and ovicaprid associations of the developing littoral *maquis*.

Temperate forest Mesolithic

North of the Alps and Pyrenees, the zone later occupied by the expanded Temperate forest was initially a cool or cold corridor bounded by the northern Baltic ice-cap and the southern glaciers of the Alps and Pyrenees, a zone of tundra, open steppe and forested steppe warmed only at the juxtaposition of the Atlantic currents and the warm Mediterranean, one on either side of the Dordogne isthmus. As conditions ameliorated, this area of low biomass, exploited by large migratory herbivores and containing wide human territories, was increasingly colonized from the south by pioneer Temperate deciduous forest *c.* 10,000-9,000 B.C. and gradually became an area of high biomass, with a very high edible productivity exploited by numerous herds of small herbivores and probably broken up into a mosaic of small, productive Mesolithic territories. The 'reindeer' economies, which had dominated the French plain and the German Wald as far north as the Hamburg swamps, either migrated or adapted in the face of the advancing pine and birch mixed forest and the growing potential of the maturing Post-Glacial landscape and forests. Whatever form the coastal seal and salmon hunting facies of the Magdalenian took, it must have contributed to the later coastal economies exploiting the rapidly growing marine and littoral potential of the Atlantic zone.

The pioneer birch and pine woodland quickly gave way to a thicker Late Boreal mixed forest with increasing hazel and oak communities, reaching a climax in a dense oak, hazel, alder, lime and elm forest in the warm, wet phase of the Post-Glacial climatic optimum between *c.* 6,000-4,000 B.C. (Fig. 4). This canopy, of many deciduous species and of great structural complexity, covered most of the Atlantic and Northern European plain and extended as far as southern Sweden and the mixed deciduous and coniferous stands east of the Baltic. The structure of this entire forest was determined by the annual loss of leaves in the autumn and the cessation of fresh green growth for a long snowy winter of three to five months. The colossal annual rain of leaves and organic detritus produced a dense ground-layer of damp humus and dead rotting and decaying trunks, dominated by large quantities of fungi, mosses and liverworts, many of them edible and available the year through. Above this enriched ground

Figure 4. Deciduous woodland, Doubs, France. Note the break in the canopy caused by the river and its seasonally flooded margins.

Figure 5. Pedunculate oakwood, Hampshire, England. Note the complex structure of the deciduous forest layers and the extensive field layer of bracken (*Pteridium aquilinium*). Both from Riley and Young, *World Vegetation*.

layer rose the field-layer of abundant herbaceous plants and small sparse stands of grasses, dominated by perennials and vegetatively spreading root and tuber plants like bracken (*Pteridium aquilinium*). Bracken spreads by means of long rhizomes that grow horizontally to produce dense and continuous stands, often extending over many acres in the field-layer, where its large leaf area makes it the most efficient interceptor of the limited amount of light that penetrates the upper forest layers (Fig. 5) (Riley & Young 1968:13).

This productive field-layer of bulbs, roots, rhizomes and tubers was shaded by a shrub-layer of hazel, berry-bearing bushes, brambles and shrubs up to fifteen feet high. Above this the tree-layer completed the structure in which the oak, elm and ash crowns formed an almost continuous shady canopy at between 25-100 feet, broken only by artificial herbaceous glades or natural ones around lakes, rivers, swamps and outcrops (Fig. 4). The complex ecological structure of two to four layers and diverse associations of tree and plants, bound by climbers and brambles, utilized every gleam of sunlight at every level in minutely integrated schedules of fruition and leaf-shedding, which differ slightly from one species to another. The detailed structure of the forest was spatially correlated with the varying dampness, acidity and nature of the underlying soils and, since these were highly varied across the old glacial terrain, this provided a great horizontal diversity of communities to be seasonally exploited, as well as the vertical one through the forest layers.

It is quite apparent, from the European Temperate forest structure, that Mesolithic man must have lived in and through the englobing forest habitat and its richly productive ecology. The humus-enriched soils provided ample browsing and grazing for an equally abundant wild life of deer, aurochs and boar, limited, in the main, by the annual constraint of the long cold European winter. However, for most of the year, the complex deciduous forest produced a great quantity and variety of seasonal vegetal foods, especially roots, foliage, fruits and nuts, supported by a vast range of ancillaries, from the important fungi to edible barks, sap-sugars and mosses, the variety of Atlantic seaweeds, and the special littoral root and herb associations of the coastal estuaries and shores. Throughout the forest, the abundant Post-Glacial lakes, swamps and many major rivers and streams added a rich network of additional resources on a scale quite unknown in the Mediterranean.

The contrast between the established Temperate forest and its resources and even the undegraded Mediterranean woodlands and their associations must always have been rather striking. The number of Temperate forest edible vegetal species is nearly one-third richer (250-450 species): edible perennials, roots, tubers and rhizomes dominate the resource spectrum together with the edible leaves, shoots, buds, flowers, berries, fruits and nuts. In contrast, the edible seeds of the sparse stands of grasses and the few pulses seem to have been insignificant: there were far fewer indigenous pulse and grass species; they occurred widely scattered, or in limited glades; they were comparatively unpredictable and low-yielding in the tiered wet-forest context; and ripened late in a short season, to be hotly competed for by grazers and abundant bird life. Although the Temperate forest provided fewer and noticeably less nutritious edible nut species, nevertheless varieties of acorns and hazel-nuts provided a very abundant but fluctuating and moderately nutritious background, with Swiss Pine (*Pinus cembra*) kernels and beech-nuts in southern areas.

The major problem for the gatherer-hunter-fisher in the Temperate forest zone will have been that of over-wintering in an ecology that had effectively shut down for several months. Marine, littoral, river, marsh and lake resources offered one winter-base solution with the combination of the still-productive green water-plants and rhizomes of the reed associations (*Scirpus, Phragmites, Menyanthes*) or the sea-shore root and leaf communities (*Atriplex, Beta, Crambe, Echinophora, Brassica, Eryngium*); waterside solutions to which many of the forest mammals also resorted. The alternative was to mimic the squirrel by storing roots, nuts, dried berries and dried fruits such as the crab apple; this, in turn, meant an intensive period of communal autumn gathering, preparation and storing in pits and baskets, which then must serve as a base-area for the rest of the winter. There is growing evidence that in especially advantageous sheltered areas, with freshwater springs and catchments that produced large quantities of storable resources within a small radius, extensive winter base-camps were established for large groups on this basis – including the expected range of irregular storage pits, root-roasting pits, nutting stones, winter huts (perhaps of turf), access to water and, perhaps, originally the composite slicers, graters, wooden mortars, throwing-sticks and digging-sticks discussed earlier.

Putative winter base-camps of this type, marked by large flint-scatters, pits and structures, are found from Britain to Poland and southern France, mainly in sheltered southerly locations on light or sandy soils, once thought to have been thinly forested. However, the tight correlation of these large Mesolithic sites and particular loamy sands, sandy gravels or greensands is very reminiscent of the Danubian I interest in the loess soils. It is well illustrated by the important Horsham group occupying the Wealden ridge linking Britain to France, between the warming Atlantic to the south and the North Sea (Fig. 6). Radial territories from this common core could conveniently run across several ecological zones, north to the Thames valley marshes and estuary, or south to the lost Sussex and Hampshire coastline on the sheltered South Channel bay.

The modern evidence suggests that these sandy gravels and comparable soils in adjacent Europe, in fact, carried varieties of oak/hazel/bracken associations. Indeed, these warm light soils provide both ideal growth conditions for bracken, and the richest and most productive soil conditions for hazel-nut production, in Western Europe (Riley & Young 1968: Fig. 6; Howes 1948:182-3; Masefield *et al.* 1971:26). This immediately emphasizes the unique importance of the great edible productivity of the oak/hazel/bracken/bramble/fungus associations on these soils – producing a vast localized and storable autumnal yield of edible acorns, hazelnuts, bracken rhizomes, blackberries and edible fungi. The average annual productivity of bracken-root alone (*Pteridium aquilinum*) ranges between 20-50 tonnes per sq. km. and it is edible, after treatment, throughout the year; it stores well and formed the major subsistence basis of the Maori gathering economy (Shawcross 1967; Hedrick 1972:470). The annual productivity of edible acorns, hazel-nuts, berries and fungi must also be calculated in tens of thousands of kilograms in this environment (Howes 1948; Brothwell & Brothwell 1969:86).

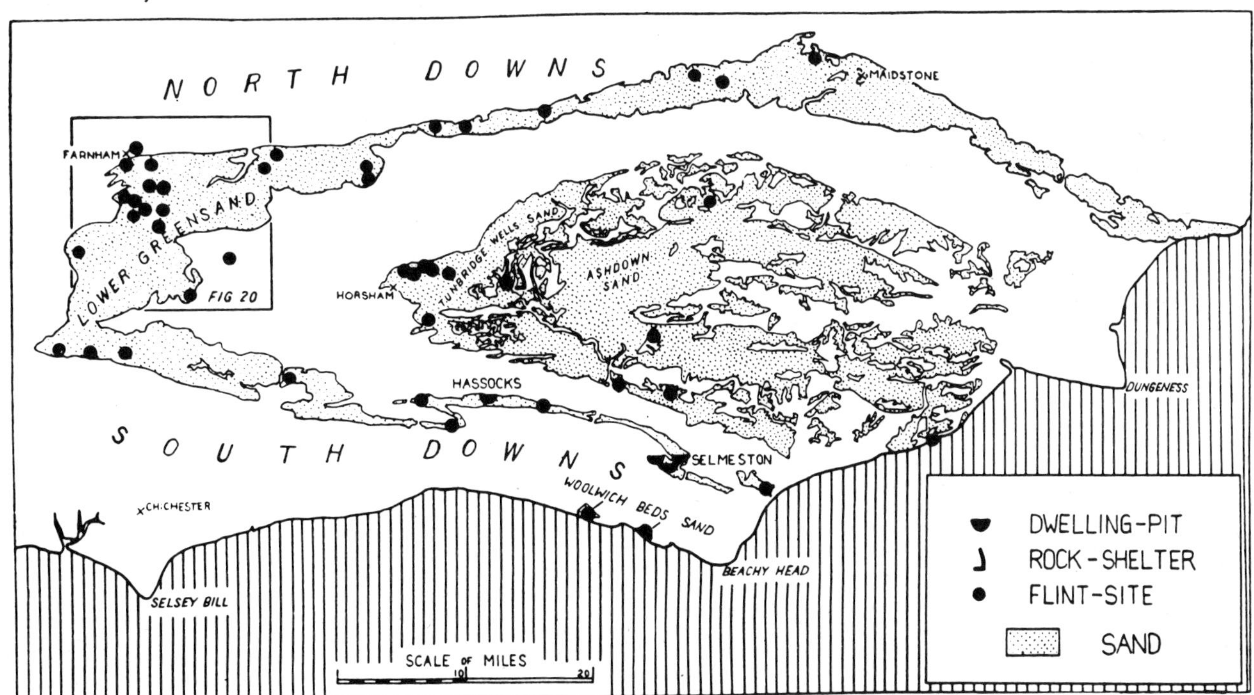

Figure 6. Distribution map of sites of the Horsham group *c.*6,000-4,000 B.C. showing the strong correlation between the site locations and the sandy-loam soils with the most productive combination of bracken, acorns and hazel nuts, along the freshwater spring line. The Horsham sites are now far more numerous but although sites have significantly been found outside the sandy-loam terrain the overwhelming correlation with these soils remains and is reinforced. The coastline indicated is modern (map after Clark & Rankine 1937-8, *P.P.S.*, 5, 93).

The key contribution, however, will have been the easy storage and complementary nutritional value and reliability of nuts and roots. In a forest economy based on nuts and roots the cycle of low nut-productivity years may be counterbalanced by root reserves, especially if several different species of nut and root are gathered. The roots are naturally rich in carbohydrates, some sugars and a little protein, whilst acorns and hazel-nuts provide valuable fat, protein and other elements. The fungi, too, may be dried and stored to provide important protein and vitamin resources; for example, laboratory animals fed on mushrooms as their protein put on 30% more weight than those fed on cheese (Brothwell & Brothwell 1969:90). Particularly important after a lengthy winter diet of roots, nuts and fungi will have been the vital anti-scorbutic value of the many early herbaceous spring greens widely available in the deciduous forest. Naturally, over and above this bulk of vegetal diet will have been the mammal meat, fish, shell-fish and wildfowl resources that would be taken whenever and wherever the opportunity offered.

In warm wet temperate shady forests a major proportion of the total edible productivity is locked up in the large subterranean growth of many varieties of roots. The natural subsistence emphasis would fall therefore, on forest root perennials and vegetatively reproducing tuberous plants, as opposed to the Mediterranean prominence of the annuals and sexually reproduced seeds. The superabundance of Temperate forest edible roots demanded exploitation and simultaneously solved three subsistence problems:

(i) They provided the most reliable minimally fluctuating staple, the year through and year by year, and bridged the critical winter gap;
(ii) They filled the carbohydrate and protein gap left by the low availability of grass and pulse-seeds in the Temperate forest;
(iii) They stored easily, harvested easily and reproduced speedily and simply, requiring little special effort or equipment.

Hardly any gatherer-hunter-fisher group that has exploited vegetatively reproducing roots and tubers can have been ignorant of the superficial basis of that reproduction and its simple control – the broken tip of the rhizome normally growing again to produce a new plant. A similar broad knowledge may be assumed for the elementary control of forest ecology by fire-setting, to open up the canopy for grazing, allowing the hazel and other shrubs to nut and fruit effectively, making the herbaceous plants flourish and stimulating the root growth of bracken and related root-plants in a prototype of slash-and-burn agricultural practice (Simmons 1969). In short, the probability is that the late Mesolithic exploitation of the Atlantic Temperate deciduous forest already closely approached varieties of asexual horticulture and forest husbandry based on limited fire-setting, pruning and clearing, long before slash-and-burn agriculture centred on annual grass-seeds was able to penetrate this habitat.

The Mesolithic/Neolithic transition

The discussion, so far, has attempted to show that traditional interpretations of the archaeological data from Mesolithic Europe between *c.* 10,000-4,000 B.C. have been artificially limited by the complexities of weak conventional assumptions, inherent sampling biases and reinforcing stereotypes. Following the work of Higgs and Jarman, man, plant and animal relationships may be seen as intricate and fluctuating rather than as a single progressive sequence from simple to advanced, from hunting to domestication. There is increasing reason to believe that a very wide range of plants and animals have been associated with man in complex and changing subsistence inter-relationships in the past, in which some measure of crop and herd control and resource management, manipulation and husbandry were already practised. In middle and southern European latitudes, ecological inference and an alternative interpretation of the data would suggest that the great bulk of gatherer-hunter-fisher diet would be drawn from the natural abundance of reliable and diverse vegetal sources. In the Mediterranean, it would naturally embrace a pulse/bulb/grass-seed and nuts dietary base, supplemented by hunting and marine gathering. The pulses and grass-seeds were probably harvested together, using the various forms of microlithic-toothed reaping-knives, and amongst this wide range of productive grass and pulse species were probably some of the ancestors of later intensively domesticated strains in the process of closer control and selection. Amongst the animals culled, it appears that in some areas the red deer and in others the ovicaprids, cattle, pigs and even rabbits may already have occupied a specially controlled relationship amounting to elementary husbandry; supplementary props to a gathering-hunting-fishing economy.

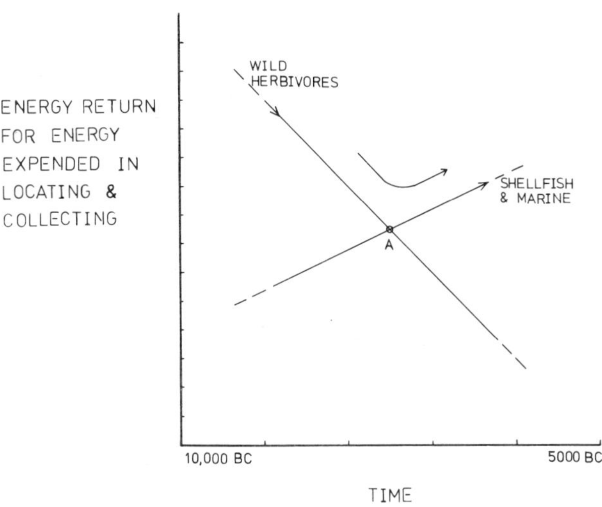

Figure 7. Schematic model suggesting a cross-over point (A) at which Mediterranean gathering-hunting-fishing coastal/inland strategies, with higher altitude summer camps in the interior, gave way to littoral systems with coastal summer camps as the return for energy expended on shellfish and marine food husbandry overtook the falling return from diminishing deer, cattle and horse herds. Experimental ovicaprid and cereal husbandry increasingly displaced the role of marine foods after *c*.5,000 B.C.

By contrast, in the European Temperate forest zone, the subsistence basis was probably focused on various root/foliage/fruit and nut combinations exploited in techniques which perhaps in some areas already approximated to simple forest horticulture. The genetic traces of the early husbandry of these root staples are less dramatic, because asexual reproduction gives rise to a limited variability and gene interchange; whilst the sexually reproducing seed crops have a relatively free gene interchange and, therefore, a naturally high plasticity, variability and rate of change, leading to the appearance of complex hybrids, novel crosses and new forms with no wild parallel. An abundant mammal fauna probably provided ample meat supplies with less need for advanced husbandry techniques, except in winter; in the north the scavenging dog had been domesticated early, perhaps as an over-wintering resource; and perhaps, in similar circumstances, the omnivorous pig may already have been closely controlled around its abundant natural marsh habitat in the Crimean/Dnestr/Danube delta. Otherwise, meat and vegetal resources were widely drawn from the abundant littoral and marine resources of the Atlantic coast and from the productive network of Post-Glacial lakes and rivers.

However, a series of environmental changes brought wider influences to bear on these two, rather differently based, subsistence patterns in which the developing instability of the Mediterranean systems *c.* 7,000-6,000 B.C. ultimately impinged on the more stable Temperate forest régimes. The elements of this hypothesis can be sketched as follows, although once again we must stress the inevitability of local divergences relating to strongly localized conditions:

(i) *c. 8,000-6,000 B.C. Southern Mediterranean preadaptive and pre-Asiatic phase.* The southernmost economies of coastal Iberia, Italy and Greece adapted to the expanding evergreen ecology, leading to a more intensive exploitation and husbandry of the remaining plant-foods, especially the grasses, legumes, vine and possibly the fig, olive and various bulbs (*Allium* spp. etc.). The diminishing herds of large herbivores were supplemented by increasing recourse to marine resources and more intensive exploitation and husbandry of the remaining small, gregarious and small-territory animals that were easier to manipulate (shell-fish, dog, pig, rabbit, ibex/ammotragus/ovicaprids). The freshly inundated and colonized littoral, under warmer conditions than at present, provided optimal conditions for marine shell-fish, crustacea and fish productivity. The overall trend was towards a more static population, strongly tied to littoral resources, exploited from more sedentary critical sites that allowed direct manipulation of the small-range animal herds and year-through husbanding of the local trees, grasses, legumes and bulbs and possibly already included sporadic re-sowing.

(ii) *c. 7,000-6,000 B.C. Northern Mediterranean transformation.* The subsistence patterns of the middle and northern parts of the Mediterranean peninsulas were transformed from south to north under the growing pressure of coastal inundation, which slowly reached a critical threshold, combining with the fall in edible productivity of the reduced littoral that remained. This collapse of the early Mediterranean mixed-forest transhumant systems in a chain reaction was initiated by the regionally critical loss of up to two-thirds of the already slender littoral with its high directly-edible productivity, which provided the critical winter browsing and grazing areas for man and the hunted herbivores. This loss was doubled by the accompanying south to north displacement of the residual mixed deciduous and Mediterranean littoral woodland by the expanding sclerophyllous and xerophytic ecology with a much lower edible productivity for man and beast. The combined result was a major quantitative decrease in primary vegetal resources and herbivore carrying capacity in the most critical 'overwintering' sectors of the transhumant schedules of man and mammals. Long-distance interior/coast transhumant systems were, therefore, increasingly replaced by littoral systems of the southern type, as southern ecology spread north, and the return for energy-expenditure on increasing marine foods, especially shell-fish, for the first time compensated fully for the decreasing yield of hunted herbivores, especially red deer (Fig. 7). Since the summer and autumn exploitation of coastal marine resources was seasonally incompatible with the simultaneous inland montane exploitation of migrant herbivore herds, the earlier preference for the latter strategy gradually gave way to the former and the northward spread of a largely littoral system of semi-sedentary groups practising pre-Asiatic forms of Mediterranean plant and animal husbandry.

(iii) *6,000-5,000 B.C. Mediterranean interconnection and integration.* The rising importance of marine resources was probably responsible for the appearance of the first reliable sea-going canoes *c.* 6,500-6,000 B.C. This technological innovation was advantageously involved in the more extensive exploitation of marine resources and distant island and coastal resources (deep-sea and migratory fish, tunny, deeper shell-fish beds; large fish-hooks appear). In addition to its importance for population responses to potential resources, the sea-going canoe was instrumental in the rapid interchange of successful local, East Mediterranean and Asiatic plant and animal domesticates through the networks between previously isolated communities. The unpopulated Mediterranean islands were now reached and colonized and their raw materials like obsidian widely distributed (Cyprus, Crete, Malta, Sardinia, Corsica, the Balearics). The domestic sheep and goat gradually replaced the waning shell-fish as a main protein source; emmer, einkorn and barley similarly displaced less productive local cultivars. The widespread use of plain and impressed ceramics developed to handle sedentary storage and the regular cereal-gruel and stew basis of the newly integrated and productive economy. Whether the 'domesticated' olive, vine and fig were part of the indigenous local development, as it now seems they might have been, or whether they were among the later exotics, has yet to be decided. A new and productive subsistence pattern had been developed by the selective integration of a diverse range of pre-existing husbandry practices and staples, drawn from a wide pool of formerly different, disconnected, localized, gatherer-hunter-fisher husbandry patterns.

(iv) *6,000-5,000 B.C. Mediterranean expansion and northern penetration.* A single new strategy may, and usually does, solve different problems in different places and the probability is that the causal factors behind the adoption of controlled food production practices were very different from place to place, but not altogether unrelated. In the Balkan zone, especially in southern and coastal Bulgaria, it is doubtful if the pattern of littoral-loss and ecological change took the same form that it did in the Mediterranean peninsulas. However, the Balkan zone was certainly an area of high edible-food productivity under natural conditions. The eastern Balkans were exceedingly rich in edible plant species, partly because of the varied climate, the soils, the rainfall and the ecological diversity, but mainly because the area had always been a southern inter-glacial refuge for both European and Asiatic steppe species (see Newbigin 1968:212). On these grounds, we must suspect that a substantial early gatherer-hunter-fisher population underlies the momentarily more impressive Neolithic cultures. Given that the predominant terrain was a mixture of alkaline and acid outcrops, low alluvial swamps and high mountain plateaux, the ecology also ranged from deciduous oak/beech/elm forest through extensive grassy and lightly-wooded steppe to a Mesomediterranean woodland with walnut and hazel trees. Against this context, the work of Dennell (1974) suggests a local development not unlike that of the southern Mediterranean with local gatherer-hunter-fishers developing increasingly complex forms of plant and animal husbandry based on the changing local grassland ecology and perhaps already embracing local legumes, fruits, cereals, pigs, ovicaprids and cattle.

It would seem that it was from the broad base of the Balkan peninsula, with its vegetal wealth and Mesomediterranean climate that a successfully integrated cattle/sheep/goat/cereal economy penetrated what, up till then, had been thinly occupied areas of Eastern Europe – the mixed oak, pine, hazel, elm, lime and birch woodlands of the Middle Danube plain. The new Starčevo/Körös/Criş subsistence pattern allowed the previously marginal dry loess soil bands to be taken into very productive exploitation for the first time. The restricted gatherer-hunter-fisher communities strung along the Danube and Tisza margins seem, on the Lepenski Vir evidence, to have been absorbed within a well adapted composite economy utilizing both the old and the new resources and techniques.

Beyond the Balkan-like ecology and cultures of the eastern triangle of continental forested steppe conditions lay the mixed deciduous forest of the Baltic-Carpathian arc to the north and the fringes of the great Temperate maritime oak forest of the Atlantic plain to the west. Along the highly productive glaciated, river- and lake-dotted Northern plain lay a belt of inter-related and long-stabilized 'Epi-Gravettian' gatherer-hunter-fisher communities. These already closely similar and closely linked forest economies are now brought into focus for the first time when they too develop their own, pointed-base, oval-bowl, ceramic assemblages from the Bug-Dnestr culture in the south, through the Polish Masovian, Zedmar, Narva to the Ellerbek and Ertebølle assemblages in the north. This chain of 'ceramicized' gatherer-hunter-fishers continued their forest economy, with little change beyond some domestic pigs and their new pottery until, at a later date, they developed their own northern agricultural pattern in the indigenous and emergent TRB and Corded-ware culture groups.

On the western frontier the highly successful emergent Danubian I economy and life style solved the initial problems of the fertile, but wetter and more heavily forested, loesses; and these, too, were brought into productive occupation before 4,000 B.C. The low-density centre of the saucer-like Mesolithic population distribution had been finally and productively penetrated by subsistence methods based on a combination of exotic and traditional pursuits, techniques and staples, in which the low natural edible-productivity of the local glade communities were replaced by highly productive artificial associations. However, surrounding the new population expansion and infilling within this central core lay the encircling chain of long established, well-adapted and, by the standards of the time, numerous gatherer-hunter-fisher populations of the Baltic-Carpathian belt to the north, the Temperate maritime forest to the west and in the Alpine valleys to the south. It was in these areas that a substantial continuity of population and subsistence practices persisted in a set of highly distinctive, regionally peculiar culture-groups, within which it may be suspected that a number of idiosyncratic practices are merely late and more substantial manifestations of very much earlier traditions.

Nevertheless, under the influence of environmental, ecological and demographic changes, the 'new' techniques and resources gradually displaced some of the older and no longer competitively productive practices in the much changed environment of fourth-millennium Europe. The productive climax of the Maritime mixed-oak forest was lost and many of the Post-Glacial lakes, rivers and coasts were long past their productive maturity. The maximum growth of the forests had been reached before *c.* 4,000 B.C. and the forest declined, and became more open, as the climate became more continental and as the cumulative result of four thousand years of human interference. The onset of sub-Boreal conditions presented the challenges of a changed European ecology to a new population structure, equipped with greatly modified technology and subsistence practices.

Conclusion

This frankly speculative and theoretical essay has attempted to avoid the prison of conventional interpretations of limited data samples, in order to explore alternative possibilities. Only when the range of alternative models has been defined may we usefully test between them in a series of carefully selected, detailed analyses on restricted data. It is, after all, the duty of speculation, hypothesis and theory to outrun current fact and thereby direct and focus the next stages of research. Speculation is both essential and productive if it obeys the cardinal injunctions that it must predict and that some of those predictions must ultimately be testable. As it happens, the hypotheses developed here are not utterly speculative. They rest on the theoretical implications of recent ecological, ethnographic, demographic, economic and archaeological work and fit the evidence available as effectively as more conventional interpretations, which are no less speculative. The basic assumptions and concepts upon which any study rests are ultimately metaphysical speculations, in the philosophical sense, and we develop new archaeological explanations as much by changing our metaphysical assumptions as from our changing data.

In conclusion, then, this essay identified a number of testable points. If microliths and blades were hafted in graters we might expect a transverse, as opposed to a longitudinal, wear pattern. If roots were important, we might expect certain distribution consequences for human communities (Fig. 6) and methods capable of recovering root and leaf fibre from decomposed faeces could provide a direct test. Suitable excavations in key areas like dry Almerian Spain and wet Temperate Atlantic Europe would also try the adequacy of the ecological and subsistence inferences. If the early coastal Mediterranean Mesolithic economies transformed from south to north, in the manner sketched, then carbon-dating should provide a direct test of this generalization.

Finally, the essay develops some interesting unconventional interpretations:

1. Mesolithic artefacts and subsistence patterns are not incompetent attempts at later Neolithic artefacts and patterns, or degenerate efforts at Upper Palaeolithic products; Mesolithic artefacts and subsistence patterns were well designed and well adapted for what could best be done to achieve an adequate food supply from certain environments, using that technology.

2. Microlithic equipment had many diverse and interchangeable functions but, taken globally, it is tempting to suggest that some especially abundant and diversified microlithic equipment may relate to phases of intensive vegetal resource exploitation and therefore, by definition, to incipient phases of plant domestication.

3. Some of the subsistence economies of the Mesolithic in the western maritime oak mixed forest may have approached limited, fire-controlled *asexual* horticulture and arboriculture, based on vegetatively reproducing *root* staples, forest *perennials*, controlled nut and fruit trees, backed up by shell-fish, dog and pig husbandry, rather than by 'conventional' hunting, fishing and gathering routines: this wet temperate forest economy would more closely resemble the root-based forest horticulture of South America, Central Africa, Australasia and New Zealand, complete with wooden pestles, mortars, bark-beaters and graters; recent forest horticulture surviving only where the forest itself has survived in a productive form.

4. One may contrast this with the *sexual*, *seed-based* subsistence patterns of the broad Mediterranean zone from North Africa to Iran, centred on grass and pulse *annuals* with hard tough seed-cases that need to be reaped with Microlithic harvesting-knives, ground between stones and stored in pits. A contrast may thus be noted between the extremely early southern appearance of extensive microlithic equipment, grinding-stones, storage baskets and pits (as at Shanidar, by 15,000-10,000 B.C.) from Iran to North Africa in the dry Mediterranean grass and woodland zone, as opposed to the soft, fibrous root, nut and fruit grating and slicing equipment of the northern deciduous forest zone (Solecki 1973; Clark 1971).

REFERENCES

Birdsell, J.B. (1957) Some population problems involving Pleistocene Man. *Population studies: animal ecology and demography. Cold Spring Harbor Symposia in Quantitative Biology*, 22, 47-69.

√Brothwell, D. and Brothwell, P. (1969) *Food in Antiquity*. London.

Camps-Fabrer, H. (1966) Matière et art Mobilier dans la Préhistoire Nord-Africaine et Saharienne. *Mémoires du centre de recherches anthropologiques, préhistoriques et ethnographiques (Algérie)*, No. V.

Cassels, R. (1972) Human ecology in the prehistoric Waikato. *Jour. Polynesian Soc.*, 81, 196-247.

Clark, J.D. (1971) A re-examination of the evidence for agricultural origins in the Nile valley. *P.P.S.*, 37, 34-79.

Clark, J.G.D. (1952) *Prehistoric Europe: the economic basis.* London.

Clark, J.G.D. (1972) *Star Carr: a Case Study in Bioarcheaology*. Addison-Wesley Modular Publications No. 10. Reading, Mass.

Clarke, D.L. (1968) *Analytical Archaeology.* London.

Clarke, D.L. (ed.) (1972) *Models in Archaeology.* London.

Deacon, H.J. (1972) A review of the Post-Pleistocene in South Africa. *South African Arch. Soc.*, 1, 26-45.

Dennell, R.W. (1974) *Neolithic and Bronze Age economies in Bulgaria.* Unpublished dissertation, Cambridge University.

Flannery, K.V. (1969) Origins and ecological effects of early domestication in Iran and the Near East. In Ucko, P.J. and Dimbleby, G.W. (eds.), *The Domestication and Exploitation of Plants and Animals*, 73-100. London.

Hedrick, U.P. (ed.) (1972) *Sturtevant's Edible Plants of the World.* New York.

Higgs, E.S. (1966) The climate, environment and industries of Stone Age Greece: Part II. *P.P.S.*, 32, 1-29.

Higgs, E.S. (ed.) (1972) *Papers in Economic Prehistory.* London.

Higgs, E.S. and Jarman, M.R. (1969) The origins of agriculture: a reconsideration. *Antiquity*, 43, 31-41.

Hill, A.F. (1952) *Economic Botany*. New York.

Howes, F.N. (1948) *Nuts: Their Production and Everyday Uses.* London.

Jacobi, R.M. (1973) *The British Mesolithic.* Unpublished dissertation, Cambridge University.

Jolly, C.J. (1970) The seed-eaters: a new model of hominid differentiation based on a baboon analogy. *Man*, n.s. 5, 5-26.

Kooijmans, L.P.L. (1972) Mesolithic bone and antler implements from the North Sea and from the Netherlands. *Berichten van de Rijksdienst voor het Oudheidkundig Bodemonderzoek*, 20-21, 27-73.

Lawton, J.H. (1973) The energy cost of food gathering. In Benjamin, B., Cox, P.R. and Peel, J. (eds.), *Resources and Population*,

Lee, R.B. (1968) What hunters do for a living, or, how to make out on scarce resources.. In Lee and DeVore (1968), 30-48.

Lee, R.B. and DeVore, I. (eds.) (1968) *Man the Hunter.* Chicago.

Masefield, G.B., Wallis, M., Harrison, S.G. and Nicholson, B.E. (1971) *The Oxford Book of Food Plants.* London.

Newbigin, M.I. (1968) *Plant and Animal Geography.* London.

Phillipson, J. (1966) *Ecological Energetics.* London.

Riley, D. and Young, A. (1968) *World Vegetation.* London.

Renfrew, J.M. (1973) *Palaeoethnobotany: The Prehistoric food plants of the Near East and Europe.* London.

Shawcross, K.A. (1967) Fern-root and the total scheme of 18th century Maori food production in agricultural areas. *Jour. Polynesian Soc.*, 76, 330-52.

Simmons, I.G. (1969) Evidence for vegetation changes associated with Mesolithic man in Britain. In Ucko, P.J. and Dimbleby, G.W. (eds.), *The Domestication and Exploitation of Plants and Animals*, 113-19. London.

Solecki, R.S. (1963) Two bone hafts from northern Iraq. *Antiquity* 37, 58-60.

Thomas, D.H. (1972) A computer simulation model of Great Basin Shoshonean subsistence and settlement patterns. In Clarke (ed.) (1972), 671-705.

Vayson, A. (1918) Faucille préhistorique de Solferino. *L'Anthropologie*, 29, 393-422.

Waterbolk, H.T. (1968) Food production in Prehistoric Europe. *Science*, 162, 1093-102.

White, J.P. (1969) Typologies for some prehistoric flaked stone artefacts in the Australian New Guinea Highlands. *Arch. & Phys. Anthrop. in Oceania*, 4, 18-46.

Whittaker, R.H. (1970) *Communities and Ecosystems.* London.

Wilkinson, P.F. (1973) *The Relevance of Musk-Ox Exploitation to the Study of Prehistoric Animal Economies.* Unpublished dissertation, Cambridge University.

Wilkinson, R.G. (1973) *Poverty and Progress.* London.

Yarnell, R.A. (1964) Aboriginal relationships between culture and plant life in the Upper Great Lakes region. *Anthrop. Papers*, 23, Mus. Anthrop., Michigan.

Yde, J. (1965) *Material Culture of the Waiwai.* The National Museum, Copenhagen, Roekke X.

IAIN DAVIDSON

Les Mallaetes and Mondúver: the economy of a human group in prehistoric Spain

The Cretaceous limestone massif of Mondúver rises to 840 metres above the present level of the Mediterranean near Gandía, only ten km. from the coast. The steep cliffs of its sides overlook the flat valleys of Valldigna and Marchuquera, near sea level, and various small *poljen* (flat-bottomed depressions extending over several metres) at about 400 m. filled with red earth (Rosselló Verger 1968) exploited by the villages of Barig and La Drova with irrigated market garden crops and oranges, or with almonds, apples, olives and plums. Irrigation water is taken from the spring-line in the cliffs to the south of the villages. Other springs abound on the mountain of Mondúver and at the foot of the northern slopes near Simat: they have a combined flow of 480 litres per second (Leandro 1908). The slopes, the rough ground and the plateau south of Barig was, until recently, grazed by 1,500 adult head of breeding sheep and mountain goats, but protection of pine plantations and the easy alternatives offered by a cash economy have, in the last thirty years, persuaded the herders to abandon the mountain goat as a source of subsistence.

The Mondúver caves

The cave of Parpalló, near La Drova, has been known since the end of the last century as a potential source of treasure, and a real source of tinder flints (Vilanova Piera 1893). It was visited by Breuil (Breuil & Obermaier 1914), who first recorded an engraved plaque at the site and recognized the importance of the cave as a prehistoric habitation site, but the richness of Parpalló in remains of prehistoric man was not revealed until the excavations of Pericot García (1942). It was Pericot García also who showed that the karstic system of the Mondúver mountain contained many caves (Les Maravillas; Les Mallaetes; Barranc Blanc; Rates Penaes etc.) with related prehistoric deposits, some of which were excavated during the years after the 1939-45 war. These caves revealed in their summary publication (Plá Ballester 1946; Jordá Cerdá 1949; Fletcher Valls 1953; 1956; Fortea Pérez 1973; Gurrea Crespo & Penalba Faus 1952) that Parpalló was unique in many respects. Nowhere else in the area, nor in the whole of Mediterranean Spain, has there been found an archaeological site so rich in art, bone tools, faunal remains or stone tools.

Pericot excavated almost all of the earth at Parpalló during his three seasons of excavations, and re-use of the cave by shepherds and visits by tourists have damaged such little deposit as remained. There is, therefore, little hope of excavating further material to explain why the cave is unique. The writer has recently examined the fauna collected by Pericot as part of a forthcoming study of the prehistoric economy of human groups in Mediterranean areas. The material from the site, however, cannot by itself provide a complete answer. Parpalló can be understood only in the context of its position on the Mondúver mountain, and in relation to the other caves nearby.

The cave of Les Mallaetes can be contrasted with Parpalló. Most notably, in a sequence of Upper Palaeolithic layers, there are not two dozen artistic representations on stone plaques, while in contemporary layers at Parpalló there are nearly 6,000 engraved or painted stone surfaces, as well as engraved bone. Comparison of the stone-tool assemblages emphasizes the similarities on the one hand, and the presence of earlier and later stratified industries at Les Mallaetes, on the other.

The description of the lowest industry at Les Mallaetes as Aurignacian is based on a bone point and a dagger of rib bone (Jordá Cerdá 1954). Fortea, in recent excavations, was unable to confirm or deny the description (references in this paper to the stratigraphy of Les Mallaetes, as observed in the recent campaign of excavations by the University of Salamanca and the Servicio de Investigaciones Prehistóricas de Valencia, are based on information provided by Fortea). The industries are described as Gravettian, Solutrean and Solutreo-Gravettian and are said to be similar to those described at Parpalló. They are defined, respectively, by the presence of large backed points, bifacial flaking and *puntas de muesca* or notched points. The chronological relationships of these industries to those with similar names in southern France has not yet been established.

In the description of the Magdalenian assemblages of Parpalló, the emphasis was on its numerous bone and antler tools and the 'impoverishment' attributed to the stone-tool industry (e.g. Fortea Pérez 1973:493) is in part due to neglect of this raw material. Jordá Cerdá (1954) and Fletcher Valls (1956a; 1956b; 1972) believed that the Epi-Gravettian industries that followed the Solutreo-Gravettian at Les Mallaetes were contemporary with the Magdalenian industry at Parpalló. To others, the scarcity of bone and antler points at Les Mallaetes constituted such a strong difference that the two industries themselves could not be contemporary. Fortea observed a stratigraphic hiatus and argues that the Epi-Palaeolithic industry at Les Mallaetes is therefore later than the Magdalenian at Parpalló (1973:314 ff.).

The upper levels of Les Mallaetes contain stratified Neolithic and Bronze Age pottery, but the pottery of Parpalló is all from mixed deposits in the galleries. Nevertheless, the two caves together give a complete sequence from Gravettian industries to deposits of the Bronze Age. In this context the quibble over the relationship between the Magdalenian of Parpalló and the Epi-Palaeolithic of Les Mallaetes is not important. Both before and after the disputed industries, the two caves were occupied contemporaneously. The relationship between the two caves is therefore something to be considered in a long time-context, and what we can observe are *trends* through the sequence. Differences between the sites should be seen in the context of these trends.

Cultural discussion is therefore deferred until such relationships have been worked out, and the present paper will discuss the sequence of occupations of Les Mallaetes as they throw light on the economic exploitation of the mountain of Mondúver. Any consideration of how contemporary human groups could live simultaneously in both caves throughout the year without competing to the disadvantage of one group, or co-operating to such an extent that they must behave as parts of a single group, suggests that the evidence of such an occurrence provided by explanations of archaeological remains in cultural terms is inadequate. The problem can be discussed independently of cultural explanation by adopting an economic approach, which considers the exploitation of the territories available from these sites, since their territories relate them to each other in space (Fig. 1).

Territories

The definition of site territories is still in its infancy, and many problems remain to be solved. Vita-Finzi and Higgs (1970) adopted as a territorial boundary the distance reached after two hours' walk from the habitation site. On flat terrain this distance approximates to the 10 km. radius of activity recorded by Lee (1969) for Bushman travel from their camps and this distance of 10 km. has also been used by Grahame Clark in his recent reconsideration of the economy of Star Carr (1972). Table 1 shows different functions for the size of territories for both the sites of Parpalló and Les Mallaetes, calculated by each of these methods, and the two sets of distances are also marked on the diagrammatic map (Fig. 2). It is clear from Table 1 that there is little advantage to be gained from exploiting both of the sites, either in competition or in co-operation. The combined 10 km. territories of the two caves are only 13% greater than that for each site. This only represents a 6.5% advantage for each site, which is equivalent

Table 1 Comparison of catchment areas

Basis on which area of territory is calculated	*Areas in '000 hectares*	
	Parpalló	*Les Mallaetes*
10 km. radius, both sites combined	36.1	36.1
10 km. radius, each site separately	31.4	31.4
10 km. radius, divided at mid-line	18.1	18.1
5 km. radius	7.85	7.85
2 hrs. walking distance	7.8	7.6
2 hrs. walk, divided at mid-line	5.2	5.3
2 hrs. walk, shared area	4.7	4.7
10 km. radius, unshared area	4.7	4.7
2 hrs. walk, unshared area	3.1	2.8
5 km. radius, unshared area	2.1	2.1

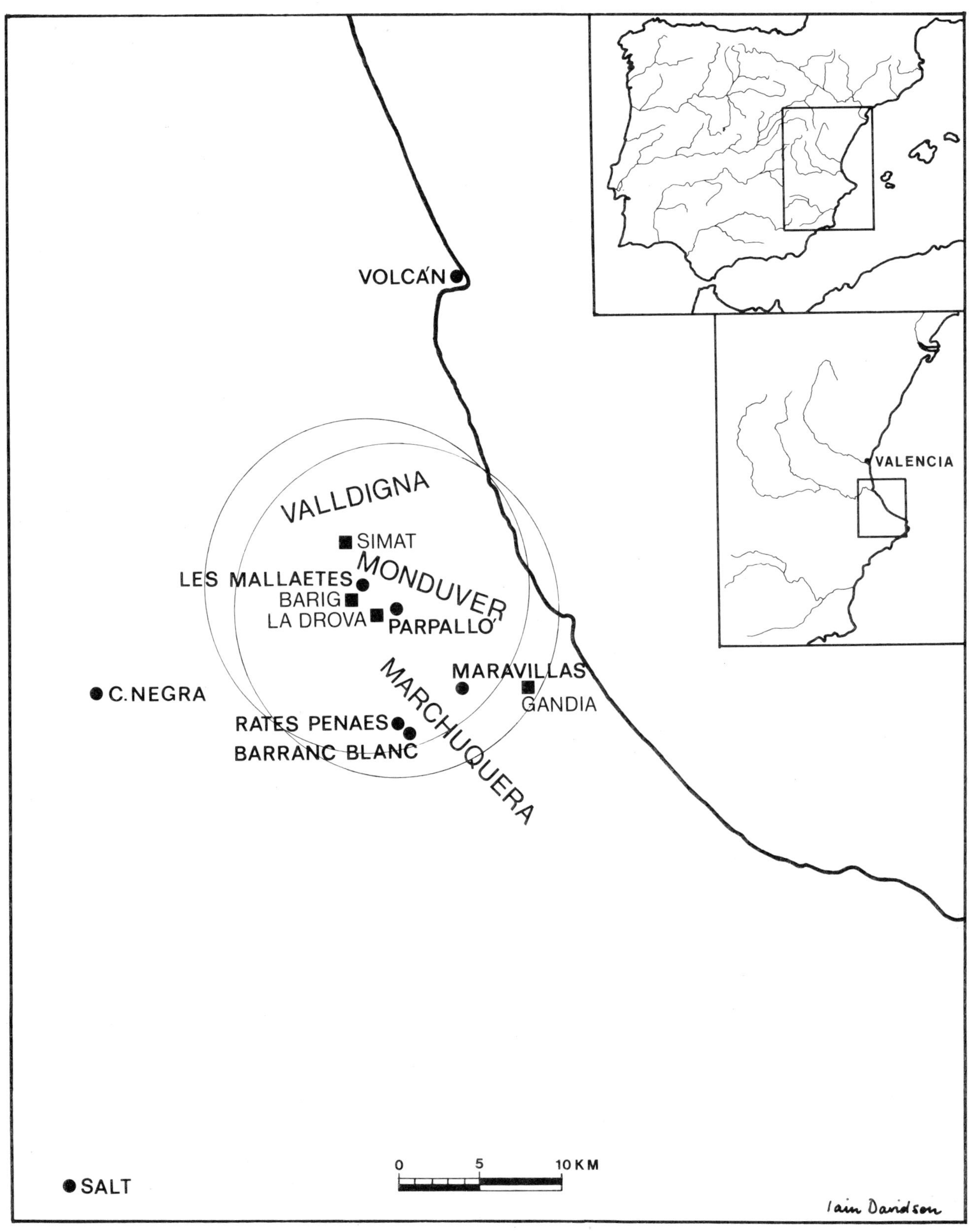

Figure 1. Map to show location of the sites. Circles are drawn round Les Mállaetes and Parpalló with 10 km. radii.

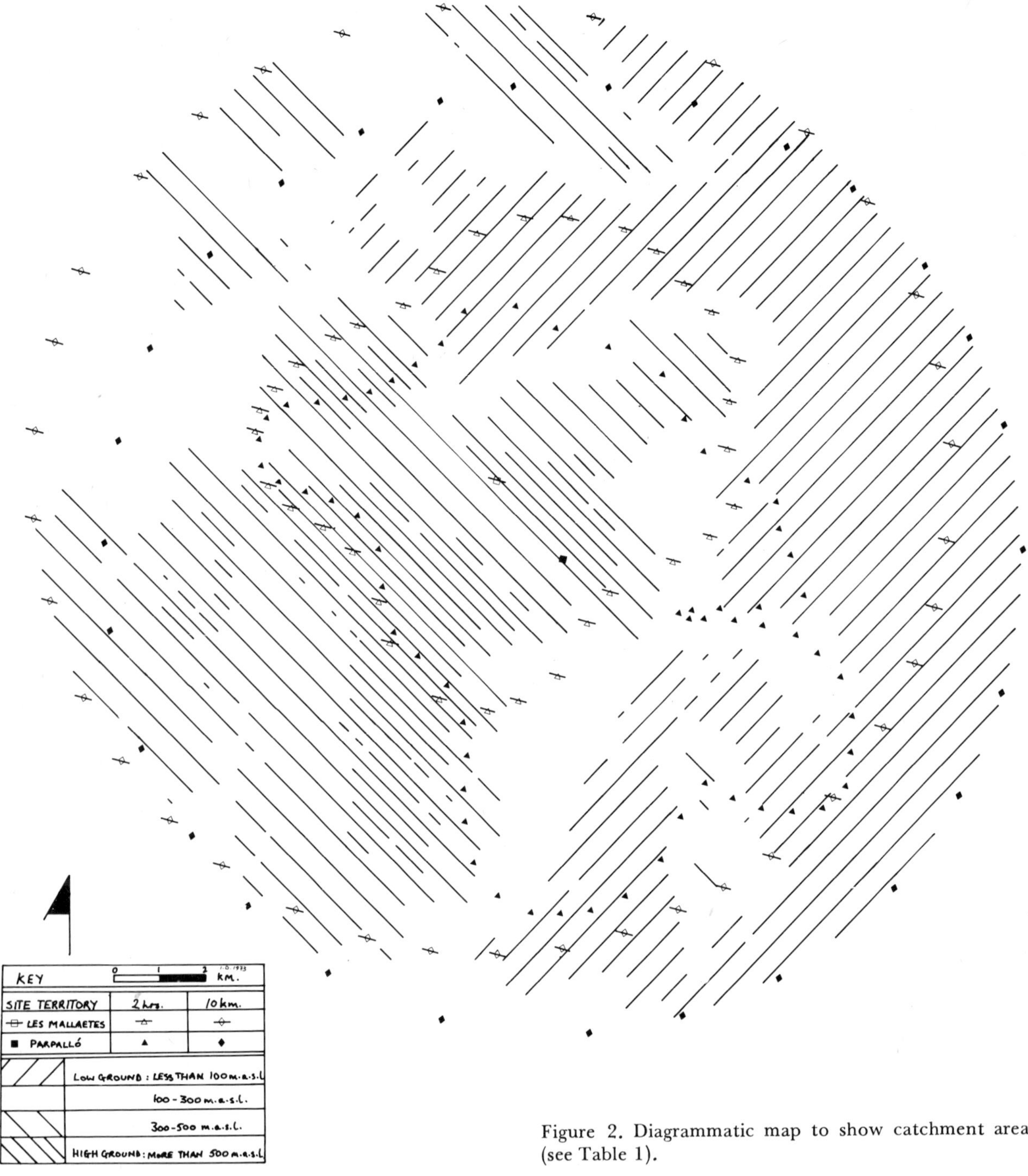

Figure 2. Diagrammatic map to show catchment areas (see Table 1).

to a resource for one extra person in a group of fifteen.

If the caves were not occupied contemporaneously and throughout the year, it is possible that they were occupied at different times or only for part of the year. As even the most complete recovery of evidence and detailed isotopic dating cannot establish that the two sites were occupied in the same century, let alone within the same year, the first alternative cannot be pursued.

However, examination of the economy of each site, so far as this is represented by the remains of the animals killed and eaten by its inhabitants, can establish, with a certain degree of probability, that the two sites may have been part of a single economic system, or show this to be impossible. This type of evidence *can* throw light on the second, alternative, hypothesis which we are considering, that each of the caves was inhabited only for part of the year.

If weighting is added to emphasize the extra energy expended as work in killing and retrieving animals at greater distances from the site, the true importance of local resources will be revealed. The same resources may be available within the territories of the two sites, calculated at 2 hrs. or 10 km., but at 15 min. or 1 km. the resources may be quite different. If they are also complementary in the sense that when one is a useful resource, the other is not, then there may be good reasons for the same human group to occupy each site, for different purposes and at different times.

Les Mallaetes: the fauna

The conclusions in this paper are drawn from detailed statistics of samples examined and reported on from Les Mallaetes, here compared with information provided by a preliminary examination of the Parpalló collections. Tables 2 and 3 show the various quantities and animal bone ratios for the various species, calculated for eleven stratigraphic units in the 1970 excavations at Les Mallaetes. Calculations are based on the number of bones of each species of animal (Table 2) and on estimates of the minimum number of individuals of each species (MIND) which takes into account age differences (Table 3). Details of the individual specimens, species descriptions and measurements will be published *in extenso* in the forthcoming excavation report for the site.

The Mondúver faunal community

The individual species at Mondúver (Tables 2 and 3) do not differ from those described elsewhere in Mediterranean Spain for this period (Davidson 1972a; 1972b). It is a community of species all but one of which are found today in the Peninsula in different places. Of the non-farmyard animals, only Spanish ibex, boar and rabbit are found in Valencia province today. The one extinct animal present is the steppe ass,

Table 2a Animal bones (numbers) at Les Mallaetes

Bone species	*Total*	*EN*	*NE*	*EP*	*PdM*	*B&T*	*SG*	*SGT*	*S 1*	*S 2*	*S T*	*AT*	*G*	*AU*
Oryctolagus cuniculus	295	08	06	28	08	37	05	50	67	47	114	4	28	56
Capra (+ Ovis)	234	40	23	27	10	12	07	29	55	36	91	2	17	04
Cervus elaphus	94	01	02	10	03	07	05	15	11	07	18	3	39	06
Equus	07	00	—	01	01	01	—	02	03	—	03	—	—	01
Bos primigenius	06	01	—	—	—	01	—	01	01	02	03	—	01	—
Sus scrofa	05	02	01	—	—	—	01	01	01	—	01	—	—	—
Felis sp.	03	—	—	—	—	—	—	—	—	—	—	—	03	—
Total	644	52	32	55	22	58	18	98	138	92	230	9	88	67

Table 2b Animal bones (percentages) at Les Mallaetes

Bone species	*Total*	*EN*	*NE*	*Ep*	*PdM*	*B&T*	*SG*	*SGT*	*S 1*	*S 2*	*S T*	*AT*	*G*	*AU*
Oryctolagus cuniculus	45.81	15.38	18.75	42.42	36.36	63.79	27.78	51.02	48.55	51.09	49.57	44.44	31.82	83.58
Capra (+ Ovis)	36.34	76.92	71.88	40.91	45.45	20.69	38.89	29.59	39.86	39.13	39.57	22.22	19.32	5.97
Cervas elaphus	14.60	1.92	6.25	15.15	13.64	12.07	27.78	15.31	7.97	7.61	7.83	33.33	44.32	8.96
Equus	1.09	—	—	1.52	4.55	1.72	—	2.04	2.17	—	1.30	—	—	1.49
Bos primigenius	0.93	1.92	—	—	—	1.72	—	1.02	0.72	2.17	1.30	—	—	—
Sus scrofa	0.78	3.85	3.13	—	—	—	5.56	1.02	0.72	—	0.43	—	—	—
Felis sp.	0.47	—	—	—	—	—	—	—	—	—	—	—	3.41	—
Total	100.02	99.99	100.01	100.00	100.00	99.99	100.01	100.00	99.99	100.00	100.00	99.99	100.01	100.00

Key: EN: Eneolithic. NE: Neolithic. EP: Epi-Palaeolithic. PdM: Solutreo-Gravettian with Puntas de Muesca. B&T: Solutreo-Gravettian with Barbed and Tanged arrowheads. SG: Solutreo-Gravettian, unspecified. SGT: Solutreo-Gravettian Total. S 1: Solutrean, Trench 1. S 2: Solutrean, Trench 2. ST: Solutrean Total. AT: Atypical industry. G: Gravettian. AU: Aurignacian. (These cultural descriptions are based on information received from Dr. Fortea)

Table 3a Minimum numbers of individuals represented by the animal bones at Les Mallaetes

Bone species	*Total*	*EN*	*NE*	*EP*	*PdM*	*B&T*	*SG*	*SGT*	*S 1*	*S 2*	*S T*	*AT*	*G*	*AU*
Oryctolagus cuniculus	64	01	02	06	02	11	02	15	16	10	26	02	05	07
Capra (+ Ovis)	64	17	07	06	04	02	03	09	15	06	21	01	02	01
Cervus elaphus	14	01	01	02	01	01	01	03	01	01	02	01	03	01
Equus	05	–	–	01	01	01	–	02	01	–	01	–	–	01
Bos primigenius	05	01	–	–	–	01	–	01	01	01	02	–	01	–
Sus scrofa	04	01	01	–	–	–	01	01	01	–	01	–	–	–
Felis sp.	01	–	–	–	–	–	–	–	–	–	–	–	01	–
Total	157	21	11	15	08	16	07	31	35	18	53	04	12	10

Table 3b Minimum numbers of individuals (percentages) represented by the animal bones at Les Mallaetes

Bone species	*Total*	*EN*	*NE*	*EP*	*PdM*	*B&T*	*SG*	*SGT*	*S 1*	*S 2*	*S T*	*AT*	*G*	*AU*
Oryctolagus cuniculus	40.76	4.76	18.18	40.00	25.00	68.75	28.57	48.39	45.71	55.56	49.06	50.00	41.67	70.00
Capra (+ Ovis)	40.76	80.95	63.64	40.00	50.00	12.50	42.86	29.03	42.86	33.33	39.62	25.00	16.67	10.00
Cervus elaphus	8.92	4.76	9.09	13.34	12.50	6.25	14.29	9.68	2.86	5.56	3.77	25.00	25.00	10.00
Equus	3.18	–	–	6.67	12.50	6.25	–	6.45	2.86	–	1.89	–	–	10.00
Bos primigenius	3.18	4.76	–	–	–	6.25	–	3.23	2.86	5.56	3.77	–	8.33	–
Sus scrofa	2.55	4.76	9.09	–	–	–	14.29	3.23	2.86	–	1.89	–	–	–
Felis sp.	0.64	–	–	–	–	–	–	–	–	–	–	–	8.33	–
Total	99.99	99.99	100.00	100.01	100.00	100.00	100.01	100.01	100.01	100.01	100.00	100.00	100.00	100.00

Equus hydruntinus, discovered previously at Parpalló and Volcán (Davidson 1972b), and identified here by a lower molar found in the Solutreo-Gravettian levels with *puntas de muesca.* The tooth shows the V-shaped outline of the enamel fold between the metaconid and metastylid, characteristic of *E. hydruntinus.* The identification confirms that of the other two sites, and agrees with Wernert's (1956) reclassification of the supposed *Equus cazurroi* specimen found at San Juliá de Ramis, and his identification of a specimen from Cueto de la Mina as *Equus hydruntinus.*

In southern Italy, at the Late Palaeolithic cave of Romanelli, specimens of *E. hydruntinus* are abundant in all layers above layer E, though they decrease in number towards the top of the stratigraphical succession (Blanc 1920; 1928). The charcoal of Scots pine, *Pinus cf. silvestris*, also occurs in all except the uppermost layer at Romanelli (Follieri & Riello 1970), and this may be taken as confirming the full glacial character of the assemblage, as it is a tree that is not found in Italy today at less than 1,000 metres above present sea level.

In Greece also, Higgs and Webley (1971) associate *Equus hydruntinus* with the cold *Artemisia* steppe behind the Late Palaeolithic cave of Kastritsa. This steppe was snow-covered in winter, though the prevailing south-east winds on the slopes of the Pindus range, which lowered the contemporary percentages of *Artemisia* pollen in the diagram from the Ioánnina lake deposits a few miles away may also have reduced the depth of winter snow.

We can be certain, then, that the presence of *E. hydruntinus* in the Spanish sites indicates steppe conditions much colder than today during the occupations of Les Mallaetes and Parpalló. The identity of the rest of the Mondúver fauna with the modern fauna of the Peninsula is a measure rather of the tolerance of these species, than of the temperate nature of the Late Palaeolithic climate.

The species of the Mondúver community

Rabbits, *Oryctolagus cuniculus*, are found today from Gibraltar to the north of Scotland, a distribution whose origins are said to be in southern France and Spain. (The very name of Spain is said by some to originate in the Phoenician word for rabbits.) The main factors limiting the distribution of rabbits are rainfall and predation. In Australia, it has been shown that rabbit densities decline as one moves towards the dry desert (Tomlinson 1961), and it was the lack of natural predators in the Australian context which allowed the catastrophic plague of rabbits to develop there. In the cold steppe environment rabbits would have a lower population density than those known in Australia or Britain, but they must still have had a serious effect on the vegetation, even allowing for their natural predators (fox, wild cat, lynx, raptorial birds etc.) and the inroads made by man.

The grazing of the ibex, *Capra ibex pyrenaica*, would be least affected by rabbits, as much of the grazing grounds of the animal would be inaccessible. The steep slopes and cliffs of many parts of the mountain provided an ideal refuge for them from their land predators. Ibex are said to be usually limited to Alpine habitats (Donner & Kurtén 1958; G.A. Clark 1971; 1972; Freeman 1971; 1973) but the presence of ibex bones in the deposits at Gorham's Cave (Zeuner & Sutcliffe 1964) and at Ermittia (Altuna 1972) shows that they certainly descended on occasions to near sea level. The restriction of their habitat by herded goats, and the presence of steep rocky areas in many mountains beyond the tree-line, may account for much of the present-day limitation of the ibex to Alpine areas (Davidson 1972a; 1972b). It is important to note that Couturier (1962:1123-32) and Galindo (1965) indicate that these animals, both in the Alps and in Spain, tend to seasonal movement that involves seeking cooler pastures in summer.

Sheep, *Ovis aries*, and a small horned goat, *C. hircus*, both appear for the first time accompanied by pottery in the two uppermost layers at Les Mallaetes. The relative numbers of these animals are difficult to estimate, as there is such a small sample: only 84 bones from a minimum of 32 animals in these two layers. Not more than five bones, from both layers, may be attributed morphologically to sheep (Boessneck *et al.* 1964; Boessneck 1969), and these could represent a single individual in each layer.

All species of *Capra* are rocky-ground dwellers, and the small goat represented here would thrive on the cliffs, scarps and rocks as easily as the ibex. Sheep, on the other hand, are not at home in such terrain: one of the reasons given by the local inhabitants on Mondúver today for selling up one's mountain goats and taking to a flock of sheep was that sheep do not prosper in such difficult terrain. They are, in this respect, more like deer in their preferences: you can follow a deer track with confidence, but not a goat track. It is not, therefore, important behaviourally that there were two *Capra* species, and we treat them both together for the purposes of this discussion.

The problem of distinguishing between sheep and goat (*Capra* ssp.) is a more serious one, given their very different behaviour; but, since only a minimum of three individuals from the two layers can be positively attributed to either, it is felt to be more realistic to group *Capra* ssp. and *Ovis* sp. together.

The migration of red deer, *Cervus elaphus*, is well documented (Darling 1956), though there is little evidence on this from Spain. Deer tend to avoid snow rather than cold, but they also look for the best pastures. In addition, migration enables them to reduce the effect of parasites.

Horse, *Equus* sp., and cattle, *Bos primigenius*, also tend to exploit only the gentler slopes. These species are not adapted to locomotion on the steep scarps of a mountain, and their movements in an area depend on the natural routes. They might never have reached the high ground on Mondúver, and if they did, are unlikely to have climbed higher than Barig, at 400 metres above sea level. In the summer, these animals probably obtained access to more convenient pastures further inland, returning to the sheltered valleys of Valldigna and Marchuquera in winter.

The bones of the wild boar, *Sus scrofa*, are very rare in all Late Palaeolithic sites in Valencia, though these animals abound in the hills today, where they are generally found in the dense maquis vegetation and on the edges of fields. Freeman (1973) has suggested that the danger associated with killing wild boar prevented their exploitation in Palaeolithic times. That these animals were at least present at Parpalló is shown by the two drawings on a plaque found at the site (Pericot García 1942:211, Fig. 418). They are rare, too, at the Cueva del Volcán (Davidson 1972a; 1972b) though, if it is correct to postulate a marshy environment for the catchment area of this cave, the boar should have preferred the wallows available in such surroundings.

Is the archaeological fauna representative?

It is important to establish that there are no obvious omissions from the samples of animal bone available for study. Vinnicombe (1972a; 1972b) and Carter (1969), for example, have shown that, in Africa, eland may be under-represented in the refuse from inhabited caves, despite both its known ritual significance and its importance in the Bushman economy. In the case of the Spanish sites, the representative character of the fauna can be substantiated only by comparison with other local records for the region. The Mousterian fauna of the area is known from three sites: the Cova Negra, Játiva (Royo Gomez 1947; Pérez Ripoll, pers. comm.) and Salt, Alcoy (unpublished field observations). Only three species from these sites are different from Les Mallaetes: an elephant, a rhinoceros and chamois.

The elephant found at Cova Negra was first identified as *Elephas iolensis*, but is now recognized as being a specimen of *Elephas antiquus* whose juvenile teeth seemed to represent a dwarf variety (Villalta & Crusafont 1953). Such post-Eemian survivals of *E. antiquus* are rare outside Spain (Crusafont & Truyols 1960) and its absence from the Late Glacial fauna at Les Mallaetes is most economically explained by its prior extinction.

The taxonomy of the rhinoceros from Cova Negra awaits re-classification by Pérez Ripoll. Post-Mousterian examples of this species are unknown in Mediterranean Spain. An Upper Palaeolithic engraving at Los Casares, in central Spain, is said to represent a hornless woolly *Rhinoceros tichorhinus* (Breuil 1952:388, Fig. 507), more correctly *Coelodonta antiquitatis*, though the drawing is not easily distinguished in poor lighting from that of a boar. The best explanation of the lack of rhinoceros in Les Mallaetes and Parpalló, as for the lack of elephants, is that the species was extinct in this region.

Chamois, *Rupicapra rupicapra*, the third of these additional species, has also been identified at Parpalló, (Sos 1947; Pericot García 1942:268 and 235, Fig. 551). The writer has identified chamois from Mousterian layers at Salt and also from the Cueva d'en Pardo, where it occurs in layers not defined by any industry, and Pérez has reported the species from Cova Negra. At Parpalló, however, the identifications were those of teeth, and when these were re-examined they were found to be the deciduous teeth of *Capra* sp., and not the permanent teeth of *Rupicapra* sp. as had first been supposed. There is thus no trace of chamois among the bones at Parpalló, and the single engraving of the species found at the cave cannot be regarded as conclusive evidence for the presence of this species with Upper Palaeolithic industries in Valencia.

Among the later fauna represented at the Mondúver caves caprine, bovine and equine species are known in their domestic forms. Red deer and roe deer, *Capreolus capreolus*, were killed at least until the Iron Age, but the roe deer is not known before the Neolithic of Coveta de l'Or.

There are no sheep known in Spain until the Neolithic. Walker (1971; 1972; 1973) has stated that I had identified sheep in pre-pottery layers at Les Mallaetes. This is incorrect: the specimens in question could not be distinguished from ibex.

There are, thus, grounds for believing that no animal was present at Les Mallaetes that could have contributed significantly to the diet, which is not represented in the bone collection. The same arguments apply to the bone collection at Parpalló, where additional evidence is afforded by the art. The only animal whose bones are found in any quantity, but does not appear in the drawings, is the rabbit. Whatever the relationship between diet and art, we cannot prefer a hypothesis that provision of food was determined by species represented neither in food wastes, nor in the art, the only available description of the environment. We must conclude, therefore, that the food remains from Les Mallaetes and Parpalló adequately represent the diet and the economy of the inhabitants of these caves. We must now discuss one peculiarity of the faunal assemblages at Mondúver, the strong representation of rabbits in this district.

Rabbits and economy

Pericot García (1968) and others (for instance Maluquer de Motes 1971) have emphasized the importance of rabbits in the faunal remains of the Late Palaeolithic of Mediterranean Spain. Numerically, they were obviously of great importance in the caves discussed here, and in the Cueva del Volcán their numbers reached enormous proportions (Davidson 1972a; 1972b), but their importance in the diet has probably been exaggerated, as is shown by the tables for meat weight (Tables 4 and 5) or calories (Table 6) compiled for these sites. There are also a number

Table 4a Bone meat (in kilograms) at Les Mallaetes

	Each	*Total*	*EN*	*NE*	*EP*	*PdM*	*B&T*	*SG*	*SGT*	*S 1*	*S 2*	*S T*	*AT*	*G*	*AU*
Oryctolagus cuniculus	0.9	265.5	7.2	5.4	25.2	7.2	33.3	4.5	45.0	60.3	42.3	102.6	3.6	25.2	50.4
Capra (+ Ovis)	25.0	5850.0	1000.0	575.0	675.0	250.0	300.0	175.0	725.0	1375.0	900.0	2275.0	50.0	425.0	100.0
Cervus elaphus	50.0	4700.0	50.0	100.0	500.0	150.0	350.0	250.0	750.0	550.0	350.0	900.0	150.0	1950.0	300.0
Equus	100.0	700.0	—	—	100.0	100.0	100.0	—	200.0	300.0	—	300.0	—	—	100.0
Bos primigenius	240.0	1440.0	240.0	—	—	—	240.0	—	240.0	240.0	480.0	720.0	—	240.0	—
Sus scrofa	72.0	360.0	144.0	72.0	—	—	—	72.0	72.0	72.0	—	72.0	—	—	—
Felis sp.	10.0	30.0	—	—	—	—	—	—	—	—	—	—	—	30.0	—
Total	497.9	13345.5	1441.2	752.4	1300.2	507.2	1023.3	501.5	2032.0	2597.3	1772.3	4369.6	203.6	2670.2	550.4

Table 4b Bone meat (percentages) at Les Mallaetes

	Total	*EN*	*NE*	*EP*	*PdM*	*B&T*	*SG*	*SGT*	*S 1*	*S 2*	*S T*	*AT*	*G*	*AU*
Oryctolagus cuniculus	1.99	0.50	0.72	1.94	1.42	3.25	0.90	2.21	2.32	2.39	2.35	1.77	0.94	9.16
Capra (+ Ovis)	43.84	69.39	76.42	51.92	49.29	29.32	34.90	35.68	52.94	50.78	52.06	24.56	15.92	18.17
Cervus elaphus	35.22	3.47	13.29	38.46	29.57	34.20	49.85	36.91	21.18	19.75	20.60	73.67	73.03	54.51
Equus	5.25	—	—	7.69	19.72	9.77	—	9.84	11.55	—	6.87	—	—	18.17
Bos primigenius	10.79	16.65	—	—	—	23.45	—	11.81	9.24	27.08	16.48	—	8.99	—
Sus scrofa	2.70	9.99	9.57	—	—	—	14.36	3.54	2.77	—	1.65	—	—	—
Felis sp.	0.22	—	—	—	—	—	—	—	—	—	—	—	1.12	—
Total	100.01	100.00	100.00	100.01	100.00	99.99	100.01	99.9	100.00	100.00	100.01	100.00	100.00	100.01

Table 5a Meat weight (in kilograms), based on minimum number of individuals, at Les Mallaetes

	Each	*Total*	*EN*	*NE*	*EP*	*PdM*	*B&T*	*SG*	*SGT*	*S 1*	*S 2*	*S T*	*AT*	*G*	*AU*
Oryctolagus cuniculus	0.9	57.6	0.9	1.8	5.4	1.8	9.9	1.8	13.5	14.4	9.0	23.4	1.8	4.5	6.3
Capra (+ Ovis)	25.09	1600.0	425.00	175.0	150.0	100.0	50.0	75.0	225.0	375.0	150.0	525.0	25.0	50.0	25.0
Cervus elaphus	50.0	700.0	50.0	50.0	100.0	50.0	50.0	50.0	150.0	50.0	50.0	100.0	50.0	150.0	50.0
Equus	100.0	500.0	—	—	100.0	100.0	100.0	—	200.0	100.0	—	100.0	—	—	100.0
Bos primigenius	240.0	1200.0	240.0	—	—	—	240.0	—	240.0	240.0	240.0	480.0	—	240.0	—
Sus scrofa	72.0	288.0	72.0	72.0	—	—	—	72.0	72.0	72.0	—	—	—	—	—
Felis sp.	10.0	—	—	—	—	—	—	—	—	—	—	—	—	10.0	—
Total		4355.6	787.9	298.8	355.4	251.8	449.9	198.8	900.5	851.4	449.0	1300.4	76.8	454.5	181.3

Table 5b Meat weight (percentages) based on minimum number of individuals, at Les Mallaetes

	Total	*EN*	*NE*	*EP*	*PdM*	*B&T*	*SG*	*SGT*	*S 1*	*S 2*	*ST*	*AT*	*G*	*AU*
Oryctolagus cuniculus	1.32	0.11	0.60	1.52	0.71	2.20	0.91	1.50	1.69	2.00	1.80	2.34	0.99	3.47
Capra (+ Ovis)	36.73	53.94	58.57	42.21	39.71	11.11	37.73	24.99	44.05	33.41	40.37	32.55	11.00	13.70
Cervus elaphus	16.07	6.35	16.73	28.14	19.86	11.11	25.15	16.66	5.87	11.14	7.69	65.10	33.00	27.58
Equus	11.48	—	—	28.14	39.71	22.23	—	22.21	11.75	—	7.69	—	—	55.16
Bos primigenius	27.55	30.46	—	—	—	53.35	—	26.65	28.19	53.45	36.91	—	52.80	—
Sus scrofa	6.61	9.14	24.10	—	—	—	36.22	8.00	8.46	—	5.54	—	—	—
Felis sp.	0.23	—	—	—	—	—	—	—	—	—	—	—	2.20	—
Total	99.99	100.00	100.00	100.01	99.99	100.00	100.01	100.01	100.01	100.00	100.00	99.99	99.99	100.00

Table 6 Calorific values (percentages) calculated from bone meat percentages at Les Mallaetes

	*Cal/100 g.**	*Total*	*EN*	*NE*	*EP*	*PdM*	*B&T*	*SG*	*SGT*	*S 1*	*S 2*	*S T*	*AT*	*G*	*AU*
Oryctolagus cuniculus	120	1.7	0.5	0.7	1.8	1.3	2.6	0.7	1.9	2.1	1.9	2.0	1.5	0.7	8.3
Capra (+ Ovis)	125	39.1	62.8	74.8	49.0	48.5	23.8	31.8	31.8	49.4	42.4	46.4	21.5	13.4	17.0
Cervus elaphus	150	37.7	3.8	15.6	43.5	34.8	36.6	54.8	39.5	23.7	19.7	22.0	77.0	73.6	61.2
Equus	100	3.7	–	–	5.8	15.5	6.4	–	7.0	8.6	–	4.9	–	–	13.6
Bos primigenius	200	15.4	24.1	–	–	–	30.6	–	16.8	13.8	36.1	23.4	–	12.4	–
Sus scrofa	120	2.3	8.7	9.0	–	–	–	12.6	3.0	2.5	–	1.4	–	–	–
Felis sp.	0	–	–	–	–	–	–	–	–	–	–	–	–	–	–
Total		99.9	99.9	100.1	100.1	100.1	100.0	99.9	100.0	100.1	100.1	100.1	100.0	100.1	100.1

*Figures based on Food Industries Manual and F.A.O. Nutritional Studies No. 15 (1957).

of reasons why it is unlikely that rabbits ever contributed more greatly in the diet than the meat and calorie figures suggest. It is unlikely that human behaviour was ever influenced by the presence or absence of rabbits as it must have been by the movements of deer or ibex.

In order to substantiate this statement we must examine the evidence more closely. For the purpose of this discussion, estimated values are required for human calorie-intake needs to compare with the estimates of the food value of rabbits. This has been calculated on the F.A.O. (1957) figures for mean human calorific requirements, for persons of various ages, which are regarded as 2,750 calories per person per day in areas where the mean annual temperature is 5°C. A group of twenty people in these circumstances would need a total of 55,000 calories. Table 7 gives estimates of the diet-value of the different species, based on this evidence.

The natural history of rabbits outside Britain and Australia is not well studied. Such statistics as we have been able to compile are based on these two countries and are, therefore, likely to be exaggerated. Despite the fact that most reports are discussions of infestation, direct statistics are minimal and very few population rates are quoted. Quantities of rabbits per acre were more usually estimated in losses of grain or grazing, rather than in densities of live rabbits. Meldrum (1959), however, quotes figures for animals slaughtered on 1,600 acres (647.5 hectares). The numbers declined rapidly each year after an initial slaughter of 16,000, or ten per acre (24.7 per hectare). Lockley (1964:73) suggests that there may exist a maximum population density of 32 per acre (79 per hectare). Phillips (1955) observed autumn densities of 3-9 per acre (7.4-22.2 per hectare), which agrees quite well with such calculations as we have made on more indirect evidence, derived from behavioural records.

It is well known that animal populations can be estimated from ecological studies of the behaviour of certain animal species. For example, Mykytowcz (1968), Myers (1961) and others have observed that rabbits are definably territorial. They mark the boundaries of their territory by scent from glands in the anal area or below the chin. Phillips has conducted experiments to record rabbit movements, and define the distance between recaptures of marked animals. We illustrate here a graph compiled from the figures recorded in this experiment. In this graph (Fig. 3), the curve recording animal movement falls off sharply at about 75 yards. Mykytowcz points out that rabbits do move outside their marked territory, but show unease as interlopers. It seems, therefore, that the recorded fall-off of animal movement could be

Table 7 Estimated diet-values

	Calories per 100 g.	*Meat weight per animal kg.*	*Calories per animal*	*Animals per person per day*	*Animals per group per year*
Oryctolagus cuniculus	120	0.9	1,080	2.54	18,250
Capra (+ Ovis)	125	25.0	31,250	0.088	640
Cervus elaphus	150	50.0	75,000	0.037	275
Equus	100	100.0	100,000	0.0275	200
Bos primigenius	175	240.0	420,000	0.0065	50
Sus scrofa	120	72.0	86,400	0.032	245

considered as due to such a restriction, and that 75 yards defines the limits of the territory of these rabbits. This would give a group territory size for rabbit populations of approximately 3.85 acres. Mykytowcz suggests a group size of 8-10 rabbits and Myers of 2-3 male rabbits with 3-5 females, which gives a common population figure of 8. Such a population would represent densities in non-stress conditions of 2 to 2.5 per acre (5 to 6.5 per hectare). For purposes of discussion, therefore, we will assume for Mondúver mountain, population densities of three rabbits per acre (7.41 per hectare), these figures being calculated on the high densities quoted for Australia and Britain.

The next problem to solve in estimating the value of these animals as a food-source for man is that of possible rabbit slaughter rates. Phillips suggests a viable rate of 30-40% of the surviving population – in our case one death per acre. Thus, from Table 7, it would be necessary to kill rabbits from 18,250 acres (7,300 hectares) to provide sufficient calories for a group of twenty for one year. This falls within the range of territories previously defined for Les Mallaetes and Parpalló (see page 484).

However, rabbit-catching is a time-consuming occupation, as efforts to control rabbits before myxamatosis showed. Phillips cites trappers setting traps, collecting and resetting them, who collected 27 rabbits per man-day. Thompson and Armour (1951) compared various methods of trapping, snaring, poisoning, gassing or hunting, and found a maximum success rate of 1.5 rabbits per man-hour, though some methods were down to 0.5 per man-hour, and this during a plague. The low success rate of 0.5 per man-hour would suggest that to provide a staple food-source based entirely on rabbit meat would require 36,500 hours of rabbit-collecting per year, or five hours per person per day for the group of twenty (which includes children).

The labour involved in collecting this rabbit meat from the edge of the area that must be exploited to support such a group would involve two hours' walking in each direction, making a total of nine hours per person per day for at least part of each year. One feels that there must be less time-consuming ways of providing food for the Palaeolithic population at Mondúver.

Clearly, a purely rabbit-based economy is a possibility, but no more. It becomes progressively more unlikely when it is remembered that the figures are all based on high densities in Australia or Britain. In Late Pleistocene Spain, the presence of predators (as, for example, the cat in the Gravettian occupation at Les Mallaetes), combined with the rainfall régime in the Pleistocene which must have been reduced even below the modern low level for the region (Butzer 1972:311), must undoubtedly have limited the rabbit population to well below the so-called plague levels. Rabbit densities high enough to support these artificially high population levels would, in any case, have had a disastrous effect on the vegetation, as has happened in Australia.

Rabbits would compete for food with any of the species represented at the Mondúver sites except the ibex, which had some special resources available to it because of its agility. This relationship is illustrated by the statistics for the Spanish caves, if we take the bones from the excavations as representative of the contribution of each species to the diet of their inhabitants. At Les Mallaetes (if we exclude the top layer),

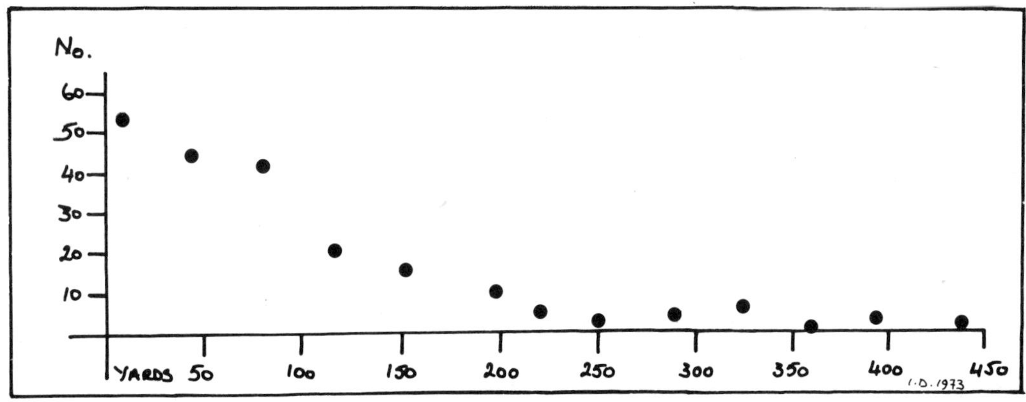

Figure 3. Rabbit recapture distance, West Wales.

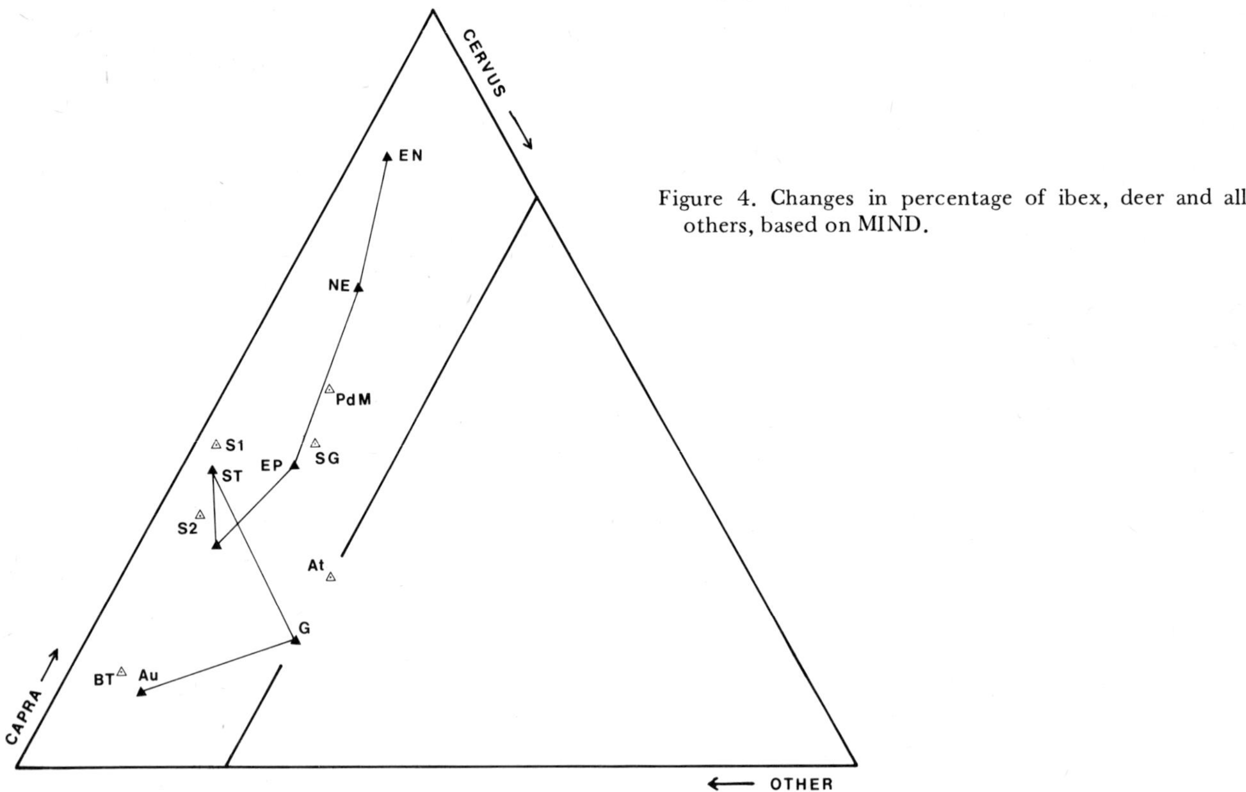

Figure 4. Changes in percentage of ibex, deer and all others, based on MIND.

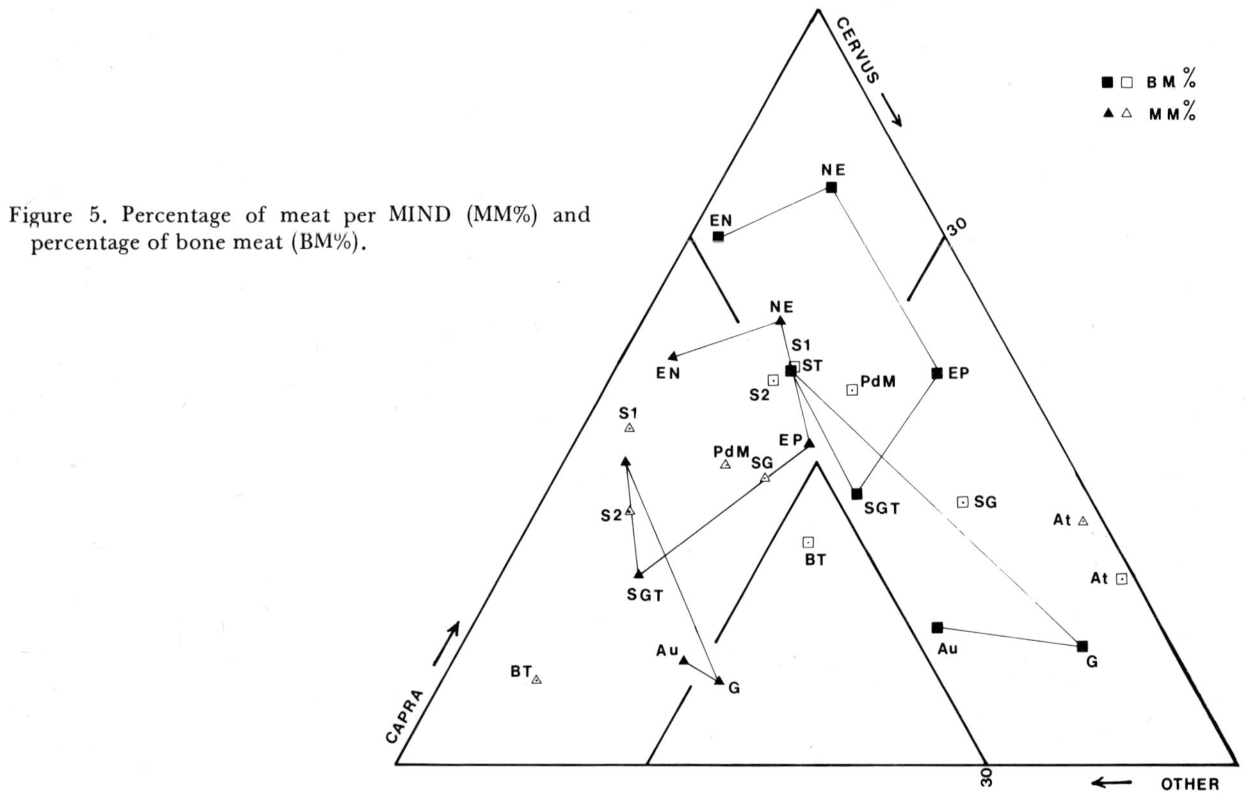

Figure 5. Percentage of meat per MIND (MM%) and percentage of bone meat (BM%).

for every rabbit present in the collection there are, on average, 2.67 (calculated on MIND – minimum no. of individuals) or 1.01 (calculated on bones) specimens of other animals represented. The other animals would, clearly, provide more meat (60.9 kg. per kg. on MIND; 43.8 kg. per kg. on bones) than the rabbits and of these the greatest contributors are, consistently, ibex and deer.

Ibex economy

We illustrate three diagrams, based on the figures in Tables 2 to 5, to show the faunal situation throughout the sequence of human occupation at the cave of Les Mallaetes. In Figs. 4 and 5, percentages of the different food animals are plotted in three parts in the triangles representing diets, which are divided up respectively in terms of ibex, deer and all others. We are here concerned with analysis of the human economy at the cave, and only those species shown to be most important in terms of numbers or of meat are of much interest for this purpose. Fluctuations in the numbers of cattle and horse are not necessarily important for the study of the exploitation of ibex or deer. In addition, the minimal size of the sample means that any species represented as rare may owe its presence or absence to chance in the sampling.

The first triangle (Fig. 4) shows changes in percentage of MIND. The diagram is dominated by rabbits. There is an increase of ibex with time, and a small variation in the percentage of red deer. In this illustration, therefore, there is good support for the hypothesis that ibex shows a linear increase in representation with time, and others a linear decrease, while the deer remain constant and low in value.

The second triangle (Fig. 5) shows, on the one hand, the percentage of meat per MIND (MM%) and, on the other, the percentage of bone meat (BM%). It is of interest to see that, in broad terms, the percentage of bone follows the percentage of MIND (and for that reason is not shown) but that MM% and BM% show different features. There also appears to be little general difference if calorific values are substituted for meat weights.

While the MM% statistics show an increase in importance of ibex through time, together with a decrease of others and small fluctuations in the representation of deer, BM% shows the same trend of increase among the ibex against constant representation of others and decrease of deer in the same levels of the cave. The differing results presented by the two diagrams stress the problems of interpretation of numbers in small samples, particularly where the animals concerned have significantly different body weights. In the present case, what stands out is that the only trend that is consistent, throughout all manipulations of the data, is that of an increase through time in the importance of ibex at Les Mallaetes. We can show this increase in another way by considering the ratio of ibex to deer meat weights (Fig. 6). Despite some fluctuations, this diagram would appear to confirm an overall trend for the ibex (*Capra* sp.) to increase in importance as a food animal through time.

The economy of Les Mallaetes

The evidence from faunal remains provides no simple argument that allows one to prove the seasonality of occupation of a prehistoric site. It is much easier to show that a site was occupied at a certain season than that it was not occupied outside that season. However, if two sites are linked together in a single economic system, for one reason or another, if one is then able to show that one site was used in summer and the other in winter, this entails a high probability that the first was not 'preferred' in winter and the second not in summer. What evidence of seasonality is available in the Mondúver caves?

At Les Mallaetes, there is no great development of antler tools, though these are common at Parpalló. The bone tools illustrated by Fortea are of bone, not antler (1973:168, 176, 186, 190). At Parpalló, the antler is both shed and from killed animals, indicating occupation both before and during the spring shedding. The antlers are worked in the groove-and-splinter technique (Clark 1953). The evidence would tend to indicate a winter occupation at Parpalló and a summer occupation at Les Mallaetes; similar evidence is provided by a study of ibex teeth.

Habermehl (1961) and Couturier (1962) suggest that heavy wear on the deciduous third molar of ibex is common in the summer of the second year of growth of this species, shortly before it is replaced by the permanent premolar. This stage of growth is common among ibex in the Solutrean at Les Mallaetes (three certain

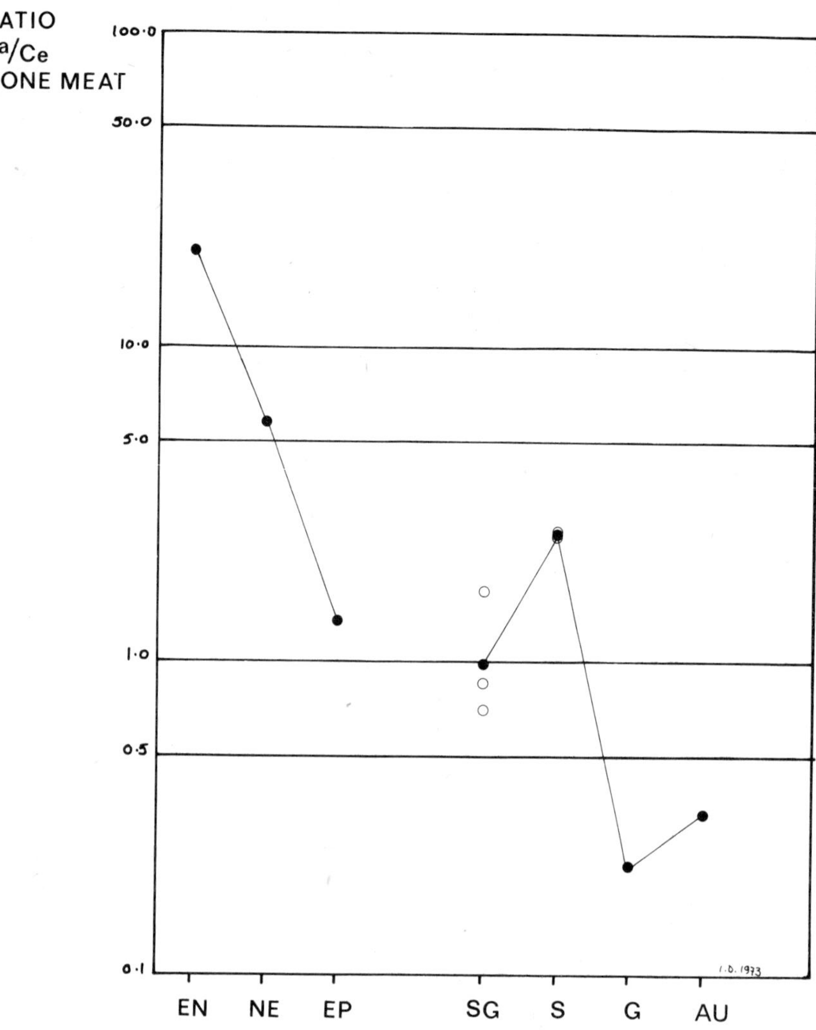

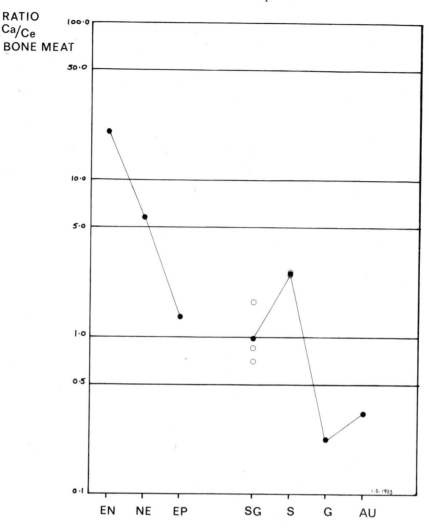

Figure 6. Ratio of ibex to deer meat by weight, on logarithmic scale.

specimens out of fifteen, and two others probable) and also again in the top layer at the same cave (where it is associated with Eneolithic pottery) and in all cases heavy wear occurs on the ibex teeth. Caution has to be exercised in using such data alone, since dental wear may vary greatly in the diverse environments considered by the two authorities and the present study, but all other seasonal indicators from all layers in the tooth-eruption sequence may also be taken to indicate a summer occupation, if anything, at Les Mallaetes. The worn deciduous third molar is never so common in Parpalló.

The cave micro-environments are also indicative of seasonality of occupation. It is certain that the use of fires allowed considerable modification of cave environments but, in the long term, and we are considering a period perhaps of 20,000 years, there is no advantage in heating a cold cave in winter if nearby there is a cave that provides a comfortable winter environment without a fire.

Now, Les Mallaetes faces west-south-west and the sun does not enter the open part of the shelter before two or three o'clock in the afternoon. In winter the insolation is then so short that the cave barely warms up. In addition, the prevailing winds blow from the south-west during the period from November to March (Fontavella 1952). Shelter from the wind is even more difficult to achieve than from cold. Les Mallaetes, at 800 metres above sea level, is also cooler than Parpalló, which is only 450 metres above the Mediterranean. Air temperatures tend to decrease by 0.55-0.8°C per 100 m. rise in altitude (Butzer 1972:77). Temperature inversions are not to be expected at these latitudes. Thus, Les Mallaetes must have been consistently 1.9-2.8°C cooler than Parpalló in winter. The lower cave faces south and has a narrower entrance. It receives more sun and is easier to protect from winds. The great frequency of hearths noted by Pericot García (1942:24) at Parpalló also contrasts strongly with their comparative scarcity at Les Mallaetes.

All these lines of evidence seem to suggest that Les Mallaetes was occupied in summer, and not in winter, and that Parpalló was occupied in winter. In this context, the long-term increase in the importance of ibex and goat in the bones at Les Mallaetes can be seen as a development of an economic specialization, taking advantage of the presence of these animals in cooler higher pastures in summer. If such a hypothesis is correct, Freeman's (1973) suggestion that ibex may be exploited only by game-drives would seem less likely. Such dependence on an animal that today is said to flee at the sight of man points to a stable economic relationship. We suggest that simple hunting was not the most appropriate mechanism for preserving high population, both man and animal. In these circumstances, the evolution of the relationship between the two species over a long period of time would suggest that perhaps some type of loose herding must have developed in successive periods. Under these conditions, the ibex would not flee from man, any more than domestic goats do today.

Finally, it is worth considering the implications of this seasonal interpretation of the economies of Parpalló and Les Mallaetes in relation to the cultural evidence from these sites. The most important observation is that the bone points so characteristic of the Magdalenian of Parpalló are actually made of antler (Pericot García 1942:37). If Les Mallaetes were occupied in summer, then the antler of deer would not be suitable for fashioning javelin points, as it is 'in velvet'. Just such an observation was made by Grahame Clark (1972) in his study of the site economy at Star Carr.

It will be seen that the argument presented here leaves open the question of the contemporaneity of the Parpalló Magdalenian and the Les Mallaetes Epi-Palaeolithic cultures. This need not necessarily affect the interpretation that we have put forward for these two sites. It must be remembered that the upper layers of Parpalló were badly disturbed by treasure hunters and flint-seekers; the earth was exploited for fields and terraces. An upper layer with Epi-Palaeolithic could have existed, so that the economic link between the two sites could have continued. At all events, the economic framework here presented allows for functional differences between the two sites, and seeks to show that one site on the mountain of Mondúver had a developing economy culminating in a specialization on goat and ibex exploitation in summer. The rest of the human economy of Mondúver mountain in prehistoric times has to be viewed in this context.

REFERENCES

Altuna, J. (1972) Fauna de mammíferos de los yacimientos prehistóricos de Guipúzcoa. *Munibe*, 24, 1-4.

Blanc, G.A. (1920-28) Grotta Romanelli. *Archivio per l'Antropología e la Etnología*, 50, 65-103; 58, 365-411.

Boessneck, J. (1969) Osteological differences between sheep (*Ovis aries* Linné) and goat (*Capra hircus* Linné). In Brothwell, D.R. and Higgs, E.S. (eds.), *Science in Archaeology*, 331-58. London.

Boessneck, J., Müller, H-H. and Teichert, M. (1964) Osteologische Unterscheidungamerkmale zwischen Schaf (*Ovis aries* Linné) und Ziege (*Capra hircus* Linné). *Kühn-Archiv.*, 78, 1-129.

Breuil, H. (1952) *Quatre cents siècles d'art pariétal.* Montignac.

Breuil, H. and Obermaier, H. (1914) Travaux en Espagne. *L'Anthropologie*, 25, 233-53.

Butzer, K.W. (1972) *Environment and Archaeology.* London.

Carter, P.L. (1969) Moshebi's shelter: excavation and exploitation in Eastern Lesotho. *Lesotho Notes and Records*, No. 8.

Clark, G.A. (1971) The Asturian of Cantabria: subsistence base and the evidence for Post-Pleistocene climatic shifts. *Amer. Anthr.*, 73, 1244-57.

Clark, G.A. (1971) El Asturiense de Cantabria. *Trabajos de Prehistoria*, 29,

Clark, J.G.D. (1953) The groove and splinter technique of working reindeer and red deer antler in Upper Palaeolithic and Early Mesolithic Europe. *Archivo de Prehistoria Levantina*, 4, 57-65.

Clark, J.G.D. (1972) *Star Carr: A case study in Bioarchaeology.* Addison-Wesley Modular Publications No. 10. Reading. Mass.

Coutourier, M. A-J. (1962) *Le Bouquetin des Alpes.* Grenoble.

Crusafont, M. and Truyols, J. (1960) Possible rasgos endémicos en la fauna post-villafranquiense española y sus consecuencias. *Estudios Geológicos*, 16, 99-101.

Darling, F.F. (1956) *A Herd of Red Deer.* London.

Davidson, I. (1972a) The animal economy of la Cueva del Volcán del Faro, Cullera, Valencia, Spain. *Trans. Cave Res. Group Gt. Britain*, 14 (1), 23-32.

Davidson, I. (1972b) The Fauna from La Cueva del Volcán del Faro (Cullera, Valencia): a preliminary discussion. *Archivo de Prehistoria Levantina*, 13, 7-21.

Donner, J.J. and Kurtén, B. (1958) The faunal and floral succession of C. del Tóll, Spain. *Eiszeitalter und Gegenwart*, 9, 72-82.

F.A.O. (1957) *Calorie Requirements.* F.A.O. Nutritional Studies No. 15. Report of the Second Committee on Calorie Requirements, Food and Agriculture Organization of the United Nations. Rome.

Fletcher Valls, D. (1953) Rótova (Valencia). Covacha de Barranc Blanc. Cova de Rates Penaes. *Noticiario Arqueológico Hispánico*, 1, 1-3, 10-16.

Fletcher Valls, D. (1956a) Estado actual del estudio del Paleolítico y Mesolítico valencianos. *Rev. Archivos, Bibliotecas y Museos*, 62 (3), 841-76.

Fletcher Valls, D. (1956b) Problèmes et progrès du Paléolithique et du Mésolithique de la Région de Valencia (Espagne). *Quartär*, 7/8, 66-90.

Fletcher Valls, D. (1972) Algunas consideraciones sobre el estado actual de los estudios de prehistória en la región valenciana. *VIII Asemblea de Coronistas del Reino de Valencia.*

Follieri, M. and Riello, M. (1970) Documents paléobotaniques de Grotte Romanelli (Terra d'Otranto, Italie Meridionale). *Actes du VIIe Cong. Int. des Sci. Préh. et Prot., Prague 1966*, 2, 1320-3.

Fontavella, V. (1952) *La Huerta de Gandía.* Zaragoza.

Fortea Pérez, J. (1973) *Los complejos microlaminares y geométricos del epipaleolítico mediterráneo español.* Salamanca.

Freeman, L.G. (1971) Significado ecológico de los restos de animales. In González Echegaray, J. and Freeman, L.G. (eds.), *Cueva Morín: Excavaciones 1966-8*, I, 419-37. Santander.

Freeman, L.G. (1973) The significance of mammalian faunas from palaeolithic occupation in Cantabrian Spain. *Amer. Antiquity*, 38 (1), 3-44.

Galindo, F. (1965) La Capra pyrenaica hispánica de los puertos de Beceite (Teruel). *Teruel*, 33, 5-76.

Gurrea Crespo, V. and Penalba Faus, J. (1952) Exploraciones en la comarca de Gandía. *Archivo de Prehistoria Levantina*, 3, 41-56.

Habermehl, K.H. (1961) *Altersbestimmung bei Haustieren, Pelztieren und beim jagdbaron Wild.* Berlin-Hamburg.

Higgs, E.S. and Webley, D. (1971) Further information concerning the environment of Palaeolithic man in Epirus. *P.P.S.*, 37, Part 2, 367-80.

Jordá Cerdá, F. (1949) Las formas microlíticas y geométricas de las estaciones valencianas. *Saitabi*, 7, 33-4 & 143-57.

Jordá Cerdá, F. (1954) Gravetiense y Epigravetiense en la España mediterránea. *Caesaraugusta*, 4, 7-30.

Leandro, P. (1908) *Hidrografía Subterránea.*

Lee, R.B. (1969) !Kung Bushman subsistence: an input-output analysis. In Vayda, A.P. (ed.) *Environment and Cultural Behaviour*, 47-79. New York.

Lockley, R.M. (1964) *The Private Life of the Rabbit* (Survival Book no. 2). London.

Maluquer de Motes, J. (1972) Proceso histórico-económico de la primitiva población peninsular. *Publicaciones eventuales no. 20 del Inst. de Arq. y Prehist. Univ. de Barcelona.*

Meldrum, G.K. (1959) Rabbit control in Tasmania: design and administration. In *The Rabbit problem in Australia Conference 1958*, 17-26.

Myers, K. (1961) Rabbit biology and behaviour and their bearing on control. *Rabbit Control Symposium, Sydney 1960*, 26-33.

Mykytowycz, R. (1968) Territorial marking by rabbits. *Scientific American*, 218 (5), 116-26.

Pericot García, L. (1942) *La Cueva del Parpalló.* Madrid.

Pericot García, L. (1968) La vida económica de España durante el Paleolítica superior. In Tarradell, M. (ed.) *Estudios de economía antigua de la Peninsula Iberica.* Barcelona.

Plá Ballester, E. (1945) 'Cova de les Maravelles' (Gandía). *Archivo de Prehistoria Levantina*, 2, 191-202.

Phillips, W.M. (1955) The effect of commercial trapping on rabbit populations. *Ann. appl. Biol.*, 43, 247-57.

Rosselló Verger, M. (1968) El Macizo del Mondúver Estudio geomorfológico. *Estudios Geográficos*, 29, 423-74.

Royo Gómez, J. (1947) Cova Negra de Bellús. In *Estudios sobre las cuevas paleolíticas valencianas* (Trabajos varios del S.I.P. de Valencia no. 6).

Sos, V. (1947) Avance a una clasificación de la fauna del Parpalló. In *Estudios sobre las cuevas paleolíticas valencianas* (Trabajos varios del S.I.P de Valencia no. 6), 43-55.

Thompson, H.V. and Armour, C.J. (1951) Control of the European rabbit (*Oryctolagus cuniculus* L.). An experiment to compare the efficiency of gin trapping, ferreting and cyanide gassing. *Ann. appl. Biol.*, 38, 464-71.

Tomlinson, A.R. (1961) A review of rabbit control in Western Australia. *Rabbit Control Symposium, Sydney 1960*, 70-82.

Vilanova Piera, J. (1893) *Memoria geognóstico-agrícola y protohistórica de Valencia.* Madrid.

Villalta, J.F. de and Crusafont Pairó, M. (1956) Los *Elephas* del cuaternario de Levante español. *Actes du IV Cong. Inter. du Quatern.*, 421-5.

Vinnicombe, P. (1972a) Myth, motive and selection in Southern African rock art. *Africa*, 42 (3), 192-204.

Vinnicombe, P. (1972b) Motivation in African rock art. *Antiquity*, 46, 124-33.

Vita-Finzi, C., Higgs, E.S. *et al.* (1970) Prehistoric economy in the Mount Carmel area of Palestine: site catchment analysis. *P.P.S.*, 36, 1-38.

Walker, M.J. (1971) Spanish Levantine rock art. *Man*, n.s. 6, 553-89.

Walker, M.J. (1972) Cave dwellers and artists of the Neothermal period in south-eastern Spain. *Trans.*

Cave Res. Group Gt. Brit., 14, 1-22.

Walker, M.J. (1973) Aspects of the Neolithic and Copper Ages in the basins of the rivers Segura and Vinalopó, south-east Spain. D.Phil. thesis.

Wernert, P. (1956) *Equus cazurroi* Cabrera 1919 o *Equus (Asinus) hydruntinus* Regalia 1907, en el Abrigo del Cueto de la Mina (Asturias). In Jordá Cerdá, F. (ed.) *Libro Homenaje al Conde de la Vega del Sella.* Oviedo.

Zeuner, F.E. and Sutcliffe, A. (1964) Preliminary report on the Mammalia (Appendix I to Waechter, J.d'A. Excavations of Gorham's Cave, Gibraltar, 1951-1954). *Bull. Inst. Arch. Univ. of London*, 4, 213-6.

JOHN EVANS

Village, town, city: some thoughts on the prehistoric background to urban civilization in the Aegean and Italy

In concluding the discussion of *Ecological Zones and Economic Stages*, which forms the first chapter of *Prehistoric Europe*, Grahame Clark devoted a paragraph to the relation between the ancient urban civilization of the Mediterranean and the Mediterranean zone of climate and ecology. Noting that the two were virtually co-terminous at the end of the first millennium B.C., he attributed this fact to 'the remarkably complete and perfect exploitation' (by the Mediterranean peoples) 'of the special features of the Mediterranean vegetation', and went on to stress the fundamental importance of the cultivation of the olive, vine and fig, once this had been introduced, as a major factor in enabling the early Mediterranean societies to transcend the restricted possibilities offered by the region for ordinary mixed farming based on cereals and stock-breeding. The addition of these plants to the subsistence economy permitted the eventual emergence of large permanent centres of population, but at the same time made it correspondingly difficult to transplant the resulting cultural product outside the boundaries of the region to which they are native. The historical importance of this for Europe was, he concluded, that 'it needed all the power of Rome to break through the boundaries established by ecology and to incorporate within the sphere of the Empire a substantial area of deciduous forest, a feat which marks for us the conventional end to prehistoric times' (Clark 1952:21).

The twenty or more years of intensive archaeological research that have passed since these words were written have not substantially modified the main historical point that he made, though recent work north of the Alps has blurred the outline a little. There is now a strong possibility, to put it no higher, that settlements of genuine urban character may have been on the point of emerging in various parts of temperate Europe of their own accord in the two centuries that preceded the Roman expansion (Piggott 1965:261; Alexander 1972:847). If so, their development was cut short by Roman military conquest and the subsequent artificial establishment of towns on the Roman model; though there is a growing feeling that many of the mediaeval towns in the part of the temperate zone of Europe that was subject to Rome may owe more to prehistoric traditions than to their Roman predecessors (Alexander 1972:848). This emphasis on the unequal, and in many instances very indifferent, success that even the immense determination and persistence of the Roman empire-builders met with in their attempts to transplant the Mediterranean city to a neighbouring ecological zone merely serves to highlight the dependence of the city on a social and cultural organization closely integrated with the geographical, climatic and vegetational peculiarities of a very special environment.

In the Mediterranean region itself these highly developed urban settlements were such a characteristic and very striking feature of the Graeco-Roman civilization of the late first millennium B.C. that it is easy to assume that they were simply a natural and inevitable expression of the social instincts of the population of those countries, and it is often taken for granted that there existed some psychological predisposition in Mediterranean man to derive a special satisfaction from congregating in large groups. 'The civilization of the Greeks and Romans was essentially urban', says one sober text-book on Greek and Roman life and thought; 'the practice of clustering together in cities . . . for the social and economic advantages of city life made a strong appeal to the Greeks and Italians' (Cary & Haarhoff 1966:103). Certainly the joyous gregariousness displayed by the modern inhabitants of those countries lends an aura of credibility to such a remark and there may, indeed, be more than a grain of truth in it. But cities are extremely complex products of historical processes and the interaction of societies with their environment. There are no natural city-dwellers and natural countrymen. The history of the last two hundred years, in particular, has made it plain that large cities may develop anywhere with great rapidity when the conditions are right, and that under the resulting pressures the habits and life-styles of ages can change out of all recognition within a couple of generations.

Actually, the towns and cities of the last few centuries B.C. in Greece and Italy, though numerous, were mostly relatively small, certainly by comparison with our modern cities. 'The area of most Greek and Roman cities', says the text-book quoted above, 'did not exceed 400 acres', or about 160 hectares '(the size of Hyde Park) and did not contain more than 50,000 inhabitants' (Cary & Haarhoff 1966:103). A few specially favoured centres such as Athens, Syracuse and Rome grew much larger than this, the first two having probably about a quarter of a million inhabitants at their peak, while Rome rose to over a million during the Empire. But on the whole these were exceptional.

Small as this average Greek or Italian town of the end of the first millennium B.C. may seem to us, however, it looks as though it was very much larger than even the largest settlement that had been known in southern Europe until a few centuries before this date. Many Mediterranean settlements of the second, and even of the third, millennium B.C. are often referred to by archaeologists as towns and that label is probably the most appropriate one to apply to them, but it must be remembered that even the largest of these clearly belong to a different order of magnitude from the more important towns and the cities of the Archaic and later periods in Greece and Italy. Now that we know, through radiocarbon dating, that the earliest farming villages were established in Greece by 6,000 B.C. and in Italy not more than a millennium later, we can see that several thousand years elapsed before urban settlements of any size appeared in either country. During the whole of this interval the average settlement does not seem to have become very much larger, and some Neolithic settlements were larger than Bronze Age ones that are called towns. The eventual emergence of cities in the first millennium B.C. was relatively rapid, taking only a few centuries, and it was a process that seems in many ways to owe more to contemporary conditions than to previous developments in either country though, of course, these had created the cultural milieu in which it began. It is in the belief that the significance of these facts has not yet been sufficiently appreciated that I shall attempt here to summarize, however inadequately, the existing evidence for settlement-size in the Aegean and Italy from the sixth to the mid-first millennium B.C.

For such a discussion, nomenclature poses an initial problem. It is necessary to use terms such as village, town and city, which in general usage are very vague and nebulous concepts and so require to be more specifically defined if they are to be useful. This is a hazardous business, however, since the extensive debates among human geographers, anthropologists and historians, as well as archaeologists, on this subject in recent years have not provided any universally accepted criteria. Rather, it has become evident that there are many standpoints from which the classification of settlements can be approached, and that the criteria used will vary according to the approach and the goals proposed (Wheatley 1972:602). Many of those that have been suggested, such as function and social structure and even, recently, the verbal usage or attitude of mind of the local population,[1] are either not directly, or not at all, accessible to the prehistoric archaeologist. Population size and density, unfortunately, are little more helpful, not simply because of the lack of totally, or even adequately, explored sites but rather because of lack of uniformity in the practice of demographers (Wheatley 1972:620). For the archaeologist the most convenient and objective measure is the extent of ground covered, if it is known or can be estimated.[2] But it ignores many other important factors and when density of occupation varies widely between settlements, as in Europe, it is almost useless by itself. Other observable features must therefore be taken into account, where possible.

I shall accordingly use the terms village, town, city, to denote the remains of settlements that not only display a gradation in size, with of necessity much overlapping, but can be distinguished also by means of other important characteristics, such as the presence or absence of indications of social or economic distinctions within the community and evidence for the existence and scale of public works. By a village I understand a settlement that usually covers only a fairly small area of ground, though it may sometimes consist of dispersed dwellings and so appear rather large; that has a population of hundreds rather than thousands of individuals; that offers little or no evidence of economic specialization or marked social distinctions within the group; and that possessed little or nothing in the way of public works. There may be a boundary ditch, fence or wall, but normally not large-scale defences. By a city, on the other hand, I mean here simply a very extensive settlement with a total area of not less than about a hundred hectares, and often much more, that has a correspondingly large population showing evidence of a wide range of social status. There must also be evidence for industrial and commercial activities carried on by highly specialized groups, and for public works on a monumental scale along with, generally, some other indications of conscious organization and planning on a large scale. A town may be anything between these extremes; not necessarily larger than a village in area or population, but showing signs of having housed a community that was somewhat more complex in its social and economic structure, and some evidence of community planning and enterprise. Like the city, it is often wholly or partially enclosed by massive defensive walls. Obviously, there is room for a considerable amount of overlapping and ambiguity between these categories. None of the criteria used are in any way absolute; all the diagnostic features may not be recognizable in individual instances. Inevitably, the assignment of some sites to a particular category will be a somewhat subjective judgement, particularly since most sites have been only incompletely excavated. Nevertheless, where sufficient work has been done or where the general plan can be made out without excavation, it is usually possible to make a reasonably acceptable judgement. The attempt to assign sites to such categories is useful, since they give in shorthand form some indication of the scale and complexity of the community in question and, collectively, of the society of a region at a particular time and of its potential in terms of cultural achievement.

During the long period of about two or three millennia, from the introduction of food-producing techniques to about 3,000 B.C., the situation in the area under consideration is a relatively simple one. No settlements are known that, on the criteria just outlined, could be ranked higher than villages. At the same time there is evidence for considerable variety, both in the size of the numerous village settlements known and in the kinds of buildings to be found in them and the way these are arranged. There is evidence that trade in various materials was carried on, sometimes over quite long distances, but no evidence of any settlements that depended solely on it for their existence.

In Greece, the open settlements that have been investigated, and indeed most of those known, are mounds. This means that what is seen on the surface represents the final state at the end of occupation, modified by any changes that have occurred since. It tells us nothing about the development. Even where excavations have been carried out, we normally have more information about the latest phases than about the earlier ones, since it is very costly in time and money to open up large areas of the deeper levels. Quite apart from the difficulties of recovering information about house-plans and the relations between buildings from the earlier stages of a settlement, however, it is possible to get a rough idea of the extent of the occupied area at different times by making a number of small soundings at suitable points, but this has rarely been attempted. I have recently tried to do it at Knossos, with results that indicate a steady expansion in the size of the settled area from only about a quarter of a hectare in *c.* 6,000 B.C. to about three hectares by *c.* 4,000 B.C. and perhaps as much as five hectares in *c.* 3,000 B.C. (Evans 1971). Knossos, however, was exceptional in the Aegean in attaining such a size at that time, and it would be of great interest to know something of the growth-patterns of more typical Neolithic settlements. As far as can be judged from sites where investigations have taken place, the initial settlements may have been considerably smaller than the latest ones, but there are few details available. At all stages, however, the average Neolithic village in the Aegean seems to have covered less than a hectare, often very much less, and very rarely more (Renfrew 1972:238).

Even so, the density of population was not great, since the Aegean Neolithic villages are not close-packed, like the generality of Near Eastern ones, but are composed of a number of free-standing buildings spaced at varying intervals, sometimes with a common orientation. This is the common European pattern (Piggott 1965:4). Little is known of the buildings of the earliest phases, but on the mainland there seem to have been substantial buildings of basically square or rectangular plan from a very early stage, while in the Late Neolithic the apsidal plan is known. Houses consist of one or two rooms, rarely of more than two. The megaron plan seems to have been used from the Middle Neolithic at least, sometimes indicating a sizable building with several rooms, which may have been the dwelling of an important villager, perhaps a headman (Sinos 1971:19). The central square building at Nea Nikomedeia has been thought to be a shrine (Rodden & Rodden 1964:604-7). In Crete there is manifest a clear tendency for building units to consist of an agglomeration of rectangular rooms of various sizes, and this goes back to an early stage of the settlement at Knossos (Evans 1971:107, 110), perhaps to the beginning. The units were clearly separated from each other by intervals of several metres and some, at least, may have had a roughly rectangular perimeter. It is interesting that the house-plans of Neolithic Crete clearly foreshadow the basic principle that was developed there, in both domestic and palace architecture, throughout the third and second millennia B.C. On the mainland, the apsidal and megaron plans crop up again in the late third and second millennia B.C. and are found yet again in the early first millennium, but were apparently in eclipse during most of the third millennium. In the Cyclades, the building found at Saliagos (Evans & Renfrew 1968:22-6, Fig. 10) somewhat resembles the Cretan ones in the complexity of the plan, but it is larger and the evidence for raised wooden floors, among other things, suggests a separate Cycladic tradition. Estimates of the number of people likely to have been brought together in these Aegean villages must take into account the relatively low density of occupation. It seems unlikely that the largest village exceeded a few hundred individuals, though the unique settlement at Knossos may have housed considerably over a thousand people in its latest stages.[3]

It is less easy to generalize about the Neolithic settlements of Italy than those of the Aegean, but open settlements seem to have been generally less permanent, though there are exceptions to this. There is certainly more regional variety; evidence for actual structure is often hard to obtain, and when found is often hard to interpret. Nothing more elaborate is attested, however, than simple huts with a wattle-and-daub superstructure, and it seems that the preference for circular or oval plans that was to persist in Italy into the Iron Age was already well established. The extraordinary Apulian ditched villages, of which so many are now known from air photographs, are a special type and seem to have been extremely prodigal in their use of land. At Passo di Corvo (Bradford & Williams-Hunt 1946:196), one of the largest, the inhabited part covers the enormous area of about forty hectares, but this does not necessarily imply a large population. Like the others, it seems to have consisted of a series of 'compounds', delimited by penannular ditches enclosing areas mostly with a diameter of 15-25 m., within which the huts were set. The hundred or so of these compounds at Passo di Corvo need not have contained more than one family apiece and they may not all have been inhabited at the same time, so that it does not seem necessary to postulate a population of more than 1,000 people for this village at any one time, and it may well have been less. The average settlement was very much smaller than this. In Sicily, similar ditched enclosures also enclosed much smaller areas, about three hectares at Stentinello, for instance (Bernabò Brea 1954: Fig. 2; the measurements originally given by Orsi 1890:178 seem to be considerably exaggerated). On the Lipari acropolis, the inhabited area cannot have been more than about four hectares, though nothing is known of the structure or density of the huts there. Little is known yet about the size of settlements or of the kinds of houses in use in north Italy. Four or five settlement areas of timber-floored houses were found at Molino Casarotto, but it is uncertain whether all of these were in use at the same time, or whether there was any solid superstructure (Barfield 1971:41). In any case, this type of settlement may have been seasonal and related to the villages on the margin of the Po plain, where clay floors and hearths have sometimes been reported.

Despite the marked differences in the form of the Neolithic villages known in the Aegean and in Italy, it is unlikely that there was any great difference in the level of social and economic organization attained by the farming communities of the areas during this period. There seems to have been very heavy reliance on food production in the form of mixed farming based on cereals and stock-breeding wherever this was possible, though in some areas (e.g. northern Italy) fishing, hunting and gathering remained important because of special conditions. The characteristic settlements, however, are open villages of up to a few hundred inhabitants, with few signs of marked social distinctions and little or no indication of economic specialization.

Though there are, in the Aegean during the fourth millennium, some signs that presage future developments, nevertheless it is only in the third and second millennia B.C. that major differences can be seen between the two areas in their general level of cultural attainment. From the mid-third millennium, Italy falls rapidly behind developments in the Aegean; and from then on, the divergence grows more marked until the collapse of the Mycenaean civilization towards the end of the second millennium. The evidence for the remarkable progress made by the population of the Aegean in developing more complex forms of society has recently been brilliantly and exhaustively studied by Professor Renfrew (1972), who has used many different kinds of evidence to demonstrate the great variety of inter-related processes that interacted to produce this result. Here, however, I am concerned only with the size and nature of the most complex settlement-units that appear to be a characteristic feature of each stage of this story.

While the seeds of later developments may have been germinating slowly since as early as the beginning of the fourth millennium B.C., it is not until the third millennium that it becomes evident that a society has emerged that is oriented quite differently from the Neolithic farming communities. The effect is first noticed in the character rather than in the size of the settlements. Instead of standing separately, as in the Neolithic settlements, houses are now huddled together along narrow irregular streets and are often separated only by party walls.[4] They are, in this respect, more like Near Eastern settlements than the Aegean villages of the preceding period. The change may have been due, as much as anything, to the desire to concentrate the population for convenience of defence, since many settlements are sited in naturally defensible spots, where space was limited, or were surrounded by artificial defences. Though one effect of this is that more people were living in less space than during the Neolithic period, it is not on account of population size, any more than area occupied, that these settlements have generally been called towns in the archaeological literature. Many of them were very small – less than a hectare in area – and the largest cover only about two hectares (Renfrew 1972:238). They are towns rather by virtue of the evidence that many of them have produced for the presence of specialist craftsmen, potters, lapidaries, cloth-workers etc. and because of the defensive walls and the existence, in some of them, of monumental buildings such as the House of the Tiles, the *Rundbau* at Tyrins, the hill-top house at Vasilike etc. While the development of vine and olive cultivation about 3,000 B.C. (Renfrew 1972:281, 285) was important in itself and for the future, it was obviously not a pre-condition for the existence of communities of this size. Rather, it was an element in the growth of economic complexity.

On the mainland, these promising developments seem to have suffered a check towards the end of the third millennium B.C., from which recovery was slow (Caskey 1964:37-8). Some towns, such as Lerna, were destroyed and though most of them were re-occupied, it seems to have been at a lower cultural and organizational level. In many areas (including the Cyclades) the numbers of known Middle Bronze Age settlements are noticeably less than those of the Early Bronze Age; commerce fell off, and defence seems to have been the over-riding preoccupation. Significantly, Messenia, an area of good farming land and situated in the remote south-west, shows a substantial increase in the number of settlements at this time, but they are all hill-top fortresses (McDonald & Simpson 1969:174) like Malthi, which has more the character of a small defended village than a town (Valmin 1938). Separate houses, with space between and often apsidal in plan, are found in many settlements of this period, though not in all (Sinos 1971:84).

In the Late Bronze Age the main development took a rather different line, with the development of the palace and citadel sites which, though they were certainly centres of power, administration and economic activity on a large scale, do not seem to have resulted in really large-scale concentrations of population.[5] Most of the population seems rather to have been dispersed around the countryside in a large number of relatively small groups with more of a village than an urban character. At Miletus, indeed, a walled Mycenaean town covering about six hectares is now known, but the excavators remark that it had more the character of a Cretan town (the wall being late) and that it was probably originally a Cretan foundation (Cook & Blackman 1971:44).

In Crete, where there was no disruption, towns did develop in the second millennium, but the ones that have been explored, and almost certainly the majority of the others, were very small, while the true character of the others is doubtful. In east Crete, a few of the small towns are quite well-known from excavation, and the relevant facts about them have recently been assembled and evaluated by Dr Branigan (1972). The evidence suggests that they were even smaller in the Middle Minoan than in the Late Minoan period; Pseira, for instance, probably covered only 7,000 sq. m. in the earlier period, but grew to at least 1.5 hectares in the later period, with perhaps some suburban development beyond the peninsula as well. The best-known of Minoan towns, Gournia, covered roughly the same or a slightly larger area in the Late Minoan period,[6] while Palaikastro, which is more difficult to assess because of incomplete excavation, perhaps extended to 5.5 hectares. Populations probably ranged from about 400 for Late Minoan Pseira to about 1,500 or 2,000 for Palaikastro in the same period.[7] None of these was a big centre of power or administration, though Gournia boasted a palace during the earlier part of its existence, but it seems reasonable to class them all as towns rather than villages. The houses were crowded together as in the towns of the Early Bronze Age, but Branigan notes evidence for more and less prosperous inhabitants (perhaps even landlord and tenant), for some simple planning in the lay-out and construction of the streets and, at Gournia and Palaikastro, for other public works in the form of drainage systems. Both of these last imply community organization and, probably, a central control. Again, as expected at this date, there is evidence for specialist crafts such as cloth-working, dyeing, carpentry and metal-work.

The character of the settlements centred on the large palaces is much more enigmatic. The palaces certainly represent highly organized communities in themselves, though they do not cover any very large area; only Knossos, the largest, exceeds one hectare. The built-up areas that surrounded the palaces of Knossos and Mallia, however, were very much larger than this. At Knossos, the area that Evans designated the Inner Town spread over at least 40 hectares, while outside this he indicated a broad zone of less intense habitation (Evans 1928:562 and site-plan opp. 547). The area covered by habitation at Mallia is little less than the Inner Town at Knossos (Demargne & Gallet de Santerre 1953: Pl. I). Both these settlements have, so far, been only patchily investigated and it is impossible to tell how densely settled they really were. It cannot be determined at present whether they really formed a single urban unit, or were made up of scattered groups of houses and mansions not closely linked together. In any case, there were very few settlements on this scale, and after the disappearance of the palaces there was nothing comparable. During Late Minoan III there were more settlements in Crete than ever before, probably, but all on a small scale. The situation in the Cyclades is not materially different. Towns such as Phylakopi seem to have covered not more than about two hectares (Atkinson *et al.* 1904: Plan); Akrotiri may have been larger but, in the present state of the excavations there, it is impossible to tell by how much.

Thus, the existence of any really large urban settlements in the Aegean during the Bronze Age remains unproven, and Renfrew's estimate of an extent of one to four hectares for the typical major settlement of this period remains credible, though the upper figure may be a bit low. If this is correct, then populations of the order of 1,000 to 2,000 at most are the largest that can be envisaged, except possibly at one or two special centres like Knossos. While these may reasonably be classed as urban communities because of the characteristics manifested by the settlements they lived in, nevertheless they are near the bottom of the scale in size. Despite this, Minoan and Mycenaean society attained a high degree of complexity in organization, and its cultural achievement was remarkable. Yet, despite all the differences that have been noted between Crete and the mainland, it seems to have been the palace community, rather than the urban community, that was at the hub in each case and, once the palace community was destroyed, both rapidly reverted to a much simpler state. This is seen in Crete after the early-fifteenth century and, more dramatically, in the whole of the Aegean after *c.* 1200 B.C.

During the corresponding period of two millennia, no such spectacular development can be observed in Italy. It can be said that, with a few possible exceptions in the Late Bronze Age, there is no settlement known during the whole of this period that deserves to rank as more than a village. Despite the changes that are very evident in the archaeological record during the third millennium B.C., there is nothing to suggest that the economic and social changes raised the social and technological level much above what it was before. At the beginning of this period, the settlement of the Diana stage on the Lipari acropolis spread down into the plain below, and there is some evidence that copper-smelting was carried on there (Bernabò Brea 1966:48). But there is nothing else to suggest any fundamental change. Little is known of settlements outside the Aeolian islands, but the size of the cemeteries does not indicate that they can have been large, nor do they provide any evidence of marked social distinctions. In Malta, the development of the temples belongs to this period, but this would seem to have been a rather lopsided development of a particular aspect of life erected on a very simple economic and technological base. Apart from the enigmatic model of what appears to be part of the plan of a complex building from Tarxien (Evans 1971: Pl. 47), there is nothing to indicate the existence of other than simple village settlements during this period.

The evidence available for settlements in Italy during the second millennium is much more considerable, but it goes to show that the typical one was still a village rather than anything that can reasonably be called a town. They seem still to have been normally made up of separate single-roomed huts, circular, oval or rectangular, with little or no sign of any attempt at overall planning, and almost equally little to suggest any strongly developed social stratification, though in some settlements it has been possible to recognize one hut that is notably larger than the rest, or which differs in plan and content (e.g. the Lipari acropolis site in the Cape Graziano phase, and the Milazzese settlement in the Middle Bronze Age) (Bernabò Brea 1966:98, 116). The size-range seems to be from less than one to about three hectares in all parts. There seems to be a certain amount of evidence for more or less specialized industrial activity, particularly metal-working, in the lakeside and *terramara* settlements of the north, and some of these also functioned as trading posts, but they do not seem quite to deserve the name of towns. In peninsular Italy it is very clear that the Apennine settlements are simply villages, the main feature in this region being the full development of a mixed farming economy in which, however, transhumant stock-breeding played a very important part (Puglisi 1959; Barker 1972). There seems to be little indication that trade or specialized industry of any kind was of any great importance in this area until after about the middle of the thirteenth century B.C. The only exception is the development of a very localized bronze industry in southern Tuscany (Trump 1966:101).

From the thirteenth century on there may have been a few small centres of more or less urban character in Apulia. Dr Ruth Whitehouse has recently put up strong arguments in favour of regarding Scoglio del Tonno, Porto Perone and a few others in this light (Whitehouse 1973:618-20). They all grew out of Apennine villages, and are certainly not larger in size (mostly under one hectare). Their claim to be regarded as towns rests on their transformation at this time into centres of specialized manufacture and trade, defended by stone walls, and probably partly supported on the produce of neighbouring village communities. Mycenaean sherds have been found in all of them and Dr Whitehouse suggests that their metamorphosis was connected with Mycenaean trading activities. The distinction she makes between these sites and the ordinary Apennine villages must be admitted to be a real one, and they are not significantly smaller than many Aegean towns of the period. However, this does raise the question of the status of some of the north Italian sites once more; clearly, all these sites lie very much on the borderline between village and town, and it would be pedantic to labour the point. Perhaps 'proto-urban' would, as Dr Whitehouse suggests, be a useful label. Sites with similar Mycenaean imports in the Aeolian islands seem to be more clearly villages, however, since they lack evidence for any kind of industrial development or trading activities of their own. It is difficult at present to judge the situation in Sicily, because of the lack of excavated sites, but the current investigations in the Thapsos settlement seem to show that this site at least was very large.[8] After about 1250 B.C., large communities of a similar order of magnitude to this certainly came into existence at a number of places, but they continued to develop well into the first millennium B.C., so I shall return to them a little later.

As a generalization, it can be said that during the third and second millennia B.C. the nucleated settlements of the Aegean and the central Mediterranean remained very small, covering at the most a few hectares and not exceeding a maximum population of about two thousand. The few larger aggregates attested in the Aegean during the later Bronze Age seem invariably to be connected with palaces and the available evidence seems to indicate that they had a rather special character, which was not like that of the densely populated Near Eastern city.

Not until the first half of the first millennium B.C. do we begin to find anything in the area under discussion which can be compared with such a city. The course of their development is still far from well understood, largely owing to the difficulty of obtaining information about the early stages in the life of cities that underwent massive redevelopment in subsequent periods and, in many cases, are still inhabited today. Developments in the eastern and western halves of the region are again disparate, though closely interconnected in the later stages. In the Aegean, the Archaic period of Greek civilization is separated from the Mycenaean and Minoan world by the profound gulf of the Dark Age, the period of recession that set in with the decline of the Mycenaean civilization, and from which it took several centuries to recover. There can be no reasonable doubt about the reality of this recession, whatever there may be about its causes. Apart from the gradual withering away of the Mycenaean cultural tradition after the destruction and abandonment of the major palaces, there was clearly a catastrophic decline in the population of Greece over a period of a few centuries, as demonstrated by the progressive reduction in the number of sites known to have been inhabited in each century from the thirteenth to the eleventh B.C. (Snodgrass 1971:364).

Recovery, as after the catastrophe of the late third millennium B.C., was at first slow. It began sooner among the emigrants to Ionia than on the mainland, where it seems to have gathered momentum only in the course of the eighth century B.C., a time when there seems to have been something of a population explosion. Even the earlier Archaic towns were probably not very large, however. Old Smyrna, for instance, does not seem to have exceeded six hectares in area (the size of the promontory on which it was built) before the seventh century B.C., when there was great development outside the walls, so that it eventually spread over about 25 hectares in all (Cook 1959:15). Cook estimates a population of only a little over 2,000 for the eighth-century town; during the seventh century, however, houses were less densely packed within the walls which, perhaps, then contained only half that number, while a larger number of people inhabited the new suburbs (Cook 1959:19). The eighth-century town of Emporio in Chios seems to have occupied about 15 hectares (not counting the acropolis, which contained only the megaron hall) but the houses seem to have been pretty well scattered over the hill-side (Boardman 1967). Some other Ionian towns were probably considerably larger than Smyrna in the early Archaic period. Cook has made some calculations about the settlement located on the promontory of Ilica, which may be the site of the earliest Erythrae. This promontory is about four times larger in area than the one on which Old Smyrna was built but, allowing for part of it having produced no remains and the obvious absence of any necessity for crowding, Cook suggests that it might have had only about twice the population of Old Smyrna (Cook 1959:21-2). Others may have been considerably larger than this again, but evidence is lacking. Moving westwards, Zagora on Andros has close-set houses grouped in a regular orientation, but it is not yet possible to give an estimate of its total size and population (Cambitoglou 1967:75). In Crete, several hill-top towns are known: two of them, Vrokastro and Kavousi, apparently survivals of earlier refuge settlements; while two others, Lato and Dreros, seem to have been new foundations but on similar sites. It is difficult to ascertain the original character and extent of these two, however, because of later building. Some coastal settlements are also known.

On the mainland, once again, excavation does not, so far, permit an estimate to be made of the size and population of any of the main centres of Classical Greece during the Archaic period (Martin 1956:76). At Athens, however, the occupied area seems to have been quite extensive to the south, north-west and north-east of the Acropolis by the seventh century B.C., engulfing earlier cemeteries. There does not seem to have been any crowding (Martin 1956:76).

In the west, some of the Greek colonies eventually grew to a great size, but as usual it is often very difficult to say what they were like in the early stages. The island part of Syracuse, Ortygia, which was occupied from the beginning, has an area of about fifty hectares, and there was also some occupation right from the start on the mainland, from which the name of the Greek city was derived (Dunbabin 1948:50). Judging by the positions of the early cemeteries, the area of occupation on the mainland could have been as large again as that on the island, but what its real extent was, and what the density of population was, is not known at present. At Taras, on the mainland, the initial settlement was again on an island, which offered a surface area of about thirty hectares, but in this case the mainland was not occupied before the sixth century (Dunbabin 1948:89, n. 5).

The information about the size of Greek towns in the eighth and seventh centuries is thus far from satisfactory, but it seems to indicate that most were still relatively small, though already bigger than almost anything previously known in the Aegean, and had a real urban character both in the structure of the populations and in the nature of their public spaces, buildings and defences. Among the reasons that contributed to the development of these towns were the development of close relations with the surrounding countryside; a good proportion of the citizens lived outside the urban area and supplied it with their produce. They were already small *poleis* on the model which the Greeks continued to develop in the city-states of Classical times. Another factor was the development of industry and wide-ranging trading networks. It now seems clear that trade was a prime factor in the early spread of Greek colonization to the west, as well as eastwards, whatever part land-hunger and other causes may have played (Buchner 1966:12).

By the sixth century B.C., however, many Greek towns must have attained a very considerable size; they became, in fact, cities in the sense in which I am using that word here. Some of them seem already to have been organized on some variant of the orthogonal plan, later regarded as the invention of Hippodamus of Miletus (see Castagnoli 1956: 13-14). The walls of sixth-century Athens may not have enclosed as large an area as after the Persian wars, but they seem to have been rebuilt partly on the old line, despite Thucydides' reference to enlargement of the circuit 'on every side' (Gardner 1904:49-50). Miletus may, at the same time, have already covered an area of perhaps as much as 150-200 hectares (Cook & Blackman 1971:44), and some of the western cities were in process of becoming very large indeed. The explorations by the University of Pennsylvania on the site of Sybaris seem to suggest that the sixth-century city may have been spread out over the enormous area of seven square kilometres (Bullitt 1972:213), while others, such as Syracuse and Taras, which had become very large indeed by the fifth century, must have been already well on the way to this. It seems reasonable to say that cities covering 100-200 hectares and having populations of 20,000 or more must have been relatively common in the Greek world by this time.

Although there is evidence of an expansion of urn-field burial rites and pottery through Italy in the later second millennium B.C., there is nothing to suggest upheaval or recession of the kind that afflicted the Aegean. There seems in fact to have been quite a lot of continuity in the passage from the second to the first millennium, and further development during the earlier first millennium built on this. The decline of Mycenaean trading clearly had some effect in slowing down the pace, particularly in the south, though some of the small trading towns in Apulia continued to flourish and carried on a commerce that had now switched to markets on the opposite side of the Adriatic. In the proto-Villanovan phase some sites in the Po valley evidently grew to a relatively large size, as at Frattesini, where the remains cover about fourteen hectares (Barfield 1971:100). In Sicily, the centres of the Pantalica culture continued to develop down to, and in some cases contemporary with, the earlier stages of the Greek colonization. At Pantalica itself, the prehistoric town probably had an area of about twenty hectares (Bernabò Brea 1954:189, Fig. 22; 1966:157 says twenty *acres*, but this seems to be a translation error). This, and the roughly five thousand collective tombs in the four main necropoleis that surround the settlement, suggest that, allowing for its life of about five centuries, the population may well have been in excess of 5,000 and possibly nearer 10,000. A centrally placed building of large blocks, measuring 36 m. by 10 m. and containing several square or rectangular rooms, one of which contained moulds for bronzes, may very well have been the palace of the ruler, who perhaps controlled the metal production. Other Sicilian centres were not so large, to judge by the numbers of tombs, but nevertheless larger than any previous settlements in Sicily. Greek colonization curtailed the natural development of these towns, though some of them continued to be urban centres.

In peninsular Italy, the most striking development in this period, apart from that of the Greek colonies, is the rise of the Etruscan cities which, under Greek influence, developed with remarkable rapidity out of the preceding Villanovan villages. In the eighth century future great cities like Veii seem still to have consisted of small clusters of circular, oval or rectangular huts housing only a few hundred people (Strong 1968:67); yet only two centuries later they had transformed themselves, through Greek interest in the mineral resources of their region, particularly iron, and the stimulus provided by the contact with Greek culture, into cities that extended over areas of 100-200 hectares. At least one was already surrounded by defensive walls (Strong 1968:66), and all dominated large areas of the surrounding countryside. In this process, the early part of the sixth century B.C. seems to have been a period of particularly rapid growth. Marzabotto, the Etruscan colony south of Bologna, was founded probably about the end of the sixth century B.C. and, though never an important centre, it was laid out on an orthogonal plan and must originally have covered about a hundred hectares (Heurgon 1964:139). Spina, another Etruscan site of much greater importance that was founded about the same time, is much larger, covering about 350 hectares (Strong 1968:75). In the Po valley there were, of course, also important Villanovan centres, of which Bologna was the largest, that seem to have developed on the basis of transalpine trade, rather than through relations with the Greeks like the rest of Italy.

The problem of the probable population of the Etruscan cities has been much discussed, and estimates have ranged from Mengarelli's suggestion of 80,000 for Caere (1927:145) to more recent attempts to argue for 10,000 or less (Wolstenholme & O'Connor 1959:81). The great discrepancy between these estimates reflects chiefly the deficiency of archaeological exploration within Etruscan settlement sites, as opposed to tomb exploration. Heurgon (1964:146-8), however, taking up the suggestion of Fotï, has tried to use the tombs themselves to arrive at a probable estimate for the population of Caere. Basing his experiment on a small, but fairly completely explored, area of the Banditaccia cemetery, he arrived at the conclusion that the lowest average figure must be about 25,000, which is particularly interesting since it agrees exactly with Nogara's earlier estimate (1937:46) based on the area occupied by the remains of the city. Nogara's estimate should also be a minimal one, since it supposes a population density of only about 150 per hectare, which is quite low. There is, as yet, little evidence for the density of population in Etruscan cities but, since there were probably quite a lot of monumental buildings and open spaces, the density supposed by Nogara's estimate may not be too far from the truth.

Thus, it seems that urban units that covered areas of 100 hectares and upwards, and had populations of 10,000 or more, first came into existence in Greece and Italy during the period from about 700 to 500 B.C., and their rise can be linked with the development of the city-state. A major factor in determining their size and degree of prosperity was usually the extent and fertility of the land they controlled, but mineral resources, industries and trading potential were also often of great, and sometimes crucial, importance.

It was the developments of the Archaic period that provided the spring-board for the subsequent blossoming of Mediterranean civilization and assured the acceleration of its cultural progression. Among other things, the development of the Archaic cities precipitated the transformation, and eventual dissolution, of the earlier kin-based social organization whose role structures 'restricted individual capacities for independent action because they subsumed and regulated all the essential requirements, interests and rights of individuals' (Smith 1972:572). Rashevsky (1968:109-10) has recently stressed the importance for cultural change and development of conditions in which nonconformity of any kind can survive and spread. The high-density conditions of urban living are most favourable to this but, since natural nonconformists are relatively rare, it is not enough to have only one or two in a community: it must be large enough to contain a group sufficiently large to support and encourage one another. If one assumes that only one individual in a hundred is likely to be such a person, then a population of the order of 10,000 is needed to furnish a group of about a hundred. Though the supposed proportion used in Rashevsky's example is, of course, arbitrary and the process itself is presented in an over-simplified and schematized way, it nevertheless highlights the significance of the Archaic Greek and Italian cities in the development of Mediterranean civilization. Before them, there had been no community in this part of the world in any way comparable in potential for cultural advance; it is a situation that has a parallel in the appearance of the first cities in Mesopotamia during the proto-Literate period. This had been followed by rapid advances in all aspects of civilized life; but the Mediterranean cities were, perhaps, even more fortunate in that the instability of their political organization during several centuries encouraged innovation and experiment. This social milieu was highly favourable to independence of thought and action and thus, for the first time, gave full scope for the display of the latent abilities of the population.

REFERENCES

Adams, R. McC. (1966) *The Evolution of Urban Society: early Mesopotamia and prehispanic Mexico.* London.

Alexander, J. (1972) The beginnings of urban life in Europe. In Ucko, P.J., Tringham, R. and Dimbleby, G.W. (eds.), *Man, Settlement and Urbanism*, 843-50. London.

Atkinson, T.D. *et al.* (1904) *Excavations at Phylakopi.* London.

Barfield, L. (1971) *Northern Italy before Rome.* London.

Barker, G. (1972) The conditions of cultural and economic growth in the Bronze Age of Central Italy. *P.P.S.*, 38, 170-208.

Beaujeu-Garnier, J. and Chabot, G. (1967) *Urban Geography*. London.

Bernabò Brea, L. (1954) La Sicilia prehistórica y sus relaciones con Oriente y con la Península Ibérica. *Ampurias*, 15-16, 137-213.

Bernabò Brea, L. (1966) *Sicily before the Greeks.* London.

Boardman, J. (1967) *Greek Emporio.* London.

Bradford, J. and Williams-Hunt, P.R. (1946) Siticulosa Apulia. *Antiquity*, 20, 191-200.

Branigan, K. (1972) Minoan settlements in east Crete. In Ucko, P.J., Tringham, R. and Dimbleby, G.W. (eds.), *Man, Settlement and Urbanism*, 751-9. London.

Buchner, G. (1966) Pithekoussai, oldest Greek colony in the West. *Expedition*, 8 (4), 4-12.

Bullitt, O. (1972) *The Search for Sybaris.* London.

Cambitoglou, A. (1967) Zagora. *Ergon tes Archaiologikes Hetaireias*, 1966, 75.

Cary, M. and Haarhoff, T.J. (1966) *Life and Thought in the Greek and Roman World.* London.

Caskey, J.L. (1964) Crete, Greece and the Aegean Islands in the Early Bronze Age. *Cambridge Ancient History*, Vol. 1, Ch. 26.

Castagnoli, F. (1956) *Ippodamo di Mileto e l'urbanistica a pianta ortogonale.* Rome. (For English trans: *see* Caliandro, V. (1971) *Orthogonal Town Planning in Antiquity*. London.)

Clark, J.G.D. (1952) *Prehistoric Europe: The Economic Basis.* London.

Cook, J.M. (1958-9) Old Smyrna, 1948-51. *Ann. Brit. School at Athens*, 53-4, 1-34.

Cook, J.M. and Blackman, D.J. (1971) Archaeology in Western Asia Minor. In *Archaeological Reports* (Society for the Promotion of Hellenic Studies), 1970-71, 33-62.

Demargne, P. and Gallet de Santerre, H. (1953) *Fouilles Executées a Mallia: Exploration de Maisons et Quartiers d'Habitation.* Paris.

Dunbabin, T.J. (1948) *The Western Greeks.* Oxford.

Evans, Sir A.J. (1928) *The Palace of Minos* II. London.

Evans, J.D. (1971) *The Prehistoric Antiquities of the Maltese Islands.* London.

Evans, J.D. and Renfrew, C. (1968) *Excavations at Saliagos, near Antiparos.* London.

Gardner, E.A. (1904) *Ancient Athens.* London.

Heurgon, J. (1964) *Daily Life of the Etruscans.* London.

Jones, E. (1966) *Towns and Cities.* London.

Martin, R.E. (1956) *L'Urbanisme dans la Grèce Antique.* Paris.

McDonald, W.A. and Simpson, R.H. (1969) Further exploration in the Southwestern Peloponnese 1964-68. *Amer. Jour. Arch.*, 73, 173.

Mengarelli, R. (1927) Caere e le recenti scoperte. *Studi Etruschi*, 1, 145.

Nogara, B. (1937) *Gli Etruschi e la loro Civiltà.* Milan.

Orsi, P. (1890) Stazione neolitica di Stentinello. *Bull. di Paletnologia Italiana*, 16, 177-200.

Piggott, S. (1965) *Ancient Europe.* Edinburgh.

Puglisi, S. (1969) *La civiltà appenninica. Origine delle comunità pastorali in Italia.* Firenze.

Rashevsky, N. (1968) *Looking at History through Mathematics.* Cambridge, Mass. and London.

Renfrew, C. (1972) *The Emergence of Civilization: the Cyclades and the Aegean in the third millennium B.C.* London.

Rodden, R.J. and Rodden, J.M. (1964) A European link with Chatal Hüyük: the 7th millennium settlement of Nea Nikomedeia in Macedonia. *Illus. London News*, 244, 604-7.

Sinos, S. (1971) *Die vorklassischen Hausformen in der Ägais.* Mainz.

Smith, M.G. (1972) Complexity, size and urbanization. In Ucko, P.J., Tringham, R. and Dimbleby, G.W. (eds.), *Man, Settlement and Urbanism*, 567-74. London.

Snodgrass, A.M. (1971) *The Dark Age of Greece: an archaeological survey of the 11th to 8th century B.C.* Edinburgh.

Strong, D. (1968) *The Early Etruscans.* London.

Trump, D.H. (1966) *Central and Southern Italy before Rome.* London.

Valmin, M.N. (1938) *The Swedish Messenia Expedition* (Skrifter utgivna av Kungl. Humanistiska Vetenskapssamfundet i Lund no. 26).

Voza, G. (1972) Thapsos: primi risultati delle più recenti ricerche. *Atti XIV Riunione Scientifica dell' Ist. Ital. di Preist. e Protost.* Firenze.

Voza, G. (1973) Thapsos: resconto sulle campagne di scavo del 1970-71. *Atti XV Riunione Scientifica dell' Ist. Ital. di Preist. e Protost.* Firenze.

Wheatley, P. (1972) The concept of urbanism. In Ucko, P.J., Tringham, R. and Dimbleby, G.W. (eds.), *Man, Settlement and Urbanism*, 601-37. London.

Whitehouse, R. (1973) The earliest towns in Peninsular Italy. In Renfrew, C. (ed.), *The Explanation of Culture Change: Models in Prehistory*, 617-24. London.

Wolstenholme, G.E.W. and O'Connor, M. (eds.) (1959) *C.I.B.A. Symposium on Medical Biology and Etruscan Origins.* London.

NOTES

1. 'A town is when people feel themselves to be in one' (Beaujeu-Garnier & Chabot 1967). 'A town is what is implied by the *local* people when they call a locality a town' (Jones 1966). These authors are quoted by Alexander 1972.

2. Adams (1966) has used this successfully for Mesopotamian settlements, where the density of habitation was probably fairly uniform.

3. Renfrew's (1972:251) estimate of about 200 people to the hectare, scaled down from Frankfort's of 400 to the hectare for Near Eastern sites, seems a reasonable estimate.

4. The settlement sites of the third millennium B.C. that have been extensively excavated are, however, all in the islands. A number of the mainland settlements have separate houses, but generally set close together or actually side by side (Sinos 1971: 30-3).

5. 'The Early Mycenaean period certainly witnessed dramatic social, political and economic changes, even if (in Messenia at least) there was no rapid increase in local population, and no large-scale immigration from outside. The developments most obvious to us now are vastly improved means of producing and acquiring movable wealth (mainly royal ?), and the appearance of specialized occupations and skills, evidenced by such phenomena as wide foreign trade and tholos tombs. In addition, there is a distinct possibility that literacy had begun to establish itself at local capitals. Traits of the sort described above are usually linked with what the culture historians call "incipient urbanization". But if urbanization requires (among other features) a really sizeable concentration of population at administrative centres, it is questionable whether the term can properly be applied to Mycenaean civilization at any stage' (McDonald & Simpson 1969:175).

6. The estimates of Branigan and Renfrew (1972:238) differ by one hectare. My estimate from the plan would agree with Renfrew's.

7. Branigan notes that calculations based on Renfrew's criteria, which were not the ones he used, give closely comparable results.

8. Preliminary reports suggest a settlement of about 20 hectares in area, with a large complex building, compared by the excavator to that at Gla, in the centre. Traces of fortification walls with bastions have also been found (see Voza 1972; 1973).

ANTHONY HARDING

Bronze agricultural implements in Bronze Age Europe

In *Prehistoric Europe: the Economic Basis* Professor Grahame Clark devoted two chapters (IV and V) to prehistoric farming. In one, he examined the question of forest clearance and methods of cultivation, including plough-types; in the other, he was concerned with crops and harvesting, livestock and salt extraction. One aspect that he hardly touched upon, since it is largely typological, concerns the tools with which agriculture was carried on in the later prehistoric period.[1] Until the end of the Neolithic the evidence for the existence and form of such tools is extremely scanty, and one may assume that organic materials were used for their manufacture; with the advent of the use of bronze for agricultural implements, however – a use that started in the Early Bronze Age (Holste 1940) – much more is preserved to us, so that it should be possible to see the entire range of tools that went to make up a Bronze Age agricultural tool-kit.

K.D. White (1967) has recently defined the agricultural tools that were in use during the Roman period, and since many of these categories must have been identical with those of the pre-Roman world, it is worth mentioning them here. I follow White in excluding ploughs and harrows from consideration, since they come properly under the heading 'machine'. This reduces the field to: spades and shovels; mattocks and hoes, and perhaps axes; knives and sickles; forks; saws; and shears. Of these, we may quickly dispose of shears, because they do not appear before the late pre-Roman Iron Age; for forks there is very little evidence, unless the 'trident' from Shaft-grave IV at Mycenae is one (Petrie 1917: Pl. LXVII, 50) – a piece that recalls the 'flesh-hooks' of the British and Irish Bronze Age, though the purpose of these is quite unknown. Saws and knives, of which there are plenty, refer more to viticulture and carpentry than to agriculture in the strict sense. The first three groups, then, comprise the bulk of the agricultural implements to be dealt with.

The spade, which is used for cutting sods of earth, is by its very nature a wet-soil implement: it would be possible to use such a tool in the south European area only in the wet season. While spades are used for turning soil over, shovels are for transporting loose soil, not usually for digging. Both implements would more likely be used for the cultivation of vegetables than of cereals, and for other purposes such as trench-digging, clay-extraction and so on. It is probable that many such implements were in wood and have not survived: White (1967:27) lists as one type the *pala cum ferro*, or wooden spade shod with iron; this is a long-lived type that can still be found today and was undoubtedly derived from pre-Roman wooden prototypes. One may presume that wooden spades were standard, yet the evidence that this was so is scanty enough. The most notable is the 'spade' as known from its marks in negative at Gwithian, Cornwall (Thomas 1970), though it was, in fact, reconstructed as a 'Cornish shovel', not as a spade proper. Its function was interpreted as the clearing of accumulations of sand, rather than digging or trenching for agricultural purposes; the blade was irregularly D-shaped and the handle long and straight (Fig. 5:1).

Though evidence for wooden spades in the Bronze Age does not seem to be known from the Swiss Lakes, north Italian sites like Castione have produced coarse simple wooden shovels (Keller 1866:229, Pl. LXIV). This is entirely what one might expect from sites so rich in organic remains; the only surprise is that there are not more. Other prehistoric spades are known from Denmark: these are earlier and made in one piece (Thomas 1970, with refs.). Another organic material used for spades and shovels is bone: ox scapulae occur commonly on flint-mining sites (Clark 1952:178, Fig. 102).[2]

It is clear that bronze was not in general use for spades in most of Continental Europe; in the Aegean, on the other hand, they were usually

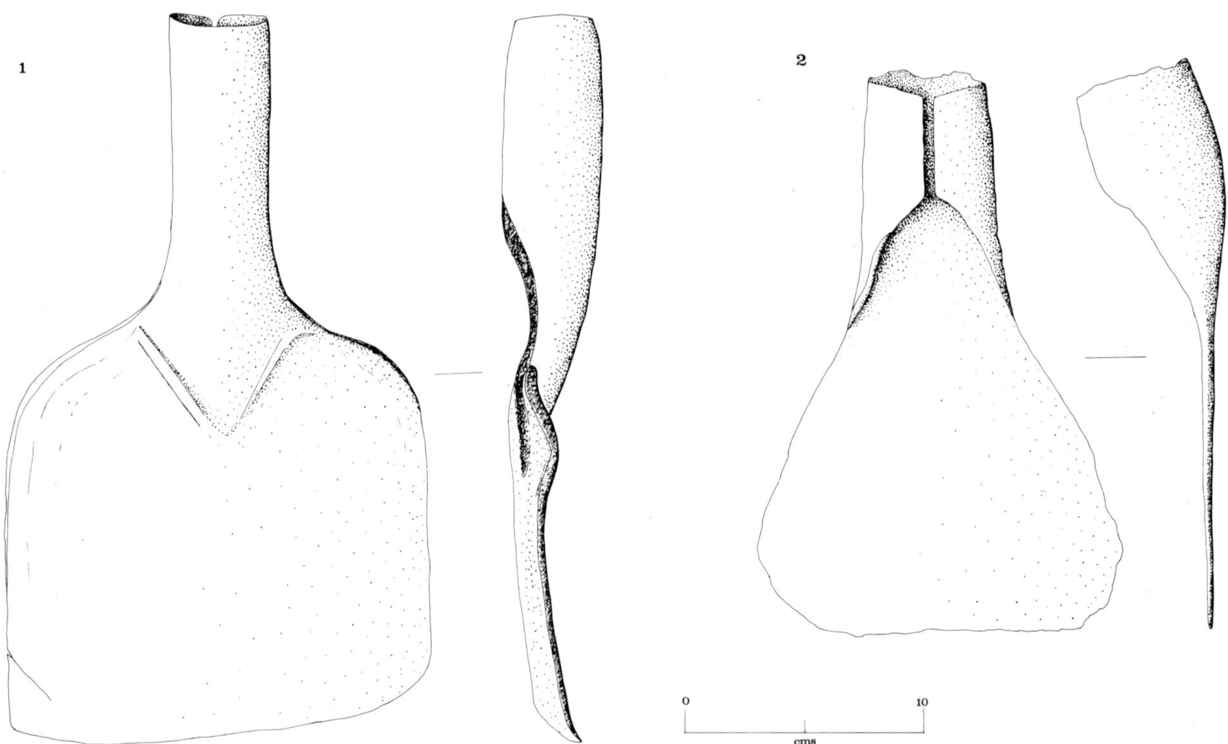

Figure 1. Cypriot shovels. 1: Nitovikla (Ashmolean Museum). 2: Enkomi, Founder's Hoard (British Museum).

made of bronze. The examples we possess come mainly from Cyprus but are also known elsewhere (Catling 1964:78-9, Pl. 3 a-d; Cape Gelidonya: Bass 1967:94, Fig. 107; Anthedon: Spyropoulos 1972:52). These pieces have a split tubular socket and splaying blade; they too were used as shovels, not spades, no doubt because of the unsuitability of Aegean soils for digging. The wide blades of these pieces would make pushing into the ground extremely hard (Fig. 1). A similar function can thus be suggested for our first group of implements, spades and shovels, in both southern and northern areas, even though the materials used were different. Few implements survive, and it cannot be ruled out that the digging spade was used, especially in areas with damper soils; but at present we have no evidence for its use before the Roman period.

The second group, mattocks and hoes, relates to another and more important form of tillage: breaking up the soil by quick blows from a narrow-bladed instrument. In the Aegean, to judge by the quantity of surviving pieces, this was numerically the commonest form, though some of the objects included here may have been plough-shares. Others were undoubtedly used as mattocks (those with hammered or cast tubular socket and transverse blade) or in some other way. The best Aegean series of hoes comes from Cape Gelidonya (Bass 1967:88ff.) where seven types were distinguished, corresponding in the main to those known from Cyprus and the Greek mainland (Catling 1964:79-82). I have included in this group Catling's type C, which he interprets as a plough-share. Most of these pieces have simple, more or less pointed, flattish blades, and roughly hammered sockets (Fig. 2, 1); they were cast in the shape of a squat T and hammered round. Catling's tool types B, C and D show varieties of what is essentially the same implement – broad and splaying, medium and straight, narrow and pointed – and it is likely that all three were used for breaking the ground, though the widest (type B, Fig. 1, 2) may be a shovel. The narrow variety, the pick, would be used for very hard earth (this type was also well represented at Cape Gelidonya), the wide variety for well-tilled soil and so on.

Outside the Aegean, there is a marked lack of tools of this kind – that is to say, tools that were *obviously* hoes. The main exception to this is in the Ukraine: Tallgren (1926) listed 28 in the area nearly fifty years ago, and the number has probably increased greatly since then. In

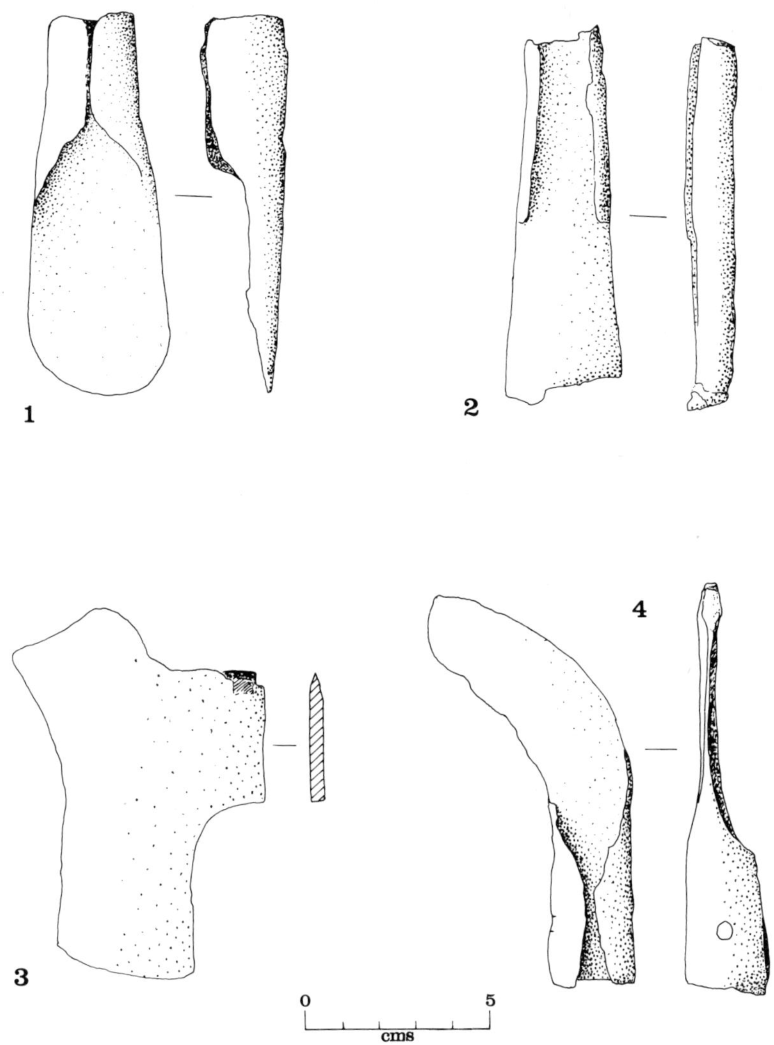

Figure 2. Implements from the Enkomi Founder's Hoard (BM).

general, the types are similar to those known in the Aegean area. The shaft-hole mattock (with the blade set at an acute angle to the shaft) is, according to Deshayes (1960: II, 95ff.), a Near Eastern form, and so may be disregarded here. It does show, however, the angle at which our split-socket hoes were probably mounted.

In Italy, a group of socketed bronze objects from a hoard found between Manciano and Samprugnano in 1885 are interpreted by Peroni as small hoes or shovels (*palettine*): they have a short squat body with a stout socket and rounded blade (*Inv. Arch.* I.5, 10, nos. 7-49). The sides of the implements are reinforced, so that only the blade itself is sharp. These are too small to have been spades; a use as hoes is much more likely. Peroni quotes possible parallels from the Larnaud hoard (Chantre 1875-6:126 ff., Pl. XLVI, 6) and the Stockheim hoard (Müller-Karpe 1959: Pl. 157, 10). In Britain, a socketed object from a hoard of doubtful homogeneity at Hawkstone, Weston, Shropshire, may also be a hoe or pick (*Nat. Index Brz. Impl.*, Fig. 5, 2). In general, however, such tools are extremely rare in continental and western Europe. How, then, did the farmers of the Bronze Age break up their soil?

The complementary process to breaking the ground is reaping, and this demands another tool, the sickle. It is in this category that we have the largest body of evidence: bronze sickles are known from all parts of Europe, and in considerable quantities. They also come in several varieties, and we may first inspect these.

Though both tanged and socketed sickles are known in Cyprus, the former is the standard Aegean form, and Catling thought the socketed type was a local Cypriot development (Fig. 2, 4). The fullest discussion of Aegean sickles is by Spyropoulos (1972:98ff.): his list supplements those of Deshayes (1960:II, 147ff.) and Catling 1964:83-5). Most of these sickles have a simple flat tang, riveted, and a slightly curving blade: it is this that distinguishes them from knives. There is no evidence about the angle of hafting, and one wonders whether they were not mounted at right-angles, in the manner of 'European' sickles, so that the cutting edge could be pulled towards the body, rather than used as a slashing instrument (see Steensberg 1943:14).

In continental Europe three main forms of sickle are found: in the east, with a distribution extending far into Asia, the hook sickle (*Hakensichel; faucille à crochet*; Fig. 3, 1); and in most other parts of Europe the knob or rivet sickle (*Knopfsichel* and *Lochsichel; faucille à bouton*) and the tanged sickle (*Zungensichel; faucille à languette*). In the north-west, especially in Britain, the socketed type is also found (Fig. 6, 2), and other distinctive local types are known in different areas.

In addition to these main sickle types, there are also implements best described as bill-hooks. In Cyprus these may be socketed or tanged (Catling 1964:85); in Syria (Deshayes 1960: II, Pl. XLVII, 12, no. 2865) and Europe (Müller-Karpe 1959: Pl. 171, B1, from Winterlingen), they are tanged. This tool is most plausibly seen as for pruning trees or vines, and similar implements may be found in use for the purpose today. The most distinctive feature is the strongly reinforced back, often with a wide projection. The example from Enkomi (Fig. 2, 3) is completely flat; its only sharp edge is at the top of the projection. It is not, therefore, similar to Catling's other example, from Mathiati, which is socketed; but like the example in negative on the Mathiati mould, the tang would probably have been hammered out and rolled over into a socket (Catling 1964:85; 272-3; Pl. 50b).

It is noticeable that the scythe was not used in any part of Europe before the Iron Age. Its introduction must have led to a revolution in harvesting: the experiments of Steensberg (1943:20ff.) showed how much faster reaping can be carried out with a scythe than with a sickle. Nor were our Bronze Age sickles, it seems, used like modern sickles, for slashing the standing corn; the curvature of many of the tanged sickles is too great for a slashing blow to be delivered comfortably, and the blade could not be kept sufficiently sharp for its effective use in this manner. They were used rather for hacking at the stems of a clump of straws held in the left hand. My own experiments with these implements, however, made me think that the slashing technique could have been used in some cases, for hay if not for corn.

I mentioned above the three main types of Bronze Age sickle; it is clear from the association of all three in Hungarian and other hoards that they were all contemporaneous, and that they did not, therefore, have the same function. Two of these types, with the addition of a fourth, the socketed, are also known from Britain (Fig. 6), though not in direct association; of particular interest is the tanged variety, rare in Britain, and known from an example from the Thames at Taplow (*B.M. Bronze Age Guide* 1920: Fig. 47; Fox 1941:157, no. 2) and two others from the same area. In different parts of Europe, then, we have similar groups of different types of sickle, and it is legitimate to infer from this that two or three different reaping processes are involved, though we cannot identify them with any certainty. No account has been taken here of differing type distributions, for which much detailed information will be necessary – not only on the bronzes themselves, but also on production and mining centres, soil and vegetation types, and so on. The forthcoming volume in the *Prähistorische Bronzefunde* series on Romanian sickles by Petrescu-Dimbovita may provide us with a chance to carry out an analysis of this sort.

If we now endeavour to reconstruct the set of agricultural tools that a Bronze Age farmer would have needed, we may do so fairly easily for the Aegean (Figs. 1-2) and for south Russia (Fig. 3). Each 'kit' is intended to include a shovel or spade; a mattock or hoe; and a sickle and/or bill-hook. More tentative would be our reconstruction of the Italian set; and when we come to continental Europe, we reach an impasse. There are sickles galore, but very few hoes.

I suggest that it is inconceivable that the farmer would not have had tools for breaking the ground other than the plough, which is

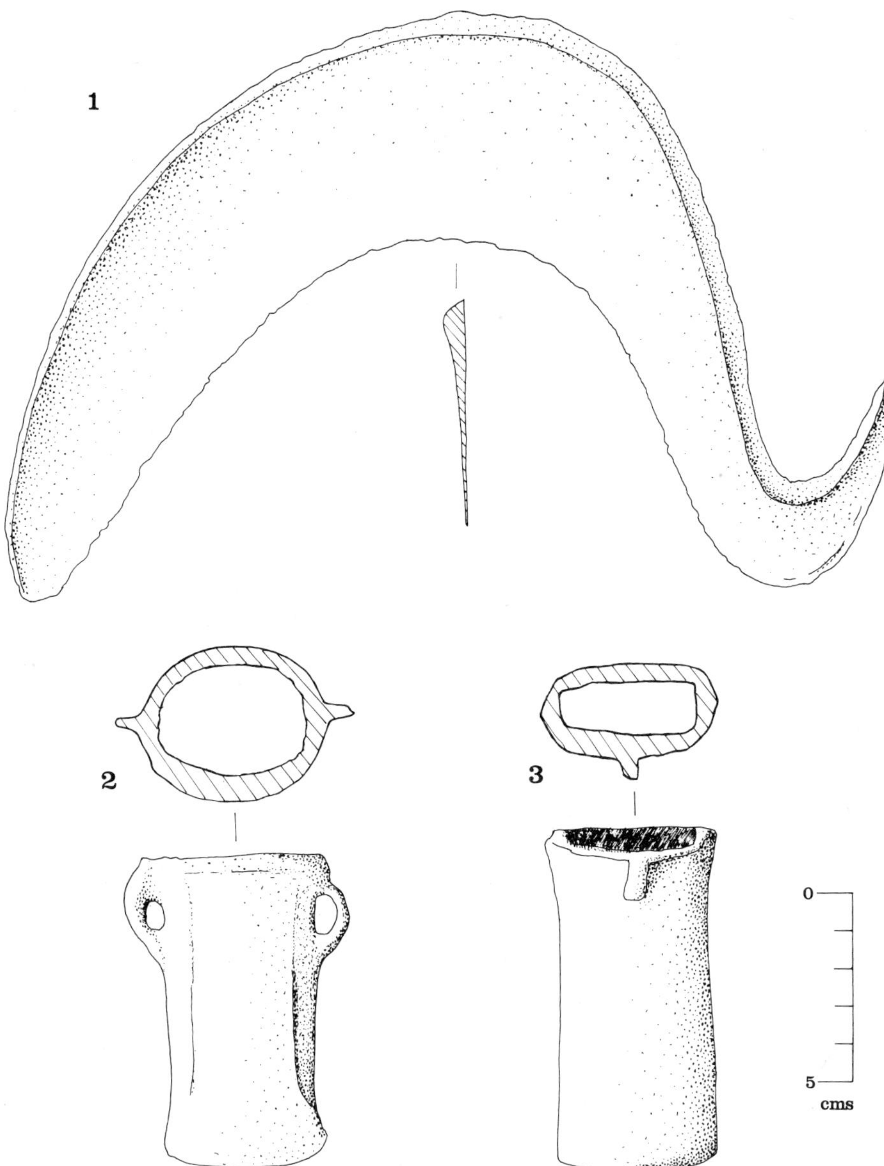

Figure 3. Agricultural Implements from Eastern Europe. 1: Hooked sickle, Transylvania; 2-3: Socketed axes, south Russia. (BM).

attested even before the Bronze Age. It would follow from this hypothesis that either such tools have not survived, or that they have survived but have not been recognized for what they are. If the latter is the case, which element of the bronze hoards that we possess would they be? They should be numerous, strong, and have a cutting edge that is not so wide that a significant penetration of the earth cannot be achieved. The only objects that can begin to fulfil such requirements are axes – flat axes, flanged axes, palstaves, socketed axes and winged axes.

These implements have traditionally been associated with carpentry and tree-felling. But were such huge quantities of axes really necessary for carpentry in the Late Bronze Age, and were there still so many trees that needed felling for the continuance of agriculture after two thousand years or more? The socketed axe is much the most frequent element in, at any rate, British Late Bronze Age hoards, outnumbering other types by as much as ten or more to one, and a similar situation obtained with palstaves in the Middle Bronze Age. If carpentry was so important, why are there not more of the obvious carpentry tools – chisels, gouges and, especially, saws? It would be foolish to suggest that axes were never used by the woodman and carpenter, but they were surely more versatile than has hitherto been supposed and formed, among other things, a major part of the farmer's tool-kit, being used for breaking the ground. Does this theory bear investigation?

In the first place, it would have been necessary to mount the axes 'adze-wise', i.e. with the cutting edge at right-angles to the line of the hafting. This alone causes difficulty: all previous reconstructions have hafted these axes 'axe-wise' (e.g. Evans 1881:155, Fig. 186) and the presence of a single loop on the side of most socketed axes, many palstaves, and all winged axes, suggests that a symmetrical hafting of this nature may be correct. Indeed, some axes, like the example quoted, were said to have been found hafted in this manner. The purpose of the loop is then to prevent the haft from splitting when a mis-hit blow caused the axe to move upwards, by lashing a cord from loop to handle. Supposing, however, the axe was mounted adze-wise, the loop and cord could either be a means of preventing the axe from becoming lost in the ground when it was wedged there particularly tightly, or else simply a safety device to prevent the axe from flying off its hafting.

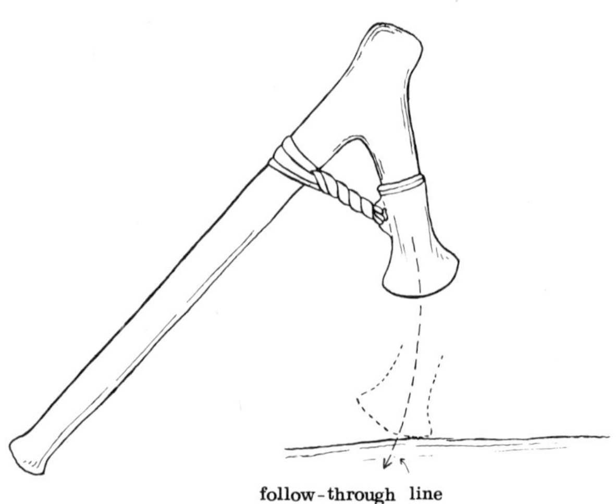

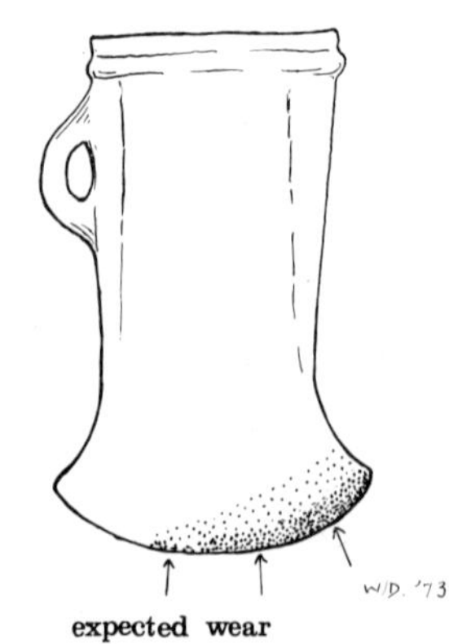

Figure 4. Diagram illustrating expected wear patterns on a socketed axe mounted axe-wise.

There are, in addition, two arguments in favour of an adze-wise rather than an axe-wise hafting. In the first place, one would expect uneven wear on the axe-blade – more wear on the far side (opposite the loop) than the near side, because of the line of follow-through – if it had been mounted axe-wise (Fig. 4). Wear of this sort is, indeed, found on some axes, but so is wear on the edge *nearest* the loop, and yet another group, though obviously used, have symmetrical wear or none at all. The latter group were presumably mounted adze-wise. Secondly, in the case of double-looped axes – as known from Spain and south Russia and, less commonly, elsewhere (Tallgren 1926:183ff.; Evans 1881:142-3) – and axes with the loop on the face, not the side (Fig. 3), there can be little doubt that an adze-wise hafting is required if symmetry is to be preserved. It may be, of course, that only those axes with symmetrical loops were hafted adze-wise; but, surely, if *some* axes were mounted in this way, others may have been. One should remember, too, that very many palstaves have no loop at all, so that there are no intrinsic reasons for supposing that the objects were mounted one way rather than the other.

It is in any case possible that axes could have been used for tillage mounted axe-wise: Kramer (1966: Fig. 3) shows a socket-hafted hoe of the Mossi in the Sudan mounted in this way. It would clearly be possible to break the ground with an axe, though one would presumably have to work in a sideways fashion rather than by proceeding backwards or forwards.

Deshayes, it is worth noting (1960: I, 133ff.; II, 64-5), refers to tools like socketed axes as *outils à tranchant transversale et douille moulée.* One would certainly not want to insist on an adze-wise mounting in every case, or even a majority of cases; the suggestion is simply that some axes – particularly those with straight blades – were mounted and used in this way. The great variety in size, shape and decorative

Table 1 Bronze hoards containing sickles

Province	*References (see Appendix)*	*Hoards with sickles*	*Hoards without axes*	*Sichelhorte*
Ukraine	1, 2 etc.	45 (-3)*	6	4
Romania	3, 4, 5, 6	46 (-12)	5	3
Bulgaria	7	3	2	1
Jugoslavia	4, 8, 10	54	7	1
Hungary	3-6 & 9-12	131 (-54)	6 (?)	1 (?)
Slovakia	4, 13	36	4	1
Moravia	14, 15 etc.	20	3	1
Austria	10, 16 etc.	22	3	1
Bohemia	6, 15, 17, 18	46	8 (?)	0 (?)
Denmark	19	35	16	0
N. Germany/ Poland	3, 20	74 (-1)	24	?
C. Germany	6 etc.	80 (-4)	37	20
S. Germany	10 & 21-23	117 (-8)	44	16
Italy	3, 10, 24	18 (-5)	9	0
France	3 & 25-28	66 (-5)	9	1
Britain	3, 28	28	5	0
Total		821	188	50

* Minus figures in brackets indicate the number of hoards whose associations are not known to me.

treatment on these tools makes it clear that, in any case, they performed a variety of functions and, further, that different axe types were used for different purposes: why else would socketed axes and palstaves, or socketed and winged axes, be current at the same time?

Further light is shed on the subject by examination of the associations of these pieces in bronze hoards. Table 1 provides some statistics, albeit in crude form, concerning the occurrence of sickles in European hoards. In the third column are the total numbers of hoards or other associated finds containing sickles; in the fourth, finds of this type that did *not* also contain axes in some form. Sickles are agricultural tools, beyond dispute; a definite association with axes would speak for a similar attribution for that type also. The figures are based on a search of the most accessible syntheses for each area, and are not intended to be in any way exhaustive: the degree of completeness varies from very low (S. Russia; N. Germany) to quite high (Slovakia; Britain). In addition, the associations of many finds are not mentioned in the publications consulted, so that the figures in the 'without axes' column are correspondingly vague. In the last column are listed those hoards that consisted, mainly or entirely, of sickles (either a small number, all sickles, or a larger number of sickles with some other pieces as well): these are von Brunn's *Sichelhorte* (1958:56ff.; 1968:218ff.) and some of them may be subtracted from the 'without axes' totals because a hoard that contains nothing but sickles, even though not associated with axes, is also not associated with anything else.

The main association, other than with axes, is with ornaments. Von Brunn (1968:220-1) provides clear figures for the occurrence of sickle and ornament hoards, and in central Germany sickle finds were divided between these two types of hoard. Why they should be found together with bracelets and rings, and nothing else, is not known; yet the association is so consistent as to be significant. Cake metal was found in only a small number of cases, nor was scrap metal present: these hoards had already passed through the hands of the manufacturer. But such associations are unusual, compared with those found in the rest of Europe. In Denmark and north Germany the local variant, the *Ruckenzapfensichel*, is often found in graves of periods IV and V as well as in hoards (less frequently), without axes. But elsewhere the figures in Table 1 point unequivocally to an association between the two types (though not, of course, in reverse: only a small fraction of those hoards with axes also contain sickles). Even if we include the German and Danish finds,

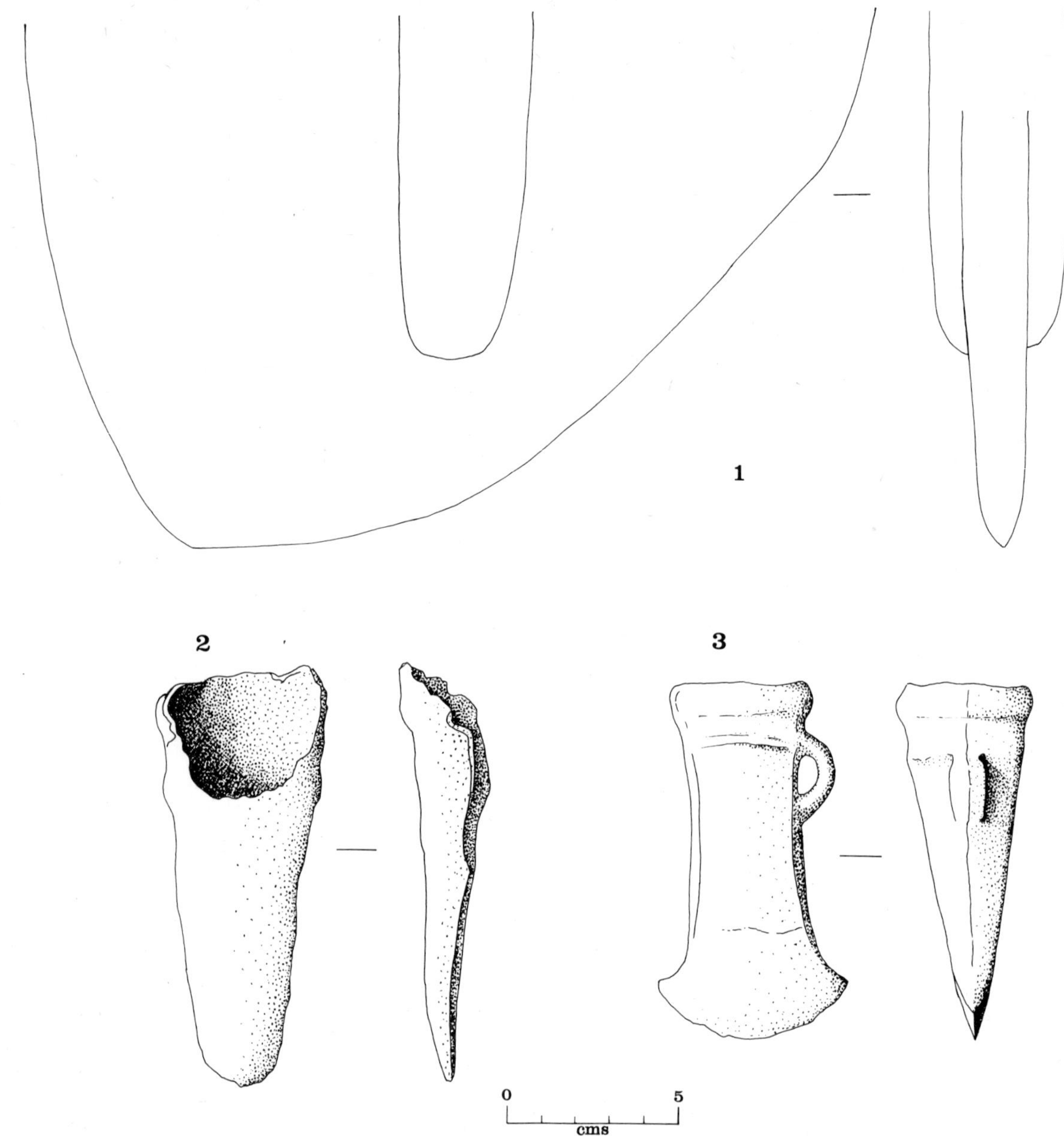

Figure 5. Agricultural implements from Britain. 1: Gwithian shovel (extrapolated reconstruction, after Thomas 1970). 2: Hawkstone, Salop (Nat. Index Br. Imps). 3: Socketed axe (BM).

well over three-quarters of the hoards with sickles also contain axes.

Now, this may be no more than a co-incidence, caused by the very fact of their being found in hoards, many of which belonged to founders and so included all the principal types of their repertoire. But certain closed finds give this theory the lie: for instance, the hoards of Nedachlebice and Syrovín in Moravia (Podborský 1970:29) and Cösitz in central Germany (Brunn 1968:312, Pl. 24) where sickles and socketed axes alone were found in a pottery vessel; Plašťovce and Plešany in Slovakia (Novotná 1970:111), Sicu in Croatia (Holste 1951: Pl. 9, 29-38) and many others, where *only* sickles and axes were found. The sum of evidence shows that this is more than a chance association. In any case, sickles are not often found in scrap hoards; the majority, certainly those found in *Sichelhorte*, are fully functional objects, sometimes not even finished.

On the basis of the available evidence, then, I

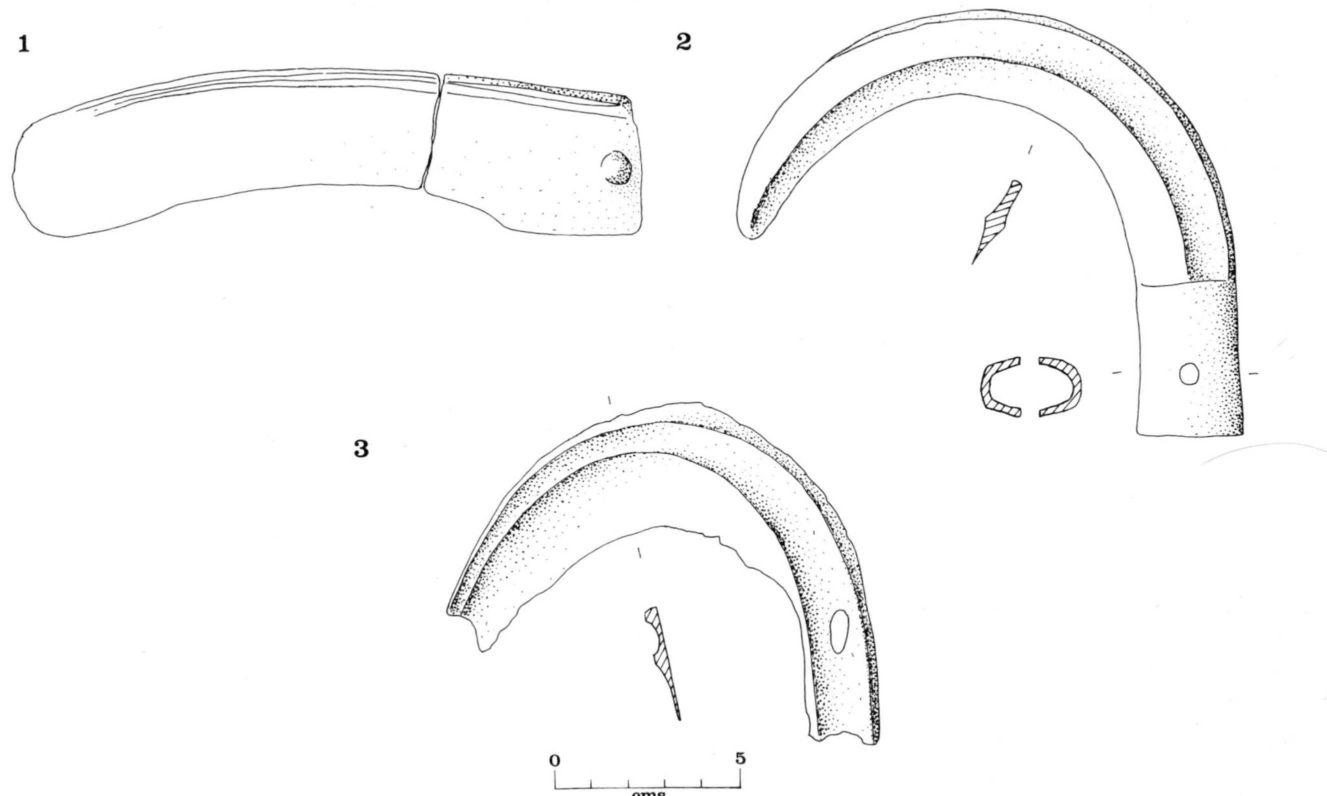

Figure 6. British Bronze Age sickles. 1: Knobbed, Minnis Bay, Kent. 2: Socketed, R. Thames at Sion Reach. 3: Tanged, R. Thames at Taplow (all BM).

propose to reconstruct the missing west European 'tool-kit' as shown in Figs. 5 and 6. Axes in one form or another – preferably with straight, not convex, cutting edge – provide the necessary implement for soil-cultivation, while spades like that from Gwithian, and sickles of various types, form the other components. This suggestion will inevitably be challenged, but I feel it is worth making, if only to provoke reaction and thereby stimulate thought. The absence of hoe-like implements is a large gap in an otherwise well-filled dossier; but the soil must have been tilled somehow.

The basic agricultural tool-kits, then, as reconstructed in Figs. 1-3 and Figs. 5-6, were probably similar in composition in every area of prehistoric Europe. Differing emphasis on stock-raising and crop-growing would naturally influence the forms and relative quantities of each of the types concerned, but each main type is consistently represented. I have tried to reconcile the absence of hoes with the embarrassing quantity of axes; the abundance of sickles must speak for the importance of crop-growing and, for this, Bronze Age farmers would have needed also an abundance of tilling implements.

Acknowledgments

I should like to thank the following for much help and advice in the preparation, and comments on an earlier draft, of this paper: J. Bouzek, C. Burgess, H.W. Catling, D.G. Coombs, I.H. Longworth and G. de G. Sieveking. Fig. 1 (1) was kindly provided by A.G. Sherratt; parts of Fig. 3, 5 and 6 by Mrs K. Hughes (courtesy British Museum); and Fig. 4 by W. Dodds.

Appendix: References for Table 1, p. 519

1. Tallgren 1926.
2. Bernjakovič, K. (1960) Bronzezeitliche Hortfunde vom rechen Ufergebiet des oberen Theisstales (Karpatoukraine, U.S.S.R.). *Slovenská Archeológia* 8: 325-92.
3. *Inventaria Archaeologica* by countries.
4. Holste 1951.
5. Hänsel, B. (1968) *Beiträge zur Chronologie der Mittleren Bronzezeit im Karpatenbeckens.* Bonn.
6. Brunn 1968.
7. Mikov, V. (1933) *Predistoričeski selišča i nachodki v B'lgarija.* Sofia.
8. Vinski, Z. and Vinski-Gasparini, K. (1956) Prolegomena k statistici i Kronologiji prethistorijskih ostava u Hrvatskoj i u vojvodanskom prodručju Srijema. *Opuscula Archaeologica* 1: 57-109.
9. Hampel, J. (1886-96) *A Bronzkor emlékei Magyarhonban.* Budapest.
10. Müller-Karpe 1959.
11. Mozsolics, A. (1967) *Bronzefunde des Karpatenbeckens.* Budapest.
12. Pátek, E. (1968) *Die Urnenfelderkultur in Transdanubien.* Budapest.
13. Novotná 1970.
14. Podborský 1970.
15. Kytlicová, O. (1964) *Archeologické rozhledy* 16: 516-56.
16. Pittioni, R. (1954) *Urgeschichte des österreichischen Raumes.* Wien.
17. Richlý, H. (1893) *Die Bronzezeit in Böhmen.* Wien.
18. Plesl, E. (1961) *Lužická kultura v severozápadních Čechách.* Praha.
19. Broholm, H.C. (1946) *Danmarks Bronzealder* vol. III. København.
20. Sprockhoff, E. (1956) *Jungbronzezeitliche Hortfunde* . . . Mainz.
21. Torbrugge, W. (1959) *Die Bronzezeit in der Oberpfalz.* Kalmünz, Opf.
22. Behrens, G. (1916) *Bronzezeit Süddeutschlands.* Mainz.
23. Hennig, H. (1970) *Die Grab- und Hortfunde der Urnenfelderkultur aus Ober- und Mittelfranken.* Kalmünz, Opf.
24. Säflund, G. (1939) Le Terremare . . . Leipzig.
25. Briard, J. (1965) *Les Depôts Bretons et l'âge du bronze atlantique.* Rennes.
26. Sandars, N. (1957) *Bronze Age Cultures in France.* London.
27. Déchelette, J. (1928) *Manuel d'archéologie préhistorique* . . . vol. II: Appx. I. Paris.
28. Coombs, D.G. (1971) *Late Bronze Age Metalwork in the South of England* vol. IV. (Unpublished dissertation, university of Cambridge.)

REFERENCES

Bass, G. (1967) Cape Gelidonya: a Bronze Age shipwreck. *Trans. Amer. Phil. Soc.*, n.s. 57, part 8.

Brunn, W.A. von (1958) Der Schatz von Frankleben und die mitteldeutschen Sichelfunde. *Praehistorische Zeitschrift*, 36, 1-70.

Brunn, W.A. von (1968) *Mitteldeutsche Hortfunde der jüngeren Bronzezeit.* Berlin.

Catling, H.W. (1964) *Cypriot Bronzework in the Mycenaean World.* Oxford.

Chantre, E. (1875-6) *Études paléoethniques dans le bassin du Rhône, Âge du Bronze.*

Clark, J.G.D. (1952) *Prehistoric Europe: the Economic Basis.* London.

Darbishire, R.D. (1874) Notes on Discoveries in Ehenside Tarn, Cumberland. *Archaeologia* 44, 273-92.

Deshayes, J. (1960) *Les Outils de bronze de l'Indus au Danube* (2 vol.) Paris.

Evans, Sir J. (1881) *Ancient Bronze Implements.* London.

Fox, Sir C. (1941) The Non-socketed Bronze sickles of Britain. *Arch. Camb.* 46, 273-92.

Holste, F. (1940) Frühbronzezeitliche Sicheln aus Süddeutschland. *Germania* 24, 6-11.

Holste, F. (1951) *Hortfunde Südosteuropas.* Marburg – Lahn.

Keller, F. (1866) *The Lake Dwellings of Switzerland.* London.

Kramer, F.L. (1966) *Breaking Ground.* Sacramento.

Müller-Karpe, H. (1959) *Beiträge zur Chronologie der Urnenfelderzeit nördlich und südlich der Alpen.* Berlin.

Novotná, M. (1970) *Die Bronzehortfunde in der Slowakei.* Bratislava.

Petrie, Sir W.M.F. (1917) *Tools and Weapons.* London.

Podborský, V. (1970) *Mähren in der Spätbronzezeit und an der Schwelle der Eisenzeit.* Brno.

Spyropoulos, Th. (1972) *Hysteromykenaikoi Helladikoi Thesauroi.* Athens.

Steensberg, A. (1943) *Ancient Harvesting Implements. A study in archaeology and human geography* (Nationalmuseets Skrifter, Ark.-Hist. Raekke no. 1). København.

Tallgren, A.M. (1926) La Pontide Préscythique après l'introduction des métaux. *Eurasia Septentrionalis Antiqua* II.

Thomas, C. (1970) Bronze Age Spade Marks at Gwithian, Cornwall. In Gailey, A. and Fenton A. (eds.), *The Spade in Northern and Atlantic Europe*, 10-17. Belfast.

White, K.D. (1967) *Agricultural Implements of the Roman World.* London.

NOTES

1. Clark 1952:104 – the ancient fields of Jutland were first marked out by digging (presumably with spades); 110-11 for sickles and their hafting.

2. Dr Ian Longworth tells me that Professor Steensberg believes the 'paddle' from Ehenside Tarn (Darbishire 1874:289, no. 26) was a spade. It is illustrated in the B.M. Guide, *Later Prehistoric Antiquities of the British Isles* (1953), 11-2, Fig. 2, no. 4.

MICHAEL JARMAN

Prehistoric economic development in sub-Alpine Italy

The work of Grahame Clark as a pioneer in the study of prehistoric economies is too well known to require elaborate mention here. Since the publication of *Prehistoric Europe: The Economic Basis*, his has been a primary influence promoting the consideration of economic data as a vital aspect of prehistoric studies. As these interests develop it is becoming increasingly evident that they can offer more to archaeology than a purely narrative description of the 'way of life' of prehistoric communities and appendices full of sterile statistical information.

What is now emerging is that the study of palaeoeconomy can identify for us some of the factors that were of long-term importance in the regulation of human development, and it can thus help us to analyse mechanisms of change in a way that goes beyond the narrative concerns of culture-history and palaeoethnography. A primary quality of any science is the search for regularities or 'laws' and, if it is to be possible to develop a scientific study of past human behaviour, an effort must be made to augment the archaeological concern for the particular and the individual with a conscious search for long-term trends and regularities that transcend the fluctuations of historical or anthropological 'noise'.

This paper studies the economic exploitation of a series of sites in sub-Alpine Italy and uses these analyses of individual sites as a basis for an interpretation of the nature of prehistoric economic development in this area. The sites concerned are all in the area bounded on the south by the northern margin of the Po plain, by the Lago di Garda on the west, the latitude of Trento on the north, and the Berici Hills on the east (Fig. 1). Molino Casarotto (Barfield 1972)[1] is a lakeside settlement in the Berici Hills, where excavation has yielded remains of a number of pile-structures and abundant Neolithic early *Bocca Quadrata* pottery. Rivoli (Barfield 1972) is a hill-top site in the Adige valley north of Verona. There are several phases of occupation, but most of the pottery is of late *Bocca Quadrata* type, and only material of that age is considered in this paper. Isera (Barfield 1972), in the Adige valley to the north of Rivoli, is a late Neolithic site. Monte Tondo (Broglio 1968) is an early-to-middle Bronze Age hill-top site in the Berici Hills. Torri (Aspes & Fasani 1969) is also in the Berici Hills, on a hill-top overlooking the Fimon lake basin. The site contains middle and late Bronze Age pottery. Fondo Tomollero (unpublished) is a lakeside settlement in the Fimon lake basin (Berici Hills), with middle-to-late Bronze Age pottery. Fiavè (Perini 1971), the most northerly of the sites dealt with here, is north of Lago di Garda and west of Trento. The site, at over 600 metres, is a lakeside settlement primarily of Middle Bronze Age date.

With the growing interest in osteoarchaeology, much has been written recently on the problems of analysis and interpretation of prehistoric faunas (Chaplin 1971; Payne 1972; Uerpmann 1973). A particularly contentious point has been the way in which the relative proportions of different species should be calculated, but the view taken here is that none of the available techniques can be considered ideal, and that they share a disadvantage in that they give an illusion of precision that the nature of the archaeological data will not support. In this paper, total numbers of identified bones are given for each species as one index of relative importance, a second table giving the numbers of a variety of anatomical elements attributable to the primary species. This provides a rough check that the relative proportions of species are not being grossly distorted by factors such as the presence of disproportionate numbers of antler-fragments of deer, or the absence of small bones such as the distal phalanges or the carpal bones of the caprines. It also supplies a reminder that our data can only deal realistically with major differences and changes, and not with minor variations.

A category of information much used for

1. See also Bagolini, Barfield & Brogli 1973.

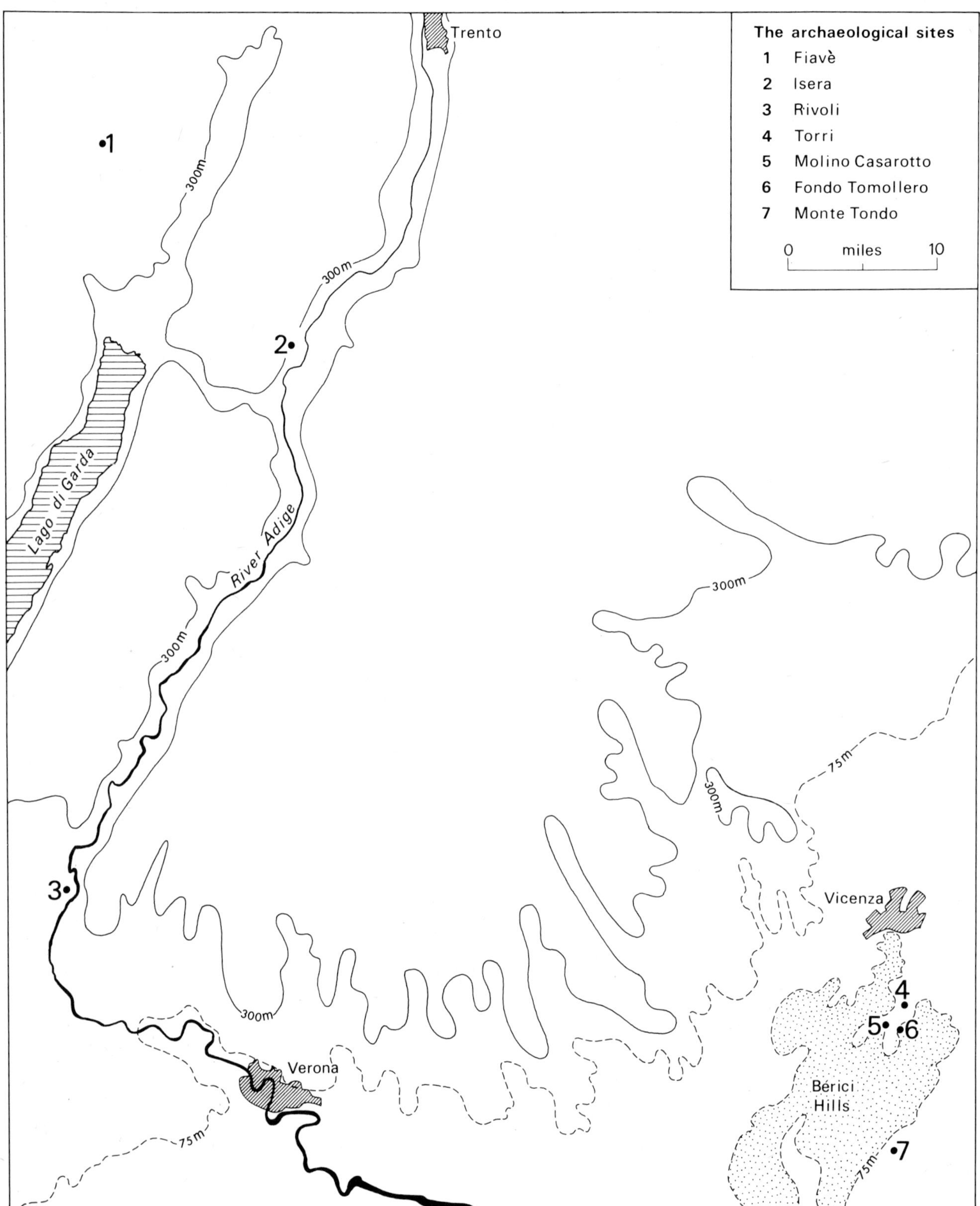

Figure 1. Map showing the area and sites discussed in the paper.

palaeoeconomic studies is the cropping pattern of the exploited species. Given a large and well preserved collection, it can be possible to age a sufficient number of specimens fairly accurately and thus to build up a mortality curve. When one is dealing with relatively small and fragmented collections, as with most of those considered in this paper, one is faced with a large number of specimens that can only be aged to within very broad limits, which is of little use for economic interpretation. Consequently, two tables have been calculated for each sample: one giving the percentage of animals certainly alive at a given age, the other giving the percentage of animals certainly dead at a given age. Thus, a specimen known to have died when between 18 and 60 months old would be registered as certainly alive until 18 months, and certainly dead after 60 months.

The botanical collections were made by the use of froth-flotation equipment (Jarman, Legge & Charles 1972) at the sites where this was possible. I am grateful to H.N. Jarman for all preliminary studies of the plants, and to the excavators of the sites, and their sponsoring institutions, for making available to me the data on which this paper is based.

Molino Casarotto

The economic bases at Molino Casarotto were red deer and pig, as far as animal protein was concerned, with water-chestnuts providing the bulk of the plant food. As can be seen from Table 1, a variety of other animal species is present, but among those only roe deer exceeds *c.* 1% of the total number of bones identified. Table 2 indicates that the proportions of the main animals seen in Table 1 are broadly similar for a number of different anatomical elements, and that the different parts of the body are present in approximately the ratio found in the living animal. The apparent over-representation of red deer metapodia is probably due to these bones being easy to recognize, even when split into small fragments, and the apparent under-representation of third molars is at least partly due to their absence in young animals.

Table 1 Species representation at Molino Casarotto (the figures in parentheses concern specimens tentatively referred to the taxon in question)

Species	*Number*		%
Cervus elaphus	2947	(166)	49.8
Sus scrofa	2285	(61)	37.5
Capreolus capreolus	275	(41)	5.0
Bos taurus	52	(2)	
Ovis/Capra	24	(3)	
Ovis	3	(1)	
Large Artiodactyla	8		1.8
Small Artiodactyla	17		
Equus caballus	1	(2)	
Vulpes vulpes	1		
Meles meles	59	(6)	
Canidae	1		1.8
Carnivora indet.	42	(6)	
Castor fiber	4		
Rodentia indet.	3		0.1
Lagomorpha indet.	2		
Anura indet.		(2)	
Emys sp.	14	(2)	
Chelonia indet.	3	(1)	3.9
Pisces	206	(1)	
Aves	11	(2)	
Total	6254		99.9

The fish bones have yet to be fully studied, but they certainly include pike. It does not appear that fish were an important resource, in spite of the lakeside situation of the site. While it is possible that they were exploited from an adjacent site, the fish not being brought to Molino Casarotto, there is no evidence to support such a hypothesis, and the excavated material does not suggest any concentration

Table 2 Numbers of selected anatomical elements from the main species at Molino Casarotto (only the medial metapodia of *Sus* have been included)

	Humerus	*Radius*	*Femur*	*Tibia*	*Meta-podia*	*Upper third molar*	*Lower third molar*
C. elaphus	85	115	113	134	487	36	42
Sus scrofa	123	73	85	100	234	40	44
C. capreolus	14	19	10	27	45	6	8
Bos taurus	—	1	—	—	3	3	3
Ovis/Capra	3	3	—	5	4	3	—

upon fishing. Nor can it be argued that the absence of fish bones is due to failure in preservation or retrieval, as bone is well preserved at the site, and excavation and collection of bone were done with care. Apart from the fish, the exploitation of lacustrine resources is indicated by the water-chestnuts and the presence on the site of freshwater mussels. The large hearth, which was one of the main features of the site, incorporated a midden that comprised alternate layers of freshwater mussel shells and water-chestnut shells. In spite of the large number of shells, if one takes into account the quantity of mussels required to produce the nutritional equivalent of a single large mammal such as a red deer, it seems unlikely that they were more than a casual source of food.

Among the plant remains, water-chestnuts were overwhelmingly the most important food plant. Hazel-nuts and grape-pips occurred sporadically, and wheat in very small quantities.

The red deer

As we have seen, red deer was one of the two staple meat crops exploited and, taking into account the meat yield of the food species involved, probably provided in the order of half the animal protein intake.

It is becoming evident (Jarman 1972a) that the red deer was a species of great economic importance for many millennia in much of Europe, and that it was, at least on occasion, exploited in a controlled and sophisticated fashion. At Molino Casarotto, the importance of deer as a staple food makes it likely that their exploitation was more complex than a random process of hunting, and there is some evidence to support this suggestion. Most of the red deer killed were immature or young mature individuals (Table 3), at least 50% being three years old or younger when killed. At least 21% were fawns, of which more than half were new-born and could have been at the most a few weeks old, as they had incompletely erupted or unworn deciduous premolars. By contrast there are very few old, and no senile individuals at all, in the sample. A maximum of 1% could have been older than ten years; only one individual certainly survived this age. It is not satisfactory to make a simple equation between the presence of a high proportion of young individuals and the exploitation of a domestic animal (Jarman & Wilkinson 1972); but where, as at Molino Casarotto, an age-biased sample is being extracted to an economic advantage, one may be justified in inferring the existence of a close or controlled exploitative relationship. The advantages of cropping the young heavily, and still maintaining a primarily young herd, have been pointed out elsewhere (Jarman 1972a).

Table 3 Cropping pattern of red deer at Molino Casarotto

Age in years	*Cumulative percentage certainly dead*	*Cumulative percentage certainly alive*
0	–	100.0
1	21.0	68.5
2	38.1	51.6
3	46.7	44.4
4	50.2	38.1
5	56.9	15.0
6	60.8	8.8
7	65.9	1.8
8	65.9	0.5
9	95.7	0.2
10	95.7	0.2
11	98.9	0.2
12	98.9	–
13	99.1	–
14	99.6	–
15	99.6	–
16	100.0	–
Number	433	433

It is probable that at Molino Casarotto, as at other sites such as Seeberg Burgäschisee-Sud (Jarman 1972a), a high percentage of males were killed, more of the females being conserved for breeding. It has not been possible, so far, to calculate the sex-ratio of the deer crop at Molino Casarotto on the basis of the available bones, so there is as yet no numerical confirmation of this hypothesis. However, about 7% of all the red-deer specimens were pieces of antler, indicating at least a substantial presence of males in the crop, and while antler was in use as a raw material, there is little indication of its special collection for industrial purposes. Furthermore, wherever the sex-ratio of the deer crop has been ascertained at sites where they form a staple resource, there is shown to have been a preferential exploitation of males.

The pigs

The second primary source of animal protein at

Table 4 Frequency table of lengths in m.m. of pig third molars

	33.0-33.9	34.0-34.9	35.0-35.9	36.0-36.9	37.0-37.9	38.0-38.9	39.0-39.9	40.0-40.9	41.0-41.9	42.0-42.9	43.0-43.9	44.0-44.9	45.0-45.9	46.0-46.9	47.0-47.9	48.0-48.9
Upper third molar	3	2	2	6	4	8	9	1	1	1	1	—	—	—	—	—
Lower third molar	—	—	4	1	5	6	4	3	5	5	—	2	4	—	—	1

Table 5 Cropping patterns of pigs

	Molino Casarotto		*Rivoli*		*Monte Tondo*		*Torri*		*Fondo Tomollero*		*Fiavè*	
Age in months	*Cumulative percentage certainly dead*	*Cumulative percentage certainly alive*	*Cumulative percentage certainly dead*	*Cumulative percentage certainly alive*	*Cumulative percentage certainly dead*	*Cumulative percentage certainly alive*	*Cumulative percentage certainly dead*	*Cumulative percentage certainly alive*	*Cumulative percentage certainly dead*	*Cumulative percentage certainly alive*	*Cumulative percentage certainly dead*	*Cumulative percentage certainly alive*
0	—	100.0	—	100.0	—	100.0	—	100.0	—	100.0	—	100.0
3	9.0	86.0	0.3	99.1	—	100.0	7.1	92.9	22.2	77.8	4.2	96.0
6	14.8	83.1	2.9	89.0	3.0	98.3	7.1	85.8	33.4	55.6	12.5	77.1
9	14.8	76.5	3.2	79.8	3.0	98.3	7.1	71.5	44.5	55.6	22.9	64.7
12	22.3	70.0	16.6	70.7	6.1	84.5	21.4	71.5	44.5	55.6	33.4	60.4
18	34.7	54.1	31.0	36.4	30.0	63.8	28.6	21.4	44.5	33.4	50.0	41.7
24	48.4	22.4	53.0	7.9	48.5	48.3	50.0	—	66.6	22.2	75.0	12.5
30	50.1	12.6	62.9	4.4	81.9	10.3	50.0	—	77.8	—	93.9	6.2
36	58.5	8.5	69.2	1.7	94.0	3.4	57.2	—	89.0	—	93.9	4.2
48	69.7	8.2	77.8	—	100.0	—	85.8	—	100.0	—	100.0	—
60	100.0	2.6	98.3	—	100.0	—	100.0	—	100.0	—	100.0	—
72	100.0	0.9	98.7	—	100.0	—	100.0	—	100.0	—	100.0	—
84	100.0	—	100.0	—	100.0	—	100.0	—	100.0	—	100.0	—
Number	311	340	342	341	33	58	14	14	9	9	48	48

Molino Casarotto was the pig, and a difficulty arises when we try to analyse the way in which it was exploited. Many European Neolithic and later faunas contain some pig-bones that are thought to come from domestic populations and others that are thought to come from wild populations. The basis for this view is the belief that wild and domestic pigs can be separated osteologically from each other on grounds of their size, and that where specimens occur which are the same size as modern wild pigs it is inferred that the prehistoric pigs were also wild, and therefore hunted. The foundation for this view is questionable, however (Higgs & Jarman 1972; Jarman & Wilkinson 1972), and while it would clearly be absurd to suggest that there were no wild pigs in the vicinity of European Neolithic sites and that none of the pigs represented in the collections could have been hunted, it is equally absurd to accept uncritically the hypothesis that all large Neolithic pigs were wild and were exploited in a completely different fashion from the smaller, domestic pigs.

At Molino Casarotto, the pigs bridge the accepted size-ranges of wild pigs and Neolithic domestic pigs from such sites as Seeberg Burgäschisee-Sud. Furthermore, there is no indication that we are dealing with two separate populations of pigs as regards size, as no strongly bi-modal tendency is apparent in the size-distribution of the bones. This is illustrated in the dimensions of the third molars (Table 4). There is a number of possible explanations of the evidence. It could be that there are two populations present, sufficiently close in size for the dichotomy to be masked; or the two groups could be blurred by the presence of feral, hybrid or 'proto-domestic' forms; or there could be but a single population present, whose size-variation encompasses part of the 'typical wild' and 'typical domestic' ranges. There is certainly no positive evidence to suggest that two different modes of pig-exploitation were in operation, and it is suggested here that the pig population was treated essentially as a single unit.

The slaughter of pigs was concentrated upon the first-year and second-year individuals. About 25% of the total kill came from first-year animals, at least a further 25% being yearlings. A few specimens came from old individuals, in their seventh year or older, but these form a negligible proportion of the crop (Table 5).

The cattle and caprines

These two groups warrant a brief mention, not because of their economic importance at Molino Casarotto but because of their importance elsewhere as economic resources, and because of their customary association with certain other traits as indicators of a 'Neolithic culture'. Judged according to the accepted zoological criteria, there is no question but that both cattle and caprines were present at Molino Casarotto in their domestic form. Measurements of the cattle teeth indicate a large animal (maximum length of lower third molar: 38.8-38.9 mm.; maximum length of upper third molar: 29.3-30.3 mm.), but considerably below the accepted size-range of *Bos primigenius*. As far as the caprines are concerned, there is no indication that either of the indigenous north Italian caprinae (*Capra ibex* and *Rupicapra rupicapra*) is involved, and the specimens thus presumably come from introduced domesticates. The measurable specimens indicate a moderate-sized animal (maximum width of distal tibia: 23.0-24.7 mm.; maximum length of calcaneum: 49.0 mm.), and all specimens allowing a distinction between sheep and goat to be made were of sheep. There are far too few data to give any adequate impression of the way in which the cattle and caprine populations were exploited, but both the cattle and the caprines seem to have been slaughtered primarily in the second, third or fourth year.

Site-location and territory

Techniques recently developed (Vita-Finzi & Higgs 1970; Jarman 1972b) for defining and studying the exploitation territory of archaeological sites have proved illuminating in the analysis of prehistoric economies. Fig. 2 shows the two-hour exploitation territory of Molino Casarotto, delimiting the area likely to have been habitually exploited from the site by a mobile economy. As can be seen, the area accessible is considerably affected by the steep slopes of the hills and the presence of the Lago di Fimon. It is difficult to ascertain accurately the extent of the lake in Neolithic times, as peat-formation and hill-wash have obscured the old land-surface. It is known, however, that the site of Molino Casarotto was on the edge of the Neolithic lake, and from this it can be inferred that, at that time, the lake was of approximately

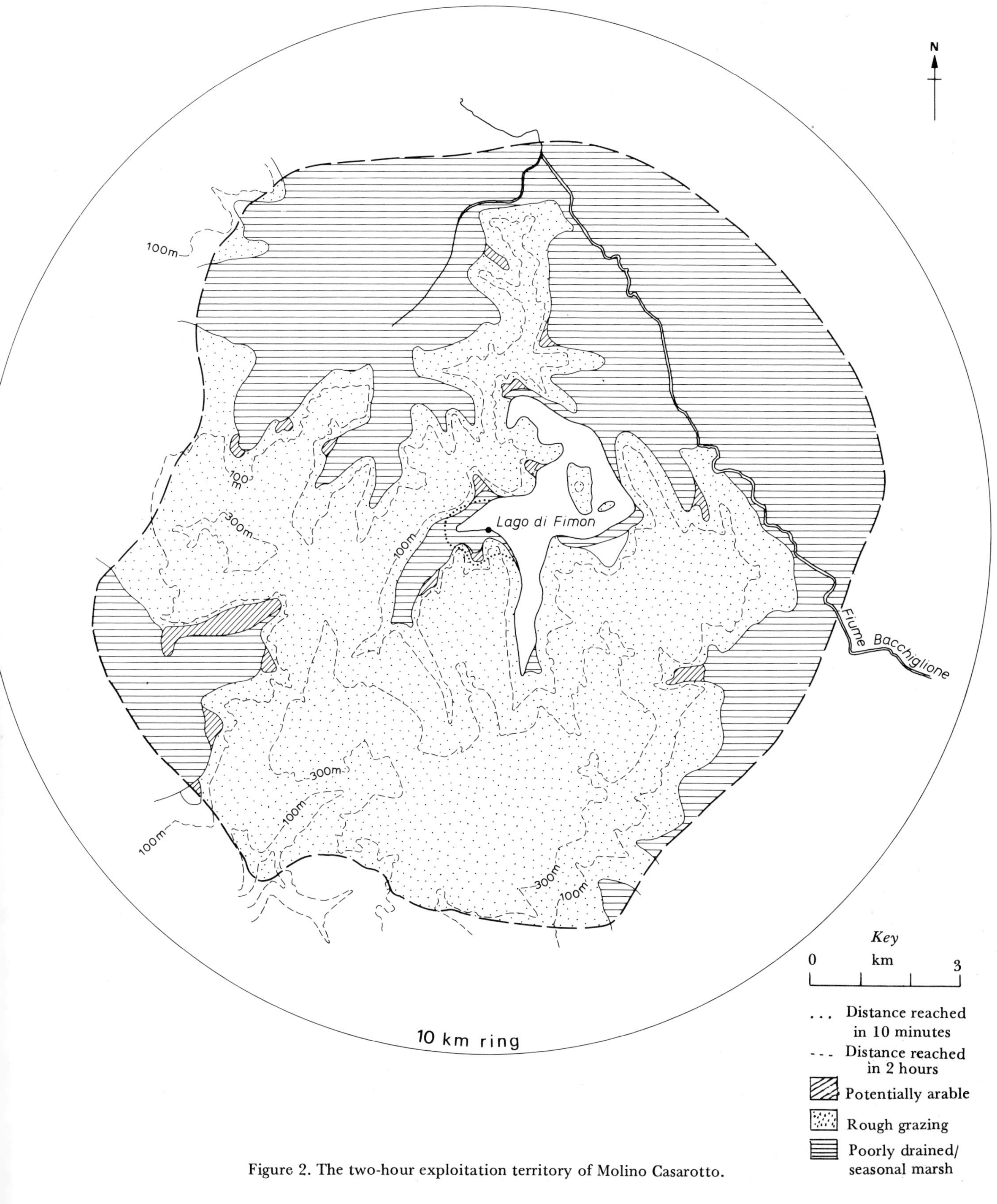

Figure 2. The two-hour exploitation territory of Molino Casarotto.

the size indicated in Fig. 2.

The Berici Hills are characterized by steep slopes and, although they rise to only modest altitudes (maximum *c.* 450 m.), the topography is complex and a considerable limiting factor upon movement. Today the steep slopes, and much of the rolling tops, of these hills are covered with thick deciduous scrub. Slope and thinness of soil are primary limiting factors in the modern exploitation of the district. The flatter areas of the hill-tops produce maize, vines and fodder crops, the steeper slopes carrying pasture and woodland. The drained valley-bottoms and lake-beds are the most productive areas, supporting intensively cultivated maize, lucerne, vines and wheat.

During the Neolithic occupation, as has been noted, the Lago di Fimon would have been considerably larger than at present, and presumably some, at least, of the other valley-bottoms would also have been marsh or open water. In addition, it can be expected that a far higher proportion of the hill-tops and slopes would have carried woodland than today, as much of the clearance is linked to the recent, and continuing, population increase. To some extent, the decrease in territory was offset by the fact that much of the area would have been mature deciduous woodland, which tends to be more open than the dense bushy scrub that has resulted from repeated modern cutting and clearance. Four primary habitats would thus be available for exploitation from the site: (1) the lake; (2) marshy lake margins (seasonal fluctuations in water-level would provide a relatively large area of seasonal marsh, apart from the belt around the summer lake level); (3) alluvial fans (these may also have provided small patches of better-drained lowland soil, as in the Val de Marca); and (4) deciduous woodland.

The economy

A possible view of the economy practised at Molino Casarotto is of a basically 'Mesolithic' economy of hunting and gathering practised by people with a 'Neolithic' material culture. This could be explained as the result either of the adaptation by Neolithic immigrants to local conditions or the acceptance by aboriginal Mesolithic people of some aspects of Neolithic culture. The presence of the 'typical Neolithic' traits of small cattle, caprines and cereals can, in this way, be referred to some unexplained process of 'acculturation'. One may wonder, however, whether this is an illuminating way in which to pose the problem.

It is quite clear why no Neolithic mixed-farming economy was in operation at the site. Almost no suitable arable soil is available in the territory; and, while minimal amounts of cereals could probably have been grown at the valley-edge on alluvial fans, the rarity of cereals in the botanical remains is entirely to be expected. The lake itself seems to have provided the only vegetable staple, the water-chestnut, which still grows today around the margins of the lake. The nutritional value of the water-chestnut is limited, but it would have contributed carbohydrate and acted as a basic filler. Equally understandable is the small importance of cattle and caprines, neither of which is at home in a heavily-wooded environment.

When we consider the two protein staples (deer and pig), we are faced with a choice of hypotheses. It can be argued that they were exploited by hunting, except for the smallest pigs which, according to the usual zoological criteria, must have been domestic. These latter could either be representative of a small local domestic population (with the bulk of the supply coming from hunted individuals), or the domestic pigs may have been imported from elsewhere. As we have noted, however, there is no evidence to support this rather complex theory, and a simpler explanation, that would also account for the available evidence, is that there was a single pig population, all exploited in essentially the same way. Given that members of this population do show an apparent size-deviation from a 'wild standard', one possible explanation of this fact is that human economic behaviour patterns may have partially caused this anomalous population. Other mechanisms could be involved (Jarman & Wilkinson 1972), but a plausible interpretation is that there was a human exploitation pattern that relied on a closer degree of control over the pig herds than formerly, perhaps coupled with attempts to maintain a high pig-population. Whatever the specific mechanisms of pig management in operation, they permitted the extraction of a predominantly young crop, a way that is encountered in many prehistoric economies of taking advantage of the very high reproductive rate of pigs.

As far as the deer are concerned, the situation is similar but simpler. It is not customary to consider deer in any other light than as a wild animal, but there are advantages in at least considering the possibility that they may have been herded. This is a hypothesis that cannot be elucidated by customary osteological techniques, but such analyses do show that the deer at Molino Casarotto were cropped in a way comparable with many 'fully domestic' herbivore populations of later date. Given their great importance to the success of the human community at Molino Casarotto, it seems most unlikely that no attempt would be made to control in some way the availability and profitability of the deer and pig populations. Furthermore the existence, in the collection, of species such as cattle and sheep that certainly required sophisticated economic manipulation, indicates that techniques of control must have been known to the human population, even if the cattle and sheep were imported from elsewhere.

A further question of some importance is the role of Molino Casarotto within the exploitation pattern of the area as a whole. Consideration of this is hampered by the scarcity of data from contemporary occupation sites, but there are at least some indications. The site is likely to have been primarily occupied in the summer, the winter site or sites being elsewhere. Several lines of evidence lead to this hypothesis. Until the recent drainage of the lake-basin, the lower Val de Marca, several metres higher than the site, was frequently flooded in winter. With the higher lake-level of Neolithic times and the absence of drainage ditches, it seems most unlikely that the site could have been effectively used in winter. It is thought that the site was located just at the (presumably summer) water's edge, and any rise in lake-level would create difficulties. Summer occupation is attested by significant numbers of new-born individuals of both red deer and pig – approximately 13% and 9%, respectively, of the aged teeth. It is also known that the water-chestnut ripens, and is best harvested, in September. This information thus gives us a minimum period of occupation for Molino Casarotto from about June to September. The presence of two shed red-deer antlers may be held to extend this period to include the spring, from about April onward, but the use of antler as a raw material complicates this issue, as it is always possible that occasional pieces may have been collected elsewhere, or in the previous season. It is impossible to disprove winter occupation on the osteological evidence; the most that can be said is that the evidence is consonant with the hypothesis that the site was not occupied earlier than March/April, or later than September/October. Some of the animals slaughtered could have been cropped during the intervening winter period, but not necessarily so.

If the view is accepted that Molino Casarotto was a summer site, then the question must be posed as to where the complementary winter site or sites were located. This question may be answered best in terms of where the deer and pig, the basic food resources, are likely to have moved. The only major area biologically complementary to the Berici Hills, within a reasonably short distance, is the Po plain, the fringe of which is included within the territory of Molino Casarotto. It seems most improbable, however, that this would have provided satisfactory winter habitation for either deer or man. Little is known of the Holocene geomorphology of the Po valley, but it appears fairly certain that much of it was wetter than it is under today's extensive drainage system. In winter, flooding and extended marsh seem probable and, while pigs are reasonably well-adapted to such conditions, this would have offered insufficient advantage to occasion a movement from the Berici Hills.

It seems more probable that the human movement was a small-scale one, either higher up into the hills or possibly just to the foot of the slopes above the flood level. In spite of the proximity of the Alps, the Berici Hills rarely get serious snow in the winter and there would be no barrier to the area's carrying a substantial permanent deer and pig population. Red deer are usually a mobile species for a number of reasons, which include the factors of food-supply, shelter, flies and other parasites. However, when no overriding factor necessitates long-distance movement, there is no reason why the major requirements of the animals could not have been provided within the relatively small area of the Berici Hills. In the absence of winters of sufficient severity to force the deer down into the low-lying areas, it seems most likely that this was the case.

Table 6 Species representation at Rivoli (the figures in parentheses concern specimens tentatively referred to the taxon in question)

Species	*Number*		*%*
Sus scrofa	880	(33)	30.5
Bos taurus	642	(41)	22.7
Ovis/Capra	553	(65)	
Ovis	24	(8)	22.3
Capra	10	(4)	
Cervus elaphus	185	(24)	6.9
Capreolus capreolus	37	(7)	1.5
Cervidae indet.	2		
Rupicapra rupicapra		(1)	15.4
Large Artiodactyla	266		
Small Artiodactyla	194		
Ursus arctos	8	(3)	
Canis lupus		(1)	
Meles meles		(1)	0.7
Carnivora indet.	5		
Castor fiber	1		
Lepus sp.		(1)	
Total	2996		100.0

Rivoli

At Rivoli pigs, cattle and caprines were the major suppliers of animal protein, with red deer a substantial element but of less importance (Jarman, in press). As can be seen from Table 6, the overall faunal spectrum is similar to that at Molino Casarotto but contains a larger number of carnivore species and lacks fish. Again, despite a wide representation of species, the economic concentration is on relatively few important animals. As at Molino Casarotto, the primary species are represented by all parts of the body, no significant bias due to conditions of deposition, preservation or recovery being observable (Table 7).

The pigs

Most of the measurable pig bones fall within the size-range of domestic pigs but, as at Molino Casarotto, some specimens are well within the wild size-range (Table 8). Here again, in the absence of any clear indication that two distinct populations are in evidence, each exploited in different ways, it seems more reasonable to treat the pigs as a single group. Most of the pig crop came from individuals in their second or third year (Table 5) with relatively few first-year animals or animals older than thirty-six months. It is to some degree surprising that more first-year animals were not slaughtered, and that the female-to-male ratio is apparently as high as two to one. This latter fact seems to imply that there was little need to conserve females for breeding, but it is possible that males formed the bulk of the younger part of the supply, as the juveniles are usually difficult to sex.

The cattle

Cattle are frequently divided into presumably wild and domestic populations according to size but, in spite of the fact that a few of the Rivoli cattle bones fall within the wild size-range, there is no firm evidence that more than one population is involved (Table 9). The killing pattern shows a peak of mortality in the third year, with very few specimens coming from animals younger than twelve months or older than four years (Table 10). Almost all of the slaughtered animals were thus prime meat animals, having attained a high proportion of maximum body weight without having become tough with age.

The caprines

Both sheep and goats are certainly present at Rivoli, with sheep apparently the more common by a considerable margin. Apart from one probable piece of chamois horn-core, all the caprine bones come from domestic sheep and goat. A relatively small proportion of the kill was of first-year animals, the crop consisting

Table 7 Numbers of selected anatomical elements from the main species at Rivoli (only the medial metapodia of *Sus* have been included)

	Distal humerus	*Distal radius*	*Proximal tibia*	*Distal tibia*	*Astragalus*	*Distal metapodia*	*Third molars*
Sus scrofa	27	10	3	23	25	50	36
Bos taurus	15	15	18	29	30	35	51
Ovis/Capra	37	11	10	32	19	19	83
C. elaphus	12	7	10	18	13	12	4
C. capreolus	7	—	—	3	8	1	1

Table 8 Measurements (mm.) of selected anatomical elements of pigs

	Molino Casarotto			*Rivoli*			*Monte Tondo*			*Torri*			*Fondo Tomollero*			*Fiavè*		
Measurement	*Range*	*Mean*	*No.*	*Range*	*Mean*	*No.*	*Range*	*Mean*	*No.*	*Range*	*Mean*	*No.*	*Range*	*Mean*	*No.*	*Range*	*Mean*	*No.*
Upper third molar: maximum length	33.0-43.3	37.8	38	31.0-37.5	33.5	11	31.3-36.0	33.7	2	–	–	–	29.7	–	1	28.8-32.9	30.9	4
Lower third molar: maximum length	35.0-48.9	40.3	40	33.2-36.8	34.9	12	32.8-38.0	35.4	2	–	–	–	29.8-36.8	33.3	2	28.8-31.7	30.2	6
Distal humerus: trochlear width	32.3-40.7	37.2	26	30.6-34.1	31.8	8	–	–	–	36.9	–	1	–	–	–	26.0-28.8	27.8	3
Proximal radius: maximum width	33.0-39.1	36.0	18	28.8-40.6	33.5	8	–	–	–	25.1-27.2	26.4	2	–	–	–	25.8	–	1
Distal tibia: maximum width	33.9-40.2	37.6	20	30.2-43.0	33.4	9	26.2-32.9	30.8	5	–	–	–	–	–	–	25.3-28.1	26.5	3
Astragalus: maximum length	41.0-55.0	49.7	15	41.5-54.0	47.5	7	39.0-53.5	44.2	3	38.1	–	1	41.5	–	1	37.0-40.5	38.6	8

Table 9 Measurements (mm.) of selected anatomical elements of cattle

	Molino Casarotto			*Rivoli*			*Monte Tondo*			*Torri*			*Fondo Tomollero*			*Fiavè*		
Measurement	*Range*	*Mean*	*No.*	*Range*	*Mean*	*No.*	*Range*	*Mean*	*No.*	*Range*	*Mean*	*No.*	*Range*	*Mean*	*No.*	*Range*	*Mean*	*No.*
Upper third molar: maximum length	29.3-30.3	29.9	3	27.5-32.0	29.7	14	27.3	–	1	28.3	–	1	26.3	–	1	24.0-30.4	27.6	24
Lower third molar: maximum length	38.8-38.9	38.8	2	35.6-39.6	37.8	8	–	–	–	–	–	–	–	–	–	31.9-38.6	34.4	15
Proximal radius: articular width	–	–	–	70.0-89.9	76.8	11	63.3	–	1	–	–	–	–	–	–	59.0-74.8	66.5	12
Distal radius: epiphyseal width	70.2	–	1	–	–	–	76.0	–	1	–	–	–	58.9	–	1	59.8-71.4	66.8	6
Proximal metacarpal: maximum width	–	–	–	56.8-66.4	61.0	5	51.4-52.5	52.0	2	43.3–46.5	44.4	2	–	–	–	43.7-57.5	51.6	14
Distal metacarpal: epiphyseal width	–	–	–	52.0-64.5	56.7	6	–	–	–	41.2	–	1	–	–	–	41.6-50.6	45.0	5
Distal metacarpal: maximum width	–	–	–	68.7	–	1	–	–	–	48.5	–	1	56.2	–	1	45.7-57.7	51.3	3
Distal tibia: maximum width	–	–	–	57.1-68.9	63.4	15	55.5-57.5	56.5	2	48.8-57.2	51.8	3	47.2-49.6	48.4	2	51.0-61.6	56.1	7
Astragalus: maximum length	68.0	–	1	62.0-74.0	67.9	13	57.0-61.0	59.0	3	57.0-61.0	58.9	7	51.0	–	1	53.5-68.0	59.1	25
Distal metatarsal: maximum width	52.8-54.3	53.5	2	–	–	–	52.1	–	1	–	–	–	–	–	–	43.4-59.1	48.8	7

Table 10 Cropping patterns of cattle

Age in months	*Rivoli*		*Monte Tondo*		*Torri*		*Fondo Tomollero*		*Fiavè*	
	Cumulative percentage certainly dead	*Cumulative percentage certainly alive*	*Cumulative percentage certainly dead*	*Cumulative percentage certainly alive*	*Cumulative percentage certainly dead*	*Cumulative percentage certainly alive*	*Cumulative percentage certainly dead*	*Cumulative percentage certainly alive*	*Cumulative percentage certainly dead*	*Cumulative percentage certainly alive*
0	—	100.0	—	100.0	—	100.0	—	100.0	—	100.0
6	1.9	92.9	—	100.0	4.5	69.8	20.0	80.0	18.7	80.1
12	4.4	80.8	—	84.7	9.1	61.0	20.0	80.0	21.5	63.4
18	7.6	62.0	14.3	73.1	31.8	43.5	20.0	60.0	31.3	53.9
24	13.7	45.2	42.8	42.3	40.9	43.5	40.0	40.0	40.6	49.2
36	45.1	32.8	85.7	23.1	45.5	39.1	80.0	—	58.5	34.5
48	76.9	6.6	100.0	7.7	45.5	4.3	80.0	—	68.1	12.5
60	100.0	1.5	100.0	3.8	59.0	4.3	100.0	—	90.8	9.0
72	100.0	0.5	100.0	—	100.0	4.3	100.0	—	100.0	—
Number	366	412	7	26	22	23	5	5	214	232

Table 11 Cropping paterns of caprines

Age in months	*Rivoli*		*Monte Tondo*		*Torri*		*Fondo Tomollero*		*Fiavè*	
	Cumulative percentage certainly dead	*Cumulative percentage certainly alive*	*Cumulative percentage certainly dead*	*Cumulative percentage certainly alive*	*Cumulative percentage certainly dead*	*Cumulative percentage certainly alive*	*Cumulative percentage certainly dead*	*Cumulative percentage certainly alive*	*Cumulative percentage certainly dead*	*Cumulative percentage certainly alive*
0	—	100.0	—	100.0	—	100.0	—	100.0	—	100.0
3	0.2	97.0	—	100.0	—	97.9	3.6	96.4	5.6	93.5
6	4.6	91.3	3.8	98.6	2.2	74.0	10.7	75.0	8.9	86.1
9	7.8	76.4	3.8	92.9	2.2	67.4	17.9	71.4	12.1	80.7
12	12.8	57.1	3.8	79.8	26.1	28.3	17.9	64.2	13.9	65.9
18	33.4	42.2	61.5	42.1	39.2	28.3	64.2	17.9	40.0	46.4
24	41.6	38.1	69.2	39.2	41.4	28.3	78.6	14.3	53.3	26.0
30	50.9	25.9	88.5	7.3	43.5	21.7	78.6	—	61.3	18.8
36	53.8	10.0	92.3	7.3	43.5	13.0	82.1	—	71.1	9.7
48	83.1	0.8	96.1	1.4	74.0	2.2	93.0	—	84.0	4.3
60	100.0	—	100.0	—	97.9	—	100.0	—	96.4	3.3
72	100.0	—	100.0	—	100.0	—	100.0	—	97.0	—
84	100.0	—	100.0	—	100.0	—	100.0	—	97.2	—
96	100.0	—	100.0	—	100.0	—	100.0	—	100.0	—
Number	437	520	26	69	46	46	28	28	686	690

mostly of second- and third-year animals (Table 11). As with the cattle, the majority of the crop is thus of prime meat animals, with no evidence for the maintenance of a considerable milk or wool herd, a factor which would have encouraged the retention of more animals to a greater age.

The red deer

As has already been pointed out, there is no logical objection to the suggestion that red deer may have been exploited in much the same way as modern farmyard animals and, in so far as we can tell from the available evidence, the culling pattern is consonant with such a suggestion. Few deer-teeth were recovered at Rivoli, but almost all came from young adults, few very young and no very old individuals being represented in the sample. The general pattern of exploitation is thus very similar to that of the other major meat-producing animals.

Site location and territory

The site is on the Rocca di Rivoli; on the west side of, and directly overlooking, the Adige valley. Steep cliffs on both sides of the river take the east side of the river virtually beyond the limit of effective exploitation, and the territory is thus roughly kidney-shaped, truncated to the east by the Adige (Fig. 3). On the assumption that the faunal spectrum, and the presence of cereal impressions in daub, indicated a basically 'mixed farming' economy, a one-hour exploitation territory was defined. (For the arguments suggesting this limit as appropriate to basically sedentary economies, see Vita-Finzi & Higgs 1970; Jarman 1972b.) Another feature of the Rivoli territory is that it is relatively small, due to topographic distortion, and that the area accessible within ten minutes from the site (of particular importance for agricultural economies) is greatly restricted. About half the territory is, today, rough grazing or woodland

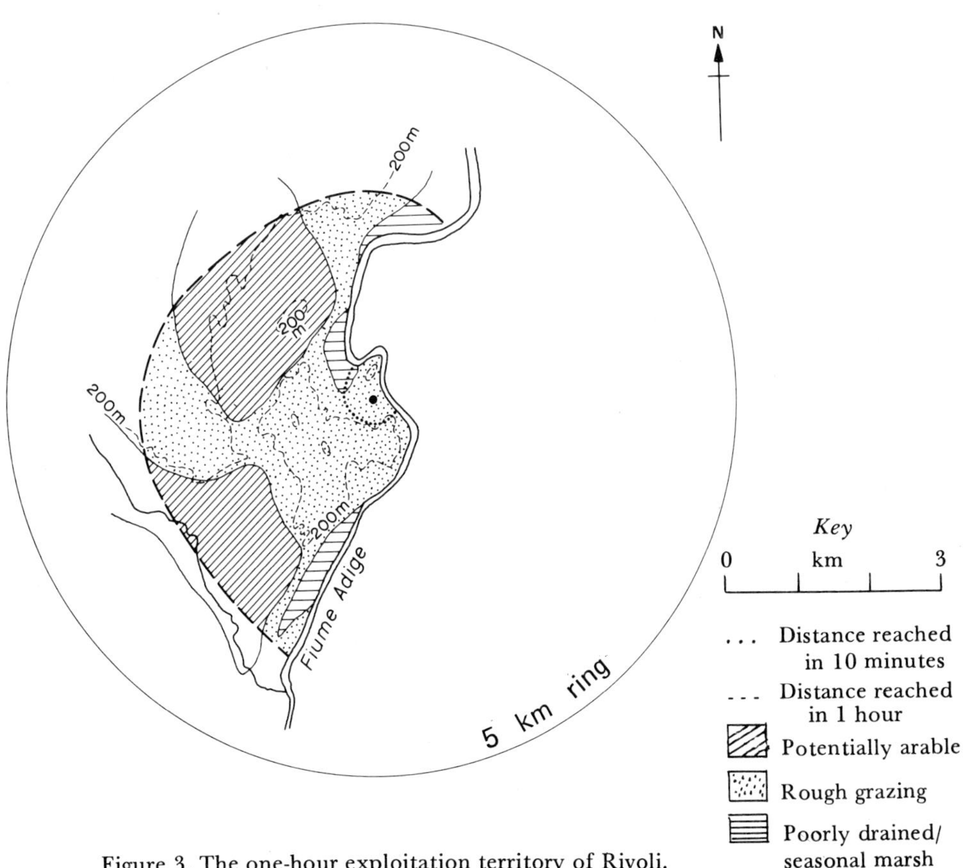

Figure 3. The one-hour exploitation territory of Rivoli.

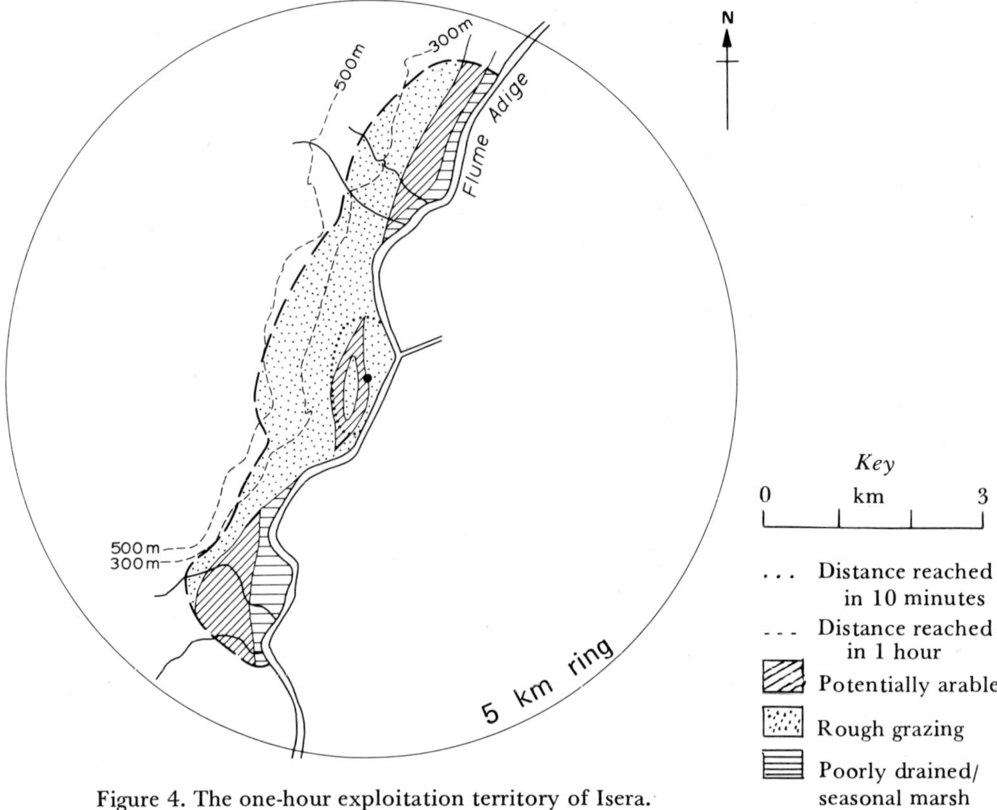

Figure 4. The one-hour exploitation territory of Isera.

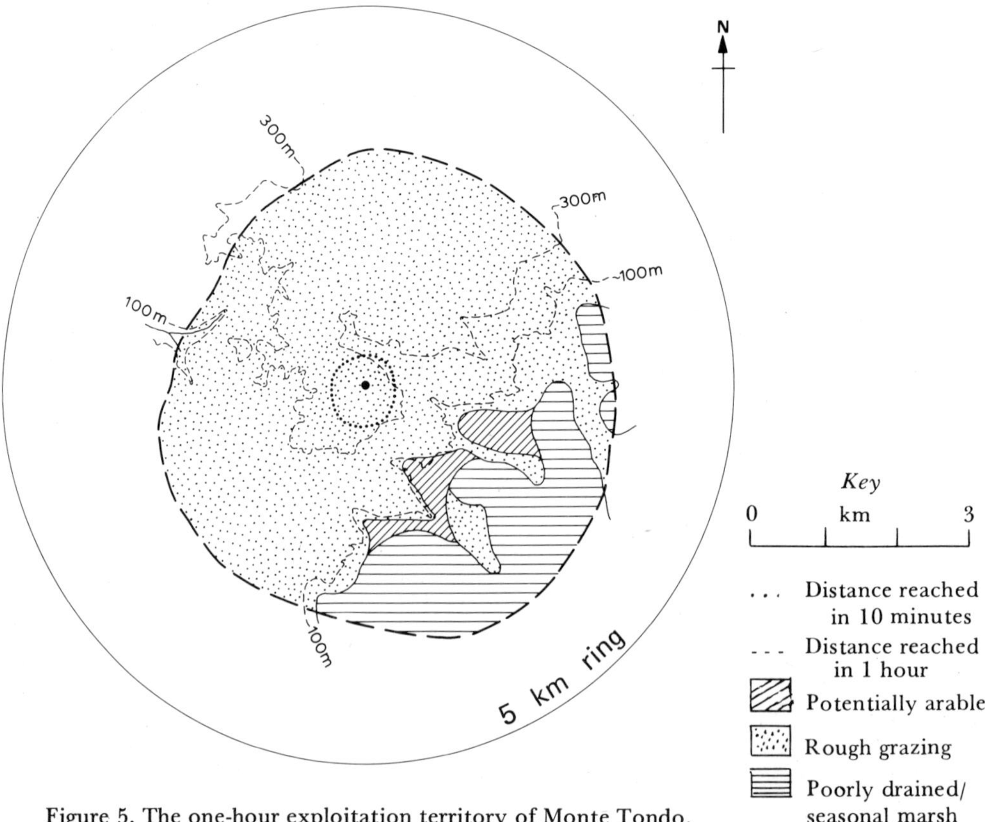

Figure 5. The one-hour exploitation territory of Monte Tondo.

and must have been so in the past, most of the remainder being at present arable. However, a considerable proportion of the arable would have carried soils too heavy, or too waterlogged, for such a mode of exploitation under Neolithic conditions, and none of it is closely adjacent to the site.

The economy

The effect of the site's location, close to the Adige, in curtailing the exploitation territory, has already been noted, and it suggests that a primary function of the site may have been a strategic or defensive one; at the same time the importance of the Adige as a route to the Brenner encourages this suggestion, as does the observation that any site whose primary function was as a subsistence settlement would certainly have been better located on the main patch of arable soil, as is the modern village of Rivoli. The relatively low proportion of first-year individuals in the crop of the main food-species may also point to this conclusion.

Isera

The economic base at Isera rested upon caprines, cattle, pig and red deer, as at Rivoli (Table 12). Each of these species was present in broadly equivalent proportions, although the small size of the collection must make this a tentative assessment. Again, there is reasonable representation of the various parts of the body, although caprine teeth were more common than expected and red-deer teeth were under-represented (Table 13). Apparent over-representation of caprine teeth and under-representation of deer-teeth were also observed at Rivoli, and this is a frequent feature of such European prehistoric faunal collections.

Little can be inferred as to the exploitation pattern from so small a sample, but such evidence as there is points to a cropping pattern similar to that at Rivoli, possibly with a higher proportion of first-year caprines and pigs (Jarman 1970).

The exploitation territory is also similar to that of Rivoli, as the site is adjacent to the west bank of the Adige. The primary difference in the two territories is that Isera is located in a relatively flat area and, although well above the river, is not so elevated as to make the river bank inaccessible or to encourage the interpretation of the site as of strategic importance. The ground rises very steeply to the west, considerably restricting movement in that direction. Little of the area can, even today, be considered as other than of marginal arable potential, although extensive terracing has allowed a certain amount of cereal and vine cultivation. Under Neolithic conditions virtually the whole territory must have been of rough-grazing potential, with the possible exception of a small area adjacent to the site (Fig. 4). Thus it seems justifiable to assume that pastoralism formed the primary economic base of the inhabitants, in spite of the fact that no botanical information was recovered.

Table 12 Species representation at Isera

Species	*Number*	%
Cervus elaphus	81	29.7
Bos taurus	75	27.5
Sus scrofa	65	23.8
Ovis/Capra	52	19.0
Total	273	100.0

Table 13 Numbers of selected anatomical elements from the main species at Isera

	Humerus	*Radius*	*Tibia*	*Meta-podia*	*Teeth*
C. elaphus	3	3	2	3	3
Bos taurus	4	1	2	1	6
Sus scrofa	–	1	–	–	4
Ovis/Capra	–	1	1	1	5

Monte Tondo

At Monte Tondo, the economy was based upon caprines, pigs and cattle, in approximately equal proportions, although the cattle may have been slightly less numerous than the pigs and caprines (Table 14). Red deer is the only other species of any economic significance, the remainder of the small collection including a dog, hare and horse. Different parts of the body are all relatively well represented, and there is no indication of systematic bias in the anatomical elements recovered (Table 15).

Table 14 Species representation at Monte Tondo (the figures in parentheses concern specimens tentatively referred to the taxon in question)

Species	*Number*		%
Sus scrofa	350	(18)	34.1
Bos taurus	254	(14)	24.9
Ovis/Capra	277	(6)	
Ovis	5	(2)	27.3
Capra	2	(2)	
Cervus elaphus	44	(39)	7.7
Cervidae indet.	2		
Large Artiodactyla	52		5.1
Equus sp.		(1)	
Canis familiaris	1	(3)	
Carnivora indet.	3		
Lepus sp.	1		0.9
Chelonia indet.	1		
Aves	1		
Total	1078		100.0

The pigs

As was the case at Molino Casarotto and Rivoli, the pigs bracket the size-ranges of domestic and wild populations as these are usually defined (Table 8), and one could treat them as two separate populations. However, in the absence of evidence for two economic (as opposed to zoological or taxonomic) groups, they have been treated here as a single exploited population. The cropping pattern is unusual in that there is a very low proportion of first-year animals, almost all being slaughtered in their second or third year (Table 5). This is unusual for pigs, as their high rate of reproduction encourages a heavy cropping of immature age-groups.

The cattle

Within the small sample of measurable cattle bones, there is none that falls within the size-range of *Bos primigenius*, the impression being of a relatively small animal (Table 9). As far as can be judged on the available data, the pattern of exploitation is the familiar one of the major part of the crop being sub-adult and young adult individuals. None of the cattle was certainly slaughtered in the first year of life, and only one specimen certainly came from an individual of older than five years (Table 10).

The caprines

Again, in the absence of evidence for chamois or ibex, it seems certain that all the caprines were domestic, husbanded animals. Both sheep and goat were present, the former possibly outnumbering the latter. The cropping pattern, like that of the pigs, is unusual for its low proportion of first-year animals, almost all the crop being second- or third-year animals, with one specimen from an individual in late maturity (Table 11).

Site location and territory

The site is located near the summit of the hill of Monte Tondo, towards the eastern edge of the Berici Hills. The one-hour territory is relatively small, the perimeter varying from *c.* 2.5 km. to *c.* 4.0 km. from the site, the constricting topographic influence of the steep-sided hills being seen especially to the west of the site (Fig. 5). The environment of the territory at the time of occupation would have been much the same as that described at Molino Casarotto, but occupation and exploitation of the area during the intervening period are almost certain to have occasioned a degree of forest clearance, thus leading to a more open and less completely wooded environment. In addition, some areas may have started to degenerate, because of exploitation, from mature woodland to thick deciduous scrub. Today, only a small proportion of the territory is used as arable, most of it being pasture and woodland. The only considerable area of arable is to the south-east of the

Table 15 Numbers of selected anatomical elements from the main species at Monte Tondo (only the medial metapodia of *Sus* have been included)

	Humerus	*Radius*	*Tibia*	*Metapodia*	*Upper third molar*	*Lower third molar*
Sus scrofa	12	7	13	25	6	9
Bos taurus	5	6	5	20	3	2
Ovis/Capra	12	7	12	14	7	7
C. elaphus	—	1	1	5	—	—

site, on the edge of the Po valley. During the Bronze Age occupation still less would have been available for cultivation, and there are no areas of good arable accessible within ten minutes from the site.

Economy

No plant remains were recovered from the samples analysed by flotation. The deposits were shallow throughout the site, and it is thus possible that poor preservation is partly responsible for the lack of plant remains, but it also seems probable that plant foods were of little importance in the diet. The evidence from the exploitation territory makes it very unlikely that agriculture played a significant part in the economy; even today the Berici Hills remain low in agricultural potential, and although some cultivation was no doubt possible in Bronze Age times, this must necessarily have been of minor importance. The only areas where agriculture could have supplied significant resources would have been on the fringes of the lake-basins or on the edge of the Po plain. It was noted above that the cropping patterns of the pigs and caprines were unusual in the very low proportions of juvenile individuals. There is nothing to suggest that the site had a special function, such as that postulated for Rivoli, and some other explanation must be sought for the data. While it is quite possible that the situation springs from a 'cultural preference' for mature meat, one should not ignore the economic aspects of the situation. The over-wintering of virtually the whole crop of relatively fast-breeding and fast-growing species, such as pig and sheep, is an expensive stock-rearing system, as it puts considerable pressure on grazing resources and thus limits the acceptable reproductive rate and reduces turnover. In almost all subsistence pastoral exploitation, a high percentage of each year's male crop is a surplus that it is most economic to slaughter fairly young, in order to conserve grazing resources for the more productive females. Possible explanations of the Monte Tondo situation are either that the site was occupied seasonally, the first-year animals being cropped primarily elsewhere; or that Monte Tondo was a unit within a more complex economy, and that first-year animals were usually sold or exchanged for a different form of economic wealth.

Table 16 Species representation at Torri (the figures in parentheses concern specimens tentatively referred to the taxon in question)

Species	*Number*		%
Ovis/Capra	142	(9)	
Ovis	6	(1)	38.3
Capra	1	(1)	
Sus scrofa	105	(2)	25.6
Bos taurus	86	(15)	24.1
Cervus elaphus	4	(5)	2.4
Capreolus capreolus	1		
Large Artiodactyla	20		4.8
Canis familiaris		(3)	
Carnivora indet.	1		1.7
Lepus sp.	1		
Rodentia indet.	2		
Chelonia indet.	3		
Reptilia indet.	1		3.1
Pisces	4		
Aves	5		
Total	418		100.0

Torri

The animal economy at Torri was based upon pig, cattle and caprines, which between them accounted for nearly 90% of the identified bones. Caprines were clearly the most numerous of these, with pigs and cattle occurring in approximately equal numbers (Table 16). Red and roe deer both occurred, but in minute proportions. As Table 17 shows, there is a considerable degree of variation in the representation of different parts of the body, but this

Table 17 Numbers of selected anatomical elements from the main species at Torri (only the medial metapodia of *Sus* have been included)

	Humerus	*Radius*	*Femur*	*Tibia*	*Metapodia*	*Upper third molar*	*Lower third molar*
Ovis/Capra	5	11	4	12	27	2	3
Sus scrofa	6	4	1	1	4	—	1
Bos taurus	3	1	—	4	17	1	1

seems more likely to be attributable to the small sample-sizes and to the greater ease with which fragments of certain bones are recognized than those of others, than to a significant bias in the bones deposited at the site.

The pigs

On the available data, the pigs were the smallest in body-size of those yet considered, none of the measured bones exceeding the size-range of domestic pigs (Table 8). Only a small sample of teeth could be aged, and of those none certainly came from an individual of older than two years, while none of the individuals could have been older than five years. Most of the mortality probably came in the second and third years (Table 5).

The cattle

Like the pigs, the cattle were small-sized, consistently smaller even than those of Monte Tondo, with none in the size-range of *Bos primigenius* (Table 9). Most of the cattle were killed as young adults, with a few certainly being slaughtered as calves and one individual surviving at least until six years old (Table 10).

The caprines

Both sheep and goat occur in the caprine sample with sheep, again, probably substantially greater in numbers. There is no indication that either ibex or chamois is present. The majority of the caprine population was cropped young, at least 25% of the sample being first-year animals. None of the specimens came from an individual certainly over four years of age, and most of the crop was taken from animals in the first three years of life (Table 11).

Site location and territory

The site is located on the crest of a small spur, adjacent to the modern village of Torri d'Arcugnano, at the eastern edge of the Berici Hills. To the south the site overlooks the basin of the Lago di Fimon, while to the east and north-east there is more low-lying ground, which merges eventually into the edge of the Po plain. To the west and beyond the lake to the south, lies the main mass of the Berici Hills. In Bronze Age times the lake had been considerably reduced in size, presumably at least partly because of silting and peat formation. The bottom of the hill-slopes and any areas of the lake basin above flood-level would still have provided potential arable areas within an exploitable distance of the site, the other principal resource being the rough grazing provided by pasture and woodland (Fig. 6). Much of the lake-basin would have been marshy, at least seasonally, and would have been of little value except as a supplementary source of food for the pigs.

The economy

Despite the lack of any botanical evidence from Torri it is reasonable to suggest, from the territorial analysis, that a significant element in the economy may have been provided by cereals. It is instructive to compare the site territory of Torri with that of Monte Tondo in relation to the other economic evidence. The Monte Tondo territory contains virtually exclusively rough grazing, and it was inferred that the site may only have been occupied for part of the year. As we have noted, there may well have been an important arable component in the Torri economy, and the animal cropping patterns do not suggest a seasonal occupation; indeed, the evidence so far as it goes suggests the reverse, as there are several specimens that must have come from animals slaughtered during their first summer, and others from animals slaughtered in winter or spring. Of course, such evidence cannot be held to demonstrate year-round occupation, but it is an indication of a probable major difference between the economies of Torri and Monte Tondo. It seems not unlikely that the proximity of Torri to the lowlands and the existence of areas suitable for cereals in the neighbourhood may be, to some extent, the controlling economic factors.

Fondo Tomollero

The basis of the animal economy at Fondo Tomollero was the pig, cattle and caprines. As far as can be judged from the small available sample, caprines were numerically the most important, accounting for over 40% of the identified specimens, with pigs the next most frequent, and cattle contributing only about

Table 18 Species representation at Fondo Tomollero (the figures in parentheses concern specimens tentatively referred to the taxon in question)

Species	*Number*		%
Ovis/Capra	118	(6)	
Ovis	6	(6)	45.4
Capra	3	(6)	
Sus scrofa	79	(5)	26.2
Bos taurus	38	(5)	13.4
Cervus elaphus	7	(1)	4.7
Capreolus capreolus	4	(3)	
Large Artiodactyla	3		1.2
Small Artiodactyla	1		
Emys sp.	9		9.1
Pisces	20		
Total	320		100.0

13% (Table 18). This general picture is borne out by Table 19, which indicates also that different parts of the body are all reasonably well represented in the collection. Small samples of deposit were analysed by froth flotation to give a picture of the plant resources; wheat is certainly present in the collection, as are stones of the cornelian cherry (*Cornus mas*).

The pigs

In so far as can be judged from the very few available measurements, the pigs are approximately comparable in size to those of the Bronze Age sites discussed above. There is none that falls within the range of wild pigs (Table 8). Of the nine teeth giving some indication of age, none was from an individual of certainly older than two years, and all but one specimen came from individuals certainly less than three years old (Table 5).

The cattle

The cattle, too, appear to be small, on the available data, measurements being as small as or smaller than those from the Bronze Age sites already discussed. Only five teeth could be aged, all of which could have been from animals in their first or second year, and none of which came from an individual of greater than five years in age (Table 10).

The caprines

Sheep and goat are both present in approximately equal proportions, and there is no indication of the presence of ibex or chamois. The cropping pattern shows high mortality in the first two years of life; no specimen must have derived from an individual older than two years, and none of them could have come from an individual of greater than five years in age (Table 11).

Site location and territory

The site is located in the basin of the Lago di Fimon, about 2 km. south of Torri and about 1 km. south-east of Molino Casarotto. Clearly, therefore, the one-hour territory of Fondo Tomollero overlaps considerably with that of Torri (Fig. 6) and, in fact, it is entirely contained within the two-hour territory of Molino Casarotto. The position of the site, in an area that was almost certainly under the lake in Neolithic times, indicates the degree of shrinkage of the lake. The economic potential of the Fondo Tomollero territory would have been comparable with that of Torri, the lowland situation providing the opportunity for some arable exploitation in the better-drained areas, the remainder of the territory providing rough grazing on the pasture and woodland, with some marsh land adjacent to the lake.

The economy

As we have noted, the arable potential of the territory was certainly exploited to some degree, cereals being the primary food-plant found.

Table 19 Numbers of selected anatomical elements from the main species at Fondo Tomollero (only the medial metapodia of *Sus* have been included)

	Humerus	*Radius*	*Femur*	*Tibia*	*Meta-podia*	*Upper third molar*	*Lower third molar*
Ovis/Capra	12	15	5	4	19	3	1
Sus scrofa	5	3	2	6	6	1	2
Bos taurus	2	1	2	7	2	1	1

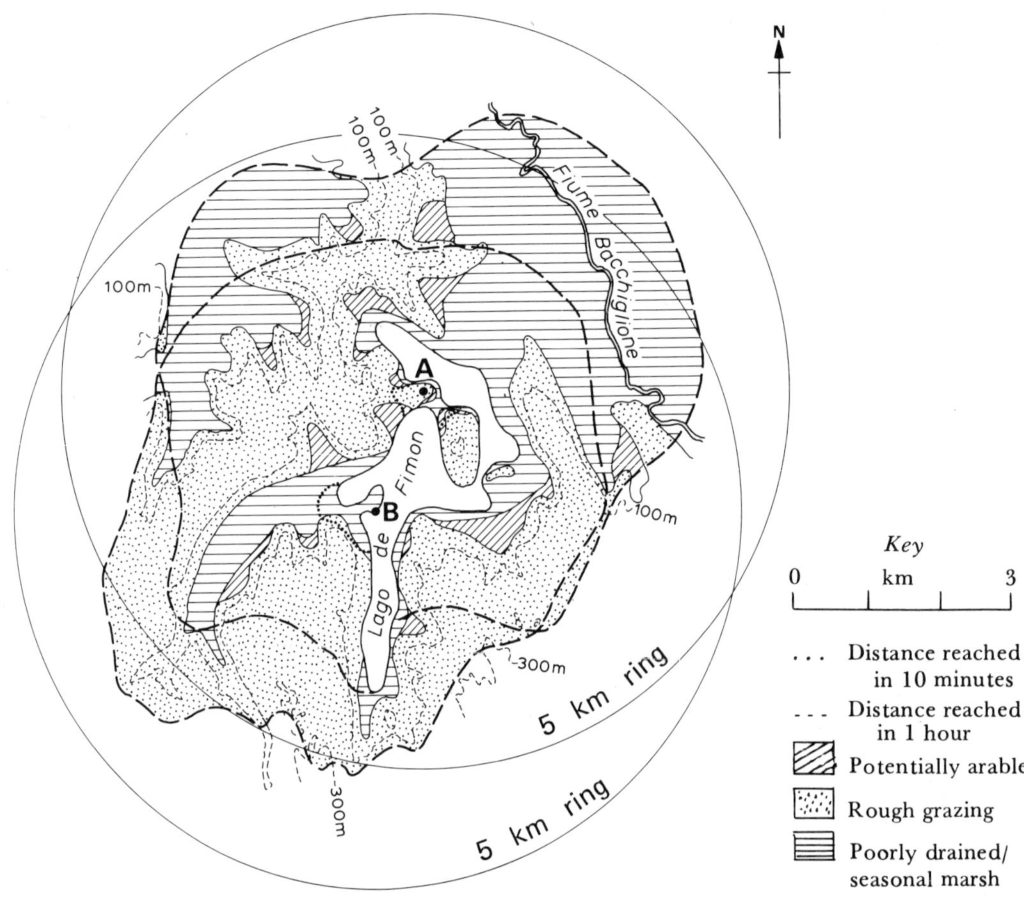

Figure 6. The one-hour exploitation territories of Torri (Site A) and Fondo Tomollero (Site B).

Indeed, it appears that by the period of occupation at Fondo Tomollero, cereals had taken over the role previously occupied by water-chestnut, for in spite of the lake-side situation of the site no water-chestnut remains whatsoever were found. Their absence is unlikely to have been caused by a serious decline in availability, as water-chestnut remained very plentiful in the lake until a few years ago. Similarly, it is not possible to explain it in terms of the season at which the site was occupied. The presence of new-born individuals of all the major economic animal species indicates clearly summer occupation of the site; and, if we are correct in assuming that cereal agriculture formed a part of the subsistence base, this would also have involved summer occupation. It will be remembered that this was also the period during which Molino Casarotto was thought to have been occupied, and that at Molino Casarotto water-chestnuts were by far the commonest of the food-plants exploited. It seems probable, therefore, that cereals had taken over the economi and dietary functions of the water-chestnuts that they replaced.

The evidence for summer occupation at this site has already been outlined; it is also worth noting that there is little evidence for winter occupation. The arguments against winter occupation at Molino Casarotto apply equally to Fondo Tomollero; and the annual cropping patterns fit the suggestion that Fondo Tomollero was primarily a summer site: while a substantial proportion of the animals must have been slaughtered in summer, there is none that unequivocally must have been slaughtered in winter.

Again, the question arises of where the inhabitants of Fondo Tomollero spent the winter, and again the obvious answer is that the complementary sites would be either on the edge or at the top of the Berici Hills. It was noted that, at the hill-top site of Monte Tondo, there were good reasons for inferring that the site was part of a system of exploitation, rather than self-sufficient, and that its inhabitants may have been elsewhere for part of the year. It is tempting to suggest that sites of the nature of Fondo Tomollero and Monte Tondo may have been associated, providing between them the annual territory of a single human population (Vita-Finzi & Higgs 1970).

Fiavè

In spite of the relatively long list of species at Fiavè, the animal economy is based almost exclusively upon cattle and caprines, with the pig a significant, but only minor, element. Both red and roe deer are present in small numbers, and it is noteworthy that chamois is also certainly represented (Table 20). Fiavè is the most northerly and the highest of the sites considered here and the presence of chamois is presumably related to its situation. Similarly, the probable chamois at Rivoli is likely to have come from the high crags close to the site. Plant remains were extremely well preserved at Fiavè, and a large sample is in the course of study. Among the cereals, emmer wheat was substantially the commonest, six-rowed barley also occurring. A large pulse, probably *Pisum*, was present, as was a small pulse, probably either *Vicia* or *Lathyrus.* A variety of fruits was also found, including hazel nuts, apples, cornelian cherry, blackberry and raspberry.

Table 20 Species representation at Fiavè (the figures in parentheses concern specimens tentatively referred to the taxon in question)

Species	*Number*		%
Ovis/Capra	2176	(256)	
Ovis	169	(104)	51.9
Capra	73	(47)	
Bos taurus	1400	(156)	28.5
Sus scrofa	317	(18)	6.5
Rupicapra rupicapra	9	(8)	
Cervus elaphus	71	(5)	2.2
Capreolus capreolus	22	(7)	
Caprinae	92	(6)	1.8
Large Artiodactyla	125		8.8
Small Artiodactyla	356		
Canis familiaris	9		
Vulpes vulpes		(2)	
Canidae indet.	1		
Ursus arctos	3		
Carnivora indet.	3	(1)	0.4
Lepus sp.	1		
Anura indet.	1		
Pisces	1		
Aves	2		
Total	5441		100.1

As Table 21 shows, there are some irregularities in the representation of different anatomical elements at this site; but it is difficult to interpret these as other than chance vagaries of preservation and identifiability. Thus, it might, on the face of it, be tempting to correlate the high representation of the hind-limb bones of pig to the disproportionate consumption of the choice cut, the ham. However, the bones of the shoulder and hip are present in the collection in almost equal numbers; and, in addition, the astragalus, difficult to butcher from the distal tibia and usually left in articulation with it, is represented by less than half the number of tibiae. The over-representation of cattle metapodia is probably due to their great robustness and ease of identification; and the disparity between the representation of the proximal long-bones (the humerus and femur) and the distal long-bones (the radius and tibia) is difficult to interpret satisfactorily in terms of butchery practice or utilization of different joints.

The pigs

As already noted, the pigs were a subsidiary element in the economy. They are of small size, none of the specimens approaching the size-range of wild pigs (Table 8). On the available

Table 21 Numbers of selected anatomical elements from the main species at Fiavè (only the medial metapodia of *Sus* have been included)

	Humerus	*Radius*	*Femur*	*Tibia*	*Meta-podia*	*Upper third molar*	*Lower third molar*
Ovis/Capra	83	201	90	195	218	82	120
Bos taurus	51	56	43	57	198	28	18
Sus scrofa	14	4	23	24	21	5	12

evidence, the Fiavè pigs appear to have been smaller in average body-size than any of those considered above, but the sample from Torri is so small that it is not possible to confirm this. Mortality is concentrated on the immature age-groups, with over 30% of the aged sample coming from first-year individuals, and 75% from first or second year individuals. There is no specimen from an individual certainly older than four years (Table 5).

The cattle

The cattle are relatively small in size, comparable with those of the other Bronze Age sites (Table 9). A relatively high proportion of the crop (more than 40%) was slaughtered in the first two years of life, about 60% being cropped over the first three years; 9% of the specimens are from individuals certainly surviving until five years of age, none certainly surviving longer than this (Table 10).

The caprines

Both sheep and goat are present in the caprine sample, and the presence of chamois at the site must raise the question of possible contamination of the sheep/goat sample. Special consideration was given to this possible source of error during the analysis, however, and there are such large numbers of specimens that are unquestionably attributable to sheep or goat that this possibility can be ignored as far as economic interpretations are concerned. The relatively good sample of caprine bones allows a reasonable estimate to be made of the relative importance of sheep and goat. Sheep are clearly the more numerous, and although the ratio in the sample as a whole is about two to one, the ratio in the population was probably more of the order of three to one, as the figure is distorted by the presence of horn-cores in female as well as male goats, only the males carrying horns in the sheep. The horn-cores of the goats were evidently collected for some industrial purpose, as nearly half of them – indeed, almost all that were complete enough to give any indication on the subject – had been cut carefully from the skull.

At Fiavè, as at the other sites discussed, the caprine-cropping pattern must necessarily be viewed as a composite picture of both sheep and goat, as there is no way of telling the teeth apart. Nor is it at all unlikely that the cropping pattern would have been different for the two species, as the goat may have been primarily a milk provider, the sheep primarily a meat provider. However, there are likely to have been features in common; in particular, the slaughter fairly early in life of males not needed for breeding and the elimination of barren females. Given this, and the dominance of sheep over goat at all the sites where there is evidence for the ratio, one may hope that at least a general impression of the sheep–cropping pattern is obtained.

More than 50% of the caprines were slaughtered during the first two years of life, a particularly large number of specimens coming from individuals of 12-18 months in age. More than 70% of the specimens came from individuals certainly younger than three years, and no specimen came from an animal certainly older than five years (Table 11).

Site location and territory

The site was located on the edge of a small lake in an upland basin, the enclosing hills rising steeply all around it. This is evident in the small size and distorted shape of the one-hour exploitation territory, clearly indicating the severely limiting effect of the topography (Fig. 7). Under today's conditions, the flat bottom of the basin is exploited largely as arable, with maize and cattle-fodder the primary crops. Although it has shrunk since the Bronze Age there remains a small lake that, with an area of marsh and water meadows around it, takes up the remainder of the basin. The lower gentler slopes of the surrounding hills are almost exclusively rich pasture, much of which is cut for hay. The higher slopes carry coniferous forest, with some pasture in the less precipitous areas, and bare rock in the steepest. In the past, a higher proportion of the basin would have been lake and marshland but, as the archaeological evidence shows, a proportion must have been available for cereal cultivation. The hill slopes have probably not changed greatly: the more accessible ones would then, as now, have provided extensive pastures; the remainder of the territory being under woodland, a high percentage of which at least would have been coniferous, to judge from the wood employed in the construction of the site.

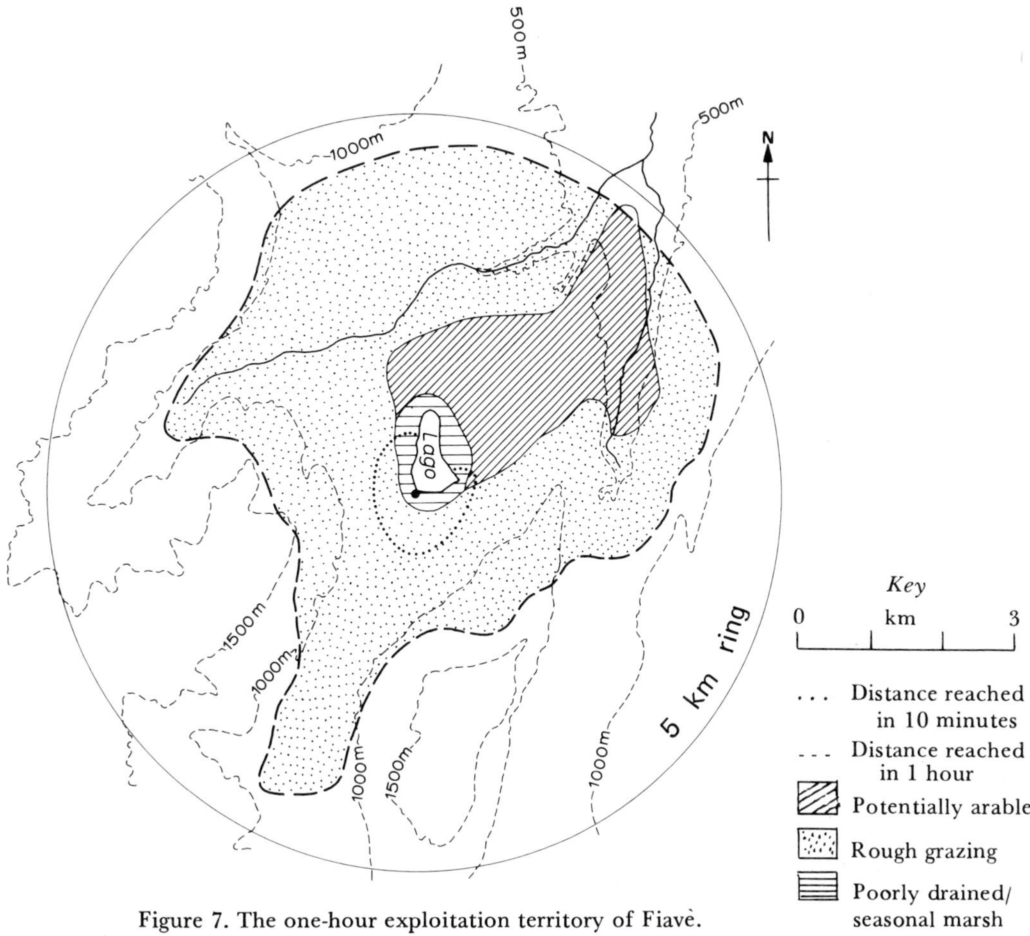

Figure 7. The one-hour exploitation territory of Fiavè.

The economy

The organic remains indicate that both animal and plant resources were of importance at Fiavè. As is usually the case, however, it is difficult to assess their relative economic significance. Territorial analysis is one useful aid, as it gives an indication as to the most likely or the most advantageous policy. Today, when there is no need for the village to be self-sufficient, the economy is almost wholly animal-oriented, as the maize is largely grown for animal consumption; thus the arable element in the territory, as well as the pasture, is geared to the needs of pastoralism. In the past, when the settlement was probably obliged to be self-supporting as far as subsistence requirements are concerned, there would have been considerable incentive to cultivate a large enough area to supply the carbohydrate needs of the community. Indeed, the plant remains indicate that developed and well-adapted agriculture was probably in use, with the frost-resistant emmer providing the human cereal staple, the pulses and barley being grown in rotation. It seems likely that, if the small pulse proves to have been cultivated, it at least was grown as animal fodder like the modern lucerne. Agriculture is always likely to have been a subsidiary element of the economy, however, as the altitude, the relatively short growing season and the humid summers all militate against successful cereal agriculture.

Another difference between the present-day situation and that of the Bronze Age is that today cattle provide the economic basis, pigs occurring in small numbers and sheep not at all. Two important factors here are the recent development of food concentrates that permit more cattle to be over-wintered than formerly, and the present legal prohibition upon the pasturing of sheep in the area (presumably for forest protection). In the past, shortage of winter fodder was a factor severely limiting the numbers of cattle it was possible to keep, there being a potential surplus of summer grazing. A likely objective of cattle husbandry would have been to pasture them away from the site as much as possible during the summer, reserving the pastures adjacent to the site for winter use as hay or foggage.

Enough snow falls in the area at the present day to allow its use as a ski resort, and there is no reason to suppose that significantly less would have fallen during Bronze Age times. In view of this, it is tempting to argue that the area was occupied during the summer only, thus overcoming the limiting factor of the snowfall by means of transhumance. This does not appear to have been the case, however; each of the three primary economic species gives evidence of having been cropped throughout the year at the site and, while a short absence is not impossible, it seems unlikely that the site was unoccupied for any prolonged period of the year. In the Bronze Age it is perhaps most likely that, as is the case today, some of the animals were taken away from the village during the summer to exploit the high pastures leaving, however, a large proportion of the herds in the vicinity of the site. The large number of cattle killed as calves and yearlings is likely to be a reflection of the pressure upon winter fodder resources, few animals being maintained over the winter. If we are correct in thinking that Fiavè was occupied in the winter, and that no major movement to the lowlands was undertaken, this suggests that, by Bronze Age times, population pressure in the whole area was such that no substantial surplus of lowland winter grazing was available. The distance it would have been necessary to travel to the lowlands is moderate by the standards of many mobile pasturalists, and is unlikely to have been a deterrent. Certainly more animals could have been carried in the Fiavè area if winter grazing had not been a limiting factor, and transhumance is such an established pattern of human behaviour in these circumstances that it seems likely that it would have taken place were it possible. It is during the Bronze Age that the upland zone in which Fiavè lies was occupied extensively for the first time, and this too may be taken as an index of rising population pressure.

Conclusions

The individual analyses of the palaeoeconomies that we have discussed can lead to a general consideration of the nature of human prehistoric development, as well as to specific information about particular communities. The influence of two important factors can be perceived in the prehistoric economies of northern Italy: the impact of individual site pressures and opportunities consequent upon particular site locations, and coherent long-term trends springing from the mechanisms of economic development.

Clearly, the nature of the immediate surroundings of a site has a significant influence upon the economy practised by its human population, and thus upon its potential for development. This is one of the primary assumptions of the technique of territorial analysis. The pressures are both direct, in that the environment can embody absolute limitations on the nature of the economies that it is possible to practise with the available technology; and indirect, in that while the environment can offer a choice of practicable economic alternatives, the long-term evolutionary pressure, generated and maintained largely by potential or actual population growth, is overwhelmingly in favour of the more productive as opposed to the less productive system (Higgs & Jarman 1975).

In the analyses discussed above, the virtual absence of caprines and of cereals at Molino Casarotto can be seen as a result of direct environmental pressure; it is quite clear that these species were known, and as they were resources introduced to the area by man, which could not have survived competition from the better adapted indigenous species without human intervention, techniques for their control were also presumably known. Their exploitation as effective economic resources was prevented, however, by environmental constraints that severely limited the use that could be made of them. Similar considerations apply to the probable absence of a significant cereal element in the economies of Rivoli, Isera and Monte Tondo.

Indirect pressures, favouring the development of more productive economies, lead to the growth of long-term regularities, norms of economic progress that can be seen to have general, as well as local, validity. A major trend of this nature observable in our data is the increasing reliance on a highly productive combination of resources, most of which were brought into the area by human agencies, in replacement of the indigenous Holocene plant and animal resources that formed the economic bases up to, and during, the period of occupation of Molino Casarotto. Despite individual variations stemming from local conditions, it can be seen that, by the Middle Bronze Age, the population of the area was economically dependent upon the farmyard animals and cereal crops common today. These species have the advantage over the indigenous ones that they can be integrated into a highly productive subsistence economy, but it must be noted that this is only at the cost of the creation of a labour-intensive system (Jarman 1972a). The Bronze Age economy, capable of supporting a greatly increased population relative to that of the Early Neolithic, could be maintained only by the increased input of labour that the rise in population had made available.

A further important factor in this development is the role of technological change. Today, the intensive agriculture that is the most important economic element in the exploitation of the Po plain and the valley bottoms within the Berici Hills is made possible only by the use of a sophisticated technology. Not only are mechanical aids necessary for effective cultivation of the heavy lowland soils, but their exploitation relies on the creation and maintenance of an extensive drainage system. Prehistoric technological advances must have increased the potential of the resources accessible to human development. Ploughs and ards, for instance, would certainly have increased the range of soils that could be cultivated, opening up for exploitation heavier but more productive soils than could be exploited with hand tools. Ards were widespread in Europe in the Bronze Age and one has recently been found at Fiavè. It seems certain that this development is linked to the population increase and expansion in areas of settlement witnessed in our area, as in many others, at this time.

Another long-term trend of interest is the tendency to size-decrease in pigs and cattle (Tables 8 and 9). Although the sample sizes are, in many cases, too small to demonstrate the course of these changes in detail, it is at least evident that there is a considerable fall in the average size of both these species from the Neolithic to the Bronze Age, and it seems likely that similar changes took place within the Neolithic (between Molino Casarotto and Rivoli) and within the Bronze Age itself (i.e. between Monte Tondo and Torri). This tendency to size-reduction is a commonplace in European faunal collections between the Mesolithic and the Iron Age, yet it has received little attention except in terms of the standard explanation of the Mesolithic to Neolithic change, as the result of domestication. As the trend continues, in most cases, well beyond the Neolithic, it is likely that the causative factors also continued. A major change taking place in Europe, at this time, seems to have been a considerable population increase, which was coupled with the introduction of cereal agriculture, major forest clearance and the development of intensive herding economies. These, and the sustained population pressure, are likely to have occasioned attempts to maintain the maximum population of herd animals on the available grazing resources. It seems more than likely that this could have stimulated continuing reduction in body-size of the animals concerned, as herd-sizes remained the same or increased, while grazing resources declined because of the additional areas given over to arable agriculture. The vast increase in the importance of the sheep is also relevant here, as it probably represents, to a large extent, the replacement of woodland by permanent pasture.

One index of the rise in population in northern Italy is the increase in the number of sites between the Early Neolithic and the Bronze Age, another being the extension of the primary area of settlement. At Molino Casarotto there are a number of individual sites, spaced out along the edge of the lake. It is possible that these represent the contemporaneous occupations of different family groups but, considering their close proximity and the scale of the available resources, it is more likely that they represent successive occupations by a single group. So far one site probably of comparable age is known from the Berici Hills, and it is noticeable that virtually the whole of the Berici Hills could be utilized by two human groups exploiting two-hour territories. This is not to say that undiscovered Neolithic sites do not exist in the area, for there must certainly be some. However, it does indicate the likely scale of the human population of the time. By the Bronze

Age, a minimum of three sites is known from the Lago di Fimon area alone, many others (including Monte Tondo) occurring elsewhere in the hills. Similarly, although the Alpine foothills in the Fiavè area were likely to have been exploited, at least occasionally or on a seasonal basis, during the Neolithic, it is not until the Bronze Age that really substantial sites are found and, as we have seen, there are reasons for thinking that Fiavè, and probably similar sites such as Ledro, were permanent occupation sites. As already suggested, this too can best be explained in terms of population pressure in the area as a whole.

REFERENCES

Aspes, A. and Fasani, L. (1969) Torri di Arcugnano (Prov. di Vicenza). *Riv. Sci. Preist.*, 24, 364.

√Bagolini, B., Barfield, L.H. and Brogli, A. (1973) Notizie preliminari delle ricerche sull' insediamento neolitico di Fimon-Molino Casarotto (Vicenza) 1969-1971. *Riv. Sci. Preist.*, 28, 161-215.

√Barfield, L.H. (1972) *Northern Italy Before Rome.* London.

Broglio, A. (1968) Monte Tondo (Prov. di Vicenza). *Riv. Sci. Preist.*, 23, 407.

Chaplin, R.E. (1971) *The Study of Animal Bones from Archaeological Sites.* London and New York.

Higgs, E.S. and Jarman, M.R. (1972) The origins of animal and plant husbandry. In Higgs, E.S. (ed.), *Papers in Economic Prehistory*, 3-13. London.

Higgs, E.S. and Jarman, M.R. (1975) Palaeoeconomy. In Higgs, E.S. (ed.), *Palaeoeconomy*, 1-7 London.

Jarman, H.N., Legge, A.E. and Charles, J.A. (1972) Retrieval of plant remains from archaeological sites by froth flotation. In Higgs, E.S. (ed.), *Papers in Economic Prehistory*, 39-48. London.

Jarman, M.R. (1970) Isera (Trentino) Cava Nord: fauna report. *Stud. Trentini di Sci. Nat.*, Sez. B., 47, 78-80.

Jarman, M.R. (1972a) European deer economies and the advent of the Neolithic. In Higgs, E.S. (ed.), *Papers in Economic Prehistory*, 125-47. London.

Jarman, M.R. (1972b) A territorial model for archaeology: a behavioural and geographical approach. In Clarke, D.L. (ed.), *Models in Archaeology*, 705-32. London.

Jarman, M.R. (in press) *Rivoli: the Fauna.*

Jarman, M.R. and Wilkinson, P.F. (1972) Criteria of animal domestication. In Higgs, E.S. (ed.), *Papers in Economic Prehistory*, 83-96. London.

Payne, S. (1972) On the interpretation of bone samples from archaeological sites. In Higgs, E.S. (ed.), *Papers in Economic Prehistory*, 65-81. London.

Perini, R. (1971) Una nuova palafitta a Fiavè – Carera (Trentino – Giudicarie Esteriori). *Stud. Trentini Sci. Nat.*, Sez. B., 48, 84-123.

Uerpmann, H-P. (1973) Animal bone finds and economic archaeology: a critical study of 'osteo-archaeological' method. *World Arch.*, 4, 307-22.

Vita-Finzi, C. and Higgs, E.S. (1970) Prehistoric economy in the Mount Carmel area of Palestine: site catchment analysis. *P.P.S.*, 36, 1-37.

JOHN NANDRIS

Some factors in the Early Neothermal settlement of south-east Europe

It seems appropriate here to make some brief observations about factors affecting human settlement in south-east Europe during the Early Neothermal period, in that many of the themes in question are ones to which Professor Grahame Clark has always drawn attention. The fact that they are of universal application and continuing relevance is in itself a better testimony than this short note.

A systematic treatment would fall under four headings, which comprise the media within which the processes of change affecting early man took place. These are the environmental, the economic, the technological and the biosocial media. About some of these, archaeology is empowered to say more than about others, and in any case their separation is an artificial matter. In reality they are mutually interdependent, and the processes of change themselves, largely those of differentiation and diffusion, are simultaneous in their operation. An understanding of rates of change, and of the ways in which changes in the media continually deflect one another from climax, can be arrived at only when the material of which prehistory is constituted has been placed securely in the primary field of reference of that study, which is spatial and temporal. For this reason an external frame of reference for dating is important to prehistoric studies. Many of our endeavours have still to achieve some sort of descriptive validity in these fields, and it can be said that explanatory ambitions often outrun this basic limitation.

In the first place the applicability of the term 'Neothermal' must be noted. The regions in question, like many others, were never subjected to glaciation. Together with important chronological differences between the successions, there and in north-west Europe, this discredits the notion of a 'Post-Glacial' period. Instead, the period of rising temperatures during the Anathermal culminating in the maxima of the Altithermal is here referred to inclusively as the 'Early Neothermal'. It was a period of very great importance for history, for it saw the emergence of a mode of behaviour characteristic only of the Neothermal. The conspicuous evolutionary success of the Neolithic mode need not be laboured, especially for Europe, although no one has done more to divert the efforts of prehistorians from eurocentrism than Grahame Clark. We are all now aware of the potentialities of distant areas of the globe for our understanding of this mode, for placing the European developments in a more realistic perspective, and for outlining possible priorities (such as, for example, that of Jōmon pottery in the technological medium). Nevertheless, to the best of our knowledge, the mode in question remains characteristically Neothermal. For this reason, a global view should see it comprehensively as a mode of human behaviour moving within all the media, reciprocating their changes, and not solely in the terms of one medium, usually the economic one. Thus one can hope to assess how universally valid the idea is of a distinctively Neothermal mode of behaviour; or, conversely, how far this was localized in its origins, and exactly where lay the evolutionary superiority that ensured it a widespread diffusion and domination. It is also worth noting that this behavioural mode did not constitute, initially, a fundamental break with the earlier and contemporary Mesolithic, in that sites still drew their subsistence, whether seasonally or not, from an immediately surrounding catchment area. The fundamental change in this respect came with what is known as urbanization. Pre-adaptations for this emerged during the course of village settlement, just as those for village settlement were found among hunter-fisher communities, in areas such as the Danube gorges, particularly favourable to hunter-fisher climax.

The history of Neothermal times could be

said, from a more local and environmental point of view, also to be that of the rise and subsequent decline of the European forest. This fact is, in itself, sufficient to demonstrate the mutual interdependence of processes of change. The vegetational decline seems to have been largely anthropogenic, starting not long after the inception of afforestation, and certainly before its climax. It was linked intimately with the polycyclic changes that produced the present patterns of soil profiles and distributions as well as the ecologically despoiled face of Europe which, like many of the products of domestication, is characterized among other things by a reduction in variety. A reciprocal effect, here, is the way in which certain species have been favoured by man's activity – for example, the spread of *Picea* in Switzerland from the Atlantic climatic phase onwards (Markgraf 1970:249).

The way in which present-day appearances are a complex resultant of such interdependent processes operating over a long period of time will be self-evident to an ecologist and should not be unfamiliar to any archaeologist. Nevertheless, it deserves emphasis. The necessary attempts have recently been made to take archaeological settlements out of the unreal museological and typological environment in which they have lain for so long, and to place them in a behavioural environment composed of resource zones located within the catchment area of the site. The field methods for this are, it may be said, bound to yield results. The question may therefore be raised, not only whether this is in itself a good thing, but also whether there is any short cut to the arduous conventional work of palaeoenvironmental and chronological reconstruction that is necessary for a soundly based interpretation. Is it really the case that the recognition of even physiographic changes 'demands little beyond practice' and that 'a lack of formal training . . . and innocence of formal preconceptions' are advantageous? (Higgs & Vita-Finzi 1972:34).

Clearly, there are varying degrees of difficulty involved. Where animal behaviour in relation to a relatively unchanged topography is involved, the difficulties may be less than where more mutable edaphic and vegetational features are essential to the interpretation. The difficulties do not invalidate 'site catchment' as an invaluable technique of research, any more than they do in the case of radiocarbon dating or palynology. But just as, in both these cases, qualifications and objections became apparent after a certain stage, so with the behavioural approach to sites it is better that the difficulties should be made explicit earlier, rather than later. This should in no way negate the achievements of the approach in putting forward intelligible results for discussion. The best method in such brief examinations as the present one which, in any case, runs the risk of being accused of superficiality, would seem to be to take one or two examples of changes operating in various media in the south-east European area, and to view them for their own sakes as well as for any light that they may shed on the difficulties of instantaneous palaeoenvironmental and palaeoeconomic reconstructions.

The fundamental problem might be said to be that of placing sites in relation to their contemporary resources. Like many a simple problem, this is too basic to be shrugged off. It can also become complex immediately there are two or more coeval sites within a resource zonation. External frames of reference are essential, namely a dating frame for the sites, and a framework of environmental developments also dated externally. The 'customary archaeological procedure' (Vita-Finzi & Higgs 1970:6) of taking similarities to indicate contemporaneity confuses two different levels of interpretation, since the customary notion of contemporaneity in archaeology is too permissive to allow the refinement of explanations that may have to discount, or to claim explicitly, the simultaneous exploitation of the same resource zones by coeval sites. Whether they are, or are not, contemporary is clearly fundamental both to the exploitation and the explanation; but it can readily be agreed that 'we have no means of telling which sites were, in fact, precisely contemporaneous' (Higgs & Vita-Finzi 1972:29).

One of the most influential factors in interpretations of the past is inevitably, and unfortunately, an almost subconscious acceptance of modern surface appearances. We may be conscious of this element in our own critical make-up, and yet be unable fully to eradicate it. That it extends to notions of human behaviour, and of the reaction of early man to environing nature and to other human groups, is only too clear in some of the explanations offered for this behaviour. Aside from that sphere of interpretation, however, what immediately concerns us here is the fundamental nature of some of the environmental changes that have taken place, especially in the geomorphological, hydrological, vegetational and faunal fields, and the difficulty of crediting a merely superficial inspection of these with a durable explanatory value. Some brief examples of these changes can be given from the south-east European area, and the fact that many of them are relatively recent does not invalidate the argument that we are dealing often with an anthropogenic palimpsest in which only traces may remain of the relata of the original site.

In the geomorphological field, soil formation, and sometimes the deleterious impact on it of the Neolithic mode, were very influential on human settlement and economy. During Neothermal times, the story of European soil formation was unfolding contemporaneously with that of human settlement. It can be misleading, therefore, to plot sites against soil, especially on maps with classifications drawn up for quite different purposes. Effects of aggradation, also, are sometimes prominent. At Gura Baciului, near Cluj (Vlassa 1972), First Temperate Neolithic (FTN) burials and signs of settlement were found underneath some two metres of fine-grained deposits, superficially resembling loess but probably attributable to hill wash. In the Mediterranean area, Vita-Finzi has drawn attention also to important geomorphological changes (Vita-Finzi 1969). In central/south-east Europe an alternative effect is seen on *Bandkeramik* sites, in which the surface layer of the settlement is seldom, if ever, uneroded. The various pedological and geomorphological changes may affect both the discovery of sites and their interpretation, in the latter case even after excavation.

In the hydrological field, the Hungarian Basin drained by the Tisza and the Danube, and their tributaries, is one of the best general examples of man's protracted interference. This was most effective from the eighteenth century A.D. in the regulation of the Tisza and other rivers, lowering the water-table by several metres, with important consequences for soil erosion by deflation, and for the vegetation. The FTN sites in the region were related to areas of well drained soils (Nandris 1970a) with a relatively low water-table, and very frequently also to the flood-plain/terrace boundaries. These boundaries were altered completely by the drainage, so that this relationship (which is not always to a prominent terrace line) is obscured. Neither the use of recent maps nor the field-walking of the area at the present day could be relied on to reveal it.

As an example of the sort of physical changes that should be studied in relation to archaeological sites, Starčevo itself will suffice. According to Stefanović von Vilovo (1883), the bank of the Danube in the region of Starčevo and Pančevo shifted 645 metres in the 48 years between 1834 and 1882. This represents a rate of 1.34 km. in a century, considerably more than the average rate posited for shifting induced by the Košava, although this wind may here have played its part. At this rate, it will be noted that Starčevo *could* lie beside the Danube within three centuries (Fig. 1). The position of the river during the FTN occupation has never been established. It seems clear that, at one time, the Danube ran along the direct course, now taken by the Tamiš, from Opovo to Pančevo, the line of which is continued by the terrace on which Starčevo lies. The effect of the Košava, blowing from the south-east in spring and autumn, is certainly to deflect the Danube away from, rather than towards, Starčevo. In itself, however, it could constitute an influential reason for choosing some sites for settlement, rather than others. Starčevo lies on the edge of the flood-plain terrace, facing away from the Košava. Microclimatic and microenvironmental features are influential for individual sites, and it is one of the contributions of the field techniques of site catchment to have emphasized this point. Many sites, in particular the Mesolithic sites of the forest zone of Europe, may have been located in relation to features of ephemeral topography, such as forest clearings, that are difficult to assess.

Some fifty kilometres upstream of Starčevo, the Tisza joins the Danube at Titel, which lies on a plateau surrounded by old river channels (Fig. 2). The Danube formerly flowed north of this plateau and joined the Tisza at Kamen, as it still does in flood. The position of sites, such as Perlez and Mužlja, on the terraces fringing the flood-area of the Tisza and Begej, should also be noted here. A Roman camp near Titel apparently lay on high ground on the right bank of the Tisza; it subsequently became an island, and now lies on the left bank (Schweiger-Lerchenfeld 1896:126). The dry area on the

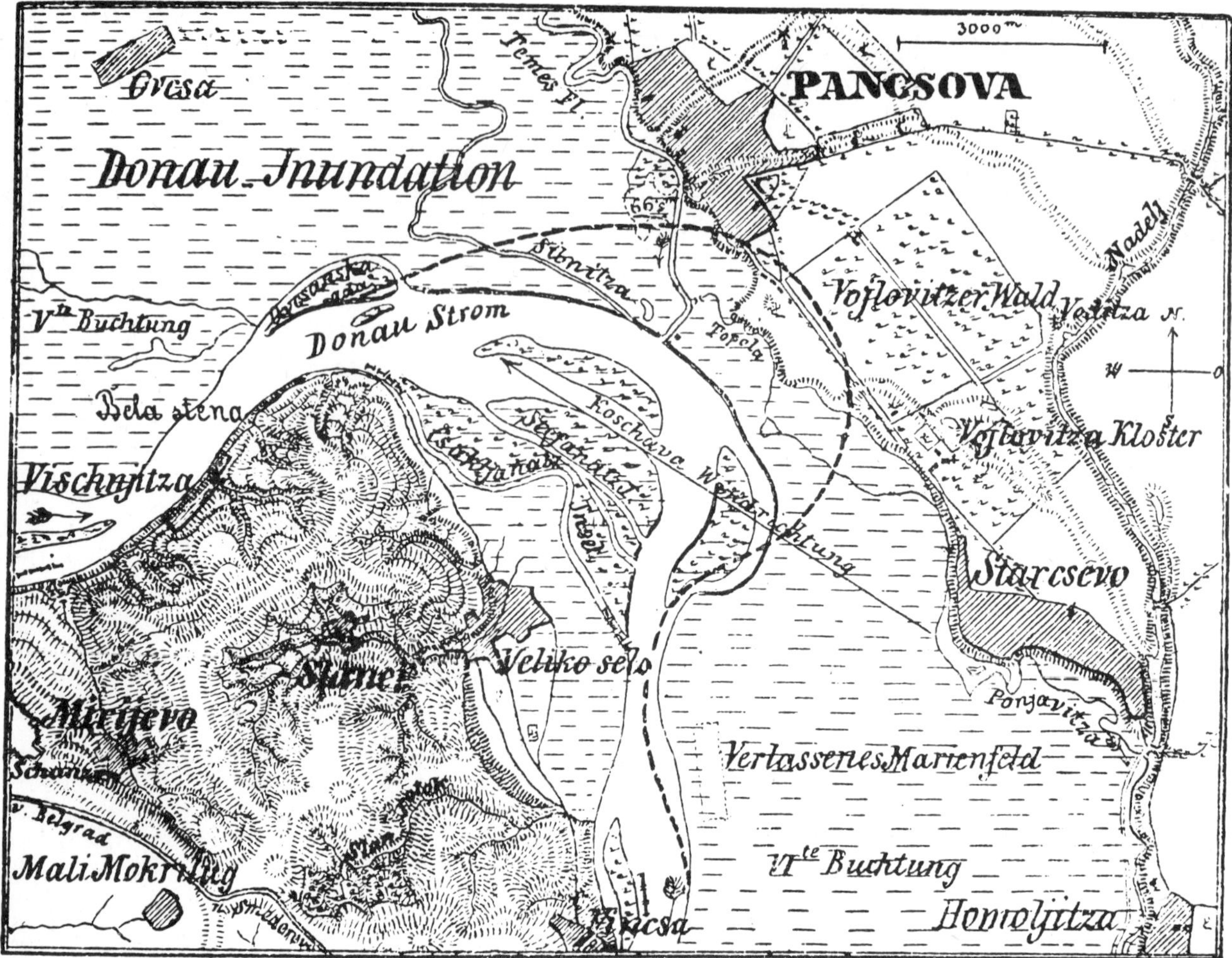

Figure 1. Bending of the Danube, induced by the Košava, in the neighbourhood of Starčevo. The Vinča site is just off the map, to the south. (Schweiger-Lerchenfeld 1896: 527)

flood-plain between and south of Titel and Perlez, on which Knićanin (Rudolfsgnade) now lies, was created artificially at the beginning of the seventeenth century. With changes such as these in mind, the dangers of pronouncing on the location and catchment areas of sites on the basis of 'an eye for country' are evident. It ought to be added that it is equally indiscriminate to posit a wholesale destruction of sites by geomorphological processes.

Climate is another field in which the relationship between past and present conditions is of great importance, and cannot be superficially assessed. Indeed, the present climatic pattern of a region may, all too easily, receive subconscious acceptance, as a norm within which to locate prehistoric settlement. It is also possible that assessment of the environment of a site, during one or two days at a certain season of the year, may give a misleading impression. Nor can every year, in itself, be taken as widely representative of the norms for the region. It is clear that even minor climatic shifts may have considerable explanatory value, especially in marginal regions. Within Europe, minor oscillations within the Altithermal in alpine regions are already attested, and other subdivisions will, no doubt, appear. The best assumption palaeoclimatology can offer at present would seem to be one of marginal variations locally, in the broad patterns established during the Anathermal. Quasi-modern zonations may have been present during the Altithermal, allowing for the conditions of higher temperature and precipitation then extant. This assumption would certainly seem to underlie Sielman's study of regional climatic factors functionally related to the distribution of German *Bandkeramik* settlement (1972). His study also underlines the point that a valid external assurance of dating is

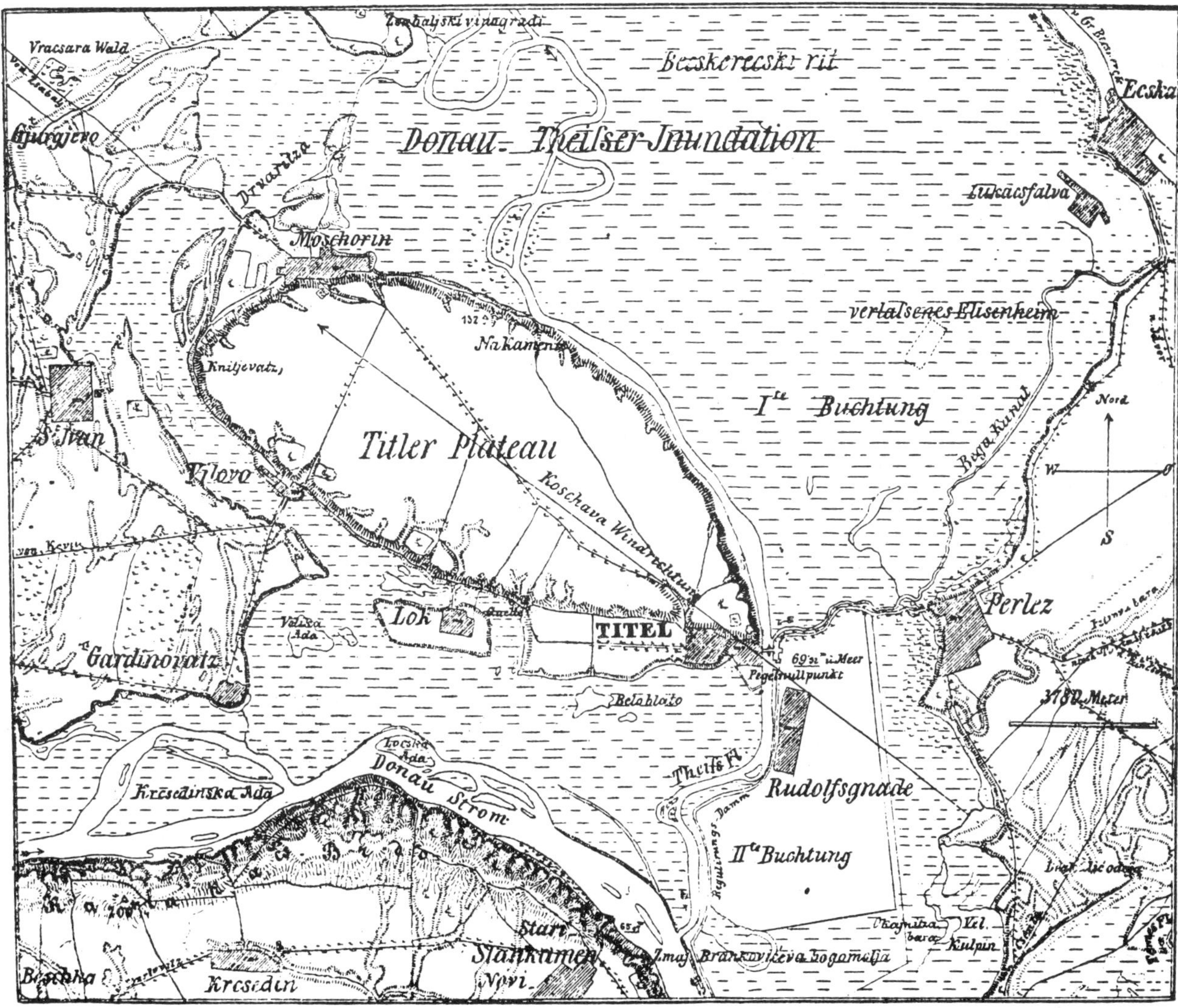

Figure 2. Old course of the Danube around the Titel Plateau. (Schweiger-Lerchenfeld 1896: 526)

necessary before one can make explanatory correlations between, for example, the 'earliest' *Bandkeramik* sites and environmental zonations, whether climatological or otherwise. To some extent, this primary assumption of marginal variation would seem to be justifiable in cases of established Neothermal environmental features where we can, indeed, find correlations that make sense. For example, the south-east margins of FTN settlement in Romania (Moldavia and Muntenia) do not encroach on the present steppe boundaries; nor does the southern Bug culture, while the later Cucuteni-Tripolje settlement of Moldavia and the Ukraine is limited within the forest-steppe zone, in a similar fashion.

While emphasizing that, with rainfall, seasonal distribution is perhaps even more important than annual means, it is possible to offer a zonation of south-east Europe, based primarily on modern mean annual precipitation, but one which has some explanatory validity, at least from Altithermal times. This is shown in the map (Fig. 3), which is to a large extent self-explanatory.

This proposed zonation can be correlated with archaeological developments in several senses. It gives a basis for the importance of the Macedo-Bulgarian region as a transitional large-scale ecotone in Early Neolithic times (Nandris 1970b). It was through this region that an adaptive continuum was afforded for the penetration from Mediterranean and Near Eastern regions into Temperate Europe of the

Figure 3. Regional zonation of south east Europe. First Temperate Neolithic and Early Greek Neolithic sites related to rainfall. Transition from Mediterranean into Temperate Europe via the Macedo-Bulgarian 'ecotone' region, bounded by wet (western) and dry (eastern) littorals. The northern and western extension of the First Temperate Neolithic zone leads into the Central European *Bandkeramik* regions. The Maritsa basin falls under markedly Mediterranean climatic influences.

- ● First Temperate Neolithic and early Greek Neolithic sites (after Nandris 1968 and 1968a).
- 1. Macedo-Bulgarian ecotonal region.
- 2. Wet Littoral, and Carpathian/Central annual rainfall >750 mm.
- 3. Dry littoral (steppe), annual rainfall <500 mm.
- 4. Transition to Central European Bandkeramik regions.
- 5. North-easterly extension of FTN (Cris), and Southern Bug culture.

Neolithic mode. The respective littorals, dry in the east and wet in the west, are the scenes of archaeological developments quite distinct from those of the other zones. The Temperate zone of south-east Europe makes the transition to Central Europe in its northern and western regions, where it can be linked ecologically with the *Bandkeramik* regions propounded by Sielman.

Faunal and vegetational changes have been as far-reaching as any others, but it is hardly necessary to list those declines and changes in European species that are common knowledge. Allusion has already been made to the fact that reduction in variety may be one of the most significant effects of domestication. What is of relevance here is the relationship of early man to his contemporary assemblages of plants and animals. It must seem clear that this can be estimated only from excavation, coupled with palaeoeconomic and palaeoenvironmental techniques. Even then, there may be less tangible resources, not to mention culturally induced illogicalities, that affect the interpretation of an occupation. When calculation is made of yields from the main resources, whether of protein from meat-weights or of crop-yields, it is worth emphasizing less obvious food sources, which may make feasible more extended occupations or different patterns of behaviour from those envisaged on the basis of the main resources alone. The use of forest fruits and minor plants of various sorts is attested from the Mesolithic through Early Neothermal times, and then strikingly by Tollund man, and into the present day; among these must be included e.g. mushrooms. The occurrence of edible mollusca in FTN contexts, notably *Helix pomatia* and *Unio*, is very common, and it is probable that snails formed an important part of the diet. In the fourth-millennium Lengyel culture in Poland, *Unio pictorum* may even have been stored for consumption (Wiślański 1970:74). The way in which the shells of *Helix pomatia* occur in pits at, for example, the FTN levels of Lepenski Vir, would seem to indicate that they were food refuse, rather than merely natural deposits. The large numbers of *Unio* shells in Criş FTN contexts has been emphasized by Necrasov (1961:265), and both species are present at Gura Baciului in the FTN (Vlassa 1972). They are also found in other Later Neolithic contexts in south-east Europe, but these and other occurrences in the FTN suffice to demonstrate their presence from the inception of the Neolithic. *Helix pomatia* and *Cepaea hortensis* are both found in the Late Boreal Mesolithic of Mücheln-Möckerling (Mania & Toepfer 1971).

It may also be worth noting some of the more obvious examples of vegetational distributions that are closely linked to a long perspective of human interference, if only to make the point that less obvious ones might escape cursory inspection in the field. One of these is afforded by *Triticum monococcum*, which was cultivated extensively at altitudes of 300-900 metres in the Apuseni mountains and the Maramureş, in western and northern Transylvania (Borza 1945), and indeed probably in other areas of south-east Europe. However, we are not dealing with the relics of either a prehistoric or a natural situation. The altitude zonation and refuges here are not so much those of plants as of Dacian populations cultivating this grain after the Roman withdrawal in A.D. 271 and under successive foreign incursions into lowland Romania. The Romanian name, *alac*, that is used for the grain in the Transylvanian regions mentioned, betrays the Latin nomenclature (*alica, halicastrum*); and its occurrence in Asturia, Sardinia and Sicily under this name can be used to support the idea of its effective introduction into Dacia by the Romans, through legions and mercenaries from Mediterranean regions. It is not necessary to pursue the example any further to make the point that any attempt to link apparently feral occurrences in the south-east European region of *Triticum monococcum* with prehistoric times must be made cautiously, and that this is simply a paradigm (in the basic English and not in the jargon sense, if any, of that term) of a situation that may apply to other and less obvious factors. In this example, the interplay of the environmental, bio-social and economic media is also evident. The simultaneous operation of long-term processes of change in a number of media makes single-factor explanations unsatisfactory even at the generalized level for which prehistoric explanation is valid.

Since the above discussion refers largely to environmental change, and its interpretation in an archaeological context, a final point of importance, relating specifically to south-east Europe, should be made here. We do not yet have anything like the detail available in north-west Europe for the framework of environmental developments since the beginning of the Neothermal. Enough is, however, available to make it clear that the ecological and climatic successions did not follow the course of development implied by the zonal names, such as Atlantic, Boreal etc., given by Blytt and Sernander. To use this terminology for south-east Europe is equivalent to using the detailed terminology developed for the French Palaeolithic as if it had the same meaning in other parts of the world. At the outset of environmental reconstruction in south-east Europe, it may be unavoidable to use these climatic terms, but it should be made clear that they are only a stand-by, in expectation of the emergence of a sequence resting on independent pollen and radiocarbon analyses. This terminology, too, cannot be used as a short cut to palaeoenvironmental reconstruction.

REFERENCES

Borza, A. (1945) Alacul (*Triticum monococcum*) la Români. *Buletinul Grădinii Botanice si al Muzeului Botanic* (Cluj), 25, 93-119 and Pl. III (map) – V.

Higgs, E.S. and Vita-Finzi, C. (1972) Prehistoric economies: a territorial approach. In Higgs, E.S. (ed.), *Papers in Economic Prehistory*, 27-46. London.

Mania, D. and Toepfer, V. (1971) Zur jungquartären Landschaftageschichte und mesolithischen Besiedlung des Geiseltales. *Jahresschrift mitteldeutsche Vorgeschichte*, 55, 11-34.

Markgraf, V. (1970) Palaeohistory of the spruce in Switzerland. *Nature*, 228, 249-51.

Nandris, J.G. (1968) *The Prehistoric Archaeology of South-East Europe*. Ph.D. dissertation, Cambridge University.

√Nandris, J.G. (1970a) Ground water as a factor in the First Temperate Neolithic settlement of the Körös region. *Zbornik Narodnog Muzeja* (Belgrade), 6, 59-71.

√Nandris, J.G. (1970b) The Development and Relationships of the Earlier Greek Neolithic. *Man*, 5, 192-213.

Necrasov, O. (1961) Study of wild and domestic fauna of the early Neolithic Criş culture (in Russian, with Romanian and French summaries). *Analele Ştiinţifice (Ştiinţe Naturale)* (Iaşi), 7, fasc. 2, 265-74.

Schweiger-Lerchenfeld, A.F.v. (1896) *Die Donau*. Wien, Pest, Leipzig.

Sielman, B. (1972) Die frühneolithische Besiedlung Mitteleuropas. *Die Anfänge des Neolithikums vom Orient bis Nordeuropa (Fundamenta A/3)*, 5a, 1-65.

Vilovo, J.S.v. (1883) *Ungarns Stromregulirungen*. Vienna.

Vita-Finzi, C. (1969) *The Mediterranean Valleys: Geological Changes in Historical Times*. London.

Vita-Finzi, C. and Higgs, E.S. (1970) Prehistoric economy in the Mount Carmel area of Palestine: site catchment analysis. *P.P.S.*, 36, 1-37.

Vlassa, N. (1972) Cea mai veche fază a complexului cultural Starčevo-Criş in România. *Acta Mvsei Napocensis*, 9, 7-28. (For German trans., see *Praehistorische Zeitschrift*, 47.)

Wiślański, T. (ed.) (1970) *The Neolithic in Poland*. Wrocław.

ANDREW SHERRATT

Resources, technology and trade: an essay in early European metallurgy

Introduction

Early European metallurgy has been a topic of debate since the beginning of the study of prehistory. As a fundamental division in the Three-age framework and a crucial contribution to chronology through typological sequences, it was a focus of interest from the mid-nineteenth century onwards. More recently, the application of rapid techniques of micro-analysis has provided a massive body of quantitative data on the composition of early metal objects and new opportunities for interpretation, while the large body of surviving material continues to offer itself as a major source of information – not only about chronology but also about the way of life of Copper and Bronze Age communities.

The abundance of copper and bronze objects from these periods leaves no doubt about their importance in the prehistoric economy, and the reasons for growth in the use of metal are clearly essential in this case to our understanding of economic change in primitive society. The process usually invoked to explain the spread of metallurgy is one of discovery, followed by diffusion of knowledge about the techniques involved, leading to a wide-spread use of metal because of its superiority for manufacturing tools and weapons. The change in technology would thus have led to a breakdown of economic self-sufficiency, and a consequent reliance on trade as a fundamental mechanism. At the same time, increasing productivity of agriculture would have begun to produce a surplus that served both to finance this increased scale of trading activity and to support the specialists concerned.

In its original conception (Childe 1958), this model sought to connect the appearance of metallurgy in Europe with the activities of prospectors from urban societies (in the Near East) whose concentration of capital had fostered the growth of the industry. More recently the re-appraisal of European chronologies has suggested a more active role for south-east Europe, and attention has turned to the background of technological skills in high-temperature firing available to Neolithic bakers and potters (Renfrew 1969). But, whatever the circumstances of discovery, emphasis still rests on metallurgical *knowledge* as the key factor in the explanation, with the assumption that, once discovered, metal became common because of its self-evident usefulness or inherent attractiveness. Both in Childe's account of this process (1956:115-20) and in Renfrew's discussion (1972:308, 483) of the growth of metallurgy in the Aegean, economic change is seen as the *result* of technological change, both through increased efficiency and through its stimulation of 'new needs'.

It may be doubted, however, whether the advantages conferred by a knowledge of the technical processes of metalworking could by themselves have had such far-reaching effects. Early metal tools were not, in practice, more efficient than stone ones, nor are early metal weapons likely to have been decisive in battle. Are there, then, less obvious reasons why a relatively rare raw material such as copper should have achieved so wide a circulation in the third and second millennia? And was this circulation different, in scale or character, from existing networks distributing materials such as fine stone?

The inevitable bias given by a material subject-matter often leads the archaeologist to a view of prehistory in which technology appears as the main element of progress. On the other hand, Professor Clark (1965) has stressed the need to come to terms with the social role of material objects, and to treat prehistoric societies in a total ecological context. From this standpoint, it may be possible to reach a view of the artefactual evidence that relates it to long-term processes of economic and social change, rather than treating technology as an independent sector producing revolutionary repercussions throughout society.

'Stone Age economics'

A key issue in this discussion is the contrast often drawn between the relative self-sufficiency of Neolithic life and the variety of raw materials required for the more complex technical processes of the Bronze Age. If there is a difference in trading activity between the two periods, however, it cannot be summarized as simply as this. Even in the Neolithic there were inherent limitations on self-sufficiency.

This point soon becomes evident from a consideration of site locations. The distribution of a population dependent on agriculture is determined largely by the soils on which its crops are grown, the most suitable zones for cultivation being naturally those with deep soil and an abundant water-supply. In order to make use of these locations, however, another set of resources is required – hard stone for tools, for example, or supplies of salt to offset dietary deficiency. By and large, such resources occur in different environments, and only a limited number of agricultural settlements have direct access to them. For instance, a distribution such as that of the early Neolithic *Bandkeramik* in central Europe (Clark 1952: Fig. 45), with its concentration on open loess-covered plains, implies a constant import of materials from sources peripheral to the main concentration of population.

In any case, there are good reasons why, in small-scale societies, individual settlements and clusters of villages should not be isolated from wider contacts. Single units of settlement are naturally vulnerable to the possibility of local disaster, whether due to poor harvest or disease. A continuous exchange of population from village to village creates a network of relationships that can distribute inequalities in local production and provide a wider pool of assistance. As a background to the distribution of rarer materials, a continuous movement of personnel and subsistence products between villages must be envisaged. It is this network which provides the basic carrier for the kinds of material that survive archaeologically in Neolithic contexts.

An important effect of this is the pattern of 'random walk' followed by individual objects in the course of such exchanges. Although there may be a general direction of drift in one class of material as it moves towards an area of scarcity, there is a large number of jumps between the source and the ultimate area of consumption. This lack of a direct link between producers and consumers at some distance from the source implies a strong spatial limit on effective demand with this kind of system. A distribution channel for a particular material is thus likely to have the following structure:

1. *Source* – not necessarily in an area of agricultural production, though accessible from it. Activities: unearthing of material, preliminary reduction of bulk.
2. *Production zone* – settlements concerned in the active exploitation of the material. Activities: working up into an exchangeable form.
3. *Direct contact zone* – area of settlements linked directly to production zone by face-to-face contact. Effective supply as result of close kinship links.
4. *Indirect supply zone* – area of settlements without direct access to the production zone, receiving supplies through intermediaries.

Anthropologists have stressed the basic contrast between the mechanisms connecting zones (3) and (4) with their supplies. Sahlins (1965) has noted the way in which exchanges with close kinsmen, who may be expected to provide assistance, are less concerned with material equivalence than those that take place across tribal boundaries, where a more direct return is sought. Brookfield & Hart (1971:315), discussing Melanesian evidence, have drawn the contrast between *transfer*, where goods are easily balanced by services, and *trade*, where goods are rarely exchanged for non-material favours. Rappaport (1968:106) has suggested that production will be sensitive to demand from within the area of direct contact, but not outside it. In a situation where each village is producing a similar range of subsistence goods, there will be an especially sharp division between those able to supply food and services direct to the producers and those beyond this range. Only in the case of particularly important materials is this friction overcome, by the exchange of high-value objects between certain individuals in different local groups (Sherratt 1972:506).

This lack of direct articulation between supply and demand must have been a characteristic limitation on Neolithic economies, as Rappaport points out for the primitive farming groups of the New Guinea highlands. The problem is to avoid a situation in which an extensively needed commodity is under-exploited because of the lack of items to exchange for it. In overcoming this, the circulation of non-utilitarian goods plays a vital role in mobilizing demand. Items of adornment or display that are exchangeable for essential commodities, and can themselves be accumulated, encourage continuity in the production of basic materials even when local needs are filled. They thus act as a kind of 'fly-wheel' for the whole system.

Not only do items not directly concerned with subsistence activities contribute to the maintenance of the system, but essential commodities, such as fine stone, also have non-material functions. Speaking again of the New Guinea highlands, Strathern notes that 'in their area of production axes circulate as items of exchange value, in ceremonial exchange, death compensation, bride-wealth, payments in the settlement of disputes, and they had a similar role in the Enga area' where they were distributed. While ordinary working axes may be given in these contexts, particularly large and fine specimens are considered appropriate for ceremonial and bride-wealth presentations, and in the case quoted by Chappell (1966:98) these may be up to five times the size of working axes. (Such an axe 30 cm. in length would require about three weeks' work in grinding.)

The goods in circulation thus carry important symbolic values in a way that is often explicitly organized. Commodities may be accumulated and exchanged in specified quantities for particular situations such as marriage alliances. Such artefacts are not generally exchangeable, as with a true currency, but act as 'standardized entitlements to a series of social prerogatives' (Douglas 1967:135).

The wider effects of this social aspect of material goods are twofold. In the first place, the system is continuously generating demand both for the commodities with direct symbolic value and for those exchangeable with them, thus helping to overcome the limitations on supplies of useful materials that arise from the lack of direct articulation between producers and consumers. The use of necessary items, such as axes, in ceremonial contexts also ensures a reservoir of raw material in case of shortage. In the second place, by linking the movement of goods with the distribution of marriage partners, the system contributes to demographic equilibrium by adjusting the spatial distribution of women and goods (Rappaport 1968:108-9).

This tentative sketch of the working of a simple economic system is a starting point for the analysis of the prehistoric European situation. In opposition to the idea that 'a Stone Age community was, at least potentially, self-sufficing' and that 'the objects of Stone Age trade were always luxuries . . . at least things that men could have done without' (Childe 1951:35), it suggests that continuous circulation was a basic pre-condition of such societies, extending even beyond simple material needs.

To be fully satisfactory, however, something beyond a static model is necessary if it is to cope with the evident changes within the prehistoric economy. In the first place, changes occur as new sources of raw materials are discovered and old ones are exhausted. Such changes are especially likely as the area under exploitation itself expands and peripheral groups come into contact with a wider environment. Secondly, any growth in population will also increase effective demand, making worth while intensification in the effort involved in unearthing raw materials and the development of larger-scale operations. Perhaps even more important are changes in the sphere of subsistence economy underlying the patterns of distribution in rarer materials. Once again, ethnography provides a clue to the processes involved.

Coastal Melanesia, in particular, shows a high development of long-distance trading links, some of them of extraordinary complexity. For some of the groups involved, participation in these networks is essential, not only at the level of raw materials but also in terms of basic subsistence products. Hogbin (1951) quotes examples from the Huon Gulf of New Guinea where groups survived only by producing pottery and importing food-stuffs, and Malinowski noted the division, within the Trobriand Islands, between the richer agricultural part and the poorer areas of the interior that manufacture wooden dishes, baskets and pots to exchange with it for food. In these cases, the occupation of such poorer areas is possible only because of a continuing output of non-subsistence products. One consequence of the extension of settlement to marginal environments is the need for a class of products that stimulate the mobility of subsistence goods.

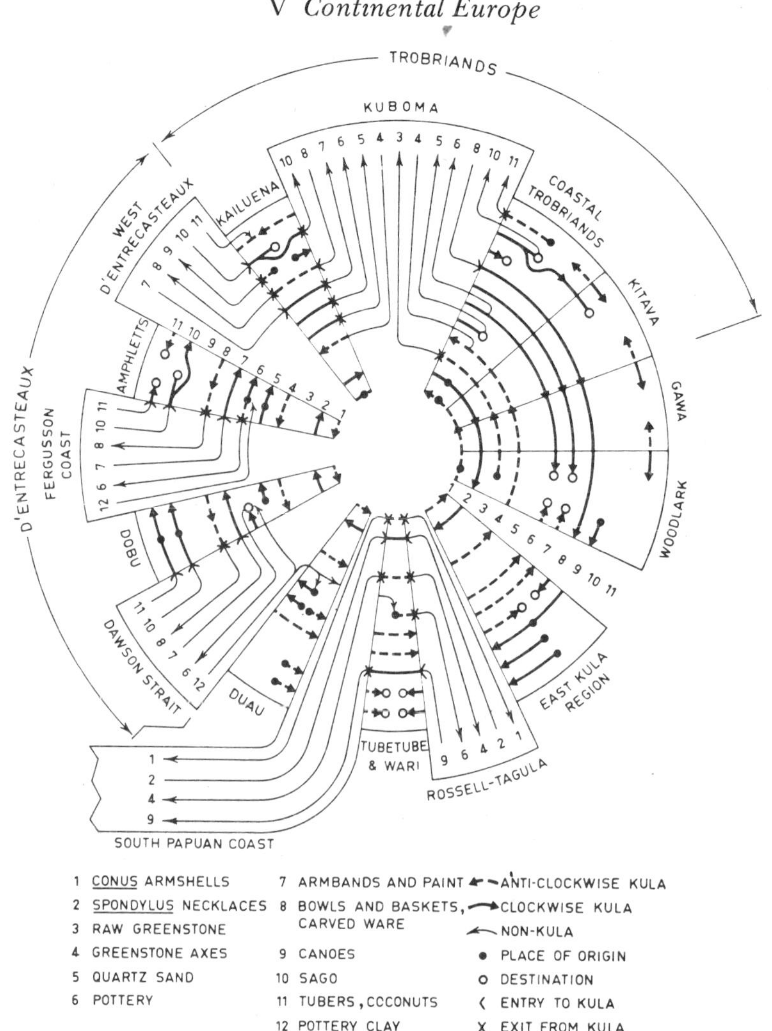

Figure 1. A reconstruction of the flows of products around the Kula Ring; from Brookfield and Hart 1971.

Brookfield & Hart (1971:320-32), in a stimulating discussion of the problem, interpret the complex cycles of inter-island exchange in Melanesia as part of a 'flywheel' mechanism to keep products on the move and so to articulate several kinds of specialization within the chain (see Fig. 1). Such regional differentiation allows areas of lower subsistence potential to survive alongside better-endowed ones. Indeed, the fact that transactions still occur in a series of individual jumps means that opportunities open up for middleman trading, and some areas well connected in the network can survive even without specialist products of their own (e.g. Siassi).

In contrast to the relatively simple situation postulated above for the *Bandkeramik*, with its concentration on a single productive zone and occasional expeditions for raw materials outside this, the colonization of a wide range of landscapes leads to a situation in which various groups are actively pumping rarer materials and products into the system. The contrast stems, not from a disparity in technology and raw material requirements but from the difference in settlement ecology between the two cases.

One further feature of the Melanesian case may be mentioned – the social mechanisms involved. The actual operation of the trading process is in the hands of individuals: participation in the network depends on the ability to create stocks of trade articles and to manipulate social and ceremonial relationships. 'Leadership and the political structure of groups are not set apart from the sphere of commerce; the rewards of the successful entrepreneur are the highest rewards of power and prestige which the society has to offer; he cannot dominate the political situation without first dominating the market ... This kind of fluidity is not a matter of individuals moving up and down rapidly from one recognized position to another. It is much more an instability in the relationship of actual positions, since each outstanding leader creates his own leadership' (Douglas 1967:125).

In such systems, which have come to be known as 'big man' systems (Sahlins 1963), richer individuals provide nodes of concentration for circulating goods, without a rigidly hierarchical social structure divided on class lines. The accumulation of subsistence products is a temporary matter, and the climb to prestige is expressed in possession of the items of display, such as valued ornaments, which act as indicators or 'counters' of success. Although the majority of transactions is concerned with subsistence products, the system runs on the movement of symbolic items and these provide a material reading of varying status positions. This situation, one of regional economic differentiation articulated by individuals in small communities, must have been the condition of much of later prehistoric Europe before the emergence of urban centres. How far are such processes reflected in the artefactual record?

The movement of materials in Neolithic Europe

The patterns of movement, even in inorganic raw materials, are a field of research hardly yet systematically explored, but some idea of the scale involved can be gained from the major commodities often recognized and from the few areas where detailed studies have been made.

The Neolithic economy required both the cutting and scraping tools for fine work that had been essential to previous hunting economies, and a range of more massive implements for forest clearance and the manufacture of wooden tools. Higher population densities, moreover, demanded a much greater bulk of raw materials. For heavy axes and chisels, either large blocks of flint were necessary or else crystalline massive rocks, mostly of highland occurrence. These included ancient sedimentary rocks such as greywackes; igneous rocks either formed at great depth, such as diorite, or nearer the surface, such as dolerite; and direct volcanic products, such as lavas (e.g. andesite and trachyte); or consolidated fall-out products (tuffs), and metamorphosed forms of these and other rocks such as amphibolite or schist. The more deeply formed varieties have larger crystals and are hard to flake, while those more rapidly cooled are more likely to approach flint in their flaking properties. Apart from flints and cherts, almost all of the rocks used for heavy tools occur in regions of low agricultural potential, either in ancient massifs or more recently up-thrust blocks.

In different areas, the distribution of agricultural land might be adjacent to such regions or far removed. In the Balkans, with tectonic basins surrounded by highland areas, there were many local sources of such rocks in the crystalline massif and volcanic deposits in the Tertiary fold-chains (Sherratt 1972:518). In addition, siltstones and cherts were used from later sedimentary deposits, while the extensive Cretaceous deposits of north-west Bulgaria provided large quantities of the characteristic brown flint that had been exploited since the Palaeolithic.

The same pattern, on a larger scale, is represented in the Carpathian Basin. Surrounded on all sides by young fold-mountains with local volcanic activity, the basin itself consists of two parts: in the western area of Transdanubia, flint and chert, along with hard intrusive rocks, occur in the Mesozoic formations of the Bakony mountains; but to the east of the Danube neither these nor massive rocks are locally available, and an area of around 50,000 sq. km. provides only river-pebbles. This deficiency is compensated for by the richness of the surrounding mountains in raw materials and their direct river links with the Danube Basin. To the north, the volcanic range of the Mátra-Bükk-Zemplén mountains could provide not only trachyte and related rocks for heavier tools but also, in the parts near Tokaj, bombs of obsidian: to the east, Transylvania offered a variety of eruptive rocks within easy access of the plains. Obsidian, as in the Near East, was particularly widely traded.

In the loess plains sought by early agriculturalists further north, inorganic raw materials again came mostly from areas peripheral to the main concentrations of population. Around the clusters of *Bandkeramik* settlement, sources of hard rocks were plentiful, for instance, in the ancient massif of Bohemia, at various points along the Rhine rift and the Middle Rhine highlands, and in the central German highlands.

There was no useful obsidian in these areas, but cherts from pre-Cretaceous rocks were available, and on the edge of the North European Plain the *Bandkeramik* spread as far as the flint sources in the Low Countries and Little Poland. Local exchange cycles brought these different sources into relationship: for instance, hard volcanic rocks, such as trachyte, tephrite and basalt from the Koblenz region, moved in the reverse direction to the flint of the Belgian Hesbaye; while the occurrence of import sherds shows how important were the major rivers in articulating such systems (Clark 1952:251). The recently investigated site at Müddersheim indicated a supply distance for stone of up to 10 km. for bulky sandstone objects, 30-40 km. for basalt, and up to 70 km. for flint. Circulation throughout the *Bandkeramik* system occasionally brought stray pieces from further afield, such as the fragments of Silesian amphibolite found at Müddersheim (Schiczel 1965).

This last source – Sobotka (Zobten) near Wrocław – seems to have been particularly important as settlement pushed further into the North European Plain in the Rössen and *Stichband* periods, and a very high proportion of the bored shoe-last adzes was made of this material (Schwabedissen 1966).

As new regions were explored, fresh sources were discovered, and particularly desirable raw materials achieved a circulation over hundreds of kilometres. The results of petrographic studies in the British Isles show how a primary use of local sources was supplemented by the products of distant factories as the network of inter-regional relations grew. Thus, in south-western Britain, early sites show a dominance of Cornish products, with Welsh and north-west British materials appearing in this area in large numbers in the Middle Neolithic. Less attractive products continued to be worked on a small scale and locally distributed: the Mynydd Rhiw quarry site (Houlder 1961) with an associated flint

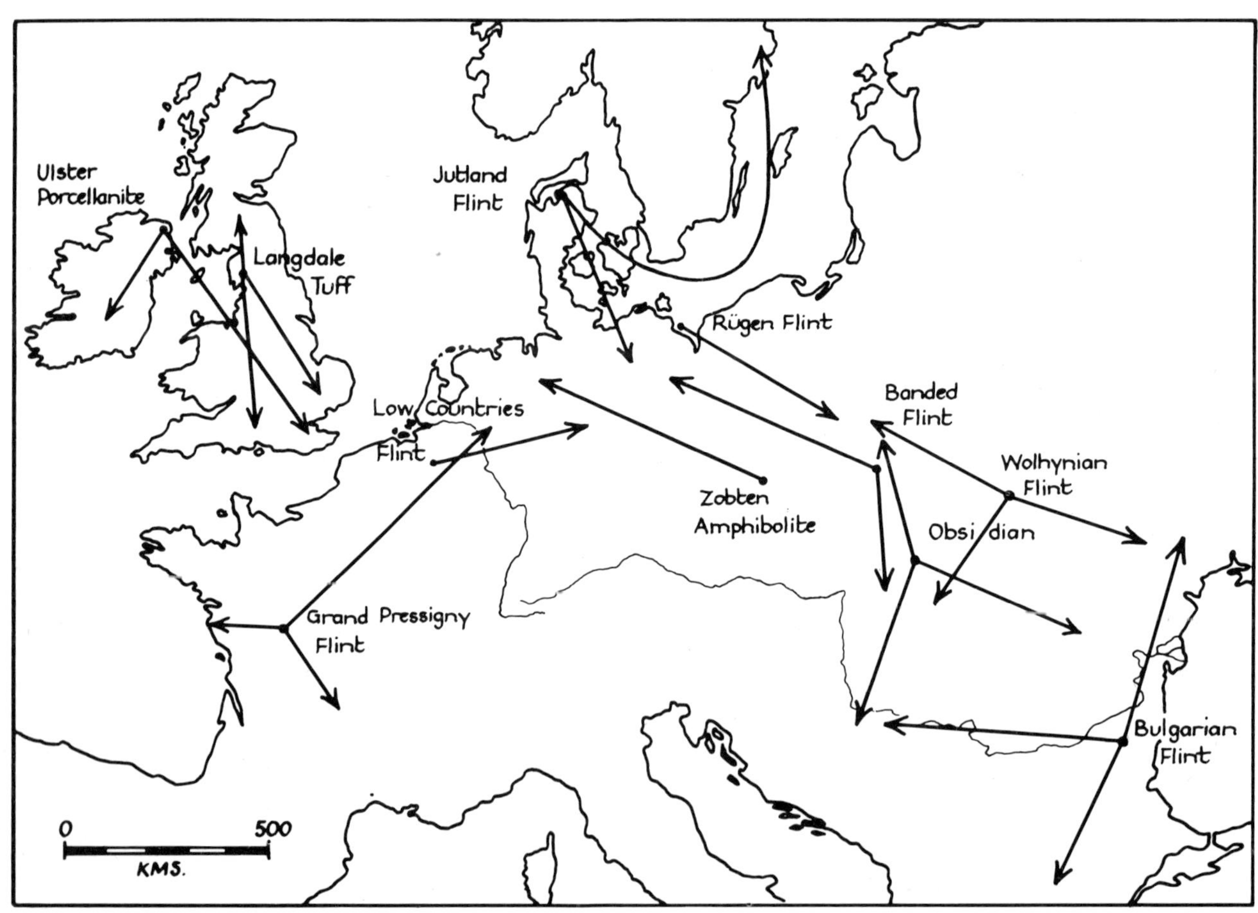

Figure 2. The major widely-traded materials of fourth and third millennium Europe.

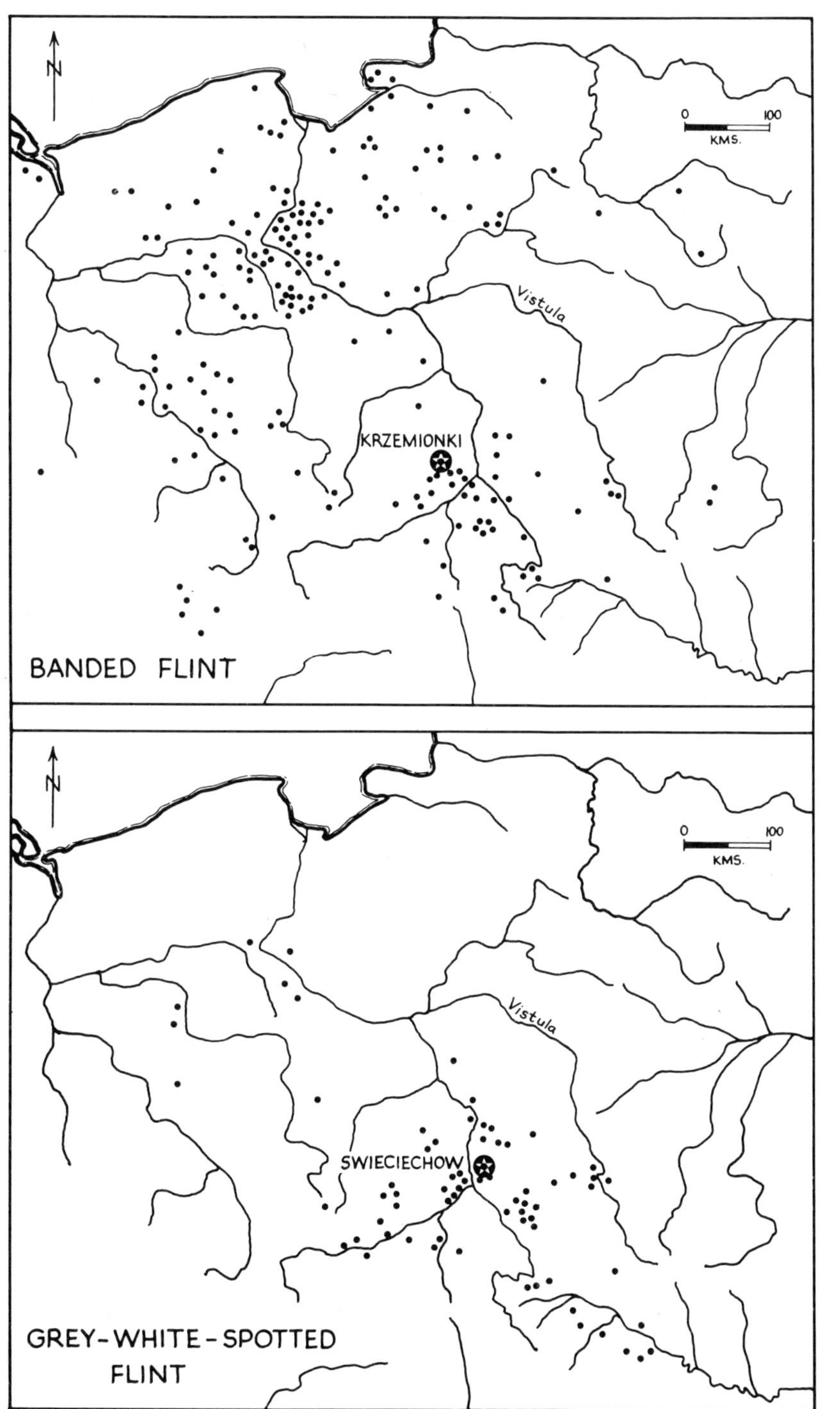

Figure 3. The distributions of two kinds of Polish flint; after Sulimirski 1960.

assemblage implies no more than small-scale seasonal exploitation in times of slack agricultural work, in which the winning of raw materials could be combined with hunting forays. On the other hand, it is clear that more highly organized production was becoming profitable for the commodities widely in demand.

The later-fourth and third millennia in many parts of Europe saw this rationalization and intensification of production on a large scale (see Fig. 2). The honey-coloured flint of Bulgaria achieved a wide distribution within the Balkans, up to the north of the Black Sea, and into the southern half of the Carpathian Basin. Obsidian continued to be traded in large quantities, and is found on a very high proportion of the sites of this period, both within the Carpathians and beyond, especially in southern Poland. This last area seems to have had – at least in certain phases such as Early Lengyel – a particularly intense exchange with the area of north Hungary and Slovakia just across the mountains, reflecting the complementary character of resources on either side. Going south to balance the obsidian were flint and, probably, salt as well: there are salt-pans from mid-fourth millennium Lengyel contexts near Krakow in Little Poland (Jodłowski 1971). Supplies of flint became particularly important as settlement increased in the North European Plain from *Trichterbecher* times onwards, for although flint was widely scattered in glacial deposits it was mostly of poor quality, due to frost cracking. As in north-west Bulgaria, large-scale working and trading took place in response to demand from neighbouring areas lacking, or with inferior, raw materials.

To the west, areas of good flint potential occurred widely in France and the Low Countries within the Cretaceous deposits between the Seine and the Maas; but to the north and east, such sources were more scattered, occurring in north Jutland, Scania, the island of Rügen, south Poland and further east in Wolhynia. Among the south Polish sources, various characteristic types can be distinguished (Sulimirski 1960), mainly from the Upper Vistula region. These include the chocolate-coloured Upper Astartian flint from the Świętokrzyskie (Holy Cross) mountains; Lower Astartian banded flint from Krzemionki, used for axes; greyish, white-speckled Turonian flint from Świeciechów, used for blades; and a banded Jurassic chert from near Krakow. (*Krema*, incidentally, is a common Slav place-name element meaning 'flint'; e.g. Kremikovci, Bulgaria.) Attempts have been made to map the distribution of these types of flint from visual identifications. The Świeciechów variety shows a restricted local circulation but the banded Krzemionki variety was exported in bulk, especially to the Middle Vistula/Notec/Middle Warta area, and examples are known from

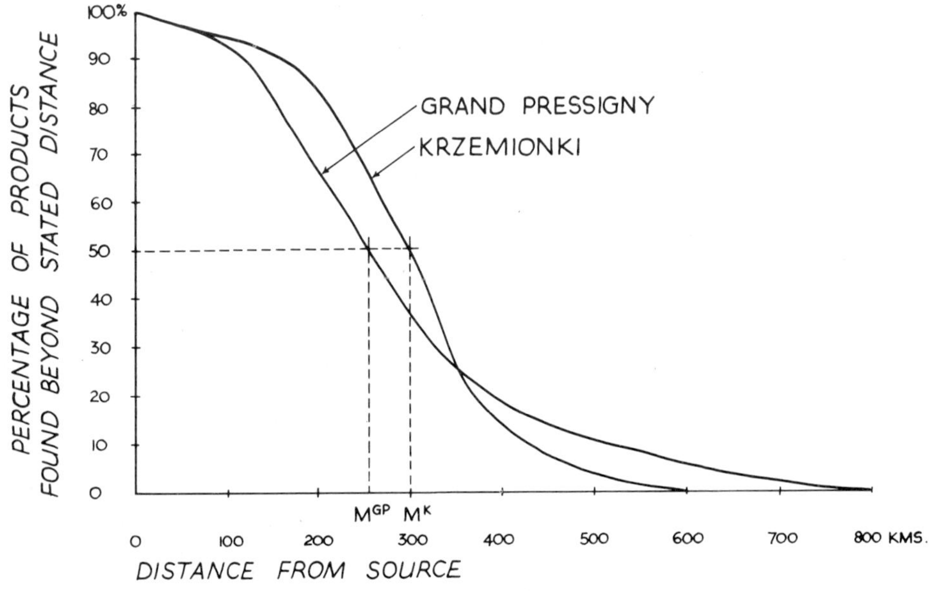

Figure 4. The distance from source of finds made from two varieties of flint.

beyond the Carpathians in Slovakia (see maps, Fig. 3).

Such distributions can be summarized as curves showing the percentages of objects at given distances from the source (see Fig. 4). Half of the known finds of Świeciechów flint lie within 100 km. of the source, while for the banded flint 50% are within 300 km., and 75% within 350 km. Finds of both types are mainly of third-millennium date, though both start in the later-fourth millennium. Something of the same order of magnitude would hold for the other widely-traded commodities shown in Fig. 2. An interesting feature of the Rügen flint distribution (see Fig. 5) is the way different products have a characteristic range of distributions.

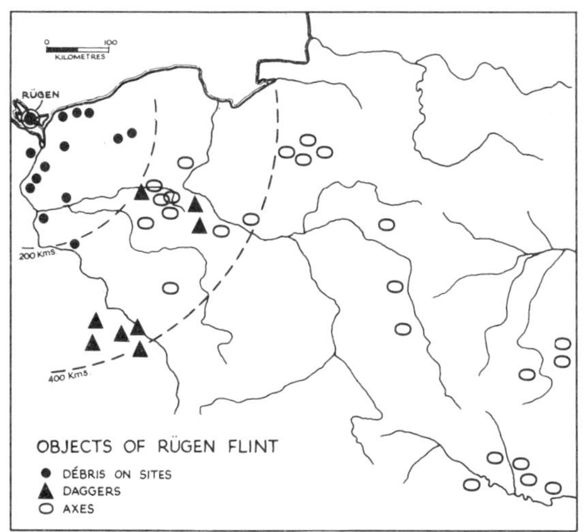

Figure 5. The differential dispersal of three types of product from the same source; after Sulimirski 1960.

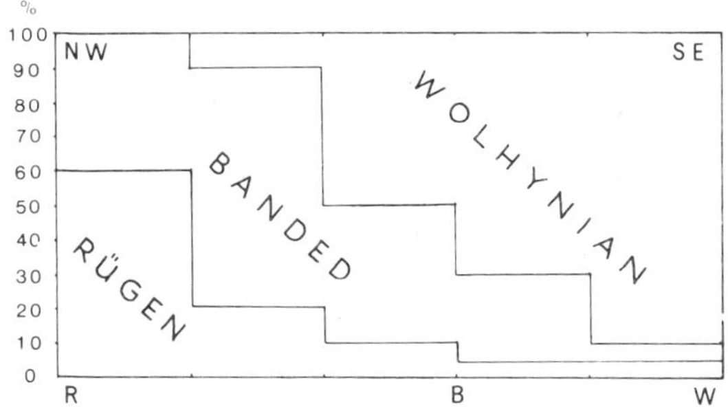

Figure 6. Approximate percentages of finds of three types of flint in a SE-NW transect across Poland. Each division represents a 100 km.^{2} sample cell: R, B and W mark the positions of sources. Note the effects of competition. Calculated from maps in Sulimirski 1960.

Of the western sources, the most easily recognizable and widely-traded variety is the well known iron-rich flint of Grand Pressigny, used in the later-third millennium for large blades hafted as daggers (see below). This shows a distribution on a similar scale to that of the banded flint, with 50% within 250 km. and 75% within 350 km., despite the fact that stray finds occasionally occur up to 800 km. away. An analysis of the direction of movement (Fig. 7) indicates three major components: up-river, down-river, and across-country north-eastward. The distribution map shows that the down-river component splits at the coast to go either to Brittany or to the Gironde – in neither case more than 200-300 km. by sea. The largest component is the overland route to centres of population on the Loire and the Seine, and beyond into the Low Countries (Fig. 7). Finds become noticeably more scattered on this axis beyond the 350 km. limit. It is an indication of the special desirability of this material that its main axis of movement should be into areas with local supplies of good flint.

Although there are several sources of bias and inaccuracy in the maps used above, they do give some idea of the scale of later Neolithic trade. While many products were of merely local significance, demand was sufficient to move large volumes of particularly desirable goods over several hundred kilometres. While the banded flint went mainly to a single cultural area, the Grand Pressigny distribution is significantly inter-cultural. Both show the 'pull' of nearby population clusters, but spread beyond these to remoter areas. (Compare, for instance, the banded-flint distribution map with the one of Globular Amphora culture settlements in Wiślański 1970:Fig. 56.)

Trading systems on this scale clearly required a considerable quantity of raw material, and a particular expression of the expansion in demand, by the later-fourth millennium and after, is the development of large-scale mining for various materials. Small operations had been undertaken even in Upper Palaeolithic times, as is shown by the two-metre deep pits for colouring material at Lovas in western Hungary. Such workings must have become very common in the Neolithic and, undoubtedly, many more sites remain to be discovered. Typical, for instance, are the 2-3 m. horizontal 'drifts' for jasper in the hard Jura limestone of the Isteiner

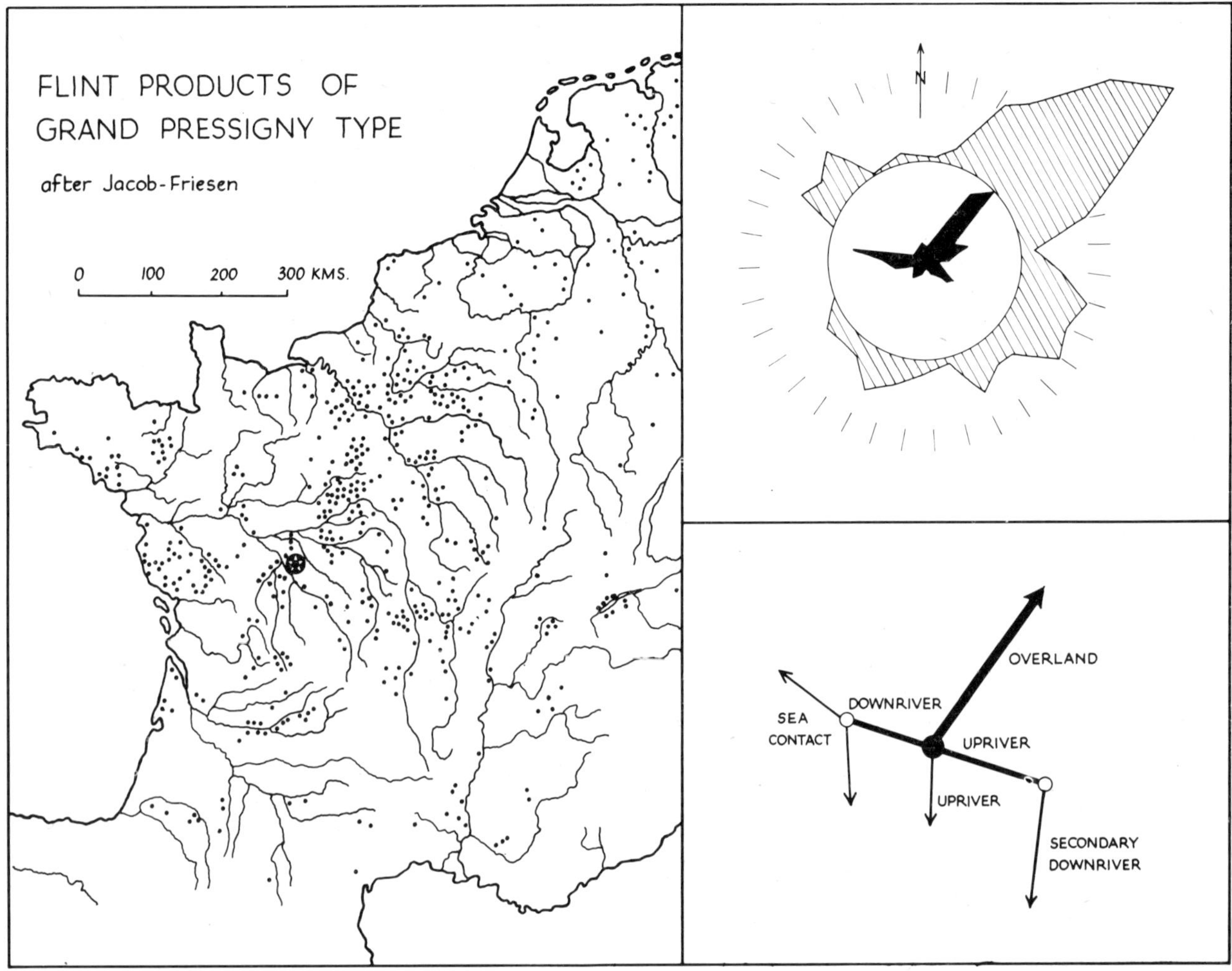

Figure 7. The distribution of products of Grand Pressigny flint, analysed by direction of movement. The black inner zone of the orientation diagram (top right) includes finds within 200 km., the hatched outer zone covers finds beyond this.

Klotz, north of Basle (Schmid 1952), the mass of small shafts for limnoquartzite near Miskolc, in north-west Hungary, and the network of 3 m.-deep channels following vertical flint boundaries at Sumeg, in western Hungary (Vértes 1964). All these are probably of third-millennium date, and the last one certainly so. Somewhat larger are the series of shafts for Jurassic chert (radiolarite) at Mauern, near Vienna, some of which reach 8 m. in depth and have lateral galleries (Kirnbauer 1958). With the wide-spread shallow workings alongside, these would have yielded around 1,000 tonnes of usable stone, perhaps at the rate of a few tonnes per year. The workings seem to belong to a Lengyel culture local group, and this material was widely used between the Alps and the Danube. That such efforts were not restricted to mining stone is shown by the extensive system of underground galleries at Šuplja Stena, near Belgrade, for the extraction of cinnabarite (red mercuric sulphide), used as a paint. The galleries are definitely dated by finds of Baden pottery to the mid-third millenium, but finds of cinnabarite at the nearby *tell* of Vinča suggests an earlier beginning (Milojčić 1943).

None of these, however, compares with the scale of flint-mining in northern Europe, where shafts were sunk through the relatively soft chalk to up to 15 m. in depth, with lateral galleries following the horizontal seams. These are found in all the areas where flint could be won direct from the chalk, and range in date from early third-millennium examples, such as the Hov mine in Jutland producing thin-butted axes, to early second-millennium ones like the

Aalborg mine 80 km. away, producing especially daggers and sickles (Becker 1959). Where flint was widely available within a region, activity was not concentrated in one place: where opportunities were rarer, very large operations took place. The extensive use and limited natural occurrence of banded flint is reflected in the scale of mines at Krzemionki Opatowskie, where between 700 and 1,000 shafts, some as much as 11 m. deep, are known in a rather barren area some 10 km. away from the nearest centres of settlement, where the working-up took place. Such an industrial scale of production (in the Krzemionki case perhaps twice that of Grimes Graves in East Anglia), as much as the wide distribution of the products, indicates the organization that underlies such a pattern, in which at least groups of villages were gaining special advantages from their nearness to raw materials.

The large volume of material required in northern Europe is partly related to the size of woodworking tools. There is a general decrease in the size of axes further south, where small quadrangular or shoe-last forms were most usually mounted in antler sleeves. In addition, the very large size of some northern examples suggests that the contrast may be exaggerated by non-utilitarian factors. In the New Guinea case mentioned in an earlier section, the ceremonial axes are clearly distinguished by their size, being over 25 cm. in length as opposed to the working axes, which are generally less than 15 cm. Thin-butted axes in Scandinavia and north Germany occasionally occur up to over 40 cm. in length, weighing around 4 kg., clearly in excess of ergonomic requirements. In northern Europe, the large axe had a symbolic role beyond its immediate technical function, and is notable as one of the few representational elements in Megalithic art. Large ceremonial forms, if that is what they are, certainly travelled over long distances; the far-flung Langdale axe from Langwood Fen, in Cambridgeshire, is 28 cm. long (Fell 1964) and it would be interesting to discover whether the larger forms generally moved further than the smaller 'working' forms. The existence of a complete spectrum from simple working tools to purely symbolic forms is impressively demonstrated by the larger and finer jadeite examples, where use in ceremonial presentations was a sufficiently powerful motive to necessitate the exploitation of a specific raw material – though this explicit differentiation between tool and symbol may be a fairly late feature. The aesthetic qualities of Langdale tuff and banded flint may, in a similar way, have contributed to their major distributions, and the cross-cutting character of the British stone axe distributions (Clark 1965: Fig. 1) indicates how one rock was traded against another.

Besides axes that are simply a variation of working forms in a different size or material, other forms appeared in the Late Neolithic that are linked to status through their use as weapons. This is most clearly seen south of the Carpathians, as early as the mid-fourth millennium, where working axes are rather small and axes over 10-15 cm. in length are almost entirely shaft-hole forms and best described as 'battle-axes', since they are clearly intended for fighting or display rather than more mundane tasks. Such stone battle-axes occur in the north from *Trichterbecher* times onwards, becoming increasingly elaborate and distinctive. These axes seem to belong to a stage in the development of a more explicit symbolism of social status, the extension of a phenomenon traceable from the Early Neolithic. The occurrence of various items as common grave-goods allows some observations to be made on this process. An interesting feature of certain classes of artefact is their association with a specific sex and age-range (see Fig. 8), suggesting that their possession was limited to individuals of a particular status – even if items such as axes could, no doubt, be borrowed by younger men for specific tasks. Such a social dimension of utilitarian objects is well known in anthropological literature, and it is likely that the exchanges that distributed objects such as axes took place only between men of comparable rank.

In the Nitra cemetery example, *Spondylus* ornaments reinforce the pattern of axe distribution: in other contemporary cases further north, however, they occupy a converse position, associated with female and juvenile burials (Pavuk 1972; Kahlke 1954). A particularly elaborate *Bandkeramik* female inhumation grave at Erfurt (*Inventaria Archaeologica* D 85) for example, had eighteen beads and eleven pendants of this shell at the neck, two discs on the breast, and a ring on each upper arm.

Besides the shaft-hole axe, another personal

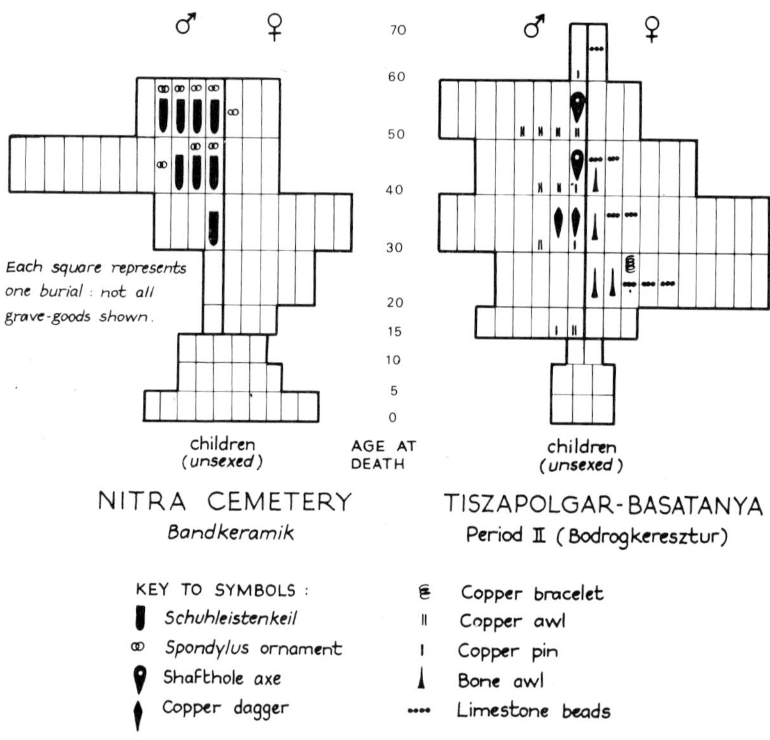

Figure 8. The association of grave-goods by age and sex; a comparison of fifth and later fourth millennium examples. Data from Pavuk 1972 and Bognár-Kutzián 1963.

weapon that began to achieve a widespread symbolic significance was the dagger. As early as the fourth millennium in Bodrogkeresztúr contexts (Bognár-Kutzián 1963:318 'Group 1'), large dagger-blades of up to 18 cm. in length often accompany male burials. This is another feature that was greatly emphasized in the third millennium of northern Europe. It is significant that one of the most extensively traded materials of the time should be the Grand Pressigny flint, whose characteristic cores were carefully prepared to produce especially long blades, at great cost in flint. Some of the most extensively developed systems of distribution in these stone-using communities were, thus, those connected with status items.

The development of a range of 'socio-technic' items, such as the battle-axe, was a characteristic feature of the artefactual history of the later fourth and third millennia, both north and south of the Carpathians and, as Tabaczynski has said (1972:59), should be considered 'nicht nur als Ausdruck der Verbreitung neuer Ideen . . . sondern auch als eine archaeologischer Hinweis auf die fortschreitende gesellschaftliche Aufgliederung'. The evidence of stonework thus shows a growing scale of trade during the Neolithic, not only in essential products but also in increasing flows of symbolic artefacts. The rise in demand for essentials relates directly to the growth of population, but the indirect results of this are also of importance for the movement of materials in general. From the cultural and environmental uniformity of the earliest Neolithic, expansion and differentiation produced a mosaic of regional groupings and economic zones of great complexity, ranging from farmers on the rich loess-lands or more pastoral groups in sandy areas, to the specialized fishing villages of the Rzucewo culture on the sandspits of the Vistula estuary. The opportunity for fruitful exchange between these groups was thus much greater than in the situation of initial colonization. The basic exchange channels could usefully carry a much greater volume of subsistence products and, with them, other material items to balance and regulate the flow. The significance of material counters in such situations has been emphasized by Vayda (1966) in discussing the Pomo Indians of central California, where shell beads were exchanged for food between communities concentrating on different staple foods that were in surplus at different seasons. Beads accumulated from a fish

Table 1. Selected occurrences of various copper ores in Romania: data from Rădulescu & Dumitrescu 1966.

		Age of ore deposits		*Crystalline Schist*						*Mesozoic*						*Banat Phase*					*Neogene*												
		Location		Bălan (r. Ciuc)	Băile Borsa (r. Viseu)	Crucea (r. Vatra Dornei)	Lipova (r. Lipova)	Muncelul Mic (r. Ilia)	Cîrli Baba (r. Vatra Dornei)	Mina Altîn Tepe (r. Istria)	Gemenea (r. Cîmpalung)	Căşăneşti (r. Brad)	Mircea Vodă (r. Tulcea)	Patirs (r. Lipova)	Tulgheş (r. Gheorghieni)	Băiţa Bihorului (r. Beius)	Moldova Moua	Oraviţa Ciclova-Romana	Sasca Montană (r. Oraviţa)	Dognecea (o. Reşiţa)	Ilba (o. Baia Mare)	Cavnic (r. Lapuş)	Baia Sprie (o. Baia Mare)	Săcărîmb (r. Ilia)	Deva	Întregalde (r. Alba)	Baia Mare	Stănija (r. Brad)	Hondol (r. Ilia)	Ruda Barzia (r. Brad)	Baia de Arieş (r. Cîmpeni)	Bucium (r. Cîmpeni)	Băiuţ (r. Lapuş)
Ore Type	*Chemical Formula*	*Colour*	*Approximate Cu Content*																														
Pure Copper																																	
Native Copper	Cu	Copper	c. 100%	x						x	x		x		x		x	x	x	x	x	x	x		x	x	x		x		x		
Copper Oxides																																	
Tenorite	$Cu O$	black	c. 80%	x									x	x			x	x	x	x	x	x				x						x	
Cuprite	$Cu_2 O$	red	c. 90%	x							x				x		x	x	x	x	x					x	x						
Copper Carbonates																																	
Azurite	$2Cu CO_3 . Cu (OH)_2$	blue	c. 55%	x			x	x	x	x	x	x	x			x	x	x	x	x	x	x	x		x						x	x	
Malachite	$Cu CO_3 . Cu (OH)_2$	green	c. 55%	x			x	x	x	x	x	x	x			x	x	x	x	x	x	x		x	x	x		x	x	x	x	x	
Copper Silicate																																	
Crysocolla (*Kupferpecherz*)	$Cu Si O_3 \ H_2 O$	blue	c. 35%						x			x	x			x	x	x	x	x				x		x							
'Fahlerz'																																	
Tennantite	$Cu_3 \ As \ S_{3\text{-}4}$	grey	c. 55%					x																					x				
Tetrahedrite	$Cu_3 \ Sb \ S_{3\text{-}4}$	grey	c. 55%	x		x		x			x				x	x	x	x	x	x	x	x			x		x	x	x	x	x	x	
Enargite	$Cu_3 \ As \ S_4$	grey	c. 50%												x				x														
Bournonite	$Pb \ Cu \ Sb \ S_3$	grey	c. 15%		x	x					x										x	x	x	x			x	x	x	x	x		
Copper Sulphate																																	
Chalcanthite	$Cu SO_4 \ 5H_2 O$	blue	c. 25%	x			x			x						x	x		x	x			x		x		x	x					
Copper Sulphides																																	
Covellina (*Kupferindig*)	$Cu S$	blue	c. 65%	x	x	x		x		x	x		x	x				x				x	x										
Chalcocite (*Kupferglanz*)	$Cu_2 S$	grey	c. 50%	x	x	x				x				x		x	x	x	x	x		x	x	x	x	x		x	x		x	x	
Bornite (*Buntkupferz*)	$Cu Fe S_4$	'peacock'	c. 65%	x		x				x		x				x	x	x	x	x			x		x			x			x		
Chalcopyrite (*Kupferkies*)	$Cu Fe S_2$	yellow	c. 35%	x	x	x	x	x	x	x	x	x	x	x	x	x	x	x	x	x		x	x	x	x	x	x	x	x	x	x	x	
Copper/Arsenic																																	
'Whitneyite'	$Cu As$	reddish-white																								x							
Domeykite	$Cu_3 As$	grey-white																								x							
Algodonite	$Cu_{6\text{-}7} As$	grey-white																								x							
Pseudomalachite	$2Cu As O_4 . 2Cu (OH)_2$	green														x																	
Pure Arsenic																																	
Native Arsenic	As	white																x				x	x	x		x	x		x	x			
Arsenic Oxide																																	
Arsenolite	$As_2 \ O_3$	grey																				x		x									
Arsenic Sulphides																																	
Orpiment	$As_2 \ S_3$	yellow														x	x		x			x	x	x			x						x
Realgar	$As_2 \ S_2$	red																	x			x	x	x			x		x				x
Arsenopyrite	$Fe \ S \ As$	white			x	x		x			x				x			x	x	x		x	x				x	x	-	x	x	x	x
Tin Oxide																																	
Cassiterite	$Sn \ O_2$	black			x																												

surplus, for instance, could be exchanged later with the donor community for inland products, when these in turn were in surplus.

The actual distribution of population on the ground also encouraged and necessitated contact. While Early Neolithic groups in central Europe showed a strong orientation towards the river network and flood-plain edge, the spread of settlement to drier interfluvial regions implied more frequent face-to-face contact between clusters of villages, and a more richly networked overall pattern (Kruk 1973). With more extensive grazing, the maintenance of a wide set of relationships with surrounding communities was not merely possible but essential to a smooth running of the system. Indeed, the wide-spread distribution of certain ceramic styles, such as the bell-beaker complex, indicates the growing intensity of inter-regional contacts. All these factors promoted an increased turnover in goods, a general quickening in local transactions that increased the power of such networks to carry rarer materials. Such traded items served to emphasize the rank and authority of those who could obtain them.

The role of copper

To understand the part that copper played in these developments, the distribution and character of its sources must first be appreciated. In the first place, copper ores are – like many of the types of harder stone used for axes – basically of highland occurrence, being 'concentrated in areas of structural complexity and igneous activity' (Park & Macdiarmid 1970). Such deposits are commonly formed by *hydrothermal injection* in periods of tectonic movement, when hot solutions from deep-lying magma chambers penetrate upwards into favourable structural and lithological environments. Many such deposits were formed, for instance, during the Alpine mountain-building phase, and such ores are wide-spread in the Tertiary fold-chains of southern Europe (Sherratt 1972:518). Somewhat different ore-complexes, formed at deeper levels, are found in the ancient crystalline massifs such as Bohemia or the Rhodope block: these may also contain copper, often lead, and occasionally tin.

A further factor of importance is the degree to which secondary changes have occurred as a result of weathering. Where an ore vein reaches the surface, a characteristic sequence of 'weathering horizons' develops, as a result of the leaching downwards of impurities. At the top is a zone of pure (*native*) copper, stable because of a thin surface coating of oxide. Below this develop successively zones of oxide and carbonate ores (see Table 1 for common minerals) and, below this, a zone of enrichment where impurities accumulate at the water-table. While the higher ore minerals are mostly brightly coloured, those of the enrichment zone are characteristically grey and are collectively referred to by the German miners' term of *fahlerz.* These are sulphide ores, containing also appreciable quantities of arsenic, antimony, often silver and sometimes lead. (Depending on whether arsenic or antimony dominates, these form crystals of the minerals tennantite and tetrahedrite respectively – though owing to chemical replacement within the same crystal structure, tetrahedrite-type crystals may represent either compound: this is important in linking ores with analysed objects.) Finally, below these secondary products, lies the zone of original unaltered sulphide ore, usually chalcopyrite. Secondary sulphides not containing iron may also occur higher up in the series. All sulphide ores require an additional roasting process before smelting, to get rid of the sulphur; and, in addition, the iron-containing pyrite ores present problems with slag. The common secondary ores all have a much higher copper content than the unaltered primary deposits.

The formation of secondary minerals is not inevitable, and ores in different areas show this to varying degrees. In the Alps, for example, unaltered sulphide ores are usual; while in the Carpathians and the Balkans large deposits of secondary minerals were formed, including native copper. Various factors (Pittioni 1957:8-9) affected this and, in particular, the effects of glaciation in the Alps, in contrast with the more continuous conditions of development further south. As Pittioni (1957:10) remarks, 'die kulturgeschichtliche Bedeutung dieser lagerstättenkundlich-klimageschichtlichen Feststellungen kann nicht eindringlich genug betont werden'. The most important factor in the early development of copper metallurgy was the availability of a well-developed series of ores from the pure native form, through the easily smelted oxide and carbonate forms, down to

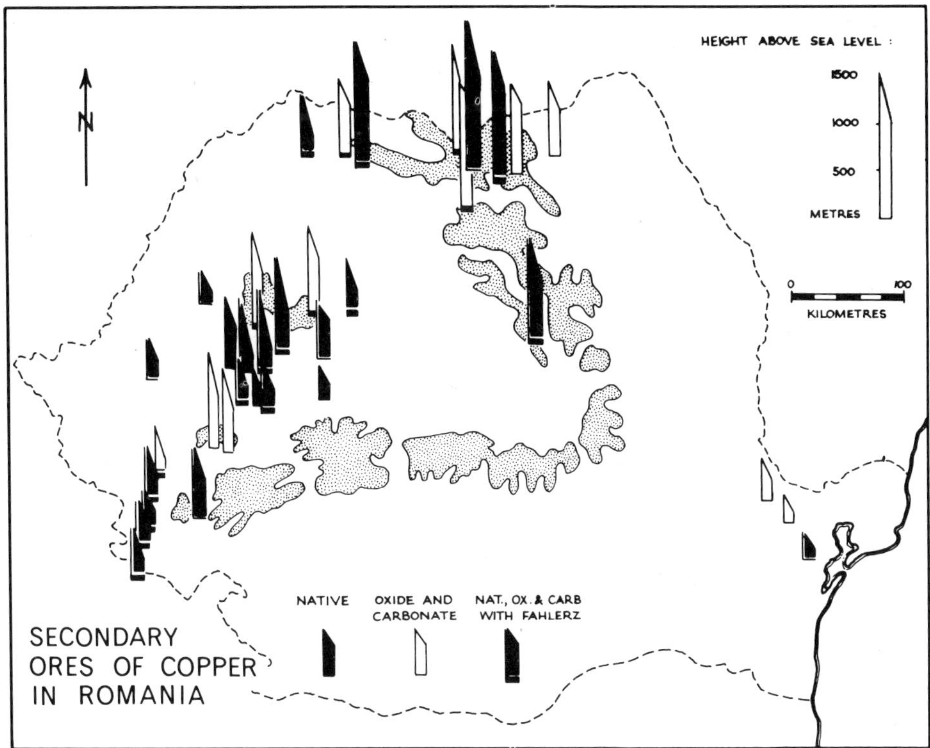

Figure 9. Relative accessibility of copper ores in Romania as indicated by the heights of different sources above sea level. Data from Rădulescu and Dimitrescu 1966.

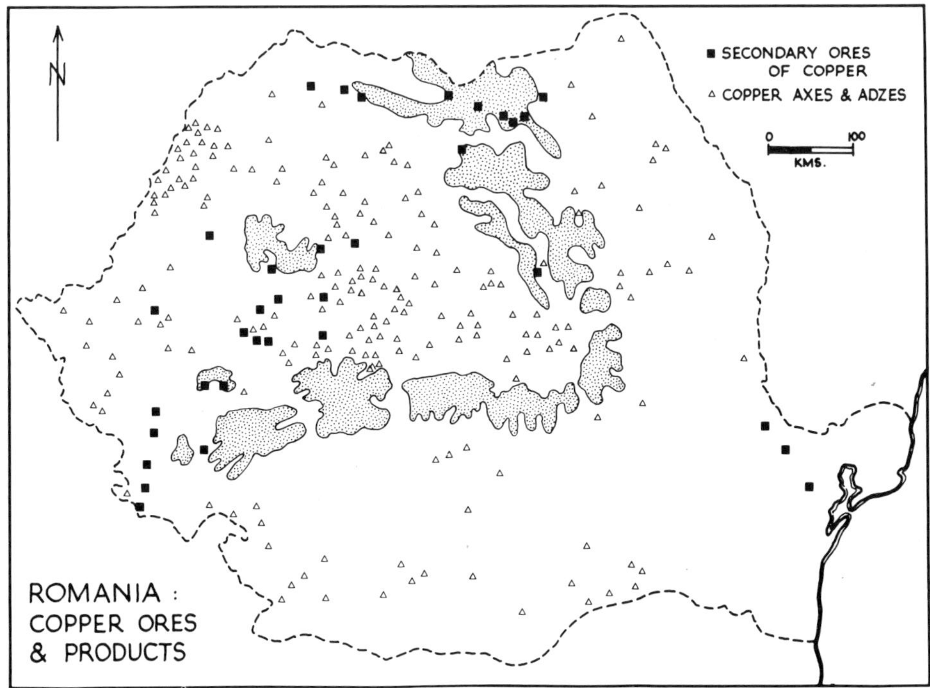

Figure 10. The distribution of copper axes of the fourth and third millennia in Romania, compared with potential ore-sources. Data from Vulpe 1973, Maczek *et al.* 1953.

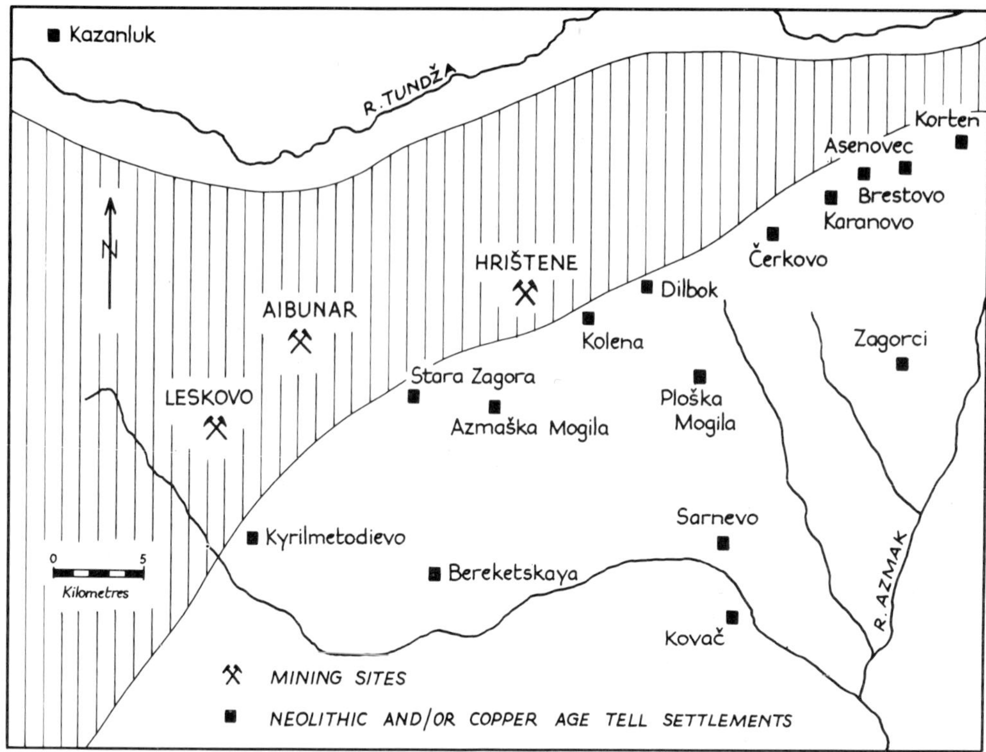

Figure 11. Settlement and resources in part of Central Bulgaria during the Copper Age.

enriched and, finally, unaltered sulphides; and, above all, the occurrence of such deposits in locations not too distantly removed from the early centres of population. In the Balkans and the fringes of the Carpathian Basin especially – as indeed in other centres of early development such as Anatolia and Spain – the exploration of nearby upland regions brought agricultural populations, familiar with the controlled use of heat in firing pottery, into early contact with the brightly-coloured secondary ores of copper.

Some idea of the overall distribution of copper ores within the Carpatho-Balkan and Dinaric chains is given in Fig. 15. Within this, however, there are important differences in accessibility, and these seem to have been major controlling factors in the development of local metallurgy. An attempt has been made in Fig. 9 to give a visual impression of the variety within Romania. Two major groupings suggest themselves – a north-east group to the east of Baia Mare, and a south-west group from the Iron Gates to the Munţii Metalici where the densest concentrations occur. The altitudes of these two groups indicate that the latter are much more accessible, and the distribution of copper artefacts (see Fig. 10) strengthens the impression that these were, in fact, important sources in the fourth and third millennia (see below). This is further emphasized by their proximity to known settlements on the Mureş and Lower Danube, and the potential of these two waterways as distribution links.

A similar situation obtained in parts of Bulgaria. Fig. 11 shows the position of sources exploited in the later fourth millennium (Chernih 1972; also below), in relation to the area of dense prehistoric settlement around Stara Zagora, where a series of important sites, including Azmak and Karanovo, occur along the spring-line at the edge of the basin. In this region, occupied from Early Neolithic times in the later sixth millennium, metal ores as well as hard stone sources occur within 5-10 km. of long-lived *tell* settlements.

In addition to areas that had this intimate association from such an early date, expansion of settlement brought about similar conditions over a wider area. One example will suffice to illustrate what must have been a widespread process. The Tertiary limestones of Serbia were extensively colonized in the Vinča period (Sherratt 1972:531). In the area around Šabac shown in Fig. 12, Starčevo occupation of the

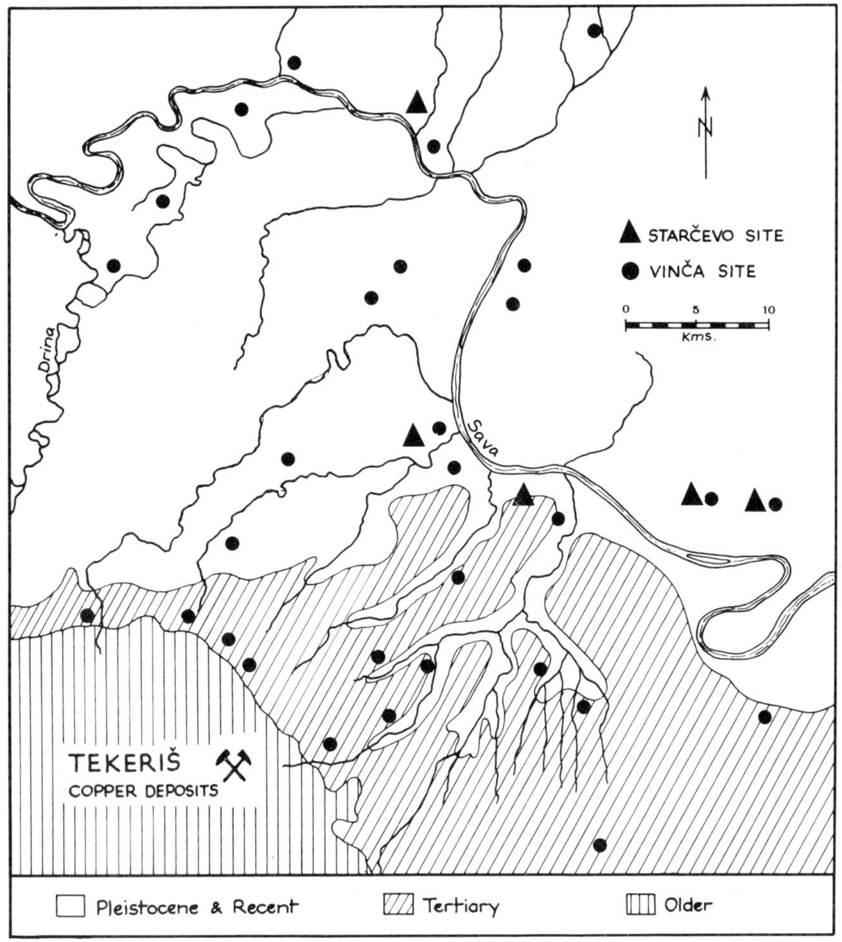

Figure 12. The spread of settlement in the fourth millennium in the region around Šabac, northern Jugoslavia. Sites marked 'Vinča' include also ones with Lengyel affinities.

fifth millennium concentrates along the Sava; but, in the course of the fourth millennium, settlement pushed into the fringes of the uplands. Copper ores are known, not from the limestone area itself, but from the older rocks behind it, for instance at Tekeriš (Maczek *et al.* 1953). Such deposits would again have been within a 5-10 km. range from the nearest settlements.

These three situations may be contrasted with the spread of settlement into those regions of the Alps where metal ores occur. In the Mühlbach-Bischofshofen area near Salzburg, for instance, which was the scene of extensive mining and smelting activity in the second millennium, the ores lie between 1,000 and 1,500 metres above sea level. This is comparable with the group in north-east Romania, and such areas would have seen little human activity before the Bronze Age. Initial Neolithic settlement concentrated on the loess lowlands (see Fig. 13), spreading in the fourth and early third millennia into the lake districts of the Alpine foreland, and only in the second millennium, with the development of transhumance, were the high pastures systematically used (Pittioni 1973). As the copper deposits in this area were, in any case, mainly sulphide ores requiring a longer roasting process, it is not surprising that Alpine ores did not figure largely in the Copper Age.

In the case of Bulgaria, therefore, with ores that must have been known as curiosities for a millennium before copper-working began, a limiting factor in terms of technology can, indeed, be inferred. The transition from light-coloured painted pottery fired in an oxidizing atmosphere to the dark-coloured reduced wares that became fashionable in south-east Europe and Anatolia in the later fifth millennium probably indicates the critical change involved. (Until more tests are made to

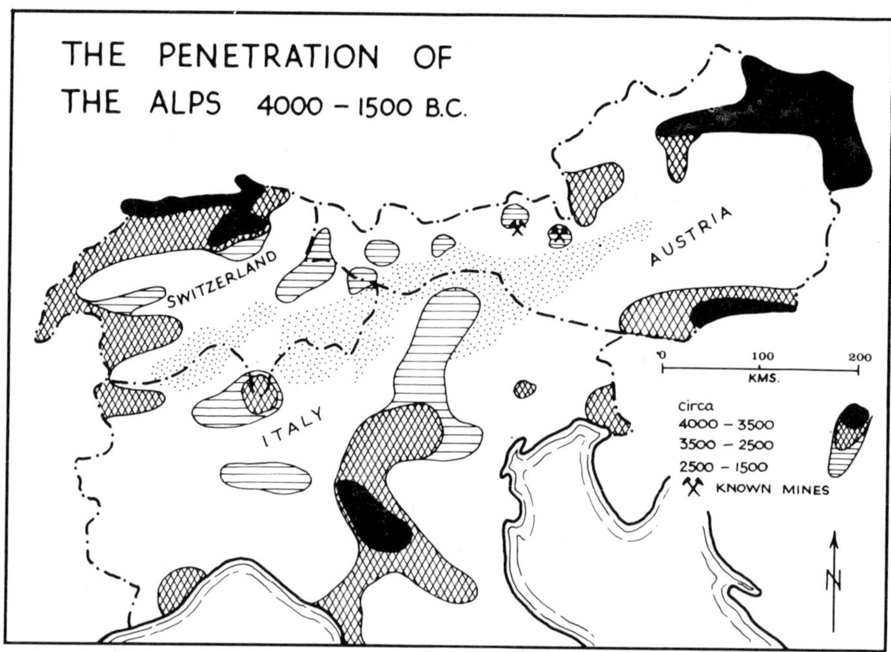

Figure 13. A schematic attempt to illustrate the extension of upland settlement in the Alps as indicated by archaeological finds; compiled from various sources.

determine the temperature at which early pottery was fired, it cannot be definitely stated that the need to fix graphite paint was an essential factor (Frierman 1969), and such a specific association is unlikely.) The Macedno-Bulgarian region, therefore, where settlement began as early as the sixth millennium in a landscape in which fertile alluvial basins lay scattered among mountains rich in stone and metal, was an area where resources waited for an appropriate technology; but outside this, factors of location and, ultimately, of ore-type were more critical. For resources requiring considerable labour to extract and process them at source, it is unlikely that extensive exploitation could take place within a primitive farming context unless these activities could be integrated within a yearly subsistence cycle. Only where settlement was nearby, or when seasonal movements of stock took men as a matter of routine into the area of occurrence, could such a process begin.

The earliest use of copper is, in fact, very hard to determine, as the kinds of small object made in the experimental stages are rarely found except by careful sieving of excavated deposits. For this reason, the date of the earliest metallurgy is likely, in many areas, to be pushed further back than current evidence allows. In south-east Europe, well-associated finds of beads, probably made from native copper, from the Boian culture cemetery of Cernica (Cantacuzino & Morinz 1963) give a *terminus ante quem* in the earlier fourth millennium, while a find of a copper awl has been claimed in a fifth-millennium Criş context, though this is disputed. The earliest well-dated heavy objects probably made from smelted copper occur early in the second half of the fourth millennium, when the simpler forms of flat and shaft-hole axes make their appearance, along with armrings and bracelets.

The typological sequence of copper shaft-hole axes, beginning with simple axe-hammers that were a direct translation of contemporary stone forms, is now well known (Bognár-Kutzián 1963; Schubert 1965 *inter alia*). Some of the earliest associated finds are the three examples from different houses in the early Gumelniţa settlement at Hotnica in Bulgaria, of the so-called Vidra type (Bognár-Kutzián 1972: 144). The Vidra form is typical of the area covered by the Gumelniţa culture in Bulgaria and south Romania. A local form of flat axe has a complementary distribution (see Fig. 14). Only slightly later are the finds from the Tibava cemetery (Šiška 1964), not far from the copper sources of east Slovakia. Here, from a sample of 41 excavated graves, come seven examples of the Čoka and Pločnik types (Fig. 14). Although

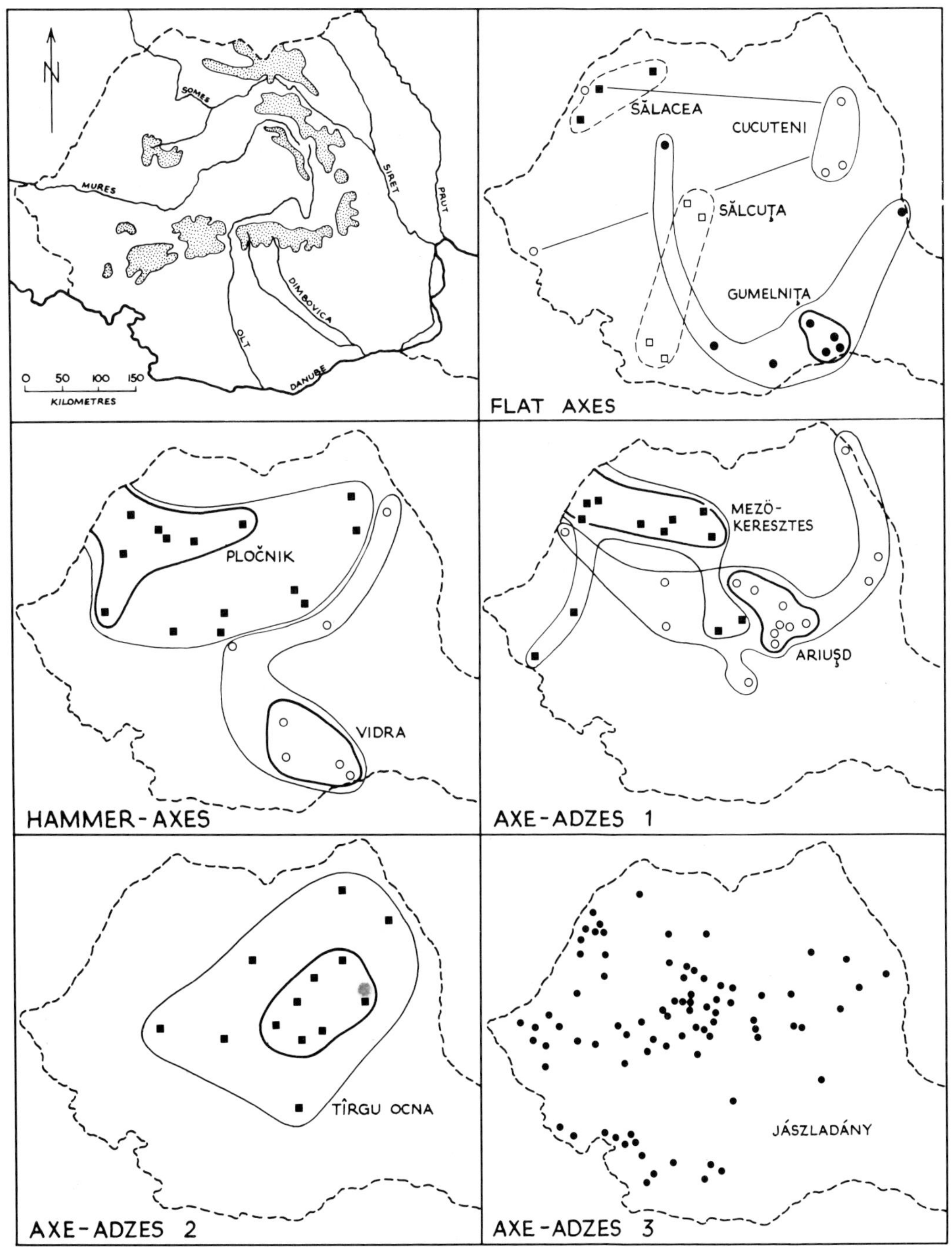

Figure 14. The distribution of various types of copper axe in Romania during the fourth and third millennia. Heavy lines enclose 50% of the finds of a given type in this country. Data from Vulpe 1973.

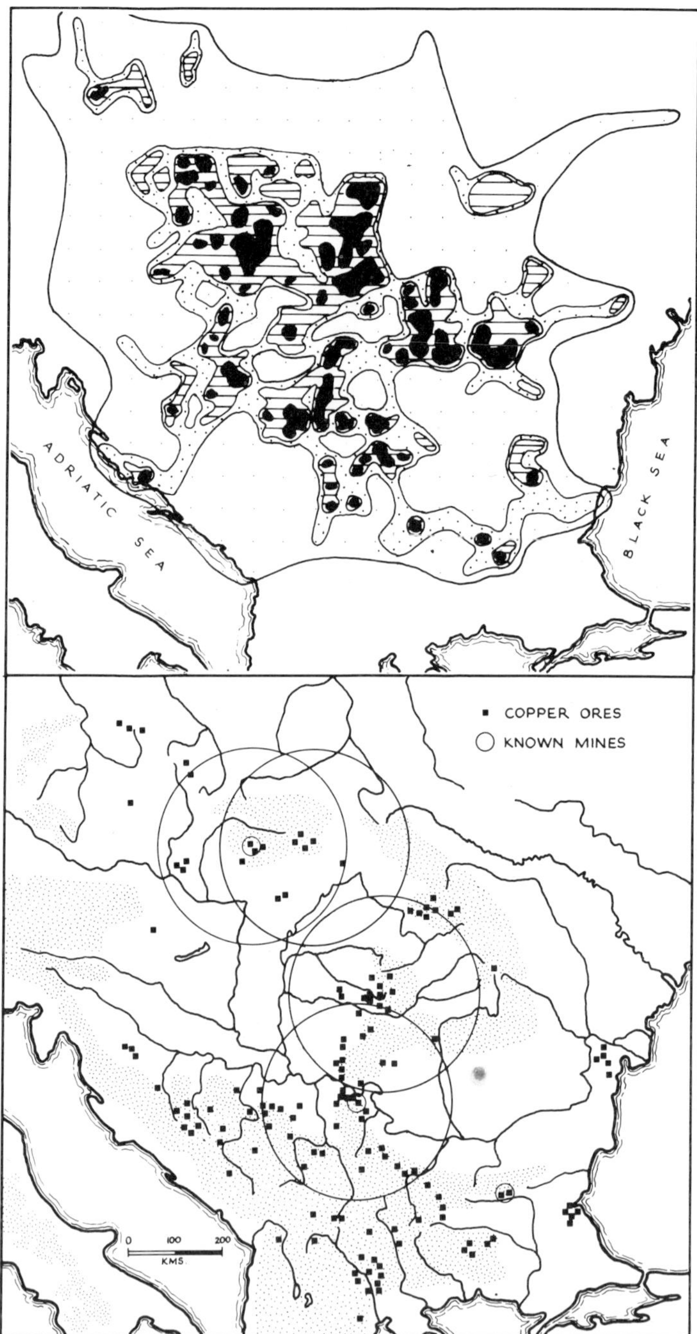

Figure 15. Top: Clusters of finds of copper axes of the fourth and third millennia shown by spatial proximity linkage. Dark masses indicate dense clusters. Data from Schubert 1965. Bottom: The distribution of copper ores and known prehistoric mines. Large circles indicate a 200 km. radius around the most important source areas. Sources from Maczek *et al.* 1954.

these forms are known from a wider area at this time, it is significant that they occur in graves only in this immediate region, which would correspond to zone (2) of the distribution model set out earlier. The metalliferous area of eastern Slovakia was, in any case, already an important supply-area for andesite and obsidian (lumps of which occur in contemporary graves at Lučky in this region), and an intermediary in the transmission of brown translucent chert and Volhynian flint (also in graves, at Tibava: Andel 1961). The copper industry at this stage was thus ancillary to the distribution of a wide range of raw materials, some of which were economically much more important.

With the widespread occurrence of mining for various rocks in mind, it is no surprise that the exploitation of copper should also involve mining activity as early as the fourth millennium. It can plausibly be related to the larger volumes of material required for heavy objects such as axe-hammers, and was probably an essential part of the process of collecting the raw material for smelting, rather than simply hammering small amounts of native copper. As with the stone-quarries, therefore, many more sites must remain to be recognized. The earliest confirmed traces of mining are the six shafts from Rudna Glava near Bor – an important copper-producing area down to the present day – where the Carpathian/Balkan arc swings through north-east Yugoslavia (Jovanović 1971). These shafts are sloping funnels, varying from two metres to half-a-metre in diameter, following the ore veins. One shaft had an access platform partly revetted by a dry-stone wall, and the shafts extend beyond the 2-3 m. to which they were explored. Fragments of pottery and a 'cult-vessel' (lamp ?) datable to the beginning of the Vinča-Pločnik phase of the early or mid-fourth millennium, were found in association with this site.

The Bulgarian sites near Stara Zagora, noted above and shown on Fig. 11, have also yielded traces of mining (Chernih & Radunčeva 1972). Pottery of Copper Age and Early Bronze Age types has been found in association at the site of Aibunar, though the mine at Hrištene, which has a wide funnel entrance and a shaft nearly 25 m. in depth, may belong to a later period. Other traces of prehistoric mining activity have been discovered at Špania Dolina, near Banska Bistrica in western Slovakia (Točik & Vladar 1971), identified by large stone hammers grooved for withy hafts of a kind known elsewhere in Bronze Age contexts. (See map for these sites: Fig. 15.)

The scale of copper-working and trading grew appreciably, towards the end of the fourth millennium and at the beginning of the third. Typologically, this is indicated by the appearance of larger and more elaborate forms of axe-hammers, usually formed by flattening and fanning out the 'hammer' end. In some cases this method was used to produce an actual working edge, and thus an axe-adze (e.g. Jászladány type); in others, it simply produced a more elaborate terminal (e.g. Mezökeresztes type). Some examples of the latter – a local development in the upper Tisza area – are up to 32 cm. in length, indicating the abundance of copper supplies available. These developments took place in the Carpathian Basin rather than in the Balkans, where supplies seem to have been less plentiful and simpler forms continued. The Jászladány type is by far the commonest and most wide-spread of the stray finds (Fig. 14), as well as being put into graves in the consuming area (zone 3) in the eastern Carpathian Basin. It was probably produced at a number of centres. Despite the large amounts of metal in circulation, however, there is no reason to believe that the trading mechanisms that distributed them were any more sophisticated than those involved in carrying stone supplies further north. The distribution map (Fig. 15) for copper axes shows a concentration largely within the Carpathian Basin, and this pattern can be accounted for as the output of a number of sources on its edge whose scale of production was well below that documented for banded flint, for instance. While the use of copper added another new and desirable raw material, it caused no revolution in the sphere of trade.

The development of copper-working in the later fourth and third millennia was the result of the availability of easily-smelted ores in locations already well known. The numerous analyses of hammer-axes, adze-axes and flat copper axes from this period (Patay *et al.* 1963; Junghans *et al.* 1968) show a consistent pattern almost without impurities, except for traces of silver. This would be compatible with the use either of native, oxide or carbonate ores, but it is likely that the bulk of copper came from the widely distributed (Table 1) ores, malachite and azurite, pieces of which have been found on a number of sites in Yugoslavia (e.g. Fafos: Jovanović 1971). Over a wide area, from Macedonia and Bulgaria in the south to Slovakia in the north, the extensive deposits of ores of this kind allowed a simple metallurgy to flourish on an impressive scale. Although smelting was probably confined to areas immediately adjacent to the sources, re-melting probably took place over a wider area, and large objects traded outwards from the sources would, no doubt, at some stage have been broken down, as occasion demanded, into a multitude of smaller forms. No specialized ingots of comparable size are known. The processes involved in the manufacture of finished products are of a simple kind, involving only a one-piece open mould and a good deal of hammering (Coghlan 1961; Charles 1969).

There is some evidence, even from the fourth millennium, of the production of arsenical alloys. One of the Tibava hammer-axes (SAM No. 3354) contains 1.15% of arsenic, and sporadic values of up to 4% occur in objects from the later Copper Age. Such occurrences in no way imply the kind of regular trade in additives suggested by consistently high tin values in the Bronze Age. As can be seen from Table 1, native arsenic and its oxides and sulphides occur commonly in association with the kinds of copper deposit under discussion. Indeed, the green pseudo-malachite mineral with a high arsenic content, similar in appearance to the pure copper carbonate, is occasionally found, and could well have been added quite accidentally. It is also, of course, likely that the effects of adding associated arsenic minerals came to be appreciated and, with the development of closed-mould casting in the later third millennium (see below), the use of this additive became standard practice in south-east Europe (Chernih 1971) and the Aegean (Charles 1967), where tin supplies were sporadic.

The ores that sustained the output of massive copper axes were naturally limited in extent, and there are indications that by the later third millennium they were in short supply. Copper axes were no longer put in graves, and settlement finds are few. Some continuity was maintained in the north-west part of the basin where axes are found occasionally in Baden contexts in Austria and in Slovakia, and pieces of sheet metal were put in graves. Significantly, one or two pieces from this period are of *fahlerz*, and while small amounts of purer copper ore remained (probably in relatively inaccessible areas) to be used sporadically for the next half-millennium, its main phase of use was over. The final stages of the third millennium marked a time of scarcity and experiment.

A curious situation then came about: at a time when raw-material supplies in the Carpathian Basin were short, contacts across the Pontic steppes with the Caucasian school of metallurgy (Chernih 1966) introduced a new range of forms, such as the single-bladed axe (Mozsolics 1967), associated with the technique of closed casting in a two-piece mould. At the same time, local copper-working began over a much wider area of central and north-west Europe. This occurred in areas metallurgically entirely distinct: lacking extensive deposits of purer secondary ores, their industries developed on the basis of a supply of *fahlerz* copper.

By the beginning of the second millennium, therefore, especially in Bohemia and central Germany but also further west, a second florescence of copper-using was under way. It is this '*fahlerz* boom' which has marked the Early Bronze Age of central Europe in general, and the Aunjetitz culture in particular, as a phenomenon of special interest to the prehistorian (Childe 1957). Based initially on open-mould casting, this central European school later followed the Carpathian Basin in adopting the two-piece mould, at the same time taking local tin as a standard additive to improve closed castings in the same way that arsenic was adopted in the Balkans.

Spectrographic analysis, of little use in identifying specific sources for the purer metals of the Copper Age, has proved of great value in distinguishing several varieties of *fahlerz* (Otto & Witter 1952; Junghans *et al.* 1960; 1968). The assemblages of the central European Early Bronze Age are dominated by a limited number of groups, chiefly 'A' or Singen metal and the so-called *ösenhalsring* metal (Waterbolk & Butler 1965). Neither can be definitely attributed to a specific source: 'A' metal probably covers several sources including, possibly, some in the Harz mountains; but *ösenhalsring* metal shows a significant geographical patterning. Its concentration on the Upper Danube and in Moravia has been related both to a Slovakian and to an

Alpine origin (Neuninger & Pittioni 1963; Bath-Bílková 1973) but, whichever is correct, two features stand out – the large quantities that occur as ingots in hoards, and the contrast between the frequency of these in Moravia and the trickle of this metal that reached the Carpathian Basin. Only appreciably later did a local *fahlerz* ($F_{A/B}$ or 'Otomani metal') become widespread in the Basin and allow a full expression of the forms that had developed there in the period of intervening scarcity (Schubert & Schubert 1967).

What, then, was the social and historical significance of these changes in the availability of metal, and how do these relate to the questions set out in the opening section? In the first place, the development of a technology of copper-smelting from the purer secondary ores had few wider effects upon contemporary society. It was a local expression of processes widespread in Later Neolithic Europe – the exploration of the landscape, an intensified exploitation of raw materials, and a limited widening of trade networks. It added a new prestige material that was used in much the same way as stone and shell elsewhere. The earliest hammer-axes are a direct translation of the stone forms elsewhere called 'battle-axes', and are clearly the equivalents of these as deposits in graves. It was used for daggers – in phase II of the Tiszapolgár cemetery associated with somewhat younger adult males than the shaft-hole axes (Fig. 8) – in place of stone blades, and it was used for armbands and beads in place of shell. Its importance was largely symbolic: the medium was the message.

The spread of metal-using further north in the second millennium was equally associated primarily with prestige uses. Again, the axe – in this case, the local flat form rather than a shaft-hole type – and the dagger were among the first applications, along with ornaments and the pins that were at this time becoming fashionable in place of buttons. There are, however, new features that are of significance for the social structure of the Bronze Age proper. The rich grave of Thun-Renzenbühl in Switzerland (Fig. 16; Strahm 1972) epitomizes both old and new features. Axe and dagger retain their symbolic role, reinforced by a headband and belt-terminal which themselves have antecedents in the later Copper Age. Cloak-pins of specific regional types no doubt

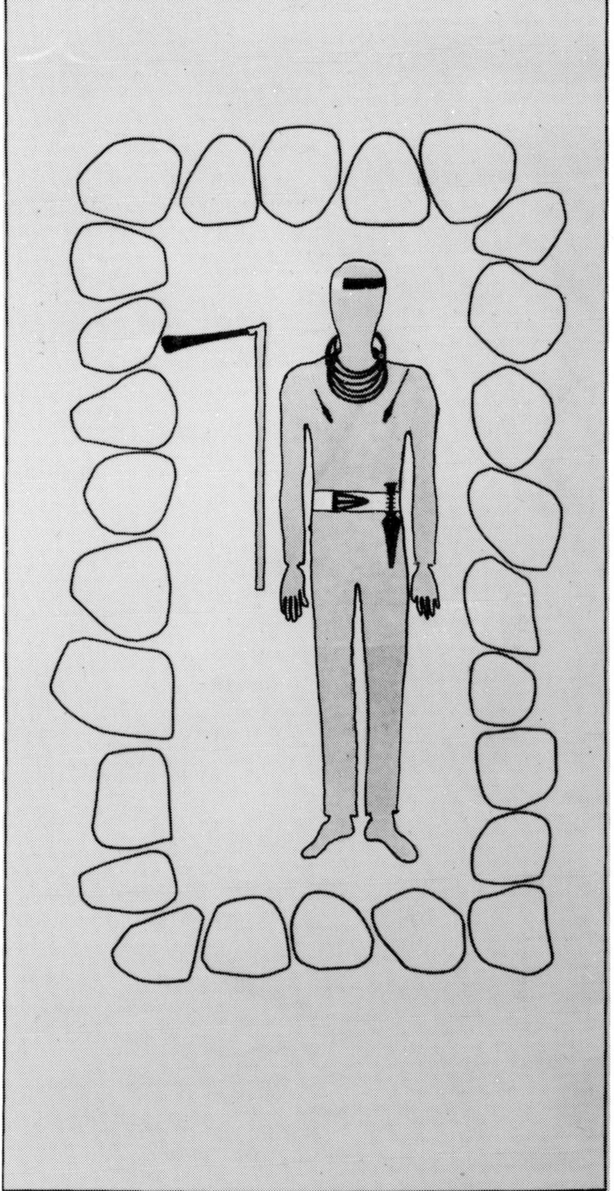

Figure 16. The rich grave of Thun-Renzenbühl, Switzerland; from Strahm 1972.

proclaim local loyalties, but the six neck-rings introduce a new element of special importance. Such neck-rings (*ösenhalsringe*) were evidently both traded as ingots and worn as ornaments. They occur in hoards of up to 600 (Schubert 1966) and are clearly counters as much as symbols of individual authority. In the Copper Age, groups of more than two or three axes found together are rare, and the 'hoard' of 13 flat axes from the Pločnik settlement is unique. This is consistent with their inferred use as indicators of ascribed status. With the *ösen-*

halsringe we have for the first time an element of accumulation, the achieved position of a 'big man' superadded to other inequalities. Slightly later than the *ösenhalsringe* are the massive axe-hoards of the Saale region, such as that of Gröbers-Bennewitz, with 300 flanged axes, or the Dieskau II hoard including also daggers and halberds (Brunn 1959). Such collections are typical of the mixture of ingot-counters and display equipment that dominates European Bronze Age hoards down to the occurrence of industrial collections ('smiths' hoards') which mark the system of rapid re-cycling necessary when bronze was used as a workaday material (Rowlands 1971).

It is unlikely that the goods that survive archaeologically moved in isolation: the greater concentration of metal in the Early Bronze Age, which for the first time saw the extensive import of metal objects to large areas, such as Denmark and north Germany, without local resources, must indicate also a greater mobility in other commodities, probably including subsistence products and textiles. The greater mobility offered by extensive transhumance and sea-faring, the wide-spread use of the horse, all helped to make possible a wider network of exchange and trade. In the Aegean, the sudden flowering of inter-regional contacts in the later third millennium (Renfrew 1967) surely indicates the beginning of the type of complex maritime exchange-cycles so familiar to ethnographers (Fig. 1).

The division of prehistory into Stone, Bronze and Iron Ages has had a remarkably long life since the scheme was first put forward in 1832. Seen as symptomatic of underlying ecological and social changes, rather than simply as a technological advance, the beginning of the Bronze Age retains its significance as a critical point in European development.

Acknowledgments

I should like to thank Dr D.L. Clarke and Professor Colin Renfrew for provoking many of the thoughts in this essay. The second section, as the title implies, owes much to the writing of Professor M.D. Sahlins. The drawings were prepared from my originals by Mrs Pat Clarke.

REFERENCES

Andel, K. (1961) Tibava – Eneoltyczny zespoł osadniczy u stóp Wychorlatu. *Acta Archaeologica Carpathica*, 3, 39-59.

Bath-Bílková, B. (1973) K problému původu hřiver – Zur Herkunftsfrage der Halsringbarren. *Památky Archeologické* 64, 24-41.

Becker, G.J. (1959) Flint mining in Neolithic Denmark. *Antiquity*, 33, 87-92.

Bognár-Kutzián, I. (1963) *The Copper Age cemetery of Tizapolgár-Basatanya* (Achaeologia Hungarica, n.s. 24).

Bognár-Kutzián, I. (1972) *The Copper Age Tiszapolgár culture in the Carpathian Basin* (Archaeologia Hungarica, n.s. 48).

Brookfield, H.C. and Hart, D. (1971) *Melanesia: A Geographical Interpretation of an Island World.* London.

Brunn, W.A. von (1959) *Die Hortfunde der frühen Bronzezeit aus Sachsen-Anhalt, Sachsen und Thüringen.* Berlin.

Cantacuzino, G. and Morinz, S. (1963) Die Jungsteinzeitliche Funde in Cernica (Bukarest). *Dacia*, n.s. 7, 27-89.

Chappell, J. (1966) Stone Axe Factories in the highlands of East New Guinea. *P.P.S.*, 32, 96-121.

Charles, J.A. (1967) Early arsenical bronzes – a metallurgical view. *Amer. Jour. Arch.*, 71, 21-6.

Charles, J.A. (1969) Metallurgical examination of south-east European copper axes (Appendix I in Renfrew 1969). *P.P.S.*, 35, 40-2.

Chernih, E. (1966) *Istoriya Drevneishei Metallurgii Vostochnoi Evropi.* Moscow.

Chernih, E. (1971) Spektralen analiz na metalnite nachodki ot praistoricheskoto selishche do s. Ezèro. *Archeologiya*, 13, 55-61.

Chernih, E. and Radunčeva, A. (1972) Starite medni roodnitsi okolo gr. Stara Zagora. *Archeologiya* 14, 61-7.

Childe, V.G. (1951) *Social Evolution.* London.

Childe, V.G. (1956) *Man Makes Himself* (3rd. ed.). London.

Childe, V.G. (1957) *The Dawn of European Civilization* (7th ed.). London.

Childe, V.G. (1958) *The Prehistory of European Society.* Harmondsworth, Middlesex.

Clark, J.G.D. (1952) *Prehistoric Europe: the Economic Basis.* London.

Clark, J.G.D. (1965) Traffic in stone axe and adze blades. *Economic History Review*, 18, 1-28.

Coghlan, H.H. (1961) Some problems concerning the manufacture of copper shaft-hole axes. *Archaeologia Austriaca*, 29, 57-75.

Douglas, M. (1967) Primitive rationing: a study in controlled exchange. In Firth, Sir R.W. (ed.), *Themes in Economic Anthropology*, 119-47. London.

Fell, C.I. (1964) The Cumbrian type of polished stone axe and its distribution in Britain. *P.P.S.*, 30, 39-55.

Frierman, J. (1969) The Balkan Graphite Ware

(Appendix II in Renfrew 1969). *P.P.S.*, 35, 42-3.

Hogbin, H.I. (1951) *Transformation Scene: The changing culture of a New Guinea village*. London.

Houlder, C.H. (1961) The excavation of a Neolithic stone implement factory on Mynydd Rhiw, Caernarvonshire. *P.P.S.*, 27, 108-143.

Jacob-Friesen, K.H. (1959) *Einführung in Niedersachsens Urgeschichte*. Hildesheim.

Jodłowski, A. (1971) *Eksploatacja Soli na Terenie Małopolski w Pradziejach i we Eczesnym Średniowieczu*. Krakow.

Jovanović, B. (1971) *Metalurgija Eneolitskog Perioda Jugoslavie*. Belgrade.

Junghans, S., Sangmeister, E. and Schröder, M. (1960) *Metallanalysen kupferzeitlicher und frühbronzezeitlicher Bodenfunde aus Europa*. Berlin.

Junghans, S., Sangmeister, E. and Schröder, M. (1968) *Kupfer und Bronze in der frühen Metalzeit Europas*. Berlin.

Kahlke, D. (1954) *Die Bestattungssitten des Donauländischen Kulturkreises der jüngeren Steinzeit*. Berlin.

Kirnbauer, F. (1958) Das jungsteinzeitliche Hornsteinbergwerk Mauer bei Wien. *Archaeologia Austriaca*, Beiheft 3, 121-42.

Kruk, J. (1973) *Studia Osadnicze nad Neolitem Wyzyn Lessowych*. Warsaw.

Maczek, M., Preuschen, E. and Pittioni, R. (1953) Beiträge zum Problem des Ursprunges der Kupfererzverwertung in der Alten Welt (II). *Archaeologia Austriaca*, 12, 67-82.

Milojčić, V. (1943) Das vorgeschichtliche Bergwerk 'Šuplja Stena' am Avalaberg bei Belgrad (Serbien). *Weiner Prähistorische Zeitschrift*, 30, 41-54.

Mozsolics, A. (1967) *Bronzefunde des Karpatenbeckens*. Budapest.

Neuninger, H. and Pittioni, R. (1963) Frühmetallzeitlicher Kupferhandel im Voralpenland. *Archaeologia Austriaca*, Beiheft 6, 1-39.

Otto, H. and Witter, W. (1952) *Handbuch der ältesten vorgeschichtlichen Metallurgie in Mitteleuropa*. Leipzig.

Park, C.F. and Macdiarmid, R.A. (1970) *Ore Deposits*. San Francisco.

Patay, P., Zimmer, K., Szabó, Z. and Sinay, G. (1963) Spektrographische und metallographische Untersuchung kupfer- und frühbronzezeitlicher Funde. *Acta Archaeologica Hungaricae*, 15, 37-64.

Pavuk, J. (1972) Neolithisches Gräberfeld in Nitra. *Slovenská Archaeológia*, 20, 5-105.

Pittioni, R. (1957) Urzeitlicher Bergbau auf Kupfererz und Spurenanalyse. *Archaeologia Austriaca*, Beiheft 1, 1-76.

Pittioni, R. (1973) Almwirtschaft. In *Reallexikon der Germanischen Altertumskunde*. Berlin.

Rădulescu, D. and Dimitrescu, R. (1966) *Mineralogia Topographică a României*. Bucharest.

Rappaport, R.A. (1968) *Pigs for the Ancestors*. New Haven, London.

Renfrew, A.C. (1967) Cycladic metallurgy and the Aegean Early Bronze Age. *Amer. Jour. Arch.*, 71, 1-20.

Renfrew, A.C. (1969) The Autonomy of the South-East European Copper Age. *P.P.S.*, 35, 12-47.

Renfrew, A.C. (1972) *The Emergence of Civilization: the Cyclades and the Aegean in the Third Millennium B.C.* London.

Rowlands, M.J. (1971) The archaeological interpretation of prehistoric metalworking. *World Arch.*, 3, 210-24.

Sahlins, M.D. (1963) Poor man, rich man, big-man, chief: political types in Melanesia and Polynesia. *Comparative Studies in Society and History*, 5, 285-303.

Sahlins, M.D. (1965) On the sociology of primitive exchange. In Bantock, M. (ed.) *The Relevance of Models for Social Anthropology*. London.

Sahlins, M.D. (1972) *Stone Age Economics*. Chicago and New York.

Schietzel, K. (1965) *Müddersheim*. Cologne and Graz.

Schmid, E. (1952) Vom Jaspisbergbau an der Kachelfluh bei Kleinkems (Baden). *Germania* 30, 153-8.

Schubert, E. (1965) Zu den südosteuropäischen Kupferäxten. *Germania*, 43, 274-95.

Schubert, E. (1966) Zur Frühbronzezeit an der Mittelren Donau. *Germania*, 44, 264-86.

Schubert, F. and Schubert, E. (1967) Spektralanalytische Untersuchungen von Hort- und Einzelfunden der Periode B III (Appendix in Mozsolics 1967, 185-203).

Schwabedissen, H. (1966) Ein horizontierter 'Breitkeil' aus Satrup. *Palaeohistoria*, 12, 409-68.

√Sherratt, A.G. (1972) Socio-economic and demographic models for the Neolithic and Bronze Ages of Europe. In Clarke, D.L. (ed.), *Models in Archaeology*, 477-542. London.

Šiška, S. (1964) Gräberfeld der Tiszapolgár Kultur in Tibava. *Slovenská Archaeológia*, 12, 352-6.

Strahm, C. (1972) Das Beil von Thun-Renzenbühl. *Helvetia Archaeologica*, 3, 99-112.

Sulimirski, T. (1960) Remarks concerning the distribution of some varieties of flint in Poland. *Swiatowit*, 22, 281-307.

√Tabaczynski, S. (1972) Gesellschaftsordnung und Güteraustausch im Neolithikum Mitteleuropas. *Neolithische Studien*, vol. 1, Berlin.

Točik, A. and Vladar, J. (1971) Prehlad badania v problematike vyvoja Slovenska v dobe bronzovej. *Slovenská Archaeológia*, 19, 369-422.

Vayda, A.P. (1966) Pomo trade feasts. *Humanités, Cahiers de l'Institut de Science Economique Appliquée*.

Vértes, L. (1964) Eine prähistorische Silexgrube am Mogyorósdomb bei Sumeg. *Acta Archaeologica Hungaricae*, 16, 187-215.

Vulpe, A. (1973) Incepturile metalurgiei aramei in spaţiul Carpata-Dunarean. *Studii şi Cercetări di Istoria Veche*, 24, 217-37.

Waterbolk, H.T. and Butler, J.J. (1965) Comments on the use of metallurgical analysis in prehistoric studies. *Helinium*, 5, 227-51.

√Wiślanski, T. (ed.) (1970) *The Neolithic in Poland*. Wrocław.

ANN SIEVEKING

Settlement patterns of the later Magdalenian in the central Pyrenees

The interest of the Pyrenees in the Upper Palaeolithic is that here there are a number of rich sites which are closely grouped and belong to a limited period of time. Many of the most spectacular were dug for Édouard Piette in the last century but are still of value because the data lost in these early and unscientific excavations are here more than compensated for by the fact that they are very rich in portable art. Like burials, this is evidence that has some value beyond material culture; it should be possible to deduce social groupings from it, even perhaps the intellectual pre-occupations of its makers. In the Palaeolithic such an extra dimension to the archaeological evidence is very rare. Technologies may represent environments or specific occupations, and the observed differences between one and another may be more apparent than real, but art is the product of a thought process, depending less on outside factors. For example, one habitation site may contain a great many harpoons, another a quantity of flint scrapers: the two assemblages are technologically different and will give the impression of two culturally differentiated groups of users although, in fact, one may represent a fishing station, the other a skin and meat processing site, both belonging to the same human group. Art forms, though (one hopes) are more constant and reflect the immediate environment less closely. Palaeolithic art is not simply decorative but, in so far as we can understand it, an embodiment of beliefs, perhaps religious, perhaps superstitious. It is a fundamental cultural determinant of the people who practised it; in fact, we may regard it as a language, the phrases of which we can easily recognize from place to place but which, at the present day, we can no longer actually read. However, even the phrases may help. The comparison of art forms will give a better indication of social grouping and connections between sites than bone and flint debris in the occupation levels. The following survey is an endeavour to use the art evidence to reinforce and supplement deductions drawn from the usual geological and archaeological material.

The Pyrenean bloc is an unstable zone of the earth's crust and has been subjected to repeated vigorous folding. Under the force of the Alpine folding the most recent beds, which were still relatively plastic, folded without breaking, but the old rigid base broke and dislocated, and in the region of these fractures thermal sources sprang up and metalliferous beds were formed. The upheaval affected the central and eastern regions more than the west. Today, the ancient granites can be seen in the heart of the chain, flanked by schists and limestones that heat and compression have often transformed into marbles. Altogether, these deposits form a mountainous belt that rises and expands from west to east, finishing in a fall of nearly 3,000 m. in view of the Mediterranean. The east-west belt is now deeply eroded by valleys, running at right angles to the watershed, which have produced a nearly perfect fish-backbone pattern.

Geographically, the French Pyrenees are divided into three major natural regions, differentiated by structure, climate and vegetation as Central, Atlantic and Mediterranean. The central area is that with the most dramatic scenery and its structure is characterized by zones of latitudinal relief. Driving south from Toulouse, one encounters first the Petits Pyrénées, modest in height and folded, next the *Zone de l'Ariège*, with pointed limestone peaks, and then the main axial zone of granites and schists. The region was heavily glaciated and the glaciers reached down as far as those places that are now Lourdes, Luchon and Tarascon. It was, of course, the action of these glaciers, grinding a smooth way through the narrow valley bottoms, that made such valleys accessible to large herd animals and man, and determined the physiognomy of the mountains themselves. Today, the peaks attract rainfall and the rivers running down from them are extensively harnessed for hydro-electric power. It is in the limestone foothills of the central Pyrenees (*Zone de l'Ariège*) and the outlying Petits Pyrénées that caves and rock-shelters are found and it is this region which is rich in archaeological sites. The Palaeolithic sites that we know to date are almost entirely restricted to the limestone, though they do not occur in all limestone areas. For example, they occur only in the central and west Pyrenees, not in the east, and only on the north-facing French slopes, not on the southerly Spanish side.

In the west, the Pyrenees are no longer a chain, strictly speaking, although there are sufficient peaks to hinder communication between France and Spain except by passes as famous as Ibaneta and Roncevaux. The topography of the Pays Basque, to quote Michelin, is 'in general, gentle and confused'; it is a region of little hills and innumerable valleys, while, towards the coast, the Landes dunes and pine forests reach beyond the mouth of the Adour almost to Biarritz. There are three major Upper Palaeolithic sites in the Landes, all found on small limestone outcrops that provide caves or shelters.

The east Pyrenees have, to date, produced no archaeological sites of Magdalenian age. There is plenty of limestone here and plenty of water but whether the lack of late Palaeolithic sites is a cultural fact, or simply due to lack of search, one cannot at present determine.

There are three sites, or groups of sites, in the west Pyrenees; apart from these, the remaining twenty-seven Middle and Late Magdalenian sites considered here are in the central region. Geographically, their distribution is based on the rivers, both because the flat-bottomed glaciated valleys are easily accessible and because the land between these is so hostile. The valleys are divided by steep ridges of rocks and peaks which, at the end of the last glaciation, were probably still heavily covered with ice and snow. Such hills do not invite settlement; in many cases they do not even allow a passage across. When you stand on the *Col de Mente* and look west, you can count seven parallel sharp-backed spines running from the High Pyrenees down towards the plain and it is very clear that, if it were not for modern road building and blasting, communication could in most places only be on a north-south line, up and down each valley. Not all the Pyrenean valleys were cut out by glaciers and those that were not have no Palaeolithic occupation. The people, or rather the animals they hunted, chose the open valleys with a flat floor and a hope of good vegetation. Many of these occupied valleys are small and the stretches that show most human settlement are often the narrow bottle-necks, particularly where high-level caves give a view across the valley and up and down its course. The settlements around Tarascon and Arudy show this pattern clearly. Whether thermal springs with hot water, such as those at Ussat, were also an attraction to Palaeolithic people, one cannot say. Probably, except for the fact that Piette went to Luchon for his health, they have had no bearing on the archaeology of the Pyrenees.

The local distribution of Middle and Late Magdalenian sites in the Pyrenees is determined by the river pattern, a factor that seems to determine the distribution of Magdalenian sites over a wider area also. The early Magdalenian stages are found at their most rich in the Dordogne and Poitou regions, but in Magdalenian IV the emphasis shifts to the Pyrenees which, at this stage, has the richest and most numerous sites. The Dordogne/Vezère region remains as a second centre, however, and sites such as Laugerie Basse and La Madeleine are the equal of any in the Pyrenees; their art objects are also strikingly similar, both in style and subject (Fig. 2). There can be no doubt that the objects from these sites and the Mas d'Azil in the Pyrenees, for example, or Gourdan, although they may not have belonged to an identical group of people, must have belonged to groups who were related or in very close contact (Figs. 2-6). It has been suggested that the Dordogne and Pyrenean finds represent the north and south migratory limits of a single group of people but (for reasons that it is more relevant to examine later) this is probably an over-simplified view of the case. However, if you look at the relief map of south-west France (Fig. 1), it does appear that the Pyrenean sites, together with Bruniquel, in Tarn-et-Garonne, and the Dordogne group, form a half ring around the Garonne drainage basin, more usually known as the Basin of Aquitaine. All are found in the limestone foothills beside the river valleys, and all the rivers drain out north or westwards; the

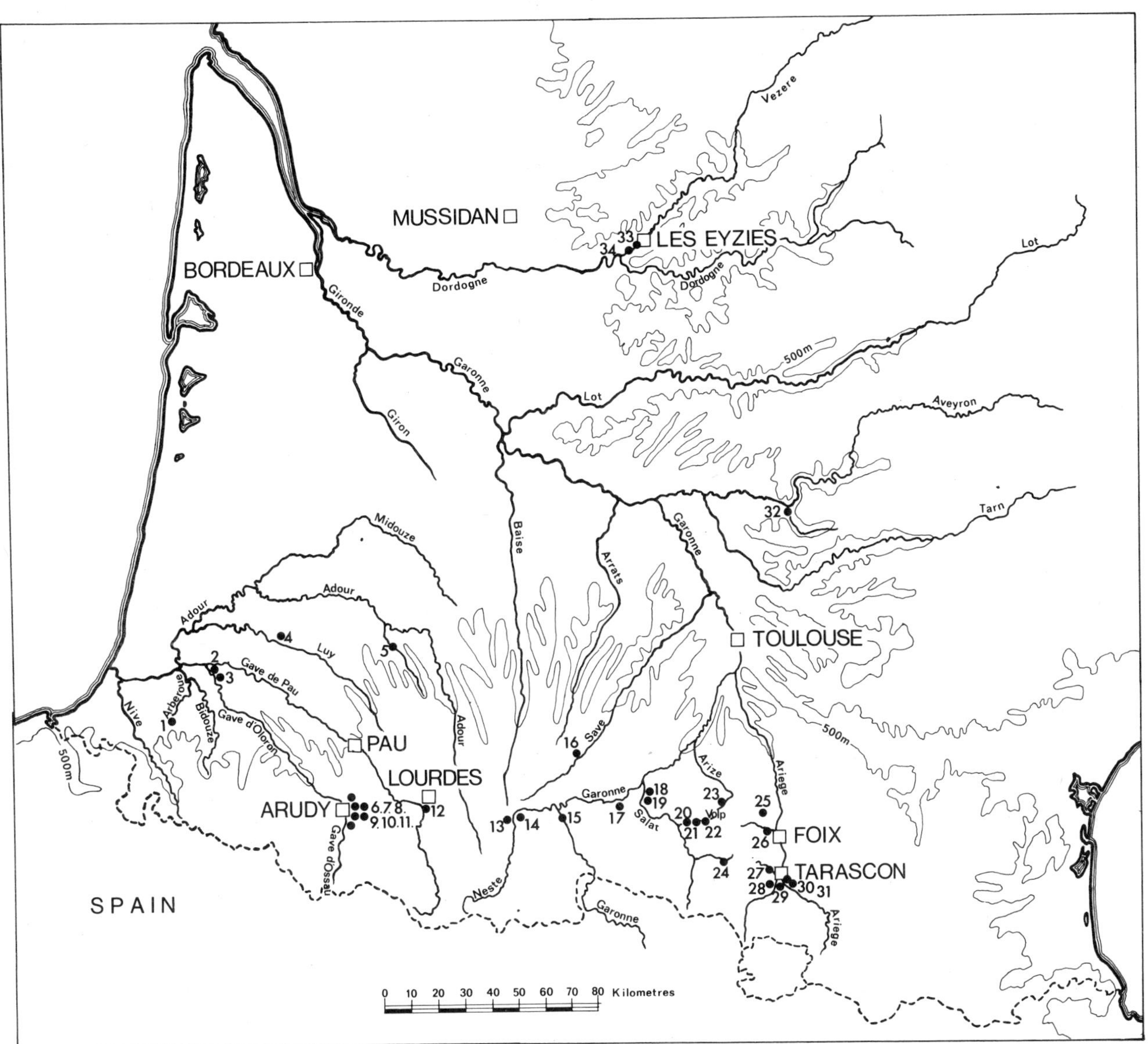

Figure 1. Later Magdalenian settlement patterns in the central Pyrenees and related districts in the Basin of Aquitaine.

1. Isturitz
2. Duruthy
3. Pastou
4. Brassempouy
5. Aurensan
6. Ste Colombe
7. Espalungues
8. St-Michel
9. Pöeymau
10. Malarode
11. Vignalats
12. Lourdes
13. Labastide
14. Lorthet
15. Gourdan
16. Lespugue
17. Montespan
18. Marsoulas
19. Tarté
20. Enlène
21. Trois Frères
22. Tuc d'Audoubert
23. Mas d'Azil
24. Massat
25. Portel
26. Labouiche
27. Bedeilhac
28. La Vache
29. Niaux
30. Les Églises
31. Fontanet
32. Bruniquel
33. La Madeleine
34. Laugerie Basse

Nos. 17 and 29 are decorated caves with no associated habitation deposits.

Garonne joining the Tarn and the Lot to become the Gironde, as does the Dordogne also in its estuary. The only reasonable lines of communication in the Pyrenees follow the rivers, and traffic thus tends to run not east and west but north and south following, principally, the Garonne and its tributaries (Appendix I). In fact, if this pattern of river communications is followed around the semi-circle of limestone foothills, it includes not only the Pyrenean sites but Bruniquel, Laugerie and La Madeleine as well. By river-ways there is quite an easy geographical connection between the Pyrenees and the Dordogne. The drainage pattern of the east Pyrenees, however, has nothing to do with the Garonne – it tends eastwards towards the Mediterranean, which may, in some degree, account for the lack of Magdalenian sites in this area.

Looking at the Pyrenees in the twentieth century, one sees a topography very little different from that of the period from about 10,800 B.C. to 8,800 B.C. It is in climate and vegetation that the differences lie. In the last phase of the Würm glaciation, the Pyrenees were free enough of ice to allow herds of large animals to graze in the valleys, even if only intermittently. The vegetation must have been that now described as Arctic Tundra, though it was probably much richer than tundra vegetation of the present day, which is confined to latitudes that suffer from a long dark arctic winter. Late-glacial Denmark had an abundant heliophyte vegetation (Degerbøl & Krug 1959); vegetation much farther to the south in the Pyrenees must have been as rich, or richer. The presence of reindeer, bison and other grazing species that live in herds suggests that such vegetation was herbaceous, however, with very few trees. Living-site deposits show that of all animal species eaten reindeer was greatly preferred, though bison, horse, ibex and deer were also killed upon occasion. In some living sites 90% of the bone debris is reindeer, but it would be wrong to conclude from this that reindeer formed 90% of the contemporary fauna. In an environment that had a plentiful supply of animals, hunters could eat which species they chose, or could most easily catch. The preference for reindeer in Magdalenian IV is so marked that these people are often described as 'the reindeer hunters'. They ate reindeer; they used the antler and bone for weapons and carving; and one supposes they used the skin for clothing and for the innumerable uses that, in the absence of other fibres, leather might have been put to, either cut into strips or sheets and knotted, or stitched.

There is, however, no present-day community that exists solely by hunting, with the exception of the Eskimo whose economy is an adaptation to extreme conditions (Balikci 1968). Gathering is a more reliable way of life than hunting and more productive for less effort. Lee (1968) calculated in the case of the !Kung Bushmen that it was from two to four times as productive as hunting. 'Hunting is a high-risk, low-return subsistence activity, while gathering is a low-risk, high-return subsistence activity.' Meat, however, perhaps because of the difficulty in obtaining it, is valued more highly by the Bushmen than vegetable foods. Such a subsistence strategy seems applicable to hunter-gatherers everywhere at the present day and can be considered as 'a persistent and well-adapted way of life'. It seems reasonable to apply this concept to the Upper Palaeolithic also, since the continuity in art forms and the substantial occupation deposits show an economy that was maintained in a remarkable state of equilibrium for a very long period of time. By analogy with modern primitive societies, this economy was highly successful in terms of adaptiveness and persistence, and it would be reasonable to assume that it was based upon the more flexible and reliable gathering-and-hunting pattern than upon the relatively hazardous hunting-only basis. Among modern primitive groups, meat usually forms no more than 35% of the diet (Lee 1968); it may be the preferred food, but it is generally not the staple one. Roots, berries, fruits, nuts and fish are the staple gathered foods.

At present, we have no macroscopic plant or pollen records for any inhabited Pyrenean cave (with the exception of Duruthy, but it is not very detailed here and the evidence is not yet published) and thus no evidence of what fruits, berries or nuts the Upper Palaeolithic people may have eaten but, although the evidence is largely conjectural, it seems probable that salmon was an important part of their diet. There is very little fish-bone debris recorded from these caves; perhaps significantly, salmon bones have been found at Duruthy, Sordes (Arambourou: pers. comm.) and at Les Églises in modern excavations; and a nearly complete salmon skeleton was found lying on the floor, together with other food remnants, in the newly discovered gallery at Fontanet in Ariège (Simonnet 1971; Clottes & Simonnet 1974). In the early excavations, animal bones and flints were perhaps saved and fragile fish bones either ignored or missed. Piette, like most early excavators, did not in fact supervise the excavations done for him. He visited the sites, but left the workmen to dig them out in his absence. Salmon, trout and eels are drawn and sculpted, particularly on the miniature art pieces of the Magdalenian, which suggests that they were eaten. That there is not a great number of these drawings is not particularly significant since reindeer, which is known from occupational debris to be the animal species most often eaten, is one of the least represented in the art of the period. Perhaps more significantly, small harpoons, which are tools that seem suitable for salmon fishing, are found in quantity at this period and the fundamental theme in their decoration, when they are decorated, is the fish (Breuil & St-Périer 1927).

To look at this question from another point of view, these Pyrenean rivers along which the Magdalenian sites are clustered are also those which, until the nineteenth century, had some of the richest salmon runs in Europe. The Gironde used to have huge runs of salmon which were spawned in the headwaters of the Garonne, and the Adour, the Gave d'Ossau, the Gave de Pau and the Gave d'Oloron were all excellent salmon streams. In the last hundred years, hydro-electric and mill dams have ruined the salmon fishing in all but a few of these rivers. Many dams were built without fish-ladders and, in any case, hydro-electric dams are too high for such ladders, so the spawning grounds in the upper reaches of the rivers have been abandoned. Salmon are also very sensitive to pollution and hot water or chemicals will very soon drive them from a river. Today, we are accustomed to heavily depleted salmon streams where a few fish make a brief seasonal appearance but, to give some idea of the quantity of fish such rivers used to support, it has been calculated that, at the end of the eighteenth century, 8,000-10,000 fish were caught *on every day* of the three-month fishing season in Spain. Not surprisingly, that total fell sharply by the middle of the nineteenth century. In addition to this, to quote Netboy (1968): 'Any productive watercourse is populated at a given time by salmon of various ages and states of development.' Large and small fish enter the estuary at different times and move to the spawning beds with greater or less speed; there will be young fish going downstream, adults going upstream, and spawned-out fish lying in pools or going slowly down to the sea again, so that there is an almost continuous supply of fish, although the best period for fishing will be when the adult fish go upstream to spawn. It is inconceivable that Palaeolithic people should have lived, as they did, beside such a marvellous supply of food and not taken advantage of it. In fact, the degree of settlement indicated by their living sites (Duruthy, for example, has deposits 40 m. deep) suggests that they must have done so. Hunting requires a high degree of mobility, while those people whose economy is settled at least for a season of some duration, have a local, gathered and rich food supply, and salmon is a classic instance of this. It has been suggested (Watanabe 1968) that one of the principal reasons for the Ainu maintaining a permanent year-round residence is that salmon is an important part of their diet.

It is not possible to prove that the Upper Palaeolithic people in the Pyrenees ate a lot of salmon, but it seems very probable that they did so, both from the location and the duration of their settlements. In addition harpoons, which are usually associated with fishing, are common in these settlement deposits. In any case, the concept of a reindeer-based economy perhaps needs re-examining. The valleys of Tarascon and Arudy, for example, which have a great density of Magdalenian sites, are not very large and reindeer, it appears, were not the only herds that grazed there; there were also bison and horses. Even if the vegetation were rich, it does not seem possible that a herd of reindeer large enough to supply meat as a staple diet, without suffering decimation, could have found pasturage there. One wonders how many reindeer were killed and how important a part of the diet they did, in fact, form. One should, perhaps, conclude that when reindeer bone is found in a cave deposit, to the exclusion of almost all other bone, it means only that when meat was eaten, it was reindeer meat, but not necessarily that it formed a large proportion of the diet. In other regions this may have been so but, in the particular geographical context of Tarascon or

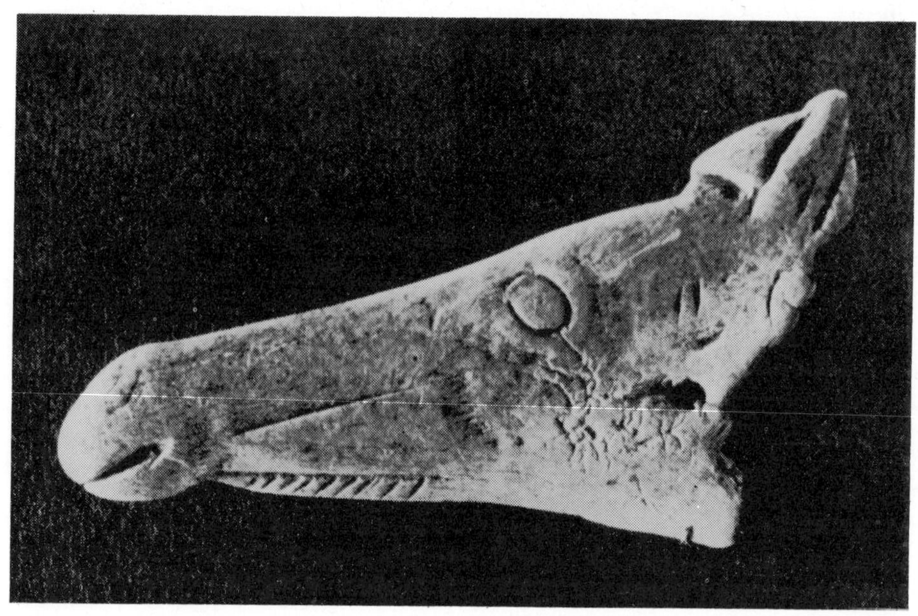

a

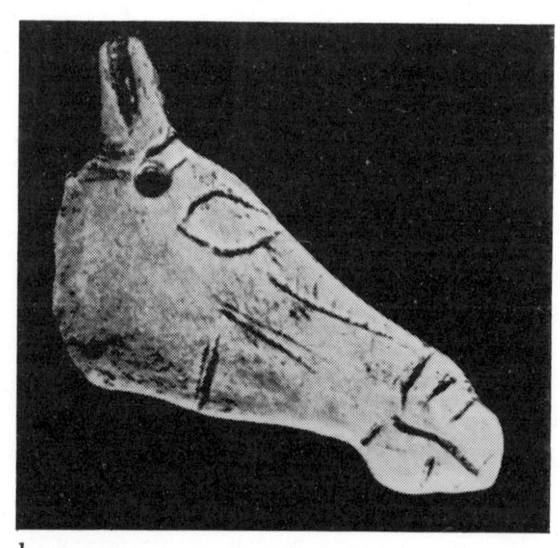

b

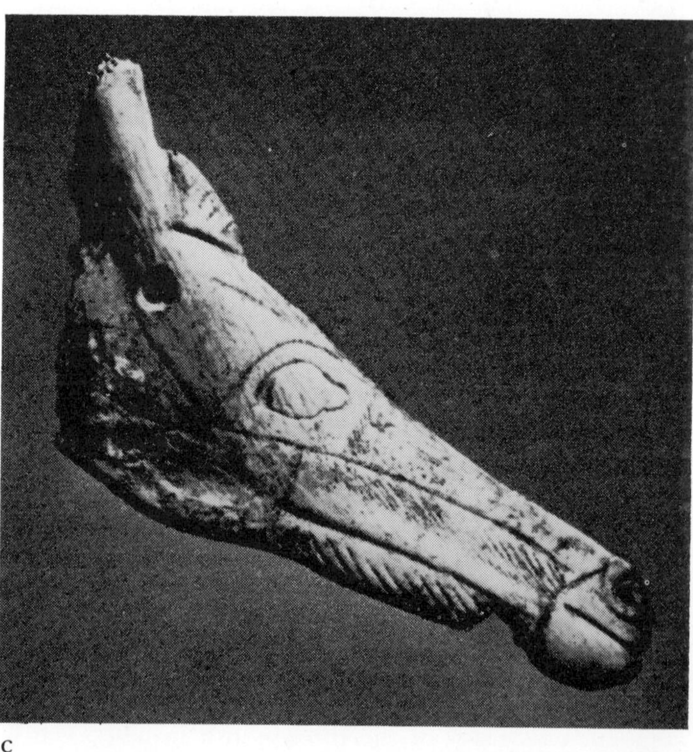

c

Figure 2. Hyoid bone horse-head pendants – Magdalenian IV in date. (a) Laugerie Basse; (b) Le Portel; (c) Isturitz. These are silhouettes with fairly schematic indications of features such as the eye and beard.

a b

Figure 3. Bison heads – Magdalenian IV in date. (a) La Madeleine; (b) Isturitz. The drawing of eye, muzzle and beard, with small chevrons, is very similar.

Arudy, a reindeer-dependent economy seems an unrealistic proposition. The smallness of the valleys and the density of the Palaeolithic sites suggests that people living there would have exploited a number of resources, rather than selecting one; or that, if one was depended upon more than others, this would have been a food in greater supply, such as salmon.

Settlement depends on food supply and it is difficult, for a period as remote as the Palaeolithic, to calculate the degree and duration of settlement in any one place. Certain evidence in cave deposits, such as the state of reindeer antler and teeth, may indicate at which period of the year the cave was used. The state of both reindeer and salmon remains at Duruthy shows the site to have been occupied from September to March (Arambourou: private communication) and reindeer antler at Isturitz seems to place this as a winter occupation also. St-Périer (1920) on the Isturitz antler has been criticized, but current opinion (Sturdy, private communication; 1972; Gaare 1968; Hustich 1951; Sbodnikov 1958; Vibe 1957) tends to readmit his conclusions). Conversely, higher sites in valleys of the Central Pyrenean foothills were more probably occupied in spring and summer. Many of the animal species found in the occupation deposits and drawn in the caves nearby, such as reindeer, bison or deer, are migratory; in all probability, at this period (within the last glaciation) and at this altitude, frost and snow would have driven them downstream to more open pasture in the winter and, had the hunters remained behind, they would have had to adapt their economy to a different food supply. There is no evidence that they did do this and the probability is that they followed the reindeer and other animals downstream.

There are two other categories of evidence that further support the idea of seasonal settlement in the Pyrenees during the Magdalenian; one is the presence of exotic objects in a deposit, such as the amber horse-head and the sea-shell and jet pendants found at Isturitz, or the representation of a sole from Lespugue; the other is the small size of so much of the portable art. A simple technology, with few or small goods (Sahlins 1968:186) is characteristic of people whose economy is nomadic. Conversely, a factor that contributes to year-round settlement is the storage of food. For example, meat

Figure 4. Fragments of horse-head spear-throwers – Magdalenian IV in date. (a) Bruniquel; (b) Isturitz. Two examples of a type of thrower known in some number from the Dordogne, Pyrenees and Kesslerloch in Switzerland.

and fish may be dried or frozen to be eaten in the lean months of the year, but there is little evidence that this was done in the Upper Palaeolithic except, perhaps, at sites such as Kostenki in the U.S.S.R. People whose existence is nomadic usually do not store food because of the obvious trouble in transporting it, and people who have a varied food supply usually do not need to. The evidence we have suggests that the Upper Palaeolithic people in the Pyrenees moved about, perhaps following herds of animals or contacting them at particular spots such as river crossings on the migratory routes, rather than maintaining a year-round settlement in one particular cave.

From an anthropological point of view the question is the same whether studying contemporary hunter-gatherers or those of the Pleistocene: how many people of what ages and sexes, in what specified biological and social relationships, reside or camp together for what defined periods, and for what reasons? (Birdsell 1968:229). The evidence that we have for the Upper Palaeolithic is very limited and for most of these questions the answers are conjectural. The basic facts are that some Magdalenian hunters lived, for some period of the year at least, in caves in the valleys of the Pyrenean foothills; that when there, they ate reindeer and used the antler and bone for tools and carvings; and that, on the evidence of the art pieces they left behind, they travelled widely outside this area. Art in the Vezère region in Magdalenian IV is so similar to that of the Pyrenean caves that one must either suppose that these two regions represent the north and south migratory limits of identical groups of people, or that the groups from each region were in periodic close contact. The first explanation is the least likely for a number of reasons. Firstly, animals and people tend to migrate in order to exploit two different environments and the Pyrenean and Dordogne valleys represent the *same* environment, each consisting of flat-bottomed bottle-necked valleys occurring at comparable altitude in limestone foothills. There would be little point in leaving the Pyrenean caves for those of the Vezère,[1] but to move from either region to the Garonne plain would provide a different habitat for both animals and men. Secondly, there is some evidence that caves in the Dordogne region were occupied at all periods of the year, so they do not provide a complementary alternate pattern for the Pyrenean settlements and, thirdly, the sites in the west Pyrenees must be taken into account. The art pieces from Isturitz, Duruthy and Brassempouy show as close a relationship to those of the Dordogne as do the Central Pyrenean pieces (Figs. 2 and 3), but geographically it is hard to fit them into a north-south migration pattern operating between these last two areas; if the points of contact were in the

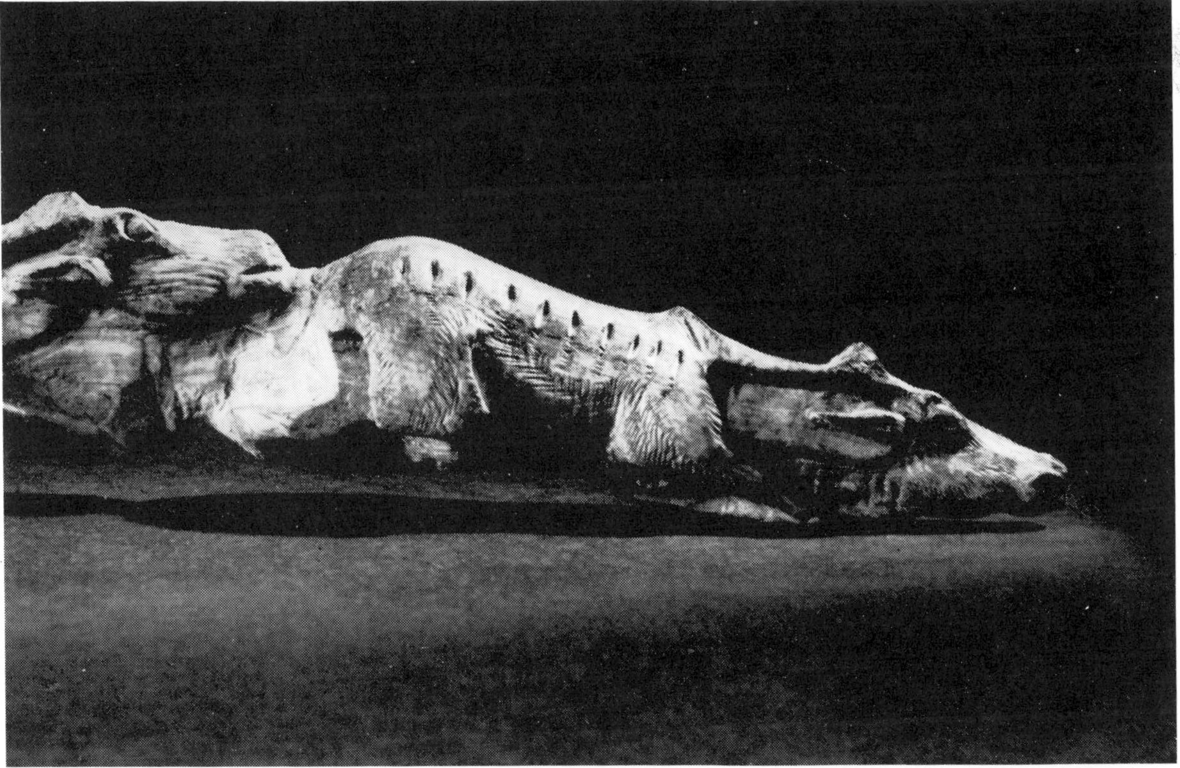

a

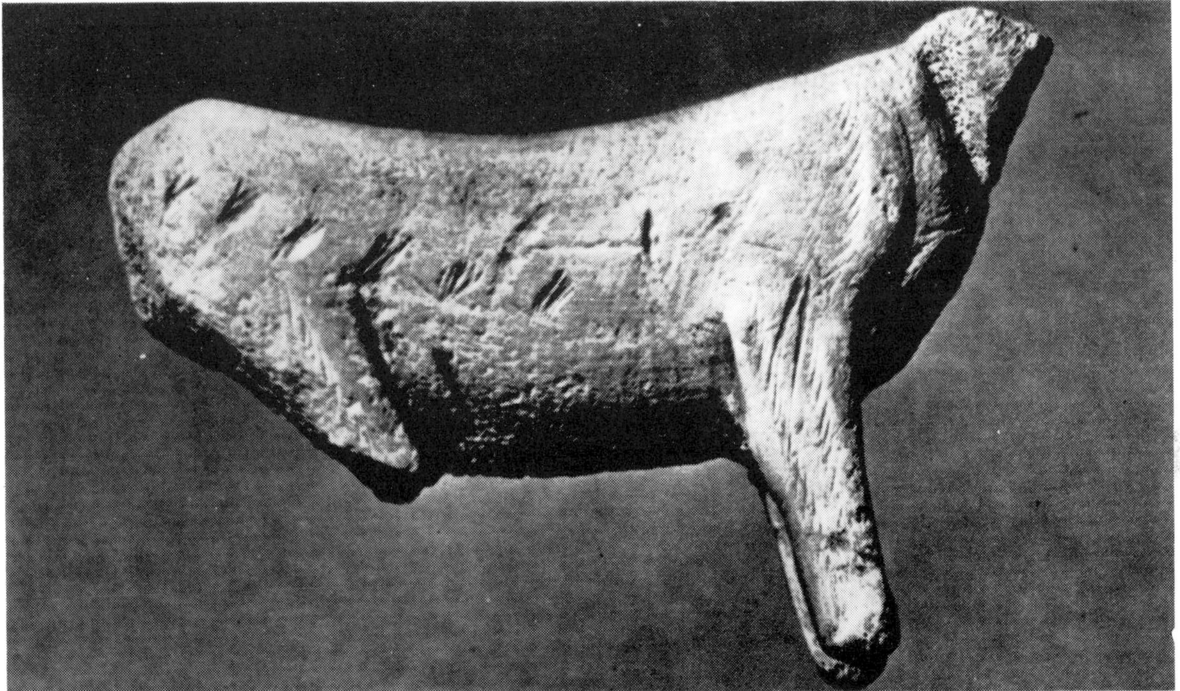

b

Figure 5. Reindeer – Magdalenian IV in date. (a) Bruniquel; (b) Arudy – this piece was probably the weight on a spear-thrower. The depiction of the animals' coats is very similar.

Garonne plain, however, it would be more feasible.

From the Garonne plain to the Dordogne or the Pyrenees is still a considerable distance for inter-related groups to cover. One might have expected that, if the Pyrenean valleys represented the high-altitude summer pastures, the lower stretches of the same rivers, perhaps in the Toulouse plain or the region at the confluence of the *Gaves*, would represent the winter limits of the territorial pattern. If this were the case, objects indicative of cultural identity, such as the miniature art pieces, should show a similar territorial grouping. The characteristic forms at Arudy, for example, might be re-encountered at Duruthy and those from Mas d'Azil at other sites lower down the Garonne, but the number of instances where this is so are so few as to be the exception rather than the rule. There is one particular design of Magdalenian IV date, a wavy line composed of fine hatching with additional notching at the edge (Chollot 1964: No. 48716), which is confined to the west Pyrenean sites; and one motif of Magdalenian V or VI date, that of an animal's head spouting blood, that is peculiar to the east (Trois Frères Begouen collection; La Vache-Robert collection; Leroi-Gourhan 1968, Pl. 216, *lower*). None of the other distinctive series is distributed in this way. The famous spirally-decorated half-rods (Fig. 7), for example, are confined to western sites, except that there is a very good example from Massat in Ariège, while the *Fâon à l'Oiseau* spear-throwers (Garrod 1955: Fig. 3), which are a distinct series of copies, are found at Mas d'Azil, Bedeilhac and Labastide in the east, but also at Arudy and perhaps Isturitz in the west, and a possible fragment occurs at Bruniquel on the Aveyron as well. To make the distribution even more confusing, there are very

a

b

Figure 6. Horse heads with 'bridle' markings – Magdalenian IV in date. (a) Mas d'Azil; (b) Arudy. The very conventionalized coat markings on these heads, looking like bridles or halters, at one time inspired a claim for the very early domestication of the horse.

Figure 7. Fragments of half-rods with spiral decoration – Magdalenian IV in date. (a) Lourdes; (b) Lourdes; (c) Arudy; (d) Isturitz. This is a decorative motif confined to the Pyrenees.

few categories confined even to the Pyrenees, and types found in the Dordogne or at Bruniquel are as likely to be duplicated in the west Pyrenean groups as in the east (Figs. 2-8). In fact, the spirally-decorated half-rods do not appear in the Dordogne, neither does the cervid-and-wolf motif (Fig. 8), nor the animal head gushing blood, both of which are late in date; but from the seventeen categories of related designs (see Appendix II), here tentatively constructed according to the subject of decoration, tool type, basic material or technique employed, these are the only ones with a specifically Pyrenean distribution. The conclusions to be drawn are that the geographical area of interrelated people is much larger than one might have expected, and that there must have been a lot of cross traffic as well as riverine communication in south-west France during the later stages of the Magdalenian.

Looking at a map (Fig. 1), it is easy to see how groups of people from Les Eyzies, for example, might join groups from the central Pyrenees, since they lived on rivers (the Vezère and the Garonne) that converge in their lower courses and both are on the edges of the same natural basin or ring. It is altogether more difficult to account for the very close parallels between Laugerie, for example, and Isturitz. The expected distribution pattern would have had two zones, one based upon the drainage system of the Garonne and the other upon the Adour,

Figure 8. Wolf-and-cervid motif – Late Magdalenian in date – V or VI. (a) El Pendo; (b) Lorthet; (c) Mas d'Azil – this piece is rather worn, but it is still possible to distinguish the wolf's head above the cervid, in the same position as on the Lorthet piece.

but the art forms in no way support this. The pattern, or lack of it, suggests that there must have been great flexibility of social grouping in south-west France at this period (Magdalenian IV); either a considerable movement of actual groups or close contact between groups, one being intermediate between two others. (In this context, the Magdalenian IV levels at Duruthy present an interesting problem. At this stage there are twelve levels of occupation here, each separated by a sterile zone. Arambourou thinks that each sterile zone indicates a gap of about thirty years, but why the occupation of this site should have followed this intermittent pattern is puzzling. Animal migration follows an annual pattern so that, in the absence of any other explanation for the sterile layers, the gaps in the Duruthy sequence must be taken to represent human choice.)[2] This overall distribution is particularly characteristic of Magdalenian IV. Geographical zones become more differentiated in the late Magdalenian and certain styles in art become regionally restricted: at this stage art generally is less rich and there are fewer data for comparison, but nevertheless a certain homogeneity remains, a continuation in some degree of the universality recognized in portable art of Magdalenian IV date.

In effect, the long-distance connections between particular art forms, such as those from Laugerie and Isturitz, are endorsed by the lack of local distribution patterns. The topography of the Pyrenees is such that each valley is segregated from its neighbour; the lack of local distribution groups is, therefore, not surprising, but the range of contacts outside this area is. The communications between the Dordogne and the Pyrenees are not unique, however. Kesserloch, in Switzerland, has a Magdalenian IV with art forms that are almost exact parallels of types found in the Dordogne. It is difficult to see how traffic could have been continuous between these two areas, but it may have been so, or Kesserloch may mark a pioneering offshoot from the Dordogne, of a different type.

No present-day hunting-gathering group exists in quite the conditions that prevailed in the Upper Palaeolithic, and ethnographic parallels must be used with care but, if they are not employed at all, any understanding of the period will be very restricted. Few general deductions can be made about present-day hunter-gatherers, fewer still of these may be applied to the Pleistocene, but some very few may be (Price 1973). One such observation is that all known twentieth-century hunting-and-gathering people who live in small groups congregate from time to time in larger numbers; it may be to conduct ceremonies (Gould 1971), to hunt communally, or to find wives outside their own family group. This seems to be a universal phenomenon and can reasonably be accepted for the Upper Palaeolithic people, particularly as in this instance the distribution of miniature art pieces in south-west France suggests just such a record of meetings and exchanges.

Further general ethnographic deductions (Birdsell 1968:229) are that hunting-and-gathering groups are generally about twenty-five in number, this unit being large enough to function successfully, in a social sense (for hunting, taking care of children and so forth) and small enough not to strain local resources; that such groups are exogamous; that they are often patrilineal and patrilocal; and that in order to keep their numbers in equilibrium there must be some form of population control – it is usually suggested that this is infanticide. Where a large resource of food is found, either locally or seasonally, though, the size of the local group may be much larger. Both salmon runs and the occurrence of herds of migratory animals are known to affect the size of present-day groups in this way, so that it would be unwise to insist on this as a permanent group size for the Pyrenean hunters. However, the extent of most cave deposits does suggest groups of a small size. These Palaeolithic hunters were probably exogamous also – inbreeding is often biologically disastrous and the fact that these people left an archaeological record of such duration suggests that they were physically stable. Again, the equilibrium shown in the archaeological record indicates a balanced population. The human reproductive cycle is fairly rapid and modern primitive people often limit the number of their children by killing those they cannot rear. Nomadic groups, in particular, cannot carry many babies along with them.

It is beyond the scope of archaeological evidence to suggest whether Palaeolithic people were patrilocal or patrilineal; it is also very difficult to deduce larger, usually tribal, groupings. Some anthropologists think a tribal grouping of 500 people to be the norm and that a tribe is distinguished by dialectical homogeneity, but there is less agreement among anthropologists on the size of the tribe than there is on the size of the family unit within it. However, a tribe cannot really be much less than 500 in number (Washburn & Lancaster 1968:293), though it may be much more. It requires something of the order of 100 pairs to keep a population in the sex ratio of 50/50, in fact a population of about 500 people. One must assume that 'nothing is more crucial for evolutionary success than the orderly production of the number of infants that can be supported'. A tribe will not generally cover an area larger than that in which its members can communicate by foot, but trying to make estimates of tribal size in the Palaeolithic is not very rewarding. It is clear that groupings larger than a family unit did exist, but to suggest that the whole of south-west France represents one tribal unit is probably much too comprehensive and we have no evidence for any other regional groupings. However, whether as one or a group of tribes, the art forms suggest that this area was in some respects a single social unit.

There is ample archaeological evidence of settlement in the Pyrenees, preserved in the very substantial Magdalenian cave deposits; there is also climatological and faunal evidence that these settlements were seasonal and it seems reasonable to suggest that the plains alongside the lower reaches of rivers such as the Garonne and Adour were the alternative, probably winter, habitat of the Pyrenean hunters, but there is at present almost no archaeological evidence to support this thesis. Such habitation sites must have been in the open air and, in addition to the problem of where to look for them, there is the greater one of preservation. Open-air structures are easily destroyed, if not by flood or weather, then, almost certainly, by subsequent agriculture. This seems to be a perfect case of the visibility or invisibility of people in the archaeological record. The Pyrenean caves represent the Palaeolithic at its most visible, the search area for cave sites is limited and their contents remain undisturbed; while the sites one conjectures for the Garonne plain are the least visible, for there was probably no continuity of occupation in an open-air site, and the scattered deposits have had little chance of survival. However, it is not impossible that open-air Magdalenian sites may be found there, for Dr Gaussen has found several in the Mussidan region (Gaussen 1965; Bordes & Gaussen 1969; Bordes 1970). Mussidan is 75 km. to the west of Les Eyzies, beyond the area of caves and shelters, and in a much more open topography. Dr Gaussen's sites occur on gentle hill spurs, near rivers or streams, and show neatly demarcated paved areas, presumably house floors, associated with scattered flints. Paving was perhaps laid to keep the floor dry, as appears to have been the case at Duruthy (Arambourou 1962; Arambourou & Genet-Varcin 1965; Bordes 1970, 1972). The deposits at Duruthy are not in caves; they are simply built up at the foot of the limestone cliff, which offers some shelter, and in certain periods the site appears to have been very wet. There are successive pavements laid here, put down (in M. Arambourou's opinion) to stop the floor from slipping, and in the Magdalenian VI level there is a very sizable post-hole also, indicating support for a roof.

A study of the miniature art pieces in the later Magdalenian shows that the hunters of the central Pyrenees, the Landes and the Dordogne had very close cultural connections; in fact, the duplication of the art objects suggests this was a region covered by a tribal or extended family network. Environmental evidence suggests the Pyrenean hunters followed a nomadic pattern of life, settling seasonally in the Pyrenean valleys and moving northwards with the migrating herds in the colder months of the year. A survey of the actual cave sites may give some idea of the conditions under which these hunters lived in the Pyrenees – the observations that follow are based on twenty-four caves in the central and west Pyrenees (Appendix III) including all the classic sites for the Magdalenian except Lespugue (due to a number of mischances, I never visited Lespugue), and Gourdan, which has been totally quarried away (you can still stand on the bluff that projects above the Garonne but the hill-face behind, that contained the cave, has gone).

The primary reason for living in a cave must be shelter; any cave that is not too low-roofed or subject to flooding will serve this purpose: if there is a choice of sites, those with the most strategic position usually have the deepest deposits indicating the most use. Caves in a very high position, a long way from the river, or caves that are very low, are less often used but there are exceptions to this rule; for example, Malarode in the Arudy region is almost at the top of a valley and Cagibi, at Tarascon, is on the present flood plain of the river. Of the twenty-four sites considered here, eighteen (see Appendix III) command a good view of the countryside around (as did Gourdan), while the remaining six have a limited range, though a short walk or a scramble from any of them, with the exception of Cagibi and perhaps Labastide, would bring you to a good view-point. The aspect of the cave itself seems to matter little: the idea that people preferred the sunny south-facing caves has no support here, for the majority in fact face north.

The preference for caves that command a good view is probably connected with hunting, or what might almost be described as herding. Sturdy (1972) has pointed out that in a modern reindeer economy in west Greenland 'in naturally defined grazing areas, with limited access and exit points, it is adequate to wait at these points and thus block the "neck" of the grazing areas'. The distribution of occupied cave sites around Arudy, for example, which lies in the valley of the westward-flowing Gave d'Ossau, is very reminiscent of this. The Palaeolithic site of St-Michel-d'Arudy is on a small limestone outcrop that stands a little way out on the flat valley floor and has an all-round view; Espalungue and Pöeymau in the hills behind both command much the same view from a slightly higher altitude and different angles, while Vignalats (which has a big deposit as yet unexcavated) is on the river to the north. There is a site in the hill of Ste Colombe, another limestone outcrop to the north of St-Michel, and so forth. The hills behind the present town of Arudy stand in a semi-circle, through a narrow gap in which the Gave d'Ossau flows from the south, while the plain below is bounded to the north and east by a big loop of the river. When you drive out over further hills to the north, you realize it is a closed terrain where hunters could very easily watch herds of big game moving about, more particularly if the vegetation were open, rather than wooded as much of it is today. Reindeer or bison could easily be followed in such an enclosed territory and were perhaps driven into the narrow valley-heads to be caught. In northern Europe, in historic times (Hvarfner 1965:319), reindeer have been caught in pits, sometimes combined with fences; or driven into enclosures, again with fences leading to them; or simply captured on rocky hillsides (reindeer are at a disadvantage on rocks and screes, though bison are more agile), or by driving over a cliff face. Palaeolithic hunters may have used any of these methods and perhaps bull-roarers, such as those found at Lorthet and Mas d'Azil (Chollot 1964), were used to scare and drive the animals. There are further examples of the importance of caves as view-points; for instance, the limestone outcrop at Mas d'Azil is a good vantage point, for here the Arize river opens out on to a small plain to the south, surrounded by hills, while Bedeilhac has a panoramic view of the Sarnat valley running up into the hills with the Col de Port at the head. Or one may cite La Vache, which is situated at a point where the Vicdessos river is very narrow, or Fontanet, which is high on the side of the Ariège with a clear view both up and down the valley.

The position of a cave appears to be important for hunting, or for watching game; obviously a cave must not be too far from water and it provides shelter. This last is generally taken to mean that Palaeolithic people camped at the entrance of a cave, using the daylight as in a rock shelter, but there are a surprising number of instances in the Pyrenean caves that contradict this concept. This is a distinction that applies to large, rather than small, caves since in shelters and small caves without long galleries there is no question of choice. In the group of twenty-four caves considered here, eight are very large: Bedeilhac and Mas d'Azil are vast; Labastide, like Mas d'Azil, is an underground river tunnel; Les Églises, Isturitz and Espalungue are spacious and extensive; and Fontanet and La Vache, though their main halls are not so big, have long lateral galleries. All of these caves have occupation sites right inside the cave. In Bedeilhac the occupation debris is at the entrance of the Vidal gallery, just at the limit of the daylight, and inside this gallery also, in the dark. At Mas d'Azil there is occupation debris at both openings of the underground river tunnel, but also a great deal in the catacombs of interior caves on the right bank, which are quite dark; at Labastide a hearth, ringed with engraved limestone plaques, was found by Norbert Casteret inside the subterranean river tunnel; at Espalungue there was debris at the cave mouth, but more in the huge dark hall at the end of the gallery behind this; and at Fontanet and La Vache there are occupation deposits in the dark lateral galleries. The gallery at La Vache has a long low entrance-passage and a quantity of hearths in the hall at the end of this (Nougier & Robert 1968). It is a fairly low hall with no apparent chimney and smoke must have been a problem, but perhaps it eventually crept out down the passage-way.[3] The main hall here was also used. A new gallery has just been found 600 m. inside the cave at Fontanet, with paintings and engravings on the wall and living-debris lying undisturbed on the floor beneath (Delteil, Durbas & Wahl 1972). It is here that there is a salmon skeleton and there are stones collected into hearths, as at La Vache. It is very difficult to reach this gallery in Fontanet from the only entrance known at present and it is presumed that the original Magdalenian entrance was easier; it was probably further to the south, perhaps now hidden under the big rock scree there. At Les Églises the habitation deposits are at the back of the huge 'ecclesiastic' hall, and for most of the day are in the dark, but for an hour or two each afternoon the sunlight shines through a small opening at the top of the scree and the light that it throws on to the whitish limestone face opposite is reflected down on to the habitation deposits below. Isturitz, also, is not all absolutely dark (St-Périer 1930). The original Palaeolithic entrance faces north and is high. Light from this would have hit the carved stalagmitic column in the centre of the left-hand gallery and must also have given a little light to the living area there, but the right-hand gallery with further deposits must have been quite dark, for the south entrance is modern.

With regard to the period when such cave interiors were used: Bedeilhac, Mas d'Azil and Isturitz have occupation debris belonging to the periods of Magdalenian IV, V and VI; Labastide is considered, because of its art pieces, to be Magdalenian IV; Espalungue was one of Piette's original excavations and Magdalenian IV was certainly present there, perhaps some material from the later periods also; Les Églises and La Vache are both later Magdalenian in date, probably Magdalenian V; and Fontanet has not been excavated yet, though some of the engraving here does suggest Magdalenian IV. In general, all three stages are represented in a number of Pyrenean caves, although Magdalenian IV is the most common and has the richest deposits. Magdalenian IV may, very tentatively, be equated with the Bølling oscillation, a little less cold than the periods preceding and following it. The period of maximum cold seems to coincide with Magdalenian V and early VI. It would be tempting to suggest that cold conditions forced the late Magdalenian hunters into the more protected interior galleries of these caves, but the evidence does not support this. Magdalenian IV people also lived in the cave interiors. Les Églises and La Vache were occupied in very wet periods; in fact the deposit at Les Églises was repeatedly flooded. It was a spring encampment containing, almost exclusively, ibex bone (Clottes: private communication).[4] At La Madeleine, in the Dordogne, there is no flooding of the shelter in Magdalenian VI and it was, perhaps, drier in the Pyrenees also at this stage. The lower cave at Massat, for example, which is very near the river, was used in Magdalenian VI.

There are not many distinctions that can be made between Magdalenian IV and the late stages of this culture in the Pyrenees. Occupation deposits of the later stages are less thick, less frequent and less rich in art (though La Vache and Lorthet are exceptions to this last rule), which suggests that in the periods of Magdalenian V and VI there were fewer hunters in this region and that environmental modifications had slightly affected the affluence of the economy. Generally, however, the same caves were inhabited at all stages, in the same manner. There is clear archaeological evidence for a seasonal occupation at Les Églises (Clottes: private communication), which is a late Magdalenian site (probably Magdalenian V), but Magdalenian IV occupations were, in all probability, seasonal also. However, the animals eaten were not always the same. Magdalenian IV hunters had a great preference for reindeer, which the later hunters did not, or perhaps could not, indulge. In the Late Magdalenian, ibex was eaten at Les Églises and red deer at Isturitz. It appears that the reindeer had by this time left the Pyrenees and moved further north. This adaptation to a different fauna is interesting. The expected reaction to the disappearance of the reindeer might have been the disappearance of the hunters in their wake, but this did not happen. The archaeological record at Isturitz, for example, shows that the people there adapted themselves to a different food supply or, more strictly perhaps, to a different element in that part of their diet that was formed by meat. This was apparently also done in Spanish Calabria. In that area, although reindeer is recorded in domestic sites, it is much less common than the red deer. The social flexibility that was characteristic of Magdalenian IV seems to have persisted, though, for the sites that show a close relationship to the art of El Pendo and El Valle, in Spain, are not in the west but in the central Pyrenees; in particular, there is the cervid-and-wolf series of engravings that come from Lorthet, Mas d'Azil and El Pendo (Fig. 8).

The survival of hunting-and-gathering communities can depend on their adaptability. This may be expressed in patterns of food collecting, in methods of hunting, or even in social relationships. The Netsilik Eskimo (Balikci 1968:78), for example, survive in an extremely harsh environment by their adaptability: each seasonal hunt has an alternative. 'If the fall caribou hunts with spears from kayaks failed, the bow and arrow was used. In winter musk ox hunting could be substituted for sealing' and so forth. Group structure, in these conditions, had to be flexible also. In the archaeological data for the later Magdalenian we have a record of more than 2,000 years of a successfully adapted hunting economy in the Pyrenees and south-west France; the fact of its survival is the principal testimony to its success. To be successful these people must have had assets, rather than luck, and these might have been skill in hunting and fishing, perhaps, and a social pattern of marriage and child-rearing that ensured the health and replacement of each tribe. The art that they left behind them not only indicates a very widely based social group with, apparently, very flexible patterns of personal or material interchange but also is, in itself, evidence of leisure, of technical skill and aesthetic achievement. When present-day anthropologists speak of the original affluent society, it is not surprising that they turn to the French Upper Palaeolithic to illustrate this: 'a people can enjoy an unparalleled material plenty, though perhaps only a low standard of living' (Sahlins 1968:85). Upper Palaeolithic art, whether from caves or domestic sites, is also a clear illustration of the fact that a simple technology need not indicate simplicity of thought, either in religion or social structure.

A great many of the conclusions in this paper are conjectural. It is to be hoped that they represent probabilities rather than guesses but, in justification, one can only say that there seems to be little point to archaeological data if one cannot build some picture from it.

Acknowledgments

I am very grateful to M. le Comte Louis Begouen, Mme la Comtesse de St-Périer, M. Georges Simonnet, M. Arambourou, M. Robert and M. Vézian for allowing me to study their private collections; to M. Clottes, M. Arambourou, M. Georges Laplace and M. Robert for kindly spending much time showing me their sites, and again to M. Louis Begouen for allowing me to visit the Volp caves. Without their help and generosity this work would not have been possible. The fieldwork for this paper was carried out with the aid of a grant from the British Academy, to whom I am much indebted.

Appendix I: Geographical groupings of Magdalenian IV Pyrenean sites

La Vache and Niaux are on the Vicdessos river, which joins the Ariège.

Les Églises and Labouiche are both on small rivers that join the Ariège.

The Ariège joins the Garonne, in the plain.

Lorthet and Labastide are on the Neste, which is a tributary of the Garonne.

Gourdan is on the bend of the Garonne, near where the Neste joins it.

Lespugue is on the Save, which joins the Garonne in the plain.

Massat is on the Arac, which joins the Salat and then joins the Garonne.

Montespan is on the Garonne.

Marsoulas and Tarté are on the Salat, which joins the Garonne.

Les Trois Frères, Le Tuc d'Audoubert and Enlène are on the Volp, which joins the Garonne.

Mas d'Azil is on the Arize, which joins the Garonne.

The Arudy group is on the Gave d'Ossau; this runs out west, joining the Gave d'Oloron, which flows past Duruthy and Pastou (the junction is below Duruthy).

Isturitz is at the head of the Arberoue, which joins the Bidouze and then the Adour, below the junction of the Adour and the two *Gaves.*

Lourdes is on the Gave du Pau, north of the Gave d'Oloron, which it joins.

Aurensan is on the upper part of the Adour, which runs round in a bend, joining the two *Gaves* (d'Oloron and Pau).

Brassempouy is on a small tributary that joins the Luy, which joins the Adour not far above its junction with the *Gaves.*

There are in reality two major geographical groups of sites, one (A) based upon the Garonne and the other (B) based on the Adour and the two *Gaves.* Each group is subdivided geographically as shown in the following table. A 1 and B 1 are the most easterly of the sub-groups; A 5 and B 4 are the most westerly.

A 1	A 2	A 3	A 4	A 5
La Vache	Mas d'Azil	Lespugue	Gourdan	Lorthet
Les Églises	Marsoulas	(The head-		Labastide
Niaux	Tarté	waters of		
Fontanet	Massat	the Save		
Bedeilhac	Enlène	extend		
Labouiche	Trois Frères	almost		
	Tuc d'Audoubert	back to		
	Portel	Lorthet &		
	Montespan	Labastide)		

B 1	B 2	B 3	B 4
Aurensan	Lourdes	Arudy	Isturitz
		Duruthy	Brassempouy
		Pastou	

Appendix II: Categories of miniature portable art of similar design

The examples are divided according to tool type (Nos. 1 and 2), subject of decoration (Nos. 3 to

12), basic material (No. 13), and technique employed (Nos. 14 to 17). These pieces are described and illustrated in Leroi-Gourhan 1968; Graziosi 1960; Chollot 1964; Piette 1907; Zervos 1959; and Garrod 1955.

1. *Weighted Spear-throwers* (showing several different types of motif)

   Mas d'Azil: Three horse heads; Galloping bison; *Fâon à l'Oiseau.*
   Trois Frères: Two fighting ibex; Three birds.
   St-Michel d'Arudy: *Fâon à l'Oiseau*; Two very mutilated horses.
   Bedeilhac: *Fâon à l'Oiseau.*
   Isturitz: Bouquetin figure; Perhaps a *Fâon à l'Oiseau* piece also.
   Bruniquel: Mammoth; Leaping horse.
   Laugerie Basse: Reindeer.
   La Madeleine: Hyena; Bison licking its flank; One other bison.

   The *Fâon à l'Oiseau* group comprises Mas d'Azil, Bedeilhac, Arudy, perhaps Isturitz, a miniature from Labastide and a possible fragment from Bruniquel.

2. *Unweighted Spear-throwers* (most usually horse heads)

   Mas d'Azil (Ibex).
   Gourdan: Three examples.
   Isturitz.
   Bruniquel: One musk ox (eight in all).
   Laugerie Basse.
   La Madeleine: Simplified types of horse form (four).

3. *Cervid-and-wolf motif*

   Lorthet.
   Mas d'Azil.
   El Pendo.

4. *Breast Beads* (very interesting because they are a continuation of an older tradition)

   Marsoulas.
   Gourdan.
   Brassempouy.
   Duruthy.
   Isturitz.
   Sergeac: Abri Castanet.

5. *Heads spouting blood*

   Massat: Bear's head.
   Trois Frères: Horse or cervid.
   La Vache: Head of feline.
   Bruniquel (?): A possibility, but very stylized.

6. *Sexual motifs*

   Vulvas
   Bruniquel (?): The same piece as the possible head spouting blood.
   Duruthy.
   La Madeleine.

   Phalli (*bâtons de commandement* in the shape of phalli)
   Bruniquel.
   Gorge d'Enfer.
   El Pendo.
   Mas d'Azil (?).

7. *Spiral-decorated Half-rods*

   Isturitz.
   Duruthy.
   Lespugue.
   Lourdes.
   Arudy.
   Massat.

8. *Diamond geometric patterns*

   Marsoulas.
   Lourdes.
   Lorthet (?): Not a very convincing example.
   Gourdan: But very simple.
   Laugerie Basse.

9. *Wavy-band decoration with edge notching*

   Brassempouy.
   Duruthy: Four or more examples.
   Isturitz.
   Lourdes: Two examples.

10. *Snakes or Eels*

    'Snakes' are often drawn on the same object as fish, or are found in the same site. However, in natural conditions eels are more commonly found with fish than are snakes, so that the drawings may well be of eels.

    Gourdan.
    Lorthet: Two examples.
    Lespugue.
    Isturitz: A possible example.
    Montgaudier.
    Teyjat.

Laugerie Basse: A possible example, not complete.

11. *Birds*

Isturitz.
Duruthy.
Labastide: Two or more examples.
Lourdes: Three examples.
Gourdan: Two examples.
Mas d'Azil.
Trois Frères: Two examples.
Raymonden: Baton shaft.

12. *Fish*

Gourdan: Shaft and fish-tail pendants.
Duruthy.
Lorthet: Spatula; Sole silhouette; Baton with salmon and reindeer; One very stylized piece.
Isturitz: Tail; Thrower with salmon; Stylized piece.
El Pendo: Two fish silhouettes, one with criss-cross design.
Marsoulas: Fish pendant.
Lespugue: Fish silhouette.
Lourdes: Salmon.
Labastide: Several salmon.
Mas d'Azil: Contour découpé – three fish tails; Salmon on rib bone.
Fontanet: Pendant, or perhaps bull-roarer.
La Roche, Lalinde: Fish or bull-roarer.
Laugerie Basse: Contour découpé salmon; Baton with salmon and another broken; Several engravings, stylized fish with criss-crossings.
Les Eyzies, Grotte de Rey: Two spatulae.
Bout de Monde: Spatula.

13. *Engraved limestone blocks*

Isturitz.
Gourdan.
Mas d'Azil.
Bedeilhac: Mud and schist blocks.
Lourdes.
Lorthet: Sandstone.
Labastide.
Bruniquel.
La Madeleine.
Laugerie Basse & Haute.
Limeuil.
Arudy: Very few.

14. *Free-standing carving*

Lourdes: Ivory horse.
Mas d'Azil: Horse head.
Isturitz: Feline; Separate heads; Numerous bodies.
Bedeilhac: Similar, smaller group.
Duruthy: Horse heads; Horse.
Laugerie Basse: Horse head; Sitting fawn; Salamander.

15. *Free outline drawings* (usually of complete animals on reindeer palms or large bone surfaces)

Isturitz: Pony.
Brassempouy: Pony's head.
Duruthy: Ibex, legs incorrect.
Labastide: Half a horse, legs wrong.
Mas d'Azil: Grazing ruminant, probably horse.
Laugerie Basse: Bison, in death throes, hind foot wrong; Bison hind-quarters; Ibex, with wrongly drawn hind legs.

In this group four animals have their hind legs drawn wrongly; usually such drawings are very rare.

16. *Contours découpés heads* (usually hyoid bones)

Brassempouy.
Isturitz: Thirty examples.
Le Portel.
Arudy.
Gourdan: Ibex.
Mas d'Azil: Fourteen horses.
Lorthet.
Lourdes.
Bedeilhac.
Labastide: One horse; One bison; Eighteen ibex.
Laugerie Basse: Five examples.

17. *Contours découpés discs* (Sieveking 1971)

Arudy: Five.	
Aurensan: Two.	Trois Frères: Two.
Duruthy: One.	Tuc d'Audoubert: One.
Enlène: Two.	Bruniquel: Eight.
Gourdan: One.	Combarelles: Two.
Isturitz: Sixty-eight.	Cromagnon: Three, but atypical.
Labastide: One.	Gros Roc: One.
Lorthet: Three.	Laugerie Basse: Eight.
Lourdes: One.	La Madeleine: Two.

Mas d'Azil: Forty-one.	Raymonden: Two. La Tuilière: One.

There are not many connections between these groups: holes, as an edge decoration, are confined to Mas d'Azil and La Madeleine; delicate denticulated edge notching is found at Mas d'Azil and Bruniquel. Mas d'Azil and Bruniquel are further linked by the use of a single side-hole and arrow design, but these two characteristics are not peculiar to these sites alone.

The lists of pieces in these seventeen categories are far from exhaustive: they are simply designed to demonstrate the variety of objects found and their unrestricted distribution.

Weighted spear-throwers, free outline drawings, contours découpés, spiral-decorated half-rods, diamond geometric and wavy-band decoration are all characteristic of, and restricted to, Magdalenian IV while both the cervid-and-wolf motif and the heads spouting blood are late Magdalenian, V or VI.

Appendix III: List of caves in the Central and West Pyrenees studied for their position and aspect

* Bedeilhac	Cagibi	* Tarté	* Pöeymau
* La Vache	Massat	Lorthet	* Malarode
* Fontanet	* Le Portel	Labastide	Vignalats
* Les Églises	* Enlène	* Lourdes	* Duruthy
* Mas d'Azil	* Trois Frères	* Espalungue	* Isturitz
* Herm	* Marsoulas	* St-Michel d'Arudy	Brassempouy

* Those marked with an asterisk command a good view.

REFERENCES

Arambourou, R. (1962) Sculptures magdaléniennes découvertes à la grotte Duruthy. *L'Anthropologie*, 66, 458-68.

Arambourou, R. and Genet-Varcin, C. (1965) Nouvelle sépulture du magdalénien final dans la Grotte Duruthy à Sorde-l'Abbaye (Landes). *Annales de Paléontologie (Vertébrés)*, 51, 129-50.

Balikci, A. (1968) The Netsilik Eskimos: adaptive processes. In Lee and DeVore (eds.), 1968, 49-55.

Begouen, Comte H. (1926) L'art mobilier dans la caverne de Tuc-d'Audoubert, (Ariège). *Institut fur Prähistoriche und Ethnographische Kunst*, 1926, 219-28.

Begouen, Comte H. (1936) *Les Grottes de Montesquieu-Avantès*. Toulouse.

Birdsell, J.B. (1968) Some predictions for the Pleistocene based on equilibrium systems among recent hunter-gatherers. In Lee and DeVore (eds.), 1968, 229-40.

Bordes, F.H. (1970, 1972) Informations archéologiques: circonscription d'Aquitaine. *Gallia Préhistoire*, 13, 485-511; 15, 487-97.

Bordes, F.H. and Gaussen, J. (1969) Un fond de tente magdalénien près de Mussidan (Dordogne). *Mélanges Rust.*

Breuil, H. and St-Perier, R. de (1927) *Les Poissons, les bactraciens et les reptiles dans l'art quaternaire* (Archives Inst. Paléontologie Humaine Mémoire 2). Paris.

Clottes, J. and Simonnet, R. (1974) Une datation radiocarbone dans la Grotte Ornée de Fontanet. *Bull. Soc. Préhist. Française*, 71, 106-7.

Chollot, M. (1964) *La Collection Piette*. Paris: Musée des antiquités nationales.

Degerbøl, M. and Krug, H. (1959) The reindeer in Denmark. *Biologiske Skrifter*, 10 (4), 1-165.

Delteil, J., Durbas, P. and Wahl, L. (1972) Présentation de la Galerie Ornée de Fontanet. *Préhistoire Ariégeoise* (Bull. Soc. Préhistoire de l'Ariège), 27, 11-20.

Gaare, E. (1968) A preliminary report on winter nutrition of wild reindeer in the Southern Scandes, Norway. *Symposia Zool. Soc. London*, 21, 109-15.

Garrod, D.A.E. (1955) Palaeolithic spear-throwers. *P.P.S.*, 21, 21-35.

Gaussen, J. (1965) Le Paléolithique supérieur de la Basse Vallée de l'Isle. *Bull. Soc. Hist. et Arch. du Périgord*, Numero spécial, 47-54.

Gould, R.A. (1971) The uses and effects of fire among the western desert aborigines. *Mankind*, 8, 14-24.

Graziosi, P. (1960) *Palaeolithic Art*. London.

Hustich, I. (1951) The lichen woodlands in Labrador and their importance as winter pastures for domesticated reindeer. *Acta Geographica* (Helsinki), 12 (1), 1-48.

Hvarfner, H. (1965) Pitfalls. In Hvarfner, H. (ed.), *Hunting and fishing*, 319-32. Luleå.

Lee, R.B. (1968) What hunters do for a living, or, how to make out on scarce resources. In Lee and DeVore (eds.), 1968, 30-48.

Lee, R.B. and DeVore, I. (eds.) (1968) *Man the Hunter.* Chicago.

Leroi-Gourhan, A. (1968) *The Art of Prehistoric Man in Western Europe.* London.

Meroc, L. (1969) Les grottes de Montmaurin. In Taillier, F. (ed.), *Livret-guide de l'excursion A6.* VIII Congrès INQUA, Paris, 1969, 28-30.

Netboy, A. (1968) *The Atlantic Salmon: A Vanishing Species?* London.

Nougier, L.R. and Robert, N. (1968) Scene d'initiation de la grotte de la Vache à Alliat (Ariège). *Préhistoire Spéléologie Ariégeoises* (Bull. Soc. Préhistorique de l'Ariège), 23, 13-98.

Piette, E. (1907) *L'Art pendant l'âge du renne.* Paris.

Price, T.D. (1973) A proposed model for procurement systems in the Mesolithic of north-western Europe. In Kozłowski, S.K. (ed.), *The Mesolithic in Europe*, 455-76. Warsaw.

Sahlins, M.D. (1968) Discussion in Lee and DeVore (eds.), 1968, 85-9.

St-Périer, R. de (1920) Les migrations des tribus Magdaléniennes des Pyrénées. *Revue Anthrop.*, 30, 136-41.

St-Périer, R. de (1930) *La Grotte d'Isturitz. I* (Archives Inst. Paléontologie Humaine Mémoire 7). Paris.

St-Périer, R. de (1936) *La Grotte d'Isturitz. II* (Archives Inst. Paléontologie Humaine, Mémoire 17). Paris.

Sbodnikov, V.M. (1958) Wild reindeer of the Taimyr peninsula and the regulation of its exploitation. In *Problems of the North* (trans. from *Problemy Severa*), Nat. Res. Council of Canada, 2, 176, Ottawa.

Sieveking, A. (1971) Palaeolithic decorated bone discs. *Brit. Mus. Quarterly*, 35, 206-29.

Simonnet, G. (1971) Informations archéologiques: Circonscription de Midi-Pyrénées. *Gallia Préhistoire*, 14, 393-420.

Skuncke, F. (1969) *Reindeer Ecology and Management in Sweden* (Biol. Papers Univ. of Alaska 8).

Sturdy, D.A. (1972) The exploitation patterns of a modern reindeer economy in west Greenland. In Higgs, E.S. (ed.), *Papers in Economic Prehistory*, 161-8. London.

Sturdy, D.A. (1975) Some reindeer economies in prehistoric Europe. In Higgs, E.S. (ed.) *Palaeoeconomy*, 55-96. London.

Vibe, C. (1967) Arctic animals in relation to climatic fluctuations. *Meddelelser om Grønland*, 170 (5), 1-227.

Washburn, S.L. and Lancaster, C.E. (1968) The evolution of hunting. In Lee and DeVore (eds.), 1968, 293-303.

Watanabe, H. (1968) Subsistence and ecology of northern food gatherers, with special reference to the Ainu. In Lee and DeVore (eds.), 1968, 69-77.

Zervos, C. (1959) *L'Art pendant l'âge du renne en France*. Paris.

NOTES

1. The Dordogne and Vezère caves are at a lower altitude than those of the central Pyrenees and so might be considered as a winter alternative to the latter, but the fact that they are considerably further north probably nullifies this difference.

2. It is known that lichen pastures, if seriously overused and trampled, may take thirty years to recover (Sturdy 1975). The gaps in the human occupation at Duruthy may be the record of such a history of overgrazing and regeneration.

3. Alternatively, the retention of smoke may here indicate its use: this gallery could perhaps have been a smoke-house for drying meat or fish, rather than a living area.

4. In M. Clottes' opinion, it would have been impossible to use Les Églises in the winter. It is a very cold cave – at the present day, temperatures of −7°C have been recorded there in December. The occupation layers at Les Églises are interspersed with layers of sand, indicating that summer meltwater streams flooded the site. These facts, in conjunction with the state of the ibex bone, suggest a short, spring occupation.

DAVID TRUMP

The collapse of the Maltese temples

That archaeology must set as its main objective the translation of changes in the material record into human history has been stressed by many. Even if we cannot recover the individual from the prehistoric past, we can and must make every effort to recover the society of which he formed a part (Clark 1953). In other words, we must look for the people behind the relics, since only thus have we any chance of explaining observed changes in the record. A historical typology of the artefacts is not enough.

Whether or not it is possible to proceed further, to determine regularities or patterns in those changes, and whether or not it is legitimate to describe such regularities as laws, I do not propose to discuss here. Instead, I intend to take a single archaeologically well documented event in the prehistoric past and re-examine it, partly for its intrinsic interest, partly for the light it can throw on the procedures available to us and their limitations, and partly, perhaps mainly, to illustrate the difficulties even a comparatively simple case may present.

The great stone temples of Malta have, not surprisingly, attracted attention from a very early date. In the seventeenth century they were attributed to giants (Abela 1647); in the nineteenth, to the Phoenicians. By the early years of the present century, a less romantic but more credible origin for them was being sought (Mayr 1908). No clear answer was possible until the careful investigation of the Tarxien Temple site by Sir (then Dr) Themistocles Zammit in 1915-16 (Zammit 1930). This not only revealed the content of the temple culture, its richness and complexity, but also threw light on its end.

Into the 'metre of sterile silt' that filled its ruins had been dug a cremation cemetery, the ashes and jars of which were accompanied by flat axes and daggers of bronze. With the possible exception of a small gold inlay in a stone bead, no metal has ever been discovered in the temple culture levels.

Even more significantly, a few of the interments were of inhumed skeletons, the skulls of which were markedly brachycephalic, in contrast to the many skulls known from the temple period that were equally markedly dolichocephalic. Similar contrasts could be observed between the pottery styles of the two groups, their beads, their figurines, not only in general form but in every detail. Indeed, every recoverable aspect of their respective cultures differed.

Subsequent work on other sites has supported fully the Tarxien evidence. At Borg in-Nadur in 1923-27, it was shown that a temple had been desecrated and used by squatters (Murray 1923-9) though, owing to the shallowness of the deposits, little information could be added on the actual process of cultural displacement. A similar result was obtained at Skorba in 1961. Though no sterile layer, like that at Tarxien, separated the two occupations here, it was noted that damage to the stone blocks of the temple preceded the construction of Bronze Age additions (Trump 1966).

The evidence so far is unanimous in suggesting that there was a complete replacement of culture and race, between the period when the temples flourished and the period when their ruins were re-used for other purposes. Zammit (1930:177) sums up well the stratigraphic evidence that he observed: 'the great importance of the Tarxien discoveries lies probably in the clear separation of the Age of Metal from that of the Stone Age by a metre of sterile silt, during the formation of which the Tarxien plateau was apparently deserted by its former inhabitants'. And Evans (1959:168) draws the cultural conclusion: 'the remarkable civilization . . . after a long and unbroken development that can be traced through many centuries, finally disappears from view with great suddenness, and without leaving a trace in the material culture of Malta during the succeeding centuries. In its place we find the remains of what appears to have been in all respects a cruder and less advanced culture, except for its possession of some simple metal tools and weapons'.

There is less unanimity over the lapse of time involved. Zammit envisaged a long gap between the two occupations, as the quotation shows. Unfortunately, in 1915 soil studies were a thing of the future, and Zammit's 'silt' was shovelled away without samples being preserved, still less analysed. His description of the deposit does not tally with other known natural deposits from Malta, but even if we dismiss it as artificial, the problem of its source, as well as its purpose, remains. Zammit's assumption that the silt was a slow, natural, probably wind-borne, deposit is easily understandable. It is neither supported by, nor contradicted by, other evidence.

Evans's argument for suddenness is based partly on cultural, partly on chronological grounds. He traces cultural connections between both temple and cemetery period material and the Castelluccio culture of south-east Sicily (Evans 1953:83, 86-7). The most notable examples are the bossed bone plaque fragment from Tarxien and the sherds of thickened-lip, or Thermi, bowls (Evans 1956). Since the Castelluccio culture is not thought to have had a long life (Bernabò Brea 1957:109-15), any gap between temple and cemetery must be of shorter duration, shorter by the period of overlap of temples with its beginning and cemetery with its end. But the Thermi bowl evidence has been weakened by the discovery that these bowls were apparently being introduced into Malta over a much longer period (Trump 1966:46), whether direct from the Aegean, from the site of Ognina near Syracuse where they were the characteristic ware (Bernabò Brea 1966), or from some other, and unknown, source. We are left with typological parallels in the handles and decoration of Tarxien and Castelluccio pots which, in themselves, carry no great weight.

Chronologically, too, some difficulties have appeared. Evans, impressed by parallels with Middle Minoan Crete, as well as those with Castelluccio, would extend the temple period well into the second millennium B.C., a view that he maintained in 1971 (Evans 1971: 223-4). Faience beads and pottery parallels would equally push the start of the cemetery back before 1500, probably well before. On the other hand, the radiocarbon dates, particularly since tree-ring calibration (Renfrew 1972b), would place the start of the cemetery period not in the second millennium but well back in the third. However, leaving aside the controversy of when the change occurred, the impression of rapidity of change is barely affected.

Summing up the factual evidence as it stands at present, we see an advanced culture, producing remarkably sophisticated architecture and sculpture for religious purposes at a remarkably early date, collapsing with what looks like catastrophic suddenness. It was succeeded by an immigrant culture, brought by a new people who absorbed nothing from their predecessors on the island. A few sites were re-used, but for new purposes. The break in tradition was absolute, with only a single minor exception – that both peoples had contacts with the makers of the Thermi bowls, wherever they lived.

This extraordinary state of affairs cries out for explanation, if prehistory is to be anything more than a simple catalogue of changes in material culture. Many explanations have been offered, based on political, social, economic or religious changes. All are possible: unfortunately at this stage none is provable.

Zammit (1930) preferred war, and Evans (1959:168) inclined the same way, while mentioning other possibilities. The cemetery people were revealed as foreigners, and armed, so the interpretation followed naturally. There is no other evidence of warfare until several centuries later, when settlements moved to naturally or artificially defended sites (Evans 1959:181; Trump 1961:260). And it would seem doubtful that a policy of complete racial extermination, difficult enough in modern circumstances, could have been pursued to a successful conclusion at so early a date. Surely one would expect some of the earlier population to escape death, if only in slavery. Even in this unhappy state they would have continued to exert at least some slight influence, both cultural and racial. There is absolutely no sign of this.

A variant of this theory would suggest that the prime factor was social instability, leading perhaps to insurrection and civil war, the cemetery people appearing on the scene only after internal strife had cleared the way. Evidence has been adduced from developments in the temple architecture for an increasingly restrictive priesthood (Trump 1966:51). This evidence is, frankly, slight and there is nothing concrete to support the view that the tendency, even if it existed, was resented. A revolt against an entrenched theocracy, disastrous to both sides and followed by renewed immigration, is certainly a possibility, but virtually unprovable.

A similar argument could be used without the need for the war-like débâcle. By this, we might postulate a similar centralized theocratic control, suffering from internal weaknesses. The later eastern temple at Skorba was of appreciably poorer workmanship than the western one, and had apparently been abandoned and used for the dumping of rubbish from the still functioning western temple, before it was destroyed. The level between the floor and the remains of the burnt roof contained great quantities of temple-period pottery, with none of later date. Had the organization broken down, both culture and population could have collapsed with it, whether or not there was any external threat. A similar interpretation has come into favour as an explanation of the collapse of Mycenaean civilization in Greece.

Disease provides another possible answer. That it would have left remarkably little impression on the archaeological record may be regarded either as an advantage or a disadvantage when advancing it as a theory. The Black Death killed a third of the population of England in the fourteenth century, with remarkably little archaeological trace. But disease, even less than war, does not exterminate, as that example shows. It is difficult to imagine a plague more disastrous than that of myxomatosis in rabbits in the last two decades, but there were survivors even of this. In a human population, despite renewed immigration after the disease abated, some physical traces of the earlier people would be expected to continue.

Economic factors offer a whole new range of possible interpretations. The number and size of the temples in their latest, Tarxien, phase necessitated a large labour force and so a substantial population. A necessary implication in a small island like Malta is an intensive use of land for food production. It is worth repeating that the evidence is strongly against a labour force recruited from outside the island, or even external economic support (Trump 1966:51). Overseas contacts at this period, while certainly existing, were slight.

Another resource in heavy demand for the programme of temple building was timber, primarily for roofing. The identification of charcoal samples from the burnt roof of the eastern temple at Skorba as olive could argue that there was already a serious scarcity of other timbers; but there may of course, have been some religious sanction for the use of olive (Trump 1966: App. V). In either case, timber in great quantities, and size, was being used for roofing the temples (Trump 1972: 29-30). Pollen samples from a Bronze Age cistern at Luqa (M.A.R. 1959-60:3; 1960:4-5; 1961:5, 8) showed that by that period the vegetation of Malta was virtually identical with that of the present day – a few pines, but for the greater part grasses, herbs and Mediterranean scrub. Where, then, did the timber for the temples come from? And in answering that, may we also have a possible answer to our original question?

If deforestation, together with over-exploitation of Malta's scanty soil cover, led to an ecological crisis, compounded of soil exhaustion and erosion, then the whole economic basis of the temple culture would be destroyed. Collapse would be the inevitable result. But once more, would that collapse be total? Would there be no survivors to blend their genes with those of the newcomers, or to bequeath some cultural trait – the sanctity of the temple sites if not their elaborate ceremonials, or some detail of pottery production if not the traditional forms and decoration?

All the interpretations offered so far postulate a unique crisis in Malta's past, but that is not essential. There is no need to call on any factor that cannot be observed at work in the island at the present day. Recent meterological records show that there is so much variation in precipitation from year to year that the average rainfall figures quoted are virtually meaningless (Bowen-Jones *et al.* 1961). One year of near-drought would cause little more than inconvenience. Such years come on average once in every ten years or so, and are randomly distributed. Every few centuries it would be possible to have perhaps as many as five successive years of drought, the effects of which would be much more serious than five separate years. Principles of water conservation at the period under discussion, and indeed until very recent times, were rudimentary. The only water cistern securely dated to the temple period is at Hal Saflieni, associated with the Hypogeum (Evans 1971:47). One in the forecourt of Tarxien probably belongs with the temple, though it was cleaned out for re-use in Roman times (Evans 1971:118). A group above Mnajdra, the Misqa Tanks, may be associated with that site, another temple complex. Few, if any, of these would contain much water after even one season of seriously deficient rainfall; after several, they would inevitably be dry, and the island's few natural springs reduced to, at best, a trickle. The consequences for the human population can easily be pictured.

One might take this climatic hypothesis further, at the risk of finding onself on shakier ground. It has often been suggested that there is a positive correlation between climatic instability and deforestation. Once more the finger of blame comes back to point to man himself.

One more theory should be mentioned, easy though it may be to scoff at it. This can best be summed up by the word 'ritual' which will, inevitably and rightly, arouse scepticism and raise eyebrows. If the human population abandoned the island completely, as would appear to be the case from the evidence, should one look for a practical, logical explanation in terms that would suit a modern situation? The example of the Cargo Cults of the south-west Pacific shows that other explanations are perfectly possible. Given the evidence for a strong religious driving force and an influential priesthood, a revered 'prophet', by playing on the religious fervour of the people, could have persuaded them to abandon their homeland, leaving it completely deserted. He would have found this even easier if he could quote signs of divine disfavour, such as some of those already suggested – hostile attack, crop failure, drought, disease. Such a theory would be greatly strengthened by the discovery of immigrant Maltese material of this date at some other point on the Mediterranean coastline, but it is not disproved by its absence. Suggestions of Maltese influence in the Ozieri culture of Sardinia (Bray 1963) are receiving little corroboration from further work (Trump & Loria, forthcoming).

Taking these various hypotheses individually, one is forced to the conclusion that none, in isolation, is entirely convincing. However, the last paragraph suggests that some combination of any or all of the factors discussed above may offer credible explanations of the observed circumstances. Indeed, any one can be given the major emphasis, with greater or lesser support from any one or more of the others.

At the present moment, this appears to be as far as any suggested explanation of the collapse of the Maltese temples can be taken. We have a large number of possible alternatives, and though there is a fair amount of circumstantial evidence, it is quite inadequate to make a reasoned choice between them. For some, notably for the religious hysteria theory, it is difficult to see what evidence could be hoped for; for the others, there is no likelihood of proof. What, if anything, can be done about this?

There would seem to be three courses open to us. One is to dismiss the problem as insoluble, with the implication that it is of no interest, or at least not worth any further expenditure of effort. In view of the manifest difficulties, this is certainly tempting, but scarcely satisfactory. It is also possible to regard the problem as insoluble from the evidence at present available to us, with the pious hope that further relevant evidence will, in due course, come to light; in other words, to postpone further consideration of the problem indefinitely, rather than dismiss it outright. Such a solution is hardly more helpful. It may, however, be the best allowed us by circumstances. More satisfactory, if at all practicable, is the third approach, to define the needs and, by deliberate research, set out to meet them.

The primary requirement for any further advance is obviously not so much new theories as new evidence, though the possibility of new theories must never be ignored. It is this that renders inapplicable to archaeological work the Holmesian principle that, when all impossibilities are excluded, whatever remains, however improbable, must be the truth. We can never be certain that all the possibilities are before us. And, as our example has shown, we may be unable to reject categorically any, let alone all but one, of those possibilities.

To return to the theories already under review, Renfrew (1972a) has rightly stressed the importance of 'testability' in any hypothesis, implying that it may give a good measure of its usefulness – 'usefulness' note, not 'accuracy'.

Only a favourable result from the test can increase our faith in the latter, and even then most tests can yield at best one of only two results – disproved or not disproved. By this standard, none of our hypotheses can be considered very useful, though some are undoubtedly less so than others. Any tests, again, require new evidence.

First, we may take the cultural evidence. If the latest phases of the temple period and the earliest of the cemetery period could be isolated, more meaningful comparisons could be made between them, supporting or confuting the argument for the completeness of cultural change at this moment. Other useful comparisons would also become possible. That between the terminal and climax phases of the temple period could be expected to throw valuable additional light on the suggestion of cultural decline at this period, a highly significant factor in the situation (Trump 1963). The relevant settlements are particularly needed: hitherto they have remained obstinately elusive. Comparison between the initial cemetery phase and comparable material outside Malta could also perhaps tell us more about its origins. Though the Thermi-bowl element is better understood than when Evans wrote in 1956, the lack of a convincing specific source for the Tarxien Cemetery culture is as great now as it was then.

Secondly, there is the chronological evidence. Any interpretation of the collapse of the temple culture and its replacement by that of the Bronze Age cemeteries depends heavily on the rapidity of the change. Unless far closer links can be found between both cultural groups and Castelluccio than has yet been done, or is indeed likely, this must mean absolute, or at least chronometric, dating. Renfrew (1972b) has commented on the greater length of the cemetery period resulting from the recalibration of the radiocarbon dates. It could be argued that this might allow sufficient time for all the changes noted above to have taken place locally. Even if presently available evidence is strongly against this, the possibility must be kept in mind. But, once again, subdivision of both temple and cemetery phases would be highly desirable here. A C14 date for the cemetery period would be of far greater value for this argument if we could show, on archaeological grounds, that it fell right at the beginning of the phase. Equally, a date for the temples would increase in relevance the later in their phase it could be placed. We cannot date the change directly, so the more narrowly we can bracket it the better.

Thirdly, there is the environmental evidence. The Tarxien silt is apparently gone beyond recall, and the proven temple-period cistern deposits likewise. Should similar opportunities become available, now that the techniques have been developed to deal with them, they must obviously be seized and exploited to the full. A pollen sample from immediately before the collapse would be invaluable. Once again, a settlement site could be expected to be the most instructive.

Some indication of where the new evidence should be sought would be more helpful than mere discussion of the sorts of evidence that we should like to obtain. Unfortunately in this context such cannot be offered. The need for relevant settlement sites, for example, has been realized for many years now, and a number of field-workers, myself among them, have attempted unsuccessfully to locate them. There can be no harm, however, in calling attention to their potential in the hope that a more skilled, or simply luckier, investigator may discover them. Or, like so many important archaeological discoveries in the past, they may emerge as chance finds in the course of other, non-archaeological, activities: so may cultural layers of the critical phases in the story, or deposits with significant environmental evidence. However they come to light, any of these would be of enormous benefit to our understanding of Malta's cultural, social and economic prehistory, and in a small way to our understanding of human culture processes and our methods of recovering them.

REFERENCES

Abela, G.F. (1647) *Della descrittione di Malta, Isola nel Mare Siciliano, con le sue antichità ed altre notizie.* Malta.

Bernabò Brea, L. (1957) *Sicily before the Greeks (Ancient Peoples and Places 3).* London.

Bernabò Brea, L. (1966) Abitato neolitico e insediamento maltese dell'età del bronzo nell'isola di Ognina (Siracusa) e i rapporti fra la Sicilia e Malta dal XVI al XIII sec. a.C. *Kokalos*, 12, 40-69.

Bowen-Jones, H., Dewdney, J.C. and Fisher, W.B. (1961) *Malta: Background for Development.* Durham.

Bray, W. (1963) The Ozieri Culture of Sardinia. *Rivista di Scienze Preistoriche*, 18, 155-90.

Clark, J.G.D. (1953) *The Study of Prehistory.* Cambridge.

Evans, J.D. (1953) The prehistoric culture sequence in the Maltese archipelago. *P.P.S.*, 19, 41-94.

Evans, J.D. (1956) The 'Dolmens' of Malta and the origins of the Tarxien cemetery culture. *P.P.S.*, 22, 85-101.

Evans, J.D. (1959) *Malta (Ancient Peoples and Places 11).* London.

Evans, J.D. (1971) *The Prehistoric Antiquities of the Maltese Islands.* London.

M.A.R. (1959-60 etc.) *Annual Report of the Museum Department for the year* 1959-60 etc. Malta.

Mayr, A. (1908) *The Prehistoric Remains of Malta.* Valetta.

Murray, M.A. (1923-9) *Excavations in Malta.* London.

Renfrew, C. (1972a) The New Archaeology. *The Listener*, 27 January 1972, 106.

Renfrew, C. (1972b) Malta and the calibrated radiocarbon chronology. *Antiquity*, 46, 141-4.

Trump, D.H. (1961) The later prehistory of Malta. *P.P.S.*, 27, 253-62.

Trump, D.H. (1963) A prehistoric art cycle in Malta. *Brit. Jour. Aesthetics*, 3.

Trump, D.H. (1966) *Skorba and the Prehistory of Malta.* London.

Trump, D.H. (1972) *Malta: an Archaeological Guide.* London.

Trump, D.H. and Loria, R. (forthcoming) *Report on the excavation of Sa Ucca di Su Tintirriolu, Mara (Sassari), 1971.*

Zammit, Sir T. (1930) *Prehistoric Malta: The Tarxien Temples.* London.

Index of Authors

General Index